Throughout the book, in the documents and in the annotations, are fresh
contributions to an understanding of th

There is heretofore unknown information about the Treaty of Logstown, and
there is a full r   tation of the tre
between P
the P

The white cancellation lines which seem to dim the type on many pages in Part I of this book (for instance pp. 72, 73, 88, 89, 240, and others) indicate places where the one who penned the original manuscript lined through words or phrases or entire sentences. To make these white cancellation lines the printer scored the type face with a cutting tool. Since often the scribe lined through only parts of a line, to us this device seemed better than to design and manufacture new type characters or print separately ruled lines by photomechanical means. The cancelled lines are printed to give a true presentation of the manuscript.

EDITOR, UNIVERSITY OF PITTSBURGH PRESS

GEORGE MERCER PAPERS
RELATING TO THE
OHIO COMPANY OF VIRGINIA

GEORGE MERCER PAPERS
IS ONE OF A LIST OF BOOKS
IN THE CULTURAL HISTORY OF
WESTERN PENNSYLVANIA
MADE POSSIBLE THROUGH
A GRANT FROM
THE BUHL FOUNDATION
OF PITTSBURGH

The Seal of the Ohio Company

Delineated for the First Time
by Theodore Bowman
from Specifications Contained in the
George Mercer Papers, page 6.

George Mercer Papers

RELATING TO THE OHIO COMPANY
OF VIRGINIA

Compiled and Edited by

Lois Mulkearn

1954
UNIVERSITY OF PITTSBURGH PRESS

Copyright, 1954, University of Pittsburgh Press
Library of Congress Catalog Card Number: 53-5387

Printed in the United States of America

IN MEMORY OF

LATHROP COLGATE HARPER

BOOKMAN AND FRIEND

1867—1950

FOREWORD

IN the middle of the eighteenth century there was great uneasiness in the Ohio Country. France wanted this rich fur-bearing territory for her own, and the adjoining English colonies of Virginia, Pennsylvania, and New York were awake to this threat of encroachment from the north. France needed a short route from Canada to Louisiana and was eager to develop the rich country of the Illinois; she wanted to break the contact which the Shawnee were maintaining between the Miami-Huron and the Iroquois-English partnerships; and she greatly feared that the English, by their encroachments into the Miami Country would cut the French supply lines. It was not surprising that Duquesne was ordered in 1752 to drive the English out of the Ohio Country and to keep them east of the Alleghenies.

It is true that the English, with their listening post at Oswego and their friendship with the Iroquois, were able to get prompt reports of French troop movements through to Pennsylvania and Virginia and thence by messengers to Croghan and Trent on the frontier, but the aggressiveness of the French fur traders, the building of their string of forts in the Ohio Country, and their alliances with the Indian enemies of the Iroquois made the threat of their southwestern advance ever more serious.

While Sir William Johnson and his Mohawks watched from Fort Johnson and such Pennsylvania frontiersmen as Croghan and Weiser reported developments to Philadelphia, the Colony of Virginia, too, felt an interest in the struggle for the valley of the Beautiful River, for Virginia considered the Ohio Country within the boundaries set forth in *her* royal charter. The Virginians believed that the treaty of Lancaster guaranteed their hold on the territory, for by its terms they were enabled to take up lands under the charter by purchase from the Indians or by securing their consent to white encroachment; and since their allies, the Iroquois, held all tribes under subjugation as far west as the Illinois, the way seemed clear to the English for an easy exploitation of western lands under British ownership.

The French, on the other hand, believed the Ohio Country to be *theirs* by right of discovery and exploration. They explained to the Indians that they could trade with either the English or the French as they chose, but that they could only trade with the English on English territory and with the French on French territory, and that since the

Foreword

Beautiful Valley was, as they maintained, French territory, the Indians could not meet the English fur traders there and the English must be driven out.

Because of this French threat, there was, of course, official encouragement both within the colony and in England when a group of prominent land speculators, mostly Virginians and including two of George Washington's brothers, organized the Ohio Company and petitioned the King for an "additional royal instruction" authorizing Lieutenant Governor Gooch to grant them half a million acres of frontier lands in what is now the southwestern part of Pennsylvania, nearly all of West Virginia, and parts of Maryland and Virginia. The Company was primarily interested in subdividing, selling, and leasing land to settlers but, in order to be sure of favorable consideration in England, they offered to open a fur trade with the Indians, to settle a given number of people on their lands, and to build forts for their protection from the French.

The English were inclined to encourage the enterprise since it would obviously hamper the French and since the chief London stockholder and promoter of the Company was John Hanbury who had been head of the powerful company of the Staples, later the Hamburg Company, and was a British army contractor of importance. However, Lieutenant Governor Gooch was a shrewd politician and did not want to be blamed for touching off a war over the controversial Ohio lands. So he wrote for specific instructions from the Crown regarding the requested Ohio Company grant, and the promoters of the Company wrote to Hanbury asking him to lobby for the petition.

To further this program Christopher Gist was sent on two expeditions to explore the territory and select the land to be included in the grant. Although the Ohio Country was already familiar to many fur traders of the adjoining colonies, there had been no carefully written description of the region until Gist's journals and the maps resulting from his explorations became known in England through Hanbury and the company's petitions. However, because of the encroachments of the French, the delaying tactics of the English authorities, the inability of the colonies to work together, and the jealousies and entanglements of the rival land companies which quickly sprang up in the wake of the Ohio Company, the purposes of the proposed grant were never realized and the whole scheme was finally wiped out by the Revolutionary War.

Though this great plan for the development of half a million of the finest acres of American land failed, its preliminary exploration

Foreword

and exploitation pointed the way to the later development of the West; it had no little influence in the final defeat of French interests in North America; and its surviving documents and letters, its journals and maps provide us with innumerable details of our early frontier history.

Were it not for three fortunate circumstances we might never have had available the true story of the Ohio Company: the bulk of the Company's papers, here completely published for the first time, luckily was preserved by William Darlington as early as 1876 and now forms an important part of the Darlington Memorial Library of the University of Pittsburgh; Mrs. Lois Mulkearn, librarian of that precious collection of Midwestern historical sources, is probably the best available scholar for the interpretation of the papers; and the University of Pittsburgh Press, fortunately, through a grant from The Buhl Foundation is able to publish this great source work in a manner worthy of its historical importance.

The editing of these papers was a task of unusual difficulty. It called for great accuracy and a clear and logical mind to cope with the intricacies of Indian diplomacy and English legal precedent; a wide knowledge of supplementary sources, making possible the inclusion in the annotations of extracts from hundreds of relevant documents gathered from many scattered depositories, for interpreting the Ohio Company or for properly placing its activities in the history of the times. This editorial task called not only for a thorough knowledge of the general history of the region but also for an intimate acquaintance with the obscure personalities living on the frontier, many of whom have had no previous biographer. It called for a firsthand knowledge of the terrain, even to the present-day exploration of eighteenth century trails, natural rock shelters and sites; and endless patience, persistence, and determination in the face of perplexing and annoying difficulties.

Though notes are used only to explain the position of the Ohio Company in the historic events of its time, and there is no attempt at complete histories of events or biographies of individuals, there are almost a thousand of these annotations and most of them are citations from primary sources. This means, of course, that the personalities and events are explained and evaluated by contemporaries or in the light of contemporary history rather than from the point of view of our day, and that is good editorial policy. Wherever possible, the present location and past history of each document is given so that the reader can verify the editor's references and explore the sources still further if he so desires. The chronology is of great aid to the

Foreword

student for it gives almost a day-by-day record of events and the voluminous bibliography locates an amazing array of rich resources which will be of great service to every future student of this period of our history.

A study of the annotations makes one wonder which is the more important, the original papers or the notes which explain and enrich them. From the notes we learn the prominent position of the Six Nations in the international intrigue of the frontier; we see the Indians as logical thinkers, generally honest and always shrewd in their presentation of arguments at the treaties, as normal human beings with a special skill in oratory and diplomacy—and not as the distorted romantic figures of Cooper or Mrs. Sigourney. We watch them with admiration at the treaties of Lancaster, Logstown, Winchester, and Carlisle. We see, both through French and English eyes, the political and military struggle for the control of the frontier, and we watch the contest, blow by blow. We follow the migrations of the Hurons, the Wyandots, and the Shawnee.

There are annotations sometimes several pages in length on such important frontier characters as George Croghan, who is here shown to have been active at Cuyahoga (Cleveland) in 1744, several years earlier than previously believed possible, and so in an early position of influence on the fur trade route from the west through the Ohio Country to Fort Duquesne. There are, too, long notes on Gist, La Force, Trent, Andrew Montour, King Beaver, Half King, and Shingas. The student reads with interest the long descriptions of Logstown, Lower Shawnee Town, or Fort Duquesne, and finds hitherto unintelligible maps and documents clarified, such as the "Articles of Agreement and Copartnership of the Ohio Company" by which the company was governed for twenty years, from 1751 to 1771, and which explains the agitation of the individual partners who wanted desperately to get patents for their half million acres before the agreement should expire on May 23, 1771.

The grateful student who uses these notes will readily see what painstaking scholarship has gone into the editing of this important historical work—scholarship of a high order which is the equivalent of more than one doctorate.

The University of Pittsburgh and its Darlington Librarian are to be congratulated on this further evidence of their abilities in the field of historical scholarship and publication. All students of the old American frontier are greatly in their debt.

R. W. G. VAIL

INTRODUCTION

THE OHIO COMPANY

IN accordance with known extant evidence it may be said that the Ohio Company functioned officially as a partnership under some "Articles of Agreement" from late in 1747 to May 23, 1771; however, the members continued to sue individually for land grants in the name of the Ohio Company for many years after their written articles of agreement had expired.

The original design of the partners was to exploit a half million acres of land "on the branches of Allagany" and to open up a "Trade with the several nations of Indians" who lived there. Later, they desired to be incorporated and made Indian trade incidental to land exploitation.

Indian traders from several English colonies, Maryland, Virginia, and Pennsylvania in particular, had traded with the Indians west of the Allegheny Mountains for about twenty years before the Company was organized; yet permanent white settlements had not been projected prior to its organization.

Lawrence Washington, first chairman or manager of the Company, circulated the petition for organization, probably prepared the partners' first petition for a land grant and caused it to be transcribed by the Clerk of the Executive Council; Thomas Cresap lobbied in Williamsburg for the grant; and on October 20, 1747, Thomas Lee, second leader of the Company, presented the first petition to the Governor and Council of Virginia.

Four days after the Governor and Council postponed action on their petition a committee representing the entire membership of thirteen wrote to John Hanbury asking him to lobby their cause in England and offering him a share in the Company. Hanbury accepted the offer, thereby increasing the number of partners to fourteen, six less than the limit of membership agreed upon. Capital stock for the Company was set at £6,000 sterling.

In July, 1749, Lieutenant Governor Gooch, having received special instruction from the King, granted the Company permission to take up 200,000 acres of land in the unsettled part of Virginia west of the Alleghenies. The Company had by this time attained full membership, twenty.

Introduction

By May 23, 1751, they had built at least one storehouse; had entered into the Indian trade; had purchased land of the Fairfaxes (New Store Tract); had ordered the purchase of 500 acres of land from Thomas Bladen, governor of Maryland; had employed Thomas Cresap and Hugh Parker to reconnoiter lands on the Ohio; had sent Christopher Gist on a similar expedition; had ordered a road to be cut from Wills Creek to the Monongahela; had applied to the College of William and Mary for a licensed surveyor to survey their land; had resolved to try to purchase about 100,000 acres of land from Maryland, North Carolina, and Pennsylvania; had entered into an agreement with Christopher Gist "for the greater Encouragement of the first Setlers upon Company's Lands"; had ordered John Hanbury to contract with German Protestants to immigrate to this country; had sent John Hanbury specifications for a Company seal, authorizing him to have it engraved on steel; and had entered into formal "Articles of Agreement and Copartnership for the space of twenty years."

By these articles the agreement was binding "during the term of Twenty years from henceforth next ensuing and fully to be compleat and ended." Stock was forty shares, each partner holding two shares. Each of the twenty partners was entitled to two shares of stock and by such ownership was given the right to two votes at annual meetings. No person was permitted to hold less than one share, or one-fortieth part of the capital stock. The maximum for investment was set at £150 sterling per share; assessments were not to exceed £15 sterling for each share. Also each new member was required to "enter into bond of the penalty of £100,000 that he or his heirs & assigns keep all & even the Articles, Covenants, Agreements, Rules & Orders." Dissolution of the partnership on May 23, 1771, was as follows: "That at the End & Expiration of the said Copartnership all the Lands belonging to the said Company shall at the joint Charge and Expence of the then Partners & Proprietors to be defrayed & born in proportion to their several & respective Shares & Interests therein be surveyed laid off & divided into forty several Shares or Lots are equal in value as the same can be done having respect to the quantity & quality. . . . "

At the same time the common stock of the Company was to be divided among the partners in proportion "to their several & respective Rights & Interests." The majority vote of the partners could alter, revoke, or change all or any of the "Articles of Agreement."

There is ample evidence throughout the papers that the "Articles" were adhered to, that the Company recognized the expiration date, May 23, 1771, and also that they were not renewed. George Mercer,

Introduction

in his negotiation for the purchase of the late Arthur Dobbs' share, recognized May 23, 1771, as the date of expiration of the Company's official existence. George Mason in his Memorial to the Virginia Assembly in 1778 stated that the "Articles of Agreement" had expired.

Full membership, attained by June 21, 1749, was soon reduced to fifteen. George Fairfax, John Carlyle, Francis Thornton, William Nimmo resigned, and Hugh Parker died. Later, George Mason, John Mercer, and Robert Dinwiddie, three very important members, were admitted into the partnership; Arthur Dobbs, Samuel Smith, and Capel Hanbury, English members, also joined. As of May 23, 1751, there were five English members, three Marylanders, and twelve Virginians.

Ordering of the seal, information unique to one variant of the minutes of the meetings of the Company, evidences the fact that the members of the partnership wished to form a corporation. Had they been successful in this endeavor, the Ohio Company would have been the first American incorporated land company to operate in the American Colonies. However, there is no record that the seal was ever cut, nor did the Company ever succeed in obtaining a clear title to even an acre of land granted them by order of the Crown.

That land business became the chief interest of the Company is shown in the orders and resolutions of the committee and of the membership general. Indian trade, a self-imposed stipulation in the John Hanbury petition of January 11, 1749, was incidental; merely if their petition were granted, they promised to open a fair and adequate trade with the Ohio Indians.

As early as 1750 the Company entered into an agreement with their agent, Christopher Gist, to seat fifty families, on part of their grant in what is now Fayette County, Pennsylvania. Gist did establish a settlement near Connellsville and contracted for additional families to seat the land. The rapid succession of interferences by rival land companies and French incursions soon put an end to that venture. Gist, however, retained the legal right to land in the region. In 1785 Pennsylvania honored Virginia land titles to Thomas Gist, "in the right of his father Christopher Gist." At the same time Richard and Nathaniel Gist obtained clear Pennsylvania titles to many acres in the vicinity of the former Ohio Company settlement. All their Pennsylvania patents were obtained on "Virginia Certificates."

Shortly after the settlement in Fayette County was established the Company widened its horizon by drawing up plans for a fort and a town to be situated on the Ohio at the mouth of Chartiers Creek, the town to be named Saltsburg. By this name they hoped to induce

Introduction

German Protestants to settle there. The plan for settlement is given in detail in the George Mercer papers—the size of the lots, the number of public lots, the establishment of a school for Indian children, the size and construction of the houses to be built, also the civil services required of each citizen. The Company voted a £400 budget for the project.

This venture was not even as successful as the one in Fayette County, for the French took possession of the region before the plot was even surveyed. With the exception of the Company's projected settlement (1763) on lands purchased from Maryland, not granted by the Crown, the Ohio Company never planned further settlements. In truth, it could not have done so, for the Treaty of Easton (1758) and subsequent orders from the Crown through the military prevented any private enterprise west of the Alleghenies.

As a land company the partners failed completely, but they should be considered the initiators of organized effort in colonial expansion west of the Allegheny Mountains, and they should be credited with a measure of the ultimate victory of England over France in North America.

From 1745, when George Croghan's success in Indian trade was considered by the French to be a dangerous threat to their complete control over the Hurons and the Miami Indians, the French increased the tempo of their activities in the West. They knew that English influence in the Miami Country would be a barrier athwart their communications' line between Canada and Louisiana via the Great Lakes, the Maumee, the Miami, and the Illinois rivers.

Céloron's alarming report of the rapid deterioration of French influence among the Ohio and Western Indians whom he visited in 1749 stirred the French to increase activity there. The governor of New France instituted a three-year program of fort building which, when completed, would provide an adequate barrier against English colonial expansion west of the Allegheny Mountains. Had it not been for Ohio Company influence and activity, the French "three-year plan" might have been a success. The rapid progress made by the Ohio Company injected into the French program an element of time incongruous to their blueprint. The fort which they planned to build at Logstown was the last link in a chain of forts stretching from Louisburg on the Atlantic Ocean to Quebec, to Montreal, to Presqu'isle, thence along the Allegheny, Ohio, and Mississippi rivers to Louisiana on the Gulf of Mexico. In April, 1754, when the French army under Contrecoeur came down the Allegheny to join an advance guard under La Force, already established at Logstown, they

Introduction

found the Virginians at the forks of the Ohio. Had William Trent not been at Redstone on Ohio Company business, Virginia would not have "had possession" at the forks of the Ohio when the French arrived. Contrecoeur routed the English on April 16, 1754, and on April 17 began to build Fort Duquesne almost twenty miles from his advance supply base and the intended fort site, Logstown.

England's persistence in her attempt to regain her foothold on the Ohio forced France into active warfare before she had had sufficient time to secure her lines of supply, chiefly the one leading from Canada. Therefore, unfortunate for the French, but fortunate for the English, the Frenchmen at Pittsburgh were neither able to improve and garrison adequately their rudely constructed fort nor to provide sufficient supplies for the Indians to keep them steadfast in the French interest.

The Ohio Company, immobilized by French possession of the land which it intended to settle, was dormant from 1754 to 1759. After the reoccupation of the Ohio Country by the British the Company renewed its activities, only to be stopped completely by Bouquet's Proclamation of October 30, 1761. Hoping in some way to circumvent the restrictions against white settlements west of the Alleghenies, they gave Bouquet the opportunity to buy into the Company. The Colonel refused, and by his own confession issued his famous proclamation for the express purpose of preventing the Ohio Company from exploiting their grant. When all their efforts failed in Virginia, the members sought royal approbation of their intended activities, but the King's Proclamation of 1763 stopped their pleas even before they were presented.

THE WALPOLE OR GRAND OHIO COMPANY

The period 1765 to 1770 was a time of intense activity on the part of Virginians, Pennsylvanians, and Englishmen in regard to western expansion in North America. During this time the citizens of Augusta County, Virginia, sought relief from the restrictions of western expansion imposed upon them by the King's Proclamation of 1763; the Ministry, itself, toyed with the idea of establishing self-maintained buffer states between the American Colonies and hostile Indians; Pennsylvania traders sued for reparations for losses suffered during the past conflict; veterans of the Virginia militia sought fulfillment of Governor Dinwiddie's promise made to them by proclamation on February 19, 1754; the Mississippi Company sued for an outright grant, enormous acreage along the Ohio; and a junto of influential

Introduction

Pennsylvanians and Englishmen, the Grand Ohio Company, presented the first offer ever made the Crown to buy land in America, and to establish and maintain the government of the territory under the Crown. The claim of the Ohio Company which had blazed the trail to the "Golden West" was insignificant when compared with the schemes of the Mississippi Company and the Grand Ohio Company. Also, influential John Hanbury, who had piloted the Ohio Company successfully through its first years, was dead. Perhaps George Mercer, the young and inexperienced Virginian who had decided against the Crown in the "Stamp Act Affair," was the wrong person to succeed Hanbury in the important position as agent or lobbyist for the Company in England.

From the beginning the Grand Ohio Company seemed assured of success. George Mercer realized that on May 23, 1771, according to the terms of the Ohio Company's "Articles of Agreement and Copartnership," each member of the Ohio Company would receive his quota of land owned by the group in partnership. Therefore, on May 9, 1770, without the Company's approbation of his intended action, he merged the Ohio Company's interests with those of the powerful Walpole or Grand Ohio Company which momentarily expected royal sanction of their great purchase. The Ohio Company's one thirty-sixth of the entire Walpole Grant of some two and one-half million acres would be their land to divide, May 23, 1771. In addition, George Mercer, personally, obtained Arthur Dobbs' stock in the Company. By having the transfer antedated in order to validate his right to it under the "Articles of Agreement," he became the largest stockholder in the Walpole Company.

First blocked by Lord Hillsborough, then by Edward Thurlow's antagonism, and finally by the strained relations between the mother country and her American Colonies, the Grand Ohio or Walpole Company's adventure ended in oblivion. Although usually attributed to political machinations, the failure of the Grand Ohio Company's scheme may be laid, at least in part, at Benjamin Franklin's doorstep. Franklin, commenting to Joseph Galloway, August 22, 1772, aired his dislike for Hillsborough and also intimated that life might be "more easy" for him, since Lord Dartmouth, Hillsborough's successor, "heretofore express'd some personal Regard for me." The Ministry's displeasure occasioned by Franklin's publication of the Hutchison letters caused him to be removed from his post as Deputy Postmaster General for the Colonies. As for Attorney General Edward Thurlow's disastrous delay in preparing the Grand Ohio Company's patent, Franklin, in quoting Thomas Walpole, states that Thurlow objected

Introduction

to preparing the patent because he, Franklin, was "unworthy the Favors of the Crown." In an endeavor to overcome Thurlow's antagonism and thus obtain the patent, Franklin, at Thomas Walpole's suggestion, sent his letter of resignation from the Company to Walpole, January 12, 1774. Information about Thurlow's refusal to prepare the patent is found in Franklin's memorandum written on July 14, 1778, on the letter of resignation. Evidently Walpole returned the letter to him.

In Virginia the other members of the Ohio Company refused to recognize George Mercer's act of merger with the Grand Ohio Company, and although the partners were not bound by formal articles of agreement, they pursued approval of their land grant in Virginia. In 1775, finally, 200,000 acres of land located in the present state of Kentucky were surveyed for them, but a technicality concerning licensing of the surveyor again blocked their success. After the Revolution certain Ohio Company members unsuccessfully pursued their request for recognition of their grant. On June 17, 1779, the Virginia Assembly passed a land law which vested in the state "the exclusive right of pre-emption from the Indians, of all lands within the limits of its own chartered territory." All deeds for lands within those limits which had been purchased from the Indians by the Crown were declared void; the lands, "to enure for ever, to and for the use and benefit of the Commonwealth." George Mason, who had labored unceasingly to obtain a clear title from Virginia, had lost.

George Mercer had failed in England; George Mason now had failed in Virginia.

THE DARLINGTON COLLECTION

The collection of papers in the Darlington Library which is published here comprises the bulk of the correspondence between the Ohio Company in Virginia and their respective representatives in London. Evidence within the papers reveals that only a small amount of the correspondence is missing from the collection. When George Mercer, who had been their agent in London since 1763, began to prepare the *Case of the Ohio Company* for publication, he requested the official correspondence of the Company from Charlton Palmer, their solicitor and former agent. Charlton Palmer's answer reveals that Palmer also had had in his possession the official papers which the Company had sent to their first representative in London, John Hanbury. Communications sent to Palmer and to Hanbury are in the collection. After George Mercer's death they may have been sent

Introduction

from England to his brother, James Mercer, who also held stock in the Ohio Company.

It is a matter of speculation as to their exact location from then until 1876 when they were purchased by William McCullough Darlington, of Pittsburgh, Pennsylvania. According to a letter from Morven M. Jones of Utica, New York, to Lyman C. Draper, October 9, 1884, he "disposed of those *old Gist* and other *papers* in the Spring of 1876 to a Gentleman of Pittsburgh Pa—Thro' a N. Y. old book dealer we met & had an interview in that City and he tempted me with a Sum I could not in my then condition decline—I was enable to recruit Some Six months in Europe that year." Mr. Jones further informed Mr. Draper that the gentleman was quite reticent to speak of his plans about the papers; yet Mr. Jones was of the opinion that the gentleman had procured in England some long printed sheets of part of a work, probably relating to the Ohio Company. This statement may refer to the printed *Case;* however, "No long printed sheets" were found in the collection when it was given to the University. William R. Mercer is the source for the information that Mr. William Darlington was the gentleman from Pittsburgh who purchased this collection from Morven Jones. Writing to Mr. Draper September 29, 1894, he cautioned Mr. Draper that should he (Draper) write to Mr. Darlington, not to mention William Mercer's name, for he was anxious "at some future day when he feels *disposed to gratify me* to inspect the bundle of *Mercer papers* in his possession many of which I have been informed relate more to family than business matters." Also, it is from this letter one learns that Mr. Darlington intended to write a history of the Ohio Company.

Correspondence between William R. Mercer and Mrs. Mary Darlington, widow of William Darlington, in 1905, adds another link in the provenance of these papers. Mr. Mercer informed Mrs. Darlington that he understood her late husband had purchased these papers through autograph dealer Burns of New York, and that his friend, Plumer Smith, was present during the transaction. Mr. Mercer, after reassuring Mrs. Darlington that he was not the least bit interested in correspondence pertaining to business affairs, asked if she would look among the papers and send him any family papers of his great-grandfather, John Mercer. W. R. Mercer's letter to James Garnett written the same year reveals that Mrs. Darlington did send him copies of Mercer letters, and that he cautioned Mr. Garnett, as he had cautioned Mr. Draper more than ten years before, not to mention his name to Mrs. Darlington else "My Chances of Ever procuring another line from her would be utterly Spoilt." There is in the Virginia His-

· xviii ·

Introduction

torical Society a manuscript containing extracts from some correspondence between John Mercer and his son George, the original of which is in this collection. Probably the Virginia manuscript is the one sent by Mary Darlington to William R. Mercer.

When Christopher Gist's journals were published by Mr. Darlington in 1893 he published several important Ohio Company papers, cited only as "Ohio Company papers."

When the Darlington Memorial Library was organized in 1936 the above notice in the published Gist journals and the letter from William R. Mercer to Mary Darlington of 1905 were the only clues that such a collection of papers existed. Shortly after the death in 1940 of Frank C. Osborne, attorney for the late William Darlington, Mrs. Osborne, in sorting the papers in his office safe in October, sent two bundles marked "William M. Darlington" to the Historical Society of Western Pennsylvania. Mr. Franklin F. Holbrook, director of the Society, realizing that these bundles of papers were a part of Mr. Darlington's library willed to the University of Pittsburgh, sent the papers to the Darlington Memorial Library.

As for their location after George Mercer's death in 1784 to 1876, Kate Mason Rowland in the *William and Mary Quarterly,* Vol. 1, 198-99, states that the papers owned by Mr. Morven Jones were at one time in the possession of Charles Fenton Mercer, nephew of George Mercer, son of James. Mrs. Rowland adds that Charles Fenton Mercer, a bachelor, had during the latter part of his life made his home with his niece, Judith, wife of the Reverend John Page McGuire. When Charles Mercer died in 1858 the papers were left in the possession of the McGuire family. The Reverend Mr. McGuire was headmaster of the Episcopal High School located in Alexandria, Virginia; his residence was "Howard." Mrs. Rowland also stated that when Alexandria was taken by the Union soldiers in 1861, the "Trunks of old papers which Mr. McGuire had been forced to leave in the house were soon broken open and their contents in part thrown upon the camp fires"; also, that "A shoe-box full of them was carried away by a Federal soldier and sold to a dealer in such wares, living in the Mohawk Valley, New York, who paid fifty dollars for the lot, and, through him, doubtless, they have found their way since into the collections of autograph seekers throughout the country." The list of papers sold to Mr. Morven Jones, and other papers which he had seen in the Mohawk Valley in 1880, contain few items which are in the University's collection of George Mercer papers. If Mrs. Rowland's information be accurate this collection in the Darlington Memorial Library is not part of the spoils of war taken from "How-

Introduction

ard," because Mr. Jones, himself, wrote that he sold his collection to Mr. Darlington in 1876. In addition, Mrs. McGuire states in her diary that the books which were in the attic of her home were boxed and stored in their dining room before they fled the oncoming Union soldiers in 1861. Mrs. McGuire also wrote in her diary that nothing was taken from her home or was destroyed excepting her sewing machine, which the soldiers must have considered an instrument of war. It seems that Mrs. McGuire and her friends made clothing for the army. According to Morven M. Jones' statement published in the *American Historical Record,* III, 82, he had in his possession in 1874 the bulk of the "George Mercer Papers" published in this volume.

Another unwritten story of the whereabouts of some of the papers confiscated in Alexandria may be found in a letter in the New York Historical Society. Information from material in that collection reveals that a surgeon, one Brigadier Grant, took and sent home for safekeeping a collection of historical papers found in the house of a "rebel school teacher whose father-in-law was a confederate general." As late as 1940 a descendant of Brigadier Grant presented the letter from which this information was gleaned along with several colonial manuscripts to the New York Historical Society. Since there is nothing in the Darlington Memorial Library which gives full provenance of the whereabouts of the papers prior to Mr. Darlington's purchase of them, it is not possible to make a definitive statement on the subject; only these few pertinent facts can be presented.

THE PRINTED CASE

The *Case of the Ohio Company,* printed in Part II of this book, is a reduced but complete facsimile of the original in the New York Historical Society. A full discussion of its history and provenance is printed on pages 393-398.

METHODS OF PRESENTATION HERE

Ample evidence within the collection and in collateral material used in this study made it possible to arrange the "George Mercer Papers" according to archival rules. During its existence the Company employed, consecutively, three different agents to represent it in England. George Mercer, the last agent, had Ohio Company papers given him by Charlton Palmer, who in turn had the official records given him by John Hanbury, the Company's first agent in London. Therefore, there are several communications in the papers and the

Introduction

printed *Case* which are either variants or duplicates. The "Chronology of Communications," pp. xxvii-xxxviii, is designed to bring together under date of origin the "enclosures," and these duplicates or variants of single communications.

Incidents contemporary with the date of origin of the papers are historical facts of today. Some contemporary opinions brought to light by this collection add immeasurably to the sum total of known information about accepted historical facts; whereas others expressed are very biased, most personal, and therefore, quite worthless. This combination of contemporary presentation of historical incidents and comments made thereon by irascible individuals made annotating item after item serially throughout the collection infeasible.

By an editorial device used in annotating, repetitious statements are kept at a minimum; also widely divergent contemporary opinions and interpretations of governmental orders, etc., are brought together and treated as an entity. In the papers a given item may be mentioned, alluded to, or commented upon by different persons as many as twenty times, and for as many different reasons; nevertheless it is considered only once in the annotations. For example: The Treaty of Lancaster is mentioned, alluded to, and interpreted many times; yet in each instance the superior figure which indicates an annotation is "287." Annotation number 287 is an exposition of background information, preliminary negotiations for the treaty, the treaty negotiations, and the effects of the treaty—all phases which are mentioned in the papers. This device avoiding repetition means that the superior figures are not always in sequence as they appear in the text proper.

Although each letter or document here printed is relevant to the history of the Ohio Company, there are several letters in the collection which contain much extraneous material, valuable for the social and economic history of mid-eighteenth century Virginia, or for Mercer family history. Since the premise of this work is the Ohio Company, all such extraneous material, although printed in Part I, is unnoticed in the annotations. The *Case* in facsimile is accompanied by a commentary, designed to clarify general statements, to rectify obvious errors, and to justify or to disqualify the many biased assertions which it contains.

Since the authorities for statements made in the annotations are for the most part contemporary letters and journals, the individual items cited are printed in a special section of the bibliography, "Calendar of Communications."

Introduction

ACKNOWLEDGMENTS

The editor wishes to thank the members of the New York Historical Society, who by their director, R. W. G. Vail, gave her permission to include a facsimile of *The Case of the Ohio Company* in this work.

Appreciation is here expressed for assistance in the preparation of the manuscript given by Mary May, Perra Rose, Helene K. Bole, Lillian E. Holbrook, and Laura Mulkearn Sitz; also, for the splendid co-operation of the history faculty and Lorena A. Garloch, assistant University librarian. In addition, the editor expresses deep gratitude for the valuable assistance received from the personnel of the following libraries: American Philosophical Society; Carnegie Library of Pittsburgh; College of William and Mary; Colonial Williamsburg; Detroit Public Library; Duke University; Harvard University; Henry E. Huntington Library and Art Gallery; Historical Society of Pennsylvania; Library of Congress; Massachusetts Historical Society; New York Historical Society; New York Public Library; Pennsylvania Historical and Museum Commission; Pennsylvania State Library; Philadelphia Free Library, including Ridgway Branch; Quebec Literary and Historical Society; Seminary of Quebec; Virginia Historical Society; Virginia State Library; William L. Clements Library, University of Michigan.

Greatest appreciation, however, is extended to Dr. A. L. Robinson, University librarian, to Dr. John W. Oliver, head of the history department in the University, to Agnes L. Starrett, University editor, to members of the Advisory Board, and to Dr. R. W. G. Vail, all of whom were main sources for constructive criticism, valuable suggestions, and much needed encouragement. Sincere thanks, too, go to Chancellor R. H. Fitzgerald of the University and to Dr. C. F. Lewis of The Buhl Foundation for faith in the project—to the University and to The Buhl Foundation for making possible the research and its publication.

Lois Mulkearn

University of Pittsburgh
Pittsburgh, Pennsylvania
January 21, 1952

TABLE OF CONTENTS

FOREWORD	vii
INTRODUCTION	xi
LIST OF ILLUSTRATIONS	xxv
CHRONOLOGY OF COMMUNICATIONS IN THE GEORGE MERCER PAPERS AND THE *CASE* (FACSIMILE)	xxvii

PART I GEORGE MERCER PAPERS IN THE
DARLINGTON MEMORIAL LIBRARY

Résumé of the Proceedings of the Ohio Company, October 24, 1747–May 24, 1751.	1
Christopher Gist's First and Second Journals, September 11, 1750–March 29, 1752.	7
George and James Mercer's Land Release to John Tayloe and Presley Thornton, November 25, 1759.	40
John Mercer's Letter to Charlton Palmer, July 27, 1762.	46

ENCLOSURES

1. Case of the Ohio Company, 1762. 49
2. Orders and Resolutions of the Ohio Company and the Committee of the Company, June 20, 1749–September 9, 1761. 140
3. Pennsylvania's Act for Preventing Abuses in the Indian Trade, for Supplying the Indians, Friends and Allies of Great Britain, with Goods at More Easy Rates, and for Securing and Strengthening the Peace and Friendship Lately Concluded with the Indians Inhabiting the Northern and Western Frontiers of this Province, April 8, 1758; A Supplement to the Act . . . April 17, 1759. 153

George Mercer's Field Notes for the Charlottesburg Survey, *ca*. March–May, 1763.	165
Orders and Resolutions of the Ohio Company and the Committee of the Company, October 20, 1748–July 4, 1763.	167
George Mercer's Appointment and Instructions as London Agent for the Ohio Company, July 4, 1763.	182

· xxiii ·

Table of Contents

Statement of Account of the Ohio Company with Arthur Dobbs, 1763.	183
John Mercer's Letter to Charlton Palmer, April 17, 1764.	184
George Mason's Letter to Robert Carter, January 23, 1768.	185
John Mercer's Letter to George Mercer, December 22, 1767–January 28, 1768.	186
John Mercer's Letter to George Mercer, March 3, 1768.	221

ENCLOSURES

1. Boundaries Proposed by the Ohio Company, February 26, 1768.	229
2. Case of the Ohio Company, 1754.	233
3. Resolutions of the Committee of the Ohio Company, October 17, 1760 and September 7-9, 1761.	287
4. Record of Land Grants made in Virginia, 1745-53.	289
5. Petitioners for Land on the Ohio, 1745-53.	292
6. Fragment of the Case of the Ohio Company, 1762.	295
7. Resolution of the Committee of the Ohio Company, July 4, 1763.	296
8. Fragment of John Mercer's Letter to George Mercer, January 28, 1768.	296
John Mercer's Letter to George Mercer, March 9, 1768.	297
Charlton Palmer's Letter to George Mercer, December 27, 1769.	310
Thomas Walpole's Memorandum to Osgood Hanbury, February 7, 1770.	311
Conway Richard Dobbs' Letter to George Mercer, March 26, 1770.	311
James Mercer's Letter to Several Members of the Ohio Company, January 9, 1772.	312
George Mason's Letter to James Mercer, January 13, 1772.	315
Pearson Chapman's Letter to James Mercer, January 13, 1772.	318
Thomas Ludwell Lee's Letter to James Mercer, January 13, 1772.	318
Thomas Ludwell Lee's Letter to James Mercer, January 19, 1772.	320

Table of Contents

Philip Ludwell Lee's Letter to James Mercer, January 21, 1772.	320
James Mercer's Letter to Several Members of the Ohio Company, Together with Their Replies to His Letter, *ca.* January 21, 1772.	321
James Scott to James Mercer, January 11, 1772.	321
Richard Lee to James Mercer, January 21, 1772.	323
James Mercer to Philip Ludwell Lee, January 21, 1772.	323
George Mercer's Draft on Samuel Wharton, August 5, 1772.	324
Samuel Wharton's Letter to George Mercer, August 20, 1772.	324
Statement of Account of Thomas Walpole with George Mercer, in Behalf of the Grand Ohio Company, February 26, 1776.	325
Statement of Account of Samuel Wharton with George Mercer, in Behalf of the Grand Ohio Company, July 17, 1777.	326
PART II THE CASE OF THE OHIO COMPANY	329
PART III COMMENTARY ON THE CASE OF THE OHIO COMPANY EXTRACTED FROM ORIGINAL PAPERS	393
PART IV ANNOTATIONS	461
BIBLIOGRAPHY	675
INDEX	705

LIST OF ILLUSTRATIONS

	FACING PAGE
THE SEAL OF THE OHIO COMPANY	Title Page
JOHN MERCER'S MAP OF OHIO COMPANY LANDS MADE BEFORE NOVEMBER 6, 1752	72
GEORGE WASHINGTON LETTER	84
ORDERS AND RESOLUTIONS OF THE OHIO COMPANY AND THE COMMITTEE OF THE COMPANY, OCTOBER 20, 1748–JULY 4, 1763	166
OHIO COMPANY MAP MADE BY GEORGE MERCER, 1753	226
CASE OF THE OHIO COMPANY, 1754	232

Chronology of Communications

(¶ Indicates separate documents, all other entries are analytics)

1745, April 26	Order of the Virginia Executive Council granting John Robinson and others 200,000 acres of land on the Green Briar River.	248
	Same, *Case of the Ohio Company,* facsimile. p. 1.	
	Order of the Virginia Executive Council granting John Smith and others 50,000 acres of land in that part of Orange County which will be Augusta County.	248
	Same, *Case* . . . , facsimile. p. 1.	
	Order of the Virginia Executive Council granting James Patton and others 100,000 acres of land in Augusta County.	249
	Same, *Case* . . . , facsimile. p. 1.	
	Order of the Virginia Executive Council granting Henry Downes and others 50,000 acres of land west of the Green Briar River.	249
	Same, *Case* . . . , facsimile. p. 1.	
November 4	Order of the Virginia Executive Council granting John Blair, William Russell and Company 100,000 acres of land west of the Lord Halifax line.	249
	Same, *Case* . . . , facsimile. p. 2.	
1747, April 22	Order of the Virginia Executive Council granting William McMahan and others 60,000 acres of land adjoining the grant of John Blair.	249
	Same, *Case* . . . , facsimile. p. 2.	
October 24	Résumé of the minutes of a meeting of the Ohio Company.	2
	Ohio Company's letter to John Hanbury.	2
November 6	Record of Sir William Gooch's letter to the Board of Trade requesting "Instructions as to granting Lands on the Western side of the Great Mountains."	1

· xxvii ·

George Mercer Papers

1748, January 19	Record of the Board of Trade's letter to the Duke of Newcastle referring Gooch's request of November 6, 1747, to the King in Council.	1
February 10	Record of the King in Council referring Gooch's request to the Committee of Council for Plantation Affairs.	1
June 16	Record of Gooch's letter to the Board of Trade.	1
September 2	Record of the Board of Trade's report to the Committee of Council.	1
October 20	Orders and minutes of a meeting of the Committee of the Ohio Company.	167
	Résumé of the minutes of a meeting of the Committee of the Company.	3
1749, January 11	Petition of John Hanbury to the King in Council in behalf of the Ohio Company.	246-248
	Same, *Case* . . . , facsimile. pp. 2-3.	
	Record of presentation of John Hanbury's petition to the King in Council.	1
	Record of the King referring the Hanbury petition to the Committee of Council for Plantation Affairs.	1
February 9	Record of the Committee of Council referring the Hanbury petition to the Board of Trade.	1
	Record of the Committee of Council referring the Board of Trade's report of December 13, 1748, and their "additional Instruction to S. William Gooch" back to them for further consideration.	1
23	Record of the Board of Trade's report to the Committee of Council on the Hanbury petition, January 11, 1749; also their "additional Instruction" to Gooch.	1
	Extract from the Board of Trade's report on the Hanbury petition, *Case* . . . , facsimile. pp. 3-4.	
	Orders of the Committee of the Ohio Company.	167-168
	Résumé of the minutes of a meeting of the Committee of the Company.	3

· xxviii ·

Chronology of Communications

February 24 Record of the Committee of Council's approbation of the Board of Trade's report and the "additional Instruction" to Gooch, February 23.   2

March 4 Record of the Board of Trade's "Letter to S. William Gooch with the Additional Instruction."   2

16 Record of the King in Council ordering the draught of the additional instruction to Gooch prepared for his signature.   2

June 20 The Ohio Company's letter to
John Hanbury.   140-141
Same.   168-169

21 Orders and minutes of a meeting of the Ohio
Company.   141-142
Same.   168-170
Résumé of the minutes of a meeting of the Company.   3-4

July 12 Order of the Virginia Executive Council granting Bernard Moore and others 100,000 acres of land on the Mississippi River.   250
Same, *Case* . . . , facsimile. p. 4.
Order of the Virginia Executive Council granting John Lewis and others 800,000 acres of land in one or more surveys west and north of the Virginia-Carolina boundary.   250
Same, *Case* . . . , facsimile. p. 4.
Order of the Virginia Executive Council granting Peyton Randolph and others 400,000 acres of land in one or more surveys on the New or Woods River.   250
Same, *Case* . . . , facsimile. p. 4.
Order of the Virginia Executive Council granting William Winston and others 50,000 acres of land on the western side of the Ohio and eastern side of the Mississippi River.   250-251
Same, *Case* . . . , facsimile. p. 4.
Order of the Virginia Executive Council granting a renewment of their grant to John Tayloe and others for 100,000 acres of land in Augusta County on the three

· xxix ·

George Mercer Papers

July 12	branches of the Mississippi River, one known as Woods River and the other two to the westward thereof.	251
	Same, *Case* . . . , facsimile. p. 4.	
September 25	Minutes of a meeting of the Ohio Company.	170-171
	Résumé of the minutes of a meeting of the Company.	4
1750, January 29	Orders and resolutions of the Committee of the Company.	171
	Résumé of the minutes of a meeting of the Committee of the Company.	5
March 27	Résumé of the minutes of a meeting of the Company.	5
29	Orders of the Committee of the Company.	142
	Résumé of the minutes of a meeting of the Committee of the Company.	5
September 11	Order and resolution of the Committee of the Company.	171-173
	Résumé of the minutes of a meeting of the Committee of the Company.	5
	Instructions given Christopher Gist by the Committee of the Company.	7-8
	Same.	97-98
	Same.	172
	Same, *Case* . . . , facsimile. p. 5.	
	Agreement made with Christopher Gist by the Committee of the Company for the greater encouragement of the first settlers upon the Company's lands.	172-173
December 3	Orders and resolutions of the Committee of the Company.	173
	Résumé of the minutes of a meeting of the Committee of the Company.	5-6
1751, *ca.* February 1	Account of the festival at Lower Shawnee Town.	121-122
	Same.	304-305
	Same, *Case* . . . , facsimile. App. p. 12.	
22	Unauthorized treaty between the Wawiagtas and Piankashaws and Pennsylvania by George Croghan and Andrew Montour.	138-139
	Same, *Case* . . . , facsimile. App. p. 23.	

Chronology of Communications

May 19   Christopher Gist's first journal, September 11,
      1750–May 19, 1751.   8-31
   Same, *Case* . . . , facsimile. App. pp. 1-12.
   Christopher Gist's first journal, October 31,
      1750–May 19, 1751.   98-121

   Extracts from Christopher Gist's first journal,
      November 25, 1750–May 19, 1751.   252-266

  22   Resolutions of the Ohio Company.   142-143

¶   24   Résumé of the Proceedings of the Ohio
     Company, October 24, 1747–May 24, 1751.   1-7

  24   Résumé of the minutes of a meeting of the
     Company, May 21-24, 1751.   6-7
     Resolutions and minutes of a meeting of the
     Company, May 21-24, 1751.   173-175

July 15   Record of a meeting of the Committee of the
     Company.   175

  16   Instructions given to Christopher Gist by the
     Committee of the Company.   31-32
     Same.   175
     Same.   252
     Same, *Case* . . . , facsimile. p. 5.

October 26   Order of the Virginia Executive Council
     granting renewments of land grants to
     John Blair and others and to William
     McMahan and others.   51
     Same.   251
     Same, *Case* . . . , facsimile. p. 6.

1752, March 29   Christopher Gist's second journal, July 16,
     1751–March 29, 1752.   32-40
     Christopher Gist's second journal, November 4, 1751–March 29, 1752, *Case* . . . ,
     facsimile. App. pp. 13-16.
     Same, extracts, November 4, 1751–
     February 21, 1752.   122-127
     Same, extracts, November 4, 1751–March 12,
     1752.   266-269

¶   29   Christopher Gist's first and second journals,
     September 11, 1750–March 29, 1752.   7-40

April 28   Instructions given Christopher Gist by the
     Ohio Company.   52-54
     Same.   176
     Same.   269-271

George Mercer Papers

April 28	Same, *Case* . . . , facsimile. pp. 6-7.	
	An instruction about cutting a road to the Monongahela given Christopher Gist by the Company.	147
	Additional instructions on a separate piece of paper given Christopher Gist by the Company.	176-177
June 13	Minutes of Virginia's conference with the Indians at Logstown, June 1-13, 1752.	127-138
	Same.	273-284
	Extracts from the minutes of Virginia's conference with the Indians at Logstown, June 1-13, 1752.	54-66
	Same, *Case* . . . , facsimile. App. pp. 17-22.	
	Indian Deed confirming the release of lands by the Six Nations to Virginia at Lancaster in 1744, *Case* . . . , facsimile. App. pp. 21-22.	
September 19	Order of the Committee of the Ohio Company.	175-176
October 6	Extract from the *Virginia Gazette* containing intelligence of an attack on the Twightwee by the French.	68
	Same, *Case* . . . , facsimile. p. 8.	
November 6	Petition of John Mercer and 13 partners to the Virginia Executive Council for 140,000 acres of land on the Ohio.	240
	Petition of the Ohio Company to the President and the rest of the Virginia Executive Council for permission to survey their land in several tracts.	66-68
	Same.	271-273
	Same, *Case* . . . , facsimile. pp. 7-8.	
22	Resolutions of the Ohio Company.	143-144
23	Resolutions and minutes of the Company, November 22-23.	176
1753, February 6	Minutes of a meeting of the Committee of the Company which includes their answer to John Pagan, regarding the encouragement the Company might give to German Protestants who may settle upon their lands.	144-147
	Same.	176

Chronology of Communications

April 10   Extract of William Trent's letter to Governor Hamilton of Pennsylvania, as printed under date line May 3 in the *Pennsylvania Gazette,* August 15.   71
         Same.   242-243
         Same, *Case* . . . , facsimile. p. 9.

May 22   Message from the Governor of Pennsylvania to the Pennsylvania Assembly, printed in the *Virginia Gazette,* August 16, 1753, *Case* . . . , facsimile. p. 12.

    26   William Fairfax's letter to William Trent.   78-79
         Same, *Case* . . . , facsimile. p. 10.
    31   Robert Dinwiddie's letter to William Trent.   73-74
         Same.   284-285
         Same, *Case* . . . , facsimile. pp. 10-11.

June 9   William Fairfax's letter to William Trent.   79-80
         Same, *Case* . . . , facsimile. p. 11.

¶   15   Record of land grants made in Virginia, 1745-1753.   289-291

¶   Petitioners for land on the Ohio, 1745-1753.   292-294
         Orders of the Virginia Executive Council granting Richard Corbin and others 190,000 acres of land.   251

July 10   Robert Dinwiddie's Speech to the Half King.   286
         Same, *Case* . . . , facsimile. pp. 11-12.

    25   Resolution of the Committee of the Ohio Company.   147-149

    27   Resolutions, orders and minutes of a meeting of the Committee of the Company, July 25-27, 1753.   178-179
         Instructions given to Christopher Gist by the Committee of the Company.   149-150
         Same.   179

ca. August 20   Speech of the Half King to the French Commandant at Fort Le Boeuf, as repeated by the Half King to George Washington, November 25, 1753, *Case* . . . , facsimile. p. 23.

September 1   William Fairfax's letter to William Trent.   80
         Same, *Case* . . . , facsimile. p. 12.

    26   Nathan Walthoe's letter to William Trent.   81
         Same, *Case* . . . , facsimile. p. 13.

George Mercer Papers

October 31	Robert Dinwiddie's letter to the Commandant of the French forces on the Ohio. Same, *Case* . . . , facsimile. pp. 13-14.		74-75
November 1	Robert Dinwiddie's address to the Virginia Assembly, *Case* . . . , facsimile. p. 13.		
2	Orders of the Committee of the Company. Same.		150 179
December 15	French Commandant, Le Gardeur de St. Pierre de Repentigny's, answer to Robert Dinwiddie, English translation. Same, *Case* . . . , facsimile, p. 14.		75-76

¶ 1754   Case of the Ohio Company, to be sent to John Hanbury.   233-296

January 27	Captain William Trent's commission from Robert Dinwiddie. Same, *Case* . . . , facsimile. pp. 14-15.	82-83
27	Robert Dinwiddie's letter to William Trent. Same, *Case* . . . , facsimile. p. 15.	81-82
February 14	Extract of Robert Dinwiddie's speech to the Virginia Assembly, *Case*..., facsimile. p. 16.	
19	A Proclamation for Encouraging men to Enlist in his Majesty's Service for the Defence and Security of This Colony, by Robert Dinwiddie. Same, *Case* . . . , facsimile. p. 17.	77
	Extract of William Trent's letter (February 19, 1754) to George Washington, copied from the *Virginia Gazette,* March 29, 1754. Same, *Case* . . . , facsimile. p. 16.	84
23	Extract of Christopher Gist's letter to George Washington, copied from the *Virginia Gazette* of March 29, 1754, *Case* . . . , facsimile. p. 16.	
March 5	Extract from an Address of the Maryland House of Delegates to Governor Horatio Sharpe.	83-84
April 16	Claude Pierre Pécaudy sieur de Contrecoeur's summons to the Commander of the King of Great Britain's Troops at the Mouth of the River Monongahela. Same, *Case* . . . , facsimile. pp. 18-19.	86-87

Chronology of Communications

April 18
[i.e. ca.
April 16] George Washington's letter to
 Thomas Cresap. 85
 Same, *Case* ... , facsimile. pp. 17-18.

 18 A Speech from the Half King to the Governors of Virginia and Pennsylvania. 88
 Same, *Case* ... , facsimile. p. 19.

May 9 Extract from the *Virginia Gazette,* reporting
 fall of fort on the Ohio. 85-86
 Same, *Case* ... , facsimile. p. 18.

 16 Advertisement from the *Virginia Gazette*
 announcing the method of taking up lands
 in the Colony. 89-90
 Same, *Case* ... , facsimile. pp. 19-20.

June 14 Original French and English translation of
 Ononraguite's, chief of St. Louis, letter to
 Myndert Schuyler. 243-244
 English translation only. 70
 Same, *Case* ... , facsimile. p. 9.

August 30 Extract from the *Pennsylvania Gazette,* as
 reprinted in the *Virginia Gazette*. 70
 Same. 243
 Same, *Case* ... , facsimile. p. 9.

1755 *Analysis of a General Map of the Middle
 British Colonies in America* ... , extracts,
 Case ... , facsimile. App. pp. 25-26.

1757, December 22 Orders and resolutions of the Committee of
 the Company, December 20-22, 1757. 179

¶ 1758, April 8 Pennsylvania's Act for Preventing Abuses in
 the Indian Trade, for Supplying the Indians, Friends and Allies of Great Britain,
 with Goods at More Easy Rates, and for
 Securing and Strengthening the Peace
 Lately Concluded with the Indians Inhabiting the Northern and Western
 Frontiers of this Province, April 8, 1758. 153-156

1759, April 17 A Supplement to Pennsylvania's Act ... of
 April 8, 1758. 156-165

 July 7 Resolution of the Committee of the Company, July 6-7, 1759. 179

George Mercer Papers

	ca. September	John Mercer's letter to Francis Fauquier. Same, *Case* . . . , facsimile. pp. 21-22.	93-95
¶	November 25	George and James Mercer's land release to John Tayloe and Presley Thornton.	40-45
	1760, October 17	Resolutions and order of the Committee of the Company.	150-151
		Same.	179-180
		Same.	287
	1761, September 7	Resolutions of the Committee of the Ohio Company.	151
		Same.	180
		Same.	287-288
¶	9	Orders and resolutions of the Ohio Company and the Committee of the Company, June 20, 1749–Sept. 9, 1761.	140-153
		"Petition of the Committee of the Ohio Company, in your Majesty's colony and dominion, in behalf of themselves, and the rest of their partners," *Case* . . . , facsimile. pp. 25-26.	
		Resolutions of the Committee of the Company, September 7-9, 1761.	287-288
¶		Resolutions of the Committee of the Company, October 17, 1760 and September 7-9, 1761.	287-288
		Committee of the Company's letter to Robert Dinwiddie.	151-152
		Same.	180
		Same, *Case* . . . , facsimile. p. 26.	
	10	Committee of the Company's letter to Capel and Osgood Hanbury.	152-153
		Same.	181
		Same, *Case* . . . , facsimile. p. 26.	
	October 30	"Proclamation of Henry Bouquet Esq, colonel of foot, and commanding at Fort Pitt and dependencies," *Case* . . . , facsimile. p. 29.	
¶	1762, ca. July	Fragment of the Case of the Ohio Company.	49-139
¶		Same, one-half manuscript page.	295-296
¶	27	John Mercer's letter to Charlton Palmer.	46-48
¶	1763	Statement of Account of the Ohio Company with Arthur Dobbs.	183

Chronology of Communications

	March 2	Resolution of the Committee of the Company.	181-182
¶	ca. April or May	George Mercer's field notes of the Charlottesburg survey.	165-166
¶	July 4	Orders and resolutions of the Ohio Company and the Committee of the Company, October 20, 1748–July 4, 1763.	167-182
¶		George Mercer's appointment and instructions as London Agent for the Company.	182-183
		Resolution of the Committee of the Company.	296
		"Petition of the Committee of the Ohio Company to the King's most excellent Majesty," *Case* . . . , facsimile. pp. 30-31.	
		Resolution of the Ohio Company.	182
		Resolution of the Committee of the Company.	296
¶	1764, April 17	John Mercer's letter to Charlton Palmer.	184-185
	1765, June 21	"Memorial of George Mercer on behalf of the Ohio Company in Virginia, to the King's most excellent Majesty in Council," *Case* . . . , facsimile. pp. 32-33.	
	1767, June 26	"Report of the Board of Trade to the Committee of Council for Plantation affairs," *Case* . . . , facsimile. pp. 33-34.	
	October 15	"Memorial of George Mercer on behalf of the Ohio Company in Virginia, &c., to the King's most excellent Majesty in Council," *Case* . . . , facsimile. pp. 34-35.	
	ca. November	Joseph Barker's letter to John Mercer.	199-200
	1768, January	John Tayloe's letter to John Mercer.	211
¶	23	George Mason's letter to Robert Carter.	185-186
¶	28	John Mercer's letter to George Mercer, December 22, 1767–January 28, 1768.	186-220
¶		Same, fragment.	296
	February 26	George Mason's letter to John Mercer.	231-232
¶		Boundaries proposed by the Ohio Company, when their grant is renewed.	229-232
¶	March 3	John Mercer's letter to George Mercer.	221-229
¶	9	John Mercer's letter to George Mercer.	297-310

· xxxvii ·

George Mercer Papers

	1769, December 18	"The Memorial of George Mercer, on behalf of the Ohio Company, to the Right Honourable the Lords Commissioners for Trade and Plantations," *Case* . . . , facsimile. pp. 35-36.	
¶	27	Charlton Palmer's letter to George Mercer.	310
¶	1770, February 7	Thomas Walpole's note to Osgood Hanbury.	311
¶	March 26	Conway Richard Dobbs' letter to George Mercer.	311-312
¶	1772, January 9	James Mercer's letter to several members of the Ohio Company.	312-315
	11	James Scott's letter to James Mercer.	321-322
¶	13	Thomas Ludwell Lee's letter to James Mercer.	318-319
		Same.	322
¶		George Mason's letter to James Mercer.	315-318
		Same.	321
¶		Pearson Chapman's letter to James Mercer.	318
		Same.	322
¶	19	Thomas Ludwell Lee's letter to James Mercer.	320
		Same.	322
	21	Richard Lee's letter to James Mercer.	323
		James Mercer's letter to Philip Ludwell Lee.	323
¶		Philip Ludwell Lee's letter to James Mercer.	320
		Same.	324
¶	after January 21	Composite—James Mercer's letter to several members of the Ohio Company, and their replies.	321-324
¶	August 5	George Mercer's draft on Samuel Wharton.	324
¶	20	Samuel Wharton's letter to George Mercer.	324-325
¶	1776, February 26	Statement of account of Thomas Walpole with George Mercer, in behalf of the Grand Ohio Company.	325
¶	1777, July 17	Statement of account of Samuel Wharton with George Mercer, in behalf of the Grand Ohio Company.	326

PART I

PART I

GEORGE MERCER PAPERS
IN THE
DARLINGTON MEMORIAL LIBRARY
UNIVERSITY OF PITTSBURGH

Résumé of the Proceedings of the Ohio Company
October 24, 1747—May 24, 1751[1]

Sr William Gooch wrote[2] to the Board of Trade for his Majesty's Instructions as to granting Lands on the Western side of the Great Mountains.   1747, Novr 6

Monson, R. Plumer, B. Leveson Gower & Dupplin inclose an Extract of it to the D. Newcastle[3] and desired him to lay it before his Majesty.   1747/8 Jan.[y] 19

Upon which the same was by the King in Council referred[4] to the Lords of the Committee of Council for Plantation Affairs.   1747/48 Feb. 10

J. Pitt, J. Grenville & Dupplin report,[5] and mention another Letter[6] which they received from S.[r] William Gooch dated June 16, 1748 in which he mentions a Petition by some Persons in partnership for 200,000 Acres, which they expected to seat with Strangers, and to build a Fort, without which or some such work for their defence it would be dangerous for them to venture out so far.   1748, Sept 2.

The Petition[7] of John Hanbury in behalf of himself and thirteen others names and their Associates by the name of the Ohio Company was presented to the King in Council and by him referred[8] to the Committee of Council for Plantation Affairs.   Jan.[y] 11. [1749]

The Lords of the Committee of Council referred[9] the said Petition to the Lords Commissioners for Trade & Plantations, together with their Report[10] dated December 13 last, and an additional Instruction to S.[r] William Gooch for their further Consideration.   Feb. 9

Dunk Hallifax, J. Pitt, Dupplin, T. Robinson & Fran. Fane report,[11] and purpose or further Encouragement to the Company, and annex an additional Instruction to the Lieutenant Governor.   23.

· 1 ·

George Mercer Papers

	24.	The Lords of the Committee of Council report[12] their Approbation thereof to his Majesty.
Mar. 16.		The King in Council ordered[13] that the D. Bedford should cause the said draught of the additional Instruction to be prepared for his Majesty's Signature Copy of the said Instruction.
	4.	Copy of Dunk Hallifax, J. Pitt, J. Grenville, Fran. Fane & Dupplin's Letter[14] to Sr William Gooch with the Additional Instruction.

Such were the Proceedings in England[15]—The following passed here.

1747, Oct. 24.[16] Sir

In order to carry on our design of taking up a large tract of 500,000 Acres of Land on the branches of Allagany and settling a Trade with the several nations of Indians according to our Agreement in Company. We desire you to offer John Hanbury Esqr Merchant in London to be a Partner with us and to engage him to sollicit our Petition to his Majesty, and the charge that Mr Hanbury is at we promise to pay according to our proportions in the Company's Stock. We are
To the Honble Thomas Lee Esqr

                  Your humble Servants
                  Thomas Cresap
                  Agustine Washington
                  George Fairfax
                  Lawrence Washington
                  Francis Thornton
                  Nathaniel Chapman

It was proposed that there should be twenty Partners Mr Hanbury preferred the Petition in the names of

John Hanbury of London Mercht in behalf of himself and of
Thomas Lee Esqr a Member of your Majesty's Council and one of the Judges of the Genl Court in Virginia.
Thomas Nelson Esqr also a Member of your Majesty's Council.
Colo Cressup .... instead of Thomas Cresap of Maryland
Colo William Thornton .... Francis Thornton[17]
William Nimmo
Daniel Cressup .... Daniel Cresap of Maryland[18]
John Carlisle
Lawrence Washington
Agustine Washington
George Fairfax
Jacob Giles .... of Maryland
Nathaniel Chapman &

In the Darlington Memorial Library

James Woodrop Esq[rs] all of Virginia... James Wardrop of Maryland & others their Associates.

1748 Oct. 20. Lawrence Washington, James Wardrop, James Scott Clk, and John Carlyle being appointed a Committee with very full Powers met and Colo Cresap having applied to the Governor for a Grant to no purpose[19] they agreed that sending for a Cargo should be posponed till a Grant could be obtained here or in England and upon notice of such Grant each Member should advance £100 Sterling to be remitted to Mr Hanbury. And it was recommended to the Company to give Mr Wardrop necessary instructions to send to Mr Sledmant[20] Mercht in Rotterdam to procure foreign Protestants to settle the Lands.

[1749] Feb. 23. L. Washington, Scott, Chapman & Carlyle, met and ordered the £100 Sterl. to be paid by the 15th of April to said Chapman[21] to be delivered to Thomas Lee Esqr and by him remitted[22] to Mr Hanbury with an Invoice for a Cargo,[23] as the former order to postpone it till a Grant was obtained might be construed as a delay on the Company's side.

But this Call being made and a general meeting of the Company appointed to be at Stafford Courthouse.

1749. June 21. Thomas Lee Esqr Thomas Cresap, Lawrence Washington, Agustine Washington, Jacob Giles and Nathaniel Chapman six of those named in the Petition and John Tayloe Esqr Presley Thornton Esqr James Scott Clk. Richard Lee, Philip Ludwell Lee, Gawin Corbin & Hugh Parker, seven others of the Company met and proceeded to Business, when Letters from George Fairfax John Carlyle & Francis Thornton desiring to resign were received and agreed to. Colo Thomas Lee then acquainted the Company that Mr Secretary Nelson[24] desired him to inform the Company that he desired to be excused and that he did not intend to be one of the Company, and Mr William Nimmo had told him that he never intended to be one, or any further concerned than lending his name to Majr Washington[25] to be used in the Petition which was enter'd, and the Company being thus reduced to fifteen, the thirteen present Mr Hanbury in England and Mr Wardrop absent agreed to receive Mr George Mason then present as a Partner upon paying his Share and then they unanimously agreed to make up the four deficient Shares till four other Partners should desire to be admitted, and in Consequence advanced £125 Sterl. each which was remitted[26] to Mr Hanbury for a Cargo.

They then advised Mr Hanbury of the Proceedings of the meeting and desired him to offer the D of Bedford a Share, if he chose to be concerned upon the terms of our Association, as Mr Hanbury had wrote us that we were obliged to his Grace for his Assistance in obtaining his Majesty's Instruction and his declaration of the advantage he conceived it would be of to Great Britain and this Colony, for that not withstanding we expected a great deal of interested opposition and should think ourselves happy in having such a patron at the head of the Company. They however wrote M̄r Hanbury that they hoped he could procure[27] proper directions to the Government here to afford us all the Encouragement they could in our Settlement by making such reasonable presents to the Indians as had been by the policy[28] of the Government all along allowed upon extending. the Frontiers Westward of all the Northen Colonies, which not withstanding their Grant of those Lands to the King they always expected when those Lands come to be settled.

They then agreed with H. Parker for the Carriage of all their Goods from the falls of Potomack to their general factory on the River Ohio and for all the back Carriage from thence at 12/. for every hundred weight, and employed Parker as their factor on such terms as the Company and he should agree upon, but he and Colo Cresap were at the Company's charge immediately to employ such persons as they thought fit to clear all such Roads[29] between those places as should be most for the Company's Advantage.

They desired[30] the Ohio Indians might be invited to a Treaty and an Interpreter[31] might be employed by Virginia and M̄r Parker their Factor be put in the commission of the Peace for Augusta County,[32] and that he should use all lawful Endeavours to prevent the Northern Indian Traders from passing through Virginia with their Skins without a Licence as the Colledge of William & Mary were thereby defrauded of the duty[33] to a very great amount, they added Colo Philip Lee, and M̄r Mason to the Committee.

Sept. 25.   Thomas Lee, Tayloe, Thornton, Corbin, R. Lee, Scott met as the company within the Terms of our Agreement.

George Mason at Chapman's request appointed Treasurer in his room, They chearfully accept Arthur Dobb's Esq̄r and M̄r Samuel Smith Mercht as two of the company on M̄r Hanbury's recommendation and impower M̄r Hanbury to agree with German or other Protestants to seat their Lands, to get an Explination about the Fort, which was misapprehended, as to presents to the Indians and that the Line between Virginia and Pennsylvania should be run[34] on the same terms as that between Virginia and Carolina[35] being under the same Circumstances.

That Colo Cresap or M̄r Parker may discover[36] the parts beyond the Mountains that the Company may know where to Survey their Lands to prevent any complaint that they prevented others.

In the Darlington Memorial Library

J. Scott, Mason, Wardrop. Committee.   1750. Jany 29
Approve of Cresap and Parker's Purchase[37] on the North Branch of Potomack opposite to Will's Creek as it is the most convenient place to begin their Trade at, and recommend taking up and purchasing adjoining Lands that may be convenient. Order each Member to pay the Treasurer £30 Curt before the tenth of March next.[38]

T. Lee, Tayloe, A. Washington, R. Lee, Corbin, Thornton, L.   Mar. 27.[39]
Washington, Scott, Mason, Giles. Compa:
Capel Hanbury and Robert Dinwiddie Esqr admitted Partners on paying their respective Shares, and that George Mason at the company's risque draw on John Hanbury for the five English Members Quotas' His own, Dobbs, Smith, C. Hanbury, and Dinwiddies. Approve last Committees Proceedings.

L. Washington, Parker, Chapman, Scott, Giles, A. Washington,   29.
Mason. Committee.
Parker to agree with Cresap for board of himself and two Servants and to build a Storehouse[182] on his Plantation for the Company till buildings at the Mouth of Will's Creek can be conveniently erected.

T. Lee. R. Lee and Corbin now absent having agreed to send Christopher Gist to the Ohio with a Cargo,[40] it is agreed to and Parker is to furnish him with a proper Cargo and twelve Men Horses and Provisions at the Company's Expence.[41]

Chapman, Scott, Mason, R. Lee Committee   Sept. 11.
Gist to have £150 for searching and discovering the Lands on the Ohio and adjoining branches of the Mississippi as low as the great Falls,[42] and if his Services merit more, he shall be handsomely rewarded. Mason to advance him £30. and Parker to supply him with Arms, Ammunition and all other necessaries.

And as he engaged to Settle 150 or more Families on the Company's Lands contiguous one to the other, within two years from this day they agreed to allow each Family 100 Acres for every person not exceeding four in Family, and 50 Acres for every one exceeding four.[43]

L. Washington, Scott, Mason, Parker. Committee   Dec. 3.
Each Member to pass George Mason £30 Sterl.[44] to remit for a supply of Goods. George Mason to Correspond with J. Hanbury in all matters relating to the Company and apply to the Exr of Thomas Lee Esqr deced for all the Company's papers in his hands.

That it is absolutely necessary to have proper Articles[45] to bind the Company that Mason write to Hanbury on that head, and that he, Scott & Chapman or any two of them, apply to John Mercer to consider and draw such Articles and desire him to attend the next general meeting of the Company at Stafford Courthouse the third Tuesday in May next.

George Mercer Papers

A Seal[46] sent for by the Company to M.r Hanbury.
A large Steel one—the devise proposed. Three Deer passant and regardant in a proper field—The crest—A Beaver—The Supporters—two Indians—one with a Bow & Arrows—the other with a Riffle gun—the Motto underneath—Pax et Commercium.

This is only a Proposal, if not agreeable to the Rules of Heraldry, the Members of the Company in England are desired to make such Alterations as they think proper.

1751, May 21. to 24.   Thornton, R. Lee, A. Washington, L. Washington, Chapman, Giles, Scott, Cresap, Mason. Comp.a Mercer added.

John Mercer admitted as a Partner on advancing his twentieth part of the whole Expence and he having prepared Articles for the Company, they were considered and approved of, and Thornton, R. Lee, A. Washington, L. Washington, Chapman, Scott, Mason, Giles, Cresap & Mercer executed the same and ordered a Counter part should be sent to M.r Hanbury to be executed by him & the Members he recommended, and he was desired to have a sufficient number printed[47] that every Partner might have a Counterpart of them duly executed and those in Virginia and Maryland who had not signed were to be applied to, for that purpose.[48]

Then George Mason was appointed Treasurer with all the Powers in those Articles.[49] And L. Washington, Chapman, Scott, Mason, & Mercer were appointed a Comittee untill the next general meeting.

That M.r Hanbury should be desired to apply to the E. Grenville[50] for a Grant of 50,000 or more Acres of Land on or near the Line dividing Virginia & Carolina, to Lord Baltimore[51] for 10,000 or more Acres in different Tracts near the back Line between Pennsylvania & Maryland, and to M.r Penn[52] for 10,000 or more Acres on or near Rays Town[53] on the Juniatta or its branches 15 or 20,000 Acres on Loweathanning & Kiskomineto Creek[54] or as much of them as may be in Pennsylvania. 5000 Acres on Chomohonan[55] and 4000 Acres at the three forks of Youghyageni,[56] which if to be got upon reasonable terms they think it necessary for Security of their Settlements and extending their Trade with the Indians. To acquaint him that the mention of the Fort & Garrison if to be construed as some people now talked would wholly destroy our Undertaking, and must have proceeded from his or S.r William Gooch's misapprehension of the Company's Proposals, and ought to be clearly explained & settled, or we must give it up.[57]

It seems to have been M.r Hanbury's misapprehension or owing to want of due consideration of the words Fort & Garrison which were too vague & interminate. S.r William Gooch's Letter as mentioned in

In the Darlington Memorial Library

the Report of the Lords of Trade of Sept. 2. 1748[5] very properly expressed it, they proposed to built a Fort without which or some such work for their defence, it would be dangerous for them to venture out so far.

Here I am obliged to stop for want of time. If another opportunity offers I will supply the remainder.

Christopher Gist's First and Second Journals
September 11, 1750—March 29, 1752[58]
For
The Honble Robert Dinwiddie Esquire
Governor & Commander
of
Virginia

INSTRUCTIONS given Mr Christopher Gist by the Comittee of the Ohio Company the 11th Day of September 1750.[59]

You are to go out as soon as possible to the Westward of the great Mountains, and carry with you such a Number of Men, as You think necessary, in Order to search out and discover the Lands upon the River Ohio, & other adjoining Branches of the Mississippi down as low as the great Falls[42] thereof: You are particularly to observe the Ways & Passes thro all the Mountains you cross, & take an exact Account of the Soil, Quality, & Product of the Land, and the Wideness & Deepness of the Rivers, & the several Falls belonging to them, together with the Courses & Bearings of the Rivers & Mountains as near as you conveniently can: You are also to observe what Nations of Indians inhabit there, their Strength & Numbers, who they trade with, & in what Com'odities they deal.

When you find a large Quantity of good level Land, such as you think will suit the Company, You are to measure the Breadth of it, in three or four different Places, & take the Courses of the River and Mountains on which it binds in order to judge the Quantity: You are to fix the Beginning & Bounds in such a Manner that they may be easily found again by your Description; the nearer in the Land lies, the better, provided it be good & level, but we had rather go quite down the Mississippi than take mean broken Land. After finding a large Body of good level Land, you are not to stop, but proceed farther, as low as the Falls of the Ohio,[42] that We may be informed of that Navigation; And You are to take an exact Account of all the larger Bodies of good level Land, in the same Manner as above directed, that the Company may the better judge where it will be most convenient for them to take their Land.

You are to note all the Bodies of good Land as you go along, tho there is not a sufficient Quantity for the Company's Grant, but You need not be so particular in the Mensuration of that, as in the larger Bodies of Land.

You are to draw as good a Plan[60] as you can of the Country You pass thro: You are to take an exact and particular Journal of all your Proceedings, and make a true Report thereof to the Ohio Company.

1750. In Complyance with my Instructions from the Committee of the Ohio Company bearing Date the 11th Day of September. 1750

Wednesday Octr 31 Set out from Colo Thomas Cresap's[61] at the old Town[62] on Potomack River in Maryland, and went along an old Indian Path[63] N 30 E about 11 Miles.

Thursday Novr 1 Then N 1 Mile N 30 E 3 M here I was taken sick and stayed all Night.

Friday 2 N 30 E 6 M, here I was so bad that I was not able to proceed any farther that Night, but grew better in the Morning.

Saturday 3 N 8 M to Juniatta,[64] a large Branch of Susquehannah, where I stayed all Night.

Sunday 4 Crossed Juniatta and went up it S 55 W about 16 M.

Monday 5 Continued the same Course[65] S 55 W 6 M to the Top of a large Mountain called the Allegany Mountain, here our Path turned, & we went N 45 W 6 M here we encamped.[66]

Tuesday 6 Wednesday 7 and Thursday 8 Had Snow and such bad Weather that We could not travel for three Days; but I killed a young Bear so that we had Provision enough.

Friday 9 Set out N 70 W about 8 M here I crossed a Creek of Susquehannah[67] and it raining hard, I went into an old Indian Cabbin[68] where I stay'd all Night.

Saturday 10 Rain and Snow all Day but cleared away in the Evening

Sunday 11 Set out late in the Morning N 70 W 6 M crossing two Forks[69] of a Creek of Susquehannah, here the Way being bad, We encamped and I killed a Turkey.

In the Darlington Memorial Library

Monday 12   Set out N 45 W 8 M crossed a great Laurel Mountain.[70]

Tuesday 13   Rain and Snow.

Wednesday 14   Set out N 45 W 6 M to Loylhannan[71] an old Indian Town on a Creek of Ohio called Kiscominatis, then N 1 M NW 1 M to an Indian's Camp on the said Creek.

Thursday 15   The Weather being bad and I unwell I stayed here all Day: The Indian to whom this Camp belonged spoke good English and directed Me the Way to his Town, which is called Shannopini Town:[72] He said it was about 60 M and a pretty good Way.

Friday 16   Set out S 70 W 10 M.[73]

Saturday 17   The same Course (S 70 W) 15 M to an old Indian's Camp[74]

Sunday 18   I was very sick, and sweated myself according to the Indian Custom in a Sweat House, which gave Me Ease, and my Fever abated.

Monday 19   Set out early in the Morning the same Course (S 70 W) travelled very hard about 20 M to a small Indian Town of the Delawares called Shannopin on the SE Side of the River Ohio,[75] where We rested and got Corn for our Horses.

Tuesday 20 Wednesday 21 Thursday 22 and Friday 23   I was unwell and stayed in this Town to recover myself; While I was here I took an Opportunity to set my Compass privately, & took the Distance across the River, for I understood it was dangerous to let a Compass be seen among these Indians; The River Ohio is 76 Poles wide at Shannopin Town: There are about Twenty Families in this Town: The Land in general from Potomack to this Place is mean stony and broken, here and there good Spots upon the Creeks and Branches but no Body of it.

Saturday 24   Set out from Shannopin's Town, and swam[76] our Horses across the River Ohio, & went down the River S 75 W 4 M, N 75 W 7 M W 2 M, all the Land from Shannopin's Town is good along the River, but the Bottoms not broad; At a Distance from the River good Land for Farming, covered with small white and red Oaks and tolerable level; fine Runs for Mills &c.

Sunday Novr 25   Down the River W 3 M, NW 5 M to the Logg's Town;[77] the Lands these last 8 M very rich the Bottoms above a Mile wide, but on the SE Side, scarce a Mile wide, the Hills high and steep. In the Loggs Town, I found scarce any Body but a Parcel of reprobate Indian Traders, the Cheifs of the Indians being out a hunting: here I was informed that George Croghan[78] & Andrew Montour[79] who were sent upon an Embassy[80] from Pensylvania to the Indians, were passed about a Week before me. The People in this Town began to enquire

· 9 ·

George Mercer Papers

my Business, and because I did not readily inform them, they began to suspect me, and said, I was come to settle the Indian's Land, and they knew I should never go Home again safe; I found this Discourse was like to be of ill Consequence to me, so I pretended to speak very slightingly of what they had said to me, and enquired for Croghan (who is a meer Idol among his Countrymen the Irish Traders) and Andrew Montour the Interpreter for Pensylvania, and told them I had a Message to deliver the Indians from the King, by Order[81] of the President of Virginia, & for that Reason wanted to see Mr Montour: This made them all pretty easy (being afraid to interrupt the King's Message) and obtained me Quiet and Respect among them, otherwise I doubt not they woud have contrived some Evil against me—I im'ediately wrote to Mr Croghan, by one of the Trader's People.

Monday 26   Tho I was unwell, I prefered the Woods to such Company & set out from the Loggs Town down the River NW 6 M to great Beaver Creek where[82] I met one Barny Curran a Trader for the Ohio Company, and We continued together as far as Moskingum[83] The Bottoms upon the River below the Logg's Town very rich but narrow, the high Land pretty good but not very rich, the Land upon Beaver Creek the same kind, From this Place We left the River Ohio to the SE & travelled across the Country

Tuesday 27   Set out from the E Side of Beaver Creek NW 6 M, W 4 M; up these two last Courses very good high Land, not very broken, fit for farming

Wednesday 28   Rained, We could not travel.

Thursday 29   W 6 M thro good Land, the same Course[84] continued 6 M farther thro very broken Land; here I found myself pretty well recovered, & being in Want of Provision, I went out and killed a Deer.

Friday 30   Set out S 45 W 12 M crossed the last Branch of Beaver Creek[85] where one of Curran's Men & myself killed 12 Turkeys.

Saturday Decr 1   N 45 W 10 M the Land high and tolerable good.

Note by Mr Gist's Plat he makes these 2 Courses N 45 W 10 M, & N 45 W 8 M, to W 8 M and N 45 W 6 M.

Sunday 2   N 45 W 8 M the same Sort of Land, but near the Creeks[86] bushy and very full of Thorns.

Monday 3   Killed a Deer, and stayed in our Camp all Day.

Tuesday 4   Set out late S 45 W about 4 M here I killed three fine fat Deer, so that tho we Were eleven in Company, We had great Plenty of Provision.

Wednesday 5[87]   Set out sown the Side of a Creek called Elk's Eye[88] Creek S 70 W 6 M, good Land but void of Timber, Meadows upon the Creek, fine Runs for Mills.

In the Darlington Memorial Library

Thursday 6   Rained all Day so that we were obliged to continue in our Camp.

Friday 7   Set out SW 8 M crossing the said Elk's Eye Creek to a Town of the Ottaways,[89] a Nation of French Indians; and old French Man (named Mark Coonce)[90] who had married an Indian Woman of the six Nations lived here; the Indians were all out a hunting; the old Man was very civil to me, but after I was gone to my Camp, upon his understanding I came from Virginia, he called Me the Big Knife:[91] There are not above six or eight Families belonging to this Town.

Saturday 8   Stayed in the Town.

Sunday 9   Set out down the said Elk's Eye Creek[88] S 45 W 6 M to Margarets Creek[92] a Branch of the said Elk's Eye Creek.

Monday Dec.r 10   The same Course (S 45 W) 2 M to a large Creek.

Tuesday 11   The same Course 12 M killed 2 Deer.

Wednesday 12   The same Course 8 M encamped by the Side of Elk's Eye Creek

Thursday 13   Rained all Day.

Friday 14   Set out W 5 M to Moskingum[83] a Town of the Wyendotts. The Land upon Elk's Eye Creek is in general very broken, the Bottoms narrow The Wyendotts or little Mingoes are divided[93] between the French and English one half of them adhere to the first, and the other half are firmly attached to the latter. The Town of Moskingum consists of about one hundred Families. When We came within Sight of the Town, We percieved English Colours hoisted on the King's[94] House, and at George Croghan's;[95] upon enquiring the Reason I was informed that the French had lately taken several English Traders,[96] and that M.r Croghan had ordered all the White Men to come into this Town, and had sent Expresses to the Traders of the lower Towns,[97] and among the Pickweylinees;[98] and the Indians had sent to their People to come to Council about it.

Saturday 15 & Sunday 16   Nothing remarkable happened.

Monday 17   Came into Town two Traders belonging to M.r Croghan, and informed Us that two[99] of his People were taken by 40 French Men, & twenty French Indians who had carried them with seven Horse Loads of Skins to a new Fort[100] that the French were building on one of the Branches of Lake Erie

Tuesday 18   I acquainted M.r Croghan and Andrew Montour with my Business[81] with the Indians, & talked much of a Regulation of Trade with which they were much pleased, and treated Me very kindly.

From Wednesday 19 To Monday 24   Nothing remarkable.

George Mercer Papers

Tuesday 25 This being Christmass Day, I intended to read Prayers, but after inviting some of the White Men, they informed each other of my Intentions, and being of several different Persuasions, and few of them inclined to hear any Good, they refused to come. But one Thomas Burney[101] a Black-Smith who is settled there went about and talked to them, & then several of them came; and Andrew Montour invited several of the well disposed Indians, who came freely; by this Time the Morning was spent, and I had given over all Thoughts of them, but seeing Them come, to oblige All, and offend None, I stood up and said, Gentlemen, I have no Design or Intention to give Offence to any particular Sectary or Religion, but as our King indulges Us all in a Liberty of Conscience and hinders none of You in the Exercise of your religious Worship, so it woud be unjust in You, to endeavour to stop the Propagation of His; The Doctrine of Salvation Faith, and good Works, is what I only propose to treat of, as I find it extracted from the Homilies of the Church of England, which I then read to them in the best Manner I coud, and after I had done the Interpreter told the Indians what I had read, and that it was the true Faith which the great King and his Church recom'ended to his Children: the Indians seemed well pleased, and came up to Me and returned Me their Thanks; and then invited Me to live among Them, and gave Me a Name in their Language Annosanah: the Interpreter told Me this was a Name of a good Man that had formerly lived among them, and their King said that must be always my Name, for which I returned them Thanks; but as to living among them I excused myself by saying I did not know whether the Governor woud give Me Leave, and if he did the French woud come and carry me away as they had done the English Traders, to which they answered I might bring great Guns and make a Fort, that they had now left the French, and were very desirous of being instructed in the Principles of Christianity; that they liked Me very well and wanted Me to marry Them after the Christian Manner, and baptize their Children; and then they said they woud never desire to return to the French, or suffer Them or their Priests to come near them more, for they loved the English, but had seen little Religion among Them: and some of their great Men came and wanted Me to baptize their Children; for as I had read to Them and appeared to talk about Religion they took Me to be a Minister of the Gospel: Upon which I desired Mr Montour (the Interpreter) to tell Them, that no Minister coud venture to baptize any Children, until those that were to be Sureties for Them, were well instructed in the Faith themselves and that this was according to the great King's Religion, in which He desired his Children shoud be instructed, & We dare not do it in any other Way, than was by Law established, but I hoped if I coud not be admitted to live among them, that the great King woud send Them proper Ministers to exercise that Office among them, at which they seemed well pleased; and one of Them went and brought Me his Book (which was a Kind contrived for Them by the French in which the Days of the Week were so marked that by moving a Pin every Morning they kept a pretty exact Account of the Time) to shew Me that he understood Me, and that He and his Family always observed the Sabbath Day.

Wednesday Decr 26   This Day a Woman,[102] who had been a long Time a Prisoner, and had deserted, & been retaken, and brought into the Town on Christmass Eve, was put to Death in the following Manner: They carried Her without the Town, & let her loose, and when she attempted to run away, the Persons appointed for that Purpose pursued her, & struck Her on the Ear, on the right Side of her Head, which beat her flat on her Face on the Ground; they then stuck her several Times thro the Back with a Dart, to the Heart, scalped Her, & threw the Scalp in the Air, and another cut off her Head: There the dismal Spectacle lay till the Evening, & then Barny Curran desired Leave to bury Her, which He, and his Men, and some of the Indians did just at Dark.

From Thursday Decr 27 To Thursday Jany 3, 1751   Nothing remarkable happened in the Town.

Friday Janry 4   One Teafe (an Indian Trader) came to Town from near Lake Erie, & informed Us, that the Wyendott Indians had advised Him to keep clear of the Ottaways[89] (these are a Nation of Indians firmly attached to the French, & inhabit near the Lakes) & told Him that the Branches of the Lakes are claimed by the French; but that the Branches of Ohio belonged to Them, and their Brothers the English, and that the French had no Business there, & that it was expected that the other Part[93] of the Wyendott Nation woud desert the French and come over to the English Interest, & join their Brethren on the Elk's Eye Creek, & build a strong Fort and Town there.

From Saturday 5 To Tuesday 8   The Weather still continuing bad, I stayed in the Town to recruit my Horses, and tho Corn was very dear among the Indians, I was obliged to feed them well, or run the Risque of losing them as I had a great Way to travel.

Wednesday 9   The Wind Southerly, and the Weather something warmer: this Day came into Town two Traders from among the Pickwaylinees[98] (these are a Tribe of the Twigtwees) and brought News that another English Trader[103] was taken Prisoner by the French, and that three French Soldiers had deserted and come over to the English, and surrendered themselves to some of the Traders of the Pick Town,[98] & that the Indians woud have put them to Death, to revenge their taking our Traders, but as the French Prisoners had surrendered themselves, the English woud not let the Indians hurt them, but had ordered them to be sent under the Care of three of our Traders and delivered at this Town, to George Croghan.

Thursday 10   Wind still South and warm.

Friday 11   This Day came into Town an Indian from over the Lakes & confirmed the News we had heard.

Saturday 12   We sent away our People towards the lower Town[104] intending to follow then the next Morning, and this Evening We went into Council in the Wyendott's King's House[93]—The Council had been put off a long Time expecting some of their great Men in, but few of them came, & this Evening some of the King's Council being a little disordered with Liquor, no Business coud be done, but We were desired to come next Day.

Sunday Janry 13   No Business done.

Monday 14   This Day George Croghan,[78] by the Assistance of Andrew Montour,[79] acquainted the King and Council of this Nation (by presenting them four Strings of Wampum) that the great King over the Water, their Roggony (Father) had sent under the Care of the Governor of Virginia, their Brother, a large Present of Goods[105] which was now landed safe in Viginia, & the Governor had sent[81] Me to invite Them to come and see Him, & partake of their Father's Charity to all his Children on the Branches of Ohio In Answer to which one of the Chiefs stood up and said, "That their King and all "of Them thanked their Brother the Governor of Virginia for his "Care, and Me for bringing Them the News, but they could not give "Me an Answer[106] untill they had a full or general Council of the "several Nations of Indians which coud not be till next Spring: & "so the King and Council shaking Hands with Us, We took our "Leave.

Tuesday 15   We left Moskingum, & went W 5 M, to the White Woman's Creek, on which is a small Town; this White Woman was taken away from New England, when she was not above ten Years old, by the French Indians,[107] She is now upwards of fifty, and has an Indian Husband and several Children—Her Name is Mary Harris, she still remembers they used to be very religious in New England, and wonders how the White Men can be so wicked as she has seen them in these Woods.

In the Darlington Memorial Library

Wednesday 16   Set out SW 25 M, to Licking Creek[108]—The Land from Moskingum to this Place rich but broken—Upon the N Side of Licking Creek about 6 M from the Mouth, are several Salt Licks,[109] or Ponds, formed by little Streams or Dreins of Water, clear but of a blueish Colour, & salt Taste, the Traders and Indians boil their Meat in this Water, which (if proper Care be not taken) will sometimes make it too salt to eat.

Thursday 17   Set out W 5 M, SW 15 M, to a great Swamp.

Friday 18   Set out from the great Swamp SW 15 M.

Saturday 19   W 15 M to Hockhockin[110] a small Town with only four or five Delaware Families.

Sunday 20   The Snow began to grow thin, and the Weather warmer; Set out from Hockhochin S 5 M, then W 5 M, then SW 5 M, to the Maguck[111] a little Delaware Town of about ten Families by the N Side of a plain or clear Field about 5 M in Length NE & SW, & 2 M broad, with a small Rising in the Middle, which gives a fine Prospect over the whole Plain, and a large Creek on the N Side of it called Sciodoe Creek All the Way from Licking Creek to this Place is fine rich level Land, with large Meadows, fine Clover Bottoms, & spacious Plains covered with wild Rye: the Wood chiefly large Walnuts and Hickories, here and there mixed with Poplars Cherry Trees and Sugar Trees.

From Monday 21 To Wednesday 23   Stayed in the Maguck Town.

Thursday 24   Set out from the Maguck Town S about 15 M, thro fine rich level Land to a small Town called Harrikintoms[112] consisting of about five or six Delaware Families, on the SW Sciodoe Creek.

Friday 25   The Creek being very high and full of Ice, We coud not ford it, and were obliged to go down it on the SE Side SE 4 M to the Salt Lick Creek—about 1 M up this Creek on the S Side is a very large Salt Lick,[113] the Streams which run into this Lick are very salt, & tho clear leave a blueish Sediment: The Indians and Traders make Salt for their Horses of this Water, by boiling it; it has at first a blueish Colour, and somewhat bitter Taste, but upon dissolved in fair Water and boiled a second Time, it becomes tolerable pure Salt.

Saturday 26   Set our S 2 M, SW 14 M

Sunday 27   S 12 M to a small Delaware Town of about twenty Families on the SE Side of Sciodoe Creek—We lodged at the House of an Indian whose Name was Windaughalah[114] a great Man and Chief of this Town, & much in the English Interest—He entertained Us very kindly, and ordered a Negro Man that belonged to him to feed our Horses well; this Night it snowed, and in the Morning tho the Snow was six or seven Inches deep, the wild Rye[115] appeared very

George Mercer Papers

green and flourishing thro it, and our Horses had fine Feeding.

Monday Jan.ry 28   We went into Council with the Indians of this Town, and after the Interpreter[79] had informed them of his Instructions[80] from the Governor of Pensylvania, and given them some Cautions in Regard to the French, they returned for Answer as follows. The Speaker with four Strings of Wampum in his Hand stood up, and addressing Himself as to the Governor of Pensylvania, said, "Brothers, We the Delawares return You our hearty Thanks for the "News You have sent Us, and We assure You, We will not hear the "Voice of any other Nation for We are to be directed by You our "Brothers the English, & none else: We shall be glad to hear what "our Brothers have to say to Us at the Loggs Town in the Spring, & "to assure You of our hearty Good will & Love to our Brothers We "present You with these four Strings of Wampum
This is the last Town of the Delawares to the Westward—The Delaware Indians by the best Accounts I coud gather consist of about 500 fighting Men all firmly attached to the English Interest, they are not properly a Part of the Six Nations, but are scattered about among most of the Indians upon the Ohio, and some of them among the six Nations, from whom they have Leave to hunt upon their Lands.

Tuesday 29   Set out SW 5 M, S 5 M to the Mouth of Seiodoe Creek opposite to the Shannoah Town,[116] here We fired our Guns to alarm the Traders, who soon answered, and came and ferryed Us over to the Town—The Land about the Mouth of Seiodoe Creek is rich but broken fine Bottoms upon the River & Creek—The Shannoah Town is situate upon both Sides the River Ohio, just below the Mouth of Seiodoe Creek, and contains about 300 Men, there are about 40 Houses on the S Side of the River and about 100 on the N Side, with a Kind of State-House of about 90 Feet long, with a light Cover of Bark in w.ch they hold their Councils—The Shanaws are not a Part of the six Nations, but were formerly at Variance with them, tho now reconciled: the are great Friends to the English who once protected[117] them from the Fury of the six Nations, which they gratefully remember.

Wednesday 30   We were conducted into Council, where George Croghan[78] delivered sundry Speeches from the Government of Pensylvania[80] to the Chiefs of this Nation, in which He informed them, "That two Prisoners[118] who had been taken by the French, and had "made their Escape from the French Officer at Lake Erie as he was "carrying them towards Canada brought News that the French offered "a large Sum of Money to any Person who woud bring to them the "said Croghan and Andrew Montour the Interpreter alive, or if dead

· 16 ·

"their Scalps; and that the French also threatened these Indians and "the Wyendotts with War in the Spring" the same Persons farther said "that they had seen ten French Canoes loaded with Stores for a "new Fort[119] they designed on the S Side Lake Erie.

Mr Croghan[78] also informed them of several of our Traders having been taken, and advised them to keep their Warriors at Home, until they coud see what the French intended which he doubted not woud appear in the Spring—Then Andrew Montour[79] informed this Nation as He had done the Wyendotts & Delawares "That the King of Great "Britain had sent Them a large Present[105] of Goods, in Company with "the six Nations, which was under the Care of the Governor of Vir- "ginia, who had sent[81] Me out to invite them to come and see Him, "& partake of their Father's Present next Sum'er" to which We received this Answer—Big Hannaona[120] their Speaker taking in his Hand the "several Strings of Wampum which had been given by the English, "He said "These are the Speeches received by Us from your great "Men: From the Beginning of our Friendship, all that our Brothers "the English have told Us has been good and true, for which We "return our hearty Thanks" Then taking up four other Strings of Wampum in his Hand, He said "Brothers I now speak the Sentiments "of all our People; when first our Forefathers did meet the English "our Brothers, they found what our Brothers the English them to be "true, and so have We—We are but a small People, & it is not to Us "only that You speak, but to all Nations—We shall be glad to hear "what our Brothers will say to Us at the Loggs Town in the Spring,[121] "& We hope that the Friendship now subsisting between Us & our "Brothers, will last as long as the Sun shines, or the Moon gives Light— "We hope that our Children will hear and believe what our Brothers "say to them, as We have always done, and to assure You of our hearty Good-Will towards You our Brothers, We present You with these four Strings of Wampum" After the Council was over they had much Talk about sending a Guard with Us to the Pickwaylinees Towns[98] (these are a Tribe of Twigtwees) which was reckoned near 200 Miles, but after long Consultation (their King[122] being sick) they came to no Determination about it.

From Thursday Jan 31 to Monday Feby 11   Stayed in the Shannoah Town, while I was here the Indians had a very extraordinary Kind of a Festival, at which I was present and which I have exactly described at the End[123] of my Journal—As I had particular Instructions from the President of Virginia to discover the Strength & Numbers of some Indian Nations to the Westward of Ohio who had lately revolted from the French, and had some Messages to deliver them from Him, I resolved to set out for the Twigtwee Town.[98]

Tuesday 12   Having left my Boy to take Care of my Horses in the Shannoah Town, & supplied myself with a fresh Horse to ride, I set out with my old Company viz George Croghan Andrew Montour, Robert Kallandar, and a Servant to carry our Provisions &c NW 10 M.

Wednesday 13   The same Course (NW) about 35 M.

Thursday 14   The same Course about 30 M.

Friday 15   The same Course 15 M. We met with nine Shannoah Indians coming from one of the Pickwaylinees Towns, where they had been to Council, they told Us there were fifteen more of them behind at the Twigtwee Town, waiting for the Arrival of the Wawaughtanneys,[124] who are a Tribe of the Twigtwees, and were to bring with them a Shannoah Woman and Child to deliver to their Men that were behind: this Woman they informed Us had been taken Prisoner last Fall, by some of the Wawaughtanney Warriors thro a Mistake, which had like to have engaged these Nations in a War.

Saturday 16   Set out the same Course[125] (NW) about 35 M, to the little Miamee River[126] or Creek

Sunday 17   Crossed the little Miamee River, and altering our Course We went SW 25 M, to the big Miamee River, opposite the Twigtwee Town.[98] All the Way from the Shannoah Town[116] to this Place (except the first 20 M which is broken) is fine, rich level Land, well timbered with large Walnut, Ash Sugar Trees, Cherry Trees &c, it is well watered with a great Number of little Streams or Rivulets, and full of beautiful natural Meadows, covered with wild Rye, blue Grass and Clover, and abounds with Turkeys, Deer, Elks and most Sorts of Game particularly Buffaloes, thirty or forty of which are frequently seen feeding in one Meadow: In short it wants Nothing but Cultivation to make it a most delightfull Country—The Ohio and all the large Branches are said to be full of fine Fish of several Kinds, particularly a Sort of Cat Fish of a prodigious Size; but as I was not there at the proper Season, I had not an Opportunity of seeing any of them—The Traders had always reckoned it 200 M, from the Shannoah Town to the Twigtwee Town, but by my Computation I coud make it no more than 150—The Miamee River being high, We were obliged to make a Raft of old Loggs to transport our Goods and Saddles and swim our Horses over—After Firing a few Guns and Pistols, & smoaking in the Warriours Pipe, who came to invite Us to the Town (according to their Custom of inviting and welcoming Strangers and Great Men) We entered the Town with English Colours before Us, and were kindly received by their King,[127] who invited Us into his own House, & set our Colours upon the Top of it—The Firing of Guns held about a Quarter of an Hour, and then all the white Men and

In the Darlington Memorial Library

Traders that were there, came and welcomed Us to the Twigtwee Town—This Town is situate on the NW Side of the Big Miamee River about 150 M from the Mouth thereof; it consists of about 400 Families, & daily encreasing, it is accounted one of the strongest Indian Towns upon this Part of the Continent—The Twigtwees are a very numerous People consisting of many different Tribes[128] under the same Form of Government. Each Tribe has a particular Chief or King, one of which is chosen indifferently out of any Tribe to rule the whole Nation, and is vested with greater Authorities than any of the others—They are accounted the most powerful People to the Westward of the English Settlements, & much superior to the six Nations with whom they are now in Amity: their Strength and Numbers are not thoroughly known, as they have but lately traded with the English, and indeed have very little Trade among them: they deal in much the same Com'odities with the Northern Indians. There are other Nations or Tribes[129] still further to the Westward daily coming in to them, & 'tis thought their Power and Interest reaches to the Westward of the Mississippi, if not across the Continent, they are at present very well affected to the English, and seem fond of an Alliance with them[130]—they formerly lived on the farther Side of the Obache, and were in the French Interest, who supplied them with some few Trifles at a most exorbitant Price—they were called by the French Miamees; but they have now revolted[98] from them, and left their former Habitations for the Sake of trading with the English; and notwithstanding all their Artifices the French have used, they have not been able to recall them.

After We had been some Time in the King's[127] House Mr Montour told Him that We wanted to speak with Him and the Chiefs of this Nation this Evening upon which We were invited into the long House, and having taken our Places Mr Montour began as follows—
"Brothers the Twigtwees as We have been hindered by the high
"Waters and some other Business with our Indian Brothers, no Doubt
"our long Stay has caused some Trouble among our Brethren here,
Therefore We now present You with two Strings of Wampum to
"remove all the Trouble of your Hearts, & clear your Eyes, that You
"may see the Sun shine clear, for We have a great Deal to say to You,
"& We woud have You send for one of Your Friends that can speak
the Mohickon[131] or the Mingoe Tongues well, that We may under-
"stand each other thoroughly, for We have a great Deal of Business
"to do"—The Mohickons[132] are a small Tribe who most of them speak English, and are also well acquainted with the Language of the Twigtwees, and they with theirs—Mr Montour then proceeded to

deliver Them a Message[133] from the Wyendotts and Delawares as follows "Brothers the Twigtwees, this comes by our Brothers the "English who are coming with good News to You; We hope You will "take Care of Them, and all our Brothers the English who are trading "among You: You made a Road for our Brothers the English to come "and trade among You, but it is now very foul, great Loggs are fallen "across it, and We woud have You be strong like Men, and have one "Heart with Us, and make the Road clear, that our Brothers the "English may have free course and Recourse between You and Us— "In the Sincerity of our Hearts We send You these four Strings of "Wampum, to which they gave the usual Yo Ho—Then they said they wanted some Tobacco to smoak with Us, and that tomorrow they woud send for their Interpreter.

Monday Feby 18   We walked about viewed the Fort which wanted some Repairs, & the Trader's Men helped Them to bring Loggs to line the Inside.

Tuesday 19   We gave their Kings and great Men some Clothes, and Paint Shirts, and now they were busy dressing and preparing themselves for the Council—The Weather grew warm and the Creeks began to lower very fast.

Wednesday 20   About 12 of the Clock We were informed that some of the foreign Tribes[129] were coming, upon which proper Persons were ordered to meet them and conduct Them into the Town, and then We were invited into the long House; after We had been seated about a Quarter of an Hour four Indians, two from each Tribe (who had been sent before to bring the long Pipe, and to inform that the rest were coming) came in, & informed Us that their Friends had sent these Pipes that We might smoak the Calamut Pipe of Peace with Them and that they intended to do the same with Us.

Thursday Feby 21   We were again invited into the long House where Mr Croghan made them (with the foreign Tribes) a Present[80] to the Value of £100 Pensylvania Money, and delivered all our Speeches to Them, at which they seemed well pleased, and said, that they would take Time and consider well what We had said to Them

Friday 22[134]   Nothing remarkable happened in the Town.

Saturday 23   In the Afternoon there was an Alarm in the Town which caused a great Confusion and running about among the Indians, upon enquiring into the Reason of this Stir, they told Us that it was occasioned by six Indians that came to war against Them, from the Southward; three of them Cutaways,[135] and three Shanaws (these were some of the Shanaws who had formerly deserted from the other Part of the Nation, and now live to the Southward)[136] Towards

In the Darlington Memorial Library

Night there was a Report spread in Town that four Indians, and four hundred French, were on their March and just by the Town: But soon after the Messanger who brought this News said there were only four french Indians coming to Council, and that they bid him say so, only to see how the English woud behave themselves; but as they had behaved themselves like Men, He now told the Truth.

Sunday 24 This Morning the four French Indians came into Town and were kindly received by the Town Indians; they marched in under French Colours, and were conducted into the long House, and after they had been in about a Quarter of an Hour, the Council sate, and We were sent for that We might hear what the French had to say to them The Pyankeshee King[137] (who was at that Time the Principal Man, and Com'ander in Chief of the Twightwees) said, He woud have the English Colours set up in this Council as well as the French, to which We answered he might do as he thought fit. After We were seated right opposite to the French Embassadors, One of Them said, He had a Present to make Them, so a Place was prepared (as they had before done for our Present) between Them and Us, and then their Speaker stood up, and layed his Hands upon two small Caggs of Brandy that held about seven Quarts each, and a Roll of Tobacco of about ten Pounds Weight, then taking two Strings of Wampum in his Hand, He said, "What he had to deliver Them was "from their Father (meaning the French King) and he desired they "woud hear what he was about to say to Them;" then he layed them "two Strings of Wampum down upon the Caggs, and taking up four "other Strings of black and white Wampum, he said, "that their "Father remembring his Children, had sent them two Caggs of "Milk,[138] and some Tobacco, and that he now had made a clear Road "for them, to come and see Him and his Officers; and pressed them "very much to come; then he took another String of Wampum in "his Hand, and said, "their Father now woud forget all little Dif-"ferences that had been between Them, and desired Them not to be "of two Minds, but to let Him know their Minds freely, for He woud "send for Them no more To which the Pyankeshee King replied, "it was true their Father had sent for them several Times, and said "the Road was clear, but He understood it was made foul & bloody, "and by Them—We (said He) have cleared a Road for our Brothers "the English, and your Father have made it bad, and have taken "some of our Brothers Prisoners, Which We look upon as done to Us, "and he turned short about and went out of Council" After the French Embassador had delivered his Message He went into one of the private Houses, and endeavoured much to prevail on some

· 21 ·

Indians, and was seen to cry and lament (as he said for the Loss of that Nation.

Monday Feby 25 This Day We received a Speech from the Wawaughtanneys and Pyankeshees (two Tribes of the Twigtwees) "One of the Chiefs[139] of the former spoke Brothers, We have heard "what You have said to Us by the Interpreter and We see You take "Pity upon our poor Wives and Children, and have taken Us by the "Hand into the great Chain of Friendship, therefore We present You "with these two Bundles of Skins to make Shoes for your People, and "this Pipe to smoak in, to assure You that our Hearts are good and "true towards You our Brothers; and We hope that We shall all "continue in the Love and Friendship with one another, as People with one Head and one Heart ought to do; You have pityed Us as You always did the rest of our Indian Brothers, We hope that Pity "You have always shewn, will remain as long as the Sun gives Light, "and on our Side you may depend upon sincere and true Friendship "towards You as long as We have Strength"—This Person stood up and spoke with the Air and Gesture of an Orator.

Tuesday 26 The Twigtwees[98] delivered the following Answer to the four Indians sent by the French—The Captain of the Warriors stood up and taking some Strings of black and white Wampum in his "Hand he spoke with a fierce Tone and very warlike Air—"Brothers "the Ottaways,[89] You are always differing with the French Yourselves, "and yet You listen to what they say, but We will let You know by "these four Strings of Wampum, that We will not hear any Thing "they say to Us, nor do any Thing they bid Us"—Then the same Speaker with six Strouds two Match-Coats, and a String of black Wampum (I understood the Goods were in Return for the Milk and Tobacco) and directing his Speech to the French said, "Fathers, You "desire that We may speak our Minds from our Hearts, which I am "going to do; You have often desired We shoud go Home to You, "but I tell You it is not our Home, for We have made a Road as "far as the Sea to the Sun-rising, and have been taken by the Hand[140] "by our Brothers the English, and the six Nations, and the Delawares "Shannoahs and Wyendotts, and We assure You it is the Road We will go; and as You threaten Us with War in the Spring,[141] We tell "You if You are angry We are ready to receive You, and resolve to "die here before We will go to You; And that You may know that "this our Mind, We send You this String of black Wampum". After a Short Pause the same Speaker spoke again thus—"Brothers the Ottaways, You hear what I say, tell that to your Fathers the French, "for that is our Mind, and We speak it from our Hearts.

In the Darlington Memorial Library

Wednesday 27 This Day they took down their French Colours, and dismissed the four French Indians, so they took their Leave of the Town and set off for the French Fort.[142]

Thursday 28 The Crier of the Town came by the King's Order and invited Us to the long House to see the Warriors Feather Dance;[143] it was performed by three Dancing-Masters, who were painted all over with various Colours, with long Sticks in their Hands, upon the Ends of which were fastened long Feathers of Swans, and other Birds, neatly woven in the Shape of a Fowls Wing: in this Disguise they performed many antick Tricks, waving their Sticks and Feathers about with great Skill to imitate the flying and fluttering of Birds, keeping exact Time with their Musick; while they are dancing some of the Warriors strikes a Post, upon which the Musick and Dancer's cease, and the Warrior gives an Account of his Achievements in War, and when he has done, throws down some Goods as a Recompence to the Performers and Musicians; after which they proceed in their Dance as before till another Warrior strikes ye Post, and so on as long as the Company think fit

Friday March 1 We received the following Speech from the Twigtwees[98] The Speaker stood up and addressing himself as to the Governor of Pensylvania with two Strings of Wampum in his Hand, He said—"Brothers our Hearts are glad that You have taken Notice "of Us, and surely Brothers We hope that You will order a Smith[101] "to settle here to mend our Guns and Hatchets, Your Kindness makes "Us so bold to ask this Request. You told Us our Friendship should "last as long, and be as the greatest Mountain, We have considered "well, and all our great Kings & Warriors are come to a Resolution "never to give Heed to what the French say to Us, but always to hear "& believe what You our Brothers say to Us—Brothers We are obliged "to You for your kind Invitation[80] to receive a Present at the Loggs "Town, but as our foreign Tribes are not yet come, We must wait for "them but You may depend We will come as soon as our Women "have planted Corn to hear what our Brothers will say to Us— "Brothers We present You with this Bundle of Skins, as We are but "poor to be for Shoes for You on the Road, and We return You our "hearty Thanks for the Clothes which You have put upon our Wives "and Children"—We then took our Leave of the Kings and Chiefs, and they ordered that a small Party of Indians shoud go with Us as far as Hockhockin;[110] but as I had left my Boy & Horses at the lower Shannoah Town,[116] I was obliged to go by myself or to go sixty or seventy Miles out of my Way, which I did not care to do; so we all came over the Miamee River together this Evening, but Mr Croghan[78]

& Mr Montour[79] went over again & lodged in the Town, but I stayed on this Side at one Robert Smith's[144] (a Trader) where We had left our Horses—Before the French Indians had come into Town, We had drawn Articles of Peace and Alliance between the English and the Wawaughtanneys and Pyankeshees; the Indentures were signed sealed and delivered on both Sides, and as I drew them I took a Copy[134]—The Land upon the great Miamee River is very rich level and well timbered, some of the finest Meadows that can be: The Indians and Traders assure Me that the Land holds as good and if possible better, to the Westward as far as the Obache[145] which is accounted 100 Miles, and quite up to the Head of the Miamee River, which is 60 Miles above the Twigtwee Town,[98] and down the said River quite to the Ohio which is reckoned 150 Miles—The Grass here grows to a great Height in the clear Fields, of which there are a great Number, & the Bottoms are full of white Clover, wild Rye, and blue Grass.

Saturday March 2 George Croghan[78] and the rest of our Company came over the River, We got our Horses, & set out about 35 M. to Mad Creek (this is a Place where some English Traders[118] had been taken Prisoners by the French.)

Sunday 3 This Morning We parted, They for Hockhockin,[110] and I for the Shannoah Town,[116] and as I was quite alone and knew that the French Indians had threatened Us, and woud probably pursue or lye in Wait for Us, I left the Path, and went to the South Westward down the little Miamee River or Creek, where I had fine travelling thro rich Land and beautiful Meadows, in which I coud sometimes see forty or fifty Buffaloes feeding at once—The little Miamee River or Creek continued to run thro the Middle of a fine Meadow, about a Mile wide very clear like an old Field, and not a Bush in it, I coud see the Buffaloes in it above two Miles off: I travelled this Day about 30 M.

Monday 4 This Day I heard several Guns, but was afraid to examine who fired Them, lest they might be some of the French Indians, so I travelled thro the Woods about 30 M; just at Night I killed a fine barren Cow-Buffaloe and took out her Tongue, and a little of the best of her Meat: The Land still level rich and well timbered with Oak, Walnut, Ash, Locust, and Sugar Trees.

Tuesday 5 I travelled about 30 M.

Wednesday 6 I travelled about 30 M, and killed a fat Bear.

Thursday 7 Set out with my Horse Load of Bear, and travelled about 30 M this Afternoon I met a young Man (a Trader) and We encamped together that Night; He happened to have some Bread

In the Darlington Memorial Library

with Him, and I had Plenty of Meat, so We fared very well.

Friday 8   Travelled[146] about 30 M, and arrived at Night at the Shannoah Town—All the Indians, as well as the white Men came out to welcome my Return to their Town, being very glad that all Things were rightly settled in the Miamee Country, they fired upwards of 150 Guns in the Town,[116] and made an Entertainment in Honour of the late Peace with the western Indians[134]—In my Return from the Twigtwee to the Shannoah Town, I did not keep an exact Account of Course or Distance; for as the Land thereabouts was every where much the same, and the Situation of the Country was sufficiently described in my Journey to the Twigtwee Town, I thought it unnecessary, but have notwithstanding laid down my Tract pretty nearly in my Plat.

Saturday March 9   In the Shannoah Town, I met with one of the Mingoe Chiefs,[147] who had been down at the Falls of Ohio, so that We did not see Hime as We went up; I informed Him of the King's Present,[105] and the Invitation[81] down to Virginia—He told that there was a Party of French Indians hunting at the Falls,[42] and if I went there they would certainly kill Me or carry Me away Prisoner to the French; For it is certain they would not let Me pass: However as I had a great Inclination to see the Falls, and the Land on the E Side the Ohio, I resolved to venture as far as possible.

Sunday 10 & Monday 11   Stayed in the Town, and prepared for my Departure.

Tuesday 12   I got my Horses over the River and after Breakfast my Boy and I got ferryed over[148]—The Ohio is near ¾ of a Mile wide at Shannoah Town, & is very deep and smooth.

Wednesday 13   We set out S 45 W, down the said River on the S E Side 8 M, then S 10 M, here I met two Men belonging to Robert Smith[144] at whose House I lodged on this Side the Miamee River, and one Hugh Crawford, the said Robert Smith had given Me an Order upon these Men, for two of the Teeth of a large Beast[149] which they were bringing from towards the Falls of Ohio,[42] one of which I brought in and delivered to the Ohio Company—Robert Smith informed Me that about seven Years ago these Teeth and Bones of three large Beasts (one of which was somewhat smaller than the other two) were found in a salt Lick[150] or Spring upon a small Creek which runs into the S Side of the Ohio, about 15 M, below the Mouth of the great Miamee River, and 20 above the Falls of Ohio—He assured Me that the Rib Bones of the largest of these Beasts were eleven Feet long, and the Skull Bone six feet wide, across the Forehead, & the other Bones in Proportion; and that there were several Teeth there, some of which he called Horns, and said they were upwards of five Feet long, and as much as a Man coud well carry: that he had hid one in a Branch at some Distance from the Place, lest the French Indians shoud carry it away—The Tooth which I brought in for the Ohio Company, was a Jaw Tooth of better than four Pounds Weight; it appeared to be the furthest Tooth in the Jaw, and looked like fine Ivory when the outside was scraped off—I also met with four Shannoah Indians coming up the River in their Canoes, who informed Me that there were about sixty French Indians encamped at the Falls.

Thursday 14   I went down the River S 15 M, the Land upon this Side the Ohio chiefly broken, and the Bottoms but narrow.

Friday 15   S 5 M, SW 10 M, to a Creek[151] that was so high, that We coud not get over that Night.

Saturday 16   S 45 W about 35 M.

Sunday 17   The same Course 15 M, then N 45 W 5 M.

Monday 18   N 45 W 5 M then SW 20 M, to the lower Salt Lick Creek,[152] which Robert Smith and the Indians told Us was about 15 M above the Falls of Ohio; the Land still hilly, the Salt Lick here much the same with those before described—this Day We heard several Guns which made Me imagine the French Indians were not moved, but were still hunting, and firing thereabouts: We also saw some Traps newly set, and the Footsteps of some Indians plain on the Ground as if they had been there the Day before—I was now much troubled that I coud not comply with my Instructions, & was once resolved to leave the Boy and Horses, and to go privately on Foot to view the Falls; but the Boy being a poor Hunter, was afraid he woud starve if I was long from him, and there was also great Danger lest the French Indians shoud come upon our Horses Tracts, or hear their Bells, and as I had seen good Land enough, I thought perhaps I might be blamed for venturing so far, in such dangerous Times, so I concluded not to go to the Falls; but travell'd away to the Southward till We were over the little Cuttaway River[153]—The Falls of Ohio[42] by the best Information I coud get are not very steep, on the SE Side there is a Bar of Land at some Distance from the Shore, the Water between the Bar and the Shore is not above 3 feet deep, and the Stream moderately strong, the Indians frequently pass safely in their Canoes thro this Passage, but are obliged to take great Care as they go down lest the Current which is much the strongest on the No W Side shoud draw them that Way; which woud be very dangerous as the Water on that Side runs with great Rapidity over several Ledges of Rocks; the Water below the Falls they say is about six Fathoms deep, and the River continues without any Obstructions till it empties itself into the Mississippi which is accounted upwards of 400 M—The Ohio near the Mouth is said to be very wide, and the Land upon both Sides very rich, and in general very level, all the Way from the Falls—After I had determined not to go to the Falls, We turned from Salt Lick Creek, to a Ridge of Mountains that made towards the Cuttaway River,[154] & from the Top of the Mountain We saw a fine level Country SW as far as our Eyes coud behold, and it was a very clear Day; We then went down the Mountain and set out S 20 W about 5 M, thro rich level Land covered with small Walnut Sugar Trees, Red-Buds &c.

Tuesday March 19 We set out S and crossed several Creeks all runing to the SW, at about 12 M, came to the little Cuttaway River:[154] We were obliged to go up it about 1 M to an Island, which was the shoalest Place We coud find to cross at, We then continued our Course in all about 30 M thro level rich Land except about 2 M which was broken and indifferent—This Level is about 35 M broad, and as We came up the Side of it along the Branches of the little Cuttaway We found it about 150 M long; and how far toward the SW We coud not tell, but imagined it held as far the great Cuttaway River,[155] which woud be upwards of 100 M more, and appeared much broader that Way than here, as I coud discern from the Tops of the Mountains

Wednesday 20 We did not travel, I went up to the Top of a Mountain to view the Country, to the SE it looked very broken, and mountainous but to the Eastward and SW it appeared very level.

Thursday 21 Set out S 45 E 15 M, S 5 M, here I found a Place[156] where the Stones shined like highcoloured Brass, the Heat of the Sun drew out of them a Kind of Borax or Salt Petre only something sweeter; some of which I brought into the Ohio Company, tho I believe it was Nothing but a Sort of Sulphur.

Friday 22 SE 12 M, I killed a fat Bear, and was taken sick that Night.

Saturday 23 I stayed here and sweated after the Indian Fashion, which helped Me.

Sunday 24 Set out E 2 M, N E 3 M, N, M, E 2 M, SE 5 M, E 2 M, N 2 M, SE 7 M to a small Creek,[157] where We encamped in a Place where We had but poor Food for our Horses, & both We and They were very much wearied: the Reason of our making so many short Courses was We were driven by a Branch of the little Cuttaway River (whose Banks were so exceeding steep that it was impossible to ford it) into a Ledge of rocky Laurel Mountains which were almost impassable.

George Mercer Papers

Monday 25   SE 12 M, N 2 M, E 1 M, S 4 M, SE 2 M, We killed a Buck Elk here and took out his Tongue to carry with Us.

Tuesday 26   Set out SE 10 M, SW 1 M, SE 1 M, SW 1 M, SE 1 M, SW 1 M, SE 1 M, SW 1 M, SE 5 M, killed 2 Buffaloes & took out their Tongues and encamped—These two Days We travelled thro Rocks and Laurel Mountains full of Laurel Thickets which We coud hardly creep thro without cutting our Way.

Wednesday 27   Our Horses and Selves were so tired that We were obliged to stay this Day to rest, for We were unable to travel—On all the Branches of the little Cuttaway River[154] was great Plenty of fine Coal some of which I brought in to the Ohio Company.

Thursday 28   Set out SE 15 M crossing several Creeks of the little Cuttaway River, the Land still full of Coal and black Slate.

Friday 29   The same Course SE about 12 M and Land still mountainous.

Saturday 30   Stayed to rest our Horses, I went on Foot and found a Passage thro the Mountains to another Creek, or a Fork of the same Creek that We were upon.

Sunday 31   The same Course SE 15 M, killed a Buffaloe & encamped.

Monday April 1   Set out the same Course about 20 M, Part of the Way We went along a Path up the Side of a little Creek, at the Head of which was a Gap[158] in the Mountains, then our Path went down another Creek[159] to a Lick where Blocks of Coal about 8 or 10 In; square lay upon the Surface of the Ground, here We killed a Bear and encamped.

Tuesday 2   Set out S 2 M, SE 1 M, NE 3 M, killed a Buffaloe.

Wednesday 3   S 1 M, SW 3 M, E 3 M, SE 2 M, to a small Creek[160] on which was a large Warriors Camp, that woud contain 70 or 80 Warriors, their Captain's Name or Title was the Crane,[161] as I knew by his Picture or Arms painted on a Tree.

Thursday 4   We stayed here all Day to rest our Horses, and I platted down our Courses and I found I had still near 200 M Home upon a streight Line.

Friday April 5   Rained, and We stayed at the Warrior's Camp.

Saturday 6   We went along the Warrior's Road[162] S 1 M, SE 3 M, S 2 M, SE 3 M, E 3 M, killed a Bear.

Sunday 7   Set out E 2 M, NE 1 M, SE 1 M, S 1 M, W 1 M, SW 1 M, S 1 M, SE 2 M, S 1 M

Monday 8   S 1 M, SE 1 M, E 3 M, SE 1M, E 3 M, NE 2 M, N 1 M, E 1 M, N 1 M, E 2 M, and encamped upon a small Laurel Creek.[163]

Tuesday 9 & Wednesday 10   The Weather being somewhat bad

· 28 ·

We did not travel these two Days the Country being still rocky mountainous, & full of Laurel Thickets, the worst traveling[164] I ever saw.

Thursday 11   We travelled several Courses near 20 M, but in the Afternoon as I coud saw from the Top of the Mountain the Place We came from, I found We had not come upon a streight Line more than N 65 E 10 M.

Friday 12   Set out thro very difficult Ways, E 5 M, to a small Creek.

Saturday 13   The same Course E upon a streight Line, tho the Way We were obliged to travel was near 20 M, here We killed two Bears the Way still rocky and mountainous.

Sunday 14   As Food was very scarce in these barren Mountains, We were obliged to move for fresh Feeding for our Horses, so We went on E 5 M, then N 20 W 6 M, to a Creek where We got something better Feeding for our Horses, in climbing up the Clifts and Rocks this Day two of our Horses fell down, and were pretty Much hurt, and a Paroquete which I had got from the Indians, on the other Side the Ohio (where there are a great many) died of a Bruise he got by a Fall; tho it was but a Trifle I was much concerned at losing Him, as he was perfectly tame, and had been very brisk all the Way, and I had still Corn enough left to feed Him—In the Afternoon I left the Horses, and went a little Way down the Creek, and found such a Precipice and such Laurel Thickets as We coud not pass, and the Horses were not able to go up the Mountain till they had rested a Day or two.

Monday 15   We cut a Passage thro the Laurels better than 2 M, as I was climbing up the Rocks, I got a Fall which hurted Me pretty much—This Afternoon as We wanted Provision I killed a Bear.

Tuesday 16   Thunder and Rain in the Morning—We set out N 25 E 3 M.

Wednesday 17   This Day I went to the Top of a Mountain to view the Way, and found it so bad that I did not care to engage it, but rather chose to go out of the Way and keep down along the Side of a Creek till I coud find a Branch or Run on the other Side to go up.

Thursday 18   Set out down the said Creek Side N 3 M, then the Creek turning NW I was obliged to leave it, and go up a Ridge NE 1 M, E 2 M, SE 2 M, NE 1 M, to the Fork of a River.

Friday 19   Set out down the said Run NE 2 M, E 2 M, SE 2 M, N 20 E 2 M, E 2 M, up a large Run.

Saturday 20   Set out SE 10 M, E 4 M, over a small Creek—We had such bad traveling down this Creek, that We had like to have lost one of our Horses.

Sunday 21   Stayed to rest our Horses.

Monday 22   Rained all Day—We coud not travel.

Tuesday 23   Set out E 8 M along a Ridge of Mountains then SE 5 M, E 3 M, SE 4 M, and encamped among very steep Mountains.[165]

Wednesday 24   SE 4 M thro steep Mountains and Thickets E 6 M.

Thursday 25   E 5 M, SE 1 M, NE 2 M, SE 2 M, E 1 M, then S 2 M, E 1 M, killed a Bear.

Friday 26   Set out SE 2 M, here it rained so hard We were obliged to stop.

Saturday 27 Sunday 28 & Monday 29[166]   These three Days it continued raining & bad Weather, so that We coud not travel—All the Way from Salt Lick Creek to this Place, the Branches of the little Cuttaway River were so high that We coud not pass Them, which obliged Us to go over the Heads of them, thro a continued Ledge of almost inaccesible Mountains, Rocks and Laurel Thickets.

Tuesday 30   Fair Weather set out E 3 M, SE 8 M, E 2 M, to a little River or Creek which falls into the big Conhaway, called blue Stone,[167] Where We encamped and had good Feeding for our Horses.

Wednesday May 1   Set out N 75 E 10 M and killed a Buffaloe, then went up a very high Mountain,[168] upon the Top of which was a Rock 60 or 70 Feet high, & a Cavity in the Middle, into which I went, and found there was a Passage thro it which gradually ascended to the Top, with several Holes in the Rock, which let in the Light, when I got to the Top of this Rock, I coud see a prodigious Distance, and coud plainly discover where the big Conhaway River broke the next high Mountain, I then came down and continued my Course N 75 E 5 M, farther and encamped.

Thursday 2 & Friday 3   These two Days it rained and We stayed at our Camp to take Care of some Provision We had killed.

Saturday 4   This Day our Horses run away, and it was late before We got Them, so We coud not travel far; We went N 75 E 4 M.

Sunday May 5   Rained all Day.

Monday 6   Set out thro very bad Ways E 3 M, NE 6 M, over a bad Laurel Creek E 4 M.

Tuesday 7   Set out E 10 M, to the big Conhaway or new River and got over half of it to a large Island where We lodged that Night.

Wednesday 8   We made a Raft of Logs and crossed[169] the other half of the River & went up it S about 2 M—The Conhaway or new River (by some called Wood's River) where I crossed it (which was about 8 M above the Mouth of blue Stone River) is better than 200 Yards wide, and pretty deep, but full of Rocks and Falls The Bottoms upon it and blue Stone River are very rich but narrow, the high Land broken.

In the Darlington Memorial Library

Thursday 9   Set out E 13 M to a large Indian Warrior's Camp, where We killed a Bear and stayed all Night.

Friday 10   Set out E 4 M, SE 3 M, S 3 M, thro Mountains[170] cover'd with Ivy and Laurel Thickets.

Saturday 11   Set out S 2 M, SE 5 M, to a Creek[171] and a Meadow where We let our Horses feed, then SE 2 M, S 1 M, SE 2 M, to a very high Mountain upon the Top of which was a Lake[172] or Pond about ¾ of a Mile long NE & SW & ¼ of a Mile wide the Water fresh and clear, and a clean gravelly Shore about 10 Yards wide with a fine Meadow and six fine Springs in it then S about 4 M, to a Branch of the Conaway called Sinking Creek.[173]

Sunday 12   Stayed to rest our Horses and dry some Meat We had killed

Monday 13   Set out SE 2 M, E 1 M, SE 3 M, S 12 M to one Richd Halls[174] in Augusta county this Man is one of the farthest Settlers to the Westward upon the New River.

Tuesday 14   Stayed at Richd Hall's and wrote to the President[175] of Virginia & the Ohio Company to let them know I shoud be with Them by the 15th of June.

Wednesday 15   Set out from Richd Hall's S 16 M.

Thursday 16   The same Course S 22 M and encamped at Beaver Island Creek[176] (a Branch of the Contaway) opposite to the Head of Roanoke.

Friday 17   Set out SW 3 M, then S 9 M, to the dividing Line[177] between Corolina and Virginia, where I stayed all Night, the Land from Richd Hall's to this Place is broken.

Saturday 18   Set out S 20 M to my own House[178] on the Yadkin River, when I came there I found all my Family gone, for the Indians had killed five People in the Winter near that Place, which frightened my Wife and Family away to Roanoke about 35 M nearer in among the Inhabitants, which I was informed of by an old Man I met near the Place.

Sunday 19   Set out for Roanoke,[179] and as We had now a Path, We got there the same Night where I found all my Family well.

Christopher Gist

Instructions given to Mr Christopher Gist by the Com'ittee of the Ohio Company July 16th 1751

After You have returned from Williamsburg and have executed the Com'ission[180] of the President & Council, if they shall think proper to give You One, otherwise as soon as You can conveniently

· 31 ·

You are to apply to Colo Cresap for such of the Company's Horses, as You shall want for the Use of yourself and such other Person[181] or Persons You shall think necessary to carry with You; and You are to look out & observe the nearest & most convenient Road You can find from the Company's Store[182] at Wills's Creek to a Landing at Monhongeyela;[183] from thence You are to proceed down the Ohio on the South Side thereof, as low as the Big Conhaway, and up the same as far as You judge proper, and find good Land—You are all the Way to keep an exact Diary & Journal & therein note every Parcel of good Land; with the Quantity as near as you can by any Means compute the same, with the Breadth, Depth, Course and Length of the several Branches falling into the Ohio, & the different Branches any of Them are forked into, laying the same as exactly down in a Plan thereof as You can; observing also the Produce, the several Kinds of Timber and Trees, observing where there is Plenty and where the Timber is scarce; and You are not to omit proper observations on the mountainous, barren, or broken Land, that We may on your Return judge what Quantity of good Land is contained within the Compass of your Journey, for We woud not have You omit taking Notice of any Quantity of good Land, tho not exceeding 4 or 500 Acres provided the same lies upon the River Ohio & may be convenient for our building Store Houses & other Houses for the better carrying on a Trade and Correspondence down the River.

1751   Pursuant to my Instructions hereunto annexed from the Com'ittee of the Ohio Company bearing Date 16th July 1751

Monday Novr 4   Set out from the Company's Store House in Frederick County Virginia opposite the Mouth of Will's Creek and crossing Potomack River went W 4 M to a Gap[184] in the Allegany Mountains upon the SW Fork of the said Creek—This Gap is the nearest to Potomack River of any in the Allegany Mountains, and is accounted one of the best, tho the Mountain[185] is very high, The Ascent is no where very steep but rises gradually near 6 M, it is now very full of old Trees & Stones, but with some Pains might be made a good Waggon Road; this Gap is directly in the Way to Mohongaly, & several Miles nearer than that the Traders com'only pass thro,[186] and a much better Way.

Tuesday 5   Set out N 80 W 8 M, it rained and obliged us to stop.
Wednesday 6   The same Course 3 M hard Rain.
Thursday 7   Rained hard and We coud not travel
Friday 8   Set out the same Courses N 80 W 3 M, here We encamped, and turned to see where the Branches lead to & found they

descended into the middle Fork of Yaughaughgaine[187]—We hunted all the Ground for 10 M, or more and killed several Deer, & Bears, and one large Elk—The Bottoms upon the Branches are but narrow with some Indian Fields about 2000 Acres of good high Land about a Mile from the largest Branch.

From Saturday 9 To Tuesday 19 We were employed in searching the Lands and discovering the Branches Creeks &c.

Wednesday 20 Set out N 45 W 5 M killed a Deer

Thursday 21 The same Course 5 M the greatest Part of the Day We were cutting our Way thro' a Laurel Thicket[188] and lodged by the Side of one at Night

Friday 22 Set out the same Course N 45 W 2M and cut our Way thro a great Laurel Thicket to the middle Fork of Yaughyaughgaine[187] then S down the said Fork (crossing a Run)[189] 1 M, then S 45 W 2 M over the said Fork where We encamped.

Saturday 23 Rested our Horses and examined the Land on Foot, which We found to be tolerable rich & well timbered but stony and broken.

Sunday 24 Set out W 2 M then S 45 W 6 M over the S Fork[190] and encamp'd on the SW Side about 1 M from a small Hunting Town of the Delawares from whom I bought some Corn—I invited these Indians to the Treaty at the Loggs Town, the full Moon in May, as Colo Patton[191] had desired Me; they treated Me very civilly, but after I went from that Place my Man informed Me that they threatened to take away our Guns and not let Us travel.

Monday 25 Set out W 6 M, then S 45 W 2 M to a Laurel Creek. where We encamped & killed some Deer.

From Tuesday 26 To Thursday 28 We were examining the Lands which We found to be rocky and Mountainous

Friday 29 Set out W 3 M then N 65 W 3 M, N 45 W 2 M.

From Saturday 30 To Friday Decr 6 We searched the Land several Miles round[192] and found it about 15 M from the Foot of the Mountains to the River Mohongaly the first 5 M of which E & W is good level farming Land, with fine Meadows, the Timber white Oak and Hiccory—the same Body of Land holds 10 M, S, to the upper Forks of Mohongaly,[193] and about 10 M, N towards the Mouth of Yaughyaughgaine—The Land nearer the River for about 8 or 9 M wide, and the same Length is much richer & better timbered, with Walnut, Locust, Poplars and Sugar. Trees, but is in some Places very hilly, the Bottoms upon the River 1 M, and in some Places near 2 M wide.

Saturday 7 Set out W 6 M and went to an Indian Camp and invited them to the Treaty at the Loggs Town at the full Moon in May next; at this Camp there was a Trader named Charles Poke[194] who spoke the Indian Tongue well, the Indian to whom this Camp belonged after much Discourse with Me, complained & said "my Friend "You was sent[81] to Us last Year from the Great Men in Virginia to "inform Us of a Present[105] from the Great King over the Water, and "if You can bring News from the King to Us, why cant You tell Him "something from Me? The Proprietor of Pensylvania granted my Father a Tract of Land begining eight Miles below the Forks of Brandy Wine Creek and binding on the said Creek to the Fork and including the West Fork & all its Waters on both Sides to the Head Fountain—The White People now live on these Lands, and will neither let Me have Them, nor pay Me any Thing for Them—My "Father's Name was Chickoconnecon,[195] I am his eldest Son, and my "Name is Nemicotton[196]—I desire that You will let the Governor and "great Men in Virginia know this—It may be they will tell the great "King of it, and He will make M[r] Pen or his People give Me the Land "or pay Me for it—This Trader here Charles Poke knows the Truth "of what I say, that the Land was granted to my Father, & that He "or I never sold it, to which Charles Poke answered that Chickocon- "necon had such a Grant of Land, & that the People who lived on it "coud not get Titles to it, for that it was now called Mannor Lands— This I obliged to insert in my Journal to please the Indian.

Sunday Dec[r] 8   Stayed at the Indian Camp.

Monday 9   Set out S 45 W 1 M, W 6 M to the River Mohongaly— at this Place is a large Cavity[197] in a Rock about 30 Feet long & 20 Feet wide & about 7 Feet high and an even Floor—The Entrance into it is so large and open that it lets in Plenty of Light and close by it is a Stream of fine Water.

From Tuesday 10 To Friday 13[198]   We were examining the Lands which for 9 or 10 M, E is rich but hilly as before described, on the E Side the River for several Miles there are fine Bottom a Mile wide and the Hills above them are extraordinary rich and well timbered.

Saturday 14   We had Snow.

Sunday 15   Crossed the River Mohongaly which in this Place[199] is 53 Poles wide, the Bottoms upon the W Side are not above 100 Yards broad, but the Hills are very rich both up and down the River and full of Sugar Trees,

Monday 16   Spent in searching the Land.

Tuesday 17   Set out W 5 M the Land upon this Course hilly but very rich for about a Mile and a half, then it was level with good Meadows but not very rich for about a Mile & a half more, & the last 2 M next to Licking Creek[200] was very good Land; upon this Creek

In the Darlington Memorial Library

We lodged at a hunting Camp of an Indian Captain named Oppay-molleah,[201] here I saw an Indian named Joshua[202] who spoke very good English; he had been acquainted with Me several Years, and seemed very glad to see Me, and wondered much where I was going so far in those Woods; I said I was going to invite all the great Men of the Indians to a Treaty to be held at Loggs Town, the full Moon in May next, where a Parcel of Goods, a Present from the King of Great Britain, woud be delivered Them by proper Com'issioners, and that these were the Goods[105] which I informed them of last Year,[81] by Order of the President of Virginia Colo Lee, who was since dead, Joshua informed Them what I said, and They told Me, I ought to let the Beaver[203] know this, so I wrote a Line to him by Joshua, who promised to declare it safe, and said there was a Traders Man who coud read it for him__This Beaver is the Sachamore or Chief of the Delawares It is customary among the Indian Chiefs to take upon Them the Name of any Beast or Bird they fancy, the Picture of which they always sign instead of all their Name or Arms.

Wednesday 18   Stayed at the Camp.

Thursday 19   Set out W 3 M, S 45 W 2 M, W 1 M to a Branch of Licking Creek[204]

Friday 20   Set out W 1 M, S 45 W 6 M and encamped.[205]

From Saturday 21 To Tuesday Janry 7 1752   We stayed at this Place, We had a good Deal of Snow & bad Weather—My Son had the Misfortune to have his Feet frost bitten, which kept Us much longer here than We intended however We killed Plenty of Deer Turkeys &c and fared very well. The Land here abouts very good but to the W & SW it is hilly.

Wednesday Janry 8   My Son's Feet being somewhat better, We set out S 30 W 5 M, S 45 W 3 M, the Land middling good but hilly—I found my Son's Feet too tender to travel, and We were obliged to stop again.[206]

From Thursday 9 To Sunday 19   Deer & Elk, so that We lived very well.

Monday 20   We set out W 5 M here We were stopped by Snow.

Tuesday 21   Stayed all the Day in the Camp.

Wednesday 22   Set out S 45 W 12 M, where We scared a Panther from under a Rock where there was Room enough for Us, in it We encamped & had good Shelter.

From Thursday 23 To Sunday 26   We stayed at this Place & had Snow & bad Weather.

Monday 27   Set out S 45 W 6, here We had Snow & encamped.

From Tuesday 28 To Friday 31   Stayed at this Place, the Land upon these last Courses is rich but hilly and in some Places stony.

Saturday Feby 1   Set out S 45 W 3 M, S 45 E 1 M, S 2 M, S 45 W 1 M, crossed a Creek[207] on which the Land was very hilly and rocky yet here and there good Spots on the Hills.

Sunday 2   S 45 W 3 M, here We were stopped by Snow

From Monday 3 Till Sunday 9   We stayed at this Place and had a good Deal of Snow & bad Weather.

Monday 10   Set out S 45 W 8 M—The Snow hard upon the Top & bad traveling

Tuesday 11   The same Course S 45 W 2 M, then W 1 M, S 45 W 4 M.[208]

Wednesday 12   Killed two Buffaloes and searched the Land to the N W which I found to be rich & well timbered with lofty Walnuts, Ash, Sugar Trees &c but hilly in most Places.

Thursday 13   Set out W 1 M, S 45 W 2 M, W 2 M, S 45 W 2 M, W 2 M,—In this Day's Journey We found a Place[209] where a Piece of Land about 100 Yards square & about 10 Feet deep from the Surface had slipped down a steep Hill, somewhat more than it's own Breadth, with most of the Trees standing on it upright as they were at first, and a good many Rocks which appeared to be in the same Position as they were before the Ground Slipt; It had bent down and crushed the Trees as it came along, which might plainly be seen by the Ground on the upper Side of it, over which it had passed.—It seemed to have been done but two or three Years ago—In the Place from whence it removed was a large Quarry of Rocks, in the Sides of which were Veins of several Colours, particularly one of a deep yellow about 3 Feet from the Bottom, in which were other small Veins some white, some a greenish Kind of Copperas; A Sample of which I brought in to the Ohio Company in a small Leather Bag No 1—Not very far from this Place We found another large Piece of Earth, which had slipped down in the same Manner—Not far from here We encamped in the Fork of a Creek.

Friday 14   We stayed at this Place—On the NW Side of the Creek on a rising Ground by a small Spring We found a large Stone[210] about 3 Feet Square on the Top, and about 6 or 7 Feet high; it was all covered with green Moss except on the SE Side which was smooth and white as if plaistered with Lime. On this Side I cut with a cold Chizzel in large Letters.

THE OHIO COMPANY FEBY 1751[211] BY

CHRISTOPHER GIST

Saturday 15   Set out S 45 W 5 M, rich Land but hilly, very rich Bottoms up the Creek but not above 200 Yards wide.

In the Darlington Memorial Library

Sunday 16   S 45 W 5 M Thro rich Land, the Bottoms about ¼ of a Mile wide upon the Creek.

Monday 17   The same Course S 45 W 3 M, W 3 M, S 45 W 3 M, S 20 W 3 M, S 8 M, S 45 W 2 M over a Creek[212] upon which was fine Land, the Bottoms about a Mile wide.

Tuesday Feby 18   S 10 M over the Fork of a Creek S 45 W 4 M to the Top of a high Ridge from whence We coud see over the Conhaway River—Here We encamped, the Land mixed with Pine and not very good.

Wednesday 19   Set out S 15 M, S 45 W 6 M to the Mouth of a little Creek,[213] upon which the Land is very rich, and the Bottoms a Mile wide—The Conhaway being very high overflowed some Part of the Bottoms.

Thursday 20   Set out N 45 W 2 M across a Creek over a Hill, then S 80 W 10 M to a large Run, all fine Land upon the Course—(We were now about 2 M from the River Conhaway)—Then continued our Course S 80 W 10 M, the first 5 M good high Land; tolerably level the last 5 thro the River, Bottoms which were a Mile wide and very rich to a Creek or large Run which We crossed, & continued our Course S 80 W 2 M farther & encamped.

Friday 21   The same Course S 80 W still continued 8 M further; then S 2 M to the Side of the River Conhaway, then down the said River N 45 W 1 M to a Creek[214] where We encamped—The Bottoms upon the River here are a Mile wide, the Land very rich—The River at this Place is 79 Poles broad.

Saturday 22   Set out N 45 W 4 M, W 7 M, to a high Hill[215] from whence—We coud see the River Ohio, then N 45 W 12 M to the River Ohio at the Mouth of a small Run where We encamped. The Bottoms upon the River here are a Mile wide & very good, but the high Land broken.

Sunday 23   Set out S 45 E 14 M over Letort's Creek[216]—The Land upon this Creek is poor, broken, & full of Pines—Then the same Course S 45 E 10 M and encamped on the River Side upon fine rich Land the Bottoms about a Mile wide.

Monday 24   Set out E 12 M up the River all fine Land the Bottoms about 1½ Miles wide, full of lofty Timber: then N 5 M crossing Smith's[217] Creek. The Land here is level & good, but the Bottoms upon the River are not above ½ a Mile wide—then N 45 E 8 M to a Creek called Beyansoss[218] where We encamped.

Tuesday 25   We searched the Land upon this Creek which We found very good for 12 or 13 M up it from the River.—The Bottoms upon it are about ½ a Mile wide, & the Bottoms upon the River at

· 37 ·

the Mouth of it a Mile wide, and very well timbered

Wednesday 26   Set out N 45 E 13 M to the River Ohio at the Mouth of a Creek called Lawwellaconin;[219] then S 55 E 5 M up the said Creek—The Bottoms upon this Creek are a Mile wide & the high Land very good & not much broken, & very well timbered.

Thursday 27 Friday 28 & Saturday 29   Rained and We coud not travel__Killed four Buffaloes.

Sunday March 1 And Monday 2   Set out N 30 E 10 M to a little Branch full of Coal then N 30 E 16 M to Nawmissipia or Fishing Creek[220]—My Son hunted up this Creek (where I had cut the Letters upon the Stone) which he said was not above 6 M in a streight Line from this Place—The Bottoms upon this Creek are but narrow, the high Land hilly, but very rich and well timbered.

Tuesday 3   Set out N 30 E 18 M to Molchuconickon or Buffaloe Creek[221]

Wednesday 4   We hunted up and down this Creek to examine the Land—The Bottoms are 3/4 of a Mile wide & very rich, a great many cleared Fields covered with white Clover, the high Land rich but in general hilly.

Thursday 5   Set out N 30 E 9 M to a Creek called Neemokeesy[222] where We killed a black Fox & two Bears—Upon this Creek We found a Cave under a Rock about 150 Feet long & 55 Feet wide; one Side of it open facing the Creek, the Floor dry—We found it had been much used by Buffaloes & Elks who came there to lick a kind of saltish Clay which I found in the Cave, and of which I took a Sample in a Leather Bag No 2.

Friday March 6   We stayed at the Cave—Not very far from it We saw a Herd of Elks near 30 one of which my Son killed.

Saturday 7   Set out N 30 E 7 M, to the Ohio River—The Bottoms here were very rich and near 2 M wide; but a little higher up, the Hill seemed very steep, so that We were obliged to leave the River & went E 6 M on very high Land: then N 9 M, thro' very good high Land tolerable level to a Creek called Wealin[223] or Scalp Creek where We encamped.

Sunday 8   We went out to search the Land which We found very good for near 15 M up this Creek from the Mouth of it, the Bottoms above a Mile wide & some Meadows—We found an old Indian Road up this Creek

Monday 9   Set out N 45 E 18 M to a Creek—The same Course 3 M to another Creek where We encamped—These Creeks the Traders distinguish by the Name of the two Creeks.[224]

Tuesday 10   We hunted up and down these Creeks to examine the

Land from the Mouths of Them, to the Place where We had crossed near the Heads of Them; in our Way to the Conhaway—They run near parallel at about 3 or 4 M Distance, for upwards of 30 M—The Land between Them all the Way is rich & level, chiefly Low Grounds & finely timbered with Walnuts, Locusts, Cherry Trees, & Sugar Trees

Wednesday 11 Set out E 18 M crossing three Creeks all good Land but hilly then S 16 M to our old Camp[205], where my Son had been frost-bitten After We had got to this Place in our old Tract, I did not keep any exact Account of Course and Distance, as I thought the River & Creeks sufficiently described by my Courses as I came down.

Thursday 12 I set out for Mohongaly crossed it upon a Raft of Logs from whence I made the best of my Way to Potomack—I did not keep exactly my old Tract but went more to the Eastward & found a much nearer Way Home; and am of Opinion the Company may have a tolerable good Road from Wills's Creek to the upper Fork[193] of Mohongaly, from whence the River is navigable all the Way to the Ohio for large flat bottomed Boats[225]—The Road will be a little to the Southward of West, and the Distance to the Fork of Mohongaly about 70 M[226]—While I was at Mohongaly in my Return Home an Indian, who spoke good English, came to Me & said—That their Great Men the Beaver and Captain Oppamylucah (these are two Chiefs of the Delawares) desired to know where the Indian's Land lay, for that the French claimed all the Land on one Side the River Ohio & the English on the other Side; and that Oppamylucah asked Me the same Question when I was at his Camp in my Way down, to which I had made him no Answer—I very well remembered that Oppamylucah had asked Me such a Question, and that I was at a Loss to answer Him as I now also was: But after some Consideration my Friend said "I We are all one King's People and the different "Colour of our Skins makes no Difference in the King's Subjects; You "are his People as well as We, if you will take Land & pay the Kings "Rights You will have the same Privileges as the White People have, "and to hunt You have Liberty every where so that You dont kill the "White Peoples Cattle & Hogs—To this the Indian said, that I must "stay at that Place two Days and then He woud come & see Me again, He then went away, and at the two Days End returned as he promised, and looking very pleasant said He woud stay with Me all Night, after He had been with Me some Time He said that the great Men bid Him tell Me I was very safe that I might come and live upon that River where I pleased—That I had answered Them very true for We were all one Kings People sure enough & for his Part he woud come to see Me at Wills's Creek in a Month.

George Mercer Papers

March From Thursday 12 To Saturday 28 We were traveling from Mohongaly to Potomack for as We had a good many Skins to carry & the Weather was bad We traveled but slow

Sunday 29 We arrived at the Company's Factory at Wills's Creek.

CHRISTOPHER GIST

This Day came before Me Christopher Gist & made Oath[227] on the holy Evangelists that the two Journals here unto annexed, both which are signed by the said Christopher Gist, the first containing an Account of his Travels & Discoveries down the River Ohio, & the Branches thereof, for the Ohio Company in the Years 1750 & 1751 together with his Transactions with the Indians and his Return Home. And the other containing an Account of his Travels & Discoveries down the said River Ohio on the SE Side as low as the Big Conhaway made for the s^d Ohio Company in the Years 1751 & 1752 & his Return to Wills's Creek on Potomack River (as in a Platt[60] made thereof by the said Christopher Gist and given in to the said Ohio Company may more fully appear) are just & true except as to the Number of Miles, which the said Christopher Gist did not actually measure and therefore cannot be certain of Them, but computed Them in the most exact Manner he coud & according to the best of his Knowledge. Given under my Hand this [blank] Day of [blank] 175 [blank]

George and James Mercer's Land Release to John Tayloe and Presley Thornton November 25, 1759[228]

THIS Indenture made the twenty fifth day of November in the Year of our Lord God One thousand seven hundred and fifty nine Between George Mercer and James Mercer of the County of Stafford Gentlemen of the one Part, and John Tayloe of the County of Richmond Esquire and Presley Thornton of the County of Northumberland Gentlemen of the other Part. Whereas John Mercer of Marlborough in the County of Stafford Gent. and Ann his Wife by their Deed bearing date the [twenty-fifth] day of [November] in the year of our Lord One thousand seven hundred and fifty nine for the Considerations therein mentioned Did grant bargain Sell and release unto the said George Mercer and James Mercer and to their Heirs, All that Tract or parcel of Land Situate on Potomack Run in the

· 40 ·

In the Darlington Memorial Library

said County of Stafford containing by Estimation thirteen hundred and ninty Acres be the same more or less. All those two Tracts of Land Situate on or near Four mile Run in the County of Fairfax containing by Estimation seven hundred and ninty Acres, and three hundred and seventy eight Acres purchased by the said John Mercer of Gabriel Adams and Ann Middleton be the same more or less. All that tract of Land Situate upon Pohick Run in the said County of Fairfax, containing by Estimation One thousand and seventy seven Acres granted to the said John Mercer by the proprietors of the Northern Neck of Virginia be the same more or less. All that tract of Land situate upon Seaclins branch of Goose Creek in the County of Loudoun containing by Estimation four hundred and thirty six Acres purchased by the said John Mercer of Jacob Lacewell be the same more or less, One equal moiety or half part of s[ever]al Tracts of Land situate upon or near Red Rock run Limestone run and Kittockton Creek in the said County of Loudon purchased by the said John Mercer of Benjamin Grayson Richard [Corbin or Lee] George Slater, Benjamin [Borden or Harrison] and had to the said John Mercer [and] Catesby Cocke Gent by the proprietors of the Northern Neck of Virginia and divided between them containing by Estimation in the whole seven thousand f[our hu]ndred and thirty seven and an half Acres be the same more or less, One equal moiety or half part of several Tracts of Land situate at the Bull run mountains in the said County of Loudon and Prince William purchased of George Byrne Charles Green Willoughby Newton Thomas Owsley and the Sons and Heir of Edward Feagin and granted to the said John Mercer by the proprietor of the Northern Neck of Virginia aforesaid containing by Estimation Sixteen thousand three hundred and thirty eight Acres be the same more or less. One equal moiety or half part of a Tract of Land Situate upon Shannandoah River in the County of Frederick containing by Estimation six thousand four hundred and ninty nine acres be the same more or less purchased of Benjamin Harrison Gent, by the said John Mercer, One equal moiety or half part of a Tract of Land situate upon Smiths Creek in the County of Augusta containing by Estimation two thousand nine hundred Acres be the same more or less purchased also by the said John Mercer of Benjamin Borden, One equal moiety or half part of twenty five thousand Acres of Land more or less upon the Ohio, being the said John Mercers part or Share as a Member of the Ohio Company and of the Stock of the said Company as fully and beneficially to all Intents and purposes as the said John Mercer was entitled to have hold and enjoy the same.[229] And also four Lotts or half Acres of Land in the Town of Port Royal in the County of Caro-

George Mercer Papers

line purchased by the said John Mercer of the Trustees and Feoffees of the said Town, And all and every the plantations Houses Outhouses Edifices Buildings Gardens Yards Orchards Woods Underwoods Trees Pastures Feedings Ways Waters and Water Courses Easments profits Commodities Advantages Hereditaments and Appurtenances whatsoever to the said Lands belonging or in any wise appertaining, and the Reversion and Reversion Remainder and Remainders Rents Issues and profits of all and singular the premisses And all the Esta[te]Right Title Claim Interest and demand of the said John Mercer and Ann his Wife or either of them of in or to the same or any part or parcel thereof. And the said John Mercer also by the said Deed Did grant bargain Sell assign and make over unto the said George Mercer and James Mercer and to their Heirs Executors Administrators and Assigns Fifty Negroe Slaves namely, Jack and Winney his Wife and their Children Patty and David, Joe and Amy his Wife, Marlborough and Betty Bass, his Wife, Ajax and Nan his Wife and their Children Esther and George, Oronoko and Jenny his Wife and their Children Betty Dick and Fortune, Jemmy and Grace his Wife and their Children Frances and Beck, London and Chloe his Wife and their Child Kate, Ralph and Betty Belfeild his Wife and their Children Nan and Nell, Hercules and Seraphina his Wife and their Child Peg, Sarah Moses and Isabel, the Children of Deborah, Christmas the Son of Belinda, Beauty, Old Nan, Esther and her Children Sam, Judy, Nanny, and Molley, Cook, Essex, Jason, Jupiter, Peter, George, Juno and Barbadoes. And all and every the future Issue and Increase of the said fifty Slaves and of all and every of them, By which said Deed the said George Mercer and James Mercer did Jointly and severally for themselves their Heirs Executors and Administrators covenant promise grant and agree to and with the said John Mercer his Executors Administrators and Assigns That they the said George Mercer and James Mercer their Heirs Executors and Administrators or some of them should and would well and truly pay[230] or cause to be paid One full equal moiety or half part of all and singular the Debts which the said John Mercer justly and bonafide owed or was bound or engaged for on the last day of September in the year one thousand seven hundred and fifty eight and one moiety of all Interest due or to become due for the same, And also that the said George Mercer and James Mercer their Heirs Executors and Administrators or some of them should and would immediately give and deliver to Sarah Ann Mason Mercer a Negro Girl named Sarah, and to Mary Mercer a Negro Girl named Isabel being two of the fifty Slaves beforementioned. And pay or cause to be paid unto

In the Darlington Memorial Library

the said Sarah Ann Mason Mercer and Mary Mercer, the sum of fo[ur] hundred pounds Current money of Virginia respectively on the first day of April that would be in the year of our Lord one thousand seven hundred and sixty two if they should be then living or to the husbands of one or both who should be then de[a]d which husbands have not agai[]n married. And Whereas the said John Tayloe and Presley Thornton on the fifth day of November now last past became bound together with the said George Mercer and James Mercer in [th]e penal Sum of Six thousand pounds to the said John Mercer for their the said George Mercer and James Mercers performing and fulfilling the abovementioned covenant, And the better to secure indemnify and save harmless the said John Tayloe and Presley Thornton or either of them their and either of their Heirs Executors and Administrators from all Costs, Losses Damages and Charges which they or either of them may Sustain by reason or means of their or either of them being bound and obliged as aforesaid This Indenture Witnesseth that the said George Mercer and James Mercer for the Consideration aforesaid as also for and in Consideration of five Shillings to the said George Mercer and James Mercer in hand paid by the said John Tayloe and Presley Thornton at and before the ensealing and Delivery of these presents the Receipt whereof is hereby acknowledged. They the said George Mercer and James Mercer Have and each of them Hath and by these presents Do and each of them Doth grant bargain Sell Alien release and confirm unto the the said John Tayloe and Presley Thornton (in their actual possession now being by Virtue of a Bargain and Sale to them thereof made for one whole year by Indenture bearing date the day next before the day of the date of these presents and by force of the Statute for transferring, of Uses into possession) and to their Heirs and Assigns. All those several Tracts parcels Dividends and Lotts of Land herein before mentioned and described, Together with all the Rights Members and Appurtenances thereunto belonging or in anywise appertaining, And all Houses outhouses, Edifices, Buildings, Orchards, Gardens, Lands, Meadows, Commons Pastures, Feedings Trees Woods Underwoods, Ways Paths, Waters, Water Courses, Easments, profits Commodities Advantages, Hereditaments, and Appurtenances whatsoever to the same belonging or in anywise appertaining or which now are or formerly have been accepted reputed taken known Used Occupied or enjoyed to or with the same or as part parcel or member thereof. And the Reversion and Reversions Remainder and Remainders Rents and Services of all and Singular the said premisses and of every part and parcel thereof with the Appurtenances

And all the Estate Right Title Interest Claim and Demand whatsoever as well in Equity as in Law of them the said George Mercer and James Mercer or either of them of in and to all and singular the said premisses beforementioned and of in and to every part and parcel thereof with the Appurtenances And all Deeds Evidences and Writings touching or in any wise concerning the said premisses To have and to hold all and every the beforementioned Lands hereditaments and premisses and every part and parcel thereof with the Appurtenances [to the] said John Tayloe and Presley Thornton their Heirs and Assigns to his and their only proper Use benefit and behoof forever   And the said George [Mercer and James Mercer or either of them or their or] either of their Heirs and Assigns Do Covenant and Grant to and with the said John Tayloe and Presley Thornton their Heirs and Assigns That they the said George Mercer and James Mercer now are the true and rightful Owners of all and Singular the beforementioned Lands Hereditaments and premisses with the Appurtenances, and that they now are lawfully and rightfully seised in their own Right of a good sure perfect absolute and indefeazable Estate of Inheritance in fee simple of and in all and singular the said premisses beforementioned with the Appurtenances, without any manner of Condition Mortgage Limitation of Use and Uses or other Matter cause or thing to alter change charge or determine the same And that they the said George Mercer and James Mercer now have good right full power and lawful and absolute Authority to grant bargain Sell and Convey the said Lands and premisses beforementioned with the Appurtenances unto the said John Tayloe and Presley Thornton their Heirs and Assigns to the only proper Use and behoof of the said John Tayloe and Presley Thornton their Heirs and Assigns forever according to the true meaning and intent of these presents And that it shall and may be lawful for the said John Tayloe and Presley Thornton and their Heirs and Assigns now and at all times hereafter forever peaceably and quietly to have hold Use Occupy possess and enjoy all and singular the said Lands and premisses beforementioned with the Appurtenances without the Let hindrance Molestation Interruption or denial of them the said George Mercer and James Mercer or either of them or their or either of their Heirs or Assigns and of all and every other person or persons whatsoever, and that freed and discharged or otherwise well and sufficiently saved kept harmless and indemnified of and from all former and other Bargains Sales Gifts Grants Leases Mortgages Dowers Uses Wills Intails Fines or any other Incumbrance of any kind or nature whatsoever had made committed done or suffered by the said George

In the Darlington Memorial Library

Mercer and James Mercer or either of them or any other person or persons whatsoever claiming by from or under him them either or any of them. And the said George Mercer and James Mercer for the causes and considerations aforesaid Have bargained and Sold Assigned and made over and by these presents, Do grant bargain Sell Assign and make over unto the said John Tayloe and Presley Thornton and to their Heirs Executors Administrators and Assigns All and every the Slaves herein before particularly mentioned and named, And all and every of their future Issue and Increase To hold to the said John Tayloe and Presley Thornton their Heirs Executors Administrators and Assigns as his and their own proper Slaves, Subject Nevertheless to the Proviso and Condition That if the said George Mercer and James Mercer or either of them their or either of their Heirs Executors and Administrators shall and [d]o now and at all time and times forever hereafter will and sufficiently save harmless and keep indemnified the said John Tayloe and Presley Thornton and each of them, and their respective Heirs Executors and Administrators of and from all manner of Suits Troubles Costs Losses Damages and Charges which they the said John Tayloe and Presley Thornton or either of them or either of their Heirs Executors or Administrators may or shall at any time hereafter Sustain by reason or means of their or either of them being so bound and obliged as aforesaid, And also that the said George Mercer and James Mercer and their Executors and Administrators do and shall well and truly account with and pay unto the said John Tayloe and Presley Thornton or their Executors and Administrators all such Sum and Sums of Money as the said John Tayloe and Presley Thornton or either of them may or shall at any time pay or advance for or by reason or means of the premises aforesaid That then and in such Case these presents shall cease and determine and every clause and Article therein contained be utterly Void to all intent[s and] purposes, but on the contrary [shall remain] in full force & virtue. In Witness whereof the [sai]d George Mercer and James Mercer have hereunto set their hands and affixed their Seals the day and Year first within written

Sealed and Delivered (the five Shillings being first paid)
In the presence of Us.

    R Rogers.
    J Mercer

G⁰ Mercer
Ja^s Mercer

[Endorsed]
Mercers to Tayloe & Thornton. Release.

John Mercer to Charlton Palmer,[231] July 27, 1762

You will at Length herewith receive the long expected Case[263] of the Ohio Compª & an Appendix[526] to it in order to be Printed & laid before his Majesty The Board of Trade & Such others as you may think proper reserving Two Dozen to be sent me for the members of our Company. I Flatter myself that I shall have no Occasion to Repent my Recomendation or alter my Opinion of you I have Since Recomended you to one or two of my Friends who have Appeals to manage, & who I am persuaded if they have no particular Friends of their own to Employ will apply to You. As to the Compỿs Affair I am in Hopes both you & they will find their Advantage in it, if properly Conducted it is certain you cannot Suffer by it in Point of Interest as you have already received an order on Mr Athawes (a Duplicate[232] of which is inclosed) to pay you your Demand without Limitation which however I doubt not will be as reasonable as you can afford your own Trouble tho' I wod by no means have you undervalue it. The Compy notwithstanding their Losses[233] being as willing as able to make a Handsome Satisfaction for any Service done them. The Expences you are at I am Sensible can admit no Abatement & as to them I am only to observe they must be submitted to your Prudence, with this Limitation that none requisite shod be Omitted or Extravagant, but at the same time those that were necessary shod be Generous & proportioned to the Occasioned — — — And if we cod at last after all our Losses & Expenses[234] obtain a Patent[235] or such an Instruction as cod not be Evaded here for our 500,000 Acres of Land we shod not think £1000[236] ill bestowed If a Grant cannot be obtained for our Land by natural Bounds[237] in which Case a large overplus wod be necessary to make up for the Barren & Uncultivated Lands within them as you will see by Mr Gists Journalls[238] is often the Case & especially on the River side[239] it will be Necessary to Endeavour to procure us Liberty to choose a Surveyor of unexceptionable character to Lay off our Lands according to our Grant as we shod be otherwise obliged to pay above £600 for the Surveying it according to the Extravagant rates allowed Surveyors whose Fees being Establish'd for small Surveys the Legislature omitted to Settle their Fees for large ones,[240] insomuch that I have known a Surveyor make by his Legal Fees upon some large surveys near £30. a day. And in Case we are Limited to our Quantity it wod be necessary to have Liberty to Survey it in as many parcells[241] as we please as it is Extremely difficult to find a very large Quantity of very good Land, altogether at any place, where it is so, it is plain it must be our own

In the Darlington Memorial Library

Interest to take as much as we can together if it was our whole Quantity, but it is Certain that in many places upon the River there is not to be had above 4. or 500 Acres or not so much Good Land to gether which you may See by our directions to Gist[242] We wanted to secure in order to Build Storehouses for Lodging Goods & Passangers while making our Settlements. If we cod get a Grant bounded by Muskingum River from the Mouth[243] to the Whitewomans Branch[244] & up the same by the Mohiccon Town[245] to the Head thereof & thence to the Mouth of Cayahoga Rive[246] then along Lake Erie to the Bounds of Pensylvania the South with the same to the Ohio & then down the Ohio to the Mouth of Muskingum on the Northwest side of the Ohio[247] as the same is described in Lewis Evans's Map of the Middle British Colonies[248] which you may easily procure at any of the Print Shops in London—or upon the other Side of the River from the Mouth[249] of the Kanhawa River up the sd River to the Ouasioto Mountains[250] then bounded by the sd Mountains 'till they meet[251] the Monaungahela then down that River to the Ohio & so down the Ohio to the mouth of the Kanhava or so much thereof as did not interfere with the bounds of Pensylvania, or we might run along the Ouasioto mountains to the Line bounding Pensylvania & with that Boundary to the Ohio & then down it to Kanhava. I say if we cod obtain a Grant for either of those Tracts we wod willingly give £1500 for it as it wod save us the Expence of a Survey & many other Charges besides the Trouble of frequent applications. You will observe that it is a narrow piece of Land between the Ohio & the Ouasioto Mountains which are an Impassable Chain 30, or 40 miles over & as is universally agreed Impassable by either Man or Beast even where the Kanhawa breaks[250] through them as you will perceive it does. But I am of Opinion that whatever you do it shod be as Expeditiously & as Privately as you can, as I am well Assured that we might have had a Grant long ago by natural boundaries, if it had not been for the Affirmations of Gentn of Virginia[252] (then in Londn) who Interest induced him to Assert the Grossest Falsehoods that can be imagined. I imagine Mr Montague the Agent for Virginia[253] (or rather for a Junto of the Council & Burgesses) may look upon himself as Concern'd to Interpose if he hears time enough of your Intentions. I Expected the Officers who have at length Engaged the Government to recommend their memorial[254] to his Majesty for a Grant of the 200,000 Acres according to the proclamation[255] mentioned in our Case wod have opposed us but they were so Sensible of the Obligation they were under to our Company that they Entered into their Agreement of which I inclose you a Copy as I do of several

Orders[256] &c made by our Company which may provably be of some Advantage as from them it will appear that our Co did from time to time everything that lay in their Power to Comply with everything that cod be Expected from them. If any Difficulty or obstacle shod intervene you will contrive me the Earliest Notice which if no readier opportunity offers you may do by the New York Packet which will afford you a frequent one I send You Lewis Evans's Essays[257] as I imagine you have not seen them & I look upon them to be one of the best Accounts that has ever been Publish'd of the Parts he Treats of & therefore may Enable you to understand our Case the Better. I also Send you the Two Printed Acts[258] of Assembly of Pensylvania to Support the Facts mentioned in our Case as I doubt Mr Franklin their Agent wod Contradict any thing might be Charged agst them without a Voucher. I expect Colo Lee[259] will Inclose you a Letter to the D: of Bedford & perhaps another to the E: of Egremont. It will be the Hanburys & Mr Dinwiddie's Interest to Assist you all in their Power as they hold three Shares & I am sure if their Interest won't Engage them nothing else can, it is very probable they may be able to Engage some persons of Note to Espouse our Cause but for my part I have so ill an opinion[260] of the Men that I don't care to have any Correspondence with them, & wod not Trust them in that or any thing else which was one principal reason of my recommending the management of it to your Care. You have Copies of the Letters wrote to them by the Committee but I wod not Sign[261] that to Dinwiddie.

You will receive with the other papers a Petition[262] to be presented to his majesty Mr Hanbury formerly wrote us that upon his Application to Mr Penn The E of Granville &c pursuant to one of our Instructions a Copy of which you have they told him they would Grant our Company the Lands we mentioned on the same Terms the Crown Granted us the Lands in Virginia as I imagined that Letter might be of Service I wrote to Mr Mason who informs me that he believes Colo Lee has it as it was wrote to his Father but that he wod search his Papers & if he cod find it wod Transmit it to you I have wrote to Colo Lee to desire he wod do the same. I am

                Sir your most hble Servt
                J. Mercer
                July 27th 1762.

[Endorsed]

Mr Mercers Letter with the Papers relating to the Ohio Company. July 27th 1762

John Mercer, Case of the Ohio Company, 1762[263]
Enclosure 1

First four manuscript pages are wanting

and subsistance of fifty men only with proper officers to form a regular garrison and even any building that could with any propriety be termed a fort would amount to more than all the ⟨Rights &⟩ quit rents[264] to be so remitted, and therefore they were persuaded nothing more was necessary to carry their point ⟨clear up that matter⟩ than a bare representation of the fact, in the mean time fully persuaded of the benefit that would arise to the colony by the prosecution of their scheme they resolved to proceed in it with vigour and for that end had come to the foregoing resolutions[265] within six months after the date of his Majestys instruction but satisfied of the expediency of procuring a plan and account of that part of the countrey (which might be depended upon) before they came to any Resolution as to taking up and surveying ⟨their⟩ land they employed Mr Christopher Gist (a person well acquainted with the Indians upon the Ohio) to undertake a Tour for that purpose giving him particular instructions[266] to search and discover the lands upon that river (and the adjoining branches of the Mississippi) as low as the falls[42] thereof and particularly to observe the ways and passes thro' all the mountains he crossed to take an exact account of the soil quality and product of the lands, the width and depth of the rivers and their several falls with the courses and bearings of ⟨them &⟩ the mountains, and also to enquire by all the ways and means he possibly could what ⌈nations⌉ of Indians inhabited those parts, their strength and numbers with whom they traded and in what commodities they dealt, and to endeavour to cultivate a good understanding with them and to convince them if possible of what consequence to them the friendship and alliance of the English was both in regard to their protection and trade. Of all which he was to keep a very exact and particular journal to be returned to the company upon his oath[267] together with a plan of the countrey he past through drawn in the best manner he could. And as his Majesty had sent in a parcel of goods as a present[105] for the Indians the said Gist had a commission[81] from the president of Virginia to acquaint them with it and to invite them to come to Virginia to receive it. Mr Gist set off the last of October on this difficult and dangerous undertaking and never returned till the nineteenth of May following, and on the fifteenth day of July 1751 returned his plan[60] and journal to the companys committee who judging it intirely impracticable to seat the land on the two rivers of Miamis (which the said Gist recommended) and that they must at all events take up their first two hundred thousand acres nearer in which they believed might be found to answer their expectations upon the creeks mentioned in the royal instruction,[5] they again agreed with the said Gist to view and examine the lands between Monongahela and the Big Conhaway but in the meantime conceiving it to be greatly for the companys interest as well as the governments to cultivate a friendship and correspondence with the Ohio Indians and that nothing could answer that end more effectually than procuring a commission for the said Gist to meet those Indians at the Logs town[77] at a grand council they were to hold there in the following month[268] (when they were to receive his Majestys present) and to engage Mr Andrew Montour[79] (one of the cheifs of the six nations) in the interest of the government of Virginia and the company, the said committee recommended him to the president and council[269] for that purpose and gave him the ⟨following⟩ ⌈instructions⌉[270]

After you return from Williamsburg and have executed the commission[180] of the president and council if they shall think proper to give you one, otherwise as soon as you can conveniently, you are to apply to Colo Cresap for such of the companys horses as you shall want for the use of yourself and such other person[181] or persons as you shall think necessary to carry with you and you are to look out and observe the nearest and most convenient road you can find from the companys store[182] at Wills creek to a landing on Monongahela,[183] from thence you are to proceed down the Ohio on the south side thereof as low as the Big Conhaway and up the same as far as you judge proper, and find good land. You are all the way to keep exact diary and journal and therein note every parcel of good land with the quantity as near as you can by any means compute the same, with the breadth depth courses and length of the several branches falling into the Ohio, and the different branches any of them are forked into, laying the same as exactly down ⌈in a⌉ plan thereof as you can, observing also the produce the several kinds of timber and trees and noting where there is plenty and where the timber is scarce, and you are not to omit proper observations on the mountainous barren or broken land that we may on your return judge what quantity of good land is contained within the compass of your journey. We would not have you omit taking notice of any quantity of good land, tho' not exceeding four or five hundred acres provided the same lies upon the river Ohio and may be convenient for our building storehouses and other houses for the better carrying on a trade and correspondence down that river

They at the same time ordered a copy of his journal and plan to be transmitted to Mr Hanbury expecting he would have had them printed.[271] That Mr Hanbury communicated the plan is apparent not only from those parts (of which there never had been any tolerable ₍discovery made before) being laid down according to his plan in all the maps[272] of those parts published since but from his journey being pricked off in the map of Virginia[273] and some other maps[274] published in England since that time, but as the journal never was printed₎ ⟨the same is now added⟩ ₍in the Appendix No 1₎

The Indians for some reasons (the certain grounds of which cannot be assigned) failed[268] to meet at Logs town in August 1751, according to their appointment tho' Colo Patton beforementioned went[275] there as a Commissioner from Virginia. Mr Gist therefore went out on the fourth of November following to search the lands on the South side of the Ohio according to his instructions and returning the twenty-ninth day of March 1752 delivered his journal to the companys committee ⟨which is also added⟩ in the Appendix No 2[276]

But in the mean time John Blair Esqr and others procured the following Order of Council

AT A COUNCIL HELD OCTOBER 26th 1751

Both the Orders of John Blair Esqr William Russell and Company, and William McMachon, John Mc Machon Richard McMachon Lewis Neale, John Neale Mark Calmees and Company were renewed, in the first four years further time allowed to survey &c. and in the second five years further time allowed and leave to insert the names of any person or persons whom they should find it necessary to take in as a partner or partners to promote the settling of the said Lands[277] &c

N Walthoe

Note the Order of John Blair Esqr and Company pretended to be renewed by this last recited Order had expired November 4. 1749. Mc Mahons would not have expired till April 22d 1752 but it is very remarkable that his was the single order that ever was granted for any longer term[278] than four years according to which time it would have expired the April before, and it is to be observed that there is no Alteration of the bounds of either, these Grantees not being then well enough acquainted with the situation of that part of the Countrey.

The company was satisfied that Mr Gists two tours had in a great measure removed the prejudices[279] the Ohio Indians lay under towards the inhabitants of Virginia which had been artfully propagated among them, at least by the traders,[280] if not by the government of Pensylvania who were jealous of having any partners in the skin and furr trade which they had in a manner engrossed[281] to themselves. The Indians had found that they were supplied with goods by the company[282] on much more reasonable terms than they had been by the Pensylvania traders and could not doubt of a much more powerful protection from his Majesty than they before had reason to expect, as they generally looked upon Mr Penn (whom they called their brother Onas) to be the only person who concerned himself with American affairs such at least as they were interested in their lands and trade. But as the said Gist could not obtain from any of the said Indians any answer concerning the settlement of any lands on the Ohio,[283] their resolution concerning which was referred till a general meeting and as they had agreed to meet at Logstown in the May[284] following, Mr Gist again applied to the Government of Virginia who allowed of his appearing at the treaty as an agent for the company, but appointed the Colonels Fry, Lomax, and Patton,[285] Commissioners for managing that treaty in behalf of his Majesty [Mr Gist] ⟨on this Occasion had the following⟩ [instructions from the company]

INSTRUCTIONS GIVEN CHRISTOPHER GIST GENT. BY THE OHIO COMPANY APRIL 28. 1752.[286]

Whereas the Governor has been pleased to grant you a commission empowering and requiring you to go as an Agent for the Ohio company to the Indian treaty to be held at Logs town on the sixteenth day of May next, You are therefore desired to acquaint the chiefs of the several nations of Indians there assembled that his Majesty has been graciously pleased to grant unto the Hon'ble Robert Dinwiddie Esquire Governor of Virginia and to several other gentlemen in Great Britain and America by the name of the Ohio company a large quantity of land on the river Ohio and the branches thereof thereby to enable and encourage the said company and all his Majesties subjects to make settlements and carry on an extensive trade and commerce with their brethren the Indians and to supply them with goods at a more easie rate than they have hitherto bought them. And considering the necessities of his children the [six Nations and the other Indians to the Westward of the English Settlements and the Hardships they labour under for] want of a due supply of goods and to remove the same as much as possible his Majesty has been pleased to have a clause inserted in the said companys grant obliging them to carry on a trade and commerce with their brethren the Indians and has granted them many priviledges and immunitys in consideration of their carrying on the said trade and supplying the Indians with goods. That the said company have accordingly begun the trade and imported large quantitys of goods, but have found the expence and risque of carrying out the goods such a distance from the inhabitants without having any place of safety by the way to lodge them at or opportunity of getting provisions for their people so great that they cannot afford to sell their goods at so easy a rate as they would willingly do nor are they at such a distance able to supply their brethren the Indians at all times when they are in want for which reason the company find it absolutely necessary immediately to settle and cultivate the land his Majesty has been pleased to grant them which to be sure they have an indisputable right to do as our brethren the six nations sold all the land to the westward of Virginia at the treaty of Lancaster[287] to their father the King of Great Britain and he has been graciously pleased to grant a large quantity thereof to the said Ohio company yet being informed that the six nations have given their freinds the Dellawars (Delawares) leave[288] to hunt upon the said land and that they still hunt upon part thereof themselves and as the settlements made by the English upon the said land may make the game scarce or at least drive it further back the said company therefore to prevent any difference or misunderstanding which might possibly happen between them and their brethren the Indians touching the said lands are willing to make them some further satisfaction for the same and to purchase[289] of them the land on the East side the river Ohio and Allagany as low as the great Conhaway providing the same can be done at a reasonable rate and our brethren the six nations and their allies will promise and engage their friendship and protection to all his Majesties subjects setling on the said lands, when this is done the company can safely venture to build factorys and storehouses upon the river Ohio and send out large cargoes of goods which they cannot otherwise do. And to convince our brethren the Indians how desirous we are of living in strict friendship and becoming one people with them You are hereby empowered and required to acquaint and promise our brethren in the name and on behalf of the said company that if any of them incline to take land and live among the English they shall have any of the said Companys lands upon the same terms and conditions[264] as the white people have and enjoy the same priviledges which they do, as far as is in the companys power to grant. And that you may be the better able to acquaint our brethren the Indians with these our proposals, You are to apply to Andrew Montour[79] the interpreter for his assistance[290] therein and the company hereby undertake and promise to make him satisfaction for the trouble he shall be at. If our brethren the six nations approve our proposals the company will pay them whatever sum you agree with them for, and if they want any particular sort of goods you are to desire them to give you an account of such goods and the company will immediately send for them to England and when they arrive will carry them to whatever place you agree to deliver them at. If our brethren the Indians do not approve these proposals, and do refuse their protection and assistance to the subjects of their father the King of Great Britain, You are forthwith to make a return thereof[291] to the said Ohio company that they may inform his Majesty thereof. You are to apply to Colo Cresap for what wampum[292] you have occasion of on the company's account for which you are to give him a receipt

You are also to apply to him for one of the companys horses[293] to ride out to the Logs town

As soon as the treaty is over you are to make an exact return of all your proceedings to the company[291]

From the following proceedings during that treaty ⟨in the Appendix No 3[294] it⟩ will appear that it was with great difficulty the Indians were even then brought to agree that any settlements should be made by the English upon the Ohio tho' at that very time they were under the strongest apprehensions of being attacked by the French.

⟨*Extracts from the Treaty with the Indians at Loggs Town in the year 1752.*⟩[294]

At a Council held at Logs town June 1. 1752. [In full in Journal p 20]
    Present. Joshua Fry, Lunsford Lomax, James Patton Esqrs[285]
                    Commissioners
        Mr Christopher Gist agent for the Ohio company
        Mr Andrew Montour[79] Interpreter
        Mr George Croghan[78] Commissioner for Pensylvania

The Indians addressed themselves to the Commissioners in the following Speeches[295]

Brethren. You have come a long and blind way if we had been certain which way you were coming we should have met you at some distance from the town but we now bid you welcome and we open your eyes with this string of wampum which we give you in the name of the six united nations   *Gave a string*

Brethren of Virginia and Pensylvania, I desire you will hearken to what I am going to say that you may open your hearts and speak freely to us [we dont doubt] but you have [many] things in your minds which may trouble you notwithstanding which we hope we may continue in friendship on which we give you these strings of wampum.

Gave two strings.

After which the Commissioners let the Indians know that they would give them an Answer in a few hours.

Sometime after all being met in the Council house M! George Croghan by directions[296] from the Governor of Pensylvania made a speech to the Indians letting them know that it was his desire that they should receive their brethren of Virginia kindly and presented them with a string of wampum. *Gave a string*

Then the Commissioners spoke as followeth[297]

Brethren, You sent us[298] a string of wampum which met us on the road, by which you acquainted us that you heard of our coming to visit you and welcomed us so far on our journey, yesterday we arrived at this place and this morning you took an opportunity with a string of wampum to bid us welcome to your town and to open our eyes that we might see the Sun clearly and look upon you our brethren who are willing to receive us this we take very kindly and we assure you of our hearty inclinations to live in friendship with you, to confirm this we present you with a string of wampum.

Gave a string

Brethren, in your second speech to us and our brethren of Pensylvania this day you delivered us two strings of wampum to clear our hearts from any impressions that may have been made on them by flying reports or ill news[299] and that we might speak our minds freely. Brethren we assure you of our willingness to remove all misunderstandings out of our hearts and breasts which might impede or hinder the friendship subsisting between us.

Now Brethren, We are to acquaint you that we are sent hither by the King of Great Britain our father who not forgetting his children on this side the great waters has ordered us to deliver you a large present[105] of goods in his name which we have brought with us but as we understand that you have sent for some of your cheifs[300] whom you shortly expect we will wait with patience till they come and will then faithfully deliver you the goods and open our hearts to you in assurance of which we present you with this string of wampum.

Gave a string

⟨There were⟩ some debates[301] concerning the method of proceeding in the treaty whether to demand their reasons why the belt and speech delivered last fall was not sent to Onandago,[300] or if nothing should be said of that affair till ⟨the⟩ more material ⟨business⟩[302]

obtaining leave to settle the lands &c. ⟨was settled, which it was⟩ judged the other would effectually defeat

June 2d[303] Got our goods ⟨The goods were got⟩ out and dried them but ⟨when it was⟩ found they had not received the damage that might have been expected our ⟨the⟩ fine goods none.

June 3d We had ⟨The Commissioners⟩ had conferences with Mr Trent and Mr Croghan about the likeliest method to succeed in our ⟨their⟩ negotiations ⟨&⟩ had further assurances of their assistance which I believe as Capt Trent always has been esteemed a man of honour they had waited some time from their own business to attend the treaty which they look upon as the Kings and therefore declared they will forward it independent of the interest of either province.

June 4th Two Shanea⟨wane⟩ cheifs[304] being disgusted[305] (as was said) came to us ⟨the Commrs &⟩ made a speech expressing their inclinations to be gone home, as we ⟨they⟩ were preparing an answer in conjunction with some of the six nations to stop them word was brought that a vessel with English colours was coming down the river, which proved to be the half king[306] with a cheif from the Onandago council, he was received with several discharges of small arms landed and fixed the English colours on the top of his house we ⟨the Commrs⟩ waited on him, sometime after he returned the visit with some of the cheifs drank the Kings health prosperity to the six nations the Governor of Virginia &c ⟨& the Commrs when he went away⟩ made him a present of tobacco. he seems to be a person of great dignity in his behaviour

June 9th We ⟨The Commissrs⟩ had a private conference with the half king[306] and other cheifs at Mr Croghans[78] shewed the Lancaster deed and other papers, they thanked us ⟨the Commissrs⟩ for letting them know what the Onandago council had done and blamed them much for keeping it private (as they said) for had they known it sooner, it would have prevented many disorders they said they never told them that they had sold further than the warriors road[63] at the foot of the Alligany mountain and that they would confirm whatever they had done. The Indians desired to have their guns and hatchets mended which was complied with. Big Hanoana[120] a Shanoah⟨wane⟩ cheif told us that the Piets ⟨Piques⟩[98] were upon the poise whether they should return to the French or continue steady to the English and wanted to see what encouragement the latter would give them.[307]

June 10th This day was appointed to deliver the Kings present to the Indians we made there were ⟨separate⟩ arbours ⟨made for the Commissrs &c⟩ as the Indians did for themselves, laid out ⟨where⟩ the present ⟨was laid out &⟩ a part was set aside[307] for the Piets ⟨Picques,⟩

which was well taken by the other Indians distributed the fine cloaths ⟨were distributed⟩ to the cheifs.

The Indians being met the Commissioners spoke as followeth
Present. Joshua Fry, Lunsford Lomax, James Patton Esq^rs
Commissioners
Mr Christopher Gist agent for the Ohio company.
Mr Andrew Montour Interpreter

Sachems, and Warriors of the six united nations our friends and brethren

We are glad to meet you at this place to enlarge the council fire already kindled[308] by our brethren of Pensylvania to brighten the chain and to renew our friendship that it may last as long as the Sun, the moon and stars shall give light and to confirm which we give you this string of wampum. *Gave a string*

Brethren at the treaty at Lancaster[287] in the year 1744 between the Governments of Virginia, Maryland, and Pensylvania you made a deed recognizing the Kings right to all the land in Virginia as far as it was then peopled or should thereafter be peopled or bounded by the King our father for which you received the consideration agreed on, at the same time Canosateego[309] desired the Commissioners would recommend you to the Kings further favour when the settlements should increase much further back, this the Commissioners promised and confirm'd it by a writing under their hands and seals in consequence of which a present was sent you from the King by Mr Conrad Weiser which he since informed us that he delivered you at a council held here in the year 1748.[310] Now the King your father to shew the love he bears to justice as well as his affection to you his children has sent a large present of goods to be divided among you and your allies which is here ready to be delivered to you and we desire you may confirm the treaty at Lancaster

Brethren, It is the design of the King your father at present to make a settlement of British subjects on the south East side of Ohio that we may be united as one people by the strongest ties of neighbourhood as well as friendship and by these means prevent the insults of our Enemies, from such a settlement greater advantages will arise to you than you can at present conceive, our people[311] will be able to supply you with goods much cheaper than can at this time be afforded, will be ready help in case you should be attacked and some good men among them will be appointed with authority to punish and restrain the many injuries and abuses too frequently committed here by disorderly white people.

Brethren we assure you that the King our father by purchasing your lands had never any intentions of taking them from you[312] but that we might live together as one people and keep them from the french who would be bad neighbours, he is not like the French King who calls himself your father and endeavoured about three years ago with an armed force to take possession of your countrey by setting up inscriptions[313] on trees and at the mouths of the creeks on this river by which he claims these lands tho' at their coming and for many years before a number of your brethren the English were residing in this town[314] and several other places on this river, you well remember how he scattered the Shawnese so that they were dispersed all over the face of the earth and he now threatens to cut off[315] the Twigtwees, this is to weaken you that he may cut you off also, which he durst not attempt while you are united. On the contrary the King your father will lay his hand on your heads under which protection you will always remain safe.

 Brethren the great King our father recommends a strict union between us you and our brethren towards the sun setting which will make us strong and formidable as a division may have a contrary effect, we are directed to send[307] a small present to the Twigtwees as an earnest of the regard which the Governor of Virginia has for them with an assurance of his further friendship when ever they shall stand in need. Brethren we earnestly exhort you not to be drawn by the empty deceitful speeches of the French the peculiar talent of that cunning people, but in all their attempts to shake your duty to our common father, think of what real acts of friendship have been done by the English and what by the french weigh those things in your minds and then determine who best deserves your esteem and regard, for it is not by vain unmeaning words that true friendship is to be discovered, that what we have said may make the greater impression on you and have it's full force we present you with this belt of wampum.   *Gave a belt*

 Brethren It is many years ago that the English first came over the great water to visit you on their first coming you took hold of our Ships and tied them to your strongest trees ever since which we have remained together in friendship we have assisted you when you have been attacked by the French by which you have been able to withstand them and you have remained our good friends and allies for though at some times the chain of friendship may have contracted some rust it has been easily rubbed off and the chain restored to it's brightness this we hope will always be the case and that our friendship may continue to the last posterity we give you this string of wampum.
                    Gave a string

In the Darlington Memorial Library

Brethren We are sorry for the occasion that requires us to complain to you of an injury done us by one of your people who murdered a poor woman on the new river. Murder is a great crime and by the consent of all nations has usually been punished with death this is the usage among the English whether one of our own people has been killed or one of our brethren the Indians, and it is one of the earliest commands of the great Father and maker of us all who inhabits the skies that who so sheddeth mans blood, by man shall his blood be shed. We understand you know the man that is accused of the murder and we hope you will give him up to be tried by our laws, you may be assured that he will have a fair trial and if he is not guilty he will be sent back unhurt. We must inform you that the Governor of Virginia expects you will deliver the person suspected to be guilty up to some Magistrate in Virginia whom we shall name to you that we may send him to Williamsburg for his trial. This procedure is not only proper as it is a compliance with the laws of God and nations but it is necessary to warn all hot headed men who are not guided by reason to forbear from such wicked actions by which their brethren suffer.

Brethren We desire for the future you will observe the treaty of Lancaster and whenever your young people travel through Virginia that they will take such passes[316] as are directed by the said treaty, by these passes the men will be known which will be some restraint on them as to their behaviour, it will be proper also that a man of prudence and discretion should head each party that one among them if possible should speak English and that by no means any french or french Indians be suffered to go with them We might have mentioned many other irregularities but we have forborn in hopes that for the future you will give your people such orders as will prevent our having any further occasion to complain to inforce what we have said and induce you to do us justice we present you with this belt of wampum. *Gave a belt*

The Commissioners then spoke to the allies of the six united nations who were present having first advised with the half king[306] and being joined in the speeches by him in the name of the six nations

Brethren the Delawares. We thank you for the kind reception you gave us when we came to Shenapins which we shall never forget we advise and exhort you to beware of the french councils and that you will adhere to a strict friendship with us the six nations and your brethren who live towards the sun setting which will strengthen us all and be a sure defence against our enemies to confirm you in this mind we present you with this belt of wampum *Gave a belt*

George Mercer Papers

Brethren the Shawnese, Your nation has suffered much by French devices by which you have been dispersed we exhort you that you continue[317] to keep firm hold of the great chain of friendship between us the six nations and their allies which is the likeliest means to retrieve your loss and again make you a happy people. we present you with this belt of wampum *Gave a belt*

Brethren the Wyendots. Your nation is divided[318] and part is under the directions of the French, we think it would be good policy in you that are in our interest to endeavour to bring over your brethren but if this cant be done you ought to take all the care in your power that they do not under the colour and name of friendship come into our countrey and hurt our inhabitants or if they do that you will endeavour to secure them on their return to prevent any misunderstanding we present you with this belt of wampum. *Gave a belt*

After these speeches had been delivered and interpreted to the several nations the half king[306] desired the commissioners not to depart for he said they had a great deal of business to do, he then with a ten rowed belt of wampum in his hand directing his speech to Eghuisara (which is Mr Montours[79] Indian name) said. Child remember that thou art one of our own people and have transacted a great deal of business among us before you were employed by our brethren of Pensylvania and Virginia, you are Interpreter between us and our brethren which we are well pleased at for we are sure our business will go on well and justice be done on both sides but you are not interpreter only for you are one of our council and have an equal right with us to all these lands and may transact any public business in behalf of us the six nations as well as any of us for we look upon you as much as we do any of the cheif councillors and to confirm what we have said we present unto you this belt of wampum.
Gave the belt

Then addressing himself to the Commissioners of Virginia and all the Indians present with a string of wampum in his hand he spoke as follows

Brethren. It is a great while since our brother the Buck (meaning George Croghan)[78] has been doing business between us and our brothers of Pensylvania but we understand he does not intend to do so any more,[319] so I now inform you that he is approved of by our council at Onandago for we sent to them to let them know how he has helped us in our councils here and I deliver him this string of wampum to strengthen him and to let you and him know that he is one of our people and shall help us still and be one of our council.
Gave the string of wampum

In the Darlington Memorial Library

He next spoke to the Shawnese⟨anes⟩ and told them that he took the hatchet from them and tied them with black strings of wampum to hinder them from going to war against the Cherokees he said that they struck their own body and did not know what they were doing had they not seen ₍of their own₎ people there ₍whom he wanted to get back and would it not be₎ better to be at peace to bring them back,³²⁰ he charged them not to go again to strike their own people and he said that the Governor of Virginia and Pensylvania would interest themselves in making a peace.³²¹ *Gave a black string*

Then turning to the Delawares he said, You went to the Wiandots and delivered a speech and a belt of wampum to make peace between you and the Cherokees and after you came back you let your young men go to war against the Cherokees which was very wrong after you had delivered the speech which I myself being present heard. I take the hatchet from you, you belong to me³²² and I think you are to be ruled by me and I (joining with your brethren of Virginia) order you to go to war no more. *Gave a belt of wampum*

Taking a belt of wampum in his hand he proceeded as followeth

Brethren, The Governors of Virginia and Pensylvania, some years ago we made a complaint to our brother of Pensilvania that his traders brought too much spiritous liquors amongst us and desired that there might not come such quantities and hoped he would order his traders to sell their goods and liquors at cheaper rates. In answer³²³ to our request Conrade Weiser delivered us this belt of wampum and told us we must pay but five buck skins for a keg and if the traders would not take that, that we should have it for nothing since which time there has been double the quantity brought out yearly and sold as formerly and we have made some complaints to try to stop such large quantities from being brought but as there has been no notice taken to prevent it we beleive Mr Weiser spoke only from his mouth and not from his heart and without the Governors authority³²⁴ so we think proper to return the belt. *He gave the belt to Mr Croghan*

June 11th Present Joshua Fry, Lunsford Lomax James Patton Esqrs Commissioners

  Mr Christopher Gist agent for the Ohio company

  Mr Andrew Montour, Interpreter

The Commissioners of Virginia delivered to the six nations a string of wampum and a suit of Indian cloathing to wipe away their tears for the loss of one of their cheifs³²⁵ who lately came down from the head of Ohio to Logs town and died there.

Gave the suit of cloaths and string

Afterwards the half king³⁰⁶ spoke to the Delawares, Nephews you received a speech last year[326] from your brother, the Governor of Pensylvania and from us desiring you to choose one of your wisest councillors and present him to us for a king as you have not done it we now let you know that it is our right to give you a king and we think proper to give you Shingas[327] for your king whom you must look upon as your cheif and with whom all public business must be transacted between you and your brethren the English. On which the half king put a laced hat on the head of the Beaver[203] who stood proxy for his brother Shingas and presented him also with a rich jacket and suit of English colours which had been delivered to the half king by the Commissioners for that purpose

The Commissioners addressing themselves to the Shawnese(anes) acquainted them that they understood their cheif, king Cochawitchiky[122] who had been a good friend to the English was lying Bedrid and that to shew the regard they bore to his past services they took this opportunity to acknowledge it by presenting him with a suit of Indian cloathing

Then the half king spoke as followeth.

Brother, the Governor of Virginia, You acquainted us yesterday with the Kings right to all the lands in Virginia as far as it is setled and back from thence to the sunsetting whenever he shall think fit to extend his settlements you produced also a copy of his deed from the Onandago council at the treaty at Lancaster[287] and desired that your brethren of Ohio might likewise confirm the deed. Brother the Governor of Virginia we are well acquainted that our cheif council at the treaty of Lancaster confirmed a deed to you for a quantity of land in Virginia which you have a right to and likewise our brother Onas has a right to a parcel of land in Pensylvania, we are glad you have acquainted us with the right to those lands and assure you we are willing to confirm anything our council has done in regard to the lands but we never understood before you told us yesterday that the lands then sold were to extend further to the sunsetting than the hill on the other side the Allagany hill so that we cannot give you a further answer.

Brother you acquainted us yesterday that the french were a designing people which we now see and know that they design to cheat us out of our lands you told us that the King of England designed to settle some lands on the south East side of Ohio that it might be better in our brethrens power to help us if we were in need than it is at present the great distance they live from us, we are sure the french design nothing else but mischeif for they have struck our friends the Twigtwees. We therefore desire our brothers of Virginia may build a stronghouse at the fork of Monongahela[328] [to keep such goods powder lead and necessaries as shall be wanting and as soon as] you please and as we have given our cousins the Delawares a king[327] who lives there we desire you will look on him as a cheif of that nation

Gave a large string of wampum

Brethren Our brothers that live on this river Ohio, are all warriors and hunters and like our brethren the traders all wise men. There has been a reason for many complaints for some time past but will not complain of our brethren the traders for we love them and cant live without them but we hope you will take care to send none amongst us but good men,[329] sure you know them that are fit and we hope you will advise them how to behave better than they have done we well remember when first we saw our brethren the English and we remember the first council we held with them and shall do all we can to keep the chain of friendship from rust.[330]

June 12th[331] This day the Indians gave us ⟨the Commiss^{rs}⟩ an answer concerning the land which we ⟨the Ohio Comp^a⟩ wanted to settle they desired us ⟨them⟩ to build a stronghouse or fort very soon, as we the Commiss^{rs} had asked for the lands at Mohon⟨naun⟩gahela we ⟨they⟩ imagined they ⟨Indians⟩ had given up the lands upon that river, but they only meant ground sufficient for the fort to stand upon as appeared by a private conversation with the half king who said that was all that was intended tho' he always spoke the sentiments of others and not his own for that we ⟨a proper Settlem^t⟩ could not be ⟨made⟩ without a large quantity of land

We had ⟨The Commiss^{rs} had also the following⟩ Conferences with the cheifs of the Indians as followeth

June 12th The half king[306] with a string of wampum informed the Commissioners that one Frazer a blacksmith at the town of Venango threatned to remove that they did not desire he should leave them but if he did requested another might be sent to them and he said that they had not a sufficient number of traders there to supply them with goods which the Commissioners replied that they would represent their case to the Governor of Virginia and hoped they would be supplied according to their desire

The same day the cheifs of the Shawnese⟨anes⟩ with a string of wampum thanked the Commissioners for their good advisce they acknowledged that they had been led astray by the French and had suffered for it and said they would take care not to be deceived by the French again but would keep fast hold of the chain of friendship between the English the six nations and themselves.

The Commissioners thanked them for their Attachment to the

English and desired their compliments might be made to the young king[332] of the Shawnese⟨anes⟩ who was generously gone to the assistance of the Picts, ⟨Picques⟩[333] they sent him also a laced hat and a rich jacket[334]

June 13th The half king speaking to the Commissioners said

Brethren you told us you sent us a present of goods in the year 1748[335] which you said Conrade Weiser delivered at this Town he may have told you so but we assure you we never heard of it from him, it is true he did deliver us some goods then but we understood him it was from our brother Onas, he never made mention of the great King our father[336] nor of our brother Assaragoa. Then directing his speech to the Governor of Virginia said

Brother you complained to us that some of our people had murdered a woman in Virginia it is true there has been such a thing done and brothers we know the man that did it, he is one of our six nations altho' he has lived sometime among the French we cant make an excuse for so barbarous a murder but we assure you he did it without our knowledge and we believe the evil spirit tempted him to do it we will let the Onandaga council know what has been done and we believe they will try to get him and make a satisfaction for the crime committed   *Gave a string of black and white wampum.*

Brother. We have heard what you said in regard to the Kings design of making a settlement of his people on the waters of the river Ohio, you likewise told us you had a deed for those lands signed by our council at the treaty of Lancaster we assure you of our willingness to agree to what our council does or has done but we have not the full power in our hands here on Ohio we must acquaint our council at Onandago of the affair and whatever they bid us do we will do. In regard to your request to build a stronghouse at the mouth of Mono⟨au⟩ngahela you told us it would require a settlement to support it with provisions and necessaries, it is true, but we will take care that there shall be no scarcity of that kind until we can give a full answer, altho' in all our wars we dont consider provisions, for we live on one another but we know it is different with our brethren the English.   *Gave three strings of white wampum*

The Commissioners having drawn an instrument of writing[337] for confirming the deed made at Lancaster and containing a promise that the Indians would not molest our settlements on the South East side the Ohio desired Mr Montour to converse with his brethren the other Sachems in private on the subject to urge the necessity of such a settlement and the great ₍advantage it would be to₎ them as to their trade or their security on which they retired for some time and then re-

In the Darlington Memorial Library

turned and M.r Montour said they were satisfied in the matter and were willing to sign and seale the writing which was done and witnessed by the Gentlemen then present.

The half king then spoke as follows.

Brethren, The Governors of Virginia and Pensylvania, You expressed your regard for our friends and allies the Twigtwees, and have considered their necessities at present, we return you our thanks for your care of them, we join with you and desire you will deliver them this belt, and let them know from us, that we desire them not to forget what they did in Pensylvania,[338] when they were down four years ago, and joined in a friendship with our brethren the English, we desire they may hold fast the chain of friendship and not listen to any other but their brethren the English the six nations, Delawares and Shawnese, as we will stand by them, we expect they will come down,[339] and confirm the friendship they have engaged with the English.

He delivered a belt to be sent to the Twigtwees.

The Commissioners then opened the roads to Virginia with a belt of wampum and the following speech

Brethren, We have travelled through a long and dark way to meet you at this council, we have now compleated our business with pleasure and satisfaction, both to you and us, and as we are now returning back, we do in the name of the great King your father, as also in the name of your brother the Governor of Virginia, remove all Obstacles out of the way and make clear the road, that you may, at any time, send messages to us, on any occasion and we shall be always ready to receive them kindly, and look on you as our brothers, and, in token of the sincerity of our hearts, present you with this belt of wampum. *Gave a belt*

The Commissioners added. Brethren, at the treaty of Lancaster the Commissioners informed you of a large house built among us for the education of Indian children[340] and desired that you would send some of yours we now make you the same offer but if you think it too far to send your children we desire to know whether it would be agreeable to you that teachers be sent among you. The advantages of an English education are greater than can be imagined by them who are unacquainted with it. By it we know the part of the world from whence all nations came how nations for some thousands of years back have rose grown powerful, or decayed, how they have removed from one place to another what battles have been fought, what great men have lived and how they have acted either in council or in war. In this part of the world we know from the first time the Spaniards came to it how cruelly they used the Indians then wholly ignorant of

George Mercer Papers

fire arms and we know the actions of the French against you and others. There are many other benefits arising from a good education which would be too tedious to be mentioned, but the greatest of all is that by it we are acquainted with the will of the great God, the Creator of the world and Father of us all who inhabits the skies by which the better people among us regulate their lives and hope after death to live with him forever.   Gave a string of wampum

And This Summer 1752. the French not only attacked the Twitwees pursuant to their threats (mentioned in Mr Gists Journal)[341] but exercised such Cruelties in their town as are scarcely credible[342] and at the same time took four Indian traders[343] belonging to Pensylvania then trading there and sent them prisoners to Canada from whence they were sent to old France and imprisoned at Rochelle but being released by the Sollicitation of the English Ambassadar who cloathed and sent them to England they returned from thence to Philadelphia in Capt Budden May 1753,[344] having been stripped naked and used very hardly by the French tho' they had seised their Goods to the value of above £1500. when they made them prisoners

The Ohio company were no sooner informed of the French proceedings[345] and the Indians consent that they might erect a fort and begin their Settlement than they dispatched Mr Gist to the Northward to give notice to the persons he had there contracted with[346] in the Companies behalf that they might remove as soon as they would to settle pursuant to their Agreement and on his return he assured the Company that fifty of those familys would remove that fall or the next spring it being judged improper that the whole number should settle at once as they could not be conveniently supplied with provisions and proper necessaries for so many people and afterwards at a meeting of the said Company September 17. 1752.[347] it was agreed immediately to enter for[348] and survey their first 200,000 Acres from Kiskamonettas down the South East side of the Ohio to the mouth of the big Conhaway where it was thought absolutely necessary to have some fort or place of security And as it was also judged proper to take up some small parcels of Land upon the river at convenient distances to build proper Stores and Houses for the reception of the persons removing to settle there and security of their Goods while they were building they directed a proper application should be made to the Governor and Council for that purpose and the following ⟨the following⟩ Petition was accordingly presented to them November 6. 1752. To the Honourable Robert Dinwiddie Esqr Lieutenant Governor of Virginia and the rest of the Honourable the Council

    [The Petition   of the Ohio Company sheweth]

In the Darlington Memorial Library

[That the] said company having at their great charge and expence employed persons for above these two years past to search and view the lands on the Ohio alias Alligany river as far Westward as the Twigtwee town and to cultivate trade and friendship with the several nations and tribes of Indians inhabiting those parts in order to seat the same according to the condition of his Majesties instruction communicated to this Honourable board by his Honour the late Governor, and having also at their great charge cleared a waggon road[349] from their Store house at Wills creek to one of the branches[350] of the Ohio navigable by large flat bottomed boats which is the nearest best and almost only passage through the great ridge of mountains and consequently is of great benefit to the public, your petitioners pray leave to survey and take up their first two hundred thousand acres between Romanettos alis Kiskominettos creek and the fork of the Ohio and the great Connaway alias new river alias Woods river on the south side of the said River Ohio, in as many surveys as they shall think fit your petitioners understanding the Indians are not willing any Settlements on the north side thereof should be yet made,[351] and as your petitioners make no doubt but that they shall be able not only to comply with the conditions of their first grant in one year from this time but to seat a much greater number of families than they are obliged to if your Honours would permit them to take up such small tracts of land not exceeding one thousand acres as lie in spots interspersed between the companys surveys as they shall cause to be actually seated on before the 25th of December 1753 on the terms[352] of your petitioners grant or such other terms and conditions as your honours shall think reasonable which your petitioners apprehend would be of great advantage to his Majesty and his plantations as it would be the most effectual means to encrease and secure their first settlements which the encroachments of the French and especially the new fort[353] built by them on the west end of lake Erie and on the Southside thereof the last year render necessary the same manifestly tending to interrupt your petitioners grant and your petitioners in order to settle a sufficient force must without such permission be obliged to part with all their own land to encourage the Settlement contrary to the intent and agreement of the company who did not enter into so expensive an undertaking with a view of setting up for a company of land mongers, tho' several companies of that sort now trade in this Colony but with [view] of making fortunes for their Children in a very hazardous undertaking at a very great and certain expence whereas the land mongers by procuring an order of council for a certain quantity of land make surveys at so unreasonable a distance as might include 500 times the quantity and it is presumed under their grant no person can interfere when they meet with purchasers so much land is taken up and his Majestys land is granted to his Subjects not by a purchase from himself but persons who substitute themselves his brokers and receive the full value of them.[354]

Your petitioners therefore hope that your Honours will think it reasonable they should reap some of the advantage the public will receive by their great expence and not allow private persons[355] to interfere with their bounds or to take up large tracts of the lands they have been at the charge of discovering till they may have time to apply to his Majesty and know his pleasure[356] as your petitioners are so far from setting up for an engrossing company that they are willing to receive any new members into it on the same terms they hold their several shares which from thirteen at the time[357] of his Majestys grant now amount to twenty[358] yet have not so much land among them as some persons who are so far from being at any expence or procuring any public advantage that they have made large fortunes by selling his Majestys lands.[359]   And your Petitioners shall ever pray

The following Paragraph had been printed in the Virginia Gazettee of October 6. preceding.
Williamsburg Oct. 6. We have credible Advice[360] that the six nations in alliance with the Twitwees a people much more powerful than themselves have declared War against the French and French Indians being exasperated thereto by the most horrid and shocking Cruelties imaginable exercised by the French on one of the Twitwee towns.

Several persons[361] therefore as well as the Company judging this the most favourable opportunity that could offer to secure a settlement upon the Ohio, while the Indians were so incensed and before the French had gained any possession there applied on the same sixth day of November 1752 to the Governor and Council to take up divers Tracts of land upon that river upon the Condition of seating several hundred families thereon within three years after their Entries were allowed but those Applications as well as the Companies petition were entirely disregarded. However the Company (resolved to do everything in their power) in the same month of Nov. 1752 employed one Trent[362] hereinafter mentioned as a Factor to carry on their trade and pressed Mr Gist to proceed in the settlement and Survey[363] as fast as possible and he in that fall and the next spring not only removed his own family but procured William Cromwell his Son in Law and eleven other families[364] to settle between the Yaughyaughgane

In the Darlington Memorial Library

and Monongahela where they were no sooner seated than William Russell under colour of the Order of Council of November 4th 1745 surveyed those very [lands in February 1753,365 fixing his beginning on a] branch of Redstone Creek above fifty miles due North of the head spring of Potomack the most Northern Corner of [as shown in] Fairfax's line366 (West and North West of which he was to be bounded) and finding the first course run between Cromwell's and Gists and would include Gists own Settlement he algered the course to leave Gist a handsome Settlement (as he termed it) but included all the other families who had settled there as upon the Companys Lands and under their Engagement with Gist on the Companys behalf. This proceeding was the more extraordinary as Colo Cresap one of the Company was then out to lay off a Town,367 pitch upon a proper place to build a fort and actually forbid Russell to proceed informing him not only of the land being then settled by the Company, but that without it or convenient Stages through it they could not possibly carry on their trade, as the road from their Store house on Wills creek to the Ohio (and which they had been at the expence of clearing) run directly through it, and Russell at the same time acknowledged that he had received a Letter368 from Lewis Burwell Esqr then president and Commander in Cheif of Virginia who was as he said concerned with him directing him by no means to interfere with the Ohio companys Lands [— — —]369 be proper to observe that that Gentleman during the time of his Government always declared that he would do everything in his power for that Companys Encouragement as he was satisfied that the Ohio would never be settled by any private Adventurers or any otherwise than by a Company of Interest and fortune369 but Russell declaring some other of his partners (who were also of the Council) would stand by him he persisted in his Resolution and continued his Survey which laid the Company under a necessity of entering a caveat370 against any patent issuing thereupon which was to be heard before the Governor and Council but as they never try such matters except during the General Courts in April and October or the Courts of Oyer and Terminer in June and December the Company (considering the urgent necessity of settling those parts as soon as possible) were in hopes the same would have been tried the following April or June at farthest yet to their great mortification they could not procure the Summons for Russell to be made returnable sooner than July ⟨June⟩ 1754 before which time the French got Possession.

For in January 1753 the French ⟨they⟩ not only robbed all the English Traders they found upon the Ohio but killed some and made others prisioners[371] ⟨an Account of whose Hostilities &c ... A below.⟩ encouraging the Indians in their Interest to make Slaves of them as appears by the following account [first] published in the Pennsylvania and afterwards in the Virginia Gazettee.

Philadelphia Augt 15, 1754. In January 1753 four of our Indian traders vizt Alexander Mac Genty Jabez Evans David Hendricks and William Powell (four of those named in Capt Trents Letter)[372] were taken trading on Kantucqui[373] river near the Ohio by a party of French Indians called the Caguawagas,[374] who plundered them of goods to the value of several hundred pounds and carried them to Canada, where they were made Slaves. But acquainting the Mayor of Albany[375] with their miserable situation by a letter[376] which he communicated[377] to this Government measures were taken to procure their release the Indians at first demanded a Negro boy for each of them, or as much as would buy one but at length were prevailed on by the Commissioners of Indian Affairs at Albany[378] to take less, tho the whole paid them with the charges amounted to seventy two pounds five shillings and three half pence for the four prisoners, which has been repaid by this province however the Indians it seems pretend not to be satisfied and Colonel Myndert Schuyler one of the Albany Commissioners for Indian Affairs who transacted this matter with them received lately a letter from the cheif of that nation on the subject which being translated out of French is as follows.

Falls of St Louis[379] June 14. 1754. I pray thee my brother Anagarondon ⟨⟨Colo Schuyler's Indian name⟩⟩ to acquaint the Gentlemen that I have not been satisfied for the prisoners that were delivered to you at Albany last year, my young men tell me every day that they do not like your management and that for the future they will bring no living prisoners since they do not receive as much for one of them as will buy a little slave. You know my brother that I had only ninty livres of our money. I charge Montandre with this Commission who will explain my sentiments to you, when he delivers you this letter. The least that ought to be paid for a prisoner is 400 Livres ⟨⟨about twenty pounds Sterling⟩⟩ let those that have the management of these sort of Affairs give due attention to this, otherwise I will not answer for what may happen hereafter when my young men make prisoners.

Onongraguicte cheif of the Falls of St Louis. Upon which the printer makes the following very just remark. By this insulting letter from a people with whom this province has not had the least difference, to whom we have never given the least occasion of offence, we may see the contempt in which we are held by these Savages who

In the Darlington Memorial Library

not content with plundering our people of their goods with impunity propose to make slaves of all of us they can catch or to have a sum for each sufficient to purchase a slave otherwise threatning they will not be at the trouble of saving our lives. If they are suffered to go on in this manner and make a trade of catching our people and selling them to us again for 400 Livres per head it may in time [cost us more to satisfy the demands of that handful of barbarions,] than would serve to defend the province against [all its Enemies.]

A more circumstantial Account of the French Hostilities (or more properly Murders and Robberies for as yet no Injury whatsoever had been offered to them by any of the subjects of Great Britain in any part of America) was printed in the Pensylvania Gazette as follows.

Philadelphia May 3ᵈ 1753. Extract of a Letter[372] from Capt William Trent. I take this opportunity of acquainting you of the French and Indians killing and taking our people prisoners. They have killed Finleys[380] three men near the little Pick town,[381] and we expect that he himself will be killed. Teaff[382] was robbed of two or three hundred pounds, but his men got off, fifty five French Indians have robbed us, on this side the river, below Shawnesse town, of three or four hundred pounds, and took prisoners David Hendrick, William Powell Jacob Evans and his brother,[376] and a servant belonging to us, one McGintie[383] and James Lowrey belonging to the Lowries,[384] the last made his escape after he had been a prisoner several days. Mr Croghan with an hundred horse load of skins is coming thro' the woods, on this side the river, with a few Indians, but am afraid that they will be killed or taken, by three hundred Ottawawas that were expected would surprize the town,[385] as they had information of their coming, and doubt they will follow them when they find them gone, the rest of the white men are coming up the river in a body with what Indians are below, but as there is a large body of French and Indians expected every day down the river,[386] I doubt they will never get up, poor Fortescue perished on the road, coming from the lower town. There is not one Indian or white man anywhere below the Shawnesse or Logstown, but what is coming up. This was accompanied with the following paragraph, May 24. Four of the Indian traders who were taken prisoners in the Twigtwee town last summer by the French carried to Canada and from thence sent to old France, are returned with Capt Budden having been released out of prison at Rochelle by the Sollicitation of the British Ambassador who was so good as to cloath them and send them to England the French having stripped them naked and used them very hardly.

It is to be presumed that Capt Trent gave the first notice of these

George Mercer Papers

Transactions to the Governor of Virginia as he in a Letter[387] to the Committee of the Ohio Company dated Feb. 15. 1753 says. I am sorry to hear by a ₍Letter₎ from Mr Trent[362] that some of the Twigtwees are gone over to the French[388] and that some French Officers &c are at Logstown building of houses &c and that there are many others at their Forts on the Lakes which he calls an Army but hope they are only Traders from Canada. This information I had last Week by Express which I returned and desired him to get what further Intelligence he possibly could between and May, when I shall send some powder Arms &c to Winchester a present to the Indians[389]

As this was wrote before the Caveat abovementioned was entred, it might have been imagined the Company would have met little difficulty in procuring a speedy hearing, but ⟨from the Govr & Councils referring it to such a very distant day they found⟩ that instead of protection and Encouragement which ⟨in virtue of his Ma'ties Instruction⟩[390] they had always expected from the Government here, ⟨they met⟩ upon every Application they were obliged to make ⟨here⟩ they met with nothing but ⟨Slights &⟩ Disappointments ⟨not to call it manifest Injustice.⟩ For in June 1753 when they hoped to have had their Caveat against Russell and Company determined they found themselves under a necessity of entring three[391] more ag. Richard Corbin Esqr one of the Council ⟨who had during at the Court of Oyer & Terminer held in that month⟩ procured three Orders of Council[392] in the name of himself and Company to empower them to survey 50,000 Acres of land on Fishing Creek 100,000 at the mouth of the big Conhaway and 40,000 on Buffalo Creek, All within those very bounds where the Company had on the 6th day of November preceding acquainted the Governor and Council they proposed to make their Surveys, and what the Company thought hardest was that ₍most₎ Entries were directed by their own Map[393] laid before the Council on that day by the Governor ⟨who got it into his Possession as a member of the Ohio Company & under an express promise not to use it to their prejudice as⟩ before that time neither he or they ⟨Council⟩ knew anything of the Situation of the Ohio or the names of its branches.

From the following Letter wrote about this time by the Governor to Capt Trent it seems he thought there was no great danger to be apprehended at that time from the French ⟨the Companies Factor from time to time advised[394] the Governments of Virginia & Pennsylvania of the several Transactions on the Ohio. as will appear from the following Papers, What Use was made of his Whether a proper Use was made of his timely Information must be submitted. The

John Mercer's map of Ohio Company lands made before November 6, 1752.

The copy of the original in the Public Records Office in London, made in April, 1882, for Mr. William M. Darlington.

In the Darlington Memorial Library

following L're from the Govr of Virga directed to him But it is very certain that many Persons represented them as Stories propagated by the Ohio Company without foundation, & it was long before they would suffer themselves to be undeceived, as will fully appear by the Sequel. The following Letters were sent by Govr Dinwiddie & Colo Fairfax President of the Council to the sd Trent.)[395]

Williamsburg May 31st 1753.

Sir

(2)[396] Your letter from Winchester of the 21st May was delivered me by Colo Lomax the contents thereof I have duly considered and it corresponds with the Intelligence I re'ced from Mr Montour[397] and what I have ⟨by⟩ express from Philadelphia[398] and I am sincerely sorry for the present situation of the Indians in Friendship with us and to shew them how much I have their interest at heart, I have this day wrote to Colo Fairfax to deliver[399] you all or what part you see proper of the present intended for them that is now at Winchester

I hope you will take a proper care to advise the half king[306] and the other chiefs of the Indians by a messenger[400] of your bringing them the supplies as above from me, that they may send some of their people to escort you, so that it may not fall into the hands of their Enemies, as you are thoroughly acquainted in the woods I must refer this Affair to you, and you will consider the great misfortune ₍that will attend₎ if these supplies should fall into the hands of the French Indians which I hope you will cautiously prevent.[401]

I am well pleased with the half kings speech[402] and hope they will be able to give a good account of the French and their Indians, and prevent their taking possession of the lands ⟨on⟩ of the Ohio. You may assure them of my firm Attachmt to their interest. It was not practicable yet to build the stronghouse, but when this attempt is defeated they may be assured it will be built. If they secure some of the principal of the French and send them here I shall send them to France by way of Britain

What the Delawar's told you is confirm'd by Mr Montour in regard to the French and Indians giving the six nations a large black belt, and the Answer the six nations made them.[403]

I am sorry[404] for the accot of the murders &c done by the French and hope if we have a settlement on the Ohio we shall turn the Tables on them in every thing but their barbarity. You know how to frame a speech to the Indians in[405] ₍their style, better than I can₎ assure them of my sincere friendship and readiness, at all times to assist them, deliver the present to them, as from this colony,[406] and

George Mercer Papers

tell them it is intended for the Six Nations, and the other nations of Indians, in amity with us and them. I intreat you to be as inquisitive,[407] as possible, of a the number of the French, and their Indians, of their designs, and the situation the Picts and Twightwees are now in; next year, I hope to deliver them a large present, from their father, and I propose delivering it with my own hands. I shall be glad to hear that Burney got safe to the Twightwees, though he broke my orders, in remaining so long in this colony, if he had gone directly, it probably had been of much service.[408]

I hope Pensylvania have been apprized of the present necessities of our friendly Indians, and that they have, or will send them some supplies.[409]

On your return, I expect you will send me as particular an account[410] as possible of all affairs relating to the intentions of the French, and their Indians, and that they are disappointed of their designs.

God preserve you, and grant you a safe return, and I remain with great sincerity,

Sir, your most humble servant,
My service to colonel Cresap   Robert Dinwiddie
You know dispatch is now absolutely necessary.]

[Copy of governor Dinwiddie's letter, to the commandant of the French forces on the Ohio, sent by Major Washington.[411]

SIR,

The lands upon the river Ohio, in the western parts of the colony of Virginia, are so notoriously known,[412] to be the property of the crown of Great Britain, that it is a matter of equal concern and surprize to me, to hear that a body of French forces are erecting fortresses,[413] and making settlements upon that river, within his Majesty's dominions. The many and repeated complaints, I have received, of these acts of hostility, lay me under the necessity of sending, in the name of the King my master, the bearer hereof, George Washington Esq, one of the adjutants general of the forces of this dominion, to complain to you, of the encroachments thus made, and of the injuries done to the subjects of Great Britain, in open violation of the law of nations, and the treaties now subsisting between the two crowns.

If these facts are true, and you shall think to justify your proceedings, I must desire you to acquaint me, by whose authority and instructions, you have lately marched from Canada, with an armed force, and invaded the King of Great Britain's territories, in the manner complained of; that according to the purport and resolution of your answer, I may act agreeable to the commission I am honoured with, from the King my master.

However, Sir, in obedience to my instructions, it becomes my duty to require your peaceable departure,[414] and that you would forbear prosecuting a purpose so interruptive of the Harmony and good Understanding which his Majesty is desirous to continue and cultivate with the most Christian King

I persuade my self you will receive and entertain Major Washington with the Candour and Politeness natural to your Nation, and it will give me the greatest Satisfaction, if you return him with an Answer suitable to my Wishes for a very long and lasting Peace between us. I have the Honour to Subscribe myself.
Williamsburg in Virginia   Sir Your most obedient Humble Servant.
                                              Robert Dinwiddie
October 31st 1753.

The Answer ⟨returned by Majr Washington was as follows⟩
Sir

As I have the Honour of commanding here in Chief, Mr Washington delivered me the Letter which you writ to the Commandant of the French Troops.

[I should have been glad that you had given him Orders, or that he had been inclined to proceed to,][415] Canada, to see our General,[416] to whom it better belongs than to me to set forth the Evidence and Reality of the rights of the King, my Master, upon the Lands situated along the River Ohio, and to contest the pretensions of the King of Great Britain thereto.

I shall transmit your Letter to the Marquiss Duquisne ⟨Duquesne⟩ his Answer will be a Law to me, and if he shall order me to communicate it to you Sir, you may be assured I shall not fail to dispatch it to you forthwith

As to the Summons you send me to retire, I do not think myself obliged to obey it, whatever may be your Instructions, I am here by Virtue of the Orders[417] of my General, and I intreat you Sir, not to doubt one Moment but that I am determined to conform myself to them with all the Exactness and Resolution which can be expected from the best Officer.

I dont know that in the progress of this Campaign any thing has passed which can be reputed an Act of Hostility, or that is contrary to the Treaties[418] which subsist between the two Crowns, the Continuation whereof as much interests, and is as pleasing to us as the English. Had you been pleased Sir to have descended to particularize

George Mercer Papers

[the Facts which occasioned your Complaint, I should have had the Honour of answering you in the fullest, and, I am persuaded, most satisfactory manner

I made it my particular Care to receive Mr Washington, with a Distinction Suitable to your Dignity and his Quality and great Merit. I flatter myself he will do me this Justice before you Sir, and that he will signify to you as well as I, the profound respect with which I am
      Sir Your most humble, and most obedient Servant
            Legardeur De St Piere[419]
From the Fort Sur La Riviere au Beuf,[420]
  the 15th of December 1753.

It appears from the ⟨same⟩ Journal that Capt Joncaire[421] Commander at Venango acknowledged to Major Washington that the Intent of the French Expedition was to take possession of the Ohio, and to prevent the English settling there as they had heard of some families moving out in order thereto, and that there had been 1500 Men for that purpose on this side Lake Ontario but on the death of the General[422] they were recalled except 6. or 700 who were left to garrison four forts[423] which they had built upon French Creek and the Lakes, and Monsr Legardeur de St Piere told Majr Washington enquiring by what authority he had made prisoners[424] of several English Subjects, that the Countrey belonged to the French that no Englishman had a right to trade upon those waters and that he had orders to make every person prisoner that attempted to trade on the Ohio or the Waters of it. And it is ⟨also⟩ remarkable that the half king in the account he gave Majr Washington of his speech[425] to the French Commander insisted that the Land on the Ohio belonged to the Indians (and neither to the English or French) altho' at the treaty at Logstown he and the other cheifs had agreed the English might build a fort and settle there and in consequence thereof the Ohio company had contributed[426] four hundred pounds to ⟨build⟩ a fort and Majr Washington mentions in his Journal that on the 6th and 7th of January ⟨as he returned⟩ he met 17 horses with materials and stores for the Fort and some families going out to settle there.[427]

Jan 21. 1754. A Proclamation was issued requiring the Assembly which stood prorogued to the last Thursday in April to meet on the 14th of February

And on the 19th day of the Month the following Proclamation[428] was published. Virginiass. By the Honourable Robert Dinwiddie Esqr His Majestys Lieutenant Governor and Commander in Cheif of the Colony and Dominion of Virginia

In the Darlington Memorial Library

A Proclamation For Encouraging Men to enlist in his Majestys Service for the Defence and security of this Colony

Whereas it is determined that a Fort be immediately built on the River Ohio, at the Fork of Monongahela, to oppose any further Encroachments or hostile Attempts of the French and the Indians in their Interest and for the security and protection of his Majestys Subjects in this Colony, and ⟨as⟩ it is absolutely necessary that a sufficient force should be raised to erect and support the same, For an Encouragement to all who shall voluntarily enter into the said service, I do hereby notify and promise, by and with the advice and consent of his Majestys Council of this Colony, that over and above their pay, Two hundred thousand Acres, of his Majesty the King of Great Britains Lands, on the East side of the River Ohio within this Dominion (one hundred thousand acres whereof to be contiguous to the said Fort and the other hundred thousand Acres to be on or near the River Ohio) shall be laid off and granted to such persons who by their voluntary Engagement and good behaviour in the said Service, shall deserve the same. And I further promise that the said Lands shall be divided amongst them immediately after the performance of the said Service in a proportion due to their respective merit as shall be represented to me by their Officers and held and enjoyed by them without paying any Rights, and also free from the payment of Quit rents for the term of fifteen years. And I do appoint this proclamation to be read and published at the Court houses Churches and Chapels in each County within this Colony and that the Sherifs take care the same be done accordingly

Given at the Council Chamber in Williamsburg on the 19th day of February in the 27th Year of his Majestys Reign, Annoque Domini 1754 Robert Dinwiddie
God save the King

The company were far from thinking themselves bound by such a proclamation and it would not have had all the intended effect if they had enterd a Caveat against it, but as they looked upon it as the most effectual method that could be taken at that time for the End proposed and that it was for the Advantage of the Public they unanimously agreed to acquiesce, ⟨and⟩ at the same time proposed the Mon⟨au⟩ngahela as a Boundary that the 200,000 Acres for the Officers and Soldiers should be laid off on the upper side, allowing the company as many tracts of about a thousand Acres each as should be necessary upon the main road which they had cleared from their Storehouse at Wills Creek to the Mon⟨au⟩ngahela for the building proper Storehouses at convenient Stages and providing Corn and Hay for the great number of Horses necessary to carry on their trade and make their Settlement.[429] This the principal Officers not only approved of but declared that they looked upon the Contiguity of the Companys Lands as one of the greatest Advantages that could be, as they would be thereby enabled not only to settle their Land but supply themselves with Necessaries from the Companys Stores on much better terms than otherwise they could possibly do in that part of the world ⟨&⟩ as their Land would likewise be render'd of much greater value by having the road running through it by which all persons going to or from the Ohio must pass, so that as soon as it could be settled they could not fail to meet a constant market for everything they could raise and as by this means the Fort could not fail of being plentifully and cheaply supplied from their own Settlements on the one side and the Companies on the other which would also greatly contribute to it's strength and the Security of that Frontier

Winchester 26th May 1753.[430]

Sir

I rec'ed yours of the 22 instant from Lord Fairfax's.[431] ₁I had propurse for meeting you hither last week in₁ hopes of meeting some of the Indian cheifs according to appointment but Mr Andrew Monture calling on me in his way to Wmsburg gave me the first Advice[432] of a numerous Body of French and their dependant Indians being on their Warlike March towards the Ohio, whereby Mr Monture apprehended none of the six nations Twigtwees or other of our friendly Indians would at this time venture to come hither[433] so that I imagined I had little more to do than come and see the Arms and Ammunition &c secured till further Direction from the Governor. I am accompanied by Majr Carlyle, Majr Geo. Washington and Son ⟨George Fairfax.⟩ We met Colo Lomax who showd me your Letter[434] to the Governor with the string of Wampum to confirm the Indians request of a present supply of Arms &c. which induced me to write by Colo Lomax and acquaint the Governor that as my Instructions were to deliver the Arms &c. only to the Indians upon their coming hither, Yet if the above reasons for their not coming be allowed and their present occasion worthy relief I would wait here and at Lord Fairfax's for his Honours Commands hoping I shall receive Orders[435] to deliver You &c what can be with the greatest convenience and Expedition conveyed to such of our friendly Indians as are in greatest want. If the Bearer should not find you at Colo Cresaps, I suppose he knows your mind having ₁consulted what is the best method to assist the threatened Indians so as to prevent any surprize from a watchful[436] Enemy who may get Intelligence of the Arms &c. being on the road soon after their being set forward I am persuaded I shall have the Governors directions by Thursday[437] at farthest. And if it would suit your other business should be glad to see you the Bearer tells us he left about 70 Indians at Colo Cresaps who he supposes came from the Cherokees[438] having several Scalps and some prisoners, please to relate this matter particularly that I may send it to the Governor. Wishing you and Friends all happiness

I am Sr Yr very hble Servant
W Fairfax.

Sir   Belvoir 9th June 1753.[439]

On seeing Mr Andrew Monture[440] the 1st instant and Mr Joseph Carroll the 3d inst. at Winchester and on discoursing with them concerning the present State of our Indian Affairs, they apprehended a great risque at this time to send the Arms Ammunition &c to Logs town especially as it was not known whereabouts the French Forces were on their March and might by their Spies get intelligence of and surprize any small party that conducted the said Arms &c which appearing plausible and uncertain when I might receive further Orders also to save Expences, I left the Town on Monday the 4th but with directions to Mr William Cock that if any Packet from the Governor should arrive to send it immediately by Express accordingly this morning Mr Cock sent me by an express Messenger his Honor's Letter accompanied with one from Colo Lomax. The Governor signifies his and the Councils concern that the Indians did not meet me as expected at Winchester and the more as they consider the situation of those people from the throats of the French and Indians in their Interest, therefore on the present Exigency I am directed to deliver you all or any part of the intended present now at Winchester. I have pursuant thereto wrote now to Mr Cock who has the care and custody thereof to get the Waggons bespoke and forthwith to load the same with powder and Ball as most wanted and such of the Cases or Chests of the firelocks, flints and duffels as can be conveniently stowd and carried as you may advise and direct to the Mouth of Pattersons creek where in your Letter to me you desir'd ⟨they⟩ might be sent you, and if your other affairs did not permit your coming or sending a trusty person to get one if perhaps Mr Joseph Carroll could not be engag'd to undertake the care of seeing them delivered to you the Governor proposes your giving notice to the half king timely for his sending a sufficient number of his people to Escort and be a safe guard to prevent the Enemy getting intelligence and possessing them. I heartily wish the French may fail of Success and that our friendly Indians may not be dispirited. You'l please to favour me with an Account of your proceeding relating to the above particulars, with my Complements to Colo Cresap &c. I remain your loving Friend &c.

W. Fairfax

⟨On the 10th of July &c. See C. fol 17.⟩

Winchester 1st Sept 1753[441]

Sir

I rec'ed your Epistle and observe that our brethren the Indians cannot be punctual as to times of appointment I hope when they understand our Governor cannot meet them here now on the sudden Notice, they will not be very angry and refuse to see me who am next in Rank, upon Colo Burwell ⟨the⟩ late Presidt's refusing to Act ever since the Governors arrival.[442] I am empowered under the Great Seal and fully instructed to receive and act with the Indians and have Hope I shall give satisfaction The Governor has advised me by the return of Mr Gist, that the Chicasaws, Cherokees, Catawbas, and Creeks on his acquainting[443] them by express Messenger,[444] that the French had come in a Warlike manner to dispossess the Ohio Indians and settle themselves, answered him[445] that they would heartily Join the six nations to drive the French back to Canada having also cause to strike them. The Cherokees propose sending a thousand men, You'l acquaint our brethren that the Governor is always studious of promoting their [Welfare]. I shall be glad if you and friend Mr Montour[79] will endeavour to expedite your March hither for beside Mr Croghan,[78] You have other friends that impatiently long to see you all, among them is your assured Welwisher & hble Servant.

W Fairfax.

P. S. ⟨⟨to the Indians⟩⟩ You must think it a mark of our good regard for you and Eghuieserra, ⟨⟨M. Montour⟩⟩ that we spare at this critical time Annosenough ⟨⟨Capt Trent⟩⟩[446] to be our Envoy, but hoping he may assist you in qualifying any uneasiness that might happen among his kindred the Wyendots,[447] he has been chosen to salute you, and we desire youl receive and entertain him accordingly

W Fx.

⟨The Indians complaining, notwithstanding the Supply they received, that they still were in want of Arms & Ammunition Capt Trent acquainted Colo Fx of it & thereupon soon after received the addi-

In the Darlington Memorial Library

tional Supply[448] mentioned in the following Letter directed to him by Mr Walthoe Clerk of the Council.⟩

Williamsburg Septemr 26. 1753.[449]

Sir

The Governor being informed by Colonel Fairfax that the Indians on the Ohio are still in want of powder and Lead, has been pleased to order them a fresh supply as below which are lodged with Mr Cock at Winchester waiting your Directions for conveying them to the Ohio, and you are hereby requested to give proper Orders that the same may be safely and speedily transported to Logstown.[448]

You will receive ten Barrels of powder six Cases of Shot and ₍four₎ hundred Flints there are neither pistols, nor Cutlasses in the Magazine, or some would have been sent. I am Sir your humble Servant
⟨To Capt Wm Trent.⟩   N. Walthoe
⟨The Assembly of Virginia &c See D fol. 18.⟩

Williamsburg Jan.' 27. 1754.[450]

Sir.

Your Letter of the 6th Currt I rec'ed from Majr Washington, from his report,[451] information and observations I find the French intends down the Ohio, in order to build Forts and take possession of the Lands on that river which I would very earnestly prevent. And as you think you could stop them this Winter, if properly impowered, so to do. I therefore enclose you a Capts Como to raise one hundred Men in Augusta, and in the exterior settlements of this Dominion and a blank Como for you to choose a suitable Lieut[452] to Co.operate with you, your Compa will be in the pay of this Government agreeable to the Act of Assembly[453]

Majr Washington has a Como[454] to raise one hundred Men, with them he is to join you, and I desire you March your men out to the Ohio, where a Fort is proposed to be built, when you are there, you are to protect and assist them in finishing the fort, and to be on your guard against any Attempts of the French. I doubt not the Woods men you may enlist will be provided with Guns &c

I have appointed[455] Majr Carlile at Alexandria Commissary of Stores and provisions, he will supply you accordingly with what Necessaries you may want and in Case of want of Guns[456] I have sent some to his Care to be delivered to the Commanders of either these Companies giving a receipt accordingly for them. As you have a good interest with the Indians, I am in hopes you will prevail with many of them to join you in order to defeat the designs of the French in taking their Lands from them by force of Arms.

George Mercer Papers

The Ho: of Burgesses are to meet the 14th of next Mo: when I hope they will enable me to send out 400 more Men early in the Spring to your Assistance. I wrote to the neighbouring Governors[457] for their aid and Assistance on the present Emergency, and am in hopes they will supply a good number of men &c.

I have some Cannon come in,[458] Ten I send up to the Commissary at Alexandria, they carry four pound shot I fear there will be difficulty in carrying them out as you are acquainted with the roads I shall be glad of your advice therein and communicate the same to Majr Carlile. You see the good opinion I have of your Capacity and Diligence which I hope you will exert on this occasion by keeping a good Command and strongly encourageing our friendly Indians to be on the Active. Provisions will be difficult to send regular supplies. Mr Washington says one Frazer can procure[459] large quantities of Venison Bear &c. I desire you may write him to get what he can. When you have compleated your Compa send me a list thereof and the time of their enlisting and the place of their abode. I wish you health and Success in the present Expedition, and I am sincerely
P S. enclosed is a Speech to the
half king which please deliver
in my name .

Sr Yr hble Servt
Robt Dinwiddie

Robert Dinwiddie Esqr his Majestys Lieut Governor Commander in Chief and the Admiral of his Colony and Dominion of Virginia
   To William Trent Esqr[460]

Whereas certain persons pretending to be the Subjects of his most Christian Majesty the King of France and that they act by his Commission have in an hostile manner invaded the Territories [of our] Sovereign his Majesty King George, the second, King of Great Britain, France and Ireland, and have committed divers Outrages and Violences on the persons and Goods of his Majestys Subjects in direct Violation and infraction of the Treaties at present subsisting between the two Crowns And, Whereas these Acts of hostility and Depradations have been perpetrated in that part of his Majestys Dominions which are under my Government. In order therefore to the preservation of the peace and good understanding between the two Crowns and the preservation of our Sovereigns undoubted rights and the protection of his Subjects as much as in me lies, I have thought proper to appoint and by Virtue of the power and Authority to me given by his Majesty I do hereby Constitute and appoint, You William Trent

In the Darlington Memorial Library

Esq[r] to be Commander of such and so many of his Majestys Subjects not exceeding One hundred Men as you can immediately raise and inlist, and with the said Company and the Assistance of our good and faithful friends and Allies the Indians of the six Nations and such others as are in Amity with them and us to keep possession of his Majestys Lands on the Ohio and the Waters thereof and to dislodge and drive away and in case of refusal and resistance to kill and destroy or take prisoners all and every person and persons whatsoever not Subjects of the King of Great Britain who now are or shall hereafter come to settle and take possession of any Lands on the said River Ohio or on any of the branches or Waters thereof.

And I do hereby require the said Men who shall so enlist themselves and every of them to obey you as their Commander and Captain &c. And you are to constitute and appoint such and so many Officers under you as the service shall require not exceeding one Lieutenant and one Ensign[461]

Given under my hand and the Seal of the Colony at Williamsburg the 26. day of January in the 27th Year of his Majestys reign Annoque Dom 1754.
Rob[t] Dinwiddie

Cap[t] Trent in Consequence of these Orders and Commission not only carried out at his own Expence (to the amount of £375)[462] the two several presents of Goods and Ammunition to the Indians, but between the 15th of February and 12th of April enlisted 52 Men viz[t] twenty one Feb 15th two on the 22[d] Six on the 24th one on the 25th another on the 27th two on the 5th March, two on the 6th one on the 7th two on the 16th one on the 27th one on the 29th two on the 1st of April one on the 2[d] one on the 3[d] two on the 4th one on the 7th three on the 9th and two on the 12th which he was also obliged not only to maintain but to arm several and supply them with other Necessaries from the Companies Store,[463] for notwithstanding the Governor wrote him that the Commissary would supply him and Maj[r] Washington with provisions from Alexandria they must have all starved if they had depended on him, and Col[o] Cresap and Cap[t] Trent had not procured all the provisions they possibly could in the parts adjacent. The Assembly of Maryland were so far from yielding any Aid and Assistance as Governor Dinwiddie expected that in their Address to their Governor they use these words.

We have considered the Requisition of the Governor of Virginia, and your Excellency's Message of the 2[d] Instant, with due Attention, and are fully convinced, that our own security is connected with the safety of our neighbours, and that in Case of an Attack we ought

· 83 ·

George Mercer Papers

mutually to assist and support each other, but as it does not appear to us that any Invasion or hostile attempt has been made against this or any other of his Majesties Colonies we do not think it necessary to make any provision for an armed force, which must inevitably load us with great Expence and which cannot, as we conceive, under the Restrictions of the Royal order, Signified by the Earl of Holderness'es Letter[464] to your Excellency effectually co-operate, except in Case of an Invasion, with that of any other Colony.[465]

In the same Newspaper the Virginia Gazettee of March 29, 1754. the following Account of Capt Trents situation is given in a Letter from him to Majr Washington dated February 19th at Yaughyaughgany big bottom[466]

The 17th Mr Trent arrived at the Forks of Monongahela (from the Mouth of Redstone Creek, where he has built a strong store house) and met Mr Gist, and several others, In two or three days they expected down all the people, and as soon as they came were to lay the foundation of the Fort, expecting to make out for that purpose about 70 or 80 Men. The Indians were to join them[467] and make them strong they requested him (Major Washington) to march out to them with all possible Expedition. They acquainted him that Monsieur La Force[468] (ou La Farce) had made a speech to some of our Indians, and told them that neither they nor the English there, would see the Sun above twenty days longer, 13 of the days being then to come.[469] By what Mr Croghan could learn from an Indian in the French Interest, they might expect 400 French down in that time.[470] A Messenger sent from the French Fort had Letters for the Commanders of the other Forts to march immediately and join them, in order to cut off our Indians and Whites, and some French Indians were likewise expected to join them When La Force had made his speech to the Indians, they sent[471] a string of Wampum to Mr Croghan, to desire him to [hurry] the English to come for that they expected soon to be attacked, and pressed hard to come and join them for they [needed] Necessaries and Assistance and then would strike. They further write that 60[472] French and Indians were gone against the lower Shawneese Town, to cut off the Shawneese, 200 Ottaways and Chippawas, was come to Muskingum and demanded the white people there, and shewed them the French Hatchet. The Wyendotts though not above 30 Men refused to let them kill them in their Town, but they expected every day to hear they had cut off the whites and likewise the Wyendots.[473]

April 2d 1754. Major Washington marched[474] from Alexandria with 120 men and 12 Waggons with Stores provisions &c according

A hitherto unknown George Washington letter copied by John Mercer into the Case of the Ohio Company, 1762.

In the Darlington Memorial Library

to the news paper, but it is to be doubted that account was exaggerated, as he writes the following Letter[475] on the 18th of that Month from Winchester to Colo Cresap.

Sir.   The difficulty of getting Waggons has almost been insurmountable, we have found so much inconvenience attending it here in these roads that I am determined to carry all our provisions &c. out on horse back and should be glad if Capt Trent with your Assistance would procure as many horses as possible against we arrive at Wills Creek that as little stoppage as possible may be made there. I have sent Wm Jenkins with 60 Yrds of Oznabrigs for Bags and hope you will be as expeditious as you can in getting them made and fill'd

Majr Carlyle acquainted me that a number of [kettles, tomhawks, best gun flints, and axes] might be had from the Companys Store which we are much in want and should be glad to have laid by for us, Hoes we shall also want, and several pair of Hand cuffs.

I hope all the Flower you have or can get you will save for this purpose and other provisions and necessary's which you think will be of use (that may not occur to my memory at present) will be laid by till our Arrival which I expect will be at Job Pearsalls[476] abt Saturday night or Sunday next, at present I have nothing more to add than that I am

Yr most Hble Servt
Go Washington

Capt Trent having been supplied with no provisions for his Company but what he purchased in the Neighbourhood was sensible that if he did not procure a proper supply in time they could not subsist and therefore was obliged to come down to Wills creek in order to purchase some.[477] In his absence and the day before the date of Majr Washingtons Letter the French had come from Venango and surprized the Fort of which the following account was published in the Virginia Gazettee of May 1754.

Williamsburg May 9. On Saturday last arrived in Town from Ohio, Ensign Edward Ward, of Capt Trents Company with an Indian Messenger from the Half King Lieutenant Ward informs us That on the 17th of last Month the French consisting of about 1000 Men, under the Command of Monsier Contrecoeur[478] came from Venango in 300 Canoes and 60 Battoes, with 18 pieces of Cannon to the Forks of Monongahela, where he with 33 Soldiers were in Garrison That as soon as they landed, they marched in regular order within a musket Shot of the Fort, and demanded an immediate surrender threatning on his refusal, to take it by force. The great superiority of the French

George Mercer Papers

obliged him to give it up, having obtained liberty to March out with every thing he had in the Fort, the next day with his company he set out to meet the forces ordered from Alexandria to reinforce him and at Wills Creek, met Lieutenant Colonel Washington with a Detachment of 150 Men under his Command. Colonel Washington on hearing this Account thought it unadviseable to proceed to the Forks with so small a force, but determined to March to Red stone Creek about 37. Miles from the fort, and there intrench himself till he should be joined by Colo Fry[479]

The speech[480] brought by the Indian messenger, from the Half King is full of the warmest Expressions of Friendship and Attachment to the English Interest. His honour the Governor dispatched him on Tuesday with Assurance of a vigorous Assistance.[481]

The following Copies of the Summons, and the half kings speech as well as the other particulars from Ensign Wards relation may be depended upon as genuine.

Summon by order of Contrecoeur Captain of one of the Companies of the Detachment of the French Marine [commander] in Cheif of his most Christian Majestys Troops now on the Beautiful River, to the Commander of those of the [King] of Great Britain at the Mouth of the River Mohongaly

Sir. Nothing can surprize me more than to see you attempt a Settlement upon the Lands of the King my [master], which obliges me now Sir to send you this Gentleman Chevalier Le Mercier[482] Commander of the Artillery of [Canada], Captain of the Bombardiers to know of you Sir, by vertue of what Authority you are come to Fortify [yourself] within the Dominions of the King my Master. This Action seems so contrary[483] to the last Treaty of peace [concluded at] Aix La Chapelle between his most Christian Majesty and the King of Great Britain that I do not know [to whose charge I am to lay] such a Usurpation as it is incontestible that the [Lands Situated upon] the Beautiful River [belong to his] most Christian Majesty. I am informed Sir that your undertaking has been concerted by none [but a] company[484] who have more in View the Advantage of a trade than the desire of preserving the union and [harmony] which subsists between the Crowns of France and Great Britain altho' Sir it is as much the Interest [to your nation] as ours to maintain it.

[Let] it be as it will Sir if you come into this place charged with Orders, I Sum'on you in the name of the King my [master by] vertue of my Generals Commands to retreat peaceably with your Troops from the Lands of my King and not to [return, otherwise] I find

In the Darlington Memorial Library

myself obliged to fulfil my Duty and compel you to it. I hope Sir you will not defer a Moment nor force [me to the] last Extremity. In the first case Sir Assure yourself that I will give Orders that there shall be no Hostility com-[ing from] my Detachment. I prevent you Sir from the trouble of asking me one hour of delay, or consent to receive [orders from] your Governor he can give none within the Dominions of the King my Master those which I have received [from my] General are my Laws which I cannot depart from. If on the contrary Sir you have not got Orders and only come [to trade], I am sorry to tell you, that I am obliged to Seize your Goods and Confiscate your Effects to the Use of the Indians, [our children, allies and friends, as you have no right to carry on any contraband trade.[485]

This was the reason Sir, why we arrested last year two Englishmen who traded on our territories. As for the rest, my master insists only on what is his right] nor has he the least Intention to disturb that good Harmony and Friendship which reigns between his Majesty and the King of Great Britain. The Governor of Canada can give proof of having done his utmost Endeavours to maintain that union which reigns between two friendly princes for he having heard that the Iroquois and Nipisinques, Inhabitants of the Lakes between the two mountains had struck and destroyed an English Family towards Carolina[486] barred up the road and obliged them to give up to him a little Boy the only one left alive of that Family which Mr Welrick a Merchant of Montreal has carried to Boston, and he has moreover forbid the Indians exercising their accustomed cruelties upon the English our Friends.

I could Sir bitterly complain of the means[487] taken all last Winter to instigate the Indians to take up the Hatchet and strike us, while we were striving to maintain the peace.

I am well assured Sir of the polite manner in which you will receive Mr Le Mercier as well out of regard to his Errand as his Distinction and personal merit. I expect you will send him back with one of your Officers who will bring me a precise answer as you have some Indians with you I have desired Mr Le Mercier who understands their language to inform them of my [illegible] upon this Subject [that they may be made acquainted with my intentions in regard to them.]*[488]

                               I am with great Respect Sir
Done at our Camp.   Your most humble & most Obedt Servt
April 16. 1754.   Contrecoeur

The French landed within 150 yards of the Fort from whence they

*Words supplied from J. N. Moreau's "The Mystery Reveal'd" London 1759.[489]

George Mercer Papers

sent Monsieur Le Mercier attended with Drums Colours and a strong guard to the Officer in the Fort and summoned him immediately to evacuate it. Mr Ward desired some time to send to his Lieutenant (Fraser)[490] who was within some miles which Le Mercier agreed to allow him at first but as soon as he saw the Cannon safely landed and mounted on the bank he took out his watch said it was twelve a Clock and it was not worth while waiting. He then told Mr Ward he would allow him an hour to get out his men and all their things of which he did not take a farthings worth but offered to let him pay himself out of a Chest of money for some necessaries they wanted. As our men came out the French enter'd, but behaved with great civility said it might be their fate ere long to surrender it again so they would set ⟨us⟩ a good example. They however immediately went to work removing some of the logs as they complained the Fort was not to their liking, and by break of day next morning 50 men went off with Axes to hew Logs to enlarge it.[491]

The speech[492] of the Half King &c was in these terms.

April 18th 1754. From the Fort on Ohio.

A speech from the Half King (Scruniattha)[493] and ⟨The Belt* of Wampum⟩[494] ⟨An Indian Cheif so called⟩ to the Governors of Virginia [and] Pensylvania.

Brothers the English, the Bearer is to let you know, how we were Used by the French. We have been waiting [this long] time[495] for the French to strike us, now we see what they design to do with us. We are ready to Strike them now and wait [for your] Assistance. Be strong and come as soon as possible and you shall find us true Brothers, and as ready to strike them [as you] are. We have sent these two young Men to see when you will be ready to come, and then they are to return to us and [let us] know, where you are that we may come and meet you and we desire (if it is convenient) that the Men from both [provinces] would meet at the Forks of the Road,[496] And now if you don't come to our Relief we are gone intirely and shall [never meet] [come together never] more. I believe which you [grieves my heart. To confirm this here is my wampum.] [I speak it in the deepest concern of my heart] (here he delivered a string of Wampum) ⟨Here he delivered a String of Wampum to Ensign Ward & then added⟩

The half King then said to Edward Ward (the Ensign who Commanded at the Fort which the French [obliged them to] deliver up) Now I depend upon you to go with these two young men to both Governors yourself for I [have no dependence] on those that are gone so long and have never returned or sent any word.[497]

*an Indian cheif so called.

· 88 ·

In the Darlington Memorial Library

A True Copy as delivered Edward Ward by John Davison the Interpreter.

The Government notwithstanding (Tho the French had thus taken possession with so large a force which by some Accounts were encreased to 1500 or 1600, the Governm^t) thought proper to publish the following Advertisement in the Virginia Gazettee of May 16. 1754.[498]

By Order of the Governor and Council.

The Method of taking up Lands in this Colony and the easy Terms on which they are held of the ₁Kings not₁ being well known to the Inhabitants of the Northern Provinces, may be the Reason that so few of those people ₁though₁ much straitned for good Lands, travel hither in search of a fine Soil and a greater Extent of Countrey and ₁therefore₁ the publishing the method and terms, on which they are granted here may be of use to promote the settlement and ₁cultivation of the finest lands (perhaps in the world) that lie to the westward of the Allegheny mountains, along the several branches of the Mississippi. With that view this authentic state of the rules is taking up, and patenting lands in₁[499] this Government are offered to the Public.

The expences on a tract of Land being less in proportion than on a smaller, the Calculation is here made on a tract of 1000 Acres which may be looked upon as a moderate Quantity

Whoever inclines to take up any Quantity of Land not exceeding four hundred acres, may enter for the same with the Surveyor of the County, in which the land lies who can furnish Rights for the same. But if a larger Quantity is wanted, he must petition the Governor and Council for which petition and Order of Council the Clerk of that board has.

A Fee of . . . . 0..10..9.

For entering the Order of Council in the Auditors Office
and a Certificate thereof . . . . .0.. 5..9

For 20. Rights at 5$ Sterling each or 6s3^d Currency . . . . 6.. 5...

Each Right entitles the Bearer to 50 Acres of his Majestys Land as the Consideration for which it is granted being Certificates of so much paid in for that End

Upon producing the Order of Council and these Rights to the Surveyor of the County in which the Land lies he is obliged to Survey ₁(as soon as prior₁ Entries or Orders will ₁permit)₁ for which his fee is 500 lbs of Tobacco payable beyond the mountains at 3. farthings per pound. . . . . } 1 11..3

George Mercer Papers

After the Survey is finished the party is to return the plot of the Land with the Rights to the Secretarys Office in the General Court next following and pay the fee to the Secretary for making out the patent on parchment and recording it in his office................................. } 0..10..6

And also to the Governor for the Seal and his signing it.... 1.. 1..6

So the whole charge of 1000 Acres is about 8£:4ˢ Sterling or in Virginia Currency being 5£ per Oz. Gold and 6ˢ8ᵈ per Oz Silver .... } 10..4..9

If the Survey is above 1000 Acres the Surveyors Fee is 30 lbs of Tobacco for every hundred Acres more, and excepting this and the Right money, the charge is the same on every patent above 400 Acres, but that quantity or under may be had without the fee to the Auditor, and that to the Clerk of the Council. The Patentee holds his Land in Fee simple, to him and his heirs forever from the Date of his patent upon paying yearly the easy Quit rent to his Majesty of one shilling sterling for every fifty Acres, and making in three years time an easy Cultivation on the Land.

And for a further Encouragement to settle on the Waters of Mississippi the General Assembly have (last November) Enacted, "That "whereas a considerable number of persons, as well as his Majestys "natural born subjects as foreign protestants are willing to come into "this Colony with their Families and Effects, and settle on the Lands "near the said Waters if properly encouraged. It is therefore enacted, "That all persons being protestants who shall settle and reside on "any Lands situate to the westward of the Allegany Ridge, shall be "exempted from the payment of all public, County, and parish Levies "for the term of Fifteen years next ensueing[500]

And for a further Encouragement to foreign protestants, Naturalization is made very easy and cheap to them and they are allowed all the Indulgencies of the Act of Toleration[501] here.

⟨As these are indisputably the Terms Upon which any Persons, even Foreigners, might have taken up Lands upon the Ohio even before it was in the Enemies possession⟩ it will appear that all the Advantage allowed the Ohio company was an Exemption of the Rights of 200,000 Acres of Land which would have amounted to £1000 Sterling but in lieu of this they were obliged to settle 100 families upon the Land which was after the rate of a⟨one⟩ family for ⟨every⟩ £10. What ⟨Whether⟩ the Company could gain by such an Exemption granted on such Conditions is readily ⟨any thing by such a Bargain may be⟩ submitted without mentioning that they were

In the Darlington Memorial Library

obliged ⟨by another Condition[502] of their Grant to advance near ten times[503] that sum in carrying on a Trade to supply the Indians with Goods according to another Condition of their Grant, the greatest part of which is inevitably lost by the Hostilities on the Ohio. The Advertisement however had no Effect for it is certain that the Inhabitants of the Northern Provinces had long been acquainted with the easy terms of taking up Lands in this Government the frontier Counties of Frederick and Augusta having been for the most part seated by people from those parts,[504] but it is as well known to them that no sooner was there a probability of seating that frontier than the beforementioned Mr Russell under colour of some Entries in the name of himself and some great Men whom he gave out to be his⟩ partners so harrassed those poor people who had settled there by Caveats and trials before the Governor and Council two or three hundred miles distant from their Houses that many of them removed back to their former habitations and those who were not to be tired out had at length the mortification to find that their costs occasioned by the Contestations with him exclusive of their trouble and riding many thousand miles amounted to more than Russell and his partners pretended to sell Lands for in that part of the Countrey and when many of those people (as has been mentioned) ₍contracted₎ with Mr Gist ₍in behalf of the company to settle their lands, and some of them had actually seated thereon,₎ when they found the same Mr Russell including them in his survey boasting of the Interest of his partners and setting the Ohio Company at defiance it not only prevented the rest of the people from coming according to their Agreement but some of those who had come returned to their former habitations and have given their Neighbours such Impressions of seating in Virginia that it is notorious that some thousands have since that time passed through this Colony to go to the Southward and take up worse Lands there on worse terms.[505] However not only strangers have been deterred ever since the French took possession of the Ohio from settling in those parts but some hundred families much nearer in have deserted their habitations ⟨Plantations & many of them very valuable⟩ to escape the Indians Cruelty

It would be needless as well as ungrateful to mention the several Transactions since that time during which except the defeating a party of French and taking Monsr[468] La Force and 20 other prisoners on the 28th of May 1754[506] we have met almost a constant series of Misfortunes until General Forbes happily recovered the possession and the French deserted Fort Duquesne in December 1758.[507] It is impossible to reckon up how many lives the War has cost this Colony, but our expence is too well ascertained by the Acts of Assembly which have laid us under a load of Taxes for several years ⟨ten years yet⟩ to come and which has been so much represented ⟨The share of Virg^a has notwithstandindg been so grosly misrepresented⟩ that it seems necessary to inform the public that Virginia ⟨that Colony⟩ has raised for that purpose, [from February 1754 to ⟨this time, no less than 399625£. of their currency.⟩ [It may be said that Virginia has been reimbursed 52814£. 19 s. sterling, as his late majesty was graciously pleased to allot so much to that colony, out of the money granted him, by two acts of the parliament of Great Britain, in the years 1757 and 1758, but it is as certain that 50000£. current money part thereof, has been already appropriated towards recruiting, paying, subsisting, and other expences of the Virginia regiment until the 1st of December 1761,[508] as well as what may be necessary to discharge the arrears due to the militia, and the damages done by the Indians, as settled and allowed by the last assembly.[509] So that there will be little or nothing to be deducted out of the said 399625£. advanced by that colony, for carrying on the war. A sum that when compared with the contributions of the northward provinces (among whom almost all the money that came from England as well as Virginia, and the neighbouring provinces, circulated, to their very great advantage) will be found to exceed the proportion of Virginia very largely.

The committee of the Ohio company (who were invested with the company's full power) were in hopes as soon as the possession was regained,][510] that they might have been allowed [to survey their] first 200,000 Acres and gave Mr Gist (who had ⟨with much difficulty after a long Application obtained⟩ a Commission[511] from the College for that purpose) Instructions to ⟨set about [it] immediately, that they might not be charged with the least delay,⟩ but they were given to understand that General Stanwix had assured the Indians that no settlements should for some time be made upon the Ohio,[512] & that as soon as they were allowed the Company should have Notice. But Mr Gist dying last year[513] of the Small pox and the Company ⟨Committee⟩ being informed that the Pennsylvanians and several others were preparing to survey the Lands in those parts,[514] ⟨which they their Company⟩ claim not only by his Majestys express ⟨the express words of his Majesties⟩ Instructions, but if they should is in the Government of Pensylvania ⟨which the Company cannot admit⟩ ⟨in Case they lay within the Province of Pennsylvania (which if the bounds between that Province & Virginia were truly surveyed) by Mr Penns promise to Mr Hanbury, it is presumed they would not.⟩ they applied to the

In the Darlington Memorial Library

College to procure a Commission to some other person in the room of the said Gist to survey the same, when the president and Masters informed them that tho' the power of appointing Surveyors was vested in them by the College Charter they could not grant any such Commission without the Consent of the Governor and Council[515] who had resolved that no such Commission should be granted or any Lands surveyed in those parts till they had received instructions for that purpose from his Majesty or the board of Trade.[516]

⟨The Committee being still alarmed by fresh Informations & particularly by that of Lieut Colo Stephen[517] who was just come from Pittsburg & was on his way to Williamsburg to wait on the Governor, desired one of their Members to make some proper Application to the Govr upon that Occasion who thereupon wrote the following Letter⟩[518]

Honoble Sir

As I am one of the Ohio Company, I was a good deal alarmed by Colo Stephen's Information that the Pensylvanians and other foreigners were about to survey large quantities of Land upon the Ohio, within this Government, I think I may venture to say that Company had not only a prior claim in Virtue of his Majesties Instruction but that the Considerations therein mentioned were public and valuable ones. And that they first at their own Expence made such discoveries of those parts as could be depended on, cleared the public Roads, took Possession and were about to build a fort and Warehouses for carrying on their Trade where Pittsburg now stands are facts cannot be controverted, yet when this Government thought proper to pitch on that place to build a Fort for the public defence and to issue a proclamation promising two hundred thousand Acres of Land (one hundred thousand of which were to be contiguous to the Fort) as an Encouragement to the Officers and Soldiers who should voluntarily inlist to repel the French Encroachments it is notorious that the Company readily submitted, desiring only such reasonable tracts of Land at proper Stages and convenient distances along the Road they had been at the Charge of clearing as should be judged necessary for building Storehouses and securing their Carriages employed in transporting Goods from their Storehouse at Wills creek to a proper place on the Monongahela where they proposed to build their boats, Those were adjudged by the principal Officers and persons concerned to be not only reasonable but greatly advantageous to the Proprietors ⟨of the⟩ adjoining Lands, and such was the general opinion at that time of the great Utility of the Company's Undertaking that the

Earl of Granville, Lord Baltimore and Mr Penn (according to Mr Hanburys information assured him they should have what quantities of Land they desired for securing their Settlements and extending their trade within their respective Proprietaries on the same terms they had procured the Grant from his Majesty.

 I am sensible the Company has been charged with delay in not having surveyed their Lands long since but it is too tedious a Subject to enter upon their Vindication however. I think I may venture to affirm they did every thing in their power, and if so it is certain they cannot be justly blamed, They did indeed at length procure a Commission for Mr Gist to Survey their Lands but he scarce got it before Hostilities began and he unfortunately died this last Summer[513] or I imagine he would have made a considerable progress in it this Fall, as I was afterwards informed that my Son was applying for a Commission I thought whether he obtaind it or not. I might depend upon him for timely notice when and to whom the Commission would be granted but having heard nothing from him on that head and not dreaming that the Company had any other Competitors than the Officers and Soldiers claiming under the Proclamation, with whom I made no doubt everything would be easily and amicably settled. I made myself very easy till Colo Stephen acquainted me[519] that no Commission is yet granted to any person in this Colony, and that he expects before any is, great tracts will be surveyed, and, among them, those very Lands engaged by the proclamation and others absolutely necessary to carry on the Indian trade, and this for Persons who I doubt will prove very bad Neighbours and take every measure in their power to exclude us from that Trade and every other Advantage they can deprive us of, I therefore presume your Honour will take such measures as you shall judge necessary to prevent such an Encroachment and that you will not suffer any Lands to be surveyed or taken up in those parts before the People of this Colony have their just Claims first satisfied.

 I have not yet seen the last Act of Assembly[520] past in Pensylvania relating to the Indian Trade but from a Letter of Capt Trents to Colo Lomax, it is a most insolent attempt to engross to themselves that whole Trade on the Ohio, notwithstanding that whole river is without their province and within this Colony, Yet. This they may effectually compass if they can secure those Lands they propose to survey which may properly be called the Key of the Ohio, as through these Lands are all the Roads and Passes both from North and South that lead to that River, The Consequences of which would be so fatal to this Colony that I greatly dread it and fear they depend on

In the Darlington Memorial Library

some other Interest than their own, Should they first seise ₍the₎ Possession however unjust their claim, it would be very troublesome to remove them, though in the end it should be effected so that a timely Prevention can alone answer all good purposes.

I have not time to enumerate the many disadvantages this Colony must suffer by such a Loss I must therefore beg leave to refer your[521] Honour to Colo Stephen who is so well acquainted with those parts that it would be a piece of presumption in me to undertake to do it would my time permit as he can do it ⟨so⟩ much better. I am with the greatest Regard

        Honble Sir

To the Hon'ble Fras Fauquier Esqr   Your most obedt Servt
His Ma'ties Lieut Gov.' & Commandr in
Chief of   Virginia   J Mercer

[Endorsed]   Copy to Gov.' abot surveying Ohio

The Information I reced from Colo Stephen was ⟨that⟩ the Philadelphians, under Bouquet's Protection (who it was said) was concerned with them were surveying abot Pittsburg after they had by Acts of Assembly engrossed the trade to themselves & Bouquet had presumed by Proclamation ⟨to⟩ threaten the rest of his Maties subjects with Court-martial Law for which he deserved to be hanged himself by the same Law.[522]

~~This being a true state of the Companies Case it must be submitted~~ ⟨Such is the state here contained & upon it they must submit⟩ whether they have not done everything in their power to comply with the terms of their Grant and ~~whether they~~ ⟨if so whether they⟩ should be ~~answerable~~ ⟨blamed⟩ for what ⟨they could by no means⟩ prevent.

They without the least delay employed proper persons to discover those parts (then in a manner unknown) cleared proper Roads purchased Lands built houses imported large Cargoes, cultivated a friendship with the Indians (then greatly prejudiced against the people of Virginia) and supplied them with Goods on such terms as would have secured their friendship if they could have been secure ~~of protection~~ ⟨protected⟩ from the French ⟨they⟩ began to settle the Lands by seating several families and to build their Fort as soon as the Consent of the Indians could be obtained ~~by which~~ ⟨and by these⟩ means they have sunk several thousand pounds ⟨a sum⟩ more than sufficient to have taken up and secured the whole 500,000 Acres ⟨which they petitioned for. ~~The~~—In the meantime the⟩ people of Virginia as well as the adjacent provinces in the meantime (as well as the French (in Ecaho to the French Cant) in Contrecoeur's Summons) affected to charge the War on the Ohio Company and to exclaim against their Grant, while other people many of them without one shilling advantage to the public, or one farthing Expence to themselves except half a pistole to the Clerk of the Council have made large sums of money by Surveying and Selling ⟨much more of⟩ his Majesties Lands to Strangers. ⟨The Comp ͬ are far from denying they even acknowledge & with a good deal of Satisfaction, that some of them early foresaw the Consequences of the French Encroachments on his Ma'ties American Dominions, they were sensible that as the French were imperceptibly stealing into Possession (it is notorious no public notice was taken of it) they wanted nothing but Time to carry their Point. In this very time Crisis they applied & obtained his Maties' Instruction, but intent on promoting the public Interest jointly with their own & to reconcile the Indians who complained of the Incroachments made by the Governm ͭ of Virg ͣ upon their Lands. took every method at however great an Expence to effect their Purposes. The Indians (far from being the ignorant People they are generally supposed to be in Europe) finding the English & French contending for their friendship & leave to build upon among them & beleiving they should be able to direct the Ballance hold the scales & direct the Ballance as they would with even French Policy pretended their Treaty at Lancaster did not give up their Lands to the King of Great Britain that (notwithstanding the Treaty at Lancaster) they still had the absolute Property in what they called their Lands.

An indisputable Proof of this is the Half King's Speech to the French General as communicated by himself to Col ͦ Washington at the Loggs Town Nov.' 25. 1753,[523] in these words.
Fathers &c.

But should this Authority be contested, did not the same Half King Ohio Indians inform the Virg ͣ Commissioners at the Treaty at the same place the June before that they Onondaga Council had informed the Ohio Indians that they had not never understood that the Lands sold at the Treaty of Lancaster sold any Land to the King of Great Britain West of extended further West than the Warrior's Road at the foot of the Alligany mountain. And did not the same Indians insist that the English should not [build or settle on the north side of the Ohio? Nay do they not now insist, after the glorious success that has attended his majesty's arms, upon their]ᵢ[524] Right to the Lands & that the English shall not settle upon them. And what does the Ohio Comp ͣ desire Not that his Majesty or the Nation any of

In the Darlington Memorial Library

his Subjects should enter into any Difference or Dispute with the Indians or incur one shillings Expence on their Account his Ma'tie let them hold the Lands as long as his Ma'tie pleases but when he shall think fit to extend settle his Dominions further to the West & to grant any of His Lands for that purpose to any of his Subjects, the Ohio Company are pursuaded assured his Ma'tie will not prefer any of his Subjects to their Prejudice who have not a juster Claim & at the same time they persuade themselves that none of their fellow Subjects (who ob regard that golden Rule of doing as they would be done by) would desire so unjust a Preference)[525]

Appendix[526]

A JOURNAL

of Christopher Gist's Journey began from Colo Cresap's at the Old Town on Potomack River, Maryland October 31. 1750. down the Ohio, within 15 miles of the Falls thereof; and from thence to Roanoak River in North Carolina where he arrived May 19. 1751. [No 1][527]

Undertaken on the Account of the Ohio Company, and by the Instructions of their Committee. Instructions given Mr Christopher Gist by the Committee of the Ohio Company. the 11th day of September 1750.[59]

You are to go out as soon as possible to the Westward of the great Mountains and carry with you such a number of Men as you think necessary in order to search out and discover the Land [upon the river] Ohio, and other adjoining branches of the Mississippi down as low as the [great Falls[42]] thereof. You[are] particularly to observe the ways and passes thro' all the Mountains you cross, and take an exact account of the Soil, quality, and product of the land, and the Width and Depth of the Rivers, and the several Falls belonging to them, together with the courses and bearings of the Rivers and Mountains as near as you conveniently can: You are also to observe what Nations of Indians inhabit there, their strength and numbers, who they trade with, and in what commodities they deal. [Gist's Instructi[ons]] [To discover the Nations of Indians, & their Trade]

When you find a large quanti[t]ty of good le[]vel land such as you think will suit the company you are to measure the breadth of it, in three [or four different] places, and take the courses of the River and Mountains on which it binds, in order to judge the quantity; You [are to fix] the Beginning and bounds in such a manner that they may be easily found again, by your description, the nearer in the

· 97 ·

George Mercer Papers

<small>to examine the Naviga-tion of the Ohio to the Falls</small>

land lies the better provided it be good and level, but we had rather go quite down the Mississippi, than take mean broken land. After finding a large body of good level land you are not to stop, but [proceed farther as low as the falls of the] Ohio,[42] that [we may be informed] of that Navigation, and you are to take an exact account of all the large bodies of good level land in the same manner as above directed, that the company may the better judge where it will be most convenient for them to take theirs. You are to note all the bodies of good land as you go along tho' there is not a sufficient quantity for the Company's Grant, but you need not be so particularl in the mensuration of that, as in the larger bodies.

<small>to draw a Plan of the Country, & keep a Journal</small>

You are to draw as good a plan[60] as you can of the Country you pass through, and take an exact and particular Journal of all your proceedings and make a true report thereof to the Ohio Company.

<small>Gist begins his Journey
Old Town</small>

1750. In compliance with my Instructions from the Committee of the Ohio Company bearing date the 11th day of September 1750.

Wednesday Oct. 31. . Set out from Colo Thomas Cresap's[61] at the old *Town*[62] on Potomack River in Maryland and went along an old Indian Path[63] N. 30d E. about 11 miles.

Thursday Novr 1 . Then N. 1 m—N 30d E. 3 m—here I was taken sick and stayed all night.

Friday .... 2d N 30d E. 6 m—here I was so bad that I was not able to proceed any farther that night, but grew better in the morning.

<small>Juniatta</small>

Saturday .... 3d N. 3 m—to *Juniatta*[64] a large branch of Susquehannah where I stayed all night.

Sunday .... 4th Crossed *Juniatta* and went up it S 55d W. about 16 m—

<small>Allegany Mountain</small>

Monday .... 5th Continued the same course[65] S 55d W. 6 m—to the top of *large mountain called the Alligany mountain;* here our path turned and we went N 45d W. 6 m—and incamped.[66]

Tuesday .... 6. *Wednesday* 7. & *Thursday* 8th Had Snow and such bad weather that we could not travel, but I killed a young Bear so that we had Provision enough.

Friday ... 9th Set out N. 70d W. about 8 m—here I crossed a creek of *Susquehannah*[67] and it raining hard I went into an old Indian Cabbin[68] where I stayed all night

Saturday Novr 10th Rain and Snow all day but cleared away in the Evening

Sunday .... 11th Set out late in the morning N 70d W. 6 m—crossing two Forks[69] of a creek of *Susquehannah* here the way being bad I encamped and killed a Turkey

· 98 ·

In the Darlington Memorial Library

Monday .... 12th Set out N 45ᵈ W. 8 m—and crossed a great Laurel Mountain⁷⁰ — Laurel Mountain

Tuesday .... 13th Rain and Snow.

Wednesday .. 14th Set out N 45ᵈ W. 6 m—to *Lowlhannon*⁷¹ an old Indian Town on a Creek of the Ohio called *Kishekeminetas* then N. 1 m—N W 1 m. to an Indian Camp on the said creek. — Lowlhannon Kishkeminetas

Thursday ... 15th The weather being bad, and I unwell stayed here all day. The Indian to whom this camp belonged spoke good English, and directed me the way to his Town which is called *Shannopin*⁷² he said it was about sixty miles and a pretty good way.

Friday .... 16th Set out S. 70ᵈ W. 10 m—⁷³

Saturday ... 17th The same course (S 70ᵈ W) 15 m—to an old Indian Camp.⁷⁴

Sunday ... 18th I was very sick and sweated myself according to the Indian Custom in a sweat house which gave me ease and my Fever abated.

Monday ... 19th Set out early in the morning the same course (S 70ᵈ W) travelled very hard about twenty miles to a small Indian Town of the Delawares, called *Shanoppin* on the S E. side of the River *Ohio*⁷⁵ where we rested and got Corn for our Horses. — Shanoppin

Tuesday ... 20th I was un₍well, and st₎ayed in this Town to recover myself. While I was here I took an opportunity to set my Compass priva₍tely, and took₎ the distance across the river, for I understood it was dangerous to let a compass be seen: *The Ohio is 76 ₍poles wid₎e here* there about twenty Families in this Town. *The Land in general from Potomack to this place, is mean stoney and broken, with here and there good spots upon the creeks and branches, but no body of it.* — Width of the Ohio — Land mean

Saturday ... 24th Set out fr₍om₎ Shanoppin and ₍swa₎m⁷⁶ our Horses across the *Ohio,* and went down the River S. 75ᵈ W 4 m—N 75ᵈ W 7 m—W 2 m—the land from *Shanoppin* is good along the river but the bottoms not broad; at a distance from the River good land for farming covered with small white and red Oaks, and tolerable level, fine Runs for mills &c. — Land good

Sunday ... 25th Down the river W. 3 m—N W. 5 m—to *Loggs Town:*⁷⁷ The lands for these last eight miles very rich, the bottoms above a mile wide, but on the S E. side scarce a mile, the hills high and steep. In the Town I found scarce anybody but a parcel of reprobate Indian traders, the cheif of the Indians being out hunting; here I was informed that George Croghan⁷⁸ and Andrew Montour⁷⁹ who were sent upon an Embassy⁸⁰ from Pennsylvania to the Indians, were passed about a week before me. The people here enquired my business — Logg's Town Lands very rich

· 99 ·

and because I did not readily inform them, began to suspect me and said I was come to settle the Indians Lands and said they knew I should never go home again safe. I found this discourse was like to be of ill consequence, so pretended to speak very slightingly of what they had said, and enquired for Croghan (who is a mere Idol among his Countrymen the Irish traders) and Andrew Montour the Interpreter for Pennsylvania, and told them I had a message to deliver the Indians from the King, by order[81] of the President of Virginia, and for that reason wanted to see Mr Montour; This made them all pretty easy (being afraid to interrupt the Kings message) and obtained me quiet and respect among them, otherwise I doubt not they would have contrived some evil against me. I immediately wrote to Mr Croghan by one of the trader's people

Monday... 26th   Tho' I was unwell I preferred the woods to such company and set out from *Loggs Town* down the River N W. 6 m— to *great Beaver creek* where[82] I met one Barny Curran a trader for the Ohio Company and we continued together as far as *Muskingum*.[83] The bottoms upon the river below *Loggs Town* are very rich but narrow, the highland pretty good but not very rich, the land upon *Beaver creek* of the same kind. From this place we left the *Ohio* to the S E. and travelled across the country

<small>great Beaver Creek Land good</small>

Tuesday... 27th   Set out from the E. side of *Beaver Creek* N. W. 6 m—W 4 m—upon these two last courses very good high land and not much broken fit for Farming—

Wednesday Novr 28th   Rained and we could not travel.

<small>Land very broken</small>

Thursday.... 29th   W. 6 m—thro' good land the same course[84] continued 6 m—farther thro' very broken land: here I found myself pretty well recovered and being in want of Provision went out and killed a Deer.

Friday.... 30th   Set out S. 45^d W. 12 m—crossed the *last branch of Beaver Creek*[85] where one of Curran's men and myself killed twelve Turkeys.

<small>Land high & tolerable good</small>

Saturday Decr 1st   N. 45^d W 10 m—the Land high and tolerable good

Sunday.... 2d   N 45^d W. 8 m—the same sort of Land, but near the creeks[86] bushy and very full of thorns.

Monday.... 3d   Killed a Deer and stayed in our Camp all day.

Tuesday.... 4th   Set out late S 45^d W about 4 m—here I killed three fine fat Deer so that tho' we were eleven in Company We had great plenty of Provisions.

<small>[Elk's] Eye Creek no Timber</small>

Wednesday... 5th[87]   Set out down the side of a creek called *Elk's Eye*[88] *Creek* S^o 70^d W 6 m—good land but void of Timber, Meadows, upon the Creek and fine Runs. for mills.

In the Darlington Memorial Library

Thursday .... 6th Rained all Day so that we were obliged to continue in our Camp.

Friday .... 7th Set out S N. 8 m—crossing *Elks eye creek* to a *Town* of *the Ottawas*.[89] a Nation of French Indians, an old Frenchman named Mark Coonce[90] who had married an Indian woman of the six nations lived here: the Indians were all out hunting, the old man was civil to me but after I was gone to my Camp upon his understanding I came from Virginia, he called me the Big Knife.[91] There are not above six or eight Families belonging to this Town

Ottawa's Town

Saturday ... 8th Stayed in the Town.

Sunday .... 9th Set out down the *Elks eye creek*[88] S 45^d W. 6 m—to *Margarets creek*[92] *a branch of Elk's eye Creek*.

Margaret's Creek

Monday ... 10th The same course S 45^d W. 2 m—to a large creek.

Tuesday ... 11th The same course twelve miles killed two Deer.

Wednesday ... 12th The [same course eight miles; encamped] by the side of *Elks eye creek*.

Thursday ... 13th Rained all day

Friday .... 14th Set out W. 5 m—to *Muskingum*[83] a Town of the Wiandots. The Land upon Elks eye creek is in general very broken, the bottoms narrow. *The Wiandots* or little Mingoes are divided[93] between the French and English one half of the them adhere to the first and the other half are firmly attached to the latter; the Town of Muskingum consists of about one hundred Families; When we came within sight of it we perceived English colours hoisted on the Kings house,[94] and at George Croghan's,[95] upon enquiring the reason I was informed that the French had lately taken several English Traders,[96] and that Mr Croghan had ordered all the white men to come into this Town, and has sent expresses to the Traders. of the lower towns,[97] and among the *Picqualinnees*,[98] and the Indians had sent to their people to come to council about it.

Muskingum
Lands broken
Wiandots divided

Saturday ... 15th & Sunday 16. Nothing remarkable happened.

Monday .... 17th Came into town Two Traders belonging to Mr Croghan came into Town and informed us that two[99] of his People were taken by forty french men and twenty French Indians who had carried them with seven horse loads of skins to a new Fort[100] that the French were building on one of the branches of *Lake Erie*

two Traders taken by the French

Tuesday ... 18th I acquainted Mr Croghan and Andrew Montour with my Business[81] with the Indians and talked much of a Regulation of Trade with which they were pleased and treated me very well.

Indians talk of a Regulation in the Trade

Wednesday .. 19th to Monday 24th Nothing remarkable

Tuesday ... 25th This being Christmas Day I intended to read Prayers, but after inviting some of the white men they informed each

Christmas Day Gist proposes to read Prayers

George Mercer Papers

other of my Intentions, and being of several different Perswasions, and few of them inclined to hear any good, they refused to come; But one Thomas Burney[101] a Blacksmith who is settled there went about and talked to them and then several of them came, and Andrew Montour invited several of the well disposed Indians who came freely. By this time the morning was spent and I had given over all thoughts of them, but seeing them come to oblige all, and offend none, I stood up and said, Gentlemen I have no design or intention to give offence to any particular Sect or Religion, but as our King indulges us all in a liberty of conscience and hinders none of you in the exercise of your religious worships, so it would be unjust in you to endeavour to stop the Propagation of his. The Doctrine of Salvation, Faith and good works is what I only propose to treat of, as I find it extracted from the Homilies of the Church of England, which I then read to them in the best manner I could, and after I had done the Interpreter told the Indians what I had read, and that it was the true Faith, which the great King and his Church recommended to his Children: The Indians seemed well pleased and came up to me and returned me their thanks and then invited me to live among them and gave me a name in their language. *Annosannoah*. the Interpreter told me this was the name of a good man that had formerly lived among them, and their King said that must be always my name, for which I returned them thanks but as to living among them, I excused myself by saying I did not know whether the Governor would give me leave, and if he did the French would come and carry me away, as they had done the English traders, to which they answered I might bring great guns and make a fort, that they had now left the French and were very desirous of being instructed in the principles of Christianity, that they liked me very well, and wanted me to marry them after the Christian manner, and baptize their Children; and then they said they would never desire to return to the French, or suffer them or their priests to come near them, more, for they loved the English, but had seen little religion among them; And some of their great men came and wanted me to baptize their children, for as I had read to them, and appeared to talk about religion, they took me to be a minister of the Gospel, upon which I desired Mr Montour the Interpreter to tell them, that no Minister could venture to baptize any Children, until those that were to be Sureties for them, were well instructed in the Faith themselves, and that was according to the great King's religion, in which he desired his Children should be instructed, and we dare not do it in any other way than was by Law established; but I hope if I could not be admitted to live among them,

Marginalia:
- Indians attend
- Gist reads Prayers
- Indians much pleased, give him an Indian Name
- desire to be married, & have their Children baptized.

In the Darlington Memorial Library

that the great King would send them proper Ministers to exercise that Office among them, at which they seemed well pleased and one of them went and brought me his Book, which was a kind of Almanack contrived for them by the French in which the days of the week were so marked that by moving a Pin every [morning, they kept a pretty] exact account of the time, to show me that he understood me and that he and his family always observed the Sabbath Day.

Wednesday .... 26th This day a woman[102] who had been a long time a Prisoner and had deserted and been retaken and brought into the Town on Christmas Eve, was put to death in the following manner. They carried her without the Town and let her loose, and when she attempted to run away the persons appointed for that purpose pursued her, and struck her on the Ear, on the right side of the head, which beat her flat on her face on the Ground, they then struck her several times thro' the back with a Dart, to the heart, scalped her, and threw the scalp in the Air, and another cut off her head; there the dismal spectacle lay till the Evening and then Barney Curran desired leave to bury her which he and his Men and some of the Indians did just at dark. A Woman Prisoner put to Death

Thursday ... December 27th 1750 to Thursday January 3d 1751. Nothing remarkable happened in the Town.

Friday ... 4th One Taafe an Indian Trader came to Town from near *Lake Erie* and informed us that the *Wiandots* had advised him to keep clear of the *Outawais*[89] (a nation of Indians firmly attached to the French living near the lakes) and told him that the branches of the Lakes were claimed by the French; but that all the branches of the Ohio belonged to them and their brothers the English, and that the French had no business there, and that it was expected that the other part[93] of the Wiandots would desert the French and come over to the English interest, and join their brethren on *Elk's eye creek* and build a strong Fort and town there . Wiandots Advice [illegible] Declaration [illegible] English [illegible] -der

Saturday ... 5th The weather still continuing bad I stayed in the Town to recruit my horses and tho' corn was very dear among the Indians I was obliged to feed them well or run the risque of losing them as I had a great way to travel

Wednesday ... 9th The wind southerly and the weather something warmer this day came into Town two traders from among the *Picqualinnees*[98] (a tribe of the Tawightwis) and brought news that another English trader[103] was also taken Prisoner by the French, and that three french Soldiers had deserted and come over to the English, and surrendered themselves to some of the Traders of the Pick town,[98] and that the Indians would have put them to death, to re- An English Trader taken Prisoner Three French Soldiers desert; the English Traders protect Them from the Indians

· 103 ·

George Mercer Papers

venge their taking our Traders, but as the French Indians had surrendered themselves to the English they would not let the Indians hurt them, but had ordered them to be sent under the care of three of our Traders, and delivered at this Town to George Croghan.

Thursday Jan. 10th   Wind still at South and warm.

Friday .... 11th   This day came into Town an Indian from near the Lakes and confirmed the news we had heard.

<small>Wiandot Council</small>   Saturday .... 12th   We sent away our People toward the lower Town[104] intending to follow them the next morning and this evening we went into council in the Wiandot Kings house,[93] the council had been put off a long time expecting some of their great men in, but few of them came, and this evening some of the king's council being a little disordered with liquor no business could be done, but we were desired to come next day.

Sunday ... 13th   No business done

<small>Acquaints the Indians the King had sent them a Present</small>   Monday ... 14th   This day George Croghan[78] by the assistance of Andrew Montour[79] acquainted the king and council of this nation (by presenting them four strings of wampum) that the great King over the water their *Roggony* (Father) had sent under the care of the Governor of Virginia their brother a large present of goods,[105] which were now landed safe in Virginia, and the Governor had sent me,[81] to invite them to come and see him, and partake of their fathers charity, to all his children on the branches of Ohio.

<small>Indians would not give an Answer till a full Council should assemble</small>   In answer to which one of the Cheifs stood up and said, "That their king and all of them thanked their brother the Governor of Virginia for his care, and me for bringing them the news, but they could not give me an answer,[106] until they had a full or general council of the several nations of Indians, which could not be till next spring, and so the king and council shaking hands with us, we took our leaves.

<small>White Woman's Creek</small>   Tuesday ... 15th   We left *Muskingum* and went W. 5 m—to the *white womans creek* on which is a small town. This white woman was taken away from new England when she was not above ten years old by the French Indians.[107] She is now upwards of fifty, and has an Indian husband, and several children, her name is Mary Harris; she still remembers they used to be very religious in new England, and wonders how the white men can be so wicked as she has seen them in ₁these woods.₁

<small>Licking Creek Land rich but broken</small>   Wednesday. 16th   Set out S W. 25 m—to *Licking creek*,[108] the land from *Muskingum* to this place rich but broken, *upon the north side of Licking creek about six miles from the mouth are several salt* <small>Salt Ponds Salt Springs</small> *licks*[109] *or ponds formed by little streams or drains of water clear but of a blueish colour and salt taste. The Traders and Indians boil their*

· 104 ·

In the Darlington Memorial Library

meat in this water which if proper care be not taken will sometimes make it too salt to eat.

Thursday. 17th   Set out W. 5m—S W. 15 m—to a great swamp.

Friday. 18th   Set out from the great swamp S W. 15 m—

Saturday. 19th   W 15 m—to *Hockhocking*[110] a small town with only four or five Delaware families   — Hockhocking

Sunday. 20th   The snow began to grow thin and the weather warmer. Set out from *Hockhocking* S 5 m—then W 5 m—then S W 5 m —to *Maguck*[111] a little Delaware town of about ten families, by the north side of a plain, or clear field, about five miles in length, N E. and S W, and two miles broad, with a small rising in the middle which gives a fine prospect over the whole plain, and a large creek on the north side of it, called *Sioto Creek;* all the way from *Licking creek* to this place is fine rich level land with large meadows and fine clover bottoms; with spacious plains, covered with wild Rye: the wood cheifly large Walnuts and Hickories, here and there mixed with poplars, Cherry trees, and sugar trees.   — Maguck / Land very rich wth fine Meadows and Variety of fine Timber

Monday 21st to Wednesday 23d   Stayed in the *Maguck Town.*

Thursday 24th   Set out from *Maguck Town* S about 15 m—thro' fine rich level land to a small town called *Hurricane Tom's*[112] consisting of about five or six Delaware families on the S W. of *Sioto creek.*   — Land rich & level / Hurricane Tom's

Friday 25th   The creek being very high and full of Ice we could not ford, and were obliged to go down it on the S E side S E. 4 m—to the *salt lick creek, about a mile up this creek, on the South side is a very large salt lick*[113] *the streams which run into this lick are very salt and tho' clear leave a bluish sediment the Indians and traders make Salt for their horses of this water by boiling it, it has at first a bluish colour and somewhat bitter taste but upon being dissolved in fair water and boiled the second time it come to tolerably pure salt.*   — Salt Springs / Indians make Salt

Saturday Jan. 26th   Set out S 2 m—S W 14 m—

Sunday ... 27th   S. 12 m—to a small *Delaware town* of about twenty families on the S E. side of *Sioto creek.* We lodged at the house of an Indian whose name was, *Windaughalah,*[114] a great man and cheif of this town and much in the English interest, he entertained us very kindly, and ordered a Negro Man that belonged to him, to feed our horses well, this night it snowed, and in the morning tho' the snow was six or seven Inches deep, the wild Rye[115] appeared very green and flourishing thro' it, and our horses had very fine feeding.   — Sioto Creek / Snow 6 Inches deep wild Rye green above it

Monday 28th   We went into council with the Indians of this town, and after the Interpreter[79] had informed them of his Instructions[80] from the Governor of Pensylvania, and given them some cautions in

· 105 ·

Message from the Govr of Pennsylvania

regard to the French, they returned for Answer as follows. the Speaker with four strings of wampum in his hand stood [up] and addressing himself as to the governor of Pennsylvania said, "Brothers we the Delawares return you our hearty thanks for the news you have sent us, and we assure you, we will not hear the voice of any other nation, for we are to be directed by you our brothers, the English, and by none else; we shall be very glad to hear what our brothers have to say to us at the Logg's town in the spring, and do assure you of our hearty good will and love to our brothers. we present you with these four strings of wampum." This is the last town of the Delawares to the westward. The Delaware Indians by the best accounts I could gather consist of about five hundred fighting men all firmly attached to the English interest: they are not properly a part of the six nations but are scattered about, among most of the Indians upon the Ohio, and some of them among the six nations, from whom they have leave to hunt upon their Lands.

Indians promise to be firm to the English

Delawares 500 fighting Men, not Part of the six Nations but have Leave to hunt on their Lands

Tuesday 29th Set out S W. 5 m—S 5 m—to the mouth of *Sioto Creek* opposite to the *Shawnee town*;[116] here we fired our Guns to alarm the Traders, who soon answered and came and ferried us over. The Land about the mouth of *Sioto Creek* [is rich, but broken, fine bottoms upon] the river and creek. The *Shawane town* is situated on both sides of the *Ohio,* just below the mouth of *Sioto creek* and contains about three hundred men, there are about forty houses on the South side of the River, and about a hundred on the North side, with a kind of State house of about ninety feet long, with a light cover of Bark, in which they hold their councils: The Shawanes are not a part of the six nations, but were formerly at Variance with them tho' now reconciled, they are great friends to the English, who once protected[117] them from the fury of the six nations which they gratefully remember.

[Land] rich but broken

Shawane Town situated, contains 300 Men

Shawanes not a Part of the six Nations, great Friends to English who protected them from the six Nations

Wednesday 30th We were conducted into council where George Croghan[78] delivered sundry speeches from the Government of Pensylvania[80] to the cheifs of this nation in which he informed them "That two prisoners[118] who had been taken by the french, and had made their escape from the french Officer at lake Erie, as he was carrying them toward Canada, brought news that the French offered a large sum of money to any person, who would bring to them the said Croghan, and Andrew Montour alive, or if dead their scalps; and that the French also threatned those Indians and the Wiandots with war in the spring. The same persons farther said that they had seen twenty french canoes loaded with stores for a new fort[119] they designed on the south side Lake Erie. Mr Croghan also informed them that

Messages from the Govr of Pennsylvania

In the Darlington Memorial Library

several of our traders had been taken, and advised them to keep their warriours at home, until they could see what the French intended, which he doubted not would appear in the spring. Then Andrew Montour informed this nation as he had done the Wiandots and the Delawares. "That the King of Great Britain had sent them a large present of Goods in company with the six nations, which was under the care of the Governor of Virginia, who had sent me[81] out, to invite them to come and see him, and partake of their fathers present[105] next summer. To which we received this Answer. *Big Hanoahansa*.[120] their speaker taking in his hand the several strings of wampum, which had been given by the English said." These are the Speeches received by us from your great men, from the beginning of our friendship all that our brothers the English have told us has been good and true for which we return our hearty thanks: Then taking up four other strings of wampum in his hand he said, Brothers I now speak the sentiments of all our people. When first our forefathers did meet the English our brothers, they found what our brothers the English told them to be true and so have we; We are but a small people, but it is not to us only that you speak, but to all nations; We shall be glad to hear what our brothers will say to us at the Loggs town, in the spring[121] and we hope that the Friendship now subsisting between us and our brothers will last as long as the Sun shines or the moon gives light. We hope that our Children will hear and believe what our brothers say to them, as we have always done, and to assure you of our hearty good will towards you our Brothers, we present you with these four strings of wampum." After the council was over they had much talk about sending a Guard with us to the *Picqualinnees town*[98] (these are a tribe of the *Tawightwis*) which was reckoned near 200 miles, but after a long consultation their King[122] being sick they came to no determination about it.

acquaints the Indians the King had sent them a Present

Indians Answer

Thursday 31st to Monday Feb. 11th   Stayed in the *Shawane town*. While I was here the Indians had a very extraordinary Festival at which I was present and which I have exactly described at the end[123] of my Journal. As I had particular Instructions from the President of Virginia to discover the strength and number of some Indian nations to the westward who had lately revolted from the French, and had some messages to deliver them from him I resolved to set out for the *Tawightwi town*.[98]

Page 15

resolves to go to the Tawightwis

Tuesday 12th   Having left my boy to take care of my Horses in the *Shawane town,* and supplied myself with a fresh horse to ride, I set out with my old company vizt George Croghan Andrew Montour Robert Kallender and a Servant to carry our Provision &c. N W. 10 m—

· 107 ·

George Mercer Papers

Wednesday 13th   the same course N W. about 35 m—
Thursday 14th   the same course about 30 m—
Friday .. 15th   the same 15 m—we met with nine Shawane Indians coming from one of the *Picqualinnees towns* where they had been to council, they told us there were fifteen more of them behind at the *Tawightwi town* waiting for the arrival of the Wawiaghtas[124] (a tribe of the Tawightwis) who were to bring with them a Shawane woman and child to deliver to their Men that were behind. This woman they informed us was taken prisoner last fall by some of the Wawiaghta warriors thro' a mistake which was like to have engaged the nations in war.

Saturday 16th   Set out the same course[125] N. W about 35 m—to the *little Mineami river*[126] *or creek.*

Sunday 17th   Crossed the *little Mineami* and altered our course S W 25 m—to the *big Mineami River* opposite to the *Tawightwi town.*[98] All the land from the Shawane Town[116] to this place (except the first twenty miles which is broken) is fine rich level land well timbered with large Walnut, Ash, Sugar trees, Cherry trees &c. and is well watered, with a great number of little streams & rivulets, and full of beautiful natural meadows, covered with wild Rye, blue grass, and clover, and abounds with Turkeys, Deer, Elks, and most sorts of Game, particularly Buffaloes thirty or forty of which are frequently seen feeding in one Meadow; in short it wants nothing but cultivation to make it a most delightful country. The Ohio and all the large branches are said to be full of fine fish of several kinds particularly a sort of cat fish of a prodigious size but as I was not there at a proper season I had not an opportunity of seeing any of them. The traders had always reckoned it 200 miles from the *Shawane town* to the *Tawightwi town;* but by my computation I could make it no more than 150. The *Mineami river* being high, we were obliged to make a Raft of old logs to transport our goods and Saddles and swim our horses over; After firing a few guns and Pistols, and smoking in the Warriors pipe, who came to invite us to the Town, according to their custom of inviting and wellcoming strangers, and great men, We entered the town with English colours before us, and were kindly received by their King,[127] who invited us into his own house, and set our colours upon the top of it. The firing of the Guns held about a quarter of an hour and then all the white men and traders that were there, came and welcomed us to the *Tawightwi town.* This Town is situate on the N W side of the *Big Mineami River* about 150 miles from the mouth thereof, it consists of about four hundred families and is daily increasing, it is accounted one of the strongest Indan

sidenotes:
Land very rich with fine Meadows & Streams Variety of Timber and Abundance of Game

The Ohio abounds with Fish

smoaks the Pipe of Peace

is kindly received by the Tawightwi King

towns upon this part of the continent. The Tawightwas are a very numerous people consisting of many different tribes[128] under the same form of Government, each tribe has a particular chief, or King, one of which is chosen indifferently out of any tribe, to rule the whole nation, and is vested with greater Authorities than any of the others. They are accounted the most powerful nation, to the westward of the English settlements, and much superior to the six nations with whom they are now in Amity. Their strength and numbers are not thoroughly known as they have but lately traded with the English and indeed have very little trade among them; they deal in much the same commodities as the Northern Indians: There are other nations or tribes[129] still further to the westward daily coming into them, and it is thought their power and interest, reaches to the westward of the Mississippi, if not across the continent; they are at present very well affected to the English and seem fond of an alliance[130] with them; they formerly lived on the farther side of the *Wabash* and were in the French interest, who supplied them with some few trifles, at a most exorbitant price, they were called by the French *Mineamis*, but they have now revolted[98] from them, and left their former habitations, for the sake of trading with the English and notwithstanding all the Artifices the French have used, they have not been able to recall them. After we had been sometime in the king's house, Mr Montour told him that we wanted to speak with him, and the cheifs of this nation this evening, upon which we were invited into the long house, and having taken our places, Mr Montour began as follows. "Brothers the Tawightwis as we have been hindered by the high waters, and some other business with our Indian brothers, no doubt our long stay has caused some trouble among our brothers here, therefore we now present you with two strings of wampum to remove all the trouble of your hearts, and clear your eyes that you may see the Sun shine clear for we have a great deal to say to you; and we would have you send for one of your friends that can speak the Mohickon[131] or the Mingoe Tongues well, that we may understand each other thoroughly, for we have a great deal of business to do. The Mohiccons[132] are a small tribe who most of them speak English and are also well acquainted with the language of the Tawightwis, and they with theirs. Mr Montour then proceeded to deliver them a message[133] from the Wiandots and Delawares as follows.

"Brothers the Tawightwis this comes by our brothers the English who are coming with good news to you. We hope you will take care of them and all our brothers the English who are trading among you. You made a Road for our brothers the English to come and trade

Remarks on the Tawightwi Town & Nation

C 9

Montour tells the King he had come on business to him. Montour speaks to the Tawigtwis

Speech from the Wiandots & Delawares to the Tawightwis

George Mercer Papers

among you, but it is now very foul, great logs are fallen across it, and we would have you be strong, like men, and have one heart with us, and make the road clear, that our brothers the English may have free course and recourse between you and us. In the sincerity of our hearts, we send you these four strings of wampum, to which they gave their usual Yo Ho. then They then said they wanted some Tobacco to smoak with us, and that tomorrow they would send for their Interpreter.

Monday 18th We walked about, and viewed the Fort, which wanted some repairs, and the traders men helped them to bring logs to line the inside.

Tuesday 19th We gave their kings and great men some cloaths paint and shirts, and they were busy dressing and preparing themselves for the council. The weather grew warm and the creeks began to lower very fast

Wednesday 20th About twelve of the clock we were informed that some of the foreign tribes[129] were coming, upon which proper persons were ordered to meet them, and conduct them to the Town, and then we were invited into the long house. After we had been seated about a quarter of an hour, four Indians, two from each tribe, who had been sent before to bring the long pipe, and to inform us that the rest were coming, came in, and informed us that their friends had sent those pipes, that we might smoak the Calumet pipe of peace with them, and that they intended to do the same with us.

Croghan delivers a Present & Messages Thursday 21st We were invited again into the long house, where Mr Croghan made them with the foreign tribes a present to the value of one hundred pounds Pensylvania money, and delivered all our speeches to them, at which they seemed well pleased, and said that they would take time and consider well what we had said to them.

Friday 22d[134] Nothing remarkable happened.

Saturday 23d In the Afternoon there was an Alarm, which caused great confusion and running about among the Indians; upon enquiring the reason of this stir, they told us, it was occasioned by six Indians that came to war against them from the Southward, three of them Cuttawas,[135] and three Shawanes; these were some of the Shawanes who had formerly deserted from the other part of the nation, and now lived to the Southward:[136] towards night there was a report spread in town, that four Indians and four hundred French, were on their March and [just by the town, but] soon after the messenger who brought the news, said there were only four french Indians coming to council, and that they bid him say so, only to see how the English would behave themselves, but as they had behaved themselves like men he now told the truth.

· 110 ·

In the Darlington Memorial Library

Sunday Feb. 24th This morning the four French Indians came into Town and were kindly received by the Town Indians. They marched in under french colours, and were conducted into the long house, and after they had been in about a quarter of an hour, the council sat and we were sent for that we might hear what the French had to say. The *Piankasha* king[137] who was at that time the principal man and commander in cheif of the *Tawightwis,* said he would have the English colours set up in this council, as well as the French, to which we answered he might do as he thought fit; after we were seated right opposite to the French Ambassadors, one of them said he had a present to make them, so a place was prepared, as they had before done for our present, between them and us, and then their speaker stood up and laid his hands upon two Keggs of brandy that held about seven quarts each, and a Roll of tobacco of about ten pounds weight, then taking two strings of wampum in his hand he said "What he had to deliver them was from their Father (meaning the French King) and he desired they would hear what he was about to say." then he laid the two strings of wampum upon the Keggs and taking up four other strings of black and white wampum he said "That their father remembering his children had sent them two Keggs of milk,[138] and some tobacco, and that he had now made a clear road for them to come and see him, and his Officers and pressed them very much to come and see him" Then he took another string of wampum in his hand and said "Their father would now forget all little differences that had been between them, and desired them not to be of two minds, but to let him know their minds freely, for he would send for them no more" To which the *Piankasha* king replied it was true their father had sent for them several times, and said the road was clear, but he understood it was made foul and bloody and by them. "We, said he, have cleared a road for our brothers the English, and your Fathers have made it bad, and have taken some of our brothers ₍₁prisoners, which we₎ look upon as done to us," and he turned short about and went out of council. After the French Ambassador had delivered his message, he went into one of the private houses, and endeavoured much to prevail on some Indians there, and was seen to cry and lament which was as he said for the loss of that nation.

Monday 25th This day we received a speech from the *Wawiaghtas* and *Piankashas* two tribes of the *Tawightwis,* one of the cheifs[139] of the former spoke, "Brothers we have heard what you have said to us by the Interpreter, and we see you take pity upon our poor wives and children, and have taken us by the hand into the great chain of friendship, therefore we present you with these two bundles of skins,

Marginalia:
₍Fo₎ur French Indians come in
French Present to the Indians
French Speech
Piankasha King's Reply to the French
Wawiaghta Speech

· 111 ·

George Mercer Papers

to make *shoes* for your people, and this pipe to smoak in, to assure you our hearts are good and true towards you our brothers, and we hope that we shall all continue in true love and friendship with one another, as people with one head and one heart ought to do. You have pitied us, as you always did the rest of our Indian brothers. We hope that that the pity you have always shewn will remain as long as the Sun gives light, and on our side you may depend upon sincere and true friendship towards you, as long as we have strength," this person stood up and spoke with the Air and gesture of an orator.

Tuesday 26th   The *Tawightwis*[98] delivered the following answer to the four Indians sent by the French. The Captain of the Warriors stood up, and taking some string of black and white wampum in his hand, he spoke with a fierce tone, and very warlike air. "Brothers the *Owtawais*,[89] you are always differing with the French yourselves, and yet you listen to what they say, but we will let you know by these four strings of wampum that we will not hear anything they say to us, or do anything they bid us do." Then the same speaker with six strouds, two Matchcoats, and a string of black wampum, (I understood the goods were in return for the milk and tobacco) directed his speech to the French and said, "Fathers you desire that we will speak our minds from our hearts, which I am going to do. You have often desired we should go home to you, but I tell you it is not our home, for we have made a road as far as the Sea, to the Sun rising, and have been taken by the hand[140] by our brothers *the English, and the six nations, and the Delawares, Shawanes, and Wiandots,* and we assure you that is the Road we will go: And as you threaten us with War in the spring,[141] we tell you if you are angry we are ready to receive you and resolve to die here, before we will go to you, and that you may know that this is our mind, we send you this string of black wampum" After a short pause the same Speaker spoke again thus. "Brothers the *Owtawais* you hear what I say, tell that to your fathers the French for that is our mind, and we speak it from our hearts.

Wednesday Feb 27th   This day they took down the French colours, and dismissed the four french Indians, so they took their leave of the Town and set off for the French fort.[142]

Thursday 28th   The Cryer of the Town came by the kings order, and invited us to the long house to see the *Warriors feather dance;*[143] it was performed by three dancing masters who were painted all over of with various colours, with long sticks in their hands, upon the ends of which, were fastened long feathers of Swans, and other birds, neatly woven in the shape of a fowls wing; in this disguise they performed many antick tricks, waving their sticks and feathers about with great

· 112 ·

In the Darlington Memorial Library

skill, to imitate the flying and fluttering of birds, keeping exact time with their musick; while they are dancing some of the Warriors strikes a Post, upon which the musick and the dancers cease, and the Warrior gives an account of his Atchievments in war, and when he has done throws down some goods as a recompence to the performers, and musicians, after which they proceed in their dance as before, till another Warrior strikes the post, and soon as long as they think fit.

Friday March 1st We received the following speech from the *Tawightwis*. The speaker stood up. and addressing himself as to the Governor of Pensylvania, with two strings of wampum in his hand, he said "Brothers our hearts are glad that you have taken notice of us; and surely brothers we hope that you will order a Smith[101] to settle here to mend our Guns, and hatchets: you kindness makes us so bold as to ask this request. You told us our friendship should last as long, and be as the greatest mountain. We have considered well, and all our great kings ₍and warriors₎ are ₍come to a resolution, never₎ to give heed to what the French say to us, but always to hear, and believe what you our brothers say to us. Brothers we are obliged to you, for your kind invitation[80] to receive a present at the Loggstown, but as our foreign tribes are not yet come, we must wait for them, but you may depend we will come, as soon as our women have planted corn, to hear what our brothers will say to us. Brothers we present you with this bundle of skins, as we are but poor, to be for shoes for you on the road, and we return you our hearty thanks for the cloaths which you have put upon our Wives and children.

We, then took our leave of the kings and cheifs, and they ordered that a small party of Indians should go with us, as far as *Hockhocking*;[110] but as I had left my boy and horses at the *lower Shawane town*,[116] I was obliged to go by myself, or to go sixty or seventy miles out of my way, which I did not *care* to do; so we all came over the *Mineami River* together this Evening, but Mr Croghan and Mr Montour, went over again and lodged in the town, but I stayed on this side at one Robert Smiths[144] a trader, where we had left our horses. Before the French Indians had come into town, we had drawn Articles of peace and alliance, between the English and *Wawiaghtas*, and *Piankashas*. the Indentures were signed, sealed and delivered on both sides, and as I drew them I took a copy.[134] The land upon the great *Mineami river* is very rich, level, and well timbered, some of finest meadows that can be. The Indians and traders assure me that the land it holds as good and if possible better to the westward as far as the *Wabash*. which is accounted 100 miles, and quite up to the head of the *Mineami river* which is sixty miles above the *Tawightwi town*,[98]

Tawightwis' Speech to the Govr of Pennsylvania

Articles of Peace ₍between₎ the English ₍and Wawiaghtas & Piankashas, Page Land on the great Mineami River very fine & the same for several Miles on the Wabash &c

· 113 ·

George Mercer Papers

and down the said river quite to the Ohio, which is reckoned 150 miles. The grass here grows to a great height in the clear fields, of which there are a great number, and the bottoms are full of white clover, wild Rye and blue grass.

<small>many clear Fields wth fine Grass White Clover, wild Rye & blue Grass</small>

<small>9 C Mad Creek</small>

Saturday 2d George Croghan, and the rest of our company, came over the River; we got our horses and set out travelled about thirty-five miles 35 m to *mad creek,* this is a place where some English traders[118] had been taken prisoners by the French.

Sunday March 3d We parted, they for *Hockhocking,*[110] and I for the *Shawane town,*[116] and as I was quite alone, and knew that the French Indians had threatned us, and would probably pursue, or lie in wait for us, I left the path, and went to the South westward, down the *little Mineami river or creek,* where I had fine travelling, through rich land and beautiful meadows, in which I could sometimes see forty or fifty Buffaloes feeding at once. the *little Mineami river or creek* continued to run thro' the middle of a fine meadow, about a mile wide, very clear, like an old field, and not a bush in it. I could see the Buffaloes in it above two miles off. I travelled this day about thirty miles.

<small>Land on little Mineami River very fine—saw large Herds of Buffaloes</small>

Monday 4th This day I heard several Guns, but was afraid to examine who fired them, least they might be some of the French Indians; so I travelled thro' the woods about thirty miles, 30 m, just at night I killed a fine barren cow Buffaloe, and took out her tongue, and a little of the best of her meat. The land still level rich and well timbered with Oak, Walnut, Ash, Locusts, and sugar trees.

<small>Land very fine and well timbered</small>

Tuesday 5th I travelled about thirty miles 30 m

Wednesday 6th I travelled about thirty miles and killed a fat Bear.

Thursday 7th Set out with my horse load of Bear, and travelled about thirty miles 30 m. This afternoon I met a young man a trader, and we encamped together that night, he happened to have some bread with him, and I had plenty of meat, so we fared very well.

<small>Shawane Town</small>

Friday 8th Travelled[146] about thirty miles 30 m, and arrived at night at the *Shawane town,* All the Indians, as well as the white men came out to welcome my return to their town, being very glad that all things were rightly settled in the *Mineami* country; they fired upwards of 150 Guns in the town,[116] and made an entertainment on account of the peace with the western Indians.[134] On my return from the *Tawightwi,* to the *Shawane town,* I did not keep an exact account of course or distance, for as the land thereabout was much the same and the situation of the Country was sufficiently described, in my Journey to the *Tawightwi town.* I thought it unnecessary, but have notwithstanding laid down my Tract pretty nearly in my plat.

· 114 ·

In the Darlington Memorial Library

Saturday 9th   In the *Shawane town* I met with one of the *Mingoe* cheifs[147] who had been down at the Falls of Ohio, so that we did not see him as we went up. I informed him of the King's present[105] and the invitation[81] down to Virginia; he told me that there was a party of French Indians hunting at the Falls,[42] and if I went they would kill or carry me away Prisoner to the French, for it was certain they would not let me pass; however as I had a great inclination to see the Falls, and the lands on the East side the Ohio, I resolved to venture as far as possible.

Sunday 10th   Stayed in the town and prepared for my departure.

Tuesday 12th   I got my horses over the river, and after breakfast, my boy and I got ferried over.[148] The Ohio is near three quarters of a mile wide at the Shawane town, and is very deep and smooth. *(Ohio at the Shawane Town 3/4 Mile wide & very deep, and gentle Current)*

Wednesday 13th   We set out S 45ᵈ W, down the river, on the S E side 8 m—then S 10 m—here I met two men belonging to Robert Smith[144] at whose house I lodged on this side the *Mineami river*, and one Hugh Crawford; the said Robert Smith had given me an order upon these men, for two of the teeth of a large beast,[149] which they were bringing from towards the Falls of Ohio,[42] one of which I brought in and delivered to the Ohio Company. Robert Smith informed me that about seven years ago, these teeth and the Bones of three large beasts, one of which was somewhat smaller than the other two, *were found in a salt lick*[150] *or spring, upon a small creek, which runs into the South side of the Ohio, about fifteen miles 15 below the mouth of the great Mineami river, and twenty below the Falls of Ohio;* he assured me that the rib bones of the largest of those beasts, were eleven feet long, and the scull bone six feet across the forehead, and the other bones in proportion, and that there were several teeth there, some of which he called horns, and said they were upwards of five feet long, and as much as a man could well carry; that he had hid one in a branch at some distance from the place, lest the French Indians should carry it away. The tooth which I brought in, for the Ohio Company, was a jaw tooth, of better than four pounds weight, it appeared to be the furthest tooth in the jaw, and looked like fine Ivory, when the outside was scraped off. I also met with four *Shawane* Indians coming up the river in their Canoes, who informed me that there were about sixty French Indians encamped at the Falls. *(three very large Carcasses of Beasts found on the Ohio; rib Bones 11 Feet Scull Bone 6 Feet across; Teeth 5 Feet long; Teeth Gist brought above 4 lbs weight)*

Thursday Mar 14th   I went down the river S 15 m the land upon this side the Ohio Cheifly broken and the bottoms but narrow. *(Land broken Bottoms narrow)*

Friday .. 15th   S. 5 m—S W 10 m—to a creek[151] that was so high that we could not get over that night

Saturday. 16th   S 45ᵈ W about 35 m—

· 115 ·

George Mercer Papers

Sunday 17th the same course 15 m—then N 45ᵈ W 5 m—

<small>Lower salt Lick 15 Miles from the Falls of the Ohio</small>

Monday. 18th N. 45ᵈ W 5 m—then S W 20 m—to the *lower salt lick creek*[152] which Robert Smith and the Indians told me was about 15 miles above the *falls of Ohio;* the land still hilly, the Salt lick here much the same with those before described. This day we heard several guns which made me imagine the french Indians were not moved, but were still hunting, and firing thereabouts; We also saw some traps newly set, and the footsteps of some Indians plain on the ground as if they had been there the day before. I [was now] much troubled that I could not comply with my Instructions, and was once resolved to leave the boy and horses, and go privately on foot to view the

<small>afraid to go to the Falls</small>

Falls; but the boy being a poor hunter, was afraid he would starve if I was long from him, and there was also great danger lest the French Indians should come upon our horses tracks, or hear their Bells, and as I had seen good land enough, I thought perhaps I might be blamed for venturing so far, in such dangerous times, so I concluded not to

<small>Little Cuttawa River</small>

go to the Falls, but travelled away to the Southward, till we were over the *little Cuttawa river.*[153] *The Falls of Ohio,*[42] by the best information

<small>Falls of Ohio described</small>

I could get, are not very steep. on the S E side there is a bar of sand at some distance from the Shore, the water between the Bar, and the Shore is not above three feet deep. and the stream moderately strong: the Indians frequently pass safely in their Canoes through this passage, but are obliged to take great care as they go down, lest the current which is much the strongest on the N W side, should draw them that way which would be very dangerous, as the water on that side runs with great rapidity over several ledges of Rocks. The waters below the Falls, as they say, is about six fathoms deep, and the river

<small>[400] miles from the Falls to the Mississippi</small>

continues without any obstruction, till it empties itself into the Mississippi, which is accounted upwards of 400 miles. The Ohio near the mouth is said to be very wide, and the land upon both sides very rich, and in general very level all the way from the Falls. After I had

<small>Ohio wide Lands very rich</small>

determined not to go to the Falls, we turned from salt lick creek, to a ridge of mountains that made towards the *Cuttawa river,*[154] and from the top of the mountain, we saw a fine level countrey S W. as far as our Eyes could behold; and it was a very clear day. We then went down the Mountain, and set out S 20ᵈ W. about 5 m—thro' rich level land covered with small Walnut, Sugar trees, Red buds &c.

Tuesday 19th We set out South and crossed several creeks all

<small>Lands on the Cuttawa River rich & level for a great Distance</small>

running to the S W, at about twelve miles came to the *little Cuttawa river,*[154] we were obliged to go up it about a mile to an Island which was the shoalest place we could find to cross at; we then continued our course in all about thirty miles thro' rich level land except about

· 116 ·

In the Darlington Memorial Library

two miles which was broken and indifferent; this level is about thirty five miles broad, and as we came up the side of it along the branches of the *little Cuttawa,* We found it about 150 miles long, and how far towards the S W. we could not tell, but imagined it held as far as the *great Cuttawa river,*[155] which would be upwards of 100 miles more, and appeared much broader that way, than here, as I could discern from the tops of the mountains. [Great] Cuttawa River

Wednesday 20th We did not travel. I went up to the top of a mountain to view the country: To the S E it looked very broken, and Mountainous, but to the Eastward and S W. it appeared very level.

Thursday 21st Set out S 45d E. 15 m—S 5 m—here I found a place[156] where the Stones shined like high coloured brass; the heat of the Sun drew out of them a kind of Borax, or Salt Petre, only something sweeter, some of which I brought into the Ohio company, tho' I believe it was nothing but a sort of Sulphur. finds a Kind of Borax

Friday. 22d S E 12 m—I killed a fat bear and was taken sick that night.

Saturday 23d I stayed here, and sweated after the Indian manner which helped me.

Sunday 24th Set out E. 2 m—N E 3 m—N 1 m—E 2 m— S E 5 m— E 2 m—N 2 m—S E 7 m—to a small creek[157] where we encamped, in a place where we had but poor food for our horses, and both we, and they were very much wearied, The reason of our making so many short courses was, we were driven by a branch of the *little Cuttawa river,* whose banks were so exceeding steep that it was impossible to ford it, into a ledge of Rocky laurel mountains which were almost impassable.

Monday March 25th Set out S E 12 m—N 2 m—E 1 m—S 4 m—S E 2 m—we killed a a Buck elk here, and took out his tongue to carry with us.

Tuesday 26th Set out S E. 10 m—S W 1 m—S E 1 m—S W 1 m—S E 1 m—S W 1 m— S E 1 m—S W 1 m—S E 5 m—killed two Buffaloes and took out their tongues, and encamped. These two days we travelled through Rocks and mountains full of laurel thickets, which we could hardly creep through, without cutting our way. Laurel Thickets

Wednesday 27th Our horses and selves were so tired that we were obliged to stay this day to rest, for we were unable to travel, *on all the branches of the little Cuttawa river*[154] *was great plenty of fine coal* some of which I brought in to the Ohio company. Plenty of fine Coal on the Cuttawa

Thursday 28th Set out S E. 15 m—crossing several creeks of the *little Cuttawa river the land still full of Coal and black Slate.* Coal & Slate

Friday 29th the same course S E about 12 m—the land still mountainous.

· 117 ·

George Mercer Papers

Saturday 30th Stayed to rest our horses. I went on foot, and found a passage through the mountains, to another creek or a fork of the same creek that we were upon.

Sunday 31st the same course S E. 15 m—killed a Buffaloe and encamped.

Monday April 1st Set out the same course about 20 m—part of the way we went along a path up the side of a little creek, at the head of which, was a gap[158] in the mountains, then our path went down another creek[159] to a lick, *where blocks of coal about eight or ten Inches square lay upon the surface of the ground;* here we killed a Bear and encamped.

<small>Blocks of Coal 8 Inches square on the Surface of the Earth</small>

Tuesday 2d Set out S 2 m—S E 1 m—N E 3 m—killed a Buffaloe

Wednesday 3d S 4 m—S W 3 m—E 3 m—S E 2 m—to a small creek[160] on which was a large Warriors camp that would contain seventy or eighty Warriors; their captain's name or title was the Crane[161] as I knew by his Picture or Arms painted on a tree.

Thursday 4th I stayed here all day to rest our horses; I plotted down our courses, and found I had still near 200 miles home upon a streight line

Friday 5th Rained and we stayed at the Warriors Camp.

Saturday 6th We went along the Warriors road[162] S 1 m—S E 3 m—S 2 m—S E 3 m—E 3 m—killed a Bear

Sunday 7th Set out E 2 m—N E 1 m—S E 1 m—S 1 m—W 1 m—S W 1 m—S 1 m—S E 2 m—S 1 m—

Monday 8th S 1 m—S E 1 m—E 3 m—S E 1 m—E 3 m—N E 2 m—N 1 m—E 1 m—N 1 m—E 2 m—and encamped on a small laurel creek.[163]

<small>Country mountainous with Laurel Thickets</small>

Tuesday 9th & Wednesday 10th The weather being bad we did not travel these two days, the countrey being still Rockey mountainous and full of laurel thickets; the worst travelling[164] I ever saw.

Thursday 11th We travelled several courses near 20 miles, but in the afternoon, as I could see from the top of a mountain the place we came from, I found we had not come upon a streight line more than N 65d E. 10 m—

Friday 12th Set out through very difficult ways E 5 m—to a small creek.

Saturday 13th The same course E upon a streight line tho' the way we were obliged to travel was near twenty miles; here we killed two Bears, the way still Rockey and mountainous.

Sunday 14th As food was very scarce in these barren mountains, we were obliged to move for fresh feeding for our horses, in climbing up the Clifts and Rocks this day two of our horses fell down, and

· 118 ·

were pretty much hurted, and a Paroquet, which I had got from the Indians on the other side of the Ohio, where there are a great number, died of a bruise he got by the fall; tho' it was but a trifle I was much concerned at losing him, as he was perfectly tame, and had been very brisk all the way and I had still corn enough left to feed him. In the afternoon I left the horses, and went all the way down the creek, and found such a precipice, and such laurel thickets that we could not pass, and the horses were not able to go up the mountain, till they had rested a day or two {Paroquets on the Ohio}

Monday April 15th We cut a passage through the laurels better than two miles, as I was climbing up the Rocks, I got a fall which hurted me pretty much. This afternoon we wanted provision I killed a Bear {cut a Passage thro a Laurel Thicket 2 Miles}

Tuesday 16th Thunder and Rain in the morning We set out N 25ᵈ E. 3 m.

Wednesday 17th This day I went to the top of a mountain to view the way, and found it so bad that I did not care to engage in it, but rather chose to go out of the way, and keep down along the side of a creek till I could find a branch or Run, on the other side to go up.

Thursday 18th Set out down the creeks side N 3 m—then the creek turning N W. I was obliged to leave it and go up a ridge N E 1 m —E 2 m—S E 2 m—N E 1 m—to the fork of a River

Friday 19th Set out down the Run N E. 2 m—E 2 m—S E 2 m—N 20ᵈ E 2 m—E 2 m—up a large Run

Saturday 20th Set out S E. 10 m—E 4 m—over a small creek. We had such bad travelling down this creek, that we had like to have lost one of our horses.

Sunday 21st Stayed to rest our horses.

Monday 22d Rained all day we could not travel

Tuesday 23d Set out E 8 m—along a ridge of mountains then S E. 5 m—E 3 m—S E 4 m—and encamped among very steep mountains[165]

Wednesday 24th S E 4 m—through steep mountains and thickets E. 6 m—

Thursday 25th E 5 m—S E 1 m—N E 2 m—S E 2 m—E 1 m—then S 2 m—E 1 m—killed a Bear.

Friday 26th Set out S E 2 m—here it rained so hard we were obliged to stop.

Saturday 27th to Monday 29th[166] These three days it continued rainy and bad weather, so that we could not travel. All the way from Salt lick creek to this place the branches of the little Cuttawa were so high that we could not pass them, which obliged us to go over the heads of them, through a continued ledge of almost inaccessible mountains, rocks and laurel thickets.

George Mercer Papers

Blue Stone River

Tuesday 30th Fair weather set out E 3 m—S E 8 m—E 2 m—to a *little river or creek which falls into the Big Kanhawa, called bluestone,* where we encamped and had good feeding for our horses.

Wednesday May 1st Set out N 75d E. 10 m—and killed a Buffaloe, then went up a very high mountain,[168] upon the top of which was a

remarkable Rock

Rock sixty or seventy feet high, and a cavity in the middle, into which I went, and found there was a passage through it, which gradually ascended to the top, with several holes in the rock, which let in the light; when I got to the top of this rock, I could see a prodigious distance, and could plainly discover where the Big Kanhawa river broke thro' the next high mountain. I then came down and continued my course N 75d E. 6 m—further and encamped.

Thursday 2d & Friday 3d These two days it rained, and we stayed at our Camp, to take care of some provision we had killed.

Saturday 4th This day our horses run away, and it was late before we got them, so we could not [travel] far; we went N 75d E. 4 m—

Sunday 5th Rained all day

Monday 6th Set out through very bad ways E 3 m—N E 6 m—over a bad laurel creek E 4 m

Big Kanhawa or New River

Tuesday 7th Set out E 10 m—to the *Big Kanhawa, or new river* and got over half of it to a *large Island* where we lodged all night.

Wednesday 8th We made a raft of Logs and crossed[169] the other half of the River, and went up it S. 2 m—*the Kanhawa or new river*

Kanhawa 200 yds wide-deep with many Falls — Bottoms rich but narrow-high Land broken

(by some called Woods river) where I crossed it which was about 8 miles above the mouth of the *blue stone river,* is better than 200 yards wide, and pretty deep, but full of Rocks and Falls. The bottoms upon it, and *blue stone river* are very rich, but narrow; the high land broken.

Thursday May 9th Set out E 13 m—to a large Indian Warrior's Camp, where we killed a Bear and stayed all night

Friday 10th Set out E 4 m—S E 3 m—S 3 m—thro' mountains[170] covered with Ivy, and laurel thickets

[A lake on] the Top of [a] moun[t]ain

Saturday 11th Set out S 2 m—S E 5 m—to a creek,[171] and a meadow where we let our horses feed, then S E 2 m—S 1 m—S E 2 m—to a very high mountain upon the top of which was a lake[172] or pond about ¾ of a mile long N E and S W; and a ¼ of a mile wide, the water fresh and clear, and a clean gravelly shore about ten yards wide, with a fine meadow, and six fine springs in it. then S about 4 m—to a branch of

Sinking Creek

the Kanhawa called *sinking creek*[173]

Sunday 12th stayed to rest our horses and dry some meat we had killed.

Monday 13th Set out S E. 2 m—E 1 m—S E 3 m—S 12 m—to one

· 120 ·

In the Darlington Memorial Library

Richard Halls[174] in Augusta County this man is one of the farthest Settlers to the westward up the new river.   [R. Hall the farthest settler to the west of new river]

Tuesday 14th Stayed at Richard Hall's and wrote the President[175] of Virginia, and the Ohio company, to let them know I should be with them by the 15th day of June.

Wednesday 15th Set out from Richard Halls S 16 m—

Thursday 16th The same course S 22 m—and encamped at *Beaver Island creek*[176] *a branch of the Kanhawa,* opposite to the head of *Roanoak.*   [Beaver Island Creek]

Friday 17th Set out S W 3 m—then S 9 m—to the dividing line[177] between Carolina and Virginia where I stayed all night the land from Richard Hall's to this place is broken.   [Line between No Carolina & Virginia]

Saturday 18th Set out S 20 m—to my own house[178] on the *Yadkin river:* when I came there, I found all my family gone, for the Indians had killed five people in the winter near that place, which frightened my wife and family away to *Roanoak* about 35 miles nearer in among the Inhabitants, which I was informed of by an old man I met near the place.   [Gist arrives at his own House on the Yadkin River]

Sunday 19th Set out for *Roanoak*[179] and as we had now a path, we got there the same night where I found all my family well.

Christopher Gist

An Account of the Festival at the Shawane Town mentioned in my Journal page 7.[528]   [Shawane Festival]

In the Evening a proper Officer made a public Proclamation, that all the Indians Marriages were dissolved, and a public Feast was to be held for the three Succeeding Days after, in which the women (as their Custom was) were again to choose their Husbands.   [Indian Marriages dissolved]

The next Morning early the Indians breakfasted, and after spent the Day in dancing till the Evening, when a plentiful feast was prepared, after feasting they spent the night in Dancing.

The same way they passed the two next days till the Evening, the Men dancing by themselves, and then the Women in turns round Fires, and dancing in their manner in the form of the figure 8 about 60 or 70 of them at a Time. The women, the whole time they danced, sung a Song in their Language, the Chorus of which was, I am not afraid of my Husband.

I will choose what Man I please.

Singing those Lines alternately.

The third day in the Evening, the men being about 100 in number, danced in a long string following one another, sometimes at length, at other times in a figure of 8 quite round the fort, and in and out of the long house, where they held their Councils, the Women stand-

George Mercer Papers

ing together as the Men danced by them; and as any of the Women liked a Man passing by, she stepped in, and joined in the Dance, taking hold of the Man's Stroud, whom she chose, and then continued in the Dance till the rest of the Women stepped in, and made their choice in the same manner; after which the Dance ended and they all retired to consummate

<small>₍Ind₎ian Women ₍choose₎ Husbands</small>

M<u>r</u> Gists second Journal[529]–*begin another Page*

Pursuant to my Instructions, from the Committee of the Ohio Company bearing date July 16th 1751.

Monday Nov<u>r</u> 4th ₍Set out from the Company's Store House in Frederick₎ County Virginia, opp₍osite₎ *the mouth of Wills Creek*, and crossing *Potomack River* went W 4 m—to *a Gap*[184] in the *Allegany Mountains* up ₍on the₎ S W. fork of the said Creek. *This Gap is the nearest to Potomack River of any in the Allegany Mountains and* ₍is₎ *accounted one of the best, tho' the mountain*[185] *is very high the ascent is no where very steep, but rises gradually* ₍near₎ *six miles; it is now very full of old Trunks of Trees and stones, but with some pains might be made a very good Wa*₍ggon₎ *Road. This Gap is directly in the way to Monaungahela, and several miles nearer than that the Traders co*₍mmonly₎ *pass thro'*,[186] *and a much better way.*

<small>Gap in the Allegany Mountain best here</small>

Tuesday Nov<u>r</u> 5th Set out N 80<u>d</u> W. 8 m—it rained and obliged us to stop.

Wednesday. 6th The same Course 3. m—hard rain

Thursday. 7th Rained hard and we could not travel.

Friday 8th Set out the same course N 80<u>d</u> W. 3 m—here we encamped, and turned to see where the branches lead to and found they descended into the middle fork of *Youghiogeni*.[187] We hunted all the grounds ₍for₎ ten miles or more, and killed several Deers, Bears, and one large Elk. The Bottoms upon the Branches a₍re but₎ narrow, with some Indian Fields, about 2000 Acres of good high land about a mile from the largest Branch.

<small>Bottoms narrow</small>

Saturday 9th to *Tuesday* 19th We were employed in searching the Lands, and discovering the Branches ₍Creeks &c.₎

Wednesday 20th Set out N 45<u>d</u> W. 5 m—killed a Deer.

Thursday 21st The same course 5 m—the greatest part of this day, We were cutting our way thro' a Laurel thicket,[188] and lodged by the side of one at night.

Friday 22<u>d</u> Set out the same course N 45<u>d</u> W 2 m—and cut our way through a great Laurel thick₍et₎ to the middle fork of *Youghiogeni*[187] then S. down the said fork crossing a Run[189] 1 m—then S 45<u>d</u> W. 2 m— over the ₍said₎ Fork where we encamped.

<small>Youghiogeni River</small>

In the Darlington Memorial Library

Saturday 23d   Rested our Horses and examined the Land on foot, which we found to be tolerable rich, and well timbered but stoney and broken. Land rich, stoney and broken, well timbered

Sunday 24th   Set out W. 2 m—then S 45d W. 6 m—over the South Fork[190] and encamped on the S W s₍ide₎ about a mile from a small hunting Town of the Delawares, from whom I bought some Corn, I invited ₍these₎ Indians to a Treaty at the Loggs Town, the Full Moon in May, as Colo Patton[191] had desired me; they treated ₍me₎ very civilly, but after I went from that place my Man informed me, that they threatned to take away our G₍uns₎ and not let us travel. Delaware hunting Town

Monday 25th   Set out W. 6 m—then S 45d W. 2 m—to a *Laurel Creek,* where we encamped, and killed some Deer.

Tuesday 26th to Thursday 28th   We were examining the Lands which we found to be rocky and mountainous. Lands rocky and mountainous

Friday 29th   Set out W 3 m—then N 65d W. 3 m—N 45d W. 2 m—.

Saturday 30th to Friday *December* 6th   We searched the Land several miles round,[192] and found it ₍about₎ 15 m—from the foot of the Mountains to the *River Monaungahela,* the first five miles of which E. & W. is good le₍vel₎ farming Land, with fine Meadows; The Timber White Oak, and Hiccory. The same body of Land holds ten miles S, to the upper Forks of *Monaungahela,*[193] and about ten miles North towards the mouth of *Youghiogeni;* ₍The Land₎ nearer the River for about eight or nine miles wide and the same length is much richer, and better timbered, with Walnuts, Locusts, Poplars, and Sugar trees; but is in some places very hilly the Bottoms upon the River one mile and some places near two miles wide. good farming Lands fine Meadows good Timber—

Land hilly

Saturday 7th   Set out W 6 m—and went to an Indians Camp and invited them to a Treaty at the Loggs Town at the full Moon in May next. At this Camp there was a Trader named Charles Poke,[194] who spoke the Indian tongue well. The Indian, to whom this Camp belonged after much discourse with me, complained and said "My Friend, you were sent[81] to us the last year from the great Men in Virginia, to inform us of a Present[105] from ₍the₎ Great King over the water, and if you can bring news from the King to us, why cant you tell him something from ₍Me? The Proprietor of Pensylvania granted my Father a Tract of Land begining eight Miles below₎ the fork of Brandy Wine Creek, and binding ₍on₎ the said Creek to the Fork, and including the West Fork and all its waters on both sides to the head fountain; The white people now live on these Lands, and will neither let me have them, nor pay me anything for them. My Father's name was Chickoconnecon,[195] I am his eldest Son, and my name is Nemicollon.[196] I desire that you will let the Governor, and the great Nemicollen an Indi₍an₎ complains₎ that he was kept out of some Lands granted him by the Proprietor of Pennsylvania on the Fork of Brandy-Wine Creek —

· 123 ·

George Mercer Papers

<small>desires Gist to let the Govr of Virginia know his Complaint</small> Men in Virginia know this, it may be, they will tell the Great King of it, and he will make Mr Penn, or his People give me the Land or pay me for it. This Trader here Charles Poke knows the truth of what I say, that the Land was granted to my Father, and that He or I never sold it." On which Charles Poke said that Chickoconnecon had such a grant of Land, and that the people who lived on it could get no titles to it, for that it was now called Mannor Lands. This I was obliged to insert in my Journal to please the Indian.

Sunday 8th We stayed at the Indian Camp.

<small>A large Cave on the River Monaungahela</small> Monday 9th Set out S 45d W. 1 m—W 6 m—to the *River Monaungahela*. At this place[197] is a large Cavity in a Rock, about thirty feet long, and twenty feet wide, and about seven feet high, and an even floor; the entrance into it, is so large and open, that it lets in plenty of light, and close by it, is a stream of fine water.

<small>Lands rich & hilly, & well timbered.</small> Tuesday 10th to Friday 13th[198] We were examining the Lands which for nine or ten miles East is rich but hilly as before described; on the E side of the River for several miles, there are several Bottoms very rich and a mile wide, and the Hills above them, are extraordinary rich and well timbered.

Saturday 14th We had Snow.

<small>Crossed the Monaungahela— Hills very rich, and full of Sugar Trees</small> Sunday 15th Crossed the *River Monaungahela* which is in this place[199] 53 Poles wide. The Bottoms upon the W. side, are not above 100 yards wide, but the Hills are very rich, both up and down the River, and full of Sugar-trees.

Monday 16th Spent in searching the Land.

<small>Various Sorts of Land.</small> Tuesday 17th Set out W 5 m—the Land upon this Course hilly but very rich, about a mile and an half, then it was level, with good Meadows, but not very rich, for about a mile and an half more, and <small>[Licki]ng Creek</small> the last two miles next to *Licking creek*[200] was very good Land. Upon this Creek we lodged at a hunting Camp of one Indian Captain [named] Oppaymolleah.[201] Here I saw an Indian named Joshua,[202] who spoke very good English, he had been acquainted with me several years, and seemed very glad to see me, and wondered much where I was going so far in those Woods. I said I was going to invite all the great Men of the Indians, to a Treaty to be held at the Loggs Town the full Moon in May next, where a parcel of Goods, a present from the King of Great Britain, would be delivered them, by proper Commissioners, and that these were the Goods[105] which I informed them of last year,[81] by order of the President of Virginia Colo Lee, who was since dead. Joshua informed them what I said, and they told me I ought to let the Beaver[203] know it, so I wrote a Line to him by Joshua, who promised to deliver it safe, and said there was a Trader's Man

· 124 ·

In the Darlington Memorial Library

who could read it for him. This Beaver is the Sachem, or Cheif of the Delawares; it is customary among the Indian Cheifs to take upon them the names of any Beast, or Bird they fancy, the Picture of which they always sign, instead of their Name or Arms.

Gist writes to the Beaver, Chief of the Delawares, to invite his Nation to a Treaty

Wednesday 18th Stayed at the Camp.

Thursday. 19th Set out W 3 m—S 45 W 2 m—W 1 m—to a Branch of *Licking Creek*.[204]

Licking Creek

Friday. 20th Set out W 1 m—S 45d W 6 m—and encamped.[205]

Saturday 21st to January 7th 1752. We stayed at this place and had a good deal of Snow, and bad weather, *my Son had the misfortune to have his Feet frost-bitten,* which kept us much longer here than we intended; however we killed plenty of Deer, Turkeys &c. and fared very well the Land hereabout is very good but to the W and S W. it is hilly

Gist's Son Frost-bitten

Land very good but hilly Game plenty

Wednesday 8th My Son's Feet being somewhat better, we set out S 30d W. 5 m—S 45 d W. 3 m—the Land midling good but hilly. I found my Sons Feet too tender to travel, and we were obliged to stop again.[206]

Land midling but hilly

Thursday 9th to Sunday 19th We stayed at this place and while we were here killed plenty of Bear Deer and Elk, so that we lived very well.

Game plenty

Monday 20th We set out W. 5 m—and were stopped by Snow

Tuesday 21st Stayed all day in the Camp.

exd

Wednesday Janr 22d Set out S 45 d W. 12 m—[where] we scared a Panther from under a Rock which had room enough for us in it so we encamped and had good Shelter.

Thursday 23d to Sunday 26th We stayed at this place being Snow and bad weather

Monday 27th Set out S 45d W. 6 m—here we had Snow and encamped.

Tuesday 28th to Friday 31st Stayed at this place the Land upon these last courses is rich but hilly and in some places stony.

Land rich, but hilly and stony

Saturday Feb. 1st Set out S 45 W 3 m—S 45d E. 1 m—S 2 m—S 45d W. 1 m—crossed *a Creek*[207] on which the Land was very hilly and rocky yet here and there good in Spots on the Hills

Land hilly, and rocky

Sunday 2d S 45d W. 3 m—here we were stopped by Snow.

Monday 3d to Sunday 9th We stayed at this place and had a good deal of Snow and bad Weather

Monday 10th Set out S 45d W. 8 m—the Snow being hard upon the top made bad travelling

Tuesday 11th The same course S 45d W 2, then W 1 m—S 45d W 4 m[208]—

· 125 ·

George Mercer Papers

Land rich and well timbered, but hilly.

Wednesday 12th   Killed two Buffaloes and searched the Land to the N W. which I found to be rich and well timbered with lofty Walnuts, Ash, Sugar trees, &c. but hilly in most places.

a Piece of Land 100 yds square slipped down a Hill, with the Trees &c in their former Position

Thursday 13th   Set out W. 1 m—S 45d W. 2 m—W 2 m—S 45d W 2 m—W 2 m—this day we found a place[209] where a piece of Land about 100 yards square and about ten feet deep from the Surface had slipped down a steep hill somewhat more than it's own breadth with most of the Trees standing on it upright as they were at first and a good many Rocks which appeared to be in the same position as they were before the ground slipp'd; it had bent downwards and crushed the Trees as it came along which might plainly be seen by the ground on the upper side of it over which it had passed; it seemed to have been done but two or three years ago. In the place from whence it removed was a large Quarry of Rocks in the sides of which were Veins of several Colours particularly one of a deep yellow about three feet from the bottom in which were other small Veins some white some green, a Sample of which I brought into the Ohio Company in a small leather Bag. No 1. Not very far from this place we found another large peice of Earth which had slipp'd down in the same manner, and encamped in the *Fork of a Creek.*

Cut on a large Stone—*The Ohio Company*

Friday 14th   We stayed at this place on the N W. side of *the Creek.* On a rising ground by a small Spring we found a large Stone[210] about three feet square on the top, and about six or seven feet high, it was all covered with green Moss except on the S E side, which was smooth and white as if plaistered with Lime; on this side I cut with a cold Chissel in large Letters. The Ohio Company. Feby 1751.[211] by Christopr Gist

rich Land, hilly Bottoms narrow

Saturday 15th   Set out S 45d W 5 m—rich Land but hilly, very rich Bottoms up the Creek, but not above 200 yards wide

rich Land.

Sunday 16th   S 45d W. 5 m—thro' rich Land the Bottoms about a quarter of a mile wide upon the Creek.

Bottoms wide, & fine Land

Monday 17th   The same Course S 45 W 3 m—W 3 m—S 45d W 3 m—S 20d W 3 m—S 8 m—S 45d W 2 m—over a Creek[212] on which was fine Land the Bottoms about a mile wide.

[illegible] different

Tuesday 18th   S 10 m—over the *Fork of a Creek* S. 45d W 4 m—to the top of a high Ridge from whence we could see over the *Kanhawa River* here we encamped the Land mixed with Pines and not very good.

Land very rich, Bottoms overflowed.

Wednesday 19th   Set out S 15 m—S 45d W 6 m—to the mouth of a *little Creek*[213] upon which the Land is very rich and the Bottoms a mile wide, *the Kanhawa* being very high overflowed some part of the Bottoms.

In the Darlington Memorial Library

Thursday 20th Set out N 45ᵈ W 2 m—across *a Creek* over a hill then S 80ᵈ W. 10 m—to a large Run all fine Land upon this Course, we were now about two miles from the *Kanhawa;* then continued our Course S 80ᵈ W. 10 m—the first five miles good high Land tolerably level, the last five thro' the River Bottoms which were a mile wide, and very rich to *a Creek or large Run* which we crossed and continued our Course S 80ᵈ W. 2 m further and encamped.

Land very rich

Friday 21st The same Course S 80ᵈ W. still continued 8 m—further then S 2 m—to the side of the *Kanhawa* then down the same N 15ᵈ W 1 m—to *a Creek*[214] where we encamped the Bottoms upon the River here are a mile wide the Land very rich. *The River at this place is 79 poles broad.*[530]

Kanhawa River 79 Poles wide. Land very rich.

exᵈ

Then the Commissioners spoke as followeth.[531]

Brethren, You sent us[298] a string of wampum which met us on the road, by which you acquainted us that you heard of our coming to visit you, and welcomed us so far on our journey. Yesterday we arrived at this place, and this morning you took an opportunity with a string of wampum to bid us welcome to your Town, and to open our eyes that we might see the Sun clearly, and look upon you our brethren, who are willing to receive us; this we take very kindly, and we assure you, of our hearty inclinations to live in friendship with you. To confirm this we present you with a string of wampum.

Comrs thank the Indians &c

Gave a string

Brethren in your second speech to us and our brethren of Pennsylvania this day, you delivered us two strings of wampum, to clear our hearts from any impressions that may have been made on them, by flying reports or ill news,[299] and that we might speak our minds freely. Brethren we assure you of our willingness to remove all misunderstandings out of our hearts and breasts, which might impede or hinder the friendship subsisting between us.

Now Brethren. We are to acquaint you, that we are sent hither by the King of Great Britain our father, who not forgetting his children, on this side the great waters, has ordered us to deliver you a large present[105] of goods in his name, which we have brought with us; but as we understand that you have sent for some of your chiefs,[300] whom you shortly expect, we will wait with patience till they come, and will then faithfully deliver you the goods, and open our hearts to you; in assurance of which we present you with this string of wampum.

Commissioners tell the Indians they had a Present to deliver Them from the King

Gave a string

There were some debates[301] concerning the method of proceeding in the Treaty, whether to demand the reasons why the belt and

George Mercer Papers

speech delivered last fall was not sent to Onandago;[300] or if nothing should be said of that affair, till the more material business[302] obtaining leave to settle the lands &c. was settled, which it was judged the other would effectually defeat.

June 2d[303]   The goods were got out and dried, when it was found they had not received the damage that might have been expected, the fine goods none.

<small>Commissioners confer with Mr Trent & Mr Croghan</small>

June 3d   The Commissioners had conferences with Mr Trent and Mr Croghan about the likeliest method to succeed in their negotiations and had farther assurances of their assistance.

June 4th   [Two Shawane cheifs[304] being disgusted[305] (as was said) came to the Comrs & made a speech expressing their inclination] to be gone home; as they were preparing an answer, in conjunction with some of the six nations to stop them, word was brought that a vessel with English colours was coming down the river, which proved to be the half king,[306] with a cheif from the Onandago council; he was received with several discharges of small arms, landed and fixed the English colours on the top of his house; the Commissioners waited on him, sometime after he returned the visit, with some of the cheifs, drank the Kings health, prosperity to the six nations, the Governor of Virginia &c: and the Commissioners when he went away made him a present of tobacco.

<small>Half King arrived with one of the Onondago Council His Reception.</small>

<small>Commissioners shew the Indians the Lancaster Deed &c</small>

June 9th   The Commissioners had a private conference with the half king,[306] and the other cheifs at Mr Croghans,[78] & shewed the Lancaster deed[287] and other papers: They thanked the Commissioners for letting them know what the Onandago council had done, and blamed them much for keeping it private (as they said) for had they known it sooner, it would have prevented many disorders; they said they never told them that they had sold further than the warriors road,[63] at the foot of the Allegany mountain, and that they would confirm whatever they had done. The Indians desired to have their guns and hatchets mended, which was complied with. Big Hanoana[120] a Shawane cheif told us that the Piques were upon the poise whether they should return to the French, or continue steady to the English, and wanted to see what encouragement the latter would give them.[307]

<small>Indians agree to confirm it</small>

June 10th   This day was appointed to deliver the Kings present to the Indians; there were seperate Arbours made for the Commissioners, and Indians, where the present was laid out, and a part set aside[307] for the Picques, which was well taken by the other Indians. The fine cloaths were distributed to the chiefs.

The Indians being met the Commissioners spoke as followeth.
Present. Joshua Fry, Lunsford Lomax, James Patton Esqrs
Commissioners

· 128 ·

In the Darlington Memorial Library

M?r Christopher Gist, agent for the Ohio Company
M?r Andrew Montour. Interpreter

ex?d

Sachems and Warriors of the six united nations, our friends and brethren.

We are glad to meet you at this place, to enlarge the council fire already kindled[308] by our brethren of Pennsylvania, to brighten the chain, and to renew our freindship, that it may last as long as the Sun, the moon and stars shall give light. To confirm which we give you this string of wampum. <i>Gave a string</i>

Brethren, at the Treaty at Lancaster[287] in the year 1744. between the Governments of Virginia, Maryland, and Pennsylvania, you made a deed recognizing the King's right to all the land in Virginia, as far as it was then peopled, or should thereafter be peopled, or bounded by the King our father, for which you received the consideration agreed on; at the same time Canosateego[309] desired the Commissioners would recommend you to the King's farther favour, when the settlements should increase much further back; this the Commissioners promised and confirm'd it by a writing under their hands and seals, in consequence of which, a present was sent you from the King by M?r Conrad Weiser which he since informed us that he delivered you, at a council held here in the year 1748.[310] Now the King your father, to shew the love he bears to justice, as well as his affection to you his children, has sent a large present of goods, to be divided among you, and your allies, which is here ready to be delivered to you, and we desire you may confirm the treaty of Lancaster.

<small>Commissioners tell the Indians of the Deed made at Lancaster in 1744 [and] recite the Particulars</small>

<small>Indians to [con]firm the Treaty of Lancaster</small>

Brethren. It is the design of the King your father at present, to make a settlement of British subjects on the south East side of Ohio, that we may be united as one people, by the strongest ties of neighbourhood, as well as friendship, and by these means prevent the insults of our Enemies: From such settlement greater advantages will arise to you, than you can at present conceive, our people[311] will be able to supply you with goods, much cheaper than can at this time be afforded, will be ready help in case you should be attacked, and some good men among them will appointed, with authority to punish, and restrain the many injuries and abuses, too frequently committed here, by disorderly white people.

<small>tell the Indians the King proposes to make a Settlement on the Ohio and point out it's Advantages</small>

Brethren. We assure you that the King our father, by purchasing your lands, had never any intentions of taking them from you,[312] but that we might live together as one people, and keep them from the french who [wou'd be bad neighbors] he is not like the French King who calls himself your father, and endeavoured about three years

· 129 ·

George Mercer Papers

ago, with an armed force, to take possession of your ₁Country by setting up Inscriptions³¹³ on Trees₁ and at the mouths of the creeks, on this river, by which he claims these lands; tho' at their coming, and for many years before, a number of your brethren the English, were residing in this town,³¹⁴ and several other places on this river. You remember how he scattered the Shawnese, so that they were dispersed all over the face of the earth, and he now threatens to cut you off³¹⁵ also, which he durst not attempt, while you are united. On the contrary the King your father, will lay his hand on your heads, under which protection you will always remain safe.

Brethren. The great King our father, recommends a strict union between us, you, and our brethren towards the sun setting, which will make us strong, and formidable, as a division may have a contrary effect: We are directed to send³⁰⁷ a small present to the Twightwees, as an earnest of the regard which the Governor of Virginia has for them, with an assurance of his further friendship whenever they shall stand in need. Brethren. We earnestly exhort you, not to be drawn by the empty deceitful speech of the French, the peculiar talent of that cunning people; but in all their attempts to shake your duty to our common father, think of what real acts of friendship have been done by the English, and what by the french, weigh these things in your mind, and then determine, who best deserves your esteem and regard; for it is not by vain unmeaning words, that true friendship is to be discovered. That what we have said may make the greater impression on you, and have it's full force, we present you with this belt of wampum. *Gave a belt*

send a Present to the Twigtwees

Brethren It is many years ago that the English first came over the great water to visit you: On their first coming you took hold of our Ships, and tied them to your strongest trees, ever since which, we have remained together in friendship, we have assisted you when you have been attacked by the French, by which you have been able to withstand them, and you have remained our good friends and allies; for though at sometimes the chain

exᵈ

₁of friendship may have contracted some₁ rust, it has been easily rubbed off, and the chain restored to its brightness. This we hope will always be the case and that our friendship may continue to the last posterity we give you this string of wampum. *Gave a string*

complain of the Murder of a Woman on the New River

Brethren We are sorry for the occasion that requires us to complain to you of an injury done us by one of your people, who murdered a poor woman on the new river. Murder is a great crime and by the consent of all nations, has usually been punished with death, this is

In the Darlington Memorial Library

the usage among the English, whether one of our people has been killed, or one of our brethren the Indians; and it is one of the earliest commands of the great Father and maker of us all, who inhabits the Skies, *that who so shedeth man's blood, by man shall his blood be shed.* We understand you know the man that is accused of the murder, and we hope you will give him up, to be tried by our laws; you may be assured that he will have a fair trial, and if he is not guilty he will be sent back unhurt. We must inform you, that the Governor of Virginia expects you will deliver the person, suspected to be guilty up to some Magistrate in Virginia, whom we shall name to you, that we may send him to Williamsburg for his trial. This procedure is not only proper, as it is a compliance with the laws of God and nations, but it is necessary to warn all hot headed men who are not guided by reason, to forbear from such wicked actions by which their brethren suffer. Brethren we desire for the future, you will observe the treaty of Lancaster, and whenever your young people travel through Virginia, that they will take such passes as are directed by the said treaty; by these passes[316] the men will be known, which will be some restraint on them as to their behaviour; it will be proper also that a man of prudence and discretion should head each party, that one among them, if possible, should speak English, and that by no means any french, or french Indians be suffered to go with them. We might have mentioned many other irregularities, but we have forborn, in hopes that for the future, you will give your people such orders, as will prevent our having any further occasion to complain. To inforce what [we] have said, and induce you to do us justice, we present you with this belt of wampum.   *Gave a belt* [demand the Man who comitted the Murder. / recommend to the Indians to observe the Treaty of Lancaster]

The Commissioners then spoke to the Allies of the six united nations who were present, having first advised with the half king,[306] and being joined in the speeches by him in the name of the six nations.

Brethren, the Delawares, We thank you for the kind reception you gave us when we came to Shenapins, which we shall never forget; we advise and exhort you to beware of the french councils, and that you will adhere to a strict friendship with us, the six nations, and your brethren who live towards the sunsetting, which will strengthen us all, and be asured defence against our enemies. To confirm you in this mind, we present you with this belt of wampum.   *Gave a belt* [Speech to the Delawares]

Brethren the Shawnese, Your nation has suffered much by French devices, by which you have been dispersed, we exhort you that you continue[317] to keep firm hold of the great chain of friendship, between us, the six nations, and their allies, which is the likeliest means [Speech to the Shawnese]

· 131 ·

George Mercer Papers

to retrieve your loss, and again make you a happy people. We present you with this belt of wampum. *Gave a belt*

Speech to the Wyendots

Brethren. the Wyendots. Your nation is divided,[318] and part is under the directions of the French; we think it would be good policy in you that are in our interest, to endeavour to bring over your brethren, but if this cant be done, you ought to take all the care in your power, [that they do not, under the Colour &] name of friend[ship,] come into our country, and hurt our inhabitants, or if they do, that you will endeavour to secure them, on their return, to prevent any misunderstanding. We present you with this belt of wampum.
Gave a belt

Half King tells Montour the Interpreter, that he has an equal Right with Them, being one of their Council, to transact Business, and sell Lands [Insert] Indian Deed Page

After these speeches had been delivered and interpreted to the several nations, the half king[306] desired the Commissioners not to depart, for he said they had a great deal of business to do: He then with a ten rowed belt of wampum in his hand, directing his speech to Eghuisara (which is Mr Montour's[79] Indian name) said Child remember that thou art one of our own people, and have transacted a great deal of business among us, before you were employed by our brethren of Pennsylvania, and Virginia; you are Interpreter between us, and our brethren, which we are well pleased at, for we are sure our business will go on well, and justice be done on both sides; but you are not interpreter only, for you are one of our council, and have an equal right with us, to

ex<u>d</u>

all these lands, and may transact any public business in [behalf of us, the six Nations, as well as any of us, for we look] upon you as much as we do any of the cheif councillors; and to confirm what we have said we present unto you this belt of wampum. *Gave a belt*

Then addressing himself to the Commissioners of Virginia, and all the Indians present, with a string of wampum in his hand, he spoke as follows.

George Croghan declared to be one of the Council see Indian Deed Page

Brethren, It is a great while since our brother the Buck (meaning George Croghan[78]) has been doing business between us and our brothers of Pennsylvania, but we understand he does not intend to do so any more;[319] so I now inform you, that he is approved of by our council at Onandago, for we sent to them to let them know how he has helped us in our councils here, and I deliver him this string of wampum to strengthen him, and to let you and him know that he is one of our people, and shall help us still and be one of our council.
Gave the string of wampum

He next spoke to the Shawanes, and told them, that he took the hatchet from them, and tied them with black strings of wampum to

· 132 ·

In the Darlington Memorial Library

hinder them from going to war against the Cherokees; he said that they struck their own body, and did not know what they were doing, said they had seen of their own people there whom he wanted to get back, and would it not be better to be at peace to bring them back?[320] he charged them not to go again to strike their own people and he said that the Governor of Virginia, and Pennsylvania would interest themselves, in making a peace.[321] *Gave a black string*

[forbids the Shawanes from going to [war] with the Chero [kees]]

Then turning to the Delawares he said. You went to the Wiandots and delivered a speech and a belt of wampum, to make peace between you and the Cherokees, and after you came back you let your young men go to war against the Cherokees, which was very wrong, after you had delivered the speech which I myself being present heard. I take the hatchet from you, you belong to me,[322] and I think you are to be ruled by me, and I (joining with your brethren of Virginia) order you to go to war no more *Gave a belt of wampum*

[For]bids the Delawares [from] going to War [with] the Cherokees

Taking a belt of wampum in his hand he proceeded as followeth.

Brethren. The Governors of Virginia and Pennsylvania some years ago we made a complaint to our brother of Pennsylvania, that his traders brought too much [spirituous] liquors amongst us, and desired that there might not come such quantities, and hoped he would order his traders to sell their goods, and liquors at cheaper rates. In answer[323] to our request Conrade Weiser delivered us this belt of wampum, and told us we must pay but five buck skins for a keg, and if the traders would not take that we should have it for nothing, since which time there has been double the quantity brought out yearly, and sold as formerly, and we have made some complaints to try to stop such large quantities from being brought, but as there has been no notice taken to prevent it, we believe Mr Weiser spoke only from his mouth and not from his heart, and without the Governor's authority; some[324] think proper to return the belt

[Com]plains of the [Qua]ntity, Price [of] spiritous Liquors

[Char]ges Conrad Weiser [with] having deceived [the]m

He gave the belt to Mr Croghan

June 11th Present Joshua Fry, Lunsford Lomax. James Patton Esqrs
Commissioners
Mr Christopher Gist. Agent for the Ohio Company
Mr Andrew Montour, Interpreter

The Commissioners of Virginia, delivered to the six nations a string of wampum, and a suit of Indian [Clothing, to wipe away their Tears for] the loss of one of their cheifs,[325] who lately came down from the head of Ohio to Loggstown, and died there.

[Com]missioners give a [pr]esent to wipe away their Tears

Gave the suit of Cloaths and string

Afterwards the half king[306] spoke to the Delawares; Nephews, you received a speech last year[326] from your brother the Governor of

· 133 ·

George Mercer Papers

<small>Shingas appointed</small>

Pennsylvania, and from us; desiring you to choose one of your wise councillors, and present him to us for a king; as you have not done it, we now let you know that it is our right to give you a king, and we think proper to give you Shingas[327] for your king, whom you must look upon as your cheif. and with whom all public business must be transacted, between you and your brethren the English. On which the half king put a laced hat on the head of the Beaver,[203] who stood proxy for his brother Shingas, and presented him also with a rich jacket, and suit of English colours, which had been delivered to the half king by the Commissioners for that purpose

<small>King of the Delawares</small>

The Commissioners addressing themselves to the Shawanes, acquainted them, that they understood their chief king

ex^d

<small>[Co]missioners send a Suit of Cloaths to the old Shawane King</small>

Cochawitchiky[122] who had been a good friend to the English was lying Bedrid, and that to shew the regard they bore to his past services, they took this opportunity to acknowledge it, by presenting him with a suit of Indian cloathing. Then the half king spoke as followeth.

<small>Half King's Reply concerning the Lands granted by the Treaty of Lancaster</small>

Brother the Governor of Virginia, You acquainted us yesterday with the King's right to all the lands in Virginia, as far as it is settled, and back from thence to the sun setting, whenever he shall think fit to extend his settlements: You produced also a copy of his deed from the Onandago council at the treaty of Lancaster,[287] and desired that your brethren of Ohio, might likewise confirm the deed. Brother the Governor of Virginia, we are well acquainted that our cheif council, at the treaty of Lancaster, confirmed a deed to you for a quantity of land in Virginia, which you have a right to, and likewise our brother Onas, has a right to a parcel of land in Pennsylvania; we are glad you have acquainted us with the right to those lands, and assure you we are willing to confirm anything our council has done in regard to the lands; but we never understood before you told us yesterday, that the lands then sold, were to extend further to the sun setting, than the hill on the other side the Allagany hill, so that we cannot give you a farther answer.

<small>desires the People of Virginia to build a Fort at the Forks of the Monaungahela</small>

Brother you acquainted us yesterday that the french were a designing people, which we now see, and know that they design to cheat us out of our lands; you told us that the King of England designed to settle some lands on the south East side of Ohio, that it might be better in our brethren's power to help Us if we were in need, than it is at present, at the great distance they live from us: We are sure the french design nothing else but mischeif, for they have struck our friends the Twightwees; We therefore desire our brothers of Virginia may build a strong house at the fork of Monaungahela,[328] to

· 134 ·

In the Darlington Memorial Library

keep such goods, powder, lead, and necessaries as shall be wanting, and as soon as you please: and as we have given our cousins the Delawares a king[327] who lives there, we desire you will look on him as a cheif of that nation.   *Gave a large string of wampum*

Brethren. Our brothers that live on this river Ohio are all warriors and hunters, and like our brethren the traders not all ₍wise Men; there has been Reason for many Complaints₎ for some time past ₍but₎ We ₍will not complain of our Brethren,₎ the traders, for we love them, and cant live without ₍them, but we hope you will take care to send none₎ amongst us but good men;[329] Sure you know them that are fit, and we hope you will advise them how to behave better than they have done. We well remember when first we saw our brethren the English, and we remember the first council held with them, and shall do all we can to keep the chain friendship from rust.[330]

[Marginal note: Says they₎ cannot live without the Traders, but desires Care may be taken to send none but good Men amongst them]

June 12th[331] This day the Indians gave the Commissioners an answer concerning the land which the Ohio company wanted to settle; they desired them to build a strong house or fort very soon: As the Commissioners had asked for the lands at Monaungahela, they imagined the Indians had given up the lands upon that river, but they only meant ground sufficient for the fort to stand upon, as appeared by a private conversation with the half king, who said that was all that was intended, tho' he always spoke the sentiments of others, and not his own, for that ₍*illegible*₎ a proper Settlement could not be made without a large quantity of land.

The Commissioners had also the following Conferences with the cheifs of the Indians

June 12th The half king[306] ₍with a String of Wampum, in₎formed the Commissioners that one Frazer a blacksmith at the town of Venango, threatened to remove, that they did not desire he should leave them, ₍but, if he did, they wished another₎ might be sent to them, and he said that they had not sufficient number of traders there to supply them with good₍s. To which₎ the Commissioners replied, that they would represent their case to the Governor of Virginia, and hoped they wou₍'d be₎ supplied according to their desire.

[Marginal note: Desires a blacksmith and more Traders might be sent amongst them]

The same day the cheifs of the Shawanes with a string of wampum thanked the Commissioners for their advice; they acknowledged that they had been led astray by the French, and had suffered for it, and said they wou₍'d take₎ care not to be deceived by the French again, but would keep fast hold of the chain of friendship, between the Eng₍lish,₎ the six nations and themselves.

The Commissioners thanked them for their Attachment to the English, and desired their compliments ₍might₎ be made to the young

George Mercer Papers

king[332] of the Shawanes, who was generously gone to the assistance of the Picques:[333] They [sent] him also a laced hat, and a rich jacket.[334]

ex<u>d</u>

June 13th   The half king speaking to the Commissioners said.

<small>Half King says Weiser had never delivered them the Present sent by the King; but had given Them some Goods as from the Govr of Pennsylvania</small>

Brethren, you told us you sent us a present of goods in the year 1748[335] which you said Conrade Weiser delivered at this Town, he may have told you so, but we assure you we never heard of it from him; it is true he delivered us some goods then, but we understood him it was from our brother Onas, he never made mention of the great King our father,[336] nor of our brother Assaragoa. Then directing his speech to the Governor of Virginia said.

Brother you complained to us that some of our people had murdered a woman in Virginia, it is true there has been such a thing done, and brothers we know the man that did it, he is one of our six nations altho' he has lived sometime among the French; we cant make an excuse for so barbarous a murder, but we assure you he did it without our knowledge, and we believe the evil spirit tempted him to do it.

<small>promises Satisfaction for the Murderer complained of</small>

We will let the Onandago council know what has been done, and we believe they will try to get him, and make satisfaction for the crime committed   *Gave a string of black and white wampum*

<small>Indian Reply concerning the Sale of their Lands by the Treaty of Lancaster</small>

Brother. We have heard what you said, in regard to the King's design, of making a settlement of his people on the waters of the river Ohio; you likewise told us you had a deed for those lands signed by our council at the treaty of Lancaster; We assure you of our willingness to agree to what our council does, or has done, but we have not the full power in our hands here on Ohio; we must acquaint our council at Onandago of the affair, and whatever they bid us do we will do. In regard to your request, to build a strong house at the Monaungahela, you told us it would require a settlement to support it with provisions, and necessaries; it is true, but we will take care that there shall be no scarcity of that kind, until we can give a full answer; altho' in all our wars, we dont consider provisions, for we live on one another, but we know it is different with our brethren the English.

Gave three strings of white wampum

<small>Indian Chiefs [s]ign a Deed to the king for the Lands, &c. on the Ohio</small>

The Commissioners having drawn an Instrument of writing[337] for confirming the deed made at Lancaster, and containing a promise, that the Indians would not molest our settlements on the south East side the Ohio, desired Mr Montour to converse with his [Brethren, the] other Sachems in [private,] on the subject to urge the necessity of such [a Settlement & the great Advantage it wou'd] be to them, as to their trade or their security: [On which they retir'd for some] time, and then returned; and Mr Montour said they were satisfied in the

In the Darlington Memorial Library

matter, and were willing to sign, and seal the writing, which was done and witnessed by the Gentlemen then present.   insert the Deed[532]

The half king then spoke as follows.

Brethren. The Governors of Virginia and Pennsylvania, you expressed your regard for our friends and allies the Twightwees, and have considered their necessities at present; we return you our thanks for your care of them, we join with you, and desire you will deliver them this belt, and let them know from us, that we desire them not to forget what they did in Pennsylvania,[338] when they were down four years ago, and joined in a friendship with our brethren the English; we desire they may hold fast the chain of friendship, and not listen to any other but their brethren the English, the six nations, Delawares, and Shawanese, as we will stand by them, and expect they will come down,[339] and confirm the friendship they have engaged to the English.   *He delivered a belt to be sent to the Twightwees*

Half King thanks the Commissioners for their Care of the Twigtwees

The Commissioners then opened the [Road] to Virginia with a belt of wampum and the following speech

[Brethren, we have] travelled through a long and dark way to meet you at this council; we have now compleated our business with pleasure, and satisfaction, both to you and us, and as we are now returning back; We do in the name of the great King your father, as also in the name of your brother the Governor of Virginia, remove all Obstacles out of the way and make clear the road, that you may at any time, send messages to us on any occasion, and we shall be always ready to receive them kindly, and look on you as our brothers; And in token of the sincerity of our hearts, present you with this belt of wampum.   *Gave the belt*

The commissioners open the roads, as is the custom with the Indians [to Virginia, with [a belt of w]ampum, [and invite the] Indians [to come down]

The Commissioners added. Brethren, at the treaty of Lancaster, the Commissioners informed you of a large house built among us, for the education of Indian children,[340] and desired that you would send some of yours, we now make you the same offer, but if you think it too far to send your children, we desire to know whether it would be agreeable to you, that teachers be sent among you. The advantages of an English education, are greater than

exd

can be imagined by them who are unacquainted with it. By it we know the part of the world from whence all nations came; how nations for some thousands of years back have rose, grown powerful, or decayed; how they have removed from one place to another; what battles have been fought; what great men have lived, and how they have acted either in council or in war. In this part of the world we know from the first time the spaniards came to it, how cruelly they

[Indians] reminded [of the school] in Virginia, [for the] Education [of Indians & asked to send] their [children down]
The [advantages] of Education enumerated

George Mercer Papers

used the Indians then wholly ignorant of fire arms; and we know the actions of the French against you and others. There are many other benefits arising from a good education, which would be too tedious to be mentioned, but the greatest of all is, that by it we are acquainted with the will of the great God, the Creator of the world, and Father of us all, who inhabits the skies, by which the better people among us regulate their lives, and hope after death to live with him forever. *Gave a string of wampum*

<small>Wawiagta and Piankasha Treaty</small>

The following is the Copy of the Treaty[533] with the Wawiagtas and Piankashas mentioned in Gi₍st's₎ Journal folio.

Whereas at an Indian Treaty held at the Tawightwis Town on the Big Mineamis creek being a branch of the River Ohio, on Friday the 22d day of February, Before George Croghan and Andrew Montour, Twenty men of the Wawiagtas and Piankashas two of their Indian Chiefs Vizt Takintoa Molsinoughko, and Nynickonowca, appeared in behalf of themselves and their nations, and prayed that as their Indian Brothers the Tawightwis had been lately admitted into

<small>₍De₎sire to be admitted ₍in₎to the English ₍allia₎nce</small>

the Friendship and Alliance of the King of Great Britain and his Subjects and as they are Tribes of the said Tawightwis earnestly desire to be admitted into the said chain of Friendship and Alliance of the King of Great Britain and his Subjects professing on their parts to become true and faithful Allies to the English and so forever to continue, Mishikinoughwee and Nemesgua and all of them Nations in friendship and Alliance with the English becoming earnest Intercessors with the said Chiefs on their behalfs the Prayer of the said Chiefs of the Wawiaghtas and Piankashas, was granted, a firm treaty and Alliance of Friendship was then Stipulated and agreed on between the said George Croghan and Andrew Montour in behalf of the Government of Pensylvania and the said Cheifs ₍or deputies of the Wawiaghtas and Piankasha₎ nations as by the Records of that Council held will more fully appear. Now these Presents Witness,

<small>Wawiaghtas & Piankashas received as Allies</small>

and it is hereby declared that the said Nations of Indians called the Wawiaghtas and Piankashas are accepted by George Croghan and Andrew Montour as good friends and Allies of the English Nation and they the said Nations and Subjects of the King of Great Britain shall forever after be as one Head and one Heart and live in true friendship as one people, In Consideration whereof the said Tokintoa Molsinoughko and Nynickonowca, Cheifs of the said Wawiaghtas and Piankashas Nations do hereby in behalf of said Nations

<small>promise to protect the English</small>

covenant promise and declare that the several people of the said Wawiaghtas and Piankashas Nations or any of them shall not at any time hurt injure or defraud or suffer to be hurt injured or defrauded

In the Darlington Memorial Library

any of the Subjects of the King of Great Britain either in their person or Estates but shall at all times readily do Justice and perform to them all the Acts and Offices of friendship and good Will. Item. that the said Wawiaghtas and Piankashas Nations by the Alliance aforesaid becoming entitled to the Priviledge and protection of the English Laws ₍they shall at all times₎ behave themselves regularly ₍and soberly, according to the laws₎ of the Government of Pensylvania ₍whilst₎ they live or be amongst or near the Christian Inhabitants thereof, Item ₍That none₎ of the said Nations shall at any time be aiding assisting or abetting to or with any other nation whether of Indians or others that shall not at such time be in Amity with the Crown of England and the said Government of Pensylvania, Item That if at any time any of the Wawiagtas and Piankashas Nations by means of evil minded Persons and Sowers of Sedition should hear of any unkind or disadvantageous Report of the English as if they had evil Designs against any of the said Indians in such Cases such Indians shall send Notice thereof to the Governor of the aforesaid province for the time being and shall not give Credit to the said Reports till by that means they shall be fully satisfied of the truth thereof. And it is agreed that the English shall in such Cases do the same by them. In Testimony whereof as well the said George Croghan and Andrew Montour as the Cheifs of Wawiagtas and Piankashas Nations have Smoaked the Calumet Pipe, made mutual Presents to each other and hereunto set their hands and Seals the 22ᵈ day of February in the year of our Lord 1750 and in the 24ᵗʰ Year of the Reign of George the second King ₍of₎ Great Britain France and Ireland Defender of the Faith &c.

agree to submit to English Law₍s₎, while₎ amongst the white People, ₍and₎ to assist them in War

agree to complain formally if they think they have ₍ca₎use

Signed Sealed & Delivered in the presence of:
Christr. Gist
Robt. Callender.
Thos. Henton
John Potts.
☉ Sarowashannoito a Shawane, witness present
John Peter. a Delaware Indian present.

Geo Croghan (Seal)
Andrew × Montour (Seal)
  his mark.
Tockintoa Moloinoughto ☉
Nynickonowca ☉

exᵈ

Orders and Resolutions of the Ohio Company, 1749—1761[534]

Enclosure 2

Potomack June 20, 1749[535]

Sir.

 We have received from our partner the Honourable Colo Thomas Lee a copy of the Petition[536] you presented in our behalf to his Majesty and what you wrote him of your Success.[537] We hold ourselves to be very much obliged to you for the trouble you have taken in this Affair which we make no doubt will turn out greatly to our advantage and the Nations, as we have been told that his Grace the Duke of Bedford has been much our friend in this Affair, we are very desirous that he should be at the head of our Company, and if you think proper you may be pleased in our names to offer his Grace a Share in our Stock on the terms of our common association, we shall many times want such a friend and Patron.

 It will be necessary for us to have a Letter[27] from the King to the Governor here for the time being to encourage and protect us in our trade and carrying on this great work, that our Surveyor might be appointed to make the Surveys to be examined by the Mathematical Master of the Colledge to see that no fraud be committed in the quantity of Acres so as to hurt his Majesties Revenue, and further that the Governour here be empowered from time to time to apply such reasonable Sums out of the Quit Rents[538] as will be necessary to engage the Indians to suffer us to settle those Lands peaceably which is the method taken by the Government of Pensylvania[539] and this will be the more reasonable as the Revenue of Quit rents will be greatly increased by it, and tho' the Indians Sold the Land yet they according to custom expected presents from the Crown when his Majesties Subjects came to Seat it

 We desire you to Ship us two thousand pounds worth of Goods according to the Invoice and Samples to be here by the last of November[23] at the furthest consigned to our partner the Honble Colo Thomas Lee on our Account and risque to potomack if possible, on either side, but if that can't be done, to any other River in Virginia or Maryland, but the most convenient to potomack, and that you supply us with another Cargo to be here by the first of March after or any good opportunity before, Shipped and consigned as aforesaid, We hope we shall have Effects[540] in hand for the first Cargo and before the Goods are actually paid for that our Effects will be there for the second, the Tradesmen who are likely to share great profit by our dealing with them will give us credit on your Application. We shall depend on your care and prudence in buying and dispatching our Goods which will turn to our mutual profit. Capt Washington carrys Samples and will endeavour to procure some Tradesmen[541] we shall want, and he will be able to explain to you as he has convers'd with those that are of our Company and understand the Indian trade well. We desire the Goods fully insured so that in case of loss we may be whole, and if notice of such loss comes timely to your knowledge that you reship them and be pleased to observe that it is only in case of absolute necessity that we desire the Goods to be sent to any other place than the Virginia side of Potomack, We are respectfully &c.

We consider you as one of our Company and that your Share £125[542] Sterl will be added to what we remit

To John Hanbury Esqr Mercht in London.
Orders of the Ohio Co June 21st 1749

And the said Company do further agree and Oblige themselves to bear an equal proportion of all Charges both for obtaining the Kings Grant for the Lands and for carrying on the Trade and other Contingencies here.

And the said Company do agree that Colo Thomas Cresap and Hugh Parker at the Charge of the said Company on the best terms they can for themselves and the said Company cause the necessary Roads[29] to be made and the Houses to be built for carrying on the said trade.[182]

Ordered that Nathaniel Chapman our Treasurer do pay the Ballance of the cash in his hands belonging to us, to the joint Order of Colo Thomas Cresap and Mr Hugh Parker to be laid out for our Use in making a Road &c' to Monongahala and that the said Orders shall be a sufficient discharge to the said Chapman.

That the said Hanbury be desired to Solicit to get the part of the Instruction altered[57] which Obliges the Company to build and Garrison a Fort, as it is impracticable for them to do it out of their private fortunes the thing being of a public nature and a fort there will guard the other Colonies as well as this and no particular advantage to the Company

That he endeavour to obtain an Order[27] to the Government here to make presents to the Indians it being as reasonable and useful to the public, as the presents that the Government of New York[28] are allowed to give, that he endeavour to obtain an Order to run the Line between Virginia and pensylvania on the same terms as the Carolina[35] line was run which is necessary in order to take our Grant with certainty

That Colo Cresap or Mr Parker be employed[36] to discover the parts

George Mercer Papers

beyond the Mountains, so that we may know where to Survey our Land, and that this may be done as soon as possible, or we may be complained of for keeping others from taking up the Kings Lands.[543]

<small>Orders of the Committee of the Ohio Co March 29, 1750.</small>

Whereas it appears to us that a Store house of Loggs built at Colo Cresaps[182] will both secure the Goods better and give leisure for building proper houses at Wills Creek the cheaper[544]

Ordered that Hugh Parker be empowered to agree with Colo Cresap for board of himself and two Servants, also to build a Store house on Colo Cresaps plantation, and that buildings be made at the mouth of Wills Creek as soon as conveniency will admit.[545]

<small>Of the Company. May 22. 1751.</small>

Resolved That the Compa write to Mr Hanbury on the following Heads. Viz. To apply to the Earle of Granville[50] for a Grant of fifty thousand or more Acres of Land upon the branches of the Ohio to the Westward of the great Mountains on or near the line dividing Virginia and Carolina and to the Lord Baltimore[51] for ten thousand or more Acres of Land in different tracts near the back line between Pensylvania and Maryland, and to Mr. Penn[52] for ten thousand or more Acres of Land at or near a place called Rays Town[53] upon the Juniatta or the branches thereof fifteen or twenty thousand Acres on Lowelhanning and Kiskamonito Creeks[54] which empty into the Ohio, or as much thereof as belongs to Pensylvania, five thousand Acres upon a branch of the Ohio called Chomohonan[55] and four thousand Acres at a place called the three forks of Youghogane[56] being a branch of the Ohio, the Company being of Opinion that if the same can be obtained upon reasonable terms it will be much for their Advantage and greatly contribute to the security of their Settlements and encrease of their Trade.

That the Forts being mentioned proceeded from a misapprehension of Sr William Gooch,[546] the Gent concerned proposing only a small fort for the security of their Goods and people and not a regular Fort and Garrison for the protection of the Countrey which is not only impracticable from the Situation of those parts and the difficulty of procuring Soldiers for that purpose, but if the same could be done must be attended with such a charge as no private Company could support and would amount to much more than the legal Composition of all the Companies Lands and all the profits they could even suppose to make would amount to, so that if it should be insisted on in such a sense it must in the end entirely ruin and disappoint the whole undertaking[57]

Resolved that it is necessary for the Company's Affairs to purchase a tract of about five hundred Acres of Land[547] belonging to Thomas Bladen Esq.' in Maryland opposite to the Companies Store[548] at Wills

In the Darlington Memorial Library

Creek and that Mr Lawrence Washington be impowered to agree for and purchase the same upon the Companies Account[549]

Resolved that it is necessary to have a Road cleared from the mouth of Wills Creek to the three forks of Youghogane and that Colo Cresap be empowered to agree with any person or persons willing to undertake the same so that the expence thereof does not exceed twenty five pounds Virginia currency.[29]

Resolved that it is absolutely necessary that the Company should have the Nomination and Appointment of a proper person in whom they can confide to Survey their Lands, and John Mercer is desired and empowered to apply to the President and Masters of William and Mary Colledge to procure their Consent thereto and a Commission for such person as the said Company shall agree with for that purpose.[550]

Whereas the Company hath been informed that Colo James Patton and his partners have under colour of their Grant, or Order of Council Surveyed one or more large Tract or Tracts of Land on a River by them called Houlstons[551] River which is a branch of the Hogohegee[552] and is far without their Limits and within those allowed to the Company.[553] Resolved that John Mercer be empowered to enter one or more Caveat[554] or Caveats against any patents issuing to the said Patton and his partners or any other person or persons for any of the said Lands or any other within the Limits allowed to the Ohio Company and to employ one or more Lawyer or Lawyers as he shall think proper to prosecute such Caveat or Caveats before the president and Council.[555]

Resolved that Philip Ludwell Lee, Nathaniel Chapman, James Scott, George Mason, and John Mercer be appointed a Committee for the said Company until the next general meeting, and that after having employed a Factor[556] according to the Order made at Alexandria Town last September[557] they send[558] to John Hanbury Esq.' for Goods to the amount of two thousand pounds Sterling to be bought at twelve months Credit, and the Company do agree to be answerable for the same, and that the said Committee have full power and Authority to manage and transact all Affairs on behalf of the Company in the same manner as the Company themselves might do.   *Of the Company Nov. 22. 1752*

Resolved that Mr Montour[79] be allowed thirty pistoles for his trouble at the Loggs Town in May last on Account of the Company, and that if he will remove to Virginia and Settle on the Companys Land and Use his Interest with the Indians to encourage and forward our Settlements that the Company make him a present of one thousand Acres of Land to live on, and make him a legal title to the same.

· 143 ·

George Mercer Papers

Resolved that the two Shares of M!" Dobbs and M!" Smith be disposed of[559] and not sunk in the Company, the Company being of Opinion that the Shares of the Company shall be kept up twenty[560]

Resolved that the Committee employ such Surveyors[561] as they think proper to Survey such of the Company's Lands between Kiskomanettos alias Romanettos Creek and the fork of the Ohio, and Conhaway as is fit for the Company to Survey and take up and to give all possible Encouragement to the people willing to Seat the said Lands by letting them Settle as fast as they come on the terms prescribed by the Company reserving to the Company a Tract of at least five thousand Acres at every twenty miles distance for settling their Store houses and keeping a Correspondence and Carriage by Water for the better settling the place but where broken Hills or Mountains will not allow such a quantity of Land such a Settlement must not be neglected tho' the Land does not exceed four or five hundred Acres the Company being satisfied his Majesty on a Representation of the Case[562] (which the Committee are desired to draw and transmit to M!" Hanbury) will upon the Lands being Settled grant the Company such other Lands as they shall desire

As the Company is inform'd that the Emperor of the Cherokees with his Wife Son and Attendants are on their way to receive some Goods which the Governor and Council have given them Credit for in the Companies Store it is agreed that the Goods delivered them upon that Order be charged at the lowest Rates such Goods are Sold by whole Sale to the Traders the Company deals with, and as the Company think themselves obliged to provide for them in a proper manner in Case the Government have not made a provision for that purpose for want of which they may want proper Necessaries it is Resolved that M!" Mason and M!" Chapman in Case they have no Order from the Government for their Maintenance supply them with proper Necessaries, and treat the Emperor in such handsome manner as they judge convenient, the Charge of which shall be allowed them by the Company, in full Confidence the Government will Answer it, and as several Horses may be wanted to carry out the Goods, if the Government have given any Order to the Company for that purpose the said Mason and Chapman are desired to purchase the same on the best terms they can, the charge attending it to be paid and allowed them by the Company and charged to the Government.[563]

At a Committee of the Ohio Company at M!" Mercers at Marlborough in Stafford County February 6th 1753.

On the Application of M!" John Pagan Mercht to know what Encouragement the Company would give to [any] German Protestants

In the Darlington Memorial Library

who would come into this Colony to settle their Lands on the Ohio, he being now on a Voyage to Great Britain and intending to Germany from thence in Expectation of Engaging a great number of families to remove for that purpose in Case the prejudices that have been artfully propagated among those people can be effectually removed and they can be convinced they may on equal if not better terms settle in this Colony than in Pensylvania or the other adjoining provinces. The Committee being satisfied that a large Accession of foreign Protestants will not only be advantageous to this Colony but the most effectual method of promoting a speedy Settlement on the Ohio, and extending and securing the same, before mentioning their own proposals think proper to observe.

That with regard to their religious Liberties, all foreign Protestants may depend on enjoying in this Government the Advantage of the Acts of Toleration in as full and ample manner as in any other of his Majesties plantations whatsoever, as great numbers of them have already experienced.

As to their civil Rights, they will be entitled to Naturalization[564] which will be attended with all the Priviledges and Advantages of English natural born Subjects which are too many to be here enumerated. That of electing their Representatives in the Legislature is the greatest can be enjoyed by any Subjects, And the English Laws of Liberty and property are universally allowed to be the best in the World for securing the peoples lives and fortunes against Arbitrary power or any unjust Encroachments whatsoever.

The Levies in this Government which will be better understood by the name of Taxes are of three kinds Public, County, and Parish, The first of which is imposed by Act of Assembly on every person in the Colony liable to pay Levies for defraying the public Charge of this Colony once in two or three years, the second for defraying each County's Charge by the people living therein which is annually imposed, as is the last on the parishoners for maintaining the Minister and other parochial Charges. All these are paid in Tobacco the Staple of the Countrey, but no Male under sixteen years of Age or any white Woman is obliged to contribute thereto. These however are so moderate that We can venture to affirm that taking them all together one Year with the other they don't amount to above the Value of eight shillings Sterling per poll, and no Tax or Imposition is laid on anything necessary for food or raiment or the Subsistence of Life, Officers fees of all kinds and Law charges amount to little more than one half of the Charge of that Sort in the adjoining Colonies, Nor do we know any single place in his Majesties Dominions where the Subject is supported in all his Rights at so easy an Expence, Our Militia renders Soldiers useless and We have no Ecclesiastical Courts.

The Legislature by an Act made last year hath exempted all foreign protestants coming to Settle West of our Great Mountains from paying Levies of all kinds for the term of ten Years from their Settlement As by a Copy of the Act hereto annexed.

As the Committee looks on these Advantages to be sufficient to invite any Strangers not bypassed by some Prejudice to settle in this Colony preferably to any other of his Majesties plantations, which they are very desirous of, so for a further Encouragement they propose and undertake in behalf of the Company

That as the said Company is intitled to five hundred thousand Acres of Land upon the River Ohio which is exempted from Quit rents for ten years after which term the Quit rent is no more than two Shillings Sterling yearly for every hundred Acres, Every foreign protestant coming in to Settle on the said Land shall have a good title made to him for as much as he desires at the rate of five pounds Sterling for every hundred Acres discharged of Quit rents for the same time allowed to the Company.

That all such as come in on those terms shall be supplied with Warehouses for their Goods convenient carriages for removing them to their Lands and such Quantity of Wheat Flour and Salt as they may want for their present Subsistence at the same Rates the Company pays for them, And such of them as have not ready money to pay for the Lands they desire to purchase shall be allowed two years Credit paying five per cent per Annum Interest

As no Countrey in the world is better or more conveniently watered than Virginia the most convenient Passage will be into Potomack River which is Navigable by the largest Ships within ten Miles of the Falls.[565] The Companys Store house at Rock creek[566] where they may land and have their Goods secured is sixty miles from Connococheege[567] a fine road from whence they may go by Water in the Companys Boat to their Store house at Wills Creek about forty miles and from thence the Company have cleared a Waggon Road about sixty miles to one of the head branches of the Ohio navigable by large flat bottomed boats where they proposed to build Storehouses[568] and begin to lay off their Lands. From this place there is no Obstruction to prevent such Vessels passing into the Mississippi which by the best Calculation is near a thousand miles, and as the Ohio from thence branches all the way down in numberless Branches it not only affords the convenience of making most of the Settlements by Water carriage but will enable the Settlers by the same carriage to carry on their

In the Darlington Memorial Library

Trade and supply themselves with every produce of those parts. The Rivers are Stocked with fine Fish and wild Fowl and the Woods abound with Buffaloes Elks Deer wild Turkeys and other Game of divers kind. The Land itself is universally allowed to be as good as can be far exceeding any Lands to the East of the great Mountains well Stocked with Timbers of all kinds and Stone for building, Slate Limestone Coal, Salt Springs and various Minerals. In short it is a Countrey that wants nothing but Inhabitants to render it one of the most delightful and valueable Settlements of all his Majesties plantations in America, And as the Value of those back Lands is now discovered and all the nations of Indians in those parts and for some hundred miles round are not only in Strict Amity and friendship with this Government but have faithfully promised[569] to Assist and protect the English Settlements on the Ohio which has tempted many other persons to take up Lands in those parts and people are daily going to Settle them, there can be no doubt but the Settlement in those parts will soon be a very considerable one.

The Committee further Engages in behalf of the said Company for the greater Encouragement of such foreign protestants to lay off two hundred Acres of Land for a Town to be called Saltsburg[570] in the best and most convenient place to their Settlement to be divided into Lotts of one Acre each, Eight of which to be appropriated for a Fort Church and other public buildings and every Tradesman or other person Settling and living three Years in the said Town to have one Lot forever paying the Quit rent of one farthing a Year,

           Signed by,   James Scott
                               George Mason
                               J Mercer

If Colo Cresap has not agreed with any person to clear a Road for the Company, You are with the advice and Assistance of the said Colo Cresap to agree with the proper Indians who are best acquainted with the ways Immediately to cut a Road[349] from Wills Creek to the Fork of Mohongaly[350] at the cheapest Rate you can for Goods and this you may mention publickly to the Indians at the Loggs Town or not as you can see Occasion *One of the Instructions given by the Compa to Mr Gist April 28. 1752.[571]*

Resolved that it is absolutely necessary that the Company should immediately erect a Fort for the Security and protection of their Settlements on a hill just below Shertees Creek[573] upon the South East side the River Ohio that the Walls of the said Fort shall be twelve feet high to be built of Sawed or hewn Loggs and to inclose a piece *By the Committee July 25. 1753.[572]*

George Mercer Papers

of Ground Ninety feet Square, besides the four Bastions at the Corners of sixteen feet square each, with houses in the middle for Stores Magazines &c.' according to a plan entered in the Companys Books,[574] That Colo Cresap Capt Trent and Mr Gist be appointed and Authorized on behalf of the Company to agree with Labourers Carpenters and other Workmen to build and compleat the same as soon as possible, and employ Hunters to supply them with Provisions and agree with some honest Industrious Man to overlook the Workmen and Labourers as Overseer, and that they be supplied with Flower, Salt, and all other Necessaries at the Companys Expence, That all the Land upon the Hill on which the said Fort is to be built to be appropriated to the Use of the said Fort, and that two hundred Acres of Land exclusive of Streets be layed off for a Town[570] Convenient and adjoining to the said Fort Land, in squares of two Acres each, every square to be divided into four Lotts so that every Lott may front two streets, if the Ground will so admit and that all the Streets be of *convenient width* that twenty of the best and most convenient Squares be reserved and set apart for the Companys own Use and one Square to build a School[575] on for the Education of Indian Children and such other Uses as the Company shall hereafter think proper and *that all the rest of the Lots be pisposed of*,[576] upon the following Terms. Every person taking up a Lot shall be obliged to build upon it in three Years, upon which they shall be intitled to Deeds for the same without any other Consideration than paying a Yearly Acknowledgment of one Ear of Indian Corn to the Company and furnishing an able bodied labouring Man to work sixty days if required about such Fortification, as the Company or their Agents shall judge necessary for the Defence and Security of the Inhabitants and at all such times and places as the Company, or their Agents shall judge fit and also perform all requisite Duty at the Fort by Watching and Warding one Month in the Year computed at twelve months according to the Course of Rotation to be Settled and appointed by the commanding Officer at the Fort and attending all Musters when required and in Case of any Assault attending on Notice to defend the Settlement from time to time with sufficient Arms and Ammunition, which are to be found and provided by the Companys Store keeper on every such Occasion. Provided that any professed Quaker or other protestant Dissenter not permitted by the Law of England to bear Arms instead of performing Duty in or about the Fort or Defence of the Town [may instead of that Service be allowed to take up their Lots upon working or sending an able man to work in[577]].

In the Darlington Memorial Library

M!˙ George Mason having informed the Committee that he has wrote to M!˙ Hanbury for twenty Swivel Guns⁵⁷⁸ and other Arms and Ammunition for the Use of the Fort, Resolved that the Committee do approve of the same and that the said Arms and Ammunition as soon as they arrive be delivered to Cap!˙ Trent the Companys Factor in Order to be sent out to Shertees Creek.

Instructions given M!˙ Christopher Gist by the Committee of the Ohio Company July 27th 1753.⁵⁷⁹

Whereas you have obtained a Commission from the College for Surveying our Lands, You are to provide a measuring wheel at the Companys expence and measure the Road clear'd by the Company from their Store at Wills Creek to the Fork of Mohongaly, in order to shew the exact place where Russel and his Company have Surveyed their Land.⁵⁸⁰ You are also to take an Instrument of writing under the hands of the people we have Settled certifying that they settled the Land under the Ohio Company and not under Russell and his Company, whose Claim they knew nothing of till he made his Surveys and took their plantations in. From thence you are to proceed to Shertees Creek, where you are to lay off the Town.⁵⁷⁰ You are particularly to note every Branch and remarkable place, as Indian Towns &c' with the different bearings, and where you pass any Creek or Navigable waters to try the Depths, enquire if any Falls or Interruption to the Passage, observing still to keep the best measure you can of the Courses of the River which you are not to lose. If you take the Latitude by an Instrument do it every [opportunity]. Lay off what quantity of good Land you can at Shertees Creek but don't be too eager to take much without 'tis very good. Shape your Courses as often as Necessary to leave out any bad or indifferent Lands so as it will not Cost the company more for such Nicety's then the charge they must be at for the time. Don't be in too great haste as the Company would chuse rather to pay for any lost time, than take bad Land when they can have more than they are allowed to Survey of the best. After laying off the Town Survey what Lands you think proper on Mohongaly and thence proceed down the River to make up your two hundred thousand Acres observing not to go above two miles back from the River, or Creeks you Survey on, as the Company may take the back Lands by their next Survey, take care that your Beginning and Corner trees are so marked that there may be no Difficulty in finding them. Whatever Land happens in every eighteen or twenty miles of what you Survey for the Company you must look out if a piece tho' not above two or three hundred Acres of good Land on the River can be got for the Company's Stages fit to build a Store house and where their Boats may meet some help if they should want it, and by the Setlers have their Goods secured till they can provide to remove them. No time you can take up in proper Searches, or discovering Stone Quarries, Slate, Salt springs or anything that may be of Advantage to the Settlement, will be thought by the Company to be misapplied, as they have so much confidence in you, that if they are persuaded you will not unnecessarily protract your time on which that of several others will depend, and you can't possibly under that assurance omit the most exact Information or enquiry as it may be so much overpaid by any Lucky Discovery, the Discriptions of the most Barren Lands, are not to be omitted or anything else you may judge Material. You are to keep an exact Journal of all your proceedings and make a return thereof to the Ohio Company.[581]

Orders of the Comittee of the Ohio Company 2d Novr 1753. Agreed and Ordered that each Member of the Company pay to Mr George Mason their Treasurer, the Sum of twenty pounds Current money[582] for Building and finishing the Fort at Shurtees Creek, Grubbing and clearing the Road from the Company's Store at Wills Creek to the Mohongaley which are to be finished with the utmost dispatch and for such other purposes as shall be directed by the Company. All such Members as have already paid any Sums of money to Christopher Gist last month, for the above Use the same are to to discounted out of their respective parts, or Shares of the Sum, ordered as above, and that the said Christopher Gist be chargeable with the same in the Company's Book in Order to account for it.

Ordered that the Attorney or Attorneys, employed to transact Business for the Company at Williamsburg be directed to enter Caveats against three Grants, or Orders of Council for one hundred thousand, forty thousand and fifty thousand Acres of Land, to Richard Corbin Esqr and Company the 15th day of June last past[583]

Orders 17. Octo.' 1760. Mr John Mercer having drawn up a State of the Companys Case and presented the same to the Committee

Resolved that the same be approved of and that Mr John Mercer be desired and empowered to transmit the same to Mr Sollicitor Charlton Palmer and employ him to lay the same before the proper board and make application for such further Orders and Instructions to the Government here as may be necessary to enable the Company to carry their Grant into Execution. That the Instructions to be given to the said Mr Sollicitor Palmer be referred to the

In the Darlington Memorial Library

said M:r Mercer who is hereby desired to draw up the same and in particular to desire M:r Palmer if he can obtain any further Orders or Instruction on the Companys behalf to take care that the same is expressed in the plainest and strongest terms.

[Ordered that M:r George Mason the Companys Treasurer write[232] to M:r Edward] Athawes Merchant in London to pay the said Sollicitors Bill and all other Expences attending the said Application for which the Company undertake to be answerable.

Resolved that the Hon'ble Philip Lee Esq:r be applied to on behalf of the Company to write a Letter[585] to his Grace the Duke of Bedford to inform him of the many disappointments the Company have met with in the prosecution of their Schemes from the Encroachments of the French and the Confusion occasioned thereby among the Indian Nations, but that by the great Success with which it has pleased God to bless his Majestys Arms in this part of the world they hope they shall now be able to prosecute this intended Settlement upon the Ohio, and reimburse the great expence they were at before the War in searching and discovering the inland parts of this continent at that time scarce known to any of his Majestys Subjects in America and to inform him that the Company intend to present an humble Petition[262] to his Majesty, shewing the Reasons why they have hitherto been disabled to comply with the Conditions mentioned in the royal Instructions to the late Governor Gooch and praying such further Indulgence's and Relief as his Majesty shall think reasonable, and that the Company emboldened by his Lordships former Approbation of their undertaking and his kind promise of his patronage signified to us by one of our Members the late M:r John Hanbury Merchant in London dec'ed have taken the Liberty to direct the Gentleman[586] in whose hands they have put their business to wait on his Lordship with a Copy of the said petition, and that they flatter themselves with the continuation of his Lordships Favour and patronage in all things that are consistent with Justice and the public Good.

Order of 7th Sept 1761.[584]

Sir. As We may expect a peace next Winter and have no reason to doubt, North America will be secured to the British Government, and then Liberty will be granted to his Majesties Subjects in these Colonies to Settle the Lands on Ohio. We the Committee of the Ohio Company think it a proper time as soon as peace is concluded to apply for a Grant for the Lands intended us by his Majesties instructions to Sir William Gooch and have for that purpose sent over a Petition[262] to his Majesty and a large and full State of our Case,

Lre to Governor Dinwiddie Sept 9. 1761.[261]

· 151 ·

and have employed M̄r Charlton Palmer a Man we are informed of great capacity and diligence to Solicit our Cause and endeavour by all means to get us a patent in England. He will be directed to apply to our Members in London for their Advice and Assistance and as no person knows the Affair better than M̄r Dinwiddie nor can it be imagined any of the Company have such an acquaintance or Interest with persons in power, let us beg you will please exert yourself in getting us a patent by natural bounds,[237] on the best terms possible for rather than be remitted to the Government here, who from jealousy or some other cause have ever endeavoured to disappoint us in every design we could form to settle and improve the Lands, we will agree to any reasonable consideration for such a Deed from England, but if this cannot be obtained that the most plain and positive instructions to the Governor of Virginia be procured on terms the most advantageous to the Company. We are &c.' James Scott, G Mason, Thos Lud. Lee, Richard Lee

L're to Capel and Osgood Hanbury Sept 10, 1761.

Gentn As We have reason to expect a peace soon and think it will be then practicable to prosecute our intended Settlements upon the Ohio, We have thought it absolutely necessary to employ some person in England to make application at the proper Boards on our behalf as well as to present a petition to his Majesty shewing the Reasons why we have hitherto been disabled to comply with the terms mentioned in the royal Instructions and praying some further Indulgencies and for this purpose We have transmitted to M̄r Charlton Palmer a full State of the Companys Case and have directed him to confer with you upon the Subject.

We have met with so many Discouragements from the Government in Virginia (many of the Council being concerned in large Entrys of Land themselves) that rather than have any further Altercation here we would willingly pay any reasonable Consideration for a patent in England by natural Bounds, which we hope will not be thought unreasonable when the expence We have been at is considered, and the great benefit that will result to the publick from our Discovery's and there cannot be a stronger proof of the publick principles upon which the Company have acted than that they have expended a much larger Sum in searching and discovering the inland parts of this Continent to the Westward than the Composition of all our Lands would have amounted to according to the common Rules of granting Lands in the inhabited parts of the Colony and it is notorious that till our discovery the Countrey upon the Ohio, and the fatal consequences of the French Incroachments then were altogether unknown or unattended to, the Inhabitants even of this Colony being uttterly unacquainted with the Geography of that Countrey as is plain from all the late Maps published either here or in England which are actually laid down from the Journals and discoverys of our Agents but if a patent cannot be obtained in England, We then hope that by a fresh Instruction to the Governor of Virginia, We may have our time for settling the Lands prolonged[587] [the Article of the Fort] altered or at least mitigated that [We may be allowed to contract with a Surveyor of our own without being liable to the high fees] settled by Law, and that we may be permitted to Survey [our Lands in small Tracts.[588] We think there cannot be any just Objection] to prolong our time for making Settlements, as the Encroachments of the French and the War have hitherto render'd it impossible to proceed in them, and We are at this time told that the Governor has Instructions to grant no Lands upon the Ohio for fear of giving Offence to the Indians. Upon the whole we make no doubt of your assisting and supporting us in everything that you judge conducive to our common Interest and are, Gentlemen &c. James Scott, J Mercer, G Mason, Thos Lud. Lee, Richard Lee

Richard Rogers of Stafford County Gent. this day made Oath before me One of his Ma'ties Justices of the Peace for the said County, That the several Copies contained in this & the Six preceding Pages are true Copies by him taken from the Original Book[589] belonging to the Ohio Company wherein the Orders made at the several meetings of the said Company or their Committees from the first Erection of the said Company have been regularly enter'd. Given under my hand & Seal at Stafford County this 26th day of July 1762.[590]

J Mercer

R Rogers[591]
[Endorsed]
Copy of Orders & Resolutions of the Ohio Company.

Acts of Pennsylvania about the Indian Trade, 1758—1759[592]

Enclosure 3

An act for preventing Abuses in the Indian Trade, for Supplying the Indians, Friends and Allies of Great Britain, with Goods at more easy Rates, and for Securing and Strengthening the Peace and Friendship lately concluded with the Indians inhabiting the Northern and Western Frontiers of this Province

WHEREAS the Indians, living and hunting near the Western and Northern Frontiers of this Province have earnestly requested that this Government would regulate the Trade with them, prevent Abuses therein, and provide that they may be furnished with a Sufficiency of the necessary Goods, by honest, prudent and Sober Men, at reasonable Rates, and that Ministers of the Gospels, Schoolmasters and other Sober and Virtuous Men may be sent among them, to civilize and instruct them in the Christian Religion, the Granting of which Requests may not only be productive of much Good to these poor people, but tend to Strenghten and secure the peace and Friendship lately concluded between them and the English and induce other and more distant Nations to seek our Alliance, withdraw themselves from the French, and effectually secure their Affections to the British Interest, and open a Trade with us, to the great Advantage and better Security of these Colonies and encreasing the Demand for the Manufactures of Great Britain And Whereas by encouraging Ministers of the Gospel, Schoolmasters, and other prudent and virtuous Men, to reside among the Indians and learn their Language and Customs, they may be civilized and instructed in the Christian Religion, and this Government may from Time to Time be supplied with faithful Interpreters and Agents, for the Management of publick Affairs with those people, from whence many Advantages may arise both to them and to us, And Whereas, it is absolutely necessary in order to effectuate the good purposes aforesaid, and prevent the Abuses complained of, that the Indian Trade and the power and Liberty of Supplying the Natives with Goods Wares and Merchandizes should be taken into the Hands of the Government in the Manner herein after directed Be it therefore Enacted by the Honourable William Denny Esqr Lieutenant Governor under the Honourable Thomas Penn and Richard Penn Esquires, true and absolute proprietaries of the province of Pensylvania and Counties of New Castle, Kent and Sussex, upon Delaware, by and with the Advice and Consent of the Representatives of the Freeman of the said province in General Assembly met and by the Authority of the same, That Edward Pennington William Fisher, John Reynall, Joseph Richardson, William West, Joseph Morris, Amos Strettell, Thomas Willing, and James Child, shall be and are hereby nominated and appointed Commissioners for Indian Affairs, which said Commissioners or a Majority of them, or of the Survivors of them shall have full power and Authority to do Execute and perform the several Duties and things enjoined and required of them by Virtue of this Act, during the continuance thereof anything herein contained to the contrary notwithstanding, and shall once in every year adjust and settle their Accounts with the Assembly of this province for the time being and shall be allowed for their Trouble One a quarter per Centum on the Sales purchase of the Goods, and one and a quarter per Centum on the Sales of the Returns, and no more, And that there shall be for each particular place appointed by the said Commissioners for carrying on the Trade aforesaid, as often as there may be Occasion, during the Continuance of this Act, three Suitable persons nominated and recommended for Agents by the said Commissioners for Indian Affairs, and returned in Writing under the Hands and Seales of the said Commissioners, to the Governor for the time being for his Approbation and Commission, And if the said Governor will not, within five days next after such Return, commissionate one of them so nominated and returned, the Person first so named in the Return shall be Agent, and serve in that Office without any further or other Commission, And in Case any Agent or Agents chosen and Commissionated by Virtue of this Act should refuse to serve, die, be removed by the Commissioners for Misbehaviour, or surrender upon their said Trust and Office the said Commissioners shall in like manner shall proceed to chuse three more suitable persons to supply his place and return them in manner aforesaid to the Governor for the time being for his Approbation, and if the Governor will not, within five days next after such Return, commissionate one of them so nominated and returned, the person first named in the Return shall be the Agent and serve in that Office, without any further or other Commission, which Agent or Agents shall reside in such Fort or Forts, place or places, as he or they from time to time shall be directed and instructed by the Governor and Commander in Cheif of this province, by and with the Approbation of the said Commissioners for Indian Affairs, or a Majority of them, or of the Survivors of them which said Commissioners, or a Majority of them, or of the Survivors of them, shall constantly furnish and supply them the said Agents with an Assortment of Indian Goods which they the said Agents shall exchange and barter with the Indians for their Peltry at such Rates as shall be from time to time settled and directed by the said Commissioners for Indian Affairs, And the said Agent or Agents so chosen and appointed as aforesaid, shall in all his or their Transactions and Dealings with the Indians in the way of trade or barter, conduct him or themselves according to the Directions of this Act, and such Instructions consistent therewith, as he or they shall receive from the Commissioners aforesaid for Indian Affairs, which Commissioners shall with such Sums as shall be granted and appropriated for that purpose, purchase from the Importers or import, as shall be most conducive to the benefit of the said Trade, and send out to the said Agent or Agents the necessary Assortment of Goods and Merchandizes for carrying on the Indian Trade, and shall receive the Peltry that shall be sent in as Returns for the same, and Sell or dispose thereof by themselves, or such other persons as they shall appoint in Lots by way of publick Auction or Vendue, in the city of Philadelphia or in such other place as they shall think proper within this province, to the highest Bidders, any Law Usage or Custom to the contrary in any wise notwithstanding giving at least ten days Notice in the publick News papers of such Sale, together with the particular Assortments and quantities thereof, and the time and place where the said Auction or Vendue is to be held, in which purchases and Sales they shall use their utmost care Circumspection and Diligence for the publick Interest.

And be it further Enacted by the Authority aforesaid, That the said Commissioners or any or either of them shall not directly or indirectly buy, Sell, barter, exchange or trade, with any Indian or Indians on his or their own Account, or on the Account of any other person or persons whatsoever, nor suffer any person under his or their direction so to do, during the Continuance of this Act, but for the Account of the province only, and in the manner directed by this Act under the penalty of One hundred pounds for every such Offence, to be recovered in the same manner the other Fines and penalties inflicted by Virtue of this Act are directed to be recovered one half thereof to the Informer, or the person that shall Sue for the same and the other half part to be applied to the Uses of the said Indian Trade.

And Whereas the Commissioners appointed by An Act intituled, "A Supplement to the Act intituled An Act for granting the sum of "sixty thousand pounds to the Kings Use, and for striking fifty five "thousand pounds thereof in Bills of Credit, and to provide a Fund "for sinking the same, and for granting to his Majesty the Additional "sum of one hundred thousand pounds with the approbation of the "Governor, did appropriate and lay out in sundry Good Wares and Merchandizes, in order therewith to trade with the Indians, the sum of One thousand pounds part of the said One hundred thousand pounds granted to the Kings Use, and did appoint John Carson to reside at Fort Augusta, and did deliver and consign to him the said

Goods Wares and Merchandizes, to Sell and barter the same on Account of the province with the Indians.

Be it therefore farther Enacted by the Authority aforesaid, That the said John Carson, his Executors or Administrators, shall, and they are hereby enjoined and commanded, whenever thereto required, to deliver up to them the said Commissioners for Indian Affairs, all and singular of the said Goods, Wares and Merchandizes that have or shall come to their Hands Custody or power, or be delivered to him or them for the purposes aforesaid, which shall remain in his or their hands not Sold or bartered as aforesaid at the time such Request shall be made, and shall also transmit and deliver to them the said Commissioners for Indian Affairs, the money and Peltry which he or they have or shall receive of the Natives therefor, and shall behave and Account with them in all things, as the Agents to be appointed by Virtue of this Act are enjoined and required to account and behave under the penalty of One thousand pounds, to be recovered by the Commissioners for Indian Affairs in the same manner as the other Fines and penalties inflicted by this Act are herein after directed to be recovered, and shall be by them applied to the Uses of the said Trade

And the better to enable the said Commissioners for Indian Affairs to carry on the said Trade, to supply the said Agents from time to time with the necessary Goods, Wares and Merchandizes, and to execute and perform all and every the Duties enjoined and required of them by this Act. Be it Enacted, by the Authority aforesaid, That it shall and may be lawful for any person or persons whatsoever to advance and lend to the said Commissioners for Indian Affairs, any Sum or Sums of money not exceeding in the whole the Sum of Four thousand pounds lawful money of this province, which Sum or Sums of money the said Commissioners for Indian Affairs, are hereby Authorized and impowered to borrow and receive for the Uses, Intents, and purposes aforesaid, And the said Lenders shall have and receive for the Use and forbearance of their respective Loans during the Continuance of this Act and until the same shall be paid off and discharged, Interests not exceeding six per Centum per Annum, And that every such Lender shall immediately have and receive a Note and Certificate in Writing of and for the Sum lent, with the Interest thereof, signed by the said Commissioners for Indians Affairs, which Note and Certificate shall be registred in a Book to be kept by them for that purpose, And that the said Lenders shall be paid by the said Commissioners for Indian Affairs, yearly and every year, the Interest Monies arising on their respective Loans, out of the profits and Gain accruing of and from the said Trade, and if not sufficient profit or Gain, then out of the Capital Stock, And that at the Expiration of five years of and from the publication of this Act they the said Commissioners shall pay off and discharge all and every the said Loans and principal Sums to the several and respective Lenders, out of the Monies remaining in their Hands.

And in Order more effectually to assure and secure to the Lenders their respective Sums of money that shall be so lent and advanced, and to the several persons employed in the said Trade, their respective Rewards and Wages, Be it further Enacted by the Authority aforesaid, That if, by any Accident, Chance of War or other Casualty whatsoever, it should so happen that the Capital Stock, and the Profits, Gain and Advantages arising from the said Trade should at the Expiration of five Years from and after the publication of this Act, be found short and insufficient, upon a Settlement as aforesaid with the Assembly, to Satisfy and discharge the said several Loans with the Interest thereon accruing and to bear and maintain the other Charges and Expences of the said Trade, the same shall be paid and satisfied by an equal and proportionable Rate and Tax, to be laid, assessed and levied on all the Estates, real and personal within this province in the same manner, by the same persons, under the same pains and penalties, and in the same proportions in the several Counties, as the Sums of Money heretofore granted to the Kings Use, and directed to be raised and levied on the real and personal Estates of the Inhabitants are, or shall be at that time assessed, raised and levied, And that the Assembly of this province for the time being, upon such insufficiency and defect appearing to them, on the Settlement of the Commissioners Accounts as aforesaid, shall forthwith certify the same to the Commissioners of the several Counties in Writing under the hand of their Speaker, in order that the same may be laid assessed and levied in manner aforesaid And when so levied shall be paid into the hands of the respective County Treasurers, who shall forthwith pay the same over to the Commissioners for Indian Affairs for the purposes aforesaid

And be it further Enacted by the Authority aforesaid, That all and every person and persons to whom any money shall be due for Loan by Virtue of this Act, after Note and Certificate entered on the Book of Registry as aforesaid, his her or their Executors Administrators or Assigns, by proper Words of Assignment to be endorsed on his, her or their Certificate, may assign, transfer, or make over, all his, her or their Right, [Find Interest and benefit of such Note and] Certificate, to any other person and persons, which Assignment shall entitle such Assignee, his her or their Executors Administrators or Assigns to the Benefit thereof, and payment thereon, and such Assigned may in like manner Assign again and so, toties quoties, and afterwards it shall not be in the power of such person or persons who have or hath made such Assignment, to make Void, release or discharge the same or the monies thereby due.

And be it further Enacted by the Authority aforesaid, That in Settling the Rates of Exchanging and Bartering with the Indians, no greater Advance shall be put on the Goods to be furnished them, than may be in the Judgment of the Commissioners aforesaid sufficient to bear and defray the necessary Expences of transacting, carrying on and managing the Trade, and of paying the Interest money aforesaid, and for supporting such protestant Teachers of the Gospel to instruct the Indians in the principles of the Christian Religion, Schoolmasters and other persons to take care of, and direct them in their temporal Affairs, as shall be most agreeable to them, which said Teachers Schoolmasters and others so to be supported shall be appointed and commissionated by the Governor and Commander in Cheif of this province, and before they are commissionated by the Governor and Commander in Cheif of this province for the purposes aforesaid they shall take the Oaths appointed to be taken in and by an Act passed in the first year of his late Majesty King George entituled "An Act for the Further Security of his Majestys person and "Government and the Succession of the Crown in the Heirs of the "late princess Sophia, being protestants and for Extinguishing the "hopes of the pretended prince of Wales, and his open and secret "Abettors" or if conscientiously Scrupulous of taking an Oath, an Affirmation instead thereof, and shall also make, repeat and Subscribe the Declaration in the said Act mentioned, And if upon final Settlement of the Accounts at the Expiration of this Act it should appear that there is a Surplus of profit, the same shall be paid into the hands of the privincial Treasurer for the time being, and disposed of in such Manner and to such purposes as shall be hereafter directed by Act of General Assembly of this province

And be it further Enacted by the Authority aforesaid, That every Agent so appointed and employed as aforesaid before he takes upon himself the Office and Trust appointed and required by this Act shall take an Oath or Affirmation before some Justice of the peace of this province, for the faithful discharge of his Duty, and the trust reposed in him by Virtue of this Act, and shall also enter into, and duly execute, and Obligation with sufficient Sureties to his Majesty and his Successors, and in such penal Sum as the said Commissioners for Indian Affairs shall require, that he will well and truly discharge and execute his Trust, and likewise observe such Orders, Instructions and Directions, consistent with this Act, as shall be sent to him from time to time by the said Commissioners for Indian Affairs and that he will neither directly or indirectly, buy, Sell, barter exchange or trade with any Indian or Indians on his own Account or on the account of any other person or persons whatsoever, nor suffer any person under his Direction so to do, but for the Account of the province only, and that he will not employ any person or persons as Assistants in trading with the Indians, but such as shall be well recommended as honest, Sober and prudent persons, and approved of by the said Commissioners for Indian Affairs, And the said Agent or Agents shall keep fair and just Accounts of all his or their Transactions and Dealings in the premisses and deliver fair Transcripts thereof into the hands of the said Commissioners for Indian Affairs at least once a Year, and shall also settle and adjust the same yearly, or oftner, if required with the said Commissioners, and shall have, for his her or their Care and trouble in negotiating and transacting the business hereby committed to him or them, and such as shall or may be employed as is herein before directed, in carrying on the trade with the Indians, and other Services relating thereto, such Rewards or Commissions as the Commissioners aforesaid for Indian Affairs shall judge reasonable and allow.

And be it further Enacted by the Authority aforesaid, That if any such Agent or Assistant or person employed by him, shall presume to demand higher or greater prices or Rates of the Indians for any Goods Sold them, or exchanged or bartered with them, than they are fixed at, or allow the Indians less for their peltry than directed and instructed to do by the said Commissioners for Indian Affairs, such Agent or Assistant, or person employed by him shall forfeit and pay the Sum of fifty pounds for every such Offence, one half thereof to be paid to the said Commissioners for Indian Affairs, to be disposed of by them in purchasing Goods, and carrying on the said Trade, and the other half thereof to such person or persons that shall Sue or prosecute for the same, to be recovered in any of his Majesty Courts of Record within this province, where the prosecutor shall think proper to commence his Suit, by Action of Debt, Bill, Plaint or Information, wherein no Essoin, protection or Wager of Law shall be allowed to the Defendant, nor any more than one Imparleance, and the Offender or Delinquent shall thenceforth during the Continuance of this Act, be altogether disabled from holding or exercising any Office within this Government

In the Darlington Memorial Library

And be it further Enacted by the Authority aforesaid, That no person or persons whatsoever other than the said Commissioners their Agents, and their Assistants, and such as are employed by them for Account of the province, from and after the publication of this Act shall presume to Sell, exchange or barter with any Indian or Indians, any Cyder, Whiskey, Wine, Rum, Brandy or any other strong Liquor, whatsoever within this province, nor shall any person or persons other than the Commissioners their said Agents and their Assistants, Sell exchange or barter, with any Indian or Indians, any Goods Wares or Merchandizes whatsoever (Provisions only excepted) beyond the Kittocktenny Hills on any pretence whatsoever, Provided that nothing herein contained shall be construed or extended to debar any Inhabitant within the Kittocktenny Hills from Selling bartering or exchanging any Goods Wares or Merchandizes, other than Spirituous Liquors as aforesaid, with such Indian or Indians, as shall or may come to their own dwelling houses for those purposes, and that every person and persons offending in the premisses, being legally convicted thereof in any Court of Record within this province, shall forfeit and pay the sum of fifty pounds to be recovered and disposed of in manner last aforesaid, and be committed to the publick Goal during the space of six months, without Bail or Mainprize any Law or Laws of this province to the contrary notwithstanding, And the said Offence, committed out of the inhabited parts of this province as aforesaid shall be heard tried and determined in any of the Courts of this province where the person offending shall or may be arrested and apprehended.

And be it further Enacted by the Authority aforesaid, That the said Agents, to be appointed as aforesaid and every of them as often as they shall be informed, or have reason to believe that any Quantity of Strong Liquors, Goods Wares and Merchandizes are carried out and transported beyond the Kittocktenny Hills with design to Sell barter and exchange the same with the Indians, shall and they, and every of them are hereby empowered and required with their Assistants and Servants to visit all Suspected places, and search for such strong Liquors Goods Wares and Merchandizes and being found beyond the Limits aforesaid, to Seize the same as forfeited, One half thereof for the Use of the person who shall prosecute for the same, and the other half thereof to the Commissioners for Indian Affairs as aforesaid to be recovered in manner aforesaid, in any Court of Record of this province, in which the prosecutor shall think proper to file his Bill, plaint or Information, and to be disposed of by them in manner last aforesaid

And be it further Enacted, by the Authority aforesaid, that where any Agent so as aforesaid appointed, shall be removed by the said Commissioners for Indian Affairs from his Office of Agent, or surrender up his said Office, he shall deliver up to the said Commissioners for Indian Affairs all the Books, public Accounts and papers, belonging to or concerning the trade and trust committed to his care, whole and entire, and undefaced, under the penalty of five hundred pounds to be recovered in the manner, and for the Uses aforesaid, And where any Agent shall be removed by death from his said Office and trust, the Executors or Administrators of such Decedent, shall deliver in like manner all the Books and papers that shall come to their Hands, relating to the Accounts and Transactions of the said Trade to the succeeding Agent or Agents, under the like penalty to be recovered and applied in manner aforesaid

And be it further Enacted by the Authority aforesaid, That the Clause which relates to the securing and assuring the Loans to the respective Lenders, shall remain, and is hereby declared to be in force until the said Lenders shall receive their several and respective Sums of money lent and advanced with the Interest thereon accruing, and that the Residue and Remainder of this Act shall be in force for five Years from and after the publication thereof and no longer,

A Supplement, to an Act intituled An Act for preventing Abuses in the Indian Trade for supplying the Indians, Friends and Allies of Great Britain, with Goods at more easy rates, and for securing and Strengthening the Peace and Friendship lately concluded with the Indians inhabiting the Northern and Western Frontiers of this province

Whereas the late salutary and pacific Measures which have been pursued by this Government with the Indians on the Northern and Western Frontiers of this province, and the Success of his Majestys Arms in those parts have procured the Friendship and Alliance of many distant and different Tribes of Indians to the British Interest And Whereas it is absolutely necessary in order to secure and firmly establish, the peace and Friendship lately concluded with them, on the part of Great Britain, to supply the said Indians with a sufficient quantity of necessary Goods at reasonable Rates, And Whereas the Sum which the Commissioners for Indian Affairs nominated and appointed in and by the abovementioned Act, are empowered to borrow, is not sufficient to Answer the above purposes and other the good purposes mentioned and contained in the said [Settlement] of Assembly [Be it therefore] Enacted by the Honourable William Denny Esquire Lieutenant Governor under the Honourable Thomas Penn

In the Darlington Memorial Library

and Richard Penn, Esquires, true and absolute proprietors of the province of Pensylvania, and Counties of New Castle Kent, and Sussex, upon Delaware by and with the Advice and Consent of the Representatives of the Freeman of the said province, in General Assembly met, and by the Authority of the same, That it shall and may be lawful for any person or persons whatsoever, to advance and lend to the said Commissioners for Indian Affairs any further Sum or sums of money not exceeding in the whole the sum of ten thousand pounds, lawful money of this province, over and above the sum of four thousand pounds which they are by the said Act, empowered and authorized to borrow which said Sum of ten thousand pounds or so much thereof as they shall think it necessary to borrow, the said Commissioners are hereby authorized and empowered to borrow and receive for the Uses Intents and purposes contained and mentioned in this and the said recited Act, And the said Lenders shall have and receive, for the Use and forbearance of their respective Loans, during the continuance of this Act and until the same shall be paid off and discharged, Interest not exceeding Six per Centum per Annum, And that every such Lender shall have and receive a note and Certificate in Writing of and for the Sum lent, with the Interest thereof, signed by the said Commissioners for Indian Affairs which Note and Certificate shall be registred in the Book by them kept for that purpose, And that the said Lenders shall be paid by the said Commissioners for Indian Affairs Yearly and every Year, the Interest Monies arising on their respective Loans, out of the profits and Gain accruing of and from the said Trade, and if not sufficient profits or Gain, then out of the Capital Stock, and that at the Expiration and Determination of this Act, they the said Commissioners, shall pay of and discharge all and every the said Loans and principal Sums of money to the several and respective Leaders, out of the Monies remaining in their Hands.

And in order more effectually to secure and assure to the said Lenders their respective Sums of money that shall be so lent and advanced, Be it Enacted by the Authority aforesaid, That if by any Accident, Chance or War, or other Casualty whatsoever, it should so happen that the Capital Stock, and the profits, Gain and Advantage arising from the said Trade should at the Expiration of this Act, be found Short and insufficient upon a Settlement with the Assembly to Satisfy and discharge the said several Loans, with the Interest thereof, and to bear and maintain the other Charges and Expences of the Indian Trade, the same shall be paid and satisfied by an equal and proportionable Rate and Tax, to be laid assessed and levied on all Estates, real and personal, within this province, in the same manner, by the same persons, under the same pains, penalties and forfeitures and in the same proportions, in the several Counties, as the Sums of Money heretofore granted to the Kings Use, and directed to be raised and levied on all Estates, real and personal within this province are or shall be at that time assessed raised and levied, And that the Assembly of this province upon such insufficiency and defect appearing to them on the Settlement of the Account of the said Commissioners, as directed by the said Act of Assembly shall forthwith certify the same to the Commissioners of the several Counties in writing under the Hand of their Speaker, in Order that the same may be laid, assessed and levied in manner aforesaid, and when so levied, shall be paid into the hands of the respective County Treasurers who shall forthwith pay the same over to the Commissioners for Indian Affairs for the purposes aforesaid

And be it Enacted by the Authority aforesaid, That all and every person and persons to whom any Money shall be due for Loan, by Virtue of this Act, after Note and Certificate entered in the Book of Registry as aforesaid, his, her, or their Executors, Administrators or Assigns by proper Words of Assignment, to be endorsed on his, her or their Certificate may Assign transfer, or make over all his, her or their Right, Title, Interest and benefit of such Note and Certificate, to any other person or persons which Assignment shall intitle such Assignee, his her or their Executors Administrators or Assigns to the benefit thereof, and payment thereon, and such Assignee may in like manner, Assign again and so toties quoties and afterwards it shall not be in the power of such person or persons, who have or hath made such Assignment, to make void release or discharge the same or the Monies thereby due.

And be it Enacted by the Authority aforesaid, That the Sum and Sums of money which the Commissioners for Indian Affairs are hereby Authorized and empowered to borrow and receive, shall be by them made Use of applied and appropriated to and for the Uses Intents and purposes mentioned and directed in and by this Act and the said Act of General Assembly to which this Act is a Supplement, and to and for no other Uses, Intents and purposes whatsoever, and that the Accounts thereof shall be Settled and adjusted in the same manner that the other Indian Accounts of the said Commissioners are thereby directed to be Settled and adjusted, And if upon final Settlement of the Accounts at the [Expiration of this Act do approve that the] Surplus of profit, the same shall be paid into the Hands of the provincial Treasurer for the time being, and disposed of in such manner and to such purposes as shall be here after directed by Act of General

In the Darlington Memorial Library

Assembly, And that the said Commissioners for Indian Affairs shall have and receive for all Goods purchased for the Use of the Indian Trade, from and after the publication of this Act, the Sum of two and half per Centum, and on the Sales of the Returns thereof the sum of two and half per Centum, and no more, for their trouble in executing and discharging the Trust, powers and Duties enjoined and required of them by this Act, anything in the said recited Act of General Assembly to the contrary thereof notwithstanding

Be it further Enacted by the Authority aforesaid, That the Clause in this Act contained relating to the assuring and securing the Loans to the respective Lenders shall remain, and is hereby declared to be in force until the said Lenders shall receive their several and respective Sums of money by them lent and advanced as aforesaid with the Interest thereon accruing, And that the Residue and Remainder of this Act shall be in Force as long as, and during the Term of the said Act of General Assembly, to which this Act is a Supplement and no longer

[Endorsed]

Acts of Pennsylvania abot the Indian Trade.

George Mercer, Field Notes for the Charlottesburg Survey, *ca* March–May, 1763[593]

Beginning at a small Elm Tree on Poto River, at the Corner of a cleared Field & running N. a 68 Perches to the No Side of the main Street

    86½   Waggon Road to Pittsburg
    160   to 3 Stones in the middle of a Triangle formed by three Walnut Trees thence E.

a[t] 74 Poles Wills's Creek where the Mills are to be built is 26 Poles distant—& bears N 18 N. & the Creek from hence Bears N 59 W up—& the Bottom is 15 Poles Wide—and the Mills are within 6 Po: of G Braddock's Waggon Road X Wills's Creek

a[t] 94 Poles E Course X a Drain at the Head of the Bottom 124 Poles came down to Wills's Creek—(the Bottom here is 30 P.) & Power Magazine witht the Fort bears S. The Course of Wills's Creek .. S. E downwards A Pine Tree by the Side of the Drain X the Bottom S 29 W—Bottom 16 Po: wide

George Mercer Papers

Then returning to the Elm at the Beginning run the Meanders of Poto River E-46 P—N 65 E 22. P. N 38 E 40 P. to a Stake (in this last Course a 24 P. X the Mouth of a Drain close to the Edge of Water the River)—thence from the B Stake [1] N 59 ½ E 24 P. to a Blackwalnut Stump by the Side of the Gardens—then [2] E 20 Poles to the Mouth of the Gut at the E Side of the Garden—thence along the Gut N 50 E to a Stump near the Bridge Ford of Wills's Creek 24 P. thence N 12 ½ W 19 P. to a Spanish Oak on a Rock in Wills's Creek near the Mouth of the Drain mentioned in the 94 Poles Course—E—The Pine bears from hence N 29 W.

1 From hence took an Observation to determine the Width of the River Poto Stake on So Side bears a$_t$t$_t$ the Beg: of this Co: N 59 ½ E 24 Poles bears S 78 ½ E & at the End of the Course at the Stump bears S 30 E—

2 again from the Stump running E 20 Poles—Stake at the Beg. bears S 30 E—& at the Mouth of the Gut S 29 W—River is 17 ½ Poles wide—From a Stump where a Stake is drove down near the N Side of the main Street run S 18 P. to the River, struck 13 ½ P. to the E of the Stake B from whence I took my first Observation X the River— Then begun where our first Course N

(Where our first Course N from the River from the Elm intersects the N Side of the main Street—and from hence Pittsburgh Road runs in the Bottom 18 ½ Poles from the N Side of the main Street—) run E—and a$_t$t$_t$ 26 P. Bottom begins—a$_t$t$_t$ 36 Poles X Pittsburg Waggon Road—46 P—left the Bottom—52 Pole to a large Oak a$_t$t$_t$ 68 Pole X the Hill to the Beginning of the Bottom & a$_t$t$_t$ 80 P. into the Bottom & run along the Foot of the Hill 104 Po: to a Stump near the Corner of the Store House where the Artillery Waggons are kept—from hence the New Store House bears S—w^{ch}: Course strikes the N End of it at the Chimney the Stump from whence took Observation over the River a$_t$t$_t$ the W End of the Garden bears S 37 E.

At the Stump W 4 Po. near the Corner of the Store run up the Side N 20 P. from hence the Pine bears N 12 E & Pittsburg Waggon Road thro' the Bottom appears here about nearly W where the N from hence 14 Poles to the E S S E 5 S—North Bastion of Fort Cumberland[594] & from N to the S Bastion is 11 Poles—

[Endorsed]
Field Notes at the Survey of Charlottesburg at Wills's Creek near Fort Cumberland belonging to the Ohio Company, 1763.

Mount Vernon Octor the 20th 1748.

Wee the Subscribers of the Committee of the Ohio Company having met at Major Lawrence Washington's this day by appointment.

1. Have allow'd Colo Thomas Cresap's Acco for Soliciting a Grant &c at Williamsburgh... £ 12. 5. —
2. Have allowed Lawrence Washington as paid the Clerk of the Council............... 1. 1. 6
3. Ordered that Mr James Wardrope pay Colo Cresap in po of his Acco................. 10. —
4. It is the Opinion of the Committee that sending for a Cargo be Postponed 'til a Grant shall be obtained at Williamsburgh or in England.
5. It's the opinion that as soon as a Grant for the Lands is obtained and upon Notice thereof given [illegible]... the Committee with [illegible] Mr John Hanbury for One hundred pounds Sterling or Bills of Exchange payable to Mr John Hanbury to be remitted by the Committee except what shall be adjudged necessary for Wampum &c.
6. It's the opinion of the Committee that as soon as a Grant is obtained that the Members which may be Assembled at Williamsburgh shall have power to give the Committee such Instructions as may be necessary for Mr Wardrope to send to Mr Stedman in Rotterdam for procuring Foreign Protestants to settle the Land
7. That Mr James Wardrope agrees to every Article the Company has agreed to and will sign whenever the Articles of Agreement shall be brought to the Committee

Signed   Lawce Washington
               James Wardrop.
               James Scott
               John Carlyle

Cameron Feb. 23. 1748.

At a Committee of the Ohio Company,

Ordered that each Member, Pay to Nathl Chapman or Order the sum of One hundred pounds Sterling to be laid out in Goods, for carrying on the Indian Trade, the money to be paid at or before the fifteenth day of April next and the said Chapman do pass Receipts for the same.

Ordered that the several Sums when received be delivered to Thomas Lee Esqr to be by him remitted to our Correspondent in London along with the Invoice for this Trade

Ordered that the Letter of this date from the Committee to Thomas Lee Esqr & also a copy of that to each Member be inserted in the Company's Books.

               Lawce Washington
               James Scott
               Nathl Chapman
               John Carlyle

Stafford Court June the 21st 1749.

At a Meeting of the Ohio Company   Present

Thomas Lee Esqr	Philip L. Lee	Jacob Giles
John Taylor	Augustine Washington	Thos Cresup.
Presley Thornton	Gavin Corbin	Hugh Parker.
Lawrence Washington		
Richard Lee	James Scott.	Nathl Chapman

At a Meeting of the Ohio Compa June the 21st 1749.

The Resignation of Coll George Fairfax being Read is agreed to by the Compa
The Resignation of Mr Jno Carlyle being read is agreed to by the Compa

(1)

Orders and Resolutions of the Ohio Company and the Committee of the Company, October 20, 1748–July 4, 1763.

Orders and Resolutions of the Ohio Company and of the Committee of the Company, October 20, 1748—July 4, 1763[595]

Mount Vernon Octor the 20th 1748.

Wee the Subscribers of the Committee of the Ohio Company having met at Major Lawrence Washington's this day by appointment.[596]

1st Have allow'd Colo Thomas Cresaps Accot for Soliciting a Grant &c. at Williamsburgh £12.5

2d Have allowed Lawrence Washington as paid the Clerk of the Counsel[597]

3d Ordered that Mr James Wardrope pay Colo Cresap in pt of his Accot 10.

4thly It is the Opinion of the Committee that sending for a Cargo be Postponed t'il a Grant shall be obtained at Williamsburgh or in England.

5thly It the opinion that as soon as a Grant for the Lands is obtained and upon Notice thereof given to each member of the Compa they shall immediately furnish the Committee with Letters of Credit on Mr John Hanbury for One hundred pounds Sterling or Bills of Exchange payable to Mr John Hanbury to be remitted by the Committee except what shall be adjudged necessary for Wampum &c.

6thly It's the opinion of the Committee that as soon as a Grant is obtained that the Members which may be Assembled at Williamsburgh shall have power to give the Committee such Instructions as may be necessary for Mr Wardrope to send Mr Stedman[20] in Rotterdam for procuring Foreign Protestants to settle the Land

7thly That Mr James Wardrope agrees to every Article the Company has agreed to and will sign whenever the Articles of Agreement[598] shall be brought to the Committee

Signed. Lawce Washington
James Wardrop.
James Scott
John Carlyle

Cameron Feb. 23d 1748[49].

At a Committee of the Ohio Company
Ordered that each Member, Pay to Natha Chapman[21] or Order the sum of One hundred pounds Sterling to be laid out in Goods, for carrying on the Indian Trade, the money to be paid at or before the

George Mercer Papers

fifteenth day of April next and the said Chapman do pass Receipts for the same.

Ordered that the several Sums when received be delivered to Thomas Lee Esqr to be by him remitted[22] to our Correspondent in London along with the Invoice for this Trade

Ordered that the Letter[599] of this date from the Committee to Thomas Lee Esqr & also a Copy of that[21] to each Member be inserted in the Companys Books.

Lawe Washington
James Scott
Natha Chapman
John Carlyle

Stafford Court June the 21st 1749.

At a Meeting of the Ohio Company,   Present

Thomas Lee Esqr	Philip L. Lee	Jacob Giles
John Tayloe	Augustine Washington	Thos Cresup
Presley Thornton	Gawin Corbin	Hugh Parker.
Lawrence Washington	James Scott.	Natha Chapman
Richard Lee		

At a Meeting of the Ohio Compa June the 21st 1749. The Resignation of Collo George Fairfax being Read is agreed to by the Compa The Resignation of Mr Jno Carlyle being read is agreed to by the Compa The Resignation of Collo Francis Thornton decesd in his life time being read is agreed to by the Company

Colo Thomas Lee acquainted the Compa that Mr Secretary Nelson[24] told him to acquaint them that he desired to be Excused and did not Intend to be one of the Ohio Company which is Ordered to be Enter'd.

And that the Late Mr William Nimmo told him he never Design'd to be one of the Compa and only lent his name to Major Lawrence Washington in the Petition never Designing to be concern'd further.

Ordered that Mr George Mason on his Desire and Paying his Share as a Partner be admitted as a Member of the Ohio Compa

Whereas the said Compa by Resignations are reduced to sixteen they do hereby Oblige themselves to make their Capital Stock Four thousand pound sterling according to the Tenor of a Ltre this day wrote to Messrs John Hanbury and Compa Merchts in London in the following words.

Potomack June 20th 1749.

Sr

We have received from our Partner the honble Collo Thomas Lee a Copy of the Petition . . .

In the Darlington Memorial Library

Letter also in "Orders & Resolutions, 1749–1761."
Printed on pp. 140, 141.

Sir

Your most humble Servants. sign'd by Thos Lee, Law. Washington, Phil. Lud Lee, Gawin Corbin James Scott, Richard Lee, John Tayloe, Presly Thornton Augt Washington, Thos Cresap, John Giles, James Wardrop. Nath Chapman, Hugh Parker.

And the said Compa do further Agree and Oblige themselves . . .

Identical item in "Orders and Resolutions, 1749–1761."
Printed on p. 141.

And Whereas Hugh Parker one of the said Compa has agreed to Transport all the Goods Imported by the said Compa from the lower Falls of Potomack to the place of their General Factory on the River Ohio for the Consideration of twelve shillings Current money for every hundred weight and at the same Rate for every Load that he shall bring back from the Ohio to the said Falls afsd which Agreement the said Compa and the said Hugh Parker mutually agree to perform. And the said Compa for a consideration hereafter to be mentioned do appoint the said Hugh Parker their Factor at the Ohio till further Consideration[600]

And the said Compa do agree that Colo Thomas Cresap, and the said Hugh Parker . . .

Identical item in "Orders and Resolutions, 1749–1761."
Printed on p. 141.

And the said Compa further desire[30] that the Indians at the Ohio be invited to a Treaty and an Interpreter[31] provided at the Expense of the Government and that a proper Application be accordingly made and that their Factor be put in the Commission of the peace for Augusta County[32]

That Legal Endeavours be used to prevent the Pensilvania and other Traders from Trading on the Branches of the River Mississipi without a Lycence from this Government[601]

That Major Washington be desired to procure in England[602] for the Compa a Good Gun Smith and a good white Smith and a set of Tools for each and a Taylor.

Also that Major Law. Washington apply to the Governor for a Dozen or two of Muskets which he is to send round by Water to Potomack if Obtaind.[603]

That the Factor for the Company be impowered to dispose of the Goods to the Indians on the Best Terms he can, and not to dispose of any of them to the Traders but at such prices as the Company shall fixt on them and likewise on such Skins as is received in pay-

George Mercer Papers

ment.[604] It is submitted to the Factor to give such Credits[605] as appears to be Absolutely necessary for the Benefit of the Trade and not in General.

That Security be Given by the Factor, for Rendring a just and faithfull Account of his dealings and proceedings in Transacting the Companys affairs in carrying on the Skin Trade

It is Order'd that Colo Philip Lee & Mr George Mason be added to the Committee

Hugh Parker agrees with the Company that unless he can procure an Acceptable person to them to undertake and Transact their Business in carrying on the Skin trade, and render them accounts according to the Companys Instructions and Satisfaction, that he said Hugh Parker doth promise and Oblige himself to undertake and Act for them as their Factor for one year to commence from the arrival of the Goods[23] and rely on the Honour of the Company for a Recompence for his Trouble

Ordered that Nathaniel Chapman our Treasurer . . .

Identical order in "Orders and Resolutions, 1749–1761." Printed on p. 141.

[signed by]

Hugh Parker	Thos Cresap.	Thomas Lee
Natha Chapman	James Scott	Lawe Washington
Augustine Washington	John Tayloe	Gawin Corbin
	Richard Lee	Phil. Lud. Lee
	Jno Giles.	Presly Thornton

At a Meeting of the Ohio Company at the Falls of Potomack in Fairfax County Sept 25th 1749

Present

Thomas Lee Esqr	Gawin Corbin
John Tayloe	Richard Lee
Presly Thornton	James Scott.

Mr Chapman having by Letter desir'd that Mr George Mason may be appointed Cashier of the Company in his room and that he be order'd to pay to him the Company's Cash remaining in his hands The Company do agree that it be done accordingly

That the Company do unanimously agree to return Mr Hanbury thanks for Negotiating the Companys Affairs for obtaining the advantageous Instructions for making them such a Grant as they very much approve off

That they Accept Chairfully of the two Gentlemen to be Partners in the Company Vizt Arthur Dobbs Esqr and Mr Samuel Smith Mercht

In the Darlington Memorial Library

That the Company agree that M[r] Hanbury be impowered to make proposals for bringing over to seat on their Lands Germans or other protestants, obliging themselves to comply with such agreements for that purpose as the said Hanbury shall make

That the said Hanbury be desired to Solicite to get the part of the Instruction alter'd[57] which Obliges the Company to build and Garrison a Fort as it is impracticable for them to do it out of their private fortunes the thing being of a Public Nature and a Fort there will Guard the other Colonies as well as this and no particular advantage to the Company

That he Endeavour to obtain an order[27] to the Goverment here to make presents to the Indians it being as reasonable and useful to the public as the presents that the Goverment of New York[28] are allowed to give

That he Endeavour to obtain an Order to Run the Line between Virginia and Pensilvania on the same Terms as the Carolina line[35] was Run which is necessary in order to take our Grant with certainty

That Col[o] Cresap or M[r] Parker be employed to discover the parts beyond the Mountains so that we may know where to Survey our Land and that this may be done as soon as possible, or we may be complained of for keeping others from taking up the Kings Lands.

It is further agreed by the Company that the Hon[ble] Thomas Lee Esq[r] do write to M[r] Hanbury in the name of the Company as to all the matters Beforementioned, And also in relation to the proposals in M[r] Parkers Letter received this day

Copia	Sign'd by	Thomas Lee	Gawin Corbin
		John Tayloe	Richard Lee
		Presly Thornton	James Scott

At a Committee of the Ohio Company January 29th 1750.

Resolved that the Committee do approve of the purchase made by M[r] Hugh Parker and M[r] Thomas Cresap in behalf of the Company of an Entry for a Tract[37] of Land and Improvement on the North Branch of Potomack opposite the Mouth of Wills Creek.

Resolved that the same is the most convenient place to settle the Factory and begin the Trade at

Ordered that M[r] Parker apply to the Lord Fairfax to obtain a Grant[37] in the Company's name for the s[d] Lands & that he do with all possible Expedition build convenient houses & Stores[182] for the Reception of the Goods thereon.

At a Meeting of the Committee of the Ohio Company at Stafford Court house the 11th day of September 1750.

George Mercer Papers

Resolved that M:r Christopher Guist be employed to search and discover the Lands upon the River Ohio and other adjoining branches of the Missisipi down as low as the great Falls thereof and that he make a true and exact Report of the Quality and Situation of the Lands (Regard being had to the Navigation and all other particulars) to the Ohio company according to the Instructions now given him by this Committee

That the said Christopher Guist be allowed the sum of one hundred and fifty pounds, Cur:t money for making the said Discovery's (He the said Christopher Guist bearing all charges and Expences thereof) and that on his Return if it appear to the Company that his Discovery's & Services merit a larger Sum, He shall be handsomly rewarded for the same

Ordered that M:r George Mason (the Companys Treasurer) pay unto Christopher Guist the sum of thirty pounds Cur:t money to defray present Expences and that M:r Hugh Parker (the Companys Factor) supply him with Arms and Ammunition and such other things as are necessary for his Expedition for which he is to take his Receipt and transmit to the Committee with an Acco:t of the first cost.

    Copy sign'd   Thomas Lee.   Nath:a Chapman
                                                    James Scott
                                                   George Mason
                                                   Richard Lee.

Instructions given M:r Christopher Guist by the Committee of the Ohio Company the 11th day of September 1750.
    Identical with entry in Christopher Gist's Journals . . . .
    Printed on pp. 7-8.
                      Copysign'd   Nath:l Chapman
                                                    James Scott
                                                   Richard Lee
                                                   George Mason

Agreement made with Christopher Guist by the Committee of the Ohio Company the 11th day of September 1750. for the greater Encouragement of the first Setlers upon the Company's Lands.[606]

Whereas M:r Christopher Guist proposes to remove one hundred and fifty or more Family's to the Ohio Company's Land on the Branches of the Mississippi to the Westward of the great Mountains. We hereby agree and oblige ourselves that all such persons as will remove themselves to, and settle upon the said Lands contiguous to each other, within two Years from the Date hereof shall have a Fee

In the Darlington Memorial Library

simple in any Quantity of the Companys Land not exceeding fifty acres for every person they remove more than four, or one hundred Acres for every person less than four upon the following Terms.

To pay to the Ohio Company after the Rate of four pounds Sterling for every hundred Acres within three years after seating upon the Land to have their Title Deeds sign'd and acknowledged upon payment of the Consideration money. To hold their Lands five years Quit Rent free and then to pay the usual Quit Rent of Virginia. In Witness whereof We have hereunto set our Hands this 11th day of September 1750.

  Copy Sign'd James Scott Nath Chapman
         Richard Lee George Mason

At a Meeting of the Committee of the Ohio Company at Occoquon Ferry on Wednesday the 3d day of December 1750.

Ordered that the said George Mason correspond with John Hanbury Esqr concerning all matters that relate to the Company and that he apply to the Executors of the honble Thomas Lee Esqr decd for all papers relating to the Companys Affairs which are in their hands.

Resolved that it is absolutely necessary the Company should enter into more regular Articles than they have hitherto done and that the members in England should Authorize some person in Virginia to sign such Articles in their Behalf

Ordered that Mr George Mason write to Mr Hanbury on that Head, and that the said George Mason, Mr James Scott and Mr Nathaniel Chapman or any two of them apply to Mr John Mercer to consider and draw up such Articles and desire him to attend the next general meeting of the Company

At a Meeting of the Ohio Company at Stafford Court house May 21. & continued the 22d 23d & 24th days of May 1751.

Colo Thomas Cresap, one of the Executors of Hugh Parker dec'ed. having acquainted the Company that the said Hugh Parker had in his life-time charged the said Company with what he had advanced for his Share of the said Companys Stock in order to reimburse himself and vest his share in the said Company and the said Cresap declaring his consent thereto and that he could not hold the said Parkers Share as his Executor and Advance what money should be necessary from time to time for that purpose out of the said Parkers Estate which was much involved. The Company upon consideration thereof do and have hereby agreed to take and accept of the said Parkers share and to give the said Parkers Accot Credit for what he has advanced and paid upon that account.[607]

George Mercer Papers

Resolved that John Mercer of Marlborough in the County of Stafford Gent be admitted a Member of the Company and entitled to two fortieth parts or Shares of the said Companies Lands, and common Stock upon his entring into Bond to pay for the said Companies Use within twelve Months from this time his Proportion of the several Sums already advanced by the said Company

John Mercer having by the Direction of the Company prepared an Indenture with divers Covenants and Agreements to be entered into and executed by the several Members thereof for the Settling and carrying on their Copartnership, the same was read and approved of and then duly executed by Presly Thornton Richard Lee, Augustine Washington, Lawrence Washington Nathaniel Chapman, James Scott, George Mason, John Mercer, Jacob Giles, and Thomas Cresap, the ten members present and resolved that a Counter part thereof shall with all convenient speed be transmitted to John Hanbury Esq[r] in order that the same may be executed by the several Members and Partners of the said Company in Great Britain and Ireland and that the other Members living in Virginia and Maryland be forthwith applied to in order that they may execute the same, And the said John Hanbury is hereby requested to get a sufficient number thereof printed in London that every of the said partners may have a Counterpart thereof duly executed.

Resolved that George Mason Gent be appointed and continue Treasurer and Receiver of the said Company with such Powers and Authorities as are mentioned and expressed in the said Companys Articles

Resolved that Lawrence Washington Nathaniel Chapman James Scott George Mason and John Mercer be appointed a Committee for the said Company until the next General meeting.

Resolved that the Company write to M[r] Hanbury on the following Heads Vizt

To apply to the Earle of Granville . . .
> *Identical item in "Orders and Resolutions, 1749–1761."*
> *Printed on p. 142.*

That the Forts being mentioned proceeded from a misapprehension of Sir William Gooch . . .
Same.

Resolved that it will be much for the Companys Advantage to settle a plantation and Quarter on their Land at the Mouth of Wills Creek for their raising Stock and being supplied with proper Hands for the transporting their Goods and Skins by Water to and from that place and therefore that M[r] George Mason shall as soon as he can con-

In the Darlington Memorial Library

veniently purchase for the said Company's Acco$\underline{t}$ three likely able men Slaves who are used to the Countrey Business and two new Negro women upon the best terms he can for that purpose.

Resolved that it is necessary to have a Road ...
> *Identical item in "Orders and Resolutions, 1749–1761."*
> *Printed on p. 144.*

Resolved that it is necessary for the Companys Affairs to purchase a Tract of about five hundred Acres of Land belonging to Thomas Bladen Esq$\underline{r}$ ...
> *Identical item in "Orders and Resolutions, 1749–1761."*
> *Printed on pp. 142-143.*

Resolved that it is absolutely necessary that the Company should have the Nomination and appointment of a proper person ...
> *Identical item in "Orders and Resolutions, 1749–1761."*
> *Printed on p. 143.*

Resolved that upon the return of Christopher Guest it will be necessary for the Committee to meet and examine his Journal Report and proceedings with his Accounts and draw up as full and perfect a State and Report thereof as they can be laid before the next general meeting of the Company and be transmitted to the Partners in England.[608]

Resolved that the said Committee be impowered from time to time to treat of and agree upon all matters and things relating to the said Companies Affairs that may happen or arise before the next General meeting where they shall judge there is a necessity or it will be for the Companies Interest and Advantage to dispatch the same before such meeting[609]

At a Committee of the Ohio Company at the Rev$\underline{rd}$ M$\underline{r}$ James Scotts July 15$\underline{th}$ 1751.

Instructions given to M$\underline{r}$ Christopher Gist by the Committee of the Ohio Company July 16. 1751.
> *Identical with entry in Christopher Gist's Journals ....*
> *Printed on pp. 31-32.*

In Witness whereof we have hereunto set our hands the day and year above

Law$\underline{e}$ Washington
James Scott
George Mason
J Mercer

At a Meeting of the Ohio Company in Alexandria 19$\underline{th}$ of Sep$\underline{r}$ 1752. Ordered that the Committee shall make an Entery for our first two

· 175 ·

George Mercer Papers

hundred thousand Acres of Land from Kiskamonetas down the South East side of Ohio to the mouth of the big Conoway including the Land on all the branches between the abovementioned Rivers[610]

At a meeting of the Ohio Company at Stafford Court house November 22d & 23d 1752.

Resolved that Philip Ludwell Lee Nathl Chapman James Scott George Mason and John Mercer be appointed a Committee . . .
> *Identical item in "Orders and Resolutions, 1749–1761."*
> *Printed on p. 143.*

Resolved that Mr Montour be allowed thirty Pistoles . . .
> *Identical item in "Orders and Resolutions, 1749–1761."*
> *Printed on p. 143.*

Resolved that the Committee employ such Surveyors as they think proper to Survey such of the Companys Lands . . .
> *Identical item in "Orders and Resolutions, 1749–1761."*
> *Printed on p. 144.*

As the Company is inform'd that the Emperor of the Cherokees . . .
> *Identical item in "Orders and Resolutions, 1749–1761."*
> *Printed on p. 144.*

Colo Lunsford Lomax having purchased of the Executors of Lawrence Washington dec'ed the said Lawrence Washingtons Share of the Companys Lands and Stock, Resolved that the said Lunsford Lomax be admitted and received as a partner and be entitled to his two fortieth parts.[611]

At a Committee of the Ohio Company at Mr Mercers at Marlborough in Stafford County February 6th 1753.

On the Application of Mr John Pagan . . .
> *Identical item in "Orders and Resolutions, 1749–1761."*
> *Printed on pp. 144-147.*

Instructions given Christopher Gist Gent by the Ohio Company April 28th 1752.
> *Identical item in "Case of the Ohio Company." Printed on pp. 52-54.*

Given under my hand in Behalf of the said Ohio Company this 28th day of April 1752.

George Mason Treasr

Additional Instructions given Christopher Gist Gent on a Seperate Paper.[612]

Upon your Arrival at the Treaty if you find the Commissioners do not make a general Agreement with the Indians in behalf of Virginia for the Settlement of the Land upon the Waters of the Ohio and

In the Darlington Memorial Library

Mississippi or that in such Agreement there are any doubtful or ambiguous Expressions which may be prejudicial to the Ohio Company you are then to endeavour to make purchase of the Land to the Eastward of the River Ohio and Allagany and procure the Friendship and protection of the Indians in Setling the said Land upon the best Terms you can for a quantity of Goods.

You are to agree with them to deliver the said Goods at the most convenient place you can if Possible at the Forks of Mohongaly, if the Indians give you a list of Goods which they desire to be sent for in return for their Land You are to enquire and find out as near as you can the usual prices of such Goods among the Indians, that we may be as near the Sum you agree with them for as possible

You are to Engage Andrew Montour the Interpreter in the Companys Interest and get him to assist you in making a purchase of the Indians, and as the Company have great Dependance and Confidence in the said Andrew Montour they hereby not only promise to make him satisfaction for his trouble, but if he can make an Advantageous Bargain for them with the Indians they will in return for his good Offices let him have a handsome Settlement upon their Land without paying any purchase money upon the same Terms which the said Company themselves hold the Land, and without another consideration then the Kings Quit rents. If you can obtain a Deed or other written Agreement from the Indians, it must be taken in the names[613] of the Honble Robert Dinwiddie Esqr Gov'. of Virginia, John Hanbury Esqr of the City of London Mercht Capel Hanbury of the said City of London Mercht John Tayloe Presly Thornton, Philip Ludwell Lee, Thomas Lee, Richard Lee, Gawin Corbin, John Mercer, George Mason, Lawrence Washington, Augustine Washington, Nathaniel Chapman Esquires and James Scott Clerk, all of the Colony of Virginia, James Wardrop, Jacob Giles & Thomas Cresap Esqrs of the province of Maryland and their Associates Members of the Ohio Company, in the said Deed or Agreement you are to mention the Bounds of the Land as expresly as possible that no dispute may arise hereafter, and we would have the Indians clearly understand what Land they sell us, that they may have no Occasion to complain of any Fraud or underhand dealings, as is often the Custom with them

The said Ohio Company do hereby agree and oblige themselves to make you satisfaction for the Trouble and Expence you shall be at in Transacting their Affairs at the said Treaty pursuant to the Instructions by them Given you, Given under my hand in behalf of the Ohio Company this 28th day of April 1752

George Mason Treasr

If Col? Cresap has not agreed with any person to clear a Road for the Company . . .
>Identical item in "Orders and Resolutions, 1749–1761."
>Printed on p. 147.

George Mason Trasr

At a Meeting of the Committee of the Ohio Company at Stratford in Westmorland County the 25th of July 1753 & continued the 26th & 27th of the same Month

Mr Robert Carter having purchased the Shares of Col? Gawin Corbin and Col? Augustine Washington and having given Bond to the Company according to Articles it is agreed that the said Robert Carter be admitted a partner in the said Company and be entitled to the four fortieth parts formerly belonging to the said Corbin and Washington.[614]

Col? Lunsford Lomax[611] also signed and acknowledged a Bond to the Company on Account of the Share he had purchased of the Executors of Mr Lawrence Washington dec'ed.

The Committee being of Opinion that t'is highly for the Companys Advantage to endeavour to enlarge their Original Grant, and that there is no time to lie lost in doing the same, it is resolved that they do approve of the Letter and State of the Companys Case[686] now offered by Mr Mercer that the same be signed by all the Members present and transmitted to Mr Hanbury and a Copy thereof Enter'd in the Companys Books

Resolved that t'is absolutely necessary that the Company should Immediately erect a Fort . . .
>Identical item in "Orders and Resolutions, 1749–1761."
>Printed on pp. 147-148.

Mr George Mason having informed the Committee that he has wrote to Mr Hanbury for twenty swivel Guns . . .
>Identical item in "Orders and Resolutions, 1749–1761."
>Printed on p. 149.

Ordered that the Treasurer pay unto Mr Gist the sum of forty four pounds sixteen Shillings Current Money of Virginia as a satisfaction for fifty six pounds Maryland Currency paid by him for making a Road[615] from Wills Creek to Mohongaly and also the sum of Twenty pounds Current money on Account of his Journey to the Treaty at Loggs Town in May and June 1752. The Committee being of Opinion that the Allowance[616] made him by the Governor was not a sufficient Satisfaction for his trouble and expence on the said Journey

In the Darlington Memorial Library

Instructions given Mr Christopher Gist by the Committee of the Ohio Company July 27th 1753.

Whereas you have obtained a Commission from the College for surveying our Lands . . .

 Identical item in "Orders and Resolutions, 1749-1761."
 Printed on pp. 149-150.

[signed by]
      Philip Lud. Lee
      James Scott
         Comtee
      John Mercer
      George Mason

At a Meeting of the Committee of the Ohio Company November 2d 1753

Agreed and Ordered that each Member of the Company Pay to Mr George Mason their Treasurer . . .

 Identical item in "Orders and Resolutions, 1749-1761."
 Printed on p. 150.

Ordered that the Attorney or Attorneys employed to transact Business for the Company at Williamsburg be Directed to enter Caveats against the Grants, or Orders of Council for 100. Thousand 40 thousand and fifty thousand Acres of Land, to Richard Corbin Esqr & Compy the 15th day of June last past.

At a Meeting of a Committee of the Ohio Company at Mr John Mercers at Marlborough the twentieth day of December in the Year 1757, and continued the 21st & 22d days of the said month.

Ordered that a Letter be wrote to Mr John Hanbury desiring him to send the Company an Account of Sales of all the Skins and Furrs in his Hands unaccounted for and also of the Skins and Furrs shipped by Mr Christopher Gist and ordered by him to be placed to the Companys Credit[617]

At a Meeting of a Committee of the Ohio Company at Stafford Court house on Fryday the sixth day of July 1759 and continued the seventh day of the said Month

Resolved that Mr John Mercer be employed to draw up a full State of the Companys Case setting forth the Hardships We labour under and the Reasons why the Lands have not been settled and the Fort finished according to the Royal Instructions for making out our Grant and that the same be transmitted to Messrs Hanburys to lay before the proper Boards and that the Company will undertake to pay all Expences attending the same.[618]

At a Meeting of the Committee of the Ohio Company at Williamsburg on Friday the 17th of October 1760.

George Mercer Papers

M̲r̲ John Mercer having drawn up a State of the Companys Case and presented the same to the Committee

Resolved that the same be approved . . .

> *Identical item in "Orders and Resolutions, 1749–1761."*
> *Printed on pp. 150-151.*

Ordered that M̲r̲ George Mason the Companys Treasurer write to M̲r̲ Edward Athawes Mercht . . .

> *Identical item in "Orders and Resolutions, 1749–1761."*
> *Printed on p. 151.*

Resolved that the Companys Storehouse at Wills Creek be repaired[619] and put into good Order, that the Treasurer write to Colo Cresap to furnish plank and Scantlin from his Saw Mill for that purpose and that Colo George Mercer be desired and empowered to agree with Workmen to undertake the same taking Bond and Security for the performance and that the charge thereof be paid by the Treasurer on the Companys Account.

Resolved that Thomas Ludwell Lee Esq̲r̲ be chosen and appointed one of the Committee in the Room of M̲r̲ Nathaniel Chapman decd

At a Meeting of the Committee of the Ohio Company at Stafford Court house on Monday the 7th day of September 1761.

Resolved that the Honble Philip Lee Esq̲r̲ be applied to . . .

> *Identical item in "Orders and Resolutions, 1749–1761."*
> *Printed on p. 151.*

Resolved that the Committee write Messrs Hanburys and Robert Dinwiddie Esq̲r̲ informing them of our having employed M̲r̲ Charlton Palmer to transact our Business in England and desiring them to confer with him upon the Subject and give him all the Assistance and support in their power.[620]

[Letter to Governor Dinwiddie, September 9, 1761]

> *Identical item in "Orders and Resolutions, 1749–1761."*
> *Printed on pp. 151-152.*

[Signed]

We are Sir, with the greatest esteem and regard
Y̲r̲ very hble Servts

James Scott
G Mason
Committee
Thos Lud. Lee
Richard Lee

To Robert Dinwiddie Esq̲r̲
London.

Sept 9, 1761.

In the Darlington Memorial Library

[Letter to Capel and Osgood Hanbury, September 10, 1761]
Identical item in "Orders and Resolutions, 1749–1761."
Printed on pp. 152-153.

Virginia Sepr 10th 1761.

[Signed]

Gentlemen.

To Messrs Capel & Osgood Hanbury

Merchts in London.

Yr most Hble Servts
James Scott
J. Mercer
G Mason   Committee
Thos Lud Lee
Richard Lee

At a Meeting of a Committee of the Ohio Company at Stafford Court house on Wednesday the 2d day of March 1763.[621]

Resolved that about fifty Acres of the Companys Land at Wills Creek adjoining to Fort Cumberland be laid off into Town Lotts with about two hundred and fifty Acres of the adjacent high Land for out Lotts to be annexed to the Town in such manner that one such Lott shall forever belong to and be deemed an Appurtenance of the Town Lott to which it was at first annexed and on no Account seperated from it and that Colo George Mercer be impowered to lay off and dispose of the same upon the Companys Account either by Leases for three Lives with priviledge of renewing the said Leases for two lives more upon paying a fine of twenty shillings sterling for each life so renewed, or for the term of fifty years at an annual ground rent of ten shillings Sterling, or if the purchasers insist upon having a fee simple Estate in their Lotts that the said Lotts to be Sold to the highest Bidder reserving in the Deeds an Annual Ground Rent of five shillings Sterling money, that the persons who take Lotts either by Leases or Deeds be obliged to build on each Lott within three years from Their respective Titles one house at least twenty feet long and sixteen feet wide with a Brick or Stone Chimney which is always to be kept in repair under penalty of forfeiting the Lott and that no houses or buildings whatever shall be erected on the out lotts except Stables or Cowhouses and that the Usual Covenants for Distress and Re entry upon the Non payment of the reserved Rent be inserted in the said Deeds and Leases and as the Land upon which the said Lotts are to be laid off is Pattented in the name of Mr George Mason (the Companys Treasurer) the said George Mason is hereby impowered and required to execute Deeds and Leases as above mentioned to the persons purchasing and taking up the said Lotts or that he make a power of Attorney unto Colo George Mercer to execute and acknowledge the said Deeds and Leases in his name and that

John Mercer Esqr be requested to draw up a Form for the said Deeds and Leases and power of Attorney according to the abovementioned Terms.

At a Meeting of the Ohio Company at Stafford Court house on Monday July 4th 1763.

Resolved that the Company will upon the very first Notice from Colo Mercer reimburse and repay him any Sums of money which he shall judge necessary to expend in order to obtain a Grant for the Ohio Company on the terms they have now Petitioned for provided the Sum does not exceed two thousand pounds Sterling in the whole, including any money that may be advanced or raised by Charlton Palmer Esqr on this Accot[622]

[Endorsed]

Resolutions of the Ohio Company beginning October the 20th 1748 and ending July the 4th 1763.

George Mercer's Appointment and Instructions as London Agent for the Ohio Company, July 4, 1763[623]

Sir   Stafford Court House July 4th 1763

From our Knowledge of you, We trusting in your Skill, abilities & Address, do, as Members of the Ohio Company impower you to sollicit for that Company according to the following Instructions.

You are to proceed as soon as convenient to London, & upon your Arrival there communicate your Errand and Instructions to Mr Dinwiddie and Messrs Hanburys who are Members of the Ohio Company, and will assist you in every Particular for the General Advantage of the Company.

You are then to apply to Charlton Palmer Esqr our Agent with whom you are to act jointly to procure Us Leave to take up our Lands according to the Terms mentioned in our Petition[624] to his Majesty, which you now have with you; if this can not be obtained to endeavour to have us reimbursed the Money we have spent on the Faith of the late Kings former Grant to Us: If any Objections should be made to either or both of these Points you will be able fully to answer them by our state Case which Mr Palmer has, and the Papers you have with you.

It will be of great Service to Us for you to wait upon Lord Halifax and We desire you to use all possible Means to get him to be our Patron, and it will be necessary to give him a Copy of the State of

In the Darlington Memorial Library

our Case; and also at the Bottom of it a Memorandum of what we request now to be done.

You will write us we hope by every Opportunity what you have done.

At some convenient Time settle the Company's Account with Messrs Hanburys which when done inform us of, for our Guidance.

It will not be amiss in your Transactions with the great People of Business to say a great Deal in as few Words as possible, & often to them in Mind if they seem to forget Us.

We doubt not of your Oconomy in the Expences, & of your Dispatch in returning to Us; therefore wishing you Success We have the Pleasure to be   Sir
              Your real Friends &c

To Colo George Mercer	John Tayloe	J Mercer
Agent for the Ohio	Presly Thornton	Phil: Lud: Lee
Company	Lunsford Lomax	Thos Lud: Lee
		Richard Lee

[Endorsed]
Ohio Company's Instructions & Appointment, 1763.

Statement of Account of the Ohio Company with Arthur Dobbs,

1763 ^{625}

1749................£ 125....................each Share
1750................ 11:11:11..................Do
Do.................. 32:17..2..................Do..
1751................ 30:— : —.................Do
1753 Apl 7.......... 50:— : —.................Do
.... 32:8.. 2 pd in Virga £44: 9: 1 Currency at
      £ 281:17: 3

1753 Nov 2d.............................£20

 NB. Arthur Dobs has paid £200 in part of the above

  £ 125.............14 Yrs.............£ 87..10..0
    44.............13............... 28..12..0
    30.............12 .... 18.. 0..0

[Endorsed]
 Sums advanced by each Member of the Ohio Company

John Mercer to Charlton Palmer, April 17, 1764[626]

I sometime since forwarded to you a copy of the Record of the Proceedings upon the contestation of a Will between Williamson and Clifton and in November last again sent you the same under the colony seal, which I hope are come safe to hand tho' I doubt too late for Capt Dansics purposes, as by a Letter I rec'ed last week from my Son[627] dated London Jan' 25. last he complained of his not hearing from me since he went from Virginia but as he mentioned his being newly returned from Bath, I suppose the packets I sent were lying for him at Mr Athawes's where I directed them. As I am assured the Ships arrived safe at London and the Captains had a particular charge of them, I must refer you to them as to Edmundson's Dansic's and Clifton's Affairs having now scarce time to write concerning our Ohio company as upon my arrival here. I was informed Capt Walker who is to be the bearer of this was coming down the River and hourly expected in town.

When my Son Colo Mercer went from hence the committee and several other members of the company proposed furnishing you and him with Instructions relative to our grant and after we had agreed upon them I understood Colo Philip Ludwell Lee undertook upon himself to acquaint you with our resolution nor was I undeceived till September or October last before which time we were so much alarmed by the repeated accounts of the many cruel murders and ravages committed by the Indians in those parts as well as on our own frontiers[628] and the advices we receiv'd of the instructions given our governors to purchase their freindship by presents in which they were plentifully furnished with powder and ball (of which they had before by some unaccountable means provided an incredible quantity) that we were in the utmost pain for all our back-settlements, who (though we had a large quantity of powder in our magazine here) had none to defend themselves. The Indians had by some villanous correspondents, as well as the Indian traders (whom they afterwards robbed and murdered) engrossed all the ammunition in Maryland and Pensylvania by which they were enabled this last summer to do incredible mischeif and lay waste a large tract on the back of all these colonies, without mentioning the many lives lost: At the same time you may therefore suppose we must have been much surprized (to say no worse) to find by the Kings proclamation[629] that those very lands were to be reserved for these cruel butchers, and all his majesties subjects ordered to remove out of those bounds, tho' great numbers of them had purchased and obtained patents from the crown for those

In the Darlington Memorial Library

very lands they were ordered to remove from, Indeed those bounds include all the lands particularly mentioned in the instruction for our grant or grants except we should under the general terms go further Westward for it which I am persuaded no English subjects will ever venture to do in some centuries if the Indians are to possess the part assigned them by that proclamation.

 Colo Mason wrote me the 6th of last December that he had by several opportunities wrote to Mr Athawes to pay you and Colo Mercer £290 Sterling on the companies account which I suppose has been complied with since which in one of Jan' 11th last after having seen the Kings proclamation he declares his opinion to be that the proclamation was an express destruction of our grant and that we ought not to be concerned with any lands in those parts except we could have some effectual and real security, against the Indians and therefore advised that we should sollicit to be recompensed for the great trouble and expence we had been at,[630] for what has past since I must refer you to my Letter to yourself and Colo Mercer and subscribe myself

       Sir
        Your most obedt humble Servt
         J Mercer
         April 17, 1764.

[Endorsed]
Extr 1764.
 Mr Mercer's Letter to Mr Palmer dated April 17th 1764 concerning Instructions which were to have been sent to Mr Palmer & Col Mercer, with Remarks on the King's Proclamation of Octr 1763 & proposing to ask a Recompense in Lieu of the Grant of Lands, as the King's Proclamation was thought an absolute Prohibition of the Grant.
 [Endorsed] Mr Mercer's Letter to Mr Palmer

George Mason to Robert Carter, January 23, 1768[631]

Sir   Gunston Hall Janry 23d: 1768.

 The Ohio Company being informd[632] that their Case is referred by order of his Majesty in Council to the Consideration of the Governor & Council of Virginia,[633] who are to Make a Report[634] thereon, I have at the Instance of several Members, wrote to his Honour the Governor to desire the Favour of him to inform us of the purport of the sd Order,[635] & What is expected from the Company in Consequence thereof. I have taken the Liberty Sir to inclose the Letter

· 185 ·

under Cover to You, & must beg the Favour of You to make such Inquirys & procure such Copys as You think necessary for the Company's Information, as well as to forward any Answer the Governor thinks fit to favour us with.

There is to be a Meeting of the Company at Stafford Court House on Tuesday the 23d: of February next, Where We expect to have the pleasure of Your Company: I Inclose an Advertisement[636] to give Notice of it: Which You'll please to have inserted in the Virginia Gazette: one is already sent to the printer at Annapolis.

I received Your Favour of the 11th Decem.r last, & wish it was in My Power to oblige You wth: the Sum You desire; but I had some little Time before let out what Cash I had bye Me upon Maryland Bonds, with a Promise to the Gentlemen who borrowed it not to call for it soon, unless I made some large purchase: if I shou'd be lucky enough to receive any considerable Sum next Summer, I will let You know it. I beg my Compliments to Your Lady, & am Sir Yr most obdt Hble Sert

G Mason

[Addressed]
To The Honble Robert Carter Esquire, Williamsburg
[Endorsed]
Geo: Mason's Lettr recd fry 1768. 1st Letter.

John Mercer to George Mercer, December 22, 1767— January 28, 1768[637]

Dear George

I have now before me your several Letters of March 27, May 8, Sept 26 & Dec. 11, 1766 & July 8 Sept 18, 1767 being all that came to my hands since you last Left Virginia[638] & which I am now to answer, but previous thereto, as you complain in that of July 8, last of not having heard from me in 18 months before, I ought in the first place to account for that. I might acquit myself by alledging, that from your Letters, as they came to hand, I was at a Loss where to write to you, or at you, yet [as] I wou'd somehow or other, have got over that Objection, if there had been no other. But your Letter, which, to my great surprize, informed me of your Intentions of going to England, before I had an opportunity of one days conversation with you (tho I fully approved of your Resolution & Reasons) having assured me that you would not stay in England an hour longer, that was necessary to justify your own conduct & Indemnify your Securities, it could not be expected I should write any to you in England after that, of Jan. 8, which you acknowledge the receipt of. Yours of May 8 & March 27 came to my hands the same day & by the same messenger, & not before the middle of Augt but the Print & box of Politicks, with your explanatory notes mentioned in them, have never yet made their apperance. Somebody has had honesty enough to appropriate them to another purpose than you intended. But as I found by that of May 8, explained by yours to your brother to which you referred me, that your affections were engaged, I made no doubt but they would detain you long enough in England to expect an Answer wch I fully intended. your next of Sept. 26 came to my house, but at what time I can't tell, I can only say that I never saw it till June last, when posting my Law papers, I found it put up in one of the holes along with them, which I then found too late to answer. That of Decr 11, came to hand just before the April General Court, when, as the Insurers were not agreed, I directed your brother to bring a Suit to stop Copithorn's Effects here till [I] coud be satisfied whether I cou'd have justice done me at home. Yours of July last informing me that you expected to sail in August & be here in October General court arriving but just before it, you coud not expect an answer, but as your last informs me, you shall not leave England till April (& I doubt not then) I am in hopes you may receive my answer to all of them, as I shall endeavour to get the most expeditious passage for this from hence & send a duplicate by the Post (as soon as the Ice will permit it to pass) for the New York Packet.

I chose to give You this Account of all your Letters together that you might compare them with an account of my situation. My business had latterly so much encreased, together with my slowness in writing, & Rogers, tho a tolerable good clerk, was so incapable of assisting me out of the common road, that when you saw me at Williamsburg, I was reduced, by my fatigue, to a very valetudinary State, which you may believe the succeeding winter very little contributed to releive, in fact, it encreased to that degree, that it was with great difficulty I could prepare my papers for carrying on my business in the general court, which, though your brother had undertaken to carry on, yet he coud not do without my assistance, & which was the more necessary, as his failing in any of my business for want of Proper instructions, might ruin his own business & credit, whereas his acquiting himself, with a good degree of reputation, under such a load of business, as he had upon his hands, would add greatly to both, & which, I can with pleasure assure you was his case; but this I was obliged to do myself, Rogers contriving to stay & keep my carriage in town & on the road a fortnight after I got home; as he was ashamed to see me, he staid no longer on the plantation, than to tell them he was so much out of order, that he must go to his own house till he got well; he went & I have never seen him since. However I stuck so constantly to business, without proper exercise, that on the 23d of Septr I was obliged to take to my bed, your papers to carry down to the general court, but tho I was for a day or two capable of talking to him, tho unable to get up & assist him, my distemper grew so violent that Doctor Mercer[639] woud not suffer anybody to speak to me. In this Situation Jemmy[640] was obliged to enter my office where, thro' Roger's neglect my papers were in the worst order they ever had been in, & forced to tumble over again & again for the papers he wanted. I don't know when he went away, but was told that when he did so, it was without the least expectation of ever seeing me again, as I had been several days under a strong delerium & had the rattles. It however pleased God, with Doctor Mercer's[639] assistance, tho he had given me over, to restore me to my family, contrary to all expectation; but such a severe schock, in the condition I was, coud not at once be repaired, I mended a good deal in November, but in the beginning of December got cold, attended with a fever which in sometime fell into my left leg & at length affected both. Tho I looked upon this as a trivial matter yet I have since found by experience it was a very serious one, as I have been several times confined to my bed for some days by them. The Governor very kindly (as I am satisfied it was so intended) advised your brother to dissuade me from drying up the humour, but as I was satisfied my constitution was not yet so far impaired as to require the assistance of Issues, I determined to get them well as soon as I cou'd, but through impatience & scratching, I lengthened out their cure till about a month ago. About the last of October past I was again alarmed with a cold & fevers, but calling Dr Mercer in time to my assistance I not only got clear of them, but recovered such a State of health, that I think I may safely aver that I have not been in a better one any time these twenty years past, & tho I am not so young, my youngest daughter (who is christned Mary, Elinor Beatrix, after two dead & one living, Aunts) was born the 20th day of last January. So that I have still six young children to provide for. Your Sister Fenton has got a better person to take that care off my hands, she got the start of you, being married on the ninth day of July last to Mr Muscoe Garnett of Essex county, a match every way so agreeable to me that I solemly declare I dont know one that coud have offerd in Virginia or Maryland that I shoud have preferr'd before it, & tho she then seem'd indifferent, I am very much mistaken, if she

In the Darlington Memorial Library

is not now as well pleased with it as I am. He is in possession of a very large fortune, of an agreeable person, good natured, sober, industrious, well acquainted with his plantation affairs, & I think I may venture to affirm, entirely clear of every modest Vice. My wife & I went to visit them last month & staid in Essex a fortnight, where we had the pleasure to find that they live very genteely, & what is better very happily with every prospect of being an happy & very affectionate couple; they are now here, & I have had the happiness this Christmas to have all my children, except you & your brother James, together. I did not mention that Mr Garnett did not enquire about her fortune, a thing, in my circumstances, very material, tho I solemnly declare that had not the least weight in obtaining my consent (tho a strong indication of his affection) which I woud not have given to a man of the greatest fortune with whom I beleived she would be unhappy.

This naturally leads me to give you a very disagreeable account of the situation the distresses of the countrey have reduced me to. The purchase of about 40 Negroes to enable me to make Grain sufficient to carry on my brewery with my own hands swelled the Expence of that scheme to about £8000, a large part of which was unpaid, for payment of which I depended on the Brewery itself & the great number of Debts due to me. But the late Treasurer's[641] death threw the whole countrey into a flame as it was quickly discovered that there was £100,000 deficient in the Treasury; as a great part of it was lent out, I am persuaded that had proper measures been taken, & the Debtors & Creditors been called together, matters might have been so settled that a very great part of the deficiency might have been set off & discounted among them to mutual advantage, but a direct contrary method was fallen upon, many people were loud to procure Justice for the Public, & among them, some who were suspected to have shared part of the money, for it was soon known that the Treasurer had kept no books or such bad ones, as to his own private affairs (& indeed those of the Treasury were greatly complained of) that his Admrs cou'd not discover, what debts were due to him (he died in a happy time I should have said lucky, the secret which must have ruined his credit & broke his heart was undiscovered & I beleive unknown to him) but from the discovery made by his Admrs from such bonds as were found & his loose papers, among which it was found endorsed on an old Letter a memorandum that he had lent Colo B . . .d[642] £15,000. This occasioned the Admrs to threaten all the Debtors with Suits & as there was no money in the Merchts & Hucksters hands, the Gazettes were filled wth Advertisements of Lands & Negroes to be sold, which however cou'd not be done but upon credit, in which case there are many people still thoughtless enough to contract debts, without any prospect, I beleive I may say, without any thought, of paying them. But the mischeif did not stop here, it alarm'd the Merch^ts and every body else that had money due to them & they brought & threatened to bring Suits, so that, to add to the misfortune, the debts will be encreased many thousand pounds by Law charges. Among the rest of the Treasurer's Debtors, the Adm^rs threaten'd Mr Ja^s Hunter, as my Security, with a Suit in the Court of York or the Hustings, where they might get a Judgment against him in two or three months, but as he insisted that by the words of the bond, there was to be twelve months notice given before any suit could be brought, they told him that the Treasurer had given him notice in April 1765. That he told them he admitted, but that he could prove (& he beleived some of themselves, Peter Randolph, Pendleton & Lyons knew it of their own knowledge.) that after you arrived in the October court, the speaker told him not to regard that notice for that he had agreed to discharge me & my Securities & to take you & your brother as his paymasters, that as you had met such a disappointment he would wait for his money till you coud pay him. Pendleton upon this applied to your brother, who told him that as he did not know when you wou'd be in, but was sensible the money must be paid among us, he would talk to me, & we shou'd fall upon some measures to raise it as expeditiously as the circumstances of the countrey wou'd admit, in consequence of which when he talk'd with me & told me that he intended to sell his Lands & negroes (reserving only the church quarter & his household slaves) & to stick wholly to his practice (which his plantation affairs greatly interrupted) We agreed to advertise his & my parts of the Shannondoah & Bull run lands with his Slaves, the sale of which he fixed to be this month. But as such an Advertisement might alarm our very good friends, Col^o Tayloe & Col^o Thornton, I agreed to execute a Release to them of the bond they had given me as Securities for your & his paying £3000 of my debts.[643]

I have mentioned my expectation of discharging my debts by those due to me & my brewery, how they failed I am now to inform you. I did not apprehend Mr King's death (of which I informed you at Williamsburg) to be so great a loss as I have since found it. I had contracted with one Wales, a young Scotch Brewer, recommended to me by Col^o Philip Lee, who, before Mr King's arrival, had put me to £100 Expence to alter my malt house (which Mr King assured me was done to great disadvantage, but as Wales affirmed that he had some years the charge of a brewhouse at Edinburgh & could brew as good beer as Mr King, I was on his death, inclined to trust him; he

In the Darlington Memorial Library

had began to malt, but before he had brewed any, one Bailey arrived with a Letter of Recommendation from Wadman, in which he informd me that upon hearing of his Uncle King's death, & expecting it would disappoint me of brewing that Season, he had sent a boat and hands on board a Ship in which Bailey had taken his passage to England & prevailed on him to return & take charge of my brewery, assuring me that from 14 years acquaintance, that he was as capable as his Uncle King to comply with the contract he had made with you & which King had shown him, & for further Satisfaction referred me to Colo Tayloe's recommendation which was in these terms.

The Bearer Wm Bailey served me five years upon high wages as a gardener, in which time he brewed me as good beer as I would wish to drink & it was preferred by some gent, of distinction & good taste to very good Burton & other English ales I had at the same time. I beleive he understands every part of brewing &c and I know him to be a most obliging orderly well behaved man of strict honesty, virtuous principles & pious disposition being a constant communicant. He left my service from choice & I shoud be glad to know him so well fixed, as in your business, to which I cordially wish Success with the sincerity of a real friend &c

You may readily believe I did not hesitate to employ Bailey on such a recommendation, more especially as he agreed with King in blaming the alteration of the malt house & besides found great fault with Wales's malting, Wales on the other hand insisted that he coud make as good beer from his malt as Bailey could from any of his making & desired he might brew his own as he supposed if Bailey was to brew it, he would to justify the bad character he had given it, spoil the beer, this I thought reasonable & Bailey agreed to it, yet though Bailey found as much fault with Wales's brewing as he did with his malting, that brewed by Wales was the only beer I had that Season fit to drink, though Bailey brewed as much, as, if good, would have sold for £500, he carried a small Schooner's load of it to Norfolk & lodged it with one Mr Hepburn there for sale, who after some months wrote me that he had sold but two casks & as the charge of storage was running on & he could sell no more from its bad character, desired I would send for it, if I thought it worth while. I did so, as I expected I coud make something by distilling it, but there I was again disappointed & the whole besides my trouble was lost. The quantity brewed by Wales was so small that it barely paid his wages of £40 & the charge of his & his wive's maintenance was so much out of my pocket, Thus my brewery for 1766 instead of discharging any part of my debts, encreased them: that for 1767 turn'd out very little better, my crop of barley according to my brewer's accot produced but 550 bushels of malt, a considerable part of the beer & ale proved bad, which Wales excused by alledging great part of the barley sprouted in the field as we had an extreme wet harvest. I had however in order to provide a sufficient quantity of barley against the next season sown 550 bushels. But as I was rather a loser than gainer by brewing the 550 bushels & Wales not only rece'd his wages but had his own & his wive's maintenance clear, I let him know that I was determined not to continue my brewery any longer upon such terms, he thereupon proposed to be answerable for any beer or ale that shou'd prove unmerchantable in consideration of being allowed five percent of the net proceeds of all that was sold over and above what was used in the family & have a dozen casks for your brother, Mr Selden & our Parson. As I those those terms reasonable I accepted them & was in hopes to have a very beneficial brewery the present year, but as for some years I have met nothing but disappointments, my expectation of making ten thousand bushels of barley (which I insist was no unreasonable one, if proper care had been taken in sowing reaping & getting it in) has failed & I am now told I shall not have two thousand & not above one half of that malted & a great part not threshed. What is brewed is, I beleive very good & I should be satisfied if I have 2000 bushels of malt as it wou'd turn out near £800. Wales complains of my Overseer & says that he is obliged to wait for barley, coals & other things that are wanted which, if timely supplied with he could with six men & a boy manufacture 250 bushels a week which would clear £200. In short, I find that the brewery cannot be carried on to effect without appropriating a proper number of hands to provide everything wanted in due time. I have land & hands enough & all Necessaries to carry it on to the utmost extent. My Overseer is a very good one & I beleive as a planter equal to any in Virginia, but you are sensible few planters are good farmers & barley is a farmer's article. Your brother is extremely prejudiced against the brewery, he says there are many articles to be provided, that if any of them fail, the whole must, but in that he is manifestly mistaken. If barley is made I know no other necessary article but hops that can fail, if mine should tho I shall have enough in a seasonable year to answer my own wants, there are enough to be procured all over the continent, his next objection extends to every thing else but his favourite article wheat, he says when my beer is made I must trust it out, & the pay for it, will come in (for want of cash circulating) like Lawyers fees whereas wheat is a ready money article with the merchants & merchant mills, who will contract for it, for a certain number of years, he instanced Colo Washington, who he said he understood, made 8000 bushels last year with 20 hands under a contract with Col͟o Tucker. If he did not expect cash would in sometime circulate, he has made a bad choice for a Livelihood in depending upon Lawyers fees for one. I think beer & ale are much more likely articles to produce Cash when it does circulate. It is affirmed that Virginia imports beer & ale to the am͟t of upwards of £30,000 Sterl. yearly (which is more than ten such breweries, as mine, coud brew) little of what is imported is sold by any ordinary keep͟r who cannot import it on his own account, as there is little to be got by it, when purchased here whereas mine at 10ᵈ & 15ᵈ a gallon, to which I have reducᵈ it upon the fall of exchange, will afford every ordinary keeper, as much, if not more, profit, than any other liquor he sells. As you know how much our Ordinaries abound & daily encrease (for drinking will continue longer than anything but eating) it will open a large field, as I imagine in a little time their consumption would equal, if not exceed our present imports. That price (exclusive of risque) is less than I beleive beer & ale can be imported for, then I affirm that barley is much easier raised & yeilds a much greater encrease than wheat, & that every bushel of barley will yeild more profit than a bushel of wheat does among the contractors, for if I did not misunderstand your brother, Col͟o Washington is determined to fling up his contract (Tucker being dead insolvent) & fall upon something else, so that I beleive your brother must have been misinformed as to Washington's making such a crop last year, as I don't know any other he can make equal to it. However I have been persuaded by your brother & some others, contrary to my own Judgment, to suffer my overseer to make a trial of some wheat this fall. I wish it may not turn out like my last barley crop, but stipulated that at least so much barley should be sown, as wou'd afford me seed, if I was encouraged to resume my brewery, & brew for the family use, that they may have drink with their victuals, tho I may not be able to make cloaths enough. You may think me very tedious on this article, but it concerns me greatly, as I have expended so much money upon it, as would make me now perfectly easy & contented if I had it in my pocket, besides the additional expence & improvements to those I had formerly made on 52 acres of land, have rendered them unsaleable, if I shoud be reduced to the most necessitous circumstances, for a tenth part of what they cost me, unless the brewery is prosecuted which in my firm opinion, woud quickly retrieve all my losses & misfortunes, that mine shoud alone fail, when such estates have been made by them on every other part of the British dominions in Europe, & even in every province of America where they have been attempted, must seem incredible. The only objection can with reason be started against me is, that I shoud not have advanced such a Sum at once, but proceeded by degrees & carried it on hand in hand with our usual plantation affairs which might have contributed to the expence & enabled me to encrease it yearly, as Woodford & Fras Thornton have done, for it seems they, not deterred by my misfortunes, are attempting the same by degrees. Woodford who brews himself, says that for these two or three years, since he began to brew to the value of £100 or 150 a year without any great prejudice to his other plantation affairs, that what he can brew in his small copper is bespoke before he brews it, & he could dispose of much more if he coud make it. Fra Thornton, I suppose, encouraged by Woodford's success & my disappointmt has commenced brewer this year at the falls tho I imagine he has no copper, or only a very small one, as Mr Jas Hunter informed me that for want of a good one, he had bought two or three of Mr Dick's crackd potash kettles, which he purchased at the price of old iron, as it seems that after the smallest crack they will not do for potash, but will boil any thing else, yet from such beginnings I doubt not but their profits will induce them to extend them in time to considerable breweries. My rule has always been that every thing I attempted ought to be set about in earnest & not carried on by peicemeal my business & practice prevented my superintending it, without which I am now satisfied no business will prosper: All was therefore entrusted to overseers, they were supplied with every thing they demanded, as I neither wanted money or credit, and fatally beleived, till the cussed Stamp act year that, I never shoud want either; that undeceived me & the deceit appeared more plainly every day, my situation prevented me from discovering the circumstances I was in till it was out of my power to retrieve them, my Overseer was discharged by Mr King. I was recommended to one Mr Monroe who promised me at the general court to come & take charge of my plantation; he had for some years managed Mr McCarty's estate to great advantage during his minority, but as he had himself removed to his plantation & thought he was capable to manage his own affairs & that it would be a good amusement & he should save the expence of an head overseer, he joined in recommending Mr Monroe to me. When I returned home I expected to have found him there but was disappointed. Mr McCarty's friends dissuaded him from parting with him, but upon my writing to Mr McCarty & insisting upon Mr Monroe's engagement he came over & promised to come after the Christmas holidays, your brother and Mr Selden having not without difficulty, agreed with him for £90 a year. I waited for him with impatience till the 16th of Jan. when he came up & found but 8 barrels of corn upon my plantation, not enough at any of my Quarters to maintain my people, a great part of my Stock dead (among them some of my English colts & horses in the 2 last years to the amo of £375.10.—) & the rest of them dying, which would infallibly have been their fate if it had not been for the straw of 1000 bushels of barley & the grains from the brewhouse, which, except the corn & a little wheat was the only article made the preceding year at all the plantations tho there were exactly 100 tithables on them. In short I was obliged to buy above £100 worth of corn & shoud have been obliged to buy as much more, if Mr Monroe had not planted a great many pease & other things besides 3000 lb of Rice which I got from Norfolk & proved much cheaper than corn at 12/6 ℔ barrel. Convinced of his integrity & regard to my interest, unable to attend to any other affairs myself than those I have mentioned, I have been forced to submit the entire management of all the plantation affairs to him, but a difference arising between him & Wales this last year has been of great disadvantage to me. He intended to have left me last year & was difficultly persuaded to stay. I cant yet tell whether he will continue another, he told your brother in October that he would not, having a good plantation of his own & several negroes, on which your brother proposed to get me an overseer from Jas river among the farmers, but having failed in that, Mr Monroe has since given me some reason to think he may stay. If he does, I have thro the doubt & perplexity I have been in, so poor a crop that I must endeavour to piece it out as well as I can, he is very fond of tending tobacco & says he could make 50 or 60 hhds besides grain. Had I known a little sooner that Semple would give £12 a year for men & £8 for women, besides cloathing them, paying their levies & taxes & allowing them 6 lb of meat a week, it is certain he shoud have had mine, as I shoud by their hire have made more without care charge or trouble, than I coud by any crop they can make. I have been the longer upon this subject, because if I am not mistaken you approve of the brewery & I beleive you must be satisfied that with care & perserverance it woud in time turn out to as great, if not greater advantage than any thing I coud fall on to employ my own people about, every thing now is completely fixed. I used to be obliged to wait for grinding my malt, when I depended on my windmill, but I have now a hand mill fixed in my brewhouse loft that will grind 50 bushels of malt (my coppers complement) every morning they brew. I can make my barley & hops, have coopers of my own, & beleive some of my own negroes coud coud malt & brew tho I shoud choose to employ an expert brewer &

malster. Surely with so many advantages it is impossible I shoud fail, if I persevere, & I cant with patience think of giving them up & losing all my expences; it is or shoud be, with such advantages, in my power to undersell all who shoud interfere with me, & had not equal advantages, but as I have observed there is & will be a demand for more than can be brewd here in sometime tho I doubt not that some years hence the countrey will be supplied wholly with beer & ale brewed here, to make my brewery complete, bottles are wanting & vessels to carry & deliver the beer, these I was in hopes to have been able to have compassed them myself, but as I find it otherwise I should be glad to take in a partner upon reasonable terms which would enable me to fix every thing on a proper & sure footing. A Glass house to be built here must I am satisfied turn to great profit, they have some in New England & New York or the Jerseys & I find by some resolves the New England men are determined to encrease their number. The vessels would be hired out to the shipping when they were not wanted for the brewery. As to the terms of a partnership I should be satisfied with the advance of £2500 Sterl (the repaymt of which should be secured to Satisfaction) during the partnership, which I would not have to exceed 5 or 7 years) the Interest of which is in lieu of rent for his moiety of the brewhouse, malthouse, which are of brick & stone each 100 feet long, Cellars, Cooper's house & all the buildings, copper & utensils whatsoever, used about the brewery, all which are in good repair, indeed they have been so lately built, they can't be otherwise, but if any thing is objected to, it shall be put into good order at my Expence. As to every thing else, it is to be carried on at the joint expence, except my partner should send in a Person to look after his interest, whom he ought to pay, but, in that case, I would let him have a neat warm house, which I built for Mr Wales & his wife, without paying any rent; but if you & he should agree to employ a Person to malt & brew, I will pay a moiety of his wages. As to the hands wanting to carry on the brewery, I will supply any number at the same price I can hire such to other people or take the same price Semple now gives, a moiety of which he must pay me. As to Barley & hops I will undertake to furnish the quantity wanted not exceeding 8000 bushels of barley & hops in proportion, the barley at 3s currt hops at ⅓ the current price equal to 2/4 9/10 & 1/. Sterl. If he should choose to supply his moiety of the barley & hops if as good a quality as mine, I woud not object to it. It may be proper to mention, tho you must know it, that beer & ale in Virginia is sold by the only measure used here, that is, wine measure. People conversant in brewing are able to calculate the profit, when they know the price of barley & hops. I don't mention cask, because a penny a gallon is allowed separately for that article which I would supply on those terms, or if he would allow the moiety of £20 a year for each of the two coopers wages & a moiety of their maintenance & the cost of the staves, hoops &c he may have a moiety of their produce. If bottles could be sent in cheap in good hampers, the profit would be such encreased & as I am sure the Brewery might be greatly extended in a little time, another copper might be set up & a glass house undertaken, I am sure to the greatest advantage, which is the principal reason of my insisting on such an advance, the profit would encrease in proportion. It is impossible at this distance to foresee or answer objections but as I can rely on you I woud willingly comply with any terms you shall think proper to enter into on my account, if you meet any body willing to engage in it, remembering that the advance is the one thing necessary, for I have so great a dislike to all partnerships, nothing but my inability to carry it on my self coud induce me to enter into one. But to demonstrate that it is purely for the sake of carrying on my brewery & establishing it, I would rent out all my houses and conveniences at a reasonable rent, & the person or compy who took it might carry on the brewery as they thought proper by importing malt, as they did long at Philadelphia & New York, tho I think it might be made cheaper here, & in that Case I woud rent them as much land & as many hands as they wanted, which woud be cheaper & better than any they coud bring or send in, except a principal brewer & malster, or I would contract to supply a quantity of barley yearly at the price mentioned. They would have the trade open without any competitor & you can point out well how Marlborough is situate for it. But as I have been at such an immense expence, I must have £2500 Sterl in advance out of which I woud discount the rent & everything I supplied them with, which shoud be as cheap as any body. Malt shoud be imported the first year or till a quantity coud be provided here. I am but just now told that Ben Grymes & Dansie are entering into a partnership to carry on a brewery at Fredericksburg, it must surely be a very extraordinary one as it is to be done without money or credit. Grymes after bringing our very good friend Colo Thornton to be bound for him for so many thousand pounds that Colo Thornton has publickly declared he must be obliged to sell all his estate below, removed himself to Williamsburg, gave up all his Estate which is to be sold in May, but it was so involved by prior mortgages that Colo Thornton will get a very small part of it; he has got a very proper partner in Dansie, as I dont think there is a greater villain breathing: After serving him every way in my power for above 15 years greatly to my own prejudice he is endeavouring to cheat me, as he has done every body, I beleive, that ever trusted him. I bought about 20 negroes from him, for which I paid & was bound for him to more than their value & tho I have had them three years, in possession he now denies the sale & pretends I hired them, but what Mr James Hunter knows of the affair, with some Letters of his own & his wife (who has discovered herself to be as vile a woman as he is a man) will, I make no doubt expose their villany.

I come now to money affairs. I reced in 1764 £1548..4..3½ & in 1765 £961..5..4½ but since I quitted my practice I reced in 1766 no more than £108..16..1 of which I borrowed £24.10.— & 7..1..6 was re'ced for the Governor's fees. £20..8..4 I got for Opinions &c and from the brewery £28..3.. the remaining £28..16.. is all I received out of several thousands due for all my old & new debts. In 1767 I reced £159..9..3 of which borrowed £5..15..— the governor's fees £10..7..6 reced for opinions &c £49..6..— from the brewhouse £66..14..— the remaining £27..6..9 for debts. The two years receipts deducting the money borrowed & the governors fees amounting to no more than £221..1..4 of which £94..14..3 was from the brewery & (in 1766 I gave a collector £20 besides his board ferrage & expences & finding him horses & his whole collection during the year turned out to be £27..2..10. In the two years my taxes levied and quit rents amounted to £199..8..1 which would have left a ballance of £1. 13. 3 in my favour in that time from the brewery & my practice (if it could be so called) & all my debts, in great part of which you and your brother are jointly & equally interested. What then remained to support me & a family consisting of about 26 white people & 122 negroes? Nothing but my crops, after that I had expended above £100, for corn only to support them, besides rice & pork to near that value & the impending charge of £125 for rent, of £140 to overseers yearly, remained, & £94..14..3 out of those crops, as I have already mentioned, proceeding from the brewery, was swallowed up in taxes (tho the people in England say we pay none, but I can fatally prove that my estate from which I did not receive sixpence has, since the commencement of the war paid near a thousand pounds in taxes only) So that you must be satisfied there could be nothing left to pay any debts after cloathing my people (which was not done but on most extravagant terms, the merchants notwithstanding the fall of exchange 40 ℔ Cent in December 1765 keeping up their very bad goods at the same exorbitant prices they sold them when the exchange was at the highest) This being a true state of the case you must be satisfied that I have been reduced to the strictest oeconomy indeed

In the Darlington Memorial Library

almost to the want of necessaries, I should have said cloaths, for victuals & drink I thank God, we have not wanted, & it is not probable that we ever shall, & few cloaths woud have served myself, as I seldom go abroad. I was however reduced to Doctr Franklyn's account of our situation, & obliged to wear my old cloaths over again & must in them have made my visit into Essex, if your brother had not very unexpectedly sent me up a new suit from Williamsburg just before I set off. As he knew of the Journey, & my condition I suppose he was ashamed of it, tho I was not, but that expedient would not answer with my wife & children, the last especially, as they grow very fast & don't take much care of their cloaths. I am satisfied you will find them grown out of your knowledge. Roy being as tall as I am; however in the depth of my difficulties (which I dont yet doubt, by the assistance of divine providence, to get clear of) my children afford me the greatest satisfaction. You & your brother are I bless God, in such a situation, as should satisfy me, especially if you should receive an adequate recompence for the time you lost in the army & your tedious attendance in England. Your sister Selden is happily settled. Your sister Fenton's behaviour, very deservedly, acquired her such a character very early as left me no doubt of procuring her such a match as would make her happy, & which has succeeded so as not to disappoint my warmest wishes. My six youngest children are such as I woud wish them and I have the pride or vanity (if it deserves that name) to beleive they cannot be exceeded, if matched, by any six children, of their ages, of any father in his British Majesties dominions; and as their parts seem to be as promising as their persons, I shoud not doubt if I could give them a proper education, tho I coud not give them fortunes, they might be able to make their way in the world. The girls might do very well under their mother's direction, but the boys cannot do without a Tutor. Roy & Jack have made a greater proficiency than coud have been expected from the opportunities they have had, [if] indeed Jack can be said to have had any. I sent Roy to the Revd Mr Bouchier in Caroline & proposed to have sent Jack (who was then too small) the next year, but Roy being taken sick and sent home & having a great disinclination to return, that scheme was disappointed, and tho I have endeavoured all in my power, & your brother advertised last general court for a tutor I have hitherto failed. The advertisement procured several applications, your brother rec'ed the following which I could not help sending you an exact copy of,
Sir

    I see by the Papers that you want a Teacher who understands the

Mathematicks and if you can wait about 8 Months I shall if Life & Health permit then be at your service if you are not supplied before and we can agree. And as I have always Born a great Character where ever I have Tawght and am Capable of Teaching Arithmetick as far as 30 Rules beyond the Single Rule of Three Direct as likewise Plane and Mercators Sailing by the Meridional parts and how to turn all Sides of any Plane Right Triangle Radius with the Nature of the Theorems used in Oblique Plane Triangles with a great Variety of Geographical & Astronomical Problems all of which I shall be able fully to make appear when I come down I hope you will not Notice my mean Writing. And as I am at a great Distance I should be glad you would let me know by the first opportunity whether it will be worth my while to come down or not and you will greatly oblige your Humble Servant now Teaching School at Mr Burgess Walls near the Mouth of Wagua Creek in Brunswick County.

Joseph Barker

P. S.   If I come I shall bring a great Character from under the Hands of Several Gentlemen for whom I have tawght.

Among others a Scotch schoolmaster of John Graham's recommended a young countreyman of his, to whom he gave a great character, who he said, he woud engage should come in, if I woud employ him. Their stated wages I beleive you know is £20 a year which I imagine is the great inducement to so many of our countreymen to send for & employ so many of them in that way, but they generally have a parish in view at the end of the time contracted for & so many have succeeded that way that I am persuaded none now come abroad but in full assurance of one. Tho I must own myself prejudiced against them, yet I shoud have agreed that Graham's schoolmaster should have wrote for his friend if your last letter had not informed me that you shoud not leave England till April. I have known several of them who understood & were capable of teaching the latin Authors, some of them Greek (whose language was so uncouth that Catesby Cocke used to swear they translated one strange language into a Stranger, & I have known some of them who understood the mathematicks, but I never knew one of them who upon his first arrival did not surprize the company he was introduced to by his awkward & unpolished behaviour. They are almost to a man bred Presbyterians & tho none of them scruple to become Episcopalians for a Parish, their religion is to be much questioned I mean whether they have any or no, for it is very certain I have known some without either religion or morals, & I attribute it to George Mason's tutor that I have long doubted with a good deal of concern, that he had very little improved in either. My opinion of a Tutor, is, that besides instructing his pupil in such branches of learning as he is designed for, he should also be particularly careful of his Religion, morals & behaviour, in short he shoud be a gentleman his knowledge in the mathematicks I should prefer to Greek Hebrew or any other learned languages, which would be of little use here whereas the other is of the greatest use not only here but every where else & may enable a man of ingenuity to make his fortune in any part of the world. As therefore I am satisfied that upon a proper enquiry many might be found in England who woud fully answer my purpose & who might by it better their own situation, I am to inform you that you cannot lay a greater obligation upon myself, my wife & our children than by taking some pains to procure us as good a tutor as you can get, the terms I must wholly submit to yourself but you may assure him from us that he will be treated as a gentleman & that no extraordinary care he may take with his young pupils will be overlooked, but will meet with a suitable return & regard. What I mean by that you may hint at; his principal pupil will be Roy who, notwithstanding his growth, was but 14 last Sept. Jack will be 9 next May, Anna 7 last Sept. Maria 6 last Dec^r & Robert 3 at the same time, the youngest can expect no benefit from his instruction during the time of his contract which ought not to be for less than four years. Now without insisting on the surprizing progress of the child in France of five years old that the publick prints mention. I have my self known & heard of some children who have been, very young, brought on by proper instruction very surprisingly (George Johnston of Alexandria's son was one instance) I agree more than ordinary care and perhaps patience may be requisite, but I must be beleive[d] it would have a good natured man the greatest satisfaction to find his pains had taken a proper effect, & I am persuaded my son Jack might by that means improve very fast. My children, to my great interruption choose to write before they know their letters. I cant quit my pen & ink & leave the room ever so short a time but one or other of them take that advantage to improve their talents. Jack could write his name very prettily in print characters, after a copy, before he learned his Letters & took a strong turn to drawing any thing he saw, he now writes so well, from some copy books that he challenges his brother Roy, & this last year I having a Survey of the Neck which lasted a fortnight & which Jack was very desirous of attending, Mr Brent or some other generally carried him behind them. I never perceived that he took any particular notice of what passed, till to my great surprize I found that after it was over he set abot drawing a plat of it, which you will agree, when you see it, has many things very remarkable in it & such as coud hardly be beleived a child of his age coud have done, without communication with or instruction from any person whatsoever, for he had set about it privately, & just finished it, when his bro. Roy surprizd him took it away & brought it to me. Bob has for some time began to apply his talents that way, but is obliged to do it by stealth, as when he applies to me, I refuse to let him have a pen & ink, therefore, as if he determined you shoud have a proof of his inclinations he contrived to scribble the superscription of his sister Selden's letter, which she delivered me to inclose to you tho we were both in the room. I have mentioned my own children, besides which there are three others, a boy not yet seven & two girls younger, for whose education with my children, I am very much concernd, they are the children of Mr Thos Hill deced by my wive's youngest sister, a very deserving & agreeable widow whom he has left in very indifferent circumstances, as she was obliged to sell a great many of his negroes to pay his debts, I mention them all particularly, that the person you engage may not pretend, as Mr Phipps did that tho' he undertook to instruct my children he intended boys only, & I or my wife might teach the girls. As I have mentioned Phipps, it must remind you that a tutor's good nature & agreeable temper are absolutely necessary both for his own ease & that of the whole family. I am confident if you meet such an one, he will live in the family very comfortably & find every body in it disposed to render his situation easy & agreeable. I need not say more on the subject. I have already said so much that you perceive how much I have it at heart. It is indeed the only thing that can make the latter part of my life happy. I have passed forty years of it, thro' a greater multiplicity of business & had more clients than I am persuaded any one man ever did in the same time or perhaps in his life, in another month I shall have passed my grand climacteric, and, I thank God, without gout stone or any other distemper, and if it was not for my wife & children I can truly say that tho in a perfect state of health & with the use of all my faculties (except hearing) I coud be perfectly content, if it pleased God, to quit the Stage at the end of that period, but as I am like to live several years yet, & indeed the welfare of my wife & children much depends upon it, I shall look upon myself as commencing a new Era & begin it by settling all my accounts & getting out of debt, as soon as possible, if to be done no other way by selling as much of my estate as will do it, for I yet have more than enough to do all the world justice. When that is done and I can say what I have is my own (however little that may be) I shall then & not till then, think myself happy. I have sometime, on account of my deafness, refused to act as a Justice, which I shoud not have done otherwise, as I have the satisfaction to know that I have done my county some service in that station, & I hope to be soon rid of my old causes, I shall then have nothing to do, but live quietly at home & if I get a good tutor for my children can enjoy my wife & family, & tho perhaps not in superfluity, yet with what is infinitely more desirable with satisfaction & content. We have these two years sufferd so much that I am sure my wife is as well inclined, as I am, to use all the frugality & oeconomy that can be commendable for the good of our children, & shall still be able to apply to some business that will contribute to our support & for the rest trust to that Providence that never failed us.

You will now think it high time I shoud come to the answer of your letters, that of the advice of the repeal of the stamp act was, as you expected extremely agreeable to me & every one of your friends to whom it was communicated, & your behaviour much approved of, except in the Lee family, which occasioned some bickerings in the public papers which probably might as well have been let alone, but as your brother thought your character reflected on, his regard to you, engaged him to enter the lists: his antagonist was backed by so many anonymous scoundrels, that I was drawn in during his abscence at the springs in Frederick to answer I did not know whom tho it since appears Dr Arthur Lee was the principal, if not the only assassin under different vizors, & he was so regardless of truth that he invented & published the most infamous lies as indisputable facts: on your brother's return I got out of the scrape but from a paper war it turned to a challenge, which produced a skirmish, in which your bro. without receiving any damage broke the Doctors head, & closed his eyes in such a manner as obliged him to keep his house sometime; the Doctor's second, one Griffin, a boy of six feet high, who, after beating at old Flood's mortar, went to London & returnd soon after, calling himself Doctor, tho not yet F. R. S. in bro. Doctor's vindication published a partial account of the challenge, which was understood as a second one. I don't beleive your bro. was to be intimidated by this overgrown bully, but his friends insisted that he shoud not take any further notice of it than to publish a true account of the affair, which he did, & many of the most material parts of it was confirmd by unexceptionable witnesses. The F. R. S. Doctor, whose pride woud not permit him to acquiesce took such liberties with some of the gent. of the town who took your brother's part, as gave general offence, in so much that they burn'd him in effigy before his own door, & if he had confind himself to his house it is very probable that they woud have tossed him into the fire. In short he has lost his credit (if he had any to lose) and, what I dare say he values much more, his practice is much hurt, as will very probably dwindle to nothing as his immoderate pride & self-conceit will not suffer him to open his eyes & see how much, how very much, he is fallen into contempt. His Vanity & itch of scribbling still continue & our prints are yet disgraced with his performances; his essay on honour, has been answered by an essay on pride which has produced other performances of authors to me unknown, & when they will end, God only knows. Such have been the effects of our free press which instead of answering the modest purposes for which it was originally designed, has been Shamefully prostituted to publish the grossest lies & most infamous calumny

Your mentioning that you had leave for a month to go to Ireland, which gave me some hopes of hearing from thence something more of what you just hinted upon Mr White's Information. I have not had a letter from thence since those you delivered me. I had wrote to my sister Phipps in Jan. 1766. as long a letter almost as this & desired her to procure from Mr White as full a state of the case as he was able to draw, with two of the principal Irish lawyers opinions upon it, desiring if they were in my favour that they might be retained & assuring her that if I come from them & some opinions from England (for which purpose I desired her to inclose a copy of the case & opinions to Mr Palmer) be satisfied that it would be worth my while I would take a trip with my family to Dublin & attend the event of the cause, but my letters went by one Patterson, Bramley's apprentice who went home after a small estate and neither he or the vessel he went in (belonging to Stephen West in Maryland) have been heard of since. I should have wrote again to my sister, but as I had nothing to inform her of but what woud have made her uneasy, & I imagined she might look upon any complaint of my circumstances as a tacit demand of that concern, which I gave her a power to receive the profits of, & which I would not willingly deprive her of, I chose to be silent & let the estate in Ireland rest where it is, tho if, upon enquiry, I coud be satisfied of my right to it, it woud be imprudent to let the matter wholly drop. I for my own part never expect to be a penny the better for it, but I shoud desire that you or some of my children shoud, & if you coud find that it was worth while I woud make you such a conveyance of it as shoud be advised. Except my education I never got a shilling of my fathers or any other relation's estate, every penny I ever got has been by my own industry, & with as much fatigue as most people have undergone, & out of that

In the Darlington Memorial Library

I contributed very considerably towards the recovery of my father's estate & the settlement of my bro. James, & I can truly say that I never had any expectation of reaping the least pecuniary advantage from the death of any relation, till I rec'ed my uncle Fenton's letter by Mr Cockburne. From the stile of that letter & Mr Cockburne's assuring your sister Selden, that my uncle was worth 60 or £70,000 & had no child, & that his wife was nearly his own age, I must own that I coud not help conceiving some hopes, that when he came to die he woud in disposing of so large a fortune, have taken some notice of his heir at law, which I look upon my self to be, as I don't know of any of his & my mother's sisters living or having left any issue. His inviting me to a correspondence, which I was once fond of establishing, if he had encouraged it, I looked on as an attempt toward a reconciliation, as he understood by my mother that I resented his not answering my letters. It was unlucky he had not lived till you got home, for I cannot beleive but that some undue influence or practice was made use of to induce him to make such a will. He must have been sensible, that he & his family had been under great obligations to my father, who not only kept him but two of his sisters Ann & Mary & his bro Swift, for some years before their father's death, as part of his family, this I remember & know to be true, but I suppose, as the will is proved, my aunt beleives all to be secure & that she has nothing to do with the heir at law. I beleive it is not necessary to call upon him in order to establish a will against him, except in the case of a real estate, & whether he had any, I have not understood, tho I think you mentioned his having some plantations in Jamaica, however as I suppose you may at a small expence get a copy of the will & advise upon it, I shoud for my own satisfaction be glad to know how far I am barred by it. I have inclosed a letter to my Aunt, open, which if you approve you may seal & deliver, otherwise commit to the flames.

Colo Tayloe's furnishing you, in the genteel manner you mention, with a letter of credit, was a proof that you had one friend in Virginia, for generally the cash is the truest proof of friendship, tho I am persuaded you had many others, who, if equally able, woud have supplied you with the same proof of it, which brings me to yours of May 8, in which you blame your bro. & Mr Hunter; you certainly have not two [more] sincere friends in the world than they are, you judg'd from the place you were then in, or Virginia, when all the money was carried to your quarters for the supply of the army, & must have concluded from thence that there could be no doubt of raising money at that time among us. I have already informed you how much I was able to raise, your brother I will agree was not in so bad a situation, but I can venture to affirm that he did all his power & perhaps was more uneasy than you were that he coud not answer your expectations. As to Mr Hunter you must partly know, that his negro consignments obliged him to be punctual in his remittances whether he rec'ed the money or not from the purchasers. They fell so short, that he was obliged to draw on his bro. William for more thousands than he coud pay & was therefore obliged to return his bills, therefore to maintain his credit, as he had many thousand pounds due on account of negroes, abot £5000 advanced for Jno Campbell Esqr (now in Jamaica to raise the money) about £3000 for Spotswood's estate, & above £6000 an Ironwork in Maryland in partnership with one Gantt, & as he was erecting a forge with four hammers above the falls, with a merchant mill &c to make the race of wch he was obliged to employ near 200 men, & for which Fras Thornton hath brought an action against him in Spotsylvania court for ten thousand pounds damage for stopping the water to his mill, he was obliged to borrow money of Colo Corbin: I looked upon it that Mr Hunter had picked up a valuable friend, who had chosen an opportunity to assist, with his large fortune, a valuable member of society, by enabling him to bring his works to perfection & retrieve his credit, but how much was I deceived, when upon a visit from our worthy friend about a month ago, he inform'd me that he had been obliged, to secure Corbin by a bill of sale of his whole estate, which I had never heard of before, & that he had urgently pressed him ever since April to advertise it for sale, I suppose to become the purchaser of it, as he was then sensible that it was almost brought to perfection & could not cost Hunter, so little as £200 a month

I can now inform you with great pleasure that his four hammers are at work, so that I am in hopes he will be able to get quit of all the Harpies that waited to prey upon him, but he assured me that tho one of his hammers [went to] began to work, in September he had not yet received five pounds for Iron tho the best article in the country to produce cash. If that will not satisfy you that there is no cash circulating among us, I can add that he assured me that he was disappointed of sending his brother to the general court after his return from Maryland, meerly by the want of cash to bear his expences, & for my own part, I can affirm that for the two last years, I never was master of five pounds for five days, I may almost say, for five hours. Yet our assembly [was not] brought to think of any expedient to relieve so general a distress: the council seems always averse to every proposal of that sort. As some of them have got a good deal of money, they will not allow that any body else shoud have any, the true reason,

In the Darlington Memorial Library

I believe is that they make all the advantage they can of theirs, & woud willingly engross so valuable an emolument in their own hands. I am surpriz'd that none of the money'd men or companies, at home, have thought of setting up a bank among us, as it is certain such a thing might be established on undoubted security & annually receive an Interest of five percent paid in London. Colo Lomax proposed a scheme, which, I think, wanted no great amendment, but Thomson Mason, who wants to be thought a very considerable man, tho I believe he wants money as much as the rest of his countryman opposed it, because he had drawn up a very inconsistent one of his own, but as your brother is of opinion, that Thomson's head is turnd, I cant help concurring with him; if he can be a leader, he does not seem to regard who, or of what sort, are his followers.

Your trip to Bath when explained by your brother, pretty fully convinced me, that you were taken in, & was the first intimation that I had, that you did not intend suddenly into Virginia. The young lady's letter prepossess'd me in her favour, her candour, good sense & affection to her father & offer to accompany you, with his consent, into so strange & distant a countrey, left me no room to doubt of her regard for you, or, that if you cou'd obtain that consent, you must be happy in such a choice: And I was well pleas'd to find that you considerd my consent either worth asking or having such instances of duty or affection not being very common in these times. I assure you it gave me great pleasure to hear that you had succeeded, & that it would give me a title to claim so near a relation to a young lady of such merit, whom for the future I shall call my daughter, but I think it an omission that you never mentioned her name before your last letter to your brother, on occasion of Mr Russell's having her thanks for his generous offer, but before that time we had it in the gentlemans magazine for August. Robt Brent informd me at Fredericksburg fair, upon Mr Carroll's authority, as he said, that it was Miss Smith of Scarborough, & so it passed till the magazine changed it into Miss Neville of Lincoln; it matters little now, as you have furnished her with a third name. It was however no small mortification to me & the rest of your friends that we were disappointed of your company at Marlborough this Christmas, & I doubt we may meet a second disappointment, as it is not improbable that by April my daughter may be in a condition, improper for so long a voyage. You may however assure her from me, that whenever we have the happiness to meet, she will find the most cordial & affectionate welcome & that her new relations will contribute every thing in their power to repair the loss of those she left behind her.

George Mercer Papers

Yours of Sept. 26 was next in point of time, but did not come to hand, as I before mentioned till June last. On New years day 1767 a sloop of Mr Ritchie's that came around from Rappa for a load of tobacco stopped at my landing; his negro skipper brought me a letter from Mr Mills, in which he informed me that, understanding there was a parcel of bottles for me, on board a ship in Corotoman, he had prevailed on Mr Ritchie's skipper, who was coming round & was to pass my house to call & take them in, on a promise to indemnify him to his master & that I shoud give him something for his trouble. He accordingly landed 30 hampers of a groce each & I gave him ten shillings & Mr Ritchie at June fair received from me £3..15..— for the freight, but as I never understood either from whence or from whom they came, or what they cost, I remained entirely ignorant of it, till I by meer accident, looking for some papers found your letter. I still was in the dark, as to what they cost, tho you informed me they came from Sedgley & Hilhouse, but I own that I cou'd not be satisfied till I had recourse to Mr Mill's letter, & found that he had not mentioned either the ship's, master's or owner's name, or that he had the least concern with any of them. The Ship must have been then long sailed, if she had been in the countrey, it was out of my power to procure good bills or good tobacco, without money as I had neither of them myself, & I coud then too, only have guess'd at the price from the twelve groce formerly shipped, which were charged me £10..4..— to discharge which, I got Andrew Edwards, one of the Inspectors at Cave's to purchase 2 hhds of good tobacco for me, as I made none myself: he bought me two, which he said were good: I am sure they cost me £17..11..—. Sedgley & Hilhouse said, they were bad, & gave me £6..18..—. for them, which brought me £3..6..— in debt, had I shipped tobacco enough to discharge it, at the same rate, it woud have cost me £25..19..— & my bottles have stood in 43s..3d a groce besides carting from Fredericksburg, which was at least as expensive as Ritchie's freight & would add half a crown more to each groce. The pounds, shillings & pence woud be much cheaper, but you formerly wrote me, that they would not ship bottles on the trifling commission to be got that way, & nothing but a tobacco consignment woud procure them, and that upon the very first trial, convinced me that I had better be without bottles, than to have them, upon such terms: It was that induced me to consign my tobacco to Copithorn; he undertook to be a yearly ship to Potomack & to deliver my bottles or any thing else, at my own landing, clear of freight, & gave assurances of rendring as good accounts as others from that part. And I shoud have had the advantage that he coud not have

In the Darlington Memorial Library

pretended that my tobacco was not good, because as I did not propose to make any myself I shoud have supplied him with cash to purchase my quota of 20 hhds of such as he liked at Alexandria where he proposed to load; and he cou'd not have proposed to continue, much less, to encrease his interest, without tolerable accounts. He by some mistake, got two hhds short of the 20 I intended the 18 he had cost me within a trifle of £10 a hhd, & as I had no opportunity of writing for insurance I took his word that he woud do it, as he was to do for some others & intended to insure on his own account, it therefore gave me some satisfaction when you wrote me that I was insured, for I had some suspicion, that as he went in the ship himself, he might have neglected it, as in case he had miscarried with the ship, he would have been out of the way of being called to an account, but on his safe arrival might have made an advantage of charging insurance to all, those who order'd it. I am in hopes the insurers will have come to an agreement before you come away, and in that case I shoud be glad you woud receive my insurance. I imagine this will be a sufficient authority, if the insurers are men of honour, especially as you are known at Bristol & it is not new in my power to send you a formal one. I never heard any thing about bottles from Aitchison & Parker or any body else, but upon your recommendation Messrs Sedgeley & Hilhouse & Mr Mollison may command any of my services, where they may think it will avail them, tho I am so far out of the way of their correspondence that at present I can't see how it can be in my power to serve them. I shoud before this time have made my acknowledgments to Mr Montague[644] & his family for their obliging civilities to you, if my perpetual hurry & confusion woud have allowed me time, pray let them know that I bear the most grateful & respectful remembrance of them & that nothing could give me a greater pleasure than to receive any of their commands, if it shoud be in my power to serve them or any of their friends. You mention another particular friend of yours under the name of the Undersecretary for the No America department, without considering that we at this distance scarcely know the names of the principal Secretaries, they are so frequently shifting.

You mention your intention to visit Mr Lutwidge. I was in hopes that you had got the money from him before that time, more especially as you complain so much for want of money in your former letters. Dr Riddell says, if you had not undertaken it he coud have got his part of it long ago, by means of a brother of his, who, he says, is an attorney of note in or near Whitehaven. Mr Lutwidge here bears a character, the very reverse of his father's, so that I did not doubt, but if you saw him, you coud have got the money, but if you leave England without it, I expect it will be lost. The whole except Riddell's share of his demand, (which he alone, of all creditors, contrary to his promises, reserved, at the execution of the assignment.) belongs to you, your brother & myself. I imagined, as you did not see him, that you woud have wrote to him, soon after your arrival, to have known his resolution & communicated it to me, as you did not, I cant tell what to say it. The Justice of the decrees is indisputable. Thomas Lutwidge's own letters not only proved the partnership with his father, but his father's injustice in protesting his apprentice & factor, Wilson's bills drawn on him with full power & for effects, to the full value, purchased by Wilson for Lutwidge's account & which he actually received, upon the most trifling pretences. The interest from the time of the decrees is considerable, but that you were left to give up or insist on, but why shoud I mention that, when you had absolute power to settle the whole as you thought fit. I think something ought to be done it before you leave England, you may, if you think proper, advise with Mr Palmer about it. I woud not lose the whole, if I coud help it, tho I had rather do so than engage in a troublesome & expensive suit for so small a Sum, if it was of value sufficient, I coud trust it upon its merits to a new trial in any court in England, but shoud it be necessary to send over a compleat record of all the proceeds here they are so voluminous that I doubt it woud amount to as much as the demand & I suppose that cost woud be lost.

As you have mentioned nothing lately of any ill consequences from the fall off your horse, I hope you received no other damage by it then your sickness & the consumption in your purse consequent upon it. I heartily participated in both, but as it was an accident that might have been attended with much worse consequences, I congratulated you on escaping them.

Your next from Bath, complaining of mine & your brothers not writing, I hope I have fully answered, as to myself, & as to your brother he insists & I believe truly, that you must be mistaken, because you have answered more than one of his letters within the time you assign. He avers & I believe he has wrote several, tho they have not come to hand. It is certain that so many have miscarried in his & my correspondence with you since you first went to England, that I am satisfied some villains have watched for & intercepted them, tho I am confident they were not able to discover any treason in them that letter came very opportunely to prevent the sale of the Shannondoah land and pursuant to your desire, I & my wife & your brother executed a conveyance to you of the whole tract, which together with my wifes

In the Darlington Memorial Library

privy examination & acknowledgment of it, was recorded the last general court, the deed bearing date the first of June to precede your marriage.

Yours of Sept 18 came to hand only Dec. 14. that was the first notice of your not leaving England, as you proposed, in August: I kept a good look out all October & part of November for every ship coming up Patomack, as you mentioned coming, in one of Russell's, & we were unwilling to go to Mr Garnett's, least you should arrive in our abscence. I was not in the least surprizd, on the receipt of yours, to find that he had disappointed you, tho he did not me, in the opinion I had of the London Merchts When you mentioned his offer to you, I made no doubt but that he proposed some extraordinary advantage from it, but why shoud it be thought strange, when there is not one man in a thousand, who does not act from views of interest. It is upwards of two years since I gave notice[645] to the members of the Ohio Company, that my health & business woud not longer allow me to concern myself in their affairs which they had entirely flung upon my hands. Mr Mason not having been at the two last meetings, nor have I seen him above once since you first left the countrey. I however sent copies of that part of your letter relating to the compa to him, Colo Tayloe, P Lee & R Carter, but I coud not tell what to make of that part, where you mention a report to be made by the governor, as I never heard any thing of it before, your letter of Sept. 6, in which you mention it more plainly, not having come to hand till Jan. 3d long since I began to write to you, which was on Dec. 22, after dispatching those copies, but I have had so many interruptions, & write so slowly that I have now been above three weeks about it, & dare say it will take me a week to make a duplicate. Phil Lee was in Maryland. I reced the following answer from Colo Tayloe.

Mr Mercer [resigns] the Ohio Company 2 yrs since he could no longer take upon him the Management of their Business.

Dear Sir

I am an entire stranger to any of the affairs relative to the Ohio Compa since Colo Mercer left us, & fear that is too generally the case with the rest of the members. I will cheerfully attend any meeting, of which I can have timely notice on so important a crisis of our affairs, but fear any resolutions or instructions may be sent too late to find Colo Mercer in London, who I coud wish to engage the families he mentions, I mean the whole, if the requisite sum did not exceed the abilities of the company. Your exertions merit the thanks of every member, therefore tender mine, & your son's care deserves reward, as well as thanks, in my private opinion.

Col. Tayloe [says] he deserves Thanks & Rewards, & if the Company lose their Grant it must proceed from Idleness and Inattention— & therefore they would have no Right to expect any Redress or Reimbursement.

I know not any thing now in my power to serve them or wou'd cheerfully do it. I never knew of the steps mentioned being taken against

· 211 ·

George Mercer Papers

us, & conclude, as you do, in respect to our governor. (I never heard of the petition to the house of Burgesses,646 & had wrote Colo Tayloe that if the governor had rece'd any such orders, as you mentioned, I thought he ought to have called upon the compa for information, without which he coud not make a just report, & I had mentioned my having recommended Colo Thos Lee, as most convenient to have supplied my place.) I wish Colo Thos Lee's application & diligence equal to his abilities, I shoud then think of him as you do, but indolence & carelessness, with extravagance are the true characteristics of Virginians, & if we now lose the advantages of the Ohio grant, the loss will follow from these sources, & deservedly fall on us, & as it will proceed from our own fault, we cannot ask or expect any redress or reimbursement of our expences. I am sorry, truly sorry to tell you, I hear Colo Presley Thornton is ill with the gout in his head, the badness of yesterday & to day, occasioned yours finding me at home. his was Jan. 4th

Govrs Report

I find however that he & Richd Lee had on the 8th wrote to Colo Mason to call a meeting, for on the 12th to my great surprize, I rec'ed a letter from him inclosing their's & desiring me to acquaint him with their motives, which from their letter he found they rec'ed from me. I had given my letter to him to my head overseer Dec 23d & he promised it a safe & immediate passage, but it, as it seems, miscarried. I sent him however another copy & pressed a meeting at all events tho I doubt it may be too late for you to receive any information from us, in which case I suppose it will be proper to write, in your absence, to Mr Palmer, but we may, at least push the governor, as you advise, to make his report. My share is so small647 that I coud undertake to settle my quota of the families my self. I coud engage a sufficient number of people who woud willingly go with two good hands each to settle there & I have carpenters & a very good Smith of my own to build for them & shoud want nothing but nails. I yesterday hired Mr Semple 21 negro men, 1 woman & 3 boys & 2 white servants, the man at £12, woman at £6, & boys at £5 the year. He allows each 6 ℔ of meat a week, finds them bedding tools &c pays their levies & taxes & is to return them completely cloathed. I shoud have been glad I coud have got clear of all the rest upon as good terms, for I am sure those I keep, tho the best will not yield as much profit & therefore I am under some concern to think that you are going to be so deeply concernd in the planting way, as your orders to your brother to purchase 50 negroes for you, convinced me. I have lost many thousand pounds by it, but as my practice so wholly engrossed me, I never cou'd attend to consider the matter thoroughly till I quitted that, & I am

· 212 ·

now convinced that every man, who will not carefully attend his own business, (I might say, in every thing else, as well as planting) will lose by it. Few people keep regular accounts & therefore don't know what their crops stand them in, & they often imagine them clear gains, after the overseer's share deducted, when if everything else, that ought as properly to be deducted, was so, they wou'd find, they did not amount to the interest, of their money. Every negroes cloaths, bedding, corn, tools, levies & taxes will stand yearly at least in £5. You ought to charge the interest of the amount of the value of the land & slaves, the overseers, I cant judge how much they will stand you in, but it will be a heavy article, & a reasonable allowance shou'd be made for the risque of the slaves lives. I have found it a very heavy article. All the slaves I now have, accounting those you and your brother had upon the division, do not make up the number I bought, tho I have had 98 born. Your sister Selden attributes it to the unhealthiness of Patomack Neck, which there may be something in, if, as she says, you & your brother have 26 children of 3 of your negro women living. I thank God, however that my own family has been generally as healthy, as other people's, & I am very glad that you and your brother have had so much better luck with your negroes, than I have had with mine; but upon the whole, you will find, that, under so heavy an expence, there can be no great profit by our ordinary crops of corn & tobacco: indeed Colo Lewis thinks that land will answer extremely well for hemp & yield a large profit, & wanted to buy the part adjoining to him, & was treating for the purchase of it with your brother, if I woud have consented that he shoud have had it, for his share, but I convinced him by the plat that it coud not be done, without cutting my part into pieces, for a straight course from the corner of the back land to the river, would not have given me a moiety, which coud not have been done, but by shaping a course that woud have taken a good part of the low grounds; the best of those, that scoundrel Snickers has been pillaging these several years, under pretence of paying 1000 lb tobo yearly rent which however, he has never yet paid, but by crediting it on a piece of paper. He has on the contrary rec'ed every penny of the rents ever since you left the countrey, & insisted he had your authority for it. In my distress last year, I sent my clerk to him for the ballance of his account which he had that spring sent me by your brother amounting to about £100 & 10,000 lb of crop tobo he did not send me a farthing but wrote me word that you owed him as much for money advanced for your quarters, that if I woud not take payment in your hands, he woud be down the tenth of August & pay me, but he neither came, wrote or sent me a farthing to this time.

Mr Dick extremely surprized me, when he said, that passing thro our land he discovered a house that he did not expect to see there, as he coud very well have put up with such an one to live in himself & he concluded that you had got some gent. overseer, who coud not find a house upon the land good enough for him & had run you to that extraordinary expence, but upon his enquiry from the first person he had met, he was informed that it was Mr Snicker's quarter, he says he then found that he had cut down so much of the low grounds & cut down sold & destroyed so much timber, that if the land had been his, he woud not have suffered it for £300. And such at last, was his insolence, that when your brother sent him word by Mr Wormley, that he must remove, for that now the whole land belonged to you & he intended to put some of your hands to that place, he sent back word, that no man in Virginia shoud remove him till you came in, & intimated that you dared not do it then, as he had you under his thumb. Jemmy, upon that, went up, determined to remove him, at the risque of his life, but when he came [here the] last day of the old year to see Mr Garnett & his wife, before they went home, he told me he effected it, without bloodshed or battery, but he agrees that Snickers had fully indemnified himself for his house, by supplying your quarters with corn, & that his quarter, as it was called, was above £500 damage to you, him & myself. He however has not yet paid any of the rents, which must lie till you come in.

I now, upon the closest review, cannot find any part of your letters unanswer'd, & you have the fullest account I am able to give you of the family affairs till this 15th of Jan. except that Mr Selden return'd from Hampton this day fivenight & informd me that he had seen Capt Munford, who acknowledgd your generosity in sending him 20 guineas, & said that he had sent some of your things round, but then had several of them on board, wch he woud send by the first opportunity. Mr Selden also informed me that your marriage settlement in nine skins of parchment was come in & was in [the] hands of Mr Nicholas, who I suppose, you have heard was our treasurer, (& who, I believe is the best they coud have pitched on in Virginia & I am assured, is better, than any they woud have sent if they coud have sent us one from England) I wish another part of his information may be true, wch is, that one reason of your staying this winter in England, was your discovery of an addition of £3000 to my daughter's fortune. I wish it as an additional convenience to both of you, & I shoud not be sorry that you both had a greater regard to that convenience than I ever had, tho I was not born to, or been conversant with thousands. Even after all I have sufferd for want

In the Darlington Memorial Library

of money, I contemn it, as much as any man living can do, except for its immediate convenience. I am satisfied there is not any real happiness to be found in the enjoyment, I should have said, the possession of millions, & that old Darby with Joan, by his side, possessed more real pleasure & satisfaction than those possessed of the largest hoards. It is in your & my daughter's power with advantage, to lay for a foundation, those pleasing endearments of youth, which neither sickness or time can decay, & which, I pray God, may be yr fa [te.]

I have now done, except adding, that if you shoud be by any means detained in England, you woud not omit to send me a tutor for my children by the first opportunity & I shoud be glad you woud send me a quantity of nails (which may be done cheapest from Bristol) 50 yds of haircloth [a] yard wide for my malt kiln, a drill plow with brass Seed boxes for wheat, turnips, lucarn pease &c if you approve of it when you see it. Stephen Wood Wheeler at Lionlane end advertises them from 4 to 8 guineas & without brass work for about 20$. I shoud particularly want a box for barley which I suppose is inc[lud]ed in the &c but if you should chuse to bring in one for your own use, I coud have one made by [our slave] people here capable to do it. I had [in 1765 from] Fullagar & Todd at the golden ball near the India house, Leadenhall street, kersey double breasted jackets at 4/3 & welted ones at 5/3 & drab breeches at 20d a pair, they pleased the negroes better & proved warmer & more serviceable than their usual cotton cloaths, which besides the trouble of making came to near double their price, the breeches tho were not proper for winter, when they shoud have woolen ones. I thought Wm Hunter had been long enough in Virginia, and wrote to him for 40 mens & 30 womens suits, but he improperly sent in those breeches for the men, & nothing but check & brown linnen for the women, who require to be as warmly cloathd as the men in winter. I expected before this a complete set of slops, bedding, great coat, shirt, shoes, stockings & hat from Mr Balfour with their first cost & the name of the person who supplies him, as he deals very largely in them to supply the sailors & assures me they are vastly the best & cheapest cloaths for our negroes, but the ice & bad weather prevent my vessel's return which I expected before Christmas, as it is not come I can't be a judge of what I should chuse, but as I believe Fullagar & Todd will supply you as cheap as anybody & I am persuaded it is the cheapest & best way you can cloath your people, & you will have the opportunity of seeing all the slops they deal in, & you are a proper judge which of them my be best for negr[oes]. I presume you will, before you leave England, contract for a yearly supply, in which I shoud be glad to be included. Jordan insists that a jacket of 6/6 with a warm flannel jacket the second year will last well two years, but most negros are so careless of their cloaths & rely so much on a yearly supply that I think such jackets as I had are cheapest & last the year very well, great coats are necessary for such as go by water, or are obliged to be much out after the stocks, carting &c. I have parted with so many of my people this year that 20 of the common jackets & 25 of the welted for my tradesmen & white servants will supply my wants this next fall, five of the best sort are for tall fellows & seven of the worst for boys between 12 & 16. I shall with them want 45 pair of breeches, but they shoud be woolen, 1 doz great coats, 5 doz of stockings & 1 dozen & half for boys & girls, 4 doz strong felt hats & 600 Ells of ozenbrigs. We shall make Virg^a cloth enough to cloath the women & children, but shall want 50 warm blankets & 2 doz of the Russia drab breeches. I compute that they will very little exceed £60 tho I can affirm that I have paid near £200 to supply the want of them these two years past. I have now dispatched my family affairs in wch you will perceive there is not a shilling for my self wife or children, tho I shoud be glad if you coud conveniently add on the family account 112 yds of sheeting for the family not too fine & 84 yds of such as is fit for comp^a for tho formerly we had as great plenty as anybody of such things, the last two years woud not [ad]mit of repairing our wear & tear, so that my wife is ashamd of her old sheets when any strangers come to the house, we still have as many good beds as any body & my wife yearly saves so many feathers, that she has promised your brother as many as he wants for you, she did not think the ticks good enough for you, being such as we coud get out of the Stores, & were necessary to save the feathers in.

I come now, in the conclusion to mention my own particular wants, I shoud be very desirous that you woud procure me the remainder of the modern universal history & the cuts of the whole which were promised together when they were finished. I have 6 of the folio volumes & 27 of the 8vo edition, one of them I design to part with, but think it might be better done if it was complete, & I would chuse to have the cuts of each bound together, as Mr Osborne sent me in those of the ancient part of that work. If you are not supplied with them & woud chuse to have them one of the Setts is at your service, that is, if you will accept them. the folios are plainly bound in a light coll^d leather letterd on the back on red leather <u>Modern History</u> with the figures 1 to 6. in the next division, a double gilt line on each side of the division & this figure gilt in the middle of each compartment

In the Darlington Memorial Library

I have likewise as neat a set of the ancient Universal history as can be in 7 vol. folio, bound in 9 as the first & last volumes were too large to bind in one. they are also at your service upon the same terms. they are very neatly bound & gilt in dark leather letterd on red leather <u>Universal History</u> & underneath VOL. I to VII. the gilding on the back as described at the end of my Letter. I shoud not have mentioned it but that if you shoud chuse them, you shoud have the supplement. I have a complete set of the 8º edition [neither] published afterwards with many additions which made a supplement to the folio one necessary I imagine if you don't chuse them they might be sold without the supplement, but probably better with it, & in that it shoud be bound & gilt as near as might be to the rest. I also want the London magazine for 1764, 5, 6 & 7. bound in a light leather sprinkled with Ink but not much letterd on red <u>London Magazine</u> the binding & cover with a double gilt line & the <u>year</u> in the next compartment to the lettering, & Nº 26. 36. 37 & as many more of the universal magazine as are published bound & covered with marble paper and leather backs letterd on red leather <u>Universal Magazine</u> & the number of the volume in figures in the next compartment. I sent the 26th volume home with one of the London Magazines as patterns to bind those I sent for to complete my sets, but they kept the books I sent & sent those I ordered in rough half bound, so that I was forced to send them to Williamsburg & pay extravagantly for the binding & lettering. John Buchanan once sent me 4 vol of the gentlemans magazine to complete my Set of the London one & wrote me word that his scoundrel bookseller who was concerned in the gentlemans magazine, assured him that it was the best. I should be glad you coud get a bookseller who woud yearly furnish me with the continuation of the London & Universal magazines as they are completed, bound as I have directed, it woud save me some trouble & expence & if your correspondent would take them in, I might depend upon having them duly for I dont expect ever to have a correspondent in London & indeed woud not desire one but for the sake of getting such things as are not to be got here. I have 4 vol of the Museum Rusticum which you sent in rough bound in marble paper with red leather backs letterd <u>Museum Rusticum</u> & numberd 1. 2. 3. 4 I would be glad to have the rest of the Sett & the court kalendar sent yearly. As I have not hitherto had time to space to apply so much of it as I woud, to acquire a thorough knowledge of the Bible & notwithstanding I have collected a great many valuable notes, am often at a very great loss to have some parts of it explaind & some others cleared up. I shoud therefore be glad to have the best commentary you can procure me, there are so many of them advertised, that one woud believe the people of England were contrary to their common character, extremely religious, the character the author of each gives to his performance is much to be questioned & I would as little rely on the bookseller's. I, for my part, shoud prefer Dr Dodd's, on account of the great helps, he says, he has been favour with, but as you are on the spot, if you can upon information, that you coud depend on, procure me a better, I should be glad of it, but I would have the fullest, to avoid sending for any other. And as your sister Fenton was fond of Swifts works & I gave her my sett, I woud willingly have another which you may get at Wm Johnstons in Ludgate street in 18 vol. complete for 36/. I omitted to take notice that they are very careless in binding their magazines & omit many of the cuts, which to their customers abroad is extremely injurious, as their Proprietors have their property secured & I presume no bookseller sells them but on their account. I think that in justice they ought to make good the deficiencies, which I have noted underneath & expect they will furnish you with. I should stop here if I did not think Donne's new Introduction to the Mathematicks with the Schoolmasters Repository added advertised at 6/. Thomas's British Negotiator at 3/6 & the History of inland Navigations especially the D of Bridgewater's at 2/6 woud be useful to my Sons & perhaps to my self. And as the girls depend of your bringing them in some books, I shoud have added Bob. Newbery at the Bible & Sun in St Paul's churchyard can best furnish you at the cheapest rate with books best adapted to the real instruction as well as amuse₍me₎nt of children from two to six feet high.

I reced last Tuesday morning at Mr Selden's, a note from your brother advising me that a Ship was to sail on Saturday for Bristol for from Hobbs's hole by which he intended to write & that I could get passage for my Letter which I despaired of the Posts being stopped by the Ice & the Ship's froze up, Fahrenheits Thermometer was on the 18th Instant at 21, eleven degrees below Frost & the River froze over that night at my house, but is now clear again. I immediately came home & have been writing ever since, but so slowly that for fear of my messenger's not getting to Hobbs's hole I am obliged to dispatch him without the letter to my Aunt. Mr Cuninghame who assures me the New York packet is stoppd promises me a conveyance of a duplicate by a Ship of his that will sail in about a fortnight, which I doubt may be too late to meet you, shoud that as well as this, come to hand, except the last part that may be added, you may fling it behind the fire. I doubt you will be tired of this, & wish I had not yet broke Silence. My Blessing on you & my daughter accompanies the sincerest

In the Darlington Memorial Library

wishes of my wife children & family (with their most affectionate love & regard) for both your healths & happiness, & that this new year may be exceeded by every other in the encrease of your pleasure & mutual satisfaction. I am

  Dear George
    Your most affectionate father & sincerest friend
      J Mercer
      Jan. 28 1768
      began Decr 22. 1767.

Wanting in the London Magazines.
Anno 50.	Manufacture of Silk in China in fol	560
51.	View of Richmond Hill	98
	George Pr of Wales	229
54	Isle of Man	7
55.	Pembrokeshire	104
	Roads & Precipices in Norway	224
	Mattock Bath	480
61.	South prospect of the City of New York	400
62	Plan of the town & fort of Grenada	640
63.	Poetical Essays from fol. 436. to	445.

Wanting in the Universal Magazine
[Stricken out. Illegible]

10	Sr Edwd Coke	106
15	Mrs Midnight's Animal Comedians	91
[13]	The Touraco Bird	301
18	The Carnation	301
24	Mr Worlidge's drill plow	257
27	Sr Edwd Hawke	82
28	Capt Cornwalls monument	40
29	Appleby castle	113
	Mount Vesuvius	150
31	South America	169
32	Catoptrics	92
33	Scarborough	225
34	Lt Colo Townshend's monument	97
	Sr Isaac Newton's monument	241
35	The Countries 30 ms round London	137
	Lt Gen Hargrave's monument	256
	Geo Fred Handel's monumt	361

George Mercer Papers

My overseer this [T]uesd[ay] [in]forms me that underst[anding] I was wishing [that] as soon as it [was possible] that Windmill Sails [should be secured] because they cannot get them here but at the most [extravagant charges and] they [can] not be made but at Norfolk.

I must therefore request you to procure me a Sett. My millwrights directions were

$$\left.\begin{array}{l}\text{The Drivers 3 foot 6 inches broad}\\ \text{The leaders 3 .... 3 ....}\end{array}\right\} \text{23 feet long.}$$

A Suit I had made at Norfolk by those dimensions proved too long, something, they should be of Duck No 2.

[Endorsed by George Mercer]

Letter from my Father dated Jany 28th 1768.—reced at Bristol April 20th 1768.

Contains Abstract of a Letter from Col. Tayloe about the Ohio Business G M deserves Thanks & *Reward*

Never heard of the Petition of the General Assembly.

Approves of pressing the Govr to make a Report about the Company's Claim. &c Informed the Compa 2 yrs before he could no longer take upon him the Management of their Business.

[Endorsed]

About the Ohio Company with an Extract of a Letter from Col. Tayloe.

[Addressed by John Mercer]

To Colo George Mercer of Virginia not at I N 5 London

Recommended to the Care of Mr Archibald Ritchie Mercht, or Doctor Mortimer at Hobbs's Hole to request either of them to deliver it to the Capt of a Bristol Ship which I am inform'd sails next Saturday & to request him immediately on his Arrival to put it into the Post Office.

[Printed postmark]   BRISTOL SHIP LRE

[Weight]   1 oz.

John Mercer to George Mercer, March 3, 1768[648]

Dear George

Since my last which cost me above a months time to begin & end & which I had Mr Ritchie's Assurance should be delivered to the Captain of a Bristol Ship lying at Urbanna that was consigned to Mr Mills & ready to sail, I was alarmed by a Letter from Parson Boucher to your brother acquainting him that he reced a Letter from his Sister advising she was to be in with Capt Fox who told her you & my daughter were to be Passengers with him & that he expected to sail in February, if so I was satisfied I had bestowed my Labour in vain, tho nothing concerned me so much as to think my Sons must have continued, God knows how much longer without a Schoolmaster which is a matter principally at my heart & which I flatter myself I shall not be disappointed in. Your brother was much concerned to hear it as he thought it would be much to advantage to receive his Letter before you left England. On the other hand your & my daughter's Stay in England is greatly regretted by all your friends.

We went to Fredericksburg the 13th of last month & were detained by bad weather till the 19th while there I discovered by the Gazettes[636] that a meeting of the Ohio Compa at Stafford Courthouse was appointed on the 23d I had by quitting my warm winter quarters & changing my cloaths got a violent cold & was all the next morning ill at Mr Hunter's (where we lay that night & where Mr Dick & his family came to dine with us the next day) In the Evening we all crossed to Fredericksburg & agreed to divide our quarters tho Mr Dick objected to it Mr Selden & his wife went to your Brothers the rest of us to Mr Dick's for there nine within the Coach, & five without it & Mr Selden rode. It rained the next day but in the morning, your Brother, who I am sorry to say it, is or affects to be a Valetudinarian, sent to enquire how I was & to inform me that Mr Seldon was very ill. It very luckily happened Doctr Mercer[639] was sent for just as he was setting off to visit a patient 30 miles off where he intended to have staid that night but on visiting Mr Selden he found him so ill with a Pleurisy that after blooding him & prescribing for him he promised to visit him the next morning & was as good as his word. He was blooded every day we staid & we were obliged to leave him & his wife behind us, indeed We got clear of the greatest part of our Load, my wife self & Jack being all that returned to Marlborough in the Coach & the Coachman postilion & a boy without.

On the 20th I reced yours[649] of Nov 25th past with the Kalendar List of the Army & some Newspapers by your two Servants who as my

horseboat was lost were brought over in a Canoe so that I did not
see your horse & mare but they told me that they were well & in good
order & the next day they set off to your Brother's. As they assured me
you would not leave London till May, I doubted not but you would
have time to be advised of the proceedings of our meeting as I was
informed Capt Anderson would sail from Leedstown the beginning
of March. They told me Capt Greig would send up your things the
week after in a Sloop which is not yet arrived, when she comes they
shall be taken care of. They were so sooner gone than I set about
collecting the necessary papers for the meeting the next day, but I
had scarce got into my Office before Mr Wm Brent with Messrs Hen
Rozer & Daniel Carroll of Maryland arrived to get me to draw some
deeds of great Consequence & were to be met by Robt Brent who, as
the day proved bad failed to meet. I don't remember that this ever
failed to be the Case, when I was preparing to write to you. I should
have told you however that they brot me yours[650] of the 15th Novr
by Johnson but I have not yet heard of the box of papers you mention
by him. Next day it rained again & I was preparing to set off in it,
when Robt Brent arrived about 12 aClock very wet & dirty. He complained he had never seen such roads & dissuaded me from going,
assuring me that Colo Mason was at his Brother's & would not be
down that day. As I had still a bad cold & was satisfied going out in
such weather would encrease it, I was prevailed on to stay at home
but sent my man to the Courthouse to see if any body was there & to
assure them that if there was the least probability of ₁arriving₁ I
would be there the next day let the weather be ₁ever₁ so bad & I sent
by him your Pacquets to George Mason & the Committee he returned
with the Papers a Letter from Richd Lee informing me that he was
the only Person & that he should stay the next day & expected Colo
Tayloe but he sent me at the same time a Letter from Phil Lee ex-
cusing his Attenda because he was obliged to be at Westmorland court
that he could see no Use of a meeting till you came in for that the
Ministry would not look at a Paper relating to our Affairs till all the
Elections were over in England which would not be before the middle
of Summer. Colo Robert Carter had sent up a Sailor on foot least his
horse should tire with a condition to forfeit his hire if he was not at
the Publicans at Stafford Courthouse on the Monday night directed
to me or Colo Mason but the outside was covered with directions that
if neither of Us was there any of the Ohio company that was was to
break it open read his Letter & then seal the Pacquet & forward it by
his Express to one of Us, this fell to Dicks Share & the Express was
willing to trust my man with it as he was on horseback. I found it

In the Darlington Memorial Library

contained your Packet[651] to me & the Committee dated Oct 10. sent from the Secretary of State's Office inclosed to the Govr so 4 mo 14 days on its passage. His own Letter was in Answer to one of Colo Mason's desiring him to have the meeting advertised in the Gazette's & inclosing one to the Govr desiring to be informed if he had received any Instruction relative to the Ohio Company (as he had reced such information) & hoping if he had that he woud as soon as he coud conveniently let him know what particulars he would desire to be satisfied in that he might be able to give him the fullest & earliest satisfaction in his power. The Councellor[652] says that he delivered his Letter to the Govr but as his Honr made it a rule never to open papers after Candles were lighted his Letter[653] & a very large Pacquet from the Secretary of States Office remained sealed till Sol's rays re-illuminated our clouded Atmosphere.

It seems the Councillor does not observe that Rule for the first part of his Letter by the date seems to have been wrote that night towards the middle it is dated the next day, & he says it was a Letter from the Secretary of State's Office to the Govr upon matters of weighty consequence & among them that Letter directed to me which the Govr was desired to forward, that nothing transpired for that the Govr seemed cautious of communicating anything till he had advised with his Council. But that by private Letters from London it was said that there was talk of some Governmts being fixed on the Ohio[654] & it was talked that in some little time several queries would transpire, among them the following

Who were the first promoters or advisers of the Ohio Company?

Did the Company ever pay the Indians any Consideration for the Land?

Did the late King ever promise that Company land in those parts? if they said he did they would be required to produce his warrant with some others of equal importance which he says he should be glad to know how to answer?

Is it not surprizing these should be made questions at this time of day? 20 Years after so publick a transaction & is it not more so that they should be made by a man[655] who holds two Shares in that compa? And that they are only in Embryo & that it will be some time before they transpire? And that they ought to be concealed with the strictest Secrecy from every person who was not one of the Company. But enough on that head.

But it seems Colo Mason got to Stafford Courthouse that night after my man came away, for when I got up next morning I found his man had come with a Letter to me after I went to bed. I then made little doubt of a meeting for I concluded Colo Tayloe was upon the Road & I had discovered that Thos Lee Had been appointed one of the Committee in Octr 1760 in Chapman's room,[656] tho I had forgot it, & indeed all the Compa seem to be guilty of something of that kind, if it may not more properly be called a mistake or both in the principal condition of our first grant. You write that you coud if the Compa would supply you with money, bring in the whole 500 families that we are obliged to settle. Colo Tayloe writes that he should choose it, yet in my last Letter to you I overlooked it & when I mentioned seating my half share I reckoned 121½ Families where as our whole complement for the 500000 acres is only 250 families, 200 for the first 200000 acres & after the same proportion 150 for the other 300.000.[657] this reduces that heavy Article of Expence to one half. Had they met there had been 3 of the Committee which would have been binding on the Compa But alas Colo Thos Lee who could not forget he was one of the Committee was in Westmorland & Dick Lee who saw him there could not prevail on him to come up, nor did Colo Tayloe appear consequently we three who did coud do nothing, but agree that I was to write to you & we agreed to some bounds[658] which Colo Mason had put into writing for my direction. I made my Clerk copy your two Letters to the Committee at Richd Lee's request to carry down to the Gent below which I gave him but as he had not time to copy the Boards report which my daughter had transcribed ten times better than those you sent me by the Boards own Clerks. I was forced to carry her copy, which they read & commended extremely, he soon left us which we were very glad of for we coud not talk before him of anything that coud promote the company's interest which he would begrudge to advance ones shilling for & he had no right to expect we should communicate our Sentiments to him, we waited for his departure & then talked the matter over and when we were ready to part & were putting our papers Colo Mason enquir'd if I had his memorandum of the bounds, I coud not find it on which we searched every paper over & found Dick according to his old Custom had pocketed it, It was so long since we had a meeting that I had forgot that he never failed to make collections of that sort, Colo Mason was however able to supply this the Loss but it cost him above two hours to do it & by that time Mr Seldon was come home & we went to dine with him & I returned home that night by water the roads being worse than I had ever known them but my trip encreased my cold prodigiously. I could not dispatch Mr Brent & his company till Saturday after breakfast after five days attendance, but as my Clerk was able with some directions now & then to do their business I have

In the Darlington Memorial Library

been almost every hour since employed about your dispatches. As you mentioned its being necessary to send over the treaty at Logstown & some other papers, it set me on searching every paper I had relating to the Companies affairs by which I discovered the mistake as to the 500 families, & found that you had already every material paper sent home in the Case from the cursory view I took of 'em I could not help lamenting our Case had not been printed which I had recommended. I must beleive that it would have been of the greatest advantage to the Comp{a} & have convinced all the World that We had been very hardly used, it would at least have saved me an incredible deal of trouble & saved Councillor Carter's Queries from transpiring, or if they did every body might have answerd them with or without book. But lest the Case may have been flung by long ago as usless as most of my papers on that head have been I have picked out the best copy[659] I could of it & sent you all the papers[660] I have that I thought could be of any Service & I must still recommend it to you, whether it would not be proper to print it in some shape or other, you may alter it as you think fit, the facts are all true & supported by sufficient Vouchers.[661] The unreasonable Grants[662] made [hereunder] feigned names in trust for Councillors[663] who did not advance a shilling but proposed to sell the Lands has been the sole Cause of all the Companies disappointm{ts} the Attorney[664] when he went to England was taxed with his Grant, he told me himself that he would not for £1000 have suffered his name to have been made use of if he had known what would have happened, & I am sure he told me it was for some other person who would not have it known that he was concerned in such Jobbs. But what can be said for Richd Corbins 3 grants[665] for 190000 acres within the bounds of the Company's grant & who were his Company when he did not know when he entered the Council Chamber I should have said Room for it was in the right hand room in the Govr house that there were such Lands or Creeks in the world & would not have known it then if it had not been for my Map[666] which I let the Govr have as a member of the Ohio Company upon his promise not to shew it to anybody without my consent, yet when I was called in Colo Corbin & Colo Ludwell were measuring the distances & taking notes in writing. I told them that was not fair the Map belonged to me as of my own drawing & my Instructions by which I drew it cost the Company above £600, they delivered it to me but they had done their business, their Entries were entered in the Council Books before they left the Room so that Corbin & Co in 3 hours time without a shilling charge or Expence except the Clerk of the Council's fee (which I suppose he dard not charge him) had leave to take up more land than

· 225 ·

the Ohio Company could obtain in 20y&rs; Sollicitation & after £10.000 Expence

See the Board of Trade's Report June 25, 1754,[667] what they had from Beverly (one of his Ma'ties Council) M&r; Hanbury had notice before He went home how far he was concerned in Interest that he had taken up 130.000 Acres in Augusta[668] which he proposed to settle with People from the Northward by selling & leasing it & that it was Beverley's Jackall Russel[669] (who was bred a poor boy in old Beverley's family) that interrupted & drove off the Ohio Companys Settlers sealed by Gist to encourage Beverely's Market, that Beverley finding a great part of his tract barren employed that same Russel as his Attorney to convey it & defraud the King of his Quitrents, that he conveyed 16,000 acres to one man, an Overseer not worth a groat, that Beverely on pretence of the Sale which was recorded on Russel's Acknowledgm&t; of the deed refused to pay the quitrents which were several years in arrear, the Sherif could hear of no such man at last he was told there was a man of that name in the County who was Overseer to a commonplanter, the Sherif who knew nothing of the quality of the land insisted he could not be the person he enquired for who was owner of 16000 acres of Land, his Informer agreed he could not but the Sherif sometime after meeting him enquired if he held any Land with a County He told him that Russell had told him he had given him 16000 acres, the Sherif said then he was the man he wanted, & that he demanded so many years arrears of quitrents which amounted to £16 Sterl' a year, the man said, he had nothing to pay & woud not be concerned with the Land. This the Company undertook to prove if M&r; Hanbury had occasion to mention it if Beverley concerned himself in opposing their grant. It was said Col&o; Grymes upon the discovery charged Beverley with & made him pay the quitrents (which is to be doubted) but had it been so would that have excused the fraud or ought such a man (tho one of his Majesty's Council) to be credited to the prejudice of a Comp&a; whose undertaking was of the greatest national advantage. And who have had their pockets picked by such villanious & fraudulent practices. Is the Ohio Company such a Set of despicable & meanspirited wretches that if a Councillor does them injustice they dare not complain of him, yet so it seems by old Hanbury's behaviour & so it should by his Son & Cousin's behaviour who pretend to bully the Company by withdrawing their allpowerful Influence if the Company will not submit to be cheated by them. This however is to yourself & you must act as you think fit.

Since I began to mention Dick Lee I recollected that looking over all my Papers I can not be certain that I had seen my daughters copy of the Board's report since my return home & upon search am now

Ohio Company map made by George Mercer, 1753, showing the extent of the Russell & Company survey, Gist's settlement, and the location of the proposed Ohio Company fort and town at Chartiers Creek (McKees Rocks).

The copy of the original in the Public Record Office in London, made in April, 1882, for Mr. William M. Darlington.

In the Darlington Memorial Library

satisfied that he pocketed that to. It is a strange that a man who pretends to be a Gent should be guilty of such mean scandalous tricks, especially as I had promised him a copy of it as soon as my clerk had time to make one. I must be obliged to send for it & shall be very free with the Gent. It is a misfortune that the notice was so ₁sent₁, as it allows a good Excuse to some of the members who I am persuaded had not timely if any, noti₁ce₁ the₁Paper came up to Fredericksburg Tuesday night & the Meeting was to be the next Tuesday & the whole time the weather very bad. I since received a Letter[670] from Colo Mason relating to a mistake in the bounds in his first draft you have copies of both.[658] I had on comparing the first bounds with Evans's map & your own /// plan[671] thought to have wrote to you about some alteration but from those & your own knowledge of the place I must think any thing I could say would have useless. I also send you a former letter[670] of his on the subject of taking up our lands in tracts of 20000 acres the breath to be one third of the length. In short you have every light I can give you but I had not time to make a list of the several papers for my Letters should have gone over the creek last night & tho I sat up till twelve aclock I coud get no further than finishing the last side, you will therefore judge in what hurry I am obliged to make up this & the rest of my Papers to get them to King George court to day. I send you inclosed a Copy of the Committees order[672] to reimburse you & you will with the other Papers receive an imperfect copy of my former Letter[673] to you wch if you have rec'ed will have put you out of dread for the Shannondoah Land If that shoud be the case burn this copy which will otherwise be only a needless trouble. I shall be out of Paper before you come in & would be glad of 2 reams of very good post something thicker than this. I have not yet had time to finish the Letter intended for my Aunt, if an opportunity offers in a few days I shall write again to supply what I may have omitted if I can from my memory recollect it, for I could not keep copies or memorandums tho I can now write as fast again as I could a month ago if such an Opportunity fails this is the last you may expect for I woud not advise you on any Account to stay longer than May. You need not bring in any Beer or Ale I shall send your Brother as soon as the Roads are passable some thats very good which will be fit to bottle by the time you arrive.

There has not been a meeting of the Compa or Committee since you wrote you had settled Hanbury's Accot but I am sure there will be still some Objections to it. I cant now say anything more on that head but I will endeavour to have a meeting soon & lay it before them.

Your brother confines himself too close to his house will drink

nothing strong & eats nothing but Rice, he looks well enough & everybody but himself beleives he is so, but he conceits he has a pain over his Eye. I thank God all the rest of the family are now well & not troubled with such imaginary disorders. They all desire to be most affectionately remembred to you & my daughter & impatiently long to see you both. My best blessings constantly attend you both with the most hearty prayers for your health & happiness. I am
    Dear George
       Your most affect. father & friend
         J Mercer
       March 3. 1768

 I had forgot to mention a most material Advice which I doubt will get home before this. Sr Wm Johnston & Genl Gage are doubtful of a General Insurrection of the Indians & advised[674] the Assembly of Pennsylvania of it. the reasons assurd that the frontier Inhabitants cheifly of Virg^a were contrary to the King's Proclamation daily settling on their unpurchased Lands which the Gov. Jan. 5. tells the Assembly[675] by the Line lately run appear to be in Pensylv^a The Assembly recommends[676] to the Govr to enquire into the murders of the Indians at Conestogoe[677] & Lancaster[678] in 1763 the Persons concerned being well known. The 10th of January one Frederick Stump a German killed 4 Indian men & two women in his own house near the mouth of [Middle Creek . . .] with going next day to an Indian Cabbin about 14 miles up the Creek & burning it with an Indian woman two girls & child in it all which it is said was done without any provocation, the Govr by proclamation[679] offered £200 reward for apprehending Stump. The next Pensylv^a Gazette of Feb 4th contains a Letter from one W Patterson dated Carlisle Jan. 23 giving an Acco^t that he had with a party of 19 men apprehended Stump & John Ironcutter after a desperate resistance by Stump & his friends & had delivered them Prisoners to Mr Holmes at Carlisle Goal, & he sends a copy of the Talk he had sent to the Susquehanna.

 The next Paragraph is the following. On Friday morning last (which was Jan. 29) a number of armed men (about 80, it is said) went to the Goal of Carlisle, which they entered by force & carried off the above mentioned Frederick Stump & John Ironcutter not withstanding the Opposition & Persuasion of the Magistrates & others to the contrary.[680]

 This I doubt will put an effectual Stop to all settlements on the Ohio for sometime. But I must seal & send off this & begin another [Addressed]

In the Darlington Memorial Library

To
Colo George Mercer of Virginia, now in London By Capt Anderson
[Endorsed]
March 3d 1768 Acknowledging the Receipt of the Report of the Lords for Trade & inclosing
Bounds proposed by the Ohio Company to take up their Lands.
[Endorsed]   Ohio 1768
Letter from my Father dated March the 3d 1768 reced 4th June, acknowledges The Receipt of the Report of the Lords for Trade June 26th 1767 see printed Case O. Compa Pages 33 & 34. sent in the Govrs Pacquet Octr 10th
Incloses Bounds of Lands which the Company desire to purchase.

Boundaries Proposed by the Ohio Company
February 26, 1768[681]
Enclosure 1

I think the following or some such Proposals would be proper on behalf of the Ohio Company.

If the Instructions from his late Majesty are insisted on, and the Company are thought to deserve no further Favours in Consideration of the great Charge they have incurred the Discoveries they have made, and the Informations they have from time to time given to the Government; then we ought at least to have Liberty to Survey our 500,000 Acres in as many different Tracts as we please, the words Grant or Grants plainly bearing that Meaning and being no way inconsistent with the Laws and Customs of Virginia, where the Patentees have never been obliged to make large Surveys for any particular Quantity, but if the words "Grant or Grants" are to be understood in the limitted Sense recommended[241] some time ago by the Board of Trade, and we are obliged to take the Lands in Tracts not less than 20,000 Acres, the breadth to be $\frac{1}{3}$ the length, We have been deceived by an unnatural Construction of the Words in the Royal Instructions[13] into a very heavy and useless Expence, as such Grants would not be worth our Acceptance, and what his late Majesty out of his Bounty, intended as a Favour and Encouragement to the Petitioners, would be turned into a real Injury, as we could have taken up the Lands upon better Terms here, without making any Application in England as many others have done in very large Quantities on this side the Allighany Mountains. Our Proposal was to take our

Lands on the other side the Allighany Mountains in a Country then unknown, which we have since discovered and opened a Road of Communication to it, at our own private Expence.

The first Adventurers in such an Enterprise as this have certainly a just Right to the Prefference in taking up the Lands they at so great Expence discovered; When the Ice is once broke, and the Settlement made practicable, those who came after will readily take such Lands as the first Adventurers refused, which in fact will be more valuable than the very best are now and the very additional Expences attending small Surveys will sufficiently restrain the Company from making more Surveys than they find absolutely necessary. As there is not the same necessity for the Company's building a Fort now as formerly, and as a Fort[682] we had begun, and a great many other of our Buildings[725] and Effects were destroyed by the War; We have reason to hope that Article will be remitted; and also that the Company may be indulged with appointing and employing a Surveyor of their own; the legal Fees to Surveyors of the Counties being exceeding high, nor would the Surveyor of Augusta County (at several hundred Miles distance from the place, tho it now falls within his District) be able to execute it, consistent with the duty's of his Office in that part of his County that is already inhabited—the only Reason why it may be thought to belong to his Office is, that the County of Augusta has no Bounds to the Westward; but as this is to be a new Settlement, and at present disjoined[683] from Virginia he can't be thought to be injured by such Appointment.

The Proprietor of the Northern Neck has always exercised the right of appointing his own Surveyor for taking up Lands not withstanding there was a commissioned Surveyor in each County, whom he has employed or not as he thought convenient.

If it should be thought proper to grant greater Indulgencies to the Company, and recompence them with a more extensive Grant, then I should think a Grant upon the following, or some such Terms, and by the following Boundaries might answer.

To begin on the River Mohongahaly where the Pensylvania line crosses the said River [illegible] with the Pensylvania Line a due West Course to the River Ohio, and down and with the River Ohio to the Mouth of the great Canhaway, alias Woods River or New River, and up the said Canhaway River binding with the same to the Mouth of the Green Briar River, and from thence by a streight Line to the Beginning on the River Mohongahaly. In consideration of which the Company to pay a yearly Acknowledgment in Lieu of Quitrents, to purchase the Lands of the Indians at their own Expence,

In the Darlington Memorial Library

and procure their Countenance and Protection to the Inhabitants, and to Settle 500 Families on the Land within seven years from the date of their Patent. In this Case it might be proper for the Ministry to recommend it to Sir William Johnston to use his Interest and good Offices with the Indians in assisting the Company to make a Purchase of the Lands;[684] which they would propose to do in plain and express Terms, without the least Fraud or Deception, that the Indians may have no Cause[744] to complain hereafter that they had been imposed upon, as has too frequently been the Case, and been attended with very fatal Consequences.

It is to be observed that these Bounds mentioned in our first Petition, and his late Majesty's Instructions without interfering with the Bounds of M<u>r</u> Penn's Grant, or without going to the Westward of the River Ohio; which would at present give great Umbrage both to the six Nations and the Western Tribes of Indians.

The Line[685] lately run by the Commissioners between the Proprietors of Maryland and Pensylvania will cross the Mohongahaly, and strike the Ohio many Miles below Pitsburg, consequently include all the Lands the Ohio Company had Settled, and though both the Proprietors of Maryland and Pensylvania promised[52] the late M<u>r</u> Hanbury that they would grant to the Company any vacant Lands, convenient to them, which might fall within their respective Provinces; Yet we don't know how far such Promises are now to be relied on; which is the Reason for ascertaining the Boundaries as before mentioned, to avoid a possibility of any Dispute. The Lands are also so convenient to Virginia, that they may well be under the same Government at least for the present. [one line illegible.]

It will be best to obtain a Grant in England instead of referring Us to the Governor and Council for the names of the present Company should lie inserted to prevent Disputes with such as were merely nominal, and have [not] advanced a single Shilling, nor been at the least Trouble.

Dear Sir.   M<u>rs</u> Moncures 26<u>th</u> Feb.' 1768

Since I parted with you I have upon reflecting on the Bounds proposed in my Memorandum for the Ohio Grant, apprehended that in one particular I am wrong, I have mentioned "Beginning on the River Mohongahaly where the Pensylvania Line crosses the said River; and runing with the Pensylvania Line a due West Course to the Ohio River" Now as we are not certain where M<u>r</u> Penns five Degrees of Longitude will end, this description may be disadvantageous to us, if his five Degrees of Longitude reach over the Ohio upon extending his lower West Course then I am right; but on the contrary, if his five degrees of Longitude are out before his lower West Line reaches the Ohio, then I apprehend Mr Penn must run a North Course from the end of his West Line; which will strike the Ohio River much higher up than to continue the West Course would do, and take in some very valuable Lands that the Bounds I before mentioned would leave out. It is indeed said that the five degrees of Longitude on his lower West Course will reach over the Ohio; but as this is not absolutely certain, We should be cautious in our Descriptions. I therefore think it will stand much better thus, "Beginning on the River Mohongahaly where the Pensylvania Line crosses the said River, and running with the Line or Boundaries [of] Pensylvania to the Ohio River &c" as before, this will answer in either Case. As I desire Mr Daniel to whose care this is directed to [you] immediately. I hope it will come to your hands before you dispatch your Letters to England; for I think the Alteration very material, for some other Reasons which I have not now time to mention.

G. Mason

P.S. Or as Mr Penn's Bounds are yet so uncertain, perhaps the Boundaries of a Grant to the Ohio Company would be better expressed as follows

"Beginning upon the East side of the River Ohio or Allaghany "where the Pennsylvania Line crosses the said River, and running "down and with the said River Ohio to the Mouth of the Great Con- "haway River, alias New River or Woods River, and up and with the "said Great Conhaway River to the Mouth of the Green Briar River, "from there by a streight Course to the nearest part of the Boundaries "of Pennsylvania, and with the Boundaries or Lines of Pennsylvania "to the Beginning upon the Ohio River"

All that Country or tract of Land bounded on the West and North West by the Ohio or Allaghany River; on the South and South West by the Great Conhaway River, otherwise called New River or Woods River; on the East and South East by the Green Briar River and the Allaghany Mountains, on the North East by the Monongahaly River and the Boundaries of Pennsylvania to the Ohio or Allaghany River.
[Endorsed]

Boundaries proposed by the Ohio Company when their grant is renewed.

The Case of the Ohio Company

By the treaty of Lancaster, as well as by deed bearing date the second day of July one thousand seven hundred and forty four, the northern Indians, by the name of the six nations (who claimed all the lands west of Virginia and also to and on the waters of the Missisippi and the lakes by right of conquest from the several nations of Indians who formerly inhabited that country and had been extirpated by the said six nations) did yield up, make over and forever quit claim to his Majesty and his successors, all the said lands west of Virginia, with all their right thereto as far as his Majesty should at any time thereafter be pleased to extend the said colony.

The year after some inhabitants of Virginia applied to the governor and council for grants of some lands in those parts, and in consequence thereof, at a council held the twenty sixth day of April one thousand seven hundred and forty five, leave was granted to John Robinson Esq. John Smith, James Patton, and Henry Downes (who had severally petitioned in the names of several other persons as well as themselves) to take up the hundred thousand acres of the westward of the Ohio, and on the fourth day of November following like leave was granted to John Blair Esq. William Russell and Company to take up One hundred thousand acres, lying to the westward of the line of Lord Fairfax on the waters of Potomack, and Youghyough gane, and altho the governor and council (who had been long sensible of the great importance of a settlement west of the great ridge of mountains and therefore for their encouragement) had allowed them four years time to survey their respective lands for which no rights were to be paid, till the return of the plans to the secretaries office, yet nothing was done in consequence of any of those orders of council, or any other applied for till William McMachen upon a petition in his own name and the names of nineteen other persons had on the twenty seventh day of April one thousand seven hundred and forty seven, leave to take up sixty thousand acres joining to the grant of John Blair Esq. and others and upon the waters of Potomack, west and north west of the line of Lord Fairfax, and on the branches of Youghyough gane and Monongaly, and they were allowed five years to survey the same and to pay rights on the return of their plan to the secretaries office. But these grantees as well as the former, lay by with their orders of council however they had some pretence, as Blairs grant upon which they were to bind never had been surveyd.

In the year one thousand seven hundred and forty eight, Thomas Lee Esq. one of his Majestys Council of Virginia who had been one of the commissioners at the treaty of Lancaster being well satisfied that no settlement would ever be effectually carried on in those parts by any private adventurers formed the first proposals of effecting it by a company which gave rise to the Ohio company. He was sensible that the chief complaints made by the Indians at that treaty were that they had been defrauded of their lands by the people of Pensilvania in particular, and had been extremely ill used by the traders from thence and New York who had ingrossed the whole peltry trade and were in general fellows of the most profligate characters, and who instead of supplying them with necessaries, sold them great quantities of spirituous liquors which not only debauched and enervated their people but involved them in continual quarrels and animosities and at the same time afforded the traders an opportunity of cheating them in their traffick. This last had been for some years a constant article of complaint and of not wholly disregarded was far from meeting any effectual redress. He therefore very rightly judged that there was no other way to fix the Indians firmly in the British Interest, but by a fair and well regulated trade. For the sake of this, he concluded, they would not be averse to the English extending their settlements to the westward, but without it, he was sure they would never permit any such thing. With this view he laid his proposals before the governor, who approving thereof recommended them to the right honourable the Lords commissioners of trade and plantations. at the same time the members of that company in Virginia and Maryland, judging that such trade could not be well carried on without taking in as a partner, or partners, one or more merchant or merchants of fortune and character, in Great Britain acquainted John Hanbury of London merchant with their proposals and intentions, and he readily approving them, preferred a petition to his Majesty in behalf of himself and others of the said company, a Copy of which is in the Appendix No. 1.

Which petition being referred by the right honourable the lords of the committee of his Majesties council, to the said commissioners of trade and plantations, they were pleased to report as their opinion that it would be for his Majesties service to grant the said petition for that the settlement of the country lying to the westward of the great mountains as it was the center of the British Dominions would be for his Majesties interest and the advantage and security of Virginia and the neighbouring colonies as by means thereof a more extensive trade and commerce might be carried on with the nations of Indians inhabiting those parts and it would likewise be a proper step towards checking the incroachments of the French by interrupting a part of their communication from their lodgments upon the great lakes to the river

Case of the Ohio Company, 1754.

Case of the Ohio Company, 1754[686]

Enclosure 2

By the treaty of Lancaster,[287] as well as by deed bearing date the second day of July one thousand seven hundred and forty four, the northern Indians, by the name of the six nations (who claimed all the lands west of Virginia and also to and on the waters of the Mississippi and the lakes by right of conquest from the several nations of Indians who formerly inhabited that countrey and had been extirpated by the said six nations) did yeild up, make over and forever quit claim to his Majesty and his successors, all the said lands west of Virginia, with all their right thereto as far as his Majesty should at any time thereafter be pleased to extend the said colony

The year after some inhabitants of Virginia applied to the governor and council for grants of some lands in those parts, and in consequence thereof, at a council held the twenty sixth day of April one thousand seven hundred and forty five, leave was granted[706] to John Robinson Esqr John Smith, James Patton, and Henry Downes (who had severally petitioned in the names of several other persons as well as themselves) to take up three hundred thousand acres of land upon the waters of the Ohio, and on the fourth day of November following like leave was granted[707] to John Blair Esqr William Russell and Company to take up One hundred thousand acres, lying to the westward of the line of Lord Fairfax on the waters of Potomack and Youghyoughgane, and altho' the governor and council (who had been long sensible of the great importance of a settlement west of the great ridge of mountains and therefore for their encouragement) had allowed them four years time to survey their respective lands for which no rights were to be paid, till the return of the plans to the secretaries office, yet nothing was done in consequence of any of those orders of council, or any other applied for till William Mc Machon upon a petition in his own name and the names of nineteen other persons had on the twenty seventh day of April one thousand seven hundred and forty seven, leave[708] to take up sixty thousand acres joining to the grant of John Blair Esqr and others and upon the waters of Potomack, West and North West of the line of Lord Fairfax, and on the branches of Youghyoughgane and Monongaly and they were allowed five years to survey the same and to pay rights on the return of their plan to the secretaries office. But these grantees as well as the former lay by with their orders of council however they had some pretence, as Blairs grant upon which they were to bind never had been survey'd

George Mercer Papers

In the year one thousand seven hundred and forty eight,[687] Thomas Lee Esqr one of his Majestys Council of Virginia who had been one of the Commissioners at the treaty of Lancaster being well satisfied that no settlement would ever be effectually carried on in those parts by any private adventurers formed the first proposals of effecting it by a company which gave rise to the Ohio company. He was sensible that the cheif complaints made by the Indians at that treaty were that they had been defrauded of their lands by the people of Pensilvania in particular, and had been extremely ill used by the traders from thence and New York who had ingrossed the whole peltry trade and were in general fellows of the most profligate characters, and who instead of supplying them, with necessaries, sold them great quantities of spiritous liquors which not only debauched and enervated their people but involved them in continual quarrels and animosities, and at the same time afforded the traders an opportunity of cheating them in their traffick. This last had been for some years a constant article of complaint and if not wholly disregarded was far from meeting any effectual redress. He therefore very rightly judged that there was no other way to fix the Indians firmly in the British Interest, but by a fair and well regulated trade. For the sake of this, he concluded, they would not be averse to the English extending their settlements to the westward, but without it, he was sure they would never permit any such thing. With this view he laid his proposals before the governor, who approving thereof recommended them to the right honourable the Lords commissioners of trade and plantations, at the same time the members of that company in Virginia and Maryland, judging that such trade could not be well carried on without taking in as a partner, or partners, one or more merchant or merchants of fortune and character in Great Britain acquainted John Hanbury of London Merchant with their proposals and intentions and he readily approving them, preferred a petition[7] to his Majesty in behalf of himself and others of the said company a Copy of which is in the Appendix No 1.[688]

Which petition being referred[9] by the right honourable the lords of the committee of his Majesties council, to the said commissioners of trade and plantations, they were pleased to report[11] as their opinion that it would be for his Majesties service to grant the said petition for that the settlement of the countrey lying to the westward of the great mountains as it was the center of the British Dominions would be for his Majesties interest and the advantage and security of Virginia and the neighbouring colonies as by means thereof a more extensive trade and commerce might be carried on with the nations of Indians inhabiting those parts and it would likewise be a proper step towards checking the incroachments of the French by interrupting part of their communication from their lodgments upon the great lakes to the river Mississippi by means whereof the British settlements were exposed to their incursions and that of the Indians in their interest, which benefits would be further extended under the said companys proposal, And therefore his Majesty was pleased by his instruction[13] to the governor of Virginia dated March the sixteenth one thousand seven hundred and forty eight nine to direct such grant or grants to be made to the said company with such exemptions and upon such conditions as was prayed almost in the very terms of the petition, Which instruction no sooner arrived and was made publick in Virginia than divers persons procured orders of council for one million and three hundred and fifty thousand acres of land on the very day[689] the said instruction was produced in council, among others James Patton (who had suffered the time allowed in his beforementioned order of council to run out) procured leave in the name of some of the persons formerly mentioned as his partners to renew the same for one hundred thousand acres and two years longer time were allowed them to compleat their surveys. Copies of which Orders are in the Appendix No 2.[690]

The Ohio company that they might comply with their proposals in the most effectual manner had upon the first notice of their petition being granted, directed[23] Mr Hanbury to ship them a cargo of two thousand pounds sterling value to be in the countrey by the last of November one thousand seven hundred and forty nine at the farthest and another cargo by the first of March after which were accordingly sent in for the carrying on the Indian trade. They also agreed that necessary roads[29] (one in particular to Monongahela) should be forthwith made and proper houses built,[182] but being sensible it would be in vain to attempt to make any settlements upon the Ohio, without the approbation and consent of the Indians settled there they directed that a proper application[30] should be made to the government of Virginia to invite those Indians to a treaty, and wrote Mr Hanbury to endeavour to obtain orders[27] from his Majesty for making a present to the said Indians as had been done by the government of New York[28] and other governments to the Northward upon the like occasions and to have the line between Virginia and Pensilvania run (in the same manner as that between Virginia and Carolina[35] had been) to enable the company to lay off their first two hundred thousand acres of land with certainty. He was at the same time desired in order to avoid any misunderstanding to procure an explanation of his Majesties instruction concerning the fort and garrison which were to be built and maintained by the company concerning which they apprehended their proposals had been mistaken.[57] They knew that the protection of their property would necessarily oblige them to build a fort and employ a force sufficient to guard their stores and servants from being plundered or no trade could possibly be carried on in such an unsettled part of the countrey, this they imagined their trade in its first beginning would not bear the expence of and therefore petitioned his Majesty to give up his quit rents (which amounted only to twenty pounds per annum) for ten years towards defraying that charge as they had prayed for the rights to be remitted on condition of seating an hundred families on the land. They well knew that one years pay and subsistence of fifty men only with proper Officers to form a regular garison, and even any building that could properly be called a fort would amount to more than both the rights and quit rents of the whole five hundred thousand acres of land would come to as may appear by the Estimate in the Appendix No[691]

And therefore they were persuaded nothing more was necessary to carry their point than a bare representation of the fact in the mean time fully persuaded of the benefit that would arise to the colony by the prosecution of their scheme they resolved to prosecute it with vigour, and for that end came to the foregoing resolutions[265] within six Months after the date of his Majesties instruction, but satisfied of the expediency of procuring a plan and account of that part of the countrey (which might be depended upon) before they came to any Resolution as to taking up and surveying the companys land they employed Mr Christopher Gist (a person well acquainted with the Indians upon the Ohio) to undertake a Tour for that purpose giving him particular instructions[266] to search and discover the lands upon that river (and the adjoining branches of the Mississippi) as low as the falls[42] thereof and particularly to observe the ways and passes thro' all the mountains he crossed, to take an exact account of the soil, quality, and product of the lands, the width and depth of the rivers and their several falls with the courses and bearings of the rivers and mountains, and also to enquire by all the ways and means he possibly could what nations of Indians inhabited those parts their strength and numbers with whom they traded and in what commodities they dealt, and to endeavour to cultivate a good understanding with them, and to convince them, if possible, of what consequence to them the freindship and alliance of the English was both in regard to their protection and trade, Of all which he was to keep a very exact and particular journal to be returned to the company

In the Darlington Memorial Library

upon his oath,[267] together with a plan of the countrey he past thro' drawn in the best manner he could. And as his Majesty had sent in a parcel of goods as a present[105] for the Indians the said Gist had a commission[81] from the President of Virginia to acquaint them with it, and to invite them to come to Virginia to receive it, Mr Gist set off the last of October on this difficult and dangerous undertaking and never returned till the nineteenth of May following and on the fifteenth day of July one thousand seven hundred and fifty one returned his plan[60] and journal to the companys committee, who judging it intirely impracticable to seat the land on the two rivers of Miamis and the falls of Ohio (which the said Gist recommended) and that they must, at all events take up their first two hundred thousand acres nearer in, which they beleived might be found to answer their expectations upon the creeks mentioned in the royal instructions,[5] they again agreed with the said Gist to vein and examine the lands between Monongahela and the Big Conhaway but in the meantime, conceiving it to be greatly for the companys interest, as well as the governments to cultivate a friendship and correspondence with the Ohio Indians and that nothing could answer that end more effectually than procuring a commission for the said Gist to meet those Indians at the Logs town,[77] at a grand council they were to hold there in the following month[268] (and then they were to receive his Majesties present) and to engage Mr Andrew Montour (one of the cheifs of the six nations) in the interest of the government of Virginia, and the company, the said committee recommended him to the president and Council [269] for that purpose and gave him proper instructions a copy of which is in the Appendix N° 3.[692] they at the same time ordered a copy of his journal and plan to be transmitted to Mr Hanbury expecting he would have had them printed.[271] That Mr Hanbury communicated the plan is apparent not only from those parts (of which there never [had been any thorough discovery made before) being] laid down according to his plan in all the Maps[272] of those parts published since but from his journey being pricked off in the map of Virginia[273] and some other maps[274] published in England since that time, but as the journal never was printed some extracts from thence are annexed in the Appendix N° 4[693] which will account for several things that have since happened.

The Indians for some reasons (the certain grounds of which cannot be assigned) failed[268] to meet at Logs town in August one thousand seven hundred and fifty one according to their appointment tho' Col^o Patton beforementioned went[275] there as a Commissioner from Virginia, Mr Gist therefore went out on the fourth of November following to search the lands on the South side of the Ohio, according to his instructions and returning the twenty ninth day of March one thousand seven hundred and fifty two delivered his journal to the companys committee from whence some extracts are made in the Appendix No 4[694]

The company was satisfied that Mr Gists two tours had in a great measure removed the prejudices[279] the Ohio Indians lay under towards the inhabitants of Virginia which had been artfully propagated among them, at least by the traders,[280] if not by the government of Pensylvania who were jealous of having any partners in the skin and furr trade which they had in a manner engrossed[281] to themselves. The Indians had found that they were supplied with goods by the company[282] on much more reasonable terms than they had been by the Pensilvania traders and could not doubt of a much more powerful protection from his Majesty than they before had reason to expect, as they generally looked upon Mr Penn (whom they called their brother Onas) to be the only person who concerned himself with American affairs such at least as they were interested in their lands and trade, But as the said Gist could not obtain from any of the said Indians any answer concerning the settlement of any lands on the Ohio[283] their resolution concerning which was referred till a general meeting and as they had agreed to meet at Logs town in the May[284] following Mr Gist again applied to the Government of Virginia who allowed of his appearing at the treaty as an agent for the company, but appointed the Colonels, Fry, Lomax and Patton[285] Commissioners for managing that treaty in behalf of his Majesty. Mr Gists instructions from the company are annexed in the Appendix No 5.[695] But as only one[696] of the Commissioners is now living who long after purchased a share in the Ohio company, and he had the misfortune to differ from his two Colleagues[697] who were largely concerned in great tracts of land to the Southward, No other part of the proceedings on that treaty than the speeches (about which there can be no controversy) is entered in the Appendix No 7[698] but from thence it will appear that it was with great difficulty the Indians were brought to agree that any settlements should be made by the English upon the Ohio, tho' at that very time they were under apprehensions of being attacked by the French.

The company were no sooner informed of the Indians resolution than they dispatched Mr Gist to the Northward to give notice to the persons he had there contracted[346] with in the companies behalf that they might remove as soon as they would to settle the land pursuant to his Majesties instructions, ⟨their Agreement⟩ and on his

In the Darlington Memorial Library

return he assured them ⟨the Compa⟩ that fifty of those families would remove ⟨that fall or⟩ the next spring as it was thought ⟨judged improper that⟩ the whole number ⟨should⟩ settle at once as they could not be ⟨supplied with proper provisions &⟩ necessaries, and afterwards at a meeting of the said Company September ⟨17. 1752⟩ the seventeenth one thousand seven hundred and fifty two it was agreed immediately to enter for[348] and survey their first two hundred thousand acres from Kiskamonettas down the South east side of Ohio to the mouth of the Big Conhaway where it was thought absolutely necessary to have some fort or place of security, And as it appeared absolutely also necessary to take up some small parcels of Land upon the river at convenient distances to build proper Houses for the reception of the persons removing to settle there and securing their goods while they were building they [illegible] November one thousand seven hundred and fifty two presented a Petition to the Governor and Council to enable them to do so on any terms the Governor and Council should think reasonable but upon an express Condition of actually seating such land before December the twenty fifth one thousand seven hundred and fifty three. This petition a Copy of which is in the Appendix No 6, was not only rejected but it was so little regarded that there was not any notice taken of it in the minutes of the council [proceedings] and therefore the company thought proper to procure an attested copy of it from their clerk, ⟨directed a proper Application should be made to the Gov' & Council for that purpose & at the same time contributed £400 towards building the Fort which was to be set about with the utmost Expedition & accordingly the following Petition was presented to the Govr & Council November 6, 1752 Insert it[699] At the same time several other Persons, judging this was the only time to obtain a Settlement upon the Ohio, before the French could get the Poss'ion which it would be extremely difficult, if not impossible to effect afterwards, applied to the Governor & Council for leave to take up several large tracts of land upon Condition of seating many hundred families thereon within three years after their Entries allowed, and as the following Paragraph had been &c As in the other Copy⟩ as they ⟨who⟩ were now fully convinced ⟨⟨as they had often before experienced⟩⟩ that instead of that protection and encouragement ⟨which⟩ they had always expected from the government here ⟨in Consequence of his Ma'ties Instruction⟩ they had the misfortune to have all their proceedings either misunderstood or misrepresented, The rejection of such a petition at that time was the more surprising as in the Virginia Gazettee of October the sixth one thousand seven hundred and fifty two was the following paragraph. (Indeed the Governor & Council then insisted that the Company was obliged to take up their 200000 Acres in one tract, altho the Entry of his Maties Instruction in the Council books & as in the following words At a Council—to—making settlem.ts thereon And it is remarkable that the Gov & Council had in express terms given Leave to all the greatest part of the Persons who had enterd for Lands the same day the Instruction was communicated to the Council to take up the Lands granted to them [in] one or more Surveys—an Indulgence they now refused to the Compa) Williamsburg October 6. We have credible advice[360] that the six nations, in alliance with the Twitwees a people much more powerful than themselves have declared war against the French and French Indians being exasperated thereto by the most horrid and shocking cruelties imaginable exercised by the French on one of the Twitwee towns.[342] The Company looked upon this stroke given the Twitwees in consequence of the French threats and their taking our traders on the Ohio both mentioned in Gist's journal as a full declaration of their intentions and were therefore satisfied that if a settlement was not gained on the Ohio before the French had time to take possession of it, it would be impossible to effect it several persons[361] who were of the same opinion and imagined they could procure a great number of families to settle those parts applied to the Governor and Council on the [same sixth] day of November one thousand seven hundred and fifty two desiring grants of large quantities of land bounded on the Ohio companies. On the condition of seating so many families thereon within a certain time one of which [Entries of] John Mercer for himself and thirteen partners desires a grant of 140,000 acres of land bounded on the Ohio companys land's when their quantity is laid off on such terms as the Governor and Council shall think reasonable to grant the same and will engage to settle one hundred and forty families in three years after the entry is allowed. Jno Mercer, Williamsburg Novr 6. 1752. Copy N Walthoe Cl Con. Whether the Governor and council were of the same opinion that some others pretended to be that these were only reports raised by the company to serve their ends (tho' none of those sagacious gentlemen ever pretended to point out what ends or in what manner they could be served by such reports) cannot be certain, tho' it is so that no more notice was taken of any of those entries than was of the companies petition however the company not to be wanting to themselves pressed Mr Gist to proceed in the settlement and survey[363] as expeditiously as possible and he in the next spring settled his own family with William Cromwells his brother in law and eleven other

In the Darlington Memorial Library

families[364] between the Yaugyaughgane and Monongahela, where they were no sooner seated than William Russell under colour of the order of council of November the fourth one thousand seven hundred and forty five granting leave to John Blair Esqr the said Russell himself and Company to take up one hundred thousand acres of land lying to the westward of the line of Lord Fairfax on the waters of Potomack and Yaughyaughgane surveyed those very lands in February one thousand seven hundred and fifty three[365] beginning on a branch of red stone creek above fifty miles due North from the headspring of Potomack the most Northern part of Lord Fairfax's line[366] and finding his first course run between Cromwells and Gists and would include Gists own settlement as Russell knew him to be the companies surveyor and thought it too barefaced an attempt on their property he altered his course to leave him as he termed it a handsome settlement but included the other eleven families who had settled there as upon the companies lands and under their engagement with Gist on the companies behalf. This proceeding was the more extraordinary as Colo Cresap one of the company was then out with several persons to lay off a town[367] contiguous to the fort (which the company had agreed to build on Shurtees creek and raised four hundred pounds for that purpose) and gave Russell notice to desist as the land was actually seated by the company no ways answered the description mentioned in the order of council which he conceived was void because as it allowed but four years to survey that expired November the fourth one thousand seven hundred and forty nine and could not be renewed as it was termed by the order of council of October the twenty sixth one thousand seven hundred and fifty one, two years after but Russell declaring his partners did not value the company persisted in his resolution and continued his survey, and Colo Cresap expecting such a peice of flagrant injustice would be no sooner complained of than redressed, suffered him to proceed tho' it is notorious that Russell dared not to have disputed his orders at that time and place, had he ordered him immediately to depart. The company upon receiving an account of this extraordinary proceeding in a regular manner enter'd a caveat[370] in April General court and made no doubt but they might have had a summons for Russell to appear as soon as possible as the Governor had that court received an express from the Ohio to give him account that the French Indians had carried off four Indian traders[376] belonging to Philadelphia in the month of January who were carried to Canada and made Slaves as appears by a letter and paragraph published in the Virginia Gazettee of August 30th 1754 hereinafter mentioned—

but how great was the companys surprize when instead of such a Summons as they desired they could not procure one returnable before June one thousand seven hundred and fifty four so much out of the ordinary course of proceedings that the company has never been able to learn that any other summons was ever delayed longer than the usual return which is to the Court of Oyer and Terminer following, and therefore the companys in the usual course should have been returnable to June one thousand seven hundred and fifty three, but at that time when at the farthest they hoped for a redress of the injury they had complained of another of the Council Richard Corbin Esqr in the name of himself and company procured three orders of Council to impower them ⟨them or rather him⟩ to survey fifty thousand acres of Land on fishing creek one hundred thousand acres at the mouth of the big Conhaway and forty thousand on Buffalo creek all within those very bounds the Ohio company had on the sixth of November preceding acquainted the Governor and Council they proposed to make their Surveys, and what the company thought hardest was that those entries were directed by their own map[393] laid before the council on that day by the Governor who was entrusted with it only as he was a member of the Ohio company and engaged his word not to shew it for before that time neither he or any of the council knew anything of the situation of the Ohio, or the names of any of it's branches. Before this time May 3. 1753. the following Extract of a Letter from Capt Trent was published in the Pensylvania and afterwards printed in the Virginia Gazettee. Philadelphia May 3. Extract of a Letter from Capt William Trent.[362] I take this opportunity of acquainting you of the French and Indians killing and taking our people prisoners. They have killed Finleys[380] three men near the little Pick town,[381] and we expect that he himself will be killed. Teaff[382] was robbed of two or three hundred pounds, but his men got off, fifty five French Indians have robb'd us on this side the river below Shawnesse town of three or four hundred pounds, and took prisoners David Hendrick, William Powell, Jacob Evans, and his brother,[376] and a servant belonging to us, one M'Ginte[383] and James Lowrey, belonging to the Lowries,[384] the last made his escape after he had been a prisoner several days. Mr Croghan with an hundred horse load of skins is coming thro' the woods on this side the river with a few Indians, but am afraid that they will be killed or taken by three hundred Ottawawas, that was expected would surprize the town,[385] as they had information of their coming, and doubt they will follow them when they find them gone the rest of the white men are coming up the river in a body with what Indians are below, but

In the Darlington Memorial Library

as there is a large body of French and Indians expected every day down the river,[386] I doubt they will never get up, poor Fortescue perished on the road coming from the lower town. There is not one Indian or white man anywhere below the Shawnesse or Logs town but what is coming up. This was accompanied with the following paragraph, May 24. Four of the Indian traders, who were taken prisoners in the Twigtwee town last summer by the French carried to Canada, and from thence sent to old France, are return'd with Cap.' Budden, having been released out of prison at Rochelle, by the Sollicitation of the British Embassador, who was so good as to cloath them, and send them to England, the French having stripped them naked, and used them very hardly.

From hence it appears that the French began their hostilities in the summer one thousand seven hundred and fifty two and that they immediately stirred up the Indians in their alliance to make slaves of the English or murder them is put out of dispute by the following letter and account first published in the pensilvania & afterwards in the Virg^a Gazettee Philadelphia Augt 15. In January 1753. four of our Indian traders viz. Alexander MacGenty, Jabez Evans, David Hendricks and William Powell (four of those named in Capt Trents letter[372]) were taken trading on Kanticoqui[373] river near the Ohio, by a party of French Indians called the Cagnawagas,[374] who plundered them of goods to the value of several hundred pounds, and carried them to Canada, where they were made slaves, But acquainting the Mayor of Albany[375] with their miserable situation, by a letter[376] which he communicated[377] to this Government measures were taken to procure their release the Indians at first demanded a Negro boy for each of them, or as much as would buy one, but at length were prevailed on by the Commissioners of Indian affairs at Albany[378] to take less, tho' the whole paid them, with the charges amounted to seventy two pounds five shillings and three half pence for the four prisoners, which has been repaid by this province however the Indians it seems pretend not to be satisfied, and Colonel Myndert Schuyler one of the Albany Commissioners for Indian affairs, who transacted this matter with them received lately the following letter from the cheif of that nation on the subject vizt (Copy Literatim), Au Sault St Louis 14.[379] Juin 1754.

[Illegible, see translation which follows]

du prisonnier que je vous estremy a Aurange. Lanne derniere, Mes juennes Gens me dise tous le Jour qu'l ne sont poin couten, de votre Fasson Dagir et qua lavenir ils nameuneron plus les Hommes vivans, puis quon ne leur donne pas. Suelement de quoy avoir un petit

· 243 ·

Esclave Sauvage, Tu cest mon Frere que je n'est pas on que quartrevingt dix Livres de notre Argent. Je charge Montandre de cette Commission, ilt expliquer a mes Sentimens ou te remettan ma Lettre. Le Moins qu'on paye un prissonier cest quarte cent Livres, Faits faire Attention a cieux qui ont ces sortes ₍des₎ Affaires autre le mains sans quois je ne repons poin de Evenement qui pourrais arriver a lavenir losque mes juenes Gens feron dis prissonier

Ononraguite Chef du Sault S⸰ Louis.

Translated into English, Falls of S⸰ Louis June 14. 1754.

I pray thee, my brother Anagarondon (Anagarondon is Col⸰ Schuyler's Indian name) to acquaint the Gentlemen, that I have not been satisfied for the prisoners that were delivered to you at Albany last year. my young men tell me every day that they do not like your management and that for the future they will bring no living prisoners, since they do not receive as much for one of them as will buy a little slave. You know my brother that I had only ninty livres of our money, I charge Montandre with this Commission, who will explain my sentiments to you, when he delivers you this letter. The least that ought to be paid for a prisoner is 400 Livres (about twenty pounds sterling) let those that have the management of these sort of Affairs, give due attention to this, otherwise I will not answer for what may happen hereafter when my young men make prisoners

Onongraguiete cheif of the Falls of S⸰ Louis.

Upon which the printer makes the following very just remark, By this insulting letter from a people with whom this province has not had the least difference, to whom we have never given the least occasion of offence, we may see the contempt in which we are held by these savages, who not content with plundering our people of their goods with impunity propose to make slaves of all of us they can catch, or to have a sum for each sufficient to purchase a slave, otherwise threatning they will not be at the trouble of saving our lives. If they are suffered to go on in this manner and to make a trade of catching our people, and selling them to us again for 400 Livres per head, it may in time cost us more to satisfy the demands of that handful of barbarians, than would serve to defend the province against all its Enemies.

That Governor Dinwiddie had timely notice and was fully apprized of the French proceedings and the dangerous situation of our freindly Indians upon the Ohio before these three orders[392] of council were obtained by Col⸰ Corbin appears from his letter[396] of May 31. 1753 to Cap⸰ Trent which with several other original papers are to be found in the Appendix N⸰ 8[700] which the company is persuaded will fully evince the great disregard shewn to them upon every occasion and the great inconsistence of the Governors conduct in throwing every bar in their way and preventing their settling those lands at the same time he was inviting foreigners to do it. Some of the persons who removed from the Northward to settle the companies land finding the company was not able to obtain any immediate redress, not only returned back to their former habitations but stopped the other families that were about to remove, and this step with some other instances of the same kind has prejudiced the Northward people to that degree that it is to be feared no promises or offers that the government of Virginia can make will ever be able to remove their prejudice or engage their confidence, and hence it is that some thousands from the Northern provinces have since passed thro' this colony to procure worse lands and on much worse terms to the Southward.

The Ohio company resolved however not to give up their interest without taking all legal steps for their redress, and therefore were no sooner informed of those three orders of council[392] obtained by Colo Corbin than they ordered caveats[391] to be entred against them. They employed persons to build their fort and sent to England for proper Guns, Arms, and Ammunition for it. The Assembly of Virginia meeting the first of November following the Governor in his speech[701] laid before them by his Majestys orders the Necessity of a mutual assistance and recommended to them to grant such supplies as the exigency then required, but tho' he tells them the French attempts had been strongly noticed and attended to at home and there judged to be of great consequence to his Majesties dominions and his subjects here, it seems pretty clear that neither he or the Assembly thought the danger very pressing as he tells the Assembly he intends to meet the cheifs of the different tribes of Indians the next May[702] at Winchester and hopes then to make a firm strong and lasting alliance with them and they thought an Act[703] to exempt the settlers on the branches of Mississippi from levies for fifteen years, and a duty on wheel carriages and some other small duties to be raised the year following and which would altogether yield a very inconsiderable sum, was a sufficient provision for the then exigency, nay it is certain that it was affirmed in Williamsburg during the sitting of the Assembly that there was not a french man upon or near the Ohio,[704] nor did the contrary opinion prevail or obtain any credit till the return of Majr Washington who was dispatched on the last of October to enquire into the particulars, and returned to Williamsburg January 16. 1754. Upon his return and report the Governor thought proper to pitch upon the place where the company proposed building their fort.

Appendix

No 1.   To the Kings most Excellent Majesty.[705]

The Humble Petition[7] of John Hanbury of London Merchant in behalf of himself and of Thomas Lee Esqr a member of your Majestys Council and one of the Judges of the Supream Court of Judicature in your Majestys Colony of Virginia, Thomas Nelson Esqr also a member of your Majestys Council in Virginia, Colonel Cressup Colo William Thornton, William Nimmo, Daniel Cressup John Carlysle Lawrence Washington, Augustine Washington, George Fairfax, Jacob Giles Nathaniel Chapman and James Woodrop. Esquires all of your Majestys Colony of Virginia and others their Associates for setling the Countries upon the Ohio and extending the British trade beyond the mountains on the western Confines of Virginia

Most humbly Sheweth,   That by the treaty of Lancaster and also by deed bearing date the 2d day of July 1744. the northern Indians by the name of the six nations (who claimed all the lands west of Virginia and also to and on the waters of the Mississippi and the lakes by right of conquest from several nations of Indians who formerly inhabited that countrey and have been extirpated by the said six nations) did yeild up and make over and forever quit claim to your Majesty and your successors all the said Lands west of Virginia with all the right thereto, so far as your Majesty should at any time thereafter be pleased to extend the said colony

That most of the nations of Indians west of the mountains and upon the lakes and the river Ohio have enter'ed into Alliance with your Majestys Subjects and with the six nations in freindship with the British Colony's and have desired your Majestys subjects the Inhabitants of Virginia to send them British goods and manufactures as they incline to trade solely with your Majestys subjects.

That by laying hold of this opportunity and improving this favourable disposition of these Indians they may be forever fixed in the British Interest and the prosperity and safety of the British Colonies be effectually secured and which your petitioners are ready and willing to undertake

That your petitioners beg leave humbly to inform your Majesty that the lands to the west of the said mountains are extremely fertile the climate very fine and healthy and the waters of Mississippi and those of Potomac are only separated by one small ridge of mountains easily passable by land carriage so that by the convenience of the Navigation of the Potomac and a short land carriage from thence to the west of the mountains and to the branch of the Ohio and the

In the Darlington Memorial Library

lake Erie British goods may be carried at little expence and afforded reasonably to the Indians in those parts, in case the lands to the west of the said mountains were setled and a fort erected in some proper place there for the protection and encouragement of your petitioners and others your Majestys subjects in adventuring their persons and fortunes in this undertaking in which if your petitioners meet with that success they have great reason to expect it will not only be made the best and strongest Frontier in America but will be the means of gaining a vast addition and increase to your Majestys subjects of that branch of the peltry and furr trade which your petitioners propose by means of the settlement herein after mentioned to carry on with the Indians to the westward of the said mountains and on the said lake and rivers and will at the same time greatly promote the consumption of our British manufactures enlarge our commerce encrease our shipping and Navigation and extend your Majestys Empire in America, and in a short space of time very considerably encrease your Majestys revenue of quit rents, as there is little room to doubt but that when this settlement is once begun by your petitioners but that a great number of foreign protestants will be desirous of setling in so fertile and delightful a countrey under the just and mild Administration of your Majestys government especially as they will be at little more charge than the transporting themselves from their native countrey.

That your petitioners for these great and national ends and purposes and in order to improve and extend the British trade amongst these Indians and to settle these countreys in so healthy and fine a climate and which are your Majestys undoubted right have enterd into partnership by the name of the Ohio company to settle these countries to the west of the said mountains and to carry on a trade with the Indians in those parts and upon the said lakes and rivers, But as the effecting the same and more especially the erecting a sufficient fort and keeping a garrison to protect the infant settlement will be attended with great expence

Your Petitioners who are the first adventurers in this benefecial undertaking which will be so advantageous to the Crown in point of Revenue, to the nation in point of trade, and to the British colonies in point of strength and security, Most humbly pray that your Majesty will be graciously pleased to encourage this their said undertaking by giving instructions to your governor of Virginia to grant to your petitioners and such others as they shall admit as their Associates a tract XM, XM, of five hundred thousand acres of land betwixt Romanettos and Buffloes creek on the south side the river Alligany otherwise the Ohio, and betwixt the two creeks and the yellow creek on the north side of the said river or in such other parts to the west of the said mountains as shall be judged most proper by your petitioners for that purpose, And that two hundred thousand acres part of the said five hundred thousand Acres may be granted immediately without rights on condition of your Petitioners seating at their proper expence a hundred familys upon the lands in seven years, the lands to be granted free of quit rents for ten years on condition of their erecting a fort and maintaining a garrison for protection of the settlement for that time Your petitioners paying the usual quit rents at the expiration of the said ten years from the date of their patent And your petitioners further pray that your Majesty will be graciously pleased to send your said governor a further instruction that as soon as these two hundred thousand acres are settled and the fort erected that three hundred thousand acres more residue of the said five hundred thousand acres may be granted to your petitioners adjoining to the said two hundred thousand acres of land as first granted with the like exemptions and under the same covenants and to give all such further and other encouragements to your petitioners in this their so useful and public an undertaking as to your Majesty in your great wisdom shall seem meet, And your Petitioners will ever pray.

       Signd.   John Hanbury

No 2.   At a Council April 26th 1745.[706]

On the petition of John Robinson Senr Esqr Thos Nelson Junr Esqr John Robinson Junr Esqr William Beverley, Robert Lewis, Beverley Robinson, Henry Wetherburne, John Lewis, John Crag, William Lewis John Wilson and Charles Lewis, leave is granted them to take up 100,000 acres lying on Green Briar river, north west and west of the Cow pasture and new found land and that four years time be allowed them to survey and pay rights for the same upon return of the plans to the secretaries Office

           N. Walthoe Cl Con.

On the petition of John Smith, Zachary Lewis, William Waller, Benjamin Waller, and Robert Green, leave is granted them to take up 50,000. acres in that part of Orange which will be in the County of Augusta when that County shall take place on the River and branches of Roanoke and the branches of James River and that four years time be allowed them to survey and pay rights for the same upon return of the plans to the secretaries office

           N Walthoe Cl Con'

In the Darlington Memorial Library

On the Petition of James Patton Robert Slaughter, John Graeme, John Belfeild, John Tayloe Jun[r] William Greene, Richard Barnes, James Gordon, James Wood, George Buchanan, Geo. Robinson, James Bowie, Robert Jackson, W[m] Parks, John Preston, Robert Gilchrist, Richard Winslow, John Roberts, John Weatheraland, James Johnston leave is granted them to take up 100,000. acres lying in Augusta County on the three branches of Mississippi river, the one known by the name of Woods river, the other to the westward thereof and of the waters of the said River the said land lying to the westward of a former order of council granted to Zachary Lewis Gent and others, and that four years time be allowed them to survey and pay rights for the same upon return of the plans to the secretaries office

N Walthoe Cl Con.'

On the Petition of Henry Downes, John Blair Jun[r] John Willis, George Taylor, Edward Spencer Robert Slaughter, Thomas Slaughter, William Jackson, Alexander Dunlap, James Ewin, and Edward Fuller leave is granted them to take up 50,000. acres lying West of the Cow pasture or Green Bryar River and that four years time be allowed them to survey and pay rights for the same upon return of the plans to the secretaries office

N Walthoe Cl Con.'

At a Council held November the 4th 1745.[707]

On the Petition of John Blair Esq[r] William Russell and Company leave is granted them to take up one hundred thousand acres of Land lying to the westward of the line of L[d] Fairfax on the waters of Potomack and Youghyoughgane and to be allowed four years time to survey and pay rights for the same upon return of the plans to the secretaries office

N. Walthoe

At a Council held April 22[d] 1747.[708]

On the Petition of William M[c]Machon, John M[c]Machon, Richard M[c]Machon, Lewis Neal, John Neal Mark Calmees and Company leave is granted them to take up sixty thousand acres of Land adjoining to the Grant of John Blair Esq[r] and others and upon the waters of Potomack West and North West of the line of L[d] Fairfax and on the branches of Youghyoughgane and Monongaley and to be allowed five years time to survey and pay Rights for the same upon return of the plans to the secretaries office

N Walthoe

George Mercer Papers

At a Council held July 12th 1749.[709]

On the Petition of Bernard Moore, Benja Hubbard, Philip Aylett, Thomas Dansie, John Snelson, George Carrington, James Power, Duncan Graham, William Taylor, and Job Thomas, Leave is granted them to take up and Survey 100,000. Acres of Land on the Waters of Mississippi River beginning at ten trees marked, P. T. C. standing in the forked branch of the said River, known by the name of new River and so down the said River and the waters of the said Mississippi and to be allowed four years time to survey and pay rights for the same upon return of the plans to the Secretaries Office.

N Walthoe Cl Con.'

On the Petition of John Lewis Esqr Thomas Walker, John Meriwether, Charles Lewis, James Power, Peter Jefferson, Charles Dick, Charles Barrett, Joshua Fry, Thomas Turpin, John Harvey, Thomas Meriwether, Thos Meriwether Junr John Baylor, Samuel Waddy, Robert Barret, Henry Willis, Peachy Gilmer, John Lewis, James Maury, Thomas Lewis, Peter Hedgman, John Moore, Robert Martin, Henry Tate, Richard Jones, William Wood, Samuel Dalton, Francis Thornton, Francis Thornton Junr John Thornton, John Peirce, William Stevenson, Nicholas Lewis, Nicholas Meriwether William Hudson, Francis Meriwether, Humphry Hill and John Dixon, Leave is granted them to take up and survey 800,000. Acres of Land in one or more Surveys beginning on the bounds between this Colony and North Carolina and running to the westward and to the north so as to include the said quantity and they are allowed four years time to survey and pay rights for the same upon the return of the plans to the secretaries office

N Walthoe Cl Con

On the Petition of Peyton Randolph, Alexr McKensie, Robert Tucker, John Tucker, George Gilmer Benja Waller, William Parks, Armistead Burwell, Edmund Pendleton, John Willoughby, John Maddison, John Shelton, John Garland, Thomas Williamson, Maximilian Calvert, Cornelius Calvert, Paul Loyall and George Logan, leave is granted them to take up and survey 400,000. Acres of Land, in one or more surveys, lying on new River commonly called Woods river and the Waters thereof and four years time allowed them to survey and pay rights for the same upon return of the plans to the secretaries office

N Walthoe Cl Con.'

On the Petition of William Winston Junr Isaac Winston Junr Peter

In the Darlington Memorial Library

Fontane Junr Edmund Winston and Samuel Red, leave is granted them to take up and survey 50,000 acres of land beginning at old fort between Ohio and Mississippi Rivers running up the western side of Ohio and Eastern side of Mississippi, in one or more surveys between the said Rivers, and four years time allowed them to survey and pay rights for the same upon return of the plans to the Secretaries office.

N. Walthoe Cl Con

On the petition of John Tayloe, William Parks, and James Wood in behalf of themselves & company leave is given them to renew their Grant for one hundred thousand acres of Land lying in Augusta County on the three branches of the Mississippi River the one known by the name of Woods river and the other two to the westward thereof and on the waters of the said River and two years longer time allowed them to compleat their surveys.

N Walthoe Cl Con.'

At a Council held October 26th 1751.[710]

Both the Orders of John Blair Esqr William Russell and Company, and William McMachon, John McMachon, Richard McMachon, Lewis Neal, John Neal, Mark Calmees and Company were renewed, in the first four years further time allowed to Survey &c.' and in the second five years further time allowed and leave to insert the names of any person or persons whom they should find it necessary to take in as a partner or partners to promote the setling of the said Lands[277] &c.'

N. Walthoe

At a Council held June 15th 1753.[711]

On the Petition of Richard Corbin and Company leave is granted them to take up and survey fifty thousand acres of land on the waters of Mississippi beginning at the mouth of fishing creek and four years time is allowed them to survey and pay rights for the same upon return of the plans to the secretaries office

To the same One hundred thousand acres on the waters of Mississippi beginning at the mouth of the new River otherwise the Big Canaughway on the same terms.

To the same forty thousand Acres on the waters of Mississippi beginning at the mouth of Buffalo creek on the South side thereof on the same terms.

N. Walthoe

George Mercer Papers

No 3   Instructions given to Mr Gist 16. July 1751.

After you return from Williamsburg and have executed the commission[180] of the president and council if they shall think proper to give you one, otherwise, as soon as you can conveniently, you are to apply to Colo Cresap for such of the companys horses, as you shall want, for the use of your self and such other person[181] or persons as you shall think necessary to carry with you, and you are to look out and observe the nearest and most convenient road you can find from the companys store[182] at Wills creek to a landing on Monongahela,[183] from thence you are to proceed, down the Ohio, on the South side thereof as low as the Big Conhaway and up the same, as far as you judge proper and find good land, you are all the way to keep an exact Diary and journal and therein note every parcel of good land with the quantity, as near as you can by any means compute the same with the breadth depth courses and length of the several branches falling into the Ohio, and the different branches any of them are forked into, laying the same as exactly down in a plan[60] thereof as you can, observing also the produce, the several kinds of timber and trees and noting where there is plenty and where the timber is scarce, and you are not to omit proper observations on the mountainous barren or broken land that we may on your return, judge what quantity of good land is contained within the compass of your journey. We would not have you omit taking notice of any quantity of good land, tho' not exceeding four or five hundred acres provided the same lies upon the river Ohio and may be convenient for our building storehouses and other houses for the better carrying on a trade and correspondence down that river

No 4   Extracts from Mr Gists Journal.[712]

Sunday Novr 25th In the Logs Town[77] I found scarce anybody but a parcel of reprobate Indian traders the cheif of the Indians being out hunting, here I was informed that George Croghan[78] and Andrew Montour[79] who were sent upon an embassy[80] from Pensilvania to the Indians, were passed about a week before me, the people in this town began to enquire my business, and because I did not readily inform them they began to suspect me and said I was come to settle the Indians lands, and they knew I should never go home again safe. I found this discourse was like to be of ill consequence to me, so I pretended to speak very slightingly of what they had said to me, and enquired for Croghan (who is a mere Idol among his countreymen the Irish traders) and Andrew Montour the Interpreter for Pensilvania and told them I had a message to deliver the Indians from the King by order[81] of the president of Virginia and for that reason wanted to see M.r Montour. This made them all pretty easy (being afraid to interrupt the Kings message) and obtained me quiet and respect among them, otherwise I doubt not they would have contrived some evil against me. I immediately wrote to M.r Croghan by one of the traders people, tho' I was unwell I preferred the woods to such company and set out from the Logs town down the River Northwest six miles to great Beaver creek.[713]

Friday Dec.r 14.th Set out West five miles to Moskingum[83] a town of the Wyendots, the land upon Elks Eye creek is, in general, very broken, the bottoms narrow. The Wyendots or little Mingoes are divided[93] between the French and English one half of them adhere to the first, and the other half are firmly attached to the latter. The town of Mouskingum consists of about one hundred families, when we came within sight of the town we perceived English colours hoisted on the kings[94] house and at George Croghans,[95] upon enquiring the reason, I was informed that the French had lately taken several English traders,[96] and that M.r Croghan had ordered all the white men to come into this town and had sent expresses to the traders of the lower towns[97] and among the Pickiveylinees,[98] and the Indians had sent to their people to come to council about it

Saturday 15.th Nothing remarkable happened.

Monday 17. Came into town two traders belonging to M.r Croghan, and informed us, that two[99] of his people were taken by forty frenchmen and twenty french Indians who had carried them with seven horse loads of Skins to a new fort[100] that the French were building on one of the branches of Lake Erie

Tuesday 25.th This being Christmas day, I intended to read prayers, but after inviting some of the white men, they informed each other of my intentions, and being of several different perswasions and few of them inclined to hear any good, they refused to come, but one Thomas Burney[101] a blacksmith, who is settled there went about and talked to them, and then several of them came, and Andrew Montour invited several of the well disposed Indians who came freely. By this time the morning was spent, and I had given over all thoughts of them, but seeing them come to oblige all and offend none, I stood up and said, Gentlemen, I have no design or intention to give offence to any particular sect or religion but as our King indulges us all in a liberty of conscience, and hinders none of you in the exercise of your religious worship so it would be unjust in you to endeavour to stop the propagation of his, the doctrine of salvation, faith and good works, is only what I propose to treat of, as I find it extracted from the Homilies of the Church of England, which I then read to them in the best manner I could, and after I had done the Interpreter told the Indians what I had read, and that it was the true faith which the great King and his Church recommended to his children, the Indians seemed well pleased and came up to me, and returned me their thanks, and then invited me to live among them and gave me a name in their language Annasonah, the interpreter told me, this was the name of a good man that had formerly lived among them, and their king said that must be always my name, for which I returned them thanks, but as to living among them I excused my self by saying I did not know whether the governor would give me leave and if he did the French would come and carry me away as they had done the English traders, to which they answered I might bring great guns and make a fort, that they had now left the French and were very desirous of being instructed in the principles of christianity that they liked me very well and wanted me to marry them after the christian manner, and baptize their children, and then he said they would never desire to return to the French or suffer them or their preists to come near them more, for they loved the English but had seen little religion among them, and some of their great men came and wanted me to baptize their children, for as I had read to them and appeared to talk about religion they took me to be a minister of the gospel upon which I desired Mr Montour the interpreter to tell them that no minister could venture to baptize any children until those that were to be sureties for them, were well instructed in the faith themselves and that was according to the great Kings religion in which he desired his children should be instructed, and we dare not do it in any other way than was by law established, but I hoped if I could not be admitted to live among them that the great King would send them proper ministers to exercise that office among them, at which they seemed well pleased and one of them went and brought me his book, which was a kind contrived for them by the French in which the Days of the Week were so marked that by moving a Pin every morning they kept a pretty exact of the time, to show me that he understood me that he and his family always observed the Sabbath day.[714]

Friday Jan.' 4. 1751 One Teafe an Indian trader came to town from near lake Erie and informed us that the Wyendotts Indians had advised him to keep clear of the Ottaways,[89] these are a nation of Indians firmly attached to the French and inhabit near the lakes, and told him that the branches of the lakes are claimed by the French, but that all the branches of the Ohio belonged to them, and their brothers the English, and that the French had no business there, and that it was expected that the other part[93] of the Wyendott nation would build a strong fort and town there.[715]

Wednesday Jan.' 9. The wind southerly and the weather something warmer, this day came into town two traders from among the Pickolinnees,[98] these are a tribe of the Twigtwees, and brought news that another English trader[103] was also taken prisoner by the French and that three Soldiers had deserted and come over to the English and surrendered themselves to some of the traders of the Pick town[98] and that the Indians would have put them to death to revenge their taking our traders, but as the french Indians had surrendered themselves the English would not let the Indians hurt them but had ordered them to be sent under the care of three of our traders and delivered at this town to George Croghan.[716]

Saturday Jan' 12, We sent away our people towards the lower town[104] intending to follow them the next morning and this evening we went into council in the Wyendotts kings house,[93] the council had been put off a long time expecting some of their great men in, but few of them came, and this evening some of the kings council being a little disordered with liquor no business could be done, but we were desired to come next day[717]

Monday Jan.' 28 We went into council with the Indians of this town and after the interpreter[79] had informed them of his instructions[80] from the governor of Pensilvania and given them some cautions in regard to the French they returned for answer as follows, The speaker with four strings of wampum in his hand stood up and addressing himself as to the governor of Pensilvania said "Brothers We the Delawares return you our hearty thanks for the news you have sent us, and we assure you, we will not hear the voice of any other nation for we are to be directed by you our brothers the English and none else, We shall be very glad to hear what our brothers have to say to us at the Logs town in the spring and do assure you of our hearty good will and love to our brothers. We present you with these four strings of wampum." This is the last town of the Delawares to the westward. The Delaware Indians by the best accounts I could gather consists of about five hundred fighting men all firmly attached to the English interest. they are not properly a part of the six nations but are scattered about among most of the Indians upon the Ohio, and some of them among the six nations from whom they have leave to hunt upon their lands.

Tuesday Jan.' 29th Set out South west five miles to the mouth of Sciodoe creek opposite to the Shannoah town[116] here we fired our guns to alarm the traders who soon answered and came and ferried us over to the town. The land about the mouth of the Sciodoe creek is rich but broken, fine bottoms upon the river and creek. The Shannoah Town is situate on both sides the river Ohio, just below the mouth of the Sciodoe creek and contains about three hundred men there are about forty houses on the south side of the river and about a hundred on the north side with a kind of state house of about ninety feet long with a light cover of bark in which they hold their councils. The Shanaws are not a part of the six nations but were formerly at Variance with them tho' now reconciled. They are great freinds to the English who once protected[117] them from the fury of the six nations which they gratefully remembered.

Wednesday 30th We were conducted into council where George Croghan[78] delivered sundry speeches from the government of Pensilvania[80] to the cheifs of this nation in which he informed them, "That two prisoners[118] who had been taken by the French and had made their escape from the French officer at Lake Erie as he was carrying them towards Canada brought news that the French offered a large sum of money to any person who would bring them the said Croghan and Andrew Montour alive, or if dead their scalps and that the French also threatned these Indians and the Wyendotts with war in the spring, the same persons farther said that they had seen twenty french canoes loaded with stores for a new fort[119] they designed on the south side of Lake Erie," Mr Croghan[78] also informed them that several of our traders had been taken and advised them to keep their warriours at home until they could see what the French intended which he doubted not would appear in the spring. Then Andrew Montour[79] informed this nation as he had done the Wyendotts and Delawares "That the King of Great Britain had sent them a large present[105] of goods in company with the six nations which was under the care of the governor of Virginia who had sent[81] me out to invite them to come and see him and partake of their fathers present next summer," To which we received this answer, Big Hanoana[120] their speaker taking in his hand the several strings of wampum, which had been given by the English he said, "These are the speeches received by Us from your great men, from the beginning of our freindship all that our brothers the English have told us has been good and true for which we return our hearty thanks," Then taking up four other strings of wampum, in his hand he said, "Brothers, I now speak the sentiments of all our people when first our forefathers did meet the English our brothers they found what our brothers the English told them to be true and so have we, we are but a small people and it is not to us only that you speak but to all nations, we shall be glad to

In the Darlington Memorial Library

hear what our brothers will say to us at the Logs town in the spring,[121] and we hope that the freindship now subsisting between us and our brothers will last as long as the Sun shines or the moon gives light. We hope that our children will hear and beleive what our brothers say to them as we have always done and do assure you of our hearty good will towards you our brothers. We present you with these four strings of wampum." After the council was over they had much talk about sending a guard with us to the Pickalinnees town[98] (these are a tribe of the Twigtwees) which was reckoned near two hundred miles but after long consultation their king[122] being sick they came to no determination about it

From Thursday 31 Jan.' to Monday February 11th   Stayed in the Shonnoah town, while I was here the Indians had a very extraordinary festival at which I was present and which I have exactly described at the end[123] of my journal as I had particular instructions from the President of Virginia to discover the strength and numbers of some Indian nations to the westward of Ohio, who had lately revolted from the French, and had some messages to deliver them from him I resolved to set out for the Twigtwee town[98]

Tuesday Feb. 12   Having left my boy to take care of my horses in the Shannoah town and supplied myself with a fresh horse to ride, I set out with my old company Viz! George Croghan, Andrew Montour Robert Kallender and a servant to carry our provision &c.' North west ten miles.

Wednesday 13th   The same course about thirty five miles

Thursday 14.   The same course about thirty miles

Friday 15.   The same course fifteen miles, we met with nine Shannoah Indians coming from one of the Pickalinnees towns where they had been to council they told us there were fifteen more of them behind at the Twigtwee town waiting for the Arrival of the Waughwaughtanneys[124] a tribe of the Twigtwees and were to bring with them a Shannoah woman and a child to deliver to their men that were behind. This woman they informed us was taken prisoner last fall by some of the Wawaugtanney warriors thro' a mistake which was like to have engaged these nations in war.

Saturday Feb.16.   Set out the same course[125] North West about thirty five miles to the little Miamee river[126] or creek

Sunday 17.   Crossed the little Miamee river and altering our course South West twenty five miles to the big Miamee River opposite the Twigtwee town.[98] All the way from the Shannoah town[116] to this place except the first twenty miles which is broken, is fine rich level land well timbered with large walnut, ash, sugar trees, cherry trees,

· 257 ·

&c.' it is well watered with a great number of little streams rivulets and full of beautiful natural meadows covered with wild rye blue grass and clover and abounds with Turkeys, deer, elks, and most sorts of game particularly Buffaloes thirty or forty of which are frequently seen feeding in one meadow. In short it wants nothing but cultivation to make it a most delightful countrey. The Ohio and all the large branches are said to be full of fine fish of several kinds particularly a sort of Cat fish of a prodigious size but as I was not there at a proper season I had not an opportunity of seeing any of them the traders had always reckoned it two hundred miles from the Shannoah town to the Twigtwee town but by my computation I could make it no more than one hundred and fifty the Miamee river being high we were obliged to make a raft of old logs to transport our goods and saddles and swim our horses over after firing a few guns and pistols, and smoking in the warriors pipe, who came to invite us to the town according to their custom of inviting and welcoming strangers and great men, we entered the town with English colours before us, and were kindly received by their king[127] who invited us into his own house and set our colours upon the top of it, the firing of the guns held about a quarter of an hour and then all the white men and traders that were there came and welcomed us to the Twigtwee town, this town is situate on the northwest side of the big Miamee river about one hundred and fifty miles from the mouth thereof, it consists of about four hundred families and is daily increasing, it is accounted one of the strongest Indian towns upon this part of the continent, the Twigtwees are a very numerous people consisting of many different tribes[128] under the same form of government each tribe has a particular cheif or king one of which is chosen indifferently out of any tribe to rule the whole nation and is vested with greater authoritys than any of the others, they are accounted the most powerful nation to the westward of the English settlements and much superior to the six nations with whom they are now in Amity their strength and numbers are not thoroughly known as they have but lately traded with the English and indeed have very little trade among them, they deal in much the same commodities with the northern Indians, there are other nations or tribes[129] still further to the westward daily coming in to them, and it is thought their power and interest reaches to the westward of the Mississippi if not across the continent, they are at present very well affected to the English and seem fond of an alliance with them,[130] they formerly lived on the farther side of the Oubache and were in the French interest who supplied them with some few trifles at a most exorbitant price, they were called by the French

Miamees but they have now revolted[98] from them and left their former habitations for the sake of trading with the English and notwithstanding all the Artifices the French have used they have not been able to recall them

After we had been some time in the kings[127] house Mr Montour told him that we wanted to speak with him and the cheifs of this nation this evening upon which we were invited into the longhouse and having taken our places Mr Montour began as follows. "Brothers the Twigtwees as we have been hindered by the high waters and some other business with our Indian brothers no doubt our long stay has caused some trouble among our brothers here therefore we now present you with two strings of wampum, to remove all the trouble of your hearts and clear your eyes that you may see the sun shine clear, for we have a great deal to say to you and we would have you send for one of your freinds that can speak the Mohickon[131] or the Mingoe tongues well that we may understand each other thoroughly for we have a great deal of business to do." The Mohickons[132] are a small tribe who most of them speak English and are also well acquainted with the language of the Twigtwees and they with theirs. Mr Montour then proceeded to deliver them a message[133] from the Wyendotts and Delawares as follows. "Brothers the Twigtwees this comes by our brothers the English who are coming with good news to you, we hope you will take care of them and all our brothers the English who are trading among you, you made a road for our brothers the English to come and trade among you but it is now very foul great logs are fallen across it, and we would have you be strong like men and have one heart with us and make the road clear that our brothers the English may have free course and recourse between you and us, in the sincerity of our hearts we send you these four strings of wampum," to which they gave their usual Yo Ho, then they said they wanted some tobacco to smoak with us and that tomorrow they would send for their interpreter

Monday 18th We walked about viewed the fort which wanted some repairs and the traders men helped them to bring logs to line the inside.

Tuesday Feb. 19th We gave their kings and great men some cloaths paint and shirts, and now they were busy dressing and preparing themselves for the council, the weather grew warm and the creeks began to lower very fast

Wednesday 20th About twelve of the clock we were informed that some of the foreign tribes[129] were coming upon which proper persons were ordered to meet them and conduct them to the town, and then were invited into the longhouse after we had been seated about a quarter of an hour four Indians two from each tribe who had been sent before to bring the long pipe and to inform us that the rest were coming came in and informed us that their freinds had sent these pipes that we might smoak the calamut pipe of peace with them and that they intended to do the same with us.

Thursday 21. We were again invited into the longhouse where M.̲r Croghan made them with the foreign tribes a present[80] to the value of one hundred pounds pensilvania money and delivered all our speeches to them at which they seemed well pleased and said they would take time and consider well what we had said to them.

Friday 22.[134] Nothing remarkable happened in the town

Saturday 23.̲d In the afternoon there was an alarm in the town which caused great confusion and running about among the Indians upon enquiring the reason of this stir they told us that it was occasioned by six Indians that came to war against them from the southward three of them Cutaways[135] and three Shanaws, these were some of the Shanaws who had formerly deserted from the other part of the nation and now lived to the southward[136] towards night there was a report spread in town that four Indians and four hundred French were on their march and just by the town but soon after the messenger who brought the news said there were only four french Indians coming to council and that they bid him sayso only to see how the English would behave themselves, but as they had behaved like men he now told the truth.

Sunday 24.th This morning the four french Indians came into town and were kindly received by the town Indians, they marched in under french colours and were conducted into the longhouse and after they had been in about a quarter of an hour the council sat, and we were sent for that we might hear what the French had to say to them. The Pyankeshee king[137] who was at that time the principal man and commander in cheif of the Twigtwees said he would have the English colours set up in this council as well as the French, to which we answered he might do as he thought fit, after we were seated right opposite to the French embassadors one of them said he had a present to make them so a place was prepared as they had done before for our present, between them and us, and then their speaker stood up and laid his hands upon two caggs of brandy that held about seven quarts each and a roll of tobacco of about ten pounds weight, then taking two strings of wampum in his hand he said. "What he had to deliver them was from their father meaning the French king and he desired they would hear what he was about to say to them" then he

In the Darlington Memorial Library

laid those two strings of wampum down upon the caggs and taking up four other strings of black and white wampum he said "That their father remembering his children had sent them two caggs of milk[138] and some tobacco and that he now had made a clear road for them to come and see him and his officers and pressed them very much to come and see him" then he took another string of wampum in his hand and said "Their father would now forget all little differences that had been between them and desired them not to be of two minds but to let him know their minds freely for he would send them no more" To which the Piankashee king replied it was true their father had sent for them several times and said the road was clear but he understood it was made foul and bloody by them, We (said he) have cleared a road for our brothers the English and you fathers have made it bad and have taken some of our brothers prisoners which we look upon as done to us." And he turned short about and went out of council, after the French embassador had delivered his message he went into one of the private houses and endeavoured much to prevail on some Indians and was seen to cry and lament as he said for the loss of that nation

Monday 25th This day we received a speech from the Wawaughtanneys and Piankashees, two tribes of the Twigtwees one of the cheifs[139] of the former spoke "Brothers we have heard what you have said to us by the interpreter and we see you take pity upon our poor wives and children, and have taken us by the hand into the great chain of freindship therefore we present you with these two bundles of skins to make shoes for your people, and this pipe to smoak in to assure you our hearts are good and true towards you our brothers, and we hope that we shall all continue in true love and freindship with one another as people with one head and one heart ought to do you have pitied us as you always did the rest of our Indian brothers, we hope that that pity you have always shewn will remain as long as the sun gives light, and on our side you may depend upon sincere and true freindship towards you as long as we have strength." This person stood up and spoke with the air and gesture of an orator.

Tuesday Feb.' 26. The Twigtwees[98] delivered the following answer to the four Indians sent by the French, the captain of the warriors stood up and taking some strings of black and white wampum in his hand, he spoke with a feirce tone and very warlike air, "Brothers the Ottaways[89] you are always differing with the French yourselves and yet you listen to what they say, but we will let you know by these four strings of wampum that we will not hear any thing to say to us or do anything they bid us do." Then the same speaker with six strouds two match coats and a string of black wampum (I understood the goods were in return for the milk and tobacco) directed his speech as to the French and said "Fathers you desire that we will speak our minds from our hearts which I am going to do. You have often desired we should go home to you, but I tell you it is not our home for we have made a road as far as the sea, to the sun rising and have been taken by the hand[140] by our brothers the English and the six nations, and the Delawares, Shannoahs and Wyendotts, and we assure you that it is a road we will go, and as you threaten us with war in the spring[141] we tell you if you are angry we are ready to receive you and resolve to die here before we will go to you, and that you may know this is our mind we send you this string of black wampum" After a short pause the same speaker spoke again thus. "Brothers the Ottaways you hear what I say, tell that to your fathers, the French, for this is our mind and we speak it from our hearts.

Wednesday 27. This day they took down their French colours and dismissed the four french Indians so they took their leave of the town and set off for the French fort.[142]

Thursday 28. The crier of the town came by the kings order and invited us to the longhouse to see the warriors feather dance,[143] it was performed by three dancing masters, who were painted all over with various colours with long sticks in their hands upon the end of which were fastned long feathers of swans and other birds neatly woven in the shape of a fowls wing in this disguise they performed many antick tricks waving their sticks and feathers about with great skill to imitate the flying and fluttering of birds keeping exact time with their musick while they are dancing some of the warriors strikes a post upon which the music and dancers cease and the warriors gives an account of his Atcheivments in war, and when he has done throw's down some goods as a recompence to the performers and musicians after which they proceed in their dance as before till another warrior strikes the post and so on as long as they think fit

Friday March the 1st We received the following speech from the Twigtwees[98] the speaker stood up and addressing himself as to the governor of Pensilvania with two strings of wampum in his hand he said "Brothers our hearts are glad that you have taken notice of us, and surely brothers we hope that you will order a smith[101] to settle here to mend our guns and hatchets, your kindness makes us so bold to ask this request. You told us our freindship should last as long and be as the greatest mountain, we have considered well and all our great kings and warriors are come to a resolution never to give heed to what the French say to us, but always to hear and beleive what you our brothers say to us. Brothers we are obliged to you for your kind invitation[80] to receive a present at the Loggs town, but as our foreign tribes are not yet come we must wait for them, but you may depend we will come as soon as our women have planted corn to hear what our brothers will say to us. Brothers we present you with this bundle of skins as we are but poor to be for shoes for you on the road, and we return you our hearty thanks for the cloaths which you have put upon our wives and children" We then took our leaves of the kings and cheifs and they ordered that a small party of Indians should go with us as far as Hockhockin,[110] but as I had left my boy and horses at the lower Shannoah town[116] I was obliged to go by myself or to go sixty or seventy miles out of my way, which I did not care to do so we all came over the Miamee river together, this evening but Mr Croghan[78] and Mr Montour[79] went over again and lodged in the town but I stayed on this side at one Robert Smiths[144] a trader where we had left our horses. Before the french Indians had come into town we had drawn articles of peace and alliance between the English and Wawaughtanneys and the Piankashees the indentures were signed sealed and delivered on both sides, and as I drew them, I took a copy.[134] The land upon the great Miamee river is very rich level and well timbered, some of the finest meadows that can be, the Indians and traders assure me that the lands hold as good and if possible better to the westward as far as the Obach[145] which is accounted one hundred miles, and quite up to the head of the Miamee river which is sixty miles above the Twigtwee town[98] and down the said river quite to the Ohio, which is reckoned one hundred and fifty miles The grass here grows to a great height in the clear feilds of which there are a great number and the bottoms are full of white clover wild rye and blue grass.

Saturday 2. George Croghan[78] and the rest of our company came over the river, we got our horses and set out about thirty five miles to Mad creek, this is a place where some English[118] had been taken prisoners by the French.

Sunday March 3d This morning we parted they for Hockhockin[110] and I for the Shannoah town[116] and as I was quite alone and knew that the French Indians had threatned us and would probably pursue or lye in wait for us, I left the path and went to the Southwestward down the little Miamee river or creek where I had fine travelling thro.' rich land and beautiful meadows in which I could sometimes see forty or fifty buffaloes feeding at once. The little Miamee river or creek continued to run thro' the middle of a fine meadow about a mile wide very clear like an old field and not a bush in it. I could see the Buffaloes in it above two miles off. I travelled this day about thirty miles.

Monday 4th This day I heard several guns but was afraid to examine who fired them, lest they might be some of the French Indians so I travelled thro' the woods about thirty miles just at night I killed a fine barren cow buffaloe and took out her tongue and a little of the best of her meat, the land still level rich and well timbered with oak walnut ash, locust and sugar trees.

Tuesday 5th I travelled about thirty miles.

Wednesday 6th I travelled about thirty miles and killed a fat bear.

Thursday 7th Set out with my horse load of bear and travelled about thirty miles this afternoon I met a young man a trader and we encamped together that night he happened to have some bread with him and I had plenty of meat so we fared very well.

Fryday 8th Travelled[146] about thirty miles and arrived at night at the Shannoah town all the Indians as well as the white men came out to welcom my return to their town being very glad that all things were rightly settled in the Miamee countrey they fired upwards of one hundred and fifty guns in the town[116] and made an entertainment in honour of the late peace with the western Indians.[134] In my return from the Twigtwee to the Shannoah town I did not keep an exact account of course or distance for as the land thereabouts was much the same and the situation of the countrey was sufficiently described in my journey to the Twigtwee town I thought it unnecessary but have notwithstanding laid down my tract pretty nearly in my plat.

Saturday 9th In the Shannoah town I met with one of the Mingoe cheifs[147] who had been down at the falls of Ohio so that we did not see him as we went up. I informed him of the Kings present[105] and the invitation[81] down to Virginia he told me that there was a party of French Indians hunting at the falls[42] and if I went they would certainly kill me or carry me away prisoner to the French for it is certain they would not let me pass, however as I had a great inclination to see the falls and the lands on the East side the Ohio I resolved to venture as far as possible

Sunday 10th I stayed in town and prepared for my departure

Tuesday 12th I got my horses over the river and after breakfast my boy and I got ferried over,[148] the Ohio is near three quarters of a mile wide at Shannoah town and is very deep and smooth.

Wednesday 13th We set out South forty five west down the said river on the South East side eight miles then South ten miles, here I met two men belonging to Robert Smith[144] at whose house I lodged on this side the Miamee river and one Hugh Crawford the said Robert

Smith had given me an order upon these two men for two of the teeth of a large beast[149] which they were bringing from towards the falls of Ohio,[42] one of which I brought in and delivered to the Ohio company Robert Smith informed me that about seven years ago these teeth and bones of three large beasts one of which was somewhat smaller than the other two were found in a salt lick[150] or spring upon a small creek which runs into the south side of the Ohio about fifteen miles below the mouth of the great Miamee river, and twenty above the falls of Ohio, he assured me that the rib bones of the largest of these beasts were eleven feet long and the scull bone six feet wide across the forehead and the other bones in proportion and that there were several teeth there, some of which he called horns and said they were upwards of five feet long and as much as a man could well carry that he had hid one in a branch at some distance from the place lest the French Indians should carry it away, the tooth which I brought in for the Ohio company was a jaw tooth of better than four pounds weight it appeared to be the furthest tooth in the jaw and looked like fine ivory when the outside was scraped off. I also met with four Shannoah Indians coming up the river in their canoes who informed me that there were about sixty French Indians encamped at the falls.

Thursday 14th I went down the river south fifteen miles, the land on this side the Ohio, cheifly broken and the bottoms but narrow.

Friday 15th South five miles South West ten miles to a creek[151] that was so high that we could not get over that night

Saturday 16th South forty five West about thirty five miles.

Sunday March 17th The same course fifteen miles then North forty five West five miles

Monday 18th North forty five west five miles, then South west twenty miles to the lower salt lick creek[152] which Robert Smith and the Indians told us was about fifteen miles above the falls of Ohio, the land still hilly, the salt lick here much the same with those before described. This day we heard several guns which made me imagine the French Indians were not moved, but were still hunting and firing thereabouts, we also saw some traps newly set and the footsteps of some Indians plain on the ground, as if they had been there the day before. I was now much troubled that I could not comply with my instructions and was once resolved to leave the boy and horses and go privately on foot to view the falls but the boy being a poor hunter was afraid he would starve if I was long from him and there was also great danger lest the French Indians should come upon our horses tracks or hear their bells and as I had seen good land enough, I thought perhaps I might be blamed for venturing so far in such dangerous times so I concluded not to go to the falls but travelled away to the Southward till we were over the little Cuttaway river.[153] The falls of Ohio[42] by the best information I could get are not very steep, on the South East side there is a bar of land at some distance from the shore the water between the bar and the shore is not above three feet deep and the stream moderately strong the Indians frequently pass safely in their canoes, thro' this passage but are obliged to take great care as they go down lest the current which is much the strongest on the Northwest side should draw them that way which would be very dangerous as the water on that side runs with great rapidity over several ledges of rocks. The waters below the falls as they say is about six fathoms deep, and the river continues without any obstructions till it empties itself into the Mississippi which is accounted upwards of four hundred miles The Ohio near the mouth is said to be very wide and the land upon both sides very rich and in general very level all the way from the falls. After I had determined not to go to the falls we turned from Salt lick creek to a ridge of mountains that made towards the Cuttaway river,[154] and from the top of the mountains we saw a fine level countrey South west as far as our eyes could behold and it was a very clear day, we then went down the mountains and set out South twenty west about five miles through rich level land covered with small walnut sugar trees red buds &c.[718]

Saturday May 18th Set out South twenty miles to my own house[178] on the Yadkin river when I came there I found all my family gone for the Indians had killed five people in the winter near that place which frightened my wife and family away to Roanoke about thirty five miles nearer in among the inhabitants which I was informed of by an old man, I met near the place.

Sunday 19th Set out for Raonoke[179] and as we had now a path we got there the same night where I found all my family well.

No 5   Extracts from Mr Gists second Journal.

Monday Novr 4th 1751. Set out from the companys storehouse in Frederick County in Virginia opposite the mouth of Wills creek and crossing Potomack river went west four miles to a gap[184] in the Allegany mountains upon the South west fork of the said creek. This gap is the nearest to potomack river of any in the Allagany mountains and is accounted one of the best, tho' the mountains[185] is very high the ascent is no where very steep but rises gradually near six miles it is now very full of old trunks and stones but with some pains might be made a very good waggon road this gap is directly in the way to Mohongahela and several miles nearer than that the traders commonly pass through[186] and a much better way.[719]

Sunday 24th Set out West two miles then South forty five west six miles over the south fork[190] and encamped on the Southwest side about a mile from a small hunting town of the Delawares from whom I bought some corn. I invited these Indians to a treaty at the Logs town the full moon in May as Colo Patton[191] had desired me, they treated me very civilly but after I went from that place my man informed me that they threatned to take away our guns and not let us travel.

From Saturday 30 to Friday December 6th We searched the land several miles round[192] and found it about fifteen miles from the foot of the mountains to the river Mohongahela, the first five miles of which East and West is good level farming land with fine meadows the timber white oak and hickory the same body of land holds ten miles South to the upper forks of Mohongahela[193] and about ten miles North towards the mouth of Yaughaughgane the land nearer the river for about eight or nine miles wide and the same length is much richer and better timbered with walnut, locusts poplars, and sugar trees but is in some places very hilly, the bottoms upon the river one mile and some places two miles

Saturday Decr 7th Set out West six miles and went to an Indian camp and invited them to a treaty at the Logs town at the full moon in May next, at this camp there was a trader named Charles Poke[194] who spoke the Indian tongue well. The Indian to whom this camp belonged after much discourse with me complained and said "My friend you were sent[81] to us the last year from the great men in Virginia to inform us of a present[105] from the great King over the water, and if you can bring news from the King to us, why cant you tell him something from me. The proprietor of Pensilvania granted my father a tract of land beginning eight miles below the fork of Brandywine creek and binding on the said creek to the fork and including the west fork and all it's waters on both sides to the head fountain, the white people now live on these lands and will neither let me have them nor pay me any thing for them, my fathers name was Chickoconecon.[195] I am his eldest Son and my name is Nemicotton.[196] I desire that you will let the governor and great men in Virginia know this, it may be they will tell the great King of it and he will make Mr Pen or his people give me the lands or pay me for it. This trader here Charles Poke knows the truth of what I say that the land was granted to my father and that he or I never sold it," to which Charles Poke answered that Chickoconecon had such a grant of land and that the people who lived on it could get no titles to it for that it was now called Mannor lands. This I was obliged to insert in my journal to please the Indian

Sunday the 8th   We stayed at the Indian camp.

Monday 9th   Set out South forty five west one mile, West six miles to the river Mohongahela, at this place[197] is a large cavity in a rock about thirty feet long and twenty feet wide and about seven feet high and an even floor the entrance into it is so large and open that it let's in plenty of light and close by it is a stream of fine water

From Tuesday 10th to Friday the 13th[198]   We were examining the lands which for nine or ten miles East is rich but hilly as before described, on the East side of the river for several miles there are several bottoms very rich and a mile wide and the hills above them are extraordinary rich and well timbered.[719]

Sunday Decr 15th   Crossed the river Mohongehela which in this place[199] is fifty three poles wide the bottoms upon the west side are not above one hundred yards wide but the hills are very rich both up and down the river and full of sugar trees.

Tuesday 17th   Set out West five miles the land upon this course hilly but very rich about a mile and half then it was level with good meadows, but not very rich for about a mile and half more and the last two miles next to licking creek[200] was very good land. Upon this creek we lodged at a hunting camp of an Indian captain named Oppaymolleah.[201] Here I saw an Indian named Joshua[202] who spoke very good English, he had been acquainted with me several years and seemed very glad to see me and wondered much where I was going so far in those woods. I said I was going to invite all the great men of the Indians to a treaty to be held at the Logs town, the full moon in May next where a parcel of goods a present from the King of Great Britain would be delivered them by proper commissioners and that these were the goods[105] which I informed them of last year[81] by order of the President of Virginia Colo Lee who was since dead, Joshua informed them what I said and they told me I ought to let the Beaver[203] know this, so I wrote a line to him by Joshua who promised to deliver it safe and said there was a traders man that could read it for him. This Beaver is the Sachemore or cheif of the Delawares it is customary among the Indian cheifs to take upon them the name of any beast or bird they fancy the picture of which they always sign instead of their Name or arms.[720]

Friday 14. Feb. 1752   We stayed at this place on the North west side of the creek on a rising ground by a small spring we found a large stone[210] about three foot square on the top and about six or seven feet high it was all covered with green moss except on the South East side which was smooth and white as if plaistered with lime, on this side I cut with a cold chissel in large letters.[721]

THE OHIO COMPANY FEB. 1751.[211] BY CHRISTOPHER GIST.

In the Darlington Memorial Library

Thursday March 12th   I set out for Mohongahela crossed it upon a raft of logs from whence I made the best of my way to Potomack. I did not keep exactly my old track but went more to the Eastward and found a much nearer way home and am of opinion the company may have a tolerable good road from Wills creek to the upper fork[193] of Mohongahela from whence the river is navigable all the way to the Ohio for large flat bottomed boats,[225] the road will be a little to the Southward of west and the distance to the fork of Mohongahela about seventy miles,[226] while I was at Mohongahela in my return home an Indian who spoke good English came to me and said that their great man the Beaver and captain Oppamyluah, (these are two cheifs of the Delawares) desired to know where the Indians land lay for that the French claimed all the land on one side the river Ohio, and the English on the other side and that Oppamyluah asked me the same question when I was at his camp in my way down to which I had made him no answer, I very well remembered that Oppamyluah asked me such a question and that I was at a loss to answer him as I now also was but after some consideration, my freind said I we are all one Kings people and the different colour of our skins makes no difference in the Kings subjects. You are his people as well as we are if you will take land and pay the Kings rights you will have the same priviledges as the white people have and to hunt you have liberty everywhere so that you dont kill the white peoples cattle and hogs, to this the Indian said I must stay at that place two days and then he would come and see me again, he then went away and at the two days end returned as he promised and looking very pleasant said he would stay with me all night after he had been with me some time he said that the great men bid him tell me I was very safe that I might come and live upon that river where I pleased that I had answered them very true for we were all one Kings people sure enough and for his part he would come to see me at Wills creek in a month.

No 5.   Instructions given Christopher Gist Gent
         by the Ohio Company April 28th 1752.[286]

Whereas the Governor has been pleased to grant you a commission empowering and requiring you to go as an Agent for the Ohio company to the Indian treaty to be held at Logstown on the sixteenth day of May next You are therefore desired to acquaint the cheifs of the several nations of Indians there assembled that his Majesty has been graciously pleased to grant unto the Honble Robert Dinwiddie Esquire Governor of Virginia and to several other gentlemen in Great

George Mercer Papers

Britain and America by the name of the Ohio company a large quantity of land on the river Ohio, and the branches thereof thereby to enable and encourage the said company and all his Majesties subjects to make settlements and carry on an extensive trade and commerce with their brethren the Indians and to supply them with goods at a more easy rate than they have hitherto bought them, and considering the necessities of his children the six nations and the other Indians to the Westward of the English settlements and the hardships they labour under for want of a due supply of goods, and to remove the same as much as possible his Majesty has been pleased to have a clause inserted in the said companys grant obliging them to carry on a trade and commerce with their brethren the Indians and has granted them several priviledges and immunitys in consideration of their carrying on the said trade and supplying the Indians with goods. That the said company have accordingly begun the trade and imported large quantitys of goods, but have found the expence and risque of carrying out the goods such a distance from the inhabitants without having any place of safety by the way to lodge them at or opportunity of getting provisions for their people so great that they cannot afford to sell their goods at so easy a rate as they would willingly do, nor are they at such a distance able to supply their brethren the Indians at all times when they are in want, for which reason the company find it absolutely necessary immediately to settle and cultivate the land his Majesty has been pleased to grant them which to be sure they have an indisputable right to do as our brethren the six nations sold all the land to the westward of Virginia at the treaty of Lancaster[287] to their father the King of Great Britain, and he has been graciously pleased to grant a large quantity thereof to the said Ohio company yet being informed that the six nations have given their freinds the Dellawars leave[288] to hunt upon the said land, and that they still hunt upon part thereof themselves and as the settlements made by the English upon the said land may make the game scarce or at least drive it further back, the said company therefore to prevent any difference or misunderstanding which might possibly happen between them and their brethren the Indians touching the said lands are willing to make them some further satisfaction for the same and to purchase[289] of them the land on the East side the river Ohio, and Allagany as low as the great Conhaway providing the same can be done at a reasonable rate, and our brethren the six nations and their allies will promise and engage their freindship and protection to all his Majesties subjects setling on the said lands, when this is done the company can safely venture to build factorys and storehouses upon the river Ohio and

In the Darlington Memorial Library

send out large cargoes of goods which they cannot otherwise do. And to convince our brethren the Indians how desirous we are of living in strict freindship and becoming one people with them, You are hereby empowered and required to acquaint and promise our brethren in the name and on behalf of the said company that if any of them incline to take land and live among the English they shall have any of the said companys lands upon the same terms and conditions[264] as the white people have and enjoy the same priviledges which they do as far as in the companys power to grant. And that you may be the better able to acquaint our brethren the Indians with these our proposals, You are to apply to Andrew Montour[79] the interpreter for his assistance[290] therein and the company hereby undertake and promise to make him satisfaction for the trouble he shall be at. If our brethren the six nations approve our proposals the company will pay them whatever sum you agree with them for, and if they want any particular sort of goods you are to desire them to give you an account of such goods and the company will immediately send for them to England and when they arrive will carry them to whatever place you agree to deliver them at. If our brethren the Indians do not approve these proposals and do refuse their protection and assistance to the subjects of their father the King of Great Britain You are forthwith to make a return thereof[291] to the said Ohio company that they may inform his Majesty thereof. You are to apply to Colo Cresap for what wampum[292] you have occasion of on the companys account for which you are to give him a receipt

You are also to apply to him for one of the companys horses[293] to ride out to the Logs town.

As soon as the treaty is over you are to make an exact return of all your proceedings to the company[291]

No 6   The Ohio Companys Petition[348]

To the Honourable Robert Dinwiddie Esquire Lieutenant Governor of Virginia, and the rest of the Honourable the Council

The Petition of the Ohio company Sheweth.

That the said company having at their great charge and expence employed persons for above these two years past to search and view the lands on the Ohio alias Alligany river as far Westward as the Twigtwee town and to cultivate trade and freindship with the several nations and tribes of Indians inhabiting those parts in order to seat the same according to the condition of his Majesties instructions communicated to this Honourable board by his Honour the late governor and having also at their great charge cleared a waggon road[349] from their storehouse at Wills creek to one of the branches[350] of the Ohio navigable by large flat bottomed boats, which is the nearest best and almost only passage through the great ridge of mountains and consequently is of great benefit to the public your petitioners pray leave to survey and take up their first two hundred thousand acres between Romanettos alias Kiskominettos creek and the fork of the Ohio and the great Connaway alias new river alias Woods river on the south side of the said river Ohio in as many surveys as they shall think fit your petitioners understanding the Indians are not willing any settlements on the north side thereof should be yet made,[351] and as your petitioners make no doubt but that they shall be able not only to comply with the conditions of their first grant in one year from this time but to seat a much greater number of families than they are obliged to if your Honours would permit them to take up such small tracts of land not exceeding one thousand acres as lye in spots interspersed between the companys surveys as they shall cause to be actually seated on before the 25th of December 1753 on the terms[352] of your petitioners grant or such other terms and conditions as your honours shall think reasonable which your petitioners apprehend would be of great advantage to his Majesty and his plantations as it would be the most effectual means to encrease and secure their first settlements which the encroachments of the French and especially the new fort[353] built by them on the west end of lake Erie and on the South side thereof the last year render necessary, the same manifestly tending to interrupt your petitioners grant and your petitioners in order to settle a sufficient force must without such permission be obliged to part with all their own lands to encourage the settlement contrary to the intent and agreement of the company who did not enter into so expensive an undertaking with a view of setting up for a company of land mongers, tho' several companies of that sort now trade in this Colony but with a view of making fortunes for their children in a very hazardous undertaking at a very great and certain expence whereas the land mongers by procuring an order of council for a certain quantity of land make surveys at so unreasonable distance as might include 500 times the quantity and it is presumed under their grant no person can interfere When they meet with purchasers so much land is taken up and his Majestys land is granted to his subjects not by a purchase from himself but persons[354] who substitute themselves his brokers and receive the full value of them.

Your Petitioners therefore hope that your Honours will think it reasonable they should reap some of the advantage the public will receive by their great expence and will not allow private persons[355]

In the Darlington Memorial Library

to interfere with their bounds or to take up large tracts of the lands they have been at the charge of discovering till they may have time to apply to his Majesty and know his pleasure[356] as your petitioners were so far from setting up for an engrossing company that they are willing to receive any new Members into it on the same terms they hold their several shares which from thirteen[357] at the time of his Majestys grant now amount to twenty[358] yet have not so much land among them as some persons who are so far from being at any expence or procuring any public advantage that they have made large fortunes by selling his Majestys lands.[359]

     And your Petitioners shall ever pray

No 7. At a Council held at Logs town June 1st 1752.[294]
       Present
Joshua Fry, Lunsford Lomax, James Patton Esqrs[285] Commissioners.
  Mr Christopher Gist agent for the Ohio company
  Mr Andrew Montour.[79] Interpreter.
  Mr George Croghan,[78] Commissioner for Pensylvania

The Indians addressed themselves to the Commissioners in the following speeches.[295]

Brethren, You have come a long and blind way if we had been certain which way you were coming we should have met you at some distance from the town, but we now bid you welcome and we open your eyes with this string of wampum which we give you in the name of the six united nations   *Gave a string*

Brethren of Virginia and Pensylvania, I desire you will hearken to what I am going to say that you may open your hearts and speak freely to us, we dont doubt but you have many things in your minds which may trouble you notwithstanding which we hope we may continue in freindship on which we give you these strings of wampum
            Gave two strings.

After which the Commissioners let the Indians know that they would give them an answer in a few hours.

Sometime after all being met in the Council house Mr George Croghan by directions[296] from the Governor of Pensylvania made a speech to the Indians letting them know that it was his desire that they should receive their brethren of Virginia kindly and presented them with a string of wampum.   *Gave a string*

Then the Commissioners spoke as followeth.[297]

Brethren, You sent us[298] a string of wampum which met us on the road, by which you acquainted us that you heard of our coming to visit you and welcomed us so far on our journey, yesterday we arrived at this place and this morning you took an opportunity with a string of wampum to bid us welcome to your town, and to open our eyes that we might see the sun clearly and look upon you our brethren who are willing to receive us this we take very kindly and we assure you of our hearty inclinations to live in freindship with you to confirm this we present you with a string of wampum, Gave a string,/ Brethren in your second speech to us and our brethren of Pensylvania this day you delivered us two strings of wampum to clear our hearts from any impressions that may have been made on them by flying reports or ill news[299] and that we might speak our minds freely. Brethren we assure you of our willingness to remove all misunderstandings out of our hearts and breasts which might impede or hinder the freindship subsisting between us.

Now Brethren, We are to acquaint you that we are sent hither by the King of Great Britain our father who not forgetting his children on this side the great waters has ordered us to deliver you a large present[105] of goods in his name which we have brought with us but as we understand that you have sent for some of your cheifs[300] whom you shortly expect we will wait with patience till they come and will then faithfully deliver you the goods and open our hearts to you in assurance of which we present you with this string of wampum.

Gave a string

We had some debates[301] concerning the method of proceeding in the treaty Colo Patton insisted strongly whether to demand their reasons why the belt and speech delivered last fall was not sent to Onandago[300] as he directed Mr Gist and I[722] opposed it, I thought or if nothing should be said of that affair till we had fully compleated what was more material,[302] obtaining leave to settle the lands &c which we judged the other would effectually defeat.

June 2d Got our goods out and dried them but found they had not received the damage that might have been expected our fine goods none.

June 3d We had conferences with Mr Trent and Mr Croghan about the likeliest method to succeed in our negotiations had further assurances of their assistance which I beleive as Capt Trent has always been esteemed a man of honour, they had waited some time from their own business to attend the treaty which they look upon as the Kings and therefore declared they will forward it independent of the interest of either province

June 4th Two Shanoa cheifs[304] being disgusted[305] (as was said) came to us made a speech expressing their inclinations to be gone home, as we were preparing an answer in conjunction with some of

In the Darlington Memorial Library

the six nations to stop them word was brought that a vessel with English colours was coming down the river, which proved to be the half king[306] with a cheif from the Onandago council, he was received with several discharges of small arms, landed and fixed the English colours on the top of his house we waited on him; sometime after he returned the visit with some of the cheifs drank the Kings health, prosperity to the six nations the Governor of Virginia &c. made him a present of tobacco, he seems to be a person of great dignity in his behaviour

June 9th We had a private conference with the half king[306] and other cheifs at Mr Croghans,[78] shewed the Lancaster deed[287] and other papers, they thanked us for letting them know what the Onandago council had done and blamed them much for keeping it private (as they said) for had they known it sooner, it would have prevented many disorders, they said they never told them that they had sold further than the warriors road[63] at the foot of the Alligany mountain and that they would confirm whatever they had done. The Indians desired to have their guns and hatchets mended which was complied with, Big Hanoana[120] a Shanoah cheif told us that the Picts were upon the poise whether they should return to the French or continue steady to the English and wanted to see what encouragement the latter would give them.[307]

June 10. This day was appointed to deliver the Kings present to the Indians we made arbours as the Indians did for themselves, laid out the present, a part was set aside for the Picts[307] which was well taken by the other Indians distributed the fine cloaths to the cheifs

The Indians being met the Commissioners spoke as followeth

Present. Joshua Fry, Lunsford Lomax, James Patton Esqrs
Commissioners

Mr Christopher Gist agent for the Ohio company

Mr Andrew Montour, Interpreter

Sachems, and Warriors of the six united nations our freinds and brethren.

We are glad to meet you at this place, to enlarge the council fire already kindled[308] by our brethren of Pensylvania to brighten the chain and to renew our freindship that it may last as long as the sun, the moon and stars shall give light and to confirm which we give you this string of wampum   *Gave a string*

Brethren, At the Treaty at Lancaster[287] in the year 1744, between the Governments of Virginia, Maryland, and Pensylvania, you made a deed recognizing the Kings right to all the land in Virginia, as far as it was then peopled or should thereafter be peopled, or bounded by the King our father, for which you received the consideration agreed on. At the same time Canosateego[309] desired the Commissioners would recommend you to the Kings further favour when the settlements should encrease much further back, this the Commissioners promised and confirm'd it by a writing under their hands and seals in consequence of which a present was sent you from the King by Mr Conrad Weiser which he since informed us that he delivered you at a council held here in the year 1748.[310] Now the King your father to shew the love he bears to justice as well as his affection to you his children has sent a large present of goods to be divided among you and your allies which is here ready to be delivered to you and we desire you may confirm the treaty at Lancaster

Brethren, It is the design of the King your father at present to make a settlement of British subjects on the South East side of Ohio, that we may be united as one people by the strongest ties of neighbourhood as well as freindship and by these means prevent the insults of our Enemies, from such a settlement greater advantages will arise to you than you can at present conceive, our people[311] will be able to supply you with goods much cheaper than can at this time be afforded, will be ready help in case you should be attacked and some good men among them will be appointed with authority to punish and restrain the many injuries and abuses too frequently committed here by disorderly white people, Brethren We assure you that the King our father by purchasing your lands had never any intentions of taking them from you,[312] but that we might live together as one people and keep them from the french who would be bad neighbours, he is not like the French King who calls himself your father and endeavoured about three years ago with an armed force to take possession of your countrey by setting up inscriptions[313] on trees and at the mouths of the creeks on this river by which he claims these lands tho' at their coming and for many years before a number of your brethren the English were residing in this town[314] and several other places on this river, you well remember how he scattered the Shawnese so that they were dispersed all over the face of the earth and he now threatens to cut off[315] the Twigtwees this is to weaken you that he may cut you off also, which he durst not attempt while you are united. On the contrary the King your father will lay his hand on your heads under which protection you will always remain safe Brethren, the great King our father recommends a strict union between us you and your brethren towards the sunsetting which will make us strong and formidable, as a division may have a contrary effect, we are directed to send[307] a small present to the Twigtwees as an earnest of the regard which the Governor of Virginia has for them with an assurance of his further freindship whenever they shall stand in need. Brethren we earnestly exhort you not to be drawn by the empty deceitful speeches of the French the peculiar talent of that cunning people but in all their attempts to shake your duty to our common father, think of what real acts of freindship have been done by the English and what by the French, weigh these things in your minds and then determine who best deserves your esteem and regard, for it is not by vain unmeaning words that true freindship is to be discovered, that what we have said may make the greater impression on you and have i'ts full force we present you with this belt of wampum. *Gave a belt*

Brethren, It is many years ago that the English first came over the great water to visit you, on their first coming you took hold of our Ships and tied them to your strongest trees ever since which we have remained together in freindship we have assisted you when you have been attacked by the French by which you have been able to withstand them and you have remained our good freinds and allies for though at some times the chain of freindship may have contracted some rust it has been easily rubbed off, and the chain restored to its brightness, this we hope will always be the case and that our freindship may continue to the last posterity we give you this string of wampum.

Gave a string

Brethren. We are sorry for the occasion that requires us to complain to you of an injury done us by one of your people who murdered a poor woman on the new River. Murder is a great crime and by the consent of all nations has usually been punished with death this is the usage among the English whether one of our own people has been killed or one of our brethren the Indians, and it is one of the earliest commands of the great Father and maker of us all, who inhabits the skies that who so sheddeth mans blood, by man shall his blood be shed. We understand you know the man that is accused of the murder and we hope you will give him up to be tried by our laws, you may be assured that he will have a fair trial and if he is not guilty he will be sent back unhurt. We must inform you that the Governor of Virginia expects you will deliver the person suspected to be guilty up to some Magistrate in Virginia whom we shall name to you that we may send him to Williamsburg for his trial This procedure is not only proper as it is a compliance with the Laws of God and Nations, but it is necessary to warn all hot headed men who are not guided by reason to forbear from such wicked actions by which their brethren suffer.

Brethren, We desire for the future you will observe the treaty of

Lancaster and whenever your young people travel through Virginia that they will take such passes[316] as are directed by the said treaty, by these passes the men will be known which will be some restraint on them as to their behaviour, it will be proper also that a man of prudence and discretion should head each party that one among them if possible should speak English and that by no means any French or french Indians be suffered to go with them. We might have mentioned many other irregularities but we have forborn in hopes that for the future you will give your people such orders as will prevent our having any further occasion to complain to inforce what we have said and induce you to do us justice we present you with this belt of wampum. *Gave a belt*

The Commissioners then spoke to the allies of the six united nations who were present having first advised with the half king[306] and being joined in the speeches by him in the name of the six nations.

Brethren the Delawares, We thank you for the kind reception you gave us when we came to Shenapins which we shall never forget, we advise and exhort you to beware of the French councils and that you will adhere to a strict freindship with us the six nations and your brethren who live towards the sunsetting which will strengthen us all and be a sure defence against our enemies to confirm you in this mind we present you with this belt of wampum, *Gave a belt*

Brethren the Shawnese. Your nation has suffered much by French devices by which you have been dispersed we exhort you that you continue[317] to keep firm hold of the great chain of freindship between us the six nations and their allies which is the likeliest means to retreive your loss and again to make you a happy people we present with this belt of wampum *Gave a belt*

Brethren the Wyendots. Your nation is divided[318] and part is under the directions of the French, we think it would be good policy in you that are in our interest to endeavour to bring over your brethren but if this cant be done you ought to take all the care in your power, that they do not under the colour and name of freindship come into our countrey and hurt our inhabitants or if they do that you will endeavour to secure them on their return to prevent any misunderstanding we present you with this belt of wampum *Gave a belt*

After these speeches had been delivered and interpreted to the several nations the half king[306] desired the Commissioners not to depart for he said they had a great deal of business to do, he then with a ten rowed belt of wampum in his hand directing his speech to Eghuisara (which is Mr Montours[79] Indian name) said, Child Remember that thou art one of our own people and have transacted a

In the Darlington Memorial Library

great deal of business among us before you were employed by our brethren of Pensylvania and Virginia, you are Interpreter between us and our brethren which we are well pleased at for we are sure our business will go on well and justice be done on both sides but you are not interpreter only for you are one of our council and have an equal right with us to all these lands and may transact any public business in behalf of us the six nations as well as any of us for we look upon you as much as we do any of the cheif councillors and to confirm what we have said we present unto you this belt of wampum.

Gave the belt

Then addressing himself to the Commissioners of Virginia and all the Indians present with a string of wampum in his hand he spoke as follows.

Brethren, It is a great while since our brother the Buck (meaning George Croghan)[78] has been doing business between us and our brothers of Pensylvania but we understand he does not intend to do so any more,[319] so I now inform you that he is approved of by our council at Onandago for we sent to them to let them know how he has helped us in our councils here and I deliver him this string of wampum to strengthen him and to let you and him know that he is one of our people and shall help us still and be one of our council.

Gave the string of wampum

He next spoke to the Shawnese and told them that he took the hatchet from them, and tied them with black strings of wampum to hinder them from going to war against the Cherokees, he said that they struck their own body and did not know what they were doing had they not seen of their own people there whom he wanted to get back and would it not be better to be at peace to bring them back,[320] he charged them not to go again to strike their own people and he said that the Governor of Virginia and Pensylvania would interest themselves in making a peace[321] *Gave a black string*

Then turning to the Delawares he said, You went to the Wiendots and delivered a speech and a belt of wampum to make peace between you and the Cherokees and after you came back you let your young men go to war against the Cherokees which was very wrong after you had delivered the Speech which I myself being present heard. I take the hatchet from you, you belong to me[322] and I think you are to be ruled by me and I (joining with your brethren of Virginia) order you to go to war no more. *Gave a belt of wampum*

Taking a belt of wampum in his hand he proceeded as followeth—
Brethren, The Governors of Virginia and Pensylvania, some years ago we made a complaint to our brother of Pensylvania that his traders

brought too much spiritous liquors amongst us and desired that there might not come such quantities and hoped he would order his traders to sell their goods and liquors at cheaper rates. In answer[323] to our request Conrade Weiser delivered us this belt of wampum and told us we must pay but five buck skins for a keg and if the traders would not take that, that we should have it for nothing since which time there has been double the quantity brought out yearly and sold as formerly and we have some complaint to try to stop such large quantities from being brought but as there has been no notice taken to prevent it we beleive M.r Weiser spoke only from his mouth and not from his heart and without the Governors authority some[324] think proper to return the belt.   *He gave the belt to M.r Croghan.*

  June 11.th   Present. Joshua Fry, Lunsford Lomax, James Patton Esq.rs
        Commissioners.
     M.r Christopher Gist agent for the Ohio
     Company
     M.r Andrew Montour, Interpreter.

  The Commissioners of Virginia delivered to the six nations a string of wampum and a suit of Indian cloathing to wipe away their tears for the loss of one of their cheifs[325] who lately came down from the head of Ohio to Logs town and died there

       Gave the suit of cloaths and string

  Afterwards the half king[306] spoke to the Delawares, Nephews you received a speech last year[326] from your brother the Governor of Pensylvania and from us desiring you to choose one of your wisest councillors and present him to us for a king, as you have not done it we now let you know that it is our right to give you a king and we think proper to give you Shingas[327] for your king whom you must look upon as your cheif and with whom all publick business must be transacted between you and your brethren the English. On which the half king put a laced hat on the head of the Beaver[203] who stood proxy for his brother Shingas and presented him also with a rich jacket and suit of English colours which had been delivered to the half king by the Commissioners for that purpose

  The Commissioners addressing themselves to the Shawnese acquainted them that they understood their cheif king Cochawitchiky[122] who had been a good freind to the English, was lying Bedrid, and that to shew the regard they bore to his past services they took this opportunity to acknowledge it by presenting him with a suit of Indian cloathing

  Then the half king spoke as followeth

  Brother, the Governor of Virginia, You acquainted us yesterday

In the Darlington Memorial Library

with the Kings right to all the lands in Virginia as far as it is setled and back from thence to the sunsetting whenever he shall think fit to extend his Settlements you produced also a copy of his deed from the Onandago council at the treaty at Lancaster[287] and desired that your brethren of Ohio might likewise confirm the deed. Brother the Governor of Virginia we are well acquainted that our cheif council at the treaty of Lancaster confirmed a deed to you for a quantity of land in Virginia which you have a right to and likewise our brother Onas has a right to a parcel of land in Pensylvania, we are glad you have acquainted us with the right to those lands and assure you we are willing to confirm anything our council has done in regard to the lands, but we never understood before you told us yesterday that the lands then sold were to extend further to the sunsetting than the hill on the other side the Allagany hill so that we cannot give you a further answer.

Brother. You acquainted us yesterday that the French were a designing people which we now see and know that they design to cheat us out of our lands you told us that the king of England designed to settle some lands on the South East side of Ohio that it might be better in our brethrens power to help us, if we were in need than it is at present at the great distance they live from us we are sure the French design nothing else but mischeif for they have struck our freinds the Twigtwees. We therefore desire our brothers of Virginia may build a strong house at the fork of Monongahela[328] to keep such goods powder lead and necessaries as shall be wanting and as soon as you please and as we have given our Cousins the Delawares a king[327] who lives there we desire you will look on him as a cheif of that nation.

Gave a large string of wampum

Brethren. Our brothers that live on this river Ohio are all warriors and hunters and like our brethren the traders all wise men. There has been a reason for many complaints for sometime past but we will not complain of our brethren the traders for we love them and cant live without them but we hope you will take care to send none amongst us but good men[329] sure you know them that are fit and we hope you will advise them how to behave better than they have done, we well remember when first we saw our brethren the English and we remember the first council we held with them and shall do all we can to keep the chain of freindship from rust[330]

June 12th This day the Indians gave us an answer concerning the land which we wanted to settle they desired us to build a strong house or fort very soon, as we had asked for the lands at Monongahela I we imagined they had given up the lands upon that river, but they only

George Mercer Papers

meant ground sufficient for the fort to stand upon as appeared by a private conversation with the half king who said that was all that was intended tho' he always spoke the sentiments of others and not his own, for that we could not be without a large quantity of land

We had Conferences with the cheifs of the Indians as followeth.

June 12th 1752. The half king[306] with a string of wampum informed the Commissioners that one Frazier a blacksmith at the town of Venango threatned to remove that they did not desire he should leave them but if he did requested another might be sent to them and he said that they had not a sufficient number of traders there to supply them with goods, to which the Commissioners replied that they would represent their case to the Governor of Virginia and hoped they would be supplied according to their desire

The same day the cheifs of the Shawnese with a string of wampum thanked the Commissioners for their good advice they acknowledged that they had been led astray by the French and had suffered for it and said they would take care not to be deceived by the French again but would keep fast hold of the chain of freindship between the English the six nations and themselves.

The Commissioners thanked them for their Attachment to the English and desired their compliments might be made to the young king[332] of the Shawnese who was generously gone to the Assistance of the Picts[333] they sent him also a laced hat and a rich jacket[334]

June 13th The half king speaking to the Commissioners said,

Brethren You told us you sent us a present of goods in the year 1748[335] which you said Conrade Weiser delivered at this Town he may have told you so but we assure you we never heard of it from him, it is true he did deliver us some goods then but we understood him it was from our brother Onas, he never made mention of the great King our father[336] nor of our brother Assaragoa. Then directing his speech to the Governor of Virginia said, Brother you complained to us that some of our people had murdered a woman in Virginia it is true there has been such a thing done and brothers we know the man that did it, he is one of our six nations altho' he has lived sometime among the French we cant make an excuse for so barbarous a murder but we assure you he did it without our knowledge and we beleive the evil spirit tempted him to do it we will let the Onandago council know what has been done and we beleive they will try to get him and make a satisfaction for the crime committed

Gave a string of black and white wampum—

Brother We have heard what you said in regard to the Kings design of making a settlement of his people on the waters of this river Ohio, you likewise told us you had a deed for those lands signed by our council at the treaty of Lancaster we assure you of our willingness to agree to what our council does or has done but we have not the full power in our hands here on Ohio, we must acquaint our council at Onandago of the affair and whatever they bid us do we will do. In regard to your request to build a stronghouse at the mouth of Monongahela you told us it would require a settlement to support it with provisions and necessaries, it is true, but we will take care that there shall be no scarcity of that kind until we can give a full answer, altho' in all our wars we don't consider provisions, for we live on one another but we know it is different with our brethren the English.

Gave three strings of white wampum

The Commissioners having drawn an instrument of writing[337] for confirming the deed made at Lancaster and containing a promise that the Indians would not molest our settlements on the South East of side of the Ohio desired Mr Montour to converse with his brethren the other Sachems in private on the subject to urge the necessity of such a settlement and the great advantage it would be to them as to their trade or their security on which they retired for some time and then returned and Mr Montour said they were satisfied in the matter and were willing to sign and seal the writing which was done and witnessed by the Gentlemen then present. The half king then spoke as follows.

Brethren, The Governors of Virginia and Pensylvania, You expressed your regard for our freinds and allies the Twigtwees, and have considered their necessities at present, we return you our thanks for your care of them, we join with you and desire you will deliver them this belt, and let them know from us, that we desire them not to forget what they did in Pensylvania,[338] when they were down four years ago, and joined in a freindship with our brethren the English, we desire they may hold fast the chain of freindship, and not listen to any other but their brethren the English, the six nations, Delawares, and Shawnese, as we will stand by them, we expect they will come down,[339] and confirm the freindship they have engaged with the English. He delivered a belt to be sent to the Twigtwees.

The Commissioners then opened the roads to Virginia with a belt of wampum and the following speech

Brethren, We have travelled through a long and dark way to meet you at this council, we have now compleated our business with pleasure and satisfaction, both to you and us, and as we are now returning back, we do in the name of the great King your father, as also in the name of your brother the Governor of Virginia, remove all Obstacles out of the way, and make clear the road that you may at any time, send messages to us, on any occasion, and we shall be always ready to receive them kindly, and look on you as our brothers, and, in token of the sincerity of our hearts, present you with this belt of wampum.   *Gave the belt*

    The Commissioners added. Brethren, At the treaty of Lancaster the Commissioners informed you of a large house built among us for the education of Indian children[340] and desired that you would send some of yours we now make you the same offer but if you think it too far to send your children we desire to know whether it would be agreeable to you that teachers be sent among you. The advantages of an English education are greater than can be imagined by them who are unacquainted with it. By it we know the part of the world from whence all nations came, how nations for some thousands of years back have rose grown powerful, or decayed how they have removed from one place to another what battles have been fought, what great men have lived, and how they have acted either in council or in war. In this part of the world we know from the first time the Spaniards came to it how cruelly they used the Indians then wholly ignorant of fire arms, and we know the actions of the French against you and others. There are many other benefits arising from a good education which would be too tedious to be mentioned but the greatest of all is that by it we are acquainted with the will of the great God, the Creator of the world and Father of us all who inhabits the skies, by which the better people among us regulate their lives and hope after death to live with him forever.   *Gave a string of wampum*

No 8.   Governor Dinwiddies letter to Capt Trent.[396]
Sir   Williamsburg May 31st 1753.

    Yr letter from Winchester of the 21st May was deliver'd me by Collo Lomax, the contents thereof I have duly considered and it corresponds with the Intelligence I rec'ed from Mr Montour,[397] and what I have express from Philadelphia[398] and I am sincerely sorry for the present situation of the Indians in Freindship with us and to shew them how much I have their interest at heart I have this day wrote to Collo Fairfax,[399] to deliver you all or what part you see proper of the present intended for them that is now at Winchester.

    I hope you will take proper care to advise the half king[306] and the other cheifs of the Indians by a messenger[400] of your bringing them the supplies as above from me, that they may send some of their people to escort you, so that it may not fall into the hands of their enemies, as you are thorowly acquainted in the woods, I must refer this affair to you, and you will consider the great misfortune that will attend if these supplies should fall into the hands of the French Indians which I hope you will cautiously prevent.[401]

I am well pleased with the half kings speech[402] and hope they will be able to give a good Accot of the French and their Indians, and prevent their taking possession of the lands of the Ohio. You may assure them of my firm Attachmt to their interest. It was not practicable yet to build the stronghouse, but when this attempt is defeated, they may be assur'd it will be built. If they secure some of the principal of the French and send them here I shall send them to France by way of Britain

What the Delawar's told you, is confirm'd by Mr Montour in regard to the French and Indians giving the six nations a large black belt and the answer the six nations made them.[403]

I am sorry[404] for the accot of the murders &c done by the French, and hope if we have a settlement on the Ohio, we shall turn the Tables on them, in every thing but their barbarity. You know how to frame a speech to the Indians in their stile better than I can, assure them of my sincere freindship and readiness at all times to assist them, deliver the present to them as from this colony[406] and that it is intended for the six nations and the other nations of Indians in Amity with us and them. I intreat you to be as inquisitive[407] as possible of the number of the French and their Indians of their designs and the situation, the Picts and Twigtwees are now in, next year I hope to deliver them a large present from their father, and that I propose delivering it with my own hands. I shall be glad to hear that Burney got safe to the Twigtwees, tho' he broke my orders in remaining so long in this Colony, if he had gone directly it probably had been [of much] service[408]

I hope Pensylvania have been appriz'd of the present necessities of our freindly Indians and that they have or will send them some supplies[409]

On yr return I expect you will send me as particular an accot[410] as possible of all affairs relating to the intentions of the French and their Indians and that they are disappointed of their designs.

God preserve you and grant you a safe return & I remain with great sincerity

Sr Yr most hble Servt
Robt Dinwiddie

My Service to Collo Cressup.
You know dispatch is now absolutely necessary

George Mercer Papers

Governor Dinwiddies directions to Mr Gist concerning the Indians July 10. 1753.[723]

To the Half King, King Shingas, and Sachems of the six nations on the Ohio Friends and Brethren, The Governor of Virginia wishes you all health and happiness

We received your message by your brother Mr Thomas Burney, and are heartily sorry for the Attempts of the French, and their Indians to disturb your peace, and by force endeavour to build forts on the Ohio without your consent   The present we sent you by Mr Trent [we hope] came [safe] to your hands, and will [ena] ble you to defeat their designs. Some of the heads and cheifs of the Twigtwees being arrived at the Logs town on the Ohio, we are preparing a small present to be sent them to Winchester, and to be delivered to them by the Honourable William Fairfax Esqr one of our council on the 20th day of next month being a small testimony of the regard we bear to them as being our Freinds and allies to the six nations, next May we shall expect the cheifs of the six nations and the Twigtwees at Winchester to receive a considerable present sent by your Father his Majesty the King of Great Britain, in the meantime we are preparing a suit of cloaths for the half king, and king Shingas which shall be sent to Winchester together with the small present to the cheifs of the Twigtwees who are now at the Ohio. I further assure you that I shall be always ready to assist you with powder and arms upon all necessary occasions when in my power, and it will be my cheif care to keep the chain of Freindship subsisting between us bright and intire as long as the Sun and moon shall continue

I remain with true affection
Your loving Brother
Robt Dinwiddie

Williamsburg July 10th 1753.

This comes by our freind and your brother Mr Christopher Gist, to whom we refer you, and to whom you may give Faith

[Endorsed: Appendices]

Resolutions of the Committee of the Ohio Company, October 17, 1760 and September 7-9, 1761.[724]

Enclosure 3

At a Meeting of the Committee of the Ohio Company at Williamsburg on Friday the 17th of October 1760.
Mr John Mercer having drawn up a State of the Companys Case and presented the same to the Committee
Resolved that the same be approved . . .
> *Identical item in "Orders and Resolutions, 1749–1761."*
> *Printed on pp. 150-151.*

Ordered that Mr George Mason the Companys Treasurer write to Mr Edward Athawes Mercht . . .
> *Identical item in "Orders and Resolutions, 1749–1761."*
> *Printed on p. 151.*

Resolved that the Companys Store house at Wills Creek be repaired and put into good Order . . .
> *Identical item in "Orders and Resolutions, 1748–1763."*
> *Printed on p. 180.*

Ordered that the Treasurer make enquiry into the damages[725] done to the Companys Houses and Lands in Virginia and Maryland and if the same can be proved, that Suits be brought against the person or persons who appear to have been principally concerned therein
Resolved that Thomas Ludwell Lee Esqr be chosen and appointed one of the Committee . . .
> *Identical item in "Orders and Resolutions, 1748–1763."*
> *Printed on p. 180.*

[signed]   Phil Lud. Lee ⎫
               G Mason   ⎬ Committee
               J Mercer   ⎭

At a Meeting of the Committee of the Ohio Company at Stafford Court house on Monday the 7th day of September 1761. (being the Day of the Companys annual meeting) and continued to Wednesday the 9th day of the same Month
Resolved that the Honble Philip Lee Esqr be applied to . . .
> *Identical item in "Orders and Resolutions, 1749–1761."*
> *Printed on p. 151.*

George Mercer Papers

Resolved that the said Letter be signed with the names of all the Members in Virginia and Maryland now living

Resolved, that the Committee write to Messrs Hanburys and Robert Dinwiddie . . .

Identical item in "Orders and Resolutions, 1748–1763." Printed on p. 180.

[signed] James Scott

J Mercer

G Mason   } Committee

Thos Lud. Lee

Richard Lee

[Endorsed]
Resolutions of the Ohio Company, 1760–1761

In the Darlington Memorial Library

Record of Land Grants, Made in Virginia, 1745–1753.[726]

Enclosure 4

		Acres	No		Yrs [allowed]
1745 April 26.	John Robinson Esqr & others	100,000	12	on Green Bryar River No Wt & Wt of the Cow Pasture & New foundland	4
	John Smith &c.	50,000	5	on Roanoke River & Branches & James River Branches.	4
	James Patton &c.	100,000	20	on 3 branches of Mississippi 1 Woods R. 1 Wt of it & on the Waters of sd River.	4
	Henry Downes &c.	50,000	11	Wt of the Cow Pasture on Green Bryar R.	4
		300,000			
Nov. 4	John Blair Wm Russel & Co	100,000	2	Wd of L. Fairfax's Line on the Waters of Potomack & Youghyoughgane	4
1747. April 22	Wm Mcmahon &c.	60,000	20	joyning Blair & on the Waters of Potomack Wt & N Wt of Ld Fairfax's Line & on the branches of Youghyoughgane & Monongaly	5

· 289 ·

1749 July 12	Bernard Moore &c.	100,000	10	beginning in a fork of New River & down that River & on the Waters of Mississippi............ 4
	John Lewis &c.	800,000	39	beginning on the Line between Virgª & Carolina & running Wt & No............ 4
	Peyton Randolph &c	400,000	18	on New River & its Waters....... 4
	Wm Winston &c.	50,000	5	beginning at old Fort between Ohio & Mississippi R. running up the Wt side of Ohio & Et side of Mississippi............ 4
		1,350,000		
1752 Nov. 3	Lunsford Lomax petitioned for	200,000	10	
	Wm Trent	200,000	10	
	Andrew Montour	80,000	4	
	John Mercer	140,000	14	620,000 on settling 140 families in 3 years after the Entry allowed & on such terms as the Govr & Council thought fit.

In the Darlington Memorial Library

1753 June 15	Richard Corbin & Co.	50,000		
	Do.	100,000		
	Do.	40,000	190,000	
			2,620,000	
1749 July 12	Ohio Company		20 500,000	
			3,120,000	
	Renewed			
1749 July 12	Patton's in name of John Tayloe	100,000	....	2 years longer time allowed. Expired April 26, 1749.
1751 Oct 26	Blair &c.	100,000	....	4 Do......Nov. 4, 1749
	Mcmahon &c.	60,000	....	5 Do......not expired till April 22, 1752.

· 291 ·

Petitioners for Land on the Ohio, 1745–1753.[727]
Enclosure 5

Robinson John Esqr	Moore Bernard	Lewis John Esqr	Randolph Peyton
Nelson Thos Jun' Esqr	Hubbard Benja	Walker Thos	McKenzie Alexr
Robinson Jno Jun' Esqr	Aylett Philip	Dick Charles	Tucker Robt
Beverley Wm	Dansie Thos	Barrett Charles	Tucker John
Lewis Robert	Snelson John	Fry Joshua	Gilmer George
Robinson Beverley	Carrington George	Turpin Thomas	Walter Benja
Wetherburn Henry	Power James	Harvie John	Parks Wm
Lewis John	Graham Duncan	Meriwether Thos	Burwell Armistead
Craig John	Taylor Wm	Meriwether Thos jun'	Pendleton Edwd
Lewis Wm	Thomas Job 10	Baylor John	Willoughby John
Wilson John &	Downes Henry	Waddy Samuel	Maddison John
Lewis Charles 12	Blair John Jun'	Barrett Robert	Shelton John
Smith John	Willis John	Willis Henry	Garland John
Lewis Zachary	Taylor George	Gilmer Penchey	Williamson Thos
Walter Wm	Spencer Edwd	Lewis John	Calvert Maximilian

In the Darlington Memorial Library

Walter Benjᵃ &	Slaughter Robert	Maury James	Calvert Cornelius
Green Robᵗ 5	Slaughter Thomas	Lewis Thoˢ	Loyal Paul &
Patton James	Jackson Wᵐ	Hedgman Peter	Logan George 18
	Dunlop Alexʳ	Moore John	Winston Wᵐ Junʳ
Graeme John	Ewin James &	Martin Robert	Winston Isaac Junʳ
Belfield John	11	Pate Henry	Fontaine Peter Junʳ
Tayloe John Junʳ	McMachon	Jones Richard	Winston Edmund
Green Wᵐ	McMachon	Wood William	Red Samuel 5
Barnes Richᵈ	McMachon	Dalton Samuel	Hanbury John
Gordon James	Neal Lewis	Thornton Francis	Lee Thoˢ Esqʳ
Wood James	Neal John	Thornton Fraˢ Junʳ	Nelson Thoˢ Esqʳ
Buchanan George	Calmees Mark	Thornton John	Cresap Thomas
Robinson George	Butler Wᵐ	Pierce John	Thornton Wᵐ
Bowie James	Neal Wᵐ	Stevenson Wᵐ	Nimmo Wᵐ
Jackson Robert	Glover Wᵐ	Lewis Nichᵒ	Cresap Daniel
Parks Wᵐ	Parrett Hugh	Meriwether Nichᵒ	Carlisle John
Preston John	Rice Patrick	Hudson Wᵐ	Washington Lawʳ

· 293 ·

Gilchrist Robert
Winstow Richard
Roberts John
Weatherhall Jas &
Johnston James.

Calvert Robert
Calvert Isaiah
Parrett Leonard
Walter George
Harding George
Harding Henry
Helms Leonard
Bruce John &
Carter James

20

Meriwether Fras
Hill Humphry
Dixon John
Meriwether John
Lewis Charles
Power James &
Jefferson Peter

Washington Augt
Fairfax George
Giles Jacob
Chapman Nathl
Wardrop James
Tayloe Jno
Thornton Presley
Lee Philip Ludwell
Lee Richard
Corbin Gawin & Jas
Scott.

39

Case of the Ohio Company, 1762[728]

Enclosure 6

told Maj.^r Washington enquiring by what authority he had made prisoners of several English Subjects, that the Countrey belonged to the French, that no Englishman had a right to trade upon those waters & that he had orders to make every person prisoner that attempted to trade on the Ohio or the Waters of it. And it is remarkable that the half king in the account he gave Maj.^r Washington of his Speech to the French Commander insisted that the Land on the Ohio belonged to the Indians & neither to the English or French. altho at the Treaty at Logs Town he & the other cheifs had agreed the English might build a fort & settle there & in Consequence thereof the Ohio Company had contributed four hundred to erect a fort & Maj.^r Washington mentions in his Journal that on the 6th & 7th of January he met 17 Horses with Materials & Stores for the Fort, & some families going out to settle.[427]

Jan. 21. 1754. A Proclamation was issued requiring the Assembly which stood prorogued to the last Thursday in April to meet on the 14th of February, when the Governor in his Speech informed them

Leave as much room as his last Speech in Novr took.

and on the 27th (19) day of the month the following Proclamation was published[428]

Virginia ss

By the Honble &c   to God save the King.

The Company were far from thinking themselves bound by such a Proclamation, & it would-not have had all the intended effect, if they had enterd a Caveat against it, but they looked upon it as the most effectual method that could be taken at that time for the End proposed, & that it was for the Advantage of the Public, they unanimously agreed to acquiesce, but at the same time proposed the Monongahela as a Boundary, that the 200,000 Acres for the Officers & Soldiers should be laid off on the upper side, allowing the Company as many tracts of about a thousand Acres each as should be necessary upon the main road which they had cleared from their Storehouse at Will's Creek to the Monongahela, for the building proper Storehouses at convenient Stages, & providing Corn & Hay for the great number of Horses necessary to carry on their trade & make their Settlement.[429] This the principal Officers not only approved of, but declared that they looked upon the Contiguity of the Company's Lands as one of the greatest Advantages that could be; as they would be thereby enabled not only to settle their Land but supply themselves with necessaries from the Companies Stores on much better terms, than otherwise they could possibly do in that part of the World, as their Land would likewise be rendred of much greater value by having the Road running thro' it by which all Persons going to or from the Ohio must pass, so that as soon as it could be settled they could not fail to meet a constant market for everything they could raise, & as by this means the Fort could not fail of being plentifully & cheaply supplied from their own Settlements on the one Side & the Companies on the other, which would also greatly contribute to its Strength & the Security of that Frontier.

But previous hereto, Colo Fairfax wrote the following Letters to Wm Trent [Letters printed on pp. 78-80.]

See the other Paper

Resolution of the Committee of the Ohio Company July 4, 1763[729]

Enclosure 7

At a Meeting of Committee of the Ohio Company at Stafford Court House on Monday July 4th 1763.

Resolved that the Company will upon the very first Notice from Colo George Mercer reimburse and repay him any Sums of Money which he shall judge necessary to expend in Order to obtain a Grant for the Ohio Company on the Terms they have now petitioned for—provided the Sum does not exceed Two thousand Pounds Sterling upon the whole including any Money that may be advanced or raised already by Charlton Palmer Esqr on this Account

J Mercer

John Mercer to George Mercer, January 28, 1768[730]

Enclosure 8

(which he alone of all the creditors, contrary to his promise, reserved at his Execution of the Assignment) . . .

I should be very desirous that you would procure me the

Fragment of complete letter which is printed on pp. 186-220.

John Mercer to George Mercer, March 9, 1768[731]

Dear George

I have again taken up my pen before my Letter got over the creek. I am apprehensive the Affair in Pensylvania will be attended with many unhappy Consequences. The massacre at Lancaster was a most scandalous & bloody one & tho many of the persons principally concerned in it were well known, so was their power too. The assembly then sitting trembled for themselves in Philadelphia, and were rejoiced to hear they were returned without paying them a visit, & dared not then to make any enquiry into the matter. The truth of the Case was that the back settlements in Pennsylvania were cheifly made by Germans & among them many Irish all of whom had purchased their Lands at excessive high rates on those Lands which Penn purchased of the Indians for a trifle, & which they always complained of. At the Treaty at Lancaster May 12. 1757, Govr Denny says in his first Speech[732] that Teedyuscung frankly acknowledged that one reason why the Indians blow fell heavier on Pennsylvania was that their brother (Onas) Penn had fraudulently possessed himself of some of their Lands, without having first purchased, or given any consideration for them. Old Penn his Descendts & Councillors were all Men who understood their Interest & would suffer nothing to come into Competition with with it They engaged Weiser the Indians Idol Interpreter early in their Interest & he was a proper tool for them. If you have the Minutes of the Conferences at Easton in October 1758[733] & those at Harris's ferry & Lancaster in 1757[734] from which I made the first quotation you will be convinced of the truth of it. They successively engaged Croghan & Montour as they form'd their Interest with the Indians encrease & by their means found they could lead & cheat the Indians as they pleased They early found the Advantage of extending their Province by tricking purchases of their Indians Lands & improving by engrossing their Skin & fur trade thro' the Colony of Virginia to the prejudice of Wm & Mary College who did not receive a penny of the duties they were entitled to. They were sensible that that trade was held on a very precarious footing that as soon as the Virginians should come to understand that it could not be carried on thro their Countrey, they might be in danger of its being shared with if not entirely lost to, them. They therefore took every Opportunity of instilling into the Indians the firmest assurances that their brother Onas was their only friend, that all the other English were either professed Enemies to them or not to be trusted. With such a People as the Indians these Suggestions worked every thing they hoped for. They ravaged the frontiers of Maryland & Virginia. The injured Inhabitants who in self defence killed or took one of them prisoners, were looked on by the Indians as their professed Enemies determined to extirpate them. Onas, imagining his Schemes might be carried too far proposed to become Mediator between the Gov.r of Virginia or more properly between his Majesty & the Indians & his Council, had address enough not only to prevail on the Gov.r of Virg.a to accept of his Negotiation but to employ Onas's Scoundrel Interpreter Weiser as the Plenipotentiary.[735] In Consequences of which, Weiser in his Report[736] annexed to the Conferences at Harris's Ferry & Lancaster in 1757, intituled The Report of Conrad Weiser, the Indian Interpreter, of his Journey to Shamokin on the Affairs of Virginia & Maryland, his Mediation for accommodating the differences between the Indians of the six nations & the s.d Provinces delivered to the Governor (of Pennsylvania) in Council the 21st day of April 1743, begins, The 9th of April 1743 I arrived at Shamokin by Order of the Gov.r of Pennsylvania to acquaint the neighbouring Indians & those on Wyoming, that the Gov.r of Virg.a was well pleased, with his Mediation & was willing to come to an agreement with the Six nations about the Land his people were settled upon, if it was that they contended for & to make up the matter of the late unhappy Skirmish in an amicable Way.

It is to be particurlarly noticed that there was not a man in Virginia then settled to the Westward of the great ridge of mountains, nor was there an entry made for one acre of land there till 1745[737] and in 1722 an Act of Assembly[738] passed in Virg.a to make death for any tributary Indian to cross Potomack or pass to the Westward of those mountains or for any of the five nations (for at that time they were so called) to hunt or travel in or thro' any part of Virg.a on the S.o side of Potomack or on the East side of the s.d Ridge of mountains without proper licenses. It was therefore impossible the Indians cou'd have any just cause of complaint ag.t any man in Virg.a because his own life was forfeited by Law by his very being there. I agree that the Law directed & they ought to have been tried. Sometime before Jonst Hyle & Benj.a Borden who were settled in Pennsylvania[739] obtained each a Grant of 100 000 Acres of Land in Frederick & Augusta on Condition of settling 100 families each in that frontier on the E.t side of the mountains & from whence I have been informed & beleive it to be true that they thought it more convenient to send for a gimSlet or any tool they wanted, than to any part of Virginia w.ch they were then wholly unacquainted with These 200 families were to remove from Pennsylvania & had subscribed as partners to the Expences of a grant.

In the Darlington Memorial Library

Indeed the frontiers were erected into new Counties only in 1720, & by the advantages allowed them settled very fast All that time there were only 25 Counties in Virginia & now there are 57. The new Counties then erected were Brunswick, Hanover, King George & Spotsylvania. All frontiers as was Henrico, & since that time have been erected 28 other all but one of them, Caroline, out of the frontiers, Vizt Caroline & Goochland in 1727 Pr William in 1730, Amelia & Orange in 1734 Augusta & Frederick in 1738 Fairfax & Louisa in 1742, Albemarle in 1744 Lunenburg in 1746 Chesterfield, Culpeper, Cumberland & Southampton in 1748 Dinwiddie & Halifax in 1752, Bedford, Hampshire, Pr Edward & Sussex in 1753, Loudoun in 1757 Fauquier in 1759 Amherst & Buckingham in 1761. Charlotte & Mecklenburg in 1764 & Pittsylvania in 1766, but I mistook Southampton & Sussex are not frontiers however the frontier Counties are 30 out of the 57 & erected in 1720 & since. In the very beginning of their Settlemt they were attacked by the Indians & Capt Mcdowell & several others were killed. It was supposed the Indians had been set on by the Pensylvanians.[740] I then knew nothing of that part of the Countrey or the different Interests of the Colonies but from what I have known of them since I am as well satisfied, as if I had been privy to their Consultations that it really was so.

But to proceed. The Indians in their Speech say. Brother Onas. We thank you for the Concern you shew for the misfortune that befel our Warriors in Virginia—It was a very prudent & good advice they (your old & wise men) gave you to become Mediator betwixt Us your brethren & the Virginians your neighbours—Therefore Brother Onas, go on with courage in your mediation, we assure you we will not violate or do anything contrary to your Mediation[741]—But if I was to take notice of every thing remarkable I should transcribe the whole You may certainly get them in London if you have them not yourself. I would send you mine if I knew by what Conveyance this is to go.

The next thing I shall take notice of is. That our Government was so imposed upon by brother Onas's Councillors & his Scoundrel Interpreter that they trusted Weiser with the King's present[742] to the Ohio Indians with regard to which the Half King in his Speech at the Loggs town in 1752, says. Brethren. You told us you sent a present of Goods in the year 1748 which you say Conrad Weiser delivered us at this town. He may have told you so, but We assure you we never heard it from him. It is true he did deliver us Goods then, but we understood him it was from our Brother Onas. He never made mention of the Great King our Father nor of our brother Assaragsa (the Govr of Virga)[743]

Was there ever so villainous a peice of treachery fraud & presumption not to call it treason, to bestow the King's Goods with which he was intrusted in direct violation of that trust, & to a quite different purpose than his Matie intended them. To attribute the King's bounty to the generosity of Onas, who always affected to make the Indians beleive he was the only white man able to protect them & all others were their Enemies of which you may see many more Instances in Weisers Report just mentioned.

But the next fact in my Opinion actually amounted to High treason. It is the treaty between Croghan, Onas's Plenipotentiary with the Wawiaghtas & Piankashas March 1750. Tho Gist was present & signed as a Witness & tho Croghan knew that the King had sent in a large quantity of Goods as a present to the Ohio Indians & he himself had informed the Wyandot King & Council the 15th day of Janry before that Gist had been sent out by the Govr of Virginia to invite the Indians to meet & receive it, yet he acted Conrad Weiser over again invited the Indians to the Logs town in Onas's name & from whom he had carried out a present of Goods to the value of £100 Pensylva money, to receive the Kings Goods, & tho the French had their Ambassadors (as they were called) treating with the Indians in the French King's name & inviting them to a treaty Croghan never since mentioned the King of England but concluded & signed a treaty of Peace & War in the name of Onas by which the Indians were bound to assist the Pensylvanians, as much against any other of his Maties Subjects as against either French or Indians. Gist took a Copy of it which I sent you & could not get time to take a Copy but as I read it this morning I think I may venture to say that will make out part of the Charge & Gist's Journal a fair Copy of which containing the Speeches was sent to Mr Hanbury will make out the rest.

I must now return to the Conferences at Harris's ferry & Lancaster in 1757 where were present 199 Mohawks Oneidas Tuscaroras, Onondagoes, Cayugas, Senecas, Nanticokes, Delawares & Connestogoes, & here Onas's friend George Croghan opens the Conferences with a Speech which begins thus.
Brethren

I am sent here by the Honble Sr Wm Johnson, to represent him at this meeting & I desire you all to give Attention to what I am going to say to you in behalf of your brother Onas & the wise men of this Government (Pennsylva)

And it is remarkable that in the Acct of the whole transaction between Croghan & the Indians before the Arrival of the Govr of Pennsylva (from April 1st to May 9.) his Maties name is not mentioned except April 23, when Croghan says, 6 Onondago Warriors applied to him for Liberty to go to Fort Cumberland to join the Southward Indians who they understood were going to War against his Maties Enemies at Ohio, he says, I granted their request & fitted them out for their Journey—A most gracious condescension—as I dont doubt he paid himself to his utmost content for whatever he supplied 'em with. Nor had Croghan even mentioned his Master Sr William Johnson, as his Maties Agent.

It is true the Govr in his first Speech to the Indians mentions Sr Wm under that Character also mentions the Indians having differences with the English in other Colonies, as well as Pennsylva & acknowledged as I before noticed that Teedyuscung complained of Onas's defrauding them of their Lands, but still the Conferences seem to be carried on purely in the name & for the separate Interest of Onas till May 17 when Croghan says he spoke to the Indians in the name of the Honble Sr Wm Johnson Bart his Maties sole Agent & Superintendant of the Affairs of the six nations & their Allies & dependts when he tells them, the meeting was appointed upon Teedyuscung's complaint. That the Kings Subjects that settled Pennsylva & the neighbouring provinces by Law were not allowed to buy any of the Indians Lands & had not done it & if those who only had a right from the Crown to purchase their Lands had done them any Injustice the Pensylvanians were present & willing to make them Satisfaction but if they or any pe or the people of any other provinces refused to do so, Sr Wm would represent their Case to his Ma'tie & procure them Satisfaction. And therefore insists to know all their complaints agt any of his Ma'ties Subjects.[744]

This would have been a proper & ought to have been the first Speech at opening the Conferences, which had then held 47 days & ended the 3d day after but then it might have appeared that the King of Great Britain had been a greater Man than Onas, but it is to be remarked that the Honble Colo John Stanwix had been present at the meeting the day before, was then present, & attended the next meeting on the 19th which was the last. And I presume Croghan & the Govr of Pennsylva too, might be apprehensive that Colo Stanwix might be alarmed had the Conferences been still carried on in the name of Onas only.

May 19. Little Abraham, a Mohawk Sachem, in his Answer to Sr Wm & the Govr of Pennsylvania joyntly as he said each of their Speeches was to the same purpose, told them, That their Complaints were, That a Delaware head man[745] was killed tried & hanged at Amboy for killing a Gent who was his friend, his gun going off by

George Mercer Papers

accident as he was going to shake hands with him thro a fence. 2d Some Shawnese going to war called at a house in Carolina where the Inhabitants rose & took them on Accot of some mischeif done there about that time & carried them to Charles town where they were imprisoned & their cheif man, called The Pride, died.[746] 3d That they the 6 nations after conquering the Delawares removed them & gave them Lands to plant & hunt on at Wyoming & Juniata, on Susquehannah, but the Pennsylvanians, covetous of Lands[747] made plantations there & spoiled their hunting grounds, on which they complained to the 6 nations who looked over the Lands & found their Complaint true. That the French to whom they were drove back took advantage of it, & told them tho the French built trading houses on their Land they did not plant it they had their provisions from over the great water but the English planted all the countrey, drove them back so that in a little time they wou'd have no Land. By these Arguments the Delawares joined the French.

You may now find that Onas's undertaking in 1743 to be a Mediator for the Govr of Virga & sending Weyser as Plenipotentiary to Shamokin & Wyoming, was a Shamokin imposition, too easily swallowed by the Gov'. of Virga who rather ought to have been applied & to have become Mediator, as his Ma'ties Governor between his Subject Penn & his Pennsylvanians, & the Indians & not in Weisers & the Indians Stile, for Onas to become Mediator between the Indians— Onas's brethren & the Virginian's Onas's Neighbours, who it seems were no ways concerned in the quarrel,[748] which Little Abraham here shews to be about the Lands at Wyoming & Juniata, which the Pennsylvanians had unjustly settled upon, as the Indians complained. Penn had made a purchase from the Indians in these parts, in 1740[749] as mentioned in Evans's map, the Consideration & bounds of which it seems was disputed, & tho the next year[750] at Easton Teedyuscung, when he saw the six nations deed, for those Lands & therefore acknowledged it being signed by Natimus[751] a Delaware cheif—who he says had 44 dollars for his Share & gives it up & but still maintain'd a claim[752] for other Lands between Tohiccon Creek & the Kittochtinny Hills—Is it not notorious that every foot of all those Lands were far within the bounds of Pennsylvania where no Virginian ever had or could have any concern & consequently could have nothing to do with the disputes. But now little Abraham having discovered the true ground of the dispute, it is confirm'd by Weisers own report in 1743. Tho Onas had artfully drawn his own head out of the Collar & slipped it over that of the Govrs of Virginia & Maryland & Weiser had in Onas's behalf duped the Indians & made them swallow every thing

In the Darlington Memorial Library

he advanced. Shickallemo[753] after thanking Onas for his mediation[735] & encouraging him to be strong in it, tells the Gov[r] of Maryland that the Indians accepted the Invitation he had given them kindly being recommended by the Gov[r] of Pennsylv[a] which he would not have done if not satisfied of the Gov[r] of Maryland's good Intention—Yet thro all this Fraud & disguise the Indians coud not help discovering their true Cause of Complaint, they say. Brother Onas—The Dutchman on Schooniady (Juniata) claims a right to the Land, merely because he gave a little Victuals to our Warriors who stand very often in need of it. This string of Wampum serves to take the Dutchman by the Arm & throw him over the big mountains within your borders (We (the six nations) have given the R. Schooniady, for a hunting place to our Cousins the Delaware Indians & our Brethren Y[e] Shawanese, & we ourselves hunt there sometimes. We therefore desire you will immediately by force remove all those that live on the s[d] River of Schooniady[754]

Note. I think I remember a Proclamation[755] of to this purpose but have not time to search for it, however I dont doubt that the Dutchman after paying Penn for his Land & submitting to the Contributions laid on him from time to time by the Indian Warriors was taken by the Arm & thrown over the big mountains, tho perhaps not within Penn's borders. The Speech[756] then rambles to the Ohio from thence to Shamokin & at last concludes with the Indians killed in Virginia [Weiser's] mediation in publick—but he has informed Us, that Shickallemos people prepared a handsome Indian dinner, after which Weiser gave them about six pounds of tob[o] to smoak & that by way of discourse on his asking Shickallemo why the Six nations had not come down to treat with the Gov[r] of Maryland, he told him that till the Gov[r] of Virginia washed off the blood & dressed the wound the six nations would not be reconciled to him, & he beleived there woud be a war but Weiser might assure the Gov[r] of Pennsylvania the Warriors woud not come through the inhabited part of Pennsylvania but direct their Course directly to Virginia over the Big Island[757] in the North West Branch of Susquehanna.

You know the treaty at Albany[758] when Lee & Beverley were Commissiones was in the next year, 1744. In 1745 some very vague Entries, one of which was Patton's, were made for some Lands West of the great Mountains. The Ohio Comp[a] was formed in 1748 & the King sent in a present to the Indians, as had been usual when any of the Governments were about extending their Settlem[ts] Westw[d] but as Virginia had no Concern in the Indian trade carried on upon the Ohio which by that time had been mostly engrossed by the Penn-

· 303 ·

sylvanians, there was not a man in the Colony proper to be employed to go out to deliver it, so that they employed their old Plenipotentiary Weiser to deliver it & he as has been observed, betrayed them & delivered it in the name of Onas. In 1750 Gist went out to search the Land & to discover what Indians were settled there, the nature of their trade & to acquaint them that the King had sent them a large present[105] of Goods which were safely arrived in Virg^a & to invite them[81] to come & receive them. When he came to Loggs town Oct 25 he was told that Croghan[78] & Montour[79] were passed it a week before on an Embassy from Pennsylvania,[80] & as he was there told that he was come to settle the Indians Lands & would never got home again he was obliged to avail himself of his Acquaintance with Croghan & Montour, & told the people he wanted to see them having a message to deliver the Indians from the King by order of the President of Virginia & wrote to Croghan (Montour not being able to read) by one of the Traders people by this means he afterwards passed quietly & with less apprehensions from the Ohio Indians, than from the rascally Pennsylv^a traders, whom he rightly describes as a parcel of the most profligate wretches. He was everywhere rec'ed by the Indians in the kindest & most friendly manner. At the Shawane Town he says he was present at an extraordinary festival, of which he gives the following account.

In the Evening a proper officer made a publick proclamation that all the Indians marriages were dissolved, & a public feast was to be held for the three succeeding days after which the women (as their custom was) were again to choose their husbands. The next morning early the Indians breakfasted & after spent the day in dancing till the evening, when a plentiful feast was prepared, after feasting they spent the night in dancing.

The same way they spent the two next days, till the evening, the men dancing by themselves, and then the women in turns round fires and dancing in their manner in the form of the figure 8 about 60 or 70 of them at a time, the women the whole time they danced, sung a Song in their own the Chorus of which was, I am not afraid of my husband. I will choose what man I please. singing those lines alternately.

The third day in the evening, the men, being about 100 in number danced in a long string following one another sometimes at length, at other times in a figure of 8 quite round the fort & in & out of the long house where they held their councils, the women standing together as the men danced by them, & as any of the women liked a man passing by, she stepped in & joined in the dance, taking hold of the man's stroud, whom she chose, and then continued in the dance till the rest of the women stepped in & made their choice in the same manner. After which the dance ended & they all retired. A young woman was chosen to lead the dance each day and at the conclusion ten or twelve made choice of their former husbands. The whole was conducted with order, decency & good humour without the least quarrel confusion or disturbance. This festival is kept at the End of every seven years, & was now held in the beginning of February 1750/1.

Gist went from hence to the Tawighti Town, being he says particularly instructed by the President of Virginia to discover the Strength & numbers of some Indian nations to the Westward who had lately revolted from the French. This is the Eng. Tawightgi Town[98] as laid down in Evans's map, about a degree distant nearly South from the Fr. Tawighti Town,[142] but you see Gists tract exactly pricked down in Evans's map & the distances mentiond in it prove that it was taken exactly from Gist's Journal & I beleive it will be allowed that except that I made off & sent to Mr Hanbury, Evans's map was the first that ever appeared that coud give any tolerable Accot of the Ohio. Gist gives the Countrey for a great Extent round the Tawighti town the most extraordinary character & recommended it to the Ohio Compa to take up their Land there but it's great distance & the absolute necessity of securing a proper Communication with it by securing strong Storehouses at convenient distances renderd that impracticable till they could find what Encouragement we should meet both here & at home. Instead of that we met every discouragemt coud possibly be flung in our way. You have in the Appendix as much of Gists two Journals as concerns us, you will there find the 24th Feb. while Gist was present, four French Indians came to declare war agt the Tawightis, if they woud not return, but in this critical Situation Onas's Ambassadors acted in his, & not the Kings name, enterd into a treaty, on which I have already made ample remarks. The poor Tawightis, relying on Onas's protection set the French at defiance, what Protection or Assistance did Onas afford, the French next year made good their Threats & most inhumanly massacred & destroyed them, which the Indians very properly & justly made another Article of their Complaint in 1758 at Easton & at the same time equally charge it against the Govr of Virga with this additional aggravation. The Govr of Virga took care to settle on our Lands for his own benefit, but when we wanted his Assistance agt the French, he disregarded us.[759] How far the Govr of Virga was to blame in this matter, or the Virginians about the two Seneca Warriors that were killed & the boy taken prisoner at Green Briar in 1755 which they at the same time made another Article of Complaint,[760] tho there was not the least mention of that the year before when they were required in Sr Wm Johnson's name to acquaint him with every ground of their Complaints[761] will appear. The Pennsylvanians had for some generations even from Penn's first Settlemt of his Countrey, maintained a correspondence with the Indians & constantly employed Interpreters who always had a great Influence over them, by which means the Pensylvanias had it in their power & had address enough whenever the Indians were dissatisfied, to excuse themselves & Lay the blame on their Neighbours, Whatever Indian trade was carried on from Virginia was to the Southward & that was long dropped, so that there was not a man in Virginia acquainted with the Indians or their trade [illegible] a treaty[762] with the Indians of the six nations at Philadelphia, they six years before agreed to release (as the printed treaty in Colden's History says, vol 2 fol 1) their claim to all the Land on both sides Sasquehannah, as far So as Pennsylva extended & to the Northwd to the Endless mountains or Kittochtinny hills for which they then received a large quantity of valuable Indian Goods for the Lands on the E. side of that River but then declined to receive any Considn for those on the W. side chusing to refer it till another visit (From the particulars the whole Consideration did not exceed £500 Sterl) They acknowledge it is the full according to agreemt but if divided among only those present they would each have but a small portion, but if those left behind who were equally entitled to a share were considered there would be extremely little therefore desired if they had the Keys of the Proprietors chest they would open it & take out a little more for them.[763] Besides they complained they were not well used as to the Lands they had not sold, the Pennsylvanians daily settled tho no right to the Nd of Kittochtinny Hills, renewed their complaints agt the Settlemts at Juniata, as far as Manatiay, & added that some Part W. of Susquehanna & So of Pennsylva had been taken up by some People who had not paid for it, that the Govr had promised to write to that Person who had authority over those People & to procure his answer, & desired the Govr would press him to send a positive answer if he would pay the worth of it, Yes or No. if he said Yes they would treat with him, if no they were able to do themselves Justice & would do it by going to take paymt themselves.[762]

It shoud seem they had never heard of Virga or Maryland before,[764] or if they had, they had a very despicable Opinion of them & upon this it seems Onas became Mediator in 1743 which has been taken notice of, but it appears from the Govrs answer that he did not think Virga

In the Darlington Memorial Library

at all concerned.[765] In Answer to their complaint abot the Lands at Juniata he tells them, some magistrates were sent to remove them. But they interrupted him & said, They did not do their duty, So far from removing the people they made Surveys for themselves & were in league with the trespassers therefore desired more effectual methods might be used & honester persons employed—which he promised, & then informed them that President Logan had wrote to the Govr of Maryland but had received no Answer & that he would write again to the him & advised them in the meantime not to use any violence.[766]

In June & July 1744 The Commissrs from Virga & Maryland met at Lancaster & with the Govr of Pennsylva held another treaty with the Six nations, & tho the six nations said they had come at the Invitation of the Govr of Maryland, the Govr of Pennsylva told them that at their last treaty it was understood that [their] claim was upon Maryland only, but it had since appeared by some Letters formerly wrote by President Logan to the late Govr of Maryland that [illegible] some Lands in the back parts of Virga If the Indians did not know[767] they had any claim agt the Governmt of Virga till Mr Logan found out one for them everybody must be satisfied that Mr Logan well knew that the Govr of Virginia, & not of Maryland was the proper person to have been acquainted, but Logan as well as others of Penn's Councillors & Interpreters made Virga the Cat's paw & endeavoured to represent the Virginians as the Indians greatest Enemies[768] who not only wanted their Lands but to extirpate them but it is too tedious to dwell on particulars, it is enough to observe, that the Govr of Pennsylva had in his hands a present of Goods to the value of £100 Sterl' lodged by the Govr of Virga after the Engagemt in Frederick between the Indian & the Militia, wch was agreed to be buried in oblivion,[769] but as a French war was apprehended it was thought necessary to engage the Six nations firm to their friendship & therefore tho they had shewn the Indians claims were groundless both agt Maryland & Virginia yet out of regard[770] to them they were willing to give them any reasonable satisfaction to release all their claims to the Lands in both Governmts which they readily consented to, accordingly all their cheifs on the 30th June & 2d July signed a Release to Ld Baltimore[771] in consideration of £200 in Goods & £100 in Gold all those Lands lying two miles above the uppermost fork of Potomack near where Thos Cresap has a hunting or trading cabbin by a North line to the bounds of Pennsylva but if such Limits shall not include every Settlement or Inhabitant of Maryland then such other Lines & Courses from the sd two miles above the forks to the outermost Inhabitants or Settlements as shall include every Settlemt & Inhabitant in Maryland & from thence by a North Line to the Bounds of Pennsylva The Virga Commiss^rs then told them that they would give them £200 in Goods & £200 in Gold on executing a deed recognizing the King's right to all the Lands that are or shall by his Ma'ties Appointm.t in the Colony of Virga which they agreed to accept but desired the Commissioners to represent their Case to the King in order to have a further Consideration when the Settlement increased much further back, which they promised & gave them a writing under their hands & Seals to that purpose on which they executed the deed July 2 & the Virga Commiss^rs at their request ordered them Rum & Provisions on their Journey home & their Goods to be carried where they directed. They then all renewed the Treaties & brightened the Covenant Chain & the Govr of Pennsylva in behalf of that Province made them a Present of Goods to the value of £300 the Commission^rs of Maryland with £100 in Gold those in Virga with £100 more in Gold & delivered them the Goods sent from Virga that cost £100 Sterl' besides which they reced from Virga at this meeting £500 Pennsylva money.

In Aug.t & Sept. 1746 there was another Treaty[772] with them at Albany at which only the Gov.r & some of the Council of New York & their Commiss^rs for Indian Affairs & some Commissioners met, the Govr after his Speech told the Indians that the King had ordered him to make them a Present & that the Governm.t of Virga had sent them one & the Indians desired they might be delayed till the next day as they were going with the Commiss^rs of Boston to their Lodgings to receive their present. It is mentioned in the printed Account of the Treaty.

The next day, the presents from the King being exposed on one part, and those from Virga separately near them, it was agreed by the People of Albany who had seen many public presents given to the Six nations on treaties with them, that this was the most valuable ever given

The Governors Speech on giving them, is then inserted—And the Account proceeds.

What his Excellency said, having been interpreted by a Mohawk Sachem, the Sachem added of his own head—You now see how you are here treated, really like Brethren, the Governor of Canada does not treat his Indians so, they are set on like his dogs & they run on without thought or consideration: You see what a noble present is made to you; if the Governor of Canada should seize all the goods in that country, it would not be in his power to make you such a present.

In 1748 another Present was sent from Virginia to the Logs town which as has been said Weiser delivered to them in the name of Onas.

In the Darlington Memorial Library

In 1750 another large Present was sent in by the King but the Indians being prevented by the French from coming in to receive it, it was sent out to them,[105] the carriage alone cost above £150 Virg[a] currency.[773]

Yet those rascally Indians on the Ohio who have no right to sell any Lands (if any had been unsold) pretend they never reced any Consideration.

When I had got this far my Clerk returned with my Packet & an Acc[t] that Anderson would not sail in Six weeks on which I laid aside all my papers by concluding it was impossible to get any of them to you in time. I had been all along so interrupted & every thing out of my memory that you will find this a most confused Epistle. I dont however doubt but you will find enough to convince you that the Virginians have been not only duped but most villainously used by Penn who according to my Notion has done so many things contrary to the duty of a Subject as woud forfeit his Charter. He might settle the bounds[685] between him & Lord Baltimore but how dare he or his Gov[r] or Commiss[rs] presume to stir or survey a foot farther without the Kings permission as his Gov[r] now tells his Assembly those Lands at Pittsburg belong to Philadelphia You may perhaps make some advantage of it however confused & I could rectify it if I had time but I cant add another word. On hearing of the Gov[rs] death[774] I sent today to your Bro for the News & complained of my having spent 10 days to no purpose my Packet being returned . He wrote me that M[r] Cunninghame dined with him & was in his way to Williamsburg from whence he would procure my Packet & secure & immediate Passage by a ship of his own & that he would wait till tomorrow at breakfast for it. Your Brother sent my messenger immediately back with this Information so that I cant detain him longer him to tell you my wife will be particularly obliged to you if you can procure her a good Weaver skilfull in as many branches of the business in the Linnen & woollen way as may be but he must bring in proper Looms &c & she desires you to send her 4 lb of raw silk to stripe fine cotton with black blue green red & yellow. With which I must conclude with my blessing & all the families best wishes to you & my daughter.

     Dear George
      Your most affect father & friend
        J Mercer
        March 9 1768

[Endorsed]
    Ohio 1768

George Mercer Papers

Letter from my Father dated March the 9th 1768. [John M] Chiefly concerning Mr Penn & the People of that Province— their Behavior in Respect to the Indians & People of Virginia.
 [To Col. Geo. Mercer]

Charlton Palmer to George Mercer
December 27, 1769[775]

Sir

What is meant by that part of the Petition which says "That the Compys Agent is provided with indisputable proofs under the Colony Seal."[776] I do not understand as I do not know that I ever had any such proofs. All the papers I rec'ed except what I gave you I delivered to Mr Jackson[777] (who then lived in the Temple but now in Southern plan Buildings Chancery Lane) which I understood were redelivered to you.

Possibly he may have those proofs yet, but suppose he is out of Town these Holidays. I will call upon him as soon as he comes to Town and if you go thet way it would not be amiss to call upon him yourself.

But the two Vols of the Virginia Laws which your Father was so obliging to send me afford sufficient proof of what are the Expences of Surveys as enacted by those Laws & the Manner of Surveying.

vide. Fees. 19 Dec. 2d 1746 Cap. 6.
Surveyors. 22 Dec. 2. 1748 Cap. 19.

I apprehend by these acts the whole of what is meant by this Clause sufficiently appears which are a better proof than any other under the Colony Seal and my Books are at your Service when ever you please to want them

                    I am   Sr
                    Your very humble

Philpot Lane
                    Servt

27 Decr 1769
                    Charlton Palmer

[Addressed]
   For Colo Mercer   Holles Street   Cavendish Square
[Endorsed]
   Dec. 27, 1769   Charlton Palmer to Col. Geo Mercer
   Mr Palmer in [illegible] wrote him asking [illegible] der the Colony Seal [illegible] mentioned in the [illegible]

Thomas Walpole's Note to Osgood Hanbury
February 7, 1770[778]

M̄ Walpole presents his Compliments to M̄ Hanbury, & begs leave to acquaint him & the rest of the Gentlemen concern'd in the Ohio Company, that M̄ Walpole having met the Gentlemen concerned with him in an Application to Government for Lands in America, M̄ Walpole is authorised to assure the Ohio Company, that M̄ Walpole & associates having no Intention to interfere with any Persons who have had any legal Grants[779] from Government, if the Ohio Company think it right to prosecute their Pretentions, M̄ Walpole & those concerned with him can have no Objection thereto.
Wednesday 7th feby 1770
[Endorsed] 1770. Note from M̄ Walpole in Behalf of himself and Associates for the Purchase of Lands on the Ohio—saying they asked for no Lands from Persons who had legal Claims[779]—& laughing at the Ohio Company's Opposition

Conway Richard Dobbs to George Mercer
March 26, 1770[780]

Sir   Dublin 26th March 1770

I am favoured with yours[781] of the 8th Inst it was sent to the Country and returned to Dublin which occasioned my Receiving it So late

As Well as I can recollect (not having a Copy of his Will with me) My Father did not dispose of his Share in the Ohio Company by Will so that probably it comes to me as his Heir, I am also his Only Acting Executor here.

I have hitherto been entirely Ignorant of the State of that Company, Having never received any Information, untill You did me the Honour to write to me on that Subject, I must therefore beg a little time to consider, before I determine what I shall do with my Share in it; I propose going to England next Month and shall take the earliest Opportunity of paying my Respects to you in Person

It gives me Pleasure to Hear that You are appointed Lieut Govr of North Carolina,[782] and You have my best Wishes that You may meet with every thing that can make that Situation agreable to you

My Brother is lately Marched from Fort William in the Highlands

George Mercer Papers

of Scotland, to Berwick on Tweed I am Sure He will be Happy to hear of your Appointment, I am
       Sir
        Your Most Obedient
         Humble Servant
         Conway Richd Dobbs

[Addressed]
 To George Mercer Esq— Holles Street, Cavendish Square, London [care of] Richd Jackson Free [Post mark] $\frac{2}{A\ P}$ N

[Endorsed]
 March 26th 1770 Mr Dobbs, concerning his Share of Lands in the Ohio Company's Grant, and the Money due from him.

James Mercer to several members of the Ohio Company, January 9, 1772[783]

Sir

 At the last General Court I rec'ed a Letr[784] from my Brother addressed to the Ohio Company, left open for my perusal, in which he greatly complains of the Silence & neglect of the Company, ever since he went to England contrary to their Ingagements at parting— the consequence of their Silence he says has left in him in an State of uneasy suspense as he cou'd not say whether they were bound to abide by a compromise[785] he had made on behalf of the Ohio Company with the C a Company formed by Mr Walpole & others, stiled the Grand Company,[786] who had having petitioned for a Tract of Country including the Lands desired by the Ohio Compy and who having being united with such of the nobility & Ministry as promised Success, left little hopes of the Ohio Company's succeeding in their Claim upon so slight an Interest an Intersist aside private one as that of the Grand Company as theirs—the consequence of which Silence left this Silence he adds leave him in this further disagreeable State as to oblige him to advance moneys agreeable to the Terms of the Grand Company without any certainty of ever being reimbursed by the Ohio Company, as if the Grand Company Grant shou'd miss shou'd fail in obtaining their Grant the Ohio Company might then say they disapproved of the union, when on the other & thereby leave him to bear the the Loss whereas, shou'd the Grand Compy succeed, whereby the Ohio Company attended with Union wou'd to be prove very advantagious, the Ohio Company might then claim the benefit of it without ever having

· 312 ·

run the risque ever advanced or even risqued one shilling. Things being thus circumstanced (very unequally as every Body must allow) my Brother adds that at that time (the 15th of Aug^t) he had incurred a Forfeiture of the grant of the Ohio Comp^y Share in the Grand Company by failing to pay 450£ Ster^l a Sum that that share was chargeable with; by which, agreeable to the Terms of the G^d Comp^y the share was sold, but my Brother writes he prevailed on a Friend to purchase it for his Use, in order to indemnify himself, for the advances he had been at & was likely to be at on that acc^t, but that he will consider himself as a Trustee holding for the Ohio Company or such members of it as shall shew they intend to act fairly and who shall, while the Fate of the Grand Company's Grant is in suspence, agree to be bound by his Acts, & shall directly remit him their proportion of the Money he was then actually in advance together with a reasonable Sum for the expences he must necessarily be in advance for expences incurred on the Ohio Company's Business—the Sum then in advance exclusive of these expences he sets at 1350£ Ster^l besides the 450 £ p^d after the repudiation Forfeiture observing however that more must be furnished at the Completion of the Grand Company's Grant which was finally to be determined on the 25th Day of Oct:[787] then following. This Let^r I delivered to Col^{os} Lee Tayloe & Carter, they being on the Spot as members of the Court, the second readily consented to abide by any measure my Brother had takren taken or shou'd pursue for the Comp^y, the others had their Scruples, & all agreed a meeting shou'd be called, promising themselves to appoint & advertize it as soon as they shou'd know when it might be, not to interfere with the coming Elections; as they neglected to do so, & as I feared the results Resolutions of the 20th of Oct: on the Subject of the Grand Company, might soon be expected to arrive here, when it wou'd be too late for the Companys agreeing or disagreeing to abide by my Brothers Proceedings, I took it upon me to request & advertize a meeting on the 15th of Dec^r[788] at the Stafford Court House the usual place of meeting, strengthening my Request of a meeting, with an assurance that was with the advice of three of the Comp^y who were members of the Genl Court, who being well known to be equally Interested with any of the Comp^y I well hoped a meeting might be had, but to my Surprize not a Soul (Col^o Th^o Lee excepted) attended nor was a single Let^r of my Brothers forwarded[789] by those who had them, tho they cou'd not know but the rest of the members wou'd have met & wanted a Sight of them. Under those Circumstances I am obliged to ask the agrem determinations of the members of the Comp^y seperately at the expence of an express, the Bearer; each Comp^y member

George Mercer Papers

can bind himself as much singly as much to his benefit in this Lease as if in Company at a legal meeting; for, for such as do assent to do Justice, my Brother agrees to hold such a share as that member wou'd have been entitled to had the Ohio Company's Interest in the Grand Company never been forfeited as allready mentioned.

What my Brother defines to be Justice in this Case, is, that while the members of the Compy are ignorant of the Fate of the Grand Company's Grant, they shall say, will they, aye or nay, be bound by his transactions for the Company, and accept of the benefit of his Compromise of with the Grand Company in Lieu of their Claim as members of the Ohio Company besides this he requires that expects that each member who agrees to his measures will immediately remit his proportion of the expence of them such measures which he sets at 150 £ Sterl at the least for each share. How far the Company are bound in Law & Honor to abide by my Brothers Conduct, and to remit him his advances will appear from the Orders of that Company entered on their Journals at a meeting held the 4th July 1763[790] purposely for my Brothers to form his Rule of Conduct when they parted with him a true Copies of which are inclosed[791]—It is to be observed that Mr Charlton Palmer never expended a shilling for the Ohio Compy since my Brothers arrival in England as so that the whole was my Brother might well advance 2000 £ on the Credit of the Company's order. How far the his Powers will authorize the compromise he has made must be the Subject of a future Question shou'd it ever grow into a dispute, but at present I think I may observe that If his known Integrity will not acqu't of any him of every species of ingenuity on this Occasion, that I may safely appeal to what any member who suspects the force of the obligation just mentioned (if any such there be) will readily admit, that is, his Interest! which being is greater than any member of the Ohio Company being proprietor of one Share & a half[792] Share in that Company What he has accepted in lieu of his & the other members Claim I can't say, but I understand he has long ago & fully given the fullest satisfaction very fully mentioned the particulars to in Lers[793] to the Compy which as there has been no meeting I presume are in the Hands knowledge of but few of the members, therefore for the Information of those who are strangers to these Lers It may not be superfluous to add that in his Lers to me he says it is a 36th part part of the Grand Company's Grant which will equall if not exceed the Quantity the Ohio Company asked expected, that as there ——— Proprietors Share of this Grant ——— to ——— mentioned in the is to be a distinct Government[794] the Shares in this Grant may reap such advantages which they cou'd not have

· 314 ·

In the Darlington Memorial Library

done had the Ohio Company succeeded in their own Grant, in fine, that he esteemed their Share to be worth 20,000 £ Sterl.

Having thus fully stated all that I can suggest for your forming a true Judgt on the Subject proposed for yr determination, I am to request that you will by the Bearer let me know that determination, if if in the affirmative I hope you will send me by the same Hand your a Bill for at least 250 £ Sterl. that I may remit it to my Brother before he leaves London, when I dare say he will stand in great need, if only to pay off Scores made for the use of the Ohio Company, As the Bearer is hired by the Day, dispatch will save money to the Ohio Company or my Brother.

      I am Sir
       Yr humble Servant
        Jas Mercer

A Copy for Colo George Mason
   the Revd Mr Jas Scott
   Mr or Mrs Chapman
   Lunsford Lomax
   Richd Lee

James Mercer to Colonel George Mason, The Revd Mr Jas Scott Mr or Mrs Chapman, Lunsford Lomax, Richd Lee, [January, 1772].
[Endorsed]
 Copy Letter to Ohio Company

George Mason to James Mercer, January 13, 1772[795]

Dear Sir,   Gunston Hall Janry 13th 1772

I last night received your Favour of the 9th[783] Instant by Express; the subject of which is of such Importance to the Ohio Company that I think a Meeting of the Company absolutely necessary; and have therefore appointed one at Stafford Court House on Tuesday the 11th of Febry next;[796] which is as soon as the Members in Virginia & Maryland can have notice of it by the public papers; at which Time and Place I hope to have the pleasure of seeing you; & must beg the Favour of you to bring with you the Ohio Company's Order Book; which was left many years ago in the Hands of your Father, & has never been in my possession since. I shou'd have attended the Meeting last Month advertized[788] by you; but did not see the Advertisement, or know any thing of the Matter, until the night before the Day you had appointed; altho' any thing that cou'd have been done then, wou'd have been too late for the Determination of the new Company's Grant; which you say was fixed to the 25th of October last.

If Colo Mercer has Cause to complain of the Ohio Company's Neglect or Silence, it is not my Fault: I imediatly ordered such money to be paid as the Company directed; and your Father was, I think upon the Terms proposed by himself, appointed[797] to correspond with Mr Palmer & Colo Mercer. Since your your Father's Death, I have not received any Letter from Colo Mercer, till last winter; when I received two or three; some of them was a Year after their Dates, and all of them some Time after Colo Mercer had assured me He shou'd take Ship for Virginia; otherwise I shou'd imediatly have answered them; and that I have not done it since, is owing to the same Cause. Colo Mercer being constantly expected here. The last Time I saw you (I think in February last at Colchester, since which I have not had a Line from Colo Mercer) you told me He had been detained only on a particular Occasion, & was expected here early in the Spring; and you wrote me from the last General Court, that He had taken his passage in Capt Anderson, & his arrival expected every Day.

The Sentiment of the Ohio Company in general upon the Subject of your Letter, I am not acquainted with; but as you desire to know the opinion of each particular Member imediatly, whilst the Success or Fate of the Grand Company (as it is called) is still unknown to us; I think myself obliged to give you mine, in the most explicit & candid Manner, as well on Account of my Interest in the Ohio Company, as on the Score of private Friendship. I can by no Means approve the Bargain[798] Colo Mercer has made with the Grand Company; nor do I think his Instructions or powers from the Ohio Company authorized Him to make such a one : and making all due Allowances for the superior Interest of the Grand Company, I had much rather have trusted to the Faith of Government, upon his late Majesty's Instructions, than have withdrawn our Caveat[799] against the Grand Company's Grant, upon the Terms Colo Mercer did.[798] It appears to me, from what Colo Mercer wrote, that He might have had our first 200,000 Acres guaranteed to us, upon the Terms of the royal Instructions, to Sir William Gooch—that is in as many Surveys and within what Limits we chose: this wou'd have been ten thousand acres to each[800] of us, and cou'd we have been permitted Entrys & Deeds for that quantity paying the usual Quit-Rents of Virginia, with the Indulgence of ten Years Exemption, without any further charge or Trouble, I shou'd have prefer'd it infinitely to what is now done: altho We shou'd then have lost more than one half the Land we had

In the Darlington Memorial Library

a right to expect from the Royal Promise;[801] upon the Faith of which we had expended so large a Sum of Money. One thirty sixth Part of the Grand Company's Grant may be an Object of Consequence to one or two men; but that divided again into twenty Parts, wou'd reduce each of our Shares to a seven hundred & twentieth Part of the said Grant, & render it so trifling as not to be worth our Regard; at least I can not think it worth mine: and rather than advance the Sum of one hundred & fifty Pounds Sterling (the Quota now required by Colo Mercer from each Member) or even half of it, upon so distant, and (to me) inconsiderable a Prospect, I wou'd submit to lose every Shilling I have already advanced. In such a Case, I shou'd think (with the old Proverb) the first Loss the best, and avoid involving my Family in a Scheme, which might give them much Trouble & Vexation, & even if it succeeded, cou'd never produce them much Profit. These Sir are my real Sentiments, upon the most mature Deliberation I am capable of; and I am sure you will pardon the Freedom with which I have given them.

What Expences the Ohio Company may have incur'd incurr'd in England I know not; having never seen any Acct of them; except Mr Charlton Palmer's Bill for about Fifty Guineas; but as nothing has been obtain'd from Government for us, I can have no Idea of their being very considerable.

As you will have a speedier & safer Conveyance to Wmsburg, than I can have from hence, I take the Liberty of inclosing you two advertizements, for Rind's & Purdie's & Dixon's Papers; which please to order them to insert imediatly; having no small Money just now bye Me, I must beg the Favour of you to pay the Printers for publishing the Advertisements, & charge the same to me; I will repay you the first Time I see you. I have also troubled you with a Letter to Mr Walles, desiring Him to transmit me, under Cover directed to your Care, a Copy of Mr Hanbury's Acct as settled by Colo Mercer in London; that it may be laid before the Company; who, I hope will take proper Measures to discharge it: when you receive it, you will be so kind to forward it to me by some safe Hand. I must also intreat you to bring with you to the meeting a Copy of your Father's Acct with the Ohio Company; for as it is so very difficult to procure a meeting of the Company; whenever there is one, these things shou'd be finally setled.

To   I am
James Mercer Esqr   Dr Sir
    in   Your affecte Kinsman & Hble Sert
Fredericksburg   G Mason

This Express)
        P.S.

Upon looking into the Virginia Gazette, I find the Assembly is to meet on the 6th of February; which wou'd prevent a meeting of the Ohio Company at the Time proposed: I have therefore altered it, & fixed the meeting of the Company on Monday the 30th of March; and as I shall have Time enough to send the advertisements myself, I have not troubled you with them.

                                                    G. M.

Pearson Chapman to James Mercer
January 13, 1772[802]

                              Maryland Pomonkey 13th 1772.

Sir

I have had very little Opportunity of being acquainted with the Ohio Company's Grant Affairs; leest do not care to ingage in the Grand Company's Grant at so great an Expence, when our share in it appears so inconsiderable, and we know Nothing of the Grand Company's Scheme, or what may be the Consequence of our binding ourselves by Articles which we are Strangers to.

                        I am Sir your very Hum. Sert
                            Pearson Chapman

Thomas Ludwell Lee to James Mercer
January 13, 1772[803]

Dear Sir

I should not have so long delayed to answer your letter concerning the Ohio Company, had not the design of seeing you in Fredericksburg prevented me, which expectation, tho' constantly indulged, hath by the intervention of various accidents, been hithertoo disappointed.

Had I been furnished with certain lights, which one would imagin easy to be supplied from the other side the water, the question, tho' perhaps important, would quickly have been decided.

I shall proceed to explain, by way of quiry, in what manner I think the information defective. — — — What benifits do the Grand Company propose to themselves? What progress have they made in the attanement of those ends? Have they actually obtained a grant from the crown? What quantity of land may they probably have within their bounds? What plan is formed for the improvement of those advantages they may have acquired? Is this new country to be erected into a separate government? Who is to be at the charge of its support? What will be the probable expence? What are the terms of union proposed between the Ohio Company and Grand Company? Is the connection to remain indissoluble, and the distant members subjected to every resolve of contribution, or sentense forfieture, without consultation, or adviseor — — —

You will agree with me Sir, that something of this sort is necessary; and that a man is but indifferently qualified to determine with respect to a scheme, of which he knows neither the nature, nor the conditions upon which he shall be admitted to a participation of the benifits that may be derived from it. A set of wealthy men acting in England upon a large scale, might very quickly exhaust the slender finances of a Virginia fortune; and the designing amongst them, by taking advantage of this, and of the distance of the virginians, at any time might draw them under a sentence of forfieture, by imposing a necessity of paying large sums in short times. — — — Of this we have already a specimen in the order for a sum to be paid, on pain of forfieture, in twenty days, without any exception in favour of those who were absent so far.

These evils could be no otherwise obviated, but by having an agent in England, with a genteel appointed ment, and furnished too with what ever sum of money might at any moment be called for. This as it would be very unsuitable to the condition of many here, so would it make the project, tho expensive enough perhaps to the members in England, doubly so to the members in Virginia.

Thus Sir have I stated those doubts, and unfolded those motives, by which I am forced to hesitate with respect to my concurrence in a plan whose state is so obscure, and whose consequences are so involved, that I am at present utterly unable to conclude any thing thing certain concerning them. The negro's you wrote for should have been sent e'er this, had I had such at present to hire.

Your book of Architecture is sent by the boy & I am much obliged to you for the loan of it.

I am Dear Sir
with much esteem
yr very hble Sert
Thos Lud: Lee
Janry 13th 1772

Thomas Ludwell Lee to James Mercer
January 19, 1772[804]

Jan'y 19th 1772

Dear Sir

I am glad to find you have recovered sufficient health to venture into the country, & hope it will continue to be improved.

In my letter relating to the proposed union with the Grand Company I designed a candid declaration of my sentiments, & the resolution I had in consequence taken.

As you think something more explicit necessary, I shall add, that it does not suit my circumstances to be connected with that company. If you have brought my bond over, I can now discharge it with conveniency.

I am D'r Sir
Y'rs always

Thos Lud: Lee

[Addressed]

To James Mercer Esq.

Philip Ludwell Lee to James Mercer
January 21, 1772[805]

Stratford, Jan'y 21, 1772

Since receiv'g y'r Lett'r I have a message from The Treasurer of the Comp'a informing of the time of meeting w'ch I will attend to do every thing I ought to do, until w'ch time you know from the articles of the opinion of those members you last consulted nothing can be done; by a letter w'ch I have from y'r Father some time before his death he is of opinion that even the Com'it'ee can do nothing of importance without a majority of the Co: in Virg'a & Maryl'd w'ch I will shew you at the meeting:—I sh'd have surely been at the meeting in Dec'r had I known it, but I did not notice the paper 'til some time after the day, that was y'r fault, had you sent down to me as you promised w'n I saw you last this mistake w'd have been prevented.

I have the pleasure to wish you the joys of the season & am,

Sir, y'r scly Fr'd, & Ca.
Phil. L. Lee.

[Addressed]

To Mr. James Mercer, in Fredericksburg.

James Mercer to several members of the Ohio Company
Copy of a circular letter and replies by the several members of the Company, *ca.* January 21, 1772[806]

Sir

At the last General Court . . .

> *Letter, same as the first draft with corrections, all in James Mercer's handwriting. Printed on pp. 312-315.*

The foregoing is a Copy of the General Letter sent by Express to Colo George Mason, The Reverand Mr James Scott, Colo Thos Lee, Mr Pearson Chapman Mr Lunsford Lomax & Mr Richard Lee

Gunston Hall Jany 13th 1772

Dear Sir

I last night received your favour . . .

> *Letter, same as holograph, George Mason to James Mercer, printed on pp. 315-318.*

James Scott to James Mercer, January 11, 1772[807]

Sir

I am favoured with yours late this Evening which I answer immediately, that the Express may go as Early in the morning as he pleases.

I was not a little surprised with the contents of your letter, and before I can give any answer to the Demand of One Hundred and fifty pounds Sterl. I should be glad to have a meeting of the Ohio Company that We may examine your Brothers Letters and Accounts: Colo Mercer hath no doubt sent an account to shew us for what such a large Sum as 3,000 £ Sterl. is demanded. I was not at the meeting when the Orders you sent were made, but if I remember Right We expected for the 2,000 £ to get a Grant in England by the natural Bounds Petitioned for, that We might be at no farther expence or be under a necessity of applying to the Governor and Council here. Many Members declared if the Lords of Trade insisted on Granting our Lands in two Surveys only, they would not have it and instructed your Brother to insist on the natural Bounds, or a Liberty at least of taking it up in small Grants; and I suspect from the uncertainty of this 36th part no Person so little acquainted as I am with the new Colony will risque any more Money. I am certain few Members of the Company have a greater opinion of Colo Mercer than I and at a general meeting you will not find me one of the most backward to encourage that Gentleman, altho at this time it would be no very easy matter for me to raise the Sum of 150 £ Sterl. as two of my Sons have lately and so still make large demands on me, yet to save the five hundred pounds already laid out on Government Credit I would endeavour to raise this further Sum did I see a reasonable prospect of securing the whole, but as I have not seen a single Letter nor heard of anything your Brother hath done for the Company but what the printed papers[808] you sent me shew, I must beg a meeting of the Ohio Company and be better informed before I proceed farther. I am at a loss to know who the Members of the Company are to whom your Brother hath wrote the many Letters you mention the Companys Secretary to whom all Letters concerning the Company shou'd be directed hath I believe received none of a publick nature or I shou'd probable have heard of them: I hope Mr Mason will on the receipt of yours immediately call[809] a meeting of the Company, where We shall be informed of everything, and the sooner that is done the better, meantime I am Sir

Your most humble Servant
James Scott
Westwood Jany 11th 1772

To James Mercer Esq
in Fredericksburg

Dear Sir

    I should not have so long delayed ...
Letter, same as holograph, Thomas Ludwell Lee to James Mercer, January 13, 1772. Printed on pp. 318-319.

Dear Sir   Jany 19th 1772

    I am Glad to find you have received sufficient Health ...
Letter, same as holograph, Thomas Ludwell Lee to James Mercer, January 19, 1772. Printed on p. 320.

Maryland Pomonkey 13th 1772

Sir

    I have had very little opportunity of being acquainted with the Ohio Company affairs ...
Letter, same as holograph, Pearson Chapman to James Mercer, January 13, 1772. Printed on p. 318.

Richard Lee to James Mercer, January 21, 1772[810]

Sir   Lee Hall Jany 21st 1772

The Relation in which I stand to the Ohio Company forbids me by every kind of principle from doing any thing by which the Gentlemen concerned may be effected without their previous knowledge and approbation.

You will find me Sir in March next very readily disposed to Comply with whatever shall be the result of the united Councils of the Company. The late advertisement for the meeting of the Company I never saw untill the time appointed for the meeting was expired

To   I am Sir
Mr James Mercer   Yr humble Servt
at Fredericksburg.   Richard Lee
by his Express

James Mercer to Philip Ludwell Lee
January 21, 1772[811]

Honble Sir

As I was disappointed in the expected pleasure of meeting with you or any one of the Ohio Company agreeable to my Advertizement (except your Brother Colo Thomas) I am now in obedience to my Brothers request to ask the Companys determinations seperately, and at the Expence of an Express as your Honour saw my Brothers Letter on which I form my Conduct. It is needless for me to say what are my Brothers Requisitions, I am therefore only to request your explicit Answer thereto, by the Bearer: intreating as he is on high Wages and the Season may protract his return, that your Honour will be pleased to give him all the dispatch you can-If you approve of my Brothers measures, I hope it will be convenient for you to assist in the Remittance he requires which will be at least 150 £ Sterl. a share; your Bill for this Sum to reach him before he leaves London will I am Confident be a seasonable relief to one, who has already stretched his Credit to the amount of 1750 £ in advance for the Company exclusive of his own proper expences-I have the Honour to wish you the Compliments of the Season and to subscribe myself

                         Your Honours
To   Most Obedt & very hble Servt
The Honble Philip Ludwell Lee   Js Mercer

George Mercer Papers

Stafford Jany 21s. 1772

Sir

Since receivg your Letter . . .
Letter, same as holograph, Philip Ludwell Lee to James Mercer, January 21, 1772. Printed on p. 320.

[Endorsed]
    Copies of Letters
    James Mercer to the
    Members of the Ohio
    Compy with the answers
    relating to Colo Mercer.

Draft of George Mercer on Samuel Wharton
August 5, 1772[812]

due Novr 5/8th.

£ 250—   London   August the 5th 1772.

Three Months after Date pay to my Order Two hundred and fifty Pounds, Value received, as advised.

To   Geo: Mercer
    Samuel Wharton Esq.r
                      Accepted
    New Suffolk Street
         London   SamL Wharton

[Endorsed]
    Geo: Mercer
    Recd London Novr 8 1772 of Samuel Wharton Esqr the full Contents of the within Draft.
                                      Edwd Blackshaw

Samuel Wharton to George Mercer
August 20, 1772[813]

Dear Sir

I do myself the pleasure to inform you, That on the 14th Instant his majesty, in Council, was pleased to approve of, and order[814] to be carried into Execution, The Report[815] of the Committee of the privy Council, In favor of the Grant of Lands to Mr Walpole and his associates:—and That a new Government should be established thereon. Mr Walpole proposed calling a general Meeting of the Company, To

In the Darlington Memorial Library

communicate this agreeable news to them:—But upon Enquiry,—most of the Gentlemen are at present out of Town, and Therefore it is apprehended best, To defer the proposed meeting, 'till towards the middle of October, When it is Probable, most of the Partners will be in London:—In the mean Time, I shall be much Obliged to you, To signify to me, Whether it is your Desire, That Mr Walpole & myself should continue our solicitation to the final accomplishment of the Business.

       I am, with the sincerest Regard, Dr Sir
        y.'r faithful & most Obt Servant
London August 20 1772   Saml Wharton
 George Mercer Esqr
[Addressed]
  To George Mercer Esqr   Holles Street   Cavendish Square
[Endorsed]
  Letter from Mr Wharton. The King approved of the Report of the Comee of Council, and ordered a new Province to be erected on Ohio, 14th August 1772.

Statement of account of Thomas Walpole, in behalf of the Grand Ohio Company, with George Mercer February 26, 1776[816]

Dr_____George Mercer Esq: to Thomas Walpole
1776
Feb' 26 To your Proportion of Expences incurred <u>on the River Ohio</u> in North America, & paid by <u>George Croghan</u>[817] Esq, relative to the Land applied for by myself, & Associates, (of which you are one,) as per Account. at £ 11:9:9—2 Shares   £ 22.19.6
George Mercer Esqr   Thomas Walpole
[Endorsed]
  26th February 1776 The Honble Thos Walpole for Expences paid on the Ohio for the Vandalia Purchase two Shares
             £ 22.19..6

Statement of Account of Samuel Wharton, in behalf of the Grand Ohio Company, with George Mercer July 17, 1777[818]

Dr   George Mercer

1776

February 26   To 2 Shares or 2/72d Parts belonging to the Ohio Company of the Expences incurred on the River Ohio in North America, and paid by George Croghan Esqr—debited in the Honorable Thomas Walpole his Account at £ 11. 9. 9 Share................£ 22 : 19 : 6

To your 1. Share or 1/72d Part of the foregoing Expence for the Share which you hold in your own Right...................... 11 : 9 : 9

August 17   To 2 Shares or 2/72d Parts belonging to the Ohio Company of the Charges and Expences incurred from 20th of February last, to this Day, upon the Application for a Grant of Lands on the River Ohio in North America at £ 7: 10 Share......... 15 : 0 : 0

To your 1 Share or 1/72d Part of the foregoing Expence for the Share which you hold in your own Right................ 7 : 10 : 0

17   To 2 Shares or 2/72d Parts belonging to the Ohio Company of sundry Charges at the Publick Offices, and Those of Mr Dagge at £ 5 : 17 : 4 Share.................... 11 : 14 : 8

To your 1 Share or 1/72d Part of the sundry Charges at the Publick Offices and Those of Mr Dagge at £ 5 : 17 : 4 Share.......... 5 : 17 : 4

£ 74 : 11 : 3

Errors Excepted
      London July 17 1777.
          S. Wharton

[Endorsed]
    A/c agst the Ohio Co. & Col Geo Mercer in favor of S Wharton the Grand Co 1776–7

PART II

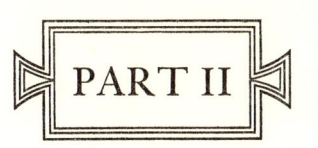

(1) *Dated Dec 18 1769*
George Mercer

THE
CASE
OF THE
OHIO COMPANY,

EXTRACTED FROM ORIGINAL PAPERS.

IT was generally reputed that, by the treaty of Lancaster, as well as by deed, bearing date July 2, 1744, the northern Indians, by the name of the Six Nations, (who claimed all the lands west of Virginia, and also to, and on the waters of the Missisippi and the lakes, by right of conquest from the several nations of Indians who formerly inhabited that country, and had been extirpated by the said Six Nations) did yield up, make over, and for ever quit claim to his majesty, and his successors, all the said lands west of Virginia, with all their right thereto, as far as his majesty should at any time thereafter be pleased to extend the said colony.

The year after, some inhabitants of Virginia applied to the governor and council for grants of some lands in those parts; and in consequence thereof, at a council held April 26, 1745, several persons were allowed to take up and survey 300,000 *acres* thereof, by virtue of the following orders.

In 1745 some inhabitants of Virginia apply to the governor and council for grants of lands.

N°. 1. On the petition of John Robinson senior Esq, Thomas Nelson junior Esq, John Robinson junior Esq, William Beverley, Robert Lewis, Beverley Robinson, Henry Wetherburne, John Lewis, John Craig, William Lewis, John Wilson, and Charles Lewis, leave is granted them to take up 100,000 *acres* lying on Green Briar River, north west and west of the Cow Pasture and Newfoundland, and that *four years* time be allowed them to survey and pay rights for the same, upon return of the plans to the secretary's office.
N. Walthoe, Cl. Con.

100,000 acres to 12 persons, and 4 years allowed to survey.

N°. 2. On the petition of John Smith, Zachary Lewis, William Waller, Benjamin Waller, and Robert Green, leave is granted them to take up 50,000 *acres* in that part of Orange, which will be in the county of Augusta, when that county shall take place, on the river and branches of Roanoke, and the branches of James River, and that *four years* time be allowed them to survey and pay rights for the same, upon return of the plans to the secretary's office.
N. Walthoe, Cl. Con.

50,000 acres to 5 persons, and 4 years allowed to survey.

N°. 3. On the petition of James Patton, Robert Slaughter, John Græme, John Belfield, John Tayloe junior, William Green, Richard Barnes, James Gordon, James Wood, George Buchanan, George Robinson, James Bowie, Robert Jackson, William Parks, John Preston, Robert Gilchrist, Richard Winslow, John Roberts, John Weatheral, and James Johnson, leave is granted them to take up 100,000 *acres*, lying in Augusta county, on the three branches of Missisippi river; the one known by the name of Wood's River, the other two to the westward thereof, and on the waters of the said River, the said land lying to the westward of a former order of council, granted to Zachary Lewis Gent and others ; and that *four years* time be allowed them to survey and pay rights for the same, upon return of the plans to the secretary's office.
N. Walthoe, Cl. Con.

100,000 acres to 20 persons, and 4 years allowed to survey.

N°. 4. On the petition of Henry Downes, John Blair junior, John Willis, George Taylor, Edward Spencer, Robert Slaughter, Thomas Slaughter, William Jackson, Alexander Dunlop, James Ewin, and Edward Fuller, leave is granted them to take up 50,000 *acres*, lying west of the Cow Pasture, or Green Briar River, and that *four years* time be allowed to survey and pay rights for the same, upon return of the plans to the secretary's office.
N. Walthoe, Cl. Con.

50,000 acres to 11 persons, and 4 years allowed to survey.

A And

(2)

And on the 4th of November following, John Blair Esq, William Ruffel and company, obtained another in these words.

100,000 acres to John Blair Esq and company, and 4 years allowed to survey.

N°. 5. On the petition of John Blair Esq, William Ruffel and company, leave is granted them to take up 100,000 *acres of land*, lying to the westward of the line of Lord Fairfax, on the waters of Potomack and Youghyoughgane, and to be allowed *four years* time to survey and pay rights for the same, upon return of the plans to the secretary's office.

N. Walthoe, Cl. Con.

4 years allowed to return surveys contrary to the usual method of granting lands.

Yet although the governor and council, who had been long sensible of the great importance of a settlement, west of the great ridge of mountains, had for their encouragement allowed them (contrary to the usual method of granting of lands) four years time to survey their respective grants, for which the rights (amounting to 5 l. sterling for every thousand acres) were not to be paid, till the return of the plans to the secretary's office, nothing was done in consequence of any of those orders of council, or any other applied for, till William M'Mahon, on April 22, 1747, obtained the following.

In 1747, 60,000 acres to William M'Machon and comp. and 5 years allowed to survey.

N°. 6. On the petition of William M'Mahon, John M'Mahon, Richard M'Mahon, Lewis Neale, John Neale, Mark Calmees and company, leave is granted them to take up 60,000 *acres of land*, joining to the grant of John Blair Esq and others, and upon the waters of Potomack, west and north west of the line of Lord Fairfax, and on the branches of Youghyoughgane and Monongaley, and to be allowed *five years time* to survey and pay rights for the same, upon return of the plans to the secretary's office.

N. Walthoe, Cl. Con.

Grant, No. 5.

But these grantees, as well as the former, lay by with their order of council, though they had some pretence, as Blair's grant upon which they were to bind, never had been surveyed.

In 1748, Tho. Lee, Esq. one of his Majesty's council, proposed the scheme of forming the Ohio company. Indians at the treaty of Lancaster had complained of being defrauded of their lands by the people of Pennsylvania, and being ill treated by their traders, and those of New York, who then engrossed all the peltry trade; and being in general fellows of profligate characters, introduced spirituous liquors among them, and then cheated them of their skins; it was proposed to fix the Indians to our interest, that a fair and well regulated trade should be established among them. Proposals laid before the governor, who approved of them, and recommended them to the Right Honourable the Lords of Trade. The members in America propose to have some partners in England, and John Hanbury Esq, of London, joined them. John Hanbury Esq petitions the king, in behalf of himself and others in Virginia, whose names are mentioned.

In the year 1748, Thomas Lee Esq one of his majesty's council of Virginia, (who had been one of the commissioners at the treaty of Lancaster) being well satisfied, *That no settlement would ever be effectually carried on in those parts, by any private adventurers, formed the first proposals of effecting it by a company, which gave rise to the Ohio company*. He was sensible, *That the chief complaints, made by the Indians at that treaty, were, that they had been defrauded of their lands, by the people of Pennsylvania in particular, and had been extremely ill used by the traders from thence, and New York, who had engrossed the whole peltry trade, and were, in general, fellows of the most profligate characters, and who instead of supplying them with necessaries, sold them great quantities of spirituous liquors, which not only debauched and enervated their people, but involved them in continual quarrels and animosities, and at the same time afforded the traders an opportunity of cheating them in their traffick. This last had been for some years a constant article of complaint, and if not wholly disregarded, was far from meeting any effectual redress*. He therefore very rightly judged, *That there was no other way to fix the Indians firmly in the British interest, but by a fair and well regulated trade*; for the sake of this he concluded, *they would not be averse to the English extending their settlements to the westward*, but without it he was sure, *they never would permit any such thing*. With this view he laid his proposals before the governor, who approving thereof, recommended them to the Right Honourable the Lords Commissioners for Trade and Plantations: at the same time the members of that company in Virginia and Maryland judging, that such trade could not be carried on, without taking in as a partner or partners, one or more person or persons of fortune and character in Great Britain, acquainted John Hanbury of London merchant, with their proposals, and he readily approving them, preferred the following petition to his Majesty, in behalf of himself and others of the said company.

To the King's Most Excellent MAJESTY,

The humble petition of John Hanbury of London merchant, in behalf of himself, and of Thomas Lee Esq, a member of your Majesty's council, and one of the judges of the supreme court of judicature in your Majesty's colony of Virginia, Thomas Nelson Esq, also a member of your Majesty's council in Virginia, Colonel Cressap, Colonel William Thornton, William Nimmo, Daniel Cressap, John Carlyle, Lawrence Washington, Augustine Washington, George Fairfax, Jacob Giles, Nathaniel Chapman, and James Woodrop Esquires, all of your Majesty's colony of Virginia, and others their associates, for settling the countries upon the Ohio, and extending the British trade beyond the mountains, on the western confines of Virginia.

Most humbly sheweth,

Indians by treaty at Lancaster, and deed, 2d July, 1744, yield all their lands westward of Virginia to the king and his successors.

That by the treaty of Lancaster, and also by deed bearing date the 2d day of July 1744, the Northern Indians, by the name of the Six Nations, (who claimed all the lands west of Virginia, and also to and on the waters of the Mississippi and the lakes, by right of conquest from several nations of Indians, who formerly inhabited that country, and have been extirpated by the said Six Nations) did yield up and make over, and for ever quit claim to your Majesty and your successors, all the said lands west of Virginia, with all their right thereto, as far as your Majesty should, at any time thereafter, be pleased to extend the said colony.

That

(3)

That most of the nations of Indians west of the mountains, and upon the lakes and the river Ohio, have entered into alliance with your Majesty's subjects, and with the Six Nations in friendship with the British colonies, and have desired your Majesty's subjects, the inhabitants of Virginia, to send them British goods and manufactures, as they incline to trade solely with your Majesty's subjects. *Indians desire the people of Virginia to send them British manufactures, as they wished to trade solely with British subjects.*

That by laying hold of this opportunity, and improving this favourable disposition of these Indians, they may be for ever fixed in the British interest, and the prosperity and safety of the British colonies be effectually secured, which your petitioners are ready and willing to undertake.

That your petitioners beg leave humbly to inform your Majesty, that the lands, to the west of the said mountains, are extremely fertile, the climate very fine and healthy, and the waters of Missisippi, and those of Potomack, are only separated by one small ridge of mountains, easily passable by land carriage; so that, by the convenience of the navigation of the Potomack, and a short land carriage from thence to the west of the mountains, and to the branches of the Ohio and the lake Erie, British goods may be carried at little expence, and afforded reasonably to the Indians in those parts, in case the lands to the west of the said mountains were settled, and a fort erected in some proper place there, for the protection and encouragement of your petitioners, and others your Majesty's subjects, in adventuring their persons and fortunes in this undertaking; in which, if your petitioners meet with that success they have the greatest reason to expect, it will not only be made the best and strongest frontier in America, but will be the means of gaining a vast addition and increase to your Majesty's subjects, of that branch of the peltry and furr trade, which your petitioners propose by means of the settlement herein after-mentioned, to carry on with the Indians to the westward of the said mountains, and on the said lake and rivers; and will, at the same time, greatly promote the consumption of our British manufactures, enlarge our commerce, increase our shipping and navigation, and extend your Majesty's empire in America; and, in a short space of time, very considerably encrease your Majesty's revenue of quit-rents, as there is little room to doubt that when this settlement is once begun by your petitioners, a great number of foreign protestants will be desirous of settling in so fertile and delightful a country, under the just and mild administration of your Majesty's government, especially as they will be at little more charge than the transporting themselves from their native country. *Lands fertile, and climate healthy. Waters of Potomack and the Missisippi only separated by a small ridge of mountains. Goods could be transported at a small expence, and sold to the Indians reasonably. Settlement over the mountains would make a strong frontier, and increase the consumption of British manufactures, as it would secure the furr trade to Great Britain. Increase shipping and the king's revenue of quit-rents. Foreign protestants would remove to so fertile a country.*

That your petitioners, for these great and national ends and purposes, and in order to improve and extend the British trade amongst these Indians, and to settle these countries in so healthy and fine a climate, and which are your Majesty's undoubted right, have entered into partnership, by the name of the Ohio company, to settle the lands to the west of the said mountains, and to carry on a trade with the Indians in those parts, and upon the said lakes and rivers; but, as effecting the same, and more especially the erecting a sufficient fort, and keeping a garrison to protect the infant settlement, will be attended with great expence; Your petitioners, *who are the first adventurers in this beneficial undertaking, which will be so advantageous to the crown, in point of revenue, to the nation in point of trade, and to the British colonies in point of strength and security,* most humbly pray; *That your Majesty will be graciously pleased to encourage this their said undertaking, by giving instructions to your governor of Virginia, to grant to your petitioners and such others, as they shall admit as their associates, a tract of 500,000 acres of land, betwixt Romanettos and Buffaloes Creek, on the south side of the river Allegany, otherwise the Ohio, and betwixt the Two Creeks and the Yellow Creek, on the north side of the said river, or in such other parts, to the west of the said mountains, as shall be judged most proper by your petitioners for that purpose; and that 200,000 acres, part of the said 500,000 acres, may be granted immediately without rights, on condition of your petitioners seating, at their proper expence, an hundred families upon the lands in seven years; the lands to be granted free of quit-rents for ten years on condition of their erecting a fort, and maintaining a garrison, for protection of the settlement for that time; your petitioners paying the usual quit-rents, at the expiration of the said ten years, from the date of their patents.* And your petitioners farther pray, *That your Majesty will be graciously pleased to send your said governor a farther instruction, that as soon as these 200,000 acres are settled, and the fort erected, that 300,000 acres more, residue of the said 500,000 acres, may be granted to your petitioners, adjoining to the said 200,000 acres of land first granted, with the like exemptions, and under the same covenants, and to give all such farther and other encouragement to your petitioners, in this their so useful and publick an undertaking, as to your Majesty, in your great wisdom, shall seem meet.* And your petitioners will ever pray. Signed, John Hanbury. *The Ohio company formed; and undertake to settle the country. The company petition for 500,000 acres of land within certain boundaries to the westward of the mountains. 200,000 acres to be granted immediately on certain conditions. The remaining 300,000 acres to be granted when the terms for settling the 200,000 are complied with.*

This petition being referred, by the Right Honourable the Lords of the Committee of his Majesty's Council, to the Right Honourable the Lords Commissioners for Trade and Plantations, they were pleased to report as their opinion, *That it would be for his Majesty's service to grant the said petition; for that, the settlement of the country lying to the westward of the great mountains, as it was the centre of the British dominions, would be for his Majesty's interest, and the advantage and security of Virginia, and the neighbouring colonies; as, by means thereof, a more extensive trade and commerce might be carried on with the Indians inhabiting those parts; and it would likewise be a proper step towards checking the incroachments of the French, by interrupting part of their communication, from their lodgements upon the great lakes to the river Missisippi, by means whereof the British settlements were exposed to their incursions, and that of the Indians in their interest;* which benefits would be farther extended, under the said company's proposal: and therefore his Majesty was pleased, by his instruction to the governor of Virginia, dated March 16 1748-9, to direct such grant or grants to be made to the said company, with such exemptions, and upon such conditions, as *Petition referred by the Right Honourable the Lords of the Privy Council to the Lords of Trade; they report it for his Majesty's service to grant it, and assign their reasons. The king was pleased March 16, 1748 9, to direct the governor of Virginia to make*

(4)

as was prayed, almost in the very terms of the petition. This instruction no sooner arrived and was made publick in Virginia, than divers persons procured orders of council for 1,350,000 acres of land, on the very day it was produced in council; among others James Patton (who had suffered the time allowed in his before-mentioned order of council to run out) procured leave, in the name of some of the persons formerly mentioned as his partners, to renew the same for 100,000 acres, and two years longer time were allowed them to compleat their surveys; copies of which orders follow.

<small>the grant on the terms and conditions which the company had prayed. The day this instruction was produced in council in Virginia, divers persons procure orders for 1,350,000 acres; and Patton allowed to renew his order, No. 3. for 100,000 acres which had been forfeited, and two years granted for a survey. See order of council, No. 11.</small>

At a council held July 12, 1749.

N°. 7. On the petition of Bernard Moore, Benjamin Hubbard, Philip Aylet, Thomas Dansie, John Snelson, George Carrington, James Power, Duncan Graham, William Taylor, and Job Thomas, leave is granted them to take up and survey 100,000 *acres of land*, on the waters of Missisippi river, beginning at ten trees marked P. T. G. standing in the fork of a branch of the said river known by the name of New River, and so down the said river and the waters of the said Missisippi river; and to be allowed *four years* time to survey and pay rights for the same, upon return of the plans to the secretary's office.

N. Waltoe, Cl. Con.

<small>1749.—100,000 acres to 10 persons, and 4 years allowed to survey.</small>

N°. 8. On the petition of John Lewis Esq, Thomas Walker, John Meriwether, Charles Lewis, James Power, Peter Jefferson, Charles Dick, Charles Barrett, Joshua Fry, Thomas Turpin, John Harvey, Thomas Meriwether, Thomas Meriwether junior, John Baylor, Samuel Waddy, Robert Barrett, Henry Willis, Peachy Gilmer, John Lewis, James Maury, Thomas Lewis, Peter Hedgman, John Moore, Robert Martin, Henry Tate, Richard Jones, William Wood, Samuel Dalton, Francis Thornton, Francis Thornton junior, John Thornton, John Pierce, William Stevenson, Nicholas Lewis, Nicholas Meriwether, William Hudson, Francis Meriwether, Humphrey Hill, and John Dixon, leave is given them to take up and survey 800,000 *acres of land, in one or more surveys*, beginning on the bounds between this colony and North Carolina, and running to the westward, and to the north, so as to include the said quantity, and they are allowed *four years time* to survey and pay rights for the same, upon the return of the plans to the secretary's office. N. Walthoe, Cl. Con.

<small>800,000 acres to 19 persons, in one or more surveys, and 4 years allowed to survey.</small>

N°. 9. On the petition of Peyton Randolph, Alexander Mackensie, Robert Tucker, John Tucker, George Gilmer, Benjamin Waller, William Parks, Armistead Burwell, Edmund Pendleton, John Willoughby, John Maddison, John Shelton, John Garland, Thomas Williamson, Maximilian Calvert, Cornelius Calvert, Paul Loyal, and George Logan, leave is granted them to take up and survey 400,000 *acres of land in one or more surveys*, lying on New River commonly called Wood's River, and the waters thereof; and *four years* time allowed them to survey and pay rights for the same, upon return of the plans to the secretary's office.

N. Walthoe, Cl. Con.

<small>400,000 acres to 18 persons in one or more surveys, and 4 years allowed to survey.</small>

N°. 10. On the petition of William Winston junior, Isaac Winston junior, Peter Fontaine junior, Edmund Winston, and Samuel Red, leave is granted them to take up and survey 50,000 *acres of land*, beginning at Old Fort between Ohio and Missisippi rivers, running up the western side of Ohio, and eastern side of Missisippi, in one or more surveys, between the said rivers, and *four years* time allowed them to survey and pay rights for the same, upon the return of the plans to the secretary's office. N. Walthoe, Cl. Con.

<small>50,000 acres to 5 persons, and 4 years allowed to survey.</small>

N°. 11. On the petition of John Tayloe, William Parks, and James Wood, in behalf of themselves and company, leave is given them to renew their grant for 100,000 acres of land, lying in Augusta county on the three branches of the Missisippi river; the one known by the name of Wood's river, and the other two to the westward thereof, and on the waters of the said river and two years longer time allowed them to compleat their surveys.

N. Walthoe, Cl. Con.

<small>Grant, No. 3. (page 1.) renewed, and 2 years more allowed to survey.</small>

The Ohio company, that they might comply with their proposals in the most effectual manner, had, upon the first notice of their petition being granted, directed Mr. Hanbury to ship them a cargo of 2000 *l*. sterling value, to be in the country by the last of November 1749 at the farthest; and another cargo by the first of March after, which were accordingly sent in, for the carrying on the Indian trade; they also agreed, that necessary roads (one in particular to Monaungahela) should be forthwith made, and proper houses built; but being sensible it would be in vain to attempt to make any settlements upon the Ohio, without the approbation and consent of the Indians settled there, they made application to the government of Virginia, to invite those Indians to a treaty; and wrote Mr. Hanbury to endeavour to obtain orders from his Majesty, for making a present to the said Indians, as had been done by the government of New York, and other governments to the northward, upon the like occasions; and to have the line, between Virginia and Pennsylvania run (in the same manner as that between Virginia and Carolina had been) to enable the company to lay off their first two hundred thousand acres of land with certainty; he was at the same time desired in order to avoid any misunderstanding, to procure an explanation of his Majesty's instruction, relative to the fort and garrison which were to be built and maintained by the company, as they apprehended their proposals concerning them had been entirely misapprehended; for though they well knew that the protection of their property would necessarily oblige them to build strong houses

<small>Company order proper goods for the Indian trade.

Agree to open roads and build houses.

Apply to have the Indians invited to a treaty, and to have the usual presents sent them by the king.

To have the boundary between Virginia and Pennsylvania established, and an explanation of the king's instruction concerning the fort, which had been misapprehended.</small>

(5)

houses, and employ a force sufficient to guard their stores and servants from being plundered, or no trade could possibly be carried on, in such a remote unsettled part of the country, yet at the same time they were sensible, their trade in its first beginning, would not bear such an expence, and therefore petitioned his Majesty to give up his quit-rents, for ten years, towards defraying that charge; as they had prayed for the rights to be remitted, on condition of seating an hundred families on the land. They could not be ignorant that one year's pay and subsistance of fifty men only, with proper officers, to form a regular garrison, and even any building that could with propriety be termed a fort, would amount to much more than all the rights and quit-rents to be so remitted; and therefore they were persuaded, nothing more was necessary to clear up that matter, than a candid representation of the fact. In the mean time, fully persuaded of the benefit that would arise to the colony, by the prosecution of their scheme, they resolved to proceed in it with vigour; and for that end, had come to the foregoing resolutions, within six months after the date of his Majesty's instructions; but, satisfied of the expediency of procuring a plan and account of that part of the country, (which might be depended upon) before they came to any resolution, as to taking up and surveying their land, they employed Mr. Christopher Gist (a person well acquainted with the Indians upon the Ohio) to undertake a tour for that purpose, *giving him particular instructions, to search and discover the lands upon that river, (and the adjoining branches of the Mississippi) as low as the falls thereof, and particularly to observe the ways and passes through all the mountains he crossed to take an exact account of the soil, quality, and product of the lands, the width and depth of the rivers, and their several falls, with the courses and bearings of them, and the mountains; and also to enquire, by all the ways and means he possibly could, what nations of Indians inhabited those parts, their strength and numbers, with whom they traded, and in what commodities they dealt; and to endeavour to cultivate a good understanding with them, and to convince them, if possible, of what consequence to them the friendship and alliance of the English was, both in regard to their protection and trade: of all which he was to keep a very exact and particular journal, to be returned to the company upon his oath, together with a plan of the country he passed through, drawn in the best manner he could.* And as his Majesty had sent in a parcel of goods as a present for the Indians, the said Gist had a commission from the president of Virginia, to acquaint them with it, and to invite them to come to Virginia, to receive it. Mr. Gist set off the last of October, on this difficult and dangerous undertaking, and never returned till the 19th day of May following; and on the 15th day of July, 1751, returned his plan and journal to the company's committee, who, judging it entirely impracticable to seat the land on the two rivers of Mineamis, (which the said Gist recommended) and that they must, at all events, take up their first 200,000 acres nearer in, which, they believed might be found to answer their expectations, upon the creeks mentioned in the royal instruction; they again agreed, with the said Gist, to view and examine the lands between *Monaungahela* and the *Big Kanhawa*: but, in the mean time, conceiving it to be greatly for the company's interest, as well as the government's, to cultivate a friendship and correspondence with the Ohio Indians, and that nothing could answer that end more effectually, than procuring a commission for the said Gist to meet those Indians at the Loggstown, at a grand council they were to hold there in the following month, (when they were to receive his Majesty's present) and to engage Mr. Andrew Montour (one of the chiefs of the Six Nations) in the interest of the government of Virginia and the company; the said committee recommended him to the president and council, for that purpose, and gave him the following instructions.

After you return from Williamsburg, and have executed the commission of the president and council, if they shall think proper to give you one, otherwise as soon as you can conveniently; you are to apply to Colonel Cresap, for such of the company's horses as you shall want, for the use of yourself and such other person or persons as you shall think necessary to carry with you; and you are to look out, and observe the nearest and most convenient road you can find, from the company's store at Will's Creek, to a landing on Monongahela; from thence you are to proceed down the Ohio, on the south side thereof, as low as the Big Kanhawa, and up the same as far as you judge proper, and find good land. You are, all the way, to keep an exact diary and journal, and therein note every parcel of good land, with the quantity as near as you can, by any means, compute the same; the breadth, depth, courses, and length of the several branches falling into the Ohio, and the different branches any of them are forked into, laying the same as exactly down, in a plan thereof, as you can, observing also the produce of the several kinds of timber and trees, and noting where there is plenty, and where the timber is scarce; and you are not to omit proper observations on the mountainous, barren or broken land, that we may, on your return, judge what quantity of good land is contained within the compass of your journey. We would not have you omit taking notice of any quantity of good land, though not exceeding four or five hundred acres, provided the same lies upon the river Ohio, and may be convenient, for our building store-houses and other houses, for the better carrying on a trade and correspondence down that river.

They, at the same time, ordered a copy of his first journal and plan to be transmitted to Mr. Hanbury, expecting he would have had them printed: that Mr. Hanbury communicated the plan is apparent, not only from those parts, (of which there never had been any tolerable discovery made before) being laid down according to his plan, in all the maps of that country, published since, but from his journey being pricked off in the map of Virginia, and some other maps published in England since that time: but as the journal never was printed, the same is now added in the Appendix, page 1.

The Indians, for some reasons, (the certain grounds of which cannot be assigned) failed to meet at Loggstown in August 1751, according to their appointment, though Colonel Patton before

B

Pay and subsistance of a garrison would exceed the sum to be paid for rights and quit-rents.

These resolutions entered into within six months after the *date of the king's instructions.*

Employ Gist to explore the country. See instructions, (Appendix, page 1.)

To enquire what nation of Indians inhabited the country, their numbers, commodities best adapted to their trade, to convince them of the consequence and importance of cultivating friendship with the English, and to return a journal of his proceedings, and plan of the country.

Gist empowered by the president of Virginia to come in to the Indians to receive a present.

Set out in October, and returned in May; delivered his journal and plan in July.

Employ Gist to go out a second time to examine the lands, and apply for a commission for him to attend at the treaty at Loggstown.

Gist's instructions for his second journey. Appendix page.

To find out the nearest and best communication from the Potomack to the Monongahela.

To report the most convenient place for building store-houses, &c.

Company send Gist's journal and plan of the country to Mr. Hanbury.

His track was pricked down in all the maps published of that country.

Indians did not meet at Loggstown.

(6)

Gift sets out the 4th of November, 1751, and returned the 29th of May, 1752.

before-mentioned went there, as a commissioner, from Virginia. Mr. Gist therefore went out on the 4th of November following, to search the lands on the south side of the Ohio, according to his instructions, and returning the 29th day of March, 1752, delivered his journal to the company's committee, which is also added in the Appendix, page

But in the mean time John Blair Esq, and others, procured the following order of council.
At a council held October 26, 1751.

*1751.
Orders No. 5. and No. 6, renewed; 4 and 5 years allowed to survey.*

Both the orders of John Blair Esq, William Russell and company, and William M'Mahon, John M'Mahon, Richard M'Mahon, Lewis Neale, John Neale, Mark Calmees and company, were renewed, *in the first, four years* farther time allowed to survey, &c. and *in the second, five years* farther time allowed, and leave to insert the names of any person or persons, whom they should find it necessary to take in as a partner or partners, to promote the settling the said lands, &c.
N. Walthoe.

Order, No. 5. had expired in 1749. No. 6. the only order that had been granted, with 5 years allowed to survey.

Note, The order of John Blair Esq, and company, pretended to be renewed by this last-recited order, had expired November 4, 1749; M'Mahon's would not have expired till April 22, 1752, but it is very remarkable that his was the single order that ever was granted, for any longer term than four years, according to which time it would have expired the April before; and it is to be observed, that there is no alteration in the bounds of either, these grantees not being then well enough acquainted with the situation of that part of the country.

The company was satisfied that Mr. Gist's two tours had, in a great measure, removed the prejudices the Ohio Indians had conceived against the inhabitants of Virginia, which had been artfully propagated among them, at least by the traders, if not by the government of Pennsylvania, who were jealous of having any partners in the skin and furr trade, which they had in a manner engrossed to themselves. The Indians had found that they were supplied with goods by the company, on much more reasonable terms than they had been by the Pennsylvania traders, and could not doubt of a much more powerful protection from his Majesty, than they before had reason to expect, as they generally looked upon Mr. Penn (whom they called their brother Onas) to be the only person who concerned himself with American affairs, such at least, as they were interested in, their lands and trade. But, as Gist could not obtain, from any of the Indians, an answer concerning the settlement of any lands on the Ohio, their resolution concerning which was referred till a general meeting, and as they had agreed to

Gist allowed to attend the treaty at Loggstown, as agent for the company.

meet at Loggstown in the May following; Mr. Gist again applied to the government of Virginia, who allowed of his appearing at the treaty, as an agent for the company, but appointed Messrs. Fry, Lomax, and Patton, commissioners for managing that treaty, in behalf of his Majesty. Mr. Gist on this occasion had the following instructions from the company.

Instructions given Christopher Gist Gent. by the Ohio company, April 28, 1752.

Company's instructions to Mr. Gist, as their agent, to attend the Indian treaty.

Whereas the governor has been pleased to grant you a commission, empowering and requiring you to go, as agent for the Ohio company, to the Indian treaty, to be held at Loggstown on the 16th of May next: You are therefore desired to acquaint the chiefs of the several nations of Indians there assembled, that his Majesty has been graciously pleased to grant unto the Honourable Robert Dinwiddie Esq, governor of Virginia, and to several other gentlemen, in Great Britain and America, by the name of the Ohio company, a large quantity of land, on the river Ohio, and the branches thereof; thereby to enable and encourage the said company, and all his Majesty's subjects, to make settlements, and carry on an extensive trade and commerce, with their brethren the Indians, and to supply them with goods at a more easy rate than they have hitherto bought them : *And considering the necessities of his children, the Six Nations, and the other Indians, to the westward of the English settlements, and the hardships they labour under for want of a due supply of goods, and to remove the same, as much as possible*, his Majesty has been pleased to have a clause inserted in the company's grant, obliging them *to carry on a trade and commerce, with their brethren the Indians,* and has granted them many privileges and immunities, in consideration of their carrying on the trade, and supplying the Indians with goods. That the said company have accordingly begun the trade, and imported large quantities of goods, but have found the expence and risque of carrying out the goods, such a distance from the inhabitants, without having any place of safety, by the way to lodge them at, or opportunity of getting provisions, for their people, so great, that they cannot afford to sell their goods, at so easy a rate, as they would willingly do, nor are they, at such a distance, able to supply their brethren, the Indians, at all times when they are in want; *for which reason the company find it absolutely necessary immediately to settle and cultivate the land, his*

Company inform the Indians of the king's right to the lands to the westward of the mountains.

Majesty has been pleased to grant them, which, to be sure, they have an indisputable right to do, as our brethren, the Six Nations, sold all the land to the westward of Virginia, at the treaty of Lancaster, to their father, the king of Great Britain, *and he has been graciously pleased to grant a large quantity thereof to the Ohio company*; yet, being informed that the Six Nations have given their friends, the Delawares, leave to hunt upon these lands, and that they still hunt upon part thereof themselves, and as the settlements to be made by the English in those parts may make the game scarce, or, at least, drive it farther back; *the company, therefore, to prevent any difference or misunderstanding, which might possibly happen, between them and their brethren the In-*

Company offer to make the Indians farther satisfaction for the lands on the east side of the Ohio.

dians, touching the said lands, are willing to make them some farther satisfaction for the same, and to purchase of them the land on the east side the river Ohio and Allegany, as low as the great Conhaway, providing the same can be done at a reasonable rate, and our brethren, the Six Nations and their allies, will promise and engage their friendship and protection, to all his Majesty's subjects,
settling

(7)

settling in that country: When this is done, the company can safely venture to build factories and store-houses, upon the river Ohio, and send out large cargoes of goods, which they cannot otherwise do. And to convince our brethren, the Indians, how desirous we are of living in strict friendship, and becoming one people with them, you are hereby empowered and required, to acquaint and promise our brethren, in the name and on behalf of the company, *that if any of them incline to take land and live among the English, they shall have any of the company's lands, upon the same terms and conditions, the white people have, and enjoy the same privileges they do, as far as is in the company's power to grant*; and that you may be the better able to acquaint our brethren the Indians, with these our proposals, you are to apply to Andrew Montour the interpreter, for his assistance therein, and the company hereby undertake and promise, to make him satisfaction for the trouble he shall be at. If our brethren, the Six Nations, approve our proposals, the company will pay them whatever sum you agree with them for, and if they want any particular sort of goods, you are to desire them to give you an account of such goods, and the company will immediately send for them to England, and, when they arrive, will carry them to whatever place you agree to deliver them at. *If our brethren, the Indians, do not approve these proposals, and do refuse their protection and assistance to the subjects of their father, the King of Great Britain, you are forthwith to make a return thereof to the said Ohio company, that they may inform his Majesty thereof.* You are to apply to Colonel Cresap for what wampum you have occasion of, on the company's account, for which you are to give him a receipt. Offer to allow any Indians who chuse to settle among them the same privileges with the white men. Ordered to employ Andrew Montour as interpreter.

You are also to apply to him for one of the company's horses, to ride out to the Loggstown.

As soon as the treaty is over, you are to make an exact return of all your proceedings to the company.

From the proceedings, during that treaty, in the Appendix, it will appear that it was, with great difficulty, the Indians were, even then, brought to agree, that any settlements should be made by the English, upon the Ohio, though, at that very time, they were under the strongest apprehensions of being attacked by the French. Page 17.

And this summer, 1752, the French not only attacked the Twigtwees, pursuant to their threats, (mentioned in Mr. Gist's journal) but exercised such cruelties, in their town, as are scarcely credible, and at the same time, took four of our Indian traders, belonging to Pensylvania, then trading there, and sent them prisoners to Canada, from whence they were sent to Old France, and imprisoned at Rochelle, but, being released, by the solicitation of the English ambassador, who clothed and sent them to England, they returned from thence to Philadelphia, in captain Budden, May 1753, having been stripped naked, and used very hardly, by the French, though they had seized their goods, to the value of above 1500*l.* when they made them prisoners. In 1752 French attack the Twigtwees. Appendix, page 5. Four Indian traders taken prisoners by the French, and sent to Old France.

Treated very hardly by the French, who took 1500*l.* from them.

The Ohio company were no sooner informed of the French proceedings, and the Indians consent, that they might erect a fort, and begin their settlement, than they dispatched Mr. Gist to the northward, to give notice to the persons he had there contracted with, on the company's behalf, that they might remove, as soon as they would, to settle pursuant to their agreement, and, on his return, he assured the company, that fifty of those families would remove that fall, or the next spring, it being judged improper, that the whole number should settle at once, as, they could not be conveniently supplied with provisions, and proper necessaries, for so many; and afterwards, at a meeting of the company, September 17, 1752, it was agreed, *immediately to enter for and survey their first 200,000 acres, from Kiskaminettas, down the south east side of the Ohio, to the mouth of the Big Kanhawa,* where, it was thought absolutely necessary, to have some fort or place of security: And as it was also judged proper to take up some small parcels of land upon the river, at convenient distances, to build proper magazines, and houses, for the reception of the persons, removing to settle there, and security of their goods. While they were building, they directed that a proper application should be made, to the governor and council, for that purpose, and the following petition was accordingly presented to them, November 6, 1752. Appendix, page 3. Gist sent to inform those who had agreed to remove to the Ohio, that they might go out immediately.

Company in September 1752 agree immediately to enter for, and survey the first 200,000 acres.

To the Honourable Robert Dinwiddie Esq, Lieutenant Governor of Virginia and the Honourable the Council, Company's Petition to the governor and council of Virginia.

The Petition of the Ohio company.

Sheweth,

That the said company, having at their great charge and expence, employed persons for above these two years past, to search and view the lands on the *Ohio*, alias *Alligany River*, as far westward as the *Twigtwee Town*, and to cultivate trade and friendship, with the several nations and tribes of Indians, inhabiting those parts, in order to seat the same, according to the condition of his Majesty's instruction, communicated to this Honourable Board, by his honour the late governor; and having also, at their great charge, cleared a *waggon road, from their storehouse at Will's Creek*, to one of the branches of the *Ohio, navigable by large flat-bottomed boats*, which is the nearest, best, and almost only passage, through the great ridge of mountains, and consequently is of great benefit to the public: Your petitioners pray leave to survey and take up *their first two hundred thousand acres, between Romanettos,* alias *Kiskaminettas Creek, and the fork of the Ohio, and the great Conhaway,* alias *New River,* alias *Wood's River, on the south side of the said River Ohio,* in as many surveys, as they shall think fit, your petitioners understanding the Indians are not willing any settlements, on the north side thereof, should be yet made; and Discoveries made of the country.

Waggon Road made from Will's Creek to the waters of the Ohio.

Desire to take up their first 200,000 acres on the south side of the Ohio, as the Indians were unwilling then to allow settlements on the north side.

(8)

Hope to comply with the terms of their first grant in one year, and pray to be allowed smaller tracts, if they settle them within a year.

and as your petitioners make no doubt, but that they shall be able, not only to comply with the conditions of their first grant, in one year from this time, but to seat a much greater number of families, than they are obliged to, if your honours would permit them to take up *such small tracts of land, not exceeding one thousand acres, as lie in spots interspersed between the company's surveys, as they shall cause to be actually seated on, before the 25th of December, 1733, on the terms of your petitioners grant, or such other terms and conditions, as your Honours shall think reasonable,* which your petitioners apprehend would be of great advantage, to his Majesty and his plantations, as it would be the most effectual means, to increase and secure their first settle-

French forts built on Lake Erie and the south side thereof.

ments, which the encroachments of the French, and especially, the new fort built by them on the west end of Lake Erie, and on the south side thereof, the last year, render necessary, the same manifestly tending to interrupt your petitioners grant; and your petitioners, in order to settle a sufficient force, must, without such permission, be obliged to part with all their own lands, to encourage the settlement, contrary to the intent and agreement of the company, who did not enter into so expensive an undertaking, with a view of setting up for a company of landmongers, though several companies, of that sort, now trade in this colony, but with a view of making fortunes for their children, in a very hazardous undertaking, at a very great and certain expence, whereas *the landmongers, by procuring an order of council, for a certain quan-*

Land-mongers complained of; the method they use to take up lands.

tity of land, make surveys at so unreasonable a distance, as might include five hundred times the quantity, and it is presumed, under their grant, no person can interfere; when they meet with purchasers, so much land is taken up, and his Majesty's land is granted, to his subjects, not by a purchase from himself, but persons, who substitute themselves his brokers, and receive the full value of them.

Pray that persons may be restrained from surveying lands which the company paid for the discovery of, till the king's pleasure was known.

Your petitioners therefore hope, that your Honours will think it reasonable, they should reap some of the advantage the public will receive, by their great expence, and not allow private persons to interfere with their bounds, or to take up large tracts of the lands, they have been at the charge of discovering, till they may have time to apply to his Majesty, and know his pleasure, as your petitioners are so far from setting up for an engrossing company, that they are willing to receive any new members into it, on the same terms they ho'd their several

Company increased from 13, the number of their original members, to 20.

shares, which from thirteen at the time of his Majesty's grant, now amount to twenty, *yet have not so much land among them, as some persons, who are so far from being at any expence, or procuring any public advantage, that they have made large fortunes by selling his Majesty's lands.*

And your petitioners shall ever pray.

The following paragraph had been printed in the Virginia Gazette of October 6, preceding.

Six nations and Twig-twees reported to have declared war against the French.

Williamsburg, Oct. 6. We have credible advice, that the *Six Nations, in alliance with the Twitwees,* a people much more powerful than themselves, have declared war against the French and French Indians, being exasperated thereto, by the most horrid and shocking cruelties imaginable, exercised by the French, on one of the Twitwee towns.

Persons apply for lands, and offer to settle them in 3 years.

Several persons, therefore, as well as the company, judging this the most favourable opportunity, that could offer, to secure a settlement upon the Ohio, while the Indians were so incensed, and before the French had gained any possession there, applied on the same 6th day of November 1752, to the governor and council, *to take up divers tracts of land upon that river, upon the condition of seating several hundred families thereon, within three years, after their entries were allowed,* but those applications, as well as the company's petition, were entirely disre-

Ohio company employ Trent as their Factor.

garded. However the company (resolved to do every thing in their power) in the same month of November, 1752, employed one Trent, herein after mentioned, as a factor to carry on their trade, and pressed Mr. Gist to proceed in the settlement and survey as fast as possible,

13 families settle under the Ohio company; Russel under the order, No. 5, page 2, surveys the lands they had settled on, though far without the limits he was confined to in his order.

and he, in that fall and the next spring, not only removed his own family, but procured William Cromwell his son-in-law, and eleven other families, to settle between the *Youghiogeni* and *Monaungahela,* where they were no sooner seated, than William Russel, under colour of the order of council of November 4, 1745, surveyed those very lands in February 1753, *fixing his beginning on a branch of Redstone Creek, about fifty miles due north of the head spring of Potomack, the most northern corner of Lord Fairfax's line, (west and north west of which, he was to be bounded)* and finding the first course run between Cromwell's and Gist's, and would include Gist's own settlement, he altered it to leave Gist a handsome settlement (as he termed it) but included all the other families, who had settled there, as upon the company's lands, and under

One of the company sent out to lay off a town,—forbids Russel from proceeding on his survey.

their engagement with Gist, on the company's behalf. *This proceeding was the more extraordinary, as Colonel Cresap, one of the company, was then out, to lay off a town, pitch upon a proper place to build a fort, and actually forbid Russel to proceed, informing him not only of the land being then settled by the company, but that without it, or convenient stages through it, they could not possibly carry on their trade, as the road from their storehouse on Will's Creek, to the Ohio (and which they had been at the expence of clearing) run directly through it;* and Russel, at the same time, ac-

Russel acknowledges orders from the president of Virginia not to interfere with the company,—proceeded nevertheless with the survey.

knowledged that he had received a letter from *the Honourable Lewis Burwell Esq, then president and commander in chief of Virginia,* who, as he said, was concerned with him, directing him, by no means, to interfere with the Ohio company's lands, but declaring some other of his partners (who were also of the council) would stand by him, he persisted in his resolution, and

Caveat entered by the company.

continued his survey, which laid the company under a necessity of entering a caveat against any patent issuing thereupon, which was to be heard before the governor and council; but as they never try such matters, except during the general courts in April and October, or the courts of oyer and terminer in June and December, the company (considering the urgent ne-

Caveat not tried before the French seized on the lands in dispute.

cessity of settling those parts as soon as possible) were in hopes the same would have been tried the following April, or in June at farthest, yet to their great mortification, they could not procure the summons for Russel to be made returnable sooner than *June* 1754, before

which

(9)

which time the French got possession of the very lands in dispute: For in *January* 1753, they not only robbed all the English traders, they found upon the Ohio, but killed some, and made others prisoners; an account of whose hostilities (or more properly murders and robberies, for as yet no injury whatsoever had been offered to them by any of the subjects of Great Britain in any part of America) was printed in the Pennsylvania Gazette, as follows.

Philadelphia, May 3, 1753. Extract of a letter from captain William Trent *. " I take "this opportunity of acquainting you of the French and Indians killing and taking our people "prisoners. They have killed Finley's three men near the little Pick Town, and we expect "that he himself will be killed. Taaff was robbed of two or three hundred pounds, but "his men got off; fifty-five French Indians have robbed us, on this side the river, below *the* "*Shawnesse* town, of three or four hundred pounds, and took prisoners *David Hendrick, William Powel, Jacob Evans and his brother, and a servant belonging to us,* one *McGintie,* and *James Lowry belonging to the Lowries.* The last made his escape, after he had been a prisoner several "days. Mr. Croghan, with an hundred horse load of skins, is coming through the woods, "on this side the river, with a few Indians, but am afraid that they will be killed or taken "by three hundred *Ottawawas,* that were expected would surprize the town, as they had in- "formation of their coming, and doubt they will follow them, when they find them gone; "the rest of the white men are coming up the river, in a body, with what Indians are be- "low, but as there is a large body of French and Indians expected every day down the river, "I doubt they will never get up; poor *Fortescue* perished on the road, coming from the "lower town. There is not one Indian or white man any where below the *Shawnesse* or "*Loggstown,* but what is coming up." This was accompanied with the following paragraph, "*May* 24. Four of the Indian traders, who were taken prisoners, in the *Twigtwee* town last "summer, by the French, carried to *Canada* and from thence to *Old France,* are returned with "*Captain Budden,* having been released out of prison at *Rochelle,* by the solicitation of the "British ambassador, who was so good as to cloath and send them to England, the French "having stripped them naked, and used them very hardly."

But the insolence of the Indians in the French interest, cannot in any instance appear plainer than in the following extract from the Pensylvania Gazette, concerning the prisoners mentioned in the above letter of captain Trent.

Philadelphia, August 15, 1754. "In *January* 1753, four of our Indian traders, viz. *Alexander M'Gentie, Jabez Evans, David Hendricks,* and *William Powel,* (four of those named in captain Trent's letter above) were taken trading on *Kantucqui River* near the *Ohio,* by a party of French Indians called the *Cagnawagas,* who plundered them of goods to the value of several hundred pounds, and carried them to Canada, where they were made slaves; but acquainting the mayor of Albany with their miserable situation, by a letter which he communicated to this government, measures were taken to procure their release. The Indians at first demanded a negro boy for each of them, or as much as would buy one, but at length were prevailed on by the commissioners of Indian affairs at Albany to take less, though the whole paid them with the charges amounted to seventy-two pounds, five shillings, and three halfpence, for the four prisoners, which has been repaid by this province; however, the Indians, it seems, pretend not to be satisfied, and *colonel Myndert Schuyler, one of the Albany Commissioners for Indian affairs, who transacted this matter with them,* received lately a letter from the chief of that nation on the subject; of which the following is a translation."

"Falls of St. Lewis, June 14, 1754. I pray thee my brother Anagarondon (colonel Schyler's Indian name) to acquaint the gentlemen, that I have not been satisfied for the prisoners, that were delivered to you at Albany last year. *My young men tell me every day that they do not like your management, and that for the future they will bring no living prisoners, since they do not receive as much for one of them as will buy a little slave.* I charge Montandre with this commission, who will explain my sentiments to you, when he delivers you this letter. *The least that ought to be paid for a prisoner is* 400 *livres,* (about twenty pounds sterling) let those that have the management of these sort of affairs give due attention to this, otherwise *I will not answer for what may happen hereafter, when my young men make prisoners.*

Onongraguicté, chief of the Falls of St. Louis."

Upon which the printer makes the following very just remark. "By this insulting letter from a people with whom this province has not had the least difference, to whom we have never given the least occasion of offence, we may see the contempt in which we are held by these savages, who not content with plundering our people of their goods with impunity, propose to make slaves of all of us they can catch, or to have a sum for each sufficient to purchase a slave, otherwise threatening they will not be at the trouble of saving our lives. If they are suffered to go on in this manner, and make a trade of catching our people, and selling them to us again for 400 livres per head, it may in time cost us more to satisfy the demands of that handful of barbarians, than would serve to defend the province against all its enemies."

It is to be presumed that captain Trent gave the first notice of these transactions to the governor of Virginia, as he, in a letter to the committee of the Ohio company, dated Feb. 15, 1753, says, "I am sorry to hear by a letter from Mr. Trent, that some of the *Twigtwees* are gone over to the French, and that some French officers, &c. are at Logstown building of

Letter from Trent concerning the French proceedings. 3 men killed.

Traders plundered.

7 prisoners taken.

Return of four prisoners (who had been sent to France, and very hardly treated) to Philadelphia.

Indians demand a negro for each prisoner.

Are paid 72l. 5s. 1½ for four prisoners.

Indians say they will bring no prisoners, unless they receive the price of a negro for each.

400 livres for each prisoner.

Remarks on the foregoing letter.

Governor's intelligence from Trent.

---

* Mr. Trent had been a captain last war on the expedition against Canada.

C houses,

(10)

"houses, &c. and that there are many others at their forts on the lakes, which he calls an army, but hope they are only traders from Canada. This information I had last week by express, which I returned, and desired him to get what farther intelligence he possibly could, between this and May, when I shall send some powder, arms, &c. to Winchester, a present to the Indians."

<small>Page 8. Company complain of not meeting with proper encouragement from the government of Virginia.</small>

As this was wrote, before the caveat above-mentioned was entered, it might have been imagined, the company would have met little difficulty in procuring a speedy hearing, but, from the governor and council's referring it to such a very distant day, they found that instead of protection and encouragement, which, in virtue of his Majesty's instruction, they had always expected from the government here, they met, upon every application they were obliged to make here, nothing but slights and disappointments, not to call it manifest injustice; for in June 1753, when they hoped to have had their caveat against Russel and company determined, they found themselves under a necessity of entering three more, against Richard Corbin Esq, one of the council, who had, during the court of oyer and terminer, held in that month, procured three orders of council, in the name of himself and company, to empower them to survey 50,000 acres of land on Fishing Creek, 100,000 at the mouth of the Big Kanhawa, and 40,000 on Buffaloe Creek, all within those very bounds, where the company had, on the 6th day of November preceding, acquainted the governor and council, by their petition, that they proposed to make their surveys. And a particular hardship upon the company was, that those very entries were directed by their own map, which cost them above 500l. and which was laid before the council on that same day by the governor, to whom it was delivered in confidence as he was a member of the Ohio company; for before that time, neither he or the council, knew any thing of the situation of the Ohio, or the names of its branches.

<small>Obliged to enter three caveats

190,000 acres petitioned for within the boundaries claimed by the company in their petition (page 7.) 8 months before, and granted them by the king's original instruction. Entries made by others, from the map made at the company's expence, and by their order.</small>

<small>Trent communicated to government all proceedings on the Ohio, and his intelligence disregarded. Letters from the governor &c. in the company's hands.</small>

Captain Trent, the company's factor, from time to time, advised the governments of Virginia and Pensylvania, of the several transactions on the Ohio. Whether a proper use was made of his timely information, must be submitted: But it is very certain, that many persons represented them as stories, propagated by the company without foundation, and it was long before they would suffer themselves to be undeceived, as will fully appear by the sequel.

The following letters which were sent by governor Dinwiddie, and colonel Fairfax president of the council, to the said Trent, during these transactions, are now in the hands of the company's committee, and are an authority which cannot be contested.

SIR, Winchester, 26th May, 1753.

<small>Letter from the honourable Mr. Fairfax, one of his majesty's council, to Mr. Trent.</small>

"I received yours of the 22d instant, from Lord Fairfax's; I had prepared for setting out hither last week, in hopes of meeting some of the Indian chiefs, according to appointment, but Mr. Andrew Monture, calling on me in his way to Williamsburg, gave me the first advice of a numerous body of French, and their dependant Indians, being on their warlike march towards the Ohio, whereby Mr. Monture apprehended none of the Six Nations, Twigtwees or other of our friendly Indians, would, at this time, venture to come hither, so that I imagined I had little more to do than come and see the arms and ammunition, &c. secured, till farther direction from the governor. I am accompanied by major Carlyle, major George Washington, and son George Fairfax: We met colonel Lomax, who shewed me your letter to the governor, with the string of wampum, to confirm the Indians request of a present supply of arms, &c. which induced me to write by colonel Lomax, and acquaint the governor, that as my instructions were to deliver the arms, &c. only to the Indians, upon their coming hither; yet if the above reasons, for their not coming, be allowed, and their present occasion worthy relief, I would wait here and at Lord Fairfax's, for his honour's commands, hoping I shall receive orders to deliver you, &c. what can be, with the greatest convenience and expedition, conveyed to such of our friendly Indians, as are in greatest want. If the bearer should not find you at colonel Cresap's, I suppose he knows your mind, having consulted what is the best method to assist the threatened Indians, so as to prevent any surprize from a watchful enemy, who may get intelligence of the arms, &c. being on the road, soon after their being set forward. I am persuaded, I shall have the governor's directions by Thursday at farthest, and if it would suit your other business, should be glad to see you. The bearer tells us he left about 70 Indians at colonel Cresap's, who, he supposes, came from the Cherokees, having several scalps and some prisoners, please to relate this matter particularly, that I may send it to the governor, wishing you and friends all happiness. I am Sir your very humble servant,

W. Fairfax.

SIR, Williamsburg, May 31, 1753.

<small>Governor Dinwiddie's letter to Mr. Trent.</small>

"Your letter from Winchester of the 21st May, was delivered me by colonel Lomax, the contents thereof I have duly considered, and it corresponds with the intelligence I received from Mr. Montour, and what I have by express from Philadelphia; and I am sincerely sorry for the present situation of the Indians in friendship with us; and, to shew them how much I have their interest at heart, I have this day wrote to colonel Fairfax, to deliver you all, or what part you see proper, of the present intended for them, that is now at Winchester.

<small>Orders to deliver Indian present to Trent.</small>

"I hope you will take a proper care, to advise the half king and the other chiefs of the Indians, by a messenger, of your bringing them the supplies, as above from me, that they may send some of their people to escort you, so that it may not fall into the hands of their enemies: As you are thoroughly acquainted in the woods, I must refer this affair to you,

"and

(11)

"and you will consider the great misfortune that will attend, if these supplies should fall into
"the hands of the French Indians, which I hope you will cautiously prevent.
"I am well pleased with the half king's * speech, and hope they will be able to give a
"good account of the French and their Indians, and prevent their taking possession of the
"land on the Ohio. You may assure them of my firm attachment to their interest. It was *Governor assures the*
"not practicable yet to build the strong house, but when this attempt is defeated, they may *Indians of his friend-*
"be assured it will be built. If they secure some of the principal of the French, and send *build a fort.*
"them here, I shall send them to France, by way of Britain.
"What the Delawares told you, is confirmed by Mr. Montour, in regard to the French
"and Indians giving the Six Nations, a large black belt, and the answer the Six Nations
"made them.
"I am sorry for the account of the murders, &c. done by the French, and hope, if we
"have a settlement on the Ohio, we shall turn the tables on them, in every thing but their
"barbarity. You know how to frame a speech, to the Indians, in their style, better than I
"can; assure them of my sincere friendship and readiness, at all times to assist them, deliver
"the present to them, as from this colony, and tell them it is intended for the Six Nations, and
"the other nations of Indians, in amity with us and them. I intreat you to be as inquisitive,
"as possible, of the number of the French, and their Indians, of their designs, and the
"situation the *Picts* and *Twigtwees* are now in; next year, I hope to deliver them a large pre-
"sent, from their father, and I propose delivering it with my own hands. I shall be glad
"to hear that Burney got safe to the Twigtwees, though he broke my orders, in remaining
"so long in this colony, if he had gone directly, it probably had been of much service.
"I hope Pensylvania have been apprized of the present necessities of our friendly Indians,
"and that they have, or will send them some supplies.
"On your return, I expect you will send me as particular an account as possible of all af- *Desires Mr. Trent to*
"fairs relating to the intentions of the French, and their Indians, and that they are disap- *send him the fullest*
"pointed of their designs. *account of the French.*
"God preserve you, and grant you a safe return, and I remain with great sincerity,
                                                      Sir, your most humble servant,
"My service to colonel Cresap.   Robert Dinwiddie.
"You know dispatch is now absolutely necessary."

                                                                      Belvoir, 9 June, 1753.
"SIR,
"On seeing Mr. Andrew Monture the first instant, and Mr. Joseph Carrol the third in- *Mr. Fairfax's letter*
"stant, at Winchester, and on discoursing with them, concerning the present state of our *to Mr. Trent.*
"Indian affairs, they apprehended a great risque at this time to send the arms, ammunition,
"&c. to Loggstown, especially as it was not known whereabouts the French forces were on
"their march, and might by their spies get intelligence of, and surprize any small party, that
"conducted the said arms, &c. which appearing plausible, and uncertain when I might re-
"ceive farther orders, also to save expences, I left the town on Monday the 4th, but with
"directions to Mr. William Cock, that if any packet, from the governor, should arrive, to
"send it immediately by express; accordingly this morning Mr. Cock sent me, by an express
"messenger, his honour's letter, accompanied with one from colonel Lomax. The governor *Governor much con-*
"signifies his and the council's concern, that the Indians did not meet me, as expected, at *cerned the Indians did*
"Winchester, and the more, as they consider the situation of those people, from the threats *not come in.*
"of the French and Indians in their interest; therefore, on the present exigency, I am di-
"rected to deliver you all, or any part of, the intended present now at Winchester: I have,
"pursuant thereto, wrote now to Mr. Cock, who has the care and custody thereof, to get
"the waggons bespoke, and forthwith to load the same with powder and ball, as most wanted,
"and such of the cases or chests of the firelocks, flints, and duffels, as can be conveniently
"stowed, and carried, as you may advise and direct, to the mouth of Patterson's Creek,
"where, in your letter to me, you desired they might be sent you, and if your other affairs
"did not permit your coming or sending a trusty person, perhaps Mr. Joseph Carroll
"could be engaged to undertake the care of seeing them delivered to you; the go-
"vernor proposes your giving notice to the half king, timely for his sending a sufficient num-
"ber of his people to escort, and be a safe guard, to prevent the enemy getting intelligence
"and possessing them. I heartily wish the French may fail of success, and that our friendly
"Indians may not be dispirited. You'll please to favour me with an account of your pro-
"ceeding, relating to the above particulars, with my compliments to colonel Cresap &c. I
"remain your loving friend &c.   W Fairfax.

On the 10th of July following, the governor dispatched the following, by Mr. Gist, to *Governor sends Gist*
the half king and the other Indians, on the Ohio.   *to the Indians on the Ohio.*

"To the *Half King* *, *King Shingas* †, and Sachems of the Six Nations on the Ohio.
"Friends and brethren, The governor of Virginia wishes you all health and happiness.
"We received your message, by your brother Mr. Thomas Burney, and are heartily sorry *Governors' letter to*
"for the attempts of the French, and their Indians to disturb your peace, and by force endea- *the Indians.*
"vour to build forts on the *Ohio* without your consent. The present we sent you, by Mr.
"Trent, we hope, came safe to your hands, and will enable you to defeat their designs: some

* An Indian chief.   † King of the Delawares. See treaty at Loggstown, Appendix page .
                                                                              "of

(12)

<table>
<tr><td>Invites them to come to Winchester, to receive a present from the king.

Promises arms &c. and to preserve the chain.</td><td>"of the heads and chiefs of the *Twigtwees*, being arrived at the Loggstown on the Ohio, we are preparing a small present, to be sent them to Winchester, and to be delivered to them by the Honourable William Fairfax Esquire, one of our council, on the 20th day of next month, being a small testimony of the regard we bear to them, as being our friends, and allies to the Six Nations; next May we shall expect *the chiefs of the Six Nations, and the Twigtwees*, at Winchester, to receive a considerable present, sent by your father, his Majesty the King of Great Britain; in the mean time, we are preparing a suit of cloaths for the half king, and king Shingas, which shall be sent to *Winchester*, together with the small present to the chiefs of the *Twigtwees*, who are now at the Ohio. I farther assure you, that I shall be always ready to assist you, with powder and arms, upon all necessary occasions, when in my power, and it will be my chief care to keep the chain of friendship subsisting between us bright and entire, as long as the sun and moon shall continue.

"I remain, with true affection, your loving brother</td></tr>
</table>

Williamsburg July 10th, 1753. Robert Dinwiddie.

Recommends Gift to the Indians.

"This comes by our friend, and your brother, Mr. Christopher Gist, to whom we refer you, and to whom you may give faith."

In the *Virginia Gazette of August* 16, 1753, was printed a message, *from the governor of Pennsylvania* to the assembly of that province, then sitting, part of which is in these words,

"Gentlemen,

<table>
<tr><td>Governor of Pennsylvania's speech to his assembly.

Governor of Canada avows the hostile proceedings.

Indians assert their independence of the French.</td><td>"By the intelligence contained in the several papers now laid before you, it may be expected, that the county of Allegheny, situate on the waters of the Ohio, partly within the limits of this province, and partly within those of Virginia, already is, or will be, in a very little time, invaded by an army of French and Indians, raised for this purpose, by the governor of Canada; and that the Indians, inhabiting there, who are of the Six Nations, with a mixture of Shawanese and Delawares, friends and allies of Great Britain, will be obliged to retire and leave their country, for want of means to defend it, against this armed force, as will also the Twigtwees, lately recommended to our alliance, by the Six Nations; and that his Majesty's subjects of this and the neighbouring colonies, now carrying on a just and lawful trade, with these Indians, will be cut off, or made prisoners, and their effects seized and plundered, unless the messengers, dispatched by me to Ohio, immediately on the receiving the advices, from the governor of New York, shall have arrived time enough to give our traders and Indian allies, an opportunity of taking measures, for their own security. The advices communicated to me, by governor Clinton, are farther confirmed by Mr. Andrew Montour, who, happening lately to be at Onandago, on business of the government of Virginia, with the Six Nations, heard the message of the governor of Canada, avowing these hostile proceedings, delivered to the council there, by seven French Indians, together with the council's answer, asserting their independency, and the property of the soil, and forbidding the French, from settling their lands at Ohio, or disturbing the English traders. But your own judgment will suggest, what such prohibition can amount to, from a people, who are not, at present, in a condition to defend themselves, and who, besides, are starving, for want of the necessaries of life."</td></tr>
</table>

Colonel Fairfax, finding the Indians failed to meet him at Winchester, as he expected, wrote the following letter to captain Trent.

SIR, Winchester 1 Sept. 1753.

<table>
<tr><td>Mr. Fairfax's letter to Mr. Trent.

Southern Indians promise to assist the Six Nations against the French.</td><td>"I received your Epistle, and observe, that our brethren, the Indians, cannot be punctual as to times of appointment. I hope, when they understand our governor cannot meet them here, now on the sudden notice, they will not be angry, and refuse to see me, who am next in rank, upon colonel Burwell, the late president's, refusing to act, ever since the governor's arrival. I am empowered, under the great seal, and fully instructed to receive and act with the Indians, and have hope, I shall give satisfaction. The governor has advised me, by the return of Mr. Gist, that the *Chicesaws, Cherokees, Catawbas, and Creeks*, on his acquainting them, by express messenger, that the French had come, in a warlike manner, to dispossess the *Ohio* Indians, and settle themselves, answered him, that they would heartily join the Six Nations, to drive the French back to Canada, having also cause to strike them. The *Cherokees* propose sending a thousand men. You'll acquaint our brethren, that the governor is always studious of promoting their welfare. I shall be glad, if you and friend Mr. Montour will endeavour to expedite your march hither, for beside Mr. Croghan, you have other friends, that impatiently long to see you all, among them is your assured well-wisher and humble servant,</td></tr>
</table>

W. Fairfax.

Recommends Gift to the Indians.

"P. S. (to the Indians) You must think it a mark of our good regard for you and Eghuiserra* (Mr. Montour) that we spare at this critical time Annosannoah†, (Mr. Gist) to be our envoy; but hoping he may assist you, in qualifying any uneasiness, that might happen among his kindred, the Wyendots, he has been chosen to salute you, and we desire you'll receive and entertain him accordingly.

W. Fairfax.

*† } Appendix Page { Treaty at Loggstown.
‡ 3 Gist's journal.

The

(13)

The Indians complaining, notwithstanding the supply they received, that they still were in want of arms and ammunition, captain Trent acquainted colonel Fairfax of it, and thereupon soon after, received the additional supply mentioned in the following letter, directed to him by Mr. Walthoe, clerk of the council.

Indians ask for another supply of arms &c.

SIR, Williamsburg Sept. 26, 1753.
"The governor, being informed by colonel Fairfax, that the Indians on the Ohio, are still in want of powder and lead, has been pleased to order them a fresh supply, as below, which are lodged with Mr. Cocks at Winchester, waiting your directions, for conveying them to the Ohio; and you are hereby requested to give proper orders, that the same may be safely and speedily transported to Loggstown.
"You will receive ten barrels of powder, six cases of shot, and four hundred flints.
"There are neither pistols, or cutlasses in the magazine, or some would have been sent. I am Sir your humble servant,
To captain William Trent. N. Walthoe.

Governor orders a supply.

The assembly of Virginia did not meet till the first of November following, when the governor, in his speech to them, has these words.

Assembly of Virginia meets.

"Gentlemen of the house of burgesses,
"Since your last adjournment, I have been alarmed by several informations from our back settlements, from the Indians, and our neighbouring governors, of a large body of French regulars, and Indians in their interest, having marched from Canada, to the Ohio, in an hostile manner, to invade his Majesty's territories, and having actually built a fort, on his Majesty's land; on which, by the advice of the council, I have sent several considerable presents to the Indians, who are our allies, and in friendship with us. These people seem much surprised, at the conduct of the French, and appear full of resentment, and have assured the commissioners, sent from me, of their sincere attachment to the British interest, and the English colonies on this continent.
"As I intend to meet the chiefs of the different tribes of Indians next May, at Winchester, to deliver a very considerable present from his Majesty, I am in great hopes, then, to make a firm, strong, and lasting alliance with them. This attempt of the French, has been represented to the ministry at home, by several of the governors on this continent, and by myself, and by them it was laid before the King. His Majesty, out of his paternal love and affection, and great regard he bears to his subjects on this continent, immediately ordered one of his ships of war to come to this dominion, with his royal instructions to me, how to conduct myself, in the present situation of affairs. I also received letters to all his Majesty's governors, on this continent, with orders to dispatch the same to them immediately.
"As this affair has been so strongly noticed, and attended to at home, and there judged to be of great consequence to his Majesty's dominions, and his subjects here, I doubt not you will think it a matter that requires your immediate consideration.
"I am commanded by his Majesty, immediately to call the assembly within my government, and to lay before them the necessity of a mutual assistance, and to engage them to grant such supplies, as the exigency of the present affairs requires, which I now do, and I doubt not, but you will answer his royal expectations, by granting such sums of money, for the defeating the designs of our enemies, as the present emergency calls for.

Governor informs the assembly of the proceedings of the French.

Indians attachment to the British interest.

King sends instructions to the governors.

Governor tells them the affair was judged of the utmost importance in Great Britain.

Commanded by the king to call the assembly, and ask supplies.

But it seems neither the governor, or assembly were of opinion, that the danger was very pressing: He put off his meeting the Indians at Winchester till May, and they, instead of levying any money, only passed an act for farther encouragement of persons to settle on the waters of the Mississippi, by which instead of *ten years*, formerly allowed, they were to be exempted for *fifteen years*, from the payment of all levies. But this cannot be thought very strange, when it was solemnly affirmed, at Williamsburg, during the assembly's sitting, by the beforementioned Mr. Russell, that there was not a Frenchman upon the waters of the Ohio; nor was the contrary generally believed, till major Washington returned from thence, January 16, 1754. The motives and success of his journey appear from his journal, printed immediately after his return, by the governor's orders, from whence the following extracts are made.

Assembly do not grant supplies.

Allow 15, instead of 10 years, to settle lands on the waters of Mississippi.

Copy of governor Dinwiddie's letter, to the commandant of the French forces on the Ohio, sent by major Washington.

The governor sends major Washington to the Ohio.

SIR,
"The lands upon the river Ohio, in the western parts of the colony of Virginia, are so notoriously known, to be the property of the crown of Great Britain, that it is a matter of equal concern and surprize to me, to hear that a body of French forces are erecting fortresses, and making settlements upon that river, within his Majesty's dominions. The many and repeated complaints, I have received, of these acts of hostility, lay me under the necessity of sending, in the name of the King my master, the bearer hereof, George Washington Esq, one of the adjutants general of the forces of this dominion, to complain to you, of the encroachments thus made, and of the injuries done to the subjects of Great Britain, in open violation of the law of nations, and the treaties now subsisting between the two crowns.

Governor's letter to the French commandant.

D "If

(14)

Governor demands by what authority the French have possessed themselves of the lands of the king of Great Britain.

"If these facts are true, and you shall think fit to justify your proceedings, I must desire you to acquaint me, by whose authority and instructions, you have lately marched from Canada, with an armed force, and invaded the King of Great Britain's territories, in the manner complained of; that according to the purport and resolution of your answer, I may act agreeable to the commission I am honoured with, from the King my master.

Governor summons them to retire.

"However, Sir, in obedience to my instructions, it becomes my duty to require your peaceable departure, and that you would forbear prosecuting a purpose, so interruptive to the harmony and good understanding, which his Majesty is desirous to continue and cultivate, with the most Christian King.

"I persuade myself you will receive and entertain major Washington, with the candour and politeness, natural to your nation; and it will give me the greatest satisfaction, if you return him with an answer, suitable to my wishes, for a very long and lasting peace between us. I have the honour to subscribe myself,

Williamsburg in Virginia   Sir your most obedient humble Servant,
October 31, 1753.   Robert Dinwiddie.

The answer, returned by major Washington, was, as follows.

SIR,

French commandant's letter to the governor.

"As I have the honour of commanding here in chief, Mr. Washington delivered me the letter, which you addressed to the commandant of the French troops.

"I should have been glad, that you had given him orders, or that he had been inclined to proceed to Canada, to see our general, to whom it better belongs, than to me, to set forth the evidence and reality of the rights of the king my master, upon the lands situated along the river Ohio, and to contest the pretensions of the king of Great Britain thereto.

"I shall transmit your letter to the marquis Duquesne; his answer will be a law to me, and if he shall order me to communicate it to you, Sir, you may be assured, I shall not fail to dispatch it forthwith.

Refuses to obey the summon from the governor.

"As to the summon you send me to retire, I do not think myself obliged to obey it, whatever may be your instructions. I am here by virtue of the orders of my general; and I entreat you, Sir, not to doubt one moment, but that I am determined to conform myself to them, with all the exactness and resolution, which can be expected from the best officer. I do not know, that in the progress of this campaign any thing has passed, which can be reputed an act of hostility, or contrary to the treaties, which subsist between the two crowns, the continuance whereof as much interests, and is as pleasing to us, as to the English. Had you been pleased, Sir, to have condescended to particularize the facts, which occasioned your complaint, I should have had the honour of answering you in the fullest, and I am persuaded, most satisfactory manner.

"I made it my particular care to receive Mr. Washington, with a distinction suitable to your dignity, and his quality and great merit, I flatter myself he will do me this justice before you, Sir; and that he will signify to you, as well as I, the profound respect, with which I am

                              Sir, your most humble and most obedient servant,
From the fort sur la Riviere au Beuf,
Dec. 15, 1753.   Legardeur de St. Piere.

Commandant at Venango avows to major Washington the design of the French.

It appears from the same journal, that captain Joncaire commander at Venango, acknowledged to major Washington, that the intent of the French expedition was, to take possession of the Ohio, and to prevent the English settling there, as they had heard of some families moving out, in order thereto; and that there had been 1500 men for that purpose, on this side of lake Ontario, but on the death of their general, they were recalled, except 6 or 700, who were left to garrison four forts, which they had built upon French Creek, and the Lakes;

Monsieur St. Pierre tells major Washington the lands on the Ohio belonged to the king of France, and that he had orders to make prisoners of all English who should be found trading there. Indians say the lands belong to them. Ohio company gave 400 l. to build a fort by permission of the Indians. Major Washington meets the stores, &c. sent out by the company for the fort. Assembly to meet.

and monsieur Legardeur St. Pierre told major Washington, enquiring by what authority he had made prisoners of several English subjects, *that the country belonged to the French, that no Englishman had a right to trade upon those waters, and that he had orders to make every person prisoner, that attempted to trade on the Ohio, or the waters of it.* And it is to be remarked, that the half king, in the account he gave major Washington, of his speech to the French commander insisted, that the lands on the Ohio, belonged to the Indians (and neither to the English or French) although at the treaty at Loggstown, he and the other chiefs then present, had agreed, that the Ohio company might build a fort and settle there, in consequence whereof, they actually contributed four hundred pounds to build the fort, and major Washington, in his journal, mentions, that on the 6th and 7th days of January, as he returned, he met seventeen horses with materials and stores for the fort, besides some families going out to settle there. Captain Trent wrote to the governor by major Washington.

Jan. 21, 1754, A proclamation issued, requiring the assembly, which stood prorogued to the last Thursday in April, to meet on the 14th day of February. And in the mean time the governor sent the following commission, and letter to captain Trent.

Governor of Virginia gives a captain's commission to Mr. Trent.

Robert Dinwiddie Esq, his Majesty's lieutenant governor and commander in chief, and admiral of his colony and dominion of Virginia,

To William Trent Esq,

Whereas certain persons, pretending to be the subjects of his most Christian Majesty the king of France, and that they act by his commission, have in an hostile manner, invaded the territories

(15)

territories of our sovereign, his Majesty King George the second, King of Great Britain France and Ireland, and have committed divers outrages and violences on the persons and goods of his Majesty's subjects, in direct violation and infraction of the treaties, at present subsisting between the two crowns. And whereas those acts of hostility and depredations have been perpetrated in that part of his Majesty's dominions, which are under my government: In order therefore to the preservation of the peace, and good understanding between the two crowns, and the preservation of our sovereign's undoubted rights, and the protection of his subjects as much as in me lies; I have thought proper to appoint, and by virtue of the power and authority to me given by his Majesty, I do hereby constitute and appoint you, William Trent Esq, to be commander of such, and so many of his Majesty's subjects, not exceeding one hundred men, as you can immediately raise and enlist; and with the said company, and the assistance of our good and faithful friends and allies, the Indians of the Six Nations, and such others as are in amity with them and us, to keep possession of his Majesty's lands on the Ohio, and the waters thereof, and to dislodge and drive away, and in case of refusal and resistance, to kill and destroy, or take prisoners, all and every person and persons whatsoever, not subjects of the King of Great Britain, who now are, or shall hereafter come to settle, and take possession of any lands on the said river Ohio, or on any of the branches or waters thereof. And I do hereby require the said men, who shall so inlist themselves, and every of them, to obey you, as their commander and captain &c. and you are to constitute and appoint such and so many officers, under you, as the service shall require, not exceeding one lieutenant, and one ensign. Given under my hand and the seal of the colony at Williamsburg the twenty-sixth day of January, in the twenty-seventh year of his Majesty's reign, annoq, domini, 1754. Robert Dinwiddie.

To raise 100 men, and in conjunction with the Indians to keep possession, and act offensively if necessary.

Power to appoint a lieutenant and an ensign.

With this commission, the governor sent him the following letter, which are the only orders, he ever received, before or after, from the governor, concerning that service.

SIR, Williamsburg January 27, 1754.
Your letter of the 6th current, I received from major Washington; from his report, information and observations, I find the French intend down the Ohio, in order to build forts, and take possession of the lands on that river, which I wish very earnestly to prevent; and as you think you could stop them this winter, if properly impowered so to do, I therefore inclose you a captain's commission, to raise one hundred men in Augusta, and the exterior settlements of this dominion, and a blank commission for you to choose a suitable lieutenant to co-operate with you. Your company will be in the pay of this government, agreeable to the act of assembly.

Governor's letter to captain Trent.

Major Washington has a commission, to raise one hundred men, with them he is to join you, and I desire you to march your men out to the Ohio, where a fort is proposed to be built; when you are there, you are to protect and assist them in finishing the fort, and to be on your guard against any attempts of the French. I doubt not the woodsmen you may inlist will be provided with guns &c.

Major Washington to raise men, and join captain Trent.

I have appointed major Carlisle at Alexandria, commissary of stores and provisions: he will supply you accordingly with what necessaries you may want, and in case of want of guns, I have sent some to his care to be delivered to the commanders of either of these companies, giving a receipt accordingly for them. As you have a good interest with the Indians, I am in hopes you will prevail with many of them to join with you, in order to defeat the designs of the French, in taking their lands from them by force of arms.

Captain Trent to prevail on the Indians to join him.

The house of burgesses are to meet the fourteenth of next month, when I hope they will enable me to send out four hundred more men, early in the spring, to your assistance. I wrote to the neighbouring governors for their aid and assistance, on the present emergency, and am in hopes they will supply a good number of men &c.

House of burgesses to meet.

I have some canon come in, ten I send up to the commissary at Alexandria, they carry four pound shot, I fear there will be difficulty in carrying them out; as you are acquainted with the roads, I shall be glad of your advice therein, and communicate the same to major Carlyle. You see the good opinion I have of your capacity and diligence, which I hope you will exert on this occasion, by keeping a good command, and strongly encouraging our friendly Indians to be on the active. Provisions will be difficult to send you regular supplies of; Mr. Washington says one Frazer can procure large quantities of venison, bear &c. I desire you may write to him, to get what he can. When you have compleated your company, send me a list thereof, and the time of their inlisting, and the place of their abode. I wish you health and success in the present expedition and I am sincerely, Sir your humble servant,
Robert Dinwiddie.

Sends up 10 cannon.

Difficulty of getting provision.

P. S. Inclosed is a speech to the half king, which please to deliver in my name.

Sends a speech to the half king.

This letter and commission were forwarded by major Washington to Winchester, to be sent from thence by Mr. Cocks to captain Trent, who had just finished a strong store-house at Red Stone Creek for the Ohio company to lodge their stores designed for the Ohio, and after finishing it, he had proceeded to build their fort. When they came to hand he began to enlist the company according to his commission, but from that time found himself obliged not only to neglect the Ohio company's affairs, but to apply their stores &c. to maintain his company, and to build a fort for the country at the company's expence, and it was expected he should raise

Captain Trent builds a strong house for the Ohio company, at the mouth of Red Stone Creek on the Monongahela, and proceeds to build a fort on the Ohio.

(16)

raise a company of one hundred men without either enlisting money, (though ten pounds a man has been since allowed) provisions or arms. His situation was mentioned in the Virginia Gazette of March 29, 1754, in the following paragraph. March 14, letters from Messrs. Trent, and Gist, to major Washington give some account of their situation near the Ohio. The first letter is dated Feb. 19, at Yaughyaughgany Big Bottom, the 17th Mr. Trent arrived at the forks of Monongahela (from the mouth of Red Stone Creek, where he has built a strong storehouse) and met Mr. Gist, and several others; in two or three days they expected down all the people, and as soon as they came were to lay the foundation of the fort, expecting to make out for that purpose about 70 or eighty men. The Indians were to join them, and make them strong. They requested him (major Washington) to march out to them with all possible expedition; they acquainted him that monsieur la Force had made a speech to some of our Indians, and told them, *"That neither they nor the English there, would see the sun above 20 days longer, 13 of the days being then to come.* By what Mr. Croghan could learn from an Indian in the French interest, " They might expect 400 French down in that time." A messenger sent from the French fort had letters for the commanders of the other forts to march immediately and join them, in order to cut off our Indians and whites; and some French Indians were likewise expected to join them. When La Force had made his speech to the Indians, they sent a string of wampum to Mr. Croghan to desire him to hurry the English to come, for that they expected soon to be attacked, and pressed hard to come and join them, for they wanted necessaries, and assistance, and then would strike." They farther write, " That 600 French and Indians were gone against the lower Shawnese Town, to cut off the Shawnese; 200 Ottawas and Chipawas came to Miskingum and demanded of the white people there, and shewed them the French hatchet. The Wiandotts, though not above 30 men, refused to let them kill them in their town, but they expected every day to hear they had cut off the whites, and likewise the Wiandotts." The other letter is dated at Monongahela Feb. 23. Mr. Gist writes, " An Indian who was taken prisoner from the Chickasaws by the Six Nations some years ago, has been this year to see his friends there; in his passage up the Ohio, he fell in with a body of near 400 French coming up the river, he parted with them below the falls, and then came in company with 10 of them that were sent up to treat with the Shawnese at the lower town: On their arrival there the English traders had agreed to make prisoners of them, but the French getting a hint from some Indians, they fled away in the night without discovering their business." We have also news that 600 French and Indians are gone down to fall on the Shawnese, if they will not admit the lower army to pass up the river, to join that above; it would therefore be prudent to let the governor know this, perhaps he might send a number of Cherokees to join the Shawnese at the lower town, and defeat them, or prevent their joining those above. Pray send a line by Mr. Steuart and let us know the exact time you will be here, that we may speak truth in all we say to our friends the Indians.

Captain Trent had been hitherto able with the Ohio company's stores, and what provisions he could purchase from the Indians, and other people in those parts, to maintain his people but very indifferently, and kept them working on the fort; but as they increased (for he had inlisted only 31 men in February, 9 in March, and 12 in April) he found himself upon the point of starving; for notwithstanding the governor had wrote him in January, that the commissary at Alexandria would supply him, and major Washington with provisions, he had never received a morsel: On the 12th of April he was therefore under an indispensible necessity, to come in to Will's Creek, to procure provisions for his company, whom he left without any thing but corn, and of that barely enough to subsist on, till he could send them a supply.

The assembly met February 14th, according to the proclamation when the governor among other things, tells them in his speech, " That nothing less than a very important concern could have induced him to call them together again, after so short a recess, but the dignity of the crown of Great Britain, the welfare of all the colonies on this continent, and more especially of this dominion, engaged him to have their advice and assistance, in an affair of the greatest consequence."

" Major Washington, who was sent by me to the commandant of the French forces on the river Ohio, being returned informs me, he found that officer at a fort they had erected on a creek running into the Ohio, and that they were then preparing all necessaries for building another fort on that river; that they had two hundred and twenty canoes made, and many more rough-hewed to be made, in order to transport, early this spring, a great number of regular forces, not less than fifteen hundred men, with their Indians in friendship with them, down the river Ohio, in order to build many more fortresses on it, and that they proposed Loggstown to be the chief place of their rendezvous." Major Washington farther reports, " That he asked why they had seized the goods of our traders, and sent their persons prisoners to Canada," to which the commandant answered, " That his orders from their general the governor of Canada, were not to permit any English subjects to trade on the waters of the Ohio, but to seize their goods, and send them prisoners to Quebec. He also asked the reason of taking Mr. Frazier's house from him, which he had built, and lived in upwards of twelve years. He said that man was lucky that he had made his escape, or he would have sent him prisoner to Canada. These transactions are entirely inconsistent with the treaties subsisting between the two crowns, and contrary to my instructions from his Majesty, whereby I am directed to prevent any foreign power settling or building any fortresses on his Majesty's lands."

" Add

(17)

" Add to the aforementioned unjuſtifiable inſults of the French, the cruel and barbarous murder in cool blood, of a whole family in this dominion, man, wife, and five children, no longer ago than laſt month; and very lately a poor man on the ſouth branch of Potomack, robbed of his ſon; theſe depredations were ſaid to be done by the French Indians, but if I be rightly informed, ſome of the French ſubjects always go with the Indians on theſe incurſions, and are both privy to, and inſtigators of, their robberies and murders."
On the 19th day of February the following proclamation was publiſhed.

Complains of the murder of a family in Virginia.

Virginia ſſ. By the Honourable Robert Dinwiddie Eſq, his Majeſty's lieutenant governor and commander in chief of the colony and dominion of Virginia.
A Proclamation for encouraging perſons to enter into his Majeſty's ſervice for the defence and ſecurity of this colony.

Proclamation.

Whereas it is determined that a fort be immediately built *on the river Ohio, at the fork of Monaungahela*, to oppoſe any farther encroachments or hoſtile attempts of the French and the Indians in their intereſt, and for the ſecurity and protection of his Majeſty's ſubjects in this colony, and as it is abſolutely neceſſary that a ſufficient force ſhould be raiſed to erect and ſupport the ſame; for an encouragement to all who ſhall immediately and voluntarily enter into the ſaid ſervice, I do hereby notify and promiſe, by and with the advice and conſent of his Majeſty's council of this colony, that over and above their pay, *Two hundred thouſand acres of his Majeſty the king of Great Britain's lands, on the eaſt ſide of the river Ohio within this dominion, (one hundred thouſand acres whereof to be contiguous to the ſaid fort, and the other hundred thouſand acres to be on or near the river Ohio)* ſhall be laid off and granted to ſuch perſons who by their voluntary engagements and good behaviour in the ſaid ſervice, ſhall deſerve the ſame. And I farther promiſe that the ſaid lands ſhall be divided amongſt them immediately after the performance of the ſaid ſervice agreeable to their reſpective rank, and in proportion to their reſpective merit as ſhall be repreſented to me by their ſuperior officers, and held and enjoyed by them, *without paying any rights, and alſo free from the payment of quit-rents for the term of fifteen years.* And I do appoint this proclamation to be read and publiſhed at the court-houſes, churches, and chapels in each county within this colony, and that the ſheriffs take care the ſame be done accordingly.

Governor fixes on the ſpot where the Ohio company had begun their fort.

Promiſes thoſe who ſhall enter the ſervice 200,000 acres of land on the Ohio.

Free from rights, or payment of quit-rents for 15 years.

Given at the council chamber in Williamſburg on the 19th day of February, in the 27th year of his Majeſty's reign, annoque domini 1754.   Robert Dinwiddie.
                    God ſave the King.

The company were far from thinking themſelves bound by ſuch a proclamation, and it would not have had all the intended effect if they had entered a caveat againſt it; but as they looked upon it as the moſt effectual method that could be taken at that time for the end propoſed, and that it was for the advantage of the public, they unanimouſly agreed to acquieſce; and at the ſame time propoſed the Monaungahela as a boundary, that the 200,000 acres for the officers and ſoldiers ſhould be laid off on the upper ſide, allowing the company as many tracts of about a thouſand acres each, as ſhould be neceſſary upon the main road which they had cleared, from their ſtorehouſe at Will's Creek to the Monaungahela, for the building proper ſtore-houſes at convenient ſtages, and providing corn and hay for the great number of horſes neceſſary to carry on their trade, and make their ſettlement. This the principal officers not only approved of, but declared that they looked upon the contiguity of the company's lands as one of the greateſt advantages that could be, as they would be thereby enabled, not only to ſettle their land, but ſupply themſelves with neceſſaries from the company's ſtores, on much better terms than otherwiſe they could poſſibly do in that part of the world; and as their land would likewiſe be rendered of much greater value by having the road running through it, by which all perſons going to or from the Ohio muſt paſs, ſo that as ſoon as it could be ſettled, they could not fail to meet a conſtant market for every thing they could raiſe: And as by this means the fort could not fail of being plentifully and cheaply ſupplied from their own ſettlements on the one ſide, and the company's on the other, which would alſo greatly contribute to its ſtrength and the ſecurity of that frontier.

Company though not obliged, acquieſce in this propoſal, and agree to a boundary between themſelves and the military.

Officers approve of the company's propoſal.

The aſſembly of Virginia granted ten thouſand pounds for making proviſion for 300 men with proper officers for an expedition to the Ohio; but that of Maryland, which had been called together upon the ſame occaſion, abſolutely refuſed to contribute a ſhilling; and the buſineſs of enliſting went on ſo ſlowly in Virginia, that it was the 18th day of April before lieutenant colonel Waſhington reached Wincheſter with his diviſion, and though he had come from Alexandria it muſt appear from his following letter to colonel Creſap, that he was not overſtocked with proviſions.

Aſſembly grant 10,000l. to raiſe 300 men.

SIR,
The difficulty of getting waggons has almoſt been inſurmountable. We have found ſo much inconvenience attending it here in theſe roads, that I am determined to carry all our proviſions &c. out on horſeback, and ſhould be glad if captain Trent, with your aſſiſtance, would procure as many horſes as poſſible, againſt we arrive at Will's Creek, that as little ſtoppage as poſſible may be made there. I have ſent William Jenkins with 60 yards of Oſnabrigs for bags, and hope you will be as expeditious as you can, in getting them made and filled.

Colonel Waſhington finds great difficulty in procuring proviſions, &c.

Major Carlyle acquainted me that a number of kettles, tomhawks, beſt gun flints, and axes might be had from the Ohio company's ſtore, which we are much in want of, and ſhould be glad to have laid by for us. Hoes we ſhall alſo want.

E   I hope

(18)

I hope all the flour you have, or can get, you will save for this purpose, and other provisions and necessaries which you think will be of use (that may not occur to my memory at present) will be laid by till our arrival, which I expect will be at Job Pearsall's, about Saturday night or Sunday next, at present I have nothing more to add than that I am

Your most humble servant,
G. Washington.

As the French had in captain Trent's absence come down from Venango and surprized the fort, it may be proper in the first place to insert that account of it, published by authority in the Virginia Gazette, which was in these words.

Account of the French taking the fort, begun by captain Trent, on the Ohio.
French force.

"Williamsburg May 9th. On Saturday last arrived in Town from Ohio, ensign Edward Ward of captain Trent's company with an Indian messenger from the half king. Mr. Ward informs us, That on the 17th of last month the French consisting of about 1000 men, under the command of monsieur Contrecœur, came from Venango in 300 canoes and 6 battoes, with 18 pieces of cannon to the forks of Monongahela, where he with 33 soldiers were in garrison. That as soon as they landed, they marched in regular order within

Summon to surrender.

a musket shot of the fort, and demanded an immediate surrender, threatening on his refusal, to take it by force. The great superiority of the French obliged him to give it up, having obtained liberty to march out, with every thing he had in the fort. The next day, with his men, he set out to meet the forces ordered from Alexandria to reinforce him, and at Will's Creek met lieutenant colonel Washington with 150 men under his command; Colonel Washington on hearing this account thought it unadviseable to proceed to the forks with so small a force, but determined to march to Red Stone Creek about 37 miles from the fort, and there intrench himself, till he should be joined by colonel Fry, who had the command of the regiment, and was expected would bring up the remainder of it.

Remarks on the half king's speech.

"The speech brought by the Indian messenger, from the half king is full of the warmest expressions of friendship and attachment to the English interest. His honour the governor dispatched him on Tuesday, with a firm assurance of a vigorous assistance."

The following are copies of the summon and the half king's speech, as well as the other particulars from ensign Ward's relation published in the Gazette.

French summon.

"A summon by order of Contrecœur, captain of one of the companies of the detachment of the French marine, commander in chief of his most Christian Majesty's troops now on the Beautiful River, to the commander of those of the King of Great Britain, at the mouth of the river Monongaly.

SIR,

"Nothing can surprize me more than to see you attempt a settlement upon the lands of the king my master; and it obliges me Sir to send the chevalier La Mercier commander of the artillery of Canada, and captain of the bombardiers, to demand, by what authority Sir you are come to fortify yourself within the dominions of the king my master. This action seems

Lands on the Ohio belong to the French king.

so contrary to the last treaty of peace concluded at Aix la Chapelle, between his most Christian Majesty and the King of Great Britain, that I do not know to what to impute such an usurpation; as it is incontestible that the lands situate upon the Beautiful River belong to his most Christian Majesty. I am informed Sir that your undertaking has been concerted

Blames the company.

by none else, than a company who have more in view the advantage of a trade, than the desire of preserving the union and harmony which subsists between the crowns of France and Great Britain; although Sir it is as much the interest of your nation as ours to maintain it.

Summons Mr. Ward to retire with his troops, and promises him protection; and in case of a refusal threatens force.

"Let it be as it will Sir, if you come into this place charged with orders, I summon you in the name of the king my master, by virtue of my general's commands, to retreat peaceably with your troops from the lands of my king, and not to return, or I find myself obliged to fulfil my duty and compel you to it. And I hope Sir you will not defer a moment or force me to the last extremity: in the first case Sir, assure yourself that I will give orders that there shall be no hostility committed by my detachment. I prevent you Sir,

Governor of Virginia cannot give orders in the French king's territories.
If come to trade only, would seize and confiscate his goods.

from the trouble of asking me one hour of delay, or consent to receive orders from your governor; he can give none within the dominions of the king my master, those which I have received of my general are my laws, which I cannot depart from. If on the contrary Sir you have not got orders and only come to trade, I am sorry to tell you, that I am obliged to seize your goods, and confiscate your effects to the use of the Indians our children, allies, and friends, as you are not allowed to carry on a contraband trade; it was for this reason Sir, that last year we stopped two Englishmen who were trading upon our lands. The king my master asks nothing but his right, nor has he the least intention to disturb that good harmony and friendship which reigns between his Majesty, and the King of Great

Governor of Canada had endeavoured to maintain the peace.

Britain. The governor of Canada can give proof, of having done his utmost endeavours to maintain that union which reigns between two friendly princes; for he having heard, that the Iroquois, and Nipisingues inhabitants of the lakes, had struck and destroyed an English family towards Carolina, barred up the road, and obliged them to give up to him a little boy, the only one left alive of that family, which Mr. Welrick a merchant of Montreal has carried to Boston; and he has moreover forbid the Indians exercising their accustomed cruelties, upon the English our friends.

Complains of endeavours to excite the Indians to strike.

"I could Sir bitterly complain of the means taken all last winter, to instigate the Indians to take up the hatchet and strike us, while we were striving to maintain the peace.

"I am

(19)

"I am well assured Sir of the polite manner in which you will receive Mr. Le Mercier, as
well out of regard to his errand, as his distinction and personal merit. I expect you will
send him back with one of your officers, who will bring me a precise answer. As you have
some Indians with you, I have desired Mr. Le Mercier who understands their language, to
inform them of my resolutions upon this subject. I am with great respect Sir

Done at our camp   Your most humble and obedient servant,
April 16, 1754.   Contrecœur.

"The French landed within 150 yards of the fort, from whence they sent Monsieur Le   *French disembark near*
Mercier attended with drums, colours, and a strong guard, to the officer in the fort, and *the fort.*
summoned him immediately to evacuate it, Mr. Ward desired time to send to his lieutenant
(Frafer) who was within a few miles, which Monsieur Le Mercier agreed to allow him at
first, but as soon as he saw the cannon safely landed and mounted on the bank, he took
out his watch, said it was twelve o'clock and not worth waiting. He then told Mr. Ward
he would allow him an hour to march off his men, with all their baggage and stores, of
which he did not take a farthing's worth, but offered to let him pay himself out of a chest *Offer money for some*
of money, for some necessaries they wanted. As our men came out the French entered, *necessaries.*
but behaved with great civility, said it might be their fate ere long to surrender it again,
and they would set a good example. They immediately went to work, removing some of
the logs, as they complained the fort was not to their liking, and at break of day next
morning 50 men went off with axes to cut more logs to enlarge it.

         "The Speech of the Half King &c. was in these terms,

"April 18th. 1754 From the Fort of Ohio.

     "A speech from the Half King (Scruniattha) and (the Belt of Wampum) an Indian *Half king and Belt*
chief so called, to the governors of Virginia and Pennsylvania.   *of Wampum's speech*
                                                                                             sent down by two In-
                                                                                             dians with ensign
"Brothers the English; The bearer is to let you know, how we are used by the French. *Ward.*
We have been waiting long for the French to strike, now we see what they design to do
with us. We are ready to strike them now, and wait for your assistance; be strong and
come as soon as possible, and you shall find us true brothers, and as ready to strike them
as you are. We have sent these two young men to see when you will be ready to come,
and then they are to return to us, and let us know where you are, that we may come and
meet you, and we desire (if it is convenient) that the men from both provinces would meet
at the forks of the road. If you do not now come to our relief we are gone intirely, and
shall never meet more I believe, which grieves my heart. *To confirm this here is my
wampum.*
"Here he delivered a string of wampum to ensign Ward, and then added—Now I depend
upon you to go, with these two young men to both governors yourself, for I have no dependence on those that are gone so long and have never returned or sent any word."
"A true copy as delivered Edward Ward by John Davison the interpreter."

Though the French had thus taken possession with so large a force, which by some accounts
were encreased to 1500 or 1600 men, the government thought proper to publish the following
advertisement in the Virginia Gazette of May 16. 1754.

                   By order of the governor and council of Virginia.

"The method of taking up lands in this colony, and the easy terms on which they are *Governor and coun-*
held of the king, not being well known to the inhabitants of the northern provinces, may *cil advertise the me-*
be the reason that so few of those people, though much straitned for good lands, travel *thod, and expence of*
hither in search of a fine soil, and greater extent of country; and therefore the publishing the *Virginia.*
method and terms on which they are granted here, may be of use to promote the settlement
and cultivation of the finest lands (perhaps in the world) that lie to the westward of the Allegany mountains, along the several branches of the Mississippi. With that view this authentic state of the rules in taking up, and patenting lands in this government are offered to
the public."
"The expences on a large tract of land being less in proportion than on a smaller, the calculation is here made on a tract of 1000 acres, which may be looked upon as a moderate
quantity."
"Whoever inclines to take up any quantity of land not exceeding four hundred acres, may *Surveyor of the coun-*
enter for the same with the surveyor of the county in which the land lies, who can furnish *ty can give rights for*
rights for the same. But if a larger quantity is wanted, he must petition the governor and *less than 400 acres.*
council; for which petition and order of council the clerk of that board has,   *Must petition the go-*
                                                                                                  vernor and council
                                                                                                                            for larger quantities.

                                                                                       A fee

(20)

	l.	*s.*	*d.*
" A fee of - - - - - - - - - - - - - - - -	0	10	9
" For entering the order of council in the auditor's office, and a cer- " tificate thereof - - - - - - - - - - - - - - -	0	5	9
" For 20 rights, at 5s. Sterling each, or 6s. 3d. currency, - -	6	5	0

" Each right entitles the bearer to 50 acres of his majesty's land,
" as the consideration for which it is granted, being certificates of
" so much paid in for that end.

	l.	*s.*	*d.*
" Upon producing the order of council and these rights to the sur- " veyor of the county in which the land lies, he is obliged to sur- " vey (as soon as prior entries or orders will permit) for which his " fee is 500 pounds of tobacco payable beyond the mountains at " three farthings per pound, - - - - - - - - - -	1	11	3
" After the survey is finished, the party is to return the plot of the " land with the rights, to the secretary's office in the general " court next following, and pay the fee to the secretary for mak- " ing out the patent on parchment, and recording it in his " office, -	0	10	9
" And also to the governor for the seal and his signing it, - - -	1	1	6

Charge of taking up 1000 acres 8l. 4s. sterling.

" So the whole charge of 1000 acres is about 8 *l.* 4 *s.* sterling, or " in Virginia currency being 5 *l.* per *oz.* gold, and 6 *s.* 8 *d.* per " *oz.* silver, - - - - - - - - - - - - - - - - - -	10	5	0

" If the survey is above 1000 acres, the surveyor's fee is 30 pounds of tobacco for every
" hundred acres more; and excepting this and the right money, the charge is the same on
" every patent above 400 acres: but that quantity or under, may be had without the fee
" to the auditor, and that to the clerk of the council. The patentee holds his land in fee-

Patentee has a fee-simple in the lands from the date of his patent.
Yearly quit-rent 2s. sterling per hundred acres.

" simple to him and his heirs for ever, from the date of his patent, upon paying yearly the
" easy quit-rent to his majesty, of one shilling sterling for every fifty acres, and making in
" three years time an easy cultivation on the land."

Act of assembly of Virginia exempts protestants settling lands over the mountains, from all public demands for 15 years.

" And for a farther encouragement to settle on the waters of Missisippi the general assembly
" have (last November) enacted, That whereas a considerable number of persons, as well his
" majesty's natural-born subjects as foreign protestants, are willing to come into this colony
" with their families and effects, and settle on the said waters, if properly en-
" couraged; it is therefore enacted, *That all persons being protestants, who shall settle and
" reside on any lands situate on the westward of the Allegany ridge, shall be exempted from
" the payment of all public, county, and parish levies for the term of fifteen years next en-
" suing.*"

Naturalization easy and cheap; and allowed indulgences of the act of toleration.

" And for a farther encouragement to foreign protestants, naturalization is made very
" easy and cheap to them, and they are allowed all the indulgences of the act of toleration
" here."

As these are indisputably the terms upon which any persons, even foreigners, might have
taken up lands upon the Ohio, *it will appear, that all the advantage allowed the Ohio company*

Company's grant would have cost only 1000l. and in lieu are obliged to settle 100 families.

*was an exemption of the rights of 200,000 acres of land, which would have amounted to 1000l.
sterling, but in lieu of this, they were obliged to settle 100 families upon the land, which was after the
rate of one family for every 10 l.* Whether the company could gain any thing by such a bargain may be submitted, without mentioning that they were obliged by another condition of
their grant to advance near ten times that sum, in carrying on a trade to supply the Indians
with goods, the greatest part of which is inevitably lost, by the hostilities on the Ohio. The
advertisement however had no effect; for it is certain that the inhabitants of the northern provinces, had long been acquainted with the easy terms of taking up lands in this government,
the frontier counties of Frederick and Agusta, having been for the most part seated by people
from those parts; but it is as well known to them, that no sooner was there a probability of

Persons deterred by Russel's proceedings from settling.

seating that frontier, than the before-mentioned Mr. Russell, under colour of some entries in
the name of himself, and some great men, whom he gave out to be his partners, so harrassed
those poor people who had settled there, by caveats and trials before the governor and council,
two or three hundred miles distant from their houses, that many of them removed back to
their former habitations, and those who were not to be tired out, had at length the mortification to find that their costs, occasioned by the contestations with him, exclusive of their
own trouble, and riding many thousand miles, amounted to more than Russell and his partners
pretended to sell lands for, in that part of the country. And when many of those people (as

Page 8.

has been mentioned) contracted with Mr. Gist in behalf of the company to settle their lands,
and some of them had actually seated thereon, when they found the same Mr. Russell including them in his survey, boasting of the interest of his partners, and setting the Ohio company
at defiance, it not only prevented the rest of the people from coming according to their agreement, but some of those who had come, returned to their former habitations, and have given their
neighbours such impressions of taking up lands in Virginia, that it is notorious some thousands have since that time passed through this colony to go to the southward, and take up

worse

worse lands there, on worse terms. However not only strangers have been deterred ever since the French took possession of the Ohio, from settling in those parts, but some hundred families much nearer in, have deserted their plantations, and many of them very valuable ones, to escape the Indian's cruelty.

It would be needless as well as ungrateful to mention the several transactions since that time; during which, except the defeating a party of French, and taking Monsieur La Force and twenty other prisoners on the 28th day of May 1754, we have met almost a constant series of misfortunes, until general Forbes happily recovered the possession of the country, and the French deserted Fort Du Quesne in December 1758. *It is impossible to reckon up how many lives the war has cost this colony, but our expence is too well ascertained by the acts of assembly, which have laid us under a load of taxes for ten years yet to come. The share of Virginia, has notwithstanding been so grosly misrepresented, that it seems necessary to inform the public, that colony has raised for that purpose, from February 1754 to this time, no less than 399625 l. of their currency. It may be said that Virginia has been reimbursed 52814 l. 19 s. sterling, as his late majesty was graciously pleased to allot so much to that colony, out of the money granted him, by two acts of the parliament of Great Britain, in the years 1757 and 1758, but it is as certain that 50000 l. current money part thereof, has been already appropriated towards recruiting, paying, subsisting, and other expences of the Virginia regiment until the 1st of December 1761, as well as what may be necessary to discharge the arrears due to the militia, and the damages done by the Indians, as settled and allowed by the last assembly. So that there will be little or nothing to be deducted out of the said 399625 l. advanced by that colony, for carrying on the war.* A sum that when compared with the contributions of the northward provinces (among whom almost all the money that came from England as well as Virginia, and the neighbouring provinces, circulated, to their very great advantage) will be found to exceed the proportion of Virginia very largely.

The committee of the Ohio company (who were invested with the company's full power) were in hopes as soon as the possession was regained, they might have been allowed to survey their first 200000 acres, and gave Mr. Gist (who had with much difficulty after a long application obtained a commission from the college for that purpose) instructions, to set about it immediately, that they might not be charged with the least delay; but they were informed by general Stanwix that he had assured the Indians, that no settlements should for some time be made upon the Ohio, and that as soon as they were allowed, the company should have notice. But Mr. Gist dying last year of the small-pox, and the committee being informed that the Pennsylvanians, and several others were preparing to survey the lands in those parts, which their company claim, not only by the express words of his majesty's instructions, but by Mr. Penn's promise to Mr. Hanbury, in case they lay within the province of Pennsylvania (which if the bounds between that province and Virginia, were truly surveyed) it is presumed they would not, they applied to the college to procure a commission to some other person, in the room of the said Gist, to survey the same, when the president and masters informed them, that though the power of appointing surveyors was vested in them by the college charter, they could not grant any such commission without the consent of the governor and council, who had resolved that none should be granted, or any lands surveyed in those parts, till they had received instructions for that purpose, from his majesty, or the board of trade.

The committee being still alarmed by fresh informations, and particularly by that of lieutenant colonel Stephen, who was just come from Pittsburg, and was in his way to Williamsburg to wait upon the governor, desired one of their members to make some proper application to the governor upon that occasion, to whom he thereupon wrote the following letter.

Honourable Sir,

As I am one of the Ohio company, I was a good deal alarmed by colonel Stephen's information, that the Pennsylvanians, and foreigners were about to survey large quantities of land upon the Ohio, within this government. *I think I may venture to say, that company had not only a prior claim, in virtue of his majesty's instruction, but that the considerations therein mentioned, were public and valuable ones; and that they first, at their own expence, made such discoveries of those parts as could be depended on, cleared the public roads, took possession, and were about to build a fort, and warehouses for carrying on their trade, where Pittsburg now stands, are facts not to be controverted. Yet when this government thought proper, to pitch on that place to build a fort, for the public defence, and to issue a proclamation promising two hundred thousand acres of land (one hundred thousand of which were to be contiguous to the fort) as an encouragement to the officers, and soldiers who should enter into the service to repel the French encroachments*; it is notorious, that the company readily submitted, desiring only such reasonable tracts of land, at proper stages, and convenient distances along the road, they had been at the charge of clearing, as should be judged necessary, for building storehouses, and securing their carriages, employed in transporting goods from their storehouse at Wills creek, to a proper place on the Monongahela, where they proposed to build their boats. These terms were adjudged by the principal officers, and persons concerned, to be not only reasonable, but greatly advantagious to the proprietors of the adjoining lands; *and such was the general opinion at that time, of the great utility of the company's undertaking, that the earl of Granville, lord Baltimore and Mr. Penn (according to Mr. Hanbury's information) assured him they should have what quantities of land they desired, for securing their settlements, and extending their trade within their respective proprietaries, on the same terms they had procured the grant from his majesty.*

I am sensible the company has been charged with delay in not having surveyed their lands long since, and it is too tedious a subject to enter upon their vindication; however I think I may

F

General Forbes recovered possession of the Ohio.

Virginia contributed 399625 l. to carry on the war.
Money allotted by parliament how applied.

Gist ordered to begin surveying; prevented by general Stanwix's engagements to the Indians.

Gist dies.

Apply for another surveyor.
College forbid by governor and council to issue any new commission.

Letter from a member of the company to the governor.
Company's claim set forth, and their proceedings.

P. 17.
Lands within the company's bounds promised to the officers, &c.
Company acquiesce under the proclamation, and enter into an agreement with the officers.

Earl of Granville, Lord Baltimore, and Mr. Penn promise to grant the company lands.

(22)

may venture to affirm, they did every thing in their power, and if so, it is certain they cannot be *justly* blamed. They did indeed at length procure a commission for Mr. Gist to survey their lands, but as soon as he got it, hostilities recommenced, and he unfortunately died, though he would have made a considerable progress in it, if general Stanwix had permitted him. As I was afterwards informed that my son was applying for a commission, I thought whether he obtained it or not, I might depend upon him, for timely notice when, and to whom the commission would be granted; but having heard nothing from him on that head, and not dreaming that the company had any other competitors than the officers, and soldiers claiming under the proclamation, with whom I did not doubt every thing would be easily and amicably settled, *I made myself very easy till colonel Stephen acquainted me, that no commission is yet granted to any person in this colony, and that he expects before any is, great tracts will be surveyed, and among them, those very lands engaged by the proclamation, and others absolutely necessary to carry on the Indian trade*; and this, for persons who I doubt will prove very bad neighbours, and take every measure in their power, to exclude us from that trade, and every other advantage they can deprive us of. I therefore presume your honour will take such measures, as you shall judge necessary, to prevent such an encroachment, and that you will not suffer any lands to be surveyed, or taken up in those parts, before the people of this colony have their just claims first satisfied.

Complains of the act to regulate the Indian trade passed by the assembly of Pennsylvania. I have not yet seen the last act of assembly past in Pennsylvania, relating to the Indian trade, but from a letter of captain Trent to colonel Lomax, it is a most insolent attempt to engross to themselves, that whole trade on the Ohio, notwithstanding that river is without their province, and within this colony. *Yet this they may effectually compass, if they can secure those lands they proposed to survey, which may properly be called the Key of the Ohio, as through them, are all the roads, and passes both from north and south that lead to that river*; the consequences of which would be so fatal to this colony, that I greatly dread them, and fear they depend on some other interest than their own. Should they first seize the possession, however unjust their claim, it would be very troublesome to remove them, though in the end it should be effected; so that a timely prevention can alone answer all good purposes.

I have not time to enumerate the many disadvantages this colony must suffer by such a loss; I must therefore beg leave to refer your honour to colonel Stephen, who is so well acquainted with those parts, that it would be a piece of presumption in me, to undertake a task, would my time permit, which he can execute so much better. I am with the greatest regard,

Honourable Sir, your most obedient servant
J. Mercer.

To the honourable Francis Fauquier, Esq,
his majesty's lieutenant-governor and
commander in chief of Virginia.

Whether the Pennsylvanians are properly charged with an attempt to engross the Indian trade or not, will depend on the construction of their own acts of assembly, the first made in 1758, and the other in 1759.

Pennsylvania acts. By these acts a sum not exceeding 14000 l. is to be taken up at interest, for carrying on a trade with the Indians, under the direction of nine commissioners, or a majority of them, on account of the province during five years; at the end of which term, if the profits of the trade should prove insufficient to repay the money lent with interest, the deficiency is to be made good by a tax on all the estates real and personal within the province. Though this alone might have been sufficient to deter all private companies or traders from intermedling with the Indian trade, as the commissioners would no doubt order their agents to undersel them; Persons prohibited from trading with the Indians. See act, p. 389. Penalty, p. 389. yet to make sure work, it is enacted that no person or persons, other than the commissioners, their agents and assistants, shall sell, exchange, or barter with any Indian or Indians, any goods, wares, or merchandizes whatsoever (provisions only excepted) beyond the Kittocktenny hills, on any pretence whatsoever, under the penalty of fifty pounds, and six months imprisonment without bail or mainprize; the offence to be tried in any court of the said province, where Agents empowered to search for goods &c. p. 389. the person offending shall be arrested or apprehended. And it is also enacted, that the said agents, and every of them, as often as they shall be informed, or have reason to believe, that any quantity of strong liquors, goods, wares, and merchandizes are carried out, and transported beyond the Kittocktenny hills, with design to sell, barter and exchange the same with the Indians, shall have power, and are required with their assistants and servants to visit all suspected places, and search for such strong liquors, goods, wares and merchandizes, and being found beyond the limits aforesaid, to seize the same as forfeited.

Pennsylvanians under their law may seize the company's goods. As the Pennsylvanians insist that Pittsburg (in which neighbourhood the Ohio company's trade with the Indians had been carried on before the war) lies within their province, will not the courts of that province determine, that any of the Ohio company's servants or agents, or any Virginians selling, exchanging, or bartering with the Indians any liquors, goods, wares, or merchandizes at that place have incurred the forfeiture of fifty pounds, and six months imprisonment by their act of assembly; or rather will they not seize their liquors and goods, Pennsylvania ought not to have an exclusive trade with the Indians. as soon as they find them between the Kittocktenny hills and Pittsburg? And if the Pennsylvanians can carry on an exclusive trade with the Indians for five years, though they were not to use any methods to prejudice them against the Virginians (as was undoubtedly the case when Mr. Gist first went out on the Ohio) it is well known how difficult a matter it is, to reduce a Virginia most convenient for the Indian trade. trade to its former channel, after it has been once diverted. That the trade upon the Ohio is most convenient to be carried on from Virginia is notorious to every one acquainted with the geography of the country, and the passes through the mountains; and that it would be carried on from thence can't be doubted, except the persons engaged in it, should be subjected

to-

(23)

to inconveniences which it might not be in the power of that government to redress. And such might, and will be the case, if the Pennsylvanians are suffered by surveying, or in any manner securing (as within their province) the lands about Pittsburg, as through them, and by no other passage, the trade must be carried on upon the Ohio, whether it is from Pennsylvania or Virginia, with this very material difference, *that though the Pennsylvanians should carry their point, and secure the lands about Pittsburg, yet they would be obliged to carry on their trade upon the Ohio to the best advantage, to import their goods into the river Potomack, to be thence conveyed to the Ohio, through the very lands the Ohio company have purchased, and by the very roads they were at the expence of clearing, in order to comply with the terms of their grant.* [*Pittsburg commands all the Ohio. Must import goods into the river Potomack.*]

The committee of the Ohio company receiving no answer by colonel Stephen, but that no lands were to be surveyed in those parts, until some particular instruction should be received from his majesty, to that purpose, afterwards applied to the governor and council, but without the least effect; they even refused to grant them a certificate that any application had ever been made to them, in the company's behalf. [*Company informed by the governor that no lands will be granted till particular instructions should be received from the king, and then apply to the governor and council, who even refuse a certificate of the proceedings.*]

Under these circumstances, the company have no way left but to apply (as they did in the first instance) to his majesty, and represent their case, with such vouchers of the facts, as could not be contested. [*Company resolve to apply again to the king.*]

Such is the state here contained, and upon it they must submit, whether they have not done every thing in their power, to comply with the terms of their grant, and if so, whether they should be blamed for what they could by no means prevent? [*Company recapitulate their proceedings.*]

They, without the least delay, *employed proper persons to discover those parts (then in a manner unknown) cleared proper roads, purchased lands, built houses, imported large cargoes, cultivated a friendship with the Indians (then greatly prejudiced against the people of Virginia) and supplied them with goods, on such terms, as would have secured their friendship, if they could have been protected from the French; they began to settle the lands by seating several families, and to build the fort as soon as the consent of the Indians could be obtained, and by these means have sunk several thousand pounds, a sum more than sufficient to have taken up and secured the whole* 500,000 *acres which they petitioned for.* In the mean time, the people of Virginia as well as the adjacent provinces (in echo to the French cant in Contrecoeur's summons) affected to charge the war on the Ohio company, and to exclaim against their grant, while many of them, without one shilling advantage to the public, or one farthing expence to themselves, except half a pistole to the clerk of the council, have made large sums of money by surveying and selling much more of his majesty's lands to strangers. The company are far from denying, *they even acknowledge and with a good deal of satisfaction, that some of them early foresaw the consequences of the French eacroachments. on his majesty's American dominions, they were sensible, that as the French were imperceptibly stealing into possession, they wanted nothing but time to carry their point.* In this very crisis they applied and obtained his majesty's instruction; but intent on promoting the public interest, jointly with their own, and to reconcile the Indians, who complained of the encroachments made by the government of Virginia, upon their lands, took every method, at however great an expence, to effect their purposes. The Indians (far from being the ignorant people they are generally supposed to be in Europe) finding the English and French contending for their friendship, and leave to build among them, and believing they should be able to hold the scales, and direct the balance as they would, with even French policy pretended, that (notwithstanding the treaty at Lancaster) they still had the absolute property, in what they called their lands. [*Company charged with bringing on the war. Company foresee the French designs. Indian policy.*]

An indisputable proof of this, is the Half King's speech to the French general, as communicated by himself to colonel Washington, at the Loggstown November 25th. 2753. in these words: Fathers, I am come to tell you your own speeches, what your own mouths have declared. Fathers, You in former days set a silver bason before us, wherein there was the leg of a beaver, and desired of all nations to come and eat of it, to eat in peace and plenty; and not to be churlish to one another; and if any person should be found to be a disturber, you said, I here lay down by the edge of the dish a rod, which you must scourge them with, and if I your father, should get foolish in my old days, I desire you may use it upon me as well as others. [*Half King's speech to the French general.*]

Now Fathers, it is you that are the disturbers in this land, (by coming and building your towns) and taking it away unknown to us, and by force. [*Charges the French with taking away their lands without their consent.*]

Fathers, we kindled a fire a long time ago, at a place called Montreal, where we desired you to stay, and not to come and intrude upon our land. I now desire you may dispatch to that place, for be it known to you, Fathers, that this is our land, and not yours. [*Asserts a claim to the lands.*]

Fathers, I desire you may hear me in civilness; if not, we must handle that rod which was laid down for the use of the obstreperous. If you had come in a peaceable manner, like our brothers the English, we should not have been against your trading with us, as they do, but to come, fathers, and build great houses upon our land, and to take it by force, is what we cannot submit to.

Fathers, both you and the English are white, we live in a country between, therefore the land belongs to neither one nor t'other: The great Being above allowed it to be a place of residence for us; so, fathers, I desire you to withdraw, as I have done our brothers the English; for I will keep you at arms length, I lay this down as a trial for both, to see which will have the greatest regard to it, and that side we will stand by, and make equal sharers with us. Our brothers the English have heard this, and I come now to tell it to you, for I am not afraid to discharge you off this land. [*Denies either English or French have a right to the lands. Orders the French to withdraw.*]

But

(24)

Indians pretend to be ignorant of the English claim, &c.

But should this authority be contested, did not the Ohio Indians inform the Virginia commissioners at the treaty at the same place, the June before, that they never understood, that the lands sold at the treaty of Lancaster, to the king of Great Britain, extended farther west than the warrior's road at the foot of the Alligany mountain? And did not the same Indians insist, that the English should not build or settle on the north side of the Ohio? Nay do they not now insist, after the glorious success that has attended his majesty's arms, upon their right to the lands, and that the English shall not settle upon them? And what does the Ohio company desire? Not that his majesty or any of his subjects should enter into any difference or dispute with the Indians, or incur one shilling's expence on their account; let them hold the lands as long as his majesty pleases, but when he shall think fit to settle his dominions farther to the west, and to grant any of the lands for that purpose, to any of his subjects, the Ohio company are assured his majesty will not prefer any of his subjects to their prejudice, who have not a juster claim, and at the same time they persuade themselves that none of their fellow-subjects (who regard that golden rule of doing as they would be done by) would desire so unjust a preference.

Company only ask their right, when it is thought proper to settle that country.

Pages 1, 2.

A list of the several orders of council referred to, in the case foregoing of the Ohio company, being all they were able to procure, the clerk of the council having refused to let them have any other copies, without an order of the governor and council, alledging that he was greatly blamed for letting them have copies of the following, viz.

In 1745 John Robinson Esq, one of the council, &c. 100000 acres.
       John Smith, &c. - - - - - - - 50000
       James Patton, &c. - - - - - - 100000
       Henry Downes, &c. - - - - - 50000
       Joh Blair Esq, one of the council, &c. 100000
  1747 William M'Mahon, &c. - ' - - 60000
  1749 Bernard Moore, &c. - - - - - 100000
       John Lewis Esq, one of the council, &c. 800000
       Peyton Randolph Esq, &c. - - - 400000
       William Winston, &c. - - - - - 50000
  1753 Richard Corbin Esq, one of the council, &c. three orders for - - - } 190000

Total 2000000 acres.

There are 123 persons named as concerned in these grants for the   2000000 acres.
Of whom 40 are concerned in grants for less than 10000 acres each, viz. 228333 or 5708 } acres
         24 - - - in grants for - - 10000 - - - 240000 or 10000 } each.
The other 59 have among them the remaining - - - - 1531667 or 25960

        123   2000000

The Ohio company was according to the first scheme to consist of twenty members.

Those originally concerned, were John Hanbury of *London* merchant; Thomas Lee Esq, one of the council of Virginia; Thomas Nelson Esq, another of the council; Thomas Cresap, Daniel Cresap, Jacob Giles, James Wardrop of *Maryland*; Francis Thornton, William Nimmo, John Carlyle, Laurence Washington, Augustine Washington, George Fairfax, and Nathaniel Chapman, of *Virginia*, who are named in the petition to his late majesty. The other six were James Scott, John Tayloe, Presley Thornton, Philip Ludwell Lee, Richard Lee, and Gawin Corbin, of *Virginia*.

Afterwards

Hugh Parker *of Maryland*,
George Mason *of Virginia*,
Arthur Dobbs *of the kingdom of Ireland*,
Samuel Smith
Capel Hanbury } *of the city of London*,
Robert Dinwiddie

came in the room of

Daniel Cresap
John Carlyle
Thomas Nelson Esq,
Francis Thornton
William Nimmo
George Fairfax,

} who resigned.

And

John Mercer *of Virginia* hath since purchased the share of Hugh Parker, deceased.
Robert Carter - - - - - - - - - - the shares of Augustine Washington, and of Gawin Corbin, deceased.
Lunsford Lomax - - - - - - - - the share of Lawrence Washington, deceased.

So that the present partners are

Anno 1760.

1. John Hanbury's representatives, 2. Capel Hanbury; 3. Robert Dinwiddie; 4. Samuel Smith*, *of London*; 5. Arthur Dobbs Esq, now governor of *North Carolina*; 6. Thomas

* Messrs. Hanburys have wrote several times that Mr. Smith will not hold his share, and it is ordered to be disposed of; he was at first admitted on Messrs. Hanburys engaging to be answerable for him.

Cresap,

(25)

Cresap, 7. Jacob Giles, 8. James Wardrop's representatives, and 9. Nathaniel Chapman's ditto. *of Maryland*: 10. Philip Ludwell Lee, 11. John Tayloe, 12. Presley Thornton, and 13, 14. Robert Carter, Esqrs. *of the council of Virginia*: 15. Thomas Ludwell Lee, 16. James Scott, clerk, 17. Richard Lee, 18. George Mason, 19. John Mercer, and 20. Lunsford Lomax, *of Virginia*:

Of which eleven only are the original partners; the other nine claim by purchase.

Philip Ludwell Lee, Thomas Ludwell Lee, James Scott, George Mason, & John Mercer, are the committee; and they prepared the following petition to be presented to his Majesty.

Committee of the Ohio company.

TO THE KING's MOST EXCELLENT MAJESTY.

The petition of the committee of the Ohio Company, in your Majesty's colony and dominion of Virginia, in behalf of themselves, and the rest of their partners. Petition to the King.

Most humbly sheweth,

THAT your Majesty's late royal grandfather, (of blessed memory) was graciously pleased, by his additional instruction, to his lieutenant governor of Virginia, dated at his court at St. James's, the sixteenth day of March, in the twenty second year of his reign, for the considerations therein mentioned, to direct, and require his said lieutenant governor forthwith, to make a *grant or grants to your petitioners and their associates, of two hundred thousand acres of land, betwixt Romanetto and Buffalo Creeks, on the South-side of the river Alleghany, otherwise Ohio, and betwixt the two Creeks and Yellow Creek, on the North-side of the said river; or in such other parts to the West of the Great Mountains, in the said colony of Virginia, as should be adjudged most proper by your petitioners, for making settlements thereon, and extending the British trade in those parts, free from the payment of any rights, as also from the payment of any quit-rents, for the space of ten years, from the date of their grants; at the expiration of which term your petitioners were to pay the usual quit-rents, for so much of the said lands as they should have cultivated within that time.* Provided, that in such *grant or grants*, should be inserted a clause or clauses, declaring, that if your petitioners and their associates did not erect a fort on the said lands, and place a sufficient garrison therein, for the security and protection of the settlers, and likewise seat at their proper expence an hundred families thereon, in seven years the said grant or grants should be void. And the said lieutenant governor was thereby authorized and required as soon as the *said two hundred thousand acres should be settled, a fort erected, and a sufficient garrison placed therein, to make a farther grant or grants to your petitioners and their associates, of three hundred thousand acres more, under the like conditions and restrictions, as the first two hundred thousand acres, and adjoining thereto, within the said limits.*

200,000 acres of land within certain limits, or in such other parts to the west of the great mountains, as the company should choose.
Lands to be free from rights, and also from quit-rents for ten years; then to pay quit-rents for what should be cultivated.

300,000 acres more to be granted as above

That your petitioners upon the first notice of his majesty's said instruction, not only applied to the said lieutenant governor, for the said *grant or grants*, but at their own expence employed proper persons to discover the lands upon the Ohio, and cultivate a friendship with the Indians on that river, and advanced several thousand pounds to begin and carry on a trade with them; besides taking every other step to comply with the conditions of their said grant, according to the true intent and meaning of the said instruction, until the French encroachments upon your majesty's dominions in those parts, brought on a war, in which your petitioners effects were indifferently plundered, by their pretended Indian friends, and the French and Indian enemy; and their debtors in those parts, were for the most part either killed, dispersed, or ruined. Notwithstanding which endeavours, expences, and losses, your petitioners have hitherto been unable to obtain any grant, or grants for any part of the lands mentioned in the said instruction; but have been from time to time put off, by divers pretences, particularly, that the Indians would not suffer the said lands to be settled; though the Indians consent to settle thereon, had been obtained at the treaty at Loggs-town, in June 1752, and your petitioners caused several families to settle, and soon after set about building a fort, at the place now called Pittsburg. And although the government of Virginia pitched upon the same place, as most convenient to build a fort on, at the governments expence, and took the possession thereof from your petitioners, engaging by proclamation, to give one hundred thousand acres of land contiguous thereto, and one hundred thousand acres more, on or near the Ohio, without any rights, or paying any quit rents, for the term of fifteen years, for the encouragement of such officers and soldiers, (over and above their pay) as should enter into his majesty's service, to erect and support the said fort. Yet no other fort was ever built, or undertaken there, but that begun by your petitioners, till the same was retaken from the French, in one thousand seven hundred and fifty eight. Your petitioners having been at the whole expence of that building there, when the French took possession of the Ohio, in April 1754.

Page 17.

That your petitioners have applied to the government here several times, since the possession has been regained, for leave to survey their lands, in order to obtain their grants, but without any manner of success: And at the same time they have great reason to believe, that divers persons are soliciting for grants of the same lands from Pennsylvania, and other places; but as they are conscious, that besides the advantage of his late majesty's instruction in their favour, they cannot be justly charged with either having done, or omitted any thing, to forfeit their right under the same; they most humbly submit their case to your majesty's consideration, and pray that you will be graciously pleased, in consideration of their great losses and expences, and to avoid any farther charges or contestations, by some positive and direct instruction to your governor here, to order your petitioners may have a *grant or grants* for the

Company, on every application in Virginia, refused leave to survey their lands.

G said

said lands, upon the terms aforesaid, or such others, as to your majesty, in your great wisdom shall seem just.

And your petitioners will ever pray.

Phil. Lud. Lee,
G. Mason,
James Scott,
J. Mercer,
Thomas Lud. Lee.

The committee at the same time wrote to governor Dinwiddie, and Messrs. Hanbury, their partners in England, the following letters, dated September 9th, 1761, and which were sent over with the foregoing memorial.

Letter to governor Dinwiddie.

SIR,

As we may expect a peace next winter, and have no doubt North America will be secured to the British government, and that liberty will be then granted to his majesty's subjects in these colonies, to settle the lands on the Ohio; We, the committee of the Ohio company, think it a proper time, as soon as the peace is concluded, to apply for a grant for the lands intended us, by his majesty's instructions to Sir William Gooch, and have for that purpose sent over a petition to his majesty, and a large and full state of our case, and have employed Mr. Charlton Palmer, a man, we are informed, of great capacity and diligence, to solicit our cause, and endeavour by all means to get us a patent in England. He will be directed to apply to our members in London for their advice and assistance; and as no person knows the affair better than Mr. Dinwiddie, nor can it be imagined any of the company have such an acquaintance, or interest with persons in power; let us beg you will please to exert yourself, in getting us a patent by natural bounds, on the best terms possible; for rather than be remitted to the government here, who from jealousy, or some other cause, have ever endeavoured to disappoint us, in every design we could form to settle and improve the lands; we will agree to any reasonable consideration for such a deed from England. But if this cannot be obtained, that the most plain and positive instructions to the governor of Virginia, be procured on terms the most advantagious to the company. We are, &c. James Scott, J. Mercer, G. Mason, Thomas Lud. Lee, Philip Lud. Lee.

Letter to Messrs. Hanbury.

Gentlemen,

As we have reason to expect a peace soon, and think it will be then practicable, to prosecute our intended settlements upon the Ohio; we have thought it absolutely necessary to employ some person in England, to make application at the proper boards on our behalf, as well as to present a petition to his majesty, shewing the reasons why we have hitherto been disabled from complying with the terms mentioned in the royal instructions; and praying some farther indulgences: And for these purposes, we have transmitted to Mr. Charlton Palmer, a full state of the company's case, and have directed him to confer with you on the subject.

We have met with so many discouragements from the government in Virginia, (many of the council being concerned in large entries for land) that rather than have any farther altercation here, we would willingly pay any reasonable consideration, for a patent in England by natural bounds, which we hope will not be thought unreasonable, when the expence we have been at is considered, and the great benefit that will result to the public from our discoveries; and there can not be a stronger proof of the public principles upon which the company have acted, than that they have expended a much larger sum, in searching, and discovering the inland parts of this continent to the Westward, than the composition of all our lands would have amounted to, according to the common rules of granting lands in the inhabited parts of the colony: and it is notorious, that till our discovery, the country on the Ohio, and the fatal consequences of the French encroachments then, were altogether unknown, or not attended to; the inhabitants, even of this colony, being utterly unacquainted with the geography of that country, as is plain from all the late maps, published either here or in England, which are actually laid down from the journals, and discoveries of our agents. But if a patent cannot be obtained in England, we then hope that by a fresh instruction to the governor of Virginia, we may have our time for settling the lands prolonged; the article of the fort altered, or at least mitigated; that we may be allowed to contract with a surveyor of our own, without being liable to the high fees settled by law; and that we may be permitted to survey our lands in small tracts. We think there cannot be any just objection to prolong our time for making settlements, as the encroachments of the French, and the war have hitherto rendered it impossible to proceed in them; and we are at this time told, that the governor has instructions to grant no lands upon the Ohio, for fear of giving offence to the Indians.

Upon the whole, we make no doubt of your assisting and supporting us, in every thing you judge conducive to our common interest; and are gentlemen, &c. Phil. Lud. Lee, Thomas Lud. Lee, J. Mercer, James Scott, G. Mason.

Since

(27)

Since finishing the foregoing memorial and state of the Ohio company's case, the history of the origin and progress of the present war, as published in the London magazine has appeared, in which the author has been guilty of so many mistakes relating to the Ohio company, and some of them of so much consequence, that the committee cannot help making some observations on the following parts of it.

The author says, that in the year 1749, a company consisting of some gentlemen in Virginia, and some merchants in London, was established by charter, under the name of the Ohio company, and to this company was granted *six* hundred thousand acres of land, upon the river Ohio. That in 1751 Mr. Gist, employed by the Ohio company, was upon the Ohio surveying the lands on that river, in order to have six hundred thousand acres of the best of them, and most convenient for the Indian trade laid out, and appropriated to the company. That as the French began to seize and plunder every British trader, they found upon any part of the river Ohio, repeated complaints of their behaviour were made to our governor of Virginia, *where our new Ohio company had such weight*, that at last, towards the end of the year 1753, Major Washington was sent to the French governor of two forts, (on the South-side of the Lake Erie, and upon Beef River), to summon him to retire, and to demand a reason for his hostile proceedings; *and at the same time a resolution was taken to build a fort some where near or upon the forks of the Ohio*. That as the Ohio company, *not only had a great influence in Virginia*, but was obliged to make the utmost use of that influence, *because its very existence depended upon putting a stop to the French incroachments and pretensions upon that river*, the colony of Virginia acted with more vigour than Pennsylvania had done. Before major Washington's return, and before they had heard of the insolent answer given to him by the French commandment, *they had provided, and sent out proper people and materials for erecting a fort, at the confluz of the Ohio and Monaungabela*, which he met upon his return; but upon his report, they might have expected that the French would attack and drive away the people they had sent out, and therefore they should instantly have sent out a strong party to defend their workmen; if it had been for nothing else but to bring the French to blows, and to oblige them, before they could effect their purpose, to commit, what even they must have acknowledged to be an act of hostility. But no such thing was done, and as the people they sent out, were no way provided for war, before the designed fort was near finished, a party of French regular troops came upon them, drove them from their works, and quite out of the country without opposition, and erected a regular fort, at the very place where our people had been at work. This was touching our ministers in a tender part. The Ohio company, which by this encroachment was quite demolished, was their favourite child; almost every member of it was intimately connected with them, *and the company had been at a good deal of expence in getting the country surveyed, and in erecting a capacious warehouse for the Indian trade at Wills's Creek, and making a road to it for wheel carriages*; all which was now in danger of being lost, beside the alluring hopes of making thousands of every hundred they had, or should lay out. This our ministers could not bear; to see their friends so treated, was more insufferable, than any indignity that had been before offered to the nation, and therefore, as soon as advice of this new French encroachment was brought home, it was resolved, it seems, to send orders, or at least to give leave, to our colonies in America, to drive the French from their new fort, upon the Ohio, or at least to defend their own frontier, by force of arms, without considering how impossible it was for our colonies, in their present divided state, to do either the one or the other. The French would certainly have continued to negotiate, as long as we continued not to oppose them, in the encroachments they intended to make upon us in America, and not to disturb them in fortifying themselves in those they had already made: But luckily for us, our Ohio company had too much interest with some of our ministers, to permit either. The country about Fort du Quesne, was what they had set their hearts upon, and was indeed a most desirable morsel; but it was first to be purchased from the Indians, which before seemed to have been forgot, and it was now to be recovered from the French: Of the former the Indians themselves put us in mind, for they had openly declared their resentment of the survey before-mentioned, made by Mr. Gist; and some of those that then inhabited this very country, though formerly our friends, if not our subjects, afterwards joined the French, and were very active against us.—It was resolved to gain some sort of right by purchase from the Indians, but the great difficulty was, how to get our numerous distinct colonies to join in the execution of any one vigorous measure, and it was certain, that they would not all contribute towards the price, that was to be paid to the Indians for the purchase, as they never had a general council, or a general purse.

These are the author's words, but how little he knows of the Ohio company's affairs or interest, must be submitted, when it is certain they have not, nor never had any charter, or a grant for an acre of land, but an instruction to the governor of Virginia, to grant them at first, two hundred thousand acres, on certain conditions, and after those were complied with, three hundred thousand acres more, on the same terms; but so small has been their interest in Virginia, that they never could obtain any grant whatsoever from the government there; though could they have done it, they too well knew the danger of settling on the Ohio, without the Indians consent, and therefore they sent Mr. Gist not to survey their *six* hundred thousand acres of the best and most convenient land, but to discover the country (then very little known to any but the Indian traders, who were wretched geographers, and not to be depended on) and to conciliate the Indians to the inhabitants of Virginia, against whom they were prejudiced by the Pennsylvania traders, who engrossed, and carried on a contraband trade to the Ohio, as that river was out of their government, and a duty upon the skins and furrs they purchased, was payable to the college of William and Mary in Virginia, which they always

smuggled.

Account of the rise and progress of the Ohio company, published in the London magazine.

(28)

smuggled. Mr. Gift had such an acquaintance and influence with the Indians, that he was treated by them with great kindness, advertised of the danger of his intended journey to the Falls, from a party of French, and their Indians, whose principal business was (most probably) to intercept him; and afterwards by his address, at the treaty at Loggs-town, the Indians consent for the Ohio company to settle the lands on Monongahela, was obtained, for which purpose he was empowered by the company, to agree with the Indians for a sum, rather to conciliate their friendship, than by way of purchase; for the company well knew the Six Nations had released to his Majesty, all claim to those lands by the treaty of Lancaster. Major Washington's journey was so far from being occasioned by any interest or weight of the Ohio company, that the different informations received from the Northward, and from captain Trent, of the hostile proceedings of the French, were not only disregarded, but expressly averred to be lies, and to be raised by that company, to serve their own ends; so that the governor could not well avoid sending some person, to be satisfied of the truth of the case: But it appears, that neither he, or the assembly that met the day after the date of major Washington's commission, believed there was any great danger, or at least they could not think it very pressing, for, as he tells them, he proposed to meet the Indians at Winchester in May, before which the French got possession; therefore all the assembly thought requisite to do at that time, was to encourage people to come and settle those parts, by exempting them from paying levies for five years extraordinary, so that no such resolution, as the author mentions, was taken to build a fort at the same time major Washington was sent out; nor did the government, before he returned, or indeed ever afterwards, provide and send out proper people and materials to erect such fort. It is true indeed, that the committee of this company, being at length convinced that it was in vain to expect any countenance, much less assistance from the government of Virginia, and being sensible of the absolute necessity there was to take some speedy measures, had sent out those people, and materials the author mentions, under captain Trent, to build, first a store-house at Redstone Creek, and then, a fort at the fork of Monongahela: These, major Washington in his journal says, he met on the 6th of January 1754, and he returned to Williamsburg the 16th of that month. On the 21st a proclamation issued to call the assembly together on the 14th of February; on the 19th of which month another proclamation was published, for encouragement of those who should enter into the service, in which it is said, *that it was determined a fort should be immediately built on the river Ohio, at the fork of Monongahela*; and as it was absolutely necessary, that a sufficient force should be raised to erect and support it, therefore *two hundred thousand acres of that very land which the Ohio company always looked upon to belong to them, were promised to be distributed among such persons as should immediately and voluntarily enter that service*. But it is notorious, that notwithstanding that determination, the government of Virginia never employed a man, or paid a shilling towards building any such fort. Indeed, when Mr. Trent had built a store-house for the Ohio company at Redstone Creek, and proceeded with their workmen and materials to build the fort, some of his men, which he enlisted as soldiers worked upon it; but it is certain, the Ohio company paid every such workman's wages, till the French took possession of it.

These are the advantages the weight and interest of the Ohio company procured for them in Virginia. They were allowed to be at the sole expence of building a fort, for which their land (at least what they reckoned such) was to be taken from them, and distributed among the officers and soldiers: and afterwards, without even asking their consent, the land which they had purchased at Wills Creek, and where they had erected, as the author mentions, a capacious warehouse, for the sake of carrying on their trade, was taken possession of, as a proper place for a fort, and after the troops had occupied them as long as they found them necessary, they, through mere wantonness, shot the store-house to pieces, to try the metal of their cannon, which obliged the company at the expence of above one thousand pounds to build another there. The French burnt their other store-house at Redstone Creek.

The company had been at many other considerable expences, besides those mentioned by the author. They had likewise given very large credit to the Ohio Indians, all which was not only in danger of being lost, but was actually so, by the French incroachments: but that the Ohio company was thereby quite demolished, or that it was their interest alarmed the ministry, are facts, which the author has taken upon him to advance, without the least foundation, or regard to truth. It was owing to some other motive that the ministers interposed, and however luckily for the nation, the author has been very unlucky in procuring information, or materials for his history, as far as it relates to Virginia, except he imagines, *that abusing the ministry may atone for any defects of that kind*. However delicious the country about Fort du Quesne might be, it was not then to be purchased from the Indians. They had both by treaty and deed sold, and conveyed their right to his Majesty, so long before as the year 1744, and it was impossible they could declare their resentment of a survey that never was made. That some of them, who had been his Majesty's subjects, and indisputably friends to the English, afterwards joined the French, and were active against us, was not therefore owing to their resentment of that survey, but of the non-performance of the promises made them by the governors of the English colonies, to protect them from the French and their Indians, who, notwithstanding destroyed the Twightwee town, in 1752; and yet the English proved so dilatory, and seemed so indifferent about the Indian's defence afterwards, that they seem to have had no other way to save themselves from inevitable destruction, than submitting to, and joining the French, who were at their doors, against the English, who were not only at a great distance, but whom they found by experience, they could not depend upon. But as it may be thought those observations have already exceeded their due bounds, it is time to conclude them.

The

(29)

The company finding they could not obtain permission in Virginia to prosecute their schemes, had determined to apply to the king, to implore his royal protection; and had transmitted to England a full and impartial state of their case, with orders for an immediate application to his majesty: They, in the mean time, however, applied frequently to the governor of Virginia, who as often assured them he had never obtained any fresh instructions on their business; they therefore were prevented from attempting to proceed in any thing over the mountains, especially as a new kind of authority was about this time started, to oppose their designs; colonel Bouquet, who commanded the troops at Pittsburg, having issued the following proclamation.

Col. Bouquet issues a proclamation.

PROCLAMATION.

By Henry Bouquet Esq, colonel of foot, and commanding at Fort Pitt and dependencies.

Whereas by a treaty held at Easton in the year 1758, and afterwards ratified by his majesty's ministers, the country to the west of the Allegheny mountains, is allowed to the Indians, for their hunting ground. And as it is of the highest importance to his majesty's service, and the preservation of the peace, and a good understanding with the Indians, to avoid giving them any just cause of complaint: This is therefore to forbid any of his majesty's subjects to settle, or hunt to the west of the Allegheny mountains, on any pretence whatever, unless such have obtained leave in writing from the general, or the governors of their respective provinces, and produce the same to the commanding officer at Fort Pitt.

Persons forbid to hunt, or settle to the westward of the mountains.

And all the officers and non-commissioned officers commanding at the several posts erected in that part of the country, for the protection of the trade, are hereby ordered to seize, or cause to be seized, any of his majesty's subjects, who, without the above authority, should pretend, after the publication hereof, to settle or hunt upon the said lands, and send them with their horses and effects to Fort Pitt, *there to be tried and punished, according to the nature of their offence, by the sentence of a court martial.*

Persons who shall be found hunting, or attempting to settle, to be punished by a court martial.

Henry Bouquet.

The company, for the reasons before given, could not attempt any thing in that country; but after the proclamation of the peace in 1763, agreed, on the application of a number of people, who engaged immediately to build upon the lots, to lay off a town at Wills's Creek, on lands which they had purchased, and had been obliged to pay rights for, during the whole war, though they never received any advantage whatever from them; but on the contrary, had suffered some thousand pounds loss, as well from the demolition of the houses they had built, as the destruction of a great quantity of very valuable timber, by the king's troops, who kept possession of their lands eight years, without making the company a shilling return; and after occupying their houses, as long as they found them necessary, took such materials from them, as they could use in building barracks within the fort, which had been constructed there.

Company agree to lay off a town at Wills's Creek, on lands which they had purchased.

Troops destroy the company's store-houses, and keep possession of their lands eight years, without paying any rents, &c.

The company found, on the first notice of their intentions to establish a town at Wills's Creek, great numbers, beside those who had originally petitioned, eager to purchase the lots, as it appeared to the meanest capacity that it must in a few years become a very considerable town; being situated on the first navigable water, on the river Potomack, only seventy-five miles from the river Monongahela, to which there was a good waggon-road, through the best pass in the Allegany mountains.

Persons eager to purchase lots at Wills's Creek.

Town would soon become very considerable, being situated on the waters of Potomack, only 75 miles from Monongahela; and a good waggon road.

The company had been at the expence of laying off the lots, and preparing deeds for the purchasers, who were alarmed by a report, that if they attempted to settle or build there, the king's troops would remove them, and take possession of their houses, as they had done the Ohio company's, whenever they pleased. Though the company imagined this report had been industriously propagated to hurt their interest, and prevent this settlement, as the troops had been removed some time, and it was generally supposed would never return, yet, that they might do every thing in their power, either to remove, or clear up any objections, that might be made to their proceedings, *they sent one of their members from Virginia, to the commander in chief of the king's forces at New York, on purpose to obtain his leave to build a town on their own lands,* not suspecting a possibility of a denial, as the fort was in a ruinous condition, and only a store-keeper there, who had the charge of a few useless stores: But the general absolutely refused his consent to build there, though the company are convinced the report, which had at first alarmed the people, did not take its rise from any declaration he had made on the subject, as he said it was the first notice he had had of the company's intentions to establish a town, which however he could not give his assent to, as it was a very convenient pass, and it might hereafter be thought necessary to reserve it for the king's use. With this answer their member returned to the people, who were assembled there, on the day appointed for the sale of the lots, and they were all, after having removed with their effects some distance, with a design to establish themselves, under the necessity of seeking some other settlement, as the company would not allow any of them to remain there, in opposition to this notice, though some were willing to run every other risque, if they could obtain their permission.

Company lay off lots and prepare deeds.

People alarmed by a report that their houses, &c. would be taken from them by the troops.

Company send one of their members to the commander in chief of the troops at New York, to obtain his permission to build at Wills's Creek, on their own lands.

General refuses to give them leave.

General's reasons for his refusal.

People who had assembled to purchase the lots, obliged to return, and seek other settlements.

Being thus baffled in every attempt they made, as well to improve their property, as to accomplish more distant schemes, and comply with their engagements to government in the strictest manner; they determined to engage one of their own body to go to England, to represent

Company determined to send home one of their members, to lay their case before the king.

H present

(30)

present their grievances to his majesty. And at a meeting at Stafford Court House in Virginia in July 1763, they drew up the following petition to be presented to the king, by one of their members, whom they prevailed upon to go home on that errand.

TO THE KING'S MOST EXCELLENT MAJESTY.

Your majesty's most loyal subjects, members of the Ohio company in Virginia, being under a necessity of approaching your royal presence, beg leave, by the first opportunity that has offered, to express their most grateful acknowledgments for the blessings they begin to experience, after a long and cruel war, which though once threatening their destruction, has under your majesty's auspicious reign, by the wisdom and steadiness of your councils, been terminated in a glorious peace, that has through every quarter of the world (which have felt the weight of your majesty's arms, and experienced your lenity and moderation) rendered the name of George the third as glorious, as it is, and always will be, dear to your majesty's subjects. And when we reflect, that these blessings are like to be perpetuated to our latest posterity, of which your majesty's happy marriage with our most gracious queen, whose virtues are an honour to her crown, and the birth of his royal highness the prince of Wales, are the most happy presages; we cannot omit rendering our sincere thanks to Divine Providence, that, by showering down so many blessings, upon the beginning of your majesty's reign, has pointed it out, to be distinguished with a lustre, so far exceeding any other, in the British annals.

Instructions to Sir William Gooch, lieutenant-governor of Virginia, to make a grant, or grants to the Ohio company, within certain limits, or in such other part, or parts to the west of the great mountains, as the company shall judge most proper.

We most humbly beg leave to represent to your majesty, that your royal grandfather was graciously pleased, to give an instruction to the late Sir William Gooch, baronet, his lieutenant-governor of this colony, to make a *grant* or *grants* to John Hanbury late of London merchant, and thirteen others therein named, inhabitants of this colony, and their associates, of 200,000 acres of land betwixt Romanetto and Buffaloe Creeks, on the south side of the river Allegany (otherwise Ohio) and betwixt the two creeks, and Yellow Creek on the north side of the said river, or in such other part, or parts to the west of the great mountains, as should be adjudged most proper by them, for making settlements thereon, and extending the British trade in those parts, upon particular terms therein mentioned; which when they had complied with, the said lieutenant-governor was required, to make a farther grant, or grants to them for 300,000 acres more, within the said limits, under the like conditions and limitations as the first 200,000 acres.

Company receive partners; twenty in the the whole. Expended above 10,000l. sterling.

That the said company immediately began to provide for making their settlements; and apprehending they should be intitled to the said lands on better terms than they were usually granted to other persons, by the government here (which was the inducement for their application to his late majesty) took in some other partners, several of whom were purchasers for a full consideration, to the number of twenty in the whole; who have, upon the faith of the said instruction, expended above *ten thousand pounds sterling*, in order to comply with the terms prescribed to them: But meeting several difficulties and objections, as well from the Indians, as from the government here, who had made many large grants, and in particular of 800,000 acres to a company in this colony, they were prevented from compleating their settlement, till the French came, and took possession of the fort they were building, destroyed their houses, and drove off their workmen. The war which followed thereupon, in which the company lost the greatest part of their stock, put a full stop to all settlements in those parts, till through the success of your majesty's arms, the possession of the enemy's fort, then called Fort Du Quesne, and now Fort Pitt, was happily restored; but since that period, when we expected to have been allowed to prosecute our settlements, we have been told, that no settlement was to be made in those parts, without your majesty's express directions.

Page 19.

In 1758.

Motives that induced the company to embark in this design.

We must beg leave humbly to represent to your majesty, that the motives which first induced the company to undertake such a scheme, were not founded on narrow self-interested principles; they observed with concern and indignation, that the French were imperceptibly, and unnoticed stealing the possession of your majesty's lands, building forts thereon, and debauching, and stirring up the Indians against your majesty's subjects; and were sensible, that nothing but the speedy settlement of those parts, and an advantageous trade, to engage the Indians to the British interest, would put a stop to it; and that no such settlement could be made, or trade carried on, with any prospect of success, but by a company who were able to advance a sum adequate to those purposes. These were once publickly acknowledged to be their motives; for on the day his late majesty's instruction was produced to the governor and council here, several persons applied, and obtained orders for, taking up above a million

Lord Granville, lord Baltimore, and Mr. Penn promise the company lands on the same terms, the king granted them.

of acres of land, in those parts: and upon the late Mr. Hanbury's application to lord Granville, lord Baltimore, and Mr. Penn, for grants of large tracts of land, within their several proprietaries, for the convenience of extending the trade with the Indians, they declared they would grant them to the company, on the same terms they obtained their grant from the crown. The company humbly hope, they may be allowed some merit from the share they bore in the war, in which, most of them who had sons, and relations fit to serve their king and country,

Three of the company's sons killed in the war.
Choose colonel Mercer, one of the company, to present their petition.

enabled them, at a considerable expence to do so; and though three of them had the misfortune to lose their sons in the course of it, they had the satisfaction to know they fell gloriously, and were universally lamented, and regretted: Among these, was the brother of colonel Mercer, whom we have chosen to present our petition to your majesty, not only as he is one of our company, and acquainted with all our proceedings, but having had the honour of serving during the whole war, with so much credit, as to receive the thanks of the general assembly,

and

and being mostly employed on that quarter, he is, from his personal knowledge of the country, able to give your majesty, or your ministers, the most exact and satisfactory account of it.

We therefore humbly presume to address your majesty, that you would be graciously pleased, to give an instruction to your governor, or lieutenant-governor of Virginia, to make a *grant* or *grants* to your petitioners, and their partners, for the said five hundred thousand acres of land, upon such terms as your majesty shall judge reasonable, and that may be of real advantage to your petitioners; as the right honourable the lords of the committee for plantation affairs, upon a reference to them of the last of our petitions, have through a misinformation of some interested persons, as we apprehend, mistaken both our meaning, and that of the instruction. Mr. Beverley named in their report, at the time of his opposition, was possessed of many very large tracts of land, in different counties, and had lately obtained a grant for 120,000 acres in Augusta county, which he had advertised for sale to purchasers, who were daily coming from the northward provinces, to buy lands within this government, which they could then do, for less money than the quit-rents, in some of those provinces, amount to. As to the expence of surveys, their lordships must have been misinformed as to our laws and customs relating thereto, as well as to those established as to the manner of surveying; of both which, our agent is provided with indisputable proofs under the colony seal, to give their lordships the most convincing satisfaction. Therefore their lordship's proposed expedient, of taking up our lands in tracts of 20,000 acres each, the breadth to be one third of the length, is so far from removing all causes of complaint, and difficulty on that head, that we are persuaded no person in your majesty's colony, would accept such a grant upon those terms. These were the company's inducements to desire a grant within natural boundaries, as it would have saved them the charge of surveying, and their agent was fully impowered to settle the quit-rent, or what should be thought reasonable in lieu of it, considering how much land not fit for cultivation, would probably be included within such a boundary: an indulgence they hoped they might have been thought to have merited, from their being the first proposers of so dangerous, and expensive an undertaking, from which so many advantages were like to accrue to the public. But if such an indulgence is, in your majesty's judgment, not fit to be granted, we must intirely submit to your royal pleasure, and beg leave that we may be allowed to survey our lands, in such a manner, as other of your majesty's subjects here have been permitted to do, upon the first settlement of our frontier counties; and if that should be thought improper, we have so firm a reliance on your majesty's justice and equity, that we cannot in the least doubt, but your majesty would be graciously pleased, to order us to be repaid the money advanced by our company, with interest, which we had much rather receive than accept of a grant of land, in so distant a part of the country, upon any other terms than we have proposed. In every case the company will have the greatest satisfaction, in having done all in their power, and contributed in ever so small a share, towards the success of your majesty's arms, and the security of their country; as whatever their interest may suffer, or whatever may be your majesty's will and pleasure, we shall submit to it with the utmost satisfaction, being, with the greatest submission, what we beg leave to have the honour of subscribing ourselves,

May it please your Majesty,

Your most loyal and obedient subjects and servants,

Committee. { J. Mercer,
Philip Ludwell Lee,
Thomas Lud. Lee,
John Tayloe,
Presly Thornton,
Lunsford Lomax,
Richard Lee.

Pray the king to give an instruction to the governor of Virginia, to make them a grant, or grants for 500,000 acres of land.

Lands in Virginia may be bought for less than the quit-rent amounts to, in the northern provinces.

Proposal to survey the lands in tracts of 20,000 acres each, the breadth to be one third of the length, will not answer the purpose.

Reason why the company ask a grant within natural bounds: and their agent impowered to settle the quit-rent.

Beg to be allowed to survey in the same manner, as is customary in Virginia in new grants;

or to be repaid the money they have expended.

Their agent arrived in London in September 1763, and immediately waited on the secretary of state with this memorial, which he told him he would inform his majesty of, and that he should be commanded to attend with it, whenever his majesty would be pleased to receive it; but no orders were ever sent him on the subject: and on the 7th of October following, his majesty was pleased to issue his royal proclamation, forbidding any grants or settlements to the westward of the Allegany mountains.

This proclamation being a total bar for the present to the company's designs, their agent, hoping it was only intended to remedy some temporary inconveniences, which would of themselves be immediately removed, thought it adviseable to wait that event, and therefore took no farther steps till the year 1765, when, being informed that several families in Virginia, within the limits described by that proclamation, who had been in actual possession, obtained grants, paid quit-rents, and every demand of government for several years, had petitioned the general assembly to represent their case to his majesty, as being under that proclamation, deprived of the whole of their property, he judged it proper to present the following humble memorial, as well as that, which the company had sent over with him in 1763, to his majesty.

Agent arrives in London in Sept. 1763, and waits on the secretary of state. Proclamation forbidding grants to the westward of the Allegany mountains.

Agent took no farther steps till 1765.

Persons in Virginia petition the assembly to represent their case to the king, as being deprived of their lands by the royal proclamation.

Agent presents a memorial on behalf of the Ohio company.

TO

(32)

TO THE KING'S MOST EXCELLENT MAJESTY IN COUNCIL.

The humble Memorial of George Mercer, on behalf of the Ohio Company in Virginia,

Most humbly sheweth;

That it has been always deemed of the utmost importance to the safety of your majesty's American dominions, and to the welfare and prosperity of Great Britain, to secure to your majesty's subjects in America, an intercourse with the Indian nations, in the interior part of North America, and to acquire and keep such possession on the great rivers, and inland waters of that country, as might prevent the execution of a plan, long since laid by the crown of France, and its governors in Canada, for the absolutely cutting off that intercourse, and thereby uniting all the said Indian nations, against the British colonies.

Ohio comany raise a stock.
Apply to the king for a grant of land.

That for the purpose of effectually making such settlements, with the good-will of the Indians, and in order to secure them when made, the first members of the Ohio company, deemed it adviseable to raise a joint stock, and soon after the conclusion of the peace of Aix-la-Chapelle, to apply by petition to your majesty's royal grandfather, for such grants of land and privileges as the governor of Virginia was not empowered to make; and they were the rather induced to make this application, because as there were just grounds to apprehend, that such settlements would not remain undisturbed, either by secret practices, or by open violence on the part of the French, it would not only be necessary to expend very large sums of money, but to take no step on so delicate an occasion, but with the knowledge and approbation of his majesty's ministers.

Bounds within which the company pray to take their land.
To settle 100 families in seven years, and erect a fort.

That the said company, by the petition presented on their behalf by the late Mr. John Hanbury, did humbly pray his said late majesty, that he would be graciously pleased to encourage their said undertaking, by giving instructions to his lieutenant-governor of Virginia, to grant to the petitioners a tract of 500,000 acres of land between Romanetto, and Buffaloe Creeks on the south-side of the Ohio, and between the streams called the Two Creeks, and Yellow Creek, on the north side of the said river; and that 200,000 acres, part thereof, might be immediately granted, upon condition of settling at their expence 100 families thereon, in seven years, and upon condition of erecting a fort, and maintaining a garrison, as in the said petition mentioned; and that 300,000 acres, the remainder of the said 500,000 acres, might be granted to the petitioners, when they had complied with the terms of the first grant.

Lords report, Feb. 23, 1748-9.

That upon a reference by the lords of the committee of the council to the lords commissioners of trade and plantations, their lordships were pleased to report, That it was their opinion, that it would be for his majesty's service to grant the said petition, especially as such settlement would be a proper step, towards checking the incroachments of the French, by interrupting part of their communication, from their lodgment on the great lakes, to the river Mississippi, by means whereof, the British settlements were exposed to their incursions, and that of the Indians in their interests, which benefits would be farther extended under the said company's proposal.

16th March, 1748-9.
above 10,000l. p. 30.

That his said late majesty was thereupon pleased to give such instructions, as was prayed by the petitioners, to the lieutenant-governor of Virginia.

That the company forthwith engaged, in a very considerable expence, to the amount of many thousand pounds, for the attaining the beneficial ends of the said grants, by causing surveys to be made, settlers to be engaged, and materials for erecting a fort to be provided, and which fort was afterwards in a great measure erected, entirely at the great expence of the company.

Obstructions from the French forces.

That many unforeseen obstructions arose soon after, not only from the forces employed by the crown of France, but also from the obstacles raised to the execution of his majesty's instructions, by the lieutenant-governor, and council of Virginia; who, after they had notice of the said instructions, but before they were produced in form, granted, either upon petitions for the extending the time, to which former petitions were limited, or upon applications intirely new, 1,350,000 acres of land west of the mountains, to persons incapable of making effectual settlements, and whose grants could therefore only serve, to frustrate the ends of those, to which the company were intitled, under his majesty's instructions.

1,350,000 acres of land granted to persons incapable of making settlements.
Fort began by the company, destroyed by the French, p. 19.

That while the company were engaged in removing those difficulties, and in conciliating the affections of the Indians, residing on the Ohio, at a very considerable expence, and when they had actually began to erect their fort, and had raised a proper garrison for that service, the whole force of the French colony in Canada, was employed by the governor of that country (sensible of the great importance, and utility of the measures the company were taking, to the crown of Great Britain) to disappoint the same; and those forces, too powerful for the company to resist, effected their design, by the intire destruction of the fort began to be erected, and of all the other footing, the company had obtained in that country.

That the company, however, so long as any hopes remained, of preserving this valuable country, without a royal army, neglected no means, nor did they spare any expence, for that purpose, and were the principal occasion of such defence as was made of it, until the arrival of general Braddock.

That the obstinacy with which the country on the Ohio hath since been contended for, is a proof how well founded, and just the proposals of the Ohio company were, for the benefit of

the

the British nation; and the immense advantages resulting to the nation from the cession of this territory by the late glorious peace, will always be a permanent evidence of the truth of the allegations in their first petition.

That as soon as the peace was proclaimed, the company, notwithstanding the heavy expences they had already been at, and from which they had yet reaped no fruit, but vigilant how they might, as early as possible, improve the benefits secured by it, began to raise a new fund, in order to enable themselves to effectuate the wise intentions of his late majesty's instructions; but the governor of Virginia assuring them he was restrained from granting what they thought they had a right to claim, they conceived it their humble duty to send over your memorialist from Virginia, to intreat your majesty's royal protection, and approbation of their design. *Company on the proclamation of peace raised a new fund, but the governor not being authorized to give them permission to proceed in their design, they send one of their members to England, with a petition to his majesty.*

But that your memorialist, soon after his arrival in England, being informed of your majesty's royal proclamation, restraining all future grants and settlements within the bounds therein described; and conceiving your majesty's royal pleasure to be, that no steps should be taken under the said instructions, until farther orders from your majesty, hath been hitherto with-held thereby, from making the humble application he had directions to make to your majesty upon the case of the Ohio company; and the company, on the advice they received from your memorialist, thought themselves bound in duty altogether to acquiesce under your majesty's proclamation; yet, understanding that your majesty, in your royal wisdom, has signified that the provisions of the said proclamation were intended to be temporary only, your memorialist most humbly hopes, that there is no reason to distrust the company's want of obedience thereto, so long as your majesty shall, in your great wisdom, deem the same fit to continue in force, although the grants directed in the said instructions should be actually made. *Royal proclamation prevents an immediate application.*

Proclamation only temporary; therefore a grant prayed for.

Your memorialist therefore most humbly prays, your majesty would please to take the premises into your royal consideration, and to renew the said instructions to the lieutenant-governor of Virginia for the time being; or that in case such instructions should, by your majesty in your royal wisdom, be deemed inconsistent with the rules of policy, that ought to be observed in that country, your memorialist, not presuming to entertain a doubt on the subject, of your majesty's royal councils, most humbly prays, that your majesty would be graciously pleased to recommend to the parliament of Great Britain, the making some provision for the reimbursement of the great expences incurred by the Ohio company, as the event hath turned out for the benefit of the public only; or that the said company may receive, by a grant of land, in some other part of your majesty's American dominions, or otherwise, such compensation, as your majesty in your bounty shall be graciously pleased to bestow upon them. *Prays that the instructions to the governor may be renewed, or that it may be recommended to parliament to reimburse them their expences; or that lands may be given them in some other part of America.*

And your memorialist shall most humbly pray.

Geo. Mercer.

These memorials his majesty in council, 21st of June, 1765, was graciously pleased to refer to the right honourable the lords commissioners for trade and plantations, with directions to report what might be adviseable to be done thereupon; and their lordships, for reasons they assigned, did not take up the consideration of them till the year 1767, when the general assembly of Virginia petitioned his majesty, on behalf of the inhabitants of the county of Augusta, (who being the frontier of the said colony, were many of them by the aforesaid proclamation, precluded from returning to their farms, which they had occupied before the war,) praying that the proclamation might be withdrawn; and also that general permission might be given to the king's subjects, to take up lands, and settle the country beyond the mountains, attributing it at the same time to the company's neglect, that settlements were not established there. *Memorials referred to the lords for trade, in 1765. Did not proceed in them till 1767. Assembly of Virginia petition the king to withdraw the proclamation, p. 31.*

On seeing this petition, the company's agent immediately applied to the lords for trade, to whom it was referred, praying, as the company had always been ready, and desirous to comply with every engagement they had made to government, and as he humbly apprehended, were in no degree chargeable with neglect, (referring to the memorials then lying at their lordship's board,) that the company might either have leave immediately to proceed in their design, or that no resolution might be taken to their prejudice; and their lordships, on the 26th of June, 1767, made the following report relative to the memorials, and the company's claim. *Company's agent applies to the lords for trade. Prays the company may have leave to proceed in their settlement.*

To the Right Honourable the Lords of the Committee of his Majesty's Most Honourable Privy Council for Plantation Affairs.

My Lords,

We have had under our consideration a petition, presented to his majesty in the year 1765, by colonel George Mercer, an behalf of the Ohio company in Virginia, setting forth, amongst other things, "that on the 16th of March, 1748, his late majesty was pleased to give an in-
"struction to the lieutenant-governor of Virginia, to grant the said company, under certain
"conditions, 500,000 acres of land, between Romanettoe's and Buffaloe's Creeks, on the
"south-side of the Ohio, and between the streams called the Two Creeks and Yellow Creeks
"on the north-side of the said river; and humbly praying, for the reasons therein contained, *Petition p. 32.*

I "that

(34)

"that his majesty will be pleased either to renew the said instructions to the lieutenant-governor of Virginia for the time being, or recommend to parliament the making some provision for reimbursing the great expences incurred by the Ohio company, or that the said company may receive, by a grant of land in some other part of his majesty's American dominions, or otherwise, such compensation, as his majesty in his bounty shall be graciously pleased to bestow upon them."

This petition, my lords, was referred to this board by an order of his majesty in council of the 21st of June 1765, with directions to report to your lordships what might be adviseable to be done thereupon; but the petitioner not appearing to prosecute his suit, and that part of the country, where the lands petitioned for by the Ohio company lie, having been precluded from all settlement by his majesty's proclamation of the 7th of October 1763, it was not thought necessary, at that time, to proceed any farther upon this business.

Some late proceedings however, of the house of burgesses of Virginia, having given cause to the petitioner to suspect, that some measures may be taken there, to encourage and support persons in making settlements beyond the mountains, he has thought fit to renew his application, and to solicit some determination upon his petition; whereupon we beg leave to report to your lordships,

That a decision upon either one or other of the alternatives, suggested in the prayer of the petition does, in our opinion so much depend upon the steps which have been already taken, and the expence incurred for carrying the plan of this company into execution, upon the state of the settlements under grants from Virginia, in that part of the country, antecedent to the date of his majesty's said proclamation, and upon the effect which the encouragement of such settlements may have on the temper of the Indians, after what has been determined by that proclamation, as to make it inexpedient, if not impossible, to come to any determination upon the petitioner's request, until these circumstances shall have been fully known; and therefore we beg leave to recommend, *that his majesty's lieutenant-governor of that province should be directed to make an exact and full report thereof; submitting at the same time, whether it may not be further adviseable, that any attempt made by the legislature of Virginia, or any proposition offered to his majesty's consideration, for the encouragement of settlements in this part of the country should be discountenanced.* We are,

My Lords,

Your Lordships most obedient and most humble servants,

Whitehall,
June 26, 1767.

Clare.
John Roberts.
Wm. Fitzherbert.

Reasons assigned by the lords of trade, for not proceeding immediately, on the consideration of the petition.
Proceedings of the house of burgesses in Virginia, to encourage settlements beyond the mountains, make it necessary for the agent to renew his application.

Recommend that the governor of Virginia be directed to report what steps the company had taken. Any attempt by the assembly of Virginia to establish settlements to be discountenanced.

Report of the lords for trade sent to the governor of Virginia.
Some persons in England propose a scheme for settling lands on the waters of the Mississippi.

This report being immediately forwarded by the secretary of state to the governor of Virginia, the company's agent, at the same time, sent several copies of it to different members there, and in Maryland, recommending it to them, in the strongest terms, to lose no time in obtaining the governor's report; but finding, before it could arrive, that several persons here were petitioning for lands on the Mississippi, and its waters, even the Ohio; and as these petitioners imagined, they had reason to believe, the schemes of settlement, &c. they proposed to government, would be approved of; the Ohio company's agent, that no delay might be occasioned by their claim, and as the settlement proposed by them, would be a means of forwarding those applied for by others, presented the following humble memorial to the king.

TO THE KING'S MOST EXCELLENT MAJESTY IN COUNCIL.

Memorial of the agent for the Ohio company to the king.

The Memorial of George Mercer, on behalf of the Ohio company in Virginia, &c.

Most humbly sheweth;

That in 1765 your memorialist, as agent for the said company presented a memorial, which your majesty in council was graciously pleased to refer to the right honourable the lords commissioners for trade and plantations; and your memorialist humbly begs leave to refer, to their lordship's report of the 26th of June last in the said memorial.

Page 34.

Reference to the governor now become unnecessary.
Lord's objection to make settlements over the mountains removed.

Agent renews the company's claim.
Appendix p. 22.
Company had settled several families before the war.

That your memorialist, being informed permission will be given to your majesty's subjects to settle on the waters of the Mississippi, and the interior parts of North America, humbly conceives, the reference then recommended by their lordships, to be made to the governor of Virginia, is become less necessary, their lordships having assigned as the chief reason for this reference, their own inability, *at that time* to determine, as to the expediency of a settlement in that country. That being no longer a subject of deliberation, and your memorialist, thinking himself now fully prepared, to answer any other objection, which then occurred to their lordships (and he begs leave to lay, the report of the governor of Virginia must confirm his information) presumes, on behalf of the company, to renew their claim to the lands granted them, by your majesty's late royal grandfather; which they, at the treaty of Loggstown in June 1752, obtained the permission of the Six Nations to settle, and on which they had really established several families before the war.

Your

(35)

Your memorialist presumes to inform your majesty, that the first actual survey of that country, was made at the company's expence, and that the road from Wills's Creek to the Ohio, the route of your majesty's troops in 1754, and 1755, was not only traced out, but compleated entirely at the company's charge; that the company had built strong houses to secure the communication, from the river Potomack to the Ohio, which were used as magazines for your majesty's stores, and some of them, afterwards destroyed by the regular forces, to erect stronger fortifications. *First discoveries of the country on the Ohio made at the company's expence, and a road cleared from the Potomack to the Ohio. Company's store-houses destroyed by the troops.*

That your memorialist is encouraged to hope, the Ohio company, who were the very first adventurers, and have expended so large a sum of money, upwards of fourteen years since, on a settlement begun under the sanction of government, will not be prevented from prosecuting their design, while others of your majesty's subjects, who have lately only formed their scheme, enjoy the benefit of the company's labour, and discoveries, especially when it is considered of what great advantage their settlement must be, as well to those now proposed, in the interior parts of North America, or which may hereafter be judged necessary to establish there, as to those provinces already very populous: To the former of these, it would be a support, and at the same time secure to them, the safest and shortest communication that can ever be found, and through which only, the manufactures of Great Britain can, at a moderate expence, be transported to the Mississippi, as the whole Passage, from the navigable part of Potomack river, including eighty miles land carriage, by the Ohio company's road, may be performed in three weeks; and to the latter, it would soon become a strong barrier, and the surest protection against Indian incursions, which greatly distressed your majesty's subjects on the frontiers of Pennsylvania, Maryland, and Virginia during the last war. *The company pray to be permitted to begin their settlements at the same time that leave is granted to others. Company's settlement will be an advantage to those proposed by others, and to the provinces already settled. The best communication to the Mississippi. Passage from the Potomack to the Mississippi may be performed in three weeks. Company's settlement will be a barrier, and prevent the Indian incursions into the old settled provinces.*

Your memorialist therefore most humbly prays, your majesty would be graciously pleased, to take the case of the Ohio company into your royal consideration, and order that their grant be renewed; that they may undertake their settlements agreeable to their former engagements with government, at the same time your majesty's other subjects are permitted to pursue their plan, that the company may enjoy, in common with them, the advantage of their own discoveries and labour: Or that your majesty would be graciously pleased to recommend it to the parliament, to make provision to reimburse the company the great expences they have incurred, and of which the public have enjoyed all the benefit, as they greatly forwarded the expeditions carried on, by your majesty's regular troops, on that quarter; or such other relief, as your majesty, in your royal wisdom, shall judge best. *Prays the company's grant may be renewed. Or it may be recommended to parliament to reimburse them their expences.*

And your memorialist will ever most humbly pray, &c. &c.

G. Mercer.

His majesty's most honourable privy council, to whom this memorial was referred, waiting for the final settlement of the Indian boundary, did not take up the consideration of it, until the 20th of November 1769, and they were pleased then to refer it, with two petitions, lately preferred by several gentlemen of fortune, and interest here, praying Grants for lands on the Ohio, to the right honourable the lords commissioners for trade and plantations. But though these gentlemen in their petitions, had fixed on no particular spot to take up their lands, the Ohio company's agent was informed they had, in a map produced to their lordships, marked them out within the bounds which his majesty, the 16th of March 1748-9, had been pleased to assign the company, agreeable to their first petition: He was therefore under a necessity of opposing them, and preferred the following memorial to their lordships. *Reference of the company's memorial to the board of trade. Persons in England ask for grants of land on the Ohio; and propose to locate them within the limits assigned the Ohio company. Company's agent enters a caveat.*

To the Right Honourable the Lords Commissioners for Trade and Plantations,

The Memorial of George Mercer, on behalf of the Ohio company,

Humbly sheweth;

That the said company have expended a large sum of money, in consequence of his late majesty's royal instruction, to his lieutenant-governor of Virginia, dated the 16th of March 1748-9, directing a grant, or grants to be made to them, of 500,000 acres of land, on the waters of the Ohio, within certain limits, and on certain conditions therein mentioned; but have been prevented by sundry acts of government, and particularly his majesty's royal proclamation, of the 7th of October 1763, from prosecuting their design, and schemes of settlement. *Page 3. Company prevented by the king's proclamation from settling their lands.*

That your memorialist is informed, there are sundry petitions preferred to your lordships, praying grants of lands on the Ohio, and its waters, (even the names of which, were not known to the public, till a chart of that country was made at the company's expence) which will interfere with the grant, ordered by his late majesty, to the Ohio company:

Your memorialist therefore, most humbly prays your lordships, not to make any grant, within the limits prescribed by the royal instruction to the company; as they are, and have ever been willing, and desirous to proceed in their undertaking, and fulfil their engagements to government. And that no unnecessary delay, may be offered to the petitioners, on behalf of the Ohio company, your memorialist *Agent prays their lordships, not to make any grants within the bounds prescribed to the company, by the king's instruction.*

(56)

Is ready to prove the company's pretensions.
Company delayed above 20 years from prosecuting their schemes.

memorialist begs leave, humbly to represent, that he is fully prepared, whenever your lordships shall be pleased to command him, to justify the company's pretensions, and shew, they have, through no neglect on their part, been delayed upwards of twenty years, from executing a plan, which would have contributed as much to the public, as their own private interest.

And your memorialist will most humbly pray, &c. &c.

Dec. 18, 1769.   George Mercer.

(1)

Geo Mercer 485

APPENDIX.

TO THE CASE OF THE

OHIO COMPANY.

A JOURNAL,

OF Christopher Gift's journey began from Col. Cresap's at the *old town on Potomack river Maryland*, October 31 1750, continued *down the Ohio*, within 15 *miles of the Falls thereof*; and from thence to *Roanoak river in North Carolina*, where he arrived May 19, 1751; Undertaken on the account of the Ohio company, and by the instructions of their committee. Old town

INSTRUCTIONS given Mr. Christopher Gift by the committee of the Ohio company, the 11th day of September 1750. Gift's instructions;

You are to go out as soon as possible to the westward of the great mountains, and carry with you such a number of men as you think necessary, in order to search out and discover the lands upon the *river Ohio* (and other adjoining branches of the *Mississippi*) down as low as the *great Falls* thereof.

You are particularly to observe the ways and passes through all the mountains you cross, and take an exact account of the soil, quality, and product of the land ; the width and depth of the rivers, and the several falls belonging to them ; together with the courses and bearings of the rivers and mountains as near as you conveniently can : You are also to observe what nations of Indians inhabit there, their strength and numbers, who they trade with, and in what commodities they deal. To discover the nations of Indians, and their trade.

When you find a large quantity of good level land such as you think will suit the company, you are to measure the breadth of it, in three or four different places, and take the courses of the river and mountains on which it binds, in order to judge the quantity ; you are to fix the beginning and bounds in such a manner that they may be easily found again by your description ; the nearer in the land lies the better, provided it be good and level, but we had rather go quite down the Mississippi than take mean broken land. After finding a large body of good level land, you are not to stop, but proceed farther as low as the falls of the Ohio, that we may be informed of that navigation ; and you are to take an exact account of all the large bodies of good level land in the same manner as above directed, that the company may the better judge where it will be most convenient for them to take theirs. To examine the navigation of the Ohio to the falls;

You are to note all the bodies of good land as you go along, though there is not a sufficient quantity for the Company's grant ; but you need not be so particular in the mensuration of that, as in the larger bodies. To note all the bodies of good land.

You are to draw as good a plan as you can of the country you pass through, and take an exact and particular journal of all your proceedings, and make a true report thereof to the Ohio company. To draw a plan of the country, and keep a journal.

In compliance with my instructions from the committee of the Ohio company, bearing date the 11th day of September, 1750. Gift begins his journey.

Wednesday, October 31 1750. Set out from Col. Cresap's at the *Old Town on Potomack river in Maryland*, and went along an old Indian path, N. 30 d. E. about 11 miles. Old town.

Thursday,

(2)

Thursday, November 1. N. 1 m. N. 30 d. E. 3 m. Here I was taken sick and stayed all night.

Friday 2d. N. 30 d. E. 6 m. here I was so bad that I was not able to proceed any farther that night, but grew better in the morning.

Juniatta. Saturday 3d. N. 3 m. to *Juniatta*, a large branch of Susquehanna, where I stayed all night.

Sunday 4th. Crossed *Juniatta* and went up it S. 55 d. W. about 16 m.

Allegany Mountain. Monday 5th. Continued the same course S. 55 d. W. 6 m. to the top of a *large mountain, called the Allegany Mountain*; here our path turned, and we went N. 45. d. W. 6 m. and encamped.

Tuesday 6, Wednesday 7, and Thursday 8th had, snow, and such bad weather that we could not travel; but I killed a young bear, so that we had provision enough.

Friday 9th. Set out N. 70 d. W. about 8 m. here I crossed a creek of *Susquehanna*, and it raining hard, I went into an old Indian cabbin where I stayed all night.

Saturday, November 10th. Rain and snow all day, but cleared away in the evening.

Sunday 11th. Set out late in the morning N. 70 d. W. 6 m crossing two forks of a creek of Susquehanna; here the way being bad, I encamped and killed a turkey.

Laurel Mountain. Monday 12th. Set out N. 45 d. W. 8 m. and crossed a great *Laurel mountain*.

Tuesday 13th. Rain and snow.

Loylhannon. Kiskeminetas. Wednesday 14th. Set out N. 45 d. W. 6 m. to *Loylhannon*, an old Indian town on a creek of the Ohio, called *Kiskeminetas* then N. 1 m. N. W. 1 m. to an Indian camp on the said creek.

Thursday 15th. The weather being bad, and I unwell stayed here all day. The Indian, to whom this camp belonged, spoke good English, and directed me the way to his town which is called *Shanoppin*; he said it was about sixty miles and a pretty good way.

Friday 16th. Set out S. 70 d. W. 10 m.

Saturday 17th. The same course (S. 70 d. W.) 15 m. to an old Indian camp.

Sunday 18th. I was very sick, and sweated myself according to the Indian custom, in a sweat-house, which gave me ease and my fever abated.

Shanoppin's town. Monday 19th. Set out early in the morning the same course (S 70 d. W.) travelled very hard about twenty miles to a small Indian town of the Delawares called *Shanoppin, on the S. E. side of the river Ohio,* where we rested and got corn for our horses.

Width of the Ohio. Tuesday 20th. I was unwell, and stayed in this town to recover myself. While I was here I took an opportunity to set my compass privately, and took the distance across the river; for I understood it was dangerous to let a compass be seen : *the Ohio is 76 poles wide here.* There are about twenty familes in this town. *The land in general from Potomack to this*

Land mean. *place, is mean, stony, and broken, with here and there good spots upon the creeks and branches, but no body of it.*

Land good. Saturday 24th. Set out from *Shanoppin* and swam our horses across the *Ohio*, and went down the river S. 75 d. W. 4 m. N. 75 d. W. 7 m. W. 2. m. the land from Shanoppin is good along the river, but the bottoms not broad : at a distance from the river good land for farming, covered with small white and red oaks, and tolerable level : fine runs for mills, &c.

Logg's Town. Land very rich. Sunday 25th. Down the river W. 3. m. N. W. 5 m. to *Logg's Town*: the lands for these last eight miles very rich, the bottoms above a mile wide, but on the S. E. side scarce a mile, the hills high and steep. In the town I found scarce any body but a parcel of reprobate Indian traders, the chief of the Indians being out hunting; here I was informed that George Croghan and Andrew Montour who were sent upon an embassy from Pennsylvania to the Indians, were passed about a week before me. The people here enquired my business; and, because I did not readily inform them, began to suspect me; saying I was come to settle the Indians lands, and that I should never go home again safe. I found this discourse was like to be of ill consequence, so pretended to speak very slightingly of what they had said, and enquired for Croghan (who is a mere idol among his countrymen, the Irish traders) and Andrew Montour the interpreter for Pennsylvania; and told them I had a message to deliver the Indians from the king, by order of the President of Virginia, and for that reason wanted to see Mr. Montour. This made them all pretty easy (being afraid to interrupt the King's message) and obtained me quiet and respect among them ; otherwise, I doubt not, they would have contrived some evil against me. I immediately wrote to Mr. Croghan by one of the traders people.

Great Beaver Creek. Monday 26th. Though I was unwell, I preferred the woods to such company; and set out from Loggs Town down the river N. W. 6 m. to *Great Beaver Creek*, where I met one Barny Curran, a trader for the Ohio company, and we continued together as far as Muskingum. The bottoms upon the river below Loggs Town are very rich, but narrow; the high land pretty good but not very rich ; the land upon Beaver Creek of the same kind. From this place we left the Ohio to the S. E. and travelled across the country.

Land very good. Tuesday 27th. Set out from the E. side of *Beaver Creek*, N. W. 6 m. W. 4 m. upon these two last courses, very good high land and not much broken, fit for farming.

Wednesday 28th. Rained, and we could not travel.

Thursday 29th. W. 6 m. through good land ; the same course continued 6 m. farther, through very broken land : here I found myself pretty well recovered, and being in want of provision, went out and killed a deer.

Friday 30th. Set out S. 45 d. W. 12. m. crossed the last branch of *Beaver Creek*, where one of Curran's men and myself killed twelve turkeys.

Saturday, December 1st. N. 45 d. W. 10 m. the land high and tolerable good.

Sunday 2d.

(3)

Sunday 2d. N. 45 d. W. 8 m. the same sort of land, but near the creeks bushy and very full of thorns.

Monday 3d. Killed a Deer and stayed in our camp all day.

Tuesday 4th. Set out late S. 45 d. W. about 4 m. here I killed three fine fat Deer; so that though we were eleven in company, we had great plenty of provisions.

Wednesday 5th. Set out down the side of a creek, called *Elk's Eye Creek*, S. 70 d. W. 6 m. good land, but void of timber; meadows upon the Creek, and fine runs for mills. Elk's Eye Creek. No timber.

Thursday 6th. Rained all day, so that were obliged to continue in our camp.

Friday 7th. Set out S. W. 8 m. crossing *Elk's Eye Creek* to a *town of the Ottawas*, a nation of French Indians: an old Frenchman, named Mark Coonce, who had married an Indian woman of the six nations, lived here. The Indians were all out hunting, the old man was civil to me; but after I was gone to my camp, upon his understanding I came from Virginia, he called me the Big Knife. There are not above six or eight families belonging to this town. Ottawa's Town.

Saturday 8th. Stayed in the town.

Sunday 9th. Set out down the *Elk's Eye Creek* S. 45 d. W. 6 m. to *Margaret's Creek* a branch of *Elk's Eye Creek*. Margaret's Creek.

Monday 10th. The same course S. 45 d. W. 2 m. to a large creek.

Tuesday 11th. The same course twelve miles, killed two deer.

Wednesday 12th. The same course eight miles, encamped by the side of *Elk's Eye Creek*.

Thursday 13th. Rained all day.

Friday 14th. Set out W. 5 m. to *Muskingum*, a town of the Wiandots. The land upon *Elk's Eye Creek* is in general very broken, the bottoms narrow. The Wiandots or little Mingoes are divided between the French and English; one half of them adhere to the first, and the other half are firmly attached to the latter: the town of Muskingum consists of about one hundred families; when we came within sight of it, we perceived English colours hoisted on the king's house, and at George Croghan's, upon enquiring the reason, I was informed that the French had lately taken several English traders; and that Mr. Croghan had ordered all the white men to come into this town, and had sent expresses to the traders of the lower towns, and among the Picqualinees; and the Indians had sent to their people to come to council about it. Muskingum. Lands broken. Wiandots divided.

Saturday 15th, and Sunday 16th. Nothing remarkable happened.

Monday 17th. Two traders belonging to Mr. Croghan came into town, and informed us, that two of his people were taken by forty French men and twenty French Indians, who had carried them with seven horse-loads of skins, to a new fort that the French were building on one of the branches of Lake Erie.

Tuesday 18th. I acquainted Mr. Croghan and Andrew Montour with my business with the Indians, and talked much of a regulation of trade, with which they were pleased, and treated me very well. Talk of a regulation in the trade.

Wednesday 19th, to Monday 24th. Nothing remarkable.

Tuesday 25th. This being Christmas Day, I intended to read prayers; but after inviting some of the white men, they informed each other of my intentions; and being of several different persuasions, and few of them inclined to hear any good, they refused to come: but one Thomas Burney a black-smith who is settled there, went about and talked to them, and then several of them came; and Andrew Montour invited several of the well disposed Indians who came freely. By this time the morning was spent, and I had given over all thoughts of them; but seeing them come, to oblige all, and offend none, I stood up and said, Gentlemen, I have no design or intention to give offence to any particular sect or religion; but as our king indulges us all in a liberty of conscience, and hinders none of you in the exercise of your religious worship, so it would be unjust in you to endeavour to stop the propagation of his. The doctrine of salvation faith and good works, is what I only propose to treat of, as I find it extracted from the homilies of the church of England, which I then read to them in the best manner I could; and after I had done, the interpreter told the Indians what I had read, and that it was the true faith, which the great King and his church recommended to his children: the Indians seemed well pleased, and came up to me and returned me their thanks, and then invited me to live among them, and gave me a name in their language, Annosannoah: the interpreter told me, this was the name of a good man that had formerly lived among them, and their King said that must be always my name, for which I returned them thanks; but, as to living among them, I excused myself by saying, I did not know whether the governor would give me leave; and if he did, the French would come and carry me away, as they had done the English traders; to which they answered, I might bring great guns and make a fort, that they had now left the French, and were very desirous of being instructed in the principles of Christianity, that they liked me very well, and wanted me to marry them after the christian manner, and baptize their children; and then, they said, they would never desire to return to the French, or suffer them or their priests to come near them more; for they loved the English, but had seen little religion among them. Some of their great men came and wanted me to baptize their children, for as I had read to them, and appeared to talk about religion, they took me to be a minister of the gospel; upon which I desired Mr. Montour the interpreter to tell them, that no minister could venture to baptize any children, until those that were to be sureties for them, were well instructed in the faith themselves; and that was according to the great King's religion, in which he desired his children shou'd be instructed, and we dare not do it in any other way than was by law established; but I hoped, if I could not be admitted to live among them, that Christmas day, Gift proposes to read prayers. Indians attend. Gift reads prayers. Indians much pleased, give him an Indian name; desire a fort to be built; desire to be married, and have their children baptized.

(4)

that the great King would send them proper ministers to exercise that office among them, at which they seemed well pleased; and one of them went and brought me his book, which was a kind of almanack contrived for them by the French, in which the days of the week were so marked, that by moving a pin every morning, they kept a pretty exact account of the time, to shew me that he understood me, and that he and his family always observed the Sabbath-day.

A woman who was a prisoner put to death. Wednesday 26th. This day, a woman who had been long a prisoner, and had deserted been retaken and brought into the town on Christmas Eve, was put to death in the following manner. They carried her without the town and let her loose; and when she attempted to run away, the persons appointed for that purpose pursued her, and struck her on the ear, on the right side of her head, which beat her flat on her face to the ground; they then stuck her several times through the back with a dart, to the heart, scalped her, and threw the scalp in the air, and another cut off her head. Thus the dismal spectacle lay till the evening, and then Barney Curran desired leave to bury her, which he and his men and some of the Indians did, just at dark.

Thursday 27th to Thursday, January 3d, 1751. Nothing remarkable happened in the town.

Friday 4th. One Taaf, an Indian trader came to town from near Lake Erie, and informed us that the Wiandots had advised him to keep clear of the Outawais (a nation of Indians firmly attached to the French, living near the lakes) and told him that the branches of the lakes were claimed by the French; but that all the branches of the Ohio, belonged to them, and their brothers the English; and that the French had no business there, and that it was expected that the other part of the Wiandots would desert the French and come over to the English interest, and join their brethren on Elk's Eye Creek, and build a strong fort and town there.

Saturday 5th. The weather still continuing bad, I stayed in the town to recruit my horses; and though corn was very dear among the Indians, I was obliged to feed them well, or run the risque of losing them, as I had a great way to travel.

Wednesday 9th. The wind Southerly, and the weather something warmer: This day came into town two traders from among the Picqualinnees (a tribe of the Tawightwis) and brought news that another English trader was also taken prisoner by the French; and that three French soldiers had deserted and come over to the English, and surrendered themselves to some of the traders of the Pick town; and that the Indians would have put them to death, to revenge their taking our traders, but as the French had surrendered themselves to the Traders protect three French deserters from the Indians. English, they would not let the Indians hurt them; but had ordered them to be sent under the care of three of our traders, and delivered at this town to George Croghan.

Thursday, January the 10th. Wind still at South, and warm.

Friday 11th. This day came into town, an Indian from near the lakes and confirmed the news we had heard.

Saturday 12th. We sent away our people towards the lower town, intending to follow them the next morning; and this evening we went into council in the Wiandot king's house: The council had been put off a long time, expecting some of their great men in, but few of them came; and this evening some of the king's council being a little disordered with liquor, no business could be done, but we were desired to come next day.

Sunday 13th. No business done.

Acquaints the Indians the king had sent them a present, and invites them to come down to receive it. Monday 14th. This day, George Croghan by the assistance of Andrew Montour, acquainted the king and council of this nation (presenting them four strings of wampum) that the great King over the water, their Roggony (father) had sent under the care of the governor of Virginia their brother, a large present of goods, which were now landed safe in Virginia; and that the governor had sent me, to invite them to come and see him, and partake of their father's charity, to all his children on the branches of Ohio.

In answer to which one of the chiefs stood up and said, "That their king and all of them "thanked their brother the governor of Virginia, for his care, and me for bringing them Indians would not give an answer till a full council should assemble. "the news; but they could not give an answer, until they had a full, or general council "of the several nations of Indians, which could not be till next spring; and so the king and council shaking hands with us, we took our leave.

White Woman's Creek. Tuesday 15th. We left Muskingum and went W. 5 m. to the White Woman's Creek, on which is a small town. This white-woman was taken away from New England, when she was not above ten years old, by the French Indians. She is now upwards of fifty, has an Indian husband and several children, her name is Mary Harris; she still remembers they used to be very religious in New England, and wonders how the white men can be so wicked as she has seen them in these woods.

Licking Creek. Land rich but broken. Salt ponds. Wednesday 16th. Set out S. W. 25 m. to Licking Creek, the land from Muskingum to this place, rich but broken. *Upon the North side of Licking Creek, about six miles from the mouth, are several salt licks, or ponds, formed by little streams or drains of water, clear, but of a bluish colour, and salt taste. The traders and Indians boil their meat in this water, which if proper care be not taken, will sometimes make it too salt to eat.*

Thursday 17th. Set out W. 5 m. S. W. 15 m. to a great swamp.

Friday 18th. Set out from the great swamp S. W. 15 m.

Hockhocking Town. Saturday 19th. W. 15 m. to Hockhocking, a small town with only four or five Delaware families.

Sunday

(5)

Sunday 20th. The snow began to grow thin, and the weather warmer. Set out from *Hockhocking* S. 5 m. then W. 5 m. then S. W. 5 m. to *Maguck*, a little Delaware town of about ten families, by the North side of a plain, or clear field, about five miles in length, N. E. and S. W. and two miles broad, with a small rising in the middle, which gives a fine prospect over the whole plain, and a large creek on the North side of it, called *Sioto Creek*; all the way from *Licking Creek* to this place, is fine rich, level land, with large meadows and fine clover bottoms, with spacious plains, covered with wild rye; the wood chiefly large walnuts and hiccories, here and there mixed with poplars, cherry-trees, and sugar-trees. — *Maguck Town. Land very rich, with fine meadows and variety of fine timber.*

Monday 21st to Wednesday 23d. Stayed in the *Maguck town*.

Thursday 24th. Set out from *Maguck town*, S. about 15 m. through fine rich, level land, to a small town, called *Hurricane Tom's* consisting of about five or six Delaware families, on the S. W. of *Sioto Creek*. — *Hurricane Tom's Town.*

Friday 25th. The creek being very high and full of ice, we could not ford, and were obliged to go down it on the S. E. side, S. E. 4 m. to the *Salt lick creek*; *about a mile up this creek, on the south side, is a very large salt lick, the streams which run into this lick are very salt, and, though clear, leave a bluish sediment: the Indians and traders make salt for their horses of this water by boiling it; it has at first a bluish colour, and somewhat bitter taste, but upon being dissolved in fair water, and boiled the second time, it comes to tolerably pure salt.* — *Land rich and level. Salt Lick Creek. Salt springs. Indians make salt.*

Saturday 26th. Set out S. 2 m. S. W. 14 m.

Sunday 27th. S. 12 m. to a small Delaware town, of about twenty families, on the S. E. side of *Sioto Creek*. We lodged at the house of an Indian, whose name was Windaughalah, a great man, and chief of this town, much in the English interest; he entertained us very kindly, and ordered a Negro man that belonged to him, to feed our horses well: this night it snowed, and in the morning, *though the snow was six or seven inches deep, the wild rye appeared very green and flourishing through it*, and our horses had very fine feeding. — *Wild rye appears green above the snow which was 6 or 7 inches deep.*

Monday 28th. We went into council with the Indians of this town, and after the interpreter had informed them of his instructions from the governor of Pennsylvania, and given them some cautions in regard to the French, they returned for answer as follows. The speaker, with four strings of wampum in his his hand, stood up, and addressing himself to the governor of Pennsylvania, said, " Brothers, we the Delawares, return you our hearty thanks for the " news you have sent us, and we assure you, we will not hear the voice of any other nation; " for we are to be directed by you, our brothers, the English, and by none else; we shall " be very glad to hear, what our brothers have to say to us at the Logg's town, in the spring; " and do assure you of our hearty good will and love to our brothers, we present you with " these four strings of wampum." This is the last town of the Delawares to the westward. The Delaware Indians, by the best accounts I could gather, consist of about five hundred fighting men, all firmly attached to the English interest: they are not properly a part of the Six Nations, but are scattered about, among most of the Indians upon the Ohio, and some of them among the Six Nations, from whom they have leave to hunt upon their lands. — *Message from the governor of Pennsylvania. Indians promise to be firm to the English. Delawares 500 fighting men, not part of the Six Nations, but have leave to hunt on their lands.*

Tuesday 29th Set out S. W. 5 m. S. 5 m. to the mouth of *Sioto Creek*, opposite to the *Shawane town*; here we fired our guns to alarm the traders, who soon answered, and came and ferried us over. The land about the mouth of *Sioto Creek* is rich but broken, fine bottoms upon the river and creek. The *Shawane town* is situate on both sides of the Ohio, just below the mouth of *Sioto Creek*, and contains about three hundred men; there are about forty houses on the south side of the river, and about a hundred on the north side, with a kind of state house of about ninety feet long, with a light cover of bark, in which they hold their councils: the Shawanes are not a part of the Six Nations, but were formerly at variance with them, though now reconciled; they are great friends to the English, who once protected them from the fury of the Six Nations, which they gratefully remember. — *Shawane town. Land rich but broken. Shawane town situated, contains 300 men. Shawanes not a part of the Six Nations. English protected them from the fury of the Six Nations.*

Wednesday 30th. We were conducted into council, where George Croghan delivered sundry speeches from the government of Pennsylvania to the chiefs of this nation; in which he informed them, " That two prisoners who had been taken by the French, had made their " escape from the French officer at Lake Erie, as he was carrying them toward Canada, " brought news that the French offered a large sum of money, to any who would bring to " them the said Croghan, and Andrew Montour alive, or if dead, their scalps; and that the " French also threatened those Indians and the Wiandots with war, in the spring. The same " person farther said, that they had seen twenty French canoes, loaded with stores, for a new " fort they designed on the south side Lake Erie." Mr. Croghan also informed them, that several of our traders had been taken, and advised them to keep their warriors at home, until they could see what the French intended, which he doubted not would appear in the spring. Then Andrew Montour informed this nation, as he had done the Wiandots and the Delawares, " That the King of Great Britain had sent them a large present of goods in company with the " Six Nations, which was under the care of the governor of Virginia, who had sent me out " to invite them to come and see him, and partake of their father's present next summer." To which we received this answer, Big Hanoahansa their speaker, taking in his hand the several strings of wampum, which had been given by the English, said, " These are the speeches " received by us from your great men. From the beginning of our friendship, all that our " brothers, the English have told us, has been good and true, for which we return our hearty " thanks; then taking up four other strings of wampum in his hand, he said; Brothers, I " now speak the sentiments of all our people. When first our forefathers the English met our " brothers, they found what our brothers the English, told them to be true, and so have we; " we are but a small people, but it is not to us only that you speak, but to all nations: we shall be — *Messages from the governor of Pennsylvania. Acquaints the Indians the king had sent them a present. Indians answer.*

B   glad

(6)

"glad to hear what our brothers will say to us, at the Logg's town in the spring; and we hope that
"the friendship now subsisting between us and our brothers, will last as long as the sun shines or
"the moon gives light. We hope that our children will hear and believe what our brothers say to
"them as we have always done; and to assure you of our hearty good will towards you our bro-
"thers, we present you with these four strings of wampum." After the council was over, they
had much talk about sending a guard with us to the Picqualinnee town (these are a tribe of
the Tawightwis) which was reckoned near 200 miles; but after a long consultation, their
king being sick, they came to no determination about it.

Appendix page Resolves to go to the Tawightwis.

Thursday 31st. to Monday February 11th. Stayed in the *Shawane town*. While I was here the Indians had a very extraordinary festival at which I was present, and which I have exactly described at the end of my journal. As I had particular instructions from the president of Virginia to discover the strength and number of some Indian nations to the westward, who had lately revolted from the French, and had some messages to deliver them from him, I resolved to set out for the *Tawightwi town*.

Tuesday 12th. Having left my boy to take care of my horses in the *Shawane town*, and supplied myself with a fresh horse to ride, I set out with my old company, viz. George Croghan, Andrew Montour, Robert Kallender, and a servant to carry our provision, &c. N. W. 10 m.

Wednesday 13th. The same course, N. W. about 35 m.

Thursday 14th. The same course about 30 m.

Friday 15th The same course 15 m. we met with nine Shawane Indians coming from one of the Picqualinnee towns where they had been to council, they told us there were fifteen more of them behind at the Tawightwi town, waiting for the arrival of the Wawiaghtas (a tribe of the Tawightwis) who were to bring with them a Shawane woman and child to deliver to their men that were behind. This woman, they informed us, was taken prisoner last fall by some of the Wawiaghta warriors through a mistake, which was like to have engaged those nations in war.

Little Mineami river.

Saturday 16th. Set out the same course, N. W. about 35 m. to the *little Mineami river or creek*.

Big Mineami river. Tawightwi town.

Sunday 17th. Crossed the *little Mineami*, and altered our course S. W. 25 m. to the *big Mineami river*, opposite to the *Tawightwi town*. All the land from the *Shawane town* to this place (except the first twenty miles, which is broken) is fine rich level land, well timbered, with large walnut, ash, sugar-trees, cherry-trees, &c; well watered with a great number of little streams and rivulets; full of beautiful natural meadows, covered with wild rye, blue grass, and clover; and abounds with turkeys, deer, elks, and most sorts of game, particularly buffaloes, thirty or forty of which are frequently seen feeding in one meadow: in short, it wants nothing but cultivation to make it a most delightful country. The Ohio and all the large branches are said to be full of fine fish of several kinds, particularly a sort of cat-fish* of a prodigious size; but as I was not there at a proper season, I had not an opportunity of seeing any of them. The traders had always reckoned it 200 miles from the *Shawane town* to the *Tawightwi town*; but by my computation, I could make it no more than 150. The *Mineami river* being high, we were obliged to make a raft of logs, to transport our goods and saddles, and swim our horses over: after firing a few guns and pistols, and smoaking in the warriors pipe, who came to invite us to the town, according to their custom of inviting and welcoming strangers, and great men, we entered the town with English colours before us, and were kindly received by their king, who invited us into his own house, and set our colours upon the top of it. The firing of the guns held about a quarter of an hour, and then all the white men and traders that were there, came and welcomed us to the *Tawightwi town*. *This town is situate on the N.W. side of the big Mineami river, about 150 miles from the mouth thereof*; it consists of about four hundred families, and is daily increasing; it is accounted one of the strongest Indian towns upon this part of the continent. The Tawightwis are a very numerous people, consisting of many different tribes, under the same form of government; each tribe has a particular chief, or king, one of which is chosen indifferently out of any tribe, to rule the whole nation, and is vested with greater authorities than any of the others. They are accounted the most powerful nation to the westward of the English settlements, and much superior to the Six Nations with whom they are now in amity. Their strength and numbers are not thoroughly known, as they have but lately traded with the English, and indeed have very little trade among them; they deal in much the same commodities as the northern Indians: there are other nations or tribes still farther to the westward, daily coming in to them; and it is thought their power and interest reaches to the westward of the Missisippi, if not across the continent; they are at present very well affected to the English, and seem fond of an alliance with them; they formerly lived on the farther side of the Wabash, and were in the French interest, who supplied them with some few trifles, at a most exorbitant price; they were called by the French Mineamis, but they have now revolted from them, and left their former habitations, for the sake of trading with the English, and notwithstanding all the artifices the French have used, they have not been able to recall them. After we had been some time in the king's house, Mr. Montour told him that we wanted to speak with him, and the chiefs of this nation this evening, upon which we were invited into the long house, and having taken our places, Mr. Montour began as follows.

Smoaks the pipe of peace.

Is kindly received by the Tawightwi king.

Remarks on the Tawightwi town and nation.

Montour tells the king he had come on business to him.

* The editor has seen them of 60 pounds weight.

" Brothers

(7)

"Brothers the Tawightwis as we have been hindered by the high waters, and some busi- Montour speaks to
"ness with our other Indian brothers, no doubt our long stay has caused some trouble among the Tawightwis.
"our brothers here, therefore we now present you with two strings of wampum, to remove
"all the trouble of your hearts, and clear your eyes that you may see the sun shine clear,
"for we have a great deal to say to you; and would have you send for one of your friends
"that can speak the Mohickon or Mingoe tongue well, that we may understand each other
"thoroughly, as we have a great deal of business to do." The Mohickons are a small tribe
who most of them speak English and are also well acquainted with the language of the
Tawightwis, and they with theirs. Mr. Montour then proceeded to deliver them a message
from the Wiandots and Delawares as follows.

"Brothers the Tawightwis, this comes by our brothers the English who are coming Speech from the Wi-
"with good news to you. We hope you will take care of them, and all our brothers the andots and Delawares
"English who are trading among you. You made a road for our brothers the English to to the Tawightwis.
"come and trade among you, but it is now very foul, great logs are fallen across it, and we
"would have you be strong, like men, and have one heart with us, and make the road clear,
"that our brothers the English may have free course and recourse between you and us. In
"the sincerity of our hearts, we send you these four strings of wampum." to which they
gave their usual Yo Ho. They then said they wanted some tobacco to smoak with us, and
that to-morrow they would send for their interpreter.

Monday 18th. We walked about, and viewed the fort, which wanted some repairs, and the
the trader's men helped them to bring logs to line the inside.

Tuesday 19th. We gave their kings and great men some cloaths paint and shirts, and they
were busy dressing and preparing themselves for the council. The weather grew warm and
the creeks began to lower very fast.

Wednesday 20th. About twelve o'clock we were informed that some of the foreign
tribes were coming, upon which proper persons were ordered to meet them, and conduct them
to the town, and then we were invited into the long house : after we had been seated about a
quarter of an hour, four Indians, two from each tribe, who had been sent before to bring the
long pipe, and to inform us that the rest were coming, came in and informed us, that their
friends had sent those pipes, that we might smoak the calumet pipe of peace with them, and
that they intended to do the same with us.

Thursday 21st. We were invited again into the long house (where Mr. Croghan made them) Croghan delivers a
with the foreign tribes, a present to the value of one hundred pounds Pennsylvania money, and present and messages.
delivered all our speeches to them, at which they seemed well pleased, and said they would
take time and consider well what we had said to them.

Friday 22d. Nothing remarkable happened.

Saturday 23d. In the afternoon there was an alarm, which caused great confusion and running about among the Indians ; upon enquiring the reason of this stir, they told us, it was occasioned by six Indians that came to war against them from the southward, three of them Cuttawas, and three Shawanes ; these were some of the Shawanes who had formerly deserted from
the other part of the nation, and now lived to the southward : towards night there was a report spread in town, that four Indians, and four hundred French, were on their march and just by
the town, but soon after the messenger who brought the news said, there were only four French
Indians coming to council, and that they bid him say so, only to see how the English would
behave themselves, but as they had behaved themselves like men, he now told the truth.

Sunday February 24th. This morning the four French Indians came into town and were Four French Indians
kindly received by the town Indians. They marched in under French colours, and were con- come in.
ducted into the long house, and after they had been in about a quarter of an hour, the council
sat and we were sent for that we might hear what the French had to say. The *Piankasha* king
who was at that time the principal man and commander in chief of the *Tawightwis*, said he
would have the English colours set up in this council, as well as the French, to which we answered he might do as he thought fit; after we were seated opposite to the French ambassadors,
one of them said he had a present to make them, so a place was prepared, as they had before French present to the
done for our present, between them and us, and then their speaker stood up and laid his hands Indians.
upon two keggs of brandy that held about seven quarts each, and a roll of tobacco of about
ten pounds weight, then taking two strings of wampum in his hand he said "What he had
"to deliver them was from their father (meaning the French king) and he desired they would
"hear what he was about to say." Then he laid the two strings of wampum upon the keggs
and taking up four other strings of black and white wampum, he said "That their father French speech.
"remembering his children had sent them two keggs of milk, and some tobacco, and that he
"had now made a clear road for them, to come and see him and his officers, and pressed them
"very much to come and see him" Then he took another string of wampum in his hand
and said "Their father would now forget all little differences that had been between them,
"and desired them not to be of two minds, but to let him know their minds freely, for he
"would send for them no more" To which the *Piankasha* king replied, it was true their father Piankasha king's re-
"had sent for them several times, and said the road was clear, but he understood it was made ply to the French.
"foul and bloody, and by them. We, said he, have cleared a road for our brothers the English,
"and your fathers have made it bad, and have taken some of our brothers prisoners, which
"we look upon as done to us," and he turned short about and went out of council. After
the French ambassador had delivered his message, he went into one of the private houses, and
endeavoured much to prevail on some Indians there, and was seen to cry and lament which
was as he said for the loss of that nation.

Monday

(8)

Wawiaghta speech.

Monday 25th. This day we received a speech from the *Wawiaghtas* and *Piankashas* two tribes of the *Tawightwis*, one of the chiefs of the former spoke. " Brothers we have heard " what you have said to us by the interpreter, and we see you take pity upon our poor wives " and children, and have taken us by the hand into the great chain of friendship, therefore " we present you with these two bundles of skins, to make *shoes* for your people, and this " pipe to smoak in, to assure you our hearts are good and true towards you our brothers, and " we hope that we shall all continue in true love and friendship with one another, as people " with one head and one heart ought to do. You have pitied us, as you always did the rest " of our Indian brothers. We hope the pity you have always shewn will remain as long " as the Sun gives light, and on our side you may depend upon sincere and true friend- " ship towards you, as long as we have strength." This person stood up and spoke with the air and gesture of an orator.

Tawightwi's reply to the French speech.

Tuesday 26th. The *Tawightwis* delivered the following answer to the four Indians sent by the French. The Captain of the warriors stood up, and taking some strings of black and white wampum in his hand, he spoke with a fierce tone, and very warlike air, " Brothers the " *Owtawais*, you are always differing with the French yourselves, and yet you listen to what " they say, but we will let you know by these four strings of wampum that we will not hear " any thing they say to us, or do any thing they bid us do." Then the same speaker with six

Refuse to go among the French and say they have joined the English &c.

strouds, two matchcoats, and a string of black wampum, (I understood the goods were in re- turn for the milk and tobacco) directed his speech to the French and said, " Fathers you desire " that we will speak our minds from our hearts, which I am going to do, You have often de- " sired we should go home to you, but I tell you it is not our home, for we have made a " road as far as the Sea, to the Sun rising, and have been taken by the hand by our brothers

Tell them they are ready for war.

" the *English*, the Six Nations, the *Delawares*, *Shawanes*, and *Wiandots*, and we assure you " that is the road we will go: and as you threaten us with war in the spring, we tell you if " you are angry we are ready to receive you, and resolve to die here, before we will go to you, " and that you may know this is our mind, we send you this string of black wampum." After a short pause the same speaker spoke again thus ; " Brothers; the *Owtawais* you hear what " I say, tell that to your fathers the French for that is our mind, and we speak it from our " hearts."

Wednesday February 27th. This day they took down the French colours, and dismissed the four French Indians, so they took their leave of the town, and set off for the French fort.

Indian feather-dance.

Thursday 28th. The cryer of the town, came by the king's order, and invited us to the long house, to see the *warriors feather dance*: it was performed by three dancing masters who were painted all over of various colours, with long sticks in their hands, upon the ends of which, are fastened long feathers of swans, and other birds, neatly woven in the shape of a fowls wing; in this disguise they performed many antick tricks, waving their sticks and feathers about with great skill, to imitate the flying and fluttering of birds, keeping exact time with their musick; while they are dancing some of the warriors strike a post, upon which the musick and dancers cease, and the warrior gives an account of his achievments in war, and when he has done throws down some goods as a recompence to the performers, and musicians, after which they proceed in their dance as before, till another warrior strikes the post, and so on as long as they think fit

Tawightwi's speech to the governor of Pennsylvania.

Friday March 1st. We received the following speech from the *Tawightwis*. The speaker stood up and addressing himself as to the governor of Pennsylvania, with two strings of wampum in his hand, he said " Brothers our hearts are glad that you have taken " notice of us ; and surely brothers we hope that you will order a smith to settle here to mend " our guns, and hatchets : your kindness makes us so bold as to ask this request. You told " us our friendship should last as long, and be as the greatest mountain. We have considered " well, and all our great kings and warriors are come to a resolution, never to give heed to what " the French say to us, but always to hear, and believe what you our brothers say to us. " Brothers we are obliged to you, for your kind invitation to receive a present at the Logg's " town, but as our foreign tribes are not yet come, we must wait for them, but you may " depend we will come, as soon as our women have planted corn, to hear what our brothers " will say to us. Brothers we present you with this bundle of skins, as we are but poor, to " be for shoes for you on the road, and we return you our hearty thanks for the cloaths " which you have put upon our wives and children.

We then took our leave of the kings and chiefs, and they ordered that a small party of Indians should go with us, as far as *Hockhocking*; but as I had left my boy and horses at the *lower Shawane town*, I was obliged to go by myself, or to go sixty or seventy miles out of my way, which I did not care to do; so we all came over the *Mineami River* together this evening, but Mr. Croghan and Mr. Montour, went over again and lodged in the town, I stayed on this side at one Robert Smith's a trader, where we had left our horses. Before the French

Articles of peace be- tween the English and Wawiaghtas and Pi- ankashas, page
Land on the great Mineami river very fine, and the same for several miles on the Wabash &c.
Many clear fields with fine grass.
White clover, wild rye and blue-grass.

Indians had come into town, we had drawn articles of peace and alliance, between the English and *Wawiaghtas*, and *Piankashas*, the indentures were signed, sealed and delivered on both sides, and as I drew them I took a copy. The land upon the great *Mineami River* is very rich, level, and well timbered, some of the finest meadows that can be: the Indians and traders assure me that it holds as good and if possible better, to the westward as far as the *Wabash*, which is ac- counted 100 miles, and quite up to the head of the *Minieami River* which is sixty miles above the *Tawightwi town*, and down the said river quite to the *Ohio*, which is reckoned 150 miles. The grass here grows to a great height in the clear fields, of which there are a great number, and the bottoms are full of white clover, wild rye, and blue-grass.

Sunday 3d,

(9)

Saturday 2d. George Croghan, and the rest of our company, came over the river; we got our horses, and travelled about 35 m. to *Mad Creek*, this is a place where some English traders had been taken prisoners by the French.

Sunday 3d. We parted, they for *Hockhocking*, and I for the *Shawane town*; and as I was quite alone, and knew that the French Indians had threatened us, and would probably pursue, or lie in wait for us, I left the path, and went to the southwestward, down the little *Mineami river or creek*, where I had fine travelling, through rich land and beautiful meadows, in which I could sometimes see forty or fifty Buffaloes feeding at once. The little *Mineami river or creek* continued to run through the middle of a fine meadow, about a mile wide, very clear, like an old field, and not a bush in it. I could see the buffaloes in it above two miles off. I travelled this day about thirty miles. Land on little Mineami river very fine. Large herds of buffaloes.

Monday 4th. This day I heard several guns, but was afraid to examine who fired them, lest they might be some of the French Indians; so I travelled through the woods about 30 m. just at night I killed a fine barren cow buffaloe, and took out her tongue, and a little of the best of her meat. The land still level, rich and well timbered with oak, walnut, ash, locust, and sugar-trees. Land very fine and well timbered.

Tuesday 5th. I travelled about thirty miles.

Wednesday 6th. I travelled about thirty miles and killed a fat bear.

Thursday 7th. Set out with my horse-load of bear, and travelled about 30 m. This afternoon I met a young man a trader, and we encamped together that night; he happened to have some bread with him, and I had plenty of meat, so we fared very well.

Friday 8th. Travelled about 30 m. and arrived at night at the *Shawane town*. All the Indians, as well as the white men came out to welcome my return to their town, being very glad that all things were rightly settled in the *Mineami* country; they fired upwards of 150 guns in the town, and made an entertainment on account of the peace with the western Indians. On my return from the *Tawightwi*, to the *Shawane town*, I did not keep an exact account of course or distance, for as the land thereabout was much the same, and the situation of the country was sufficiently described, in my journey to the *Tawightwi town*, I thought it unnecessary, but have notwithstanding laid down my track pretty nearly in my plot. Shawane town.

Saturday 9th. In the *Shawane town* I met with one of the *Mingoe* chiefs, who had been down at the falls of Ohio, so that we did not see him as we went up. I informed him of the king's present and the invitation down to Virginia; he told me that there was a party of French Indians hunting at the falls, and if I went they would kill or carry me away prisoner to the French, for it was certain they would not let me pass; however as I had a great inclination to see the falls, and the lands on the East side the Ohio, I resolved to venture as far as possible.

Sunday 10th. Stayed in the town and prepared for my departure.

Tuesday 12th. I got my horses over the river, and after breakfast, my boy and I got ferried over. The Ohio is near three quarters of a mile wide at the Shawane town, and is very deep and smooth. Ohio at the Shawane town ¾ mile wide, very deep, and a gentle current.

Wednesday 13th. We set out S. 45 d. W. down the river, on the S. E. side 8 m. then S. 10 m. here I met two men belonging to Robert Smith at whose house I lodged on this side the *Mineami river*, and one Hugh Crawford; the said Robert Smith had given me an order upon these men, for two of the teeth of a large beast, which they were bringing from towards the falls of Ohio, one of which I brought in and delivered to the Ohio company. Robert Smith informed me that about seven years ago, these teeth and the bones of three large beasts, one of which was somewhat smaller than the other two, *were found in a salt lick or spring, upon a small creek, which runs into the south side of the Ohio, about fifteen miles below the mouth of the great Mineami river, and twenty above the falls of Ohio*; he assured me that the rib bones of the largest of those beasts, were eleven feet long, and the scull bone six feet across the forehead, and the other bones in proportion, and that there were several teeth there, some of which he called horns, and said they were upwards of five feet long, and as much as a man could well carry; that he had hid one in a branch at some distance from the place, lest the French Indians should carry it away. The tooth which I brought in, for the Ohio company, was a jaw tooth, of better than four pounds weight, it appeared to be the farthest tooth in the jaw, and looked like fine ivory, when the outside was scraped off. I also met with four *Shawane* Indians coming up the river in their canoes, who informed me that there were about sixty French Indians encamped at the falls. Three very large carcases of beasts found on the Ohio.

Rib bones 11 feet. Scull bone 6 feet across. Teeth 5 feet long.

Tooth Gift brought above 4 pounds weight.

Thursday 14th. I went down the river S. 15 m. the land upon this side the Ohio chiefly broken and the bottoms but narrow. Land broken, bottoms narrow.

Friday 15th. S. 5 m. S. W. 10 m. to a creek that was so high that we could not get over that night.

Saturday 16th. S. 45 d. W. about 35 m.

Sunday 17th. The same course 15 m. then N. 45 d. W. 5 m.

Monday 18th. N. 45 d. W. 5 m. then S. W. 20 m. to the *lower salt lick creek*, which Robert Smith and the Indians told me was about 15 miles above the *falls of Ohio*; the land still hilly, the salt lick here much the same with those before described. This day we heard several guns which made me imagine the French Indians were not moved, but were still hunting, and firing thereabouts; we also saw some traps newly set, and the footsteps of some Indians, plain on the ground as if they had been there the day before. I was now much troubled that I could not comply with my instructions, and was once resolved to leave the boy and horses, and go privately on foot to view the falls; but the boy being a poor hunter, was afraid Lower salt lick 15 miles from the falls of the Ohio.

C

(10)

Afraid to go to the falls.	afraid he would starve if I was long from him, and there was also great danger lest the French Indians should come upon our horses tracks, or hear their bells, and as I had seen good land enough, I thought perhaps I might be blamed for venturing so far, in such dangerous times, so I concluded not to go to the falls, but travelled away to the southward, till we were over
Little Cuttawa river. Falls of Ohio described.	the *little Cuttawa river*. *The falls of Ohio*, by the best information I could get, are not very steep; on the S.E. side there is a bar of sand at some distance from the shore, the water between the bar, and the shore is not above three feet deep, and the stream moderately strong: the Indians frequently pass safely in their canoes, through this passage, but are obliged to take great care as they go down, lest the current which is much the strongest on the N.W. side, should draw them that way, which would be very dangerous, as the water on that side runs with great rapidity, over several ledges of rocks. The waters below the falls, as they say, is about six fathoms deep, and the river continues without any obstruction, till it empties itself
400 miles from the falls, to the Mississippi. Ohio wide. Lands very rich.	into the Mississippi, which is accounted upwards of 400 miles. The Ohio near the mouth is said to be very wide, and the land upon both sides very rich, and in general very level all the way from the falls. After I had determined not to go to the falls, we turned from salt lick creek, to a ridge of mountains that made towards the *Cuttawa river*, and from the top of the mountain, we saw a fine level country S.W. as far as our eyes could behold; and it was a very clear day. We then went down the mountain, and set out S. 20 d. W. about 5 m. through rich level land covered with small walnut, sugar-trees, red buds &c.

Tuesday 19th. We set out south, and crossed several creeks all running to the S.W. at about twelve miles came to the *little Cuttawa river*, we were obliged to go up it about a mile to an island which was the shoalest place we could find to cross at: we then continued our

Lands on the Cuttawa river rich, and level, for a great distance. Great Cattawa river.	course in all about thirty miles, through rich level land except about two miles which was broken and indifferent: this level is about thirty five miles broad, and as we came up the side of it along the branches of the *little Cuttawa*, we found it about 150 miles long, and how far towards the S.W. we could not tell, but imagined it held as far as the *great Cuttawa river*, which would be upwards of 100 miles more, and appeared much broader that way, than here, as I could discern from the tops of the mountains.

Wednesday 20th. We did not travel. I went up to the top of a mountain to view the country: To the S.E. it looked very broken, and mountainous, but to the eastward and S.W. it appeared very level.

Thursday 21st. Set out S. 45 d. E. 15 m. S. 5 m. here I found a place where the stones

Finds a kind of borax.	shined like high coloured brass; the heat of the Sun drew out of them a kind of borax, or salt-petre, only something sweeter, some of which I brought in to the Ohio company, though I believe it was nothing but a sort of sulphur.

Friday 22d. S.E. 12 m. I killed a fat bear, and was taken sick that night.

Saturday 23d. I stayed here, and sweated after the Indian manner which helped me.

Sunday 24th. Set out E 2 m. N.E. 3 m. N. 1 m. E. 2 m. S.F. 5 m. E. 2 m. N. 2 m. S.E. 7 m. to a small creek where we encamped, in a place where we had but poor food for our horses, and both we, and they were very much wearied. The reason of our making so many short courses was, we were driven by a branch of the *little Cuttawa river*, whose banks were so exceeding steep that it was impossible to ford it, into a ledge of rocky laurel mountains which was almost impassable.

Monday 25th. Set out S.E. 12 m. N. 2 m. E. 1 m. S. 4 m. S.E. 2 m. we killed a buck elk here, and took out his tongue to carry with us.

Tuesday 26th. Set out S.E. 10 m. S.W. 1 m. S.E. 1 m. S.W. 1 m. S.E. 1 m. S.W. 1 m.

Laurel thickets.	S.E. 5 m. killed two buffaloes and took out their tongues, and encamped. These two days we travelled through rocks, and mountains full of laurel thickets, which we could hardly creep through, without cutting our way.
Plenty of fine coal on the Cuttawa.	Wednesday 27th. Our horses, and selves were so tired, that we were obliged to stay this day to rest, for we we were unable to travel: On all the branches of the little Cuttawa river was great plenty of fine coal, some of which I brought in to the Ohio company.
Coal and slate.	Thursday 28th. Set out S.E. 15 m. crossing several creeks of the *little Cuttawa river*; the land still full of coal, and black slate.

Friday 29th. The same course S.E. about 12 m. the land still mountainous.

Saturday 30th. Stayed to rest our horses. I went on foot, and found a passage through the mountains, to another creek or a fork of the same creek that we were upon.

Sunday 31st. The same course S.E. 15 m. killed a buffaloe and encamped.

Monday April 1st. Set out the same course about 20 m. part of the way we went along a path up the side of a little creek, at the head of which, was a gap in the mountains, then

Blocks of coal, eight inches square, on the surface of the earth.	our path went down another creek to a lick, *where blocks of coal about eight or ten inches square lay upon the surface of the ground*; here we killed a bear and encamped.

Tuesday d. Set out S. 2 m. S.E. 1 m. N.E. 3 m. killed a buffaloe.

Wednesday 3d. S. 1 m. S.W. 3 m. E. 3 m. S.E. 2 m. to a small creek on which was a large warrior's camp that would contain seventy or eighty warriors; their captain's name or title was the crane, as I knew by his picture or arms painted on a tree.

Thursday 4th. I stayed here all day to rest our horses: I plotted down our courses, and found I had still near 200 miles home upon a straight line.

Friday 5th. Rained, and we stayed at the warrior's camp.

Saturday 6th. We went along the warriors road S. 1 m. S.E. 3 m. S. 2 m. S.E. 3 m. E. 3 m. killed a bear.

Sunday 7th.

Sunday 7th. Set out E. 2 m. N. E. 1 m. S. E. 1 m. S. 1 m. W. 1 m. S. W. 1 m. S. 1 m. S. E. 2 m. S. 1 m.

Monday 8th. S. 1 m. S. E. 1 m. E. 3 m. S. E. 1 m. E. 3 m. N. E. 2 m. N. 1 m. E. 1 m. N. 1 m. E. 2 m. and encamped on a small laurel creek.

Tuesday 9th, and Wednesday 10th. The weather being bad, we did not travel these two days, the country being still rocky, mountainous, and full of laurel thickets ; the worst tra- velling I ever saw. *Country mountainous; with laurel thickets.*

Thursday 11th. We travelled several courses near 20 miles, but in the afternoon, as I could see from the top of a mountain the place we came from, I found we had not come upon a straight line more than N. 65 d. E. 10 m.

Friday 12th. Set out through very difficult ways E. 5 m. to a small creek.

Saturday 13th. The same course E. upon a straight line ; though the way we were obliged to travel was near twenty miles : here we killed two bears, the way still rocky and mountainous.

Sunday 14th. As food was very scarce in these barren mountains, we were obliged to move for fresh feeding for our horses; in climbing up the clifts and rocks this day, two of our horses fell down, and were much hurt, and a paroquet, which I had got from the Indians on the other side of the Ohio, where there are a great number, died of a bruise he got by the fall; though it was but a trifle I was much concerned at losing him, as he was perfectly tame, and had been very brisk all the way, and I had still corn enough left to feed him. In the afternoon I left the horses, and went all the way down the creek, and found such a precipice, and such laurel thickets that we could not pass, and the horses were not able to go up the mountain, till they had rested a day or two. *Paroquets on the Ohio.*

Monday 15th. We cut a passage through the laurels better than two miles ; as I was climbing up the rocks, I got a fall which hurt me much. This afternoon we wanted provision. I killed a bear. *Cut a passage through a laurel thicket two miles.*

Tuesday 16th. Thunder and rain, in the morning we set out N. 25 d. E. 3 m.

Wednesday 17th. This day I went to the top of a mountain to view the way, and found it so bad that I did not care to engage in it, but rather chose to go out of the way, and keep down along the side of a creek, till I could find a branch or run, on the other side to go up.

Thursday 18th. Set out down the creek's side, N. 3 m. then the creek turning N. W. I was obliged to leave it, and go up a ridge N. E. 1 m. E. 2 m. S. E. 2 m. N. E. 1 m. to the fork of a river.

Friday 19th. Set out down the run N. E. 2 m. E. 2 m. S. E. 2 m. N. 20 d. E 2 m. E. 2 m. up a large run.

Saturday 20th. Set out S. E. 10 m. E. 4 m. over a small creek. We had such bad travelling down this creek, that we had like to have lost one of our horses.

Sunday 21st. Stayed to rest our horses.

Monday 22d. Rained all day, we could not travel.

Tuesday 23d. Set out E. 8 m. along a ridge of mountains, then S. E. 5 m. E. 3 m. S. E. 4 m. and encamped among very steep mountains.

Wednesday 24th. S. E. 4 m. through steep mountains and thickets, E. 6 m.

Thursday 25th. E. 5 m. S. E. 1 m. N. E. 2 m. S. E. 2 m. E. 1 m. then S. 2 m. E. 1 m. killed a bear.

Friday 26th. Set out S. E. 2 m, here it rained so hard we were obliged to stop.

Saturday 27th, to Monday 29th. These three days it continued rainy and bad weather, so that we could not travel. All the way from Salt-Lick creek to this place, the branches of the little Cuttawa were so high that we could not pass them, which obliged us to go over the heads of them, through a continued ledge of almost inaccessible mountains, rocks and laurel thickets.

Tuesday 30th. Fair weather, set out E. 3 m. S. E. 8 m. E. 2 m. to a *little river or creek which falls into the Big Kanhawa, called Blue Stone*, where we encamped and had good feeding for our horses. *Blue Stone river.*

Wednesday May 1st. Set out N. 75 d. E. 10 m. and killed a buffaloe ; then went up a very high mountain, upon the top of which was a rock sixty or seventy feet high, and a cavity in the middle, into which I went, and found there was a passage through it, which gradually ascended to the top, with several holes in the rock, which let in the light ; when I got to the top of this rock, I could see a prodigious distance, and could plainly discover where the Big Kanhawa river broke through the next high mountain. I then came down and continued my course N. 75 d. E. 6 m. farther and encamped. *Remarkable rock.*

Thursday 2d, and Friday 3d. These two days it rained, and we staid at our camp, to take care of some provision we had killed.

Saturday 4th. This day our horses ran away, and it was late before we got them, so we could not travel far; we went N. 75 d. E. 4 m.

Sunday 5th. Rained all day.

Monday 6th. Set out through very bad ways E. 3 m. N. E. 6 m. over a bad laurel creek E. 4 m.

Tuesday 7th. Set out E. 10 m. to the *Big Kanhawa or new river*, and got over half of it to a *large island*, where we lodged all night. *Big Kanhawa, or New River.*

Wednesday 8th. We made a raft of logs and crossed the other half of the river, and went up it S. 2 m. *The Kanhawa or new river (by some called Wood's river)* where I crossed it, which was about eight miles above the mouth of the *Blue Stone river*, is better than 200 yards wide, and *Kanhawa 200 yards wide, deep, with many falls.*

(12)

Bottoms rich but narrow: high land broken. and pretty deep, but full of rocks and falls. The bottoms upon it, and *Blue Stone river* are very rich, but narrow; the high land broken.

Thursday 9th. Set out E. 13 m. to a large Indian warrior's camp, where we killed a Bear and staid all night.

Friday 10th. Set out E. 4. m. S. E. 3 m. S. 3 m. through mountains covered with ivy, and laurel thickets.

A lake on the top of a mountain. Saturday 11th. Set out S. 2 m. S. E. 5 m. to a creek, and a meadow where we let our horses feed, then S. E. 2 m. S. 1 m. S. E. 2 m. to a very high mountain, upon the top of which was a lake or pond about three quarters of a mile long N. E. and S. W. and a quarter of a mile wide, the water fresh and clear, and a clean gravelly shore about ten yards wide, with a fine meadow, and six fine springs in it; then S. about 4 m. to a branch of the Kanhawa called *Sinking Creek.*

Sinking Creek.

Sunday 12th. Stayed to rest our Horses, and dry some meat we had killed.

R. Hall the farthest settler to the west of new river. Monday 13th Set out S. E. 2 m. E. 1 m. S. E. 3 m. S. 12 m. to one Richard Hall's in Augusta county; this man is one of the farthest settlers to the westward up the new river.

Tuesday 14th. Stayed at Richard Hall's and wrote to the president of Virginia, and the Ohio company, to let them know I should be with them by the 15th day of June.

Wednesday 15th. Set out from Richard Hall's S. 16 m.

Beaver Island creek. Thursday 16th. The same course S. 22 m. and encamped at *Beaver Island creek, a branch of the Kanhawa,* opposite to the head of *Roanoak.*

Line between North Carolina, and Virginia. Friday 17th. Set out S. W. 3 m. then S. 9 m. to the dividing line between Carolina and Virginia, where I stayed all night. The land from Richard Hall's to this place is broken.

Gist arrives at his own house, on the Yadkin river. Saturday 18th. Set out S. 20 m. to my own house on the *Yadkin river;* when I came there, I found all my family gone, for the Indians had killed five people in the winter near that place, which frightened my wife and family away to *Roanoak,* about 35 miles nearer in among the inhabitants, which I was informed of, by an old man I met near the place.

Sunday 19th. Set out for *Roanoak,* and as we had now a path, we got there the same night where I found all my family well.

Christopher Gist.

Shawane festival. An account of the Festival at the Shawane Town mentioned in my Journal page 6.

Indian marriages dissolved. In the evening a proper officer made a public proclamation, that all the Indians marriages were dissolved, and a public feast was to be held for the three succeeding days after, in which the women (as their custom was) were again to choose their husbands.

The next morning early the Indians breakfasted, and after spent the day in dancing, till the evening, when a plentiful feast was prepared; after feasting, they spent the night in dancing.

The same way they passed the two next days till the evening, the men dancing by themselves, and then the women in turns round fires, and dancing in their manner in the form of the figure 8, about 60 or 70 of them at a time. The women, the whole time they danced, sung a song in their language, the chorus of which was,

I am not afraid of my husband;
I will choose what man I please.

Singing those lines alternately.

The third day in the evening, the men being about 100 in number, danced in a long string following one another, sometimes at length, at other times in a figure of 8 quite round the fort, and in and out of the long house, where they held their councils, the women standing together as the men danced by them; and as any of the women liked a man passing by, she *Indian women choose husbands.* stepped in, and joined in the dance, taking hold of the man's stroud, whom she chose, and then continued in the dance, till the rest of the women stepped in, and made their choice in the same manner; after which the dance ended and they all retired to consummate.

MR.

(13)

MR. GIST'S SECOND JOURNAL.

PURSUANT to my instructions, from the committee of the Ohio Company, bearing date July 16th, 1751 *.

Monday November 4th, Set out from the *company's storehouse*, in Frederick county Virginia, *opposite the mouth of Wills creek*, and crossing *Potomack* river went W. 4 m. to a gap in the *Allegany* mountains upon the S. W. fork of the said creek. *This gap is the nearest to Potomack river of any in the Allegany mountains, and is accounted one of the best, though the mountain is very high the ascent is no where very steep, but rises gradually near six miles; it is now very full of old trunks of trees and stones, but with some pains might be made a very good waggon road. This gap is directly in the way to Monaungahela, and several miles nearer than that the traders commonly pass through, and a much better way.* — Company's store called New Store. Wills Creek. Gap in the Allegany mountain best here.

Tuesday Nov. 5th. Set out N. 80 d. W. 8 m. it rained, and obliged us to stop.
Wednesday 6th. The same course 3 m. hard rain.
Thursday 7th. Rained hard and we could not travel.
Friday 8th. Set out the same course N. 80 d. W. 3 m. where we encamped, and turned to see where the branches lead to, and found they descended into the middle fork of *Youghiogeni*. We hunted all the grounds for ten miles or more, and killed several deer, bears, and one large elk. The bottoms upon the branches are but narrow; with some Indian fields, about 2000 acres of good high land about a mile from the largest branch. — Bottoms narrow.

Saturday 9th to *Tuesday* 19th. We were employed in searching the lands, and discovering the branches creeks &c.
Wednesday 20th. Set out N. 45 d. W. 5 m. killed a deer.
Thursday 21st. The same course 5 m. the greatest part of the day, we were cutting our way through a laurel thicket, and lodged by the side of one at night.
Friday 22d. Set out the same course N. 45 d. W. 2 m. and cut our way through a great laurel thicket to the middle fork of *Youghiogeni* then S. down the said fork crossing a run 1 m. then S. 45 d. W. 2 m. over the said fork where we encamped. — Youghiogeni river.

Saturday 23d. Rested our horses and examined the land on foot, which we found to be tolerable rich, and well timbered but stoney and broken. — Land rich, stony and broken, well timbered.

Sunday 24th. Set out W. 2 m. then S. 45 d. W. 6 m. over the south fork and encamped on the S. W. side about a mile from a small hunting town of the Delaware's, from whom I bought some corn. I invited these Indians to a treaty at the Loggs town, the full moon in May, as Col. Patton had desired me; they treated me very civilly, but after I went from that place my man informed me, that they threatened to take away our guns and not let us travel. — Delaware's hunting town.

Monday 25th. Set out W. 6 m. then S. 45 d. W. 2 m. to a *laurel creek*, where we encamped, and killed some deer.
Tuesday 26th, to *Thursday* 28th. We were examining the lands which we found to be rocky and mountainous. — Land rocky and mountainous.

Friday 29th. Set out W. 3 m. then N. 65 d. W. 3 m. N. 45 d. W. 2 m.
Saturday 30th, to *Friday* December 6. We searched the land several miles round, and found it about 15 m. from the foot of the mountains to the *river Monaungahela*, the first five miles of which E. and W. is good level farming land, with fine meadows, the timber white oak, and hiccory. The same body of land holds ten miles south to the upper forks of *Monaungahela*, and about ten miles north towards the mouth of *Youghiogeni*; the land nearer the river for about eight or nine miles wide and the same length is much richer, and better timbered, with walnuts, locusts, poplars, and sugar trees; but is in some places very hilly, the bottoms upon the river one mile and some places near two miles wide. — Good farming land, fine meadows, good timber. Land hilly.

Saturday 7th. Set out W. 6 m. and went to an Indian camp and invited them to a treaty at the Loggs town at the full moon in May next. At this camp there was a trader named Charles Poke, who spoke the Indian tongue well. The Indian, to whom this camp belonged, after much discourse with me, complained and said, " My friend, you were sent to
" us the last year from the great men in Virginia, to inform us of a present from the great
" king over the water, and if you can bring news from the king to us, why can't you tell
" him something from me? The proprietor of Pennsylvania granted my father a tract of
" land beginning eight miles below the fork of Brandy Wine Creek, and binding on the said
" creek to the fork, and including the west fork, and all its waters on both sides to the head
" fountain: The white people now live on these lands, and will neither let me have them,
" nor pay me any thing for them. My father's name was Chickoconnecon, I am his eldest
" son, and my name is Nemicollon. I desire that you will let the governor, and the great
" men in Virginia know this, it may be, they will tell the great king of it, and he will make
" Mr. Penn, or his people give me the land, or pay me for it. This trader here Charles
" Poke knows the truth of what I say, that the land was granted to my father, and that he — Nemicollon an Indian, complains that he was kept out of some lands, granted him by the proprietors of Pennsylvania on the fork of Brandy Wine Creek. Desires Gist to let the governor of Virginia know his complaint.

* Ohio Company's Case page 5.

D " or

(14)

"or I never sold it." On which Charles Poke said, that Chickoconnecon had such a grant of land, and that the people who lived on it could get no titles to it, for that it was now called manor lands. This I was obliged to insert in my journal to please the Indian.

Sunday 8th. We stayed at the Indian camp.

A large cave on the river Monaungahela. Monday 9th. Set out S. 45 d. W. 1 m. W. 6 m. to the *river Monaungahela*. At this place is a large cavity in a rock, about thirty feet long, and twenty feet wide, and about seven feet high, and an even floor; the entrance into it is so large and open, that it lets in plenty of light, and close by it is a stream of fine water.

Land rich, hilly, and well timbered. Tuesday 10th to Friday 13th. We were examining the lands which for nine or ten miles East is rich but hilly, as before described; on the E. side of the river for several miles there are several bottoms very rich, and a mile wide, and the hills above them are extraordinary rich and well timbered

Saturday 14th. We had snow.

Crossed the Monaungahela. Hills very rich, and full of sugar trees. Sunday 15th. Crossed the *river Monaungahela*, which is in this place fifty-three poles wide. The bottoms upon the W. side are not above one hundred yards wide, but the hills are very rich both up and down the river, and full of sugar-trees.

Monday 16th. Spent in searching the land.

Various sorts of land. Licking creek. Tuesday 17th. Set out W. 5 m. the land upon this course hilly, but very rich, about a mile and a half, then it was level, with good meadows, but not very rich, for about a mile and an half more, and the last two miles next to *Licking creek* was very good land. Upon this creek we lodged at a hunting camp of an Indian captain named Oppaymolleah. Here I saw an Indian named Joshua, who spoke very good English, he had been acquainted with me several years, and seemed very glad to see me, and wondered much where I was going so far in those woods. I said I was going to invite all the great men of the Indians, to a treaty to be held at the Loggs-town, the full moon in May next, where a parcel of goods, a present from the king of Great Britain, would be delivered them by proper commissioners, and that these were the goods which I informed them of last year, by order of the president of Virginia, Colonel Lee, who was since dead. Joshua informed them what I said, and they told me I ought to let the Beaver know it; so I wrote a line to him by Joshua, who promised to deliver it safe, and said there was a trader's man who could read it for him. This Beaver is the Sachem, or chief of the Delawares; it is customary among the Indian chiefs to take upon them the names of any beast or bird they fancy, the picture of which they always sign, instead of their name or arms.

Gist writes to the Beaver, chief of the Delawares, to invite his nation to a treaty.

Wednesday 18th. Stayed at the camp.

Licking creek. Thursday 19th. Set out W. 3 m. S. 45. W. 2 m. W. 1 m. to a branch of *Licking creek*.

Friday 20th. Set out W. 1 m. S. 45 d. W. 6 d. and encamped.

Gist's son frost bitten. Land very good, but hilly; game plenty. Saturday 21st, to Tuesday January 7th, 1752. We stayed at this place and had a good deal of snow, and bad weather, *my son had the misfortune to have his feet frost bitten*, which kept us much longer here than we intended, however we killed plenty of deer, turkeys, &c. and fared very well; the land hereabout is very good, but to the W. and SW. it is hilly.

Land midling, but hilly. Wednesday 8th. My son's feet being some what better, we set out S. 30 d. W. 5 m. S. 45 d. W. 3 m. the land midling good, but hilly. I found my son's feet too tender to travel, and we were obliged to stop again.

Game plenty. Thursday 9th, to Sunday 19th. We stayed at this place, and while we were here killed plenty of bear, deer, and elk, so that we lived very well.

Monday 20th. We set out W. 5 m. and were stopped by snow.

Tuesday 21st. Stayed all day in the camp.

Wednesday 22d. Set out S. 45 d. W. 12 m. where we scared a panther from under a rock which had room enough for us in it, so we encamped and had good shelter.

Thursday 23d. to Sunday 26th. We stayed at this place being snow and bad weather.

Monday 27th. Set out S. 45 d. W. 6 m. here we had snow and encamped.

Land rich, but hilly and stony. Tuesday 28th, to Friday 31st. Stayed at this place, the land upon these last courses is rich but hilly, and in some places stony.

Land hilly and rocky. Saturday February 1st. Set out S. 45 d. W. 3 m. S. 45 d. E. 1 m. S. 2 m. S. 45 d. W. 1 m. crossed *a creek* on which the land was very hilly and rocky, yet here and there good in spots on the hills.

Sunday 2d. S. 45 d. W. 3 m. here we were stopped by snow.

Monday 3d. to Sunday 9th. We stayed at this place and had a good deal of snow and bad weather.

Monday 10th. S. 45 d. W. 8 m. the snow being hard upon the top made bad travelling.

Tuesday 11th. The same course S. 45 d. W. 2. then W. 1 m. S. 45 d. W. 4 m.

Land rich and well timbered, but hilly. Wednesday 12th. Killed two buffaloes. Searched the land to the N. W. which I found to be rich, and well timbered, with lofty walnuts, ash, sugar trees, &c. but hilly in most places.

A piece of land 100 yards square, slipped down a hill, with the trees, &c. in their former position. Thursday 13th. Set out W. 1 m. S. 45 d. W. 2 m. W. 2 m. S. 45 d. W. 2 m. W. 2 m. this day we found a place where a piece of land, about 100 yards square and about ten feet deep from the surface, had slipped down a steep hill somewhat more than its own breadth, with most of the trees standing on it, upright as they were at first, and a good many rocks which appeared to be in the same position as they were before the ground slipped; it had bent downwards, and crushed the trees as it came along, which might plainly be seen by the ground on the upper side of it, over which it had passed; it seemed to have been done but two or three years ago. In the place from whence it removed was a large quarry of rocks, in the sides of which

(15)

which were veins of several colours, particularly one of a deep yellow about three feet from the bottom, in which were other small veins, some white some green, a sample of which I brought into the Ohio company in a small leather bag, No. 1. Not very far from this place, we found another large piece of earth, which had slipped down in the same manner. Encamped in the *fork of a creek.*

Friday 14th. We stayed at this place on the NW. side of *the creek.* On a rising ground by a small spring we found a large stone about three feet square on the top, and about six or seven feet high, it was all covered with green moss except on the SE. side, which was smooth and white as if plaistered with lime; on this side I cut with a cold chissel in large letters, The Ohio Company, February 1751, by Christopher Gift. *Cut on a large stone, The Ohio Company.*

Saturday 15. Set out S. 45 d. W. 5 m. through rich land but hilly, very rich bottoms up the creek, but not above 200 yards wide. *Rich land, hilly, bottoms narrow.*

Sunday 16th. S. 45 d. W. 5 m. through rich land, the bottoms about a quarter of a mile wide upon the creek. *Rich land.*

Monday 17th. The same course S. 45. W. 3 m. S. 45 d. W. 3 m. S. 20 d. W. 3 m. S. 8 m. S. 45 d. W. 2 m. over a creek on which was fine land, the bottoms about a mile wide. *Bottoms wide, and fine land.*

Tuesday 18th. S. 10 m over the *Fork of a creek* S. 45 d. W. 4 m. to the top of a high ridge from whence we could see over the *Kanhawa river,* here we encamped, the land mixed with pines and not very good. *Land indifferent.*

Wednesday 19th. Set out S. 15 m. S. 45 d. W. 6 m. to the mouth of *a little creek,* upon which the land is very rich, and the bottoms a mile wide; *the Kanhawa* being very high, overflowed some part of the bottoms. *Land very rich, bottoms overflowed.*

Thursday 20th. Set out N. 45 d. W. 2 m. across *a creek* over a hill, then S. 80 d. W. 10 m. to a large run, all fine land upon this course, we were now about two miles from the *Kanhawa;* then continued our course S. 80 d. W. 10 m. the first five miles good high land, tolerably level, the last five, through the river bottoms which were a mile wide, and very rich, to *a creek or large run,* which we crossed, and continued our course S. 80 d. W. 2 m. farther and encamped. *Land very rich.*

Friday 21st. The same course S. 80 d. W. still continued 8 m. farther then S. 2 m. to the side of the *Kanhawa,* then down the same N. 15 d. W. 1 m. to *a creek* where we encamped, the bottoms upon the river here are a mile wide, the land very rich. *The river at this place is 79 poles broad.* *Kanhawa river 79 poles wide, land very rich.*

Saturday 22d. Set out N. 45 d. W. 4 m. W. 7 m: to a high hill from whence we could see the *river Ohio,* then N. 45 d. W. 12 m. to *the said river at the mouth of a small run,* where we encamped. The bottoms upon the river here are a mile wide and very good, but the high land broken. *Ohio river. Bottoms rich, high land broken.*

Sunday 23d. Set out N. 45 d. E. 14 m. over *Letort's creek,* the land upon this creek is poor, broken, and full of pines, then the same course N. 45 d. E. 10 m. and encamped on *the river side* upon fine rich land, the bottoms about a mile wide. *Letort's creek, land poor; but very rich on the Ohio.*

Monday 24th. Set out E. 12 m. *up the river,* all fine land, the bottoms about a mile and an half wide, full of lofty timber; then N. 5 m. crossing *buffaloes creek,* the land here is level and good, but the bottoms upon the river are not above half a mile wide; then N. 45 d. E. 8 m. to *a creek called Beyansoss,* where we encamped. *Buffaloe creek, land good, bottoms narrow. Beyansoss creek.*

Tuesday 25th. We searched the land upon *this creek,* which we found very good for twelve or thirteen miles up it from the river; the bottoms upon it are about half a mile wide, and the bottoms upon *the river* at the mouth of it a mile wide, and very well timbered. *Land on Beyansoss creek very good, and well timbered.*

Wednesday 26th. Set out N. 45 d. E. 13 m. to the *river Ohio,* at the mouth of a *creek called Lawellaconin;* then S. 55 d. E. 5 m. *up the said creek;* the bottoms upon this creek are a mile wide, and the high land very good, and not much broken, and very well timbered. *Lawellaconin creek, land good and well timbered.*

Thursday 27th, Friday 28th, and Saturday 29th. Rained and we could not travel, killed four buffaloes.

Sunday March 1st, and Monday 2d. Set out N 30 d. E. 10 m. *to a little branch full of coal,* then N. 30 d. E. 16 m. to *Nawmissippi or Fishing creek,* my son hunted up this creek, to the place where I had cut the letters upon the stone, which he said was not above six miles in a straight line; the bottoms upon *this creek* are but narrow, the high land hilly, but very rich and well timbered. *A creek full of coal; Fishing creek. Lands hilly, but rich and well timbered.*

Tuesday 3d. Set out N. 30 d. E. 18 m. to *Molchoconiccon creek.* *Molchoconiccon creek.*

Wednesday 4th. We hunted up and down *this creek* to examine the land: the bottoms are three quarters of a mile wide, and very rich, a great many cleared fields covered with white clover, the high land rich, but in general hilly. *Land rich, but hilly.*

Thursday 5th. Set out N. 30 d. E. 9 m. to a *creek called Neumoccosy,* where we killed a black fox and two bears: upon *this creek* we found a cave under a rock, about 150 feet long and 55 feet wide, one side of it open facing the creek, the floor dry; it is much used by buffaloes and elks, who come there to lick a kind of saltish clay, which I found in the cave, and of which I took a sample in a leather bag, No. 2. *Neumoccosy creek. Black Fox. A large cave.*

Friday 6th. We stayed at the cave, not very far from it we saw a herd of elks near thirty, one of which my son killed. *Elks.*

Saturday 7th. Set out N. 30 d. E. 7 m. to the *Ohio river.* The bottoms here were very rich, and near two miles wide, but a little higher up the hill seemed very steep, so that we were obliged to leave *the river,* and went E. 6 m. on very high land, then N. 9 m. through very good high land tolerably level, to a *creek called Weeling or scalp creek,* where we encamped. Sunday *Ohio river, bottoms wide, land rich. Weeling or Scalp creek.*

(16)

Land good, bottoms wide.   Sunday 8th. We went out to search the land, which we found very good for near fifteen miles *up the creek,* from the mouth of it; the bottoms above a mile wide, and some meadows. We also found an old Indian road up the creek.

Two creeks.   Monday 9th. Set out N. 45 d. E. 18 m. to a *creek,* the same course three miles to *another creek,* where we encamped. *These creeks* the traders distinguish by the name of *the two creeks.*

Land on the two creeks very fine, and well timbered.   Tuesday 10th. We hunted up and down *these creeks* to examine the land, from the mouths of them, to the place where we had crossed near the heads of them, in our way down to the *Kanhawa,* they run near parallel at about three or four miles distance, for about thirty miles: the land between them all the way is rich, and level, chiefly low grounds, and finely timbered with walnuts, locusts, cherry trees, and sugar trees.

Crosses three creeks, and returns to the encampment, where his son had been frost bitten.   Wednesday 11th. Set out E. 18 m. crossing *three creeks,* all good land but hilly; then S. 16 m. to *our old camp where my son had been frost bitten.* After we had got to this place in our old track, I did not keep any exact account of course and distance, as I thought the rivers and creeks sufficiently described by my courses as I came down.

Road from Monaungahela to Wills's creek about 70 miles.   Thursday 12th. I set out from *Monaungahela,* and crossed it upon a raft of logs, from whence I made the best of my way to *Potomack.* I did not keep exactly my old track, but went more to the Eastward, and found a much nearer way home, and am of opinion the company may have *a tolerable good road from Wills creek, to the upper fork of Monaungahela, from*

Monaungahela river navigable for flat-bottomed boats.
Indian asks Gist where their lands were, the French claiming those on one side, the English on the other, of the river.   *whence the river is navigable, all the way to the Ohio for long flat bottomed boats: the road will be a little to the southward of west, and the distance to the fork about seventy miles.* While I was at *Monaungahela,* in my return home an Indian who spoke good English came to me, and said that their great men the Beaver, and Captain Oppamyluah (two chiefs of the Delawares) desired to know where the Indians land lay, for that the French claimed all the land on one side of the river Ohio, and the English that on the other side, and that Oppamyluah had asked me the same question when I was at his camp in my way down, to which I had made him no answer. I very well remembered that Oppamyluah had asked me such a question, and that I was at a loss to answer him, as I now also was; but after some consideration, my friend said I, We are all one king's people, and the different colour of our skins makes no difference between the king's subjects; you are his people as well as we are, if you will take land and pay the king's rights, you will have the same privileges as the white people have; and to hunt you have liberty every where, so that you do not kill the white people's cattle and hogs. To this the Indian said, that I must stay at that place two days, and then he would come and see me again; he went away, and at the two days end returned as he promised, and looking very pleasant, said he would stay with me all night: after he had been with me some time, he said that the great men bid him tell me I was very safe, that I might come and live upon that river where I pleased, that I had answered them very true, for we were all one king's people sure enough; and for his part, he would come and see me at Wills creek in a month.

Thursday 12th, to Saturday 28th. We were travelling from *Monaungahela to Potomack;* for as we had a good many skins to carry, and the weather was bad we travelled but slow.

Company's store-house at Wills creek.   Sunday 29th. We arrived at the *company's store at Wills creek.*

Christopher Gist.

EXTRACTS

(17)

EXTRACTS

FROM THE

Treaty with the Indians at Loggstown in the Year 1752.

At a Council held at Loggstown, June 1, 1752.

Present. Joshua Fry, Lunsford Lomax, James Patton, Esqrs. Commissioners.
Mr. Christopher Gist, Agent for the Ohio Company.
Mr. Andrew Montour, Interpreter.
Mr. George Croghan, Commissioner for Pensylvania.

Indian treaty at Loggs-town in 1752.

The Indians addressed themselves to the Commissioners in the following speeches.

BRETHREN, You have come a long and blind way, if we had been certain which way you were coming, we should have met you at some distance from the town; but we now bid you welcome, and we open your eyes with this string of wampum, which we give you in the name of the six united nations. *Gave a string.* *Indians welcome the commissioners.*

Brethren of Virginia and Pensylvania, I desire you will hearken to what I am going to say, that you may open your hearts, and speak freely to us; we dont doubt but you have many things in your minds which may trouble you, notwithstanding which, we hope we may continue in friendship, on which we give you these strings of wampum. *Gave two strings.* *Desire them to speak their minds freely.*

After which the commissioners let the Indians know they would give them an answer in a few hours.

Some time after, all being met in the council house, Mr. George Croghan, by direction from the governor of Pennsylvania, made a speech to the Indians, letting them know, that it was his desire that that they should receive their brethren of Virginia kindly, and presented them with a string of wampum. *Gave a string.* *Croghan recommends the commissioners, by order of the governor of Pennsylvania.*

Then the Commissioners spoke as followeth:

Brethren, You sent us a string of wampum which met us on the road, by which you acquainted us that you heard of our coming to visit you, and welcomed us so far on our journey. Yesterday we arrived at this place, and this morning you took an opportunity with a string of wampum to bid us welcome to your town, and to open our eyes, that we might see the sun clearly, and look upon you our brethren, who are willing to receive us; this we take very kindly, and we assure you, of our hearty inclinations to live in friendship with you: To confirm this we present you with a string of wampum. *Gave a string.* *Commissioners thank the Indians, &c.*

Brethren, In your second speech to us and our brethren of Pennsylvania this day, you delivered us two strings of wampum, to clear our hearts from any impressions that may have been made on them, by flying reports or ill news, and that we might speak our minds freely. Brethren, we assure you of our willingness to remove all misunderstandings out of our hearts and breasts, which might impede or hinder the friendship subsisting between us.

Now brethren, we are to acquaint you, that we are sent hither by the King of Great Britain our father, who not forgetting his children, on this side the great waters, has ordered us to deliver you a large present of goods in his name, which we have brought with us; but as we understand that you have sent for some of your chiefs, whom you shortly expect, we will wait with patience till they come, and will then faithfully deliver you the goods, and open our hearts to you; in assurance of which we present you with this string of wampum. *Commissioners tell the Indians they had a present to deliver them from the king.*

Gave a string.

There were some debates concerning the method of proceeding in the treaty, whether to demand the reasons why the belt and speech delivered last fall were not sent to Onandago; or if nothing should be said of that affair, till the more material business obtaining leave to settle the lands, &c. was settled, which it was judged the other would effectually defeat.

June 2d. The goods were got out and dried, when it was found they had not received the damage that might have been expected, the fine goods none.

June 3d. The commissioners had conferences with Mr. Trent, and Mr. Croghan, about the likeliest method to succeed in their negotiations, and had farther assurances of their assistance. *Commissioners confer with Mr. Trent and Mr. Croghan.*

June 4th. Two Shawane chiefs being disgusted (as was said) came to the commissioners, and made a speech, expressing their inclinations to be gone home; as they were preparing an answer, in conjunction with some of the six nations to stop them, word was brought, that a vessel with English colours was coming down the river, which proved to be the Half King with a chief from the Onandago council; he was received with several discharges of small arms, landed and fixed the English colours on the top of his house; the commissioners waited on him, some time after he returned the visit, with some of the chiefs, drank the king's health, *Half king arrives with one of the Onondago council. His reception.*

B

(18)

health, prosperity to the Six Nations, the governor of Virginia, &c. and the commissioners, when he went away, made him a present of tobacco.

Commissioners shew the Indians the Lancaster deed, &c.

June 9th. The commissioners had a private conference with the half king, and the other chiefs at Mr. Croghan's, and shewed the Lancaster deed and other papers: They thanked the commissioners for letting them know what the Onandago council had done, and blamed them much for keeping it private (as they said) for had they known it sooner, it would have prevented many disorders. They said, they never told them that they had sold farther than the warriors road, at the foot of the Allegany mountain, and that they would confirm what-

Indians agree to confirm it.

ever they had done. The Indians desired to have their guns and hatchets mended, which was complied with. Big Hanoana, a Shawane chief, told us, that the Piques were upon the poise whether they should return to the French, or continue steady to the English, and wanted to see what encouragement the latter would give them.

June 10th. This day was appointed to deliver the king's present to the Indians; there were separate arbors made for the commissioners and Indians, where the present was laid out, and a part set aside for the Piques, which was well taken by the other Indians. The fine cloaths were distributed to the chiefs.

The Indians being met, the Commissioners spoke as followeth:

Present. Joshua Fry, Lunsford Lomax, James Patton, Esqrs. Commissioners.
Mr. Christopher Gist, Agent for the Ohio company.
Mr. Andrew Montour, Interpreter.

Sachems and Warriors of the six united nations, our friends and brethren.

We are glad to meet you at this place, to enlarge the council fire already kindled by our brethren of Pennsylvania, to brighten the chain, and to renew our friendship, that it may last as long as the sun, the moon, and stars shall give light. To confirm which we give you this string of wampum. *Gave a string.*

Commissioners tell the Indians of the deed made at Lancaster in 1744, and recite the particulars.

Brethren, at the treaty at Lancaster, in the year 1744, between the governments of Virginia, Maryland, and Pennsylvania, you made a deed recognizing the king's right to all the land in Virginia, as far as it was then peopled, or should thereafter be peopled, or bounded by the king our father, for which you received the consideration agreed on; at the same time Canosateego desired the commissioners would recommend you to the king's farther favour, when the settlements should increase much farther back; this the commissioners promised, and confirmed it by a writing under their hands and seals, in consequence of which, a present was sent you from the king, by Mr. Conrad Weiser, which he since informed us that he delivered you, at a council held here in the year 1748. Now the king your father, to shew the love he bears to justice, as well as his affection to you his children, has sent a large present of

Desire the Indians to confirm that treaty.

goods, to be divided among you and your allies, which is here ready to be delivered to you, and we desire you may confirm the treaty at Lancaster.

Tell the Indians the king proposes to make a settlement on the Ohio, and point out its advantages.

Brethren, It is the design of the king your father at present, to make a settlement of British subjects on the South-east side of Ohio, that we may be united as one people, by the strongest ties of neighbourhood, as well as friendship, and by these means prevent the insults of our enemies. From such a settlement greater advantages will arise to you, than you can at present conceive; our people will be able to supply you with goods, much cheaper than can at this time be afforded, will be ready help in case you should be attacked, and some good men among them will be appointed, with authority to punish, and restrain the many injuries and abuses, too frequently committed here, by disorderly white people.

Brethren, We assure you that the king our father, by purchasing your lands, had never any intentions of taking them from you, but that we might live together as one people, and keep them from the French who would be bad neighbours; he is not like the French king, who calls himself your father, and endeavoured about three years ago, with an armed force to take possession of your country, by setting up inscriptions on trees, and at the mouths of the creeks, on this river, by which he claims these lands; though at their coming, and for many years before, a number of your brethren the English, were residing in this town, and several other places on this river. You remember how he scattered the Shawnese, so that they were dispersed all over the face of the earth, and he now threatens to cut off the Twigtwees; this is to weaken you, that he may cut you off also, which he durst not attempt, while you are united. On the contrary, the king your father, will lay his hand on your heads, under which protection you will always remain safe.

Brethren, The great king our father, recommends a strict union between us, you, and our brethren towards the sun setting, which will make us strong and formidable, as a division may

Send a present to the Twigtwees.

have a contrary effect: We are directed to send a small present to the Twigtwees, as an earnest of the regard which the governor of Virginia has for them, with an assurance of his farther friendship when ever they shall stand in need.

Brethren, We earnestly exhort you, not to be drawn by the empty deceitful speeches of the French, the peculiar talent of that cunning people; but in all their attempts to shake your duty to our common father, think of what real acts of friendship have been done by the English, and what by the French; weigh these things in your mind, and then determine, who best deserves your esteem and regard; for it is not by vain unmeaning words, that true friendship is to be discovered. That what we have said may make the greater impression on you, and have its full force, we present you with this belt of wampum. *Gave a belt.*

Brethren,

Brethren, It is many years ago that the English first came over the great water to visit you: On their first coming you took hold of our ships, and tied them to your strongest trees, ever since which, we have remained together in friendship; we have assisted you when you have been attacked by the French, by which you have been able to withstand them, and you have remained our good friends and allies; for though at some times the chain of friendship may have contracted some rust, it has been easily rubbed off, and the chain restored to its brightness. This we hope will always be the case, and that our friendship may continue to the last posterity, we give you this string of wampum. *Gave a string.*

Brethren, We are sorry for the occasion that requires us to complain to you of an injury done us by one of your people, who murdered a poor woman on the new river. Murder is a great crime, and by the consent of all nations, has usually been punished with death, this is the usage among the English, whether one of our own people has been killed, or one of our brethren the Indians; and it is one of the earliest commands of the great Father and Maker of us all, who inhabits the skies, *that whoso sheddeth man's blood, by man shall his blood be shed.* We understand you know the man that is accused of the murder, and we hope you will give him up, to be tried by our laws; you may be assured he will have a fair trial, and if he is not guilty he will be sent back unhurt. We must inform you, that the governor of Virginia expects you will deliver the person suspected to be guilty, up to some magistrate in Virginia, whom we shall name to you, that we may send him to Williamsburg, for his trial. This procedure is not only proper, as it is a compliance with the laws of God and nations, but it is necessary to warn all hot-headed men, who are not guided by reason, to forbear from such wicked actions, by which their brethren suffer. Brethren, we desire for the future, you will observe the treaty of Lancaster, and when ever your young people travel through Virginia, that they will take such passes as are directed by the said treaty; by these passes the men will be known, which will be some restraint on them as to their behaviour; it will be proper also that a man of prudence and discretion should head each party, that one among them, if possible, should speak English, and that by no means any French, or French Indians be suffered to go with them. We might have mentioned many other irregularities, but we have forborn, in hopes that for the future you will give your people such orders, as will prevent our having any farther occasion to complain. To inforce what we have said, and induce you to do us justice, we present you with this belt of wampum. *Gave a belt.*

Complain of the murder of a woman on the New river.

Demand the man who committed the murder

Recommend to the Indians to observe the treaty of Lancaster.

The commissioners then spoke to the allies of the Six united Nations who were present, having first advised with the Half King, and being joined in the speeches by him, in the name of the Six Nations.

Brethren, the Delawares, We thank you for the kind reception you gave us when we came to Shenapins, which we shall never forget; we advise and exhort you to beware of the French councils, and to adhere to a strict friendship with us, the Six Nations, and your brethren who live towards the Sun-setting, which will strengthen us all, and be a sure defence against our enemies. To confirm you in this mind, we present you with this belt of wampum. *Gave a belt.*

Speech to the Delawares.

Brethren, the Shawnese, Your nation has suffered much by French devices, by which you have been dispersed; we exhort you that you continue to keep firm hold of the great chain of friendship between us, the Six Nations, and their allies, which is the likeliest means to retrieve your loss, and again make you a happy people. We present you with this belt of wampum. *Gave a belt.*

Speech to the Shawnese.

Brethren, the Wyandots, Your nation is divided, and part is under the directions of the French; we think it would be good policy in you that are in our interest, to endeavour to bring over your brethren; but if this can not be done, you ought to take all the care in your power, that they do not, under the colour and name of friendship, come into our country, and hurt our inhabitants, or if they do, that you will endeavour to secure them on their return, to prevent any misunderstanding. We present you with this belt of wampum. *Gave a belt.*

Speech to the Wyandots.

After these speeches had been delivered and interpreted to the several nations, the Half King desired the commissioners not to depart, for he said they had a great deal of business to do: He then with a ten rowed belt of wampum in his hand, directing his speech to Eghuisara (which is Mr. Montour's Indian name) said child, remember that thou art one of our own people, and have transacted a great deal of business among us, before you were employed by our brethren of Pennsylvania, and Virginia; you are interpreter between us and our brethren, which we are well pleased at, for we are sure our business will go on well, and justice be done on both sides; but you are not interpreter only, for you are one of our council, and have an equal right with us, to all these lands, and may transact any public business in behalf of us the Six Nations, as well as any of us, for we look upon you as much as we do any of the chief councellors; and to confirm what we have said, we present unto you this belt of wampum. *Gave the belt.*

Half King tells Montour the interpreter, that he has an equal right with them, being one of their council, to transact business and sell lands. See Indian deed, p.

Then addressing himself to the commissioners of Virginia, and all the Indians present, with a string of wampum in his hand, he spoke as follows:

Brethren, It is a great while since our brother the Buck (meaning George Croghan) has been doing business between us and our brothers of Pennsylvania, but we understand he does not intend to do so any more; so I now inform you, that he is approved of by our council at Onandago, for we sent to them to let them know how he has helped us in our councils here, and

George Croghan declared to be one of the council. See Indian deed, p. 22.

(20)

and I deliver him this string of wampum to strengthen him, and to let you and him know, that he is one of our people, and shall help us still and be one of our council.
Gave the string of wampum.

Forbids the Shawanes from going to war with the Cherokees.

He next spoke to the Shawanes, and told them, that he took the hatchet from them, and tied them with black strings of wampum, to hinder them from going to war against the Cherokees; he said that they struck their own body, and did not know what they were doing, he said they had seen of their own people there, whom he wanted to get back, and would it not be better to be at peace to bring them back? He charged them not to go again to strike their own people, and he said that the governor of Virginia and Pennsylvania would interest themselves in making a peace.
Gave a black string.

Forbids the Delawares from going to war with the Cherokees.

Then turning to the Delawares he said, You went to the Wiandots, and delivered a speech, and a belt of wampum, to make peace between you and the Cherokees, and after you came back you let your young men go to war against the Cherokees, which was very wrong, after you had delivered the speech, which I myself being present heard. I take the hatchet from you, you belong to me, and I think you are to be ruled by me, and (I joining with your brethren of Virginia) order you to go to war no more.
Gave a belt of wampum.

Taking a belt of wampum in his hand, he proceeded as followeth:

Complains of the quantity, and price of spirituous liquors.

Brethren, The governors of Virginia and Pennsylvania, some years ago we made a complaint to our brother of Pennsylvania, that his traders brought too much spiritous liquors amongst us, and desired that there might not come such quantities, and hoped he would order his traders to sell their goods and liquors at cheaper rates. In answer to our request, Conrade Weiser delivered us this belt of wampum, and told us we must pay but five buck-skins for a keg, and if the traders would not take that, that we should have it for nothing, since which time there has been double the quantity brought out yearly, and sold as formerly, and we have made some complaints to try to stop such large quantities from being brought, but as there has

Charges Conrad Weiser with having deceived them.

been no notice taken to prevent it, we believe Mr. Weiser spoke only from his mouth, and not from his heart, and without the governor's authority; so we think proper to return the belt.
He gave the belt to Mr. Croghan.

June 11th. Present. Joshua Fry, Lunsford Lomax, James Patton, Esqrs. Commissioners.
Mr. Christopher Gist, Agent for the Ohio Company.
Mr. Andrew Montour, Interpreter.

An Indian Chief died, commissioners give a present to wipe away their tears.

The Commissioners of Virginia, delivered to the Six Nations a string of wampum, and a suit of Indian cloathing, to wipe away their tears, for the loss of one of their chiefs, who lately came down from the head of Ohio to Loggs-town, and died there.
Gave the suit of cloaths and string.

Shingas appointed king of the Delawares

Afterwards the Half King spoke to the Delawares; Nephews, you received a speech last year from your brother the governor of Pennsylvania, and from us, desiring you to choose one of your wisest councellors, and present him to us for a king; as you have not done it, we now let you know that it is our right to give you a king, and we think proper to give you Shingas for your king, whom you must look upon as your chief, and with whom all public business must be transacted, between you and your brethren the English. On which the Half King put a laced hat on the head of the Beaver, who stood proxy for his brother Shingas, and presented him also with a rich jacket, and suit of English colours, which had been delivered to the Half King by the commissioners for that purpose.

Commissioners send a suit of cloaths to the old Shawane king.

The commissioners addressing themselves to the Shawanes, acquainted them, that they understood their chief king Cochawitchiky, who had been a good friend to the English, was lying bed-rid, and that to shew the regard they bore to his past services, they took this opportunity to acknowledge it, by presenting him with a suit of Indian cloathing.

Half King's reply, concerning the lands granted by the treaty of Lancaster.

Then the Half King spoke as followeth:

Brother, the governor of Virginia, You acquainted us yesterday with the king's right to all the lands in Virginia, as far as it is settled, and back from thence to the sun-setting, whenever he shall think fit to extend his settlements: You produced also a copy of his deed, from the Onandago council, at the treaty at Lancaster, and desired that your brethren of Ohio, might likewise confirm the deed. Brother, the governor of Virginia, we are well acquainted that our chief council, at the treaty of Lancaster, confirmed a deed to you for a quantity of land in Virginia, which you have a right to, and likewise our brother Onas, has a right to a parcel of land in Pennsylvania; we are glad you have acquainted us with the right to those lands, and assure you, we are willing to confirm any thing our council has done, in regard to the lands; but we never understood, before you told us yesterday, that the lands then sold, were to extend farther to the sun-setting, than the hill on the other side the Allegany hill, so that we cannot give you a farther answer.

Brother, You acquainted us yesterday, that the French were a designing people, which we now see, and know that they design to cheat us out of our lands; you told us that the king of England designed to settle some lands on the South-east side of Ohio, that it might be better in our brethren's power to help us if we were in need, than it is at present, at the great distance they live from us: We are sure the French design nothing else but mischief, for they

Desires the people of Virginia to build a fort at the forks of the Monaungahela.

have struck our friends the Twigtwees; we therefore desire our brothers of Virginia, may build a strong house at the fork of Monaungahela, to keep such goods, powder, lead, and necessaries

(21)

cessaries, as shall be wanting, and as soon as you please; and as we have given our cousins the Delawares a king who lives there, we desire you will look on him as a chief of that nation.
Gave a large string of wampum.

Brethren, Our brothers that live on this river Ohio, are all warriors and hunters, and like our brethren the traders, not all wise men. There has been reason for many complaints for some time past, but we will not complain of our brethren the traders, for we love them, and cannot live without them; but we hope you will take care to send none amongst us but good men: Sure you know them that are fit, and we hope you will advise them how to behave better than they have done. We well remember when first we saw our brethren the English, and we remember the first council held with them, and shall do all we can to keep the chain of friendship from rust. *Says they cannot live without the traders, but desires care may be taken, to send none but good men, amongst them.*

June 12th. This day the Indians gave the commissioners an answer concerning the land which the Ohio company wanted to settle; they desired them to build a strong house or fort very soon: As the commissioners had asked for the lands at Monaungahela, they imagined the Indians had given up the lands upon that river, but they only meant ground sufficient for the fort to stand upon, as appeared by a private conversation with the Half King, who said, that was all that was intended, though he always spoke the sentiments of others, and not his own, as he knew a proper settlement could not be made without a large quantity of land.

The commissioners had also the following conferences with the chiefs of the Indians.

June 12th. The Half King with a string of wampum informed the commissioners, that one Frazer a black-smith, at the town of Venango, threatened to remove, that they did not desire he should leave them, but if he did, requested another might be sent to them; and he said that they had not a sufficient number of traders there, to supply them with goods: to which the commissioners replied, that they would represent their case to the governor of Virginia, and hoped they would be supplied according to their desire. *Desires a blacksmith, and more traders might be sent amongst them.*

The same day the chiefs of the Shawanes, with a string of wampum, thanked the commissioners for their good advice; they acknowledged that they had been led astray by the French, and had suffered for it, and said they would take care not to be deceived by the French again, but would keep fast hold of the chain of friendship, between the English, the Six Nations, and themselves. *Shawanes promise to remain firm to the English.*

The commissioners thanked them for their attachment to the English, and desired their compliments might be made to the young king of the Shawanes, who was generously gone to the assistance of the Picques. They sent him also a laced hat, and a rich jacket.

June 13th. The Half King speaking to the commissioners said:

Brethren, You told us you sent us a present of goods in the year 1748, which you said Conrade Weiser delivered at this town; he may have told you so, but we assure you, we never heard of it from him: it is true, he delivered us some goods then, but we understood him they were from our brother Onas*; he never made mention of the great king our father, nor of our brother Assaragoa †. Then directing his speech to the governor of Virginia said: *Half King says Weiser had never delivered them the present sent by the king, but had given them some goods as from the governor of Pennsylvania.*

Brother, you complained to us that some of our people had murdered a woman in Virginia: it is true there has been such a thing done, and brothers we know the man that did it, he is one of our Six Nations, although he has lived some time among the French; we cannot make an excuse for so barbarous a murder, but we assure you he did it without our knowledge, and we believe the evil spirit tempted him to do it. We will let the Onandago council know what has been done, and we believe they will try to get him, and make a satisfaction for the crime committed. *Gave a string of black and white wampum.* *Promises satisfaction for the murder complained of.*

Brother, We have heard what you said, in regard to the king's design, of making a settlement of his people, on the waters of the river Ohio; you likewise told us, you had a deed for those lands, signed by our council at the treaty of Lancaster; We assure you of our willingness to agree to what our council does, or has done, but we have not the full power in our hands here on Ohio; we must acquaint our council at Onandago of the affair, and whatever they bid us do we will do. In regard to your request, to build a strong house at the Monaungahela, you told us it would require a settlement to support it, with provisions, and necessaries; and it is true, but we will take care that there shall be no scarcity of that kind, until we can give a full answer; although in all our wars, we do not consider provisions, for we live on one another, but we know it is different with our brethren the English. *Indian reply concerning the sale of their lands by the treaty of Lancaster.*
Gave three strings of white wampum.

The commissioners having drawn an instrument of writing, for confirming the deed made at Lancaster, and containing a promise, that the Indians would not molest our settlements on the South-east side the Ohio, desired Mr. Montour to converse with his brethren the other Sachems, in private on the subject, to urge the necessity of such a settlement, and the great advantage it would be to them, as to their trade, or their security: on which they retired for some time, and then returned; and Mr. Montour said they were satisfied in the matter, and were willing to sign and seal the writing, which was done and witnessed by the gentlemen then present. *Indian chiefs sign a deed to the king, for the lands, &c. on the Ohio.*

INDIAN DEED.

Whereas, at the treaty of Lancaster, in the county of Lancaster and province of Pennsylvania, held between the government of Virginia and the Six united Nations of Indians, in the year of our Lord 1744: The honourable Thomas Lee, and William Beverley, Esqrs. be- *Deed made at the treaty of Lancaster, recited.*

* Governor of Pennsylvania. † Governor of Virginia.

F ing

(22)

ing commissioners, a deed recognizing and acknowledging the right and title of his Majesty, our Sovereign Lord the King of Great Britain, to all the lands within the colony as it was then, or hereafter might be peopled, and bounded by his said Majesty our Sovereign Lord the King, his heirs and successors, was signed sealed and delivered by the Sachems and Chiefs of the Six united Nations, then present, as may more fully appear by the said deed, reference thereto being had, We *Conogariera, Chescaga, Cononsagret, *Eaghuisara, Togrondoara, Thonarissa*, Sachems and Chiefs of the said Six Nations, now met in council at Loggs-town, do hereby signify our consent to, and confirmation of the said deed, in as full and ample a manner as if the same was here recited. And whereas his said Majesty, King of Great Britain, has at present a design of making a settlement or settlements, of British subjects, on the Southern or Eastern parts of the river Ohio, called otherwise Allegany; we in council (Joshua Fry, Lunsford Lomax, and James Patton, Esqrs. being commissioners on behalf of his Majesty) do give our consent thereto, and do farther promise, that the said settlement, or settlements shall be unmolested by us, and that we will, as far as is in our power, assist and protect the British subjects there inhabiting. In witness whereof we have hereunto set our hands and seals, this 13th day of June, in the year of our Lord God 1752.

Signed, sealed, and delivered
in the presence of

	Marks of	Seals
William Trent,	Conogariera,	(L. S.)
‡George Croghan,	Chescaga,	(L. S.)
Thomas Mc Kee,	Cononsagret,	(L. S.)
William Blyth,	(*Andrew Montour*)	
Hugh Crawford,	†Eaghuisara,	(L. S.)
Michael Taaffe,	Togrondoara,	(L. S.)
William West,	Thonarissa,	(L. S.)
Christopher Gist,		
William Preston,		
Aaron Price,		
John Taylor,		
Peter Tostee.		

Indians confirm the deed made at Lancaster. Agree to a settlement.

Promise their protection to British subjects, settling on the Ohio.

The Half King then spoke as follows:

Half King thanks the commissioners for their care of the Twigtwees

Brethren, The governors of Virginia and Pennsylvania, you expressed your regard for our friends and allies the Twigtwees, and have considered their necessities at present; we return you our thanks for your care of them; we join with you, and desire you will deliver them this belt, and let them know from us, that we desire them not to forget what they did in Pennsylvania, when they were down four years ago, and joined in a friendship with our brethren the English; we desire they may hold fast the chain of friendship, and not listen to any other but their brethren the English, the Six Nations, Delawares, and Shawnese, as we will stand by them, and expect they will come down, and confirm the friendship they have engaged to the English.   *He delivered a belt to be sent to the Twigtwees.*

The commissioners open the roads, as is the custom with the Indians, to Virginia, with a belt of wampum, and invite the Indians to come down.

The commissioners then opened the roads to Virginia, with a belt of wampum, and the following speech:

Brethren, We have travelled through a long and dark way to meet you at this council; we have now compleated our business with pleasure and satisfaction, both to you and us, and as we are now returning back, we do in the name of the great king your father, as also in the name of your brother the governor of Virginia, remove all obstacles out of the way, and make clear the road, that you may at any time send messages to us, on any occasion; and we shall be always ready to receive them kindly, and look on you as our brothers: and in token of the sincerity of our hearts, present you with this belt of wampum.   *Gave the belt.*

Indians reminded of the school in Virginia, for the education of Indians, and asked to send their children down. The advantages of education enumerated.

The commissioners added. Brethren, At the treaty of Lancaster, the commissioners informed you of a large house built among us, for the education of Indian children, and desired that you would send some of yours; we now make you the same offer, but if you think it too far to send your children, we desire to know whether it would be agreeable to you, that teachers be sent among you. The advantages of an English education, are greater than can be imagined by them who are unacquainted with it. By it we know the part of the world from whence all nations came; how nations for some thousands of years back have rose, grown powerful, or decayed; how they have removed from one place to another; what battles have been fought; what great men have lived, and how they have acted either in council, or in war. In this part of the world we know, from the first time the Spaniards came to it, how cruelly they used the Indians, then wholly ignorant of fire arms; and we know the actions of the French against you, and others. There are many other benefits arising from a good education, which would be too tedious to be mentioned, but the greatest of all is, that by it we are acquainted with the will of the great God, the Creator of the world, and Father of us all, who inhabits the skies, by which the better people among us regulate their lives, and hope after death, to live with him for ever.   *Gave a string of wampum.*

* Andrew Montour.   ‡ Page 19.   } Half King declares Montour, and Croghan, Indian Councillors.

The

The following is the copy of the treaty with the Wawiagtas, and Piankashas, mentioned in Gist's Journal, folio 8.

Whereas, At an Indian treaty held at the Tawightwi town, on the big Mineami creek, being a branch of the river Ohio, on Friday the 22d day of February, before George Croghan, and Andrew Montour, twenty men of the Wawiagtas, and Piankashas, two of their Indian chiefs, viz. Tokintoa Molfinoughko, and Nynickonowca, appeared in behalf of themselves and their nations, and prayed, that as their Indian brothers the Tawightwis, had been lately admitted into the friendship and alliance of the king of Great Britain and his subjects, and as they are tribes of the said Tawightwis, they earnestly desire to be admitted into the said chain of friendship and alliance of the king of Great Britain and his subjects, professing on their parts, to become true and faithful allies to the English, and so for ever to continue ; Mishikinoughwee, and Nemesgua, and all the nations in friendship and alliance with the English, becoming earnest intercessors with the said two chiefs on their behalfs, the prayer of the said chiefs of the Wawiaghtas and Piankashas, was granted ; a firm treaty and alliance of friendship was then stipulated and agreed on, between the said George Croghan, and Andrew Montour, in behalf of the government of Pennsylvania, and the said chiefs or deputies of the Wawiaghta and Piankasha nations, as by the records of that council held, will more fully appear. Now these presents witness, and it is hereby declared, that the said nations of Indians called the Wawiaghtas and Piankashas, are accepted by the said George Croghan and Andrew Montour, as good friends and allies of the English nation, and they the said nations, and the subjects of the king of Great Britain, shall for ever after be as one head, and one heart, and live in true friendship as one people. In consideration whereof, the said Tokintoa Molfinoughko, and Nynickonowca, chiefs of the said Wawiaghta, and Piankasha nations, do hereby, in behalf of said nations, covenant, promise, and declare, that the several people of the said Wawiaghta and Piankasha nations, or any of them, shall not at any time hurt, injure, or defraud, or suffer to be hurt, injured, or defrauded, any of the subjects of the king of Great Britain, either in their persons or estates, but shall at all times readily do justice, and perform to them, all the acts and offices of friendship, and good-will. Item, That the said Wawiaghta and Piankasha nations, by the alliance aforesaid, becoming entitled to the privilege and protection of the English laws, shall at all times behave themselves regularly and soberly, according to the laws of the government of Pensylvania, whilst they live or be amongst, or near the christian inhabitants thereof. Item, That none of the said nations shall at any time, be aiding, assisting, or abetting, to, or with any other nation, whether of Indians or others, that shall not at such time be in amity with the crown of England, and the said government of Pennsylvania. Item, That if at any time any of the Wawiaghta and Piankasha nations, by means of evil minded persons and sowers of sedition, should hear of any unkind or disadvantageous report of the English, as if they had evil designs against any of the said Indians, in such case, such Indians shall send notice thereof to the governor of the aforesaid province, for the time being, and shall not give credit to the said reports, till by that means they shall be fully satisfied of the truth thereof: And it is agreed that the English shall in such cases, do the same by them. In testimony whereof, as well the said George Croghan, and Andrew Montour, as the chiefs of Wawiaghta and Piankasha nations, have smoaked the calumet pipe, made mutual presents to each other, and hereunto set their hands and seals, the 22d day of February, in the year of our Lord 1750, and in the 24th year of the reign of George the second, king of Great Britain, France, and Ireland, defender of the Faith, &c.

Signed, sealed, and delivered
in the presence of

Christopher Gist,
Robert Kallender,
Thomas Kenton,
John Potts.

George Croghan, (L. S.)
Andrew ^{his} Mark Montour, (L. S.)
Tokintoa Molfinoughko,
Nynickonowca.

Lauwashannoito, a Shawane witness present,
John Peter, a Delaware Indian present.

Wawiagta and Piankasha treaty.

Desire to be admitted into the English alliance.

Wawiaghtas, and Piankashas received as allies.

Promise to protect the English.

Agree to submit to the English laws, while amongst the white people, and to assist them in war.

Agree to complain formally, if they think they have cause.

EXTRACTS

FROM

LEWIS EVANS'S Analysis of a General Map of the Middle British Colonies in America. Printed at Philadelphia, in 1755.

POTOMACK is navigable with large shipping to Alexandria, and for shallops fourteen miles more to the Falls; the portage thence is six miles by a good waggon road. Boats shaped like those of Delaware, and of something less dimensions, may get up to the North Mountain without obstruction, save at the Rift or Falls, in the South Mountain, which however is passable. The river runs through the North Mountain without any Fall; and from thence to Wills Creek, there are three or four Rifts passable with canoes or batteaux, when the water is not very low. The inland navigation by this river is scarce begun; *but one may foresee that it will become in time, the most important in America, as it is likely to be the sole passage from the Ocean to the Ohio.*

Probably a pass may also be found for wheel-carriages, to the North of the Falls *; and if there should, it would much improve the Portage between Potomack and Youghiogani, and reduce it to fifty miles, whereas it is now but little short of seventy. If we have the good fortune of being masters of the Ohio, the navigation of Youghiogani will be of importance, since it is passable with flat-bottomed boats, capable of carrying five tons, from the mouth, to the foot of the Rift below the Falls of the Youghiogani.

The floods in the Ohio continue of some height for at least a month or two, being guided in the time, by the late or early breaking up of the Winter. The stream is then too rapid to be stemmed upwards, by sailing or rowing, and too deep for setting †; but excellently fitted for large vessels going down: Then ships of 200 tons may go from Fort Du Quesne to the sea with safety.

Ohio carries a great uniformity of breadth; gradually increasing from two or three furlongs, at the forks to near a mile, as you go lower down; and spreading to two miles or more, where dammed by the rief of rocks, which make the falls. Thence to Mississippi, its breadth, depth, and easy current, equalling any river in Europe except the Danube, affording there, the finest navigation for large sailing vessels.

Upon the whole the navigation of this river, may be divided into four parts. First, from Canaway to Chartier's Old Town in battoes, capable of carrying four tons. Second, from Chartiers to the Big Bent, in flats, like those used in Delaware, or larger, bearing eighteen or twenty tons. These two parts must be performed in long flat-bottomed boats, as better fitted, for setting in shallow water, and rapid streams. Third, from the Big Bent to the Falls, in shallops or schooners, of ten or fifteen tons: As these are made for sailing and working to windward, they must have sharp bottoms, and deep keels; and though made broader than the flats, they will not admit such lengths, and therefore not capable of so large burdens. Fourth, from the Falls to Mississippi, in good sloops, or large schooners. The navigation of Mississippi thence to the Sea, is only fitted for light canoes or battoes against the stream; but for any vessels downwards. *Hence in process of time large ships may be built upon Ohio, and sent off to Sea with the heavy produce of the country, and sold with the cargoes.*

Monaungahela is a very large branch of the Ohio; at their junction stands Fort Duquesne. It is deep and gentle, and passable with large batteaux, beyond Red Stone Creek, and still farther with lighter craft. At six miles from the mouth, it divides into two branches; the northermost Youghiogani, passable with battoes to the foot of the Rift at Laurel Hill.

Louisa, New River and Green Briar, are fine large branches of the Canhawa; which in future times, will be of service for the inland navigation of Virginia, as they interlock with Monaungahela, Potomack, James River, Ronoak, and the Cuttawa River.

Were there nothing at stake, between the crowns of Britain and France, but the lands on that part of Ohio included in this map, we may reckon it as great a prize, as has ever yet been contended for, between two nations; but if we farther observe, that this is scarce a quarter of the valuable land, that is contained in one continued extent, and the influence that a state, vested with all the wealth and power that will naturally arise from the culture of so great an extent of good land, in a happy climate, it will make so great an addition to that nation which wins it, where there is no third state to hold the ballance of power, that the loser must inevitably sink under his rival. It is not as two nations at war, contending the one for the other's habitations; where the conquered, on submission, would be admitted to partake of the privi-

Page 23 Potomack river, it's inland navigation.

Potomack will be the only communication from the sea with Ohio.

Page 24. Portage between Potomack and the waters of Ohio, may be reduced to fifty miles. Youghiogani navigable to the Falls.

Page 26. Floods in the Ohio.

Ships of 200 tons may go from Fort Du Quesne to the sea. Breadth of Ohio in several places. Ohio equal to any river except the Danube, for inland navigation.

Page 27. Navigation of the Ohio divided into four parts. Vessels fit for each part.

Large ships may be built on Ohio, and carry the produce of the country to sea.

Monaungahela. Navigation of the Monaungahela. Navigation of the Youghiogani.

Page 29. Canhawa and its branches.

Page 31.

* Of Youghiogani.
† By the known laws of mechanics, a man *setting* a boat over a hard firm bottom, has twice the advantage of the like strength employed in *rowing*. In *rowing*, the water being moveable, receives half the motion, while in *setting*, the boat receives the whole.

G   leges

(26)

leges of the conquerors; but for a vast country, exceeding in extent, and good land, all the European Dominions of Britain, France, and Spain, almost destitute of inhabitants, and will as fast as the Europeans settle, become more so of its former inhabitants. Had his majesty been made acquainted with its value, the large strides the French have been making, for several years past, in their incroachments on his dominions, and the methods still taken to keep the colonies disunited, and of impeding the generous attempts of his most zealous subjects, it is impossible to conceive that his Majesty would have sacrificed, to the spleen of a few bitter spirits, *the best gem in his crown*. It is not yet too late to retrieve the whole, provided the British Plantations, are not thought to be grown already too large——if such an opinion prevails, an opportunity now offers of soon making them less. We may reckon the representation of the extent and power of the plantations, being great, and that such power may be dangerous to their Mother-Country, amongst the greatest of vulgar errors. Any person, who knows the nature of the soil, and the extent of our settlements, will confess, that all the land, worth the culture, from new Hampshire, to Carolina, and extended as far back as there are planters settled within three or four miles of one another, though including nine colonies, is not equal in quantity to half the arable land in England. All the Whites in the remainder of the British colonies on the continent, scarce amount to 120,000 souls. How different this from the conceits of those, who would represent some single colonies as equal to all England. The Massachusets, though made such a bug-bear, as if its inhabitants were so rich and numerous, as that they might one day be able to dispute dominion with England, is not as large as Yorkshire, nor has half so much arable land. Supposing the colonies were grown rich and powerful, what inducement have they to throw off their independency? National ties of blood and friendship, mutual dependencies for support and assistance in their civil and military interests, with England; each colony having a particular form government of its own, and the jealousy of any one's having the superiority over the rest, are unsurmountable obstacles to their ever uniting to the prejudice of England, upon any ambitious views of their own. But that repeated and continued ill usage, infringements of their dear bought privileges, sacrificing them to the ambition and intrigues of domestic and foreign enemies, may not provoke them to do their utmost, for their own preservation, I would not pretend to say; as weak as they are. But while they are treated as members of one body, and allowed their natural rights; it would be the height of madness for them to propose an independency, were they ever so strong. If they had any ambitious views, a strong colony, of a natural enemy to England, on their borders, would be the only article that would render any attempt of independency truly dangerous; and for that reason it becomes those, who would regard the future interest of Britain and her colonies, to suppress the growth of the French power, and not the English in America.

If his Majesty would be pleased to appoint a colony to be made on Ohio, with a separate governor, and an equitable form of government, a full liberty of conscience, and the same secured by Charter; not all that the French could project, would give it any impediment after a few years. The importance of such a colony to Britain would be vastly great, since the climate, and its remoteness from the Sea, would turn it immediately to raising *raw silk*, an article of vast expence to our nation, which we are at continual difficulties and disappointments in procuring. The charge of carriage of this article from the remotest parts to the Sea, is too inconsiderable to effect its value. Ohio is naturally furnished with salt, coal, limestone, grindstone, millstone, clay for glass-houses and pottery, which are of vast advantage to an inland country, and well deserving the notice I take of them in the map.

Marginal notes:
- Extent of the country on Ohio, &c. exceeds all the European dominions of Britain, France and Spain.
- The plantations in America less considerable than commonly supposed.
- Massachuset's not so large as Yorkshire.
- The interest and disposition of the colonies to be attached to England.
- A colony proposed to be established on Ohio.
- Ohio, proper for raw silk.
- Ohio abounds with coal, salt, limestone, &c. &c.

THE END.

PART III

COMMENTARY

ON

THE CASE OF THE OHIO COMPANY EXTRACTED FROM ORIGINAL PAPERS

CASE COMPILED FROM MANUSCRIPTS PRINTED IN PART I

THE George Mercer Papers printed in Part I of this book are a manuscript collection in the Darlington Memorial Library at the University of Pittsburgh. They cover most of the source material from which was compiled the printed pamphlet reproduced in Part II: *The Case of the Ohio Company, Extracted from Original Papers.*

Because the printed *Case* contains material which is not among the Mercer papers in the Darlington Library and which is hitherto unknown information concerning the history of the Company it, too, is reproduced here. The manuscript papers and the printed pamphlet belong together in a study of the Ohio Company.

The printed *Case* appears in reduced facsimile as Part II of the book. Since superior figures pointing to footnotes cannot be imposed upon a facsimile, the annotations are in commentary form.

The Commentary, Part III of the book, is intended to supply sufficient explanations and background material for the reader to interpret more easily the heterogeneous group of documents which comprise the *Case.* The Commentary is not a history of the Ohio Company; it is an elucidation and correlation of documents which epitomize the random activities of the Company.

HISTORY AND PROVENANCE OF THE *CASE*

The Case of the Ohio Company, Extracted from Original Papers is a unique pamphlet in the Rufus King Collection of the New York Historical Society. Information from R. W. G. Vail, director of the Society, reveals that the pamphlet came originally from the library of John Pownall, veteran secretary to Great Britain's Board of Trade and Plantations. Rufus King, ambassador to the Court of St. James's under George Washington, purchased it along with many other pamphlets. All of these were given to the New York Historical Society in 1906 by the grandson of Rufus King.

The New York Historical Society graciously lent the printed *Case* to the Darlington Memorial Library, University of Pittsburgh, so that it could be edited and published along with the "George Mercer Papers Relating to the Ohio Company of Virginia," the original documents from which it was compiled by George Mercer.

The pamphlet is complete with the exception of the last page which, if extant, could prove conclusively the hypothesis that the *Case* was printed for official use only, for presentation to the King in Council.

"ARTICLES OF AGREEMENT" REQUIRED REPORTS SENT TO ENGLAND

An "Item" in the formal "Articles of Agreement and copartnership for the Ohio Company for the Space of Twenty Years," dated May 23, 1751, required "that once every year as soon as conveniently may be after the general meeting of the said partners . . . a true copy of all the Proceedings of the said Company, their Committees for the year preceding shall be transmitted by the Clerk of the said Company for the time being to the aforesaid John Hanbury."

There is in the George Mercer Papers a document, identified as "A Résumé of the Proceedings of the Ohio Company, October 24, 1747–May 21, 1751," which may be the first report in fulfillment of the above requirement. John Hanbury, London member of the Company, was also the Company's solicitor. Therefore, it is logical to assume that the Company realized it was necessary to keep the London representative abreast of activities in the field.

"REPRESENTATION OF THE CASE," 1752

At the same general meeting of the Company, May 22–24, 1751, when the "Articles of Agreement . . . " were presented, approved, signed, and ordered to be transmitted to Mr. Hanbury, the Company resolved that "upon the return of Christopher Gist the Committee of the Company should meet, examine his reports and draw up as full and perfect a State and Report thereof." The report was to be submitted to the Company for approval at its next general meeting and, after approval, to be sent to Mr. Hanbury in London. The minutes of the next general meeting, November 22, 1752, show that the "Representation of the Case (which the Committee are desired to draw and transmit to Mr. Hanbury)" had not been executed;

Commentary

however, the document was prepared shortly and approved by the Committee on July 27, 1753. It was then signed by all the members present and sent to Mr. Hanbury. This actual document, the "Representation of the Case" was not located by the editor, but a document in the George Mercer Papers identified as "Case of the Ohio Company, 1754" may be an official copy of it. Also, a comparison of the 1754 petition of John Hanbury,[57] presented to the King in Council, and the before-mentioned "Minutes" of the Company show that the "Representation of the Case (which the Committee are desired to draw and transmit to Mr. Hanbury)" was undoubtedly the basis of that 1754 petition.

FRENCH AND INDIAN WAR DISRUPTS PLANS

The outbreak of French-English hostilities on the Ohio in 1754, followed by the loss of that region by the English, brought about the cessation of activities of the Company until after General Forbes regained the lost territory for the English, in November, 1758. If copies of the Orders of the Company be complete in the George Mercer Papers, the Company issued only one order from 1753 to 1759. Then, after more than five years of forced inactivity, the Ohio Company renewed its interests and vigorously explored all avenues which might lead to a legal title or patent to a huge tract of land on the Ohio. The French had been driven from the region, and Fort Pitt, an imposing English fort, now (1759) graced the "forks of the Monongahela" at what is now Pittsburgh, Pennsylvania; yet the Company to all intents and purposes had lost its great land grant "west of the Alleghenies." Henry Bouquet, upon assuming command at Fort Pitt, issued a proclamation denying ownership of western lands by the whites and proclaiming military rule in the region west of the Allegheny Mountains.

When the Committee of the Company met on July 6, 1759, John Mercer, secretary, was ordered "to draw up a full State of the Company's Case setting forth the Hardships We labour under and the Reasons why the Lands have not been settled and the Fort finished according to royal Instructions for making out our Grant and that the same be transmitted to Messrs. Hanburys to lay before the proper Boards and that the Company will undertake to pay all Expenses attending the same." John Hanbury died in 1758; hence this document was to be sent to Capel and Osgood Hanbury.

COMMITTEE ORDERS *CASE*

The *Case of the Ohio Company* . . . , of which a reduced facsimile

The Case of the Ohio Company

is printed in Part II, is the outgrowth of this order of July 6, 1759. George Mercer was its combined author and compiler. This work, in addition to a revision of John Mercer's "Case" consists of: (1) documents, extracts, and letters, the originals of which are in the George Mercer Papers printed in Part I; (2) information which could be known only by George Mercer; (3) documents presented to the King in Council; (4) miscellaneous public and private documents.

CASE APPROVED BY THE COMMITTEE

On October 17, 1760, John Mercer presented the "Case" to the Committee of the Company for their approval. Approval was given together with an order to send the document not to the Hanburys but to Charlton Palmer, a London barrister. In addition, Mercer was "empowered" to employ solicitor Palmer to represent them at the seat of government in London.

This document, which ends with the first paragraph on page 24 of the printed *Case*, was corrected and augmented greatly as late as December 1, 1761, long after it had been approved by the Committee. Almost two years after Committee approval Secretary Mercer sent it to Palmer.

GEORGE MERCER COMPILES *CASE*

Evidence that this particular manuscript was the basic document from which the printed *Case of the Ohio Company* was derived comes from two observations: (1) marginalia throughout this manuscript and the many corrections on it are in the handwriting of George Mercer, and (2) the printed *Case* follows more closely the arrangement of substantiating documents in this variant than in the other variant in the manuscript collection.

The actual manuscript as prepared for the printer was not among the George Mercer Papers nor was it located elsewhere by the editor. Thomas Pownall, who in 1776 published Christopher Gist's first *Journal*, gives notice that the *Journal* was lent him by George Mercer. This publication does not have the exact marginalia which appear in the manuscript variant of the document sent to Charlton Palmer on July 27, 1762. However, Pownall's version of Gist's first *Journal* does coincide with the Journal as printed in the *Case*. Pownall himself, therefore, must have copied either the manuscript prepared for the printer by George Mercer, or the printed *Case*.

In addition to the foregoing manuscript variant of the "Case," the George Mercer Papers contain: (1) part of a folio page of a first draft of the "Case" in John Mercer's handwriting and (2) the "Case

Commentary

of the Ohio Company, 1754."[686] Full description, provenance, and annotations accompany both documents printed in Part I (see Chronology).

It is necessary, however, to give further explanation in regard to the manner in which the printed *Case* may have been compiled. When George Mercer began to prepare it for publication in 1769 he had at hand the following materials: (1) the Resolutions of the Committee and of the Ohio Company, 1748–1763; (2) Résumé of the activities of the Ohio Company, 1747–1751; (3) Orders of the Ohio Company, 1749–1762; (4) Record of land grants; (5) Acts of Pennsylvania about the Indian Trade; (6) three variants or parts thereof of the "Case"; and (7) several business letters from his father, John Mercer, secretary to the Company. Some of this material was sent or given directly to him; other documents came through the hands of Charlton Palmer.

Naturally, Mercer had before him many more official papers other than those which are printed in this work. The petitions were for the most part of his own composition, and if he did not have copies, they were available at the Board of Trade.

There are no manuscripts in the George Mercer Papers, printed in Part I, from which the *Case* was printed from facsimile page 24, *"The Ohio Company was according..."* to facsimile page 26, *"Letter to Governor Dinwiddie,"* and from facsimile page 27 to the end, page 36. However, facsimile pages 27 and 28, as stated in the text, originated with the Committee of the Ohio Company and undoubtedly were written first by John Mercer. Internal evidence in the substance, pages 29 to 36, shows that George Mercer was the author.

Just as the Memorial of the Virginia House of Burgesses (1766) spurred George Mercer to presenting his "Proceedings of the Ohio Company" and his memorial (1767) to the Privy Council, the memorials of the Walpole Company and of Arthur Lee spurred him to action in 1769. Mercer's Memorial of December 18, 1769 (read at the Board of Trade January 3, 1770) was transmitted on January 24 "to the secretary of the Lords of the Treasury for their information as having reference to the application of Mr. Walpole and others, now before the Board." The delay by the Board of Trade to take action on Mercer's December 18 Memorial may have occasioned his decision to bring his father's "Case of the Ohio Company" up to date and to have it printed for presentation to the "King in Council for his consideration." On December 27, 1769, Charlton Palmer answered Mercer's request for all Ohio Company Papers; on May 8, 1770,

The Case of the Ohio Company

Mercer, in a Memorial to the Board of Trade, withdrew his last and therefore all his memorials to the English government in behalf of the Ohio Company.[798] Therefore, it is logical to assume that this document, *The Case of the Ohio Company, Extracted from Original Papers,* was prepared by George Mercer in the first few months of 1770 and printed before May 7, the date he associated the Ohio Company with the Walpole Company. On July 9 John Pownall refers to the printed *Case of the Ohio Company,* one fact amidst assumptions.

The *Case of the Ohio Company . . . ,* probably the outgrowth of annual reports ordered in 1751 to be sent to John Hanbury in London, was actually conceived in 1759; written between 1759 and 1761 by John Mercer; in the hands of Charlton Palmer, Richard Jackson, and George Mercer, from 1762 to 1769, respectively; revised, enlarged, and prepared for publication by George Mercer early in 1770; and printed by May. This particular copy was deposited at the Board of Trade or given to John Pownall by July 9, 1770, in whose hands it remained until his death in 1795; was in the possession of the King family until 1906, when it was given to its present owner, the New York Historical Society. Here it is published in reduced facsimile with the source material from which the greater part of the document was derived.

"Such is the state here contained, and upon it they must submit, whether they have not done everything in their power, to comply with the terms of the grant, and if so, whether they should be blamed for what they could by no means prevent." Thus wrote John Mercer in conclusion of his "Case of the Ohio Company." On July 27, 1762, he sent this document to their solicitor in London, Charlton Palmer, and instructed him to have it "Printed & laid before his Majesty The Board of Trade & Such others as you may think proper reserving Two Dozen to be sent me for the members of our Company."[231]

Although somewhat biased in behalf of the Company, the document, in addition to bringing to light opinions contemporary with opening the door of the Westward Movement, lifts the cloud of illusion and speculation which has enveloped the activities, achievements, and significance of the Ohio Company for almost two hundred years.

IMPORTANCE OF THE TREATY OF LANCASTER, 1744
Facsimile, Page 1

John Hanbury, London member of the Company and its first representative there, wrote the first paragraph, " . . . that by the Treaty of Lancaster . . . ,"[287] in his petition to the King in Council

Commentary

in their behalf, January, 1749. When John Mercer copied this phrase, more than ten years later, he substituted for Hanbury's confident words at the beginning, "Most Humbly Sheweth," the disconsolate ones, "It was generally reputed." Nevertheless, the paragraph remains a concise, simple statement of the terms of the Treaty of Lancaster (1744).

Rightfully, the Company could use this treaty as the starting post for their race westward, a race which, if won, would give the Ohio Company first place in the development of the West; for the Treaty of Lancaster established the first firm stage upon which Virginia settlements west of the mountains could be built.

A brief statement outlining the several methods by which Englishmen could obtain lands in North America and a résumé of some important steps which led to the treaty may help the reader understand more fully the importance of that Lancaster agreement and the Virginia deed signed in 1744.

INDIAN CONSENT REQUIRED TO SEAT LAND

From 1584, when Sir Walter Raleigh obtained from Queen Elizabeth "a patent for exploring and planting lands in North America not actually possessed by any Christian prince," to 1744, when the Treaty of Lancaster gave the English undisputed right to the lands west of the mountains, the method of acquiring lands in North America underwent many changes. Protestant England had to develop a criteria for granting lands different from the papal decrees which arbitrarily gave newly discovered territory to favored nations. By 1600 English royal rule and precedent had established the following three different methods for the colonization of North America.

First, "uninhabited or derelict lands" were possessed outright by the Crown. This was the status of Newfoundland. On April 27, 1610, James I of England declared that Newfoundland was "not actually possessed or inhabited by any Christian or other whatsoever"; in consequence thereof he granted that territory outright to the Earl of Northampton and others.

Second, the Crown granted to individuals or to corporate groups the right to colonize certain lands under English rule. However, before the land could be exploited the adventurers were required to purchase it or to obtain peaceful possession of it from "the original inhabitants or Indian princes." In this manner Rhode Island's charter was obtained by a company of associates; Pennsylvania was chartered to William Penn alone.

Third, lands were possessed of the Crown by right of conquest. In

The Case of the Ohio Company

this manner England, in 1664, obtained New York from the Dutch. Captain John Smith, by conquering certain Indian tribes, gained part of Virginia for the Crown; yet some of the land within Virginia's charter rights was owned by the Iroquois, an ownership derived from the right of Iroquois conquest of the southern Indians.

Theoretically, the Treaties of Breda and Westminster (1677 and 1678) gave England control over all the Iroquois lands, for the Iroquois had placed themselves under Dutch protection prior to 1677. Actually, the boundaries of the Iroquois lands were dimly outlined. Until 1684 all negotiations between English Crown colonies and the Six Nations were carried on by the governor of New York. That year Virginia came upon the scene, at a meeting of Governor Dongan of New York with the Five Nations at Albany. Lord Effingham Howard, governor of Virginia, did not enter into direct negotiations with the Five Nations at that time but was, in principle, merely a witness to transactions between Governor Dongan and the Five Nations.

HISTORY OF THE TREATY OF LANCASTER

The first definite step toward Virginia's acquisition of land by the Treaty of Lancaster was in 1701 when the Five Nations gave the English a "deed of sale of all their hereditary and conquered country for a valuable consideration."

John Huske in his *Present State of North America (1755)* outlines the hereditary country of the Five Nations set forth in this deed:

In 1672 they the Five Nations conquered and incorporated the Illinois Indians residing upon the River Illinois, which rises near Lake Michigan, and disembogues into the Mississippi. And they also then incorporated the Satanas that they formerly drove from the Lakes Ontario and Erie. And the Rivers Illinois and Mississippi make the Western Bounds of their Conquests, and of their Deed of Sale to the Crown of Great Britain in 1701. They also conquered the New-York or Hudson's River Indians, the Delaware, Susquehanah, Ohio, and other Indians in the Provinces of New-York, Pennsylvania, Maryland, and Virginia by 1673. The Twightwees, or Miamis, residing on the River Oubache or St. Jerom, they conquer's in 1685.

By this deed the English recognized Iroquois' ownership of the land within the above boundary. In reality this deed was not a transfer from Indian to white of all the lands within the boundaries mentioned. It was, after a fashion, the creation of an English protectorate over the Indian, thus giving them the exclusive right to exploit the Indian and the right to first option on the land when the Indian could be induced to sell.

Virginia's Governor Spotswood, by his interest in the lands beyond

Commentary

the Blue Ridge, was responsible for the next step toward the Lancaster Treaty. It was at the Treaty of 1722,[91] primarily a Virginia–Five Nations' affair, that a definite boundary line was first mentioned. The previous year Virginia and the Five Nations met at Williamsburg and reached a preliminary agreement in regard to the northern boundary of Virginia. This agreement was the spark which lit the fire of westward expansion in Virginia. Encouraged by prospects of a treaty with the Indians, land-hungry Virginians immediately obtained grants for 112,000 acres of land within the boundaries mentioned in the negotiations, 68,000 of which were patented by Governor Spotswood through his own personal agents. At Albany, Spotswood told the Five Nations

that they have never strictly adhered to any Treaties made with that Gov't for these 50 years past, & as they have often desired that some Deputies Might come from Virginia to Albany to Treat with them, he is now come to make such a Peace & Treaty with them in behalf of the Christians of Virginia & the Tributary Indians bordering upon that Province as shall be forever inviolable. And says that the foundation of this Peace is, that the River Potomack & the high ridge of Mountains wch extend along the Frontiers of Virginia to the Westward of the present Settlements are to be the Boundaries between the 5 Nations & the Virginians Xts & Indians—so that none of either Govt shall pass them without Passports from their respective Govrs or Commdrs in Chief. And that he expects the 5 Nations solemnly Assent to these Limits as the preliminary Article of their present Treaty wch he promises on the part of Virginia.[91]

This treaty, as interpreted by the Virginians, gave them the right to settle all the territory south of the Potomac and east of the Allegheny (not the Blue Ridge) Mountains. The Five Nations interpreted "the high ridge of mountains" to be the Blue Ridge. Nevertheless, the northern boundary, understood by both parties to be the Potomac River, did free the frontier of Indian incursions for sufficient length of time to allow Virginians to establish strong settlements west of the Blue Ridge. The Indians were alarmed when they realized the inroads which these white settlements were making on their hunting grounds. At the same time they were cringing under a restriction in the treaty which prohibited them from traveling southward over the warriors' paths to wage war on their traditional enemies, the southern Indians. In 1732 a Virginia family was massacred[735] by some northern warriors. The governor of Virginia asked Pennsylvania's assistance in apprehending the offenders. Unrest and suspicion continued to grow in the minds of the Six Nations until 1736, when the Indians took the initiative and demanded payment for lands seated by Virginians and Marylanders.

In 1736, at a conference between the Six Nations and Pennsylvania,

The Case of the Ohio Company

the Indians asked James Logan, president of the Provincial Council,

> to write to the Governors of Virginia & Maryland, who are possessed of their Lands, without ever considering the Indians for them, & request that we would take the Answer of those Governors, which next Spring some of their Nations will come to receive at the Fire kept for them in this place. That they intend to apply to the great King on the other side of the Water, & let Him know what they expect on this Head from His People.[764]

At this time Pennsylvania executed a deed of purchase of lands on both sides of the Susquehanna, one-half the purchase price to be paid at the time and one-half to be paid later. The Six Nations did not come to Philadelphia for final payment until 1742, when they renewed the accusations against Maryland only.[747] Canasatego, chief of the Six Nations, spoke in threatening tone. Although the chief's harangue was hurled against Marylanders, he asked Governor Thomas if he had written to both Maryland and Virginia concerning the encroachment on Six Nations' territory. The chief continued:

> If you have not done anything we now renew our Request, and desire You will inform the Person whose people are seated on our Lands, that that Country belongs to Us in right of Conquest—We having bought it with our Blood, and taken it from our Enemies in fair War; And we Expect as Owners of that Land to receive such a Consideration for it as the Land is worth. We desire you will press him to send Us a positive Answer; Let him say Yes or No; if he says Yes, we will treat with him; if No, we are able to do ourselves Justice, and we will do it by going to take payment on ourselves.

Trouble between the southern colonies and the Six Nations reached its zenith[735] in 1743, as a result of the late "unhappy skirmish in Virginia," when northern Indians, passing through Virginia to make war on the Catawbas, clashed with the settlers there. Several persons on both sides were killed. Pennsylvania, realizing that this affront to the Six Nations might touch off a general Indian war, exerted every effort to bring about a peace between Virginia and the Six Nations. Poor Conrad Weiser, Virginia's emissary, shuttled between Philadelphia and the Onondaga Council (present Syracuse, New York) the entire winter and spring of 1743–44. Fortunately, he was able to bring Virginia, Maryland, and the Six Nations together to treat at Lancaster in 1744.

Thomas Lee, former resident agent for the Fairfax proprietary and a member of the Executive Council, was Virginia's principal commissioner at the treaty.[287] Eagerness for possession of land by the Virginians was epitomized in Lee's disdainful and autocratic attitude toward the Indians. Lee outlined the terms of the Treaty of Albany (1722) and accused the Six Nations of breaking them; insisted that that treaty gave the Virginians a legal right to establish the settlements

Commentary

of which the Indians so loudly complained; asked the haughty Canasatego by what right he could claim as his own the lands upon which he was not permitted to walk without Virginia's permission; and accused the Indians of setting up their "right against the Great King under whose grants the people you complain of are settled." A modern writer, Paul A. W. Wallace, believes that the haughty speeches between the Six Nations and the Virginia commissioners were strategic moves on the part of both. When the conference ended each side was gleeful in gaining its objectives. Virginia had obtained a legal right to lands coveted by visionary-minded Virginia expansionists; the Six Nations were granted a certain warriors' path over which their messengers were permitted to travel north and south. When the bourse was closed the night of July 2, 1744, at Lancaster, the Virginia commissioners held in their hands a deed from the Six Nations, "recognizing the King's right to all the lands that are, or shall be, by His Majesty's appointment in the colony of Virginia." The Indians possessed goods that cost "£200 Pennsylvania currency bought with ready cash," two hundred pounds in gold and the promise of an authorized Warriors' Road north and south.

LANCASTER TREATY GIVES VIRGINIA LIMITED POSSESSION OF WESTERN LANDS

Therefore, the Company could indeed rightfully use this treaty as the starting post for their race westward. Lord Effingham Howard, Governor Spotswood, and Governor Gooch, in turn, had worked unceasingly to give character to the faint boundary line between English and Six Nations' territory. At long last, Virginia, in the King's name, had a right to "all the lands that are or shall be by his majesty's appointment in the colony of Virginia."

This release of lands at Lancaster did loose the Indian bond which limited Virginia settlements to the tidewater region; yet there was another unsettled land controversy which limited free settlement beyond the Blue Ridge in the Shenandoah Valley and along the Potomac.

VIRGINIA-FAIRFAX LAND DISPUTE

In this document John Mercer does not give cognizance to the settlement of the Virginia-Fairfax land dispute nor to the delicate French-English situation abroad, both of which played an important rôle in the western expansion of Virginia. Thomas, sixth Lord Fairfax, was proprietor of the Northern Neck of Virginia, a tract of almost six million acres of land situated between the Potomac and Rappa-

The Case of the Ohio Company

hannock Rivers. This vast tract had been given to Lord Culpepper, Lord Fairfax's forefather, as a reward for services rendered Charles II. Before the king returned from exile to the throne of England, he rewarded some of his most faithful supporters by giving them huge tracts of land in Virginia. In so doing he merely followed English precedent. The awarding of frontier lands to deserving soldiers "was the usual custom and policy of all Nations, but in more especial manner of the state of England."

The Fairfaxes interpreted "heads of the Rivers of Tappahanocke als Rappahanock and Quiriough or Patawomecke River, the courses of the said rivers as they are commonly called and known by the inhabitants, and all the islands withe the banks of those rivers," set forth in the original grant, to mean that their boundary line cornered at the first heads or springs of the Rappahannock and Potomac Rivers, respectively; while Virginia's interpretation of the western boundary, as given in the grant, was that the Potomac River head was at the junction of the Potomac and Shenandoah Rivers and that the head of the Rappahannock was at its junction with the Hedgman River. The difference between the two interpretations was about four million acres of land. By 1736 pressure of settlements in the Shenandoah Valley made it necessary for Lord Fairfax to establish a definitive boundary line for his proprietary. Therefore, he had the tract surveyed according to his interpretation of boundaries and a map with duplicate thereof delineated. One copy of this map was kept in Virginia; the other was sent to London where the case, Virginia *vs.* Fairfax, was finally decided.

It was not until April 6, 1745, that the Privy Council handed down its decision in the Virginia-Fairfax land dispute. Fairfax's interpretation of the grant was upheld; the boundaries as outlined in the map of 1736 were final. Virginia's course to the West via the great valleys of Virginia and Potomac was now outlined clearly, and the surge to the West began.

KING GEORGE'S WAR BREAKS DEADLOCK FOR VIRGINIA

James Patton gives an entirely different reason for these large land grants. If one chooses to believe Patton, it was the outbreak of King George's War in Europe and not the settlement of boundaries that prompted the Virginia Executive Council to make these great grants of lands on the Mississippi and her tributaries. In 1753 James Patton reminded John Blair that when he petitioned the government of Virginia for 200,000 acres of land on "three Branches of the Mississippi & the Waters thereof" in 1743 he received assurance from the

Commentary

Virginia Executive Council that his petition for lands would be considered if and when conditions were more favorable for settlement to the westward.

Wrote Patton:

after some time spent their Hon^rs: told me that nevertheless of their Inclination to encourage Such an undertaking they could not at that Time Grant my Pettition not knowing how the Govermt at Home would approve of their Granting Land on those Waters lest it might Occasion a Dispute betwixt them and the French who claimed a Right to the Land on those Waters, and as the distance was so great from any Part of the Atlantick Ocean, They could not conceive that any Benefit could arise to his Majesties Revenues or to the Strength of this Colony, by an handfull of Poor People that might Venture to settle on these Waters. But if a War broke out betwixt England and France, they would then Grant my Pettition.

In his letter Patton reiterated his request to the Executive Council of 1743 to enter his petition on the Council books, so that when lands would be granted he would be considered the first petitioner and thus receive first choice in lands.

War did break out in Europe and, according to his own statement, Patton was called to appear before the Executive Council where he received the grant, along with the other petitioners mentioned in this *Case*.

GOOCH FAVORS GRANT BUT FEARS INTERNATIONAL REPERCUSSIONS

Patton's explanation of the grants of 1745 being contingent upon European affairs is substantiated by Governor Gooch's reluctance to grant to "Thomas Lee and Eleven others" 200,000 acres of land on the Ohio River. In 1747, when Lee petitioned for the grant, peace between Great Britain and France was in the offing. Therefore, Governor Gooch informed the Board of Trade of the reason that he did not exercise his right under royal instructions and grant this land to the petitioners. Wrote Gooch: "As these lands lye upon some of the chief Branches of the River Mississippi, I was apprehensive such Grants might possibly give some Umbrage to the French, especially when we were in hopes of entering into a Treaty for Establishing a general Peace."

OTHER PETITIONERS FOR WESTERN LANDS

The petitioners mentioned by Mercer were not new in land speculation. Before 1745 they had obtained permission to survey an aggregate sum of more than a half million acres. To add acreage to abundant acreage was more the order of the day with them than it was unusual. The sixth petition which gives the Fairfax line as a boundary

The Case of the Ohio Company

is evidence that some petitioners were influenced by the settlement of the Virginia-Fairfax case.

JOHN MERCER'S OPINIONS BIASED
Facsimile, Page 2

Mercer's criticism of the petitioners' laxity in not surveying their lands and his criticism of the Council's leniency toward them do not coincide with the facts as he presents them in the *Case*. The Governor informed the Board of Trade that more than one year's time for survey was often allowed petitioners whose grants were large and at a great distance from the eastern seaboard. The Board of Trade was aware of John Mercer's biased thinking when they rejected in part the Ohio Company's petition of 1754. Here they stated specifically that the obstacle, insufficient time to execute surveys, which hindered the progress of the Ohio Company, was not unique to that Company alone but was an obstacle common to all land speculators in the West.

When John Mercer wrote this defense of the Ohio Company (1759-1761) he misstated some facts concerning its origin. The Company was organized by October, 1747,[16] and not in 1748. A list of land grants upon which action was postponed reveals that on October 20, 1747, Thomas Lee and eleven associates petitioned the Executive Council for 200,000 acres of land in the Ohio Country. Governor Gooch favored the petition; yet as mentioned previously, on account of the delicate French-English situation, he wished to have further direction from the Crown before he acted upon it. His letter of November 6, 1747, began negotiations which culminated in the "Additional Instruction" and which authorized him to make the Ohio Company grant. On October 24, 1747, the Company wrote to John Hanbury in London and offered him a share in their partnership. They also asked him to try to obtain an additional royal instruction to Virginia's governor, empowering him to make vast grants of land in a territory unquestionably English, according to English interpretation of the Treaty of Utrecht, and unquestionably French, according to the French interpretation of the same document.

John Mercer's letter to Charlton Palmer, July 27, 1762, in which he enclosed the manuscript from which this pamphlet was compiled, shows clearly that frustration held the writer firmly in its grip. With the return of the English to the Ohio in 1758 came the bright hope that the Ohio Company would succeed in their enterprise. Henry Bouquet's Proclamation of October, 1761, dimmed that hope, and it became even fainter in the light of reports from Adam Stephen that Pennsylvania was engrossing the Indian trade. This background leads

Commentary

one to believe it was at least righteous indignation, if not rage, that caused John Mercer to write this scathing invective against the foreign (Pennsylvania) traders. Mercer may have been reporting what Thomas Lee had heard at Lancaster; yet the language of the Treaty of 1744, as printed, does not connote that unprincipled, profligate Pennsylvania traders were the main source of contention between the Indians and the whites. Also such invectives as this from John Mercer were not unusual. Lawyer Mercer was the victim of a vile tongue and was admonished on more than one occasion for using, in the courtroom, language unbecoming a lawyer. His verbal abuse of opposing counsel had caused him to be threatened with disbarment in Virginia.

PETITION OF JOHN HANBURY, 1749
Facsimile, Pages 2-3

The petition prepared by John Hanbury, as printed here, was not corrected according to the minutes of the Company, for the minutes show that Daniel Cresap never was a member,[18] and that Francis,[17] not William, was the Thornton member. John Hanbury drew up the petition and presented it, as requested by the Company. Naturally, Hanbury who lived in England was not concerned with the Virginia-Fairfax land dispute; nor would it have been politic for him to remind the Crown that her colonies were mere pawns on the European chessboard. Therefore, it is easy to understand why he presented only the Treaty of Lancaster as the ways from which the Ohio Company could launch its ship of enterprise.

When the Company sent Hanbury information about the prospects of the success of this venture, few Virginians had traveled over the territory that the Company desired. Claims of ease of transportation, short portages, etc., were based upon wishful thinking and dreams of fortune rather than upon the actual experience of those who furnished the information. Only the scheme to obtain settlers, as outlined by Hanbury, had a real foundation. Since the 1730's the Pennsylvania Germans had been pouring into the Shenandoah Valley.[504] Now, most of this land was declared a part of the Fairfax grant, and the efficiency with which the Fairfax resident agent operated made the expense of settling there exhorbitant. If the Ohio Company could assure their settlers that they would be exempt from quitrents for ten years, they would have no difficulty in settling the "hundred families" upon the lands in "seven years."

The Hanbury petition was presented to the King in Council on January 11 and was referred[9] by them to the Board of Trade for their consideration. The Board was slightly confused when they received

The Case of the Ohio Company

it. For almost a year they had been corresponding with Governor Gooch on the same matter. Already the Board had reported[10] back to the Privy Council on Governor Gooch's request, and on December 13, 1748, at the Privy Council's request, had prepared an "additional instruction" which empowered Virginia's governor to make the grant requested by the Ohio Company. Upon conferring with Mr. Hanbury, the Board of Trade learned that the Hanbury petition and Governor Gooch's request were one and the same.[11] Therefore, on March 16, 1749, they rescinded the "additional instruction" and issued a new one in behalf of the Ohio Company. The first one of December 13, 1748, which was never sent, is the "additional instruction" most frequently cited and is printed in many other places.

George Mercer, in his report before the Privy Council on October 8, 1767, stated that the chief obstacle in the path of the Ohio Company's progress was the "very large Grants of Lands being made to private Persons on the very first Report of the Instruction in Behalf of the Comp^a being sent to the Govr" Mercer also informed the Privy Council that the members of the Company in Virginia knew of the King's approbation of their request many months before the Governor acknowledged the receipt of his royal instruction. Furthermore, he accused the Council of granting lands "to borrowed Names and private Landmongers" who could not effectively take up the lands. None of these grants coincided with or even overlapped the Company's grant. Francis Thornton and John Tayloe, members of the Ohio Company, were among the George Mercer-styled "landmongers" who received grants on July 12.

COMPANY'S ACTIVITIES INADEQUATELY PRESENTED IN THE *CASE*
Facsimile, Page 4

Although the period, 1749 to 1752, was a time of intense activity of the Company, John Mercer gives less than two pages' space to those years. Records of five meetings of the membership and six of the committee selected to transact business between membership meetings are in the Mercer manuscripts.

The first cargo was ordered from John Hanbury before October 20, 1748, at which time the Committee agreed to have shipment postponed until the grant was obtained. On June 20, 1749, the Company sent "an Invoice for a Cargo" worth £2,000 to be delivered in Virginia in November. As late as May, 1750, this cargo was still on a landing on the Potomac.[23] Another cargo arrived in Virginia in December, 1751.[558]

Commentary

At a general meeting of the Company on June 21, 1749, they employed Hugh Parker as their factor. There is no statement in the George Mercer Papers which reveals the exact time when the first storehouse was built, or who built it. However, the Frederick County, Virginia, Court case, Ohio Company *vs.* Hamer, reveals that in July, 1750, Parker engaged John Hamer to assist in hauling the Company's goods from the landing to the store. Mr. Hamer's account against the Ohio Company also shows that he did carpenter work "on the store."[182]

VIRGINIA ENGAGES CONRAD WEISER, INDIAN INTERPRETER

Thomas Lee had been a Virginia Commissioner at the conference at Lancaster in 1744. There he had promised the Six Nations' Chief, Canasatego, that he would recommend them to the King for a further consideration when Virginia settled the lands deeded to her. Lee and Weiser, since their meeting at Lancaster, had corresponded regularly. After Lee had written to the Board of Trade, requesting treaty goods in order to fulfill his pledge to the Six Nations, he wrote to Conrad Weiser, tentatively engaging him to carry the invitation treaty "belt" to Onondaga and to serve as the interpreter at the anticipated conference.[31] The treaty goods arrived in the spring of 1750, but Weiser was unable to persuade the Six Nations to come to Fredericksburg, Virginia, to receive the present.[105] Therefore, Lee employed Gist, conveniently on his way to Ohio to reconnoiter the Ohio Company lands, to invite the Ohio Indians to attend the Fredericksburg conference. Gist was equally unsuccessful.

JOHN HANBURY LOBBIES FOR THE COMPANY

Since John Hanbury held no official position in England, evidence that he acted[34] upon the Ohio Company's request—that he "endeavour to obtain orders from his Majesty, for making a present to the Indians . . . and to have the line between Virginia and Pennsylvania run"[35]— is found in correspondence between the Board of Trade and persons through whom Hanbury lobbied for the Company. Lee referred "your Lordships [the Board of Trade] to what Mr. Hanbury will lay before your Lordships more at Large, and we hope for your Lordships favourable representation to his Majestye in favour of the Ohio Company." As extra bait Lee adds,

If by these further indulgences from his Majestye, the Ohio Company are allowed to carry on their trade and make their settlements they hope to engage the Indians of the several nations soe effectually in the British Interest y^t the encroachments of the french will be prevented.

The Case of the Ohio Company

Lee's request was of no consequence[30] in the Board of Trade's decision to send treaty goods. His letter was not received at the Board of Trade until September 30, 1750, and not read until October 11, at least four months after the treaty goods arrived in Virginia. It was the powerful lobbyist, John Hanbury, who engineered the whole business in London. Although he was very busy marrying off his daughter, he did take time to procure from the Crown the contract to supply the treaty goods. He also conferred with Thomas Penn in London on the matter of settling the boundary line between Pennsylvania and Virginia. Mr. Hanbury was lukewarm on the question of this boundary line, for he informed Thomas Penn that he was of the opinion nothing should be done about it until the Indians were reconciled to the English building a fort on the Ohio. From the Penn-Hanbury discussion one learns that Hanbury, unlike the American members of the Company, favored building, not a fortified storehouse, but a fort. Hanbury's influence is evident also in Robert Dinwiddie's "Memorial" to the Board of Trade, which set forth his proposal for addition to the royal instructions by which he was to govern Virginia. Before Dinwiddie left London to assume his position as lieutenant governor of Virginia, he submitted "an humble Intimation of what may be esteemed no improper Addition."[27] Dinwiddie explained that

The cultivating a good Understanding with the Indians ought to be the daily care of every Governor on the American Continent, and is of the last Importance to Virginia—but as this Friendship is chiefly secured by annual Presents, which the french have rendered customary and are very punctual in making, it seems quite expedient that somewhat certain should be fixed to support such Gratuities on our Part.

Also, Lee agitated that the Pennsylvania-Virginia-Maryland boundary line be run. He wrote letters to Conrad Weiser, to Governor Hamilton, to Governor Ogle, and to the Board of Trade; still the issue was decided between John Hanbury and Thomas Penn in London. Richard Peters, who was much excited about the affair, relayed his concern to Thomas Penn, the proprietor in London who, in the beginning, expressed concern.

However, after Penn had conferred with John Hanbury, he closed the discussion with Peters by the following paragraph:

As to Mr Ogle & Collo Lees Letters I shall say nothing more to them, than that the Lines will be run very soon with both Maryland & Virginia, as I conceive this is the most proper time of doing it, about the Latter I shall consult the Lords of Trade with whom I am so happy to stand very well, & who will, I am sure be ready to do my Family justice, more than which I do not ask. Mr Hanbury writes Collo Lee that he thinks it will be much better to defer for sometime running the Lines, 'till the Indians are better

Commentary

satisfied with the project of building a Fort at Allegheny, but however that may be, neither Mr Lee nor Mr Hamilton can give any power to fix the Boundarys, that must be done by Commissions from the King & from us here which I shall take care of so that your intercourse with Collo Lee will not be of any immediate use, however if it shou'd be appointed on each side it may be of Service.

Hanbury quickly obtained the Indian present which Virginia needed. From 1699 the Crown had provided Indian presents to be given at conferences pertaining to land transfers.[28]

GIST JOURNALS PRINTED IN PART I
Facsimile, Page 5

Since both the first and second "Journals" of Christopher Gist in the George Mercer Papers are annotated and printed in Part I, it is unnecessary to include any discussion of them in this Commentary.

Gist's commission from the president and Council in 1751 was to carry an invitation to the Indians on the Ohio to attend a conference at Logstown in 1752. Although there is no record of such a commission to Gist in the Virginia Executive Council *Journals,* his own journal does reveal that he was authorized to extend the invitation. The authorization, however, was once removed from the source. Gist himself stated that he was acting under orders from James Patton, not Lewis Burwell.

OHIO COMPANY MAP BECOMES PUBLIC DOCUMENT, 1754

John Mercer unjustly accused Hanbury of breach in confidence. Before 1754 Hanbury was provided with a map which showed the extent of lands, encompassed by natural boundaries, which the Company wished to be permitted to enter for survey. Traced upon this map were the routes followed by Gist on his two exploratory journeys. When John Hanbury presented the Ohio Company's Memorial to the King in Council, March 28, 1754,[57] he also presented a plan showing the natural boundaries of the land desired by the Company. This map may be the one delineated by John Mercer before November 6, 1752. At present the original is in the British Museum and is reproduced from copy made for Mr. William Darlington. When the map annexed to the Hanbury Petition was presented to the King in Council it became a public document and was no longer the private property of the Ohio Company. All of the maps which the government could procure were made available to John Mitchell in 1755 when he delineated his famous map of the British Colonies in North America. The routes followed by Gist are marked on Mitchell's *Map.*

The Case of the Ohio Company

John Dalrymple, who revised the Fry and Jefferson map of Virginia in 1755, also marked Gist's route on his *Map*. Lewis Evans' *Map* (1755) gives the same information. More than likely these map makers derived their information, either directly or indirectly, from the map deposited with the Board of Trade by John Hanbury. John Hanbury could scarcely be maligned for misuse of Ohio Company property; the map became a public document.

INDIANS SET TIME AND PLACE FOR LOGSTOWN CONFERENCE, 1752
Facsimile, Pages 5-6

It is difficult to understand why John Mercer did not know that the Virginians had no appointment to meet the Ohio Indians at Logstown in 1751.[268] At this time the Virginia-Indian conference was scheduled[275] to be held at Fredericksburg, Virginia, not Logstown, on the Ohio. On his first journey into the Ohio Country, November, 1750–May, 1751, Gist carried a message from Acting Lieutenant Governor Thomas Lee to the Indians, inviting them to come to Fredericksburg, Virginia, "to meet and treat with them and receive the King's present." Since Lee's instructions to Gist have not been located, there is no way of knowing whether Lee instructed Gist to invite all the western Indians in the English sphere of influence to Fredericksburg. Evidently Gist did not speak an Indian tongue fluently, for he depended upon Andrew Montour to interpret the invitation to the Indians at Logstown. Unfortunately, Gist arrived there after George Croghan and Andrew Montour had left for the Miami Country to deliver a present and a treaty invitation in the name of Pennsylvania to the western tribes. He followed the Pennsylvania emissaries to Muskingum (Coshocton, Ohio) where, by Andrew Montour, he extended Virginia's and Pennsylvania's invitation to the Wyandots. The chiefs declined the invitation by answering, "That their King and all of Them thanked their Brother the Governor of Virginia for his Care, and Me for bringing them the News, but they could not give Me an Answer untill they had a full and general Council of the several Nations of Indians which coud not be till next Spring." Likewise at Windaughalah's Town and the Lower Shawnee Town Montour delivered invitations to the Delawares and Shawnee, respectively. Here they answered only Pennsylvania's invitation. They accepted with thanks and declared their intentions were to attend the treaty at Logstown the next spring (1751). Gist, in his journal, does not record that Virginia's invitation was extended to the Twightwees.

The following final answer to "Mr. Guests's" message was given

· 412 ·

Commentary

at the Pennsylvania-Indian Conference at Logstown in May, 1751:

Now, Brother, we expect You will consider that we are a poor People and at War with the Southward Indians, and don't know but some of our Nations may soon be struck by the French, so that it is not in our Power to go down to hear what our great Father has to say to us; But our Brothers of Pennsylvania have kindled a Council Fire here, and we expect you will send our Father's Speeches to us here, for we long to hear what our great Father the King of Great Britain has to say to us his poor children.

On June 10, 1751, George Croghan, Pennsylvania's emissary at her Indian conference at Logstown, sent his account of the proceedings of the meeting to the governor of Pennsylvania and expressed the hope that "your Honour will recommend it to the Government of Virginia to answer the Speech sent them now in answer to their own Speech sent last Fall, as soon as possible." Upon receiving this message Lewis Burwell, acting lieutenant governor, sent James Patton to the Ohio to deliver an official invitation to the Indians to attend a Virginia conference at Logstown in May, 1752. Patton set out on September 28 and returned to Cresap's on October 21.[275] While at Logstown he delivered to the Indian chiefs an invitation belt of wampum which he expected would be sent to Onondaga, the seat of Six Nations' authority. Sir William Johnson reported that the wampum which Burwell "sent to call or invite the Six Nations to the Conference was found remaining in Logstown, when the Commissioners came there last May."[300] However, Thomas Cresap wrote to Conrad Weiser that Patton, "instead of giving them modest Invitation, threaten'd them very much, at which they are greatly affronted" and paid no attention to his message. Cresap also relayed to Governor Dinwiddie Andrew Montour's interpretation of Patton's behavior. Montour said that Patton "did not do it right or others since have Interpreted it otherwise: some telling them one thing and others another, so that they are confused about it." In this same letter Thomas Cresap gave the governor some sound advice on Indian protocol. He wrote as follows:

The proper way to invite the Indians to a Treaty is, to send a Belt of Wampum, which signifies that you have something of Importance to Communicate to a Council, the time of wch should be then agreed on: and not to mention the Business till the time of that Council is come. the Remarks the Indians made on the Message from the Honble Lewis Burwell Esqr by Col^o Patton, was that he had told them his Business then, and therefore they had no occasion to come to a Council to hear the same thing over again.[275]

Whether one believes Thomas Cresap or Sir William Johnson, the result was the same. James Patton's faux pas invalidated Virginia's

The Case of the Ohio Company

conference at Logstown in 1752 before it took place. If the invitation were not accompanied by a belt of wampum, the agreement was not binding on the part of the Indians; if an invitation wampum belt were given by Patton, yet not delivered to the Onondaga Council, the agreement was likewise void. True, the Indians on the Ohio had had a separate Council Fire kindled, but the seat of Six Nations' authority remained at Onondaga and commitments made by the "hunters" meant nothing to high-ranking Iroquois chiefs. Christopher Gist, on his second exploratory trip, also invited the Indians to the forthcoming conference. His invitation, however, must have been an informal one, for he does not mention having given an invitation "belt of Wampum" to the Indians.

JOHN MERCER ACCUSES VIRGINIA OFFICIALS OF DISCRIMINATION
Facsimile, Page 6

John Mercer's complaint against the extension of time for survey, given to certain land patentees, linked with his discussion of the anticipated success of the Logstown Conference, implies that expediency in carrying out the terms of their grant was of primary importance to the Ohio Company. A clear title to 200,000 acres of land and an opportunity for the Ohio Company to obtain 300,000 acres more was contingent upon seating the land and establishing a satisfactory trade among the Indians.

His chief complaint was against John Blair, William Russell, and William McMachon. On November 4, 1745, John Blair, William Russell, and others were granted leave "to take up one hundred Thousand Acres of Land lying to the westward of the Line of Lord Fairfax on the Waters of Potomack and Youghyoughgane" and were "allowed four Years Time to survey and Pay Rights for the same upon Return of the Plans to the Secretarys Office." On April 22, 1747, William McMachon and others were granted similar leave "to take up sixty Thousand Acres of Land joining the Grant of John Blair and others," and were "allowed five years Time to a survey." No uniform length of time for the survey of grants was set by Virginia law. Four years was the usual time given in the case of large grants—small grants, one year; yet the Ohio Company were given seven years' time to return their plans to the Secretary's office. In the meantime, May 5, 1749, all surveys were prohibited "beyond the great Mountain" by Executive Council order, an order issued in favor of the Ohio Company. Six months later this ban was lifted and surveyors were allowed "to proceed in surveying any lands beyond

Commentary

the great Mountains, so that they don't interfere with the Grant of the Ohio Company."

After Gist received "Instructions" for his second journey for the Ohio Company, he went to Williamsburg to solicit another commission from the Virginia government. Therefore, John Blair, a member of the Executive Council, could have known that the Company considered taking up land on the Monongahela and Youghiogheny. Since Blair's original grant was for land on the Youghiogheny, this renewment of which John Mercer complained could have been an Ohio Company countermove.

PENNSYLVANIA-VIRGINIA INDIAN TRADE RIVALRY

In order to establish favorable trade relations with the Ohio Indians it was necessary for the Ohio Company to do something about the rivalry existing between the Pennsylvania and Virginia traders; also more and more French traders were moving into the Ohio Country. In addition, the law of supply and demand imposed a new threat to the trader. As European culture was accepted by the Indian his need for European goods increased; as the whites pushed their settlements into their hunting ground the Indians' stock in trade, furs, decreased. Therefore, they demanded cheaper goods.

Of the two colonies Pennsylvania held the more favorable position in the western Indian trade. When the tide of French influence flowed into the Miami Country in the 1740's, Virginia and Carolina traders fled before it; when it ebbed, not Virginia but Pennsylvania traders, led by George Croghan, established themselves among the Miami. Perhaps Thomas Lee's remarks to Conrad Weiser concerning the Ohio Company's projected program of Indian trade alerted Pennsylvania to competition in the field. Rivalry approaching hostility between Pennsylvania and Virginia traders on the Ohio existed in 1748 when Lee informed Weiser that "if ye Govern^t of Pensylv^a don't regulate their traders, the rascally fellows the go^e among the Indians by lyes & treachery will be Authors of much blood shed and in consequence give the French possession of the trade." Also, both Pennsylvania and Virginia realized that the French were a real threat to this lucrative business. In 1748 Hugh Parker, a Maryland trader and later a member and factor for the Ohio Company, gave offense to some Indians at Kuskuskies (New Castle, Lawrence County, Pennsylvania); in consequence thereof they killed Parker's hired man. Lee purports this outbreak was instigated by the French; William Trent's report of the episode hints that the reason for this outrage was that Parker, a Maryland trader and therefore obnoxious to the Indians,

The Case of the Ohio Company

refused to sell them rum at the price—five bucks a keg—set by Pennsylvania at the Logstown Conference in August, 1748. When Richard Peters informed Thomas Penn, the proprietor living in England, that he had learned from a reliable source that the Ohio Company had received their grant, he also expressed the fear that their activities would spur the French on to greater efforts to capture the western Indian trade, especially the Twightwee (Miami) trade. Lee's remarks to Conrad Weiser about "Mr Parker's (one of Our Company) Store" being robbed is misleading. Hugh Parker was on the Ohio at this time as factor for Lord Fairfax and his associates and not for the Ohio Company. However, it does appear that he was also scouting for the Company. He and Thomas Cresap had circulated among the Indians the information that they expected a large quantity of goods in the spring, and that they would undersell the Pennsylvania traders. At this time Parker persuaded Robert Smith, the young trader whom Gist met at Pickawillany in January, 1751, to work for the Ohio Company. Richard Peters, secretary to the proprietor, was alarmed by the news of the message Cresap and Parker had sent to the Indians. Writing to Thomas Penn in England, he remarked: "If the Trade was to remain in its present State unnoticed by the French the Traders would in a very few years be rich men, and indeed supposing the worst, as Mr Croghan is to be in the Indian Country, they cannot fail of making very considerable gain."

In July, 1749, Peters asked George Croghan to spy out the situation on the Ohio in regard to the French threat.[281] Croghan reported back to Peters that the rumors of the French encroachments must have resulted from an alarm that

Mr Cresap & Mr Parker Spread amongst ye Ingans Last fall that ye Virginians was going to Setle a Branch of Ohio Calld Yougagain & that then they wou'd Suply ye Indians with goods Much Cheaper than they Col'd be Suplyd from Pensilvaina, Butt to my Certain knowlidge that Report had nott its Desired affectt, for Instead of gaining an Interest Amongst ye Indians itt gave them an aversion to Mr Parker, for the Indians Dos nott Like to hear of there Lands being Setled over Allegany Mountain, & in particular by ye Virginians, Butt my Opinion is that they will nott Come To Ohio, Butt Rather go by Lake Erie towards Wabauce in order to Secure a very Considerable branch of Trade amongst ye Twightwees which has been out of thire hands Some years past and of Considerable advantage to this Province, & it is well known ye French will Spare no Troble to advance thire Trade, Nor No people Carries on ye Indians Trade in So Regular a manner as the French."[282]

Thomas Penn took this matter of competitive Indian trade seriously and advised Peters how to proceed so that they (Pennsylvania traders) would not be "long after the Ohio Company."[281] After Penn

Commentary

had received Peters' letter, he discussed the matter with his friend John Hanbury, whom Penn styled, "principal director of the Ohio Company." Hanbury assured Penn that "the gentlemen concerned in the Ohio Company have not in mind the carrying on an exclusive trade or the confining it to the people of Virginia but says that all the Inhabitants of all the Colonies are to have the protection of their Fort and the Assistance of their peoples."

Meanwhile, Lee continued to peck at Pennsylvania. He complained that the "insiduous behaviour, as I am informed of some traders from your Province, tending to disturb the Peace of this Colony and to alienate the Affections of the Indians from us." He accused the Pennsylvania traders of having

prevailed with the Indians in the Ohio to believe that the Fort is to be a bridle for them, and that the roads which the Company are to make is to let in the Catawbas upon them to destroy them, and the Indians naturally jealous are so possessed with the truth of these Insinuations that they threaten our Agents if they survey or make those Roads that they had given leave to make, and by this the carrying the King's Grant into execution is at present impracticable.[299]

LOGSTOWN CONFERENCE, 1752
Facsimile, Page 7

Peters kept the proprietor in England fully informed about Pennsylvania-Virginia relations. Again, as in the boundary dispute, Penn and Hanbury discussed the situation. By the spring of 1752 Hanbury's assurance to Penn that the Ohio Company did not intend to engross the Ohio Indian trade and the increased activity of the French traders drew Virginia and Pennsylvania closer together. As a result, Pennsylvania entered wholeheartedly into the Logstown Conference. James Hamilton sent a message to the Ohio Indians "telling them that the kinder they are to the Virginia People, and particularly to those who are minded to trade with them, the more agreeable it will be to me, that I wish the Indians all manner of Happiness, and shall be very glad at all times to give them amplest Proofs of my Regards for them."[296]

According to the printed Virginia Executive Council *Journals*, Christopher Gist's official position at the Logstown Conference was that of joint interpreter with Andrew Montour. John Mercer states in his "Case" that the "government of Virginia allowed of his appearing at the treaty, as an agent for the company." In each of the several manuscript variants of the minutes of this treaty, printed in Part I of this work, Gist's position is given as "agent for the Ohio Company."

The Case of the Ohio Company

It is evident that Gist, while on his second journey for the Ohio Company, carried on governmental negotiations with the Indians on the Ohio; otherwise, the discussion between the Indian chief and him concerning the ownership of lands would not have taken place. Both the Beaver and Oppaymolleah "desired to know where the Indians' Land lay, for that the French claimed all the Land on one side the River Ohio & the English on the other Side."

Mercer implies that Gist's second scouting trip was designed to pave the way for the Ohio Company to take up their lands immediately after the Conference of Logstown; also that he was given authority to treat independently with the Indians. By the Treaty of Lancaster, Virginia had been ceded this territory on the Ohio and the Indians had been promised "a further consideration" when Virginia settled those lands. The Committee's instructions to Gist show that the Ohio Company stood ready and willing to supply that "further consideration." Governor Dinwiddie must have been informed of the Ohio Company's willingness to treat separately for the land, else he would not have "allowed" Gist to act as "agent for the Ohio Company" at the meeting.

Joshua Fry and James Patton were named commissioners on December 11, 1751; Lunsford Lomax, on April 4, 1752. Governor Dinwiddie instructed them to obtain recognition of the release of lands given by the Six Nations to Virginia at Lancaster in 1744, thus insuring a peaceful settlement for the Ohio Company.[285] Although the minutes of the Conference, as given to the Ohio Company, were written by Lunsford Lomax, who purchased the late Lawrence Washington's share in the Company, there is no mention of separate dealings by Christopher Gist in behalf of the Company. Evidently it was not necessary for him to exercise his permission to treat separately with them.

The "present"[105] provided by the Crown for this treaty was in fulfillment of the promise made to the Six Nations at Lancaster in 1744, thus assuring the Ohio Company peaceful settlements on the Ohio. The frankness with which Governor Dinwiddie spoke of this ultimate goal could be interpreted hastily and rashly as an improper expenditure of government funds for personal use. Such an interpretation would be both unjust and incorrect. The crux of the situation was that the Crown had ordered Virginia to grant mortgaged lands outright to the Ohio Company. Only when the mortgage was lifted could the Ohio Company obtain a clear title to the grant. John Mercer's assertions that the Ohio Company contributed largely to the treaty and that Christopher Gist was chiefly responsible for its

Commentary

success may have emanated from the Company's *Instructions to Christopher Gist, April 28, 1752.* The Virginia Executive Council *Journals* show that Virginia paid for the transportation of the present, also the salaries of the commissioners and interpreters who served at the conference; the present was provided by the Crown. Therefore, if the above statement of John Mercer be true, it was not recorded by the Ohio Company's representative who returned the minutes of the Conference to the Committee of the Company. According to the minutes, Andrew Montour, not Christopher Gist, obtained Half King's halfhearted approval of a confirmation of the release of lands given at Lancaster in 1744. Andrew Montour received from the Company 30 pistoles "for his Trouble at Loggstown in May." Since Gist did not speak the Indian tongue fluently, he may have been responsible for the limited success of the Conference and Andrew Montour's reward may have been for his extraordinary ability as interpreter of Gist's persuasive promises.

By this time (1752) the Ohio Company was well established in the Indian trade at Wills Creek. Their store was well stocked with wampum and other supplies.[292] Thomas Cresap reported to Conrad Weiser that since the Ohio Company had imported a large quantity of wampum recently from New York, they would be able to supply Virginia with a sufficient quantity for the Logstown Conference.

The minutes of this Conference, as recorded by Lunsford Lomax, are annotated and printed on pages 54-66, this work; therefore, any résumé given here would be unnecessary duplication.

REPORTS OF TWIGHTWEE MASSACRE BY THE FRENCH REACHES VIRGINIA

Since the Twightwee or Miami were not represented at the Logstown Conference, in answer to their plea (1751), Virginia sent a portion of the present to them. William Trent was engaged[307] to carry the gift to Pickawillany (Piqua, Ohio), their chief town.

On June 21, 1752, the day that Trent and Andrew Montour began this journey, 200 French Indians under the command of Charles de Langlade swooped down upon flourishing Pickawillany. The village lay practically undefended, for most of the Indian men and boys were working in their cornfields. The French offered the Twightwee a truce, if they delivered them the English traders as captives. The Indians were defenseless, and so they pretended to acquiesce and delivered all except two Englishmen—Thomas Burney and Andrew McBryar—whom they hid. George Henry, John Evans, James Devoy, and Owen Nicholson, four of the traders taken captive, were later

The Case of the Ohio Company

sent to France and were returned to Philadelphia in May, 1753, on Captain Budden's ship, the "Myrtilla." Burney and McBryar, who had escaped, carried the news of this "outrage" to the other Indian villages in the Ohio Country.

When Trent arrived at Muskingum, June 29, he learned of the destruction of Pickawillany. In his progress to the Lower Shawnee Town (Portsmouth, Ohio) accounts of the massacre reached him at every Indian village. Thomas Burney also carried the news to the English settlements. Upon arriving at Carlisle, Pennsylvania, on August 29, he related that "in the Skirmish there was one white man and fourteen Indians killed, and five white men taken Prisoners." Burney then traveled to Williamsburg, Virginia, where he delivered a message from the Twightwee to Governor Dinwiddie, addressed by them to "Our good brother of Virginia."

This Twightwee affair of 1752 was not officially reported in Virginia until after October 6, for on that date Dinwiddie informed the Board of Trade that the Twightwee were under a French threat, that 30 of them had been killed, and that he had sent assistance to them in answer to their appeal made after the French assault in 1751. He also informed the Board that the messenger who took them this assistance or present from Logstown had not returned.[307] About a month later the Governor wrote again to the Board of Trade that Mr. Trent, the said messenger, had returned; also that Thomas Burney had delivered him the Twightwee's second urgent appeal.

OHIO COMPANY HASTENS TO VALIDATE THEIR GRANT
Facsimile, Pages 7-8

If this French assault (1752) were the motivating factor in the decision of the Ohio Company to petition the Executive Council for permission "to enter" for specific lands, the unofficial reports reached the civilian population in Virginia long before official Williamsburg heard of it.[345] As stated previously, Thomas Burney brought the news to Carlisle, Pennsylvania, on August 29.[360] At the time he expressed a willingness to go to Philadelphia to testify before the governor; yet he was not available when called upon later to do so. From Governor Dinwiddie's correspondence one learns that Burney arrived in Williamsburg sometime between October 6 and November 10, but unofficial news of the disaster was published in the *Virginia Gazette* under the date line October 6. William Trent returned from his mission on October 27. It is more plausible that fear lest the Half King's commitments regarding the erection of a

Commentary

fort on the Ohio might not be sanctioned by the Onondaga Council spurred the Company to action at this time.

COMPANY SEEKS GERMAN PROTESTANT SETTLERS

In September, 1750, the Ohio Company had entered into an agreement with Gist, "for the greater encouragement of the first settlers upon the Company's lands." One possible clue to the place from which Gist expected to obtain the settlers is found in a letter from Thomas Penn to Richard Peters. Peters accused Thomas Cresap and other members of the Ohio Company of conniving to depopulate a part of Pennsylvania. On February 24, 1751, Penn, in a letter to Peters, discussed the matter. Wrote Penn:

I am sorry to hear the people of Virginia and Maryland are so much displeased at the Justice wee do the Indians, and I fear from their way of acting with regard to those people a War will by and by break out, but I shall make Mr Hanbury acquainted with this behaviour and as principal Director of the Ohio Company he will write to the manager in Virginia to advise Cressap to another behaviour, had you sent full Affadavits of what Cressap and others have done to draw over the setlers, wee should have petitioned the King in Council, and if they continue to be troublesome I desire you will do it.

Lawrence Washington was of the opinion that he could obtain a number of German settlers from the Upper Shenandoah Valley, provided they were exempted from the tithe for the Church of England. Gist does not mention any such obstacle in his way of colonization; yet a few known facts about settlers on Ohio Company lands indicate that they—some, at least—were from northern Virginia or Maryland. When John Mercer discusses the ultimate outcome of this attempt to establish a permanent settlement, he does not state concisely from which province the settlers migrated. George Mercer recorded "they had 20 Families then settled." Among them William Cromwell, Gist's son-in-law, is the only person named. If any of the settlers had come directly from Pennsylvania, it is quite likely that George Mercer would have mentioned it.

PETITION, 1752, BLUEPRINT FOR EXPANSIVE MONOPOLY

At this time permission from the Executive Council was required in order "to enter" tracts of more than 400 acres for survey; less than 400 acres were entered directly with the official surveyor for the district. Unfortunately, the Company wished to take advantage of the modifying clause in their 1749 grant, a clause which gave them permission to take up land in any part "to the West of the said Mountains as shall be adjudged most proper by Your Petitioners."

The Case of the Ohio Company

Since specific boundaries were not given in the first permission for entry, July 12, 1749, and the separate tracts desired embraced more than 400 acres, the Company believed that it was necessary to seek Council permission "to enter" for the lands which they had selected.

The Ohio Company's petition (November 6, 1752) to Robert Dinwiddie is an extraordinary document, inasmuch as it presented a scheme for monopoly which outstripped by far the so-called "landmongers' plans." Sanction of this proposal would have given the Company a complete monopoly of the exploitation of all the territory beyond the Alleghenies and along the Ohio, from its junction with the Kiskeminitas to the mouth of the Big Kanhawha. Had the Company been given the permission to take up their half million acres of land in as many tracts as they saw fit, and their friends been permitted to take up one-thousand-acre tracts intermittently between the numerous Ohio Company surveys, they could have controlled the entire economy of the territory west of the Alleghenies. The Mercerstyled "landmongers" were interested only in profits from the sale of land. Evidently, the Ohio Company had visions of the same profits in addition to those derived from a monopoly of the economy. Mr. Mercer may have been guided in this unusual request by John Mitchell's report to the Board of Trade concerning the best method of proportioning lands west of the Alleghenies. John Mitchell recommended that small grants should be made on the same terms as the Ohio Company grant and should include all the land above the Kanhawha and between the mountains and the Ohio. Mr. Mitchell also reported that it was the opinion of those best acquainted with the subject that by this method the Ohio Country would soon be secure by settlement.

Lunsford Lomax, John Mercer, Andrew Montour, Christopher Gist, and William Trent, all linked closely to Ohio Company interests, were the "several persons" who, upon "judging this the most favourable opportunity that could offer," petitioned for an aggregate 420,000 acres of land on the Ohio. In each case a boundary line was to be in common with the Ohio Company line.[361]

When John Mercer wrote that all of these petitions "were entirely disregarded," he failed to give the Executive Council's side of the story. Already they had taken steps toward obtaining official sanction of the Six Nations' release given at Logstown. Governor Dinwiddie and the members of the Executive Council knew that the "further consideration" for land which they desired must be given to the Six Nations proper, not to a few hunters on the Ohio. Therefore, it was necessary for them to disregard those petitions.

Commentary

ONONDAGA COUNCIL'S POLICY, STRICT NEUTRALITY
IN FRENCH-ENGLISH DISPUTE

Facsimile, Page 8

"Credible advice," mentioned in the extract from the *Virginia Gazette,* October 6, 1752, that the Six Nations in alliance with the Twightwee had declared war on the French, is not substantiated by Thomas Burney's account of the destruction of Pickawillany;[360] nor is the statement verified by extant documents. The Six Nations, at this time, had not declared war on the French; in truth they never did declare it. Twice, the Twightwee sent them an urgent appeal for aid; the Six Nations never answered.

Interpolation of this newspaper extract between the Company's petition to the Governor and Council and the record of their disregard for it is intended to show the Privy Council that, while the colonial government made no attempt to stop the French aggression, the Company recognized the urgency of English possession of the Ohio Country. The inaction of Onondaga in this matter caused Virginia and Pennsylvania to hesitate to give assistance to the Twightwee. Both colonies sent emissaries to Onondaga to ascertain the disposition of the Six Nations regarding the matter. Onondaga's answer was of little comfort. The colonies, prepared to send arms and ammunition, were told by the Onondaga Council to send only "advice."

WILLIAM RUSSELL *VS.* OHIO COMPANY

On September 19 the Committee of the Ohio Company was ordered to employ a factor to carry on their western trade. When the Company met in general meeting on November 22, the Committee received from the members the additional order—"that after having employed a Factor according to the order made at Alexander Town last September they send to John Hanbury Esqr for Goods to the amount of two thousand pounds sterling to be bought at twelve months credit." William Trent,[362] who was also in the employ of the government, was the factor appointed; Christopher Gist and Thomas Cresap were the surveyors. An Ohio Company map (1753) shows the northern and southern natural boundaries as mentioned in the original entry (1749), the proposed Ohio Company "Town," and the exact location of the lands which William Russell and Company had surveyed. George Mercer's notation on the map, "I saw them (William Russell and surveyors) on Thursday 26th of April in my way to the Indian 'Towns,'" is evidence that the Russell survey was made in April, not in February, as given in the *Case.*

The Case of the Ohio Company

OHIO COMPANY MAP, 1753

This Ohio Company map[364] is extraordinary, inasmuch as it gives dual information. The Russell grant is delineated and explained in more detail than on the William Russell plat itself.[365] The extent of the Ohio Company lands, with detailed drawing "where the Company propose to erect a Town," and Mercer's explanation written on the map give more information about the rivalry of these two land companies, as well as more detailed information about the location of the Ohio Company's first venture on the Ohio than is found elsewhere. It is strange that John Mercer did not mention it.

JOHN MERCER'S APPRAISAL OF WILLIAM RUSSELL BIASED

The recitation of the activities of "unscrupulous William Russell" is strictly a one-sided account. Russell had been interested in lands "over the great mountain" since 1745 when the Blair-Russell partnership was granted 100,000 acres on the Youghiogheny. George Mercer complained about William Russell's interpretation of the location of lands granted to the Russell-Blair Company; while, at the same time, the Ohio Company had taken up lands on the Youghiogheny, a river not even mentioned in their grant. On May 5, 1749, when John Blair and associates petitioned for renewal of their grant, the Council deferred action "till his Majesty's Pleasure be known, And That the postponing thereof shall not prejudice the Right of the Petitioners." Although the Council did not sanction this renewal until October 26, 1751, the grantees, according to the promise made by the Council on May 5, 1749, did have priority of entry over the Ohio Company. If Lewis Burwell as "president and commander in chief of Virginia" warned William Russell against interfering with the Ohio Company grant, the letter[368] was written before November 21, 1751, the day Robert Dinwiddie assumed lieutenant-governorship of the colony. However, this warning was in accordance with an order of Council issued on November 6, 1749, which modified an order of May 5 that forbade any surveyor to "survey any Lands beyond the great Mountains, commonly call'd the blue Ridge, on any Entry, or Order of Council, nor receive Entries for such Lands till further Orders." After November 6 surveyors were permitted to survey lands "beyond the great Mountains" provided the surveys did not interfere with the grant to the Ohio Company.

The summation of William Russell's side of the Russell Company–Ohio Company dispute is as follows: (1) in 1745 Russell and associates were granted the right to survey 100,000 acres of land on the Potomac and Youghiogheny Rivers with four years' time allowed

Commentary

to complete survey; (2) in May, 1749, renewal of the grant was postponed without penalty, an action undoubtedly caused by uncertainty of the boundaries of the Ohio Company's future grant; (3) on October 25, 1751, the renewal requested in 1749 was given and four years' time allowed to complete survey.

When the Russell-Blair Company received this renewal of their grant they proceeded to survey in accordance with an order of the Executive Council which gave survey priority according to the date of entry. Since the governor had not granted the Company entry rights, as requested by them on November 6, he was not interfering with Ohio Company grant.

There is no record in the Virginia Executive Council *Journals* of any caveats entered by the Ohio Company against any person; yet John Mercer entered at least one, for early in 1753 James Patton informed John Blair, member of the Council and associate of William Russell, that

Mr Mercer in behalf of himself & the Ohio Company who has an order of Council for 500,000 Acres & Mr James Powers in behalf of himself and John Lewis Esqr & his Company for 800,000 acres has entered Caveats that no Patent may Issue out to me & others in the former Order for any Land surveyd on ye afforsd Waters. for what reason I am Ignorant of having to the best of my Judgment complied with every thing I undertook the noise of which Caveats has made my first settlers very uneasy not knowing what may be their Fate lest they Should have their own Improvements to Pay for, nevertheless they bought their Land from those new Caveateers."370

FRENCH-ENGLISH RELATIONS REVIEWED
Facsimile, Page 9

Extracts from newspapers of 1753 and 1754, printed on page 9 of the facsimile, disrupt the chronological pattern which John Mercer adopted in this document. Perhaps he included them as proof of the veracity of his presentation of the unjust treatment given the Company by Virginia officials. Mercer implies that the Council's disregard of the Ohio Company's constructive plans was largely responsible for the loss of the region beyond the Alleghenies to the French.

The first eight pages of the *Case* present: (1) background for the Company's grant; (2) their efforts to obtain the grant; (3) their field activities; (4) a review of swift French aggression on the Ohio; and (5) the lack of co-operation on the part of Governor Dinwiddie and several members of the Executive Council. Having presented in conclusion these newspaper extracts, proof of the precarious existence of the English who attempted to settle or trade west of the Alleghenies, John Mercer rests the Ohio Company's case against Virginia and

· 425 ·

The Case of the Ohio Company

returns to review, in chronological order, the French-English negotiations and subsequent action in 1753 and 1754.

This contemporary account of Virginia's efforts to keep control of the Ohio Valley, together with documents and letters presented as evidence of the validity of the *Case,* shows that the belated decisions made by the Crown did not keep abreast of swift French aggression. From March 16, 1749, the date of the "additional instruction" empowering the Virginia governor to grant 200,000 acres of land to the Ohio Company, to November 6, 1752, when the Company finally agreed on the boundaries of a definite tract to be surveyed, they sent Gist to reconnoiter suitable land, they perfected their organization, they built storehouses, they contracted for trade goods, they began cutting a wagon road from Wills Creek to a landing on the Monongahela, and they participated in the Virginia Conference at Logstown. Meanwhile, the French had sent Céloron on his leaden plate planting expedition, subdued the Pickawillanies, built forts on the south side of Lake Erie, and established a trading house at Logstown. The interim between 1752, when Trent was appointed the Ohio Company's factor in the field, and January, 1754, when he actually started to the Ohio with materials to build the storehouse at Redstone and a fort on the Ohio at the mouth of Chartiers Creek, the Ohio Company had had some surveying done, had established a settlement on the Youghiogheny, and had completed plans for storehouses and for a fort and town on the Ohio. At the same time the French were building Fort Machault and had completed Fort Le Boeuf, situated at the south end of the portage from Presque Isle. Also, at Le Boeuf the French had built several hundred canoes in preparation for transporting soldiers and supplies down the Ohio. La Force and an advance guard were at Logstown awaiting the arrival of these troops.

JOHN MERCER CHARGES DINWIDDIE WITH MISUSE OF COMPANY CONFIDENTIAL INFORMATION
Facsimile, Page 10

Throughout his *Case* John Mercer usually concludes a narrative of separate events with an incoherent paragraph unrelated, for the most part, to both the succeeding and preceding one. His complaint that certain members of the Executive Council were immune from injunction proceedings is a favorite subject in them. Apparently the Company's caveats against Richard Corbin as well as the one against William Russell (previously mentioned) never reached the floor of the Executive Council, for the printed *Journals* of that governing body reveal that many caveats were served at that time, some denied,

Commentary

some granted; yet no John Mercer caveat is recorded in the *Journal*.

Misuse of the Ohio Company's map by Richard Corbin was a particular source of irritation to John Mercer.[393] This map, delineated by John Mercer himself, was presented to Governor Dinwiddie on November 6, 1752, together with the Company's petition. Mercer's own description of the map identifies it as an Ohio Company map in the British Museum. After Governor Dinwiddie had disregarded their petition of November 6 the Company petitioned the King in Council to permit them to take up an enlarged grant within natural boundaries. The petition was accompanied by a "Chart." There is, in the British Museum, an Ohio Company map or chart which shows Gist's routes (first and second journeys) and the extent of lands enclosed within natural boundaries. John Mercer, secretary to the Company and author of the greater part of the *Case*, mentions three Ohio Company maps or plans: (1) Gist's plan of the routes which he followed; (2) the map of "my own making"; and (3) "your plan" (George Mercer's). The map in the British Museum coincides with Mercer's description of the "map of my own making." Since no others are mentioned, it is likely that the "chart" annexed to John Hanbury's petition of March 28, 1754, and the map mentioned in the *Case* are the same.

VIRGINIA SEEKS OHIO INDIANS' FIDELITY

Virginia, fully aware of the extent of French encroachment on the Ohio, never abandoned hope that the balance of power could be tipped in her favor, provided she could gain full support of the Miami, the Six Nations, and the lesser tribes on the Ohio. Although Captain Trent's services in 1753 and early 1754 were of inestimable value to Virginia and therefore to the Crown, it is not difficult to understand why John Mercer wrote so little about his activities. Trent had been severely criticized for his absence from the fort at the forks of the Ohio when the French swooped down upon it in April, 1754. George Washington, also, had registered complaints against the conduct of the militia under Trent's command.

STYLE OF *CASE* CHANGED

At this place in the document the author changes completely his pattern of presentation. Exposition is lacking. Events which marked the crucial year prior to French occupation of the Ohio Country are represented in the *Case* by random correspondence, most of which was sent to John Mercer by Trent in 1759.[396] Therefore, some statements concerning Trent's valiant attempt to prevent that French occupation seem necessary.

The Case of the Ohio Company

WILLIAM TRENT, MOST IMPORTANT, 1753

Trent was first employed by Virginia to carry to the Twightwee their portion of the present given at the conference at Logstown in June, 1752. Early in 1753 Dinwiddie asked him to be his particular emissary to the Indians on the Ohio. This appointment was precipitated by a letter from Trent and Thomas Cresap to Governor Dinwiddie, January 22, 1753, by which he learned of the defection of the Twightwee from the English interest, and that "15 or 16 French are come to Loggs Town, and are building Houses, &c., and that it is to be fear'd they will take possession of the River Ohio, oppress our Trade and take our Traders Prisoners, &c." During the spring and summer of 1753, Trent, the capable and willing envoy, was as the fountainhead on the Ohio from which a constant stream of information flowed to Williamsburg.

John Mercer presents for review by the Privy Council and the Board of Trade correspondence between their factor on the Ohio, William Trent, and the governor of Virginia or his representative at the Winchester Conference. Mercer may have chosen to include these letters in the *Case* in order to prove to the home government, in an unpretentious manner, that the Ohio Company's factor served his country well at this critical time—also, to imply that Governor Dinwiddie may not have taken full advantage of the services of one as capable as Trent. In reality, the letters tell very little of Trent's activities that summer of 1753, nor do they fully record Dinwiddie's efforts to thwart French aggression.

TRENT AND THE CONFERENCE AT WINCHESTER, 1753

Although the Conference of Logstown (1752) had ended with the signing of a confirmation of the Six Nations' release of lands made at Lancaster in 1744, the Executive Council regarded it as unfinished business. On November 6, 1752, they accepted the minutes of the conference and at the same time planned another attempt to obtain a clear title to the land desired by the Ohio Company. The Executive Council instructed Governor Dinwiddie to issue an invitation to the Six Nations' chiefs to come to Winchester in May, 1753, to receive a gift from his Majesty the King. This gift was in accordance with the promise made Canasatego at Lancaster in 1744. Andrew Montour, who took the message to Onondaga, returned on May 15 and reported that when he was at Onondaga seven French Indians had delivered a belt of wampum to the Indians, informing them that

the King of France, their Master, had raised a Number of Soldiers to chastise the Twightwees and drive away all the English Traders from Ohio, and take

Commentary

those Lands under their own care, because the Indians acted a foolish Part, and had not Sense enough to take care of their own Lands.[397]

Montour added that although the Indians sent the governor of Canada word they would not permit the French "to build Forts there, nor take Possession of those Lands nor drive away the English," they, nevertheless, were greatly intimidated by French braggadoccio and "would not show affection for the English by coming to Winchester."

It is evident that the Virginians had not expected the Indians' blunt refusal of the invitation, for the Executive Council had already completed arrangements for the conference to be held at Winchester the last of May.[399] The gift had been sent there and stored in William Cocke's huge warehouse; William Fairfax had been authorized to conduct the treaty.

Although not mentioned in the Executive Council *Journals,* the governor had arranged to have chiefs from the Ohio participate in the conference, and Thomas Burney carried the invitation to them. Dinwiddie was also disappointed on this score, for Burney had left Williamsburg before the end of 1752 and, by May, had not returned nor sent any word. When he did return he carried a message from the Half King at Logstown, dated June 22. By this message the Half King informed the governor that "the Head Men of the Six Nations, the Twightwees, Shawonese, and Delawares were coming down to pay you a visit," but ominous news of an impending French attack prevented their coming.[408]

Preparations for this conference seem perfunctory when compared with William Trent's contemporary activity. His trading interests on the Ohio made the French-English dispute also a matter of personal concern. Whether intentional or coincidental it, nevertheless, is a fact that George Croghan and William Trent, Pennsylvanians and partners in the Indian trade, were playing similar rôles at this time. George Croghan was Pennsylvania's chief informant on the frontier, and William Trent, at Dinwiddie's request,[411] sent him "what farther intelligence he possibly could." Trent was not mentioned in the preconference negotiations for the Winchester Conference; yet the sequence of events made him a principal not only at the meeting at Winchester, but also at an unscheduled conference at Logstown in August, 1753.

WILLIAM FAIRFAX'S LETTER TO TRENT

Fairfax's letter to Trent, May 26, is in answer to Trent's report of affairs on the Ohio as of May 16. Trent's letter of May 22 was not located; but a report of these anxious times, printed in the *Colonial*

The Case of the Ohio Company

Records of Pennsylvania, reveals that when news reached the Ohio that the French were coming en masse to take possession of the territory, Trent, by "four Strings of Wampum in behalf of the Governor of Virginia" promised the Indians material assistance if they would oppose the French. The Half King, spokesman for the Six Nations on the Ohio, accepted the offer of a "supply of arms and ammunition."[402]

DINWIDDIE CHANGES HIS MIND
Facsimile, Pages 10-11

Dinwiddie altered the original order to Colonel Fairfax and directed a part of the gift designed as the "further consideration" for the Six Nations to be sent to the Indians on the Ohio. He also reversed his opinion about the French-inspired depredations and murder of English traders. Previously, at the behest of the Executive Council, he had informed Trent and Cresap that traders' troubles on the frontier were no doubt caused by jealousy among themselves and were of no concern to the government. Now Dinwiddie expressed sympathy for them. The Governor's remark, "You know how to frame a speech, to the Indians, in their style, better than I can," is reminiscent of Thomas Cresap's advice to Dinwiddie on Indian protocol. Soon after his arrival in Virginia, Dinwiddie was made to be aware of his inexperience in Indian negotiations; in consequence thereof he often confessed this inexperience.

FAIRFAX'S LETTER TO TRENT
Facsimile, Page 11

Fairfax's letter of June 9 connotes a feeling of resignation to inevitable French success; also, of doubt whether or not Trent would be able to deliver arms and ammunition to the Indians. Trent did succeed in transporting the goods to Logstown where he held a lengthy conference with the Delaware, Twightwee, and Six Nations' chiefs. Although his valiant effort to keep the Ohio Indians in the English interest is not mentioned in this document, it was of utmost importance. Following is a résumé[410] of the proceedings.

TRENT'S INDIAN CONFERENCE AT LOGSTOWN, 1753

After a long and arduous trip from Winchester, Trent arrived at Logstown, July 11, and in addition to conducting a formal conference carried out Dinwiddie's instructions—to be "as inquisitive as possible of the number of the French and their Indians." He interrogated the Half King and numerous other Indians who were shuttling between

Commentary

Venango and Logstown; also the Canawaugus who were suspected of being solely in the French interest. Half King, notably in the English interest, added his threats to Trent's pleas for them and the Delawares to return to the Six Nations and English interests. Trent endeavored to draw off many of the French Indians from Venango, but the French refused to let them come to Logstown. He learned that traders for their firm who had been taken on the Kentucky River were imprisoned by order of French officers and that the commander of Detroit had encouraged the Indians to "kill the People of Virginia, Carolina, & Pensylvania; for he wanted to pick a quarrel with them." In order to show the dishonesty which the French practiced in their negotiations with the English, he recorded in his report of the conference that the French had promised the Delawares a share in a fictitious powder mine located near Shannopin's Town.

Christopher Gist, who on July 10 had been sent by Dinwiddie with a special letter to invite some particular Indians to the treaty, did not carry the message to Ohio himself. He sent Thomas Burney, who arrived there on August 8. Mr. Gist was delayed by Ohio Company business until July 25, when he received their instructions to proceed to the Ohio at the mouth of Chartiers Creek, there to lay out the ground for a town and fort.

Trent delivered the present on August 10 to Shingas and the Beaver (Delawares), Newcomer and the young king (Shawnee), the young Twightwee king and the Turtle (Miami), and a Wyandot chief. At the conference he spoke "in the same Manner as he (Dinwiddie) wou'd have done were he here Present." Utmost in his mind was building a trading house "on that Piece of Ground which you appointed the Commissioners last Spring, which House shall serve as a Nursery for You." Trent painted a dark picture, indeed, for all Indians who might come under French influence. He appealed to the pride of the Six Nations when he asked them if they would become slaves of the French; he warned them that, after the French had three or four strong houses built on their lands, "the Six Nations will then cease to be a People"; and he promised them that the trading house would be well stocked with warlike stores which they could draw upon, when necessary.

HALF KING GOES TO LE BOEUF; SCAROUADY, TO WINCHESTER

Trent's arguments were convincing, for the Half King, in council with the other Indians, decided to issue a third and final warning to the French to remove themselves from the Indians' land. The decision made by the Indians was that half of them would accompany

The Case of the Ohio Company

the Half King to Venango, there to warn the French off the land; while the others, 98 in all, would go with Trent to Winchester, there to receive an additional present from the English. Since they were going to Winchester, the Indians deferred their thanks for the present given them by Trent until they met Governor Dinwiddie himself. From the text of the minutes of the Winchester Conference one realizes that the Indians were aware of their advantageous position in the French-English dispute. They requested Thomas Burney to go to Virginia and to explain to the officials that after they had attended to a "little Business" of their own they would come to Winchester; they requested that the governor himself treat with them; and finally, they specified that the speeches made by the governor at the forthcoming conference be set down in writing as well as delivered orally.

GOVERNOR HAMILTON'S SPEECH TO THE PENNSYLVANIA ASSEMBLY
Facsimile, Page 12

Mercer's inclusion of a copy of Governor Hamilton's speech to the Pennsylvania General Assembly, May 22, 1753, among the group of letters and documents selected to show Trent's influence on the frontier is inharmonious, for it disrupts the sequence of the source material which relates to one event—the Virginia-Indian conferences of 1753. Mercer, who was most antagonistic to the Pennsylvanians at the time this document was written (1761–62), may have included it in order to show Pennsylvania's former disinterest in territory which she now (1762) wished to call her own. The document as it stands is incriminating evidence against Pennsylvania's loyalty to the Crown; yet at that session the Assembly voted £800 as a present to the Indians "in our Alliance." Virginia was seldom so generous with the Indians.

FAIRFAX'S LETTER TO TRENT
Facsimile, Pages 12-13

The Commissioner's impatience with Trent and his anxiety concerning the temper of the Indians, as shown in this letter of September 1, are a good barometer by which one may measure the density of the importance of this conference to Virginia. In 1744 Virginia had given the Six Nations about £400 for uncounted acres of land. Now, only nine years later, a vice-chief set over a few Six Nations' hunters and a few Indians of allied or socage tribes requested that a present be given them by none other than the governor himself; and

Commentary

the Commissioner, acting president of the Executive Council of Virginia, hoped that, in lieu of the governor's inability to come to Winchester, his presence would be satisfactory to them.

The Mr. Gist who carried the message of French aggression to the southern tribes in May was Christopher's son. Those Indians promised 1,000 warriors, but they never came. The postscript in this letter shows no avenue which might lead to the Indians' pleasure was left unexplored. Christopher Gist, it is remembered, had been adopted into the Wyandot tribe at Muskingum, Christmas, 1750.

RÉSUMÉ OF WINCHESTER CONFERENCE, SEPTEMBER, 1753

Mercer, in his writing, infers that the Indians came to Winchester, but, as in the case of Trent's conference at Logstown, he tells nothing about the conference. When at long last they arrived, September 10, they were received with pomp and ceremony. Colonel William Fairfax assembled 50 militia as an honor guard of welcome. Lord Fairfax, Colonel William Fairfax, and other gentlemen present walked up the road and shook hands with the chiefs, escorting them past the honor guard, who fired a salute. The Indians were lodged in a partially built church and all, 98 men, women, and children, were treated on their first night in Winchester to a "good Supper of Beef." Monacatootha, the Indians' chief representative at Winchester, informed the English that during the present crisis on the Ohio they would permit neither the French nor the English to build forts or strong houses there. William Fairfax's remarks on the conference were that their temper was such that he did not care "to touch upon that subject"; yet he believed that when the governor met them the next year they would cheerfully confirm the Treaty of Lancaster.

DISILLUSIONED INDIANS RETURN EMPTY-HANDED TO OHIO

Unfortunately, the Virginians, either skeptical of the Indians' fidelity or fearful lest a superior French force might overwhelm the few warriors who had come to Winchester, withheld the gift of arms and ammunition from them. Likewise, the Pennsylvanians who treated with the group at Carlisle, whence they had gone from Winchester, sent the Indians back empty-handed to the Ohio. The Indians did not understand this sort of treatment, and by the time they left Carlisle were completely demoralized. Richard Peters described the band as "poor Ohio drunken Indians" who "arrived from Carlisle, at Shannopin, full of drink and under the direction of the lowest and meanest of Indian Traders." Apparently the proprietor's secretary was lacking in sympathy for the Indians; he was more interested in obtaining land for the Penns. By letter he acquainted Conrad Weiser with his "notion of the matter." Peters wrote in part:

The Six Nations at Ohio desire the commissioners to send an account of their proceedings to Onondago. This last message is but part of their proceedings. What, then, if you should go to Onondago and tell of it with a deplorable account of the miserable circumstances of these Indians and that they cannot defend their possessions against the French, and if therefore desired, the Proprietors of Pennsylvania will buy their land and defend it for them, and then desire the sentiments of the council at Onondago on this proposal and urge the reasonableness and necessity of this motion and pray their confirmation of it, or rather approbation of it, that is of a general release of all the land between the Susquehanna and the Ohio, within the limits of this Province, for a sum of money to be paid at one time, or in annual payments for seven years to come, or less time as they should please. I think, from the circumstances of the Six Nations and of these poor Ohio drunken Indians, the thing may be brought about. But pray consider it well in all its branches, and after taking due time, say whether it be practicable or no. The more I like it, for they must sell, and will do it now better than any other time.

DINWIDDIE DECIDES TO USE ARMED FORCE AGAINST THE FRENCH
Facsimile, Page 13

Although Dinwiddie had spent the summer of 1753 in a final effort to secure the Ohio for the English, by giving presents to the Indians, he knew as early as June that nothing less than armed force could rout the French. As a result of repeated complaints of attacks on traders on the frontier he wrote to the Board of Trade informing them that Virginia's provincial government could not maintain law and order on the Ohio. "And till the line is run between Pennsylvania and this, His Majesty's Dominion, so as to ascertain our limits, I can not appoint magistrates to keep the traders in good order, as the Pennsylvanians dispute the right of this government to the river Ohio," wrote the governor. He also informed the Board of Trade that in answer to the Twightwee plea of 1752 for assistance he had sent a message to them advising that "the season of the year will not admit of sending them supplies . . . in the spring he would send them and the Six Nations their friends and allies, twenty barrels gunpowder, one hundred small arms, and some clothing, etc." His plea to the Board of Trade continued with an account of the number of the Indians on the Ohio, their eagerness for friendship with the English, their strategic position which would enable them "to hinder an intercourse of trade between the French settlements of Canada with that of the Mississippi behind our colonies," and their desire to have English forts on the Ohio. Therefore, he proposed to the Board

Commentary

of Trade "that one thousand £ from the quit-rents should be invested in goods, agreeable to the enclosed sketch of goods suitable" and that suitable ordnance for forts on the Ohio should be granted by the Crown. "Small cannon, carriages and powder, etc.; to make a beginning, twenty or thirty three pounders would do," remarked the governor. This letter placed the problem of peace between England and France in America squarely on the shoulders of the home government. In answer to Dinwiddie's plea the King in Council granted Virginia ordnance for forts on the Ohio valued at £1,196 10s. 11d.[456] The Governor also wrote for special instructions to govern his conduct in this crisis. Information had reached him that the French were actually building forts on the Ohio, on the very lands England claimed as her own. On August 28, 1753, the Earl of Holdernesse sent the several colonial governors identical instructions to follow during this critical period.[464] The King, himself, issued a special instruction to Governor Dinwiddie. Following the royal command, Dinwiddie called the House of Burgesses in session extraordinary, acquainted them of the critical situation, and asked them to pass a supply bill sufficient to support the building and maintenance of forts on the Ohio. On November 9, 1753, the committee appointed to study and make recommendations on the Governor's speech presented the following resolution to the House:

Resolved, That it is the Opinion of this Committee, that the Law now in Force, making provisions against Invasions and Insurrections, are sufficient to impower the Governor to resist any hostile Attempts or Invasions made on this Colony: But if any Invasion should Happen, and the Power given to the Governor, by those Laws, should then be found insufficient; that there ought to be such further Assistance given, as the Exigency of Affairs shall require.

JOHN MERCER UNJUSTLY ACCUSES VIRGINIA OF APATHY TOWARD FRENCH THREAT

The example cited by Mercer to show the laxity and lack of foresight of the members of the House of Burgesses cannot pass without an explanation. To pass "an act for farther encouragement of persons to settle on the waters of the Mississippi" was in fulfillment of a request made by the Board of Trade. This act provided

That all persons being protestants who have already settled, or shall hereafter settle and reside on any lands situate to the westward of the ridge of mountains, that divides the rivers Roanoke, James, and Potowmack, from the Mississippi, in the county of Augusta, shall be, and are exempted and discharged from the payment of all public, county, and parish levies, for the term of fifteen years next following, any law, usuage, or custom to the contrary thereof, in any wise, notwithstanding.

The Case of the Ohio Company

Rapid developments in the French encroachment crisis and the routine correspondence that guided the Crown colony in her government brought about this apparently incongruous legislation. The Board of Trade, in answer to Governor Dinwiddie's Memorial of 1751, proposed that in order for Virginia to obtain her much-needed increase in population, encouragement, fifteen-year exemption from all levies, should be given foreign Protestants who wished to settle in Virginia. Since the matter of parochial levies and the localities in which these settlers were most needed was a matter of provincial concern, the Board further recommended that these privileges should be given by colonial law rather than by royal instructions to the governor.

DINWIDDIE FOLLOWS ROYAL INSTRUCTIONS
Facsimile, Pages 13-14

Having complied, although unsuccessfully, with the royal instructions to provide for the maintenance of additional militia, Dinwiddie proceeded to carry out the next instruction—to issue a final warning to the French to remove themselves from his Majesty's land and find out whether or not existing treaties had been broken. Upon hearing that a special messenger was needed to take this warning to the French on the Ohio, Major George Washington, adjutant for the fourth militia district, hastened to Williamsburg and offered his services. It is to be remembered that William Trent had been asked by Dinwiddie to spy out the situation until May, 1753, and William Russell had been commissioned to go to Logstown to inquire of the French if they came to trade or to take possession of the territory. Dinwiddie informed the Board of Trade that "The Person [Russell] sent by the Commissioner to the Commandant of the French Forces, neglected his Duty & went no further than Logstown on the Ohio, reports the French were then one hundred & fifty Miles further up that River, & I believe was afraid to go to them." Governor Dinwiddie's report of William Russell's statement concerning the French on the Ohio differs from John Mercer's interpretation. In his letter to the Board of Trade he stated that "The Person sent" reported that the French were 150 miles up the Ohio, while John Mercer attributes to Russell the information, "that there was not a Frenchman upon the waters of the Ohio."

GEORGE WASHINGTON'S MISSION TO FORT LE BOEUF
Facsimile, Page 14

On October 27, 1753, the Executive Council accepted Washington's

Commentary

offer "to go properly commissioned to the Commandant of the French Forces, to learn by what Authority he presumes to make Incroachments on his Majesty's Lands on the Ohio." According to his journal of the expedition, Washington left Williamsburg October 31, the same day he received his commission from Governor Dinwiddie, and traveled alone to Fredericksburg where he engaged Jacob Van Braam as French interpreter. The two men proceeded to Alexandria for provisions, thence to Winchester for baggage and horses, then over the new road to Wills Creek. At Wills Creek, Christopher Gist, Barnaby Curran, John Maguire, Henry Stewart, and William Jenkins joined the party. Gist was the official guide; the others, servants. The party traveled overland by way of Turtle Creek and McKees Rocks, then the home of Shingas, to Logstown on the Ohio, twenty-five days' travel from Williamsburg.

At Logstown Washington conferred with the Half King and other chiefs; they informed him of the strength of the French on the Ohio. Half King reiterated his speech to the French at Venango, also the French general's reply. In August Half King and a party of Indians had gone up the river to the French camp to issue the French a third and final warning to evacuate their forts and trading posts in the region. Half King told Washington that the French general informed him the Ohio Country was French land and they intended to take full possession of it and keep it.

From Logstown Washington's party traveled to Venango where Joncaire was in command. Le Boeuf, the French headquarters a few miles up French Creek, was Washington's destination. He arrived there on December 12, at which time he delivered Governor Dinwiddie's letter to St. Pierre, the commandant. This letter to the French was circumscribed by Dinwiddie's instructions from the Earl of Holdernesse, also, by instructions from the King himself. In like manner St. Pierre's answer was circumscribed by the French minister's instructions to Duquesne, May 15, 1752. Governor Duquesne was ordered to drive the English from the Ohio, seize their goods, and destroy their storehouses. He was also instructed to keep friendly relations with the Indians by explaining to them that they could trade with the English only on English soil—not on French soil.

Great Britain claimed the land on the Ohio both by purchase and by conquest. Dinwiddie, in accordance with instructions from the King, sent an emissary to the French, asking them to evacuate any forts they had built on English territory. The French claimed the same region by right of exploration; therefore, St. Pierre, acting in accordance with instructions given him, refused to leave.

The Case of the Ohio Company

Captain Joncaire was well acquainted along the Ohio. He had been with the Céloron expedition in 1749, and later was given full responsibility for the three-year expansion program in the Ohio Country. Washington was invited "to sup" with him and twelve other French officers who lived in John Fraser's house. In his journal Washington recorded the evening entertainment as follows:

The Wine, as they dosed themselves ... gave a Licence to their Tongues to reveal their Sentiments more freely ... They told me, That it was their absolute Design to take Possession of the Ohio, and by G—— they would do it: For that altho' they were sensible the English could raise two Men for their one; yet they knew, their Motions were too slow and dilatory to prevent any Undertaking of theirs. They pretend to have an undoubted Right to the River, from a Discovery made by one La Salle 60 Years ago; and the Rise of this Expedition is, to prevent our settling on the River or Waters of it, as they had heard of some Families moving-out in Order thereto.[451]

HALF KING CHARGED WITH INFIDELITY TO THE ENGLISH

John Mercer's accusation against the Half King of duplicity is based on the Half King's speech to the French commandant. It is true that in 1752 the Half King reluctantly gave his consent for the Ohio Company to build a trading house at the "forks of the Ohio"; nevertheless, it was recognized by the Virginia Executive Council that this consent was contingent upon the Onondaga Council's approval of the Half King's action.

TRENT SETS OUT FOR OHIO COUNTRY TO BUILD COMPANY FORT

Although William Trent was in the employ of the Ohio Company from November, 1752, his activities on the frontier were never exclusively for the Company. Trent's convoy, seventeen horseloads of provisions and additional packhorses which Washington met a short distance from Wills Creek, included fourteen horseloads of Indian goods, the present given the Indians (Winchester, September, 1753).

George Croghan, writing from the Ohio on February 3, 1754, excused his tardiness in reporting in person to Richard Peters by informing him that "Mr Trent is Just Come outt with ye Virginia goods, and has brought a quantity of Toules and workmen to begin a fort, and as he Can't talk ye Indian Languidge, I am oblig^d to stay and asist him in Delivering them goods." As for the fort, Trent himself stated that the Ohio Company fort was only on paper and he had gone to the Ohio to build a fort for Virginia.

John Mercer, the Ohio Company's secretary, admitted that the government had ignored their petition "to enter" for the lands they

Commentary

wished to settle. Likewise, in September, 1753, the Ohio Indians asked the Virginians not to settle in that region. If Trent set out to build a Company fort on the Ohio, it was in open violation of the wishes of both Virginia and the Indians.

SPECIFICATIONS FOR COMPANY FORT AT CHARTIER'S CREEK

On July 25, 1753, the Ohio Company issued orders for building a fort on the Ohio at the mouth of Chartiers Creek. Specifications for the fort were as follows:

for the Security and protection of their Settlements on a hill just below Shertees Creek upon the South East side the River Ohio that the Walls of the said Fort shall be twelve feet high to be built of Sawed or hewn Loggs and to inclose a piece of Ground Ninety feet Square, besides the four Bastions at the Corners of sixteen feet square each, with houses in the middle for Stores Magazines &c.' according to a plan entered in the Companys Books, ...

However, it is to be remembered that this order was issued before the Winchester Conference took place. Therefore, the order was in accordance with the permission given at Logstown, not in violation of the denial to have English installations on the Ohio, an order which Scarouady gave at Winchester in 1753.

DINWIDDIE ORDERS MILITIA RECRUITED
Facsimile, Page 15

Facsimile pages 15-19 of the *Case* are concerned with Virginia's loss of the Ohio Country to the French and the Ohio Company's ruination by that loss.

St. Pierre's unsatisfactory answer to Dinwiddie's letter and Washington's personal report of the strength of French installations and their determined attitude toward permanent occupation of the Ohio region convinced the Governor not only that existing treaties had been broken but that expediency was necessary if the French were to be dislodged from the Western Country. He immediately set about to execute the third and final royal instruction—"to drive them out by force of arms, in the execution of which all our officers civil and military within the limits of your government are to be aiding and assisting to the utmost of their abilities." First, he called the recalcitrant House of Burgesses into special session in a second effort to obtain the necessary funds to maintain additional militia. Less than two months previous they had refused to vote such funds. For this reason John Mercer's criticism of the Governor's treatment of Trent was unwarranted. Dinwiddie's addresses made to the joint legislative meeting show that he exerted the greatest effort to obtain the funds re-

The Case of the Ohio Company

quired. Next, in pursuance of the royal command, the Governor gave a captain's commission to William Trent, instructing him to enlist from among the traders on the frontier a company of militia not exceeding 100 men. George Washington, already a military adjutant, was instructed to take command of 50 militia from Frederick County and 50 from Augusta County and march to join Trent on the Ohio.

TRENT BEGINS FORT AT THE FORKS OF THE OHIO
Facsimile, Pages 15-16

Trent was at Redstone when Thomas Cresap delivered him this commission, which not only charged him to enlist 100 men but to build a fort at the forks of the Ohio and in company with the friendly Six Nations "to keep Possession of His M'y's Lands on the Ohio and the Waters thereof and to dislodge and drive away, and in case of refusal and resistance to kill and destroy or take Prisoners all and every Person and Persons not Subjects of the King of G. B. who now are or hereafter come to settle and take Posses'n of any Lands on said River Ohio, or on any Branches or Waters thereof."

In the copy of the Governor's letter to Trent, as made in Dinwiddie's letter book, the postscript is omitted, but his speech to the Half King whom he addressed as "Good and faithful Friend Monacatootha" is copied in his letter book. Dinwiddie, by this speech, informed the chief that Major Washington and Captain Trent had been commissioned "to bring You sufficient Assistance to enable You to deliver Y'r Selves from Y'r Enemies."

Excerpts from the letters of Christopher Gist and William Trent inadequately present the extreme effort and the accomplishments of Trent and his handful of militia. In about three months, in midwinter, he had led a group of Ohio Company settlers from Wills Creek (Cumberland, Maryland) into what is now southwestern Pennsylvania; had brought supplies sufficient to erect an Ohio Company storehouse at Redstone (Brownsville, Pennsylvania); had supervised building that shelter; had brought and had delivered fourteen horseloads of Indian goods (Virginia's present) to the Indians on the Ohio; had organized a company of militia; had begun a fortification at what is now Pittsburgh; and had returned to Wills Creek to expedite the sending of additional troops and supplies to augment his meager installations on the Ohio.

TRENT RETURNS TO WILLS CREEK FOR SUPPLIES
Facsimile, Page 16

The date of Trent's departure from the Ohio has ever been a matter

Commentary

for speculation, for extant records relating to this incident treat the matter generally. So far as the study of history is concerned the date is important. After the loss of the fort he was criticized severely for having left his post when a French assault was imminent. According to this document, he was obliged to "come in to Will's Creek" on April 12. This statement can be interpreted in two different ways, either Trent left the Ohio on April 12 or Trent arrived at Wills Creek on that date. In Washington's letter to Cresap (*ca* April 16) he infers that he knew Trent was in the vicinity of Cresap's. Ensign Ward deposed that Trent had gone to Wills Creek and had obtained supplies but was detained from setting out on the return trip because Washington had sent word that he wished to see him. Ward's statement, Washington's letter to Cresap, and an extract from Washington's *Diary,* April 20, places him ready to return to the Ohio about April 18.

Trent's account with Virginia, which includes his charges for transportation of the present and reimbursement for money laid out by him, is dated April 8. Trent had purchased black and white wampum and had had a fine "belt" made to be given to the Indians when he delivered Virginia's present. Also he had paid Thomas Cresap twice for courier service. Cresap had brought Governor Dinwiddie's commands to Trent at Redstone and had taken Trent's message to Andrew Montour. Evidently Trent believed that Montour's presence was essential at this meeting, for George Croghan, at Montour's suggestion, had remained on the Ohio in order to interpret for him. It would have been difficult for Trent to compile such a carefully prepared and beautifully written document while he was still on the Ohio; however, he could have prepared it in this manner at Cresap's. Mercer's information in the *Case* has at times not been exact. If, in this event, he be correct, one must at least interpret his statement to mean that Trent arrived at Wills Creek on April 12. It was true that the Ohio Company had financed Trent's activities and that Virginia's debt was outstanding in 1762, when this part of the *Case* was written. Later, part of the debt was paid by order of the House of Burgesses and part by Governor Dinwiddie, in 1767.

JOHN MERCER'S INVECTIVES UNWARRANTED

John Mercer in turn registers resentment against each and everyone concerned in the Ohio campaign, excepting the few individuals in the employ of the Company. Since John Carlyle's appointment as commissary was made on January 27, the identical date of William Trent's commission, he could scarcely be charged with neglect of duty.

The Case of the Ohio Company

In two months' time he could not have let army contracts, obtained supplies, and had them transported to the Ohio, more than a hundred miles away.

Nor is Mercer's criticism of the House of Burgesses' and the Governor's actions in this crisis less unbiased. Dinwiddie's ulterior motive in suggesting a "soldiers bonus" in the form of land on the frontier was to have a self-supporting militia ever ready for service on the frontier.

GOVERNOR DINWIDDIE'S PROCLAMATION, FEB. 29, 1754
Facsimile, Page 17

The Executive Council, when asked to approve the Governor's "inducement for enlistment," took into consideration the Ohio Company's claim; however, the Council "being satisfy'd that there are other Lands sufficient to answer the Quantity granted to the Ohio Company" approved the issuance of Dinwiddie's proclamation, printed on facsimile page 17. The "Agreement to a boundary line between the Ohio Company and the military" and Mercer's discussion of the matter are found only in this printed document and the "Case" from which it was compiled. The agreement must have been entered into after July 4, 1763, the date of the last minutes of the Company preserved in the George Mercer Papers, for it is not mentioned in them.

The abrupt summons which the French commandant sent to the Virginia militia at their fort, Ward's capitulation, and his deposition about the unfortunate affair are so well known that it is unnecessary to comment upon them.

HERETOFORE UNKNOWN GEORGE WASHINGTON LETTER
(TO THOMAS CRESAP)
Facsimile, Pages 17-18

George Washington's letter to Thomas Cresap and the Half King's speech, printed on facsimile pages 17-18, 19, are of special interest, inasmuch as Washington's letter, it appears, is heretofore unknown and the Half King's speech, as presented, corrects an error caused, undoubtedly, by faulty French translation of Washington's diary of 1754.

Washington's letter is neither contained nor even mentioned in any compilation of Washington letters. It is a most extraordinary coincidence that this letter has survived, even in copy form; also that there is extant some information concerning its inclusion in the "Case of the Ohio Company." It was in the possession of William Trent until April 11, 1759, when he sent it with seven other items

Commentary

from Philadelphia to John Mercer in Williamsburg, probably to be used as evidence by the Company when they pressed their claim against Virginia for payment for material supplied the militia in 1754. All the letters in the packet, with the exception of this one, were addressed to Trent. The printed version of the letter differs slightly from the manuscript copy in the Mercer papers. The clause as found in the Darlington George Mercer Papers, "Hoes we shall also want, and several pair of Hand cuffs," was made to read in the printed document, "Hoes we shall also want." Evidently George Mercer did not wish to admit to the home government that there were deserters among the ranks of the Virginia militia. A recent biographer of Washington cites an item in a Washington *Account* as sole extant evidence that at least one person had deserted Washington's ranks before the Company arrived at Wills Creek. Washington, writing to Cresap for "several pair of Hand cuffs," further substantiates the biographer's assertion. As for the date, the letter was written sometime between April 10 and 17. Washington left Alexandria on April 2, arrived at Winchester April 10, spent a week there in an endeavor to procure wagons for the transportation of supplies, and arrived at Job Pearsall's April 20. The text of the letter indicates that it was written after he had concluded his week's effort to procure wagons and before he left Winchester, probably April 16 or 17.

NEW INTERPRETATION OF HALF KING'S SPEECH
Facsimile, Page 19

As a Washington "item," the Half King's speech, as preserved in both the manuscript and printed version of the *Case* is no less interesting nor less important than Washington's letter to Cresap. Heretofore, Washington's biographers, and historians who have mentioned the incident, have taken the French version of this item in Washington's diary of his first campaign to be authentic. A careful study of the chief's speech, as preserved in the Provincial Papers in the Pennsylvania State Archives and printed in the *Colonial Records of Pennsylvania*, volume 6, page 31, together with Washington's letter to Governor Hamilton, May 3, 1754, printed in the same volume, gives some cause to doubt the authenticity of the French version of Washington's *Diary*. The diary fell into the hands of the French, was translated into their language, published, and distributed throughout the Courts of Europe in an effort to brand England the aggressor in North America. The volume was retranslated into English and several editions were published; Washington's diary was extracted from the publication and edited by J. M. Toner, and later

The Case of the Ohio Company

was included in Fitzpatrick's *Diaries of Washington*. In all these presentations of the Half King's speech the last paragraph is recorded to have been directed to Washington personally. Washington himself never claimed such an important place in the Half King's confidence. Faulty French translation undoubtedly awarded him that distinction. As presented in the *Colonial Records of Pennsylvania* there is no mention that Half King addressed Washington personally; the speech as given in both the manuscript and printed copy of the *Case* shows that Half King's personal command was directed to Edward Ward and not to Washington; in the *Colonial Records of Pennsylvania* the presentation, "Delivered to me by John Davidson and Interpreter" should have been, as it appears in the manuscript in the Provincial Papers, "Delivered . . . Davidson, an Interpreter."

Different punctuation and capitalization of letters in the caption, supplied by different persons who copied or transmitted the speech, confuse its authorship. In both the George Mercer Papers and the printed *Case* Half King and The Belt of Wampum are given joint credit for authorship; the "Provincial Papers," *Colonial Records of Pennsylvania,* and the printings derived from the French version give only the Half King as the author. From the text of the letter it appears that the Half King himself sent the message.

Half King must have been thinking about George Croghan when he said, "I have no dependence on those that are gone so long and have never returned or sent any word." After Croghan had left the Ohio for his home in the East, about the middle of March, 1754, the Half King sent a runner to overtake him and deliver him the Half King's urgent appeal for help. Up to this time Croghan had "never returned or sent any word."

JOHN MERCER EXCUSES COMPANY FOR THEIR FAILURE
Facsimile, Pages 19-21

After Mercer presented the futile efforts of the Ohio Company and the reasons for their failure in the attempt to gain even a toe hold on the land granted to them, he proceeded to present for review by the home government the reasons for the Company's inability to resume operations after the French had been driven from the land along the Ohio River.

First, he reviews the Colony's discrimination against the Company. In 1745 the Executive Council had considered that settlements "westward of the Allegany mountains, along the several branches of the Mississippi" would create an effective barrier against French aggression. A lack of communication facilities and the administration of

Commentary

civil affairs were reasons for the seemingly incongruous legislation which Mercer derides. Dinwiddie in his Memorial to the Board of Trade (1751), presented even before he left England for Virginia to take up residence as lieutenant governor of Virginia, asked the Board of Trade to amend the royal instructions under which he was to govern the colony. Virginia needed more colonists, and to compete successfully with the other colonies it was necessary to make immigration most attractive. Therefore, Dinwiddie asked the Board of Trade for permission to remit parish levies and quitrents of all foreign Protestants for an extended time. The Board of Trade did not answer the Memorial for more than a year, at which time they advised the governor that remission of parish levies was a civil matter; therefore, Virginia should provide for such exemption by law and not by royal instruction. The problem did not reach the House of Burgesses until November, 1753. At that time they passed an act which exempted foreign Protestants from all parish levies for fifteen years. The advertisement which appeared not only in the *Virginia Gazette* but also in the *Pennsylvania Gazette* undoubtedly was prepared and sent to the newspapers for publication before the news reached Williamsburg that the French had taken possession of Virginia's fort on the Ohio.

As for Mercer's complaint of discrimination against the Company, he evidently did not consider that the terms for the acquisition of the land, of which he so loudly complained, were of the Company's own making and not restrictions laid down either by Virginia or by the Crown. True, settlers who returned from the vicinity of the Youghiogheny to "more inhabited parts" did so in 1754; but according to William Trent, the Company's factor, their migration was occasioned not by Mr. Russell's threats but by fear of Indian incursions against them.

John Mercer's discussion of the early settlement on Ohio Company lands near the headwaters of Redstone Creek (Fayette County, Pennsylvania) substantiates random information gleaned from correspondence between the proprietor of Pennsylvania and his resident secretary, Richard Peters. In answer to Richard Peters' complaint about the conduct of Thomas Cresap and others, Thomas Penn informed Peters that he would speak to Mr. Hanbury, the "principal Director of the Ohio Company," about the behavior of Cresap and others whom Peters accused of "draw[ing] over Setlers." However, Mercer is not clear in the matter, and the Pennsylvanians may have gone first to northern Virginia and later to the Ohio Company settlement.

The Case of the Ohio Company

According to the minutes of a meeting of the Committee of the Company, July 25, 1753, Gist had recently obtained a surveyor's commission from the College of William and Mary. This commission was not solely for the surveying of Ohio Company lands, for George Mercer, George Washington, and Robert Stewart had entered for "bonus" lands with him before he died.

JOHN MERCER'S LETTER TO FRANCIS FAUQUIER
Facsimile, Pages 21-22

Mercer's letter to Governor Fauquier was written sometime between July 25 and mid-October, 1759. Mention of Christopher Gist's death, July 25, 1759, and Adam Stephen's reply, October 27, to Fauquier's queries make it possible to give the approximate date. The minutes of the meeting of the Committee of the Company, July 6 and 7, record only a resolution to have John Mercer prepare the Case of the Ohio Company; no discussion of Pennsylvania Indian trade laws and the survey of Company land. Perhaps the gentlemen met informally to find a way to stop Pennsylvania's monopoly of trade at Pittsburgh, a monopoly reported by Colonel Adam Stephen.

The Committee had had several months in which to consider the problem, for Stephen's conversation with Mercer must have taken place in the spring of 1759. Information in the Bouquet *Papers* reveals that "after a very fatigueing march from Winchester" he arrived at Bedford on May 2, 1759, and remained on the frontier the entire summer and fall.

ADAM STEPHEN WRITES OF PENNSYLVANIA INDIAN
TRADE MONOPOLY AT FORT PITT
Facsimile, Page 22

Writing from Fort Pitt (October 27) Colonel Stephen answered Fauquier's letter by reaffirming his accusation against the Pennsylvanians, that they were engrossing the Indian trade and "pushing all possible measures to keep it in their hands." Although he added that the Pennsylvanians considered Fort Pitt within their colony, he assured the governor that the Acts of the Pennsylvania Assembly regarding the Indian trade did not affect the Virginia traders at the moment. However, Stephen predicted that it would exclude them when military restrictions were removed from around the fort. True, the Pennsylvania-Virginia boundary had not been settled; but Colonel Bouquet, in his conference with the Indians at Fort Pitt, regarded Fort Pitt and its environs as part of the Indians' hunting

Commentary

ground returned to them by the Treaty of Easton (1758). Strictly speaking, Fort Pitt was an English fort, located in Indian territory for the purpose of protecting the Indians against the French.

TRENT ACCUSES PENNSYLVANIA OF TRADE MONOPOLY

The basis for Trent's affirmation of Stephen's report, written to Lunsford Lomax, was without doubt his service on the frontier (1759) where he had ample opportunity to learn of Pennsylvania's elaborate plans to establish a government trading post at Pittsburgh. Robert Tuckniss, colonial agent appointed by the Pennsylvania Commissioners of Indian Affairs, was at Fort Loudon en route to Pittsburgh in January, 1759; Trent was also at that fort. He was deeply concerned in the Indian trade himself; therefore, if Trent's letter to Lomax should ever be located, it would perhaps show that Pennsylvania traders feared trade monopoly as much as the Virginians did.

JOHN MERCER'S INVECTIVE AGAINST HENRY BOUQUET ASTOUNDING

The copy of Mercer's letter to Fauquier preserved in the George Mercer Papers is in an unknown hand. However, the endorsement, disregarded in the printed document, is a John Mercer holograph. The endorsement, which is the epitome of the frustration experienced by the Company, is as follows:

Copy to Gov.' abot surveying Ohio The Information I reced from Colo Stephen was that the Philadelphians, under Bouquet's Protection (who it was said) was concerned with them were surveying abot Pitsburg after they had by Acts of Assembly engrossed the trade to themselves & Bouquet had presumed by Proclamation to threaten the rest of his Maties subjects with Court-martial Law for which he deserved to be hanged himself by the same Law.

Internal evidence in the letter shows that it was written in 1759. Mercer, in his endorsement, infers that the report by Stephen was given him after Bouquet's Proclamation, October 30, 1761. The endorsement dates probably from July, 1762, when the Case was sent to Charlton Palmer, but it is obvious that Mercer's letter itself was written in 1759.

CRITICISM OF PENNSYLVANIA LAWS FOR REGULATING INDIAN TRADE, 1758-59

Lack of knowledge of the exact time John Mercer compiled this section of the document clouds any interpretation of his comments on the Pennsylvania "Acts for the regulation of Indian trade." As it happened, Mercer's fears were ungrounded, for Colonel Bouquet, interested primarily in the provision of huge quantities of trade goods, encouraged private enterprise on the part of both Pennsylvanians and Virginians. Israel Pemberton, George Croghan, and William Trent had trading houses at Pittsburgh. In 1759 and 1760 Bouquet corresponded with Fauquier and with George Mercer personally, urging them to encourage Virginians to enter into the Indian trade.

Virginia had enacted regulations for trading with the Indians, had appropriated £5,000 in public funds for that purpose, and had appointed a committee to supervise the business. Fauquier agreed so heartily with Bouquet's sentiments concerning the necessity of adequate supplies for the Indians that he informed Bouquet he would "recommend it to this Committee to employ good part of this Money in the Trade wth the Indians on the Ohio; the first Time a Number of them are in Town, for they are not put under my Orders to summon them to meet on any Occasion."

SUMMARY OF *CASE*, AS WRITTEN BY JOHN MERCER
Facsimile, Pages 23-24

The conclusion of the Case proper, as found in the George Mercer Papers, is additional evidence that the original document prepared for transmission to England was completed before October, 1761, the date of Bouquet's Proclamation, else Mercer certainly would have mentioned it. The epitome of this summary is that by a full exposition of the motivation and activities of the Company, accompanied by items which verified the author's exposition, the members believed they had justified their inability to fulfill the promises they had made to the home government, whereby they would have been entitled to one-half-million acres of land "west of the great mountains"; also, they recognized as valid the Treaty of Easton (1758), whereby the land which they had hoped to own was returned to the Indians. Mention of the Half King's approval (1752) of an Ohio Company fort on the Ohio and the presentation of his speech to the French commandant a year later was the evidence presented to show doubt whether the Indians were entitled to the land returned to them.

That this section of the document written by John Mercer is a faithful exposition of the motivation and activities of the Company is not affirmed by extant contemporary evidence. As reviewed in the light of this contemporary material, including Ohio Company official papers, it stands as a mixture of fact and both biased and unbiased interpretations of isolated episodes in the colonial western expansion.

Commentary

DISINTEGRATION OF ONONDAGA COUNCIL'S
AUTHORITY OVER OHIO INDIANS
Facsimile, Page 24

A continued disregard of the integrity of the Six Nations' government may have ruined the Company's prospects by hastening the ultimate struggle between the French and English for domination of North America. George Croghan, Conrad Weiser, Thomas Lee, Robert Dinwiddie, Richard Peters, William Trent, and the Indians themselves, each in turn ignored the authority of the Onondaga Council. Undoubtedly, Croghan planted the seed of revolution against parental authority in the minds of the Six Nations' Indians whom he met on the Ohio in the early 1740's; for it was by his instigation that a representation traveled to Philadelphia in 1747 to gain Pennsylvania's recognition of them as a group separate from the Council of Onondaga. It was Conrad Weiser who persuaded Richard Peters, secretary to the Penns, to recognize them by sending him to kindle their separate Council Fire at Logstown in 1748. Thomas Lee, unsuccessful in his attempt to treat with the Onondaga Council, chose to try to keep "the Ohio Indians in the English interests." Robert Dinwiddie, who did not have an opportunity to formulate an Indian policy, continued to follow the blueprint made by his predecessor, Thomas Lee. Like Lee, Dinwiddie treated with the Ohio Indians as a separate group but knew full well that any commitments made by them were subject to approval by the Council of Onondaga. William Trent was so close to the scene of action that his efforts were stopgap efforts. By the time Trent emerged influential on the frontier the breach between "chief at Onondaga" and "hunter on the Ohio" was so wide that it could not be mended on short notice.

Thomas Penn, who did not have firsthand knowledge of colonial affairs, had an academic viewpoint of the situation. Penn disapproved of any dealings with a separate group within the Six Nations. To him the seat of authority was and remained at Onondaga. Richard Peters, his secretary, tried to carry out the Proprietor's wishes; but the Pennsylvanians voted many a separate gift for the Ohio Indians.

Mercer chose to disregard the Indian "side" of this land question, thus accusing the Half King of infidelity. Had the gentleman read carefully the minutes of the Logstown Conference which he embodied in this document, he would have been forced to admit that the Half King explained that although he gave his consent for the Company to build a fort on the Ohio, the final decision lay with the Onondaga Council. As for his speech to the French commandant,

The Case of the Ohio Company

the Half King knew full well that if the English were permitted to build a fort on the Ohio, the French would attack that fort; and to the victor, whoever he was, belonged the spoils.

SECTION OF *CASE* COMPILED BY GEORGE MERCER
Facsimile, Pages 24-36

The latter part of the *Case,* pages 24-36, appears to have been compiled by George Mercer from heterogeneous items originating with his father. Coherence is completely lacking. From the format one could conclude that George Mercer, after separating his father's "Case of the Ohio Company" from all the other Company papers in his possession, took the remainder, arranged them chronologically, added a few comments of his own, placed them after his father's *Case,* and sent the bulk, en toto, to the printer.

UNRELATED PARAGRAPH, ABSTRACTS OF GEORGE MERCER MANUSCRIPTS
Facsimile, Page 24

"A list of the several orders of Council" is derived from a John Mercer holograph in the George Mercer Papers; the summary is the work of George himself.

THE ROSTER OF MEMBERS
Facsimile, Pages 24-25

The roster of members of the Company, *information unique* to the printed *Case,* is new and valuable information about a highly controversial subject—names of the members, their number, and when certain individuals became members.

PETITION OF 1762, UNIQUE TO PRINTED *CASE*
Facsimile, Pages 25-26

On September 7, 1761, the Committee of the Ohio Company resolved to ask Philip Lee to write a letter of supplication in behalf of the Company to the Duke of Bedford. Bedford was to be informed that the Company intend to present an humble Petition to his Majesty shewing the reasons why they have hitherto been disabled to comply with the Conditions mentioned in the Royal Instructions to the late Governor Gooch and praying such further Indulgence's and relief as his Majesty shall think reasonable . . . .

John Mercer enclosed the petition mentioned in the above minute in his letter to Charlton Palmer, July 27, 1762. Since the enclosure was not among the George Mercer Papers, nor was it located else-

Commentary

where, this petition seems to have survived only by its inclusion in the printed document.

LETTERS TO LONDON MEMBERS
Facsimile, Page 26

A letter to Robert Dinwiddie and one to the Hanburys were also enclosed in John Mercer's letter to Palmer. George added his father's signature to the letter to Dinwiddie, for as found in the George Mercer Papers, it is unsigned by his father who explained to Charlton Palmer that he had so "ill an opinion" of Dinwiddie that he refused to sign the letter.

JOHN MERCER'S CRITICISM OF A CONTEMPORARY ACCOUNT OF COMPANY
Facsimile, Pages 27-28

Evidently, pages 27 and 28 were written by John Mercer; also, they are *unique to the printed document*. The article, discussed by him, appeared in the *London Magazine,* volume 28 (1759), pages 357-60. The quotation is not exact; there are a few omissions and parts are paraphrased, not quoted.

Mercer's refutation of assertions made by the author, probably John Almon, adds nothing to the history of the Company as heretofore presented by him. Although interspersed with the usual John Mercer invectives against the governor, Executive Council of Virginia, and the Pennsylvania fur traders, this refutation is a clear and concise résumé of the history of the Company.

CHARLOTTESBURG, MARYLAND, PROPOSED OHIO COMPANY TOWN
Facsimile, Page 29

The introduction to the Proclamation by Henry Bouquet is also unique to the printed pamphlet; likewise the discussion of the Company's plans to found a town at Wills Creek (Cumberland, Maryland). Undoubtedly, both were written by George Mercer. There was some information available about the Ohio Company's projected development at Wills Creek before the George Mercer Papers and the *Case* came to light. An advertisement signed by George Mercer is extant in the *Maryland Gazette* of February 17, March 3, 10, 17, 24, and April 7, 1763. By it the public was informed that

At the repeated Sollicitations of several Persons, the Ohio Company have agreed to lay off a Number of Lots for a Town at Fort Cumberland ... and

The Case of the Ohio Company

that each Purchaser may have an opportunity of attending, and choosing the Lots he may judge most convenient, they will be Sold to the Highest Bidders on Friday the 15th of April next.

In the same advertisement the Company offered for lease,

Two very good Store-Houses, opposite to Fort Cumberland, in Virginia, one 45 by 25, with a Counting-Room and Lodging-Room at one End, the other 44 by 20, with proper Conveniences for a Family to live in, two Stories high each, besides Garrets, with good dry Cellars fit for storing Skins, the whole Size of the Houses; and a Kitchen, Stable for 12 Horses, Meat-House and Dairy there are Two good Battoes, which will be given to the Person who Rents the Houses. The whole entirely new, and will be compleately finished, and fit to enter upon immediately; and the Person who takes the Store-Houses, may also have a Lease, for a Term of Years, of so much Land adjacent to them as he chooses.

In the same newspaper, June 16, another advertisement appeared in which the description of the projected town was changed to read as follows:

THE OHIO Company have ordered 300 Half-Acre LOTS to be laid off for a TOWN, to be called Charlottsburg, on Patowmack River, in the Province of Maryland, near Fort Cumberland; and an equal Number of Out Lots, contiguous to the Town, will be annexed to it.

Apparently both advertisements have been overlooked by expositors on the history of the Ohio Company.

Additional information about this project is found in the George Mercer Papers. On March 2, 1763, the Committee of the Company "resolved that about fifty Acres of the Companys Land at Wills Creek adjoining to Fort Cumberland be laid off into Town Lotts...." The name of the town, Charlottesburg, is not mentioned in the resolution; however, George Mercer's "Field notes of the Charlottsburg Survey" is in the George Mercer Papers.

Just as the new information in the George Mercer Papers reveals the first action on the part of the Company in their effort to establish a town at Wills Creek, additional new information in the *Case* furnishes the final episode of this projected enterprise. Also the fullest recitation of the confiscation and destruction of the Ohio Company's property at Wills Creek, by the military, is found in this document. The reason for George Mercer's appointment as the Company's representative in London and the record of his personal interview with Amherst is found only in the *Case*.

That George Mercer was the Company's representative sent to New York is information derived only from circumstantial evidence. The editor found no direct proof that General Amherst either conversed or corresponded with George Mercer or any other member of the Company on the matter of their right to dispose of their own

Commentary

land around Fort Cumberland. However, about the first of April George Mercer had an interview with General Amherst in New York. The date of that interview, Mercer's signature on the advertisements, and the statements in the *Case* that one of their members traveled to New York "to obtain his leave to build a town on their own lands," and that their representative returned to Wills Creek on April 15, together seem to be sufficient proof that George Mercer was the member sent to New York. Here, also, is additional evidence that George Mercer compiled the *Case* and authored the exposition interspersed among the documents printed on pages 24-36.

REVIEW OF THE COMPANY'S MEMORIALS AND PETITIONS
Facsimile, Pages 30-36

The petitions and memorials of the Ohio Company represent one phase of its activities—the acquisition of land. In order to obtain a patent or legal title to land in Virginia it was necessary to proceed in the following manner:

(1) If the amount desired exceeded 400 acres, it was necessary to obtain permission from the governor and executive council "to enter" a request with the legal surveyor to have land within the given limits surveyed. For tracts under 400 acres this entry could be made without permission from the governor and council.

(2) After having surveyed the land the surveyor was required to "enter or cause to be entered, in a book well bound, to be ordered and provided by the court of his county, at the county charge, a true, correct, and fair copy and plot of every survey by him made."

(3) Patents were then issued.

Up to the time that George Mercer merged the Ohio Company with the Walpole Company, the Ohio Company prepared for presentation to the proper authorities at least nine petitions or memorials; eight were presented, one of which was disregarded, and action was postponed on another.

To understand fully the memorials and petitions printed on facsimile pages 30-36, it may be of value to review all of them. The Company's petition of October 20, 1747, presented to the Virginia Executive Council in the name of Thomas Lee and eleven others, was not located by the editor. It is known only by the terse record that Lee and eleven others petitioned for permission to take up 200,000 acres of land "to be laid out from ye Branch called Kiskomanett's and Buffalo creeke on the south side of the River Alligany, and between the two creeks and the yellow creek on the north side

The Case of the Ohio Company

and on the main River of Alligany als. Ohio." The Executive Council postponed action on this petition. About the same time the Council informed James Patton, another petitioner, that they would not grant any western lands at this time, lest they give umbrage to the French.

Unsuccessful in Virginia, Thomas Lee and eleven others, members of the Ohio Company, engaged John Hanbury to solicit their affairs in England. On January 11, 1749, John Hanbury, member of the Company and their representative, petitioned the King in Council to issue an additional instruction to the lieutenant governor of Virginia, an authorization to grant the Company leave to take up and survey the land as outlined in the petition, printed on facsimile pages 2 and 3. Hanbury's request was granted; and so the Company obtained permission to have 200,000 acres surveyed.

By November 6, 1752, the Company, having profited by the explorations of Christopher Gist, discovered that it would be advantageous and cheaper to take up their land in small tracts. Since the additional instruction issued to Governor Gooch was interpreted to mean that the land should be taken up in a single tract, the Company thought it necessary to abide by the laws for taking up lands in Virginia. Hence they duly petitioned the governor and executive council for permission "to enter" with the surveyor sundry tracts of land of 1,000 acres, all within the bounds of their original grant. This petition is printed on pages 7 and 8. Undoubtedly, the unsettled state of Indian affairs in November, 1752, and the Company's deviation from the original intent as mentioned in the "additional instruction" were the chief reasons that this petition was "completely disregarded."

Having been unsuccessful in obtaining permission to take up only the land which they desired, the Company again changed their method of procedure and through John Hanbury, their representative in London, presented to the King in Council another petition (March 28, 1754) for instructions to be sent to Virginia's governor. This time they wished to have the governor instructed to permit the Company to circumvent the usual procedure of survey and permit them to patent a large grant circumscribed by natural boundaries. (This petition is not printed in the *Case*.) The Board of Trade advised the Privy Council that to obtain a patent for lands, circumscribed by natural boundaries, would be of no particular advantage. Sooner or later the land must be surveyed, else quitrents could not be collected. Therefore, the petition was denied. The Board, however, did compromise, and ordered the governor to permit the Company to take up lands in tracts of not less than 20,000 acres, the depth of

Commentary

each tract never to be more than one-third the length. This last stipulation was designed to prevent the Company from obtaining all the river frontage and fertile interval lands, thus leaving undesirable tracts for future settlers. Before the report of the Board of Trade reached Virginia hostilities had broken out on the Ohio, and so all activities ended.

When the English regained possession of the Ohio Country in 1758 the Company renewed their activities. John Mercer was ordered to draw up a full and complete state of the Company's case to be sent to the Company's London solicitor. About the same time the Committee prepared the petition which is printed on facsimile pages 25-26. There is no record that it was ever presented to the King in Council.

With peace came the era of martial law west of the Alleghenies. Colonel Bouquet proclaimed lands surrounding the forts to be military reservations. The Treaty of Easton and subsequent conferences with the western Indians gave them the assurance that all the land which they had sold to Pennsylvania at the Treaty of Albany in 1754 and all the land west of the mountains which they had sold to the Virginians at the Treaty of Lancaster in 1744 would be returned to them.

The Ohio Company had purchased tracts of land at Wills Creek. This land was taken over by the army, and after Fort Cumberland was built in 1754 it became a military reservation. The Company had been immobilized insofar as the acquisition of the lands on the Ohio; now, they were also prevented from exploiting lands which they had purchased outright. When George Mercer was appointed their representative in England he carried with him the petition which is printed on facsimile pages 30-31. This petition contained the rejection of the Board of Trade's "olive branch" of 1754. The Company could not accept the proposal that 20,000 acres was the minimum of land which they could have surveyed in one plot. They answered the report with alternative suggestions. If they were not permitted to take up land circumscribed by natural boundaries, the Company wished to be reimbursed for expenditures they had made. Since the roads and storehouses built by the Company had been for the advantage of the Crown, the Company had derived no benefit from them.

The King's proclamation of October 7, 1763, stopped any move projected by the Company. Therefore, this petition was not presented until June 21, 1765, at which time George Mercer presented it along with his own memorial, which is printed on pages 32-33. Mercer's

The Case of the Ohio Company

petition brought forth nothing new inasmuch as claims or desires of the Company were concerned. Since the King's proclamation was still in effect June 21, 1765, the Board of Trade did not take into consideration the Privy Council's request for a report on these memorials. When the citizens of Augusta County, Virginia, addressed the King in Council for relief from the wartime restrictions about western settlements George Mercer renewed his plea to have the Board consider these memorials.

In a letter to the Committee of the Company, October 10, 1767, George Mercer explained that he had learned only by accident that the citizens of Augusta County had addressed the King, imploring him to withdraw his proclamation of October 7, 1763, and thus reopen the Western Country for legal settlement. He also informed the Committee that it would be greatly to their advantage if they would "make the Govr thoroughly acquainted" with Ohio Company affairs, in "order that his report on the status of the Company," requested by the Board of Trade, would be favorable to their interests. Lord Shelburne, in accordance with the Board of Trade Report, had written to Governor Fauquier, October 8, 1767, requesting the information desired by the Board. Unfortunately, Fauquier died shortly after he received the letter; apparently his successor never answered.

George Mercer wrote again to the Committee, on November 21, verifying a remark in his previous letter about "some Persons here Petitioning for a New Government at the mouth of the Ohio." His memorial, printed on facsimile pages 34-35, was occasioned by "the circumstance of establishing new governments in America." According to Mercer's letter the Board of Trade was, at the time, holding preliminary hearings on the subject. When George Mercer "was called for interrogation," he answered their questions very agreeably but also took the opportunity "to mention the disappointments of the Ohio Company." During the course of this interrogation he was informed that Ohio Company affairs "were discharged from the Board's consideration until they would receive further orders from the King. Therefore, Mercer hastily prepared a memorial to be presented to the King in Council, November 26, 1767. On December 12, 1767, the Committee of Council for Plantation Affairs referred it to the Board of Trade for their consideration and report thereon; the memorial lay dormant at the Board until November 20, 1769. From October, 1767, George Mercer had tried unsuccessfully to obtain some directive from the Ohio Company to guide him in making a final disposition of Ohio Company affairs in England. The last memorial or caveat against the Walpole Company, printed in the *Case*, was

Commentary

Mercer's last memorial for the Company, except the one dated May 8, 1770, by which he withdrew this caveat and all other Ohio Company Memorials. The day previous, May 7, he had merged his Company with the interests of the rival Walpole Company. The caveat of December 18 was read at the Board of Trade on January 3, 1770, and by them transmitted to the Secretary of the Lords of the Treasury to be considered by them along with the memorial of the Walpole Company and the petition of the Mississippi Company.

One more petition not printed in the *Case* should be considered. On May 8, 1770, George Mercer withdrew his caveat of November 20 along with all other petitions which the Ohio Company had presented to the King in Council, thus resting the case of the Ohio Company *vs.* the Crown.

APPENDIX—CHRISTOPHER GIST'S FIRST AND SECOND JOURNALS
Facsimile, Pages 1-16

Copies of Christopher Gist's Journals, printed in the *Appendix* are edited in the George Mercer Papers; therefore, no additional comment is necessary.

APPENDIX—EXTRACTS FROM THE TREATY AT LOGSTOWN, 1752
Facsimile, Page 17

The treaty made between George Croghan and Andrew Montour, in behalf of the colony of Pennsylvania and the Wawiagtas and Piankashaws, was not authorized by the colony, and George Croghan was severely reprimanded for making it. Since these nations were theoretically socage tribes of the Six Nations, the Pennsylvanians feared that the Onondaga Council would be offended. Nevertheless, the treaty was faithfully adhered to by the Wawiagtas and Piankashaws. On June 15, 1762, Major Edward Ward, writing from Fort Pitt to Colonel Bouquet, relayed to him a conversation which he had had with two Indian chiefs, one a Wawiagtas and the other a Piankashaw. Both chiefs had been present at the treaty held by Mr. Croghan. In order to express the sincerity of their respective nations the Wawiagtas chief, acting as speaker for both the above tribes

laid before me the Writings of a Treaty held by Mr Croghan which Pass'd between those Nations of Indians and the Governments of Virginia and Pennsylvania in the Year 1750 and this he said was the first of their Allience with the English that they Ever held this Treaty in the greatest Esteem and that they never had Violated their Promises made in S^d Treaty tho' some of their Unthinking Young Men had been Active in the War in favour of the French but that they were but a few.

The Case of the Ohio Company

APPENDIX—EXTRACTS FROM LEWIS EVANS' ANALYSIS ...
Facsimile, Pages 25 and 26

Extracts from Lewis Evans' Analysis ... printed in the *Appendix*, facsimile pages 25-26, may have been included in this document to prove that passage into the Ohio Country was easier through Virginia than through Pennsylvania. The page numbers (e.g. *page 23*) given in the marginalia refer to the pages in Lewis Evans' *Analysis* ... from which these extracts were taken. The footnotes are also from the *Analysis*.

PART IV

Annotations

ABBREVIATIONS

Acts of the Privy Council denotes Great Britain Privy Council. Colonial series. *Acts of*

B. M. Add. MSS—British Museum Additional Manuscripts

B. T. *Journal*—Great Britain, Board of Trade and Plantations. *Journal of*

Colonial Records of Pennsylvania—Pennsylvania Provincial Council. *Minutes of*

Dinwiddie *Papers*—Dinwiddie, Robert. *The Official Records of*

Hening's *Statutes*—Virginia. Laws, Statutes, etc. *The Statutes at Large ... of Virginia*

N.Y.C.D.—*Documents Relative to the Colonial History of the State of New York*

P.R.O. C.O.—Great Britain. Public Record Office. Colonial Office

P.R.O. P.C. Register—Great Britain. Public Record Office. Privy Council Register

Pennsylvania, *Votes and Proceedings*—Pennsylvania (Colony) General Assembly. House of Representatives, *Votes and Proceedings*

Pennsylvania Magazine—Pennsylvania Magazine of History and Biography

Virginia Magazine—Virginia Magazine of History and Biography

1. Two pages, folio, in John Mercer's handwriting. There is no specific mention of the memorandum in this collection of papers; however, it may have been sent to John Hanbury in order to comply with and bring up to date an item in the "Articles of Agreement"— "that once every year as soon as conveniently may be after the general meeting of the said partners as aforesaid a true copy of all the Proceedings of the said Company, their Committees for the year preceding shall be transmitted by the Clerk of the said Company for the time being to the aforesaid John Hanbury." —"Articles of Agreement and Copartnership for the Ohio Company for the Space of Twenty Years, May 23, 1751." Photostat in the Virginia Historical Society, Richmond, Virginia.

In 1761 the Committee of the Company wrote to Capel and Osgood

Annotations

Hanbury, members of the Ohio Company and successors to the John Hanbury firm, asking them to give all possible assistance to Charlton Palmer, newly appointed London solicitor for the Company. This memorandum may have been given to Mr. Palmer who delivered all Ohio Company papers he had to George Mercer. —Committee of the Ohio Company to Osgood and Capel Hanbury, September 10, 1761; Charlton Palmer to George Mercer, December 27, 1769. See *Chronology*.

There are four separate items in this George Mercer collection which recite the activities of the Ohio Company—(1) this memorandum; (2) Resolutions of the Committee of the Ohio Company, October 17, 1760, and September 7-9, 1761; (3) Orders of the Ohio Company and the Committee of the Company, June 20, 1749–September 9, 1761; (4) Orders and Resolutions of the Ohio Company and the Committee of the Company, October 20, 1748–July 4, 1763. Each varies from the others in form, content, period covered, and phraseology. Items unique to each version are so designated.

2. Letter in Great Britain. Public Record Office. Colonial Office, 5: 1326/547-54. Printed in Kenneth Bailey, *The Ohio Company of Virginia* . . . (Glendale, Calif., Arthur H. Clark Co., 1939), p. 297; Berthold Fernow, *The Ohio Valley in Colonial Days* (Albany, N. Y., Joel Munsell's Sons, 1890), pp. 240-41, extract.

This letter was the natural outgrowth of the petition of Thomas Lee and eleven others for a grant of 200,000 acres of land on the Ohio, a petition presented to the Virginia Executive Council on October 20, 1747, and action thereon postponed at that time. —"List of Early Land Patents and Grants Petitioned for in Virginia up to 1769, Preserved Among the Washington Papers," in *Virginia Magazine of History and Biography* (Richmond, Va., The Society, 1893–date), V, 175-80, 241-44. See also *note 16*.

3. Letter to the Duke of Newcastle in P.R.O., C.O. 5: 1366/410. Extract printed in Fernow, *op. cit.*, p. 242.

4. Great Britain. Public Record Office. Privy Council, Register 2: 100/540. Order of the Committee of Council for Plantation Affairs, referring Gooch's request to the Board of Trade for their consideration, February 23, 1747 [48] in P.R.O., C.O. 5: 1327/1, endorsement, 16;—P.C., Register 2: 100/551.

5. In P.R.O., C.O. 5: 1366/411-17; printed in Fernow, *op. cit.*, pp.

Annotations

244-48. Although the order of the Privy Council was given on February 23, it was not read at the Board of Trade until April 6, when action thereon was delayed until the Board would receive further information requested from Gooch in their letter of January 19, 1748. Gooch's answer of June 16 was received at the Board on August 16. —Great Britain. Board of Trade, *Journal of the Commissioners for Trade and Plantations . . . 1742–49* (London, H. M. Stationery off., 1920), pp. 278, 336, 341, 342.

Letter, Board of Trade to Gooch, January 19, 1748, in P.R.O., C.O. 5: 1366/408-09; extract printed in Fernow, *op. cit.*, pp. 242-43.

On November 24, 1748, the Privy Council approved the Board of Trade's report of September 2 and ordered* them to prepare "instructions" empowering Gooch to grant lands on the western side of the Great Mountains in Virginia.

*Order in P.R.O., P.C. Register 2: 101/117-18;—C.O. 5: 1327/21, endorsement, 32.

6. In P.R.O., C.O. 5: 1327/7-8, endorsement, 10; extract printed in Fernow, *op. cit.*, pp. 243-44.

7. Printed on pp. 246-248, this volume; Bailey, *Ohio Company . . .*, *op. cit.*, pp. 298-301.

8. Order in P.R.O., P.C. Register 2: 101/145.

9. Order in P.R.O., C.O. 5: 1327/51-70;—P.C. Register 2: 101/84-86. Printed in Bailey, *op. cit.*, pp. 302-03; Fernow, *op. cit.*, pp. 248-55; Great Britain. Privy Council, *Acts of the Privy Council of England. Colonial series . . .*, ed. by James Munro . . . (London, H. M. Stationery off., 1908–12), IV, 55-57.

The printing in Fernow is a queer mixture of the "Order in Council" and the "Petition of John Hanbury"; therefore, useless.

This Order of Council requested the Board of Trade to determine the relationship between the Hanbury petition and the Gooch request.

10. Report and "additional instructions" to Gooch in P.R.O., C.O. 5: 1366/421-25. "Additional instructions" printed in Fernow, *op. cit.*, 255-58. These instructions were superseded by those of March 16 and were, therefore, never sent to Virginia.

11. Report of the Committee of Council on Plantation Affairs in P.R.O., P.C. Register 2: 101/189-92. Extract printed in *Acts of the*

Annotations

Privy Council, IV, 57-58. This report was based on the Report* by the Lords of Trade to the Committee of Council.

**Report in P.R.O., C.O. 5: 1366/427-33. The Lords of Trade informed the Committee of Council that the application made by Gooch was a part of the Hanbury proposal.

12. In P.R.O., P.C. Register 2: 101/191-92.

13. Order in *ibid.,* pp. 215-16; P.R.O., C.O. 5: 1327/93-94.

14. In P.R.O., C.O. 5: 1366/439-44.

15. The "Proceedings in England" appears only in this memorandum.

16. No direct reference to this letter and no copy of the letter were located by the editor. The postponement of consideration of the October 20, 1747, petition may have been the reason for the Ohio Company's decision to seek, through the influence of John Hanbury, an instruction to the governor of Virginia empowering him to grant lands on the Ohio to them. —"List of Early Land Patents and Grants Petitioned for in Virginia up to 1769...," *op. cit.*

17. The correction of the Thornton name is evidence that this memorandum, *unique to this document,* is not an exact copy of the original minutes of the Company. —"Memorial of the Ohio Company, November 20, 1778." MS in Virginia State Library, Richmond, Virginia; printed in Bailey, *Ohio Company..., op. cit.,* pp. 320-27.

18. Daniel Cresap never was a member of the Company. *Ibid.*

19. Entry for October 20, 1748, in "Resolutions of the Ohio Company and the Committee of the Company, October 20, 1748–July 4, 1763." See *Chronology;* also *notes* 2, 16.

20. Probably John Stedman, a Philadelphia merchant, sea captain, and one of the most vigorous traffickers in German Redemptionists, 1730–60. —"Christopher Saur's First Letter to Governor Morris on the Trials and Wrongs of the Early German Immigrants," March 15, 1755, in The Pennsylvania-German Society, *Proceedings and Addresses* ([Lancaster, Pa.], The Society, 1891–date), X, 238-45.

Annotations

21. Nathaniel Chapman, treasurer of the Company. A letter signed by Lawrence Washington, James Scott, Nathaniel Chapman, and John Carlyle to a member of the Company (addressee unknown) and executing this order is number 14,853, Emmett Collection in the New York Public Library.

22. Order to Mr. Hanbury. Ohio Company members to John Hanbury, June 20, 1749. See *Chronology*.

23. This cargo arrived sometime before May 27, 1750. Relative to the appointment of a factor, George Mason said that in his opinion it was better to accept Hugh Parker's questionable security than to "delay sending up the Goods any longer; for we have already give to our Rivals the Pensilvns too many Advantages over us." Mr. Mason concludes, "I wrote to stop our next Cargoe till next Spring." —George Mason to Lawrence Washington, May 27, 1750, printed in Moncure Daniel Conway, *Barons of the Potomac and Rappahannock* (N. Y., Grolier Club, 1892), pp. 280-81.

24. Thomas Nelson.

25. Lawrence Washington must have circulated the petition presented to the Virginia Executive Council in 1747, on which action was postponed, October 20, 1747. See *notes* 2 and 16.

26. The order was for £2,000 worth of goods. Ohio Company members to John Hanbury, June 20, 1749. See *Chronology*.

27. Hanbury's influence is evident in Robert Dinwiddie's Memorial to the Board of Trade, September 10, 1751, in which he proposed some additions to his instructions relative to presents for the Indians (P.R.O., C.O. 5: 1327/417-19). The memorial was not read until March 11, 1752, when Hanbury was called by the Board for consultation on the matter (B. T. *Journal*, 1749–53, p. 290). Subsequently, the Board of Trade informed Dinwiddie of their cognizance of the gravity of the Indian situation and asked him to procure means from the Virginia Legislature to provide for those presents without a new royal instruction. If unsuccessful, they wished an estimate of the sum annually required for presents for the Indians. —Board of Trade to Dinwiddie, November 29, 1752, in P.R.O., C.O. 5: 1366/516-33.

28. Report of the Lords of Trade to the Lords of the Privy Council,

Annotations

December 20, 1739, recites the history of the Crown's giving presents to the Indians on like occasions, a precedent set in 1699. Printed in *Documents Relative to the Colonial History of the State of New York* (Albany, Weed, Parsons and Company, printers, 1853–87), VI, 156-57.

29. Orders and resolutions of the Committee and of the Company are inconclusive on this matter of road building. See orders or resolutions in *Chronology* dated June 21, 1749; May 22, 1751; July 25–27, 1753; also "Additional Instructions to Christopher Gist on a separate piece of paper," April 28, 1752, and "Instructions to Christopher Gist, July 27, 1753."

30. On October 18, 1749, Thomas Lee, manager of the Company and president of the Virginia Council, wrote to the Board of Trade setting forth the necessity for a treaty with the Ohio Indians. —Letter in P.R.O., C.O. 5: 1327/195-97. This letter was not received until September 30, 1750, and read on October 11, 1750, eight months after the treaty goods arrived in Virginia. See also *note* 105.

31. By February 27, 1750, Thomas Lee had tentatively engaged Conrad Weiser to bring the Indians to Fredericksburg for a conference and to assist him as interpreter. —Thomas Lee to Conrad Weiser, February 27, 1750. Peters Papers, III, 5. MS in the Historical Society of Pennsylvania.

32. No record that this commission was given was found by the editor.

33. In October, 1705, an export duty was imposed on all furs and skins exported and carried out of Virginia by land and water "for and towards the better support and maintenance of the College of William and Mary." —Virginia. Laws, Statutes, etc., *The Statutes at Large; Being a Collection of All the Laws of Virginia from the First Session of the Legislature, in the Year 1619* . . . By William Waller Hening (v.p., v. pub., 1809–1823), III, 356-57.

34. See *note* 27. This letter from the Board of Trade to Dinwiddie, November 29, 1752, shows that with the exception of "an Explination about the fort" all these desires of the Ohio Company expressed to Hanbury were contained in Dinwiddie's Memorial to the Earl of Halifax. The Board of Trade answered the Memorial leniently and favorably. In addition, Thomas Lee, in 1749 and 1750, carried on a

Annotations

vigorous correspondence on the boundary line subject with the governors of Virginia and Maryland and the Board of Trade.

35. In 1728 the governors of the two colonies, Virginia and Carolina, met and drew up proposals for running the line. Next year the King in Council gave an order to carry out these proposals. Three commissioners for Virginia, four for North Carolina, and four surveyors, two from each colony, ran the line. The costs were paid out of the quit-rents of the respective colonies (William Byrd, *The History of the Dividing Line Between Virginia and North Carolina as Run in 1728-29* . . . [Richmond, Va., 1866], pp. 215-25). The line was continued westward in 1749. —Virginia (Colony) Council, *Executive Journals of the Council of Colonial Virginia* . . . (Richmond, Va., State Library, 1925–date), V, 269, 291, 310, 384, 412.

36. This order was not carried out successfully for " . . . in Septr following 1749 employed Gentlemen to discover the Lands beyond the Mountains to know where they shou'd make their Surveys But they not having made any considerable progress the Company in Septr 1750 agreed to give Mr. Christopher Gist £150 certain and such further handsome allowance as his Service should deserve for searching & discovering the Lands upon the Ohio . . . . " —Order of the Committee of Council referring the petition of the Ohio Company to the Board of Trade [with petition annexed], April 2, 1754, in P.R.O., C.O. 5: 1328/153-61; printed in Bailey, *Ohio Company, op. cit.*, pp. 304-09; Fernow, *op. cit.*, pp. 265-73.

37. The land was not patented until October 25, 1754, when George Mason secured patents from Lord Fairfax for lots one, five, fourteen, fifteen, and sixteen, known as the New Store Tract. —Northern Neck Grants, H, 1751–56, pp. 507, 508, 509, 510, 511. Land Office, Archives Division, Virginia State Library, Richmond, Virginia.

38. No other mention of this assessment in the different versions of the minutes of the Company.

39. The only record of this meeting of the Ohio Company.

40. It is unlikely that this order was carried out, for arrangements were not made for establishing trade by May 27, 1750. See *note 23*. Indian trade by Gist is not mentioned in his instructions for "searching and discovering the lands" issued by the Committee of the Ohio Company on September 11.

Annotations

41. No record was found concerning Gist's opening up the Indian trade on the Ohio.

42. Falls of the Ohio, at present Louisville, Kentucky.

43. A copy of the agreement between the Company and Gist is in the "Resolutions of the Ohio Company, 1748–63" (see *Chronology*, September 11, 1750). Minutes of the Pennsylvania Board of Property, June 26, 1770, and September 9, 1791, show that, according to this agreement, lands on the Monongahela were "taken up" under Christopher Gist and titles for these lands were in dispute at these late dates. —*Pennsylvania Archives*, 3rd series (Harrisburg, J. Severns & Co., 1852–56), I, 301, 757-58.

44. Information *unique to this version* of the minutes of the Company.

45. "Articles of Agreement and Copartnership for the Ohio Company for the Space of Twenty Years, May 23, 1751." See *note* 1.

46. Research at the College of Heralds, London, England, reveals that there is no record that this seal was ever made; the seal, if made, was never registered. However, it is now delineated according to these specifications and produced as the frontispiece in this work. Information concerning the seal is *unique to this document*.

47. No record of printing or of printed copies was located by the editor.

48. The photostat of the "Articles of Agreement" in the Virginia Historical Society (see *note* 1) shows the signatures of "Robt Dinwiddie, Lawrence Washington, Natha Chapman, Phil: Lud: Lee, John Tayloe, James Scott, George Mason, Presly Thornton, Gawen Corbin, J. Mercer, Richard Lee, Augst Washington, Jacob Giles, and Thomas Cresap." Since Robert Dinwiddie, who arrived in Virginia in November, 1751, signed this document and neither James Wardrop, who was in London about that time, nor any London member signed it, it is reasonable to assume that the original from which this photostat was made was never sent to London.

49. "ITEM That the said major Part of the said Partners as aforesaid at every such yearly meeting shall also have full Power & Au-

Annotations

thority to nominate appoint & agree with such of the said Partners as they shall think proper to be a Treasurer or Receiver of the said Company who is hereby authorized impowered & required to receive & pay away all such Sum & Sums of money tobacco or other Effects belonging to the said Company as the major Part of the said Company at their meetings or the Committee to be [by them] from time to time appointed shall order & direct: For all which Payments he shall be obliged to produce proper Receipts & Vouchers upon the passing his Accounts. And all Bonds Bills promissory notes Bills of Exchange & other Securities for the Payment of any money or other Effects belonging to the said Company shall be taken by such Treasurer or Receiver for the time being in his own name; FOR THE USE OF THE OHIO COMPANY and shall immediately upon his receiving the same be by him endorsed in blank, that in Case of his Death they may be delivered over to such other Treasurer or Receiver as shall be appointed by the major Part of the said Partners...."

50. The Earl of Granville told Hanbury that he would grant the Company the lands mentioned in this order on the same terms that the Crown granted them the lands in Virginia. —John Mercer to Francis Fauquier, 1759; John Mercer to Charlton Palmer, July 27, 1762. See *Chronology*.

51. *Ibid.*

52. *Ibid.* There is also extant an account of expenses incurred by Thomas Penn's solicitor in negotiating this matter. On July 6, 1754, an agreement to this effect was executed in London by Mr. Hanbury and three other members of the Ohio Company, on the one part, and Thomas Penn and Richard Penn, on the other part; "but Mr. Hanbury keeps them all, on Pretence that some *other* Terms were agreed upon." —"Thomas Penn's Expense Account." Penn MSS, "Accounts," II, 15. Historical Society of Pennsylvania.

53. Present site of Bedford, Pennsylvania.

54. Loyalhanna and Kiskiminetas in western Pennsylvania.

55. Conemaugh River. Loyalhanna Creek and the Conemaugh unite at Saltsburg, Pennsylvania, and form the Kiskiminetas River.

56. At Turkey Foot, present site of Confluence, Pennsylvania.

Annotations

57. The petition of the Ohio Company of March 28, 1754, presented to the Privy Council by Arthur Dobbs, J. Hanbury, Samuel Smith, and James Wardrop in behalf of themselves and the rest of the Ohio Company, and referred to the Board of Trade by the Committee of Council on April 2, was a plea to have "their former contract in consideration of their erecting two forts" rescinded. For this condition they wished to have substituted the condition to "enlarge their Settlmts & Seat three hundred Familys instead of One hundred by their former Contract and in Consideration of their erecting two Forts One at Shurtees Creek and the other at the Fork where the great Conhaway enters the Ohio, and maintain them at their Own Expence That Your Majesty will be graciously pleased to enlarge their Grant under the same exemption of Rights and Quit Rents as in the former Instructions . . . . " —Order of the Committee of Council to the Board of Trade [with petition annexed], April 2, 1754, *op. cit.*

58. Twenty-four pages, folio, closely written on Gerrevink watermark paper, this is a copy of the "attested copy" of the Gist journals, made for Robert Dinwiddie. John Mercer stated that he sent a copy of Gist's journals to John Hanbury (see *page 237*) and also remarked to his son, George, that the journals sent to Mr. Hanbury might be of value to him in negotiating for the Ohio Company grant (see *page 237*). Although this manuscript is the complete first and second journals, it does not appear to be the copy mentioned in John Mercer's correspondence. Internal evidence in several letters shows that part of this collection was at one time in the hands of Richard Jackson, London agent for Pennsylvania (see *page 310*). Also, there is evidence that official Ohio Company papers were at hand when members of the Walpole Company were actively engaged in soliciting their purchase. It is not unreasonable to assume that this particular copy of the journals was made from official colonial records sent to England from Virginia, and when George Mercer obtained Charlton Palmer's Ohio Company files from Richard Jackson, the copy was included by mistake (Charlton Palmer to George Mercer, December 27, 1769. See *Chronology*). Also, it is possible that this is the actual copy of Gist's journals made for Dinwiddie.

The first and second journals and extracts from the second journal appear in several places in the Mercer papers, as well as in the printed *Case of the Ohio Company* (see *Chronology*). An appendix in the *Case*, printed in 1770, is the first printing of the first and second journals. "Appendix, Number VI," "Christopher Gist's first journal," published in Thomas Pownall's *A Topographical Description Of Such*

Annotations

Parts Of North America As Are Contained In The (Annexed) Map Of The Middle British Colonies, &c. In North America (London: Printed for J. Almon, opposite Burlington House, in Piccadilly, 1776), is the second edition of the journal and not the first, as heretofore credited. Also, there is in the Darlington Memorial Library, in undistributed signature format and without title page or colophon, another printing of this document. Mr. Darlington died in 1889. It is most likely that these signatures were printed before his death. In addition, from 1876, when he purchased this collection (*page* xviii), until 1889 he prepared for publication an edited edition of the Gist journals, posthumously published by his widow in 1893 (Christopher Gist, *Journals with Historical, Geographical, and Ethnological notes* ... by William M. Darlington [Pittsburgh, J. R. Weldin & Co., 1893]). Thus the above two printings are the third and fourth editions of Gist's first and second journals, printed from original manuscripts. In 1949 a revised and enlarged edition of Pownall's *Topographical Description* was published: Thomas Pownall, *A Topographical Description of the Dominions of the United States of America*, ... Revised and enlarged edition edited by Lois Mulkearn (Pittsburgh, University of Pittsburgh Press, 1949).

To date there are five known printed editions of Gist's first journal and two editions of the second journal, derived from this George Mercer manuscript collection:

(1) Appendix in *Case* (first and second journals, derived from manuscript "Case of the Ohio Company"), 1770.
(2) Appendix in Thomas Pownall (first journal only, derived from printed *Case of the Ohio* Company, 1770), 1776.
(3) Undistributed signatures, n. pub., n. d. (derived from this manuscript).
(4) William Darlington's edition of the first and second journals, annotated (derived from this manuscript), 1893.
(5) Appendix to Pownall, annotated first journal (derived from Thomas Pownall's 1776 edition), 1949.

Several other reprints and editions have been published from printed presentations of both journals.

As for Christopher Gist (1706-1759), himself, it seems strange that he never became a member of the Ohio Company. Born in Maryland, later a resident of North Carolina, Virginia, and Pennsylvania, the major part of his activities was service for Virginia and the Ohio Company. Undoubtedly, he became acquainted with Thomas Cresap in Baltimore and through this acquaintance obtained his berth with the Ohio Company. His account of explorations for the Company is

Annotations

the first topographical description of a large area west of the Alleghenies. This firsthand knowledge of the frontier proved invaluable to the Crown in England's struggle with the French for possession of North America. In addition to the two exploratory trips made for the Company, he was their land agent who succeeded in establishing a settlement in what is now Fayette County, Pennsylvania. He served as their representative at Logstown in 1752; was their surveyor commissioned to lay out, according to their approved plan, a town and fort on the Ohio River at the mouth of Chartiers Creek; supervised cutting a road from their storehouse at Wills Creek (Cumberland, Maryland) to a landing on the Monongahela; was one of their factors who actively engaged in the Indian trade; and was in charge of their Maidstone storehouse as late as 1756. Sources for the above information are given elsewhere in the annotations and may be found readily by use of the index.

59. Given at a meeting of the Committee of the Ohio Company, September 11, 1750, when the Committee also made arrangements for Gist's current expenses, his necessary supplies, including arms and ammunition, and a minimum salary of £150, which he was to receive for his services. In addition the Committee entered into an agreement with Gist "for the greater Encouragement of the first Setlers upon the Company's Lands." See *Chronology,* September 11, 1750.

60. The original Gist plan or copies of it were not located by the editor. There is extant in the British Museum, however, a plan showing Gist's routes on his first and second trips and the proposed boundaries, as petitioned for on November 6, 1752. John Mercer states that on that day he presented a petition, on behalf of the Ohio Company, to the Virginia Council and, at the same time, lent Ohio Company member Lieutenant Governor Dinwiddie the plan for his own personal perusal. Mr. Mercer also says that "the Map belonged to me as of my own drawing & my Instructions by which I drew it cost the Company above £600 . . . " (John Mercer to George Mercer, March 3, 1768. See *Chronology*). In the John Hanbury petition of March 28, 1754 (see *note* 57) mention is made of a plan annexed to the petition. The holograph map (P.R.O., C.O. Maps, Virginia, no. 13) on which is marked the extent of Gist's two journeys, the natural boundaries for their grant, and the road from Wills Creek to a landing on the Monongahela fits the description of both of these plans. It is not unlikely that, if they were not one and the same, the plan annexed to the petition of March 28, 1754, was a copy of John Mercer's plan,

Annotations

lent to Dinwiddie on November 6, 1752. There is, in the Darlington Memorial Library, a copy made from the original by J. A. Burt for William M. Darlington, April, 1882, reproduced opposite p. 72, this work; also a photostat of the original, courtesy of Howard N. Eavenson. See also *note* 199.

61. In 1740 Thomas Cresap purchased from John Charlton 200 acres of land in Maryland, called "Indian Seat." Two years later he added by purchase 50 acres more and renamed the tract "Indian Field." Here Cresap established the frontier post, Old Town. —Kenneth Bailey, *Thomas Cresap, Maryland Frontiersman* (Boston, Christopher Publishing House, 1944), pp. 62-63.

62. Shawnee Old Town or Opessa's Town (*ca.* 1697–1730) was on the Maryland side of the Potomac where the great Warriors' Path from north to south crossed the river, on the site of Cresap's Old Town. The location is about 15 miles southeast of the present city of Cumberland and near Green Spring, Maryland. Maryland made her first treaty with the Shawnee from "the head of Potomock" in 1698. —Treaty, dated May 26, 1698, printed in *Archives of Maryland* . . . (Baltimore, Maryland Historical Society, 1884–date), XXIII, 426-31.

In 1700 and 1701 Maryland and Pennsylvania, respectively, signed "Articles of Agreement" with Chief Opessa and other Shawnee inhabiting the headwaters of the Potomac. —Ratification and confirmation of the treaty of 1698, printed in *ibid.*, XXV, 104-06; Articles of Agreement concluded and agreed upon between William Penn and certain Susquehanna and Shawnee and other nations of Indians living along the Northern Potomac River, April 23, 1701. Pennsylvania. Provincial Council, *Minutes of . . . from its Organization to the Termination of the Proprietary Government* (Philadelphia, J. Severns & Co., 1852–53), II, 14-18.

In the 1720's Opessa's Town was a haven for runaway slaves from Virginia and Maryland. By 1731 the town was abandoned and the Shawnee had moved over the Allegheny to settle on the Conemaugh and Allegheny Rivers. —Gist (Darlington Edition), *op. cit.*, p. 90; *Archives of Maryland, ibid.*, XXIII, 92-93, 429; XXV, 442-43; *Colonial Records of Pennsylvania, ibid.*, III, 211-15, 459-60; *Pennsylvania Archives,* first series (Philadelphia, Joseph Severns & Co., 1852–56), I, 301-02.

63. This was the Warriors' Path, from Frankstown, south along the

Annotations

base of Great Warriors' or Tussey Mountain, which crossed the Potomac River at Old Town. Gist traveled in the valley of Flintstone Creek through the Warriors' Gap, the pass between Warriors' Mountain and Iron Ore Ridge. —Charles Hanna, *The Wilderness Trail* ... (N. Y., London, G. P. Putnam's Sons, 1911), I, 156, 191; Robert Bruce, *The National Road* ... (Washington, D. C., National Highways Association [1916]), p. 32.

64. At Bloody Run, now Everett, eight miles east of Bedford, Pennsylvania. Here the Warriors' Path met the east-west trail known as the Raystown Path. Gist turned west and followed the Raystown Path. Gist (Darlington edition), *op. cit.*, p. 90.

65. The course lay through Alliquippa's Gap to present Bedford, to Schellsburg, across the Allegheny Ridge, reaching the top of the mountain in Allegheny Township, Somerset County, following the present boundary line between Shade and Stoney Creek Townships, Somerset County, Pennsylvania. —Hanna, *op. cit.*, I, 280-81.

66. At a sleeping place on the Raystown Path known as Edmund's Swamp near present Buckstown, Somerset County, Pennsylvania. —*Colonial Records of Pennsylvania*, V, 761; Hanna, *op. cit.*, I, 281.

67. The path led across Stoney Creek near Stoyestown, Somerset County, Pennsylvania. Stoney Creek is a tributary of the Allegheny not the Susquehanna River. —Gist (Darlington edition), *op. cit.*, p. 91.

68. Kickeney Paullin's Camp. —*Colonial Records of Pennsylvania*, V, 761. Evidently near Stoyestown, Pennsylvania.

69. The two branches of the Quemahoning Creek are of the Allegheny and not the Susquehanna watershed.

70. The great Laurel Ridge. The winding road over the mountain descended on the western side about three miles east of present Laughlinstown, Pennsylvania. —Hanna, *op. cit.*, I, 283.

71. An Indian village probably founded by the Shawnee when they moved from Opessa's Old Town to the Allegheny and Kiskiminetas Rivers in the 1730's (see also *note* 62). In 1758 Captain Harry Gordon, in preparation for General John Forbes' expedition against Fort Duquesne, built Fort Ligonier on the site of this old Indian town.

Annotations

—A. P. James, "Fort Ligonier: Additional Light From Unpublished Documents" in *Western Pennsylvania Historical Magazine* (Pittsburgh, Historical Society of Western Pennsylvania, 1918–date), XVII, 265.

On the present site of Ligonier, Pennsylvania.

72. An important Delaware Indian village located on the southeast side of the Allegheny River at the mouth of Two Mile Run, in present twelfth ward, Pittsburgh, Pennsylvania.

Shannopin, a Delaware chief, for whom the village was named, figures in Ohio Indian and Pennsylvania affairs from 1730 to 1740 (*Colonial Records of Pennsylvania,* IV, 432-34, 443-47; V, 355; *Pennsylvania Archives,* I, 254-55; 301-02, 341). Since Shannopin was no longer the Delaware chief at Allegheny in 1751 (*Colonial Records of Pennsylvania,* V, 519) and Gist does not mention him in his *Journal,* one may assume that he died sometime between May, 1748, after his attendance at the Logstown Conference of that year, and November, 1750. The name, Shannopin's Town, appears many times in official Pennsylvania correspondence from 1731 to 1754.

73. Gist's course as stated S 70 W does not coincide with the regularly traveled path to Shannopin's Town. The established trail was more nearly N 70 W. Mr. Darlington states that the trail passed through Chestnut Ridge by Miller's Run Gap, passed south of the present town of Latrobe and then directly west. —Gist (Darlington edition), *op. cit.,* pp. 91-92.

74. Cockey or Cock Eye's Cabin stood about three miles north of Penn, Allegheny County, Pennsylvania *(ibid.).* John Harris, in his account of the road to Logstown, places Cock Eye's Cabin 15 miles from Shannopin's Town. —*Pennsylvania Archives,* II, 135. In the vicinity of present Bushy Run Battlefield Park.

75. Allegheny River. In early times the French called the Allegheny River the Ohio; the English often did, too.

76. Lewis Evans states that the river at Shannopin's Town was so shallow that in very dry times it could be forded. —Lewis Evans, *Geographical, Historical, Political, Philosophical and Mechanical Essays: The First, Containing an Analysis of a General Map of the Middle British Colonies in America* . . . (Philadelphia, B. Franklin and D. Hall, 1755), p. 25.

Annotations

77. Logstown (*ca.* 1743–54) was the English stronghold on the Ohio before the French and Indian War. It was probably founded by Kakawatcheky, the Shawnee chief who migrated from Eastern Pennsylvania in 1743 or 1744 (*Colonial Records of Pennsylvania*, IV, 648, 747). By 1747 this village was inhabited by a heterogeneous group of young warriors and hunters. Delaware, Shawnee, and Six Nations were the principal tribes represented. They had, however, one tie— a common dislike for the French. The Onondaga council who ruled over the tribes represented on the Ohio had named Tanacharison, a Seneca chief, as their resident deputy or Half King. Also, Onondaga had placed as guardian over the Shawnee one Scarouady, an Oneida, known also as Monacatootha (*Colonial Records of Pennsylvania*, V, 615). In 1747 the group became so strong and so closely knit together that they issued an invitation to all the Indians in the Ohio and Miami Country to attend a general council to be held the next year. Then ten principal warriors, representing the group, made their first trek over the Alleghenies to Philadelphia, there to explain to official Pennsylvania that they no longer could abide by the parent Onondaga Council's order of "strict neutrality" in the French-English dispute. At the same time they asked for arms and ammunition with which to fight the French and solicited Pennsylvania's recognition of a separate Council Fire (*ibid.*, 145-47). Conrad Weiser, veteran Indian interpreter and emissary, persuaded the Pennsylvania authorities to recognize the integrity of this group (*ibid.*, 147-48). Therefore, it was he who kindled their first separate Council Fire on the Ohio, in 1748 and, at the same time, delivered them a gift worth £1,000. In answer to Weiser's request for "a List of their fighting Men," the deputies of all the Indian nations "settled on the Waters of Ohio" gave him ten bundles composed of 789 sticks to represent the number of warriors available.

Logstown, at that time, was the headquarters for many English traders. Weiser reported that more than 20 were in business there. After 1748 the Ohio Indians looked upon Logstown as their official rendezvous. —"Journal of Conrad Weiser, Indian Interpreter at Ohio," August 11–September 29, 1748, printed in *ibid.*, 348-58; Pennsylvania (Colony). Treaties, etc., 1748, *A Treaty Held by Commissioners, Members of the Council of the Province of Pennsylvania, at the Town of Lancaster, with Some Chiefs of the Six Nations at Ohio, and Others, for the Admission of the Twightwee Nation into the Alliance of His Majesty, &c. in the Month of July, 1748.* (Philadelphia, Printed and Sold by B. Franklin, 1748); Minutes of Virginia's Conference at Logstown in 1752, see *Chronology*, June 13, 1752.

Annotations

This village was headquarters for the Half King, or Tanacharison, Scarouady, and Kakawatcheky, aged chief of the Shawnee (*Journal of Conrad Weiser, . . . , 1748, op. cit.*). The Virginians never projected a fortification for Logstown. Their efforts of 1754 were farther up the Ohio at the mouth of Chartiers Creek (Orders of the Committee of the Ohio Company, July 25, 1753, see *Chronology*) and the forks of the Monongahela (Robert Dinwiddie, *The Official Records of . . . with an introduction and notes* by R. A. Brock [Richmond, Va., Virginia Historical Society, 1883], I, 59). After the French took possession of the English stockade at the "forks" in April, 1754, "Monacatoocha" burned the first Indian village named Logstown (George Washington, *Journal of . . . across the Allegheny Mountains in 1754 . . .* , edited, with notes, by J. M. Toner [Albany, N. Y., Joel Munsell's Sons, Publishers, 1893], p. 128). However, the name continued in history as the name of the French Shawnee village built in 1755 (Christian Frederick Post, *The Second Journal of . . .* [London, J. Wilkie, 1759], p. 57) and, after the fall of Fort Duquesne, as the headquarters for a few English traders (Hanna, *op. cit.*, I, 380-81). In November, 1792, General Anthony Wayne established winter army quarters, Legionville, near the site of old Logstown (present Ambridge, Pennsylvania). —Horatio N. Moore, *Life and Services of General Anthony Wayne* (Philadelphia, John B. Perry, 1845), p. 174.

The French looked upon Logstown, called Chiningué by them, as a strategic place for a fortification on the Ohio. Mr. Renick, a Pennsylvania trader, reported as early as 1732 that the French were building a fort of "Loggs" on or near the Ohio (*Pennsylvania Archives*, I, 309-10). There is no record that this fort was built, but it does give rise to the speculation that some sort of building made of logs may have been standing when the English traders came to this place. In a report of his mission of good will and possession for the king of France in 1749, Céloron gives the fullest account of its size and inhabitants. He reported there were 50 cabins of Iroquois, Shawnee, and Delaware, including many refugees from Shannopin's Town (Charles B. Galbreath, ed., *Expedition of Céloron to the Ohio Country in 1749* [Columbus, Ohio, The F. J. Heer Printing Co., 1921], p. 30). Father Bonnecamp, who was with him on the expedition, remarks that the village was quite new, perhaps only five or six years old (*ibid.*, 87-88). Philip Thomas de Joncaire, a French officer with Céloron, was chosen by the governor of New France to make a three-year expedition to the Ohio Country, a project which included building a fort at Logstown and gaining that group of Indians for the French interest. He left Canada in 1750, carrying a large quantity of valuable goods with

Annotations

which he hoped to purchase the good will of all the Indians from Lake Ontario to Logstown, where he arrived at the time George Croghan was conducting the Pennsylvania Indian conference in May, 1751. In the presence of the Pennsylvania commissioners he entreated the Indians to embrace the French cause and warned the English traders off the Ohio (*Colonial Records of Pennsylvania*, V, 530-31). Joncaire did not remain at Logstown, for minutes of the Virginia conference in 1752 do not mention the presence of any Frenchmen (June 1-13, 1752, see *Chronology*). The next direct report of French activities is of January 15, 1754, when some Frenchmen in the company of Scarouady and others of the Six Nations came to Logstown from Venango (*Colonial Records of Pennsylvania*, V, 732-33). Among the Frenchmen was the keeper of the King's stores (*ibid.*, 735), one LaForce, who was captured by Washington at the time of the "Jumonville skirmish." It was LaForce who issued the warning to the English and their Indian allies, "You have but a short time to see the Sun, for in Twenty Days You and your Brothers and the English shall All die" (*ibid.*, VI, 22). As stated previously, the native inhabitants destroyed their village in June, 1754 (Washington's *Journal*, 1754 [Toner edition], *op. cit.*, p. 128), but the French immediately built 30 cabins for the Shawnee who remained true to the French interest after the English rout from the Ohio. The Indians who lived there during the French regime left their homes in 1758 and 1759 to take up residence at Kuskuskies, on the Pickawillany Plains and on the Muskingum. —Hanna, *op. cit.*, I, 378-79.

78. Hated by the French, loved by the Indians, needed and respected by the English, George Croghan was perhaps the most colorful and influential frontiersman during the Colonial Period. By 1745, only four years after he emigrated from Ireland, Croghan had established residence on the Juniata Path about five miles from John Harris' Ferry (Harrisburg, Pennsylvania); had received his first trader's license; had spent a winter trading in the Ohio Country; and had begun his career as informant for Pennsylvania on Indian affairs. Heretofore, published accounts have given 1747 as the date of Croghan's entrance upon the stage of western Indian trade and diplomacy; yet extant records show that in 1745 he began to report on Indian affairs to the government of Pennsylvania. A deposition made by Peter Tostee, James Dunning, and Croghan reveals that he was trading at "Guyhawga on the borders of Lake Erie in April, 1745." By their deposition these traders gave the Pennsylvanians the first authentic information concerning the desertion of the Shawnee under

Annotations

Peter Chartier. When they were trading "down the Allegheny" they found, within 120 miles of the Shawnee town, seven or eight hundred Indians under the command of Peter Chartier, who was leading them to a place the French had given them on the second branch of the Wabash. Here the Indians robbed the traders of a canoe load of skins and perhaps other goods valued at £800. These same Indians appeared at Guyhawga while Croghan was there, April 6-23, 1745, but upon seeing that the English were under the protection of the Six Nations, they withdrew without molesting them. —"Deposition of three traders George Croghan, Peter Tostee, and James Dunning" May 14, 1745, made before Edward Shippen, mayor of Philadelphia; Governor Thomas to Conrad Weiser, May 14, 1745; Richard Peters to Thomas Penn, June 25, 1745. Peters Papers, II, 30-32, 36. MSS in the Historical Society of Pennsylvania.

This early activity of Pennsylvania traders near Lake Erie was not only the basis of French hatred for Croghan, but also the alarm which awakened the French to the fact that they must take definite steps to secure their line of communication between Canada and Louisiana. The robbery reported by Tostee, Dunning, and Croghan in May, 1745, was also reported to the French Minister by the governor-general of Canada. —Beauharnois to the French Minister, October 28, 1745, extract printed in *N.Y.C.D.*, X, 19-21.

Two years later Captain Raymond, commandant at Niagara, in a letter to the French Minister, reminded him that in 1745 he had given warning that the savages "would be corrupted and Won over by the English who trade at la Riviere Blanche [Cuyahoga River], who have no other object than to Make Themselves masters of all the upper country through the Sole medium of the Savages whose minds they have won by their address." Raymond advised the minister that the only way to stop this defection of the Indians from their interest was to deprive the savages of all communications with the English. He continued: "To succeed in this, and to Establish a lasting peace in the whole of the upper country, let Your Grace make England Agree in the next treaty of peace with This Crown, that the English shall abandon and Give up to the King forever the Complete possession of the fort of Chouegen; that they Renounce having any relation with the Five yrocoisses nations, who shall carry on no Trade directly or indirectly throughout the territory Around lakes hontario, lake herrier, lake huron, Riviere Blanche and Belle Riviere and in all their dependencies and other surrounding territories, shall Withdraw to their own country for ever Without ever being allowed to Return and carry on any Trade, or even under any pretext whatsoever."—Memoir

Annotations

of Raymond to the French Minister, November 2, 1747, printed in Wisconsin State Historical Society, *Collections of* . . . edited by Reuben Gold Thwaites (Madison, The Society, 1855–1882), XVII, 474-77.

In addition, the conspiracy of La Demoiselle, chief of the Miami, was attributed to "The instigation of The English Man" [George Croghan]. —*Ibid.*, XVIII, 58-60.

Before 1751 Croghan had at least five trading houses on the frontier: at Logstown on the Ohio, at Pine Creek on the Allegheny, at Oswegle Bottom on the Youghiogheny, at Conchake on the Muskingum, and at Pickawillany on the Big Miami. His keen understanding and his sympathy for the natives, also the trade goods with which he supplied them, established friendly relations with the Delawares, the Shawnee, the Miami, the Wyandotts, and the Six Nations in the Ohio Country.

Conrad Weiser, Indian plenipotentiary for Pennsylvania, was employed full time in keeping the Six Nations in the English orbit. Pennsylvania needed George Croghan on the frontier; it was he whom the Indians trusted, and at many conferences they refused to speak unless Croghan or his good friend, Andrew Montour, was present.

That Pennsylvania respected his ability in Indian diplomacy is shown clearly by the number of important missions assigned to him. Scarcely a conference with the western Indians took place between 1748 and 1775 that Croghan did not serve either in an active or advisory capacity. He was present with Conrad Weiser when he kindled the Council Fire at Logstown in 1748; was informant for Pennsylvania on Virginia activities in 1749; was Pennsylvania's courier to Pickawillany late in 1750; conducted the Pennsylvania-Logstown Conference in 1751; was chosen to be Pennsylvania's representative at the Virginia-Logstown conference in 1752; traveled with Trent and the Ohio Indians to Winchester and thence to Carlisle in 1753; assisted John Patten in returning the captive Shawnee to their tribesmen at Logstown in January, 1754; with the assistance of Andrew Montour delivered Pennsylvania's present at Logstown in January, 1754; assisted William Trent in delivering the Virginia present to the Ohio Indians at Logstown in February, 1754; brought to Philadelphia the ominous news that the French were establishing themselves at Logstown early in 1754; was engaged by the Virginia government to supply the Virginia militia in their spring campaign of 1754; was host to the Indians who fled the Ohio when the French took possession in April, 1754; was with Braddock in 1755; and served as deputy

Annotations

Indian agent for the Northern Department under Sir William Johnson from 1756 to 1772.

He represented the Crown at several conferences with the Indians, 1756–58, when the Delaware, Shawnee, and rebel Iroquois were drawn back into the English sphere of influence. With the reoccupation of the "Forks of the Ohio" by the British, Croghan, deputy Indian agent, established headquarters at Fort Pitt. For ten years, 1758–68, he labored for amicable relationship between the Ohio Indians and the English. The provincial trading post at Fort Pitt (1759–62) was supervised indirectly by him. He also issued licenses to individual traders and represented the Crown at several treaties held at Fort Pitt. When Henry Bouquet was ordered to raise the siege of Fort Pitt, in 1763, he received valuable assistance from Croghan. Later he assisted in the occupation of the Illinois Country (1764–66).

During Croghan's entire military and civil service career he engaged in extensive Indian trade and land speculation. In addition, he was London representative for a group of Indian traders who sought restitution in the form of land grants for their enormous losses caused by French and Indian depredations (1750–63). The Grand Ohio Company paid him for services rendered on the Ohio in 1776. —Thomas Walpole to George Mercer, February 26, 1776, and Samuel Wharton to George Mercer, August 17, 1776. See *Chronology*.

Record of these and many other activities is found chiefly in the *Pennsylvania Archives, Colonial Records of Pennsylvania,* Dinwiddie *Papers, Calendar of Virginia State Papers,* and *N.Y.C.D.* These source books are arranged chronologically, therefore details relating to activities mentioned can be located easily. Albert Volwiler's *George Croghan and the Westward Movement, 1741–1782* (Cleveland, Ohio, Arthur H. Clark Co., 1926) is the secondary source for some information given. Since Dr. Volwiler made this study a large collection of Croghan's personal papers has been acquired by the Historical Society of Pennsylvania. It is the understanding of the editor that exhaustive research on them is in progress.

79. Andrew Montour, son of the famous Indian interpretress, Madame Montour, was known to Pennsylvania officials for several years prior to his employment by that colony and by Virginia. First mention of him in Pennsylvania colonial affairs was made by Conrad Weiser. At Shamokin, in January, 1743, Weiser recorded in his journal "Andrew the son of Madame Montour, who served for Interpreter to the Delawares" ("Conrad Weiser's Report of his Journey to Shamokin," January 30–February 9, 1743, printed in *Colonial Records*

Annotations

of *Pennsylvania,* IV, 640-46), and, in 1744, he recorded: "French Andrew who went to fight the Catawbas, fell sick near James revier in Virginia, and his Company left him under the Care of Pisquedon, one of the Company. Andrew got well, and is Come backe to Shomockin, he told me he would Come down with the other two young Indians which are to Come agt the time when the Indians in Philadia prison will be tried" (Conrad Weiser to James Logan, September 29, 1744, printed in *Pennsylvania Archives,* I, 661-62). He was with Weiser again at Onondaga in 1745 (Extract of Conrad Weiser's Report of his Journey to Onontago, printed in *Colonial Records of Pennsylvania,* IV, 778-82) and was informant for George Croghan in 1749, at which time he was living on the borders of Lake Erie (George Croghan to Richard Peters, July 3, 1749, printed in *Pennsylvania Archives,* II, 31). A partial list of official assignments entrusted to him by Pennsylvania includes services for: Conrad Weiser at Philadelphia and Logstown in 1748 *(Colonial Records of Pennsylvania,* V, 290, 349); George Croghan and a special assignment from the governor at Pickawillany and Muskingum in 1750 (Gist's *Journals,* p. 9, 14, this volume. Also *note* 80); George Croghan at Logstown in 1751 *(Colonial Records of Pennsylvania,* V, 530-39); the government as interpreter at Carlisle in 1753 *(ibid.,* V, 665-84); John Patten at Logstown the year following *(ibid.,* 732-33); the Quakers at their Conference in Philadelphia in 1756 (fragment of original minutes in Darlington Memorial Library; also printed in *An Account of Conferences held and Treaties made, between ... Sir William Johnson, Bart. and the Chief Sachems and Warriours of the ... Indian Nations ...* [London, A. Millar, 1756], pp. 65-77); the government at Lancaster in 1762 *(Colonial Records of Pennsylvania,* VIII, 757-59).

He served the Virginians in different capacities. Christopher Gist employed him in 1750–51 to interpret Virginia's message to the Indians at Muskingum and Pickawillany (Gist's *Journals,* January 30 and February 17, 1751. See *Chronology*). Upon the recommendation of Thomas Cresap and Conrad Weiser the colony asked him to act as interpreter at their Logstown Conference in 1752 (Virginia Council *Journals,* V, 386). Later William Trent employed him in the same capacity when he delivered the Twightwee their portion of the Logstown present (William Trent, *Journal of ...* edited by Alfred T. Goodman ... [Cincinnati, R. Clarke & Co., for W. Dodge, 1871]). The next year, 1753, Montour assisted Trent at Logstown (P.R.O., C.O. 5: 1327/15-40); William Fairfax, at the Winchester Conference *(ibid.,* 1328/48-72); and carried two official messages from Governor Dinwiddie to the Onondaga Council (Virginia Council *Journals,* V, 427).

Annotations

Montour also assisted representatives of the Crown at Easton in 1758 (*Colonial Records of Pennsylvania,* VIII, 174-223); at Pittsburgh, in 1759 (*ibid.,* 429-35); and at Fort Stanwix, in 1768 (*N.Y.C.D.,* VIII, 111ff.).

As a soldier Montour was not too successful. On June 18, 1754, Governor Dinwiddie honored him with a captain's commission, the authorization to enlist a company of Indian scouts to serve under Colonel Innes. Later Dinwiddie remarked that Montour had exceeded his authority in expecting his recruits to be supplied with uniforms; Dinwiddie had thought of Montour's company only as Indian scouts (Dinwiddie to Governor Sharpe, December 17, 1754, printed in *Archives of Maryland,* VI, 143-47). Sharpe, in defense of Montour's misunderstanding of his commission, praised him most highly. Answered Sharpe, "For my own part I cannot help thinking him as I before hinted a well-meaning well-disposed Man & of all the Traders Interpreters or Woodsmen without Comparison the most promising & honest" (Sharpe to Dinwiddie, December 26, 1754. *Ibid.,* 148-52). However, Montour went to Fort Necessity and, much to Washington's delight, served him as interpreter (George Washington to Robert Dinwiddie, June 3 and June 10, 1754, printed in George Washington, *The Writings of . . . ,* edited by John C. Fitzpatrick [Washington, U. S. Government Printing Office, 1931–1944], I, 72, 75).

Also, he recruited among the English settlers in Pennsylvania. On December 28, 1754, John Harris informed Edward Shippen that his brother, William Harris, and many other young men from Paxtang had joined Montour's company which expected to go to Wills Creek. —Letter in *Pennsylvania Archives,* II, 230.

After serving with Braddock's army, Montour returned to Indian life and had Scarouady as his chief companion for a number of years. He went to Philadelphia with Scarouady in August, 1755, to offer the services of the Ohio Indians to Pennsylvania in their fight against the French. So important was the message they brought that Montour met the governor secretly at Conrad Weiser's; and, in the presence of only three Indians, he gave a scathing denunciation of General Braddock's behavior and pleaded with the governor to cast aside assistance from English regulars and unite his troops with the Indians. An excerpt from this plea is as follows: "But let us unite our Strength. You are very numerous, & all the English Governors along your Sea Shore can raise men enough; don't let those that come from over the great Seas be concerned any more; they are unfit to fight in the Woods. Let us go ourselves, we that came out of this Ground, We may be assured to conquer the French." (*Colonial Records of Pa.,* VI, 589).

Annotations

By this time the French had spread their influence as far east as Shamokin (Sunbury, Pennsylvania) and were reported to have planned to build a fort there. Montour, firm in the belief that the Indians could cope with the situation, raised a company of 300 of his people in order to recapture Fort Venango and thus remove the French threat. Even Washington was "greatly enraptured" when he heard that Montour had gathered a company of 300 on Long Island in the Susquehanna and that he planned to march against Fort Venango. Washington wrote to Montour and asked him to bring his Indians to Wills Creek. By his own admission Washington's letter "favours a little of flattery, etc., but this I hope is justifiable on such occasions" (Washington to Dinwiddie, October 11, 1755, printed in *Dinwiddie Papers*, II, 236-42). He did not accept Washington's invitation but continued to plan a defense against the French at Shamokin. During the winter of 1755-1756 Montour kept the Pennsylvanians informed of the hostile Indian and French activities, not only in the Shamokin region but as far west as Fort Duquesne itself.

Scarouady and Montour paid their final visit together to Philadelphia in 1756 to attend the Quaker conference. At this time Montour placed the last two of his five children under the care of Pennsylvania. Scarouady told the Pennsylvanians that he intended to go to Onondaga and live among his people. Montour went with him. With the exception of his visits in the official capacity of interpreter at treaties, Montour appears to have remained in the Onondaga Country. It has been stated that he died about 1775 on Montour's Island in the Ohio, near by Pittsburgh.

80. This mission or embassy was threefold:

(1) Montour, on July 2, 1750, had reported to Governor Hamilton that during the past two or three years several traders had been killed on the Ohio and the Indians had not been reprimanded for it. Therefore, the Governor sent a message of censure "to the Indians of the Six Nations, Shawonese, Delawares, and others living at Ohio." The message was given in charge of "Mr. Montour to deliver it, and to observe all the Forms and Ceremonies used in delivering such Messages, so that the Complaint might go with the greatest Force; and if any Expression be omitted necessary and usual on such occasions that he should supply it." —*Colonial Records of Pennsylvania*, V, 449-50.

(2) Upon Governor Hamilton's recommendation the General Assembly, in August, 1750, voted a small present (£100) for the Twightwees, in answer to their two or three different messages telling how they resisted the French and how much they would be pleased

Annotations

to receive some testimony of Pennsylvania's regard for them. Montour and Croghan were commissioned to deliver this present. —Pennsylvania (Colony). General Assembly. House of Representatives, *Votes and Proceedings of the House of Representatives of the Province of Pennsylvania ... from 15th Day of October, 1744 to September 30, 1758* (Philadelphia, Henry Miller, 1774), IV, 137, 144-45, 146.

(3) At the same session the General Assembly voted a present (£500) for the Ohio Indians and an additional one (£100) for the Twightwees. Conrad Weiser was commissioned to arrange for the transportation of goods to the Ohio as quickly as possible, and George Croghan was ordered to inform the Ohio and Miami Indians that the present would be distributed at Logstown in May, 1751. —*Ibid.*, 156, 182, 185, 187.

81. No specific record of this commission is recorded in the Gist journals. However, Thomas Lee, having been unsuccessful in his attempts to treat with the Six Nations, resorted to an attempt to treat separately with that portion of them who lived on the Ohio. Gist must have been Virginia's official emissary for on July 31, 1751, he was paid £20 "for going on a Message to the Ohio Indians" (Virginia Council *Journals*, V, 349). A few days after Christopher Gist began his journey for the Company and after Lee had received the disappointing report of the unsuccessful trip of Conrad Weiser, his emissary to Onondaga, Lee reported to the Board of Trade that, although the Six Nations in New York were hostile to the Virginians, he would "try to secure the Ohio Indians." —Paul Wallace, *Conrad Weiser, 1696–1760. a Friend of Colonist and Mohawk* (Philadelphia, University of Pennsylvania Press, 1945), pp. 319-20.

82. Shingo's (Shingas) Old Town on the Ohio, near the mouth of the Big Beaver Creek. There, in 1748, Conrad Weiser had wampum belts made for the Pennsylvania-Indian conference held at Logstown ("Journal of Conrad Weiser ... ," 1748, *op. cit.*). King Beaver and his brother Chief Shingas resided here until after Fort Pitt was built in 1759, when they declared their intentions to migrate to Kuskuskies (Hugh Mercer to Richard Peters, March 1, 1759, printed in *Colonial Records of Pennsylvania*, VIII, 305-06). A deed for land purchased from the Six Nations by Pennsylvania, dated October 23, 1784, gives a boundary as "near Shingo's old Town, at the mouth of Beaver Creek" (Pennsylvania. General Assembly, *Minutes of the First Session of the Ninth General Assembly ... Which Commenced the twenty fifth day of October, 1784* [Philadelphia, Francis Bailey, 1784], p. 320).

Annotations

Located in the vicinity of present Beaver, Beaver County, Pennsylvania.

83. On the Tuscarawas River at a point about five miles east of Coshocton, Ohio, also known as Conchake, the Wyandot Indian Town (*ca.* 1748–1753). This Indian town was founded by the rebel Wyandot or Huron Chief Nicholas who, fearing the Ottawas, fled from Detroit to Sandusky. When he deserted the French and went over to the English interest, Chief Nicholas left Sandusky and went to the banks of the Tuscarawas. —Lawrence Gipson, *The British Empire Before the American Revolution* . . . (New York, Alfred A. Knopf, 1939), IV, 173-77.

84. The course led from the east side of the Big Beaver, passing near present West Salem, Pennsylvania, to the vicinity of Lisbon, Ohio, (Gist [Darlington edition], *op. cit.,* pp. 102-03). This was the Great Trail from Fort Pitt to Fort Detroit, which followed the north bank of the Ohio River from Fort Pitt to the mouth of the Beaver, thence along the watershed to the "Crossing-Place of the Muskingum" (Bolivar, Ohio).

Bouquet, in his journal of his expedition against the Ohio Indians in 1764, mentions that somewhere between camps numbers seven and eight the "path divided into two branches, that to the southwest leading to the lower towns upon the Muskingum. In the forks of the path stand several trees painted by the Indians, in a hieroglyphic manner, denoting the number of wars in which they have engaged, and the particulars of their success in prisoners and scalps." —Hulbert names this crossing "Painted Post." Archer B. Hulbert, *Indian Thoroughfares* . . . (Cleveland, Ohio, Arthur H. Clark Co., 1902), p. 108; [William Smith], *An Historical Account of the Expedition Against the Ohio Indians, in the Year MDCCLXIV, Under the Command of Henry Bouquet, Esq.* . . . (Philadelphia, Printed: London, Reprinted for T. Jefferies, 1766), pp. 11-12.

85. The west branch of Little Beaver Creek. Thomas Hutchins, "A Topographical Plan of the Part of the Indian Country Through Which the Army under the Command of Colonel Bouquet Marched in the Year 1764." —*Map* in William Smith, *op. cit.*

86. After crossing the west branch of the Little Beaver the trail crossed the upper reaches of Yellow Creek and a series of small north-flowing tributaries of the present Big Sandy Creek, a tributary of the Tuscarawas or east branch of the Muskingum River. —*Ibid.*

Annotations

87. Interpolated on a present map of Ohio, Gist's course from November 27 to December 5 was, in general, approximately from Lisbon, Ohio, across the northwest corner of Wayne Township, Columbiana County, to Bayard, to Oneida, Carroll county.

88. Present Big Sandy Creek.

89. This town may have had its roots in the Ottawa town mentioned in Sieur Navarre's report on the Indian settlements at the White River to Pierre Joseph de Céloron, French commandant at Detroit in 1743. In this region Navarre found five or six cabins of the Ottawas who had asked the Senecas (Six Nations) "for a smallpiece of land, in order to light a little fire." Navarre adds, "The greater part of these Ottawas are bad people who only established themselves in this place in order to be able to go more easily to Chouegen (Oswego), an English trading post in the Seneca country in New York." —Navarre's "Report," as printed in Hanna, *op. cit.*, I, 317-18.

The location, White River of the French in the early 1700's, has been a controversial subject for many historians. Lawrence Gipson reviews the subject in detail and concludes that the French were referring to the region around the headwaters of the present Cuyahoga River, in Ohio (Gipson, *op. cit.*, IV, 169-71, 61*n*). Also there is evidence that this White River region coveted by the French may have included the upper reaches of the Muskingum. Pennsylvania traders who were active at Muskingum and Tuscarawas by 1750 had well-established storehouses built at the request of the Six Nations and the English *(Ohio Company Papers, 1753–1817, Being Primarily Papers of the "Suffering Traders" of Pennsylvania,* by Kenneth P. Bailey, Arcata, California, 1947, pp. 78, 102). De Longueuil, in 1744, directed the several nations of Indians living around Detroit to march to find and destroy the English traders at the White River and the Ohio (Gipson, *op. cit.*, IV, 168-69). D'Anville in his map of 1746 calls the Muskingum, the White River (Hanna, *op. cit.*, I, 332). Lewis Evans on his *A General Map of the Middle British Colonies, In America:* . . . (Published According to Act of Parliament, By Lewis Evans, June 23, 1755. And Sold by R. Dodsley, in Pall-Mall, London, & by the Author in Philadelphia) shows a portage of but one mile between the Cuyahoga and a branch of the Muskingum. He also locates the Indian town Tuscarawas on the west bank of Elk's Eye Creek, present Big Sandy.

Camp No. 12 of Bouquet's expedition was at Tuscarawas. Here Bouquet received a message that the chiefs of the Delaware and

Annotations

Shawnee were hastening there to treat with him (William Smith, *op. cit.,* pp. 12-13).

The Ottawas had deserted this village by 1755, when the Delawares from near Fort Duquesne established King Beaver's Town or Tuscarawas (Hanna, *op. cit.,* II, 183). Tuscarawas town is marked on Evans', *A General Map of the Middle British Colonies, op. cit.*

Fort Laurens of Revolutionary time was located here, near the town of present Bolivar, Ohio. Gist (Darlington edition), *op. cit.,* pp. 103-05.

The Ottawas or upper Algonquians are of the western branch of the Algonquian tribe whose early habitat was along Georgian Bay. Gradually they moved westward to the shores of Lake Superior (Frederick Hodge, ed., *Handbook of American Indians North of Mexico* [Washington Government Printing Office, 1907–10], II, 168). Although spoken of as ancient friends of the French (*N.Y.C.D.,* IX, 171), they had, according to Governor Dongan of New York, traded at Albany ever since it was founded. Dongan also relates that in 1683, for the first time in New York's history, some traders went to the far Indians called the Ottawas whose habitation was about three months' journey to the west and west northwest of Albany. These traders brought back many beaver skins and the report that the Ottawas were more inclined to trade with the English than with the French (*ibid.,* III, 510, 395). Truly a vacillating nation, the Ottawas were both friend and enemy to other Indian tribes, to the French, and to the English. They quarreled with the Hurons, then banded with English-loving Chief Nicholas against the French in 1748; they were allied with the French at Braddock's defeat and later had as their chief the infamous Pontiac.

90. Maconce, a French interpreter from Saguin's (Seguin's) trading house on the Cuyahoga River. In 1742 Sieur Navarre reported that "one named Maconce offered to deliver a letter to the English" governor to inform him of the bad behavior of the English traders. —Hanna, *op. cit.,* I, 316. Probably Jean Tafar, alias Maconts, who went with his uncle, Mr. Montour, on a mission to the far Indian nations in 1708.

91. Assarigoa, or Long Knife, the Indian name given Francis Howard, fifth Lord of Effingham, governor of Virginia, in 1684, when he treated with the Iroquois at Albany ("Conference between Governor Spotswood and the Five Nations," 1722, printed in *N.Y.C.D.,* V, 670). Hereafter all Virginians, especially the governors, were known by that Iroquois name.

Annotations

92. Present Sugar Creek which empties into the Tuscarawas at Dover, Ohio (Gist [Darlington edition], *op. cit.,* p. 105). The trail crossed in the vicinity of what was known as Broad Run, about a mile south of the town of Strasburgh. —Charles Mitchener, ed., *Historic Events in the Tuscarawas and Muskingum Valleys, and in Other Portions of the State of Ohio* (Dayton, Ohio, Thomas W. Odell, Publisher, 1876), p. 76.

93. In 1738 the Wyandot (English) or Huron (French) Indians living with the Ottawas at Detroit asked permission of the French to migrate to Montreal, for the Ottawas, resentful of a peace concluded between the Hurons and their traditional enemies, the Flatheads, had turned against the Hurons and threatened to exterminate them. This leave was granted the Hurons, but "the drunken Angouirot," the third chief of the tribe, opposed the move. Caustic remarks by the chief at Sault St. Louis (Montreal) about the peace between the Hurons and the Flatheads and fear of loss of prestige in fleeing under pressure from an enemy prevented this migration. The Huron planting grounds had for some years been at Sandusky, in the vicinity of present Venice, Ohio. Here they met English traders and by July 14, 1741, the French recognized the loss of the Sandusky Hurons. —Wisconsin Historical Society *Collections,* XVII, 280, 328, 331-32, 349-50.

In 1742 more Detroit Hurons, under the leadership of Chief Nicholas, joined Angouirot at Sandusky where the tribe was under the influence of English traders. Chief Nicholas not only weaned the Hurons away from the French orbit, but also gathered in his sphere many of the other tribes living in the Ohio Country. A massacre of French traders in 1747 and discovery of the rebel Indians' plot against Detroit caused Chief Nicholas to flee from Sandusky early in 1748 and establish himself and his band on the Muskingum (Gipson, *op. cit.,* IV, 173-85). In September, 1748, Conrad Weiser held council with the chiefs of the Wyandots at Logstown on the Ohio. The chiefs informed him that there were 100 fighting men of the Wyandots who had come over to join the English, of which 70 were left behind at another town, but they hoped that they would follow them. —"Journal of Conrad Weiser . . . ," 1748, *op. cit.*

94. Meaning the chief's house.

95. In 1750 a trading house was built by Teaffe and Callender (partners of George Croghan) "at Muskingum River which said River Runs into the Ohio." This trading house was built "by the direction

Annotations

of the Six Nations of Indians in Alliance with the English." In 1756 George Croghan valued this storehouse at £150. —*The Ohio Company, 1753–1817, op. cit.,* pp. 61, 136.

96. The four English traders were Luke Irwin [Erwin] of Philadelphia, Joseph Fortiner [Faulkner] of New York, Thomas Bourke [Burk] of Lancaster, and George Pathon [John Patten] of Wilmington. All were traders, licensed in Philadelphia. For full details read "Extract of the interrogatories of the four English traders, taken upon the territories of France," printed in *The Conduct of the Late Ministry, or A Memorial; Containing a Summary of Facts with their Vouchers, in Answer to The Observations, sent by the English Ministry, to the Courts of Europe* . . . (London, W. Bizet, 1757), pp. 92-106. See also *Case, facs.,* p. 9; *note* 98.

97. The Shawnee had several towns along the Ohio River, the principal one being Lower Shawnee Town at the mouth of the Scioto.

98. About 1672 the Miami, a western tribe of the Algonquins, were driven by the Sioux Indians from their home around Lake Superior. The next 30 years' history reveals their migrations to the River St. Joseph, to the land north of Detroit, and to the vicinity of Green Bay, Wisconsin. The struggle between the French and English for favor with the Miami began in about 1702, when a Huron chief in the English interest established himself on the River Maumee and attempted to make an alliance with the Miami of the River St. Joseph. In the same year the French governor invited savages, including the Miami, to come and settle near the French fort at Detroit. The period, 1706–08, was one of turmoil around Detroit. At one time other savages reported that the Miami were masters of the French fort. The French made peace with them in 1708. Four years later the Miami informed the French that they intended to "abandon their village and build another on the Oyou, in the fond of Lake Erie." This Miami village, located in the bend of the Maumee on the site of present Fort Wayne, Indiana, was Fort Miami (English) or Kiskakon (French). For many years the Miami wavered in their affections for the French and English. They were trading in Albany in 1719. In 1721 Charlevoix relates in his *Journal Historique* that there were three principal Miami villages, one on the River St. Joseph; another, Kiskakon, on the Maumee River that flows into Lake Erie; and the third on the Wabash which flows into the Mississippi. —Wisconsin Historical Society *Collections,* XVI, 84, 99, 127, 146, 211-13, 239, 254, 285, 382-83, 409-10.

Annotations

About 1733 some Miami from Kiskakon withdrew and established Pickawillany (French) or Twightwee Town (English) on the upper Great Miami River. The French spent much time and effort to keep them "away from the snares of the English"; nevertheless, by 1747 their chief had come under the influence of Chief Nicholas, the English-loving Huron (*ibid.*, XVII, 185-86, 210-11, 484-85, 505-06). In July, 1748, they requested an alliance with the English. The outcome was *A Treaty Held by Commissioners, Members of the Council of the Province of Pennsylvania, At the Town of Lancaster, with some Chiefs of the Six Nations at Ohio, and Others, for the Admission of the Twightwee Nation into the Alliance of his Majesty, &c. in the Month of July, 1748, op. cit.*

Chief Nicholas died in 1748, but La Demoiselle, the Miami chief at Pickawillany, continued the revolt of the Ohio Indians against the French. The Miami openly traded with the English, encouraged Pennsylvania traders, especially George Croghan, to build storehouses among them, and in their quarrel with the French sought assistance from the English governors and their Indian allies (Minutes of a Conference held with the Indians at Mr. Croghan's, May 17, 1750, printed in *Colonial Records of Pennsylvania*, V, 431-35). See also note 80.

Just as vigorously as the Miami sought an alliance with the English and their Indian allies, so did the French seek to regain this rebel band. In 1749 Céloron vainly attempted to persuade La Demoiselle and his band to return to the French fort, Miami (Kiskakon). Persuasion having failed, the French, in 1751, planned to use armed force against the Miami. Since the few Indians in the French interest claimed that there was not a French force sufficient to bring La Demoiselle to terms, the devastating 1751 foray, which was ordered by the French, never took place; but on June 21, 1752, Pickawillany was destroyed by a force of several hundred fierce Ottawas and Chippewas under the command of Charles Michel Langlade. —Gipson, *op. cit.*, IV, 199-222.

The town was located on the Great Miami at the mouth of Loramie Creek near the site of present Piqua, Ohio.

99. The two of the four traders captured (*note* 96) were Luke Irwin and Joseph Fortiner (Faulkner). —Wisconsin Historical Society *Collections*, XVIII, 112n.

100. Probably "Fort Sandoski, which is a small Pallisadoed Fort, with about 20 Men lying on the South side of Lake Erie, and was built

Annotations

the latter end of the Year 1750" ("A Journal or Account of the Capture of John Pattin," *Pennsylvania Magazine of History and Biography* [Philadelphia, Publication Fund of the Historical Society of Pennsylvania, 1877–date], LXV, 427). Near the north shore of Sandusky Bay. Hanna, *op. cit.*, II, 189.

101. Thomas Burney, itinerant blacksmith, Indian trader, courier, and soldier, may have been a blacksmith in the Ohio Country as early as 1742. Navarre (see *note* 89) reports that "forty leagues from the French house (Saguin's) going towards the River Ohio, there is an English blacksmith whom five or six families of the Loups have stopped" (Hanna, *op. cit.*, I, 316). Gist found him at his trade at Muskingum in 1750. Blacksmith and Indian trader Burney was one of the two traders who escaped from Pickawillany when the French destroyed it in 1752 (*Trent's Journal . . . 1752, op. cit.*, p. 86). Courier Burney carried a message from the vanquished Twightwee to Governor Dinwiddie (1752); brought Dinwiddie's response back to the Twightwee (1753); was the bearer of Half King's and Scarouady's message to Governor Dinwiddie (June, 1753); substituted for Christopher Gist as bearer of Virginia's special message to the Half King (August, 1753); and served regularly as courier for William Trent, George Washington, and Governor Dinwiddie in late 1753 and 1754 (*ibid.*, p. 76; *Colonial Records of Pennsylvania*, V, 635; P.R.O., C.O. 5: 1327/15-40). Militiaman Burney served under Andrew Lewis at the Battle of Fort Necessity and with General Braddock, in whose campaign he lost his life. —Washington's *Journal of 1754* (Toner edition), *op. cit.*, p. 174; *The Ohio Company, 1753–1817, op. cit.*, p. 61.

102. According to legend this woman, known as "The Newcomer," was a white captive of Eagle Feather, the Indian husband of Mary Harris. Eagle Feather was mysteriously killed in his sleep and "The Newcomer" had fled. Mary Harris willingly placed the blame on "The Newcomer." "Mary Harris insisted that the 'newcomer' killed her husband with his own hatchet, in revenge for being brought into captivity, while she, as tradition gives it, alleged that Mary did the work out of jealousy, and intended dispatching her also, but was defeated in her project by the flight of 'newcomer.'" —Mitchener, *op. cit.*, pp. 106-09.

103. Probably John Patten who was taken captive by the French in November, 1750. See also *note* 96.

Annotations

104. White Woman's Town. Named for Mary Harris, the white woman who as a child was taken captive in New England and spent a happy life among the Indians. Taken at Deerfield, February 29, 1704 (John Williams, *Redeemed Captive Returning to Zion:* . . . 6th edition [Boston, Samuel Hall, 1795], p. 108). White Woman's Town was on the south side of the White Woman's Creek or Walhonding River, opposite the mouth of Killbuck Creek. —Hanna, *op. cit.,* II, 149n. See also *note* 102.

In early times Killbuck River, now the Walhonding, was called White Woman's Creek, from the town to its entrance into the Muskingum. Mitchener, *op. cit.,* p. 107.

105. This present, applied for by Thomas Lee on October 18, 1749, was not given to the Indians until June, 1752, at the conference at Logstown. In his application to the Board of Trade on October 18, 1749, Thomas Lee reports that the Indians, having been incited by the Pennsylvania traders, were not so friendly to the Ohio Company as they were at the time their grant was given and that without treaties and presents nothing could be done with them (letter in P.R.O., C.O. 5: 1327/195-97). On June 12, 1750, Lee acknowledged the receipt of the Indian present for the Six Nations and tribes on the Ohio and, in sending Conrad Weiser with an invitation, took the best measure he could think of to bring those nations to Fredericksburg. In order to make peace between the northern and southern Indians, he also invited the Catawba to the meeting (letter in P.R.O., C.O. 5: 1327/187-89). The present sent was not in answer to Lee's plea, for his letter was not received in England until months after the gifts had arrived in Virginia (P.R.O., C.O. 5: 1327/195-97, endorsement). Such action, before Lee's letter was received, undoubtedly was in response to the Ohio Company's requesting John Hanbury to recommend this action on the part of the Board of Trade. Hanbury was so anxious that the good will of the Indians be purchased so the Ohio Company could take up their lands that "he paid the money for them before he received it and would not charge any commission for the buying of them so that there is a large quantity" (Penn to Peters, February 24, 1751. Penn MSS Supplement, Saunders-Coates, 1720–1766, p. 39, in Historical Society of Pennsylvania). The present consisted, among other things, of fine woolens and gunpowder. In fact, the goods were so fine that James Patton, one of the commissioners appointed for the Logstown Conference, advised the Executive Council that the goods were "too rich" for the Indians and should be exchanged for the more suitable Indian goods (Virginia Council *Journals,* V, 376).

Annotations

The Six Nations refused to come to Fredericksburg in 1750 (Lee to Weiser, June 21, 1750, Peters Papers, III, 9, Historical Society of Pennsylvania), and the Ohio and western Indians refused to travel to Virginia in 1751 to receive the present (Gist's Journals, January 14, 1751, printed p. 14). Finally, the western Indians sent word that they would receive the King's gift and speech at Logstown on the Ohio in 1752 (*Colonial Records of Pennsylvania*, V, 537). The present had been stored all this time at Fredericksburg, Virginia, and on December 12, 1751, the Executive Council ordered it to be removed from storage, to be exchanged for suitable goods as Patton advised, and to be forwarded by Anthony Struther from Fredericksburg, Virginia, to Frederick Town, Maryland, from whence Thomas Cresap, at the price of a pistole per hundred, transported it to Logstown on the Ohio (Virginia Council *Journals*, V, 374). The present was subjected to extreme weather conditions; yet so well protected by tarpaulins that, when it was spread beneath the arbor of Logstown, even the woolens were not damaged by rain (see p. 56). Only part of this gift was distributed there, the remainder being taken by William Trent to Pickawillany in the Miami Country (see *note* 307). William Trent and Andrew Montour loaded the goods on pack horses, and on June 21, 1752, set out from Logstown; but, before they arrived, the English village of Pickawillany was destroyed and the Miami scattered. Finally, after a round trip of almost 700 miles, Trent was able to deliver the last of this present to the widow of La Demoiselle, famous Miami chief, to his young son, and to the few remaining Miami. —Trent's *Journal . . . 1752, op. cit.*, pp. 84, 85, 92, 93 ff.

106. The answer to Gist's request was given via Pennsylvania at Logstown on May 29, 1751. There the Indians informed the Virginians that they, in view of the French threat and the fact that they were "a poor People and at War with the Southward Indians," could not travel so far afield, but would expect the Virginians to treat with them at Logstown where Pennsylvania had kindled their Council Fire. —*Colonial Records of Pennsylvania*, V, 537.

107. Two hundred Abenakis and Caughnawagas and 50 Canadians commanded by Hertel de Rouville led the raid. —Francis Parkman, *A Half Century of Conflict* (Boston, Little, Brown & Co., 1892), I, 53.

108. The trail from White Woman's Town southwest to Licking River was through Coshocton County, passing near present Dresden to Clay Lick Station, six miles east of Newark. —Gist (Darlington edition), *op. cit.*, p. 115.

Annotations

109. Colonel James Smith, while an Indian captive camped at a buffalo lick, where the Indians "in their small brass kettles made about half a bushel of salt." Smith said this buffalo lick was somewhere between the Muskingum and the Scioto. —James Smith, *An Account of the Remarkable Occurrences in the Life and Travels of . . . during his Captivity with the Indians, in the Years 1755, '56, '57, '58, & '59 . . .* (Lexington, John Bradford, 1799), p. 13.

110. On the site of present Lancaster, Fairfield County, Ohio. Formerly French Margaret's Town, the residence of Margaret Montour, relative of the famous Madame Montour and wife of Peter Quebec. The Moravian missionary, Martin Mack, in his journal of 1753 speaks of her as Madame Montour's niece, but the same year Chief Shikellamy told Governor Gordon that she was Madame Montour's daughter. French Margaret had left the Ohio before Gist's arrival. In 1745 she was at the Big Island in the West Branch of the Susquehanna (Lock Haven), on her way to Philadelphia; in 1753, at her headquarters on the Susquehanna at the mouth of Lycoming Creek (Williamsport); in 1754, at Bethlehem, en route to New York; in 1758, at the Treaty at Easton; and in 1760, near Tioga at the house of her son-in-law, a Minsi chief. —Wallace, *op. cit.*, pp. 488, 524; Hanna, *op. cit.*, II, 204-06.

Near the beginning of the eighteenth century the Delawares who occupied a greater part of New Jersey, Delaware, eastern Pennsylvania, and New York were subdued by the Iroquois. After this time they gradually moved westward, and in 1751 a group was invited by the Hurons or Wyandots to settle on the Muskingum and other streams in eastern Ohio. —Hodge, *op. cit.*, I, 385.

111. Located between Scippo Creek and the Scioto River, about three and one-half miles south of present Circleville, Pickaway County, Ohio ("Map of the Ancient Shawanoese Towns, on the Pickaway Plain" in Henry Howe, *Historical Collections of Ohio . . .* [Cincinnati, Derby, Bradley & Co., 1848], p. 402). Highway U.S. 23 from Circleville to Kentucky traverses the Pickaway Plains. Two miles from Circleville one has an excellent view of them. Elliptical in contour, they measure seven miles long and four miles in diameter at their greatest width. The upper or largest plains are 150 feet above the level of the Scioto River. —Writers' Program. Ohio, *The Ohio Guide* (N. Y., Oxford University Press [c1940]), p. 571.

112. Hurricane Tom's Town, probably the "Shawanese Salt Lick

Annotations

Town" on the Scioto, mentioned in a letter from Colonel Bouquet to Sir William Johnson, May 31, 1764 (Hanna, *op. cit.*, II, 385). On U.S. highway route number 23, which follows the Scioto River from Circleville to Portsmouth, it is 17 miles from the Pickaway Plains to Chillicothe, Ohio (Writers' Program. Ohio, *op. cit.*, pp. 752-73). Gist traveled 15 miles, according to his own measuring, from Maguck to Hurricane Tom's Town located near present Chillicothe, Ohio.

Hurricane Tom must have deserted the English cause sometime before 1756. Although, from 1750 to 1756, the English trusted him for much trade goods, he, as captain of a "gang of Indian warriors," robbed Pat Mullen, a Pennsylvania trader, of almost £100 worth of buckskins. —*The Ohio Company, 1753–1817, op. cit.*, pp. 52, 53, 111, 134.

113. When the state of Ohio was created, in 1803, Congress set apart tracts of land in this region for the use of the state. The next year the Ohio legislature provided by law for the regulation and management of the salt industry on this reserve. The Great Scioto Salt Works was located in this region, near the site of present Salt Springs, Ohio. Salt Creek, flowing west, empties into the Scioto in Jefferson Township, Ross County, Ohio. —Writers' Program. Ohio, *op. cit.*, p. 516; S. P. Hildreth's "History of an Early Voyage on the Ohio and Mississippi Rivers . . . , " printed in *The American Pioneer* (Chillicothe, Ohio, J. S. Williams, 1842), I, 97.

114. Windaughalah, or the Council Door, was a Delaware chief whose name appears in Pennsylvania history from 1748 to 1785. In 1748 he bought trade goods from James Lowry, Michael Teaffe, and John Owens, traders at Lower Shawnee Town (*The Ohio Company, 1753–1817, op. cit.*, pp. 110, 132, 146). Windaughalah also attended Indian conferences at Pittsburgh in 1759 (*Colonial Records of Pennsylvania*, VIII, 383); at Lancaster in 1762 (Pennsylvania [Colony] Treaties, etc., 1762, *Minutes of Conferences, Held at Lancaster, in August, 1762*. Philadelphia, Printed and Sold by B. Franklin and D. Hall, 1763); again at Pittsburgh in 1774 (*Pennsylvania Archives*, IV, 531-33); and at Fort McIntosh in 1785 (Pennsylvania. General Assembly, *Minutes of the First Session of the Ninth General Assembly* . . . , pp. 322-28). "Wandachales Town" is located on the east bank of the Scioto, not far from its junction with the Ohio (Lewis Evans' *A General Map of the Middle British Colonies, op. cit.*). "Wanduxales" is given the same location on Thomas Hutchins' *A New Map*

Annotations

of the Western Parts of Virginia, Pennsylvania, Maryland and North Carolina; ... (London, T. Hutchins, 1778).

115. Of this grain George Mercer gave the following description: "The Wild Rye, which grows every where in the Ohio Country, is a Species of the Rye which is cultivated by the Europeans. It has the same bearded Ear, and produces a farinaceous Grain. The Ear and Grain, in the wild State of this Plant, are less, and the Beard of the Ear is longer than those of the cultivated Rye, which makes this wild Plant resemble more the Rye-grass in its Appearance; but it differs in no other Respect from the Rye, and it shoots in its spontaneous Vegetation about the Middle of November as the cultivated Rye doth."—Thomas Pownall, *Topographical Descriptions* ... (Mulkearn edition), *op. cit.,* p. 26.

116. Lower Shawnee Town or Shawnee villages in the Scioto region figure in historical documents from 1673 to the American Revolution. William E. Meyer interprets Gabriel Arthur's account of his captivity in 1673 and 1674 to mean that there was in that early time a "Shawnee village near the present site of Portsmouth, Ohio." —U.S. Bureau of Ethnology, *Annual Reports* . . . (Washington, U.S. Government Printing Office, 1879/80–1930/31), XLII, 736.

In 1731 the Shawnee traveled to Montreal to ask Sieur Marquis de Beauharnois, the governor of New France, "to indicate the place where he wished to place them." In reply Beauharnois ordered Sieur La Joncaire to accompany them to the north bank of the Ohio (Wisconsin Historical Society *Collections,* XVII, 156). There is no direct evidence that they were directed to Lower Shawnee Town. By 1736 La Joncaire reported his mission was completed, that the Shawnee were located on the Beautiful River (Ohio), and that they would not remove themselves without the orders from the French governors who had lighted the fire for them at that place (*ibid.,* 243). Again there is no specific information that the Council Fire was lighted at Lower Shawnee Town; however, Céloron recorded that Longueuil held a conference there with the Shawnee while on his journey to Louisiana in 1739 (Galbreath, *op. cit.,* p. 45). In 1747 Kinousaki, the loyal French Huron chief, spoke of the Shawnee at Scioto (*N.Y.C.D.,* X, 162). A letter of 1748 from the French minister to Galissonière revealed that the Shawnee from around Detroit decided to leave and settle in the direction of La Belle Rivière. The letter continued, "since the war [King George's, 1744–48] they have been joined by a considerable number of savages of all nations, forming a sort of republic

Annotations

dominated by the Iroquois or Five Nations who form part of it, and that, as the English almost entirely supply their needs, it is to be feared that they may succeed in seducing them" (Wisconsin Historical Society *Collections,* XVIII, 11-12).

The Indians from English-controlled territory began their migration westward about 1730. Peter Chartier, the half-breed turncoat, who began negotiations with the French at Detroit before 1740, led a band of Shawnee from the Allegheny to French-dominated Ohio (*ibid.,* XVII, 331). This alliance lasted but a few years. Lack of French trade goods and antipathy for other Indians caused the Shawnee to desert the French at Detroit, part migrating to Scioto (Lower Shawnee Town) and the others with Chartier to the south among the Alabama Indians *(ibid.,* XVIII, 20 and 20*n*). When Gist visited Lower Shawnee Town it was inhabited by Shawnee, some of whom had remained loyal to the English and some of whom had for a time followed Chartier to the French; and by Iroquois, Delawares, and other groups of Indians allied to the English. The French, alarmed by the persuasive power of abundant English trade goods at Lower Shawnee Town, attempted to woo the Shawnee back into the French sphere of influence and so weaken the "republic" (*ibid.,* 21). Céloron tried in vain, in 1749, to induce the Shawnee to leave "St. Yotoc" (Lower Shawnee Town) and return to Detroit. He reported that the native village of 80 to 100 huts was inhabited for the most part by Shawnee, Iroquois with a few Indians from the Sault St. Louis Mission (Montreal) and the Lake of the Two Mountains, Miami, Loups (Delawares), and others from Upper Country tribes, all entirely devoted to the English (*ibid.,* 45). The Indians at Scioto remained in the English interest, and Lower Shawnee Town became a center from which English traders carried on a lucrative trade in all directions. With the fall of Fort Duquesne, George Croghan, the Lowry brothers, Michael Teaffe, William Trent, and others lost huge sums in outstanding debts of the Indians and in goods confiscated by the French. Daniel and Alexander Lowry alone placed their losses at £1,877 15*s.* 9*d.* (*The Ohio Company, 1753–1817, op. cit.,* p. 121). Although George Croghan reported the town destroyed by flood waters in 1753 (Hanna, *op. cit.,* II, 129), the Lowry brothers attributed their loss to the taking of Fort Duquesne.

The town is described as located on both the east and west banks of the Scioto at its mouth and, in part, on the south shore of the Ohio (near the site of present Portsmouth, Ohio, and Alexandria, Ky.).

117. In 1693 the Shawnee, traditional enemies of the Five Nations,

Annotations

traveled to Albany to make peace with them (*N.Y.C.D.*, IV, 43). At the same time the Five Nations informed Governor Fletcher of New York and Pennsylvania that they were pleased because the Shawnee, their enemies, had applied to Pennsylvania for protection, and because his colonies had sent them to the Five Nations to "endeavour a peace" (Cadwallader Colden, *The History of the Five Indian Nations* . . . , 3d edition [London, Lockyer Davis, 1755], I, 162-63). Evidently the peace was made, for the next year the Shawnee were admitted into friendly relations with the Five Nations (Hanna, *op. cit.*, I, 142). Hereafter the Shawnee looked upon the Five Nations as their guardians, and in 1737 informed them that since the Cayugas and Senecas had sold to Pennsylvania the lands upon the Susquehanna which they inhabited, they had asked for shelter among tribes to the westward. Intercession of colonial power did not prevent their migration, but in 1739 Pennsylvania did succeed in obtaining from the Shawnee a confirmation of the "Articles of Agreement" or treaty of amity (April 23, 1701) entered into by William Penn, the governor of Pennsylvania, and the Shawnee chiefs then living about the northern part of the Potomac River. —*Colonial Records of Pennsylvania,* IV, 346-47.

118. On May 26, 1750, Morris Turner and Ralph Kilgore, in the employ of John Fraser and James Young of Lancaster County, Pennsylvania, were taken captive by the French at Mad Creek, about 25 miles from Pickawillany. While on their way to Canada, somewhere between Niagara and Oswego they escaped, made their way south, and arrived in Philadelphia early in October, 1750, via Fort Oswego and New York. —Deposition printed in *Colonial Records of Pennsylvania,* V, 482-84.

119. Probably "Fort Sandoski, which is a small Pallisadoed Fort, with about 20 Men lying on the South side of Lake Erie, and was built the latter end of the Year 1750." —"A Journal or Account of the Capture of John Pattin." *Op. cit.*

120. Conrad Weiser, on February 4, 1743, at Shamokin met leading men of the Shawnee, "the oldest of them was Missemediqueety, a Captain of War, and a very noted Man among the Shawonese; the English call him the great Huminy" ("Conrad Weiser's Report of his Journey to Shamokin," January 30–February 9, 1743, *op. cit.*) In 1748, at Logstown, Weiser met "big Hominy & the Pride, those that went off with Chartier, but protested against his proceedings against our Traders" ("The Journal of Conrad Weiser," September 29, 1748,

Annotations

op. cit.). Big Hominy also attended Virginia's conference at Logstown in 1752 (see p. 56, this work). His outstanding debts due various Indian traders in 1756 amounted to £91 12s. 6d. (*The Ohio Company, 1753-1817, op. cit.,* pp. 47, 50, 56, 110, 119, 138). The last recorded transaction was of April 10, 1753. *Ibid.,* p. 119.

121. Since Virginia's invitation was to treat at Fredericksburg, this answer must have been directed to the Pennsylvanians.

122. Kakawatcheky was a chief among the Shawnee for at least 43 years. He ruled over the Shawnee settlements on the Delaware River from 1709 to 1728 and at Wyoming (near the present site of Plymouth, Pennsylvania) from 1728 to 1743 or 1744, when he removed to Logstown on the Ohio. Although the Shawnee were at this time under the influence of Peter Chartier, Kakawatcheky refused to desert the English cause and follow Chartier to French-dominated territory. In 1745 he and Newcomer, another Shawnee chief, were living "at Allegheny and have done great service to the traders." Richard Peters reported that Kakawatcheky had declared that they, the French and their Indian followers, "shall cut him to pieces before he will quit the friendship of the Proprietaries and that he will not remove an inch from his old place of residence nor none of his relations shall" (Peters to Penn, June 25, 1745. *Op. cit.).* From Logstown (1748) Weiser reported that Kakawatcheky was ill and childish. In his report of the Pennsylvania Logstown Conference in 1751 George Croghan stated that Kakawatcheky could not attend the conference on account of his great age. At the Virginia Logstown Conference (1752) the commissioners, understanding that the chief "Cockawichy" was bedridden, showed appreciation for his past services by presenting him with a suit of Indian clothing.

Kakawatcheky may have lived years after 1752. Paul Wallace interprets a message of 1755 "from the Adherents and Friends of Cachanatreka to the Governors of Pennsylvania and Virginia" as a message sent from the old chief himself (*Colonial Records of Pennsylvania* VI, 568). Wallace also presents "The Speech of Ackowanthio, an old Indian on the Ohio, in behalf of the Delaware Indians and others living on the Waters thereof. September 1758" as possible evidence that Kakawatcheky may have been living at that late date. —Wallace, *op. cit.,* p. 529.

123. The description of this festival is not appended to this variant of Gist's journal but was included in the copy made for the Ohio Company. Printed on pp. 121-122.

Annotations

124. Wea or Ouatonon, a subtribe of the Miami whom the Jesuits found in eastern Wisconsin in 1673. Later they moved to the Illinois Country on the banks of the Wabash River. Ouiatenon, the village on the Wabash, was also the principal headquarters for the French traders. —Hodge, *op. cit.*, II, 925. See also *note* 128.

125. The course was northwest from the mouth of the Scioto River through Scioto, Adams, Highland, Fayette, Madison, Clarke, and Champaign Counties to present West Liberty, Logan County, Ohio, a distance of about 140 miles. Gist (Darlington edition), *op. cit.* p. 123.

126. Mad River, not the Little Miami.

127. La Demoiselle or Old Britain, the famous Miami chief who led the revolt of the western Indians against the French. See *note* 98.

128. The Miami recognized four subtribes within their nation. A message from the Twightwees to the governor of Pennsylvania (1750) was sent by "The Four Miamy Nation of Indians" (*Colonial Records of Pennsylvania,* V, 437-38)—Twightwees, Weas, Piankashaws, and Tepicons. See *notes* 98 and 124. —Hodge, *op. cit.*, II, 228-29; Wisconsin Historical Society *Collections,* XVII, 485.

129. According to French reports, La Demoiselle was at this time organizing all the Indians in the Ohio Country for a general revolt against the French; and the Cahokias, Peorias, Weas, Piankashaws, Delawares, Shawnee, and the Five Iroquois Nations were to have a meeting at La Demoiselle's in 1751. The Piankashaws and Weas were Miami; the Cahokias and Peorias, Illinois; the others, tribes firmly attached to the English. —Wisconsin Historical Society *Collections,* XVIII, 111-12.

130. From 1747 to 1750 the Twightwees carried on, to this effect, a vigorous correspondence with Pennsylvania and her Indian allies, most of which is printed in *Colonial Records of Pennsylvania,* V, 308ff.

131. Refers to Algonquin language. —Hodge, *op. cit.*, I, 786, 867.

132. Mingos, a small band of Indians who left the main body of the Iroquois before 1750 and settled on the upper Ohio, gradually moving down that river and into what is now Ohio, where they mingled freely with the other tribes. —*Ibid.*, I, 867-68.

Annotations

133. Montour was the intermediary between "the tribes of Indians at Ohio and elsewhere in amity with the English" and the Twightwees. Previous messages sent via Montour are printed in *Colonial Records of Pennsylvania,* V, 308-09.

134. Although Gist makes no mention of activities, the treaty made between George Croghan and Andrew Montour, on the one part, and the Weas and Piankashaws, on the other, was witnessed by Christopher Gist on this day. —*Ibid.,* 521-24. Treaty printed on pp. 138-39.

135. Catawbas.

136. Lack of French trade goods and antipathy for the other Indian nations living in the French spheres of influence caused the Shawnee to remain in the French interest but a short time. They separated into two bands, one establishing a stronghold or sort of republic at the mouth of the Scioto (Lower Shawnee Town, 1747–1753) and the other joining the Alabama Indians to the south. See also *note* 116.

137. La Mouche Noire or Black Mouth. —Hanna, *op. cit.,* II, 265.

138. Brandy.

139. For names of chiefs see *Treaty* printed on pp. 138-39.

140. Refers to the admission of the Twightwees into the English alliance in 1748. —Pennsylvania (Colony). Treaties, etc., 1748, . . . Lancaster, . . . *for the Admission of the Twightwee Nation into the Alliance of His Majesty, op. cit.;* also printed in *Colonial Records of Pennsylvania,* V, 307-19.

141. La Jonquière's plan was to organize both French and Indians from the Great Lakes region and attack in the spring of 1751. This plan was not carried out. —*N.Y.C.D.,* X, 239. See also *note* 98.

142. The French Miami fort, Kiskakon (*ca.* 1712–1760), was located on the Maumee River on the site of present Fort Wayne, Indiana (Wisconsin Historical Society *Collections,* XVI, 185). The rebel Miami fled from this post about 1747 and established Pickawillany. In 1749, when Captain Raymond was sent as commandant to the fort, "he stopped le pied froid, the Great Chief of the Miamis Nation, and All his Band who were about to abandon that post and Go over to

Annotations

The English" (*ibid.*, XVIII, 95). Father Bonnecamp who accompanied Céloron on his 1749-journey reports that the fort was in a dilapidated state and the French were all ill of "the Fever" (Galbreath's *Céloron, op. cit.*, p. 92). John Patten, who was taken captive at Kiskakon in 1750, described the fort as "small, stock round with Pallisadoes and had at the time he was there a Capt. Lieut. & 50 Men, but that most of these men were traders, who were continually passing to & from, & by what he could learn there were but about 9 or 10 who constantly resided there" (Wisconsin Historical Society *Collections*, XVIII, 114). Kiskakon remained under French control until it was occupied by the English in December, 1760. The English lost control of it on May 10, 1763, when Indians under the influence of Pontiac routed them and destroyed the fort. —*Ibid.*, 226, 250-51.

143. "Tcitahaia, popularly known as the 'feather dance' because the dancers have canes in their hands with feathers fastened at the ends. This is distinctly a peace dance." —U.S. Bureau of American Ethnology. *Annual Reports...*, XLII, 609.

144. The young trader whom Hugh Parker endeavored to engage as a trader for the Ohio Company. In a letter to Smith Parker said he "expected to receive momentarily about 15 or 16 thousand pounds' worth of Indian goods." —*Indian treaties printed by Benjamin Franklin, 1736–1762, . . . historical & bibliographical notes by Julian P. Boyd* (Philadelphia, The Historical Society of Pennsylvania, 1938), lvi.

145. Wabash River.

146. Mr. Darlington assumed that Gist followed the Little Miami River until somewhere in Warren County, Ohio, where he turned northeast to Lower Shawnee Town. —*Gist* (Darlington edition), *op. cit.*, p. 127. See also *note* 116.

147. Tamany Buck or the Pride. Big Hominy, Tamany Buck, and Lawachkamicky (or The Pride) were the three principal chiefs residing at Lower Shawnee Town. Gist saw Big Hominy when he went to Pickawillany. —*Colonial Records of Pennsylvania*, VI, 153.

148. Gist crossed into Greenup County, Kentucky. The Great Warriors' Trail, north and south, from the Cherokee Country to Lake Erie had several branches in upper Kentucky. The trail branched

Annotations

at the Upper Blue Licks, one trail reaching the Ohio at present Vanceburg, Kentucky. From Vanceburg the trail followed the Ohio upstream to a place opposite Lower Shawnee Town. Gist crossed the Ohio at Lower Shawnee Town. The direction and distance traveled given in his journal indicate that he followed this prong of the Great Warriors' Trail to present Vanceburg. —U.S. Bureau of American Ethnology. *Annual Reports* ..., XLII, 779-80.

149. The early explorers found bones, tusks, and teeth, remains of the mammoth that inhabited this region, the valley of Big Bone Creek in Boone County, Kentucky. —Lewis Collins, *History of Kentucky. Revised, Enlarged ... and Brought Down to the Year 1874* ... (Covington, Ky., Collins & Co., 1874), II, 51-52; Gist (Darlington edition), *op. cit.*, pp. 129-30.

150. Big Bone Lick, Boone County, Kentucky.

151. Probably the north fork of the Licking River.

152. The prong of the Great Warriors' Trail from Vanceburg led to "The Great Salt Lick River" (Evans, *A General Map of the Middle British Colonies, op. cit.*) to a place in the vicinity of present Cynthiana, Kentucky. Since Gist did not remark about difficult travel, he may have traveled over this trail to the above-mentioned point. The Shawnee name for the Licking River was Salt River (U.S. Bureau of American Ethnology. *Annual Reports* ..., XLII, 792). Gist was confused in his whereabouts at the time, for the Salt River of today is south of the Kentucky River. He did not cross the Kentucky until days later; therefore, he could not have been at the place described by Robert Smith.

153. Kentucky River. Gist crossed the Kentucky River near the present site of Frankfort, Kentucky (Gist [Darlington edition], *op. cit.*, pp. 130-31). Evidently this report was not written on March 18, for he did not make the crossing until the next day.

154. Meaning Little Cuttawa, present Kentucky River.

155. Tennessee River.

156. On the Kentucky River in the vicinity of the mouth of the Red River (*ibid.*, p. 133). However, it is to be remembered that Gist was

Annotations

following the south shore of the Kentucky. The Red River flows from the northeast into the Kentucky.

157. North fork of the Kentucky River. —*Ibid.,* p. 133.

158. Pound or Stony Gap near Whitesburg, Letcher County, Kentucky (*ibid.,* p. 134). Indian trails from Virginia passed through this historic gap of the Cumberland Mountains to the headwaters of the Kentucky, Cumberland, and Big Sandy Rivers. Pound Gap is on the Virginia-West Virginia state line about 20 miles west of Norton, Virginia. —Federal Writers' Project. Kentucky, *Kentucky, a Guide to the Bluegrass State* (New York, Harcourt, Brace and Company, 1939), p. 242.

159. Pound Creek, fork of the Big Sandy River. —Gist (Darlington edition), *op. cit.,* p. 134.

160. An Indian creek, probably Crane's Nest Creek in Wise County, Virginia.

161. This must have been a camp of the Miami tribe, for the crane is the totem of the Miami. —Hodge, *op. cit.,* I, 862.

162. An Indian trail which the Indians traveled from the Big Sandy to the Bluestone River. —U.S. Bureau of American Ethnology, *Annual Reports* . . . , XLII, 770.

163. On Guesse's [Gist's] Creek or River, a branch of the Clinch, in Wise County, Virginia (Gist [Darlington edition], p. 134). Gist traveled a general course down Gist's Creek to the valley of the Clinch. —Lewis Summers, *History of Southwest Virginia, 1746–1786,* . . . (Richmond, Va., J. L. Hill Printing Company, 1903), p. 48.

164. Gist was traveling through the country that has been called the Switzerland of Virginia. This territory in and around Tazewell County, Virginia, has the appearance of a "tossed bed of mountains." —Edward A. Pollard, *The Virginia Tourist* . . . (Philadelphia, J. B. Lippincott & Co., 1870), pp. 155-56.

165. The route lay along the east side of Dividing or New Garden Ridge between Buchanan and Russell Counties, Virginia.

Annotations

166. In Baptist Valley, Tazewell County, Gist traveled the valley of the Clinch River, on the south side of the ridge dividing the heads of the Big Sandy and Clinch Rivers. He believed the Clinch River was the Kentucky. —Gist (Darlington edition), *op. cit.*, p. 134.

167. In 1753 land on the headwaters of Clinch River and on Bluestone Creek in Abb's Valley was surveyed for William Ingles. The Bluestone was in the vicinity of lands surveyed by both the Greenbrier and Loyal Land Companies. James Patton was the prime mover in the Loyal Land Company, rival of the Ohio Company. —William Pendleton, *History of Tazewell County and Southwest Virginia 1748–1920* (Richmond, Va., W. C. Hill Printing Company, 1920), p. 185.

168. Pinnacle Rock in Pinnacle Rock State Park, Mercer County, West Virginia. —Writers' Program. West Virginia, *West Virginia, A Guide to the Mountain State* (N. Y., Oxford University Press c1941), p. 473.

169. Probably at present Crump's Bottom, Virginia.

170. Peters Mountain.

171. Big Stony Creek, Giles County, Virginia.

172. Salt Pond, a lake of pure fresh water located on top of Salt Pond Mountain, about 16 miles from Christianburg, Montgomery County, Virginia. —Pollard, *op. cit.*, p. 146. —At present this lake is called Mountain Lake.

173. Draper's Meadows, a grant of land given by James Patton to William Ingles and John Draper in 1748, was in this vicinity. Sinking Creek, in Giles County, Virginia, was 15 miles from the Ingles cabin. —Robert Kincaid, *The Wilderness Road* (Indianapolis and New York, The Bobbs-Merrill Company, 1947), pp. 54-55.

174. Richard Hall lived in the vicinity of Reed Creek. Captain William Preston, while on his expedition against the Indians in 1756, spent three days ranging the Reed Creek section. This round trip to Richard Hall's was 15 miles. (U. S. Bureau of American Ethnology, *Annual Reports* . . . , XLII, p. 768). In the vicinity of Blacksburg, the western extent of old Draper's Meadows, about 10 miles west of Christianburg, Virginia.

Annotations

175. Thomas Lee.

176. Now called Reed Island Creek in Carroll County, Virginia. —Gist (Darlington edition), *op. cit.,* p. 136.

177. The pass in the mountains at the dividing line was called Flower Gap. This was not a main trail but a minor one which branched from the Great Trail into Carolina. —Kincaid, *op. cit.,* p. 162.

178. Gist's plantation was on the north side of the Yadkin River and on the west side of the stream marked Saw Mill Creek. Near the present site of Wilkesbarre, Wilkes County, North Carolina. —Gist (Darlington edition), *op. cit.,* p. 136.

179. Gist followed the south branch of the Great Warpath between the Iroquois and the Cherokee Indians. There were settlements at this village as early as March 15, 1730, for Thomas Walker on that date "bought corn of Michael Campbell for their horses." —Summers, *op. cit.,* p. 48.

180. The President and Council did not issue all the orders to Gist. He received one, at least, from James Patton. See page 33.

181. He was accompanied by his son. See page 35.

182. On March 29, 1750, the Committee of the Ohio Company authorized Hugh Parker to build a storehouse on Cresap's plantation, to be used until a suitable building was erected at the mouth of Wills Creek (Résumé of activities. See *Chronology,* March 29, 1750). John Hamer was employed by Hugh Parker for the Ohio Company in the summer of 1750, at which time he made doors for the store ("Account of John Hamer with the Ohio Company, July, 1750," MS in Darlington Memorial Library). The building erected at the mouth of Wills Creek is mentioned as the "New Store." Here the Committee was referring to the first store on Cresap's plantation near Wills Creek. See *Chronology,* Resolutions, March 29, 1750.

183. Redstone, the site of present Brownsville, later became the Ohio Company's established landing. On his journey Gist did not travel this far, but reached the Monongahela near present Jacobs Ferry and opposite the mouth of Muddy Creek. See also *note* 197.

Annotations

184. Sandy Gap, about four miles from present Cumberland, Maryland. Probably between Dan's and Piney Mountains. See *map* on page 39 in Bruce, *op. cit.*

185. This part of the Allegheny Mountain Range is called Wills Mountain.

186. The National Road (U.S. 40) out of Cumberland passes over this longer but easier route through the Narrows. —*Ibid.*, p. 41.

187. Castleman's River. Gist's trail, later Braddock's Road, was through Frostburg, Maryland, to the tributaries of the middle fork of the Youghiogheny (Castleman's) River.

188. His trail northwest was over Big Savage and Negro Mountains into Addison Township, Somerset County, Pennsylvania, to the Great Meadows, near the Great Crossings Bridge on the National Road (U.S. 40).

189. Probably Negro Glade Run.

190. Gist crossed the south fork or Youghiogheny River proper. Castleman's River is the center fork; Laurel Hill Creek, the north fork. All three branches unite at Confluence, Pennsylvania, known in colonial days as "Turkey Foot."

191. Colonel James Patton. Later Patton was sent to the Ohio to issue a formal invitation to the Indians to attend the conference at Logstown in May, 1752. He was one of the Virginia commissioners who conducted the conference.

192. Gist explored most of the region in Wharton, Georges, and South Union Townships, Fayette County, Pennsylvania, to the junction of the Cheat and Monongahela Rivers. This included the lands which he settled later which became known as Gist's Plantation. See *map* printed opposite p. 226.

193. The junction of the Cheat and Monongahela Rivers at Point Marion, Pennsylvania, was known in early times as the upper forks of the Monongahela.

194. His name appears in historical records from 1734 to 1799. In

Annotations

1734 some Indians in the Ohio Country complained to the Pennsylvania authorities about the misconduct of unlicensed traders, among whom was Charles Poke (Indian letter respecting Indian Traders, May 1, 1734. Printed in *Pennsylvania Archives*, I, 425). Sometime in the 1730's he resided near the northern bend of the Potomac River ("A Map of the Northern Neck of Virginia according to an Actual Survey Begun in the Year MDCCXXXVI, and ended in the Year MDCCXLVI. Drawn by Peter Jefferson and Robert Brook." P.R.O., Board of Trade Maps, Vol. 12, No. 16. Copy in the Darlington Memorial Library was made for W. M. Darlington in 1882 by J. A. Burt; Richard Peters to the Governor, March 12, 1754, printed in *Colonial Records of Pennsylvania*, V, 760). In his letter of August 4, 1738, from the Allegheny Chief Newcomer mentions Charles Poke and Garrett Pendergrass who were well acquainted with affairs in that region (Newcomer, king of the Shawnee, to the governor of Virginia, printed in Virginia, *Calendar of Virginia State Papers, and Other Manuscripts, 1652–1781 ...*, arranged and edited by Wm. P. Palmer [Richmond, R. F. Walker, 1875], I, 231-32). A deposition, made on November 15, 1799, by Charles Polke of Shelby County, Kentucky, is printed in Thomas Jefferson's *Notes on the State of Virginia* (New York, M. L. & W. A. Davis, 1801), p. 368.

195. Checochinican [Sheeckokinichan], a chief of the Delawares, formerly of Brandywine, but residing at Paxtang on the Susquehanna in 1718, with other Indian chiefs visited Philadelphia in order to renew the league of friendship with the English and to request the government to prohibit excessive rum trade by unlicensed Indian traders (*Colonial Records of Pennsylvania*, III, 45-47). Eight years later Checochinican represented the Delawares in a land dispute with Nathaniel Newlin who had taken up land on Brandywine Creek. This land was included in the acquisition of 1685; yet, in 1705 the Delawares repossessed the mile-wide intervales along the Creek. The land was repurchased from them for £100, part of which was paid at the time and the remainder in 1726. At this time (1726) James Logan told Checochinican that neither Nathaniel Newlin nor any other person would disturb the Indians' quiet possession of the land (Pennsylvania. General Assembly, *Votes and Proceedings*, II, 481-82). On June 24, 1729, Checochinican remonstrated anew to the Pennsylvania officials concerning possession by the English of the mile-wide intervals on the Brandywine. In his letter to Patrick Gordon the chief reminded the governor of the promise made by James Logan (*Pennsylvania Archives*, I, 239-40).

Annotations

196. Nemacolin may have been the "Memocollen" who, on August 21, 1730, complained to the justices of Lancaster County of the impositions and abuses heaped upon them by an Indian trader, Isaac Miranda *(ibid.,* 266-67). When the French took possession of the Ohio Country in 1754 Nemacolin was indebted to several Indian traders *(The Ohio Company, 1753–1817, op. cit.,* pp. 55, 94, 143). It has been stated that he was among the Indians employed by the Ohio Company to cut the first road from Wills Creek to Gist's plantation; yet, no record of this employment is recorded in the minutes of the Company, which are in this George Mercer collection of manuscripts. Likewise, it is said that his home was on the Monongahela at the mouth of Dunlap's Creek; yet Gist's statement here shows that he lived, not at the above place, but somewhere along the creek.

197. Gist reached the Monongahela several miles up the river from the mouth of Redstone Creek. The direction and distance given indicate that his place of crossing was in the vicinity of Jacobs Ferry, Fayette County, Pennsylvania.

On the north side of Wallace's Run, about a quarter of a mile from its confluence with the Monongahela, is a small defile in which there are vestiges of a cave not unlike the one described by Gist. The remaining part is about half the original size as outlined by the outcrop of rocks of the same stratum as the roof of the existing shelter. The cavity is dry and the floor is smooth, as described by Gist. Since the aperture is to the south, the December sun would have given "plenty of light." Information from Paul A. W. Wallace is that an Indian trail east in Greene County led to the Monongahela River at the mouth of Muddy Creek.

The "poor public or private road" in this vicinity, marked on the Masontown quadrangle map, may have had its origin in an Indian trail, a part of the one leading to the Monongahela at the mouth of Muddy Creek. This rock ledge would not have been too far away from the Indian trail to have been noticed by Gist; the "Stream of fine water" may have been Wallace's Run. —Observations made on a field trip, October 16, 1951.

198. Probably these three days were spent exploring the lands on the east side of the Monongahela in present Menallin and Luzerne Townships, Fayette County, Pennsylvania. In 1753 Gist took up lands in this vicinity.

199. Mr. Darlington stated that Gist crossed the Monongahela to

Annotations

the west side below the mouth of the Youghiogheny (*ibid.,* p. 141). In this explanation Mr. Darlington followed Gist's route as laid down on the map reproduced opposite p. 72. However, according to distances and directions this plan of the crossing does not coincide with Gist's information. It is reasonable to assume that the three days spent in exploring lands (see *note* 198) may have been the background for his settlement early in 1753. Therefore, according to directions given by Gist, the Monongahela crossing was near present Jacobs Ferry. See *note* 197.

200. Now Ten Mile Creek, Greene County, Pennsylvania.

201. Distance and direction recorded by Gist would place this hunting camp in the vicinity of present Jefferson, in Greene County. Oppaymolleah, a Delaware chief, attended the conference at Fort Pitt in 1768. —Pennsylvania (Colony). Treaties, etc., 1768. *Minutes of Conference Held at Fort Pitt in April and May, 1768* . . . (Philadelphia, Printed and Sold by William Goddard, at the New Printing-Office, in Market-Street, 1769), p. 4.

202. Joshua, a Delaware, is a name mentioned occasionally in historical records over a period of more than fifty years. The name appears in the Maryland colonial records in July, 1742, as one of the informants concerning an anticipated Shawnee attack on white settlements (*Archives of Maryland,* XXVIII, 266-27, 269-70). In September of the same year Joshua, an Indian, accompanied Count Zinzendorf on his journey from Bethlehem to Shamokin (William C. Reichel, *Memorials of the Moravian Church,* Philadelphia, J. B. Lippincott & Co., 1870, I, 78). Joshua and Tangoocqua, messengers from the Ohio, attended an Indian conference at Philadelphia, in December, 1759 (*Colonial Records of Pennsylvania,* VIII, 415-23). On November 26, 1779, Daniel Brodhead, in command of the western army, asked David Zeisberger, then residing on the Muskingum, to send a scout to reconnoiter around Detroit. Joshua, a very intelligent Indian, was selected to go on this mission, but excessive cold weather prevented him from making the trip ("Brodhead correspondence," printed in *Pennsylvania Archives,* XII, 192, 196, 221-22). Many years later (1805) an aged Delaware prophet, Joshua, was burned at the stake. —U.S. Bureau of American Ethnology, *Annual Reports,* XIV, 673-74.

Gist, who had been a ranger in Baltimore County in 1746, could have been acquainted with Joshua, the informant, in Maryland. Joshua's home in present Greene County is evidence that it was Gist's friend who accompanied Tangoocqua to Philadelphia in 1759. The

Annotations

other references mentioned above may be Zinzendorf's protégé, Joshua. On the basis of meagre and vague information, positive identification seems impossible.

203. Although King Beaver (Tamaqui), a noted Indian of the Turkey clan of the Delawares, played a chief's rôle in Delaware affairs on the Ohio for almost 20 years, there is no direct evidence that he held the position officially. On the contrary, some of his tribesmen, in 1762, questioned his authority to make decisions for them. However, his position, principal speaker for the tribe, seems to have had official sanction.

When George Croghan conducted the Pennsylvania-Indian conference at Logstown in May, 1751, he asked the Beaver, speaker for the Delawares, to prevail upon his tribe to "choose amongst Yourselves one of your wisest Councellors and present to your Brethern the Six Nations and me for a Chief, and he so chosen by you shall be looked upon us as your King, with whom Publick Business shall be transacted" ("A Treaty with the Indians of the Six Nations, Delawares ...," printed in *Colonial Records of Pennsylvania* V, 532-39). The Delawares, who had been without a duly appointed leader since the death of the aged and dissipated Olumapies [Sassoonan, Alummapees, Allomappis] in 1747, did not comply with Croghan's request. Therefore, in June, 1752, at the Virginia-Logstown conference the Half King, Seneca chief deputed by the Six Nations to watch over the Delawares on the Ohio, gave the tribe a chief, Shingas, the brother of the Beaver. In the absence of Shingas, the Beaver stood proxy for his brother and was presented "with a rich jacket & a suit of English Colours, which had been delivered to the Half King, by the Commissioners for that Purpose." See *Chronology*, June 13, 1752, Logstown conference.

The destruction of Pickawillany by the French in June, 1752, brought about the first critical period in Anglo-French relations on the Ohio. English activities were epitomized in the activities of William Trent, representative of both Virginia and the Ohio Company. Although Trent's negotiations, for the most part, were with the Six Nations' deputy (the Half King), the Delawares were also represented. The Beaver spoke for the Delawares at the Virginia Conference conducted by William Trent at Logstown in August, 1753, and at the Winchester Conference a month later. After the fall of Fort Necessity he represented the Delawares who had traveled east to George Croghan's home at Aughwick (Shirleysburg, Pennsylvania) to confer with the Pennsylvanians. Here, in private conference with Weiser, in

Annotations

behalf of his tribesmen, he pledged allegiance to the English. The Half King appeared to be so impressed with the Beaver's sincerity that he sent the speech "to the Six Nations by a special Messenger where it ought to be"; while in private he advised Weiser to keep the Delawares and the Shawnee at Aughwick as long as possible. —"Journal of the Proceedings of Conrad Weiser in his way to and at Aucquick . . . in . . . 1754, in August and September." Printed in *Colonial Records of Pennsylvania,* VI, 150-60.

Apparently the Half King's suspicion was well founded, for in a very short time the Delawares were leading forays against the frontier settlements. Many depositions concerning these depredations are printed in the *Colonial Records of Pennsylvania,* while other records are extant only in manuscript (*ibid.,* VI, 673 ff.); yet, the Beaver is never quite identified as having been among the marauders. Nor do the records show that he actually took the captives which he returned later to the English. Shortly after the French occupation of the Ohio Country in 1754 the Six Nations' Indians withdrew, leaving only the Delaware and Shawnee in the French orbit. After 1756 the famous Teedyscung, self-styled King of the Delawares, with residence east of the Susquehanna, established intermittent communications with the Ohio Delawares. Christian Frederick Post, Moravian missionary and emissary for Pennsylvania in 1758, was the first white man to negotiate with the Delawares on their own western soil. When, in July, Post arrived at Kuskuskies (New Castle, Lawrence County, Pennsylvania) he was cordially received by the Beaver. With Post's mission the English re-established continuous communication with the western Indians. On July 18, 1758, the Beaver, in behalf of all the western nations, sent the following message to the "Governor and People of Pennsylvania": "it is the first Message we have seen or heard from you. Brethern you have talked of that Peace and Friendship which we had formerly with you. . . . we tell you to be strong, and always remember that Friendship which we had formerly. . . . desire you would be strong and let us once more hear of our good Friendship and Peace we had formerly. . . . we desire that you make haste and let us soon hear of you again. —Thomson, *An Enquiry into the Causes of the Alienation of the Delaware and Shawanese Indians from the British Interest . . . Together with the Remarkable Journal of Christian Frederick Post . . .* " (London, Printed for J. Wilkie, 1759), pp. 157-58.

He was tribal spokesman at Bouquet's conference with "nine Chiefs of the Six Nations, Shawneese and Delaware Indians" at Fort Pitt on December 4, at which time he committed himself to carry the English message of peace to all the western tribes and to work for the return

Annotations

of the English captives. At the same time he assured Bouquet that the Delawares would send representatives to Philadelphia to treat with the Pennsylvanians. —B. M. Add. MSS, 21655, f. 19; printed in Henry Bouquet, *The Papers of* . . . , edited by Sylvester K. Stevens and Donald H. Kent (Harrisburg, Department of public instruction, Pennsylvania historical commission, 1940–41), 21655, pp. 18-21.

Shortly after the conference the Beaver visited the western nations. He returned to Fort Pitt from his mission late in February (1759) and reported to Bouquet that the western Indians would consider the English peace overture but first they must be convinced of the sincerity of the English. He also informed him that the old men would willingly make peace but the young Indians were still much in the French interest. "Two Tawas accompanied the Beaver back to Fort Pitt to know the truth, if the English had made peace with the Delawares" (Hugh Mercer to Bouquet, March 1, 1759, B. M. Add. MSS, 21644, f. 78; printed in *ibid.*, 21644, pt. I, 64-66). Colonel Hugh Mercer, commandant at Fort Pitt, was not impressed with the Beaver's sincerity, for the next day he wrote to Bouquet that "The Beaver went home yesterday pretending to know nothing of the French up the River, and assured me they were not come in Such numbers, other wise he would Know, and undoubtedly inform me, when Danger was so near.

"He at the Same time declined letting one of his young men go to spy up the River." —Letter in *ibid.*, f. 82; printed in *ibid.*, pp. 68-69.

Mercer's surmise about the Beaver was incorrect, for he did go to the other side of the lake to inform other Indian nations living there that the English had made peace with the Delawares, and on his return to Fort Pitt, July 4, 1759, delivered to the English two women, his own captives, one of which he called his mother and the other his sister ("Journal of James Kenny, 1758–59" in *Pennsylvania Magazine*, XXXVII, 427). Chief Shingas must have abdicated his position of authority before this time, for at the conference, July 9, on the roster of those attending, the Beaver is listed as King of the Delawares, but Shingas' name is among the captains and warriors. Evidently the Beaver had assumed the chief's authority, for on August 7, 1759, at another conference at Fort Pitt, it was the Beaver who ceremoniously took the hatchet away from all the Indians formerly in the French interest and buried it. His power in tribal affairs must have been limited, however, for another Delaware chief, Killbuck, continued to harass the whites. Hugh Mercer remarked to Bouquet that he had demanded satisfaction for Killbuck's depredations but that the Beaver had so little influence among his own people he presumed that nothing would be done about it. —Mercer to Bouquet, August 20, 1759, B. M. Add. MSS, 21655, f. 86; printed in Bouquet *Papers*, 21655, pp. 80-81.

The Beaver gave the western Indians' full reply to the peace mission at the conference at Pittsburgh on October 26, 1759. At that time he informed the English that the presence of the Tawas at Fort Pitt was only a partial answer to his mission and that he expected the other tribes to come in the spring and reaffirm the peace (minutes of the conference, printed in *Colonial Records of Pennsylvania*, VIII, 429-35). Statesmanlike, the Beaver moved cautiously in the final peace negotiations. In 1760, when Teedyscung traveled to the Ohio Country in order to persuade his tribesmen there to confirm the peace made at Easton in 1758, he conferred with King Beaver. The Beaver declined to answer Teedyscung on the matter, but sent word to the governor that he would come to Philadelphia, there to confer with the governor "at the place of the council fire of his grandfathers." *Ibid.*, VIII, 497-99. The Delaware king did not go to Philadelphia for the conference scheduled for May, 1761, but sent another, one Grey Eyes, as his deputy, who informed the Pennsylvanians that "the old men are preparing to come." —*Ibid.*, 618-20.

On July 5 Killbuck and the Beaver breakfasted with James Kenny, employee of the provincial store at Fort Pitt. Apparently Kenny quizzed them about their feelings toward the English. Kenny wrote in his journal that although "White Eyes & Wingenum after their return from there (the treaty at Philadelphia) seem'd mightly Pleas'd," he could not find when the chiefs themselves would go to Philadelphia to treat with the English. Kenny believed that Killbuck had an unfavorable influence on King Beaver and retarded Beaver's interest in the English by telling him that during the war the English had a price on his head and that he, Killbuck, was sure that if the Beaver went among the inhabitants to the eastward, he would be killed.

That summer of 1761 the Beaver traveled in the opposite direction and went with George Croghan to Detroit where Sir William Johnson made a treaty with the western tribes, including the Delawares. He took with him six kegs of rum and delivered them to his tribesmen at his home town, Tuscarawas, where Christian Frederick Post reported that the Indians were drunk for six days. During the Beaver's absence, Delaware George, another Delaware chief, told James Kenny that the chief reason the Beaver did not go to Philadelphia to treat with the English was that the Delawares were under three chiefs, the Beaver, White Eyes, and himself; and they could not agree among themselves on the treaty at Philadelphia.

Annotations

When Croghan, then deputy Indian agent, returned to Fort Pitt around the first of October, he brought with him for perusal Sir William Johnson's journal of his conference held with the Indians at Detroit. According to Kenny's information, Johnson liberated the Delaware from the Six Nations' yoke. The minutes of the Detroit Conference in September, 1761, printed in Sir William Johnson's *Papers* . . . (Albany, University of the State of New York, 1921–39) volume three, pages 474-501, do not bear witness to this statement of James Kenny. He also related that the Beaver had held a conference with the other nations before Sir William arrived, informing them that he, like them, had been misled by the French. The Beaver and Shingas returned from the conference at Detroit on October 12, at which time they promised George Croghan that they would go to Philadelphia in the spring. They then returned to their home at Tuscarawas for the winter of 1762–63, for Christian Frederick Post passed by way of Fort Pitt on December 26, 1762, with a message from King Beaver and Shingas to the governor of Pennsylvania "signifying that they had comfirm'd ye Peace with ye Western Nations."

Post led Beaver's delegation from Tuscarawas to Lancaster, where the long awaited treaty with the western chiefs was made. At this time there appeared to have been a challenge of the Beaver's chieftainship. It is to be remembered that William Johnson, in October, 1761, liberated the Delawares from the mastery held over them by the Iroquois. One Indian named Keecaise, a cousin of Nemacolin, informed James Kenny that "the Beaver King & ye Indians about Tuscorawas though of ye Lenappe Nation, yet are not Delawars properly, likewise that ye Beaver never was made a King by ye Indians, but by ye people of Virginia, and that Neat-hot-whelme was ye Deleware King, & Tuscologas a Half King, being half a Mingo."

Also, young Jacobs' Netotwhelmy (Newcomer, a Delaware), who was at Fort Pitt, said that his father and Tuscologas (Custaloga), the half Delaware and Mingo king, were coming to go with Beaver to Philadelphia. Newcomer and Tuscologas with their followers arrived at Fort Pitt two days after King Beaver. The chiefs held council and decided that King Beaver and his group should attend the treaty; the others would send deputies. This statement is significant, for the commitments made to Pennsylvania's governor by the Beaver were repudiated by Newcomer and Tuscologas. The governor had issued the invitation to the conference only to the Beaver. The old chief's influence had waned, for after his return to Tuscarawas he was not able to stem the tide of French influence. Newcomer had assumed full leadership and had eagerly accepted the war hatchet from the Six

Nations. When the Delawares heard that the French had laid down their arms and there was peace with England, and that the French had lost control of the Ohio Country, King Newcomer, according to Post, "was Struck dumb for a considerable time." When Post upbraided him by saying he did not like the English the Newcomer replied that the English had grown too powerful "as if they would be too Strong for God himself." —"Journal of James Kenny, 1761–1763" printed in *Pennsylvania Magazine,* XXXVII, 10, 17-18, 23-25, 34, 157, 160-61, 167, 175, 187.

Simeon Écuyer, on August 3, 1763, reported to Bouquet that King Beaver, who had been at Fort Pitt, left for Tuscarawas "with a party of warriors and that they are divided among themselves." Écuyer added that some want to continue the war, others do not. (Letter in B. M. Add. MSS, 21649, f. 286; printed in Bouquet *Papers,* 21649, pt. II, 9). The next spring the Delawares appeared to be of the same divided opinion—King Beaver still working for peace. —Deposition of Gershom Hicks, April 14, 1764, B. M. Add. MSS, 21650, f. 140; printed in Bouquet *Papers,* 21650, pt. I, 100-03.

In 1764 and 1765 it seemed that the Beaver co-operated with Colonel Bouquet and George Croghan in every way. However, there were rife many reports that the Delawares were continuing their opposition to the English. When Colonel Bouquet conferred with Custaloga and King Beaver on the Muskingum, on October 17, 1764, they readily gave the commander six hostages to stay with the English until the white prisoners were restored. Bouquet had given the Delawares twelve days to fulfill this mission; yet by February, 1765, when Beaver again conferred with George Croghan at Fort Pitt, the Delawares had returned only one captive. Croghan reported in his journal that they suspected the Delawares' sincerity (Smith, *Bouquet's Expedition, op. cit.,* 16, 23; *Colonial Records of Pennsylvania,* IX, 250-64). Of all the Indian depredations committed during those dark years, only the Sherman Valley raid has been attributed to Indians led by King Beaver. — A re-examination of Gershom Hicks, April 19, 1764, B. M. Add. MSS, 21651, f. 121; printed in Bouquet *Papers,* 21651, 7.

The last mention of King Beaver is found in the *Minutes of the Conferences held at Fort Pitt in April and May 1768* where were present 1,103 Indians, not including women and children. Here the Beaver spoke at times for the Delawares and also for the Muncies and Mohicans. Already peace had been established between his tribe and the whites at a conference held by Sir William Johnson on May 8, 1765 (treaty printed in *N.Y.C.D.,* VII, pp. 738-41). Therefore, the

Annotations

Beaver's discussions at Fort Pitt related for the most part to improvement of Indian trade.

In summation, the Beaver, brother in the Turkey tribe of the Delawares to Shingas and Pisquetomen, resided on the Ohio and held some temporal power from 1751 to 1768. Acting as principal speaker for his tribe on the Ohio, he did make sincere overtures for friendship with the English. During the three years (1755–1758) that he lived in French controlled territory, there is no recorded evidence that he actually led Indian incursions against the whites. When Fort Duquesne was taken he was living at the Delaware town of Saukonk on the Ohio at the mouth of the Big Beaver, and at Kuskuskies (Post conferred with him in July and October at Kuskuskies; Hugh Mercer stated that he lived at Saukonk early in 1759). He established Beaver's town, or Tuscarawas, late in 1759 or 1760, where he lived the rest of his life. It is stated that he died in 1771 (C. Hale Sipe, *The Indian Chiefs of Pennsylvania* [Butler, Pa., Ziegler Printing Co., 1927], p. 308). As for the Beaver's chieftainship, the editor found no record that King Beaver was ever officially appointed chief ruler over his tribe. However, there is ample evidence to show that for many years he acted in that capacity. His bias toward the English made him a most important factor in winning the Delawares back to the English interest, thus assuring English victory on the Ohio in 1758; his efforts from 1758 to 1762 were responsible for the most part for bringing all the western Indians back into the English sphere of influence; and his resistance to the anti-British faction among the Delawares may have curbed the intensity of the Indian revolt in 1763–1764.

204. Ruff's Creek, a branch of Ten Mile Creek.

205. Near New Freeport, Greene County, Pennsylvania.

206. Near the headwaters of Fish Creek, near Burton, West Virginia.

207. Gist's course, S 45 W, would lead across Fishing Creek which empties into the Ohio at New Martinsville, West Virginia. The creek mentioned would be Middle Island which comes into the Ohio at St. Mary's. The logical place of crossing would be near Middlebourne, Tyler County, West Virginia. —Gist (Darlington edition), *op. cit.*, p. 142.

208. Gist was traveling S W 45, for the most part, and parallel to the Ohio River. This course would lead over the Hughes River, a branch of the Little Kanawha.

Annotations

209. On Standing Stone Creek in Ritchie County, West Virginia.

210. Mr. Darlington stated that this stone once stood on the creek bottom of the Parish Fork of Standing Stone Creek. —*Ibid.,* pp. 142-43.

211. New style, 1752. Gist may have reached the Little Kanawha River at Elizabeth, Wirt County, West Virginia.

212. Probably a branch of Thirteen Mile Creek, a tributary of the Kanawha River. The trail southwest from Elizabeth on the Little Kanawha River would cross a branch of Big Mill Creek, Big and Little Buffalo Creeks, and the headwaters of Thirteen Mile Creek—and also traverse Wirt, Jackson, Putnam, and Mason Counties, West Virginia.

213. Big Buffalo Creek in Putnam County.

214. Ten Mile Creek, which flows into the Kanawha at Beech Hill Station, may be the creek mentioned by Gist.

215. Kanawha Ridge. —Gist (Darlington edition), *op. cit.,* p. 144.

216. LeTort's Creek does not appear on the quadrangle maps of West Virginia. Distance and direction given by Gist identify LeTort's Creek as present Old Town Creek which comes into the Ohio near present LeTort's Falls.

217. Big Mill Creek, Jackson County, West Virginia. —Gist (Darlington edition), *op. cit.,* p. 145.

218. Big Sandy Creek, Jackson County, West Virginia. —*Ibid.,* p. 145.

219. Pond Creek, Wood County, West Virginia. —*Ibid.*

220. Little Kanawha River *(ibid.).* Gist encamped on this same creek on February 14.

221. Middle Island Creek in Pleasant and Tyler Counties, West Virginia.

222. Fishing Creek which flows into the Ohio at New Martinsville, West Virginia.

Annotations

223. Wheeling Creek comes into the Ohio at Wheeling, West Virginia.

224. Buffalo and Cross Creeks. Buffalo Creek empties into the Ohio at Wellsburg, West Virginia.

225. This statement may refer to "very large wooden Canoes" which Thomas Pownall described as "Generally 30 or 40 Feet long, Three or Four Feet broad, and drawing empty 10 or 12 Inches Water, and when loaded about 18 inches." (Pownall's *Topographical Descriptions* (Mulkearn edition), *op. cit.*, p. 138, 138n.) These boats known as Durham boats were developed to carry bulk products over the rifts in the Delaware River. They followed the pattern of Indian canoes and could be rowed, poled, or sailed. —*Steelways* (N. Y., American Iron and Steel Institute), I, no. 13, p. 28.

226. Meaning the junction of Redstone Creek and the Monongahela River.

227. A fact given in *Case of the Ohio Company*. See *facs.*, p. 5. Therefore, this document was derived from an attested one.

228. Probably George Mercer's copy of this "Release," signed by George Mercer and James Mercer, each with his accompanying seal. The seal of George Mercer is slightly mutilated; that of James Mercer is in an almost perfect state. The manuscript, in John Mercer's handwriting, is badly mutilated, in 24 small pieces, having suffered from close folding. It was witnessed by R. Rogers and J[ohn]Mercer. The endorsement on the back of one of the segments is as follows: "Mercers to Tayloe & Thornton Release."

At the time this release was executed George Mercer was assistant quartermaster general under Colonel Bouquet, with headquarters at Winchester, Virginia. Letters between them show that Mercer was concerned about "Business of great Consequence to myself," which required his personal attention in Williamsburg. Mercer was absent from the post from about November 8 to November 27. —Mercer to Bouquet, September 28 and November 28, 1759. In B. M. Add. MSS, 21644, f. 417, 494; printed in Bouquet *Papers*, 21644, pt. II, pp. 121-127 and 201-02, respectively.

Execution of this "release" may have been one item of George Mercer's urgent business in Williamsburg, but his correspondence with George Washington at this time shows that the acquisition of

Annotations

"soldiers bonus lands" was uppermost in his thoughts. On September 16, Mercer wrote: "Your Proposal concerning an Entry on the Ohio I am fully of Opinion will answer; indeed it is what I had before determined upon, and am much rejoiced that you propose to be a Partner in the Scheme. I had obtained Leave to be at Williamsburg on the Meeting of the Assembly in November, with no other View, than that of securing to myself so much Land as I was entitled to by the Governor's Proclamation; which allowed Us such Terms that We cant possibly lose by it—and as I determined to go to England this Year, I thought it proper to settle that Point before I embarked. it must be of Service in Time to come—Lands on the Ohio will be valuable. You may bid Me to do any Thing you think necessary till We meet at Williamsburg, no Doubt you will be there on the Assembly, then We may surely secure it to ourselves."—Stanislaus M. Hamilton, editor, *Letters to Washington and Accompanying Papers* (Boston, Houghton, Mifflin and Company, 1901), III, 159.

This letter was written only one month after General Stanwix appointed Mercer assistant deputy quartermaster general in charge of supplies to be acquired in Virginia (Warrant in B. M. Add, MSS, 21652, f. 148; printed in Bouquet *Papers*, 21652, p. 220-21). At the time Mercer received his commission, he informed General Stanwix that he must have leave to attend to urgent business in Williamsburg. —Letter in B. M. Add. MSS, 21644, f. 464; printed in Bouquet *Papers*, 21644, pt. II, 172-75.

In addition to his application for lands and execution of this "Release" to John Tayloe and Presley Thornton, Mercer, at this time, applied for and received from the College of William and Mary a commission as surveyor of Ohio lands. —"Journal of the Meetings of the President and Masters of William and Mary College," December 10, 1759. Printed in *William and Mary College Quarterly*, 1st series (v.p., v. pub., 1892–1920), III, 129.

Perhaps it may be advantageous to some readers to have included in the annotations for this document full descriptions of the lands sold by John Mercer to his sons, George and James, who in turn signed this "Release" to John Tayloe and Presley Thornton. If this were an edited edition of George Mercer Papers, such annotations would be in order; but this volume contains only a special collection of George Mercer papers, all of which, in some manner, pertain to the history of the Ohio Company of Virginia. The editor considered detailed annotations concerning lands owned personally by the Mercers to be extraneous to this book. Therefore they are omitted.

Annotations

229. It is interesting to note that at this time John Mercer considered the grant to the Ohio Company to be 500,000 acres of land. Only 200,000 acres were granted, and the acquisition of the remaining 300,000 acres was contingent upon the fulfillment of certain requirements outlined in John Hanbury's petition of January 11, 1749 (see *Chronology*). The "Articles of Agreement," May 23, 1751 (see *note* 1), in effect for 20 years, bound this land to be owned in partnership. Only after May 23, 1771, was John Mercer entitled to his one share, 25,000 acres.

230. In 1765 John Mercer executed a release to John Tayloe and Presley Thornton of the bond given him "as Securities for your [George Mercer] & his [James Mercer] paying £3000 of my debts." —John Mercer to George Mercer, January 28, 1768. See *Chronology*.

231. A contemporary copy in Charlton Palmer's handwriting, three pages, folio. Palmer is first mentioned on October 17, 1760, as London solicitor for the Ohio Company (October 17, 1760, Resolution . . . see *Chronology*), at which time John Mercer was empowered to transmit the "Case" to him and employ him to obtain from the home government a renewal of their grant of 1749. Personal affairs or the restraining proclamations of General Stanwix and Henry Bouquet caused John Mercer to delay in carrying out the resolution of the Committee of the Company. Presence of the letter in this collection is explained in Charlton Palmer's letter to George Mercer. In answer to George Mercer's request for the official papers of the Company Palmer wrote: "All the papers I rec'ed except what I gave you I delivered to Mr Jackson (who then lived in the Temple . . .) which I understood were redelivered to you." —Palmer to George Mercer, December 27, 1769. See *Chronology*.

232. The enclosure is missing from this collection.

233. The conflict on the Ohio caused the Company to lose "the greatest part of their stock." Petition to the King drawn up in July, 1763, but not presented until 1765. See *Case . . . facs.*, p. 30, this volume.

234. The largest single expenditures for which they had received no returns were £600 for exploration and £400 for building a fort on the Ohio. See pp. 46, 239, this volume.

235. Although the request for a patent directly from the crown was

Annotations

made for the first time in the petition of 1765 (printed on *facs.*, p. 30), this statement is evidence that as early as 1762 the Virginia members of the Company believed they were "out of favor" with the colonial government.

236. The Company had, at this time, between £2,000 and £2,500 including "some pretty considerable outstanding debts, on hand at this time." —George Mercer to Henry Bouquet, December 27, 1760, B. M. Add. MSS, 21645, f. 340; printed in Bouquet *Papers,* 21645, pp. 252-54.

237. This would save the price of surveying. The Board of Trade's decision of 1754, on the Ohio Company's formal request for permission to take up lands bounded by natural boundaries, was in the negative. They ruled that in order to assess for quitrents it would be necessary to have the land surveyed; therefore, there would be no advantage for the Company. —"Board of Trade report of June 25, 1754." P.R.O., C.O. 5: 1367/76-87.

238. Gist's journals are printed on pp. 7-40, this work.

239. Gist, in his journals, does note carefully the width of the river bottoms.

240. Surveyors' fees were 500 pounds of tobacco for a survey comprising not more than 1,000 acres and 30 pounds additional for every 100 acres over the 1,000. This covered the fee for surveying large grants. —Hening, *op. cit.,* V, 340; printed also in *Case . . . , facs.,* pp. 19-20.

241. The Board of Trade had issued an instruction authorizing their grant to be taken up in parcels of not less than 20,000 acres with breadth equal to one-third the length. This, added the Board of Trade, would prevent "skimming off all the good lands." —"Board of Trade report, June 25, 1754," *op. cit.*

242. Dated July 16, 1751. See *Chronology.*

243. At present Marietta, Ohio.

244. At the Wyandot Indian town at the junction of the Walhonding and Tuscarawas Rivers, the site of present Coshocton, Ohio. The

Annotations

Walhonding River was formerly known as White Woman's Creek.

245. Mohican John's Town was a regular stopping place on the Great Trail from Fort Pitt to Detroit. It was located at the head of the Black Fork of the Mohican River (Hutchins, *Topographical* Map, 1778, *op. cit.*). Charles Hanna gives the location on the east bank of the Jerome Fork of the Mohican River about two miles below present Jeromeville, opposite the mouth of Old Town Run. —Hanna, *op. cit.*, II, 187, 207, 208.

246. At present Cleveland, Ohio.

247. The foregoing directions would on present maps include all the territory in Ohio bounded by a line drawn from Marietta up the Muskingum River to Coshocton; thence northwest along the Kokosing River to its junction with the Mohican in New Castle Township, Coshocton County; thence north along the Mohican River to Muddy Fork; up Muddy Fork of the Mohican to its source in the southwest corner of Medina County; thence northeast to Cleveland; along the south shore of Lake Erie to present Erie, Pennsylvania; then following the portages to French Creek and the Allegheny; down the Allegheny and the Ohio to Marietta.

248. Evans, *A General Map of the Middle British Colonies . . . , 1755, op. cit.*

249. At present Point Pleasant, West Virginia.

250. According to Evans' *Map* of 1755, the Kanawha River breaks through the mountains near present Charleston, West Virginia. However, in his letter to R. Dodsley (June 25, 1756, original in Library of Congress; printed in *Pennsylvania Magazine,* LIX, 295-301), Evans stated that Dr. Mitchell had convinced him he had placed "the important Pass through the Ouascioto Mountain 30 or 40 miles too far west." On present maps Kanawha Falls, or the gap in the mountains, is at the junction of the Kanawha and Gauley Rivers, present Glen Ferris, West Virginia.

251. According to the same map (Evans' 1755), no doubt the one used by Mercer, the boundary line followed the mountains to the Tygart River near present Grafton, West Virginia; thence down the Tygart to the west fork of the Monongahela at present Fairmont;

Annotations

thence followed the Monongahela to Brownsville, Pennsylvania; down the Monongahela to the Ohio River; and thence on the Ohio to Point Pleasant, West Virginia.

252. Probably refers to William Beverley to whom the Board of Trade refers in their report, June 25, 1754, on the Company's petition of March 28.

The third reason for the need of an alteration in the terms of the instructions of 1749 was that the council refused to permit them to survey the first 200,000 acres in separate tracts.

The Board of Trade stated that the reason "alledged by Mr Beverley (one of His Majesty's Council in Virginia) for the Governor & Council's refusal to permit the petitioners to survey their Lands in separate Tracts ad Libitum, was because they apprehended, that by such a Method the Intention of the Crown, in making the Building a Fort a Condition of the Grant, would be frustrated, in as much as it was reasonable to suppose the Petitioners would be induced from such Liberty to take all the best Land they could find within the Limits prescribed by the Grant; in which case the settlers might be dispersed and distant from each other, that the Fort could not Possibly afford them any Protection."

The Board of Trade, however, did soften the blow and permit the Ohio Company "to survey the whole 500,000 Acres of Land in separate Tracts of Twenty thousand Acres in each Tract ... provided that the Breadth of Each Tract be one-third of the Length of such Tract." This order was designed to assure future settlers adequate river frontage and fertile interval lands. —Board of Trade Report, June 25, 1754, *op. cit.*

253. On March 27, 1759, Edward Montague was appointed agent "to solicit and properly represent the affairs of this colony [Virginia] in Great Britain." Although Virginia, in reality the Executive Council only, had a colonial representative in London who officially looked after Virginia's interest prior to 1700, Montague was the first agent who represented the House of Burgesses. In 1770 he opposed the activities of the Grand Ohio Company, not the Ohio Company. —Ella Lonn, *The Colonial Agents of the Southern Colonies* (Chapel Hill, University of North Carolina Press, 1945), pp. 3, 33, 63, 66, 175, 176.

254. Upon application to the Board of Trade for the clarification of the status of both existing and promised grants, Governor Fauquier received instructions from the home government which forbad him

to grant lands as promised in Dinwiddie's "Proclamation" of 1754. A junto of veterans of the 1754–58 campaign who petitioned Virginia's governor in 1760 for leave to take up lands on the Ohio under the Dinwiddie "Proclamation" reported to the Board of Trade that "upon application to Your Majesty's present lieutenant governor and council of the said colony your memorialists received for answer that they were restrained by Your Majesty's late instructions from making any grants in those parts" (P.R.O., C.O. 5: 1330/328). This petition was read at the Board of Trade March 2, 1763. *Ibid.*, /323.

255. Dinwiddie's Proclamation, printed in *Case* . . . , facs., p. 17.

256. Enclosure, Orders and Resolutions, printed pp. 140-153.

257. Evans' *Geographical, Historical, Political, Philosophical and Mechanical Essays. The First, Containing an Analysis of a General Map of the Middle British Colonies in America . . . , op. cit.;—Number II Containing a Letter Representing the Impropriety of Sending Forces to Virginia . . . . Published in the New York Mercury, No. 178, January 5, 1756, With an Answer to so Much Thereof as Concerns the Public.* (Philadelphia, Printed for the Author, 1756.)

258. Although mentioned as printed acts, a manuscript copy is in this collection and is printed on pp. 153-165.

259. Philip Ludwell Lee.

260. John Hanbury, while in Virginia, took advantage of Ohio Company information given in secret to Dinwiddie as a member of the Ohio Company and, before he went home, "had taken up 130,000 Acres in Augusta which he proposed to settle with people from the North ward." —John Mercer to George Mercer, March 3, 1768. See *Chronology*.

As for Robert Dinwiddie, John Mercer accused him of duplicity in permitting Colonel Richard Corbin and Colonel Thomas Ludwell to peruse the Ohio Company map. Says Mercer, "I told them that was not fair the Map belonged to me as of my own drawing & my Instructions by which I drew it cost the Company above £600, they delivered it to me but they had done their business, their Entries were entered in the Council Books before they left the Room so that Corbin & Co? in 3 hours time without a shilling charge or Expence except the Clerk of the Council's fee (which I suppose he dare not charge him) had

Annotations

leave to take up more land than the Ohio Company could obtain in 20 y^{rs} Sollicitation & after £10,000 Expence" —John Mercer to George Mercer, March 3, and March 9, 1768. See *Chronology*.

261. Letter to Dinwiddie, as printed in Samuel Wharton, *Plain Facts* . . . (Philadelphia, printed and sold by R. Aitken, bookseller, in Market-street, three doors above the coffee-house, 1781), p. 120, and in *Case* . . . , *facs.*, p. 26, shows John Mercer's signature which does not appear in the copies in the George Mercer manuscripts.

262. Enclosure missing from this collection, but printed in *Case* . . . , *facs.*, pp. 25-26.

263. This fragmentary "Case of the Ohio Company," of 62 folio pages, the first enclosure mentioned in the foregoing letter, is in the handwriting of Richard Rogers, John Mercer's clerk. The first four pages and two pages which would have been numbered 17 and 18 are missing. The document was folded crosswise and refolded; therefore each page, as it exists today, is either in four separate pieces or very badly creased in four places; also, some of the edges are worn away. For full discussion of all matter, other than physical properties, see *Commentary*, pp. 396-398. The first four pages which are missing were probably much the same and in the same order as the material printed in the *Case of the Ohio Company, facs.*, pp. 1-5 and pp. 233-36. In order to understand this document, it is advisable first to read the *facsimile* pages 1-5. Bracketed [   ] material, *illegible* in manuscript, is supplied from printed *Case*. John Mercer corrected in his own hand the Case as transcribed by his secretary. John Mercer's corrections are identified as contained within brackets (⟨   ⟩).

264. On June 21, 1699, the Virginia Executive Council "Ordered, y^t very [every] person paying five shillings Sterl to Mr Auditor for ye use of his Maj^{ty} shall have ye same liberty to take up & patent fifty acres of land's which [he] would otherwise have had for the Importacon of any of his Maj^{ties} Subjects into this Dominion, and y^t Mr Auditor doe accordingly grant a Certificate to every such person for ye taking up and Patenting fifty acres of land for every five Shillings which shall be soe paid by him for his Maj^{ties} use, and every Surveyor unto whom such Certificate shall be produced, is hereby required to make entry & survey of such Quantity of land according to every such Certificate respectively, in like manner as ye law directs upon ye produceing a Certificate of ye Importacon of any of his Maj^{ties}

Annotations

Subjects into this Dominion." —Virginia Council *Journals,* I, 457.

Therefore, landrights in lieu of headrights, five shillings sterling for 50 acres, would be £1,000 sterling for the 200,000 acres. Quitrents for the same acreage at two shillings sterling per 100 acres would have been £200 sterling annually.

265. On June 21, 1749, John Hanbury was asked to solicit an alteration in the instruction "which obliges the Company to build and Garrison a Fort." See *Chronology,* Orders of the Company, June 21, 1749.

266. Instructions to Gist are found in several places in the George Mercer Papers. For location in this volume, see *Chronology,* September 11, 1750.

267. The original of this "Journal" is not among the George Mercer Papers; nor was it located elsewhere by the editor. However, the copy of Gist's first and second journals made for Governor Dinwiddie was from the attested "Journal." Printed on pp. 7-40.

268. No meeting on the Ohio between Virginia and the Indians was scheduled for August, 1751. James Patton was sent to the Ohio at this time to issue a correct invitation to the Indians to meet the Virginia commissioners at Logstown in May, 1752. See *note* 275.

269. No record was found of the committee's recommendation of Gist nor of this appointment by Virginia. However, contemporary copies of the minutes of the conference show that Gist served as "Agent for the Ohio Company." Printed on pp. 54-66.

270. Date of this instruction is July 16, 1751. For variants printed in this volume, see *Chronology.*

271. Mr. Hanbury did not publish the journal; nor was the manuscript, sent him by John Mercer, located by the editor.

272. The principal English maps of North America, published 1751–60, were delineated by Joshua Fry and Peter Jefferson (1751), William Douglass (1753), Lewis Evans (1755), and John Mitchell (1755). Fry and Jefferson were Virginians given a commission to delineate a map of Virginia in consequence of a directive issued by the Lords of Trade on July 19, 1750 (Virginia Council *Journals,* V, 354).

Annotations

William Douglass mapped "the British Dominions of New England." Lewis Evans, in his *Analysis,* pages two to five, does not mention Christopher Gist's "Plan" among his many sources of information. In his letter of June 25, 1756, to his publisher, R. Dodsley (*op. cit.*), in London, Evans writes of his recent conversation with Mr. Gist who "could not be well persuaded at first but I had had a Perusal of his Draught." John Mitchell's map "was Undertaken with the approbation and at the request of the Lords Commissioners for Trade and Plantations; and is Chiefly composed from Draughts, Charts and Actual Surveys of different parts of His Majesties Colonies & Plantations in America; Great part of which have been lately taken by their Lordships Orders, and transmitted to this Office by the Governors of the said Colonies and others." —*A Map of the British and French Dominions in North America, with the Roads, Distances, Limits, and Extent of the Settlements* .... By Jno Mitchell (London, printed for Jefferys & Faden, Feb. 13th, 1755).

However, John Mercer may have been correct in this accusation, for Evans, in his letter to Dodsley (*op. cit.*), stated that "Dr. Mitchell used his journal which Dr. Mercer had sent home from Virginia." On March 28, 1754, John Hanbury presented to the King in Council a petition in behalf of the Ohio Company to which was annexed a "Chart" of the Western Country, made according to information received from Gist ("Order of Council Referring the Humble Petition of the Ohio Company to the Consideration of the Board of Trade," April 2, 1754, *op. cit.*). This chart is reproduced opposite page 72, this volume. Hence it was possible that, although Lewis Evans was the source for the information, Mitchell used Gist's journals; Gist's route as "pricked out" on Mitchell's map may have been derived from the plan filed with the government and not Gist's plan which was sent to John Hanbury.

273. The Fry and Jefferson *Map* (1751), published by Thomas Jefferys. For full bibliographical information see *Bibliography.*

274. See *Bibliography* for Lewis Evans, John Mitchell, and Fry and Jefferson *Maps* printed before 1760, the approximate date of this manuscript.

275. Colonel Patton did not go to Logstown to attend a conference in 1751 but to invite the Indians to the conference of 1752 (Thomas Cresap to Governor Dinwiddie, December 27, 1751. Original in Virginia State Library; printed in *Calendar of Virginia State Papers, op. cit.,* I, 245-47). The Indians at the Pennsylvania-Logstown con-

Annotations

ference of 1751 sent a message to the governor of Virginia, informing him that they would meet Virginia at Logstown in 1752 (see *note* 106). Although there is no record in the Virginia Council *Journals* which indicates that Patton was sent on a mission at this time, there is ample evidence extant to show that he was sent by the government.

On September 28, 1751, in preparation for this trip, Patton purchased of Thomas Cresap 300 white and 1,405 black wampum, among other items. He left for the Ohio about September 15, 1751, and returned to Thomas Cresap's by October 21, 1751. The first item on an expense account presented to the Virginia government by Patton is "shoeing my horses, Sept. 16, 1751." The last entry is dated October 21, 1751, at which time he returned the 1,405 black wampum not needed at present and paid his account with Cresap in full, £7 4s. 11d. —MS account, "James Patton to Virginia, Debtor, September 16, 1751." In Virginia State Library, Richmond, Virginia, Colonial Papers.

Patton's report of his trip to Logstown must have been satisfactory, for Virginia began preparations for the treaty. At a meeting of the Virginia Executive Council on December 12, 1751, the council ordered the receiver general to pay James Patton "for his Expences on his Journy to Loggs Town and the further Sum of £78. for his Extraordinary Trouble, and Loss of two Horses." Thomas Cresap's proposal for conveying the treaty goods from Frederick Town (Maryland) to Logstown was approved; arrangements were made to forward the said goods from Fredericksburg to Frederick Town; and "Joshua Fry Esqr and Colo James Patton were this day nominated Commissioners to Negotiate a Treaty with the Indians at Loggs Town, and deliver to them his Majesty's Present, if Mr Fry declines Mr Christopher Gest is to be appointed in his room." —Virginia Council *Journals*, V, 374.

276. Printed on pp. 122-139. For variants of this journal see *Chronology*, July 16, 1751.

277. These lands were located "on the Waters of Potowmack west and North west of the Line of Lord Fairfax and on the Branches of Youghyoughgane and Mongely" and "on the Waters of Potowmack and youyougane." —"Order," printed in Virginia Council *Journals*, V, 368. This was the same vicinity which the Ohio Company had tentatively marked to be the best place to begin their settlements.

278. The Ohio Company was given seven years to seat their lands and ten years to return the survey. John Hanbury's petition in behalf of the Ohio Company, January 10, 1749. See *Chronology*.

Annotations

279. George Croghan remarked that "the Indians Dos nott Like to hear of there Lands being Setled over the Allegany Mountain, & in particular by ye Virginians." —George Croghan to Richard Peters, July 3, 1749, *op. cit*. See also *note* 282.

280. Thomas Lee complained to Governor Hamilton that the Pennsylvania traders were arousing Indian sentiment against the Virginians (see letters in *Colonial Records of Pennsylvania*, V, 423-25). On the other hand, William Trent and George Croghan complained about the unethical tactics of Hugh Parker and Thomas Cresap, who were advertising for the Ohio Company. —Letters in *Pennsylvania Archives*, II, 16, 31.

281. Before the French engulfed the region that is now the state of Ohio, Virginia, and Carolina traders were chief among the English traders in the region. In the mid-1740's the English, dominated by George Croghan, reopened this region to English traders. In his remarks about Virginia's trading activities in 1749 Croghan stated that he believed the Ohio Company trade would be directed toward Lake Erie and not on the Ohio, in order to recapture the Miami trade which had been out of Virginia's hands for "Some years past and of Considerable advantage to this Province Pennsylvania" (Croghan to Peters, July 3, 1749, *op. cit.*). Pennsylvania was indeed eager for this trade and depended much on Croghan, for Thomas Penn asked Governor Hamilton "to consider well so as to give the greatest as well as the most speedy encouragement, to Trade you can, that we may not be long after the Ohio Company" (Penn to Hamilton, July 31, 1749. Penn Letter Books, II, 270-74. MS in Historical Society of Pennsylvania). Yet, in the light of extant records the statement in this document appears unfair. True, when Virginia traders made a bid for the western Indian trade the Pennsylvania traders became alarmed. Richard Peters acquainted Thomas Penn, then in England, of this impending threat to Pennsylvania's prosperous business. Penn, in turn, conferred with John Hanbury, who assured him that the Ohio Company did not intend to engross the Indian trade and that the fort which they wished to build was not for the protection of Virginians alone but for the protection of all settlers and all traders (Penn to Peters, February 24, 1751, *op. cit.*). When some Ohio Indians, at Thomas Cresap's request, traveled to Maryland to be fully informed about the "cheap goods" from Virginia, they conferred with Mr. Peters at George Croghan's house on June 7, 1750. At the conference the secretary informed them: "As Trade is of a private Nature,

Annotations

the Indians, since you ask my Advice, ought to buy their Goods where they can be best served. The People of Maryland and Virginia who deal in this Trade may serve You as well as any Others from Pennsylvania or elsewhere, and I advise you by all Means to go to Capt Cresap's and to cultivate a good Understanding with every body who can supply You with Goods, for it is equal to this Government from whence the Indians are supplied so that there be a good Harmony kept up between them and all the King's Subjects." —Minutes of the Conference, printed in *Colonial Records of Pennsylvania*, V, 439.

282. In a letter from George Croghan to [Richard Peters], dated July 3, 1749, Croghan informed Peters that "Mr Cresap & Mr Parker Spread amongst ye Ingans Last fall that ye Virginians was going to Setle a Branch of ohio Calld Yougagin & that then they wou'd Suply ye Indians with goods Much Cheaper." No records of actual trade transactions between the Ohio Company and the Indians were located. Minutes of the Logstown Conference infer that trade had not begun by 1752, and at the Conference the Ohio Company rescinded this promise to the Indians. There they informed the Indians that, unless they obtained permission to erect storehouses in their country, they could not supply them with goods at "so easie a rate." See p. 57, this work.

283. No mention is made in Gist's journals that he pressed for such an answer from the Indians; yet Oppaymolleah's speech infers that Gist did make some overture to the Indians. See *page* 39, this work.

284. As reported in Gist's journals, the answer expected to issue from a general meeting of the Indians was the answer to Gist's invitation for the Indians to attend a Virginia treaty at Fredericksburg (see *page* 14). The Indians at the Pennsylvania conference at Logstown did set the time and place for the Virginia meeting—1752 at Logstown. —*Colonial Records of Pennsylvania*, V, 537.

285. Joshua Fry, James Patton, and Lunsford Lomax were appointed. Their commissions and instructions from Governor Dinwiddie are printed in the *Virginia Magazine*, XIII, 143-52.

286. Also, at the same time, Gist was issued secret instructions "on a separate piece of paper." See *Chronology*, April 28, 1752.

287. The Treaty of Lancaster (1744) was the culmination of eight years' negotiations between the Six Nations and the colonies, Mary-

Annotations

land, Virginia, and Pennsylvania. At a treaty made in Philadelphia in October, 1736, the speaker for the Six Nations, in private conference, informed the president of the Council and the proprietors' agent that he had had a communication from the governor of Maryland. The Indian speaker said that in Governor Ogle's letter he had informed the Indians that he, the Governor, had received a letter from the King of England who wrote that he understood the Marylanders had been unfair to the Six Nations and "ordering him to see that they should not be wronged of their Lands." According to the Six Nations' speaker, Governor Ogle added that he understood some of his people had wronged them and assured the Indians that if they would come to Maryland "they should have justice done them." The speaker for the Indians then asked James Logan, President of the Council, to write to the governors of Maryland and Virginia, informing them that people of their respective governments had settled on lands not purchased from the Indians.

The next day the speaker for the Six Nations reiterated this request before the Council and added that they wished Pennsylvania "would take the Answer of those Governments, which next Spring some of their Nations will come to receive at the Fire kept for them in this place." They also informed the Council that they intended to "apply to the great King on the other side of the Water, & let Him know what they expect on this Head from His People." The president in Council, in answer to this demand, told the Indians that the Council would do anything they could for them, but they did not fully understand the meaning of the letter from the governor of Maryland to them, and furthermore, they did not believe there was any truth in it. In addition, the Council said they did not know how the Indians could support a claim against Virginia. —Pennsylvania (Colony) Treaties, etc., 1736, *A Treaty of Friendship held with the Chiefs of the Six Nations at Philadelphia in September and October, 1736* (Philadelphia: B. Franklin, 1737), pp. 13-14.

Nevertheless, both the Pennsylvanians and the Onondaga Council knew of the strained relations between Maryland and Virginia, and the Onondaga Council. The Six Nations had been alarmed by the many rumors of action which Virginia intended to take in order to avenge the murder, in 1732, of a man and his wife in Spotsylvania County. The Pennsylvanians were aware of the incident, for Governor Gooch had solicited Governor Gordon's assistance in seeking out the Conoy Indians who committed the murder (Gooch to Patrick Gordon, July 13, 1733, printed in *Colonial Records of Pennsylvania* III, 564). Thomas Cresap, the Marylander, in direct violation of the Six Na-

Annotations

tions' rule, had endeavored to purchase Pennsylvania land from Six Nations' warriors.

Shickellamy, intermediary between the Onondaga Council and Pennsylvania, was so fearful of ruptured relations with the colonies that he requested that even the Indians' friend, John Harris, who kept the ferry across the Susquehanna, stop clearing fields on the western side of the Susquehanna at the ferry crossing lest "the Warriours of the Six Nations, when they pass that way, may take it ill to see a Settlement made on Lands which they have always desired to be kept free from any Persons settling on" *(ibid.,* 500-04). Undoubtedly, the unfortunate murders in Virginia and the Virginia-Maryland land dispute prompted this complaint.

James Logan acceded in part to the Indians' request. On December 20, 1736, he wrote the governor of Maryland, informing him that he had evaded the Indians' request when they were in Philadelphia in July; but the Indians, insisting that he intercede for them, had given Conrad Weiser, the interpreter, the enclosed message on the subject. The message was as follows: "We desire further of Our Brethren Onas and James Logan to let Us know in as short a time as possible the Answer of the two Chief Men, One living in Annapolis and the Other in Virginia, if so be that the Chief Man of Annapolis and the Chief Man of Virginia do neglect to make Us any Consideration for Our said Land, We desire Our Brethren Onas and James Logan to let the Great King over the Great Sea know of it but notwithstanding let Us know as soon as possible the Answer of Both." —*Archives of Maryland,* XXVIII, 272. The Six Nations did not return to Philadelphia for their answer until July, 1742, at which time they were insistent that they receive a positive one on the Virginia and Maryland land question. Canasatego issued the threatening statement, "Let him say Yes or No, if he says Yes, we will treat with him, if No, we are able to do Ourselves Justice, and we will do it, by going to take Payment Ourselves." —*Ibid.,* 273.

The governor of Pennsylvania responded promptly to Canasatego's request and assured him that Mr. Logan did write, but that he had received no answer. Governor Thomas wrote immediately to Maryland.

Maryland was at the time endangered by both the Shawnee and Conoy Indians who were dissatisfied with settlements which Maryland had recently made on lands in eastern Maryland. This October meeting of the Council was a scene of frantic preparation to forestall any major Indian attack. Governor Bladen expressed relief that the recently planned Shawnee attack was discovered before it took place.

Annotations

He informed the Council that it was "absolutely necessary, for the Preservation of the Lives, and Security of the Property of his Majestys Subjects within this Province, according to the Example of the Neighbouring Governments; to enter into a Treaty with the Six Nations, who, by all the Accounts I have, are not only more numerous and formidable than all the other neighbouring Indians together, but also more to be relied on, in Case of a Rupture with France." —*Ibid.*, XLII, 295. Annapolis was not the favored place for the meeting. Governor Bladen in his message to the Council recommended that, in order to avoid the excessive expense of bringing so great a number of Indians to Annapolis, two commissioners be appointed to meet and treat with the Indians either at "Albany, or such Place as may be thought more convenient to treat with the said Indians." (*Ibid.*)

Robert King and Charles Carroll were appointed commissioners according to Governor Bladen's request. Colonel Levin Gale, who was going to Philadelphia, was "desired by this Board to take Care to provide in a proper manner for the Subsistence of the said Indians in their Journey to this Province and whatever He shall expend or engage for on that Occasion to be repaid him out of the Fund of three pence p hh^d for Arms" (*ibid.*, XXVIII, 293). Mr. Chase of Maryland and Conrad Weiser, intermediary in the dispute, carried the invitation to Shamokin in the summer of 1742. Shickellamy, the Onondaga Council's representative, agreed to take the invitation from there to the Onondaga Council, "and about half way he overtook some of the Onontagers who had been at the last Indian Treaty in Philadelphia, amongst whom was Caxhayion One of the Chiefs of Onontago, who undertook to carry the Message to Onontago and manage it in the best manner and promised to bring down an Answer from the Council to Shikellimo." The Indians dallied on the way and Shickellamy did not receive the promised answer. He, therefore, decided to go to Onondaga himself, but was stopped by the alarming news of the "unhappy skirmish" in Virginia in December, 1742. Shickellamy knew that his friend, Conrad Weiser, upon hearing the same news, would set out immediately for Shamokin. Weiser went to Shamokin as the old chief expected. After they conferred on both Maryland's invitation and the massacre of the Indians in Virginia, Shickellamy decided to carry Maryland's invitation to Onondaga himself; but, on account of the recent trouble with Virginia, he doubted whether the Six Nations would go as near Virginia as Annapolis. Weiser and the chiefs then arranged for a preliminary meeting to be held at John Harris' Ferry after Shickellamy returned from Onondaga. He suggested that Maryland decide upon some place farther

Annotations

from Virginia than Annapolis, "a Place where Bread or Meal Beef or Mutton is to be had some Pipes good Tobacco, and some good Rum should not be forgot, and where they can get Bark to make little Wig Wams, all which will please them very well" (Weiser to Gale, March 9, 1743, Peters Papers, II, 5, MS in Historical Society of Pennsylvania; printed in *Archives of Maryland,* XXVIII, 293-95). Governor Bladen, apparently most anxious to conclude this treaty, employed Thomas Cresap as another emissary to carry the invitation to the Six Nations. Bladen negotiated with him to have the meeting held at his (Cresap's) plantation at Old Town. "Sconohode, King of the Keyouekeas or Sinnacas," and others who met at Cresap's house on June 15, 1743, agreed to attend a conference at that place (Thomas Cresap to Shegelema [Shickellamy], April 4, 1743, Peters Papers, I, 118; Statement of Sconohode by interpreter, Michael Webster, June 15, 1743, *ibid.,* 122; Governor Bladen to the Six Nations, March 24, 1744, *ibid.,* II, 6, MSS in the Historical Society of Pennsylvania). Weiser, having heard that Cresap was also employed in arranging for the meeting, warned that Cresap was out of favor with the Onondaga Council and also that, on account of the strained relations between Virginia and the Six Nations, the Potomac should not even be mentioned as a place for treaty-making (Weiser to Gale, March 9, 1743, *op. cit.*). Mr. Gale, acting upon the advice given in Weiser's letter, recommended to Governor Bladen that he send another message to the Six Nations informing them that the Marylanders would meet and treat with them at any place they chose in the province of Pennsylvania. —Gale to Weiser, March 10, 1743, *Archives of Maryland,* XXVIII, 295-96.

Virginia's routine arrangements for the treaty were upset completely by the Indian skirmish in December, 1742. Governor Gooch at the time of the incident asked Pennsylvania's governor to have his emissary, Conrad Weiser, mediate the dispute with the Six Nations. After much negotiating Weiser, having taken "the Hatchet out of their Head" and distributed sufficient condolence to cover their dead, brought negotiations to a close. The Six Nations consented to come to Harris' Ferry in the summer of 1744, there to meet and treat and settle all disputes with Maryland and Virginia. —"Report of Conrad Weiser . . . of his second Journey to Shamokin on the Affairs of Virginia & Maryland . . . 1743," printed in *Colonial Records of Pennsylvania,* IV, 646-50.

But Governor Gooch was dissatisfied with the time and place of meeting. He complained to Governor Thomas that Weiser had changed the time and place of treating, from Cresap's at Old Town to

Annotations

Harris' Ferry, and from May to April, 1744. Governor Gooch preferred to meet the Indians at New Town (Lancaster, Pennsylvania) or Philadelphia. He also wished to have the meeting in May and not in April. —William Gooch to George Thomas, January 11, Thomas to Gooch, January 20, and Thomas Bladen to Weiser, January 25. Peters Papers, II, 1-3. MSS in Historical Society of Pennsylvania.

No sooner had Conrad Weiser completed negotiations for the conference to be held at Lancaster than the unfortunate incident of the murder of John Armstrong and his men cast a threatening cloud over its success. It was feared that the imprisonment of the murderers, Delaware Indians, in Lancaster might embarrass the Treaty Commissioners. Weiser's influence with the Indians at Shamokin insured a peaceful setting for the meeting. —"Conrad Weiser—his Report of his Journey to Shamokin," May 2, 1744, printed in *Colonial Records of Pennsylvania,* IV, 680-85.

By May 27, the Virginia commissioners were in Philadelphia (Journal of William Black, 1744, printed in *Pennsylvania Magazine,* I, 117-32, 233-49, 404-19; II, 40-49). The Maryland commissioners, however, chose to remain at Annapolis until they were informed by Conrad Weiser that the Indians were on their way. —Peters to Weiser, June 4, 1744, Peters Papers, II, 12, MS in Historical Society of Pennsylvania.

Since neither the governor of Virginia nor the governor of Maryland attended the meeting, Governor Thomas of Pennsylvania did not wish to attend. In truth, he believed that his "interposition will be thought by the Commissioners from that Government (Virginia) rather impertinent than necessary" (*Colonial Records of Pennsylvania,* IV, 686). It was through Conrad Weiser that Governor Thomas was persuaded that his presence was very necessary at the meeting (Wallace, *op. cit.,* 184). Although this treaty is often considered to be a treaty projected for the sole purpose of land acquisition by Maryland and Virginia, the land acquisition was of minor importance. France had just declared war on England. The Six Nations, the buffer between the English and French colonies in North America, held the balance of power in the New World. Edmund Jennings, one of Maryland's commissioners at the treaty, in his letter of June 12 to Lord Baltimore expresses this idea very clearly. Wrote Jennings of the recent opening of hostilities between France and England as it concerned the forthcoming conference. "I am truly sensible . . . of the Difficultys which may occurr from the Criticall Times, which no Doubt will Drive the French to sollicit & Ingage by Every Method the Indian Friendship: This will give the Indians a Handle to insist

· 537 ·

Annotations

(If they Treat with us at all) on a Greater Sums than what is allotted by the Assembly, or that Can be Discharged at present perhaps without your Lordships assistance: But after all If we should meet, we must not part upon bad Terms: The Event of this Treaty may be of such Consequence as to draw the Indians in junction wth the French not only on our Borders, but on those of His Maj^{tys} other Dominions in America on the Continent. This, Virginia & Pensylvania are so Aware of, That The Virg^a Comiss^{rs} are now at Philadelphia ready for the Treaty, And the Governor of Philadelphia designes to attend it, In order to forme a Defensive Allyance, If it Can be effected; But perhaps we may find the Indians so Averse in this point as that a strict neutrality may be the Only Thing they will Concede to." —*Archives of Maryland,* XLII, 666.

Since the Six Nations considered that they had come to Lancaster at the request of Maryland, the first conferences were between the Indians and the Commissioners from that colony. Canasatego, in reply to the Commissioner's address, informed him that "as there is no Obstacle to a good Understanding between us, except this Affair of our Land, we, on our Parts, do give you the strongest Assurances of our good Dispositions toward you, and that we are as desirous as you to brighten the Chain, and to put away all Hindrances to a perfect good Understanding."

Canasatego lodged more than one complaint against Virginia. Just as Virginia's Commissioner, Thomas Lee, spoke in a less conciliatory tone than did Jennings of Maryland, the Indians' reply to the Virginians was less conciliatory. In reply to Lee's questions about the status of the tribes which had been conquered by the Iroquois, the speaker for the Indians answered all of them and, in addition, accused the Virginians of altering the course of the Indian "road" agreed upon between them at the Albany Treaty of 1722. "Those Things must have been done by your People in manifest Breach of your own Proposal made at *Albany,*" was his final thrust. The Virginians were also informed "that the Affair of the Road must be looked upon as a Preliminary to be settled before the Grant of Lands; and that either the *Virginia* People must be obliged to remove more Easterly, or, if they are permitted to stay, that our Warriours, marching that Way to the Southward, shall go Sharers with them in what they plant."

Finally, Maryland gave the Indians "Goods" and gold, valued at £300 Maryland currency, in exchange for "A Release in Writing of all your Claim to any Lands in *Maryland.*" Virginia in exchange for "a Deed recognizing the King's Right to all the Lands that are, or shall be, by his Majesty's Appointment in the Colony of Virginia,"

Annotations

gave the Indians "These Goods and Two Hundred Pounds in Gold, which lie on the Table." In addition the Indians gained their chief objective, the right to a Warriors' Road to the South. —Pennsylvania (Colony) Treaties, etc., *A Treaty, Held at the Town of Lancaster, in Pennsylvania ... June, 1744* (Philadelphia, B. Franklin, 1744); see also *Commentary,* pp. 398-403.

288. At the Conference of 1742, held in Philadelphia, Canasatego, the Six Nations' Chief, banished the Delawares from the Forks of the Lehigh and offered them a new home at Shamokin, or Wyoming. Many Delawares at that time migrated to the Ohio Country. When Conrad Weiser delivered the invitation for the 1744 conference at Lancaster to the Six Nations at Shamokin, a deputy of the Onondaga Council told Weiser, "We have given the River Scokooniady (Juniata) for a hunting-place to our Cousins the Delawares, and our Brethren the Shawonese, and we our Selves hunt there some times. We, therefore, desire you will imediately by force remove all those that live on the said River of Scokooniady (Juniata)" ("The Report of Conrad Weiser, ... of his second Journey to Shamokin on the Affairs of Virginia & Maryland, April 21, 1743," *op. cit.*). The Six Nations considered all land west of the Susquehanna to be their hunting grounds.

289. Virginia had purchased these lands from the Indians by the Treaty of Lancaster (1744). It is therefore difficult to understand the term "purchase" in these instructions.

290. Montour was paid £30 by the Ohio Company for this assistance. They regarded the remuneration given him by Virginia insufficient for the service rendered. —"Orders of the Ohio Company, November 22, 1752." See *Chronology.*

291. Although Gist was directed to make the return, the proceedings in the Appendix of this manuscript were reported by Lunsford Lomax. See *page* 238 and *note* 697.

292. The Ohio Company had "a large Quantity lately come from New York." —Thomas Cresap to Conrad Weiser, February 20, 1752. Weiser Correspondence I, 38, MS in Historical Society of Pennsylvania.

293. The Company owned nine horses, at least. On March 19, 1750, Hugh Parker bought for the Ohio Company five horses (two of which

Annotations

were plough horses) and four mares, among other items. Bill of sale to Hugh Parker in behalf of the Ohio Company. —Frederick County, Maryland, Deeds B, folios 343-44, 347-48, MS in Hall of Records, Annapolis, Maryland.

294. Printed on pp. 273-284, this work. Extracts from the minutes of this conference appear in several documents in the George Mercer manuscripts and in the printed *Case of the Ohio Company*. For location of these variants, see *Chronology*, June 13, 1752. The minutes, as printed in the *Virginia Magazine*, V, 143-74, are from a contemporary manuscript copy attributed to James Patton and owned by the Virginia Historical Society. The copy sent to the Board of Trade and identified at present as in P.R.O., C.O. 5: 1327/575-612 was received and read at the Board on February 28, 1753. The copy in the Public Record Office in London and the one in the Virginia Historical Society are, for the most part, identical. Different punctuation or a word change occurs occasionally. Although the proceedings at Shannopin's Town, May 29-31, which are in the Public Record Office and the Virginia Historical Society copy, are not in the George Mercer papers, notice of the variants is given by annotation.

Simultaneously, John Hanbury and Thomas Lee were requested by the Ohio Company to ask the Board of Trade to sanction a conference between Virginia and the Six Nations in fulfillment of commitments made to the Six Nations by Virginia at the Treaty of Lancaster. —"Résumé of Affairs, June 21, 1749." See *Chronology*.

Lee wrote to the Board of Trade, and John Hanbury in London acted accordingly. Conrad Weiser carried Virginia's invitation to the Onondaga Council, but the Six Nations refused to travel to Fredericksburg, Virginia, the treaty headquarters (1750); whereupon Lee sent an invitation by Christopher Gist to the Six Nations and to other tribes on the Ohio. The Ohio Indians likewise refused to come to Fredericksburg (1751). However, at the Pennsylvania Logstown Conference (1751), the Indians there assembled decided that they would confer with the Virginians at Logstown in 1752. Upon being informed of the Indians' wishes, Virginia sent James Patton to Logstown to issue them a formal invitation to the conference. Through some misunderstanding the Indians living on the Ohio, who were ruled by a deputy chief from the council at Onondaga, failed to send Virginia's formal invitation, the belt of wampum, to Onondaga.

Although it is stated in the minutes of the conference that a chief from the Onondaga Council was present, other information within the text and declarations made to Sir William Johnson belie the offi-

Annotations

cial status of that chief from Onondaga. Since the Onondaga Council officially denied knowledge of the transactions which transpired at Logstown, and Virginia herself knew that since her official invitation had not reached the Six Nations' Council Fire this Logstown confirmation of the Lancaster deed was worthless. Virginia moved immediately after the conference to make the confirmation valid by inviting the Six Nations to come to Winchester to receive a present from them. The Six Nations again refused to come. William Trent brought Ohio Indians to the conference where they repudiated their promise made so recently.

However, they were given for the second time not only the gift intended for the Six Nations but an additional quantity of arms and ammunition. William Trent delivered the present to them at Logstown in February, 1754. Hostilities began on the Ohio a few months later, and so Virginia could not test the validity of this bastard treaty. Four years spent in negotiations failed to bring about a treaty between the Six Nations and Virginia, a treaty in fulfillment of the promise made to Canasatego at Lancaster in 1744. In granting lands west of the great mountains to the Ohio Company, Virginia found herself unable to give the Company a clear land title. She had tried for four years to lift the mortgage, to give the Six Nations the "further Consideration" which had been promised them. When hostilities ceased on the Ohio in 1758, the right to grant lands in the region passed from colony to crown. Hence the Conference at Logstown availed nothing to the Company nor to Virginia. Only the Ohio Indians profited by three handsome presents.

Minutes of the conference at Shannopin's Town, May 29–31, as found in the Public Record Office, which are omitted in all variants of the minutes in the George Mercer papers, are as follows:

Friday the 29th: of May
At a Council held at Shenapin's Town
Present
Joshua Fry
Lunsford Lomax   Comissrs
James Patton
Mr Christopher Gist Agent for the Ohio Company
The Chiefs of the Delawar Indians
Mr Andrew Montour Interpreter

The Speaker of the Indians addressing himself to the Comissrs Said Brethren. You have come a long Journey, & have Sweated a great deal. We wipe off yr Sweat with this String of Wampum.   *Gave a String.*

Annotations

Brethren. You are come a long Way, & we are glad to See you. We hope You Will open y^r Hearts to us, & Speak clearly; & that You may be enable to do it, We clear y^r Voice with this String of Wampum.
Gave a String.

Brethren. You are come from far, & have heard many Stories & false Reports, about us y^r Brethren. We hope you will not keep them in y^r Mind; & that you may disregard them, we give you this String of Wampum. *Gave a String.*

Brethren. We desire you will consider our Brethren, that live towards the Sunsetting, & that you will give them y^r: best Advice; upon which we give you this String of Wampum. *Gave a String.*

Then Mr Christopher Gist, & Mr Andrew Montour, deliver'd to the Comiss^{rs} a String of Wampum, from the Council at Logs Town, to let them know, they were glad to hear of their being on the Road, & to assure them that they might come in Safety to Logs Town. The Comiss^{rs} not having any Wampum String, without which Answers could not be return'd, acquainted the Indians, that they wou'd answer their Speeches in the Afternoon, on which the Council broke up.

May the 29th in the Afternoon

The Same Persons being met the Comiss^{rs} spoke as followeth. Brethren the Chiefs of the Delawars. We have had a long & difficult Journey hither, to see our Brethren, but that has been sufficiently made amends for, by the kind reception you have given us. We assure you we are glad to meet you here in Council, & present you with this String of Wampum. *Gave a String.*

Brethren. In y^r second Speech, you clear'd our Voices, that we might speak our Minds to you. In answer to which we inform you, that the great King our Father, has sent by us a Present of Goods, to his Children the Indians, the Largest he has even given them, which we are to deliver at Logstown, whither we are going. It is the Desire of our Father, that you, & we his Children, Shou'd be Strongly united together as one People; & that it is our Inclination So to be Join'd, we confirm to you by this String of Wampum. *Gave a String.*

Brethren. In answer to y^r third Speech, We let you know, that we did hear Many Stories in our Way hither, rais'd by idle, & wicked People, to occasion a Difference between us, but we did not believe them, & now we are satisfied that they were False. If any other shou'd be spread, we shall wholly disregard them, & we hope you will do the like; & that our good Agreement may always continue; we give you this String of Wampum. *Gave a String.*

Brethren. We heartily wish well to our Brethren, who live towards

Annotations

the Sun Setting, & Shall be always ready to assist them, with our best Advice, whenever we shall be inform of their Circumstances, which in the Course of the Treaty to be held at Log's Town, we suppose, we may be. We present you with this String of Wampum.   *Gave a String.*

295. This introduction, as reported in both the Public Record Office and Virginia Historical Society copy, is as follows: "The Chiefs of the Indians then at Loggs Town having met in their Council House, by a Message acquainted the Commissioners that they had something to say to them. They went to the Place, and they and the other Company being seated, a Chief of the Six Nations stood up, & addressing himself to the Commissioners, spoke as followeth:" —*Virginia Magazine,* XIII, 158; P.R.O., C.O., 5: 1327/575-612.

296. When Andrew Montour informed Governor Hamilton that he was to be employed by Virginia as interpreter at a meeting at Logstown, he asked "his Honour's Leave and Advice how to act." Hamilton, believing that Virginia's Logstown conference was of utmost importance, gave Montour advice and "thought it best to give it him in Writing, and that it should be enter'd in the Council Books." In the form of a memorandum the governor asked Montour to convey his message "to the Six Nations and all the other Indians residing at Ohio in such a manner as you think will make the deepest Impression on them." Hamilton's desire, as expressed to Montour, was that the "kinder they [the Indians] are to the Virginia People, the more agreeable it will be to me" ("Memorandum," James Hamilton to Andrew Montour, April 18, 1752, printed in *Colonial Records of Pennsylvania,* V, 568). Evidently Montour believed that George Croghan could convey the messages from Hamilton in the best manner possible.

297. The minutes of the conference, as recorded in the "Case of the Ohio Company, 1754," and in "appendix" of this document, begin with this sentence. See *Chronology,* June 13, 1752.

298. At Shannopin's Town Andrew Montour and Christopher Gist delivered the commissioners a string of wampum sent by the Council at Logstown. —*Virginia Magazine,* V, 156.

299. The Virginia traders accused those from Pennsylvania of circulating the story that the Virginians intended to build a fort on their lands, which would be to their detriment. Lee complained to Governor Hamilton: "But your Traders have prevailed with the Indians on the Ohio to believe that the Fort is to be a bridle for them,

Annotations

and that the roads which the Company are to make is to let in the Catawbas upon them to destroy them, and the Indians naturally jealous are so possessed with the truth of these Insinuations that they threaten our Agents if they survey or make those Roads." —Lee to Hamilton, November 22, 1749, printed in *Colonial Records of Pennsylvania,* V, 422-23.

300. Half King and this chief, supposedly from Onondaga, arrived for the council on June 4. Although extant records of this treaty recite the above information, Sir William Johnson informed Governor Clinton that he "could not learn that one of the Sachims or Young Men of the Six Nations attempted even to go Virginia last year; They also declare that they have not received any of the said Present, but they heard it was given to some Indians living about Ohio, Shawaness &c: which they don't seem well satisfied at." —Johnson to Clinton, March 26, 1753. *The Documentary History of the State of New-York; ...,* edited by E. B. O'Callaghan ... (Albany, Weed, Parsons & Co., 1849-51), II, 624.

301. Variants of this document give additional information about the "debates." See pp. 238, 274, this work.

302. The chief aim of the conference was to gain Indian consent to the Ohio Company adventure. Governor Dinwiddie to the Board of Trade stated, "I shall give the Commiss^{rs} in Command to Insist on that Treaty [Lancaster, 1744] and on a Setlement on the Ohio, agreeable to his Majesties late Grant [to the Ohio Company]." —Letter of January 20, 1752, in P.R.O., C.O. 5: 1327/453-54.

303. A variant of June 2 entry gives additional pertinent information. See *Chronology.*

304. One of which was Big Hominy. See entry for June 9, this document. Exclusive of the aged, bedridden Kakawatcheky, the four principal Shawnee chiefs on the Ohio were Newcomer, Big Hominy, the Pride, and Tamany Buck. Big Hominy was present at Logstown; Trent met Newcomer at Lower Shawnee Town; the Pride, who was killed in South Carolina, was probably on the warpath to the south at this time. Therefore, the other Shawnee chief present must have been Tamany Buck.

305. The Shawnee awaited anxiously for a special message from the

Annotations

Virginians. On February 8, 1752, George Croghan wrote to Governor Hamilton informing him that the Shawnee were determined "to be revenged on the French for the thirty Men of the Twightwees that the French have killed this Winter, and they wou'd not undertake such a Proceeding without acquainting you and having your advice, which I take to be as if they wanted to be assured of your Friendship if they engaged in a War with the French." Croghan enclosed in the letter a message from the Shawnee to the governor, reiterating the long friendship and trust which existed between Pennsylvania and them, asking the governor for guidance in this matter, and assuring him that they, the Shawnee, would "be directed by you and no other." —Croghan to Hamilton, printed in *Colonial Records of Pennsylvania*, V, 568-69.

The governor answered both letters on April 24. He reminded Croghan that he well knew that the General Assembly was averse to war; therefore, he must evade the Shawnee demands or make false promises which he would not do. His answer to the Shawnee was a masterpiece in the field of diplomacy. He wrote: "The Circumstances and real Inclinations of the other Indian Nations among whom you live, with regard to these bad men the subjects of the King of France, are not so well known to me as to enable me to give you proper advice, but since I understand that his Majesty our great King over the Waters has invited you and the other Indian Nations to a Council to be held at Logg's Town this next month, and Mr. Crawford tells me all the Indians are determined to be present at this Juncture at the meeting, I think the Counsellors and Commissioners for Virginia will be better enabled on the spot to judge of what shall be proper for you and the other Indian Nations to do, and will, I doubt not, give you good and faithful advice." —Hamilton to the Shawnee, printed in *Colonial Records of Pennsylvania*, V, 571.

306. The Half King or Tanacharison, a Seneca chief, was the Onondaga Council's representative ruler over the Indians on the Ohio from about 1747 to late 1754. A "Tanarecco, Mingow" signed, by his mark, an Indian letter from the Ohio dated May 1, 1747, recommending their friends, the Miami, to the English interest (Indian letter to President and Council, May 1, 1747, printed in *Pennsylvania Archives*, I, 737). When the Twightwees were admitted into the Anglo-Six Nations alliance at Lancaster July, 1748, all the principal chiefs from the Ohio attended the conference. On the roster of those attending are the names of chiefs, commonplace in the regional history of this period. The wide variation in spelling of these names from

Annotations

time to time makes positive identification impossible. In the instance of this treaty "Suchrachery, a chief of the Seneka Nation" appears to be the Half King (Scruniattha).

The first reference to Tanacharison as the Half King appears in Conrad Weiser's journal of his conference with the Indians at Logstown in 1748 (*op. cit.*). At this time the Half King informed Weiser that he was new in the field of Indian diplomacy; therefore, in order to purchase wampum and send messengers abroad, he needed extra gifts for his Council bag.

At the Virginia Logstown conference in June, 1752 the Half King officiated at the ceremony of making Shingas king of the Delawares (see *page* 62). This conference was a Virginia–Six Nations affair. In 1744, by the Treaty of Lancaster, Virginia had recognized their ownership of the Ohio Country. She had tried unsuccessfully to fulfill a certain promise made in that treaty whereby, as Virginia extended her frontier, the Six Nations would receive "further consideration" for the land. The Ohio Company who received this grant in 1749 wished to seat their lands on the Ohio, and representatives from the Onondaga Council could not be prevailed upon to go to Virginia to confirm the release of these lands; therefore, Virginia, in the face of rapid French aggression, chose the expedient method, dealing with the Six Nations representative on the Ohio. From this time, June, 1752, to the death of the Half King, October, 1754, the history of Virginia's efforts to retain her foothold on the Ohio can be traced by a study of her negotiations with this Six Nations' deputy.

Pennsylvania entertained no thoughts of territorial claim in this region. To the Pennsylvanians, the Ohio Country was a huge trading post where furs were traded for Indian goods and the profits were a chief source of pounds (£) sterling. When the Half King reluctantly signed a confirmation of the deed executed at Lancaster (see *Case, facs.*, appendix, pp. 21-22), Virginia replaced Pennsylvania as the dominant English influence on the Ohio. Virginia now assumed the rôle of colonial domination, while Pennsylvania receded to the position of colonial assistant to the Crown.

William Trent, the Pennsylvania partner of George Croghan, was given an "in-the-field" commission to carry the Twightwees' portion of the Logstown gift to the Miami Country (see *note* 105). When he returned to Williamsburg in the fall of 1752 he was officially appointed factor for the Ohio Company (see *Chronology*, September 19, 1752). Early in 1753 Governor Dinwiddie named him unofficial representative for Virginia on the Ohio (see *Case, facs.*, pp. 9-10). From the time of the Logstown Conference until the French took possession of

Annotations

Virginia's little stockade on April 17, 1754, William Trent and the Half King were the English and Indian diplomats who worked unceasingly but unsuccessfully to build an effective barrier against French aggression.

In May, 1753, at Trent and Croghan's trading house (on the Allegheny at the mouth of Pine Creek) Trent, by four strings of wampum in behalf of the governor of Virginia, told the Half King "that he [Virginia's governor] look'd upon the Ohio Lands to belong to them the Indians, and that if the French attempted to settle them or to build any Forts, the Virginians would supply them with Arms and Ammunition." The Half King answered for the entire Six Nations' population in the region by saying: "if the French came peaceably they would receive them as Friends, but that if they came as Enemies they would treat them as such; that they hoped their Brethren the English wou'd consider how they were circumstanced and send them a supply of arms and ammunition, which if they did they did not doubt but that they wou'd be able to strike the French." Most of the Shawnee and Delaware were too drunk to give a positive answer "but several of their chief Men declared they wou'd agree to what the Half King had said." —*Colonial Records of Pennsylvania*, V, 614-16.

Although William Trent acted immediately on the question of aid for the Half King, the old chief was impatient. Only a month after he had conferred with William Trent, he sent another message to Virginia via Thomas Burney who had been on a mission to the Twightwees. In this speech, addressed to the governor of Virginia, the Half King requested him to send a representation to meet the Indians at the Forks of the Monongahela. The Half King had been informed that there were 300 Frenchmen and 10 Caughanawaga Indians within two-days' journey of Logstown. They wished to have the Virginia representation go along with them to the French, in order to find out why they came. The Half King closes this message with a remark which epitomizes his feelings toward the English. Wrote the Half King: "we do not want the French to come amongst Us at all, but very much want our good Brothers the English to be with us, to whom our Hearts are good and shall ever continue to be so." —The Half King to the governor of Virginia, June 22, 1753, printed in *ibid.*, V, 635.

Virginia sent a substantial gift of arms and ammunition to the Ohio in July. William Trent, as usual, represented Virginia, and although many Indians and their chiefs were at Logstown to partake of the bounty, it was the Half King who conferred daily with Trent.

Annotations

His facility for obtaining information is amazing. The minutes of this conference give, through the words of the Half King, a complete panorama of French activity from Presqu'Isle to Logstown. On the 24th of August the Half King and Scarouady, Six Nations' deputy over the Shawnee, resolved, according to Indian custom, to send the third and final warning to the French to stop building forts on their, the Indians', lands. The two chiefs agreed that the Half King, first deputy on the Ohio, should carry the message to the French and Scarouady, second in authority, would confer with the governor of Virginia at Winchester. Since the Half King could not attend the Winchester conference, the Six Nations requested that "whatever Speeches may be made by the Governor, may be sent in Writing, as well as what is deliver'd by Word of Mouth to our People that go down." —William Trent's "Account of his Proceedings with the six Nations of Indians & their Allies, at Logstown, July 11–September 14, 1753," *op. cit.*

The Half King was at his home at Logstown when George Washington arrived there in December, 1753. Washington had been commissioned by Governor Dinwiddie to go to the French on the Ohio, to find out if they were building military installations on English-claimed territory and, if so, to warn them to leave. At the conference the chief informed Washington of the haughty answer he had received to the Indians' third and last warning to the French. —Extract of the Half King's Speech to the French printed in *Case, facs.,* p. 23; the full "Substance of what he spoke" is printed in George Washington, *The Journal of . . . Sent by the Hon. Robert Dinwiddie* [in 1753] *. . . to the Commandant of the French Forces on Ohio . . .* (Williamsburgh Printed, London, reprinted for T. Jefferys, 1754), pp. 9-10.

When Washington left Logstown for Fort Le Boeuf, on December 30, Half King, two other chiefs, and one hunter accompanied him. George Croghan, John Patten, and Andrew Montour were at Logstown when, on January 15, 1754, Half King and his party of Indians returned from Fort Le Boeuf. "Five Canoes of French" arrived with him. Washington had returned to Williamsburg by an alternate route. Croghan reported that Half King accepted presents from the French at Logstown but remained heartily in the English interest. A speech delivered to Patten and Croghan by this chief was signed by six other chiefs of the Ohio and sent to the governors of Pennsylvania and Virginia. In the speech the Half King requested the governor of Virginia to build a "Strong House" at the Forks of the Monongahela and to maintain a garrison there; he asked the governor of Pennsylvania to build another strong house somewhere along the river

Annotations

for the purpose of housing "whatever assistance he will think proper to send us"; and he told both governors that the Six Nations "have our Hatchet in our Hands to strike the Enemy as soon as our Brethren come to our assitance." —A speech delivered by the Half King, January, 1754, printed in *Colonial Records of Pennsylvania*, V, 734.

When William Trent arrived at the Forks of the Ohio in February, to deliver the present which Virginia had allotted the Ohio Indians at Winchester in September, 1753, and to build an Ohio Company storehouse and a Virginia fort, the Half King was greatly encouraged by this show of English assistance. From this time until the fall of Fort Necessity in July the old chief assumed the rôle of advisor to the English. Ensign Ward said Half King laid the first log for the fort and was his chief advisor when he was forced to capitulate to the superior French forces. —Deposition of Ensign Ward, May 7, 1754. P.R.O., C.O. 5: 14/293.

The day after the capitulation Half King sent a message to the governors of Virginia and Pennsylvania (printed in *Case, facs.*, page 19). Ensign Ward and the Indian runners who took the message to the English settlements showed it to Washington who had just begun his march to the Ohio Country. Washington sent a copy of the message to the governor of Pennsylvania, made another copy which he later incorporated in his diary, and then dispatched Ward and the runners to Governor Dinwiddie. He answered the Half King's speech himself, promising him that assistance was on the way and asking him to come to meet his Virginia militia.

Governor Dinwiddie's answer to the Half King was relayed to the chief by Washington. On May 19 he dispatched one of the Indian runners to the chief with his, Washington's, speech in which he acquainted the Half King "with an agreeable speech which the Governor of *Virginia* has sent to you: He is very sorry for the bad usage you have received. The swollen streams do not permit us to come to you quickly, for that reason I have sent this young man to invite you to come and meet us: he can tell you many things that he has seen in *Virginia,* and also how well he was received by the most prominent men; they did not treat him as the *French* do your people who go to their Fort; they refuse them provisions; this man has had given him all that his heart could wish; for the confirmation of all this, I here give you a Belt of *Wampum*."

On May 24 Washington received the Half King's reply to his message of May 19. It was an open letter "to any of his Majesty's officers whom this May Concern." The Half King warned the English that the French had left Fort Duquesne to seek out and destroy

· 549 ·

Annotations

Washington's little army. He also informed them that he and other chiefs would join the Virginians in council within five days (Washington, *Journal of . . . 1754 . . .* [Toner edition], *op. cit.,* pp. 45-51, 66-67, 71). Coulon de Jumonville was in command of the French. Half King and the other chiefs arrived at the Indians' camp in time to confer with and assist Washington in his pursuit of the French. For a discussion of this skirmish see *note* 506. Half King remained with the Virginia militia and was with Washington at the Battle of Fort Necessity where they capitulated to the French. Later the old chief complained to Conrad Weiser that, had Washington taken his advice, the English would not have been defeated. —"Journal of the Proceedings of Conrad Weiser in his way to and at Aucquick . . . in . . . 1754, in August and September," *op. cit.,* p. 151.

This fiasco seemed to be too much for the Half King. After the battle he went to Fort Cumberland, but soon traveled east to Croghan's home at Aughwick, bringing with him many loyal Six Nations' Indians from the Ohio Country. From Aughwick he wrote in vain for Shingas and other socage Indians to leave the Ohio. He was present at the conference which Conrad Weiser held with those refugee Indians at Aughwick in August and September, 1754. Here he advised Weiser, in private, to keep the Delaware and Shawnee from returning to their homes on the Ohio. Half King did not believe in their integrity.

Perhaps the last official record of this Seneca chief is in a letter received at the Onondaga Council, September 20, in which he states that he shall live and die with the English (Daniel Claus to Richard Peters, September 29, 1754, printed in *Colonial Records of Pennsylvania,* VI, 182-83). Early in October the Half King did die among the English at John Harris'. When Harris asked the Indians where they chose to bury him and in what manner, they answered, "they looked upon him to be like one of our Selves, and as he died among us we might bury him as we thought proper; that if he was buried well it would be very good, which I did much to their Satisfaction." —Harris to Peters, October 29, 1754, printed in *ibid.,* VI, 184.

307. Appended to the minutes of the Conference at Logstown, an enclosure in Dinwiddie's letter of December 7, 1752, to the Board of Trade (P.R.O., C.O. 5: 1327/575-612), was a copy of a letter to Captain William Trent and of the speech to the Twightwees which are as follows:

Annotations

Logs Town June 13th

To Capt William Trent
Sir

We desire you to proceed with Expedition to the Picts Town, & there to deliver to the Pianquisna King, the Lac'd Hat, Cloak & Vest for his own use, & the rest of the Present, to be dispos'd of as he, & the rest of his great Men, shall think fit; & that you will endeavour to promote his Majesties Interest there.

      Joshua Fry
      Lunsford Lomax
      James Patton"

(Original letter signed by the three commissioners is in the Etting Collection, Revolutionary Papers, p. 90, Historical Society of Pennsylvania.)

Speech to the Twightwees

"Brethren the Twightwees. You join'd in a Council Chain with us, your Brethren the English, & the Six Nations of Indians, Three or four Years ago, which was agreeable to us.

The King of Great Britain has now sent, a very large Present of Goods to Logs Town, to be divided among his Children; & as you could not come thither, we have taken care to send you part.

We join with the Six Nations in advising you, to Stand fast to the Chain of Friendship, which you have already taken hold, & assure you of the Friendship, of the Government of Virginia under the Direction, of the Great King yr Father, on the other side of the Water.

      J. F.
      L. L.
      J. P.

A true Copy
by Wm Withers

The gift sent to the Twightwees was in answer to a message sent by the Shawnee via George Croghan to the governor of Pennsylvania on February 8, 1752. They informed the English of the deplorable condition of their friends, the Twightwees, who had been attacked by the French and had had 30 warriors killed. Governor Hamilton, hampered by a hostile Quaker assembly referred the Shawnee to the Virginians who were about to hold their treaty at Logstown. — A message to the governor from the Shawnee, February 8, 1752; Hamilton's answer to George Croghan and to the Shawnee, April 24, printed in *Colonial Records of Pennsylvania*, V, 569-71.

On October 6, 1752, Dinwiddie informed the Board of Trade that Virginia had sent part of the present distributed at Logstown to the

Annotations

Twightwees. —Dinwiddie to the Board of Trade, October 6, 1752, printed in Trent, *Journal of . . . 1752, op. cit.*, pp. 69-72.

308. In 1748 Conrad Weiser kindled the separate Council Fire at Logstown for the Ohio Indians. His account of this historic event is printed in *Colonial Records of Pennsylvania*, V, 348-58. See also note 77.

309. Canasatego, a Six Nations' chief, given to quick wit and great oratory. In 1743 when Conrad Weiser and John Bartram visited Onondaga on a mission for Virginia, Canasatego was the chief advisor (Wallace, *op. cit.*, pp. 161-68). Also it was he who, in 1742, banished the Delawares from their land in eastern Pennsylvania, assigning them hunting grounds and abode at Wyoming or Shamokin (*ibid.*, 130). He died in September, 1750. The entire Onondaga Council went into mourning and Pennsylvania sent condolence gifts. —"A Journal of the Proceedings of Conrad Weiser in his Journey to Onondago, with a Message from the Honourable Thomas Lee, . . . to the Indians there, August 15–October 10, 1750"; "Mr. Weiser's Journal of his Proceedings at Onondago," July 10, 1751. Printed in *Colonial Records of Pennsylvania*, V, 470-80 and 541-43, respectively.

310. According to Conrad Weiser's journal of the conference at Logstown (1748), the Indians were not told that the present was in accordance with the Treaty of Lancaster (1744). Weiser stated that in reply to the solicitation of the Ohio Indians at Philadelphia in the fall of 1747, Pennsylvania prepared a gift of arms and ammunition with which they could fight the French. Since the French and English were at peace in 1748, the province turned the war supplies "into a Civil & Brotherly Present." Weiser delivered the present in these words: "Here are the Goods before your Eyes, which I have, by your Brethern's Order, divided into 5 Shares & layd in 5 different heaps, one heap whereof your Brother Assaraguoa [governor of Virginia] sent to You to remember his Friendship and Unite with You." In acceptance the spokesman for the Indians replied, "We return you many thanks for the large Presents; the same we do to our Brother Assaraquoa, who joined our Brother Onas in making us a Present." —"Journal" printed in *ibid.*, 348-58.

However, in the acknowledgment of Governor Palmer's request for Virginia to participate in Pennsylvania's Conference at Logstown (1748), Governor Gooch replied, "I must acknowledge the Request You make is so just & equitable, considering the Share we shall have

Annotations

in the advantage of fixing the Ohio Indians steadfast in the British Interest" (Gooch to Palmer, March 7, 1748, printed in *ibid.*, 221-22). The Virginia Council's instructions, via Governor Palmer, to Conrad Weiser were: "to place either the Money or Goods, as Your Honour & he shall think most expedient, in the hands of those Indians as a free Gift from the Government of Virginia, that the Ohio Indians may know to whom they are oblig'd, and not only remember their Engagements to the Crown of Great Britain, but they & all the Indians living near that River may by Gratitude be restrain'd from doing any manner of Injury or Wrong to our Inhabitants. These are the Instructions we have thought fit to give Captain Robinson and your honest & worthy Interpreter, which we trust will be satisfactory to Your Honour & the Council of Pennsylvania." —Gooch to Palmer, May 9, 1748, printed in *Colonial Records of Pennsylvania*, V, 257-58.

311. Meaning the Ohio Company.

312. This statement is like a page from William Penn's diary. In 1701, when William Penn informed the Indians at Philadelphia that he had purchased their lands on the Susquehanna from the Onondaga Council by the Dongan Treaty (1684), he assured them that they would continue to have the same privilege to the land as his own people. To seal this agreement he gave the deed to the chiefs present, requesting them to preserve the document for three generations. Dramatically, Penn added that the fourth generation will have forgotten all differences between the races. Charles Thomson, Indian interpreter and secretary, doubted this statement and remarked that "all we know of the Contents of the Writing is from this [the above] account given by the Proprietary Agents." —Thomson, *op. cit.*, p. 8n.

313. Refers to Céloron's expedition. In 1749 Rolland Michel Barrin, Marquis de La Galissonière, governor of New France, sent Pierre-Joseph Céloron de Blainville to warn the English traders off "their lands," and to entice the disloyal Indians on the banks of the Ohio and its tributaries, back to the French King. He buried six leaden plates on the Ohio. The first plate was placed, or was to be placed, at the junction of Conewango Creek and the Allegheny River, near Warren, Pennsylvania; the second, in the Allegheny below Franklin, probably at Big Rock; the third, at the junction of Wheeling Creek and the Ohio River at Wheeling, West Virginia; the fourth, at the junction of the Muskingum and Ohio Rivers at Marietta, Ohio; the fifth, at the junction of the Kanawha and Ohio Rivers at Point

Annotations

Pleasant; and the sixth plate, at the mouth of the Great Miami on the Ohio below Cincinnati, Ohio. The first plate was at the time (1749) sent to New York's Governor Clinton by bewildered Indians who found or stole it; the second, third, and sixth ones have not been unearthed; the fourth plate was found in 1798 by some youngsters who were bathing at the mouth of the Muskingum and is now in the American Antiquarian Society, Worcester, Massachusetts; and the fifth one, found in 1846 by a boy who was playing on the Kanawha River bank, is now in the Virginia Historical Society (Galbreath, *op. cit.*, pp. 114-27; reproduction of Father Bonnecamp's *Carte du Voyage Fait Dans La Belle Riviere En La Nouvelle France M DCC XLIX* in Galbreath, *op. cit.*, pp. 10-11).

Céloron's party traveled from Montreal up the St. Lawrence to Lake Erie, to Conewango Creek, to the Allegheny River, to the Ohio, and down the Ohio to the mouth of the Great Miami River. The expedition then went up the Great Miami (13 days' travel) to Pickawillany, where they tried unsuccessfully to lead that great group of English-loving Miami Indians back to their "ancient fire at Kiskakon," the French Miami fort on the site of present Fort Wayne, Indiana. Céloron did not return by way of Detroit but traveled east along Lake Erie to Montreal. His account of this journey has been translated into English and is printed in several places. Perhaps the best and most accessible is W. O. Marshall's translation edited by G. B. Galbreath, *op. cit.*

314. Conrad Weiser's journal of his 1748 journey to Logstown records that there were 20 English traders at Logstown. —*Op. cit.*

315. In 1749 Céloron tried unsuccessfully to persuade the rebel Miami or Twightwee to return to the French interest. The same year Captain de Raymond was commissioned commander of the French Miami post, Kiskakon, where he prevented the remainder of the Miami from joining La Demoiselle at Pickawillany (De Raymond to Rouillé, October 1, 1751, printed in Wisconsin Historical Society *Collections,* XVIII, 94-98; also *notes* 142 and 98). Céloron, commandant at Detroit, was ordered in 1751 to subdue this Miami rebellion by force. When the French were unable to secure Indian reinforcements around Detroit the expedition was abandoned. Lieutenant de Longueuil, who commanded an expedition against Pickawillany in 1751, delayed action until June, 1752. Céloron reported to Governor de La Jonquière that Longueuil considered his force insufficient for successful attack and that no dependence could be placed on Indian assistance for any expedition (Longueuil to

Annotations

Rouillé, April 21 [i.e. May 17], 1752, printed in *N.Y.C.D.*, X, 245-51). That the Twightwee were alarmed by the French incursions of 1751 is shown by Governor Dinwiddie's letter of October 6, 1752. Dinwiddie informed the Lords of Trade: "I beg leave to observe that the Twightwees, a large nation of Indians to the westward of the river Ohio, have taken up the hatchet (as they term it) against the French and the Indians in amity with them; that is, that they have declared war against the French and their allies, and that they solicited the friendship of the English and the nations of Indians on the Ohio; as this application was made before His Majesty's present was divided, the commissioners (I think) prudently laid aside part of the present for the Twightwees, which was much approved of by the other nations of Indians then at Logstown, and they sent two gentlemen with that present, to be delivered to the chiefs in the name of His Majesty, the King of Great Britain." —Letter, *op. cit.*

316. By the Lancaster Treaty of 1744 the northern Indians were confined by the Potomac River and "the high ridge of Mountains which extend all along the frontiers of Virginia to the westward of the present settlements of that Colony." It was also agreed that neither northern nor southern Indians should cross that boundary without producing a passport from New York or Virginia, respectively.

317. In July, 1748, the Six Nations at Ohio interceded for the Shawnee; whereupon the Pennsylvania commissioners for the conference at Lancaster advised them to "Chastize Neucheconne and his Party in such Terms as shall a proper Severity with them, tho' the expressions are left to your discretion, and then tell the delinquent Shawonese that we will forget what is past and expect a more punctual regard to their Engagements hereafter." —Treaty . . . 1748, *op. cit.*, p. 8.

318. At the Pennsylvania Logstown Conference (1748) the chiefs of the Wyandots informed Conrad Weiser that they left the French "because of the hard Usage they received from them; That they wou'd always get their Young Men to go to War against their Enemies, and wou'd use them as their own People, that is like Slaves, & their Goods were so dear that they, the Indians, cou'd not buy them." —Journal of Conrad Weiser . . . August 11–September 29, 1748, *op. cit.*, 350. See also *note 93*.

319. There was, at this time, a breach in confidence between George Croghan and the proprietary. Twice in 1751 he had been reprimanded

Annotations

by the Pennsylvanians. The governor did not authorize the treaty between Pennsylvania and the Weas and Piankashaws at Pickawillany (printed pp. 138-39). Although "the Governor had reproved Mr. Croghan for acting in publick matters without his orders." he accepted the treaty as valid and ordered it to be entered in the Council's minutes. The second reprimand was occasioned by the Six Nations' request for Pennsylvania to "build a strong House on the River Ohio." The proprietors in England had recommended to the Pennsylvania government that a strong house—"that tho' very small it may look Fort like"—be built on the Ohio. They were willing to contribute £400 toward building and £100 annually for its maintenance. When Conrad Weiser was unable to manage the Pennsylvania conference at Logstown in May, 1751, the governor appointed Croghan and Montour to distribute the present. Croghan's "private Instruction" was appended to the general instructions for the treaty. Privately Hamilton forbad him "to make any publick mention of building a Fort, but only desiring him to sound the Indians on this Point when by themselves in private Conversation." —"An Extract from the Proprietarie's Letter [1749]"; Weiser to Hamilton, April 22, 1751; Hamilton's instructions to Croghan and Montour, printed in *Colonial Records of Pennsylvania*, V, 515, 517-18, 518-22, respectively.

In addition, trading firms with which Croghan was affiliated had been the victims of French aggression. From 1749, during three years, marauding Indians in the French interest had captured many traders and plundered their trade goods and effects. Croghan was fast approaching the brink of bankruptcy. Also, he was accused by Richard Peters of deserting Pennsylvania's interest in favor of the Ohio Company. Thomas Penn, writing to Peters on March 18, 1752, expressed displeasure with Croghan's behavior in regard to the Wea, Piankashaw treaty; showed great concern over Peters' "acct of the withdrawing of Mr. Croghan and the likelihood that Mr. Hockley would be a great sufferer by him"; and informed Mr. Peters that "the Gentlemen concerned in the Ohio Company here [London] know nothing of Mr. Croghan yet so that there may not be any foundation for the story you tell me." —Fragment of letter in Penn MSS, Saunders-Coates, p. 55. Historical Society of Pennsylvania.

320. James Glen, governor of South Carolina, in a letter to Governor Hamilton, gave the following explanation of the Shawnee's imprisonment in his province:

Upon their invasion of Catawba territory, the Six Nations who were constantly at war with the southern Indians had been accom-

Annotations

panied frequently by Caughnawauga Indians who were completely in the French interest. In the governor's opinion this was a clever ruse on the part of the French. By having offences against the whites committed in South Carolina, the French hoped to have that province seek revenge on the Six Nations. The Shawnee in question were taken captive by the South Carolina militia who were protecting the frontier and were imprisoned in the Charlestown jail (Glen to Hamilton, October 12, 1753, printed in *Colonial Records of Pennsylvania*, V, 699-700). At the conference in Winchester, September, 1753, Scarouady and Andrew Montour agreed to go to South Carolina to intercede for the Shawnee and to negotiate for the release of their tribesmen (*op. cit.*). The Ohio Indians traveled from Winchester, where they had conferred with Virginia, to Carlisle, where they made a treaty with Pennsylvania in October (Pennsylvania [Colony] Treaties, etc., 1753, *A Treaty Held with the Ohio Indians, at Carlisle, in October, 1753* [Philadelphia, B. Franklin, 1753]). During this conference the Indians were informed that their third and last representation to the French on the Ohio had been in vain; therefore, the Pennsylvania commissioners prevailed upon Scarouady and Andrew Montour to forego their mission in behalf of the Shawnee and to permit Pennsylvania to intercede with South Carolina for the return of the captives.

This concern of the Shawnee over the fate of their kinsmen was unnecessary, for already Governor Glen had effected the release of two of the captured Shawnee and had sent them to Philadelphia (Glen to Hamilton, October 12, 1753, *op. cit.*). Later John Patten was employed by the province to escort them to the Ohio whence they were taken and delivered to their tribesmen at Logstown in January, 1754. —"George Croghan's Journal," January 12—February 2, 1754, printed in *Colonial Records of Pennsylvania*, V, 731-35.

321. For years Virginia, especially, had been trying to effect a peace between the northern and southern Indians. This very treaty, in its inception, included negotiations for such a peace (*Virginia Council Journals*, V, 332). Since the Winchester Conference of 1753 was designed to give the Six Nations the gift intended for them in consequence of the commitment made at Lancaster in 1744, it did not include the southern Indians. However, the projected Winchester Conference of 1754 was to have included the Chickasaws, Cherokees, and Catawbas. —*Ibid.*, 442.

322. Refers to the subjugated status of the Delawares.

323. Weiser gave this answer, confirmed by a belt of wampum, at

Annotations

the Pennsylvania Logstown Conference, 1748. —*Colonial Records of Pennsylvania,* V, 357.

324. Conrad Weiser did not speak without authority. During Scaiohady's [Scaraouady] visit to eastern Pennsylvania, in 1747, he complained to Conrad Weiser about the excessive supply of rum furnished the Indians by the traders (Weiser to Peters, November 28, 1747, printed in *Colonial Records of Pennsylvania,* V, 166-67). On February 18, 1748, this complaint, relayed by Weiser to the Provincial Council, was answered in the form of a proclamation issued by Governor Palmer. The proclamation reminded the traders that there did exist several Acts of Assembly which prohibited the sale of rum to the Indians. To prevent abuse of the existing laws the proclamation prohibited any trader from trading among the Indians "without first obtaining a Licence from the Governor or Commander-in Chief for the time being, according to the directions given in the said Act of Assembly." Furthermore, by the proclamation, anyone who seized contraband intoxicants would receive two-thirds of the confiscated liquor as a reward. The governor would receive the other third. —"Proclamation," printed in *ibid.,* 194-96.

325. Not identified. Probably one of the Six Nations from the head of the Ohio who attended the Pennsylvania-Logstown Treaty, May, 1751. —"An Account of the Proceedings of George Croghan . . . ," May 18–30, 1751, *op. cit.,* 530.

326. On May 28, 1751, George Croghan, speaking for Governor Hamilton at the Pennsylvania Logstown Conference, said to the Delawares, "I desire you may choose amongst Yourselves one of your wisest Counsellors and present to your Brethren the Six Nations and me for a chief, and he so chosen by you shall be looked upon by us as your King, with whom Publick Business shall be transacted." —*Ibid.,* 533.

327. Shingas, brother of King Beaver and Pisquetomen, was named King of the Delawares at the Virginia Logstown conference in June, 1752. The tribe's aged chief, Olumapies, died late in 1747 (Conrad Weiser to Richard Peters, October 15, 1747, printed in *Colonial Records of Pennsylvania,* V, 136-39). Unfortunately, in his lifetime he did not appoint a successor, and Lapapitton, "an Honest, true-hearted man," refused to succeed him *(ibid.;* Weiser to Peters, July 20, 1747, printed in *Pennsylvania Archives,* I, 761-62). Since the principal men of the

Annotations

Delawares could not agree upon any other person to be their king, Tanacharison, or the Half King, by virtue of the authority vested in him as deputy over the Indians on the Ohio, named Shingas, King of the Delawares, at this conference (see *Chronology*, June 13, 1752, Conference at Logstown). Little about Shingas can be discerned from existing records, 1752–1754, for both Virginia and Pennsylvania recognized only the Onondaga Council to be the chief authority over the Indians on the Ohio. It can be said that Shingas was loyal to the English until he, with many others, was disillusioned completely about English strength at the Battle of Fort Necessity.

Shingas was at his home on the Ohio at the mouth of Chartiers Creek in November, 1753. There Washington, en route to Fort Le Boeuf, conferred with him. Washington, in his journal of that trip, stated that, although Shingas said he could not accompany him on account of his wife's illness, he believed that it was a fear of the French that prevented the chief from traveling with him. —Washington's *Journal of . . . 1753*, pp. 6-7, 15-16.

Although he was present at the conference held by William Trent at Logstown in August, 1753, and at the later conferences at Winchester and at Carlisle, it was the Beaver who spoke for the Delawares (see *note 203*). After the fall of Virginia's fort to the French, the Half King, at Washington's request, sent a message to Shingas requesting him to come to the English camp at the Great Meadows and bring with him as many of his tribesmen as possible. Shingas came and acted as advisor and scout for Washington. By the chief's special advice they, the Virginians, were instructed in the preparation of "a great war-belt to invite all the warriors who would receive it, to act independently of their king and [Onondaga] Council; and King Shingas promised to take privately the most subtle measures to make the affair succeed though he did not dare to do it openly" (Washington, *Journal of . . . 1754* . . . [Toner edition], p. 123). In this statement Shingas alluded to the adopted policy of the Onondaga Council—strict neutrality in the English-French dispute.

After Washington's defeat at Fort Necessity the Indians who had been at his camp fled first to Fort Cumberland and thence to Aughwick where Conrad Weiser conferred with them in August and September, 1754. The Delawares did not travel with the main group of Indians, for the Half King in mid-August sent three men "off for Shingass and the Delawares and the Shawonese to bring them here in ten Days." Shingas had gone over to the French; therefore he did not attend the conference. —George Croghan to James Hamilton, August 16, 1754, and "Journal of the Proceedings of Conrad Weiser

Annotations

at Aucquick in August and September 1754." Printed in *Colonial Records of Pennsylvania,* VI, 140-41 and 150-60, respectively.

By the fall of 1755 Shingas had become the chief leader of the deadly Indian incursions against the frontier settlements. This leadership earned for him the name of "Shingas the Terrible." From headquarters at Kittanning, then the chief Delaware town on the Allegheny, he led many bands of marauding French and Indians as far as the Great Cove in Pennsylvania, Fort Cumberland in Maryland, and the Virginia settlements on the south bank of the Potomac at the mouth of Patterson's Creek. Volume II of the *Pennsylvania Archives* contains many depositions and much correspondence pertaining to these Indian depredations on the frontier.

In 1756 Colonel John Armstrong led the Pennsylvania militia in a successful campaign against Kittanning (John Armstrong to Governor William Denny, September 14, 1756, printed in *Pennsylvania Archives,* II, 767-73). After its destruction the Delawares moved their headquarters to Shingas' Old Town at the mouth of Beaver Creek. Kuskuskies (New Castle, Pennsylvania) and Tuscarawas on the Muskingum (Coshocton, Ohio) were the other chief Delaware towns at this time. Christian Frederick Post, who came to the Ohio on his peace mission in July, 1758, found Shingas at Kuskuskies. There both he and his brother, the Beaver, expressed a desire to return to the English fold. —"The Journal of Christian Frederick Post in his Journey from Philadelphia to the Ohio . . . July 15–September 22, 1758, printed in Thomson, *op. cit.,* pp. 130-71.

When the English routed the French from the Forks of the Ohio, November, 1758, Shingas, reassured that he would not be punished for his depredations against the English, came to Fort Pitt to the first English conference held there in more than four years. From 1759 to 1762 he shuttled between his home at Tuscarawas and Fort Pitt. He must have relinquished his title of King of the Delawares before July 5, 1759, for at the conference held at Pittsburgh beginning on that date, Shingas' brother, the Beaver, was recognized as King of the Delawares, while Shingas was mentioned as a chief.

Nevertheless, Shingas attended most of the numerous conferences held at Fort Pitt from 1759 to 1762 (Minutes of these conferences are printed in the *Colonial Records of Pennsylvania* or are in B. M. Add. MSS, Bouquet Papers). His last official presence was at the famous Treaty of Lancaster (1762), when all the western tribes confirmed a treaty of peace made at Easton in 1758. He died in the winter of 1763–64 at his home at Tuscarawas. —Deposition of Gershom Hicks, April 14, 1764. *Op. cit.*

Annotations

Although Shingas was feared by the English, women and children who had been his captives asserted that he had always been kind to them. A personal note written to Colonel Bouquet and signed by Shingas' mark shows that in his declining years he had cast off the cloak of the roving warrior and had become a domiciliated old chief who wanted some "Shinkel Nails" which the Colonel had promised him. —Shingas to Bouquet (1763?), B. M. Add. MSS, 21655, f. 290, printed in Bouquet *Papers,* 21655, p. 261.

328. The fork of Monongahela, present Pittsburgh, Pennsylvania.

329. Excesses of Indian traders presented a problem for colonial governments. One contemporary writer remarked, "It would be too shocking to describe the Conduct and Behaviour of the Traders, when among the *Indians,* and endless to enumerate the Abuses the Indians had received and borne from them for a Series of Years. Suffice it to say, that several of the Tribes were at last weary of bearing. . . . these Traders were the Persons who were in some Sort, the Representatives of the *English* among the Indians, ..."—Thomson, *op. cit.,* 56.

330. The following additional paragraph is in P.R.O., C.O., 5: 1327/575-612; also printed in *Virginia Magazine,* XIII, 169.

"This Evening the Comissrs had a private Conference with the Half King, on the Subject of the Strong House; for it had been Alledged, that the Expression implied a Settlement of People, as well as an House. The Question being ask'd whether he meant it in that Sense or not, he answer'd in the Negative. The Comissrs then told him that a Trade could never be carried on with them, to their Advantage, unless we had a Settlement of People near to raise Provisions, & render them Plenty & Cheap, for whilst the Traders, were oblig'd to bring theirs from Pensylvania, or purchase of those who brought them for Sale, they were oblig'd to lay a great Advance on their Goods, to answer that Charge; & that if at any Time, they themselves should stand in need of Assistance, against an Enemy, it would be easier for their Brethren the English, to send Men than to Support them afterwards with Provisions."

331. This entry for June 12 is *unique to this version* of the minutes of the Logstown Conference.

332. Loapeckaway or Lapechkewe. —*Colonial Records of Pennsylvania,* V, 570; VI, 160.

Annotations

333. The Shawnee, incensed by the French attack upon the Twightwees in 1751, informed the governor of Pennsylvania that they intended to strike the French; yet they did not wish to do so unless they were assured of Pennsylvania's friendship (The Shawnee to Hamilton, February 8, 1752. *Op. cit.*). Evidently the Shawnee did not wait for an answer from the English but did send some assistance to the Twightwee. See also *note 305*.

334. In P.R.O., C.O. 5: 1327/575-612 this paragraph is continued: "A little before the Treaty began, A Traders Man about forty Miles above Log's Town, cut an Indian of the Six Nations dangerously across the Rist with a Knife, & took his Gun from him, which much exasperated the Indian, & he threatned to reveng it, on some of the Traders. To pacify him the Comiss^{rs} gave him a Gun, & Mr George Croghan one thousand of Wampum, to pay for the Cure.

On which the Indian return'd Thanks, for the Care his Brethren had taken & assur'd them they had remov'd all Anger from his Breast, & that he wou'd think no more of what had happend." Also printed in *Virginia Magazine*, XIII, 170.

The laced hat and rich jacket were not given to the young Shawnee king, but to the young Piankasha king. —Trent, *Journal of . . . 1752, op. cit.*, p. 104.

335. Pennsylvania provided £1,000 worth of Indian goods for the present and Virginia sent £200 with which to purchase treaty goods. —Pennsylvania. General Assembly, *Votes and Proceedings,* IV, 74; Virginia Council *Journals,* V, 248.

336. The crown did not contribute directly to this gift. When Conrad Weiser distributed it he stated clearly that one-fifth was given by Virginia and four-fifths by Pennsylvania. The spokesmen for the Indians, one of whom was Half King, thanked both Virginia and Pennsylvania. —Journal of Conrad Weiser . . . , 1748. *Op. cit.*

337. Printed in *Case of the Ohio Company, Appendix, facs.,* pp. 21-22, this volume.

338. At a treaty between Pennsylvania and the Six Nations at Ohio, made at Lancaster, July, 1748, the Twightwee nation was admitted into the English alliance. —*Op. cit.*

339. The King or Racoon, the Turtle or chief warrior, and several

Annotations

other Twightwee did attend the Winchester Conference, September, 1753.

340. The ninth instruction to the commissioners for this treaty, as printed in *Virginia Magazine,* XIII, 151-52, was as follows:
"9th. As the Instructions of the Indians in the principles of the christian Religion hath been the Subject of the prayers, & utmost endeavours of many pious men; and as the charitable Institution of the School at Brafferton hath not produced the Effect that was hoped for from it, by reason of the difficulty of prevailing on the Indians to send their Children so far from their parents, for the sake of a religious Education, the happy Consequences of which their natural ferocity will hardly permit them to be made sensible of. I would have you talk fully to them on this head, and if you find their prejudice against trusting their Children, so far from them too strong to be overcome, you must sound their inclinations another way, and learn if they would receive and entertain a teacher among them, if this Government would send one, to instruct them in our Language & Religion, the Benefits and advantages of which they are as capable of partaking of as we, if they desire them with a straight & willing mind." The building which housed the Brafferton School at William and Mary College is still standing.

341. Entry for February 26, 1751.

342. Refers to the destruction of Pickawillany on June 21, 1752. See *notes* 98 and 307.

343. Probably George Henry, John Evans, James Devoy, and Owen Nicholson, who on May 22, 1753, petitioned the Pennsylvania Assembly for money to carry them from Philadelphia to Cumberland County. These four traders' experiences, according to their petition, coincide with information in this paragraph. —Pennsylvania. General Assembly, *Votes and Proceedings,* IV, 242.

344. Information published as advice from Captain Budden of the "Myrtilla." —*Pennsylvania Gazette,* May 24, 1753.

345. John Mercer, writing in retrospect, may have confused the French hostilities against the Twightwee in 1751 and in 1752. This paragraph gives the background of action taken by the Committee of the Company on September 17. The French attack on Pickawillany

Annotations

(see *note* 105) was not reported by Thomas Burney until the first part of November, 1752 (Dinwiddie to the Board of Trade, October 6 and December 10, printed in Trent's *Journal . . .* 1752, *op. cit.,* pp. 69-81). William Trent arrived in Williamsburg the week of October 27, one week before Burney (*Maryland Gazette,* November 9, 1752, and December 7, 1752). However, Thomas Burney, en route to Virginia, was at Carlisle, Pennsylvania, on August 29 (Robert Callendar to Hamilton, August 30, 1752, reprinted in *Colonial Records of Pennsylvania,* V, 599-600). Therefore, it is possible that action taken by the Company on September 17 was prompted by the Twightwee affair of 1752. Nevertheless, the "French proceedings" which gave rise to this increased activity on the part of the Company may have been French attacks on the Twightwee in 1751 in which 30 Twightwee were killed. Word of this French attack, in which many more Twightwee were killed than in 1752, was sent by the Shawnee to Pennsylvania and not to Virginia. Governor Hamilton, who did not receive this information until mid-April, 1752, evaded a direct answer to the Shawnee's appeal for assistance in punishing the French for their attack upon their allies, the Twightwee. Hamilton referred them to the Virginians, who were about to hold a conference with all the Ohio Indians at Logstown (Hamilton to the Shawnee, April 24, 1752. *Op. cit.*). Since Governor Dinwiddie, on October 6, 1752, was unaware of the 1752 French attack (Dinwiddie to the Board of Trade, *op. cit.*), it is not unjust to think that fiery John Mercer, writing in 1760 or 1761, may have confused dates, especially when the incidents were similar.

346. The editor found no record of actual contracts having been made between Mr. Gist and specific persons. A resolution of the Committee of the Ohio Company, September 11, 1750, states that Gist had contracted to seat families on the Ohio Company's lands. Under this same date the minutes of the meeting record the actual agreement made between Gist and the Committee. See *Chronology* for both items.

Thomas Penn's letter of February 24, 1751, may refer to Gist's efforts to obtain German settlers in Pennsylvania. Penn wrote: "I am sorry to hear the people of Virginia and Maryland are so much displeased at the Justice we do the Indians, and I fear from their way of acting with regard to those people a War will by and by break out, but I shall make Mr Hanbury acquainted with their behavior and as principal Director of the Ohio Company he will write to the Manager in Virginia to advise Cresap to another behavior, had you sent full Affidavits of what Cresap and others have done to draw over

Annotations

Setlers, wee should have petitioned the King in Council, and if they continue to be troublesome I desire you will do it." —Penn to Peters, *op. cit.*

347. See *Chronology,* September 17, 1752.

348. Entry for the survey of land was required by law. If the survey were for more than 400 acres, it was necessary to have the approval of the Executive Council before entry could be made. Entries for survey were returned by the surveyor to the next court and entered in the records (Hening's *Statutes,* VI, 33-35). The Company's petition to Governor Dinwiddie, which follows in the text, was their request for permission to enter for the survey of their grant. See *Commentary,* pp. 421-22.

349. On June 21, 1749, the Committee of the Ohio Company ordered Nathaniel Chapman, treasurer, to give all the Company's cash in hand to Thomas Cresap and Hugh Parker, who had been commissioned to have necessary roads and storehouses built (see *Chronology,* June 21, 1749). Two years later the Committee resolved that it was necessary to have a road cut from the mouth of Wills Creek to the three forks of the Youghiogheny River, and Cresap was ordered to pay for the job not in excess of £25, Virginia currency. Evidently the Committee had not received a report on the road building since Cresap was commissioned in mid-1751, for on April 28, 1752, they instructed Christopher Gist to engage Indians who were acquainted with the trails and to have a road cut immediately from Wills Creek to the forks of the Monongahela. Before Gist engaged anyone the Committee wished him to consult with Thomas Cresap as to whether or not he had agreed with anyone to clear the road. If not, Gist was instructed to act, but only with the advice and assistance of Cresap. Although the Company, in 1751, agreed that the total cost of the road should not exceed £25, Virginia currency, Gist was reimbursed to the extent of "£ 44 16s, current Virginia money, as a satisfaction for £ 56, Maryland currency, paid by him for making a road from Wills Creek to Mohongaly." Many histories of western expansion relate the story that Nemacolin, a Delaware Indian, assisted the Ohio Company in laying out their road from Wills Creek to a branch of the Monongahela. This was the road over which Braddock traveled in 1755 on his ill-fated expedition against the French on the Ohio. There are in the orders and resolutions of the committee and of the membership general of the Ohio Company seven entries pertaining to cutting this

Annotations

road, yet none mention that Nemacolin was employed. (Orders or Resolutions dated June 21, 1749; May 22, 1751; April 28, 1752; July 25-27, 1753; and November 2, 1753. See *Chronology*.) Gist merely mentions Nemacolin in his *Second Journal*, the only reference to him in the entire George Mercer manuscript collection.

An early biographer of Michael Cresap stated that Thomas Cresap "employed an honest and friendly Indian to lay out and mark a road from Cumberland to Pittsburg. This Indian's name was *Nemacolin*." This statement was based, according to the biographer, on evidence in his possession—"a bill paid by col. Cresap, to an old fellow, for digging Sideling Hill, amounting to £ 25." (John Jacob, *A Biographical Sketch of the Life of the Late Capt. Michael Cresap* [Cumberland, Md., Printed for the Author, by J. M. Buchanan, 1826], pp. 27-28). Since Sideling Hill lies east of the road cut by the Ohio Company and on the direct line of the trail which led north from Cresap's plantation at Old Town, the above evidence most probably referred to a private transaction of Thomas Cresap.

350. Youghiogheny River. At this time the northern terminus of the Ohio Company's road was mentioned to be at the three forks of the Youghiogheny, commonly called Turkey Foot. Present site of Confluence, Pennsylvania.

351. Originally the Company desired their grant to include lands on the north side of the Ohio between Yellow Creek and Two Creeks. Petition of John Hanbury, January 11, 1749. See *Chronology*.

352. "Two hundred thousand acres part of the said five hundred thousand acres may be granted immediately without rights on condition of your Petitioners seating at their proper expence a hundred familys upon the lands in seven years, the lands to be granted free of quit rent for ten years" (Petition of John Hanbury, January 11, 1749. See *Chronology*). This would be at the rate of one family per two thousand acres.

353. Probably "a new Fort at a Place call'd Kyhogo on the West Side of Lake Eare." Andrew Montour, upon his return from the Lake Erie region late in 1751, gave Thomas Cresap this and other detailed information about French activities on the shores of the lake. —Thomas Cresap to Robert Dinwiddie, December 23, 1751. *Op. cit.*

354. Undoubtedly, John Mercer was referring to the activities of

Annotations

William Beverley and James Patton. As early as 1732 William Beverley was engaged in the land brokerage business (William Beverley to ?, April 30, 1732, printed in *Calendar of Virginia State Papers,* I, 217-18). Five years later he was corresponding with Captain James Patton of Kircubright, Scotland. On August 8, 1737, Beverley wrote, "According to your desire you have here inclosed the order of council and I should be very glad if you could import families enough to take the whole off from our hands at a reasonable price and tho' the order mentions families from Pensilvania, yet families from Ireland will do as well."

Later, on August 22, Beverley further informed Patton that re the order of Council for 30,000 acres, he, Beverley, was willing to give Patton one-fourth of the grant contingent upon Patton's paying one-fourth of the charges and his doing his "utmost endeavour to procure families to come in & settle it." Also, Beverley was willing to allow Patton's pocket expenses to be charged against the land. The balance of this letter of August 22, when viewed in the light of early land brokerage in Virginia, deserves to be quoted: "as for differences ye may arise between us I am willing to referr them as you propose tho' I can't conceive there can any arise, for we all 3 propose to make money of the Land & to y^t end I propose to hold it undivided & to sell out & make ye most we can of it, unless either of us shou'd have a mind to make a settlement there for our own use & y^n we might have what we have occasion for laid off & appropriated for ye purpose. By ye order of Council you will perceive I have been obliged to make use of Mr Barradall's name but that signifies nothing for he will convey his right to me when we have got a pattent. As for ye 1000, or 1500 acres of my land I can't agree to take goods at 60 p.c. when I can have them at a less advance here, but I expect to have money for ye Land here unless you should have any tradesmen or gardners to dispose of, & then perhaps I may be your chap, & also for ye bolting mill or machine I wrote to you about. If your relation comes in he may have the Land. As for Col^o Conway I have no depend^e on him for unless I'll vote for him to be Speaker I suppose he will do me all ye prejudice he can and I assure you y^t I cannot vote for him.

I heartily wish you success & a safe return to us." —Letters printed in *William and Mary College Quarterly,* III, 226-27.

James Patton, prior to 1753, had settled 100 families on the acreage granted him in 1745 (James Patton to John Blair, 1753, MS in Draper Collection, IQQ 75-77, Wisconsin Historical Society). Patton's manner of taking up these lands caused considerable trouble for the persons who bought small tracts from him. Colonel Patton surveyed this grant

Annotations

only as portions of it were purchased. The patents were taken out in the name of the purchaser, but as late as 1764 neither James Patton nor his executors had taken out a patent for the original grant. This was the practice of which John Mercer disapproved. —Francis Fauquier to the Lords of Trade, February 13, 1764, MS in P.R.O., C.O. 5: 1330/589-96.

355. On November 4, 1745, John Blair, William Russell, Andrew Lewis, and others were granted "one hundred Thousand Acres of Land lying to the westward of the Line of Lord Fairfax on the Waters of Potomak and Youghyoughgane" (Virginia Council *Journals*, V, 195). Andrew Lewis was surveying land included in this grant on April 26, 1753 (map of this survey in the Archives Division, West Virginia State Library, Charleston, West Virginia). John Mercer's statement here is evidence that he knew of the John Blair Company's activities along the Youghiogheny prior to the report given him by his son, George Mercer, some time after April 26, 1753. See statement on George Mercer's *Map,* printed opposite p. 26 this work.

356. At a meeting of the Company on May 22-24, 1751, the members resolved to ask John Hanbury to endeavor to procure for them a release from a stipulation in their grant—build forts and maintain garrisons within (see *Chronology*). John Hanbury embodied this request in his petition of March 28, 1754 *(op. cit.).* The French were in complete possession of the Ohio Country before the Board of Trade gave to the Privy Council their recommendation on the said petition. —Report of the Board of Trade, June 25, 1754. *Op. cit.*

357. According to the John Hanbury petition, January 11, 1749 (see *Chronology*), there were, originally, 14 members: John Hanbury, Thomas Lee, Thomas Nelson, Daniel Cresap, William Thornton, William Nimmo, Thomas Cresap, John Carlyle, Lawrence Washington, Augustine Washington, George Fairfax, Jacob Giles, Nathaniel Chapman, and James Wardrop. A correction recorded in the "Memorial of the Ohio Company, November 20, 1778" *(op. cit.)* states that Daniel Cresap never was a member of the Ohio Company. Therefore, the total was 13.

358. On May 23, 1751, the membership of the Company had been increased to 20: John Hanbury, Arthur Dobbs, Robert Dinwiddie, Capel Hanbury, Samuel Smith, Thomas Ludwell Lee (who inherited the share owned by his father, Thomas Lee), Philip Ludwell Lee, John

Annotations

Tayloe, Presley Thornton, Gawin Corbin, Richard Lee, Augustine Washington, Lawrence Washington, Nathaniel Chapman, James Scott, George Mason, John Mercer, James Wardrop, Jacob Giles, and Thomas Cresap. —"Articles of Agreement and Copartnership, May 23, 1751," *op. cit.*

359. See comments on this item, pp. 414-15, 423-27.

360. Thomas Burney and William Trent, who brought the official word of the Twightwee massacre to Governor Dinwiddie, had not arrived in Williamsburg by October 6, 1752 (Dinwiddie to Board of Trade. *Op. cit.*). However, this information is similar to that given in a letter dated "Twightwee's Town, June 21, 1752" in which the Twightwees informed the Virginians that they had taken "the Hatchet to strike the French, for spilling our Blood" (P.R.O., C.O. 5: 1327/561-64). Since Thomas Burney who carried the two letters from the Twightwees arrived in Carlisle by August 30, it is probable that unofficial information had reached Virginia before October 6. —Robert Callendar to Hamilton, August 30, 1752. *Op. cit.* See also *notes* 105 and 345.

361. Andrew Montour, Christopher Gist, Thomas Cresap, Jr., Michael Cresap, William Trent, and nine others; also Lunsford Lomax and nine others, petitioned the Executive Council for 310,000 acres of land of which 280,000 acres were to be bounded in part by Ohio Company lands. No action was taken by the Council on this petition ("List of Early Land Patents and Grants Petitioned for in Virginia up to 1769," *op. cit.*). There is also in the document cited, under date of November 4, 1752, the record of a petition by John Mason [Mercer] and 13 partners for 140,000 acres of land bounded by Ohio Company lands.

362. When the Company engaged William Trent, a Pennsylvanian, as their factor on the Ohio, they obtained the services of one of the ablest men on the frontier. Prior to his service as captain of Pennsylvania Militia in the abortive Canadian campaign of 1746, he was in partnership with George Croghan in the Indian trade. Richard Peters, writing of Trent, informed Thomas Penn that "they could have made a fortune but ambition seized him so violently that he broke up that Partnership in hopes to be a man of Figure in the Conquest & Settlement of Canada" (letter, November 24, 1748, in Penn Official Correspondence, IV, 167). Although this partnership must have been

Annotations

formed in 1744 or 1745, his name is not mentioned in extant documents relative to Croghan's trading activities on the Ohio and in the Lake Erie region during the winter of 1744-45. Although not mentioned by Weiser, it is known that Trent was with him on his journey to Logstown in 1748. Shortly after his return from the frontier Trent went to England to plead payment for his military services in 1746. Thomas Penn's comments on Weiser's journal of 1748 contain the remark that "Weiser's account of the Land is very agreeable but Capt Trent who was with him knows nothing of the matter and does not remember any quantity remarkably good." It is not recorded whether or not Trent was successful, but so pleased was Penn with the young Pennsylvanian that he bought him trade goods valued at £500 so that he could begin business anew. —Letter, February 20, 1749, in Penn Letter Books, II, 253-56.

When Trent returned to America he resumed his association with George Croghan. Undoubtedly, Croghan was responsible for the commissioners at Logstown engaging him to deliver Virginia's present to the Twightwees in 1752. After his return to Virginia from that mission the Ohio Company employed him. Trent's name is not found in the minutes of the meetings of the Company; yet John Mercer mentions him frequently in the "Case." From his correspondence with Governor Dinwiddie in 1753 one learns that he went to Wills Creek shortly after his Ohio Company appointment. During 1753 he was employed by Governor Dinwiddie, first to spy out the French activities on the Ohio, then to conduct a conference with the Indians at Logstown in August. Only by his persuasion were the Ohio Indians induced to go to Winchester to confer with the Virginians.

As for Ohio Company business, he set in motion its first broadscale expansion, the first of January, 1754. On January 6, 1754, George Washington, returning from his mission to the French on the Allegheny, met Trent and his entourage, one day out from Wills Creek on the road to Redstone. Trent, accompanied by settlers "going out to take up Ohio Company land," had as his first objective the building of an Ohio Company storehouse on the Monongahela at the mouth of Redstone Creek. There he supervised building of a "large shed, forty feet long by twenty wide, made of timbers laid upon each other and roofed with bark" (J.C.B.'s *Travels, op. cit.,* p. 60). After one month's service, for the Ohio Company exclusively, he was ordered again into service for Virginia. Thomas Cresap brought to him at Redstone a captain's commission, directing him to enlist 100 frontiersmen as a company of Virginia militia and proceed to the forks of the Ohio, there to build a fort. Governor Dinwiddie had sent only

Annotations

a captain's commission and orders to Trent—no money. Enlistment money in Virginia at that time was set at £10. The entire project was financed by the Ohio Company. When the debt remained unpaid for many years Trent sued Governor Dinwiddie personally for payment. According to John Mercer's statement, some £665 was awarded Trent and he was credited with the entire sum on the Ohio Company's books. (John Mercer to [James Tilghman], with George Mason's statement on William Trent's account, March 1, 1767. Cadwalader Papers, Historical Society of Pennsylvania.) Previously, the Colony had voted partial payment of Trent's account which included money due him for "carrying out Virginia's present" and his pay as captain of militia.

In less than three months' time, February to mid-April, Trent and his men had rendered great service to the Colony. He had traveled from Redstone, enlisting men along the way, had delivered Virginia's present to the Ohio Indians, and had planned some sort of stockade at the forks of the Ohio. Fear of starvation for his troops caused him to return to Wills Creek for supplies. At the time he was severely criticized for his absence from his command when the French came down the Allegheny en masse and forced his ensign's surrender.

Governor Dinwiddie's criticism of his administration of Ohio Company business at the New Store in 1754 is evidence that he resumed his duties as factor for the Company at Wills Creek. On September 6 the governor informed Horatio Sharpe that he had ordered Colonel James Innes to take possession of the Ohio Company's storehouse, only to reverse his opinion on September 18. In his letter of this date he informed Innes that the New Store was an "improper place"; therefore, he should build a magazine. He also accused Trent of taking "the advantage of having a high rent w'ch I dare say he has no Orders for." According to Dinwiddie, even the price of flour "at the New Store" was exorbitant; therefore, he advised Innes to purchase it from John Carlyle, who in turn would obtain that commodity from George Croghan. Trent was also accused of being "vastly impudent in regard to his Dem'd for the Timber"; therefore, Innes was instructed to have the cooper "take w't is wanted anywhere, with't asking Ques's." —Letters in Dinwiddie *Papers,* I, 303-06, 320-33, 459-61, respectively.

Apropos of the criticism of Trent at the time, it is interesting to note that Thomas Walpole in his remarks upon George Washington's Memorial of Virginia Militia stated that "Major William Trent, one of our Associates [Walpole Company] is 'the Gentleman' who had the honor to command the *first* raised troops" mustered as a force against French aggression in 1754.

Annotations

Loss of the Ohio region to the French ruined many a trader financially, and Trent was no exception. Suffering from a military disgrace, evidently an unpopular factor for the Ohio Company, and, along with George Croghan, possibly the greatest loser in the Indian trade, Trent's fortune had certainly reached its nadir in 1755. By this time he had moved his family from Maryland, where he had lived since his marriage about 1753, to eastern Pennsylvania. The war years were barren years for the Company, and Trent's active service must have ended; yet he may never have resigned his position with the Company. On September 25, 1767, he, as "factor for the Ohio Company" accepted from George Croghan £111 10s. "in full of his [Croghan's] obligation to Francis Wafer dated the twentieth day of February, 1750 [1751] given at the same time to Christopher Gist by said Wafer for the use of the Ohio Company." —MS in the Historical Society of Pennsylvania.

As for Trent, the man, he resumed his military, diplomatic (Indian) and trading career in Pennsylvania. He assisted in negotiating Indian treaties for both Pennsylvania and the Crown and was George Croghan's assistant in Indian affairs at Fort Pitt; he distinguished himself as a military man, especially at Fort Pitt in 1763; and as an individual trader, as well as a partner in several Pennsylvania trading firms, he continued to be interested in business. The Indian uprising in 1763 engulfed the stock of many traders in the Ohio Country, and as in 1754, Trent lost heavily; but the circumstances were different. On this occasion the Indians alone were the antagonists, and having subdued them, the whites sought reparations for their losses in the form of land grants. Two groups of "Suffering Traders" were formed: one, the principal losers in 1754; the other, the losers in 1763. Trent's friend, George Croghan, and Moses Franks, who represented the first group, were sent to England in 1764 to seek reparations by orders directly from the Crown. This plan failed completely. As a representative of both groups Trent attended the Conference of Fort Stanwix (Rome, New York) in 1768, and before the conference proper opened obtained from the Indians reparations for the "Suffering Traders," (1763) —a deed for land comprising, approximately, that part of present West Virginia north of the Little Kanawha and east of the Laurel Mountains. At the conference proper the Indians deeded some 2,500,000 acres of western land to the Crown, reserving for Trent the tract assigned to him and his associates. Trent was sent to England to obtain royal affirmation of this deed, also to plead for reparations for the "Suffering Traders of 1754." It is to be remembered he was a chief "sufferer" in both groups. While in England he

Annotations

personally became a member of the Walpole Company which had pledged itself to honor all bona fide grants within their great grant, providing they were made prior to January 4, 1770. The "Suffering Traders of 1763," or Indiana Company, qualified for that recognition.

Political machinations blocked royal sanction of the Walpole Grant until the Revolution, which ruined all chances for their obtaining a title to the tract under consideration. Nevertheless, Trent's tenacity was never-ending. He pursued the land grant problem in England, in the colonies, and finally in the United States. In 1792, five years after Trent's death, final decision against all English grants was handed down by the United States Supreme Court in the William Grayson and others *vs.* the Commonwealth of Virginia Case, the plaintiffs losing.

Trent's life was flecked with financial failures; yet his achievements were many. During the critical year, 1753, he was the whites' chief representative among the Ohio Indians. Probably no one ever accomplished more in so little time as did Trent, for where all others failed he succeeded in keeping aglow in the Indian camp a tiny spark of fidelity to the English. Had this not occurred, French-Indian solidarity along the Ohio undoubtedly would have taken place. —Samuel Wharton, *Plain Facts . . . op. cit.;* Sewell Slick, *William Trent and the West* (Harrisburg, Archives Publishing Co., 1947); *Ohio Company Papers, 1753–1817, op. cit;* George Lewis, *The Indiana Company, 1763–1798* (Glendale, California, The Arthur H. Clark Company, 1941); *Case of the Suffering Traders,* n.d.; *Considerations of the Agreement of the Lords Commissioners of his Majesty's Treasury, with the Honourable Thomas Walpole and the* [his] *Associates, for Lands Upon the Ohio, in North America* [London, Jan. 7th, 1774, A. B.] *Considerations on the Agreement . . .* is attributed to Samuel Wharton; however, it is signed "A. B." and may have been written by Anselm Yates Bayley.

363. Although Christopher Gist is not mentioned as surveyor, he did obtain such a commission before July 27, 1753, when he received instructions to proceed to the Ohio and to "lay out" a town and fort on Chartiers Creek at its confluence with the Ohio. He was also instructed to "provide a measureing Wheel at the Companys Expence and measure the Road clear'd by the Company . . . in order to shew the exact place where Russell and his Company have Surveyed their land." See *Chronology.*

The "George Mercer Map" reproduced in this work is evidence that Gist carried out the Committee's instructions. In Mercer's ex-

Annotations

planation of the map he states that Thomas Cresap ran at least some of the lines; he also identifies himself as one of the surveyors. However, he does not name Christopher Gist.

364. Annotations on George Mercer's map state that Gist settled 20 families and not 11; Washington, in 1753, reported several families (Washington, *Journal of . . . 1753, op. cit.,* p. 32); while Gist, in his *Journal of 1753,* does not mention a specific number (Gist [Darlington edition], *op. cit.,* p. 87). The editor was unable to trace or find the names of any of the settlers, excepting William Cromwell, Gist's son-in-law.

365. This order of council granted to John Blair, William Russell, and their associates 100,000 acres of land on the waters of the Potomac and Youghiogheny Rivers (order printed, p. 249, this work). The plan of the survey of the Blair-Russell lands is extant in the West Virginia State Archives, Charleston, West Virginia. A study of George Mercer's survey and this plan proves that the unidentified one in the West Virginia Archives is a sketch of William Russell and Company's lands on the Youghiogheny River. George Mercer's annotation on his map states that he saw William Russell surveying at this location on Thursday, April 26, 1753. —The plan in the West Virginia Archives is signed Thursday, April 26, 1753.

366. The Fairfax Stone or cornerstone of Lord Fairfax's grant is located about one-half mile from Kempton, West Virginia. At present the Fairfax Stone marks the boundary between West Virginia and Maryland. The original one stood about one mile to the south of the present marker. —Writers' Program. West Virginia, *op. cit.,* p. 370.

367. Colonel Cresap and Christopher Gist were engaged the summer of 1753 to lay off the town and fort to be built at the mouth of Chartiers Creek (site of present McKees Rocks, Pennsylvania). —Resolution, July 25, 1753. See *Chronology.*

368. This letter was in accordance with action taken by the Virginia Executive Council on November 6, 1749, when they ordered that "an advertisement be inserted in the next *Virginia Gazette,* signifying that Surveyors are now at Liberty to proceed in surveying any Lands beyond the great Mountains, so that they don't interfere with the Grant of the Ohio Company." —Virginia Council *Journals,* V, 306.

Annotations

369. The crossed-out material in this paragraph is *unique to this document.*

370. John Blair, William Russell's partner, was a member of the council at this time (Virginia Council *Journals,* V, 195). When John Mercer and James Powers, in behalf of the Ohio Company and the Loyal Land Company, respectively, entered caveats, that no patent should be issued to James Patton for any land bordering on the "three branches of the Mississippi," Patton wrote to his friend Blair, setting forth the legality of his claim. Patton informed Blair that he had already satisfied the requirements for his patent for 100,000 acres of land granted him in 1745. Priority of entry for lands was the criterion for location of lands granted by the Council. Patton's petition of 1743 was for 200,000 acres of land. Although the grant was not made until 1745, his petition was inserted in the Council books in 1743, a fact which gave him, the first petitioner, preference as to the location of any land granted west of the mountains. Patton continued his letter to Blair by asking for an Order of Council for the remaining 100,000 acres. In the discussion he added, "As to the Ohio Company who I understand Intends to survey their Lands to the Norward of the Waters of Woods River, if so it cannot Interfere with Mine." —James Patton to John Blair, 1753, *op. cit.*

371. Three of John Finley's men were killed and seven others taken captive, two of whom were imprisoned in Montreal. See *note* 376.

372. Evidently William Trent's letter to James Hamilton, April 10, 1753 (In P.R.O., C.O. 5: 1065/59; calendared in New York (State) Secretary of State, *Calendar of Historical Manuscripts, in the Office of the Secretary of State, Albany, N. Y.,* edited by E. B. O'Callaghan [Albany; Weed, Parsons and Company, 1866], part II, 603). A different version purported to be an exact copy is printed in Hanna, *op. cit.,* II, 230-31 and in Gist (Darlington edition), *op. cit.,* pp. 192-93.

The letter does not contain the names of the traders who were captured.

373. Kentucky River.

374. Caughnawaga, French Indians living near Montreal.

375. Robert Sanders. See also *note* 378.

376. On June 9, 1753, from Montreal, Alexander McGinty, Jabez

· 575 ·

Annotations

Evans, Jacob Evans, David Hendricks, William Powel, and Thomas Hyde wrote to Mayor Sanders of Albany that "We were taken from off the South Side of Allegheny River, about one hundred Miles, on the twenty-sixth of last January, and the Indians brought Four of Us along to this Place, and Two of Us they sold to a French Captain on the Road as We came" (Letter printed in *Colonial Records of Pennsylvania*, V, 627.) Apparently there were only six captives taken to Canada. Alexander McGinty, in his deposition, states that James Lowry escaped soon after he was taken prisoner. Jacob Evans and Thomas Hyde were the two who were imprisoned. —Alexander McGinty's deposition, October 12, 1753, is printed in *ibid.*, V, 663-64.

377. On July 7, 1753, Governor Clinton of New York sent the letter to Governor Hamilton, whereupon Pennsylvania immediately sent Conrad Weiser to Albany "to concert with you the proper means of affecting" their release. —*Ibid.*, 627-28.

378. The mayor of Albany (Robert Sanders at this time) was a member of the commissioners for Indian Affairs. Magistrates of the city and county of Albany had control of Indian affairs in New Netherlands and continued in the same capacity when the English gained control of the territory. In 1749 Governor Clinton transferred this control to Sir William Johnson, an act not recognized by the New York Assembly, who favored the Albany Commissioners. Sir William Johnson was not named sole superintendent of Indian affairs until 1755. —New York (Colony). *An Abridgment of the Indian Affairs ... Transacted in the Colony of New York, from the Year 1678 to the Year 1751 by Peter Wraxall,* edited with an introduction by Charles Howard McIlwain (Cambridge, Harvard University Press, 1915), introduction lxxiv-vi.

379. The Caughnawaga town near Montreal.

380. John Finley, Pennsylvania trader.

381. The Kentucky Shawnee Town, Eskippakitheki, was known to the early settlers as "Indian Old Corn Fields." The site of present "Indian Fields" about 11 miles east of Winchester, Clark County, Kentucky. —Hanna, *op. cit.*, II, 230.

382. Michael Teaffe, sometime partner in the firm of Croghan, Trent, Callender, and Teaffe. The firm's goods lost at this time were valued at £267 18s. —Volwiler, *op. cit.*, p. 46.

Annotations

383. Alexander McGinty. See also *note 376*.

384. Lazarus Lowry, founder of a trading firm, and his five sons, James, John, Daniel, Alexander, and Lazarus were among the earliest and most active traders on the frontier. Lazarus Lowry, Sr., was licensed for trading with the Indians in 1730. He and his son John were trading west of the Alleghenies before 1740; Alexander began to trade in the Ohio Country about 1744. —Hanna, *op. cit.*, I, 177-79.

385. Lower Shawnee Town.

386. The Allegheny River.

387. Letter reported in Virginia Council *Journals*, V, 418.

388. On February 10, 1753, Governor Dinwiddie, answering Cresap and Trent's letter of January 22, remarked that he was "very sorry that part of the Twightwee are gone to the French on account of lack of Powder." —Dinwiddie *Papers, op. cit.*, I, 21-24.

389. Since no representative of the Six Nations at Onondaga was present at the Logstown Conference, Governor Dinwiddie, by November 6, 1752, arranged a present-giving conference with them, to be held at Winchester in May, 1753 (Virginia Council *Journals*, V, 411). About this time he dispatched Thomas Burney to the Twightwee with a condolence message and an invitation to attend at Winchester. Now Dinwiddie enlarged the conference still further and invited the Ohio Indians.

390. Refers to "Additional Instructions" to Governor Gooch (see *Chronology*, March 16, 1749).

391. There is no record that these caveats were executed.

392. Orders in Council, June 15, 1753, are printed in Virginia Council *Journals*, V, 436-37; also in this work. See *Chronology*.

393. John Mercer states that at the time Corbin entered for these grants he did not even know "who were his Company" nor did he know "there were such Lands or Creeks in the world." John Mercer, who had drawn a map showing the extent of lands desired by the Company, gave it to Governor Dinwiddie who, according to Mercer,

Annotations

permitted Colonel Corbin and Colonel Ludwell to peruse the map, when it was intended only for Governor Dinwiddie as a member of the Ohio Company.—John Mercer to George Mercer, March 3, 1768, see *Chronology;* notes 260 and 272; *map* reproduced opposite p. 72.

394. Governor Dinwiddie requested this correspondence. See *note* 362.

395. Corrections in this paragraph were made by John Mercer. For variant of this statement, see printed *Case, facs.,* p. 10.

396. Note in manuscript: "Lre 2. fol. 16. Govr Dinwiddie to Capt Trent."

Provenance of the letter is found in a manuscript, "List of Papers sent to Mr. Mercer by Capt. Robert Stewart," which is endorsed as follows: "April 11th [1759] at night wrote Capt. Robert Stewart a letter desiring him, to deliver my Letter to Mr Mercer, which had all my paprs inclosed in it agreeable to the acct on the other side, & sent them to him by Capt Ward & requested of him in my Letter if Mr. Mercer should not be at Wmsburg to deliver them to any of the Ohio Company that might happen to be there. W. Trent" —Society Collection, Historical Society of Pennsylvania.

Listed in the document are eight letters or communications to Trent and one to Thomas Cresap. Most of the items are included in the manuscript "Case" or in the printed *Case of the Ohio Company,* this volume. Some items, at least, were also used by John Mercer in a law suit, William Trent *vs.* Robert Dinwiddie. The whereabouts of John Mercer's private papers is unknown to the editor.

397. Montour's report or formal declaration, dated May 15, 1753, is printed in Virginia (Colony) General Assembly. House of Burgesses, *Journal of . . . 1752–58,* edited by H. R. McIlwaine (Richmond, Va., 1909), pp. 515-16; copy in P.R.O., C.O. 5: 13/621-22.

398. When Governor Clinton of New York heard from Colonel William Johnson and Hitchen Holland, commissary at Oswego, that the French and French Indians in great numbers had passed Oswego en route to the Ohio, he sent the information to the governors of Pennsylvania, Maryland, and Virginia, and to George Croghan on the Ohio. —Hamilton to Dinwiddie, May 6, 1753, printed in *Colonial Records of Pennsylvania,* V, 628-30.

Annotations

399. On April 21, 1753, Colonel William Fairfax was commissioned to deliver the present to the Indians who were to assemble at Winchester (Virginia Council *Journals*, V, 419-20). This present, intended originally for the Six Nations at Onondaga, and ordered in November 6, 1752, consisted of "Twenty Barrels of powder, 40Hh^d of Lead, 100 Small Arms and Bayonets, . . . Vermilion, 5000 Flints; Three Peices of black and white Duffels for Match Coats" (*ibid.*, 412). At the same time Montour was commissioned to go to the Council of Onondaga in order to invite them to come to Winchester at the full of the moon in May. —*Ibid.*, 411.

400. Trent sent Barnaby Curran to the Ohio to inform the Indians that he would be there with a present of arms in 20 days. Also, William Russell had been sent to the Ohio by Colonel William Fairfax (Virginia Council *Journals*, V, 427). William Russell, commissioned to go to Logstown, had received written instructions "in the gov's name to desire admittance to the Commandant of the French forces and to demand by whose Commission and authority he acts." Russell was "also to gain what Intelligence he can relating to the Designs of the French & their Indians" (*ibid.*, 433). Curran, according to Trent, was abused verbally by Russell who informed the Indians that Curran's message was a lie, for Trent was not coming with a gift. Trent unjustly accused Dinwiddie of duplicity in sending another emissary to the Ohio. At the request of the Executive Council, Colonel Fairfax sent Russell; Trent was Dinwiddie's personal informant.

401. Neither Virginia's nor Pennsylvania's present was given directly to the Indians at the time of the conferences. Trent took Virginia's present to the Ohio in February, 1754 (Croghan to Hamilton, February 3, 1754, printed in *Pennsylvania Archives*, II, 119-20). Pennsylvania's gift was delivered to them by Andrew Montour at Logstown on January 28, 1754 ("George Croghan's Journal," January 12–February 2, 1754, *op. cit.*). George Croghan stated that this fact aroused suspicion among the Indians, thus lowering morale among those who were friendly to the English.

402. Refers to Half King's speech made at Croghan's trading house at Pine Creek on May 13, 1753, after John Harris had brought the news that the French were on the march (*note* 398). The Half King and other chiefs assembled listened to Croghan's and Trent's promises, and then deliberated upon them a whole night and until 2:00 P.M. the next day when Half King, in behalf of the Six Nations

Annotations

at the Ohio, addressed the English. Half King answered that if the French came peaceably, they would be treated as friends; but, if they came as enemies, they would be treated as such. Also, he expressed the hope that the English would send them arms and ammunition, and promised that, if necessary, they would strike the French. —*Colonial Records of Pennsylvania*, V, 615.

403. Montour's report, as given by him to Mr. West at Philadelphia, does not mention "a large black belt" but records that the answer of the Six Nations at Onondaga to the French Indians, sent by the governor of France to them, was that they, the Six Nations, "wou'd not suffer him to build Forts there, nor take Possession of those Lands, nor drive away the English: that those Lands belonged to the Indians, and that neither French nor English shou'd have any thing to do with them; that the Indians were owners of the Soil and independent of Both, and wou'd keep the Lands in their own hands" (*ibid.*, 608). Montour's formal declaration, made to Colonel Fairfax on his return from Onondaga, was more reserved. —Declaration, May 15, 1753. *Op. cit.*

404. In a letter of January 22, 1753, Cresap and Trent confirmed a report that a trader had been killed on the Ohio and also complained of the many abuses of the whites by the French-incited Indians. Dinwiddie, in his reply of February 10, stated that until the Pennsylvania-Virginia boundary was run he could not appoint magistrates to "restrain the many abuses" committed there (Dinwiddie *Papers*, I, 22). Cresap and Trent's letter was reported to the Executive Council in April, at which time a committee was appointed to frame an answer which was in part as follows: "That we don't think the Irregularities complained of against the Indians to be so threatening as they apprehend them; that they appear to have arisen from private Differences among the Indians and some Traders whom we suppose to be duly licenced, and think ought to apply to the Government from whence they had their Licences, and that those who have our Licence will not want our protection. That they seem to mistake our purpose in sending for the Indians to Winchester; it is not to hold a Treaty, but to deliver to them a present of Arms and Ammunition which we found they wanted. In Respect to the Dutchman, that, as the Charge against him amounts to a Felony, the Information against him should be upon Oath, on which if we can get him apprehended, it will be necessary for Mr Cresap to appear with his proofs to prosecute him at Williamsburg. Advising them to speak with Caution what they

Annotations

think on a Rupture between Us and the Indians, and to avoid giving just Occasion for such Event, as our Interest may perhaps, be more effectually secured by lenient Methods, than by violent Measures."
—Virginia Council *Journals,* V, 420-21.

405. Here two pages of the manuscript are missing. No attempt has been made to supply all the material included in these pages. Only the missing parts of letters are supplied from printed *Case, facs.,* pp. 11-14.

406. Trent delivered the present to the Indians at Logstown, not in the name of the governor, but as spokesman for the governor, by addressing them as follows: "His Honour the Governor of Virginia has sent me here to speak to You in his Name, which I shall do in the same Manner as he wou'd have done were he here Present," and continues "Brethren, Capt Trent from Ohio inform'd me of the March of a French Army to attack You; . . . Capt Trent deliver'd Your Message to me, desiring me to send you some Powder, Lead, Guns, &ca Things suitable for Your Warriors." —Trent's account of the conference at Logstown, July 11–September 14, 1753. *Op. cit.*

The Indians were so impressed by the manner in which the gift was delivered that they deferred their thanks for the present until they would go to Winchester where they expected to meet the governor and thank him in person.

407. Trent was inquisitive indeed. Minutes of this conference reveal that in addition to much time spent with Half King, Trent interrogated every Indian he met—and there were many who came to Logstown: Conewagas, Delawares, Ottawas, Chipewas, and Six Nations who had gone to the French to inquire why there were in this territory white men from the Lower Shawnee Town.

408. When Thomas Burney reported the destruction of Pickawillany to Governor Dinwiddie *(note* 105), he immediately dispatched Burney back to them with assurance of support from Virginia, a present, and promise of a supply of arms for "next May at Winchester." The governor blamed the trouble on the Ohio on the fact that Burney tarried too long before setting out for the Miami Country (Dinwiddie to Cresap and Trent, February 10, 1753, *op. cit.*). Burney did not report back to Dinwiddie until after June 22, when he was sent from Ohio to the governor of Virginia by the Half King and "Monakatootah" (Scarouady) informing him that the western In-

· 581 ·

Annotations

dians, including the Twightwee and Shawnee, could not come to Winchester. According to the message, the chiefs could not leave their homes on the Ohio, for the French were within two days' journey of Logstown and they feared immediate attack. They also requested Virginia to send someone to the Forks of the Monongahela to request of the French why they had come to build forts on the Ohio. —Half King or Monacatootha's speech, June 22, 1753. *Op. cit.*

409. On May 30, 1753, the Pennsylvania General Assembly voted £200 for the Twightwees and £600 for the other Indian nations in the English alliance. This money, payable to the governor, was to be used in the most suitable and expeditious manner (Pennsylvania. General Assembly, *Votes and Proceedings,* IV, 247). The governor, on August 29, reported to the general assembly that the Indians at Onondaga and at Ohio had not applied to him for assistance; therefore, no money had been laid out for gifts to the Six Nations. As for the Twightwees, the governor realized full well that the £200 should have been laid out in goods, but alarming news that the French were on the march to the Ohio caused the delay in sending the present. Hamilton thought that the risk of its falling into the enemy's hands was too great (*ibid.,* 251).

410. Trent returned a detailed account of his proceedings at Logstown, July 11 to September 14. —In P.R.O., C.O. 5: 1328/15-40. See also *Commentary,* pp. 430-32.

411. There was some misunderstanding concerning the messengers sent to Ohio early in 1753. Governor Dinwiddie asked William Trent to find out as much as he could until May, the time set for the Conference at Winchester (*note* 407). William Fairfax sent William Russell to Logstown to inquire of the French on whose command they were there (*note* 400); yet Governor Dinwiddie informed the Board of Trade that "the Person [William Russell] sent by the Commissioner to the Commandant of the French Forces, neglected his Duty & went no further than Logstown on the Ohio, reports the French were then one hundred & fifty Miles further up that River, & I believe was affraid to go to them" (Dinwiddie to the Board of Trade, November 17, 1753, P.R.O., C.O. 5: 1328/21). In the same letter Dinwiddie informs the Board of Trade that he had received "Orders and instructions to govern his conduct in this delicate situation." Instructions from the king directed him: "first to represent our undoubted right to such parts of the River Ohio as are within the limits of our province of

Annotations

Virginia or any other province or provinces in America, and to require the peaceable departure of any such Europeans or Indians offering to molest or hinder you from carrying on the forts you are hereby authorized and empowered to erect, but if notwithstanding such peaceable representations they should still persist in endeavouring to obstruct the execution of these our orders, our will and pleasure is that you should repel force by force and whereas we have received information of a number of Europeans not our subjects, being assembled in a hostile manner, upon the River Ohio, intending by force of arms to erect certain forts within our territory on the said river, contrary to our peace and to the dignity of our Crown, we do hereby strictly enjoin you to make diligent enquiry into the truth of this information and if you shall find that any number of persons whether Indians or Europeans shall presume to erect any fort within the limits of our province of Virginia you are first to require of them peaceably to depart and not persist in such unlawful proceedings and if notwithstanding your admonition, they do still endeavor to carry on such unlawful and unjustifiable designs, we do strictly charge and command you to drive them out by force of arms, in the execution of which all our officers civil and military within the limits of your government are to be aiding and assisting to the utmost of their abilities." —P.R.O., C.O. 5:1344/ no folio number. Therefore, Dinwiddie employed Washington who had volunteered to carry the message to the French. —Virginia Council *Journals*, V, 444.

412. By the Treaties of Breda (1667) and Westminster (1673) the English gained control over all the Dutch lands in North America. These possessions included the land of the Iroquois. The Iroquois reaffirmed their possession by the Dongan Treaty (1684) and the sale of their lands to the English in 1701. Again this English sovereignty was reaffirmed in particular at their Lancaster Treaty (1744). The terms of the Treaties of Utrecht (1713) and Aix-la-Chapelle (1748) returned to the French and English the territory in North America each had owned before the wars between them.

413. On August 11, 1753, William Trent informed the governor "that the French, whose Army consists of about One Thousand five Hundred Soldiers from old France, within three Months will have three Forts on the Ohio River, that they declare publickly they will have all the Land as far as Allegheny Hill, and will build Towns and Forts where they please." —Virginia Council *Journals*, V, 439-40.

Annotations

414. End of material supplied from printed *Case, facs.*, pp. 11-14. See *note 405*.

415. Bracketed material [ ] supplied from *ibid., facs.*, p. 14.

416. In 1752 Ange de Menneville, Marquis de Duquesne, was appointed governor general of New France in the room of La Jonquière, until Vaudreuil, the permanent appointee, would arrive in Canada. —The Minister to Vaudreuil, June 8, 1752, calendared in Carnegie Institution of Washington. Department of historical research, *Calendar of Manuscripts in Paris Archives and Libraries Relating to the History of the Mississippi Valley to 1803*, edited by N. M. Miller Surrey (Washington, D. C., the author, 1926–28), II, 1199.

417. Duquesne's instructions, approved April, 1752, included the item, "to make every possible effort to drive the English from our territory, and to prevent them coming there to trade" (Minute of Instructions to be given to M. Duquesne, printed in *N.Y.C.D.*, X, 242-44). In a discussion of the King's instructions the French minister stated that the English encroachments on the Ohio were endangering the line of communication between Canada and Louisiana. The minister added: "It is therefore necessary to act on the spot; and the only thing to be considered is the most suitable means of doing so to advantage." The minister suggested that an effective method of driving "the English away from our lands in that region," would be to seize their goods and destroy their posts. —The French minister to Duquesne, May 15, 1752, printed in Wisconsin Historical Society *Collections*, XVIII, 118-22.

418. The Treaties of Utrecht (1713) and Aix-la-Chapelle (1748). The fifteenth article of the Treaty of Utrecht recognized the domination of Great Britain over the Five Nations. Since the French claimed supremacy in the Ohio River basin by right of discovery and exploration by La Salle in 1669, they denied the later claim of the Five Nations to the territory, a claim based on Iroquois conquest. Therefore, according to French interpretation, Great Britain had no right to this disputed territory.

419. Upon the death of Pierre Paul Marin, October 29, 1753, Legardeur de St. Pierre de Repentigny assumed command of the Ohio expedition. —Jean Baptiste Ferland, *Cours D'Histoire du Canada* (Quebec, August in Cote, 1861–65), II, 504-05.

Annotations

420. This was the fort built by Marin on the Riviere au Boeufs (French Creek) at the southern terminus of the 21-mile portage between Lake Erie and a headwater of the Ohio River (*N.Y.C.D.*, VI, 836). Washington, in his journal, gives the following description of this fort: "It is situated on the South, or West Fork of *French* Creek, near the Water; and is almost surrounded by the Creek, and a small Branch of it which forms a Kind of Island. Four Houses compose the Sides. The Bastions are made of Piles driven into the Ground, standing more than 12 Feet above it, and sharp at Top: With Port-Holes cut for Cannon, and Loop-Holes for the small Arms to fire through. There are eight 6 *lb.* Pieces mounted, in each Bastion; and one Piece of four Pound before the Gate. In the Bastions are a Guard House, Chapel, Doctor's Lodging, and the Commander's private Store: Round which are laid Plat-Forms for the Cannon and Men to stand on. There are several Barracks without the Fort, for the Soldiers Dwelling; covered, some with Bark, and some with Boards, made chiefly of Loggs. There are also several other Houses, such as Stables, Smiths, Shop, &c." —Washington *The Journal of . . . sent by Robert Dinwiddie . . . to the commandant of the French Forces on Ohio, op. cit.*, p. 21.

The site of present Waterford, Erie County, Pennsylvania.

421. Philip Thomas Chabert de Joncaire, son of Joncaire the elder who established the Shawnee on the lower Ohio or the Wabash in 1736, was interpreter for Céloron on the Ohio in 1749, and was with the de Longueuil expedition in 1739. In 1750 he was chosen to lead a three-year expedition to the Ohio. Governor Clinton reported to Governor Hamilton that "Joncaire has gone with another officer to the Ohio to bring that body of Indians over to the French. He had with him a large quantity of very valuable goods to distribute among them and to the Indians along the way." Clinton's informant was Arent Stephens, the interpreter, who spoke with Joncaire at Oswego, at which time Joncaire "made no scruples to tell the intent of his journey" (Clinton to Hamilton, September 3, 1750, printed in *Colonial Records of Pennsylvania*, V, 462). Joncaire and the other officer, accompanied by 40 warriors of the Six Nations, arrived at Logstown in May, 1751, when George Croghan and Andrew Montour were conducting a conference for Pennsylvania. Both Joncaire and Croghan exhorted the Indians to be true to their respective governments. Joncaire insisted that the Indians drive the English traders off the Ohio, "in Pain of incuring the Governor of Canada their Father's displeasure." Croghan presented the Indians with a "Present of Goods

Annotations

to renew the Friendship so long subsisting between Us" (Croghan's account of this conference is printed in *ibid.*, 530-39).

422. Meaning Pierre Paul Marin.

423. Forts Niagara (Buffalo, New York), Presqu'isle (Erie, Pennsylvania), Le Boeuf (Waterford) and Venango or Machault (Franklin). —*N.Y.C.D.,* VI, 836.

424. On August 15, 1753, John Trotter and his servant, James McLaughlen, were taken captive by the French near Venango (Franklin, Pennsylvania) and sent "in Irons" to Montreal. Here they remained in jail for four days, then were transported to Quebec where they were imprisoned for 30 more days. Trotter, McLaughlen, and Jacob Evans who had been taken prisoner in Kentucky (see *note* 376) were shipped to La Rochelle, France. After another 30 days in jail, this time in Old France, they were released. They begged their way to Bordeaux. Trotter and Evans shipped to Philadelphia on the "Betty and Sally," where they arrived on March 16, 1754. "James McLaughlen was left behind at Bourdeaux for want of Conveniences in the Vessel." —Deposition of John Trotter, March 22, 1754, printed in *Pennsylvania Archives,* II, 131-32.

425. According to Washington's report, the Half King's message to the French commandant at Fort Le Boeuf was in part as follows: *"Fathers, Both you and the English are white, we live in a Country between; therefore the Land belongs to neither one nor t'other: But the Great Being above allow'd it to be a Place of Residence for us; so Fathers, I desire you to withdraw, as I have done our Brothers the English."* —Washington, *The Journal of . . .* sent by Robert Dinwiddie *. . . to the commandant of the French Forces on Ohio, op. cit.,* p. 10.

426. Each of the 20 members was ordered to contribute £20 for the building of a fort at Shurtees (Chartier's) Creek and the Ohio. Orders of the Committee of the Ohio Company, July 25 and November 2, 1753. See *Chronology.*

427. Washington, *The Journal of . . .* sent by Robert Dinwiddie *. . . to the commandant of the French Forces on Ohio, op. cit.,* p. 27.

428. In a discussion of this proclamation the Virginia Executive Council agreed among themselves that, although the bonus lands

· 586 ·

Annotations

mentioned in the proclamation had already been granted to the Ohio Company, there were "other Lands sufficient to answer the Quantity granted" them. —Virginia Council *Journals,* V, 462.

429. There is no mention of these proceedings in the minutes of any meeting of the Ohio Company preserved in this George Mercer collection.

430. *Note* in document: Lre 1. fol. 21. Colo Fairfax to Capt Trent. In 1759 this letter was sent by William Trent to John Mercer. See *note 396.*

431. Greenway Court, Lord Fairfax's manor, was located near present Whiteport, Virginia, on State Highway Route 12 about 22 miles from Winchester. Only the Land Office remains standing. —Writers' Program, Virginia, *Virginia; a Guide to the Old Dominion* (New York, Oxford University Press, 1940), p. 442.

432. Andrew Montour reported first to William Fairfax who served as scribe for Montour's declaration to the governor, May 15, 1753, printed in Virginia, *Journal of the House of Burgesses, 1752–58, op. cit.,* pp. 515-16.

433. Probably Montour gave Colonel Fairfax the same information which he had given Mr. West in Philadelphia. See *note* 403.

434. In this letter Trent must have repeated the promise which he made to the Half King at Pine Creek (Etna, Pennsylvania) on May 12, 1753, when John Harris brought the news that the French were coming en masse to take possession of the Ohio Country. Croghan and Trent conferred with the Half King, Scarouady, and other chiefs at that time. During the conference Trent informed the Half King that "if the French attempted to settle them or to build any Forts, the Virginians would supply them with Arms and Ammunition" (*Colonial Records of Pennsylvania,* V, 615). For the Half King's reply see *note* 402.

435. On May 31, 1753, the Executive Council ordered Colonel William Fairfax "to deliver to Capt Trent the Arms and Ammunition in his possession, or such part of them as shall be thought necessary to be by him conveyed in the most careful Manner to the Indians." —Virginia Council *Journals,* V, 429.

Annotations

436. Bracketed material supplied from printed *Case, facs.*, p. 10.

437. May 31, 1753.

438. In a letter to Governor Dinwiddie dated January 22, 1753, Thomas Cresap and William Trent must have informed Dinwiddie that Six Nations' warriors were going to attack the southern Indians, for on February 10 he replied: "I did not know that the Warriors of the Six Nations were gone to the So[uth] w[ar]d. I wish you c'd have inform'd me of their Design, for I sh'd be very glad to have them and the So.w'd Ind's in a confirm'd State of Peace, which will be of great Service to the British Colonies on the Con't." —Dinwiddie to Cresap, February 10, 1753. *Op. cit.* See also *note* 486.

439. *Note* in document: "Lre 3. fol. 21. Colo Fairfax to Capt Trent. On April 11, 1759, William Trent sent this letter to John Mercer. See also *note* 396.

440. On his return to Onondaga, Montour stopped at Winchester to see Colonel Fairfax. This second mission to Onondaga for Virginia in 1753 was in accordance with the Executive Council order of May 22 whereby: "his Honour would by the Return of Mr Montour inform the Six Nations by a Letter under his Hand and the seal of the Colony, that we are well pleased with their Assurances of Fidelity, and that they may depend on our Support to enable them to repel our Common Enemies, and to advise them to keep their young Warriors at Home, for Fear of a Surprize." —(Dinwiddie's letter, dated May 24, 1753, to the Six United Nations is in P.R.O., C.O. 5: 1327/651-52.) As usual, Montour stopped in Philadelphia, informed the governor of his business for Virginia and inquired if "anything was to be carried from the Governor of Pennsylvania." Hamilton asked Montour to deliver the following message to the Onondaga Council: "The French have invaded your Lands on the Ohio and are building Forts there. The Indians of your Nations settled there, with the Delawares and Shawonese, Twightwees and Owendats, are terrified and desire our assistance, which we are willing to afford them but want first to know in what Manner You will desire We shall give them Assistance, and what You wou'd chuse We should do to prevent the Country and Them from falling into the Hands of the French." Onondaga sent the same answer to Pennsylvania which they sent to Virginia. The Council wrote in part, "We love the English and we love the French, and as you are at Peace with one another do not disturb one

Annotations

another; if you fall out make up your Matters among Yourselves."
—*Colonial Records of Pennsylvania*, V, 637.

441. Letter to William Trent. On April 11, 1759, William Trent sent this letter to John Mercer. See *note* 396.

442. Lewis Burwell was president of the Executive Council and served as acting lieutenant governor during the interim between Thomas Lee's death and the arrival of Robert Dinwiddie; Colonel William Fairfax was acting president of the Executive Council.

443. Intelligence sent by the governors of New York and Pennsylvania that the French were on the march toward the Ohio (see *note* 398) was discussed at a meeting of the Executive Council on May 22, 1753. The Council ordered that a messenger be sent immediately to the Cherokees and Catawbas in order that they might "be on their Guard against the Designs of the French" (Virginia Council *Journals*, V, 428). —Letters in P.R.O., C.O. 5: 1327/653-56.

444. Henry Morris received a courier's fee of £50 "for his journey to the Cherokees and Catawbas including what he has already received and Thirty pounds to his son for a Journey to the Catawbas." —Virginia Council *Journals*, V, 442.

445. The Catawbas' answer of July 26, 1753, is printed in *Calendar of Virginia State Papers, op. cit.*, I, 248-49.

446. Christopher Gist, not William Trent. Insertion "Capt Trent" is in John Mercer's handwriting. This error is also corrected in the printed *Case*. See *facs.*, p. 12.

447. Christopher Gist was given the Indian name Annosannoah when he was adopted into the Wyandot tribe on Christmas Day, 1750. See p. 12, this volume.

448. William Trent himself transported this gift to Logstown. —"William Trent's account with Virginia, April 8, 1754." MS in Virginia State Library, Colonial Papers, 1740–1759.

449. On April 11, 1759, William Trent sent this letter to John Mercer. See *note* 396.

450. *Ibid.* As printed in Dinwiddie *Papers*, I, 55-56, the postscript is lacking.

451. Washington returned to Williamsburg on January 16, 1754. On the seventeenth he presented his report or journal to the Executive Council. Thus in one day's time he transcribed from his "rough notes" and prepared for "his Honour's Perusal" a report which is considered today a classic in its field. The "Advertisement" or preface in the printed journal gives authenticity to the account. Wrote Washington: "There is nothing can recommend it to the Public, but this. Those Things which came under the Notice of my own Observation, I have been explicit and just in a Recital of:—Those which I have gathered from Report, I have been particularly cautious not to augment, but collected the Opinions of the several Intelligencers, and selected from the whole, the most probable and consistent Account." —Washington, *The Journal of* . . . *sent by Robert Dinwiddie* . . . *to the Commandant of the French Forces on Ohio, op. cit.,* p. 2.

452. Trent appointed John Fraser.

453. At this time the assembly had not passed the supply bill. On February 14, 1754, the governor called the House of Burgesses in session extraordinary in order to inform them of the gravity of the situation on the Ohio and to request them to pass a supply bill, thus enabling him to provide additional militia to protect the frontier settlements. In answer Charles Carter, chairman of the committee appointed to consider the governor's request, presented to the Burgesses a resolution which excused his committee's inability to report favorably on an increased supply bill. Again on October 17 the governor addressed the Burgesses exhorting them to make provision for adequate defense of the colony. Accordingly, they agreed on a "Bill, intituled, An Act for raising the Sum of Twenty Thousand Pounds for the Protection of his Majesty's Subjects against the Insults and Encroachments of the French." —Virginia, *Journal of the House of Burgesses, 1752–58, op. cit.,* pp. 175-77, 201, 212-13, 221.

This act and another "for raising levies and recruits to serve in the present expedition against the French, on the Ohio" are printed in Hening's *Statutes,* VI, 435-40.

454. Since George Washington, adjutant of the fourth militia district, was already a commissioned military officer, the governor issued

Annotations

him "Instruct's to be observ'd . . . on the Expedit'n to the Ohio." Printed in Dinwiddie *Papers,* I, 59.

455. Commission printed in *ibid.,* 54.

456. Dinwiddie, in his letter of December 10, 1752, to the Board of Trade, remarked to them that since the French had built forts in the Ohio Country, "I think it's full time we should build some forts of defence." If the home government approved this suggestion, Virginia would need "some small cannon, carriages, and powder, etc., proportionable" (Letter in P.R.O., C.O. 5: 1327/531-34. Printed in Trent's *Journal . . . 1752, op. cit.,* 73-81). This foregoing portion of Dinwiddie's letter which "relates to ordnance" was referred to the King in Council who in turn referred the request to the Board of Ordnance (B. T. *Journal, 1750–53,* pp. 402, 416, 421). On August 10, 1753, there was issued an order of council directing "30 cannon to be sent for the use of the forts proposed to be built on the River Ohio in Virginia" ("Order" in P.R.O., C.O. 5: 1328/1-8). The ordnance, valued at £1,196 10s. 11d., was received in Virginia before January 29, 1754. —Dinwiddie to Board of Trade, January 29, 1754, in P.R.O., C.O. 5: 1328/97-100.

457. Letters to the governors of South Carolina (James Glen), Pennsylvania (James Hamilton), New York (James DeLancey), New Jersey (Jonathan Belcher), Massachusetts (William Shirley) and to the acting governors of North Carolina (Matthew Rowan) and Maryland (Benjamin Tasker) are printed in Dinwiddie *Papers,* I, 61-71. These letters, of much the same import, conveyed the news of French aggression on the Ohio as reported by George Washington, Dinwiddie's emissary to the French. Dinwiddie also informed the governors that he had ordered the Virginia militia to the Ohio Country.

458. In a letter of January 29, 1754, Governor Dinwiddie acknowledged the receipt of guns and ammunition from the Board of Ordnance (see *note* 456). According to his letter, the cannon were "much too large to be transported so great a Distance by Land, & in bad Roads: However," added Dinwiddie, "I shall make a Tryal of Ten, if we can get them carried to the Fort they will be very serviceable; If possible cou'd have twenty Guns something larger than Blunderbuss fix'd in Tryangles, they wou'd be very portable."

459. Washington, on his mission to the Ohio Country, conferred

Annotations

with John Fraser at his home on the Monongahela at the mouth of Turtle Creek. —Washington, *Journal of* ... sent by Robert Dinwiddie ... *to the commandant of the French Forces on Ohio, op. cit.*, pp. 6, 27.

460. Trent was at Redstone when he received this commission. His account with Virginia contains the following item: "For four Pounds paid Coll. Cresap for his going Express with the Governors Lettrs to me at Redstone Creek." —William Trent's account with Virginia, April 8, 1754, *op. cit.* See also *note* 362.

For the letter which accompanied this commission, see printed *Case, facs.*, p. 15.

461. Edward Ward was appointed ensign. Ward's deposition about the fall of the English fort was made before the Virginia governor in council on May 7, 1754, a copy sent to the Board of Trade, was received and read on July 2 (P.R.O., C.O. 5: 14/293 and was printed in Gist's *Journals* [Darlington edition], pp. 275-78). Ward's deposition is the chief source of information concerning the fall of the Virginia fort. Later, Ward made several more depositions concerning this affair.

462. Trent's account with Virginia, dated April 8, 1754, was for "Fourteen Horses Loaded with Powder, Lead and Flints," entire cost, which included Montour's services as interpreter, £76 11s. 5¼d. (William Trent's account with Virginia, April 8, 1754, *op. cit.*). He transported a gift to the Ohio Indians in July, 1753, and in January-February, 1754, he brought to the Ohio not only the goods given the Indians at the Winchester Conference, but added supplies granted them by an order of council of the last of September. See *notes* 401, 448, and 463.

463. Washington met Trent four days out from Gist's plantation on the same day that he arrived at Wills Creek. Trent was bringing to the Ohio 17 horses loaded with material and stores for the Ohio Company's fort, also the Indian present given at Winchester. See Trent's bill dated April 8, 1754; Washington, *The Journal of* ... sent by Robert Dinwiddie ... *to the Commandant of the French Forces on Ohio, op. cit.*, 27-28.

Evidently Trent also brought Ohio Company trade goods in abundance, for George Croghan suggested to Pennsylvania that he could purchase an Indian present worth £100 from the Ohio Company

Annotations

store on the Ohio. —Croghan to Hamilton, February 3, 1754, printed in *Pennsylvania Archives,* II, 119-20.

464. The instructions sent by the Earl of Holdernesse to the governors of the several colonies requested a cautiousness on the part of the colonies not displayed in the royal instructions sent to Dinwiddie alone. The circular instructions were designed "to put You upon your Guard that you may at all Events be in a Condition to resist any Hostile attempts that may be made upon any Parts of his Majesties' Dominions within your Government . . . " If a foreign power committed any "Act of Hostility," the colonies concerned were ordered to try by peaceful measures to have the enemy "desist" and, if unsuccessful, were ordered to use armed force. This was no doubt the basis of Maryland's refusal. —Holdernesse's instructions, printed in *Colonial Records of Pennsylvania,* V, 689-90.

465. The foregoing two paragraphs do not appear elsewhere in the George Mercer Papers, nor in printed *Case.* Governor Sharpe's appeal to the General Assembly and this answer are printed in *Maryland Archives,* L, 408-13, 418-19.

466. "Youghiogheny big bottom" and "Oswegle [Sewickley] bottom," the location of one of George Croghan's trading houses may be one and the same. It is known that Croghan had a storehouse at Sewickley Bottom on the Youghiogheny about 15 miles above its confluence with the Monongahela. At Robbins Station on the Youghiogheny in about this location there is a fertile bottom which is traditionally called "Queen Alliquippa's Corn fields." It is said that the Indians who resided with Queen Alliquippa at present McKeesport came to this place in summer to raise corn; also, marks attributed to sites of the tepees were shown to the editor. This broad intervale may have been the site of Croghan's establishment.

467. Shortly after William Trent arrived on the Ohio, George Croghan informed Governor Hamilton that "The Indians all Intend, as soon as y[r] honour and the Governor of Verginia begins to Build, to gether all thire Warrers to ye Pleaces where y[e] Build, and Nott suffer ye French to Come Down ye River" (Croghan to Hamilton, February 3, 1754, *op. cit.*). William Trent had received his commission, and the information that Washington's militia was ordered to proceed to the Ohio to assist in building and protecting the fort (see pp. 81-83, *note* 460). Half King was present at the English fort when the

Annotations

French came down the Allegheny. It was he who advised Ensign Ward to build a "Stockade Fort" in order to repel the impending French assault. When the French commander, Contrecoeur, demanded immediate capitulation of the English, the Half King advised the Ensign to inform the French that "he was no Officer of Rank or invested with powers to answer their Demands and requested them to Wait the arrival of the principal Commander." This request was refused by the French who took possession of the fort within the hour. Ward reported "That the Half King stormed greatly at the French at the Time they were oblieged to march out of the Fort and told them it was he Order'd that Fort and laid the first Log of it himeself." —Deposition of Ensign Ward, before the Governor [of Virginia] in Council, May 7, 1754, *op. cit.*

468. Monsieur La Force, a valued scout and interpreter for the French, was commissary of the French stores at Venango when Washington was there in December, 1753. —Washington's *Journal of . . . 1753, op. cit.*, pp. 19-20.

"On the fifteenth Five Canoes of French came down to Log's Town in Company with the Half King and some more of the Six Nations, in Number an Ensign, a Serjeant, and Fifteen Soldiers." In this manner George Croghan reported the arrival at Logstown of the advance unit of the French-Canadian army sent to secure the Ohio Valley. Croghan, Andrew Montour, and John Patten were at Logstown when the French arrived. La Force, upon finding the Indians well disposed toward the English, remained at Logstown for only one day, after which "the Officer ordered his Men on board their Canoes and set off to a small Town of the Six Nations about two Miles below the Log's Town, where he intends to stay till the Rest of their Army come down" ("George Croghan's Journal, 1754," *op. cit.*). A short time after the English left Logstown, probably around the first of March, La Force undertook to coerce the Indians by threatening them. He warned that in less than three weeks the French army would come down the river; then they and their English friends were doomed to die. —A speech made by La Force, *ibid.*, VI, 22.

La Force's next mission was to scout Washington's little army near the Great Meadows. On May 24 an Indian trader reported to Washington that La Force and several other Frenchmen were lurking about Gist's plantation. Three days later Christopher Gist corroborated the trader's statement. Early the next morning, May 28, the English and Indians encountered the Frenchmen led by Jumonville. In the skirmish 30 of the 31 Frenchmen were either killed or taken prisoner.

Annotations

La Force was one of the men captured and sent to be confined in Williamsburg. —Washington, *Journal of ... 1754 ...* (Toner edition), pp. 70-90.

Shortly after Washington's capitulation at Fort Necessity, Governor Dinwiddie, in accordance with his interpretation of the Articles of Capitulation, dispatched the French prisoners to Wills Creek, from whence they were to be escorted to Fort Duquesne to be exchanged for the two English hostages given at the capitulation. Before the French prisoners had begun their trip to the French fort, hostage Robert Stobo's letter of July 28 was received in Virginia. Although this letter was intended for Colonel James Innes, commandant at Fort Cumberland, it is evident that it was dispatched to Governor Dinwiddie. Stobo wrote, "La Force is greatly wanted here, no scouting now, he certainly must have been an extraordinary Man amongst them, he is so much regretted and wished for." The governor answered this letter by ordering Colonel Innes to return La Force to Williamsburg. In the order he charged Colonel Innes to be careful that he did not escape and to "Look on him as a cunning, designing Man and therefore require double Care."

When the French officers complained of treatment unbecoming men of their rank, Governor Dinwiddie removed the prisoners to Winchester and, as winter arrived, on to Alexandria, Virginia, where they were relieved of close confinement and given private lodgments. Although Governor Dinwiddie does not mention La Force specifically, he was undoubtedly carried along with the group. After General Braddock arrived at Alexandria the prisoners were removed from the scene of military preparations for the campaign. The officers and private soldiers were sent to England, but La Force, at the suggestion of the Virginia Executive Council, remained in prison. By this time the Virginians were convinced that he was indeed a wicked man, had robbed many settlers, was suspected of scalping some of the English, had frequently tried to escape from prison, and had tried to persuade a fellow prisoner, a deserter, to escape with him. After his collusion with the deserter, La Force was placed in close confinement in Williamsburg jail.

La Force escaped the latter part of August, 1755, only to be apprehended two days later at West Point, a few miles up the James River from Williamsburg. When he was returned to jail he was placed in double irons and chained to the floor of his dungeon. With this statement the official records of Virginia concerning La Force come to an abrupt end. —Washington to Dinwiddie, May 29, 1754; Dinwiddie to Cresap, June 1; same to James Innes, August 22 and August 30; same

Annotations

to Lord Fairfax, September 10; same to Innes, October 5; same to William Shirley, September 20, 1755; same to Sir Thomas Robinson, October 1; same to Horatio Sharpe, March 13, 1756; same to Washington, August 21, 1756; printed in Dinwiddie *Papers,* I, 176-82, 184-86, 293, 296-98, 312-13, 346-48; II, 208-10, 227-28, 367-68, 484-85, respectively: John Burk, *The History of Virginia* (Petersburg, Va., the author, 1804), III, 192-93.

Only once again is La Force mentioned in correspondence of the day. In accordance with an article of the capitulation of Fort St. George, August 9, 1757, Montcalm wrote to Lord Loudoun as follows: "I demand particularly the man named La Force, a Canadian, who ought to have been sent back according to the capitulation of Fort Necessity. I request you to have them conducted to Halifax to be exchanged for yours whom I shall send to Louisbourg." —Montcalm to Lord Loudoun, August 14, 1757, printed in *N.Y.C.D.,* X, 619-20.

469. La Force's speech and the reply given by the speaker of the Six Nations are printed in *Colonial Records of Pennsylvania,* VI, 22. The speaker replied to La Force, "You tell Us in Twenty Days We and our Brethren the English must all dye. I believe You speak true, that is You intend to kill Us if You can; but I tell You to be strong and bring down your Soldiers for We are ready to receive You in battle but not in Peace. We are not afraid of You, and after an Engagement You will Know who are the best Men, You or We."

470. Croghan gleaned this information from the Indians who were at Logstown in January, 1754, when he assisted John Patten and Andrew Montour in the return of captivated Shawnee *(note 320)* to their tribesmen. Andrew Montour's cousin, who arrived with La Force at Logstown on February first, brought the news that "the French expect Four Hundred Men every Day to the Fort above Weningo, and as soon as they come they are to come down the River to Log's town to take Possession from the English till the rest of the Army comes in the Spring." —George Croghan's "Journal," 1754, *op. cit.*

471. Since this speech was made at Logstown after Croghan and Montour had left, the Indians sent a messenger east on the trail to overtake Croghan and "ordered me to send it immediately to your Honour that you might see how they were treated by the French and desired You might send a Copy of it to the Governor of Virginia."

Annotations

—Croghan to Hamilton, March 23, 1754. *Colonial Records of Pennsylvania*, VI, 21.

472. Six hundred, not 60, French and Indians. See printed *Case, facs.*, p. 16.

473. Croghan heard this news on January 16, at Logstown. —"Journal of George Croghan, 1754," *op. cit.*

474. Washington wrote of the beginning of his march to the Ohio as follows: *"April the 2nd.* Every Thing being ready, we began our march according to our Orders, the 2nd of April, with two Companies of Foot, commanded by Captain *Peter Hog* and Lieutenant *Jacob Van Braam,* five subalterns, two Sergeants, six Corporals, one Drummer, and one hundred and twenty Soldiers, one Surgeon, one *Swedish* Gentleman, who was a voluntee, two wagons guarded by one Lieutenant, Sergeant, Corporal and twenty-five Soldiers. We left *Alexandria* on Tuesday Noon and pitched our tents about four miles from *Cameron* having marched six miles." —Washington, *Journal of . . .* (Toner edition), *op. cit.,* entry April 2, 1754, pp. 20-26.

475. This letter does not appear in any collection of the writings of George Washington nor does any biographer of him mention it. Although written to Thomas Cresap, the letter was in the hands of William Trent, who on the night of April 11, 1759, sent this and eight other letters by Captain Robert Stewart to John Mercer. This letter was among them (List of letters . . . Historical Society of Pennsylvania. See *note* 396). "And several pair of Hand cuffs" is deleted from the printed copy in *Case, facs.,* pp. 17-18.

476. Job Pearsall, one of the first settlers on the south branch of the Potomac, resided near the present town of Romney, West Virginia, along the main road between Winchester and Fort Cumberland. George Washington traveled this route and waited at Job Pearsall's for the arrival of additional troops. —Washington, *Journal of . . .* (Toner edition), *op. cit.,* entry April 19, 1754, pp. 26-30.

477. This sentence does not appear elsewhere in the George Mercer Papers nor in the printed *Case.*

478. Claude Pierre Pécaudy, Sieur de Contrecoeur, before being sent to relieve St. Pierre of his command on the Ohio, had been commandant

at Niagara and had accompanied Céloron on his expedition in 1749. After taking command of the French army at Venango, in the spring of 1754, he proceeded to the forks of the Ohio where Ensign Ward surrendered Virginia's fort to him. He remained in command at Fort Duquesne until late in 1755, when he was succeeded by Dumas. —Wisconsin Historical Society *Collections*, XVIII, 49n.

479. Colonel Fry's orders from Dinwiddie, dated March 1754, were to march to Alexandria and there take command of the forces. From thence he was to go to Wills Creek, then with the "Great Guns, Amunit's and Provisions" proceed to the Monongahela and choose the best place to erect a fort. Colonel Fry was commander in chief of the Virginia regiment. —"Instructions to Joshua Fry," printed in Dinwiddie *Papers*, I, pp. 89, 90.

480. See *Chronology*, April 18, 1754.

481. The Half King's speech was read in council May 4, 1754. The same day the council advised "his Honour in his Answer to the Half Kings Speech to Assure him we are sending many Forces out whom they may expect Very soon, to support and Protect Them, to desire him to be strong and not fear; and that our Forces shall join him and all the Indians which they can gather together at the Forks of the Road." —Virginia Council *Journals*, V, 469. See also *Case, facs.*, p. 19.

482. Le Mercier served as engineer and commissary under Marin on his 1753-expedition to the Ohio. In addition to his duties as engineer for the construction of Fort Duquesne, he had charge of the artillery and provisions for the whole detachment and was second in command of the French forces at the battle of Fort Necessity. —Marquis Duquesne to the Minister, August 20, 1753, printed in *N.Y.C.D.*, X, 255-57; ——— October 8, 1754, printed in Frontier Forts and Trails Survey, *Wilderness Chronicles of Northwestern Pennsylvania* (Harrisburg, Pa., Pennsylvania Historical Commission, 1941), p. 64; Varin to Bigot, July 24, 1754, printed in *ibid.*, pp. 80-82.

483. Refers to the fifteenth article in the Treaty of Aix-la-Chapelle, that "all Things shall remain there in the Condition they were in before the war." The French had recognized the Iroquois rights to this territory, also the English right over the Iroquois. Therefore, the English considered that French fortifications on the Ohio were not in accordance with the treaty.

Annotations

484. Meaning the Ohio Company. This statement appears to be the only direct reference to the Company's activities having been a motivating factor in the French-English dispute on the Ohio. On January 29, 1754, Governor Dinwiddie remarked to the Board of Trade that: "Under the certain right of the Crown of Great Britn His Majesty was pleas'd to grant to some of his Subjects, five hundred Thousand Acres of Land on the Waters of the Ohio, under the Name of the Ohio Company.—This Company & their Grant, is well known to the Governor of Canada, & that they have, at great Expence begun their Settlement, agreeable to their Grant, but some of their People are return'd being seiz'd with a Panick on the Threats of the French, & their seizing all they can lay their Hands on belonging to the British Subjects, & its further surmiz'd that they spirit up the Indians in their Interest, to way lay them, & Murder them." —P.R.O., C.O. 5: 1328/97-100.

485. The French insisted that the Treaty of Aix-la-Chapelle (1748) gave freedom of trade to this region, but not freedom of location for traders' headquarters; therefore, according to French interpretation Indians under their influence were at liberty to trade with the English, but only on English soil.

486. George Washington, on his return trip from Venango, met at John Fraser's a group of Indians who had returned from southward. They told him that "coming to a Place upon the Head of the great Kunnaway, where they found seven People killed and scalped (all but one Woman with very light Hair) they turned about and ran back for Fear the Inhabitants should use and make them the Authors of the Murder . . . By the Marks which were left they say they were *French* Indians of the *Ottaway* Nation, &c. who did it." —Washington, *The Journal of* . . . *Sent by the Hon. Robert Dinwiddie,* . . . *to the Commandant of the French Forces on Ohio* . . . , *op. cit.,* p. 27.

487. Refers to the activities of William Trent. Trent had brought a valuable present to the Ohio Indians in August, 1753, and had led them to Winchester to receive a still larger present. He left Wills Creek the beginning of January, 1754, with tools and ample supplies for the Indians on the Ohio. These supplies consisted of the present given them at Winchester in September and an additional one voted them the latter part of the same month. He delivered the presents in February, 1754, and by April 17 had recruited almost 100 frontiersmen to serve as militiamen whose duty it was to protect the workmen

Annotations

who had begun a stockaded fort at the forks of the Ohio. See *notes* 306, 307, 362, 406, 413, 434, and 467.

488. The bracketed [ ] material supplied from Moreau does not appear in the printed *Case*.

489. This book is an English retranslation of *Mémoire contenant le Précis des Faits, avec leurs Piéces Justificatives, Pour servir de Réponse aux Observations envoyées par les Ministers d'Angleterre, dans les Cours de l'Europe.* (Paris, De l'Imprimerie Royale, 1756.) The *Mémoire contenant . . .* is a collection of documents concerning English aggression, so-called by the French, on the Ohio. Some of the documents contained in the volume were confiscated by the French at Braddock's defeat, while others, such as Washington's *Journal of his expedition to the Ohio* may have fallen into the hands of the French at the capitulation of Fort Necessity. This journal is extant only in the French translation and English retranslation. However, many of the other documents exist in official copy form. The book, printed by order of the French King, was sent by him to the Courts throughout Europe in order to show the perfidy and aggressiveness of the English. When the volume became known to the English, it was retranslated immediately and five separate editions were published in rapid succession. For bibliographic information concerning the original French and English translations which were published, see Joseph Sabin, *A Dictionary of Books relating to America, from its Discovery to the Present Time* (New York, V. pub., 1868–1936), Nos. 15205, 41650, 47511, 47512, and 51661.

490. This request made by Ensign Ward was at the behest of the Half King. A few days previous, Ward, upon learning that a French attack was imminent, went to Fraser's plantation to ask his superior officer, Fraser, to return to duty at the fort. Since Fraser refused to return to the fort at that time, Ward could have scarcely expected his return in the face of capitulation to the French. No doubt Half King was "buying time." —Edward Ward's Deposition, May 7, 1754, *op. cit.*

491. The French Fort Duquesne (1754–58) was built of squared timbers, 12 feet thick on the land side, while the part facing the river was a stockade. Inside the enclosure were the commandant's quarters, the guardhouse, the barracks, a storehouse, and barracks for the gunners, all protected by "six pieces of cannon of six, and nine of two and three pound ball." The whole enclosure was surrounded by a

Annotations

moat. De Lery, a subengineer from Fort Detroit, came in the spring (1755) and "put the fort in the best condition he was able." Commandant Contrecoeur, in his report of May 24, 1755, to Duquesne, stated that the fort was completed. In the past year they had raised 700 minots of Indian corn and, with the clearings recently made, they expected to harvest 2,000 minots. Livestock at the fort consisted of "two cows, one bull, some horses and twenty-three sows with young." —J. C. B., *Travels in New France* edited by Sylvester K. Stevens and others (Harrisburg, Pennsylvania Historical Commission, 1931), pp. 54, 55; *N.Y.C.D.*, X, 300, 307.

On July 28, 1754, Robert Stobo, famous English hostage of the battle of Fort Necessity, smuggled a letter out of Fort Duquesne. In this letter to Colonel Innes, commander at Fort Cumberland, he estimated the strength of the garrison to be 200. On the back of the letter he made a draft of the fort. The original letter is in the Darlington Memorial Library, University of Pittsburgh. A similar letter in the Palais de Justice, Montreal, Canada, is reputed to be the original. Up to this time no one has rendered a final decision on the status of the two letters, both purported to be holographs. Printed in *Colonial Records of Pennsylvania*, VI, 161-63.

Fortunately for the French, the strength of Fort Duquesne was not tested by General Braddock in 1755. The French themselves knew that the fortification was inadequate and could not withstand strong frontal attack. It had been hastily and rudely constructed; also, the supply line from Canada was too long to afford adequate supplies for the garrison. Therefore, it is small wonder that the French were alarmed by the rumors that the English intended to attack. That spring they transferred half the militia from Detroit and a number of Indians to the Monongahela. Dumas had adopted the strategy of "delaying action" by which they harassed the English settlements to such a degree that an organized attack upon the French was impossible. In the meantime they adopted measures to strengthen the fort. The pillage from the Battle of the Monongahela attracted many Indians to the French. As the Indians became more and more successful in their forays against the English, greater and greater numbers of western tribes flocked to the fort. By 1756 supplies were being sent up the Ohio from the Illinois Country as well as over the well-established Presqu'Isle–Le Boeuf–Allegheny River supply line. In one month, October, 1755, the commandant sent 250 Indians, usually under French command, to lay waste the English frontiers. At this early date they were attacking settlements even beyond Fort Cumberland. But Dumas did not depend solely upon a delaying action to save

Annotations

Fort Duquesne. He informed Marquis de Vaudreuil that the fort could not resist any artillery attack. Therefore, if the enemy appeared, his only recourse was to go out and meet him. Since the governor's instructions to the commandant did not cover offensive action, he asked Vaudreuil for official sanction of his strategy. Vaudreuil responded by ordering all the French posts near Fort Duquesne "to forward some Indians and Frenchmen," and remarked that these reinforcements would permit Dumas to continue the forays and, if necessary, disrupt any organized attack before they reached the drawbridge of the fort.

One report to the home government, dated Montreal, June 12, 1756, contained the enlightening remark, "Fort Duquesne is not worth a straw. A freshet nearly carried it off a short time ago." An abstract of dispatches from Canada shows that, by March 23, 1756, the French claimed that they and their Indian allies, since Braddock's defeat, had killed or taken prisoners more than 700 Pennsylvanians, Virginians, and Carolinians. At this time Commandant Dumas was so flushed with victory that he "had his eye on Fort Cumberland." He was well supplied with ammunition; he had received 300 Canadian reinforcements and Vaudreuil's approval of his plan of defense of the fort. The Marquis' instruction also authorized him, if he learned that the enemy were marching against him, "he is to call his forces together again in order to proceed to meet them, as, in the present state of the fort, it would be impossible to make any resistance for any length of time were he to allow himself to be besieged in it." Materials for the defense were greatly augmented by the French from a considerable quantity of "shell, shot and bullets which had been secreted in the woods on General Braddock's defeat." This was in addition to the quantity of stores obtained at the time of the Battle of the Monongahela.

The summer report from Fort Duquesne was relayed by Marquis de Vaudreuil to the home government in August, 1756. At this time he reported the garrison of 810 men was so busy with murder on the frontier that the commandant of Fort Duquesne was "occupied for more than eight days merely in receiving scalps." This same report, however, reveals the first break in Indian-French solidarity. Almost all the Iroquois in the vicinity of Fort Duquesne had retired to the north to Fort Machault, many miles nearer the Onondaga Council. This bad news was balanced by the optimistic note that Fort Cumberland had been rendered ineffective, partly from within, partly from without. Sickness had taken a heavy toll at the fort during the winter, and the French had rendered even the road from Winchester to

Annotations

Cumberland untenable. According to French scouts, no corn was planted about the fort in the spring, no supplies had been brought to it for three months, and the garrison, preparatory to blowing up and abandoning the fort, had dug a ditch to bury their cannon. The official French reports from which the foregoing statements were derived are printed in *N.Y.C.D.*, X, 327, 408, 410, 416, 424, 425, 435-38.

According to John M'Kinney, who was a prisoner at the fort in 1756, it was more substantial than the French records reveal. M'Kinney stated that the outside structure was rectangular, 50 yards long and 40 wide with a bastion at each corner. The entrenchment around it was about seven feet high. Outside the back gate at the water side of the fort was the bakehouse and the magazine which was almost underground, built of large logs and covered over with clay. M'Kinney mentioned another building about 30 yards from the fort which contained the tools "and a great quantity of wagon-wheels and tire." An estimate of strength of the garrison as given by M'Kinney and Dumas' official report is incongruous. M'Kinney said there were about 250 Frenchmen in the fort, while Dumas' report (*op. cit.*) gave the strength to be 810 men. —"John M'Kinney's Description of Fort Duquesne," printed in *Olden Time,* edited by Neville B. Craig (Pittsburgh, Dumars & Co., 1846), I, 39-40.

By mid-1757 the French began to feel the effects of Pennsylvania's fury against the marauding French and Indians. Only a short distance from Fort Duquesne three Delawares had been killed by the English, French intelligence was that although the Delawares swore they had abandoned the English forever, they had sent representatives to make peace with the Pennsylvanians. The French were also aware of the line of frontier blockhouses that Pennsylvania had built; but the rumor most alarming to the French was that soldiers from all the English provinces had banded together for an attack on Fort Duquesne. Vaudreuil reported the situation to the home government as follows: "Fort Duquêne, in its present condition, could not offer any resistance to the enemy; 'tis too small to lodge the garrison necessary on such an occasion. A single shell would be sufficient to get it so on fire, that 'twould be impossible to extinguish it because the houses are too close. The garrison would then find itself under the painful necessity of abandoning the fort. Besides, 'tis so near the confluence of the Beautiful river with the Malangaillee, that it is always exposed to be entirely submerged by the overflowing of the rivers. M. de Ligneris is having such repairs done to that fort as it is susceptible of, regard being had to its bad situation; but that will not enable us to dispense with the erection of a new fort."

Annotations

From this time on there was a rapid deterioration in the French-Indian relations. The Delawares around Tioga "had been seduced by an English interpreter who made them considerable presents." In a memoir on the artillery of Canada, October 30, 1757, Le Mercier stated that the artillery of Fort Duquesne remained the same—the post was too small to sustain a siege. He recommended that if the king wished to secure his possession on the Ohio, it would be necessary to build a "respectable fort."

Noteworthy in the "Journal of Occurrences in Canada 1757, 1758" is a statement, as of January 28, 1758, that a cadet, arriving in Canada from Fort Duquesne, reported everything quiet and in good order, excepting the Indians. The empty storehouse at the fort, which meant no large presents for them, made the Indians reluctant to go out to fight. By the last of August, 1758, rumors of an English attack were greatly magnified. It was reported to the home government that a force of 18,000 English was marching on the French—6,000 toward Fort Duquesne, 6,000 toward Fort Machault, Le Boeuf, and Presqu'-Isle, and 6,000 against Fort Frontenac. French intelligence was at a low ebb, for on August 30, 1758, de Ligneris learned that General Forbes was expected at Loyalhaning (Ligonier), but was unable to find out whether or not the English intended to attack them in the fall. Vaudreuil's comment on this information was that it would be impossible for de Ligneris to resist an attack, and that since lack of provisions had reduced his garrison to 200 men, de Ligneris could not do much to delay it. Montcalm blamed "the two public order of Monsieur de Vaudreuil to evacuate Fort Duquesne for the loss of that strategic point in the Ohio Country." In the same report he leveled his guns of criticism at the corrupt Intendant Bigot. The French had been niggardly in supplying not only provisions, but in providing an adequate force and adequate installations at the fort. When de Ligneris in the face of the advancing English army left Fort Duquesne, November 25, 1758, he blew it up, and he and his pitifully small force of French retired to a "pretended fort" called Fort Machault. Montcalm explained to the home government the word "pretended fort" with another blast at the excesses of Bigot's favorites. The official French reports from which the above statements were compiled are printed in *N.Y.C.D.*, X, 583, 589, 656, 819, 837, 925, 960-62.

492. Heretofore this speech has been known only as recorded by George Washington who incorporated it in his journal of his march to the Ohio in 1754 (Washington, *Journal of . . . 1754* . . . [Toner

Annotations

edition], *op. cit.,* pp. 38-39). He also sent a copy to Governor Hamilton (*Colonial Records of Pennsylvania,* VI, 28-29, 31). The original of his journal has never been located, but the text of it has been preserved in a French translation in the publication, *Mémoire contenant les Précis de Faits, op. cit.* (see also *note* 489). In both the French translation and English retranslation Washington stated that the Half King directed the last paragraph of the speech personally to him. Although he did not mention this fact to Governor Hamilton, it is suggested in the last sentence of the Half King's speech as copied by Washington, "Delivered to me by John Davidson and Interpreter." The speech, as recorded in this document, reveals that Davison, the interpreter, was the Half King's scribe and that after the speech was written he gave it to Edward Ward. It was Edward Ward and not Washington, as implied in the copy sent to Hamilton, who was to go "to both governors." Two Indian messengers accompanied Ward. Undoubtedly, the Half King expected replies from both governors. Also, the French rendition of the speech, as recorded by Washington in his journal, states that if Washington approved, the Half King would go "to both the Governors, with these two young men." This interpretation, which is erroneous, may be attributed to faulty translation.

493. At times the Half King, or Tanacharison, was addressed as *Scruniyatha* or *Scruniattha.* —Hodge, *op. cit.,* I, 526.

494. Although the *Belt, Belt of Wampum,* or the *Old Belt* was the name of an Indian chief, this speech was made by the Half King himself. He sent a belt of wampum and the speech to the governors. Here the asterisk (*) is in the wrong place. "An Indian cheif so called," refers to Scruneyattha. The asterisk (*) is placed correctly after Scruneyattha in the speech as printed in the *Colonial Records of Pennsylvania,* VI, 31.

495. From 1749 to 1754 the Indians on the Ohio had lived in a state of suspense, fearing momentarily an attack by the French. Even Céloron's expedition of 1749 had been reported to them as a French army sent to occupy the Ohio Country. Reports, originating at Oswego and relayed via New York, Pennsylvania, or Virginia to the Ohio, held them in constant fear of a French attack. —*Ibid.,* V, 387-88, 431-40, 459-60, 462, 480-82, 496-98, 537-38, 568-70, 575, 599-600.

496. The logical meeting place for armed forces from Pennsylvania

and from Virginia would have been at the junction of the Great Warriors' Trail and the Raystown Path, about eight miles east of the present town of Bedford, Pennsylvania. From Governor Dinwiddie's correspondence concerning this message one learns that he interpreted the message differently. On May 4, 1754, the Governor informed Washington that he had written to Colonel Joshua Fry, "directing him also to proceed to red Stone Creek, w'ch being not far from the Place call'd the Fork of the Roads, where the Half-King proposes to meet a select Body of our friendly Ind's . . . " (letter in Dinwiddie *Papers*, I, 148-49). If this interpretation be correct, the forks of the road mentioned by the Half King was probably not far from Gist's plantation. William Scull's map of Pennsylvania (1770) indicates that the road from Cumberland forked at that place, one branch leading to the Monongahela at the mouth of Redstone Creek, the other, by a circuitous route, to Fort Pitt. These roads as marked by Scull followed the route of the Indian trails. See *Bibliography*, Map, 1770.

497. Half King must have been referring to George Croghan and the Pennsylvanians. When La Force issued his warning to the Indians at Logstown, on February 20, he sent a message to George Croghan imploring him to have Pennsylvania recognize "how they were treated by the French." Formerly the Half King had asked the two colonies to "send out a number of your People, our Brethern, to meet us at the Forks of Monongialo, and see what is the Reason for their coming, for we do not want the French to come amongst Us at all." Up to this time, April, the Virginians had sent representatives and arms to the Indians, but the Pennsylvanians had "never returned or sent any Word."—Half King to Dinwiddie, June 22, 1753; Croghan to Hamilton, March 23, 1754. *Op. cit.*

498. This advertisement was also published in the *Pennsylvania Gazette*, May 24, 1754. In February, 1752, Virginia enacted into law *An Act for encouraging persons to settle on the waters of the Mississippi,* which exempted all settlers in that region from the payment of all public, county, and parish levies for ten years. The act stated that such encouragement, exemption from colonial levies, would cause many natural-born subjects and foreign Protestants to settle the western frontier of the province, thus adding "to the strength and security of the colony in general, and be a means of augmenting his majesty's revenue of quit rents." To levy or to remit the payment of quitrents was the king's prerogative; therefore quitrents, a source

Annotations

of private income for the king, could not be remitted by colonial legislation. At the next General Assembly, November, 1753, the Burgesses, upon the suggestion of the Board of Trade, passed *An Act for further encouraging persons to settle on the waters of the Mississippi*, whereby all settlers in that remote region were exempted from paying all colonial levies for a term of 15 years. —Hening's *Statutes*, VI, 258, 355-56; *Journal of the House of Burgesses*, 1752–58, xiii-xvi.

The time required for messages to be transmitted between the colonies and England, the recess of the legislative bodies, and the rapid turn of events in regard to French encroachment on Virginia's frontiers brought about this apparent incongruous legislation. Undoubtedly, these advertisements had been prepared and sent to the newspapers before May 7, when Ensign Ward brought to Virginia the news of English evacuation and French occupation of Virginia's fort at the "forks of Monongahela."

499. Bracketed ([   ]) material is supplied from printed *Case* . . . , *facs.*, p. 19.

500. Fifteen years' exemption from all taxes was a stipulation suggested by the Board of Trade. The Board, in their letter of November 29, 1752, to Governor Dinwiddie, advised him that they were "of Opinion, that it would be greatly for the Interest and Advantage of the Colony, if foreign Protestants were exempted from all Parochial Charges and Taxes whatever for a Term of Years, not exceeding 15, from the time of their Arrival in the Province." The Board of Trade added, "as the Regulations however with respect to Parishes & Support of Ministers have their foundation in old established Laws, which have been long acquiesced in, We could wish that any Alteration of these Regulations should have the Sanction & Concurrence of the Council and Assembly there." —Letter, *op. cit.*

501. England's Acts of Toleration (1689) secured freedom of worship to all religious believers except "Papists and such as deny the Trinity."

502. According to John Hanbury's petition to the King in Council (see *Chronology*, January 11, 1749), in behalf of himself and other members of the Ohio Company, one of the chief objectives of the Company was "to improve and extend British trade amongst the Indians." In exchange for the public benefit derived from their private enterprise the Company wished to be given special concessions in regard to lands granted them by Virginia. Hence the need for

Annotations

petitioning the King for an alteration in his royal instructions to the governor.

503. George Mercer stated officially that the total investment of the stockholders was £10,000 ("Proceedings of the Ohio Company...," October 8, 1767. Shelburne Papers, L, 90-95, MS in William L. Clements Library, Ann Arbor, Michigan); unofficially he gave Colonel Bouquet the same evaluation, "Company have advanced £500 each." —George Mercer to Henry Bouquet, December 27, 1760. *Op. cit.*

504. Refers to the German and Scotch-Irish migration. John and Isaac Van Meter of New York, and John Stover, Joist Hite (Germans), and the Lewis's (Scotch-Irish) of Pennsylvania led this migration in the early 1730's. On June 17, 1730, John Van Meter of New York was granted 30,000 acres of land in the Shenandoah Valley, 10,000 of which were to be seated by his relatives and friends. The 20,000-acre grant was contingent upon his bringing 20 additional families to settle in Virginia. Isaac Van Meter of New Jersey received 10,000 acres upon which he was obliged to settle ten families within two years. Jacob Stover, at the same time, was granted 10,000 acres upon which he was to seat German and Swiss families at the rate of one family for every 1,000 acres within two years' time (Virginia Council *Journals*, IV, 223-24, 252-53). The next year Robert McKay and Joist Hite of Pennsylvania petitioned the Virginia Executive Council for 100,000 acres of land "setting forth that they & divers others Families to the number of one hundred are desirous to remove from thence & seat themselves on the back of the great Mountains within this Colony."

In 1732 William Beverley wrote to a friend: "I am persuaded that I can get a number of people from Pensilvania to settle on Shenondore, if I can obtain an order of Council for some land there..." (letter in *Calendar of Virginia State Papers*, I, 217-18). John Walter Wayland, in his *The German Element of the Shenandoah Valley of Virginia* (Charlottesville, Va., Michie Company for the author, 1907), pages 57 to 79, reprinted sufficient Virginia county records to show that migration from the northern colonies, especially Pennsylvania, was largely responsible for the rapid growth of settlements in this section of Virginia.

505. Refers to the Wachovia Tract purchased by the Moravians of Bethlehem, Pennsylvania, in 1751. The Earl of Granville who had had "set apart ⅛ part of the provinces of Carolina under certain conditions" encouraged the Moravians to settle in North Carolina.

Annotations

There, under a royal act of May 12, 1749, they would be "indulged with full liberty of conscience, and be exempted from personal military service for a reasonable compensation, and be permitted, instead of taking an oath, in cases where the laws require it, to make a solemn affirmation or declaration." As a result the Pennsylvania Moravians purchased 100,000 acres of the Granville grant in North Carolina. Bishop Spangenberg, accompanied by six men, went to North Carolina in August, 1752, met the surveyor general of the province, Mr. Churton, and had surveyed 98,925 acres in 19 separate tracts. Most of the lands lay along the Yadkin, New, and Catawba Rivers, in present Surrey County. The development was named the Wachovia Tract in honor of Count Zinzendorf who also held the title, Lord of the Valley of Wachau, Austria. —B. T. *Journal, 1741-49*, p. 40; Francois-Xavier Martin, *The History of North Carolina from the Earliest Period* (New Orleans, A. T. Penniman & Co., 1829), I, appendix xxiv-xxxviii.

506. Refers to the "Jumonville affair." As the Virginia militia under the command of Washington were nearing Turkey Foot (the junction of the three branches of the Youghiogheny River, present Confluence, Pennsylvania), he sent an Indian courier to the Half King with a message of assurance that the English were on the march and asked him to "march vigorously towards your brethern the *English*." The next day, May 20, the army encamped at Turkey Foot where they remained several days, examining the terrain which they thought especially suitable as the site for a fort. On May 24 Washington received a message from the Half King informing him that, two days before, the French had marched from Fort Duquesne and intended to engage the English wherever they found them. The Half King also informed Washington that he and other chiefs would join him in council in five days. The English, again on the move, had by this time reached the Great Meadows. There a trader informed them that the French were reconnoitering around Gist's Plantation, and that a strong detachment of French was on the march. Christopher Gist, on the twenty-seventh, confirmed this statement, by reporting that La Force and 50 Frenchmen were in the vicinity. The same evening Half King confirmed Gist's statement. Leaving a small guard at the camp, Washington marched with 40 men to seek and engage the enemy. Early next morning he arrived at the Half King's camp, where he conferred with the Indians who joined forces with him, sought out the French, and engaged them. After 15 minutes' combat the French were defeated, only one Frenchman having escaped death or imprisonment.

Annotations

Ensign Coulon de Jumonville, commander of the party, was one of the ten killed; La Force, one of the 21 prisoners taken. —Washington's *Journal* ... 1754 ... (Toner edition), *op. cit.;* see also *note* 468. —The original document, Articles of the Capitulation of Fort Necessity, is in the Palais de Justice, Montreal, Canada; printed in *Pennsylvania Archives,* II, 146-47.

507. General Forbes took possession of the abandoned Fort Duquesne on November 26, 1758. —Forbes to William Pitt, November 27, 1758, printed in John Forbes, *Writings of* ... compiled and edited by Alfred P. James (Menasha, Wis., Collegiate Press, 1938), pp. 267-68.

508. This statement is evidence that this "Case of the Ohio Company" is either the amended original approved by the committee (see *Chronology*), or a revised copy of the original approved by the committee.

509. The *Journals of the House of Burgesses, 1758–61* record awards given many persons who suffered damages at the hands of the French during the 1754–58 period.

510. End of bracketed ([   ]) material supplied from printed *Case, facs.,* p. 21.

511. Extant "Journal of the Meetings of the President and Masters of William and Mary College" (1759–61) does not show that Christopher Gist was commissioned by the College ("Journal" as printed in the *William and Mary College Quarterly,* 1st series, III, 128-32). However, George Mercer writes in a letter to Washington, September 16, 1759, "I have a copy of all our Entries We made with Gist now by Me—he told me, he had entered Them for us." Only a licensed surveyor could make entry for lands. Also, on December 10, 1759, George Mercer, probably in the room of Christopher Gist, deceased, was appointed surveyor of lands by the president and masters of William and Mary College. —"Journal" as printed in *William and Mary College Quarterly,* 1st series, III, 129.

512. Brigadier General Stanwix, at a conference with the Indians at Fort Pitt, October 24–26, 1759, told the Indians assembled that "the Original Draught of the Boundary Line Settled between us at the Treaty of Easton, by the Six Nations, was delivered them." At the same time he gave the Delawares and Shawnee a copy of the draft

Annotations

which was sent to them by Governor Denny of Pennsylvania. —Minutes of the conference, printed in *Colonial Records of Pennsylvania,* VIII, 429-35.

At the Treaty of Albany (1754) the proprietors of Pennsylvania purchased of the Indians "a large tract of land over Susquehannah, extending from the mouth of John Penn's Creek to the Ohio." The Indians received a partial payment for the entire tract, 1,000 pieces of eight for the part which had been settled already by the English. They were to receive, at a later date, payment for the rest of the land as it was settled. At the Treaty of Easton the Indians informed the proprietors that "Our Warriors or Hunters, when they heard that we had sold such a Large Tract of Land, disapproved our Conduct in Council, so now we acquaint you, that we are determined not to confirm any more, than such of the Lands as the Consideration was paid for, and are settled, tho' included in the Deed; they are our hunting Grounds, and we desire the request may be granted, and Notice taken that it was made in open Conference." The proprietors answered this request by saying that they preferred the friendship of the Indians and the public good to their own private interest. They also informed the Indians that three years previous, 1755, Sir William Johnson interceded for the Indians and at that time the proprietors "cheerfully agreed to release to you all that part of the Purchase you have reclaimed; and, by a Letter of Attorney, empowered Richard Peters and Conrad Weiser to execute a Deed to you for those Lands, on your Confirming to them the Residue of that Purchase. On this Subject, therefore, you will please to Confer with them and Settle the Boundaries between you, and that they may release the Lands to you accordingly before you leave this Place, and set your Minds at Ease." —*Pennsylvania (Colony) Treaties. Minutes of the Conference held at Easton in October, 1758* . . . (Philadelphia, printed and sold by B. Franklin, and D. Hall, 1758); also printed in the *Colonial Records of Pennsylvania,* VIII, 174-223. Citations from pp. 199 and 204, respectively.

513. Christopher Gist died of smallpox "on the road from Williamsburg" to Winchester on July 25, 1759. —Captain James Gunn to Major John Tulleken, July 31, 1759, B. M. Add. MSS, 21644, f. 266; printed in Bouquet *Papers,* 21644, pt. I, pp. 216-17.

514. At this time, 1759–60, Adam Stephen, Thomas Bullitt, George Mercer, George Washington, and Robert Stewart, all Virginia militiamen, veterans of the 1754-58 campaign, were pressing their claims

Annotations

for land on the Ohio, in accordance with Dinwiddie's proclamation of 1754 (see *Chronology,* February 29, 1754). By September 16, 1759, Christopher Gist, in behalf of George Mercer and George Washington, had entered for lands on the Ohio (George Mercer to Washington, September 16, 1759, *op. cit.*). On February 17, 1760, Mercer wrote a scathing denunciation of Stephen and Bullitt's collusion in an effort to obtain for themselves the best land on the Ohio. Before February 17 Bullitt had written to Mercer informing him that the place of surveyor was to be divided and each, Mercer and Bullitt, was to have a district. According to the description of the land given Washington by Mercer, Thomas Bullitt and Adam Stephen had carved for themselves a generous slice of land claimed by the Ohio Company (Mercer to Washington, February 17, 1760, printed in Hamilton, *op. cit.,* III, 172-75). Captain Robert Stewart, one of the group of veterans headed by Washington and Mercer, wrote to Washington inquiring "after what Steps have been taken in securing to us, those Lands which poor Cap^n Gist was to have enter'd for us, I hope the needfull is done, they surely will soon be very valuable."—Stewart to Washington, September 28, 1759, *ibid.,* 163.

Colonel Bouquet in his memorandum, "Articles necessary for the Western Department in 1760," included an item: "Establish Farmers at Bedford, Ligonier, Wetherhold, Cumberland, Crossing, Guest, F^t Burd, and Pittsburgh to raise oats, Indian Corn, Wheat, and Rye &c a Power vested in the Command^g officer to grant such Lands." —B.M. Add. MSS 21653, f. 50; printed in Bouquet *Papers,* 21653, p. 46. See also *note* 516.

515. If this statement be true, the governor and council did give consent to the president and masters of the College of William and Mary to appoint George Mercer surveyor for land on the Ohio. See *note* 511.

516. From 1759 to 1762 Governor Fauquier carried on an extensive correspondence with the Board of Trade, the governor of Pennsylvania, and Henry Bouquet, commandant at Fort Pitt. The denial for lands to be granted or surveyed in the Ohio region was occasioned by the insistence of the Virginia militiamen that the bonus lands rightfully due them under Dinwiddie's proclamation of 1754 should be granted them at this time. When Governor Fauquier refused to act contrary to the confirmed promise to the Indians under the Treaty of Easton (1758), they threatened to petition the proprietors of Pennsylvania for these lands. Here it is to be noticed that at this time the

Annotations

boundary line between Pennsylvania and Virginia had not been established. On May 7, 1760, Fauquier wrote to Hamilton, requesting him to postpone granting any lands in questionable territory until instructions should be received from the home government (letter, printed in *Journal of the House of Burgesses* 1758–61, p. 283). The Board of Trade agreed with the governor that existing treaties with the Indians denied the right of any whites to land beyond the Alleghenies and instructed the governor to refuse any entry for land until he received official instructions to do so. —Fauquier to the Lords of Trade, September 1, 1760, printed in *ibid.*, 287-89.

517. Adam Stephen may have gone to Williamsburg on the same mission as did George Mercer—to lobby for lands on the Ohio.

518. John Mercer to Francis Fauquier. The body of the letter, one and one-half folio pages, is in Richard Rogers' handwriting with complimentary close, signature, and endorsement in Mercer's own hand. His statement in the letter, "Mr. Gist . . . died this last summer," is evidence that Mr. Mercer wrote the letter in the fall of 1759 (see *note* 513). Mention in the endorsement of Bouquet's proclamation of October 30, 1761, is basis for the assumption that Mercer endorsed it when he revised the Case prior to sending it to Palmer, July 27, 1762.

519. This conversation must have taken place before September, 1759, for at that time Colonel Stephen was at Fort Ligonier en route to Fort Pitt. From October until the spring of 1761 he was in the Western Country. —George Mercer to George Washington, February 17, 1760, *op. cit.*, and Adam Stephen to Francis Fauquier, October 29, 1759, printed in Virginia, *Journal of the House of Burgesses, 1758–1761*, pp. 280-81.

520. Refers to the supplementary act, April 17, 1759, for the regulation of Indian trade, an act which augmented the one of April 8, 1758. Printed in *The Statutes at Large of Pennsylvania from 1682–1801*, compiled . . . by James T. Mitchell and Henry Flanders (Harrisburg, Pa., W. S. Ray, 1898), V, 396-400; also on pp. 153-165, this work. For discussion see *facs.*, p. 22 and *Commentary*, pp. 447-448.

521. Evidently, Governor Fauquier acted upon the advice of John Mercer and wrote to Colonel Adam Stephen for details of Pennsylvania's activity in the fur trade. Stephen, in his reply from the "Camp at Pittsburgh Octr 29, 1759," reaffirmed the statement made to Mercer.

Wrote Stephen: "The *Pensylvanians* engross it at present and are pushing all possible measures to keep it in their hands. About twenty Tuns of Skin and Furr have been bought at this place within these three months; the *Pensylvanians* say the Post is within their limits, and accordingly have made an Act of Assembly for enhancing the Trade. This does not affect *Virginia* whilst the General Commands, but were one of the *Pensylvania* Officers to Command, they would be obliged to act according to their orders from that Province. The determination is of importance to us who first engaged in *Virginia* service; as we are intituled to a considerable quantity of Land by virtue of Govr *Dinwiddie's* proclamation approved of by His Maj'ty, and I would be glad to know the sense of your honor and Council on that Head." —Stephen to Fauquier, *op. cit.*

522. Proclamation, dated October 30, printed in *Case . . . , facs.,* p. 29. Bouquet enclosed the proclamation in a letter to James Livingston, commandant at Fort Cumberland, requesting him to publish and "post up" at Fort Cumberland and to "Inform the Country People thereof, that they Do not expose themselves to certain punishment for their Trespasses & disobedience of orders." —Bouquet to Livingston, October 31, 1761. B. M. Add. MSS 21653, f. 91, printed in Bouquet *Papers,* 21653, p. 87.

Governor Fauquier, not satisfied with Bouquet's explanation of the proclamation, complained to Sir Jeffery Amherst, commander in chief in North America, who inquired of Bouquet as to the validity of Fauquier's allegations of his discrimination against the Virginians. Had John Mercer been aware of one reason for Bouquet's proclamation, it may be surmised that he would have been even more vitriolic in this denunciation. An excerpt from Bouquet's answer, dated April 1, 1762, is as follows: "I had yet another reason to make my Intentions publickly known at that time, and which I thought best not to communicate to Mr Fauquier. I had been repeatedly informed, that one Coll. Cresap, who is concerned in one of the Ohio Companies (the favorite Scheme of Virginia) was proposing by way of Subscription to Several familys to remove from the frontiers of that Colony &. Mariland, to form settlements on the Ohio: I foresaw that those poor People would be ruined by that bubble, and I was the more induced to credit that Report, from an offer made me by that same Gentleman of a share of 25,000 Acres of those Lands, which did not tempt me. —*Ibid.,* 21634, f. 112, printed in Bouquet *Papers,* 21634, pp. 81-83.

The Ohio Company had tried unsuccessfully to interest Bouquet. Thomas Cresap offered him a share in the Company; Bouquet evaded

Annotations

acceptance of the offer. Likewise George Mercer offered to sell him a share in the Company. Mercer, apparently confident that Bouquet would join them, had the necessary papers drawn up before he went to Philadelphia. —Thomas Cresap to Henry Bouquet, July 24, 1760; Henry Bouquet to Thomas Cresap, September 12, 1760; George Mercer to Henry Bouquet, December 27, 1760, in B. M. Add. MSS, 21645, f. 163; 21653, ff. 24-25; 21645, f. 340, respectively. Printed in Bouquet *Papers* 21645, pp. 122-23; 21653, pp. 23-24; 21645, pp. 252-54, respectively.

523. Half King's speech to the French general as he repeated it to Washington is printed in *Case, facs.,* p. 23.

524. Material enclosed in brackets ([   ]) supplied from *Case, facs.,* p. 24.

525. For continuance of this document as compiled by George Mercer, see *Case, facs.,* pp. 24-36.

526. In Richard Rogers' handwriting, 28 numbered folio pages, pages 19 and 20 missing. The missing material includes the latter part of Gist's second journal and the first minutes of Virginia's Logstown Conference of 1752. The marginalia were added by George Mercer. Since the marginalia are in George Mercer's handwriting and the printed *Case* was compiled by him, it is evident that this document was the basis of the printed *Case*. Likewise, the few corrections, omissions, and additions to the marginal notes, as they appear in the printed *Case,* show that the manuscript was not the printer's copy. For a full discussion of provenance, etc., see *Commentary,* pages 393-398.

527. Appendix number one, consisting of the journals of Gist's two explorations for the Ohio Company, was probably copied from his report to the Committee of the Company. (Gist's signature is copied at the end of the first journal; the latter part of the second journal is missing in the manuscript.) For complete text of both journals see *Chronology*.

528. This account does not appear elsewhere in the George Mercer manuscript collection. The "page 7" refers to the manuscript page of this particular document.

· 615 ·

Annotations

529. For variants and complete text printed in this work see *Chronology*.

530. The remainder of the journal, from Saturday, February 22, 1752, to March 29, 1753, on pages 19 and 20 of this manuscript is missing. For complete text see *Chronology*.

531. The first minutes of the Logstown Conference, page 20 of this document, are missing. For complete text and variants as printed in this work see *Chronology*, June 13, 1752; for discussion see *notes* 77, 105, 294, and *Commentary*, pp. 398-403.

532. "insert the deed" is in John Mercer's handwriting, and, according to this instruction, the deed was inserted in the printed copy. See *facs.*, pp. 21-22.

533. Although Gist's entry in his journal for February 22, 1751, does not mention this Indian conference, he witnessed the signing of the pact. Also, John Mercer stated that Gist, who was present, "took a copy of it." In 1748 Conrad Weiser, a Pennsylvanian, kindled a separate Council Fire for the Ohio Indians, at Logstown; yet the Colony's Indian policy was one of strict respect for Iroquois authority over tribes said to have been subjugated by them. The Iroquois claimed control over all the western Indians east of Illinois. Therefore, they feared that entrance into a pact with these separate western nations might offend the Six Nations. Croghan was reprimanded severely by Governor Hamilton, who in turn had been interrogated by the General Assembly when he presented the treaty to that body. —Pennsylvania. General Assembly, *Votes and Proceedings*, IV, 186. See also *note* 319.

534. Six and one-fourth folio pages in Richard Rogers' handwriting, with marginalia by John Mercer. This copy of the minutes of the Ohio Company and the committee of the Company omits all records of meetings held on September 25, 1749; January 29, September 11, and December 3, 1750; December 21-22, 1757; July 6, 1759; also the special instructions issued to Christopher Gist on April 28, 1752. For the minutes of those meetings see *Chronology*. Since the last record in this document is dated September 9, 1761, and the George Mercer collection contains no record of any meetings held between this last date and March, 1763, the editor considered this document, the enclosure mentioned in John Mercer's letter to Charlton Palmer, July 27, 1762.

Annotations

535. According to the several copies of Orders and Resolutions of the Company this letter to John Hanbury was written before the general meeting. Therefore, it must have been compiled by the committee in order to be approved at the general meeting the next day, June 21.

536. The petition of John Hanbury, January 11, 1749, is printed in the *Case, facs.,* pp. 2-3.

537. On June 1, 1749, Thomas Lee wrote to the members of the Ohio Company informing them that according to Mr. Hanbury "our Grant for 500,000 Acres is ready for the Kings sign & will be sent in his next." —Lee to members of the Ohio Company, No. 6214, MS in the Emmett Collection, New York Public Library.

538. Quitrent computed on acreage owned was the king's own private revenue (Virginia, *Journal of the House of Burgesses 1752–1758,* xiii). If quitrents were used for the purchase of treaty goods, the king himself would have been financing the crown's colony. In a similar situation Thomas Penn remarked that the use of quitrents for expenditures in Indian affairs in Pennsylvania could be likened to a governor personally contributing to the provincial coffers. Pennsylvania. General Assembly, *Votes and Proceedings,* IV, 191.

In Virginia only the commissary and attorney general's expenses were deducted from the quitrents. Usually the funds used for the purchase of treaty goods were taken out of export revenue. For the semiannual accounts in Virginia see Virginia Council *Journals,* index, "quit rents, account of; receiver general, warrants on."

539. Since English precedent bound the Penns to purchase the land within their grant from the original native inhabitants (see *Commentary,* pp. 399-400), quitrents, the proprietor's personal income, were used for the purchase of treaty goods. Although the province was supposed to pay all other expenses, the Penns frequently provided additional presents at treaties of amity when no sale of land was considered. After a study of expenditures in the year 1749 the General Assembly resolved to ask the governor to solicit the proprietor's agent for presents to the Indians, even when the sale of land was not involved. Also they wished the Penns to contribute toward the expenses incurred by the visiting Indians. In August, 1751, Thomas Penn gave his opinion on the matter. Penn informed the governor, "that they do not conceive themselves under any Obligation to contribute to

Annotations

Indians or any other Public Expenses . . . and that they purchase the Land from the Indians, and pay them for it, and that they are under no greater Obligation to contribute to the public Charges than any other Chief Governor of any other Colonies" (Pennsylvania. General Assembly, *Votes and Proceedings*, IV, 111, 154, 155-56, 191). Nevertheless, the General Assembly continued to ask the Penns to help defray the expenses of Indian affairs, and the proprietors continued to contribute to the colony's treasury.

540. A colloquialism meaning, for the most part, in Virginia's barter system, tobacco.

541. Lawrence Washington was commissioned by the Company to engage the services of a "good gun smith, a good white smith and a tailor." See p. 169.

542. The Company's stock was divided into 20 equal shares. Since there were only 16 members at this time, the £2,000, capital subscribed, divided equally among the investors amounted to this sum.

543. In the "Résumé of the proceedings of the Company" this order is dated September 29, 1749. See *Chronology*.

544. The order is *unique to this document* in the George Mercer collection.

545. For a variant, see *Chronology*, January 29, 1750. See also *note* 548.

546. Mr. Hanbury, not Sir William Gooch, committed the Company, in lieu of quitrents, to erect a fort and maintain a garrison for the protection of the families which they expected to seat on the land. This arrangement was to continue for ten years from the date of their patent (see *Chronology*, January 11, 1749, Hanbury Petition). Sir William Gooch, in his letter of June 16, 1748, to the Board of Trade "very properly expressed it, they proposed to build a Fort without which or some such work of defence, it would be dangerous for them to venture out so far." —Letter in P.R.O., C.O. 5: 1327/7-8, 10.

547. George Mason purchased from Thomas Bladen a 500-acre tract of land called Walnut Bottom, a corner of which was on a cliff of rocks at the lower end of a bottom about half a mile below the mouth of

Annotations

Wills Creek on the Maryland side. Bladen assigned the land to Mason on September 11, 1753, but the patent was not recorded until March 25, 1756. The purchase price was £20. The plat and certificate are recorded in the Commissioners Land Office, Annapolis, Maryland, books B. C. and G. S., no. 5, folio 170; the patent in *ibid.*, G. S., no. 2, folio 400.

On October 25, 1783, George Mason sold Walnut Bottom and Lime Stone Rock to Thomas Beall, who laid out Washington Town (Cumberland, Maryland) in 1785. —William H. Lowdermilk, *History of Cumberland* (Washington, D. C., James Anglim, 1878) pp. 259-61.

548. According to this statement, the Company's store on the Virginia side of the Potomac and on land known as the New Store Tract was completed before May, 1751. On January 29, 1750, the Committee of the Ohio Company approved Hugh Parker's and Thomas Cresap's purchase of land and improvement from Lord Fairfax. The committee also ordered Hugh Parker to build a store for the reception of goods. Lots one, five, fourteen, fifteen, and sixteen, a total of 1,435 acres, in Hampshire County, were granted to George Mason on October 25, 1754. See also *note 37*.

In July, 1750, John Hamer, employed by Hugh Parker, worked in the storehouse, "making a door and cut a joist and sundre other things." Also, Hamer hauled goods to the store, unloaded the boat, and helped four days with the boat (John Hamer in account with the Ohio Company by Hugh Parker, July, 1750. MS in the Darlington Memorial Library, University of Pittsburgh). On March 19, 1750, the Committee of the Company, after considering the problem of housing their trade goods, empowered Hugh Parker "to build a Store house on Colo Cresap's plantation and that buildings be made at the mouth of Wills Creek as soon as conveniently will admit" (see *Chronology*, March 19, 1750). Unfortunately, nothing in the John Hamer account indicates the location of the storehouse built at this time. The account could refer to a storehouse built at either of the two locations.

549. According to an item in the "Articles of Agreement," May 23, 1751, George Mason, treasurer of the Company, was empowered among other things to purchase land in his own name "for the use of the Ohio Company" (see *notes* 1 and 49). Lawrence Washington, who had been head of the Company after Thomas Lee's death in 1749, died before the formal articles of agreement were ratified by the Company on May 23, 1751.

Annotations

550. Although the "Journal of the Meetings of the President and Masters of William and Mary College," as printed in the *William and Mary College Quarterly*, volume three, first series, pages 60-64, 128-32, 195-97, and 262-65, does not record such a commission awarded to Gist, it is evident that in 1753 he did obtain from them a special one to survey Ohio Company lands. —Memorial of the Ohio Company, November 20, 1778, *op. cit.* See also *Chronology*, Instructions given Christopher Gist by the Committee of the Ohio Company, July 27, 1753.

551. Holston River (Tennessee).

552. Tennessee River.

553. The Tennessee and Holston Rivers were far below the Ohio Company's grant.

554. In 1753 James Patton wrote to John Blair complaining that these caveats were unfair. Mr. Patton informed the councilor, "as to the Ohio Company who I understand Intends to survey their Lands to the Norward of the Waters of Woods River, if so it cannot interfere with mine." —Letter, *op. cit.*

The foregoing order is *unique to this document*.

555. The Virginia Council *Journals* do not record any caveats entered by the Company.

556. William Trent. See *Case, facs.*, p. 8; also *note 362*.

557. Order dated September 19, 1752. See *Chronology*.

558. The first cargo was received before May 27, 1750, at which time George Mason asked John Hanbury to postpone shipment of the second cargo until the fall of 1750 (George Mason to Lawrence Washington, May 27, 1750, *op. cit.*). Another shipment of goods arrived in November, 1751 (Dinwiddie to Cresap, January 23, 1752, printed in Dinwiddie *Papers*, I, 17-19). If a second cargo were received in the fall of 1750, the one mentioned by Governor Dinwiddie would be the third, and the invoice mentioned here would be for a fourth consignment of trade goods.

559. In 1760 both Samuel Smith and Arthur Dobbs still held their

Annotations

shares in the Company. However, the Hanburys had by this time informed the committee that "Mr. Smith will not hold his share, and it is ordered to be disposed of" (*Case . . . facs.,* pp. 24-25). Arthur Dobbs' heirs held his interest in the Company as late as 1771. George Mercer endeavored to obtain Arthur Dobbs' share in 1771. To be eligible for a division of the land as outlined in their "Articles of Agreement," May 23, 1751, Mercer wished to have Conrad Richard Dobbs predate the bill of sale (The "Articles of Agreement" were effective for a space of 20 years). —Conway Richard Dobbs to George Mercer, March 26, 1770, see *Chronology;* Mercer to Dobbs, May 28, 1771, photostat in Arthur Dobbs Papers. State Department of Archives and History, Raleigh, North Carolina.

Evidently, he was successful in this endeavor, for in January, 1772, James Mercer stated that his brother George owned one and one-half shares in the Company.

560. Resolution, *unique to this document.*

561. Thomas Cresap and Christopher Gist were ordered to lay out the town and fort on Chartiers Creek. See *Chronology,* Resolution, July 25–27, 1753.

562. At a meeting of the Committee of the Company, July 25–27, 1753, John Mercer presented this Case and accompanying letter to John Hanbury for approval. The original document ordered to be transmitted to England was not located by the editor, but an item in this George Mercer collection is identified as a copy of it. "Case," printed on pp. 233-251, this work. For provenance see *Commentary,* pp. 393-95.

563. The chiefs of the Cherokees conferred with the governor on November 11, 1752. The "emperor," upon being asked what "Present would be acceptable, . . . reply's, that he . . . only requested some Clothes proper for people in their Station, and Ammunition." —Record of this meeting, which includes the emperor's address to the governor, and Dinwiddie's reply, is printed in Virginia Council *Journals,* V, 413-16.

564. By the Naturalization Act of October, 1705, the governor was empowered "to declare any alien or aliens, foreigner or foreigners, being already settled, or inhabitants in this colony, or which shall hereafter come to settle, plant, or reside therein, upon his, her or

Annotations

their taking, before him, the oaths appointed by act of parliament to be taken." This act of parliament provided an oath of allegiance for the succession of the Crown in the Protestant line and for extinguishing the hopes of all pretenders to the throne. —Hening's *Statutes*, III, 434-35.

565. The Great Falls of the Potomac, above present Washington, D. C.

566. Just below the Great Falls of the Potomac. There is among the Washington "Papers" in Library of Congress a Christopher Gist holograph, an inventory of Ohio Company goods in the Rock Creek Store House in 1756; also printed in Hamilton's *Letters to Washington*, I, 362-64.

567. Conococheague empties into the Potomac at present Williamsport, Maryland.

568. The Company planned to have a storehouse on the Monongahela River at the mouth of Red Stone Creek.

569. Refers to the Treaty of Logstown. See *Chronology*, June 13, 1752, Logstown Conference.

570. This was the town mentioned in the committee's resolution of July 25–27, 1753 (see *Chronology*). The resolution gives a full description of the projected development.

571. Gist was given general instructions, also secret ones, to govern his conduct at the conference at Logstown in June, 1752. For complete information see *Chronology*, Complete Instructions to Christopher Gist and Secret Instructions to Gist, April 28, 1752.

572. This meeting was held July 25–27 at Philip Lee's home. —John Mercer's ledger. MS in the Virginia Historical Society.

573. Originally the Company intended to erect a fortified storehouse, to begin trade, and to establish a settlement on the Ohio, on the site of present McKees Rocks, Pennsylvania. The settlement never progressed beyond the blueprint stage. When George Washington returned from his mission to the French in January, 1754, he recommended to Governor Dinwiddie that a fort should be built

Annotations

at the junction of the Allegheny and the Monongahela Rivers (Washington's *Journal* . . . 1753, *op. cit.*). Although financed with Ohio Company money, the fort at the junction of the Monongahela and Allegheny Rivers (now Pittsburgh, Pennsylvania), was a government enterprise. The Ohio Company was reimbursed for money advanced and materials supplied. —John Mercer to [James Tilghman?], March 1, 1767, and George Mason's statement on William Trent's account. Copy in the John Cadwalader Papers, Historical Society of Pennsylvania.

574. According to Thomas Cresap the fort built by William Trent for Virginia was "Fort St. George So called in the Company's Books" (Thomas Cresap to [James Tilghman, May 20, 1767], MS in the Society Collection, Historical Society of Pennsylvania). Also, Governor Dinwiddie stated that he had "raised a Co. of Men and some Artificers, and sent them to the Ohio to build a Fort in His M'y's Name, and to call it Fort Prince Geo." —Dinwiddie to Horace Walpole, September 23, 1754, printed in Dinwiddie *Papers*, I, 343-45.

575. One of the instructions given to the Virginia Commissioners at the conference at Logstown in 1752 was to offer to educate some of the Indian children at Brafferton, the charity Indian school of William and Mary College. When the Indians did not wish to send their children so far away, the Commissioners desired "to know whether it wou'd be agreeable to you that Teachers shou'd be sent among you." Instructions printed in *Virginia Magazine* XIII, 151-52. See also *Chronology*, June 13, 1752.

576. Here in this resolution begins information *unique to this document*.

577. This section of the document is badly mutilated. One line worn away completely. End of information *unique to this document*.

578. At least four of these 20 swivel guns were received by the Company. Major James Livingston reported, in February, 1762, that "The Brass Gun I mentioned in my late Return, I found at a Fort called Pearsals Fort, on the South Branch, with a Quantity of Grape Shot, and 4 Swivels, which they told me belong'd to the Ohio Company." —James Livingston to Bouquet, February 14, 1762, in B. M. Add. MSS 21648, f. 30; printed in Bouquet *Papers*, 21648, pt. I, 25.

Annotations

579. William Trent left Winchester for Logstown the latter part of June, 1753, on a mission to deliver a special gift of arms and ammunition to the Ohio Indians. At the conference held at Croghan and Trent's trading house at the mouth of Pine Creek on May 16, 1753, the Half King had requested a "supply of arms and ammunitions" (*Colonial Records of Pennsylvania,* V, 615). Virginia answered the Half King's plea by sending a gift of arms and ammunition to the Ohio. Trent arrived on the Ohio on July 10 with the gift. In November, 1752, Governor Dinwiddie sent Thomas Burney to the Twightwee with a message assuring them of English aid against the French and also promising them that Virginia would provide a handsome present to be delivered them at Winchester the next spring (1753). Thomas Burney, accused by Governor Dinwiddie of negligence, on his return trip was at Logstown, June 22, 1753. On that day the Half King sent a message by Burney to Governor Dinwiddie informing him that the French being only two or three days away from the Ohio made it impossible for the chiefs to desert their people long enough to travel to Virginia to partake of the King's bounty. In answer, Dinwiddie dispatched a "speech to the Half King and other special Chiefs on the Ohio" (printed in *Case, facs.,* pp. 11-12). This speech, dated July 10, was entrusted to Christopher Gist for delivery. In the address the governor was careful to note that the Indians should appreciate the mark of respect paid them by having Annosanoah (Christopher Gist's Wyandot name) serve as messenger to deliver his speech to them.

The speech was not delivered by Gist, but by Thomas Burney who informed Trent that pressing business delayed Gist in Virginia (Trent's Account of the Conference at Logstown, July 11–September 14, 1753). Apparently the urgent business was this commission from the Ohio Company.

580. Evidence that Christopher Gist was with Cresap when they surveyed along the Youghiogheny in 1753. Interpolated on the plat is a long note by George Mercer to whom his father attributed the map. —John Mercer to George Mercer, March 3, 1768, see *Chronology;* also *note* 365. Map reproduced opposite page 226.

581. There is no mention in the George Mercer manuscripts that Gist returned any account of his activities in the Ohio Country during the summer of 1753; nor did the editor locate such a journal elsewhere.

Annotations

582. The assessment, £20 for each share or £400 Virginia money, was the total outlay of the Company for building the fort. See also *note* 573.

583. There is no record in the Virginia Council *Journals* that these caveats were entered against Richard Corbin. For a full discussion of the matter by John Mercer, see *Chronology,* John Mercer to George Mercer, March 3, 1768.

584. This annual meeting was held at Mr. Selden's. —John Mercer's ledger, *op. cit.*

585. John Mercer, in his letter to Charlton Palmer July 27, 1762, mentioned this resolution and expressed the doubt whether or not Lee had adhered to the Company's request (see *Chronology*). The letter in question was not located by the editor.

586. Meaning Charlton Palmer.

587. According to John Hanbury's petition of January 11, 1749, the Company was allowed seven years' time in which to seat one hundred families upon their land. From Mercer's statement it is evident that they wished to have this favor extended when a new instruction was sent to the governor. So far as revisions of quitrents and the right to patent were concerned, failure to settle the land, in accordance with the Hanbury petition, was immaterial. Enrollment on quitrent roles was not made until the land was patented, and so freedom from quitrents would date from the date of the patent and not the date of the instructions to the governor.

588. On November 6, 1752, the Company first petitioned for permission to survey the land in small tracts (see *Chronology,* Petition to Dinwiddie, November 6, 1752). This same request was repeated in the "Boundaries proposed" in 1768. See *Chronology.*

589. At a meeting of the Committee of the Company, December 3, 1750, it was ordered that George Mason "apply to the Executors of the honble Thomas Lee Esqr decd for all papers relating to the Companys Affairs which are in their hands." On January 13, 1772, George Mason, in writing to James Mercer (John Mercer's son) regarding a proposed meeting of the Company, asked him "to bring ... the Ohio

Annotations

Company's Order Book; which was left many years ago in the Hands of your Father & has never been in my possession since."

See *Chronology.*

590. This is the only attested copy of any Ohio Company document in the George Mercer collection.

591. Richard Rogers, John Mercer's clerk.

592. Six pages, 9 × 15 inches, in Richard Rogers' handwriting. Pennsylvania's "Act for preventing Abuses in the Indian Trade" was enacted on April 8, 1758; the "Supplement," on April 17, 1759. —*Votes and Proceedings*, IV, 816 and V, 47. —For John Mercer's discussion of the laws, see *Case . . . , facs.*, pp. 22-23.

593. A George Mercer holograph, 7¼ × 9 inches. On March 2, 1763, the Committee of the Company resolved to have about 50 acres of their land at Wills Creek (Cumberland, Maryland) "laid off into Town Lotts with about two hundred and fifty Acres of the adjacent high Land for out Lotts." George Mercer was commissioned to make the survey and was given the power of attorney to execute the deeds when the lots were sold (*Chronology*, Resolution, March 2, 1763). That the project was begun before the committee made this resolution is evidenced by an Ohio Company advertisement in the *Maryland Gazette*, February 17, 1763. The advertisement appearing in each weekly issue of the newspaper from February 17 to April 7 announced an auction of lots "for a Town at Fort Cumberland" to be "sold to the Highest BIDDERS on Friday the 15th of April next." By the same announcement the Company offered to "LET to the highest Bidder, for a Term of Years, Two very good Store-Houses, opposite to Fort Cumberland, in Virginia." After giving a full and flowery description of the desirable location of the building sites at Fort Cumberland and the desirability of the Company's Virginia storehouses, the advertisement is concluded as follows: "and the Company are building a Saw and Grist Mill, within a Mile of the Spot proposed for the Town." A military order from General Jeffery Amherst, given to George Mercer personally, prohibited the sale of the lots on April 15. Soon afterward the Company renewed their efforts, for on June 16 another advertisement appeared in the *Maryland Gazette*. This time the public was informed that "THE OHIO Company have ordered 300 Half-Acre LOTS to be laid off for a TOWN, to be called Charlottsburg." The lots were to be sold "on

Annotations

the Premises, to the highest Bidders, on Monday the 20th of this Instant June." Apparently the Company was prevented from pursuing this enterprise and as a result the members decided to send George Mercer to England in an endeavor to find a way to circumvent the stringent military orders issued by General Amherst. —*Case...*, facs., pp. 29-30.

Mrs. Rowland, writing in the *William and Mary College Quarterly* (1st series, I, 198-200), states that a detailed plan of this survey was made. There is no mention of such a plan in the George Mercer papers.

The name, Charlottesburg, may have been given the development to honor Princess Charlotte Sophia, consort of King George III.

594. When Governor Dinwiddie learned of the defeat of Washington at Fort Necessity he ordered Colonel James Innes, in command of the South Carolina troops at Wills Creek, to call a council of his field officers and select a proper place for "building a Log Fort, and erecting a Magazine to receive 6 mo's Provisions for 12 or 14 [sic?] men." About 10 days later he wrote to Governor Hamilton informing him that "the Gov'r of M'yl'd proposes building a large Magazine for Provisions Near Wills's Creek." The same day he informed Governor Sharpe that he would order Colonel Innes to march all his forces "over the Allegany Mount's and if he cannot disposses the Enemy of the Fort, he is to build a Fort at red Stone Creek, the Crossing Place, or any other Place most convenient." Also he wrote that he would be pleased to have Sharpe build a "Magazine for Provis's anywhere near Wills's Creek, large enough to receive Provis's for 1500 Men for one Year." On August 30, Dinwiddie ordered Colonel Innes to "Take Possess'n of the Ohio Compa's Warehouse at Will's Creek for Y'r Proviss's; get your great Guns all up there, mount them for defence." Two weeks later, September 18, the governor evidently yielding to his pique against William Trent, the Ohio Company's factor at Wills Creek, ordered Innes to build a magazine. The building, completed before December 10, was inspected by Sharpe, who disapproved of it.

Of the installations Sharpe wrote to Dinwiddie that the "stoccado fort" was too small, only about 120 feet on the exterior side; also, that its location was undesirable. In addition he informed Dinwiddie that he had ordered the Maryland militia who was there to build "another much larger raised on an adjacent & more elevated piece of Ground." Innes then received word from the Virginia governor approving his suggestion to reserve a "considerable Qu'ty of Land round the Fort You have built, kept for the Public, and I wish I

Annotations

c'd get some Hands to manure Part, and plant Corn." On February 12, 1755, Dinwiddie enclosed "the Draft of the Fort and Barracks, W'ch is named Cumberl'd Fort" in a letter to Sir Thomas Robinson. From the plan (CXXII, no. 38, King's MSS, British Museum) one learns that the fort was "made of Puncheons of Wood cut 12 Foot, and set three Feet in the ground." The artillery consisted of "10 Pieces of Cannon mounted in the fort Bastions, 4 Pounder and 4 Small Swivels." The fort was 120 feet square; the parade, 96 feet long and extending toward the precipice were "officers houses." —"A Plan of Fort Cumberland on Will's Creek & Potomack River with a View of the Store Houses, belonging to the Ohio Company on the other side of the River," reproduced in Archer B. Hulbert, *The Crown Collection of Photographs of American Maps* . . . (Cleveland, O., Arthur H. Clark Co., 1904–08) II, no. 19.

When Sir John St. Clair, "quarter master general of all the Forces of the Expedition for the Ohio," inspected the installations at Wills Creek he declared that the fort was "improperly located." It "should have been 30 miles nearer the mountains," remarked St. Clair. Therefore, in preparation for the arrival of Braddock's army, he ordered "proper Lodgments" to be built; also a hospital for the regiments from Ireland. A second sketch of the fort, "a Plan of the Fort and Barracks at Mount Pleasant in Maryland" shows additional officers' barracks and a hospital. —King's MSS, British Museum, CXXII, no. 39; reproduced in *ibid.*, II, no. 20.

Prior to Braddock's campaign, Fort Cumberland was the rendezvous for the Independent Companies; for Braddock it was a base for operations. After Braddock's defeat both the morale of the militia stationed there and the installations deteriorated rapidly. Chief among the causes of this deterioration was the question of the responsibility for the fort. On June 4, 1754, Governor Dinwiddie, who considered it an English fort on provincial soil, appointed Colonel James Innes, commander-in-chief of "all the Forces already rais'd and destin'd, or that shall hereafter be rais'd, design'd and ordered on the service of the s'd Expedit'n." This commission was given by orders from the King, commanding the governor "to raise Forces, build Fortresses on the river Ohio, and to protect his [the King's] Lands on the s'd River." Later Dinwiddie and Maryland's Governor Sharpe, appointed commander-in-chief of the combined forces on the expedition (October 24, 1754), agreed to appoint Innes, camp-mastergeneral. This was in addition to his commission as commander-in-chief. It was James Innes, duly appointed general of Fort Cumberland, whom Braddock left in charge when he marched toward Fort

Annotations

Duquesne. Colonel Adam Stephen, who was given temporary command at the fort, had relinquished it to Captain John Dagworthy, favorite of Governor Sharpe and a British "regular" reduced to half pay. Dagworthy asserted that his imperial commission gave him precedent over all colonial officers; over this, he and George Washington clashed sharply. The quarrel was carried to Commander-in-chief William Shirley's headquarters in Boston. There George Washington personally pleaded his case. Shirley ordered that British officers outranked colonial officers only when "regulars" were present in the ranks (Washington Irving, *Life of Washington* [N. Y., G. P. Putnam & Co., 1856–59] I, 228). As a result of this quarrel and of Virginia's and Maryland's wrangling about responsibility for paying and provisioning the troops stationed there, in 1756 the fort was all but abandoned.

Upon his arrival in America to assume command of all the British forces, Colonel John Stanwix took Fort Cumberland under his command and reactivated it to serve as a base of supplies for Forbes' army.

George Mercer, newly appointed assistant deputy quarter-master-general under Stanwix, reported in 1759 that the fort was in a dilapidated state and that he had ordered necessary repairs to be made.

In 1762 the feud between Maryland and Virginia flared up anew. Each colony refused to pay the troops stationed there. Finally, Governor Fauquier ordered Colonel Adam Stephen to disband his Virginia regiment; Fort-major James Livingston, serving under Colonel Bouquet, was ordered to keep the Virginia militia there and was assured by him that he, Bouquet, would pay the men, if necessary. However, Colonel Stephen disregarded the Fort-major's order and evacuated his troops; whereupon Captain Écuyer sent a few men from Fort Pitt to Cumberland to take care of the King's stores. About this time the Ohio Company prepared to repossess the land upon which the fort was built. George Mercer stated that the fort had been abandoned, only a few soldiers remaining to guard the King's stores.

Undoubtedly, it was rumors of a new Indian uprising in 1763 that caused Commander-in-chief Jeffery Amherst to deny the Company the right to repossess their land and exploit it as they had planned. By August the uprising seemed imminent, and Amherst ordered Cumberland to be garrisoned. Virginia responded by sending 400 militiamen under the command of Colonel Adam Stephen. After Bouquet's success in the West (1763 and 1764) Fort Cumberland's usefulness came to an end.

In 1765 General Gage ordered the fort abandoned (Thomas Gage to Halifax, June 8, 1765, printed in Gage, *Correspondence,* I, 58-61).

Annotations

It is written that the fort was reoccupied again for a few days during the Whiskey Insurrection (1794), at which time Washington, in uniform for the last time, reviewed the troops gathered there.

The site of the fort is within the city limits of present Cumberland, Maryland.

Excepting the special sources cited within this annotation, the facts were gleaned from the following: Dinwiddie, *Papers;* Bouquet, *Papers; Archives of Maryland;* Lowdermilk, *History of Cumberland;* and Hamilton, *Letters to Washington.*

595. A John Mercer holograph, 18½ letter size pages, endorsed by George Mercer.

George Mercer was appointed London agent for the Company on July 4, 1763, and sailed for England a few days later. The last entry in the document is that of George Mercer's appointment. Therefore, it may be assumed that this copy of the proceedings of the Company was made for his use in England.

596. October 20, 1747, was the date of this group's petition, a petition upon which action by the governor and council was postponed (see *note* 2). Later it was resolved by the Company that a committee should be appointed to transact business during the interim between annual stockholders' meetings. Record of this meeting one year later is evidence that the Company held meetings and functioned along similar lines prior to the adoption of this resolution. For minutes of the Company prior to October 20, 1748, see *Chronology.*

597. It is logical to assume that this was the clerk of the Council's fee for preparing the petition of October 20, 1747.

598. No articles of agreement of this early date were located by the editor.

599. The letter is not in the minutes of the Company in the George Mercer Collection, nor was such a letter located elsewhere.

600. Evidently the appointment, if made, was a temporary one. Although not fully satisfied with the security offered by Hugh Parker, George Mason, in May, 1750, did recommend his appointment as factor for one year (Mason to Lawrence Washington, May 27, 1750, *op. cit.*). The order is *unique to this document.*

Annotations

601. A Virginia trader's license or registration assured the College of William and Mary of her legal revenue. See *note 33*.

602. Lawrence Washington went to England in the summer of 1749. George Washington to Mrs. Lawrence Washington, 1749–50, printed in Washington's *Writings* (Fitzpatrick edition), I, 18.

The Company informed John Hanbury that he should confer with Captain Washington who "carrys Samples and will endeavour to procure some Tradesmen we shall want, and he will be able to explain to you as he has convers'd with those that are of our Company and understand the Indian trade well." Ohio Company to John Hanbury, June 20, 1749. See *Chronology*.

603. No record of this application appears in the Virginia Council *Journals*, nor was such an application located elsewhere.

604. The Indian trade, like the Company's land venture, was short-lived. Although Hugh Parker was appointed factor for the Company in 1750 (see *note* 600), opening of trade on the Ohio did not get under way until November, 1752. William Trent, who was appointed at that time, took the first trade goods to the Indian Country in January, 1754. George Croghan, who was on the frontier at the time, wrote to Pennsylvania's governor informing him that Pennsylvania's present to the Shawnee at Lower Shawnee Town should be enlarged and that the extra "goods" could be purchased on the frontier. Wrote Croghan: "itt is Mr Montour's and my opinion that there should be one hundred pounds Worth More goods aded to what is in my hands, and sent to them, if ye honour Aproves of this, as there is no posebility of sending those things att this Time of ye year from Philadelphia: ye Ohio Company has a quantity of goods hear which they wo'ld sell at first Cost, if ye honour will Send a person to purchase them with Cash, which will save ye Expence of Carridge to ye Government." (Croghan to Hamilton, February 3, 1754, *op. cit.*) The date of this letter is doubtful. The date line as printed is "Febry 3d, 1753, Suppos'd to be 1754," and the endorsement Ffebry 30, 1754. However, the text of the letter shows that it was written in 1754, probably February 3.

In 1760 George Mercer, writing to Henry Bouquet, inferred that the Company's trading venture never really began. Of the Company's prospects, Mercer stated that "they have some pretty considerable outstanding Debts from the Trade they intended to prosecute." –Letter, dated December 27, 1760, *op. cit.*

A résumé of the Company's trading activities with the Indians is

Annotations

found in George Mercer's "very full State of the Company's affairs," presented before the Privy Council on October 8, 1767: "the destruction of the Fort they had begun at Pittsburgh, and another Fort or Blockhouse which they had actually completed at the Mouth of Red Stone Creek on the River Monongahela, together with some Store Houses they had built on the Comunication to Red Stone Creek, at a Place called in the Maps *Gists* on the West Side of the Mountains, and by plundering their Effects, which ruined most of the Traders they had employed, and the rest being chiefly killed, or the Indians whom they had traded with, being mostly engaged against them the Company lost all the Money they had advanced for the Trade."
—George Mercer to the Committee of the Ohio Company, October 10, 1767, MS in Library of Congress; "Proceedings of the Ohio Company," *op. cit.*

605. The factor or factors for the Company overextended this authority, for the Company, by legal action, endeavored to collect many bad debts, contracted especially in the latter half of 1750 and in 1751. Many dossiers of these suits are filed in the Frederick County (Virginia) "Court Records."

606. The following agreement is *unique to this document*. Gist did begin this project. His son-in-law, William Cromwell, some other families, and Gist himself began settlements on the broad meadows between the Youghiogheny and Monongahela in present Fayette County. Improvements on this land were destroyed by the French in 1754. Virginia (Colony) *Journals* of the House of Burgesses 1752–58, p. 223). Christopher Gist's son, Thomas Gist, was among the many Virginians whose land patents were honored by Pennsylvania when the boundary line was settled.

607. Information is *unique to this document*.

608. Resolution is *unique to this document*.

609. Same.

610. This entry for land was in the form of a petition to Governor Dinwiddie, November 6, 1752. See *Chronology*. Order is *unique to this document*.

611. Lunsford Lomax was active in Ohio Company affairs as early as

Annotations

June, 1752, for it was he who kept the minutes of the Conference at Logstown for them. See page 274 and *note* 697.

612. These additional or "secret" instructions are *unique to this document*. For further explanation see *Commentary*, p. 418, this work.

613. Evidence that the Company was a partnership and not a corporation.

614. On December 5, 1752, Gawin Corbin assigned "all Right and title" to his shares of the Ohio Company's stock to Robert Carter. On June 2, 1753, Augustine Washington received "of R. Carter three hundred and sixty Pounds Current Money" for his "Part of the Ohio Company" (MSS in the Washington Collection, Chicago Historical Society). The bond mentioned was in accordance with an item in the "Articles of Agreement," May 23, 1751, which was as follows: "And every such new Partner shall at the time of his Admission as aforesaid, enter into bond of the penalty of one hundred thousand pounds Sterling conditioned that he his Heirs Executors Administrators & Assigns shall & will on his & their several Parts & behalf well & truly observe perform fulfill & keep all & every the Articles covenants Agreements Rules & Orders there in being & subsisting between the several Partners of the said Company of which shall at any time thereafter be made in pursuance of & according to the tenor & true meaning of these Presents."

615. On June 21, 1749, the Company ordered their treasurer to "pay the Ballance of the Cash in his Hands belonging to us, to the Joint Order of Colo Thomas Cresap and Mr Hugh Parker, to be laid out for our Use in making a Road &c to Monongahela" (see *Chronology*). Later the committee of the Company resolved that "Colo Cresap be impowered to agree with any person or persons willing to undertake the same [cutting the road] so that the expence thereof does not exceed twenty five pounds Virginia currency" (see *Chronology*, Resolution, July 15, 1751). When Christopher Gist received instructions from the Company to govern his conduct at the conference at Logstown, in 1752, he received a special instruction concerning the road. If Cresap had not agreed with anyone "to clear a Road for the Company," Gist was authorized to do so. See *Chronology*, Committee of the Company's instructions to Gist, April 28, 1752.

616. On November 4, 1752, the Virginia Executive Council ordered

Annotations

the receiver general to pay "Fifty pounds to Mr Gist, for his services at the Logstown Conference." —Virginia Council *Journals*, V, 410-11.

617. Order *unique to this document*.

618. Same.

619. The storehouse was used by the Army during the campaign. George Mercer stated that when the troops "abandoned them and returned to the Fort [Cumberland], were pulled down to build Barracks, and the Timber for above a Mile round cut down and destroyed to the Amount of some hundred Pounds." —"Proceedings of the Ohio Company," October 8, 1767, *op. cit.*
   The order is *unique to this document*.

620. Order *unique to this document*.

621. Same. See also *note* 593; pp. 165-166; *facs.*, pp. 29-30.

622. Resolution, *unique to this document;* however, a companion resolution, made the same day, appears elsewhere in this collection. See *Chronology*, Ohio Company's appointment of and instructions to George Mercer, July 4, 1763.

623. One page, 7⅜ × 12 inches, in an unidentified handwriting. All the signatures appended to the document are holographic; the endorsement is in an unidentified hand.

624. Printed in *Case* . . . , *facs.*, pp. 30-31. This petition was not presented to the King in Council until 1765. *Ibid.* p. 31.

625. One page, 7½ × 9 inches. The statement of the account, the computation of interest, and the endorsement are in three different hands, all unidentified by the editor. The computation of interest is the basis for the date (1763) given the document. The text of the endorsement is indicative of the fact that this document was used for some other purpose than its original intent.
   On November 22, 1752, the Committee of the Company resolved that Arthur Dobbs' share should be disposed of and not sunk in the Company (see *Chronology*). The sale, however, did not transpire, for he still held stock in the Company in 1760. (*Case* . . . , *facs.*, pp. 24-25). For further details see *note* 559.

Annotations

626. A John Mercer holograph, one page, 8½ × 12¼ inches, with endorsement in an unidentified hand.

627. George Mercer.

628. The reduction of French Canada and the subsequent peace pact, signed February 10, 1763, between England and France had ominous forebodings for the frontier settlers and Indians alike. The Indians who had been conditioned thoroughly by French propaganda in the past years believed that English control in North America meant their subjugation and eventual annihilation. Supposedly, the Treaty of Easton (1758) protected their land from encroachment by the whites; however, the influx of settlers beyond the Allegheny Mountains increased steadily. Colonel Bouquet's proclamation of October 30, 1761 (see *Chronology*) did not stop this infringement. The rumbling of the Indians' discontent, which had never been silenced completely, grew louder and louder. The wave of economy which swept the War Office prevented George Croghan, deputy Indian agent at Fort Pitt, from giving the usual presents to the Indians, thus increasing their suspicion that the ulterior motive of the English was to drive them out of the Ohio Country. By June, 1763, a new Indian uprising on the frontier seemed inevitable. On June 20 Governor Hamilton laid before the Pennsylvania Provincial Council seven communications from responsible persons on the frontier. These letters contained "Accounts of Hostilities committed by the Western Indians, on His Majesty's Subjects within this Province and of the Suspicious Behaviour of the Indians settled on the upper parts of the Susquehanna." Among these communications were letters from Colonel Bouquet (Fort Pitt), James Burd (Fort Hunter), and Captain Ourry (Fort Bedford). By July the personnel of the forts at Presqu' Isle, Le Boeuf, and Venango had been massacred or driven from their posts by the Indians, and Pontiac had succeeded in organizing the western Indians for an attempt to drive the English back over the Alleghenies (*Colonial Records of Pennsylvania*, IX, 30-31). As for Mr. Mercer's statement concerning the Indian incursions in Virginia, there never had been a cessation of hostilities in that region after 1759. In 1761 the Shawnee raided the upper James River settlements, massacred many of the settlers, and carried off some prisoners. The Indians had two approaches to the Virginia frontier. The Scioto-Big Sandy branch of the Great Warriors' Trail by which they penetrated deep into southern Virginia and the war trail which crossed the Ohio at the mouth of the Kanawha. It was over the Big Sandy path

Annotations

that the warriors passed when they assaulted the settlements at Draper's Meadows in 1755. James Patton was killed in that foray. In 1763 the western Indians traveled over these same trails to the settlements of Big Levels, Muddy Creek, and Carrs Creek. Many Virginians were killed and taken prisoners at this time. —John Lewis Peyton, *History of Augusta County* (Staunton, Virginia, S. M. Yost and son, 1882), pp. 106-120.

629. The home government was aware that it was necessary to formulate some plan to correct the so-called abuses committed by the traders and by settlers encroaching on Indian lands. On August 5, 1763, the Lords of Trade, realizing the inadequacy of additional instructions to the colonial governors, suggested to the Ministry that the king should issue a proclamation on the subject. Lord Shelburne, then president of the Board of Trade, may have been largely responsible for the first draft of the proclamation; while Lord Hillsborough, who succeeded him in this post on September 28, was responsible for the proclamation as it was signed on October seventh by King George III. By it the King set forth the advantages for settlers in "Four Distinct and separate Governments, stiled and called by the Names of Quebec, East Florida, West Florida, and Grenada." It defined boundaries of the four divisions. Among other matters touched upon was the Indian boundary line, the item which George Mason said "was an express destruction of our grant." An excerpt from that part of the proclamation concerning Indian boundaries is as follows: "We do therefore, with the Advice of our Privy Council, declare it to be our Royal Will and Pleasure, that no Governor or Commander in Chief in any of our Colonies of Quebec, East Florida, or West Florida, so presume, upon any Pretence whatever, to grant Warrants of Survey, or pass any Patents for Lands beyond the Bounds of their respective Governments, as described in their Commissions; as also that no Governor or Commander in Chief in any of our other Colonies or Plantations in America do presume for the present, and until our further Pleasure be known, to grant Warrants of Survey, or pass Patents for any lands beyond the Heads or Sources of any of the Rivers which fall into the Atlantic Ocean from the West and North West, or upon any Lands whatever, which, not having been ceded to or purchased by Us as aforesaid, are reserved to the said Indians, or any of them."

The proclamation gave authority to the governors to grant bonus lands to both army and navy veterans of the past campaign. Also, it set forth orders in the name of the Privy Council designed to prevent frauds and abuses "in purchasing Lands of the Indians." By the King's proclamation individuals were prohibited from purchasing lands from the Indians. All purchases were to be made in the name of the Crown or the Proprietaries as the case should be. All persons employed in the "Management and Direction of Indian affairs within the Territories reserved for the use of the said Indians" were ordered to apprehend any criminals who fled from the colonies to the Indian territory and to return them to the said colony for trial. —The Proclamation as contained in "Papers Relative to the Province of Quebec," 1791, in the Public Records Office is reprinted in *Documents Relating to the Constitutional History of Canada, 1759–1791*, edited by Adam Short and Arthur Doughty (Ottawa, S. E. Dawson, 1907), I, 119-123.

By the Treaty of Easton (1758), Bouquet's proclamation (1761), and finally by this, the King's proclamation (1763), the colonial governors were expressly forbidden to grant or permit survey of former land entries within the Ohio watershed. The King's proclamation appeared not to have conveyed the meaning which the Ministry intended, especially in regard to the newly created colonies. Some of the so-called injustices inflicted upon Catholic Quebec were not rectified until the passage of the Quebec Act of 1774. Clarence W. Alvord in his "The Genesis of the Proclamation of 1763" summarized the conclusions at which he arrived after a full study of the problem. Dr. Alvord stated that the proclamation was conceived originally in order to quiet the fears of the Indians by controlling the purchase of land. The home government believed that purchase of the Indians' land in the above manner would guarantee peaceful western expansion. Article printed in Michigan Pioneer and Historical Society, *Historical Collections* . . . (Lansing, Mich. 1874–1929), XXXVI, 14-52.

Although the intent in 1763 was to purchase this territory piecemeal from the Indians, the pressure of settlers who were eager to obtain land forced them to abandon the method. By the Treaty of Fort Stanwix (1768) the Six Nations and other Indians sold "2,400,000 acres of land at the back of Virginia" to the Crown, for £10,460.7s.3d. —*Acts of the Privy Council*, V, 202, 210.

630. This thought was not contingent upon the King's proclamation of October 7, 1763. The Company's petition of July 4, 1763, set forth alternative proposals to the Privy Council. Petition printed in *Case* . . . , facs., p. 31.

631. A George Mason holograph, endorsed by Robert Carter. Two small letter pages, 7½ × 9 inches. Printed in Rowland, *op. cit.*, I, 131-32.

Annotations

632. George Mercer in a letter to his father, dated September 18, 1767, informed the Ohio Company that the Board of Trade had reserved final decision on his Memorial of November 21, 1765, until they would receive from Governor Fauquier a report on the status of the Ohio Company grant. John Mercer received this letter on December 14, after which he sent that part of his son's letter relating to the Company to George Mason, John Tayloe, Phillip Ludwell Lee, and Robert Carter. See *Chronology,* John Mercer to George Mercer, January 28, 1768.

633. Governor Fauquier was informed of the Board of Trade's decision by Lord Shelburne's letter of October 8, 1767. Fauquier did not receive this letter until February, 1768. See *Chronology,* John Mercer to George Mercer, March 3, 1768.

634. Fauquier died before he had time to make this report.

635. Since Governor Fauquier had not received Lord Shelburne's letter of October 10 before the date of this letter, George Mason could not have been officially informed by him. However, Fauquier did write to George Mason asking him "to furnish me with their answer to your Lordships several Query's (sending them a Copy of the Letter) to enable me to comply the best I can." Although Fauquier's letter to Mason was not located by the editor, John Blair's letter to Lord Shelburne, March 21, 1768, states that he, Blair, upon assuming the lieutenant governorship after Fauquier's death, found a copy of the letter to Mason in the governor's "Book of Letters" (Blair to Shelburne in P.R.O., C.O. 5: 1346/13-16). Fauquier's papers were in possession of Robert Carter in 1783. In May, 1786, Carter sent the trunk containing the papers to Francis Fauquier [Junior], in care of Edward Athawes of London. There appears to be no record of their existence today. —Robert Carter to Francis Fauquier, July 5, 1783, *Carter Letter Books,* V, 144. MS in Duke University Library, Durham, North Carolina.

Lord Shelburne's letter, styled an order by George Mason, requested Fauquier to answer certain queries concerning the origin and activities of the Ohio Company. These queries are listed in *note 653.*

636. The advertisement in Rind's *Virginia Gazette* of February 11 and 18, 1768, is as follows: "A FULL MEETING of the OHIO COMPANY is desired, on *Tuesday* the 23d day of February, at *Stafford* courthouse, on business of importance."

Annotations

637. A John Mercer holograph, nine pages, 10 × 15 inches, some sheets badly worn, broken, and worn away at the folds. The body of letter, address, and orders to the Ship Captain, all are in John Mercer's handwriting. The endorsement is by George Mercer.

The first half, which does not pertain to Ohio Company affairs, gives very interesting Mercer family information and highlights of social and economic life in Colonial Virginia. Since the editorial policy of this work is to confine the annotations to information about the Ohio Company or to pertinent collateral historical information, all extraneous information remains unnoticed.

638. When George Mercer returned to Virginia late in October, 1765, he found his position, stamp distributor, untenable. After a conference with the governor he issued a public statement that he would not execute the Stamp Act without the consent of the Assembly, and returned to England less than 10 days later. —Rowland, *op. cit.*, I, 125-26.

639. Hugh Mercer.

640. John Mercer's son James.

641. John Robinson, speaker of the House of Burgesses and treasurer of the Colony from November 30, 1738, to the time of his death in May, 1766. After his death it was discovered that he was almost £100,000 in default with treasury funds. Most of this money had been lent to his friends. At stated intervals the House of Burgesses ordered redeemed "treasurer's notes" to be burned. Before the orders were carried out Robinson made loans of them to his friends and took their promissory notes as collateral. This irregular practice came to light after Robinson's death, at which time the government called in the once canceled treasury notes. Virginians, whose economy was based largely on the barter system, had little hard money. If the government's order could have been fully prosecuted, it would have forced the colony into economic disaster. Ultimately, the Robinson estate assumed responsibility for the default, and it is said that the colony was repaid from the estate. —*Journal of the House of Burgesses, 1766–69*, pp. X-XXVI; *Virginia Magazine*, IX, 356-57.

642. Colonel William Byrd of Westover.

643. In 1759 George and James Mercer released lands to Presley

Annotations

Thornton and John Tayloe, as security for their father's debts. See *Chronology,* November 25, 1759, Release . . . .

644. Edward Montague was the first colonial agent for Virginia who represented the House of Burgesses especially. He served in this capacity from 1761–1772. —Lonn, *op. cit.,* pp. 63-66, 393.

645. Apparently no positive action was taken, for John Mercer continued until his death to be concerned with the Ohio Company affairs.

646. On November 24, 1766, the inhabitants of Augusta County presented a petition to the House of Burgesses. The petition cited the need for some definite land policy for the territory "Beyond the Mountains" and claimed that the great grants of land which had been entered for but never surveyed were deterring many German emigrants from settling "on the Waters of Ohio." They requested the House of Burgesses to address his Majesty on these matters, asking "that the grants not yet complied with may be declared void and of no Effect." —*Journal of the House of Burgesses,* 1766–69, p. 37; see also *note* 254.

647. John Mercer owned one share at this time. In November, 1759, John Mercer conveyed to his sons, George and James, a moiety of his two shares in the Ohio Company. See *Chronology,* James and George Mercer's release of lands to John Tayloe and Presley Thornton, November 25, 1759; also p. 224.

648. A John Mercer holograph, two and three-quarter pages, 9 × 15 inches. The address is in John Mercer's hand; the endorsement, by George Mercer. John Mercer's seal, attached, is in a perfect state. Again it is to be noted that only Ohio Company affairs and pertinent collateral historical information are annotated.

649. Probably the letter, George Mercer to the Ohio Company, printed in *William and Mary Quarterly,* first series, I, 200-03. The letter, dated November 21, 1767, mentions a memorial which he intended to present to the King in council "on Thursday next," November 25. In conclusion Mercer wrote: "I shall write you again as soon as I know the success of my memorial." On December 12, 1767, the King referred the memorial to the Committee of Council for Plantation Affairs *(Acts of the Privy Council,* V, 119). The Committee, however, did not refer it to the Board of Trade until Novem-

Annotations

ber 20, 1769 (Order in Council, in P.R.O., C.O. 5: 1332/299-306). Therefore, the assumption—that this letter of November 21 and the one of November 25, mentioned in the text, may be one and the same.

650. Not located by the editor.

651. This packet contained the Report of the Lords of Trade to the Privy Council, June 26, 1767. Printed in *Case* . . . , *facs.*, p. 34. See also the paragraph preceding the report.

652. Robert Carter.

653. Lord Shelburne's letter to Governor Fauquier, October 8, 1767, requested answers to the following queries:

(1) What is the Nature of the Claim which the Ohio Company have to the Lands petitioned for?
(2) What Circumstances first gave Rise to the Formation of the Company?
(3) What Sums they have expended in consequence of the first Cession of Lands made to the Company by the Indians, or His Majesty's Instructions to His Lieutenant Governor of Virginia in the Year 1749 directing him to grant them the above mentioned 500,000 Acres?

—Letter in P.R.O., C.O. 5: 1345/385-90.

654. This statement refers to activities which precede those of the Walpole Company. "On the first of October, 1767, and during the time that the Earl of Shelburne was Secretary of State for the southern department, an idea was entertained for forming, '*at the expense of the Crown*,' three *new governments* in North America, viz. one at *Detroit* (On the waters between Lake Huron and Lake Erie); one in the *Illinois Country*, and one on the *lower* part of the River Ohio." —Great Britain. Board of Trade, *Report of the Lords Commissioners for Trade and Plantation on the Petition of the Honorable Thomas Walpole and his Associates, for a Grant of Lands on the River Ohio in North America* (April 15, 1772), p. 34.

655. Meaning Councilor Robert Carter. Since these were the same queries as Lord Shelburne directed to the governor, John Mercer may have been misinformed about their origin. See also *notes* 634 and 653.

· 641 ·

Annotations

656. See *Chronology*, Resolutions of the Committee of the Company, September 17, 1760.

657. According to terms of the only "grant" the Ohio Company ever received, they were bound to seat 100 families on the first 200,000 acres, and if they did so, they were to receive an additional 300,000 acres, subject to the same terms. —Additional instruction to Governor Gooch, March 16, 1749. *Op. cit.*

658. Enclosure, "Boundaries Proposed when the grant is renewed," printed on pp. 229-232.

659. Enclosure, an office copy of the "Case of the Ohio Company," as prepared in 1753 and ordered to be sent to John Hanbury. Printed on pp. 233-251. See also *Commentary*, pp. 394-395.

660. Communications in the George Mercer Collection which were identified as enclosures in this letter are as follows:

(1) Boundaries Proposed by the Ohio Company, February 26, 1768.
(2) Case of the Ohio Company, 1754.
(3) Resolutions of the Committee of the Ohio Company, October 17, 1760, and September 7–9, 1761.
(4) Record of Land Grants—Virginia, 1745–1753.
(5) Petitioners for Lands on the Ohio, 1745–1753.
(6) Fragment of an early draft of the Case of the Ohio Company, 1762.
(7) Resolution of the Committee of the Ohio Company, July 4, 1763.
(8) Imperfect Copy of John Mercer's letter to George Mercer, January 28, 1768.

661. Refers to the Appendix to the Case of the Ohio Company which contains the documents that support John Mercer's statements in the Case proper. *Appendix,* printed on pp. 246-286.

662. Appendix, No. 2, has copies of the minutes of the Virginia Executive Council, granting lands, 1745–1753.

663. John Mercer singled out John Blair and William Beverley, especially, as persons who were guilty of many irregularities in obtaining huge land grants. See *notes* 354 and 355.

Annotations

664. May refer to James Abercromby, colonial agent for Virginia, 1754–1774. From 1754 to 1761 he represented the entire colony; from 1761 to 1774, only the governor and executive council. To "negotiate matters pertaining to large land grants" was a specific duty of the agent. (Lonn, *op. cit.,* pp. 66 and 393.) William Beverley's grant was receiving attention in England in 1754. Newly appointed colonial agent, Abercromby, may have been concerned in presenting Beverley's case to the home government.

665. Grants made by the Virginia Executive Council, June 15, 1753. These minutes of the Council are printed on pp. 248-251.

666. May refer to the original of the map reproduced opposite page 72. If not the original of it, it may be a copy made for and sent to John Hanbury together with the Company's petition of March 28, 1754. For further details, see *note* 60.

667. On June 25, 1754, the Board of Trade reported to the Committee of Council for Plantation Affairs "upon the Petition of the Ohio Company praying for an Enlargement of their Grant." Here Mr. Mercer refers to the Board of Trade's answer to their request to have their grant defined by natural boundaries and surveyed in separate tracts. The Report was as follows: "With respect to the last difficulty, The Reason alleged by Mr Beverley (one of His Majesty's Council in Virginia) for the Governor & Council's refusal to permit the Petitioners to survey their Lands in separate Tracts ad Libitum, was because they apprehended, that by such a Method the Intention of the Crown, in making the Building a Fort a Condition of the Grant, would be frustrated, in as much as it was reasonable to suppose the Petitioners would be induced from such Liberty to take all the best Land they could find within the Limits prescribed by the Grant; in which case the settlers might be so dispersed and distant from each other, that the Fort could not Possibly afford them any Protection." Report, *op. cit.*

668. William Beverley was concerned in the company that was granted "one hundred thousand Acres lying on Green Brier River, North West and West of the Cow Pasture and Newfoundland." —Virginia Council *Journals,* V, 282. The *Journals* do not record any grant for the additional 30,000 acres.

669. William Russell, who was responsible for the Blair-Russell sur-

Annotations

vey, as shown on the plan reproduced opposite p. 226. See also *note* 355.

670. Letter is incorporated in John Mercer's copy of "Boundaries Proposed . . . . " Printed on pp. 231-232.

671. Map reproduced opposite p. 226.

672. The original, not the enclosure, is in the George Mercer Papers. Printed on pp. 182-183.

673. Enclosure, fragment of letter to George Mercer, January 28, 1768. Complete letter printed in this work. See *Chronology*.

674. General Gage wrote to Governor Penn as follows: "The Accounts that I have lately received from all Quarters, are full of Intelligence of the dissatisfaction of the Indians, and of their ill disposition towards us. I am now called upon, by a Letter I have received from Sir William Johnson, expressive of his apprehensions of an immediate Rupture with the Indians, unless some means are fallen upon to pacify them, to acquaint you, that altho' several Causes for their present ill temper are suggested, yet the Insults they have received from the frontier People, chiefly from those of Virginia, and the obstinacy of the People who persist to Settle on their Lands, not only without their Consent, but in contradiction to their warmest Remonstrances, and the endeavours that have been used to remove them, I perceive to be the most immediate cause of their present discontent. . . . " —Thomas Gage to John Penn, December 7, 1767, printed in *Colonial Records of Pennsylvania*, IX, 403-04.

Gage asked Penn "to devise some effectual measures to remove these Lawless Setlers, and to obtain some Satisfaction for the ill treatment the Indians daily complain of," and offered "the assistance of his Majesty's Troops to co-operate with you." —*Ibid.*

675. Penn's message to the Assembly is printed in *ibid.*, 407.

676. In addition to the Assembly's recommendation, mentioned by Mercer, they advised a "speedy Confirmation of the boundary line agreed upon by Sir William Johnson and the Indians" and a "just satisfaction made to them for their Lands on this side of it." The Assembly also passed "An Act to remove the Persons now settled and to prevent others from settling upon any Lands in this Province not

Annotations

purchased of the Indians." —Pennsylvania. General Assembly, *Votes and Proceedings*, VI, 7-16.

677. Refers to the murder of six Conestoga Indians in their Indian town on December 14, 1763, and to the subsequent massacre of the remainder of the group in the workhouse in Lancaster, whence they had been removed for protection against the frontier mob who had ravaged their town (Edward Shippen to John Penn, December 14 and 17, 1763, printed in *Colonial Records of Pennsylvania*, IX, 89-90 and 100, respectively). Another group of Conestogas, also living under the protection of the province, was threatened. Governor Penn had provided refuge for this group of friendly Indians on Province Island, situated on the Schuykill a little below Philadelphia. The frontiersmen were so incensed with, what they termed, provincial favoritism towards the Indians that to them the only good Indian on the frontier was the dead Indian. Penn, apprehensive of the safety of the citizens in Philadelphia itself, ordered their removal to New York, where they would be under the protection of Sir William Johnson, superintendent of Indian Affairs. The rioters were never apprehended, a fact which burned deeply in the heart of the Indian, thus retarding progress in establishing a permanent peace. For full details see *Colonial Records of Pennsylvania*, IX, 89ff.

678. Mercer's recitation of the Lancaster Massacre coincides with the official reports in *Colonial Records of Pennsylvania*, IX, 414-513.

679. Proclamation of January 19, 1768, printed in *ibid.*, 420.

680. Later the sheriff and others who had custody of Stump and Ironcutter were absolved of any part in the obstruction of justice. At a meeting of the Provincial Council on May 12 the governor, John Penn, being convinced that the officers of the law involved in the Carlisle jail affair had not intended to obstruct justice, informed the officers that he would "take no further other Notice of the Matter than to admonish you ₍them₎ for the future to be very careful, in confining yourselves within the Bounds of your Jurisdiction, and not to interfere again in Matters which belong to a Superior Authority." *Ibid.*, 513.

681. In John Mercer's handwriting, 1½ pages, 9⅞ × 15 inches, endorsed by George Mercer. The document contains John Mercer's copy of George Mason's memorandum on the bounds proposed for

Annotations

the Ohio Company's land when their grant would be renewed and a copy of Mason's letter to Mercer. For John Mercer's own comments on this document see p. 227.

682. The Company lost the "Fort they had begun at Pittsburg, and another Fort or Blockhouse which they had actually completed at the Mouth of Red Stone Creek on the River Monongahela, together with some Store Houses they had built on the Comunication to Red Stone Creek, at a Place called in the Maps *Gists* on the West Side of the Mountains, and by plundering their Effects, which ruined most of the Traders they had employed, and the rest being chiefly killed, or the Indians whom they had traded with, being mostly engaged against Them the Company lost all the Money they had advanced for the Trade." —"Proceedings of the Ohio Company, about the settlement & of the Ohio." *Op. cit.*

The above statement and the assertion made in the text are incongruous with all other evidence regarding the first English fort at the forks of the Ohio. An analysis of Trent's activities in January and February, 1754, reveals that although he went to the Ohio Country for the purpose of building a fort on the Ohio at the mouth of Chartiers Creek, his intentions were thwarted by orders from Governor Dinwiddie. When he came to the Ohio, early in February, 1754, he was a commissioned Virginia militia officer under orders to erect a fort for Virginia. See *notes* 573 and 574.

683. By the King's Proclamation of 1763 the land granted the Ohio Company in 1749 was considered beyond the boundary of Virginia. See *note* 629.

684. This recommendation was the antithesis of the King's Proclamation (1763) which prohibited purchase of land from the Indians either by individuals or colonies. The Crown reserved sole right of purchase. See *note* 629.

685. Refers to the Mason and Dixon's Line established between Pennsylvania and Maryland in 1764–67. The survey extended as far west as the "second crossing of Dunkard [Creek] in Greene County." "A Plan of the Boundary Lines between the Province of Maryland and the Three Lower Counties on Delaware with Part of the Parrallel of Latitude which is the Boundary Between the Provinces of Maryland and Pennsylvania. —Original 'Parchment Map Prepared by Messrs Mason and Dixon in 1768'" is in the Maryland Historical Society, Baltimore.

Annotations

686. Six pages, 9 × 15 inches, a John Mercer holograph. The document is in very poor condition having suffered from close folding. For further description and provenance see *Commentary*, pp. 394-95.

687. Evidently an error or faulty memory on John Mercer's part. See *Chronology*, October 24, 1747.

688. Printed on pp. 246-248.

689. July 12, 1749.

690. Printed on pp. 248-251.

691. This estimate was not included in the Appendix of the *Case*.

692. Printed on p. 252.

693. Printed on pp. 252-266. For variants of Gist's first journal see *Chronology*, May 19, 1751.

694. Printed on pp. 266-269. For variants of Gist's second journal see *Chronology*, March 29, 1752.

695. Printed on pp. 269-271.

696. Lunsford Lomax.

697. James Patton and Joshua Fry were the other two commissioners. In this statement lies the provenance of authorship of this particular copy of the minutes of the Logstown Conference. In the minutes of the Logstown Conference as appended to this document the commissioner who reported the minutes stated that "Colonel Patton insisted strongly to demand their reasons why the belt and speech . . . was not sent to Onondaga . . . Mr. Gist and I opposed it" (p. 274, this work). According to these statements, Lunsford Lomax, the only commissioner who ever was a member of the Ohio Company, must have taken these minutes of the Logstown Conference.

698. Printed on pp. 273-284.

699. In the "Case," sent to Charlton Palmer, July 27, 1762, the petition to Robert Dinwiddie, November 6, 1752, is inserted at this

Annotations

particular place in the manuscript; also, printed in *Case* . . . , *facs.*, pp. 7-8.

700. Printed on pp. 284-285; *Case* . . . , *facs.*, pp. 10-11.

701. Governor Dinwiddie addressed the House of Burgesses, November 1, 1753. —Address, printed in *Case* . . . , *facs.*, p. 13.

702. When Dinwiddie excused himself for not attending the conference at Winchester, in 1753, he sent a message that he fully intended "to meet them at Winchester next summer with a handsome Present from his Majesty, and to fix a Time, the most suitable to them" (Virginia Council *Journals*, V, 440). He also wrote to the Catawbas, informing them that he was to meet with some of the chiefs of the Six Nations, Twightwees, and some of the other chiefs from the Ohio at Winchester on May 20, and that he desired "two of Y'r Chiefs to be there to receive Part of a Pres't sent by Y'r Father the K. of G. B." Likewise, he sent an invitation to the Cherokees, asking them to see that "some of the Chickasawa" came. —Governor Dinwiddie's message to the Catawba Indians, January 29, 1754; ——— to the Emperor, King of Chote, and Warriors of the Great Nation of the Cherokees, April 19, 1754; ——— to the King, Head Men, and Warriors of the Catawbas, April 19, 1754; ——— to. . . Warriors of the Cherokees, April 19, 1754, printed in Dinwiddie *Papers*, Vol. I, 60-61, 131-32, and 132-33, respectively.

Dinwiddie left Williamsburg for Winchester on May 13, 1754, and returned June 16, having spent 16 days "in great Expectat'n and Uneasiness," waiting in vain for the Indians to come to Winchester. None came (Dinwiddie to Sir Thomas Robinson, June 18, 1754, printed in *ibid.*, 201-05). The Half King sent his regrets. He could not leave "his People at this time, thinking them in great Danger." Washington who relayed the Half King's message wrote: "He says if your Hon'r has anything to say, you may communicate by me, &c., and that if you have a present for them, it may be kept to another occasion, after sending up some things for their immediate use" (Washington to Dinwiddie, May 29, 1754, *op. cit.*). The Indian chiefs from the Ohio and the Twightwee also sent messages of regret and strings of wampum. Since the "French had invaded their Lands, they c'd not at this Time leave their young Men, but that they were march'g to join our Forces under Colo. Washington's Com'd." Dinwiddie to Governor DeLancey, June 20, 1754, printed in *ibid.*, 216-18.

As for the present, it was delivered piecemeal to the Indians. "An

Annotations

Assortm't of Ind'n Goods" was sent to Washington to be delivered to the Half King and others who were with him. Abraham Smith took gunpowder and lead to the Cherokees and Catawbas. A medal was sent to the "head man of each tribe." —Dinwiddie to Washington, June 1, 1754; ———— to Major Carlyle, July 5; ———— to Abraham Smith, July 5. Printed in *ibid.*, 186-87 and 231, respectively.

About the first of December Colonel Innes treated with the Shawnee from the Ohio. By November 12 William Cocke of Winchester, with whom the remaining treaty goods had been stored, was ordered to send "the present to Colonel Innes at Fort Cumberland." Dinwiddie, in acknowledgment of the receipt of the minutes of the treaty, replied to Innes: "Y'r Treaty with the Ind's was read in Council, but I think it's not proper at this Time to publish it; the more silent we are in our Transact's, the better" (Dinwiddie to Innes, November 12 and December 12, 1754, printed in *ibid.*, 396-97, 422-23, respectively). George Croghan, writing from his home at Aughwick on December 5, informed Richard Peters that "ye Shannas, which I Menshoned was within 50 Miles of this Plese, after Treating with Coll Innes att ye Camp, Came hear and was very unesey att thire being Detaind So Long hear this Sumer, and Now was oblig^d to go home without hearing from thire Brother Onas, which was thire only Busness Down to know what thire Brother wold have them to Do, I Strowe to keep them till his honours Instructions wold Come up, Butt to No purpose, they wold by No Mains be stopt as the Winter was so far advanct and as they Seem^d to be unesey by thire Nott Receiveing any Present from this government" —Letter in *Pennsylvania Archives*, II, 212-13.

703. "An Act for further encouraging persons to settle on the waters of the Mississippi," enacted in November, 1753; "An Act for the encouragement and protection of the settlers upon the waters of the Mississippi," enacted in February, 1754. Printed in Hening's *Statutes*, VI, 355-56 and 417-20, respectively.

704. In another version of the "Case" John Mercer attributes this misinformation to William Russell. See *Case* . . . , *facs.*, p. 13.

705. The John Hanbury Petition, January 11, 1749.

706. Also printed in the Virginia Council *Journals*, V, 172-73.

707. *Ibid.*, 195.

708. *Ibid.*, 231.

Annotations

709. *Ibid.*, 296-98. The grants of July 12, 1749, are those of which John Mercer so often complained.

710. According to John Mercer, this order which allowed the petitioners additional time in which to survey their land was an act of discrimination on the part of the Executive Council. See *Case . . . , facs.*, p. 2.

711. For John Mercer's comments on the grants to Richard Corbin see *Chronology*, John Mercer to George Mercer, March 3, 1768.

712. Gist began his journey on October 31. The record of his travel from Cresap's to Logstown is omitted.

713. Omission, entries for November 26 to December 13 inclusive; December 18.

714. Omission, "From Thursday Decr 27 to Thursday Jany 3, 1751.—Nothing remarkable happened in the Town."

715. Omission, one entry which covers January 5 to 8 inclusive.

716. Omission, entries for January 10 and 11.

717. Omission, entries for January 13 to 20 inclusive, entry for January 21 to 23, and entries for January 24 to 27 inclusive.

718. Omission, entries from March 18 to May 18, which include the record of Gist's travels through Kentucky and the mountainous region of southern Virginia.

719. Omission, November 5 to 23 and December 14, "we had Snow."

720. Omission, entries for December 18 to February 13, 1752, inclusive. Entries for these inclusive dates cover Gist's travels and experiences in southwestern Pennsylvania and present northwestern West Virginia.

721. Omission, entries for February 15 to March 11 inclusive. This part of the journal records his travel south, inland and parallel to that part of the Ohio River which bounds West Virginia, and his return trip along the Ohio itself.

Annotations

722. The use of the first person personal pronoun in these minutes is evidence that this document is a copy of the original personal report made by Lunsford Lomax. See *note* 697.

723. Gist did not deliver this message in person to the Indians on the Ohio but sent Thomas Burney in his place. At this time the Company had completed plans for building a fort and trading house at the mouth of Chartiers Creek on the Ohio. On July 27 the Committee of the Company issued special instructions to Gist in regard to laying out the town, Saltsburg. See *Chronology*.

William Trent was holding a conference with Indians on the Ohio when Thomas Burney arrived on August 8 with the message. Mr. Trent, in his account of the conference, states: "Mr. Burney arriv'd here at Night, with Directions in Writing from Mr. Gist, to invite some particular Indians to the Treaty." Gist arrived at Logstown the next day. —"William Trent's Account of his Proceedings . . . at Logstown, July 11–September 14, 1753," *op. cit.*

724. In Richard Rogers' handwriting, one page, $9\frac{7}{8} \times 15$ inches.

725. According to George Mercer, the storehouse at Wills Creek was used by troops during the 1754–58 campaign, "but when they abandoned Them and returned to the Fort, were pulled down to build Barracks, and the Timber for above a Mile around cut down and destroyed to the Amount of some hundred Pounds." —Proceedings of the Ohio Company, October 8, 1767, by George Mercer, *op. cit.*

726. One-half page, $9\frac{7}{8} \times 15$ inches; text and endorsement in John Mercer's handwriting. The document is badly mutilated, in four pieces.

This document was the source for information printed in *Case* . . . , *facs.*, p. 24.

727. The same.

728. One-half page, $9\frac{7}{8} \times 15$ inches, a fragment of the "Case" of the Ohio Company, in John Mercer's handwriting. Mercer's directions within the text are evidence that it is an early, probably a first, draft of the "Case" prepared for transmission to Charlton Palmer, July 26, 1762. Compare this document with pages 41-139 and 117-332.

729. A memorandum, $7\frac{1}{2} \times 3\frac{3}{4}$ inches. In an unidentified hand-

Annotations

writing, identical with "George Mercer's appointment as London agent, and his instructions."

730. A John Mercer holograph. Two pages, 9⅞ × 15 inches, badly mutilated. Fragment of a duplicate of John Mercer's letter to George Mercer, March 3, 1768.

731. A John Mercer holograph, three and one-half pages, 9⅞ × 15 inches. Letter badly worn, having suffered from close folding. Endorsement by George Mercer.

732. Pennsylvania (Colony). *Treaties, 1757, Minutes of Conference, Held with the Indians, at Harris's Ferry, and at Lancaster, In March, April, and May, 1757* (Philadelphia, B. Franklin and D. Hall, 1757). Governor Denny's speech, p. 10.

733. *Minutes of the Conference held at Easton in October, 1758, op. cit.*

734. See *note* 732. Weiser's report "of his Journey to Shamokin on the Affairs of Virginia and Maryland...," in April, 1743, is appended to the minutes of the conference held with the Indians at Harris's Ferry and at Lancaster in 1757. —*Op. cit.*, pp. 20-22.

735. For more than ten years prior to the Treaty of Lancaster, 1744, Virginia had solicited Pennsylvania's assistance in Indian affairs. A party of Conoy Indians traveling through Virginia murdered a man and his wife in their home in Spotsylvania County. Governor Gooch sought the assistance of Pennsylvania's governor, Patrick Gordon, in his attempt to apprehend the culprits. Wrote Gooch: "Now my worthy Friend, what I have to request of you is, that you will take such Measures as you judge most effectual for bringing these Villians to Punishment, and if their Nation can be induced to deliver them up to this Government, I shall be ready to give them a handsome Reward." (Letter, July 13, 1733, printed in *Colonial Records of Pennsylvania*, III, 564.) In the letter mentioned in this text John Mercer stressed the unfortunate circumstances of December, 1742, at which time several Six Nations' warriors traveling to the southward to war against the Catawbas were murdered by Virginians; also, several Virginians were killed in the skirmish. Unfortunately, at this time negotiations were being carried on in order to bring about a peace between Virginia and Maryland, on the one part, and the Six Nations

Annotations

on the other. An endeavor to establish a peace between the northern and southern Indians was under way.

According to extant records it was neither Virginia nor Pennsylvania but the Indians themselves who named Pennsylvania intermediary between Virginia and the Six Nations. At the conference at Philadelphia, in 1736, the chief asked James Logan to write to the governors of Virginia and Maryland, asking them to make some return for land they had settled before it was purchased from them. The Indians said they would return to Philadelphia the next year, 1737, to receive the compensation sent them by those colonies. Nothing was done on the subject, and the Indians did not appear at Philadelphia until 1742, when they demanded some satisfaction from both Virginia and Pennsylvania. Before Conrad Weiser and Shickallemy had completed arrangements for a conference between the Six Nations and the colonies, Virginia and Maryland, the "skirmish" in Virginia took place. Virginia, upon hearing the report of Colonel James Patton, who was present at the attack, ordered Gooch to write to the governor of New York "representing this Affair to him that he may make an enquiry at the next meeting of the Indian Commissioners at Albany what Nations these Indians belong to & upon what pretence they Committed these Hostilities and Depredations upon our People   If they have any Demands upon us for Lands for which they pretend not to have received Satisfaccon Let us know their Demand and upon Notice of the time and place appointed for the next meeting of the Indian Commissioners this Government will send Commissioners to meet & treat with them upon that Subject And are ready to make Satisfaccon for any reasonable Demand." —Virginia Council *Journals,* V, 113.

Notice of the "unhappy skirmish in Virginia," December 18, 1742, came to Philadelphia by Thomas McGee, an Indian trader at Shamokin. On January 25, 1743, Governor Thomas proposed to the Provincial Council that in order "to prevent the flame spreading Wider," Conrad Weiser should take a message of assurance and friendship to the Onondaga Council. Weiser was sent to Onondaga. Thomas wrote to Governor Gooch, explaining "the necessity of an Enquiry therein, that Justice may be done, and the ill Consequences which otherwise might happen to the back parts of most of the British Colonies in America be prevented."

Apparently John Mercer's antipathy for the Pennsylvanians was not shared by official Virginia, for Governor Gooch responded speedily to Governor Thomas's offer to mediate the dispute. Likewise, he was well-satisfied with the results of the mediation. Writing to

Annotations

Thomas, on May 7, 1743, Gooch remarked: "Had I known of the good Understanding, and how firmly the ffriendship between Your Province and the Indians is establish'd, I should not have Troubled the Governor of New York on this Subject." —Letter, printed in *Colonial Records of Pennsylvania*, IV, 654-55.

736. "Report of Conrad Weiser . . . of his second journey to Shamokin on the Affairs of Virginia and Maryland," April 21, 1743, *op. cit.*

737. In 1743 James Patton petitioned the Virginia Executive Council for permission to take up land west of the great mountains. The petition, presented October 25, 1743, was ordered "to lye by for furrther Consideration they to be preferr'd to other Petitioners." Council action had been postponed, lest such activity might give umbrage to the French. England, on the brink of war with France, was anxious to maintain peace as long as possible; therefore, she had cautioned the provincial governors to do nothing which might disrupt amicable relations between the two countries. However, Patton was promised that if war broke out between the powers in Europe, he would be granted the land. War did break out, and in April, 1745, Patton received the first grant of land "west of the great mountains" (Patton to Blair, January, 1753, *op. cit.;* Virginia Council *Journals*, V, 134, 172-73). On the same day, April 26, 1745, land was granted to John Robinson *et. al.* and Henry Downs, *et. al.* All these grants were for land west of the "great mountains."

738. "An Act for enforcing and rendring more effectual the Treaties already made, or hereafter to be made, with foreign Indians," May, 1722, printed in Hening's *Statutes*, IV, 103-06. "A copy of this act was delivered to the great men of the five nations, under the seal of the colony, at the treaty at Albany, in September, 1722, and by them ratified." —*Ibid*.

739. On October 21, 1731, Joist Hite and Robert McKay were given permission to take up 100,000 acres of land "on the back of the great Mountains" on condition that they seat 100 families in two years; on May 5, 1735, Benjamin Borden was given a like grant, subject to the same restrictions (Virginia Council *Journals*, IV, 253, 350-51). It is to be remembered that these lands were in the Shenandoah Valley, "on the Et side of the mountains."

740. Captain McDowell and others were killed in the skirmish of

Annotations

December, 1742. James Patton, who reported the incident to the Executive Council, stated that the Indians were accompanied by "some few white Men Supposed to be French." He did not mention Pennsylvania. —*Ibid.,* V, 112-13.

741. The preceding quotations were taken at random from Weiser's journal of his trip to Shamokin, in April, 1743. —*Op. cit.*

742. Refers to Virginia's contribution (goods worth £200 sterling) to the present distributed at Logstown in 1748. See also *note* 743.

743. The Half King's speech at Logstown, in 1752, and Weiser's report of the 1748 conference are incongruous. According to his journal, Weiser gave one heap or one-fifth of the treaty goods to the Indians in the name of the governor of Virginia. Later, the Half King and two other chiefs came to Weiser's abode and returned thanks for the large presents. This particular thanks was directed to the King. The spokesman for the trio continued "the same we do to our Brother Assaraquoa (Governor of Virginia), who joined our Brother Onas in making us a present." —*Colonial Records of Pennsylvania,* V, 356, 358.

744. On September 10, 1756, Sir William Johnson wrote to the Lords of Trade about the controversy between the Six Nations and the Penns. The Lords of Trade, in turn, referred his letter to the Penns, who answered by making "some observations" on Johnson's letter. Johnson inferred that the Indians were dissatisfied with Pennsylvania's purchase of land at Albany in 1754. His belief was that although the transaction was agreeable to some of the Indians, a greater number of them were opposed to it. Even the Indians who agreed to the sale at the time were sorry for it later. In his letter Johnson suggested that "the most effectual method of producing Tranquility, to that Province would be a Voluntary, & open surrender of that deed of Sale, Fix with the *Indians* in the best manner they can, the Bounds for their Settlements, and make *them* Guaranties of it." —Letter, printed in *Documentary History of New York, op. cit.,* II, 733-37.

The Proprietors' observations on Johnson's proposal were a challenge to "all the World to shew any *one Instance* of their Conduct, that has given dissatisfaction to the Six Nations, and which they say those Nations will readily acknowledge, in any free Conference" (Communication, December 11, 1756, printed in *ibid.,* 738-41). In

Annotations

rebuttal Johnson informed the Lords of Trade that the Indians were "disgusted and dissatisfied with the extensive purchases of land, and do think themselves injured thereby." Furthermore, he stated that the Indians' hostile attitude was not toward Pennsylvania alone, but also toward some other colonies. He also expressed the opinion that Quaker intervention in colonial affairs obstructed an amicable settlement of the dispute in question. Wrote Johnson: "I believe Your Lordships will be of opinion that Indian Affairs ought to be considered and conducted upon one public Spirited plan for the good of the whole, and that either party or partial Interferings to warp them from this Salutary End is not less contrary to His Majesty's Royal & Paternal Determinations, than it will if permitted be destructive to the welfare of His Subjects and Dominions here." —Letter, September 28, 1757, printed in *N.Y.C.D.*, VII, 276-79.

Although the Proprietors insisted that the Indians were well satisfied with the terms of purchase made at Albany in 1754, they followed Johnson's advice, when the Six Nations brought this complaint to the fore at the conference held at Easton, October, 1758. Then Governor Denny reminded the Six Nations' representatives: "that at a Treaty you held with your good Friend, Sir William Johnson, three Years ago, some of your wise men told him that there were some among them who were dissatisfied with the sale of the above Lands made by them at Albany, and were desirous that part of it should be reserved for them, though the Proprietaries had purchased it fairly of them and paid One Thousand Pieces of Eight, which was all they were to receive till our People settled to the Westward of the Allegheny or Appalaccin Hills. Sir William Johnson represented this matter to the Proprietaries in your Behalf, whereupon they chearfully agreed to release to you all that part of the Purchase you have reclaimed; and, by a Letter of Attorney, empowered Richard Peters and Conrad Weiser to execute a Deed to you for those Lands, on your Confirming to them the Residue of that Purchase. On this Subject, therefore, you will please to Confer with them and Settle the Boundaries between you, that they may release the Lands to you accordingly before you leave this Place, and set your Minds at Ease." —Minutes of the Conference, *op. cit.*

Six days later Messrs. Peters and Weiser held a "private Conference with the Chiefs of the United Nations at the House of Adam Johe," at which time "The Limits of the Lands to be released by the said Proprietaries' relase, and the Indians' Deed of Confirmation were read and interpreted; and the Indians expressing their Satisfaction at every part thereof, and particularly with the Limits, as described

Annotations

in the Draught annexed to their Confirmation Deed, they were both executed in the Presence of William Logan, George Croghan, Henry Montour, Charles Swaine, and John Watson, who subscribed their Names, as Witnesses thereto." —*Ibid.*

745. On June 23, 1727, Wequalia, a Delaware Indian King, was sentenced to death for the murder of John Leonard at Perth Amboy, New Jersey, and was executed on July 8, the same year. Three chiefs and fifty other Indians attended the trial. When asked what they had to say in the matter, the spokesman replied: "We have thought of this matter, and desire you will tell Wequalia, That we neither have nor intend to do any thing in the Affair, it is he that has wronged the English, and not Us, and therefore he must himself make them Satisfaction without expecting any Assistance or hearing any more from us."

After his execution it was said of him that he had also murdered his own brother and other Indians. Only a few relatives accompanied Wequalia to the gallows, all other Indians shunned him—"refused to shew him the least Regard." —Accounts in *Weekly News Letter,* July 13, 20, 1727, and *American Weekly Mercury,* July 6, 13, 1727, as reprinted in *Documents Relating to the Colonial, Revolutionary and Post-Revolutionary History of the State of New Jersey* (v.p., v. pub., 1880–1942), XI, 129-30, 131-33, 135.

746. The Pride, influenced by Peter Chartier, deserted to the French but later returned to the English interest. See *note* 116. This foray into Carolina took place in the latter part of 1752. For details see *note* 320.

747. At the conference held in Philadelphia, July, 1742, the Six Nations' chief, Canasatego, complained of the colonial settlements west of the Kittochtinny Mountains (*Colonial Records of Pennsylvania,* IV, 579-80). The Pennsylvanians, aware of the danger in provoking the Indians, sought means to prevent further encroachment on land claimed by them and to remove the families who had already settled there. On October 5, 1742, Governor Thomas issued a proclamation warning the people against "taking up or settling any Lands in the County of *Lancaster,* to the *Westward* of the *Kittochtinny-Hills,* otherwise called the *Endless* or *Blue Mountains* ("Proclamation of Gov. Thomas Ag'st Settlers on Lands in Lancaster, 1742," printed in *Pennsylvania Archives,* I, 629-30. There is an original broadside "Proclamation" in the Darlington Memorial Library). Warnings

notwithstanding, the settlers continued to inch over the mountains. Eight years later, Richard Peters, accompanied by several magistrates, attempted to remove these settlers by force. Many families in the Juniata Valley, along Sherman Creek, in the Big and Little Coves and in the Conolloway, were evicted and their cabins burned ("Report of Richard Peters . . . of the Proceedings against sundry Persons settled in the unpurchased Part of the Province," July 2, 1750, printed in *Colonial Records of Pennsylvania*, V, 440-49). Afterwards, Peters wrote to Thomas Penn, giving him a detailed account of his journey. The letter reveals that Mr. Peters' mission was twofold—to dispossess the trespassers on Indian lands and to secure the "best spots of Land" for the Proprietors. His recitation of the plight of the settlers of the Little Cove and the Big and Little Conolloway shows that the Province was responsible for some of this trespassing. According to Peters, the settlers in these regions were there with full proprietary approval, he himself having advised the governor previously "to give the hint to some good sort of people there to settle there and to keep off Cresap." When Thomas Cresap endeavored to collect taxes for Maryland, they "disowned the Jurisdiction of Maryland, and courageously and unanimously" adhered to their right as Pennsylvanians. Since the governor had made no distinction between these and other settlers, they drew up a petition which they sent to the governor; Peters and his entourage retired without dispossessing them.

Peters also reconnoitered the land for an advantageous site for a town to be the future county seat of Cumberland County. The secretary, according to his own confession, had purchased an "abundance of Land on Yellow Breeches & Conedogwainet which would be considerably advanced in its value" if the proprietors accepted a certain site proposed by him. Peters hastened to add that he did not wish to influence the proprietor, for his land was so advantageously located that under any circumstances he was assured of its increasing in value. —Peters to Penn, July 10, 1750. Penn Official Correspondence, V, 29-35. MS in Historical Society of Pennsylvania.

748. From the text of this letter one may conclude that Mercer was referring to the "Walking Purchase" of 1737.

749. The proprietors did not purchase land from the Indians in 1740. However, it was the year which marked the zenith of their grumbling about the "Walking Purchase" of 1737. In November they had threatened violence against almost 100 families who had settled within the purchase. In answer to their threat Thomas Penn con-

Annotations

ferred with the governor and his council. After they had studied the deed, the map of the "Walk," and the haughty letter from the Delawares, they ordered Governor Thomas to write to them, "requiring them to live peaceably with the English as before, and, moreover, informing them that the whole affair would be disclosed to the chiefs of the Six Nations coming to Philadelphia in May, to which meeting the Delawares might come at their own expense." —Charles P. Keith, *Chronicles of Pennsylvania* ... (Phila., n. pub., 1917), II, 809-10.

750. Refers to the conference held at Easton in 1758.

751. Nutimus. Here Mercer refers to the Albany Purchase (1754).

752. Nutimus received forty-four dollars, his share of the purchase money (1754). Teedyuscung, speaker for the Delawares at Easton in 1758, having been shown the deed executed at Albany in 1754, remarked: "We have seen the Deed, and know it well. Nutimus, one of our Chief Men, has signified it; and here sits one of our men, named Philip Compass, who was present when the sale was made; and remembers that Nutimus, our Chief, received Forty-four Dollars as his Part, or Share of the Consideration Money. We agree to it, and acknowledge that the Land was fairly Sold. We give it up, and now confirm it. Let there be no difference, nor any thing more said about it. This is not the Land I have disputed with my Brethren, the English. That Land lies between Tohiccon Creek and the Kittochtinny Hills."

753. Shickallemy, in behalf of the Six Nations, and Weiser, Pennsylvania's emissary, arranged for the conference held at Lancaster in 1744. —Report of Conrad Weiser ..., April 21, 1743, *op. cit.*

754. Again, John Mercer has digressed from his discussion of the Easton Conference (1757). The foregoing account is a paraphrase of Shickallemy's message to the governor of Pennsylvania. —*Loc. cit.*

755. On October 5, 1742, Governor Thomas issued a proclamation against settlers taking up land west of the *Kittochtinny Hills;* on July 18, 1749, Governor Hamilton issued another of similar import. Printed in *Pennsylvania Archives,* I, 629-30 and *Colonial Records of Pennsylvania,* V, 394-95, respectively.

756. Refers to Shickallemy's speech as given by Conrad Weiser in his Report of April 21, 1743. *Op. cit.*

Annotations

757. An island in the Susquehanna River, near present Lock Haven, Pennsylvania.

758. Lee and Beverley were Virginia's commissioners at the conference at Lancaster—not Albany.

759. Thomas King, an Oneida, was the "speaker" who made this complaint. It is natural that Mercer thought this accusation against Virginia was unjust; for during those dark days of 1752, '53, and '54, both Virginia and the Ohio Company gave the Ohio Indians all the assistance possible. When Thomas Burney brought the appeal for assistance from the Twightwees to Governor Dinwiddie, Dinwiddie sent a message of assurance back to them immediately. Knowledge that the Six Nations considered themselves in authority over the western tribes caused Dinwiddie to refrain from giving them material aid until he had obtained approval from the Council at Onondaga (*Colonial Records of Pennsylvania*, IV, 84). Although this interpretation is not revealed in the minutes of the Virginia Executive Council nor in Andrew Montour's report of the Six Nations' reaction to Virginia's overtures, the Virginians could scarcely have been unaware of the jealous manner in which the Onondaga Council guarded its authority over the Ohio and western Indians. According to the Executive Council minutes, Montour was sent to Onondaga in January, 1753, and again in June to invite the Six Nations to come to Winchester to receive a present from the King. Obviously, Virginia wished not only to obtain official sanction of the confirmation of the release of lands given by the Ohio Indians at Logstown in June, 1752, but also to obtain official sanction of a policy which was the antithesis of the "policy of neutrality" maintained by the Onondaga Council. Governor Hamilton did not send a message to Onondaga by Montour in February, for he wished "to know first how the Six Nations might receive the Governor of Virginia's invitation of them to a treaty at Winchester" (*ibid.*, V, 607). However, in June Richard Peters entrusted Andrew Montour with a specific query directed to the Onondaga Council. The colonies' hesitation in giving assistance to the Twightwees is epitomized in this query which was as follows: "Brethren of the Six Nations—'The French have invaded your Lands on the Ohio and are building Forts there. The Indians of your Nations settled there, with the Delawares and Shawonese, Twightwees and Owendats, are terrified and desire our assistance, which we are willing to afford them but want first to know in what Manner You will desire We shall give them Assistance, and what You wou'd chuse We should do to prevent the Country and Them from falling into the Hands of

Annotations

the French. Brethren, We desire You will speak plainly and fully on this Head, not knowing what to do till we hear from You.'" —*Ibid.,* 635-36. The Onondaga Council, anxious not to incur the displeasure of the French, answered both Virginia and Pennsylvania: "We thank you for the Notice you are pleased to take of those Young Men, and for your kind intentions towards them. They stand in need of your Advice, for they are a great way from Us. We, on behalf of all the Indians, our Men, Women, Children, entreat you will give them good Advice. . . . We love the English and we love the French, and as you are at Peace with one another do not disturb one another; if you fall out make up your Matters among Yourselves. . . . If our Indians shou'd be struck it will be very kind to help them; it is better to help them than Us, for we are near New York and can be supplied easily from thence. Col. Johnson the Agent of that Government, has assured Us We may always have what we want there; We expect him amongst Us soon, and can ask then for any thing for ourselves, but our young Men at Ohio must have their Supply from You. We, therefore, heartily thank you for your Regards to Us and our Hunters at Ohio, which we testify by A String of Wampum." —*Ibid.,* 637.

760. At the Easton Conference, October, 1758, the speaker for the Delawares complained: "About three years ago eight Warriors were returning from War through Virginia, having Seven Prisoners and Scalps with them; at a place called Green Briar, they met with a Party of Soldiers, not less than One Hundred and Fifty, who kindly invited them to come to a certain Store, and they said they would supply them with Provisions, and accordingly they travelled two Days with them in a Friendly Manner, and when they came to the House they took their Arms from the Senecas; The head men cryed out here is Death, defend yourselves as well as you can, which they did, and two of them were killed on the Spot, and one, a young Boy, was taken Prisoner; This gave great offence, and the more so as it was upon the Warriors road and we were in perfect Peace with our Brethren. It provoked to such a Degree that we could not get over it." Since the principal item discussed by the Pennsylvanians was the return of prisoners, the speaker desired the return of this Seneca boy, Squissatego. If he were dead they wished to know and they would "be content." —*Colonial Records of Pennsylvania,* VIII, 197-98.

Governor Denny promised he would "immediately send to the Governor of Virginia to enquire after the Seneca Boy, Squissatego, who you say was left a Prisoner in his Country, and if he is alive, you may depend on his being returned to you." —*Ibid.,* 203.

Annotations

761. At a conference held at Easton in November, 1756, William Denny asking Teedyuscung, king of the Delawares, why they had turned against their friends, the Pennsylvanians, addressed him as follows: "Have we, the Governor or People of Pennsylvania, done you any kind of Injury? If you think we have, you shou'd be honest and tell us your Hearts. You should have made complaint before you struck us; for so it was agreed in our Ancient League. However, now the great Spirit has thus happily brought us once more together. Speak your mind plainly on this head, and tell us if you have any just cause of Complaint, what it is; That I may obtain a full answer to this Point." —Extract from the Minutes of a Conference held at Easton, November, 1756, printed in *Colonial Records of Pennsylvania*, VII, 320.

Teedyuscung answered Denny's question with the accusation that the Penns had deceived the Delawares. He concluded the lengthy harangue with the following speech: "Yes, I have been served so in this Province; all the Land extending from Tohiccon, over the great Mountain, to Wioming, has been taken from me by fraud; for when I had agreed to sell the Land to the old Proprietary, by the course of the River, the Young Proprietaries came and got it run by a straight Course by the Compass, and by that means took double the Quantity intended to be sold." —*Ibid.*, 326.

Governor Denny then informed Teedyuscung that he would send a full report of these accusations to Sir William Johnson, his majesty's superintendent of Indian Affairs. In addition he requested the haughty king of the Delawares to have Johnson confirm the Indians' accusations against the Penns. —*Ibid.*, 331.

Next year, at the Easton conference, Denny told Teedyuscung: "Sir William Johnson has since deputed your and our Friend, Mr. George Croghan, who is well acquainted with your Affairs and Language, to act in his Behalf, to attend this Treaty, and enquire into every Grievance you may have suffered, either from your Brethren of Pennsylvania or the neighboring Provinces."—Extract from Minutes of a Conference held at Easton, July, 1757, printed in *ibid.*, 667.

The Delawares' bill of complaints, set forth by George Croghan, is printed in *Documentary History of New York, op. cit.*, II, 761-62.

762. Refers to the conference held at Philadelphia in July, 1742. Treaty printed in Colden, *op. cit.*, II, 1-44; also, in *Colonial Records of Pennsylvania*, IV, 560-86.

763. A paraphrase of Canasatego's speech.

Annotations

In reply to his request the governor stated that since the proprietors were absent, it was impossible to "enlarge the Quantity of Goods." He explained further: "Were they here, they might, perhaps, be more generous; but we cannot be liberal for them.—The Government will, however, take your Request into Consideration, and, in Regard to your Poverty, may perhaps make you a Present. I but just mention this now, intending to refer this Part of your Speech to be answered at our next Meeting." —*Loc. cit.*

764. At the treaty held at Philadelphia in October, 1736, the Six Nations' Indians lodged a complaint against Virginia's and Maryland's encroachments on their land. At that time they informed the proprietor, Thomas Penn, that "all the Lands on Sasquehannah (Susquehanna) and at Chanandowa (Shenandoah)" were theirs. Also, they asked the Pennsylvanians to write to the governors of Maryland and Virginia "to make them Satisfaction for the Lands belonging to them [the Indians]." They expressed satisfaction with the release of land just made to Pennsylvania, but added that they had never received anything from the other governments to the southward who had settled on their land. —*Colonial Records of Pennsylvania*, IV, 570.

765. Mr. Logan informed Canasatego that according to his request (1736) he had written to the governor of Maryland *(ibid.,* 572). There is no record of any such letter (1736) in the Virginia Council *Journals.*

766. Both James Logan's letter of December 20, 1736, and the Six Nations' message, interpreted by Conrad Weiser, are printed in *Maryland Archives*, XXVIII, 271-72. Evidently, Maryland disregarded these communications, for they were not entered in the "Proceedings of the Council" until July 23, 1742. *Ibid.*

767. Canasatego was aware of the Indians' claim on lands settled by the Virginians. In the opening speech at the treaty he remarked, "As to our Brother Assaragoa, we have at this present Time nothing to say to him; not but we have a great deal to say to Assaragoa, which must be said at one Time or another." —Pennsylvania (Colony) Treaties, 1744, *A Treaty held at ... Lancaster, op. cit.,* p. 4.

As negotiations progressed it is evident that Canasatego, by this speech, meant only that the Indians wished to treat with the Marylanders first, and with the Virginians later. Governor Thomas, in his answer to the chief's address, took care of the situation of 1736 by stating that he could not write to Virginia's governor until he

· 663 ·

knew of the specific claims against the colony and that the matter had been cleared by a study of James Logan's correspondence. *Ibid.*

768. John Mercer's criticism of Pennsylvania's Indian diplomacy seems unjust. Pennsylvania's geographical location made her the colony which would suffer most from the outbreak of hostilities between the Six Nations and either the southern Indians or the Virginians. Shickallemy and Conrad Weiser were the ambassadors appointed by the Six Nations, and only through them could business be transacted. In 1733 as well as in 1743 Virginia's governor chose to use this diplomatic channel to settle disputes which arose from clashes between the Six Nations and the settlers.

769. This gift was not a settlement for damages for the death of Indians in the "late unhappy skirmish," but in accordance with Indian protocol an item by which, according to Shickallemy's request, the Virginians "washed off the blood first" and took "the Hatchet out of their Head and Dress the Wound (according to Custom he that Struck first must do it)." This ceremony was necessary before the Six Nations would speak to the governor or be "reconsiled to him, and bury their affair in the ground that it never may be seen or heard of any more so long as the World Stands." —Report of Conrad Weiser, April, 1743, *op. cit.*

Governor Thomas wrote to Governor Gooch of the success of his negotiations with the Six Nations: "Nothing now remains but to take the Hatchet out of their Heads—that is, I suppose, to send Commissioners to Albany to declare your Concern for the rashness of your remote Inhabitants, and at the same time to make them a present. This done, they will enter into a friendly Treaty with you about the Land when they Treat with the Governor of Maryland at Harris' fferry on Sasquehannah, which will be next Spring." —Thomas to Gooch, April 25, 1743, printed in *Colonial Records of Pennsylvania*, IV, 653-54.

Thomas also informed Gooch that Conrad Weiser, "The Messenger is order'd to wait your own Time for an Answer, which I shall not fail to Transmit forthwith to Shamokin in Order to its being Convey'd to the Indian Council at Onondaga." —*Ibid.*

Gooch replied to Governor Thomas: "And therefore we request that You will be pleas'd to send your honest Interpreter once more to the Indian Chiefs, and if Possible prevail with them to accept through Your Hands a present from Us of £100 Sterl. value in such Goods as you think proper, as a token of our sincere Disposition to preserve Peace and friendship with them, And as an Earnest that

Annotations

we will not fail to send Commissioners next Spring, at the Time and to the place that shall be agreed upon, to treat with them concerning the Lands in Dispute. If what the six Nations insist upon be true, that we were the aggressors, the matter has been greatly misrepresented to me, and I should be much concerned. But since, by your kind interposition, the Cure for past injuries and the Preservative against future ones is applied, I shan't controvert the ffact, and You may depend upon it no fresh Hostilities shall be Exercised against them. Had I known of the good Understanding, and how firmly the ffriendship between Your Province and the Indians is establish'd, I should not have Troubled the Governor of New York on this Subject." —Gooch to Thomas, May 7, 1743. *Ibid.*, 654-55.

770. Governor Thomas in his opening address at the Lancaster treaty gave the Pennsylvania and Maryland commissioners the following warning concerning the present negotiations with the Indians: "Some Allowances for their Prejudices and Passions, and a Present now and then for the Relief of their Necessities, which have, in some Measure, been brought upon them by their Intercourse with us, and by our yearly extending our Settlements, will probably tie them more closely to the *British* Interest." —Pennsylvania (Colony) Treaties, 1744, *A Treaty held at . . . Lancaster, op. cit.*, p. 5.

771. Release, printed in *Maryland Archives*, XXVIII, 334-35.

772. New York (Colony) Treaties, *A Treaty Between His Excellency, The Honourable George Clinton, Captain General and Governor in Chief of the Province of New-York, and of the Territories thereon depending in America . . . and the Six United Indian Nations, and other Indian Nations, depending on the Province of New-York; Held at Albany the months of August and September, 1746* (New York, James Parker, 1746).

773. This present, received in Virginia in 1750, was not distributed until June, 1752, at Logstown. On December 12, 1751, Virginia agreed to pay Thomas Cresap one pistole per hundred-weight for conveying the treaty goods from Frederick Town to Logstown (Virginia Council *Journals*, V, 374). The printed Virginia Council *Journals* do not record a separate item, payment to Thomas Cresap for his services.

774. Governor Fauquier died March 3, 1768. —Blair to Shelburne, March 21, 1768. P.R.O., C.O. 5: 1346/13-16.

Annotations

775. One page, 7½ × 9 inches, in an unidentified hand, signed by Charlton Palmer. This letter is a factor in dating the printed *Case* .... Evidently, George Mercer, after having entered a caveat against the Walpole Company (Memorial of December 18, 1769, printed in *Case* ... , *facs.*, pp. 35-36), decided to present the Ohio Company's case to the Privy Council. Lack of direct evidence makes it impossible to verify that George Mercer asked Charlton Palmer for his file of Ohio Company papers, for the purpose of preparing the *Case* for publication; however, circumstantial evidence does give credence to such speculation. George Mercer had entered a caveat against a rival land company; he had received notice that his plea would receive attention along with the memorials of the Grand Ohio Company, and the Mississippi; and his father's last letters pleaded for a printed *Case* ... in order that everyone might know that the Company was ill used by the Virginia Council and the Ministry. The *Case* was printed before July 9, 1770. —John Pownall to Thomas Walpole, July 9, 1770; P.R.O., C.O. 5: 1333/385-403.

776. This is a quotation from the petition prepared by the Committee of the Company in July, 1763. When George Mercer sailed for England, on July 8, he took this petition with him but did not present it to the King in Council until June 21, 1765. —Petition, in printed *Case* ... , *facs.*, pp. 30-31.

777. Richard Jackson was a member of the Walpole or Grand Ohio Company. This statement made by Palmer is significant, inasmuch as it indicates that the Walpole Company had access to the Ohio Company's records when they formed their company.

778. One page, 7½ × 9 inches. A Thomas Walpole holograph, probably endorsed by George Mercer.

779. Meaning patents. No land was ever patented to the Ohio Company. The only bona fide claim which the Ohio Company ever had was Governor Gooch's leave to take up 200,000 acres of land. When Richard Lee presented the Ohio Company's petition of 1772 to the Virginia Executive Council, he was informed that the petition for permission to survey was unnecessary, for the Company had had such a permission since 1749 and no prior grants excluded them.

780. A Conway Richard Dobbs holograph. Two pages, 7½ × 9 inches, endorsed by George Mercer.

Annotations

781. Letter not located. Mercer's offer to purchase Arthur Dobbs' share at this time is evidence that his statements made to the members of the Ohio Company were sincere. In an open letter to the members he spoke enthusiastically of the future successes of the Grand Ohio Company (see *Chronology,* James Mercer to several members of the Ohio Company, January 9, 1772). This letter is also evidence that as early as March 8, 1770, he had decided to cast the lot of the Ohio Company with the Walpole Company. George Mercer must have purchased the Arthur Dobbs' share; for, on May 28, 1771, he informed Conway Richard that his brother and he [Mercer] had "settled your Affair in the Manner he thought best for you."— Letter, *op. cit.*

782. He held this appointment for about a year, but never took up residence in the colony.

783. A James Mercer holograph, five and one-half pages, 7½ × 10 inches, endorsed in an unknown hand. This letter is in very poor condition; each page is in three pieces, at least. The date is from George Mason to James Mercer, January 13, 1772. See *Chronology.*

784. Probably an enclosure in George Mercer's letter to George Mason, dated August 8, 1771, in which he mentions an enclosed letter to "that *extraordinary Company*" which contained his "Resolutions As to their Concern." Although the enclosure mentioned was not located by the editor, this letter to Mason reveals that George Mercer was irked about the silence of his associates in regard to his decision to merge the Ohio Company with the Walpole Company. He complained to Mason that he had not been compensated for the time nor the money which he had spent in negotiating their affairs in England. Wrote Mercer in part: "I had wrote them that I had strained my Credit for them as far as it would stretch—but not one word of answer to all this—no money, no Credit, no approbation of my past Conduct, or orders for my future—Is this Sir treatment for an Agent, for one whom the Company reposed such a Confidence in?" —Copy of the original is No. 20624, MSS Collection, Virginia State Library.

785. Refers to George Mercer's agreement to merge the interests of the Ohio Company with those of the Walpole Company. In consideration of George Mercer's withdrawal of his caveat against them the Walpole Company agreed "to admit the Ohio Company as a Co-purchaser . . . for two shares of the said Purchase," the whole being divided into seventy-two equal shares. —Agreement, May 7, 1770,

Annotations

printed in the *American Historical Record* . . . edited by Benson J. Lossing (Philadelphia, Chase & Town, 1872–74) III, 205.

786. In 1769 the Grand Ohio or Walpole Company, later styled the Vandalia Company, was formed by a group of influential Englishmen and Americans. Thomas Walpole was the most active and influential English member; Samuel Wharton and Benjamin Franklin, the Americans. The land which they desired encompassed the grant made the Ohio Company in 1749 and the land given to William Trent and his associates (Suffering Traders, 1763) by the Indians on November 3, 1768. By 1771 the Walpole Company had recognized the Indians' deed to William Trent and associates as valid, and George Mercer had merged the Ohio Company with the Walpole Company. Thus the Walpole Company's interests encompassed the original interests of three separate groups.

On July 24, 1769, Thomas Walpole and others petitioned the King in council for permission to purchase from the Crown the land (2,400,000 acres) which the Crown had purchased from the Indians at Fort Stanwix in November, 1768. The price offered was the exact sum paid by the Crown £10,460 7s. 3d., sterling. Their petition, referred to the Committee of Council for Plantation Affairs on August 4, reached the Board of Trade on November 20. Since the transaction involved money matters, the Board of Trade suggested to the memorialists that they should seek the Treasury Board's approbation of the memorial. Having received the Treasury's approval "with respect to the purchase Money and Quit Rent," Thomas Walpole, Benjamin Franklin, John Sargent, and Samuel Wharton renewed "their application for a grant reserving the rights of present occupiers within the tract prayed for."

The next day, May 25, 1770, the Committee of Council referred the petition to the Board of Trade (*Acts of the Privy Council,* V, 202-09; VI, 471). At first Lord Hillsborough, president of the Board, approved of the plan; later he opposed it and succeeded in delaying action upon it until March 25, 1772. Although their report as printed is dated April 15—the day it was completed and ordered to be transcribed— it was not signed until April 29. By it the Committee of Council was informed that the Board of Trade "cannot recommend to your Lordships to advise his Majesty to comply with the prayer of this Memorial, either as to the erection of any parts of the lands into a separate government, or the making a grant of them to the Memorialists" (Great Britain. Board of Trade, *Report of the Lords Commissioners . . . with Observations and Remarks* [London, J. Almon, 1772] p. 32).

Annotations

The Committee of Council resolved that the petitioners "could not be heard formally against the Report of the Board of Trade." When the petitioners were "called in" to be informed of the resolution Thomas Walpole "proceeded to open the matter by reading a paper" in defence of their Memorial. The paper read by Walpole was the source of his *Observations on, and Answers to, the Foregoing Report,* a treatise of more than 70 pages published along with the Board *Report.*

Walpole's brilliant defence of the *Memorial* and information given by the parade of witnesses brought before the Committee by him caused the Committee of Council to act contrary to the Board's recommendation. On July 1, 1772, they recommended that the King act favorably upon the Petition of the Grand Ohio or Walpole Company. On August 14 the King issued "Orders for carrying into execution the proposals of the Committee report of July 1" (Acts of the Privy Council, VI, 202-09). By May 6, 1773, Lord Dartmouth, who had succeeded Hillsborough as president of the Board of Trade, observed to the King in Council that the Board had complied with his order of August 14, 1772, and had prepared "a plan for establishing a separate government on the said tract," the Walpole purchase. Chief among the recommendations in the plan was: "That the lands comprehended within the boundaries described in the said report, should be separated from the colony of Virginia, and be created by letters patent, under the great seal of Great Britain, into a distinct colony, *under the name of Vandalia.*"

The King acted upon this report on May 19, 1773, and on July 3, the Committee of Council ordered "his Majesty's Attorney and Solicitor General . . . [to] prepare and lay before that Committee, *a draught* of a proper instrument, to be passed under the Great Seal of Great Britain, containing a grant to you Memorialist Thomas Walpole and others his associates, of the lands prayed for by their Memorial. . . . " Edward Thurlow, attorney general, and Alexander Wedderburn, solicitor general, opposed the grant and succeeded in delaying action upon it until friction between the mother country and her colonies made such action infeasible, Dr. Alvord remarked: "The stubborn opposition of Thurlow and Wedderburn to the Ohio colony is even more inexplicable, if possible, than that of Lord Hillsborough" (*Mississippi Valley, op. cit.,* II, 160). Wedderburn, upon learning that Franklin had been responsible for the publication of Governor Hutchison's letters, bitterly denounced him. As a result he was relieved of his long held position as deputy post-master-general of the colonies. Lewis, *op. cit.,* p. 139.

Annotations

Recently, there has come to light a letter written by Franklin to Samuel Wharton, and at his request. By this letter of January 12, 1774, Franklin informed Wharton that since he was of the opinion that only Thurlow's opposition to him stood in the path of success of the Company, he would resign. Walpole returned this letter to him and on July 14, 1778, at Passy, France, Franklin added a memorandum which gave the reason for Thurlow's refusal to prepare the draught for the royal grant. According to Franklin, Thurlow believed that he, Franklin, was unworthy of any favors from the Crown. Franklin also stated that the resignation was but a ruse and that he was still a member of the Company.

On August 17, 1775, Samuel Wharton, believing he could not "be of any use in the further Application to Government for Lands on the River Ohio," closed the accounts of the members of the Walpole Company (Thomas Walpole to Benjamin Franklin, February 10, 1777, Franklin Papers, V, 1, no. 53). Finally, in the spring of 1775, the draught for the royal grant to the Company was prepared and presented to the Lord President of the Committee of Council, who suspended execution of the document until the revolution was over. In March, 1781, Benjamin Franklin and Samuel Wharton presented a Memorial to the United States Congress offering to pay for the land at the same rate they had offered the Crown (Wharton, *Plain Facts,* pp. 159-60). The decision as to preemption rights to lands ceded to England by the Indians had obliterated the claims of the Grand Ohio Company and other similar groups, and the plans made for the public lands acquired by the government by this decision did not include disposal of the great tracts in parcels of over two million acres each.

787. Neither the *Journals of the Board of Trade* nor the *Acts of the Privy Council* projects October 25, 1771, as a day upon which a final decision was to be made about the Walpole Grant.

788. An advertisement signed by James Mercer appears in Purdie and Dixon's *Virginia Gazette,* December 5, 1771, for "A meeting of of the Company very necessary, and as soon as may be." The meeting was advertised for Stafford Courthouse on December 16.

789. The notice included a request for "Any Member who has Letters from my Brother on the Subject of the Company is requested to bring or send them to the Meeting."

790. See *Chronology,* July 4, 1763.

Annotations

791. These enclosures are missing.

792. Evidently Arthur Dobbs' share (*note* 781) and a part of his father's interest. See *Chronology*, Release . . . 1759.

793. George Mercer, in his letter to George Mason, August 8, 1771, (*op. cit.*), remarked that he did not believe the clear thinking members of the Company could condemn him "for demanding one Clear Answer to all the Letters I have wrote for eight years past to my Friends, my Relatives, my Acquaintances, the Committee of the Company, and the Company at large, concerning the Agentcy the Company appointed me to, on the 3d of July 1763, giving me full Power and Authority to Act for them as Seemed best to me."

794. In 1767 the Earl of Shelburne, secretary of state for the southern department, sponsored "an idea of forming, '*at the the expense of the crown,*' three *new governments* in North America, viz. one at *Detroit* (on the waters between Lake Huron and Lake Erie); one in the *Illinois Country;* and one on the *lower* part of the River Ohio." —Great Britain. Board of Trade, *Report of the Lords Commissioners for Trade and Plantation, on the Petition of the Honorable Thomas Walpole and his Associates, for a Grant of Lands on the River Ohio in North America* (London [1772]), p. 34.

795. A George Mason holograph, four pages, 9 × 15 inches.

796. A notice, signed by George Mason and published in Purdie & Dixon's *Virginia Gazette,* March 5, 1772, summoned the members to a "Meeting of the Ohio Company, upon Business of the utmost Importance, at *Stafford* Courthouse, on *Monday* the 30th of this Instant (March)."

797. See *Chronology,* Resolution, October 17, 1760.

798. George Mercer withdrew the Ohio Company's caveat against the Walpole Company in lieu of two shares of their stock (see *note* 785). By his Memorial of May 8, 1770, George Mercer withdrew not only his caveat of December 18, 1769, but also all other Company memorials and petitions which they had had presented to the King in Council from time to time.

799. George Mercer's Memorial . . . , December 18, 1769, printed in *Case* . . . , *facs.,* pp. 35-36.

Annotations

800. According to the "Articles of Agreement and Copartnership ... May 23, 1751," the stock of the Company was to be held in common for twenty years, after which time the property was to be divided into 20 equal parts. Each of the 20 shareholders would have had 10,000 acres, their share of the land.

801. The Company's right to 300,000 acres additional land was contingent upon fulfillment of certain conditions set forth in the John Hanbury petition of January 11, 1749. See *Chronology*.

802. A Pearson Chapman holograph, one page, 6¼ × 8 inches. The answer to James Mercer's letter, January 9.

803. A Thomas Ludwell Lee holograph, two pages, 8 × 13 inches. The answer to James Mercer's letter, January 9.

804. A Thomas Ludwell Lee holograph, one page, 7¼ × 5¾ inches. The answer to James Mercer's letter, January 9.

805. A Philip Ludwell Lee holograph, one and one-half pages, 6 × 7½ inches. The answer to James Mercer's letter, January 9.

806. A composite, written in an unfamiliar hand, eight pages, 9 × 15 inches, endorsed in an unidentified hand. The format gives credence to the hypothesis that James Mercer compiled this document and sent it to his brother George in London.

807. The original letter is not in this George Mercer collection.

808. Probably reports of the Board of Trade.

809. George Mason advertised "A Meeting of the Ohio Company, upon Business of the utmost importance at Stafford Courthouse, on Monday the 30th of this Instant." —*Virginia Gazette,* March 5, 1772.

810. The original letter is not in this George Mercer collection.

811. *Ibid.*

812. A small piece of paper, 2⅝ × 7¼ inches. All signatures are autographs.
    At this time the Company was mustering its entire strength. On

· 672 ·

Annotations

April 15 the Board of Trade had submitted to the Committee of Council a favorable report on the Company's Memorial. The Committee of Council accepted the Board's recommendations (July 1) and submitted their report to the king, who ordered "a plan for establishing a separate government upon the said tract, in such form and manner, and under such restrictions and regulations as they should judge proper and expedient...." —Thomas Walpole, *Memorial of ...* [and others], August, 1774, *op. cit.*

813. Holograph, one page, 8¾ × 7⅜. Probably a routine letter. It is likely that Mr. Wharton would inform each member of the governmental decision on their memorial; also, solicit each member's approbation of his contemplated action on the matter.

By August 20 Lord Hillsborough who opposed the grant had resigned and the Company believed that the successful culmination of their efforts was near. Although Benjamin Franklin, who attributed Hillsborough's resignation to his humiliation by the "Committee of Council's Approbation of our Grant in Opposition to his Report," believed that Lord Dartmouth's acceptance of Hillsborough's post was the assurance of success of the Walpole enterprise; yet he warned his friend Joseph Galloway, "Don't let us yet be too sanguine [in our] Expectations of the Grant. There is a great deal before the Business is compleated, and many Things happen between Cup and Lip." —Holograph, dated August 22, 1772, in the New York Public Library.

814. In P.R.O., C.O. 5: 27/311.

815. The Board of Trade's report, dated July 1, 1772, is summarized in Thomas Walpole, *Memorial*, August, 1774, *op. cit.*, pp. 5-8.

816. One page, 9 × 15 inches, signed by Thomas Walpole, endorsed by George Mercer. This is a personal communication to George Mercer. Since the Ohio Company held the same amount of Walpole Company stock, this personal communication is included in this collection, in the absence of a like statement which must have been delivered to Mercer, the Ohio Company's representative.

817. George Croghan was the Walpole Company's representative in the West. —Alvord, *Mississippi Valley, op. cit.*, II, 113.

818. One page, 8 × 13 inches, signed by Samuel Wharton. This document is indicative of the end of Samuel Wharton's services for

Annotations

the Grand Ohio Company. The last entry in the statement, August 17, 1776, coincides with Thomas Walpole's remark to Benjamin Franklin which is as follows: "Mr. Wharton having signified to me by Letter that in the present unhappy Situation of Affairs in America he apprehends he cannot be of any use in the further Application to Government for Lands on the River Ohio, he therefore finally closed his Account on the 17^{t} August last against myself & Associates." —Holograph, February 10, 1777. Franklin Papers, V, 1, no. 53, in the American Philosophical Society, Philadelphia, Pennsylvania.

BIBLIOGRAPHY

PRIMARY SOURCES

LEGEND

§ Indicates manuscript material consulted.
BP = Bouquet, *Papers of* (Stevens and Kent edition).
CHS = Chicago Historical Society.
DHNY = *Documentary History of the State of New York.*
DP = *Dinwiddie Papers.*
GW(Fitzpatrick) = Washington, *Writings* (Fitzpatrick edition).
HSP = Historical Society of Pennsylvania, Philadelphia, Pa.
JHB = Virginia. House of Burgesses, *Journal.*
LC = Library of Congress.
MA = *Archives of Maryland.*
MHR = Maryland. Hall of Records, Annapolis, Md.
Miller-Surrey = Carnegie Institution of Washington. Calendar . . . .
NYCD = *Documents Relative to the Colonial History of New York.*
NYPL = New York Public Library, New York City.
PA = *Pennsylvania Archives.*
PCR = Pennsylvania (Colony) *Minutes of the Provincial Council.*
PM = *Pennsylvania Magazine of History and Biography.*
PPL = Philadelphia Public Library.
PRO CO = Public Record Office. Colonial Office.
VCJ = Virginia (Colony) Executive Council, *Journals.*
VHS = Virginia Historical Society, Richmond, Va.
VM = *Virginia Magazine of History and Biography.*
VSL = Virginia. State Library, Richmond, Va.
VSP = Virginia, *Calendar of State Papers.*
W(1) = *William and Mary College Quarterly*, first series.
WCL = William L. Clements Library, Univ. of Michigan, Ann Arbor.
WHC = Wisconsin (State) Historical Society, Collections.

MANUSCRIPT COLLECTIONS

Search for material relating to this study was made in the manuscripts' divisions of the libraries listed below. The manuscripts found to be pertinent are cited in the section of the bibliography, *Calendar of Communications,* which follows this section.

The libraries are: American Philosophical Society; Carnegie Library of Pittsburgh; College of William and Mary; Colonial Williamsburg; Detroit Public Library; Duke University; Harvard University; Henry E. Huntington Library and Art Gallery; Historical Society of Pennsylvania; Library of Congress; Massachusetts Historical Society; New York Historical Society; New York Public Library; Pennsylvania Historical and Museum Commission; Pennsylvania State Library; Philadelphia Free Library, including Ridgway Branch; Quebec Literary and Historical Society; Seminary of Quebec; Virginia Historical Society; Virginia State Library; William L. Clements Library, University of Michigan.

Bibliography

CALENDAR OF COMMUNICATIONS

1682 March 23   Extracts of the Opinions Rendered at the Conference Held at the House of the Jesuit Fathers on the Subject of the News Received from the Iroquois, printed in *NYCD*, IX, 168-73.

1686 *ca.*   Extract from a Letter Written to Count de Pontchartrain, printed in *WHC*, XVI, 127-30.

1687 Feb. 19   Thomas Dongan to the Earl of Sunderland, printed in *NYCD*, III, 510-12.

1700 Aug. 29   Ratification and Confirmation of the Treaty of 1698, printed in *MA*, XXV, 104-06.

1701 April 23   Articles of Agreement Between William Penn and the Indians Living Along the Susquehanna, printed in *PCR*, II, 15-18.

1702 April 19   Father Jean Mermet to Monthe de Cadillac, printed in *WHC*, XVI, 211-13.

1706 Aug. 27   Father Joseph Marest to Vaudreuil, Governor of Montreal, *ibid.*, 238-39.

1722 Sept. 12   Conference between Alexander Spotswood and the Five Nations, August 29–September 12, printed in *NYCD*, V, 669-77.

1729 June 24   Checochinican to Patrick Gordon, printed in *PA*, I, 239-40.

1730 Aug. 21   Indian Complaint Against J. Miranda, August 21, 1720 [1730], *ibid.*, 266-67.

1732 April 22   Extract of the Yearly Instructions of the King and Minister to the Governor and Intendant of New France, printed in *WHC*, XVII, 154-59.

        30   William Beverley to a Friend, printed in *VSP*, I, 217-18.

1733 July 13   William Gooch to Gordon, printed in *PCR*, III, 564.

    Oct. 14   Extract of the Official Yearly Report of Beauharnois and Hocquart to the French Minister, printed in *WHC*, XVII, 184-87.

1734 May 1   Indian Letter Respecting Indian Traders, printed in *PA*, I, 425.

1736 Dec. 20   James Logan to Samuel Ogle, printed in *MA*, XXVIII, 271-72.

1737 Aug. 8   Beverley to James Patton, printed in *W*(1), III, 226.

        22   Same to same, *ibid.*, 226-27.

1738 Aug. 4   Newcomer, King of the Shawnee to the Governor of Virginia, printed in *VSP*, I, 231-32.

Bibliography

1739   Aug. 1   Confirmation of Articles of Agreement between Penn and the Shawnee, April 23, 1701, printed in *PCR*, IV, 346-47.

Dec. 20   Report of the Lords of Trade to the Lords of the Privy Council, printed in *NYCD*, VI, 156-57.

1740   Aug. 26   Father de la Richardie to Father St. Pé, extract, printed in *WHC*, XVII, 328-29.

Oct. 1   Letter from Beauharnois to the French Minister, *ibid.*, 329-35.

1741   June 12   "Memorandum of what occurred in The Affair of the hurons of Detroit with the Outaouacs, Poutoüatamis, Sauteux and Mississagués of that Post," August 12, 1738–June 12, 1741, *ibid.*, 279-88.

14   Beauharnois to Father de la Richardie, *ibid.*, 348-50.

1742   July 12   Minutes of a Conference Held Between the Six Nations and the Shawnee and Pennsylvania, July 2–12, 1742, printed in *PCR*, IV, 560-86; also in Colden, . . . *Five Nations*, II, 1-44.

Oct. 5   "Proclamation of Gov. Thomas Ag'st Settlers on Lands in Lancaster, 1742," printed in *PA*, I, 629-30; also a broadside in Darlington Memorial Library.

Dec. 18   § Patton to Gooch. Peters Papers, I, 110, HSP.

23   § Same to same. *Ibid.*, 111.

1743   Navarre's Report to Pierre Joseph de Céloron, French Commandant at Detroit, 1743, extract, printed in Hanna, *Wilderness Trail*, I, 315-18.

Feb. 8   § Gooch to George Thomas. Peters Papers, I, 109, HSP.

9   Conrad Weiser's Report of his Journey to Shamokin, January 30–February 9, 1743, printed in *PCR*, IV, 640-46.

March 9   § Weiser to Levin Gale. Peters Papers, II, 5, HSP; printed in *MA*, XXVIII, 293-95.

10   § Gale to Weiser. *Ibid.*, I, 115; *ibid.*, XXVIII, 295-96.

April 4   § Thomas Cresap to Shegelama [Shickellamy]. *Ibid.*, I, 118.

21   Weiser's Report of his Second Journey to Shamokin on the Affairs of Virginia and Maryland, printed in *PCR*, IV, 646-50.

25   Thomas to Gooch, printed in *PCR*, IV, 653-54.

May 7   Gooch to Thomas, *ibid.*, 654-55.

June 3   § Gale to Weiser. Peters Papers, I, 119, HSP.

15   § "Statement of Sconohode, king of the Keyouekeas or Sinnacas, by Interpreter, Michael Webster." *Ibid.*, 122.

Bibliography

1744 Jan. 11 § Gooch to Thomas. *Ibid.*, II, 1.
        20 § Thomas to Gooch. *Ibid.*, 2.
        20 § Weiser to Thomas Bladen. *Ibid.*
        25 § Bladen to Weiser. *Ibid.*, 3.
   March 24 § ―――― to the Six Nations. *Ibid.*, 6.
   May 2 Conrad Weiser, Report of his Journey to Shamokin, printed in *PCR*, IV, 680-85.
       24 § Richard Peters to Weiser. Peters Papers, II, 11, HSP.
   June 4 § Same to same. *Ibid.*, 12, HSP.
       11 § Same to same. *Ibid.*, 14, HSP.
       12 Edmund Jennings to Lord Baltimore, printed in *MA*, XLII, 665-67.
       15 "Journal of William Black," May 17–June 15, printed in *PM*, I, 117-32, 233-49, 404-19; II, 40-49.
       30 Release of Six Nations Land to Maryland, printed in *MA*, XXVIII, 334-37.
   Sept. 29 Weiser to Logan, printed in *PA*, I, 661-63.

1745 May 14 § Thomas to Weiser. Peters Papers, II, 30, HSP.
       14 § Deposition of Three Traders George Croghan, Peter Tostee, and James Dunning Made Before Edward Shippen of Philadelphia. *Ibid.*, 31-32. Includes both Shippen's first draft and final copy.
       19 Extract of Weiser's Report of his Journey to Onontago, May 19, 1745, printed in *PCR*, IV, 778-82.
   June 25 § Peters to Thomas Penn. Peters Papers, II, 36, HSP.
   Oct. 28 Beauharnois to the French Minister, Extract, printed in *NYCD*, X, 19-21.

1747 May 1 Indian Letter to President and Council, printed in *PA*, I, 737.
   July 20 Weiser to Peters, *ibid.*, 761-62.
   Oct. 15 Same to same, printed in *PCR*, V, 136-39.
   Nov. 2 Memoir of M. de Raymond to the French Minister, printed in *WHC*, XVII, 474-77.
       6 § Gooch to the Board of Trade. PRO CO 5: 1326/547-54.
       28 Weiser to Peters, printed in *PCR*, V, 166-67.
   Dec. 21 Extracts from the Diary of Events for the Year 1747 Sent by the Governor and Intendant of New France to the French Minister, November 8–December 21, 1747, printed in *NYCD*, X, 137-48.

Bibliography

1748	Jan. 19	§	Board of Trade to the Duke of Newcastle. PRO CO 5: 1366/410.
	19	§	———— to Gooch. *Ibid.*, 408-09.
	Feb. 10	§	Order of the King in Council Referring an Extract of Gooch's Letter, November 6, 1747, to the Committee of Council for Plantation Affairs. PRO PC Register 2: 100/540.
	13	§	Thomas Lee to Weiser. Peters Papers, II, 89, HSP.
	18		Pennsylvania Provincial Council's *Proclamation*, Strictly Charging and Commanding no Person or Persons to Trade with the Indians Without First Obtaining a License from the Governor and the Commander-in-Chief, printed in *PCR,* V, 194-96.
	23	§	Order of the Committee of Council Referring an Extract of Gooch's Letter to the Board of Trade. PRO CO 5: 1327/1, endorsement 16; PRO PC Register 2: 100/551.
	March 7		Gooch to Palmer, printed in *PCR,* V, 221-22.
	May 9		Same to same, *ibid.*, 257-58.
	June 16	§	Gooch to the Board of Trade. PRO CO 5: 1327/7-8, endorsement, 10.
	July 28	§	Peters to Penn. Penn Official Correspondence, IV, 143, HSP.
	Sept. 2	§	Report of the Board of Trade to the Committee of Council for Plantation Affairs, on Gooch's Letter of November 6, 1747. PRO CO 5: 1366/411-17.
	29		The Journal of Conrad Weiser, Indian Interpreter to Ohio, printed in *PCR,* V, 348-58.
	Oct. 20		William Trent to Peters, printed in *PA,* II, 16-17.
	23		La Galissonière to the French Minister, printed in *NYCD,* X, 181-85.
	Nov. 24	§	Order of the Committee of Council for Plantation Affairs to the Board of Trade, Approving Their Report of September 2. PRO PC Register 2: 101/117-18; CO 5: 1327/21, endorsement, 32.
	24	§	Peters to Penn. Penn Official Correspondence, IV, 167, HSP.
	Dec. 13	§	Final Report of the Board of Trade to the Committee of Council on Gooch's Letter of November 7, 1747, with an "Additional Instruction" to Gooch. PRO CO 5: 1366/421-26.
1749			"An Extract from the Proprietarie's Letter," printed in *PCR,* V, 515.

Bibliography

Jan. 11 § Order of the King in Council Referring John Hanbury's Petition to the Committee of Council. PRO PC Register 2: 101/145.

Feb. 9 § Order of the Committee of Council Referring John Hanbury's Petition to the Board of Trade. PRO CO 5: 1327/51-70; ——— PC Register 2: 101/184-86.

20 § Penn to Peters. Penn Letter Book, II, 253-56, HSP.

23 § Report of the Committee of Council Based on a Report of the Board of Trade. PRO PC Register 2: 101/189-92.

23 § Lawrence Washington ₁and others₁ to a Member of the Ohio Company. Emmett Collection, no. 14853, NYPL.

23 § Report of the Board of Trade to the Committee of Council, on John Hanbury's Petition. PRO CO 5: 1366/427-33.

March 4 § Board of Trade to Gooch. *Ibid.*, 439-44.

16 § Order of the King in Council to Have the "Draught of the Additional Instruction" to Gooch Prepared for His Signature. PRO PC Register 2: 101/215-16; ——— CO 5: 1327/93-94.

June 1 § Thomas Lee to Members of the Ohio Company. Emmett Collection, no. 6214, NYPL.

July 3 Croghan to Peters, printed in *PA*, II, 31.

18 Hamilton's Proclamation Agreeable to the Request of the Seneca Deputies [of the Six Nations], at the last Treaty, warning settlers to remove themselves from lands west of the Blue Hills, printed in *PCR*, V, 394-95.

31 § Penn to James Hamilton. Penn Letter Book, II, 270-74, HSP.

(fall of) George Washington to Mrs. Lawrence Washington, printed in *GW*(Fitzpatrick), I, 18.

Oct. 18 § Lee to the Board of Trade. PRO CO 5: 1327/195-97.

26 § Peters to the Proprietors. Penn Official Correspondence, IV, 243-49.

Nov. 22 Lee to Hamilton, printed in *PCR*, V, 422-23.

Dec. 20 Same to same, *ibid.*, 423-24.

1750 Jan. 2 § Hamilton to Lee. Penn Official Correspondence, IV, 177.

Feb. 27 § Lee to Weiser. Peters Papers, III, 5, HSP.

March 19 § Bill of Sale of Hugh Parker in Behalf of the Ohio Company. Frederick Co., Maryland, Deeds B., ff. 343-44, 347-48, MHR.

May 17 Minutes of a Conference Held with the Indians at Croghan's, printed in *PCR*, V, 431-36.

27 George Mason to Lawrence Washington, printed in Mon-

Bibliography

cure Conway, *Barons of the Potomac and Rappahannock*, 280-81.

29   A Message from the Twightwees to Hamilton, printed in *PCR*, V, 437-38.

June 12   § Lee to the Board of Trade. PRO CO 5: 1327/187-89.

21   § ——— to Weiser. Peters Papers, III, 9, HSP.

July   § John Hamer in Account with the Ohio Company, by Hugh Parker. MS in Darlington Memorial Library.

2   "The Report of Richard Peters . . . of the Proceedings against sundry Persons settled in the unpurchased Part of the Province . . . ," printed in *PCR*, V, 440-49.

10   § Peters to Penn. Penn Official Correspondence, V, 29-35, HSP.

Sept. 3   George Clinton to Hamilton, printed in *PCR*, V, 462.

25   Sir William Johnson to Clinton, *ibid.*, 480-82.

[Oct.]   The Examinations of Morris Turner and Ralph Kilgore, *ibid.*, 482-84.

Oct. 8   Clinton to Hamilton, *ibid.*, 480.

10   "A Journal of the Proceedings of Conrad Weiser in his Journey to Onondago, with a Message from the Honourable Thomas Lee, Esquire, President of Virginia, to the Indians there," August 15–October 1, *ibid.*, 470-80.

Dec. 16   Croghan to Hamilton, *ibid.*, 496-98.
(*i.e.* Nov.)

1751   Feb. 24   § Penn to Peters. Penn Letter Book, III, 37-55, HSP.

April 22   Weiser to Hamilton, printed in *PCR*, V, 517-18.

25   Hamilton's Instructions to Croghan and Montour, *ibid.*, 518-22.

May 23   § "Articles of Agreement and Copartnership for the Ohio Company for the Space of Twenty Years, May 23, 1751," photostat in VHS.

30   "An Account of the Proceedings of George Croghan, Esquire, and Mr. Andrew Montour at Ohio, in the Execution of the Governor's Instructions to deliver the Provincial Present to the several Tribes of Indians settled there," May 18–30, 1751, printed in *PCR*, V, 530-39.

30   "A Treaty with the Indians of the Six Nations, Delawares, Shawonese, Owendatts and Twightwees, at Log's Town on Ohio," May 28–30, 1751, *ibid.*, 532-39.

July 10   "Mr. Weiser's Journal of his Proceedings at Onondago," June 27–July 10, *ibid.*, 541-43.

Bibliography

	Sept. 10	§ Robert Dinwiddie's Memorial to the Board of Trade. PRO CO 5: 1327/417-19.
	16	§ James Patton's Account with Virginia. Colonial Papers, VSL.
	28	§ Penn to Peters. Penn MSS, Saunders-Coates, p. 47, HSP.
	Oct. 1	De Raymond to Rouillé, printed in *WHC*, XVIII, 94-98.
	Dec. 27	Cresap to Dinwiddie. *VSP*, I, 245-47.
1752	Jan. 20	§ Dinwiddie to the Board of Trade. PRO CO 5: 1327/453-54.
	23	——— to Cresap, printed in *DP*, I, 17-19.
	Feb. 8	Croghan to Hamilton, printed in *PCR*, V, 568-69.
	8	The Shawnee to Hamilton, *ibid.*, 569-70.
	20	§ Cresap to Weiser. Weiser Correspondence, I, 38, HSP.
	March 18	§ Penn to Peters. Penn Papers, Saunders-Coates, p. 55, HSP.
	April	Minute of Instructions to be given to Marquis Duquesne, printed in *NYCD*, X, 242-45.
	1	§ Cresap to Weiser. Peters Papers, III, 55, HSP.
	18	Hamilton to Andrew Montour, "Memorandum," printed in *PCR*, V, 568.
	21	[*i.e. ca.* May 17] Longueuil to Rouillé, printed in *NYCD*, X, 245-251.
	24	Hamilton to Croghan, printed in *PCR*, V, 570.
	24	——— to the Shawnee, *ibid.*, 571.
	May 15	Rouillé to Duquesne, printed in *WHC*, XVIII, 118-22.
	June 8	§ French Minister [of War] to Vaudreuil, calendared in Miller-Surrey, II, 1199.
	11	Hamilton to Clinton, printed in *PCR*, V, 575.
	13	§ Joshua Fry, Lunsford Lomax and James Patton to William Trent. Etting Collection, Revolutionary Papers, p. 90, HSP; copy in PRO CO 5: 1327/575-612.
	13	§ Minutes of the Logstown Conference. PRO CO 5: 1327/575-612; variant printed in *VM*, XIII, 143-74.
	21	§ Twightwees to Dinwiddie. PRO CO 5: 1327/561-62; printed in *JHB, 1752–58*, p. 509.
	21	§ Picks and Windaws to Dinwiddie. PRO CO 5: 1328/563-64; printed in *ibid.*, p. 510.
	Aug. 30	Robert Callender to Hamilton, printed in *PCR*, V, 599-600.
	Oct. 6	Dinwiddie to the Board of Trade, printed in William Trent's *Journal, 1752* (Goodman), pp. 69-72.

Bibliography

Nov. 11   Dinwiddie's Speech to the Emperor of the Cherokees, printed in *VCJ*, V, 413-14.

29   § Board of Trade to Dinwiddie. PRO CO 5: 1366/516-33.

Dec. 5   § Robert Carter's Purchase of Gawin Corbin's Ohio Company's Stock. Washington Collection, CHS.

10   § Dinwiddie to the Board of Trade. PRO CO 5: 1327/531-34, printed in Trent's *Journal, 1752,* pp. 73-81.

1753   § James Patton to John Blair. Draper Collection, no. 1QQ, pp. 75-77, WHS.

Feb. 10   Dinwiddie to Cresap, printed in *DP,* I, 22-24.

March 26   Johnson to Clinton, printed in *DHNY,* II, 624-25.

April 10   § Trent to Hamilton. PRO CO 5: 1065/59; extract, printed in Hanna, II, 230-31.

May 6   Hamilton to Dinwiddie, printed in *PCR,* V, 628-30.

15   § Andrew Montour's "Declaration" Relative to his Journey to Onondago in Behalf of Virginia. PRO CO 5: 13/621-22; printed in *JHB, 1752–58,* pp. 515-16.

22   § Dinwiddie to the Cherokees and Catawbas. PRO CO 5: 1327/653-56.

24   § ——— to the Six Nations. *Ibid.,* 651-52.

31   § ——— to the Emperor of the Cherokees. *Ibid.,* 655.

June 2   § Receipt for Payment by Robert Carter for Augustine Washington's Shares in the Ohio Company. Washington Collection, CHS.

9   Alexander McGinty [and others] to Robert Sanders, mayor of Albany, printed in *PCR,* V, 627.

22   The Half King to Dinwiddie, *ibid.,* 635.

July 7   Clinton to Hamilton, *ibid.,* 625-26.

26   Catawbas to Dinwiddie. *VSP,* I, 248-49.

Aug. 10   § Order of the Privy Council Directing Ordinance to be Sent to Virginia. PRO CO 5: 1328/1-8.

20   Half King's Speech to the French at Fort Le Boeuf, printed in Washington's *Journal . . . of 1753,* pp. 9-10.

20   Duquesne to Rouillé, printed in *NYCD,* X, 255-57.

28?   § Royal Orders and Instructions to Dinwiddie. PRO CO 5:1344/unpaged.

28   § Holdernesse's Instructions to Dinwiddie. PRO CO 5: 211/43.

28   ——— Instructions to Hamilton, printed in *PCR,* V, 689-90.

Bibliography

Sept. 14 § "William Trent's Account of his Proceedings with the six Nations of Indians & their allies at Logstown, July 11–September 14, 1753." PRO CO 5: 1328/15-40.

17 § "William Fairfax's Narrative of the Proceedings at a Conference Held at Winchester." PRO CO 5: 1328/48-72.

Oct. 12 Deposition of Alexander McGinty, printed in *PCR*, V, 663-64.

12 James Glen to Hamilton, *ibid.*, 699-700.

Nov. 17 § Dinwiddie to the Board of Trade. PRO CO 5: 1328/21.

1754 Jan. A Speech Delivered by the Half King, printed in *PCR*, V, 734.

10 "Deposition of Stephen Coffen," printed in *NYCD*, VI, 835-37.

26 Dinwiddie's Commission of Major John Carlyle, printed in *DP*, I, 54.

27 Dinwiddie to Trent, *ibid.*, 55-56.

[Jan. 27] Instructions to be Observed by Major George Washington, on the Expedition to the Ohio, *ibid.*, 59.

29 § Dinwiddie to the Board of Trade. PRO CO 5: 1328/97-100.

29 Dinwiddie's Message to the Catawbas, *DP*, I, 60-61.

29 ———— to James Hamilton, *ibid.*, 63-64.

ca. 29 ———— to James Glen, *ibid.*, 61-63.

ca. 29 ———— to the Acting Governor of North Carolina, Matthew Rowan, *ibid.*, 64-65.

ca. 29 ———— to James de Lancey, *ibid.*, 65-66.

ca. 29 ———— to Acting Governor of Maryland, Benjamin Tasker, *ibid.*, 67-68.

ca. 29 ———— to Jonathan Belcher, *ibid.*, 68-69.

ca. 29 ———— to William Shirley, *ibid.*, 69-71.

Feb. La Force's Speech to Indians at Logstown, printed in *PCR*, VI, 22.

Six Nations' Answer to La Force, *ibid.*

2 George Croghan's Journal, January 12–February 2, 1754, printed in *PCR*, V, 731-35.

3 Croghan to Hamilton, printed in *PA*, II, 119-20.

9 Dinwiddie to James Abercrombie, *DP*, I, 71-73.

March Dinwiddie's Instructions to Joshua Fry, *ibid.*, 88-90.

ca. 12 Peters to Hamilton, printed in *PCR*, V, 760-61.

22 Deposition of John Trotter, printed in *PA*, II, 131-32.

Bibliography

22 § Deposition of Jacob Evans Before Chief Justice of Pennsylvania, William Allen. Du Simitiere Collection, Yi 966 f, no. 35, PPL.

23 Croghan to Hamilton, printed in *PCR*, VI, 21.

28 § Ohio Company's Petition to the King in Council. PRO CO 5: 1328/153-61.

April 2 § Order of the Committee of Council Referring the Petition of the Ohio Company to the Board of Trade, *ibid.*

8 § Trent's Account with Virginia. Colonial Papers, 1740–59, VSL.

18 "A Speech sent from the Half King Scruneyattha, and the Belt of Wampum to the Governor of Virginia and Governor of Pennsylvania," printed in *PCR*, VI, 31.

18 Same, printed in Washington's *Journal . . . 1754* (Toner ed.), pp. 37-39.

19 Dinwiddie to the King, Head Men, and Warriors of the Catawbas, printed in *DP*, I, 131-32.

19 ———— to the Emperor, King of Chote, and Warriors of the Great Nation of the Cherokees, *ibid.*, 132.

19 ———— to . . . Warriors of the Cherokees, *ibid.*, 133.

ca. 20 § George Washington to Hamilton. MS in Darlington Memorial Library, printed in *PCR*, VI, 28-29.

27 Dinwiddie to ————, *ibid.*, 31-32.

May 4 Dinwiddie to Washington, printed in *DP*, I, 148-49.

7 § Edward Ward's Deposition. PRO CO 5: 14/293.

19 Washington's Speech to the Half King, printed in Washington's *Journal . . . 1754* (Toner ed.), pp. 66-67.

29 Washington to Dinwiddie, printed in *DP*, I, 176-82.

June 1 Dinwiddie to Cresap, *ibid.*, 185-86.

1 ———— to Washington, *ibid.*, 186-87.

3 Washington to Dinwiddie, printed in *GW* (Fitzpatrick), I, 71-74.

10 Same to same, *ibid.*, 74-76.

18 Dinwiddie to Sir Thomas Robinson, printed in *DP*, I, 201-05.

20 ———— to James de Lancey, *ibid.*, 216-18.

25 § Report of the Board of Trade to the Committee of Council for Plantation Affairs. PRO CO 5: 1367/76-87.

July 3 § Articles of the Capitulation of Fort Necessity. Original in Palais de Justice, Montreal, Canada; printed in *PA*, II, 146-47.

Bibliography

	5	Dinwiddie to John Carlyle, printed in *DP*, I, 231.
	5	——— to Abraham Smith, *ibid.*, 231-32.
	6	§ "Thomas Penn's Expense Account." Penn MSS, "Accounts," II, 15, HSP.
	20	Dinwiddie to Innes, printed in *DP*, I, 232-34.
	24	Varin to Bigot, printed in *Wilderness Chronicles of Northwestern Pennsylvania*, pp. 80-82.
	28	§ Robert Stobo to James Innes. MS in Darlington Memorial Library; printed in *PCR*, VI, 161-63.
	31	Dinwiddie to Hamilton, printed in *DP*, I, 255-57.
	31	——— to Sharpe, *ibid.*, 258-59.
Aug.	16	Croghan to Hamilton, *PCR*, VI, 140-41.
	22	Dinwiddie to Innes, printed in *DP*, I, 293.
	30	Same to same, *ibid.*, 296-98.
Sept.	6	"Journal of the Proceedings of Conrad Weiser in his Way to and at Aucquick, by Order of His Honour Governor Hamilton," August 24–September 6, 1754, printed in *PCR*, VI, 150-60.
	6	Dinwiddie to Sharpe, printed in *DP*, I, 303-06.
	10	——— to Lord Fairfax, *ibid.*, 312-13.
	18	——— to Innes, *ibid.*, 320-22.
	23	——— to Horace Walpole, *ibid.*, 343-45.
Oct.	5	Dinwiddie to Innes, printed in *DP*, I, 346-48.
	8	Duquesne to Rouillé, printed in *Wilderness Chronicles of Northwestern Pennsylvania*, p. 64.
	25	§ Lord Fairfax's Land Patents to George Mason, for Lots One, Five, Fourteen, Fifteen and Sixteen, Known as the New Store Tract. Northern Neck Grants, H, 1751–56, pp. 507-11. Land Office, Archives Division, VSL.
	29	Daniel Claus to Peters, printed in *PCR*, VI, 182-83.
	29	John Harris to Peters, *ibid.*, 184.
Nov.	12	Dinwiddie to Innes, printed in *DP*, I, 396-97.
Dec.	5	Croghan to Peters, printed in *PA*, II, 212-13.
	10	Sharpe to Dinwiddie, printed in *MA*, VI, 136-42.
	12	Dinwiddie to Innes, printed in *DP*, I, 422-23.
	17	——— to Horatio Sharpe, printed in *MA*, VI, 143-47.
	26	Sharpe to Dinwiddie, *ibid.*, 148-52.
	28	Harris to Edward Shippen, printed in *PA*, II, 230.
1755	Jan. 15	Dinwiddie to James Innes, printed in *DP*, I, 459-61.

Bibliography

	Feb. 12	—— to Sir Thomas Robinson, *ibid.*, 493-95.
	March 15	"Christopher Saur's First Letter to Governor Morris on the Trials and Wrongs of the Early German Immigrants," printed in Pennsylvania German Society, *Proceedings and Addresses,* X, 238-39.
	July 6	Duquesne to Vaudreuil, printed in *NYCD*, X, 300-02.
	24	Vaudreuil to Machault, *ibid.*, 306-09.
	Sept. 20	Dinwiddie to William Shirley, printed in *DP*, II, 208-10.
	25	Vaudreuil to Machault, printed in *NYCD*, X, 318-27.
	Oct. 1	—— to Sir Thomas Robinson, *DP*, II, 227-28.
	11	Washington to Dinwiddie, *ibid.*, 236-42.
	Nov. 4	Dinwiddie to Shirley, printed in *ibid.*, 261-62.
1756		Abstract of Dispatches from Canada, printed in *NYCD*, X, 423-28.
		§ Inventory of Ohio Company Goods in the Rock Creek Store House. MS in Library of Congress; printed in Hamilton, *Letters to Washington,* I, 362-64.
	Jan. 2	Dinwiddie to Sharpe, printed in *DP*, II, 308-09.
	23	—— to Washington, *ibid.*, 325-28.
	24	—— to Shirley, *ibid.*, 328-31.
	25	Lewis Evans to Richard Dodsley, printed in *PM*, LIX, 295-301.
	March 13	Dinwiddie to Sharpe, printed in *DP*, II, 367-68.
	25	§ Land Certificate, Plat and Patent to George Mason for a Tract of Land Called Walnut Bottom, Commissioners Land Office, Annapolis, Maryland. Books B. C. and G. S. no. 2, folio 400, MHR.
	April 19	§ Minutes of the Conference Between the Quakers and the Six Nations. MS, fragment of original in Darlington Memorial Library; printed in *An Account of Conferences . . .* , 65-77.
	June 4	Abstract of Dispatches (February 2–8) received from Canada, printed in *NYCD*, X, 407-10.
	12	M. de Montcalm to Count d'Argenson, printed in *NYCD*, X, 413-16.
	Aug. 8	Vaudreuil to Machault, printed in *NYCD,* X, 435-38.
	21	Dinwiddie to Washington, printed in *DP,* II, 484-85.
	Sept. 10	§ Sir William Johnson to the Lords of Trade, PRO CO 5: 284 / 44; printed in *DHNY,* II, 733-37.
	14	John Armstrong to William Denny, printed in *PA,* II, 767-73.

Bibliography

	Nov. 17	John M'Kinney's Description of Fort Duquesne, printed in *Olden Time,* I, 39-40.
	Dec. 11	Proprietors of Pennsylvania's "Observations on Sir William Johnson's Letter," printed in *DHNY,* II, 738-41.
1757	July	The Delawares' Bill of Complaints, Set Forth by George Croghan, *ibid.,* 761-62.
	12	Vaudreuil to de Moras, printed in *NYCD,* X, 580-84.
	13	Same to same, *ibid.,* 588-90.
	Aug. 14	Montcalm to Lord Loudoun, *ibid.,* 619-20.
	Sept. 28	Johnson to the Lords of Trade, *ibid.,* VII, 276-79.
	Oct. 30	Le Mercier's Memoir on the Artillery of Canada, *ibid.,* X, 655-56.
1758	Aug. 31	M. Doriel to Marshal de Belle Isle, *ibid.,* 818-20.
	Sept. 22	"Journal of Christian Frederick Post in his Journey from Philadelphia to the Ohio . . . ," July 15–September 22, printed in Thomson, 130-71.
	28	Vaudreuil to M. de Massiac, printed in *NYCD,* X, 923-25.
	Oct. 20	[Adjutant Malartic], "Journal of Occurrences in the Garrisons or Camps occupied by the Regiment of Béarn," October 20, 1757–October 20, 1758, *ibid.,* 835-55.
	26	Minutes of a Conference Held at Easton with the Indians, October 7–26, printed in *PCR,* VIII, 174-223.
	Nov. 27	John Forbes to William Pitt, printed in Forbes, *Writings,* pp. 267-68.
	Dec. 4	Minutes of a Conference Held by Colonel Bouquet with the Chiefs of the Delaware Indians at Pittsburgh, printed in *BP,* series 21655, pp. 18-21.
1759	March 1	Hugh Mercer to Bouquet, printed in *BP,* series 21644, I, 64-66.
	2	——— to Peters, printed in *PCR,* VIII, 305-06.
	2	——— to Bouquet, printed in *BP,* series 21644, I, 68-69.
	April 11	§ William Trent, "List of Papers Sent to Mr. Mercer by Capt. Robert Stewart." Society Collection (William Trent), HSP.
	12	Montcalm to De Belle Isle, printed in *NYCD,* X, 960-62.
	12	——— to M. le Normand, *ibid.,* 962-66.
	July 16	Minutes of a Conference Held at Pittsburgh, July 5–16, printed in *PCR,* VIII, 383-91.
	Aug. 19	Stanwix, Warrant Appointing George Mercer, Assistant Deputy Quarter Master General for Virginia and Maryland, *BP,* series 21652, pp. 220-21.

Bibliography

	20	Hugh Mercer to Bouquet, *ibid.*, series 21655, pp. 80-81.
	31	James Gunn to John Tulleken, *ibid.*, series 21644, I, 216-17.
	Sept. 16	George Mercer to George Washington, printed in Hamilton, III, 158-63.
	28	—— to Bouquet, printed in *BP*, series 21644, II, 121-27.
	28	Robert Stewart to Washington, printed in Hamilton, III, 163-70.
	Oct. 26	Minutes of Conferences Held at Pittsburgh, October 24–26, printed in *PCR*, VIII, 429-35.
	27	Mercer to John Stanwix, *BP*, series 21644, II, 172-75.
	29	Adam Stephen to Francis Fauquier, printed in *JHB*, 1758–61, pp. 280-81.
	Nov. 8	Journal of James Kenney, December 10, 1758–November 8, 1759, printed in *PM*, XXXVII, 395-449.
	28	George Mercer to Bouquet, printed in *BP*, series 21644, II, 201-02.
1760		Bouquet, "Articles Necessary for the Western Department in 1760," *ibid.*, series 21653, 46-47.
	Feb. 17	George Mercer to Washington, printed in Hamilton, III, 172-75.
	May 7	Fauquier to Hamilton, printed in *JHB*, 1758–61, p. 283.
	July 24	Cresap to Bouquet, printed in *BP*, series 21645, pp. 122-23.
	Sept. 1	§ Fauquier to the Lords of Trade. PRO CO 5: 1330/59; printed in *JHB*, 1758–61, pp. 287-89.
	12	Bouquet to Cresap, printed in *BP*, series 21653, pp. 23-24.
	Nov. 8	George Mercer to Trent, printed in *Ohio Company Papers*, pp. 347-48.
	Dec. 27	George Mercer to Bouquet, *ibid.*, 21645, pp. 252-54.
1761	Sept.	Minutes of a Conference Between Sir William Johnson and Several Nations of Indians at Detroit, printed in Johnson, *Papers*, III, 474-501.
	Oct. 31	Bouquet to James Livingston, printed in *BP*, series 21653, p. 87.
1762	Feb. 14	Livingston to Bouquet, *ibid.*, series 21648, I, 25.
	April 1	Bouquet to Jeffery Amherst, *ibid.*, series 21634, pp. 81-83.
1763		King Shingas to Bouquet, *ibid.*, series 21655, p. 261.
	Feb. 8	Simeon Écuyer to Bouquet, *ibid.*, series 21649, I, pp. 42-45.
	March 2	§ Petition of Veteran Virginia Militia for Compensation in Western Lands to Which They Were Entitled by Gover-

Bibliography

		nor Dinwiddie's Proclamation, February 19, 1754. Read at the Board of Trade, March 2, 1763. PRO CO 5: 1330/323-30.
	June 15	Journal of James Kenney, April 13, 1761–June 15, 1763, printed in *PM*, XXXVII, 2-47, 152-201.
	July 27	Livingston to Bouquet, printed in *BP,* series 21649, I, 241.
	Aug. 3	Écuyer to Bouquet, *ibid.*, II, 7-9.
	Oct. 7	Proclamation by the King (George III), printed in Canada. Archives, Documents edited by Shortt and Doughty, pp. 119-23.
	Dec. 14	Edward Shippen to John Penn, printed in *PCR*, IX, 89-90.
	27	Same to same, *ibid.*, 100.
1764	Feb. 13	§ Fauquier to the Lords of Trade. PRO CO 5: 1330/589-96.
	April 14	Deposition of Gershom Hicks, printed in *BP*, series 21650, I, 100-03.
	19	"A re-examination of Gershom Hicks," *ibid.*, 21651, 7.
1765	May 8	Treaty of Peace Concluded with the Delawares by Sir William Johnson, printed in *NYCD*, VII, 738-41.
	11	George Croghan's Journal of Transactions with the Indians at Fort Pitt, February 28–May 11, 1765, printed in *PCR*, IX, 250-64.
	June 8	Thos. Gage to Lord Halifax, printed in Gage Correspondence, I, 58-61.
1767	March 1	§ John Mercer to [James Tilghman], with George Mason's Statement of William Trent's Account. Cadwalader Papers, HSP.
	May 20	§ Thomas Cresap to [James Tilghman]. Society Collection, HSP.
	Sept. 25	§ George Mercer's acceptance of obligation from George Croghan. MS in HSP.
	Oct. 8	§ Lord Shelburne to Francis Fauquier. PRO CO 5: 1345/385-90.
	8	§ "Proceedings of the Ohio Company & Settlement on the Ohio." Shelburne Papers, L, 93-95, WCL.
	10	§ George Mercer to the Committee of the Ohio Company. Copy by Patrick Henry in LC.
	Nov. 21	George Mercer to the Committee of the Ohio Company, printed in *W*(1), I, 200-03.
	Dec. 7	Thomas Gage to John Penn, printed in *PCR*, IX, 403-04.
1768		"Journals of the Meetings of the Presidents and Masters

Bibliography

of the College of William and Mary," printed in *W*(1), I-V, various pages.

§ John Mercer's Ledger, *ca.* 1735–68. Note—This ledger is, for the most part, an account of legal fees, names of his clients, miles traveled in his practice, and the record of meetings of the Ohio Company which he attended; also, the distance he traveled to those meetings with an account of expenses incurred while on Ohio Company business. MS on permanent loan to the Virginia Historical Society. —Ed.

March 21 § John Blair to Lord Shelburne. PRO CO 5: 1346/13-16.

1769 "Lists of Early Land Patents and Grants Petitioned for in Virginia up to 1769, preserved among the Washington Papers," printed in *VM*, V, 175-80, 241-44.

Nov. 20 § Order of the Committee of Council Referring the Ohio Company Memorial to the Board of Trade. PRO CO 5: 1332/299-306.

1770 May 7 Certificate of Admission of the Ohio Company as a Co-purchaser of Two Shares of Grand Ohio Company Stock, printed in *American Historical Record*, III, 204-05.

June 26 Minutes of the Pennsylvania Board of Property, printed in *PA,* 3rd series, I, 300-304.

July 9 § John Pownall to Thomas Walpole, "Remarks Respecting the Granting of Lands Within the Colony of Virginia." PRO CO 5: 1333/385-403.

Oct. 18 § William Nelson to the Lords of Trade. PRO CO 5: 1348/321-32.

1771 March 5 § "Observations and Answers, humbly submitted To the Right Honorable the Lords Commissioners of Trade and Plantations, by Mr Walpole and his Associates, On the Extract of the Letter from Mr Nelson, President of the Council of Virginia, To the Earl of Hillsborough; dated the 18th of October 1770." PRO CO 5: 1333/365-384.

May 28 § George Mercer to Conway Richard Dobbs. Photostat in Arthur Dobbs Papers, State Department of Archives and History, Raleigh, N. C.

Aug. 8 § George Mercer to George Mason. Contemporary copy is no. 20624, MSS Collection, VSL.

14 "Orders for carrying into execution the proposals of the Committee report of 1 July, and for apprising the Indians of the intention to form a settlement on the lands purchased from them in 1768," printed in Walpole, *Memorial,* August 8, 1774, pp. 7-12.

1772 Aug. 22 § Benjamin Franklin to Joseph Galloway. MS in NYPL.

· 691 ·

Bibliography

1774   Jan. 12 § Franklin to Samuel Wharton. MS in NYPL.

        June 29   Minute of a Meeting Held With the Indians at Pittsburgh, printed in *PA*, IV, 531-33.

1777   Feb. 10 § Thomas Walpole to Franklin. Franklin Papers, V, 1, no. 53, American Philosophical Society, Philadelphia, Pa.

        March 5 § Same to same. *Ibid.*, V, 2, no. 91.

1778   July 14 § Franklin's Memorandum on his letter to Wharton, January 12, 1774. MS in NYPL.

        Nov. 20 § "Memorial of the Ohio Company." MS in VSL.

1783   July 5   § Robert Carter to Francis Fauquier, Jr. Carter Letter Books, V, 144, Duke University Library, Durham, N. C.

1791   Sept. 9   Minutes of the Pennsylvania Board of Property, printed in *PA*, 3rd series, I, 757-58.

1799   Nov. 15   Deposition of Charles Polke, printed in Jefferson, *Notes* . . . , p. 368.

1884   Oct. 9   § Morven M. Jones to Lyman C. Draper. Draper MSS, 3C 10, WHS.

        Sept. 29 § William R. Mercer to Draper. *Ibid.*, 3C 11, WHS.

1905   Oct. 12 § ———— to Mrs. Mary Darlington. MS in Darlington Memorial Library, University of Pittsburgh.

DOCUMENTARY SOURCE BOOKS, CONTEMPORARY ACCOUNTS, NEWSPAPERS.

An Account of Conferences Held and Treaties Made, between . . . Sir William Johnson, Bart. and the Chief Sachems and Warriours of the . . . Indian Nations. . . . London, A. Millar, 1756.

ANDREWS, CHARLES M., comp. *Guide to the Manuscript Materials for the History of the United States to 1783, in the British Museum, in Minor London Archives, and in the Libraries of Oxford and Cambridge.* By Charles M. Andrews and Frances G. Davenport. Washington, The Carnegie Institution of Washington, 1908. (Carnegie Institution of Washington. Publication No. 90.)

————. *Guide to the Materials for American History, to 1783, in the Public Record Office of Great Britain. . .* Washington, The Carnegie Institution of Washington, 1912–14. 2 vols. (Carnegie Institution of Washington. Publication No. 90A.)

Archives of Maryland. . . . Baltimore, Maryland Historical Society, 1883–date. 60 vols.

BOUQUET, HENRY. *The Papers of . . . . Prepared by Frontier Forts and Trails Survey. . . .* Edited by S. K. Stevens and D. H. Kent. Harrisburg, Pennsylvania Historical Commission, 1940–41. 19 vols.

BYRD, WILLIAM. *History of the Dividing Line, and Other Tracts.* From the

Bibliography

Papers of William Byrd, of Westover, in Virginia, Esquire. Richmond, Va., 1866. 2 vols. (*Historical Documents from the Old Dominion, Nos. 2-3.*)

Canada. Archives. *Documents Relating to the Constitutional History of Canada, 1759–1791.* Edited by Adam Shortt and Arthur G. Doughty. Ottawa, S. E. Dawson, 1907–35. 3 vols.

Carnegie Institution of Washington. *Division of Historical Research. Calendar of Manuscripts in Paris Archives and Libraries Relating to the History of the Mississippi Valley to 1803.* Edited by N. M. Miller Surrey (Mrs. F. M. Surrey). . . . Washington, D. C., the Author, 1926–28. 2 vols.

Case [of the Suffering Traders, 1763]. n.p., n.pub.

COLDEN, CADWALLADER. *The History of the Five Indian Nations.* London, 3rd ed., Lockyer Davis, 1755. 2 vols.

Conduct of the late Ministry: or, A Memorial: Containing a Summary of Facts with Their Vouchers, in Answer to the Observations, Sent by the English Ministry to the Courts of Europe. . . . London, W. Bizet, 1757.

Considerations on the Agreement of the Lords Commissioners of his Majesty's Treasury with the Honourable Thomas Walpole and the [his] Associates, for Lands upon the Ohio, in North America. [London, Jan. 7th, 1774. A.B.]. Ed. note—Although this pamphlet is attributed to Samuel Wharton, it may have been authored by Anselm Yates Bayly.

DINWIDDIE, ROBERT. *The Official Records of* . . . with an Introduction and Notes by R. A. Brock. Richmond, Virginia Historical Society, 1883. 2 vols. (Virginia Historical *Collections,* vols. 3 and 4.)

The Documentary History of the State of New-York: Arranged under the Direction of the Hon. Christopher Morgan. . . . By E. B. O'Callaghan. Albany, Weed, Parsons & co., 1849-51. 4 vols.

Documents Relating to the Colonial History of New Jersey. . . . v.p., v.pub., 1880–1929. 33 vols. (*Archives of the State of New Jersey, First series,* Vols. I-XXXIII.)

Documents Relative to the Colonial History of the State of New York. . . . Albany, Weed, Parsons and Company, printers, 1853–87. 15 vols.

EVANS, LEWIS. *Geographical, Historical, Political, Philosophical and Mechanical Essays. The First, Containing an Analysis of a General Map of the Middle British Colonies in America* . . . . Philadelphia, B. Franklin, and D. Hall, 1755.

———. *Geographical, Historical, Political, Philosophical and Mechanical Essays. Number II Containing a Letter Representing the Impropriety of Sending Forces to Virginia.* . . . *Published in the New York Mercury, No. 178, January 5, 1756, With an Answer to so Much Thereof as Concerns the Public.* Philadelphia, Printed for the Author, 1756. Reprinted in Lawrence H. Gipson's *Lewis Evans.* . . . Philadelphia, Historical Society of Pennsylvania, 1939.

FORBES, JOHN. *Writings of.* . . . Compiled and edited by A. P. James. Menasha, Wis., Collegiate Press, 1938.

Bibliography

Frontier Forts and Trails Survey. *Wilderness Chronicles of Northwestern Pennsylvania....* Edited by S. K. Stevens and D. H. Kent. Harrisburg, Pennsylvania Historical Commission, 1941.

GAGE, THOMAS. *The Correspondence of General Thomas Gage....* Compiled and Edited by Clarence Edwin Carter.... New Haven, Yale University Press; London, H. Milford, Oxford University Press, 1931–33. 2 vols. (*Yale Historical Publications. Manuscripts and Edited Texts,* Nos. 11-12.)

GALBREATH, CHARLES B., ed. *Expeditions of Céloron to the Ohio Country in 1749....* Columbus, Ohio, The F. J. Heer Printing Co., 1921. (Republished with additions from the *Ohio Archaeological and Historical Quarterly,* October, 1920.)

GIST, CHRISTOPHER. *Christopher Gist's Journals with Historical, Geographical, and Ethnological Notes and Biographies of his Contemporaries, by William M. Darlington.* Pittsburgh, J. R. Weldin & Co. 1893.

Great Britain. Board of Trade. *Journal of the Commissioners for Trade and Plantations....* Preserved in the Public Record Office... London, H. M. Stationery off., 1920–38. 15 vols.

――――. Board of Trade. *Report of the Lords Commissioners for Trade and Plantations on the Petition of the Honourable Thomas Walpole, Benjamin Franklin, John Sargent, and Samuel Wharton, Esquires, and Their Associates; for a Grant of Lands on the River Ohio, in North America; for the Purpose of Erecting a New Government. With Observations and Remarks by [Thomas Walpole].* London, J. Almon, 1772.

――――. Privy Council. *Acts of the Privy Council of England. Colonial Series....* Edited by James Munro [and others]. London [etc.], H. M. Stationery Office, 1908–12. 6 vols.

HAMILTON, STANISLAUS, ed. *Letters to Washington and Accompanying Papers.* Boston, Houghton, Mifflin & Co., 1898–1902. 5 vols.

HULBERT, ARCHER B. *The Crown Collection of Photographs of American Maps,* selected and Edited by.... Cleveland, O., Arthur H. Clark Co., 1904–08. 5 vols.

[HUSKE, JOHN]. *The Present State of North America. The Discoveries, Rights and Possessions of Great Britain.* London, R. & J. Dodsley, 1755.

An Impartial History of the Late War from 1749 to 1763 [in Canada]. London, 1763. The book is attributed to John Almon.

Indian Treaties Printed by Benjamin Franklin, 1736–1762. With an Introduction by Carl Van Doren and Historical & Bibliographical Notes by Julian P. Boyd. Philadelphia, The Historical Society of Pennsylvania, 1938.

JEFFERSON, THOMAS. *Notes on the State of Virginia.* New York, 3rd American ed., M. L. & W. A. Davis, 1801.

JOHNSON, SIR WILLIAM. *The Papers of Sir William Johnson.* Prepared for Publication by the Division of Archives and History.... Albany, The University of the State of New York, 1921–52. 10 vols.

Bibliography

Maryland Gazette (Annapolis) Issues for the years 1754 and 1763.

MARSHE, WITHAM. ... *Journal of the Treaty of Lancaster in 1744, with the Six Nations.* Annotated by William H. Egle. Lancaster, Pa. The New Era Steam Book and Job Print., 1884.

Mason and Dixon Line Resurvey Commission. *Report on the resurvey of the Maryland-Pennsylvania Boundary Part of the Mason and Dixon Line.* [Harrisburg, Pa., Harrisburg Publishing Co., 1909.]

Mémoire contenant le precis des faits, avec leurs piéces justificatives, pour servir de réponse aux observations envoyées par les ministres d' Angleterre, dans les cours de l'Europe. Paris de l'imprimerie Royale, 1756.

Michigan Pioneer and Historical Society. *Historical Collections* .... Lansing, Mich., 1855–82. 20 vols.

New York (Colony). *An Abridgment of the Indian Affairs ... Transacted in the Colony of New York, from the Year 1678 to the Year 1751 by Peter Wraxall.* Edited with an introduction by Charles Howard McIlwain. Cambridge, Harvard University Press, 1915.

―――. Treaties. *A Treaty Between His Excellency, The Honourable George Clinton, Captain-General and Governor in Chief of the Province New-York, and of the Territories thereon depending in America ... and the Six United Indian Nations, depending on the Province of New-York; Held at Albany in the months of August and September, 1746.* New York, James Parker, 1746.

――― (State). Secretary of State. *Calendar of Historical Manuscripts, in the Office of the Secretary of State, Albany, N. Y.* Edited by E. B. O'Callaghan. Albany, Weed, Parsons & Co., 1866. 2 vols.

The Ohio Company Papers, 1753–1817, Being Primarily Papers of the "Suffering Traders" of Pennsylvania: by Kenneth P. Bailey. Arcata, Calif., n. pub., 1947.

Pennsylvania (Colony). General Assembly. *Minutes of the First Session of the Ninth General Assembly ... Which Commenced the twenty fifth day of October, 1784.* Philadelphia, Francis Bailey, 1784.

――― General Assembly. House of Representatives. *Votes and Proceedings of the House of Representatives of the Province of Pennsylvania Beginning the Fourteenth Day of October, 1707.* Philadelphia, B. Franklin and D. Hall, 1753. Vol. II.

――― General Assembly. House of Representatives. *Votes and Proceedings of the House of Representatives of the Province of Pennsylvania Beginning the Fifteenth Day of October, 1744 to September 30, 1758.* Philadelphia, Henry Miller, 1774. Vol. IV. There are six volumes in this set, each published separately.

――― Provincial Council. *Minutes of the Provincial Council from its organization to the Termination of the Proprietary Government.* Philadelphia [etc.], Jo[seph] Severns & Co. [etc.], 1851–52. 10 vols.

――― Treaties, etc., 1736. *A Treaty of Friendship held with the Chiefs of*

Bibliography

the Six Nations at Philadelphia in September and October, *1736*. Philadelphia, B. Franklin, 1737.

——— Treaties, etc., 1744. *A Treaty, Held at the Town of Lancaster, in Pennsylvania, by the Honourable the Commissioners for the Provinces of Virginia and Maryland, with the Indians of the Six Nations, in June, 1744.* Philadelphia, Printed and Sold by B. Franklin, at the New-Printing-Office, near the Market. 1744.

——— Treaties, etc., 1748. *A Treaty Held By Commissioners, Members of the Council of the Province of Pennsylvania, at the Town of Lancaster, with some Chiefs of the Six Nations at Ohio, and Others, for the Admission of the Twightwee Nation into the Alliance of His Majesty, &c. in the Month of July, 1748.* Philadelphia, Printed and Sold by B. Franklin, at the New Printing-Office, near the Market, 1748.

——— Treaties, etc., 1753. *A Treaty Held with the Ohio Indians, at Carlisle, in October, 1753.* Philadelphia, B. Franklin, 1753.

——— Treaties, etc., 1756. *Minutes of Conferences, Held with the Indians, at Easton. In the Months of July and November, 1756; together with Two Messages sent by the Government to the Indians residing on Sasquehannah; and the Report of the Committee appointed by the Assembly to attend the Governor at the last of the said Conferences.* Philadelphia, Printed and Sold by B. Franklin, and D. Hall, at the New-Printing-Office, near the Market. 1757.

——— Treaties, etc., 1757. *Minutes of Conferences, Held with the Indians, at Harris's Ferry, and at Lancaster, in March, April, and May, 1757.* Philadelphia, Printed and Sold by B. Franklin, and D. Hall, 1757.

——— Treaties, etc., 1758. *Minutes of the Conferences held at Easton in October, 1758. . . .* Philadelphia, Printed and Sold by B. Franklin, and D. Hall, 1758.

——— Treaties, etc., 1762. *Minutes of Conferences, Held at Lancaster, in August 1762.* Philadelphia, Printed and Sold by B. Franklin and D. Hall, 1763.

——— Treaties, etc., 1768. *Minutes of Conferences Held at Fort Pitt, in April and May, 1768,* under the Direction of George Croghan . . . with the chiefs and warriors of the Ohio and other Western Indians. . . . Philadelphia, William Goddard, at the New Printing-Office, in Market-Street, 1769.

Pennsylvania Archives. First series. Philadelphia, Joseph Severns & Co., 1852–1856. 12 vols.

——— Third series. Harrisburg, Joseph Severns & Co., 1852–56. 30 vols.

Pennsylvania Gazette, Philadelphia, 1728–1815. Issues of 1753 and 1754 were consulted.

Post, Christian Frederick. *The second journal of Christian Frederick Post, on a message from the governor of Pensilvania to the Indians on the Ohio.* London, Printed for J. Wilkie, 1759.

Bibliography

POWNALL, THOMAS. *A Topographical Description of such Parts of North America as are contained in The (annexed) Map of the Middle British Colonies, &c. In North America.* London, Printed for F. Almon, 1776.

———. Same. Revised and enlarged edition edited by Lois Mulkearn. Pittsburgh, University of Pittsburgh Press, 1949.

SABIN, JOSEPH [and others]. *A Dictionary of Books Relating to America, From its Discovery to the Present Time.* New York, J. Sabin [etc.], 1868–1936. 29 vols.

SMITH, COLONEL JAMES. *An Account of the Remarkable Occurrences in the Life and Travels of . . . during his Captivity with the Indians, in the Years 1755, '56, '57, '58, & '59.* Lexington, John Bradford, 1799.

[SMITH, WILLIAM]. *An Historical Account of the Expedition Against the Ohio Indians, in the Year MDCCLXIV, Under the Command of Henry Bouquet, Esq.* . . . Philadelphia, William Bradford, 1765.

SUMMERS, LEWIS P. *History of Southwest Virginia, 1746–1786.* . . . Richmond, Va., J. L. Hill Printing Company, 1903.

THOMSON, CHARLES. *An Enquiry into the Causes of the Alienation of the Delaware and Shawanese Indians from the British Interest, and into the Measures Taken for Recovering Their Friendship.* . . . London: Printed for J. Wilkie, at The Bible, in St. Paul's Church-yard, 1759.

Travels in New France by J. C. B. Edited by S. K. Stevens [and others]. Harrisburg, Pennsylvania Historical Commission, 1941.

TRENT, WILLIAM. *Journal of.* . . . Ed. by Alfred T. Goodman. . . . Cincinnati, R. Clarke & Co., for W. Dodge, 1871.

U. S. Library of Congress. Division of Maps. *List of Maps of America in the Library of Congress, preceded by a List of Works Relating to Cartography.* By P. Lee Phillips. Washington, Government Printing Office, 1901.

Virginia. *Calendar of Virginia State Papers and Other Manuscripts . . . . Preserved in the Capitol at Richmond.* Arranged and edited by William P. Palmer. Richmond, R. F. Walker [etc.], 1875–93. 11 vols.

——— Laws, Statutes, etc. *The Statutes at Large; Being a Collection of All the Laws of Virginia from the First Session of the Legislature, in the Year 1619.* By William Waller Hening. V. p., v. pub., 1809–1823. 13 vols.

——— (Colony). Council. *Executive journals of the Council of Colonial Virginia.* . . . Edited by H. R. McIlwaine (v. 1-4) and Wilmer L. Hall (v. 5). Richmond, D. Bottom, 1925–date. 5 vols.

——— General Assembly. House of Burgesses. *Journal of . . . 1752–58,* edited by H. R. McIlwaine. Richmond, Va., 1909.

Virginia Gazette (Hunter, Purdie & Dixon), 1751–1778, Williamsburg, Virginia.

——— (Rind, Pinkney), 1766–1776, Williamsburg, Virginia.

WALPOLE, THOMAS. *The Memorial of the Honourable . . . , in Behalf of himself and the Earl of Hertford, Earl Temple, the Right Honourable Charles Lord Camden, the Honourable Richard Walpole, the Hon-*

Bibliography

ourable Robert Walpole, Sir Harry Featherstonbaugh, Baronet, Sir George Colebrooke, Baronet, Thomas Pitt, Esq. Richard Jackson, Esq. John Sargent, Esq. and Samuel Wharton, Esq. and their Associates. [London, August 8, 1774]. Caption title.

———. *Observations on, and Answers to, the foregoing Report* [Report of the Board of Trade, April 15, 1772], being pages 34-99 of that report (London, J. Almon, 1772).

WASHINGTON, GEORGE. *The Diaries of.* . . . Edited by J. C. Fitzpatrick. Boston, Houghton Mifflin Co., 1925. 4 vols.

———. *Journal of Colonel George Washington, Sent by Robert Dinwiddie, Across the Allegheny Mountains, in 1754, to Build Forts At the Head of the Ohio.* . . . Edited, with Notes, by J. M. Toner. Albany, N. Y., Joel Munsell's sons, 1893.

———. *The Journal of Major George Washington, Sent by the Hon. Robert Dinwiddie, Esq; His Majesty's Lieutenant-Governor, and Commander in Chief of Virginia, to the Commandant of the French Forces on Ohio . . . with a New Map of the Country as far as the Mississippi.* Williamsburgh, Printed, London, Reprinted for T. Jefferys, 1754.

———. *The Writings of.* . . . *From the Original Manuscript Sources, 1745–1799.* Prepared under the direction of the U.S. George Washington Bicentennial Commission and published by authority of Congress; John C. Fitzpatrick, ed. Washington, Government Printing Office, [1931–44]. 39 vols.

[WHARTON, SAMUEL]. *Plain Facts: Being an Examination into the Rights of the Indian Nations of America to their respective Countries and a Vindication of the Grant, from The Six United Nations of Indians, to the Proprietors of Indiana.* . . . Philadelphia: Printed and Sold by R. Aitken, 1781.

WILLIAMS, JOHN. *The Redeemed Captive Returning to Zion: or, A Faithful History of Remarkable Occurences in the Captivity and Deliverance of Mr. John Williams.* . . . The Sixth Edition. Boston, Samuel Hall, 1795.

Wisconsin. State Historical Society. *Collections of* . . . edited by Lyman Copeland Draper . . . . Madison, The Society, 1855–82. 20 vols.

MAPS, PLANS.

1718   *Carte de la Louisiane et du Cours du Mississippi. Dressée sur un Grand Nombre de Mémoires entrau'tres sur ceux de Mr le Maire.* Par Guillaume Délisle de L'académie R'le. des Sciences. Paris, l'auteur, 1718.

1737   "A Map of the Northern Neck in Virginia; The Territory of the Right Honourable Thomas Lord Fairfax; Situate betwixt the Rivers Potomack and Rappahanock, According to a Late Survey; Drawn in the Year 1737 by Wm Mayo." Manuscript Map in the Darlington Memorial Library, University of Pittsburgh.

· 698 ·

Bibliography

1749 *Carte D'un Voyage Fait dans La Belle Rivière en la Nouvelle France MDCCXLIX*. Par le Reverend Pere Bonnecamps, Jesuitte Mathematicien, reproduced in Galbreath, *Expedition of Céloron*.

1752 [John Mercer's map showing the courses of Christopher Gist's two journeys and proposed natural boundaries for the Ohio Company grant as outlined in their petition to the King in Council, March 28, 1754]. MS is P.R.O. Colonial Office, Maps (Virginia), No. 13. Copy, made by J. A. Burt for William M. Darlington, April, 1882, in the Darlington Memorial Library, University of Pittsburgh.

1753 [George Mercer's map showing extent of Russell & Co. survey and location of proposed Ohio Company fort and town ordered to be built on the Ohio River]. MS is P.R.O. Colonial Office, Maps (Virginia), No. 12.

1753 *Plan of the British Dominions of New England in North America Composed from Actual Surveys*. By Dr. William Douglas. Engraved by R. W. Seale, London, 1753.

1754 Robert Stobo's Plan of Fort Duquesne, MS in Darlington Memorial Library.

1755 *A Map of the Most Inhabited Part of Virginia Containing the Whole Province of Maryland with Part of Pennsylvania, New Jersey and North Carolina Drawn by Joshua Fry & Peter Jefferson in 1751*. Engrav'd and Publish'd according to Act of Parliament by Thos Jefferys Geographer to his Royal Highness the Prince of Wales at the Corner of St Martins Lane, Charing Cross, London. In the 1755 edition the "Dalrymple tables" and the word, "most," in the title were added. An explanation on the map is as follows: "The Course of the Ohio or Alliganey River and its Branches are laid down from Surveys and Draughts made on the Spot by Mr Gist and others in the Years 1751.2.3&4."

1755 "A Plan of Fort Cumberland on Will's Creek & Potomack River with a View of the Store Houses, belonging to the Ohio Company on the other side of the River." King's MSS, Library of the British Museum; reproduced in Hulbert, *Crown Collection of American Maps*, II, no. 19. CXXII, no. 38. Reproduced in Bailey, *Ohio Company*, opp. p. 74. Probably the plan sent by Dinwiddie to Sir Thomas Robinson, February 12, 1755. —Ed.

1755 "A Plan of the Fort and Barracks at Mount Pleasant in Maryland." *Ibid.*, no. 20. This plan shows the additions ordered by Sir John St. Clair, made to accomodate Braddock's army.—Ed.

1755 *A Map of the British and French Dominions in North America, with the Roads, Distances, Limits, and Extent of the Settlements.* ... By Jno Mitchell. London, Printed for Jefferys & Faden, Feb. 13th, 1755.

1755 *A General Map of the Middle British Colonies, in America:* ... *By Lewis Evans.* 1755. Engraved by Jas Turner in Philadelphia. Published According to Act of Parliament, by Lewis Evans, June 23,

Bibliography

1755. And sold by R. Dodsley, in Pall-Mall, London, & by the Author in Philadelphia.

1758 *A General Map of the Middle British Colonies in America: viz. Virginia, Maryland, Delaware, Pensilvania. . . . By Lewis Evans. Corrected and Improved in the Addition of the Line of Forts on the Back Settlements.* By Thomas Jefferys. [London], R. Sayer & T. Jefferys, 1758.

1764 *A Topographical Plan of the Part of the Indian Country Through Which the Army Under the Command of Colonel Bouquet Marched in the Year 1764.* [By Thomas Hutchins]. Printed in William Smith's *History of Bouquet's Expedition.*

1768 *A Plan of the Boundary Lines between the Province of Maryland and the Three Lower Counties on Delaware with Part of the Parrallel of Latitude which is the Boundary Between the Provinces of Maryland and Pennsylvania.* Original "Parchment Map Prepared by Messrs Mason and Dixon in 1768" is in the Maryland Historical Society, Baltimore. Printed in Mason and Dixon Line resurvey Commission, *Report on the Resurvey of the Maryland-Pennsylvania Boundary...*, [Harrisburg, Harrisburg Pub. Co., 1909].

1770 *To the Honorable Thomas Penn and Richard Penn, esquires, True and Absolute Proprietors and Governors of the Province of Pennsylvania and the Territories Thereunto Belonging and to the Honorable John Penn, Esquire, Lieutenant Governor of the Same. This Map of the Province of Pennsylvania is Humbly Dedicated by Their Most Obedient Serv't W. Scull.* Henry Dawkins Sculp't. Philadelphia, James Nevil, for the Author, April 1st, 1770.

1778 *A New Map of the Western Parts of Virginia, Pennsylvania, Maryland and North Carolina; Comprehending the Rivers Ohio and All the Rivers Which Fall into it; Part of the River Mississippi, the Whole of the Illinois River, Lake Erie; Part of the Lakes Huron, Michigan &c and All the Country Bordering on These Lakes and Rivers.* By Thos. Hutchins. London, T. Hutchins, 1778.

SECONDARY SOURCES

BOOKS, PERIODICALS, ARTICLES, ETC.

ALVORD, CLARENCE E., "The Genesis of the Proclamation of 1763," printed in Michigan Pioneer and Historical Society, *Historical Collections,* XXXVI, 20-52.

———. *The Mississippi Valley in British Politics.* Cleveland, Arthur H. Clark Co., 1917. 2 vols.

American Historical Record . . . Edited by Benson J. Lossing. Phila., Chase & Town, 1872–[74]. 3 vols.

The American Pioneer, a Monthly Periodical, Devoted to the Objects of the Logan Historical Society. Cincinnati, Ohio, J. S. Williams, 1842–43. 2 vols.

Bibliography

BAILEY, KENNETH P. *The Ohio Company* .... Glendale, Calif., Arthur H. Clark Co., 1939.

———. *Thomas Cresap, Maryland Frontiersman*. Boston, Christopher Publishing House, 1944.

BURK, JOHN D. *The History of Virginia*. Petersburg, Va., the Author, 1804. 4 vols.

BRUCE, ROBERT. *The National Road* .... Washington, D. C., National Highways Association [1916].

CARTER, CLARENCE E. *Great Britain and the Illinois Country, 1763–1774*. [American Historical Association, 1910].

COLLINS, LEWIS. *History of Kentucky*. Revised, Enlarged ... and Brought Down to the Year 1874 by his son, Richard H. Collins .... Covington, Ky., Collins & Co., 1874. 2 vols. (First published under the title: *Historical Sketches of Kentucky* ..., 1847).

CONWAY, MONCURE D. *Barons of the Potomac and Rappahannock*. New York, Grolier Club, 1892.

EAVENSON, HOWARD N., "Who Made the Trader's Map," printed in *Pennsylvania Magazine of History and Biography*, LXV, 420-38.

FEDERAL WRITERS' PROJECT. Kentucky. *Kentucky, a Guide to the Bluegrass State*. New York, Harcourt, Brace & Co., 1939. "American Guide Series."

FERLAND, JEAN BAPTISTE ANTOINE. *Cours D'Histoire du Canada*. Quebec, Augustin Coté, 1861–65. 2 vols.

FERNOW, BERTHOLD. *The Ohio Valley in Colonial Days*. Albany, N. Y., Joel Munsell's Sons, 1890.

FREEMAN, DOUGLAS S. *George Washington*. N. Y., Charles Scribner's Sons, 1948–date. 4 vols., all published to date.

GIPSON, LAWRENCE H. *The British Empire Before the American Revolution: Provincial Characteristics and Sectional Tendencies in the Era Preceding the American Crisis* .... Caldwell, Idaho, The Caxton Printers; New York, Alfred A. Knopf, 1936–date. 7 vols., all published to date.

HANNA, CHARLES A. *The Wilderness Trail; or, The Ventures and Adventures of the Pennsylvania Traders on the Allegheny Path, with Some New Annals of the Old West, and the Records of Some Strong Men and Some Bad Ones*. New York, G. P. Putnam's Sons, 1911. 2 vols.

HILDRETH, S. P., "History of an Early Voyage on the Ohio and Mississippi Rivers," printed in *The American Pioneer*, I, 89-105, 128-145.

HODGE, FREDERICK, ed. *Handbook of American Indians North of Mexico*. Washington, Government Printing Office, 1907–10. 2 vols. (Smithsonian Institution. Bureau of Ethnology. Bulletin 30.)

HOWE, HENRY. *Historical Collections of Ohio*. Cincinnati, Derby, Bradley & Co., 1848.

HULBERT, ARCHER B. *Indian Thoroughfares*. ... Cleveland, Ohio, Arthur H. Clark Co., 1902.

Bibliography

IRVING, WASHINGTON. *Life of George Washington.* N. Y., G. P. Putnam & Co., 1856–59. 5 vols.

[JACOB, JOHN J.]. *A Biographical Sketch of the Life of the Late Captain Michael Cresap.* Cumberland, Md., the Author, 1826.

JAMES, A. P., "Fort Ligonier: Additional Light From Unpublished Documents," printed in *Western Pennsylvania Historical Magazine,* XVII, 259-85.

KEITH, CHARLES P. *Chronicles of Pennsylvania from the English Revolution to the Peace of Aix-la-Chapelle, 1688–1748.* Phila., 1917. 2 vols.

KINCAID, ROBERT L. *The Wilderness Road.* Indianapolis, The Bobbs-Merrill Co., 1947.

LEWIS, GEORGE E. *The Indiana Company, 1763–1798.* . . . Glendale, Calif., The Arthur H. Clark Co., 1941.

LIVERMORE, SHAW. *Early American Land Companies, Their Influence on Corporate Development.* N. Y., The Commonwealth Fund, 1939.

LONN, ELLA. *The Colonial Agents of the Southern Colonies.* Chapel Hill, University of North Carolina Press, 1945.

LOWDERMILK, WILLIAM H. *History of Cumberland (Maryland) From the Time of the Indian Town, Caiuctucuc, in 1728, up to the Present Day, Embracing an Account of Washington's First Campaign, and Battle of Fort Necessity, Together With a History of Braddock's Expedition.* Washington, D. C., J. Anglis, 1878.

MARTIN, FRANCOIS-XAVIER. *The History of North Carolina from the Earliest Period.* New Orleans, A. T. Penniman & Co., 1829. 2 vols.

MITCHENER, CHARLES H., ed. *Historic Events in the Tuscarawas and Muskingum Valleys, and in Other Portions of the State of Ohio.* Dayton, Ohio, Thomas W. Odell, 1876.

MOORE, HORATIO N. *Life and Services of General Anthony Wayne.* Philadelphia, John B. Perry, 1845.

PARKMAN, FRANCIS. *A Half-Century of Conflict.* Boston, Little, Brown & Co., 1892. 2 vols.

PENDLETON, WILLIAM C. *History of Tazewell County and Southwest Virginia, 1748–1920.* Richmond, Va., W. C. Hill Printing Company, 1920.

Pennsylvania Magazine of History and Biography. Philadelphia, Publication Fund of the Historical Society of Pennsylvania, 1877–date. 75 vols.

The Pennsylvania-German Society. *Proceedings and Addresses:* [Lancaster, Pa.], The Society, 1891–date. 53 vols.

PEYTON, JOHN LEWIS. *History of Augusta County,* Virginia, Staunton, Va., S. M. Yost & Son, 1882.

POLLARD, EDWARD A. *The Virginia Tourist.* Philadelphia, J. B. Lippincott & Co., 1870.

REICHEL, WILLIAM. *Memorials of the Moravian Church.* Philadelphia, J. B. Lippincott & Co., 1870.

Bibliography

ROWLAND, KATE M. *The Life of George Mason, 1725–1792.* . . . N. Y., G. P. Putnam's sons, 1892. 2 vols.

———, "The Ohio Company," printed in *William and Mary College Quarterly*, first series, I, 197-203.

SIPE, C. HALE. *Indian Chiefs of Pennsylvania.* Butler, Pa., Ziegler Printing Co., 1927.

SLICK, SEWELL. *William Trent and the West.* Harrisburg, Pa., Archives Publishing Co., 1947.

Steelways. New York, American Iron and Steel Institute, 1947–date. I, no. 13. p.28.

U.S. Bureau of American Ethnology. *Annual Reports of the Bureau of Ethnology to the Secretary of Smithsonian Institution.* Washington, U.S. Government Printing Office, 1881–1933. Forty-eight reports in 54 vols.

VEECH, JAMES. *Mason and Dixon's Line: A History, Including an Outline of the Boundary Controversy between Pennsylvania and Virginia.* Pittsburgh, W. S. Haven, 1857.

Virginia Magazine of History and Biography. Richmond, Va., The Society, 1893–date. 59 vols.

VOLWILER, ALBERT T. *George Croghan and the Westward Movement, 1741–1782.* Cleveland, The Arthur H. Clark Company, 1926. (Early Western Journals, No. 3.)

WALLACE, PAUL A. W. *Conrad Weiser, 1696–1760, Friend of Colonist and Mohawk.* Philadelphia; University of Pennsylvania Press, 1945.

WAYLAND, JOHN WALTER, *The German Element of the Shenandoah Valley of Virginia.* Charlottesville, Va., Michie Company for the author, 1907.

Western Pennsylvania Historical Magazine. Pittsburgh, Historical Society of Western Pennsylvania, 1918–date. 34 vols.

William and Mary College Quarterly. First series. v.p., v. pub., 1892–1920. 27 vols.

Writers' Program. Ohio. *The Ohio Guide.* New York, Oxford University Press [c1940]. "American Guide Series."

Writers' Program. Virginia. *Virginia, a Guide to the Old Dominion* . . . New York, Oxford University Press [1940]. "American Guide Series."

Writers' Program. West Virginia. *West Virginia, A Guide to the Mountain State.* New York, Oxford University Press [1941]. "American Guide Series."

INDEX

Abercromby, James: colonial agent for Va., 643.
Ackowanothio [Ackowanthio], an Indian: 500.
Acts of Toleration (1689): 145, 607.
Albany, mayor of: captives appeal to, 243, 576; see also Sanders, Robert.
Albemarle Co. (Va.): erected, 299.
Alexandria (Va.): Ohio Co. meets at, 175-76.
Allaquippa, Seneca queen: 593.
Allaquippa's Gap (Pa.): 474.
Allegheny River: Shawnee migrate to, 473, 475; see also Ohio River.
Amelia Co. (Va.): erected, 299.
American Antiquarian Society: French leaden plate in, 554.
Amherst, Sir Jeffery: refuses Ohio Co. permission to establish town at Fort Cumberland, 452-53, 629.
Amherst Co. (Va.): erected, 299.
Anagarondon: 70, 244, fac. 9; see also Schuyler, Myndert.
Angouirot, Huron chief: 489.
Annosannoah [Annosanah, Annasonah, Annosenough]: Christopher Gist's Indian name, 12, 80, 102, 254, fac. 12, fac. app. 3.
Armstrong, Col. John: 537, 560.
Articles of Agreement. See Ohio Co., Articles of Agreement.
Assarigoa [Assarigia, Assaragsa]: 64, 136, 282, 299, fac. 1, fac. app. 21, 488; see also Big Knife.
Athawes, Edward, London merchant: to pay Charlton Palmer and George Mercer, 46, 151, 185.
Aughwick, George Croghan's home: 512, 550; see also Shirleysburg (Pa.).
Augusta Co. (Va.): erected, 299; John Mercer's land in, 41; petition of inhabitants to the crown (1766), 640.
Aylett [Aylet], Philip: 250, 292, fac. 4.

Bailey, William: 191.
Baltimore, Lord: Ohio Co. solicits land from, 6, 94, 142, fac. 21.
Barker, Joseph: application to teach at John Mercer's, 199-200.
Barnes, Richard: 249, 293, fac. 1.
Barrett, Charles: 250, 292, fac. 4.
Barrett, Robert: 250, 292, fac. 4.
Baylor, John: 250, 292, fac. 4.
Beall, Thomas: purchases Ohio Co. land in Md., 619.
Beaver, Delaware chief: 431, 485; Christopher Gist sends message, 35, 124-25, 268, fac. app. 14; makes Shingas king of the Delaware, 62, 134, 280, fac. app. 20; recognized as king of the Delaware, 560; sketch, 512-18; speaks for the Delaware at Carlisle and Winchester (1753), 559.
Beaver (Big) Creek (Pa.): on Christopher Gist's route, 10, 100, 253, fac. app. 2, 486.
Beaver Island Creek (Va.): 31, 121, fac. app. 12; see also Reed Island Creek (Va.).
Bedford, Duke of: 48; offered share and presidency of Ohio Co., 3, 140.
Bedford (Pa.): 474; see also Fort Bedford and Raystown.
Bedford Co. (Va.): erected, 299.
Beech Hill Station (W. Va.): 519.
Belcher, Jonathan, gov. of N. J.: 591.
Belfield [Belfeild], John: 249, 293, fac. 1.
Belt of Wampum, Six Nations chief: 605.
Beverley, William: 226, 248, 292, fac. 1, 567, 608, 642, 643.
Beyansoss Creek (W. Va.): Christopher Gist's camp, 37, fac. app. 15; see also Big Sandy Creek.
Big Bone Lick (Ky.): 504.
Big Hominy [Hanoahansa, Hannaona, Huminy], Shawnee chief: 17, 56, 107, 128, 256, 275, fac. app. 5, 18, 503, 544; sketch, 499-500.
Big Island in Susquehanna River (Lock Haven, Pa.): Indian town, 495, 660.
Big Knife: Christopher Gist's Indian name, 11, 101, fac. app. 3; see also Assarigoa.
Big Mill Creek (W. Va.): 519.
Big Rock along the Allegheny River [Indian God Rock]: French leaden plate buried at, 553.
Big Sandy Creek (Ohio): 486; see also Elk's Eye Creek.
Big Sandy Creek (W. Va.): 505, 519.
Bigot, François, intendant of New France: 604.
Black Mouth, Piankashaw chief. See La Mouche Noire.
Bladen, Thomas, gov. of Md.: Ohio Co. purchases land from, 142-43, 175, 618-19; warns his Council of impending Indian attack, 535.
Blair, John: 574, 642; extract of letter from James Patton, 404-5, 425; land grants to, 51, 233, 251, 289, fac. 2, 6, 24, 414, 567, 568; land survey in Western Pa., 241.
Blair, John, Jr.: 249, 292, fac. 1.

Index

Blair-Russell Land Co. *See* Russell, William.
Bloody Run (Pa.): junction of Indian paths, 474; *see also* Everett.
Bluestone River (Va.): 30, 120, 180, *fac. app. 11,* 505.
Blyth, William, Indian trader: *fac. app. 22.*
Bolivar (Ohio): on Christopher Gist's route, 486; Fort Laurens near, 488.
Bonnecamps, Joseph Pierre de: 477.
Borden, Benjamin: Va. land grant, 298; sold land to John Mercer, 41.
Boucher, Rev. Jonathan: tutor to John Mercer children, 199, 221.
Bouquet, Col. Henry: confers with Delaware, 517; John Mercer's invective against, 95, 447; proclamation (1761), *fac. 29,* 395, 637; receives message from western Indians, 513-14; refuses membership in Ohio Co., 614-15; requests power to grant western lands, 612; route to Ohio, 486.
Bowie, James: 249, 293, *fac. 1.*
Braddock, Maj. Gen. Edward: campaign denounced by Andrew Montour, 483.
Braddock's Road. *See* Ohio Co. Road.
Brafferton Indian School in Williamsburg: 563, 623.
Brandywine Creek (Pa.): land on claimed by Delaware, 509.
Brent, Robert: 207, 222.
Brent, William: 201, 222.
Brewing industry in Va.: John Mercer's discussion, 189, 190-97.
Brodhead, Col. Daniel: 511.
Brownsville (Pa.). *See* Redstone.
Bruce, John: 294.
Brunswick Co. (Va.): erected, 299.
Buchanan, George: 249, 293, *fac. 1.*
Buck, The: 60, 132, 279, *fac. app. 19-20; see also* George Croghan.
Buckingham Co. (Va.): erected, 299.
Buckstown (Pa.). *See* Edmund's Swamp.
Budden, Richard, sea captain: 66, 71, 243, *fac. 9,* 420.
Buffalo, N. Y.: site of Fort Niagara, 586.
Buffalo Creek (W. Va.): 38, 72, 242, *fac. 3, 10, fac. app. 15,* 519, 520; *see also* Molchuconicon Creek and Middle Island Creek.
Bull Run Mts.: 41.
Bullitt, Thomas: presses claim for bounty lands, 611-12.
Burke, Thomas, Indian trader: 490.
Burney, Thomas: 420, 660; blacksmithing at Muskingum, 12, 102, 253, *fac. app. 3;* carries Indian messages to Va. and Pa., 286, *fac. 11;* 420, 569, 624; carries Va.'s messages to Indians, 74, 284, 286, 429, 577, 624, 651; escapes French at Pickawillany, 419-20; sketch, 492.

Burwell, Armistead: 250, 292, *fac. 4.*
Burwell, Lewis, president of Va. Executive Council: 69, *fac. 8,* 411, 589.
Bushy Run Battlefield Park: 475; *see also* Cock Eye's Cabin.
Butler, William: 293.
Byrne, George: 41.

Callender [Callendar, Kallandar, Kallender], Robert: 18, 107, 257, *fac. app. 6;* trading house, 489-90; witnesses treaty, 139, *fac. app. 23.*
Calmes [Calmees], Mark: 51, 249, 251, 293, *fac. 2, 6.*
Calvert, Cornelius: 250, 293, *fac. 4.*
Calvert, Isaiah: 294.
Calvert, Maximilian: 250, 292, *fac. 4.*
Calvert, Robert: 294.
Cameron: Ohio Co. meets at (1749), 167.
Campbell, John: 206.
Canasatego [Canosateego], Six Nations chief: 57, 129, 276, *fac. app. 18;* at Lancaster (1744), 538, 663-64; at Philadelphia (1742), 402, 534, 539; sketch, 552.
Carlyle [Carlile, Carlisle], John, member of Ohio Co.: 2, 3, 167, 168, 246, *fac. 2, 24,* 465, 568; at Winchester (1753), 78, 85, *fac. 10, 17;* commissary for Va. militia (1754), 81-82, 83, *fac. 15,* 441-42; petitions for land on Ohio, 293.
Carolina traders, Early: in Ohio Country, 531.
Carolina-Va. boundary line: 4.
Caroline Co. (Va.): erected, 299; John Mercer's land, 41-42.
Carrington, George: 250, 292, *fac. 4.*
Carroll, Charles: 535.
Carroll, Daniel: 222.
Carroll, Joseph: 79, *fac. 11.*
Carson, John: Pa. agent for Indian trade at Fort Augusta, 156-57.
Carter, James: 294.
Carter, Robert, member of Ohio Co.: 178, *fac. 24, 25;* George Mason corresponds, 185-86; John Mercer sends extract of son's letter, 211; John Mercer's criticism, 223, 225: Ohio Co. packet received, 222-23; purchases Gawin Corbin's stock in Ohio Co., 633.
"Case of the Ohio Co." (1754): 233-96; approved and ordered to be sent to John Hanbury, 178; description, 394-95.
"Case of the Ohio Co." (1762): 49-139, 182, 295-96; description, 395-96, 527; John Mercer ordered to draw up the "Case," send it to London to be printed, 46, 150-51, 179, 225, 398.
Case of the Ohio Co. (1770): xx, facsimile; commentary, 393-458; com-

· 706 ·

Index

piled and written in part by George Mercer, 450 ff.; provenance, 393-98; written in part by John Mercer, 448-50.
Castleman's River: 32, 33, 122, 508.
Catawba [Cutaway, Cuttaws] Indians: 20-21, 110, 260, *fac. app. 7*; Six Nations attack, 402.
Caughnawaga [Cagnawagas] Indians: 70, 243-44; *see also* French Indians.
Cayuga Indians: 300.
Céloron, Pierre-Joseph, de Blainville: expedition to Ohio Country (1749), 477, 491, 497-98, 553-54; orders expedition against Pickawillany (1751), 554-55.
Chapman, Nathaniel, member of Ohio Co.: 2, 3, 4, 5, 6, 141, 143, 167, 169, 170, 172, 173, 174, 176, 177, 180, 246, *fac. 2, 24*, 465, 468, 565, 568; petitions for land on Ohio, 294.
Chapman, Pearson, member of Ohio Co.: 318.
Charleston (W. Va.): 524.
Charlotte Co. (Va.): erected, 299.
Charlottesburg (Cumberland, Md.): 451-53, 626-27; *see also* Ohio Co. lays out Charlottesburg.
Charlton, John: Thomas Cresap purchases land from, 473.
Chartier, Peter: leads Shawnee to the French (1745), 478-79.
Chartiers [Shertees, Shurtees] Creek: proposed site of Ohio Co. fort and town, 147-49, 241, 621.
Chase, Thomas: goes to Onondaga with Conrad Weiser (1742), 535.
Cheat River (W. Va.): 508.
Checochinican [Chickoconecon, Chickoconnecon], Delaware chief: 34, 123-24, 267, *fac. app. 13-14*, 509.
Cherokee Indians: confer with Gov. Dinwiddie, 144; Half King warns Delaware not to attack, 61, 133, 279, *fac. app. 20*.
Chescaga, Six Nations chief: signs deed at Logstown (1752), *fac. app. 22*.
Chesterfield Co. (Va.): erected, 299.
Child, James: Pa. commissioner for Indian trade, 154.
Chiningué. *See* Logstown.
Chippewa [Chippawa] Indians: demand surrender of whites at Muskingum, 84.
Christmas (1750): celebrated at Muskingum, 12, 101-2, 253-54, *fac. app. 3*.
Cincinnati (Ohio): French leaden plate buried near, 554.
Circleville (Ohio): site of Maguck, Shawnee Indian town, 495.
Clay Lick Station (Ohio): 494.
Cleveland (Ohio): corner of Ohio Co. proposed boundary, 524; *see also* Cuyahoga River.
Clifton *vs.* Williamson: contestation of will, 184.
Clinton, George, gov. of N. Y.: 578.
Coal on Little Cuttawa [Cuttaway] River: Christopher Gist finds, 28, 117-18, *fac. app. 10*.
Cock Eye's [an old Indian] Cabin: 9, 99, *fac. app. 2*, 475.
Cocke, Catesby: 41, 200.
Cocke, William: 79, 81, *fac. 11, 13*.
Cohokia Indians: 501.
Cold Foot, Miami chief. *See* Le Pied Froid.
College of William and Mary: commissions surveyors, 143, 446; Pa. traders accused of evading fur tax, 297; receives revenue from fur trade, 4; *see also* Brafferton Indian School.
Conchake, Indian town: 480; *see also* Muskingum.
Conemaugh [Chomohonan] River (Pa.): Ohio Co. wants land, 6; Shawnee settle, 473.
Conestoga [Conestogoe] Indians: at treaty (1757), 300; massacred by whites, 228, 297, 645.
Conewango Creek: French plate buried on, 553.
Confluence (Pa.). *See* Turkey Foot.
Conococheaque Creek: 622.
Conogariera, Six Nations chief: signs deed at Logstown (1752), *fac. app. 22*.
Cononsagret, Six Nations chief: signs deed at Logstown (1752), *fac. app. 22*.
Conoy Indians: threaten Md. inhabitants, 534-35.
Contrecoeur, Claude Pierre Pecaudy, sieur de: at Fort Prince George (Pittsburgh), 85-87, *fac. 18-19*; sketch, 597-98.
Coonce, Mark, French interpreter: 488; Christopher Gist meets, 11, 101, *fac. app. 3*.
Copithorn, ———, London merchant: 187.
Copperas: found in Ky. by Christopher Gist, 36, *fac. app. 14-15*; *see also* Rock Quarry.
Corbin, Gawin, member of Ohio Co.: 3, 4, 5, 168, 169, 170, 171, 177, 178, *fac. 24*, 468, 633; petitions for land on Ohio, 294.
Corbin, John: 206.
Corbin, Richard: accused of unfair practices by John Mercer, 225, 526-27, 577-78; John Mercer purchases land from, 41; Ohio Co. complains about, 242; Ohio Co. enters caveats against, 72, 150, 179, 244, 245, *fac. 10*, 426-27; Va. land grants, 72, 242, 251, 291, *fac. 10, 24*.

· 707 ·

Index

Coshocton (Ohio): 523-24; *see also* Tuscarawas.
Council Door. *See* Windaughalah.
Craig [Crag], John: 248, 292, *fac. 1*.
Crane, The, Miami chief: 28, 118, *fac. 10*.
Crane's Nest Creek (Va.): 505.
Crawford, Hugh, Indian trader: 25, 115, 264-65, *fac. app. 22*.
Cresap [Cressap, Cressup], Daniel, member of Ohio Co.: 2, 246, *fac. 2, 24*, 464, 568; petitions for land on Ohio, 293.
Cresap, Michael: 566, 569.
Cresap [Cressap], Thomas, member of Ohio Co.: 2, 3, 6, 169, 170, 174, 177, 246, *fac. 2, 24*, 468, 531, 532, 565-66, 568, 623; accused of drawing German settlers from Pa., 421; advises Va. on Indian diplomacy, 413; and the Ohio Co. fort and town on the Ohio River, 69, 148, 241, *fac. 8*, 621; and the Ohio Co. road to the Monongahela River, 4, 5, 141, 565-66, 633; furnishes wampum for Logstown Conference, 54, 271, *fac. 7*; Indians visit, 79, *fac. 10*, James Patton purchases wampum from, 530; location of hunting cabin along Potomac River, 307; messenger from Gov. Dinwiddie to William Trent, 441; obtains food for Va. militia, 83, offers share in Ohio Co. to Henry Bouquet, 614-15; Ohio Co. agent for land purchased in Va., 5, 171, 619; Ohio Co. builds store at plantation, 619; petitions for land on Ohio, 293; plantation in Maryland (Old Town), 473; plantation, suggested site for Indian treaty (1743), 536; presents Ohio Co. petition for land to Va. Executive Council, xi, 167; settles Hugh Parker estate, 173; surveys on Youghiogheny River for company, 624; to explore for company, 4, 141-42, 171; transports treaty goods to Logstown (1752), 494, 665; tries to buy land directly from Indians, 533-34; unknown letter from George Washington printed, 85, *fac. 17; see also* Saltsburg.
Cresap, Thomas, Jr.: 569.
Croghan, George: accompanies Christopher Gist to Pickawillany, 18, 107, *fac. app. 6;* advocates separate Council Fire for Ohio Indians, 449; Andrew Montour informant for, 482; asks Delaware Indians to select a chief, 558; at Muskingum Indian town (1750), 11, 101, 253, *fac. app. 3;* at Pickawillany (1751), 23-24; attends Indian conference at Detroit (1761), 515; attends Indian conference at Logstown (1751), 413, 500, 512; attends Indian conference at Logstown (1752), 54 ff., 273 ff., *fac. app. 17, 22*, 413; attends Indian conference at Winchester (1753), 429; Christopher Gist writes, 10, 100, *fac. app. 2;* comments on Ohio Co. trade, 531; criticized by Half King, 606; endangered by French, 71, 242-43, *fac. 9;* gives Pa.'s present to Twightwee, 20, 110, 260, *fac. app. 7;* informs Pa. Indians want fort on the Ohio, 593; interprets for Christopher Gist at Muskingum Indian town, 14, 104, *fac. app. 4;* John Mercer's invective against, 297, 300-1; letter to Richard Peters, 416, 532; losses at Lower Shawnee town, 498; meets Joncaire at Logstown, 585; negotiates treaty with Wawiagta and Piankashaw Indians (1751), 113, 138-39, *fac. app. 23*, 502, 556; Ohio Indians ask assistance, *fac. 16;* Pa.'s envoy to Twightwee, 9, 10, 99, 100, 252, 253, *fac. app. 2;* receives information about French aggression on the Ohio, 84; remarks about Pa. and Md. traders, 531; reprimanded by Pa., 555-56; serves on the Ohio for Walpole Co., 325, 326, 673; sketch, 478-81; suggests Pa. buy Indian presents from Ohio Co. (1754), 592-93; trading house at Muskingum, 11, 101, 253, *fac. app. 3;* 489-90; trading house at Youghiogheny Big Bottom, 593; William Trent, partner, 569-70; *see also* Buck, The.
Croghan, Trent, Callender, and Teaffe, trading firm: losses, 576.
Cromwell, William: early settler on Ohio Co. land in Western Pa., 68-69, 240-41, *fac. 8*, 421.
Cross Creek (W. Va.): 520.
Culpeper Co. (Va.): erected, 299.
Cumberland Co. (Va.): erected, 299.
Curran, Barnaby: accompanies George Washington to Fort Le Boeuf, 437; buries white woman tortured by Indians, 13, 103, *fac. app. 4;* messenger for William Trent, 579; Ohio Co. trader, 10, 100, *fac. app. 2*.
Custaloga, Delaware chief. *See* Tuscaloga.
Cuttaway [Cuttawa] River: 27, 117, 266, *fac. app. 10; see also* Tennessee River.
Cuttaway (Little) River: 26, 27, 28, 116-17, 266, *fac. app. 10;* 504; *see also* Kentucky River.
Cuyahoga [Guyhawga, Kyhogo] River: 47; French fort, 566; Six Nations (1745), 478-79.
Cynthiana (Ky.): branch of Great Warriors' Trail near, 504.

Dagge, Henry: attorney for Grand Ohio Co., 326.

· 708 ·

Index

Dagworthy, Capt. John: 629.
Dalrymple, John: reviser of Fry and Jefferson map, 412.
Dalton, Samuel: 250, 293, *fac. 4.*
Dansie, Thomas: 250, 292, *fac. 4.*
Darlington, William: edits Christopher Gist's journals, 471; his copy of Ohio Co. map (1752), 411; on Christopher Gist's crossing Monongahela River, 510-11.
Davison, John, interpreter for Half King: 89, *fac. 19.*
De Lancey, James, gov. of N. Y.: letter from Gov. Dinwiddie, 591.
Delaware George, Delaware chief: 515.
Delaware Indians: answer Pa.'s invitation to conference (1751), 16, 106, *fac. app. 5;* asked to select a chief, 558; at treaty (1757), 300; freed from Iroquois yoke, 516; given king at Logstown Conference (1752), 62, 134, 280, *fac. app. 20;* greeted Virginians at Shannopin's Town, 131, 278, *fac. app. 19;* hunting grounds overrun by Pennsylvanians, 302; invited to treaty by Christopher Gist, 33, 123, 267, *fac. app. 13;* jailed at Lancaster, 537; migration, 495; reason for joining French, 302; for towns see Hockhocking, Hurricane Tom, Maguck, Windaughalah, Shannopin.
Denny, William, gov. of Pa.: speaks at Lancaster, 297.
Devoy, James, Indian trader: 419-20, 563.
Dick, Charles: 194; John Mercer visits, 221; reports on Edward Snickers to John Mercer, 214; Va. land grant, 250, 292, *fac. 4.*
Dinwiddie, Robert, lt. gov. of Va. and member of Ohio Co.: 5, 48, 177, *fac. 24,* 468, 568; appoints William Trent his personal envoy to the Ohio Indians, 582; asked to assist George Mercer in London, 182; asks additional royal instructions for governing Va., 410, 465; aware of French movements on the Ohio, 72, 244-45; comments on Six Nations warring on the southern Indians, 588; commissions William Trent captain of militia, 82-83, *fac. 14-15,* 570-71; criticism of Trent, 571; decides to use armed force against the French, 434-35; disagrees with Andrew Montour, 483; hears of Twightwee massacre, 420-21; instructs William Trent to build fort on the Ohio (Pittsburgh), 81, *fac. 15;* John Mercer criticises, 48, 305, 526-27; letter from Ohio Co., 151-52, *fac. 26;* letter to French commandant, 74-75, *fac. 13-14;* letter to Ohio Co., 72, *fac. 9-10;* letter to Six Nations Indians, 588; letters to William Trent, 73-74, 81-82, 284-85, *fac. 10-11, 15;* Ohio Co. petitions, 66-68, 271-73, *fac. 7-8;* orders militia recruited, 439-40; orders present sent to Ohio Indians, 79-80; orders to Col. Joshua Fry, 598; orders Va. fort built on the Ohio, 570-71; pleased with Half King's speech, 73, 285, *fac. 11;* Proclamation (1754), 77, *fac. 17,* 442, 526; regrets Twightwee are gone to the French, 577; rejects Ohio Co. petition, 239-40; sends George Washington on mission to Fort Le Boeuf, 436-38; sends messages to Twightwee, *fac. 11,* 577, 624; speech to the Half King, 286, *fac. 11-12;* speeches to the House of Burgesses, *fac. 13, 16-17;* sued by William Trent, 571; to attend Winchester Indian conference (1754), *fac. 13,* 648-49; writes to colonial governors, 591.
Dinwiddie Co. (Va.): erected, 299.
Dividing Ridge (Va.): 505.
Dixon, John: 250, 294, *fac. 4.*
Dobbs, Arthur, member of Ohio Co.: 4, 5, 170, 311-12, *fac. 24,* 470, 568, 620-21, 634, 667; company's statement of account (printed), 183.
Dobbs, Conway Richard: letter to George Mercer, 311-12.
Dongan, Thomas, gov. of N. Y.: 400, 488.
Dover (Ohio): 489.
Downes, Henry: 233, 249, 289, 292, *fac. 1, 24.*
Draper, John: 506.
Draper's Meadows: Indian assault, 636; location, 506.
Dresden (Ohio): 494.
Dumas, Jean Daniel: strategy at Fort Duquesne, 601-2.
Dunlop [Dunlap], Alexander: 249, 293, *fac. 1.*
Dunning, James, Pa. Indian trader: 478-79.
Duquesne, Ange de Menneville, marquis de, gov. of New France: royal instructions, 75, *fac. 14,* 584.
Durham boats: description, 520.

Eagle Feather, an Indian: 492.
Écuyer, Simeon, commandant at Fort Pitt: 517, 629.
Edmund's Swamp: 474.
Education in Va.: John Mercer's opinion, 199-202.
Edwards, Andrew: 208.
Effingham, Francis Howard, 5th lord of, gov. of Va.: 400, 403, 488.
Eghuisera [Andrew Montour]: 60, 80, 132, 278-79, *fac. 12, fac. app. 19, 22;* see also Montour, Andrew.

Index

Egremont, Charles Windham, 1st earl of: 48.
Elizabeth I, queen of England: method of granting land in North America, 399.
Elizabeth (W. Va.): 519.
Elk's Eye Creek (Ohio): 10, 11, 100, 101, 253, *fac. app. 3;* see also Big Sandy Creek (Ohio).
English colonists: Lewis Evans on national blood ties, *fac. app. 26.*
English maps of North America: 528-29.
English traders captured by Indians: 13-14, 16-17, 66, 71, 103-4, 106-7, 243, 255, 256, *fac. 7, 9, fac. app. 4, 5.*
Erie (Pa.): site of Fort Presque Isle, 586.
Erie, Lake: proposed boundary for Ohio Co. grant, 47.
Erwin, Luke: captured by Indians, 490.
Eskippakitheki, Shawnee Indian town (Ky.): 576.
Evans, Jabez, Indian trader: captured by Indians, 70, 242, 243, *fac. 9,* 575-76.
Evans, Jacob, Indian trader: captured by Indians, 71, 242, 576, 586.
Evans, John, Indian trader: captured by Indians, 419-20, 563.
Evans, Lewis, *Analysis of a General Map of the Middle British Colonies* (1755): extracts printed, *fac. app. 25-26.*
——, *Essays:* John Mercer refers to, 48.
——, *A General Map of the Middle British Colonies* (1755): 47, 227, 302, 412; distances, etc. taken from Christopher Gist's journals, 305.
Everett (Pa.). *See* Bloody Run.
Ewin, James: 249, 293, *fac. 1.*

Fairfax, George, member of Ohio Co.: 3, 168, 246, *fac. 2, 24,* 568; at Winchester Conference (1753), 78, *fac. 10;* petitions for land on Ohio, 294.
Fairfax, Thomas, 6th lord, proprietor of the Northern Neck (Va.): 41, 587; disputation of original grant, 403-4; Ohio Co. purchases land, 171.
Fairfax, William: 579, 587; at the Winchester Conference (1753), 80, *fac. 12,* 432-33, 482; letters to William Trent, 78-80, *fac. 10, 11, 12;* ordered to release Indian goods to William Trent, 73, 284, *fac. 10.*
Fairfax boundary line: 69, 233, 241, 249, *fac. 8.*
Fairfax Co. (Va.): erected, 299; John Mercer land in, 41.
Fairfax stone: location, 574.
Fairmont (W. Va.): 524-25.
Falls of Potomac: Ohio Co. meets at, 170.
Falls of the Ohio (Louisville, Ky.): 5, 7, 26-27, 97, 116, 266, *fac. app. 1, 10;*

French Indians reported at, 25, 26, 116, 264, *fac. app. 9-10.*
Faulkner, Joseph, Indian trader: captured by Indians, 490.
Fauquier, Francis, lt. gov. of Va.: corresponds with Gen. Amherst about Bouquet's proclamation, 614-15; letter from John Mercer (printed), 93-95, *fac. 21-22;* papers missing, 638; receives instructions from Board of Trade about bounty land grants, 525-26, 612-13.
Fauquier Co. (Va.): erected, 299.
Feagin, Edward, heirs of: 41.
Finley, John, Indian trader: employees taken captives, 71, 242, *fac. 9,* 575.
Fisher, William, Pa. commissioner of Indian trade: 154.
Fishing Creek (W. Va.): 38, 72, 242, *fac. 10, 15,* 519; see also Nawmissipia, Kanawha (Little) River.
Flower Gap (Va.): 507.
Fontaine [Fontane], Peter, Jr.: 250-51, 293, *fac. 4.*
Forbes, Brig. Gen. John: campaign, 91, *fac. 21,* 610.
Foreign protestant settlers sought by Ohio Co.: 144-47, 167, 171, 421.
Forks of the road: Half King to meet Virginians and Pennsylvanians, 88, 605-6.
Fort Augusta: Pa. Indian trade, 156-57.
Fort Cumberland: 166, 181-82, 301; Bouquet's proclamation posted, 614; Half King arrives, 550; Ohio Co. plans town, 451-53; sketch, 627-30; *see also* Charlottesburg, Ohio Co. storehouses, Ohio Co. town at Wills Creek.
Fort Detroit: route from Fort Pitt, 486.
Fort Duquesne: 88, 91, *fac. 19, 21,* 484, 488, 549, 598; sketch, 600-4.
Fort Kiskakon: 490-91, 554; sketch, 502-3.
Fort Laurens: 488.
Fort Le Boeuf: description, 585.
Fort Ligonier: 474-75.
Fort Machault: 586.
Fort Necessity: 550, 559-60.
Fort Niagara: 586.
Fort Pitt: 481, 513 ff., 560.
Fort Presque Isle: 586.
Fort Prince George [St. George]: 440-41, 623.
Fort Sandusky [Sandoski]: John Patten's description, 491-92, 499.
Fort Venango: 484.
Fort Wayne (Ind.): site of Kiskakon, 502.
Fortescue: dies en route from Lower Shawnee town, 71, 243, *fac. 9.*
Four Mile Run (Va.): 41.
Frankfort (Ky.): Christopher Gist crosses Kentucky River, 504.
Franklin, Benjamin: 48, 199; member of

Index

the Grand Ohio Co., 668, 669, 670, 673, 674.
Franklin (Pa.): site of Fort Machault, 586.
Fraser, John, Indian trader and lt. of militia at Fort Prince George: 63, 82, 135, 282, *fac. 15, 16, 21,* 499, 599, 600.
Frederick Co. (Va.): erected, 299; John Mercer's land, 41.
Fredericksburg (Va.): proposed site for Indian conference, 409.
French activities at Logstown: 72, *fac. 9-10,* 477-78, 548.
French and Indian War disrupts plans of Ohio Co.: 395.
French attacks on Pickawillany: 66, 68, 240, 305, *fac. 7, 8,* 563-64.
French encroachment on the Ohio reviewed by gov. of Pa.: *fac. 12.*
French forts on Lake Erie: 11, 67, 72, 101, 253, *fac. 8.*
French Indians take English captives to Canada: 241, 242, 243, 244.
French influence at Shamokin: 484.
French inform George Washington they intend to take possession of the Ohio Country: 437.
French intend to take possession of the Ohio: 76, *fac. 14.*
French leaden plates buried along Allegheny and Ohio Rivers: 58, 130, 276, 553-54.
French Margaret. *See* Montour, Margaret.
French Margaret's Town (Ohio): location, 495; *see also* Hockhocking.
French offer reward for capture of George Croghan and Andrew Montour: 16-17, 106, 256, *fac. app. 5.*
French remarks on Ohio Co. activities: 86, 599.
French send English captives to France: 66.
French soldiers desert to English traders: 14, 103-4, *fac. 4.*
French warned to leave English territory on the Ohio: *fac. 13-14.*
French-English negotiations (1753-54): 425-26.
Frontier inhabitants: fear Indian assaults (1768), 297-99; settle on Indian lands, 228.
Fry, Joshua: in command of Va. militia (1754), 86, *fac. 18,* 598; Va. commissioner at Logstown Conference (1752), 52, 54 ff., 238, 273 ff., *fac. app. 17 ff.,* 647; Va. land grant, 250, 292, *fac. 4.*
Fuller, Edward: 249, *fac. 1.*

Gage, Gen. Thomas: 228, 629, 644.
Gale, Levin: 535, 536.

Galloway, Joseph: 673.
Garland, John: 250, 292, *fac. 4.*
Garnett, Muscoe: 188-89, 214.
Gauley River (W. Va.): 524.
George II, instructions of Sir William Gooch for Ohio Co. land grant, 235, *fac. 3-4;* instructions to Robert Dinwiddie, 582-83; sends treaty goods to Va., 237, *fac. 5.*
George III; Proclamation of 1763, 184-85, *fac. 31,* 636-37.
"George Mercer Papers" in the Darlington Memorial Library, University of Pittsburgh, xvii-xx, 393.
German migration from Pa. to N. C.: 608-9.
German migration from Pa. to Va.: 608.
Gilchrist, Robert: 249, 294, *fac. 1.*
Giles, Jacob [John], member of Ohio Co.: 2, 3, 5, 6, 168, 169, 170, 174, 177, 246, *fac. 2, 24,* 468, 568; petitions for land on the Ohio, 294.
Gilmer, George: 250, 292, *fac. 4.*
Gilmer, Peachy [Penchey]: 250, 292, *fac. 4.*
Gist, Christopher: accompanies George Washington to Fort Le Boeuf, 437; and the Logstown Conference (1752), 52-54, 129 ff., 176-77, 238, 271, 273, *fac. 6-7, 17-22,* 412-13, 418, 540 ff., 647; and the Ohio Co.'s road from Wills Creek to the Monongahela River, 32, 39, 47, 50, 147, 178, 269, *fac. 5, fac. app. 16,* 565, 633; and the Wawiagta and Piankashaw Treaty, 139, 300, *fac. app. 23;* camp in cave along the Monongahela River identified, 510; camp on Allegheny Mountain, 8, 98, *fac. app. 2, see also* Edmund's Swamp; conducts religious services, 12, 101-2, 253-54, *fac. app. 3-4;* contract with Ohio Co. to settle its land, 5, 91, 172-73, *fac. 20;* cuts Ohio Co. name on rock, 36, 126, 268, *fac. app. 15;* death, *fac. 21,* 611; delayed going to Logstown (1753), 651; delivers Va.'s message to Ohio Indians (1753), 286, *fac. 12;* description of Lower Shawnee town, 497-98; description of Pickawillany, 18-19, 108-9, 257-60, *fac. app. 6;* description of southwestern Pa., 510-11; explorations for Ohio Co., 5, 50, 236-38, 252, 467, 471-73; given Wyandott Indian name, 12, 102, 254, *fac. app. 3;* invites Delaware to treaty at Logstown, 33, 34, 123, 267, *fac. app. 13, 14;* invites King Beaver to treaty at Logstown, 35, 124-25, 268, *fac. app. 14;* invites Oppaymolleah to treaty at Logstown, 35, 124, 268, *fac. 14;* invites western Indians to treaty at Logstown, 49, 237, *fac. 5;* journals of explorations, 46, 51, 98, 175, 237,

· 711 ·

Index

238, *fac. 5, 6, fac. app. 1* (editions enumerated), 471 (printed), 7-40, 97-127, 252-69, *fac. app. 1-16;* letter to George Washington (1754), *fac. 16;* licensed Va. surveyor, 446, 573-74, 610, 620; meets William Trent at Redstone, 84; no record of trading on the Ohio, 467; Ohio Co. factor at Rock Creek storehouse [Maidstone], 146, 472, 622; Ohio Co. instructions to explore, 49-50, 236-37, *fac. 5;* Ohio Co. orders for settlement along the Youghioghenny River, 68-69, 238-41, *fac. 7, 8;* Ohio Co. orders to build a town and fort on the Ohio, 147-48, 149-50, 472, 621 (*see also* Saltsburg); petitions for land on the Ohio, 422, 569; sketch, 471-72; son of, 35, 38, 125, *fac. app. 14, 15, 16;* title to lands on the Monongahela River, 468; unable to obtain Indians' permission for Ohio Co. to take up land on the Ohio, 52, 238; *see also* Annosannah, Big Knife.
Gist, Thomas: Va. land patent honored by Pa., 632.
Gist's Creek (Va.): 505.
Glen, James, gov. of S. C.: 591.
Glen Ferris (W. Va.): Kanawha Falls at, 524.
Glover, William: 293.
Gooch, Sir William, lt. gov. of Va.: viii, 403; accepts Pa.'s mediation in Indian controversy (1743), 298; asks Pa. and the Ohio Co. for assistance in negotiations with Indians, 1, 6-7, 142, 533; suggests time and place for Lancaster Conference, 537; views on granting western lands, 405.
Goochland Co. (Va.): erected, 299.
Gordon, Capt. Harry: builds Fort Ligonier, 474.
Gordon, James: 249, 293, *fac. 1*.
Graeme, John: 249, 293, *fac. 1*.
Grafton (W. Va.): 524.
Graham, Duncan: 250, 292, *fac. 4*.
Graham, John, Scotch schoolmaster: 200-1.
Grand Ohio Co.: xv-xvii, 481, 525; account with Ohio Co. (1776-77), 325, 326; George Mercer explains prospects of, 312-15; members of Ohio Co. oppose its merger with, 315 ff.; Privy Council recommends separate government, 324-25; sketch, 668-70; Thomas Ludwell Lee's queries, 318-19; *see also* Walpole Co.
Granville, Earl of: agreement with Ohio Co. for land in N. C., 6, 48, 94, 142, *fac. 21,* 469.
Grayson, Benjamin: 41.
Grayson *vs.* Commonwealth of Va.: U.S. Supreme Court decision on English land grants, 573.
Great Britain: domination of Six Nations, 583, 584; King George's War breaks deadlock for Va. in granting western lands, 404-5; methods of granting land in North America, 399-400; Ohio Co. seeks to obtain grant directly from, 231.
Great Britain. Board of Ordnance: sends ordnance for forts on the Ohio, 591.
Great Britain. Board of Trade and Plantations: 1, 2; answers Gov. Dinwiddie's memorial, 466-67; denies whites the right to settle west of the Allegheny Mts., 613; instructs Gov. Fauquier about land grants, 525-26; reports, 226, *fac. 33-34,* 523, 525, 643.
Great Britain. Privy Council: Committee for Plantation Affairs acts on Ohio Co. affairs, 1, 2; requests information about company, 222-23, *fac. 34*.
Great Huminy, Shawnee chief. See Big Hominy.
Great Scioto Salt Works: 496.
Great Warriors' Trail (Ohio & Ky.): 503-4.
Green, Charles: 41.
Green, Robert: 248, 293, *fac. 1*.
Green, William: 249, 293, *fac. 1*.
Green Spring (Md.): Opessa's town near, 473.
Greenbriar Land Co.: 506.
Greenbrier River: proposed boundary for Ohio Co. grant, 230, 232
Greenway Court: 587.
Grymes, John: 226.
Grymes and Dansie brewery (Fredericksburg): 197.

Half King [Tanacharison], Seneca chief: accuses Conrad Weiser of misrepresenting Va.'s part in Logstown Conference (1748), 136, 299, 300; arrives with French at Logstown (1754), 548, 594; at Logstown Conference (1752); *see* Logstown Conference (1752); criticizes George Croghan and Pennsylvanians, 606; Gov. Dinwiddie sends supplies to, 73, 284-85, *fac. 11;* helps Va. build Fort Prince George (Pittsburgh), 549, 593-94, 600; informs Washington of Jumonville's whereabouts, 609-10; message from Gov. Dinwiddie (1753), 286, *fac. 11-12;* message to Va. and Pa. (1754), 85-86, 88-89, *fac. 18, 19,* 443-44, 549, 604-5; names Shingas king of the Delaware, 61-62, 134, 280, 546, 558-59; refuses to confer with Gov. Dinwiddie at Winchester (1754), 648; requests Va. to build stronghouse at forks of the Ohio (Pittsburgh), 62-63,

· 712 ·

Index

64, 135, 136, 281-82, *fac. app. 20-21*, 548, 561; signs confirmation of Treaty of Lancaster, 546; sketch, 545-50; speech about Andrew Montour, 60, 132, 278-79, *fac. 19;* speech at Croghan's trading house (1753), 73, 285, *fac. 11,* 579-80; states Indians' claim to Ohio Country, *fac. 23;* Thomas Burney carries message to Va., 492; Va. answers request for aid, 598; warns French off the Ohio (1753), 76, *fac. 14, 23,* 431-32, 586.
Halifax, George Montagu Dunk, 2nd earl: Ohio Co. solicits aid from, 182-83.
Halifax Co. (Va.): erected, 299.
Hall, Richard: 31, 121, *fac. app. 12,* 506.
Hamer, John: helps build first Ohio Co. store, 409, 507, 619.
Hampshire Co. (Va.): erected, 299.
Hanbury, Capel, member of Ohio Co.: 177, 182, *fac. 24,* 461-62; John Mercer's opinion, 48; letter from the committee of the company, 152-53, *fac. 26.*
Hanbury, John, London member and representative of Ohio Co.: 2, 5, 167, 177, 293, *fac. 24;* activities as company representative in England, 4, 6-7, 141, 171, 235-36, *fac. 4-5,* 409-11, 465, 493, 528, 540, 568; agrees with Thomas Penn for land for company, 48, 92, *fac. 21,* 469; "Articles of Agreement" for the copartnership of the Ohio Co. sent to, 6; assures Thomas Penn of company cooperation on the frontier, 410, 417, 531; "Case of the Ohio Co." (1752) sent to, 178, 394-95; empowered to obtain German settlers for company, 4; John Mercer sends Ohio Co. map to, 305; John Mercer's criticism, 411-12; lands in Va., 526; letter from company printed, 140-41; petition in behalf of Ohio Co. (1749), 234-35, 246-48, *fac. 2-3,* 407-8; petition in behalf of Ohio Co. (1754), 470; reported to have given Ohio Co. map to persons in England, 237, *fac. 5;* to apply to proprietors of Pa., N. C., and Md. for land for company, 6; to have company seal made in England, 6; to order purchase in England of trade goods and swivel guns, 3, 140-41, 143, 149, 235, *fac. 4.*
Hanbury, Osgood, member of Ohio Co.: 461-62; John Mercer's opinion of, 48; letter from committee of Ohio Co., 152-53, *fac. 26;* note from Thomas Walpole, 311; to assist George Mercer in London, 182.
Hanover Co. (Va.): erected, 299.
Harding, George: 294.
Harding, Henry: 294.

Harris, John, Indian trader: 475, 534; ferry, suggested treaty site (1743), 535, 536-37.
Harris, Mary, New England white captive: 14, 104, *fac. app. 4,* 492.
Harris, William: joins Andrew Montour's scouts, 483.
Harrison, Benjamin: 41.
Harvey, John: 250, 292, *fac. 4.*
Hedgman, Peter: 250, 293, *fac. 4.*
Helms, Leonard: 294.
Hendricks, David, Indian trader: captured by Indians, 70, 71, 242, 243, *fac. 9.* 576.
Henrico Co. (Va.): erected, 299.
Henry, George, Indian trader: captured by Indians, 419-20, 563.
Hepburn ———, merchant of Norfolk (Va.): 191.
Hill, Humphrey: 250, 294, *fac. 4.*
Hill, Thomas: 202.
Hillsborough, Lord: opposes Walpole Co., 668, 669, 673.
Hite [Hyle], Joist: 298.
Hockhocking, Delaware Indian town: 105, *fac. app. 5; see also* French Margaret's Town.
Hog, Peter: with George Washington at Fort Necessity, 597.
Holdernesse, Earl of: instructions to colonial governors (1753), 84, 593.
Holland, Hitchin: reports on French activity from Oswego, 578.
Holston [Houlston] River (Ky.): 143.
Hubbard, Benjamin: 250, 292, *fac. 4.*
Hudson, William: 250, 293, *fac. 4.*
Hughes River (W. Va.): 518.
Hunter, James: 190, 194, 198, 205, 206.
Hunter, William: ironworks, 206.
Huron Indians: sketch, 489; *see also* Wyandott Indians.
Hurricane Tom's [Harrikintoms], Indian town: 15, 105, *fac. app. 5,* 495-96.
Huske, John: quoted, 400.
Hutchinson, Thomas, gov. of Mass.: Benjamin Franklin responsible for publication of letters, 669.
Hyde, Thomas, Indian trader: captured by Indians, 576.

Illinois Indians: conquered by Six Nations, 400.
Impartial History of the Late War: quotation on history of the Ohio Co. (printed), *fac. 27.*
Indian affairs (N. Y.): commissioners, 576.
Indian conferences: attended by George Croghan, 480-81.
Indian consent required in seating lands under Great Britain: 399-400.

Index

Indian forays from Fort Duquesne to English settlements: 601-3.
Indian God Rock. *See* Big Rock.
Indian hostilities on the frontier (1763): 635-36.
Indian method of counting time: 13, 103, *fac. app. 4.*
"Indian Old Corn Fields." *See* Eskippakitheki.
Indian schools proposed by Va.: 563.
"Indian Seat": tract purchased by Thomas Cresap, 473.
Indian Sweat House: 9, 99, *fac. app. 2.*
Indian trade: rivalry between Va. and Pa. traders, 415-17.
Indian traders: derogatory remarks by Charles Thomson, 561.
Indian treaties: Albany (1722), 401; Albany (1746), 308; Albany (1754), 611; Carlisle (1753), 433-34; Dongan (N. Y., 1684), 553; Easten (1756), 662; Easton (1757), 662; Easton (1758), 297, 483, 637, 661; Fort Cumberland (1754), 649; Harris' Ferry (1757), 297-98; Lancaster (1744), *see* Lancaster Treaty (1744); Lancaster (1757), 297, 300-2; Logstown (1748), 303-4, 308-9, 552-53; Logstown (1752), *see* Logstown Treaty (1752); Logstown (1753), 81, *fac. 13*, 430-32, 438-39, 547-48, 592; Philadelphia (1736), 533, 663; Philadelphia (1742), 657-58; Quaker Conference (Philadelphia, 1756), 484; Wawiagta and Piankashaw (1751), 138-39, *fac. app. 23*, 457; Winchester (1753), 245, 286, *fac. 12*, 428-30, 433-34, 541, 557, 579; Winchester (proposed, 1754), 648-49.
Indian unrest (1756): 655-57.
Indian warriors on the Ohio: enumerated, 476.
Indians at Logstown: receive warning from French, 477-78.
Indians in French interest renounced by Twightwee: 21-22, 111, 260-61, *fac. app. 7.*
Ingles, William: 506.
Ironcutter, John: 228, 645.
Iroquois land: English right of jurisdiction, 583, 584.

Jackson, Richard, Pa. colonial agent: 666; Charlton Palmer delivered Ohio Co. papers to, 310, 522.
Jackson, Robert: 249, 293, *fac. 1.*
Jackson, William: 249, 293, *fac. 1.*
Jacobs Ferry (Pa.): Christopher Gist reaches Monongahela River near, 510.
James I: grants New Foundland to Earl of Northampton, 399.
Jefferson, Peter: 250, 294, *fac. 4.*
Jefferson (Pa.): Indian hunting camp near site, 511.
Jenkins, William: accompanies George Washington to Fort Le Boeuf, 437; courier for George Washington, 85, *fac. 17.*
Jennings, Edmund: Md. commissioner at Treaty of Lancaster (1744), 537-38.
Jeromeville (Ohio): site of Mohican John's town, 524.
John, Peter, Delaware Indian: witnesses Wawiagta and Piankashaw Treaty (1750), 139.
Johnson, James: 249, 294, *fac. 1.*
Johnson, Sir William: 231, 300, 301, 306, 578, 644; comments on Logstown Conference, 413-14, 540-41; given control of Indian affairs by N. Y., 576; holds Indian conference at Detroit (1761), 515; observations on Indian unrest, 228, 655-57.
Johnston, George: 201.
Joncaire, Philip Thomas Chabert de: activities in the Ohio Country, 477-78; entertains George Washington at Venango, 76, *fac. 14*, 437, 438; sketch, 585-86.
Jones, Morven M.: owned "George Mercer Papers," xviii.
Jones, Richard: 250, 293, *fac. 4.*
Joshua, Delaware Indian: 35, 124, 268, *fac. app. 14*, 511-12.
Jumonville, Coulon de: 550, 609-10.
Juniatta [Juniatta] River: Gist at, 8, 98, *fac. app. 2.*

Kakawatcheky [Cochawitchiky], Shawnee chief: 62, 134, 280, *fac. app. 20*, 476, 500, 544; *see also* Ackowanthio.
Kanawha Falls: 524.
Kanawha Ridge (W. Va.): 519.
Kanawha [Kanhawa, Conhaway, Connoway] (Great) River (W. Va.): 37, 47, 67, 72, 237, *fac. 5, 7, 10, fac. app. 15*, 519; proposed natural boundary for Ohio Co. grant, 230, 232.
Kanawha (Little) River (W. Va.): 519.
Keecaise, Delaware Indian: 516.
Kempton (W. Va.). *See* Fairfax stone.
Kenny, James: at Fort Pitt, 514-17.
Kenton, Thomas, Indian trader: witnesses Wawiagta and Piankashaw Treaty (1751), 139, *fac. app. 23.*
Kentucky region: Christopher Gist's description of, 26-28, 116-18, 265-66, *fac. app. 10-11.*
Kentucky [Canticoqui, Kantucqui] River: English traders captured on, 70, 243, *fac. 9; see also* Cuttaway (Little) River.
Kickeney Paullin's Indian camp: 474.
Kilgore, Ralph, Indian trader: captured by Indians, 499.

· 714 ·

Index

Killbuck, Delaware chief: 514-15.
King, ———: John Mercer's brewmaster, 190, 191, 194.
King, Robert, Md. commissioner: appointed to treat with the Six Nations Indians (1742), 535.
King, Rufus: once owner of New York Historical Society copy of printed *Case*, 393-94.
King, Thomas, Oneida chief: 660.
King George Co. (Va.): erected, 299.
Kiskiminetas [Kiscominatis, Kiskamonettas, Kiskiminetas, Kiskominettos, Kiskomineto] River: 142, 469; Christopher Gist at, 9, 99, *fac. app. 2;* Ohio Co. desires land on, 6; proposed boundary for Ohio Co. grant, 66, 67, *fac. 7.*
Kittanning, Delaware Indian town: destruction of, 560.
Kittatinny [Kittocktenny] Mts. (Pa.): 161, 302, 306.
Kittockton Creek (Va.): 41.
Kuskuskies, Indian town (New Castle, Pa.): 485, 560; King Beaver receives Christian Frederick Post, 513.

Lacewell, Jacob: 41.
La Demoiselle (Old Briton), Miami chief: 480, 491, 494, 501.
La Force, Michel Pépin, called: at Logstown, 478; captured by George Washington, 91, *fac. 21,* 609-10; sketch, 594-96; speech to Indians at Logstown, 84, *fac. 16.*
La Galissonière, Rolland Michel Barrin, comte de, gov. of New France: 553.
La Jonquière, Pierre Jacques de Taffenel, marquis de, gov. of New France: 502.
Lake Erie: French forts on, 11, 67, 72, 101, 253, *fac. 8, 10, fac. app. 3;* southern shore, the proposed boundary of Ohio Co. grant, 47.
La Mouche Noire, Piankashaw chief: 502.
Lancaster (Ohio): site of French Margaret's town, 495.
Lancaster (Pa.): John Mercer comments on massacre of Conestoga Indians at, 297.
Lancaster Treaty (1744): confirmed by Indians at Logstown Conference (1752), 64-65, 136-37, 283 (printed), *fac. app. 21-22;* explained to Indians at Logstown Conference, 56-59, 62, 128-31, 275-78, *fac. app. 18;* John Mercer's criticism of Pa.'s role, 298, 302-3, 306-8; Ohio Co. cites deed as Va.'s right to land west of the Allegheny Mountains, vii, 53, 233, 246, 270, *fac. 1, 2, 3, 6,* 398-99; preliminary negotiations, 652-54, 664-65; sketches, 400-3, 532-39.
Langlade, Charles Michel: leads Indians in attack on Pickawillany, 419.
Lapechkewe, young Shawnee king: 64, 135-36, 282, *fac. app. 21,* 561.
La Salle, René-Robert Cavalier, sieur de: French claim Ohio valley by right of discovery, 584.
Laughlintown (Pa.): 474.
Laurel Hill Creek, branch of Youghiogheny River: 508.
Laurel Ridge (Pa.): trail over, 474.
Lawachkamicky. *See* Pride, The.
Lawwashannoito, Shawnee Indian: witnesses Wawiagta and Piankashaw Treaty, 139, *fac. app. 23.*
Lawwellaconin Creek (W. Va.): 38, *fac. app. 15; see also* Pond Creek.
Lee, Arthur: James Mercer controversy with, 203-4.
Lee, Philip Ludwell, member of Ohio Co.: 3, 4, 48, 143, 168, 169, 170, 176, 177, 179, 180, 183, 190, 222, 320, *fac. 24, 25,* 468, 568, 622; letter from James Mercer to, 323; receives extract of George Mercer's letter to John Mercer, 211; remiss in corresponding for company, 184; to write to Duke of Bedford on company business, 48, 151.
Lee, Richard, member of Ohio Co.: 3, 4, 5, 6, 169, 170, 171, 172, 173, 174, 177, 180, 181, 183, 222, *fac. 24;* criticized by John Mercer, 224-27; letter to James Mercer, 323; presents Ohio Co. petition to Va. Executive Council (1772), 666; sells land to John Mercer, 41.
Lee, Thomas, member of Ohio Co.: 2, 3, 4, 5, 140, 168, 169, 170, 171, 177, *fac. 2, 24, 25,* 412, 568; agitates for permanent Va. boundary lines, 410-11, 466-67; arranges for Indian conference (1749-50), 540; complains of Pa. traders, 417, 531, 544; death, 5, 268; engages Conrad Weiser as Indian interpreter, 466; founder of Ohio Co., 234, *fac. 2;* George Mason applies for Ohio Co. papers from executors, 173; informs company members their grant is approved by the king, 617; negotiates with Six Nations Indians, 409, 493-94; Ohio Co. letter to, 2; petitions Va. for Ohio Co. grant (1747), 462; remarks on Treaty of Lancaster reported by John Mercer, 234, *fac. 2;* tries to secure Ohio Indians to the English, 485; Va. commissioner to Lancaster Treaty (1744), 402-3, 538; writes to Board of Trade for treaty goods, 409-10, 466.
Lee, Thomas Ludwell, member of Ohio

· 715 ·

Index

Co.: 180, 181, 183, 224, 568; letters to James Mercer, 318-20.
Le Mercier, Chevalier; engineer of French Ohio expedition: 86, 87, 88, *fac. 18*, 598.
Leonard, John, of New Jersey: murdered by Wequalia, 657.
Le Pied Froid, Miami chief: 502-3.
Le Tort's Creek (W. Va.): 37, *fac. app. 15*, 519.
Lewis, Andrew: at Fort Necessity, 492; Va. land grant, 568.
Lewis, Charles: 248, 292, 294, *fac. 1, 4*.
Lewis, John: 248, 250, 290, 292, *fac. 1, 4, 24*.
Lewis, Nicholas: 250, 293, *fac. 4*.
Lewis, Robert: 248, 292, *fac. 1*.
Lewis, Thomas: 250, 293, *fac. 4*.
Lewis, William: 248, 292, *fac. 1*.
Lewis, Zachary: 248, 249, 292, *fac. 1*.
Lewis families of Pa.: migrate from Pa. to Va., 608.
Licking Creek (Ohio): 15, 105, *fac. app. 5*.
Licking Creek (Pa.): 34, 35, 124, 268, *fac. app. 14*; *see also* Ten Mile and Ruff's Creeks.
Licking River (Ky.): called Salt River by Shawnee, 504.
Ligneris, Capt. François le Marchand, sieur de: at Fort Duquesne, 603-4.
Ligonier (Pa.). *See* Loyalhannan, Indian town, and Fort Ligonier.
"Lime Stone Rock": Ohio Co. land in Md., 619.
Limestone Run (Va.): 41.
Liquor: price on the frontier, 61, 280, *fac. app. 20*.
Lisbon (Ohio): on Christopher Gist's route, 486.
Little Abraham, Mohawk chief: 301-2.
Little Pict, Shawnee Indian town (Ky.): English traders captured, 71, 242, *fac. 9*; *see also* Eskippakitheki.
Livingston, James, fort major at Fort Cumberland: 614, 623, 629.
Logan, George: 250, 293, *fac. 4*.
Logan, James, sec'y of Pa.: negotiates for treaty at Lancaster, 307, 534; speaks to Chief Checochinican, 509.
Logstown [Chinengué, Loggstown], Indian town: burned by Chief Monacatootha (Scarouady), 477; Christopher Gist visits, 9-10, 99-100, 252-53, *fac. app. 2*; French activities, 72, *fac. 9-10, 16*, 477-78, 548; George Croghan's trading house, 480; George Washington confers with Half King, 437; Indians informed of Va.'s message, 10, 100, *fac. app. 2*; Joncaire arrives, 585; rebuilt by French (1755), 478; sketch, 476-78; treaty (1752), *see* Logstown Treaty.
Logstown Treaty (1744): Christopher Gist invites Indians to, 33-34, 123-25, 267, 268, *fac. app. 13, 14*; Christopher Gist represents Ohio Co., 472; Christopher Gist's secret instructions from Ohio Co., 52-54; confirmation of Lancaster deed, 64-65, 136-37, 283 (printed), *fac. app. 21-22*; Half King and other Onondaga chiefs arrive, 544; Half King names Shingas, king of the Delaware, 62, 134, 546; Lancaster deed and treaty explained to Indians, 56-59, 62, 128-31, 275-78, 281, *fac. app. 18*; location of minutes, 540; minutes (additional) not in Ohio Co. copy, 541-43, 562; necessary for Va. and Ohio Co., 541; not official for Onondaga Council, 413-14; preliminary negotiations in London by John Hanbury, 409-11; preliminary session at Shannopin's town, 541-43; printed, 54-66, 127-38, 273-84, *fac. app. 17-22*; sketch, 417-19; treaty goods, 493-94; unsuccessful negotiations before 1751, 412-13; Va. commissioners do not agree, 238.
Lomax, Lunsford, member of Ohio Co.: 54 ff., 183, 273 ff., *fac. app. 17 ff.*, 632-33; appointed Va. commissioner for Logstown Conference (1744), 52, 238, *fac. 6*; kept minutes of Logstown Conference for Ohio Co., 418, 539, 647; letter from William Trent, 78, 94, *fac. 10, 22*; letter to William Fairfax, 79; opposes James Patton at Logstown Conference, 274; petitions for land on Ohio, 290, 422, 569; purchases Lawrence Washington's share in Ohio Co., 176, 178; scheme to establish a local bank, 207.
London Magazine: history of Ohio Co., printed, *fac. 27*, 451.
Long Knife. *See* Assarigoa.
Longueuil, Charles le Moyne, 2nd baron de, 487, 554-55.
Loudoun Co. (Va.): erected, 41, 299.
Louisa Co. (Va.): erected, 299.
Louisville (Ky.). *See* Falls of the Ohio.
Lower Indian towns (Ohio): 11, 14, 101, 104, 253, 255, *fac. app. 3, 4*; *see also* White Woman's town.
Lower Shawnee Indian town (Portsmouth, Ohio): 16, 84, 106, 255-56, *fac. app. 5*, 420, 490, 497-98.
Lowry, Alexander, Indian trader: 577.
Lowry, Daniel, Indian trader: 577.
Lowry, James, Indian trader: escapes from Indian captors, 71, 242, *fac. 9*, 576, 577.
Lowry, John, Indian trader: 577.
Lowry, Lazarus, and son, Indian traders: 577.
Loyal Land Co.: 506.
Loyalhanna [Loweathanning, Lowel-

· 716 ·

Index

hanning, Creek (Pa.): 6, 142, 469.
Loyalhannon, Indian town: 9, 99, *fac. app.* 2, 474-75.
Loyall, Paul: 250, 293, *fac. 4.*
Ludwell, Thomas: criticized by John Mercer, 225-26, 526-27; sees Ohio Co. map, 578.
Lunenburg Co. (Va.): erected, 299.

McBryar, Andrew, Indian trader: escapes from Pickawillany, 419-20.
Macconce. *See* Coonce, Mark.
McDowell, James: killed by Indians, 299, 654-55.
McGinty, Alexander, Indian trader: captured by Indians, 70, 71, 242, 243, *fac. 9,* 575-76.
McGuire, Rev. John Page: xix-xx.
Mack, Martin, Moravian missionary: 495.
McKay, Robert: 608, 654.
McKee, Thomas, Indian trader: *fac. app.* 22.
McKensie, Alexander: 250, 292, *fac. 4.*
McKinney, John: description of Fort Duquesne by, 603.
McLaughlin, James, Indian trader: 586.
McMachon, John: 51, 249, 251, *fac. 2, 6.*
McMachon, Richard: 51, 249, 251, *fac. 2, 6.*
McMachon, William: 51, 233, 249, 251, 289, *fac. 2, 6, 24, 414.*
Mad Creek (Ohio): 24, 114, 263, *fac. 9,* 501; *see also* Miami (Little) River.
Maddison, John: 250, *fac. 4.*
Maguck, Delaware Indian town: 15, 105, *fac. app. 5.*
Maguire, John: accompanies George Washington to Fort Le Boeuf, 437.
Maidstone (Md.): Ohio Co. storehouse at, 472.
Margaret's Creek (Ohio): 11, 101, *fac. app. 3; see also* Sugar Creek.
Marietta (Ohio): French leaden plate buried, 553.
Marin, Pierre Paul, French commandant: death, 584.
Martin, Robert: 250, 293, *fac. 4.*
Maryland: and Pa. boundary line, 231-32, 410-11; Ohio Co. wishes land grant from, 6; refuses to recruit militia, 83-84; signs treaty with Shawnee Indians, 473.
Maryland Gazette: Ohio Co. advertises sale of lots in town at Wills Creek, 451, 452, 626-27.
Mason, George, member of Ohio Co.: 3, 143, 168, 172, 177, 178, 179, 180, 222, 223-24, *fac. 24, 25,* 468, 569; appointed Co.'s cashier or treasurer, 4, 6, 170; asks James Mercer for Ohio Co. books, 315; comments on king's proclamation, 636; comments on Ohio Co. merger with Grand Ohio Co., 316-17; criticism of George Mercer, 316-17; draws up proposals for boundaries for company grant, 227; empowered to purchase land for company, 619; given power of attorney to execute company deeds, 181; inquiries about privy council queries, 185-86; letter to James Mercer, 315-17; letter to John Mercer, 231-32; letter to Robert Carter, 185-86; opinion of Hugh Parker, 465; opposes Lunsford Lomax's scheme for local bank, 207; ordered to purchase slaves for company, 175; purchases land in Md. for company, 618-19; seeks official company books from Thomas Lee executors, 5; sells company land, 619; to arrange for written articles of agreement for company, 5, 173, 174; to correspond with John Hanbury on company business, 5, 173.
Mastadon remains found in Kentucky: 25-26, 115, 265, *fac. app. 9,* 504.
Maury, James: 250, 293, *fac. 4.*
Mecklenburg Co. (Va.): erected, 299.
Memocollen. *See* Nemacolin.
Mémoire contenant le Précis des Faits, avec leurs Piéces Justificatives, Pour servir de Réponse aux Observations envoyées par les Ministers d'Angleterre, dans les Cours de l'Europe: discussion, 600.
Mercer, Ann (Mrs. John): 40.
Mercer, Anna: 201.
Mercer, Fenton: 188, 199.
Mercer, George, member of Ohio Co.: appointed lt. gov. of N. C., 311; appointed London agent for Ohio Co., 182-83; asks permission to merge company with Grand Ohio Co., 312-15; authority for size of Gist's settlement, 421; compiles *Case of the Ohio Company,* 396-98; complains of company members' negligence, 667, 671; corresponds with George Washington about land, 520-21; describes Ohio Country, 497; draft on Samuel Wharton, 324; executes company survey of Charlottesburg at mouth of Wills Creek, 165-66, 181-82, *fac. 29,* 451-53; George Mason's criticism of, 316-17; land release, 40-45; lends Christopher Gist's journals to Thomas Pownall, 396; letter from Charlton Palmer, 310; letter from Conway Richard Dobbs, 311-12; letter from Samuel Wharton, 324-25; letters from John Mercer, 186-229, 297-310; licensed Va. surveyor, 612; map, 227, 423, 424, 573-74, 624; marriage, 207, 214; memorials in behalf of company, *fac. 32-36,* 455-57; merges com-

Index

pany with Grand Ohio Co., 312-14, 667-68, 671; ordered to repair company store at Wills Creek, 180; presses claim for bounty lands, 611-12; proposals for engaging settlers for company, 224; purchases Arthur Dobbs' company stock, 621; receives company papers from Charlton Palmer, 397, 462, 522; rumors of return to Va., 221, 222; stamp collector, 630, 639; statement of account with Grand Ohio Co., 325, 326; to be reimbursed for expenses by company, 296; to settle company accounts with Hanburys, 183.

Mercer, Hugh, commandant at Fort Pitt: 188, 221, 514.

Mercer, James, member of Ohio Co.: 189, 227-28; controversy with Arthur Lee, 203-4; defense of George Mercer, 312-15; land release of, 40-45; letters from members of Ohio Co., 315 ff.; letters to members of Ohio Co., 312-15.

Mercer, John, secretary of Ohio Co.: 143, 175, 176, 177, 180, 181, 182, 183, *fac. 24, 25,* 468, 522, 640; accusation against Henry Bouquet, 447; accusation against Va. officials, 414-15; approves George Mercer's conduct as stamp collector, 186; authored case of the Ohio Co., 395-96; blames failure of company on individual members, 212; company meets at home of, 176, 179; conveys company stock to sons, 41; criticism of history of company published in England, *fac. 27-29;* criticism of Pa. Indian policy, 297 ff., 309, 406-7, 664; criticism of Robert Carter, 223; criticism of Robert Dinwiddie, 526-27; criticism of Va.'s land policy, 414-15; description of brewery of, 190 ff.; discusses Lancaster Treaty (1744), 306-8; draws up cases of the company, 150-51, 179; draws up company's articles of agreement, 6, 173, 174; excuses failure of company, 444-46; executes release of bond to John Tayloe and Presley Thornton, 190, 522; invective against Conrad Weiser, 299-300; laments case of the company, not printed (1768), 225; land sold to sons, 40-45; letter from John Tayloe, 211; letter to Francis Fauquier, 93-95, *fac. 21-22;* letters to Charlton Palmer, 46-48, 184-85, 406-7; letters to George Mercer, 186-229, 297-310; makes map for company, 225, 237, 411-12, 526-27, 577-78; names of children of, 188; negro slaves not profitable for, 212-13; on frontier affairs, 184-85; on Pa. legislation regulating Indian trade, 48; on tutoring in Va., 199-201; on Va.'s surveyor fees, 46-47; orders books, supplies, clothing for slaves from England, 215-20; petitions for land on the Ohio River, 240, 422, 569; queries about family estate in Ireland, 204-5; receives important company papers, 222-23; refuses to sign company letter to Robert Dinwiddie, 48; resigns as company secretary, 211; self-appraisal of economic status, 189-99; sells his slaves, 42; Shenandoah and Bull Run lands of, 190; solicits license for company surveyor, 143.

Mercer, John, son of John: 199, 201.
Mercer, Maria: 201.
Mercer, Mary: 42-43.
Mercer, Mary Elinor Beatrix: 188.
Mercer, Phipps: 204.
Mercer, Robert: 201, 202.
Mercer, Roy: 199, 201, 202.
Mercer, Sarah Ann: 42-43.
Mercer, Selden: 205, 213.
Mercer, William R.: correspondence about "George Mercer Papers." xviii-xix.
Mercer family (Ireland): 205.
Meriwether, Francis: 250, 294, *fac. 4.*
Meriwether, John: 250, 294, *fac. 4.*
Meriwether, Nicholas: 250, 294, *fac. 4.*
Meriwether, Thomas: 250, 294, *fac. 4.*
Meriwether, Thomas, Jr.: 250, 292, *fac. 4.*
Miami Indians: 400, 490-91, 502-3; *see also* Pickawillany, Pict, and Twightwee.
Miami (Great) River (Ohio): 24, 113-14, 263, *fac. app. 8,* 554; Ohio Co. rejects land on, 49-50, 237, *fac. 5.*
Miami (Little) River (Ohio): 18, 108, *fac. 6;* Ohio Co. rejects land on, 49-50, 237, *fac. 5; see also* Mad Creek.
Middle Island Creek (W. Va.): 519.
Middlebourne (W. Va.): 518.
Middleton, Ann: 41.
Mingo Indians on the Ohio River: 501.
Mitchell, John, mapmaker: 411-12, 422.
Mohawk Indians: 300.
Mohican [Mohickon] Indians: 19-20, 109, 259, *fac. app. 7.*
Mohican [Mohiccon] John's, Delaware Indian town: 47, 524.
Molchuconickon Creek (W. Va.): 38, *fac. app. 15; see also* Middle Island Creek and Buffalo Creek.
Molsinoughko, Wawiagta chief. See Tokintoa Molsinoughko.
Monacatootha, Oneida chief: 431-32, 476; burns Logstown, 477; *see also* Scarouady.
Monongahela [Monaungahela, Monongaly] River: Christopher Gist description of land along, 34-35, 123-24, 267, *fac. app. 13-14;* Christopher Gist discovers cave near, 34, 124, 268, *fac. app.*

Index

14; John Blair's land on, 233; Lewis Evans on navigation of, *fac. app. 25;* Ohio Co. settlement on, 69, 240-41; proposed boundary for company lands, 47, 230-32; upper forks, identified, 508.
Montague, Edward: Va. colonial agent in London, 47, 209, 525, 640.
Montandre, Caughnawaga Indian: 244.
Montour, Andrew: *fac. 11, fac. app. 2, 3, 5, 6, 8;* accompanies William Trent to Pickawillany (1752), 419-20, 494; agrees to go to S. C. to liberate Shawnee captives, 558; assists William Trent at Logstown (1754), 480; criticism of James Patton's treaty invitation to the Indians, 413; French offer reward for capture or death of, 16-17, 106, 256; Half King speaks to Eghuisera at Logstown Conference, 60, 132, 278-79, *fac. app. 19;* informant for new French fort on Lake Erie, 566; informs Va. of French troop movements towards the Ohio, 78, *fac. 10;* intermediary between Indian tribes, 502; interprets for Christopher Gist, 17, 107, 256-57, 259, *fac. app. 4, 7;* interprets for Ohio Co. and Va. at Logstown Conference, 54 ff., 143, 177, 271, *fac. app. 17 ff.,* 539; interprets Wyandott and Delaware message to Twightwee, 20, 109-10, 259, *fac. app. 7;* invited to settle in Va. by Ohio Co., 143; James Mercer comments on services to Pa., 297; makes treaty with Wawiagta and Piankashaw in behalf of Pa. (1751), 138-39, *fac. app. 23;* missions to Onondaga (1753) for Pa. and Va., 73, 79, 284, 285, *fac. 11,* 580, 587, 660-61; Ohio Co. recommends to Va., 50, 237; Pa. mission to Pickawillany, 9, 16, 99, 252, 484-85; petitions for land on Ohio River (1752), 290, 422, 569; receives Pa.'s instructions for attendance at Logstown Conference (1752), 543; sketch, 481-84; *see also* Eghuiessera.
Montour, Margaret: 495.
Moore, Bernard: 250, 290, 292, *fac. 4, 24.*
Moore, John: 250, 293, *fac. 4.*
Moravians migrate from Pa. to N. C.: 608-9.
Morris, Henry: takes Va.'s message to Cherokee and Catawba, 589.
Morris, Joseph: Pa. commissioner for Indian trade, 154.
Mountain Lake (Va.): identified, 506.
Muddy Creek (Pa.): Indian trail west, 510.
Mullen, Patrick, Indian trader: 496.
Muskingum, Wyandott Indian town: 11, 101, 253, 420, 492.
Muskingum River: 47.

"Myrtilla" (ship): English captives returned from France to Philadelphia on, 420.

Nanticoke Indians: 300.
Navarre, Sieur de: report on Ottawa town, 487.
Nawmissipia Creek (W. Va.): 38, *fac. 15; see also* Little Kanawha River, Fishing Creek.
Neal, William: 293.
Neale [Neal], John: 51, 249, 251, 293, *fac. 6.*
Neale [Neal], Lewis: 51, 249, 251, 293, *fac. 2, 6.*
Neemokeesy Creek: Christopher Gist describes land and cave along, 38, *fac. 15; see also* Fishing Creek.
Nelson, Thomas, member of Ohio Co.: 2, 3, 168, 246, *fac. 2, 24,* 568.
Nelson, Thomas, Jr.: land grant, 248, 292, 293, *fac. 1.*
Nemacolin [Nemacolon, Nemicollin, Nemicotton], Delaware chief: 34, 123-24, 267, *fac. app. 13,* 510, 566.
Neville, Miss (of Lincoln): marries George Mercer, 207.
New Castle (Pa.). *See* Kuskuskies.
New Freeport (Pa.): 518.
New Garden Ridge. *See* Dividing Ridge.
New River: 31, 120, *fac. app. 11; see also* Kanawha (Great) River.
"New Store": Ohio Co. storehouse at Wills Creek, 507; *see also* Ohio Co. storehouses.
New York: monopolizes early Indian negotiations, 400.
New York Commissioners of Indian Affairs: ransom English prisoners, 70, 243.
New York Historical Society: owns unique copy of *The Case of the Ohio Co.* (1770), xx, 393-94.
Newcomer, Delaware chief: 516-17.
Newcomer, Shawnee chief: 509, 544, 555.
Newcomer, white captive: put to death at Muskingum, 13, 103, *fac. app. 4,* 492.
Newfoundland: granted outright to Earl of Northampton, 399.
Newlin, Nathaniel: 509.
Newton, Willoughby: 41.
Nicholas, Huron chief: 486, 488, 491.
Nicholson, Owen, Indian trader: 419-20, 563.
Nimmo, William, member of Ohio Co.: 2, 3, 168, 246, 293, *fac. 2, 24,* 568.
North Carolina: George Mercer appointed lt. gov., 311.
Nutimus [Natimus], Delaware chief: 302, 659.

· 719 ·

Index

Nynickonowca, Piankashaw chief: signs treaty, 138-39, *fac. app. 23.*

Occoquon Ferry (Va.): Ohio Co. meets at, 173.
Ogle, Samuel, gov. of Md.: 410.
Ohio Co.: accepts Hugh Parker's share for credit, 173; account with Arthur Dobbs (1753), 183; account with Grand Ohio Co. (1776-77), 325-26; agreement with Thomas Penn for land in Pa. (1754), 48, 92, 469; appoints Charlton Palmer London solicitor, 46, 180, 522; appoints George Mercer London agent, 182-83, 296, *fac. 29-30*, 630; "Articles of Agreement and Copartnership for the space of 20 years, May 23, 1751," 5, 6, 173, 174, 394, 461, 468-69, 619, 672; asks Henry Bouquet to join company, 614-15; asks John Hanbury to be London representative, 2, 234, *fac. 4-5*; asks John Pagan to procure foreign Protestant immigrants to settle land, 144-47; asks Va.'s permission to take up land in small tracts, 67, *fac. 8*; business conducted by William Trent, 569-73; cannot afford to build a fort in Western Country, 171; *Case, see* "Case of the Ohio Company"; Christopher Gist recommends land on the Miami Rivers to the company, 305; Christopher Gist recommends route from Wills Creek to upper forks of the Monongahela, 39, 269, *fac. app. 16;* Christopher Gist writes to Thomas Lee, president of, 31, 121, *fac. app. 12;* cites Treaty of Lancaster as basis for their claim, *fac. 1*, 398-99; claims to western land recited by John Mercer, 93-95; complains of Va.'s renewal of land grants to others, 51, *fac. 6;* complaint against Richard Corbin, 242; contracts with Thomas Cresap and Hugh Parker to explore Western Country, 4, 171; criticism of so-called land mongers, 67-68; *fac. 8;* desires land on Va.-Carolina border, 6; desires Pa. traders be prevented from trading in Western Country, 169; duties of Committee of the company, 175; Earl of Granville's proposal for company land in N. C., 469; employs Christopher Gist as explorer, 5, 236, *fac. 5*, 472; employs Hugh Parker, first factor, 4, 169, 465; employs William Trent as factor (1752), 68, 143, *fac. 8*, 570; enters caveat against James Patton, 143, 575; enters caveat against Richard Corbin, 72, 150, 179, 245, *fac. 10*, 426-27; enters caveat against William Russell, 69, 72, 241-42, *fac. 8, 10*, 426-27; expected Indian consent to build storehouse on the Ohio, 544; expenditures, 522, 523; first factors, 4, 68, 143, 169, *fac. 8*, 465, 570; founded by Thomas Lee, 234, *fac. 2;* gov. of Va. asked to report to the Privy Council on company's status, *fac. 34;* grant had boundary north of Ohio River, 566; grant never patented, 666; grant of 500,000 acres made by Va., July 12, 1749, 291; grant, terms of, 642; hastens to validate grant (1752), 420-21; history as published in *London Magazine, fac. 27;* history by John Mercer, *fac. 27-29;* hopes to survey grant after Forbes' campaign, 91-92, *fac. 21;* imports trade goods from England, 3, 140-41, 167, 235, *fac. 4*, 408, 465, 620; in Indian trade, 631-32; instructions to Christopher Gist for exploration, 7-8, 31-32, 49-51, 97-98, 236-37, 252; instructions to Christopher Gist for Logstown Conference, 52-54, 176-77, 269-71, *fac. 6-7;* instructions to Christopher Gist to lay out a town on the Ohio (Saltsburg), 149-50; James Patton's comments on location of company land, 620; John Mercer conveys shares to his sons, 41; John Mercer excuses failure of adventure, 444-46; John Mercer, secretary, 211; John Mercer's recapitulation of proceedings, *fac. 23;* John Mercer's summary of company activities, 95-97, 221-27; lays out Charlottesburg (Md.), a town at Wills Creek, 165-66, 181-82, *fac. 29*, 451-53, 626-27; letter from James Mercer, 312-15; letter from Robert Dinwiddie, 72, *fac. 9-10;* letter to Capel and Osgood Hanbury, 152-53, *fac. 26;* letter to John Hanbury, 140-41; letter to Robert Dinwiddie, 151-52, *fac. 26;* letter to Thomas Lee, 2; Lord Shelburne's queries, 641; losses, 522, 523, 646; Lunsford Lomax records minutes of Logstown Treaty, 274, 632-33, 647; map (1753) by George Mercer, 227, 423, 424; map (1752) by John Mercer, 72, 225, 242, 305, *fac. 10*, 427, 472-73, 526-27; meetings advertised in *Virginia Gazette*, 221, 315, 638, 671, 672; members assessed, 3, 5, 76, 150, 239, *fac. 14*, 586, 625; membership reduced (1749), 168; memorials and petitions, (résumé) 453-57 (to Va. Executive Council, 1747), 167, 464, 630 (to Board of Trade by John Hanbury, 1749), 234-35, 246-48, *fac. 2-3*, 407-8, 568, 607-8, 625, 672 (to Robert Dinwiddie, 1752), 66-68, 175-76, 239-40, 271-73, *fac. 7-8*, 421-22 (to Board of Trade by John

· 720 ·

Index

Hanbury, 1754), 411-12, 470 (to the king in council, 1761), 48, *fac. 25-26*, 450-51 (to the king in council, 1763), *fac. 30-31* (to the king by George Mercer, 1765), *fac. 32-33* (to the king in council by George Mercer, 1767), *fac. 34-35*, 397, 408 (to Board of Trade by George Mercer, 1769), *fac. 35-36* (to Board of Trade, 1770), 457 (to Va. Executive Council by Richard Lee, 1772), 666 (to General Assembly of Va. by George Mason, 1778), 464; merged with Grand Ohio Co., 667, 671; names of members, *fac. 24*, 568-69; obtains treaty wampum from Thomas Cresap, 54, 271, *fac. 7*; official company papers given to George Mercer by Charlton Palmer, 397-98, 462; opposes merger with Grand Ohio Co., 315 ff.; orders and resolutions printed (résumé), 1-6, 140-53, 167-82, 287-88; orders Christopher Gist to survey land for settlement, 68-69, 240-41, *fac. 8*; orders Christopher Gist's journal sent to John Hanbury, 51, 237, *fac. 5*; orders legal appointment of surveyor, 143; orders swivel guns, 149; owns live stock, 539-40; partnership limited to 20 members, 2-3; patents land in Va., 467; pays workmen for building fort at Pittsburgh, *fac. 28*; plans disrupted by French and Indian War, 395; plans storehouses along road to the Ohio, 77-78, 295-96, *fac. 17*; prepares to take up land according to grant, 235 ff., *fac. 4-5*; Privy Council's queries about origin of claim, 223; property at Will's Creek devastated by troops at Fort Cumberland, 180, *fac. 28, 29,* 634; proposed natural boundaries between company land and soldier bounty land agreed upon, *fac. 17*; proposed natural boundaries for grant, 47-48, 224, 227, 229-32, 523, 524; purchases land in Md., 142-43, 618-19; purchases land in Va., 5; reasons for failure, viii-ix; receives Christopher Gist's plan and journal of his explorations, 49-50, 51, 237, *fac. 5*; recommends establishing Va.-Pa. boundary line, 4; reimbursed for building Fort Prince George (Pittsburgh), 623; rejects Miami Rivers site for land grant, 49-50, 237, *fac. 5*; renews activity in 1759, 395; requests John Hanbury to procure foreign protestant settlers, 171; requests plan and journal of Christopher Gist's exploration, 7, 98, 175, *fac. 1*; road from Wills Creek to Redstone on the Monongahela, 32, 39, 50, 67, 178, 269, *fac. 5, 7,* 472, 565-66, 633; role in Logstown Conference (1752), 52-54, 269-71, *fac. 6-7*; seal, 6, 468; seeks German Protestant settlers, 144-47, 167, 421; sends William Trent to build fortified storehouse on the Ohio, 438-39; settlement between Monongahela and Youghiogheny Rivers, 66, 68-69, 238-41, *fac. 7, 8, 20,* 423-24, 574; sketch, xi-xv; solicits land from Earl of Granville, Lord Baltimore, and Thomas Penn, 142; solicits Robert Dinwiddie's assistance in London (1761), *fac. 26*; solicits Va.'s permission to survey grant in small plats, 272, *fac. 7-8*; storehouses—at Thomas Cresap's, 141, 142, 409, 507; at Wills Creek, Md., 32, 180, *fac. 28,* 507, 627, 651; Rock Creek, at Maidstone, Va., 146, 472, 622; at New Store Tract, Va., 122, 171, 266, *fac. app. 13*; at Redstone on the Monongahela, *fac. 15, 28*; supplies Va. militia on the Ohio (1754), 83; swivel guns stored by Job Pearsall, 623; to employ surveyors, 144; total investment, *fac. 30*, 608; town and fort to be built on the Ohio (specifications), 147-48, 439, 574, 586, 622-23, *see also* Saltsburg on the Ohio; trade goods on the Ohio (1754), 592-93; Va.'s dilemma of land for company grant, 546; wants all Indian traders to have Va. license, 4; wants royal permission for Va. to use quitrents for Indian presents, 140; William Beverley's comments, 525.

Ohio Country: Lewis Evans on extent, *fac. app. 26*; Lewis Evans recommends separate government, *fac. app. 26*; proposed new colony, 641, 671.

Ohio Indians: accept Va.'s invitation to treat at Logstown, 52, 238, *fac. 6*, 413, 529-30; ask English to help defend Ohio Country from French aggression, *fac. 16*; ask George Croghan for Pa.'s help (1754), 84; children of, Va. offers to educate, 65-66, 137-38, 284, *fac. app. 22, see also* Brafferton Indian School; decline invitation to Winchester (1753), 582; did not come to Va. Conference at Winchester (May, 1753), 79; disillusioned about English aid after Winchester and Carlisle conferences, 433-34; favor Thomas Penn, 52, 238, *fac. 6*; fear French attack, 605; go to Philadelphia (1747), 476; go to Winchester Conference (1753), 548; reply to La Force's threats, 596; say Six Nations Indians murdered Virginians, 64, 136, *fac. 21*; send message to Twightwee (1752), 65, 137, 283, *fac. app. 22*; sign confirmation of Lancaster Treaty at Logstown (1752), 64-65, 136-37, 283, *fac. app. 22*; Trent delivers Va.'s pres-

Index

ent to (1753), 581; Va. holds conference at Logstown with (1753), 430-31.
Ohio River: Lewis Evans on navigation, *fac. app. 25;* proposed boundary for Ohio Co. grant, 47, 67, 230-32, *fac. 7-8;* Va. petitioners for land along, enumerated, 292-94; width at Shannopin's town, 9, 99, *fac. app. 2.*
Old Town (Md.): Thomas Cresap's 8, 98, *fac. app. 1,* 473; *see also* Opessa's.
Old Town Creek (W. Va.): 519.
Olumapies, Delaware chief: 512.
Onas, Pa. proprietors: 64, 136, 282, *fac. app. 21; see also* Penn, Thomas and William.
Onondaga Council: adheres to policy of strict neutrality, 423, 661; disintegration of authority over Ohio Indians, 449; *see also* Six Nations Indians and Indian treaties.
Onongraguicte, Caughnawaga chief: 70, 243-44, *fac. 9.*
Opessa's, Shawnee Indian town: 473.
Oppaymolleah, Delaware chief: 35, 39, 124, 268, 269, *fac. app. 14, 16,* 511.
Orange Co. (Va.): erected, 299.
Ordnance for forts on the Ohio: imported from England, 591.
Oswegle Bottom: George Croghan trading house, 480; *see also* Youghiogheny Big Bottom.
Ottawa, Indian town (Ohio): 11, 101, *fac. app. 3,* 487-88.
Ottawa Indians: demand surrender of white traders at Muskingum, 84; expected to attack traders at Lower Shawnee town, 71, 242-43, *fac. 9;* in French interest, 13, 103, 254-55, *fac. app. 4;* renounced by Twightwee, 22, 112, 261-62, *fac. app. 8;* sketch, 488.
Ouasioto Mts. (W. Va.): 47, 524.
Owsley, Thomas: 41.

Pagan, John: agent to contract for German Protestant settlers for Ohio Co., 144-47.
Palmer, Charlton, London solicitor for Ohio Co.: 150-51, 180, 210, 296, 314, 317; delivers Ohio Co. papers to George Mercer, 397, 462, 522; letter to George Mercer, 310; letters from John Mercer, 46-48, 184-85; to assist George Mercer in London, 182.
Parker, Hugh, member of Ohio Co.: 3, 416, 531; builds company storehouse, 5, 141, 142, 409, 507, 619; employed to transport trade goods, 4, 169; first company factor, 4, 169, 170, 465, 630; purchases horses for company, 539-40; purchases land in Va. for company, 5, 171, 619; recommended for justice of the peace for Augusta Co., 4, 169; servant killed at Kuskuskies, 415-16; shares absorbed by Ohio Co. after death, 173; to contract for company road, 4, 141, 142, 565-66; to explore for company, 4, 141-42, 171; to supply Christopher Gist with company trade goods, 5, 172; to trade with Indians only, 169-70.
Parks, William: 249, 250, 251, 292, 293, *fac. 1, 4.*
Parrett, Hugh: petitions for land on Ohio River, 293.
Parrett, Leonard: petitions for land on Ohio River, 294.
Pate, Henry: petitions for land on Ohio River, 293.
Patten, John, Indian trader: 274, 490, 492, 557.
Patterson, William: captures Frederick Stump and John Ironcutter, 228.
Patton, James: 57, 61, 128, 133, 267, 275, 280, *fac. app. 18, 20, 22,* 411, 647; inexperienced in Indian diplomacy, 413-14; invites Indians to Logstown Conference (1752), 528; killed by the Indians, 636; letter to John Blair about land grant, 425, 575; member of Loyal Land Co., 506; Ohio Co. enters caveat against, 143, 620; petitions for western lands, 654; views on Va. land policy, 404-5; Va. commissioner at Logstown Conference (1752), 33, 51, 52, 54, 123, 237, 238, 273, *fac. 5-6, fac. app. 13,* 493, 494, 529-30, 532, 540; Va. land grants, 233, 235, 249, 289, 293, *fac. 1, 4, 24,* 567-68.
Paxtang settlers: join Andrew Montour's scouts, 483.
Pearsall, Job: George Washington at home of, 85, *fac. 18,* 597; Ohio Co. swivel guns stored at home, 623.
Pendergrass, Garrett, Indian trader: 509.
Pendleton, Edward: 250, 292, *fac. 4.*
Pendleton and Lyons: 190.
Penn, Thomas: 48, 92-94, *fac. 21,* 469; assured of Ohio Co. cooperation, 531; comments on Ohio Co. activities, 416-17; discusses company with John Hanbury, 410; letter to Richard Peters, 410-11, 421; Ohio Co. desires land from, 6, 142; Ohio Indians favorable to policy of, 52, 238, *fac. 6;* on Pennsylvania German migration to Va., 564-65.
Penn, William: speech to the Indians, 553.
Pennington, Edward: Pa. commissioner for Indian trade, 154.
Pennsylvania: acts of assembly regulating Indian trade on the frontier, 48, 94-95, 153-65, *fac. 22-23,* 447-48; An-

Index

drew Montour employed by, 482; as mediator in Va.-Six Nations dispute, 302; chastizes Shawnee Indians (1748), 555; claims Fort Pitt is in Pa., *fac. 22-23;* evicts settlers west of the Susquehanna River, 658; finances Indian trade, 153-65; gives present to Twightwee, 484-85; governor's message to the general assembly (1753), *fac. 12;* Indian policy of, 616; Indian traders maligned by John Mercer, 406-7; indicted by John Mercer for Indian policy, 297 ff.; invites Delaware Indians to conference at Logstown (1751), 16, 105-6, *fac. 5;* Maryland boundary line, 231-32, 410-11; message to western Indians, 9, 100, 252, *fac. app. 2;* Ohio Co. desires land in, 6; orders against sale of rum to Indians, 558; proclamation forbidding settlements west of Kittotinny [Kittochtinny] Hills (1742), 303, 657-58; quitrents reportedly used to buy Indian gifts, 140; Richard Peters reconnoitres for county seat for Cumberland Co., 658; role in Lancaster Conference criticised by John Mercer, 306-7; sends message to Shawnee, 545; sends message to Six Nations, 588; signs articles of agreement with the Shawnee (1701), 473; trade goods transported to the Ohio Country via Potomac River, *fac. 23;* treaty with Wawiagta and Piankashaw, 139, 300, *fac. app. 23;* Va. boundary line, 4, 92-93, 171, 235, *fac. 4, 21,* 410-11; Va. trade rivalry, 415-17; votes gift to western Indians (1753), 582.

Pennsylvania, Southwestern: boundary, a concern of Ohio Co., 230-32; Christopher Gist's description of (1752), 32-33, 122, 267-68, *fac. app. 13-14.*

Pennsylvania Gazette: extracts printed from, 70, 71, 228, 242-43, *fac. 9.*

Pennsylvania Germans: settled in Va., 407.

Pennsylvania Proprietors: Indian policy of, 297-98, 305, 433-34, 617-18, 655-57; propose fort on Ohio River, 556.

Pennsylvania traders: jealous of Ohio Co., 238, *fac. 6;* killed in Ohio Country, 484; number at Logstown (1748), 476; Thomas Lee reports Indians defrauded by, 234, *fac. 2.*

Peoria Indians: 501.

Peter, John, Delaware Indian: witnesses Indian treaty, *fac. app. 23.*

Peters, Richard: 658; informs Thomas Penn of Ohio Co.'s activities, 416-17; letter to Conrad Weiser, 434; letters from Thomas Penn, 421; scheme to purchase land from the Six Nations (1753), 433-34; speaks to Indians about trade, 531-32.

Piankashaw [Pyankashee]: and Wawiagta Indian treaty with Pa., 24, 113, 138-39, 263, 300, *fac. app. 8, 23,* 457; chief renounces French Indians at Pickawillany, 21, 111, 260-61, *fac. app. 7;* young king receives gift from Va., 562.

Pickawillany [Picqualinnee, Pickwaylinees], Indian town: 17, 18, 107, 108, *fac. app. 6;* English traders captured at, 13-14, 103-4, 255, *fac. app. 4;* founding of, 491; French attack and destroy, 66, 68, 240, 305, *fac. 7, 8,* 419-20, 491, 563-64; George Croghan's trading house at, 480; traders repair fort at, 20, 110, 259.

Pickawillany Indians: Andrew Montour's mission to, 484-85; George Croghan sends message to, 11, 101, 253, *fac. app. 3;* receive present from Va., 494; *see also* Miami, Pict, and Twightwee.

Picktown. *See* Pickawillany.

Pict [Piet, Piques, Picques] Indians: 56, 128, 275, *fac. app. 18; see also* Miami, Pickawillany, and Twightwee.

Pierce, John: 250, 293, *fac. 4.*

Pine Creek (Pa.): George Croghan's trading house at, 480.

Pinnacle Rock (W. Va.): Christopher Gist visits, 30, 120, *fac. app. 11,* 506.

Piqua (Ohio): site of Pickawillany, 491; *see also* Pickawillany.

Pisquetomen, Delaware chief: 518.

Pittsburgh [Pitsburgh]: Delaware Indian town at, *fac. 23;* under Pa. jurisdiction, 231; Va. fort at, 63, 81-82, *fac. 15-16; see also* Shannopin's Indian town; Forts Duquesne, Pitt, and Prince George.

Pittsylvania Co. (Va.): erected, 299.

Pohick Run (Va.): 41.

Point Marion (Pa.): 508.

Point Pleasant (W. Va.): 525; French leaden plate buried, 553-54.

Poke, Charles, Indian trader: 34, 123-24, 267, *fac. app. 13-14,* 509.

Pond Creek (W. Va.): 519.

Port Royal (Va.): 41-42.

Portsmouth (Ohio): site of Lower Shawnee town, 497-98.

Post, Christian Frederick: Moravian missionary and Pa. envoy to Delaware Indians, 513, 515, 516.

Potomac River (Va.): 69, 241, 249, *fac. 2, 8, fac. app. 25.*

Potomac Run (Va.): 40.

Potts, John, Indian trader: 139, *fac. 23.*

Pound Creek (Va.): 505.

Pound Gap (Ky.): 505.

· 723 ·

Index

Powell, William, Indian trader: captured by the Indians, 70, 71, 242, 243, *fac. 9*, 576.
Power, James: 250, 292, 294, *fac. 4*.
Powers, James: represents Loyal Land Co., 575.
Pownall, John: owned printed "Case of the Ohio Co.," 398.
Pownall, Thomas: obtains Christopher Gist's journal from George Mercer, 396, 470-71.
Preston, John: 249, 293, *fac. 1*.
Preston, William: *fac. 22*, 506.
Price, Aaron: *fac. 22*.
Pride, The, Shawnee chief: 302, 503, 544, 657.
Prince Edward Co. (Va.): erected, 299.
Prince William Co. (Va.): erected, 299; John Mercer land, 41.

Quebec, Peter: husband of Margaret Montour, 495.
Quemahoning Creek (Pa.): 474.
Quitrents: use, 617-18.

Raccoon, Twightwee chief: attends Winchester Treaty (1753), 562-63.
Randolph, Peter: 190.
Randolph, Peyton: 250, 290, 292, *fac. 4, 24*.
Raymond, Capt. de: at Fort Kiskakon (French), 554; warns ministry of English encroachment, 479-80.
Raystown (Bedford, Pa.): 142.
Raystown Path: 474.
Red, Samuel: 251, 293, *fac. 4*.
Red Rock Run: 41.
Redstone: 507, 592; see also Ohio Co. and Trent, William.
Redstone Creek (Pa.): William Russell surveys land on a branch, 69, 241, *fac. 8*.
Reed Island Creek (Va.): 507.
Renick, ———, Indian trader: 477.
Reynall, John: Pa. commissioner for Indian trade, 154.
Rice, Patrick: 293.
Richardson, Joseph: Pa. commissioner for Indian trade, 154.
Ritchie, Archibald: 208, 220.
Roanoke (Va.): Christopher Gist's family flees to, 31, 121, 266, *fac. app. 12*.
Robbins Station (Pa.). *See* Youghiogheny Big Bottom.
Roberts, John: 249, 294, *fac. 1*.
Robinson, Beverley: 248, 292, *fac. 1*.
Robinson, George: 249, 293, *fac. 1*.
Robinson, John, treasurer of Va.: land grants to, 248, 289, 292, *fac. 1, 24*; default of, 189-90, 639.
Robinson, John, Jr.: 248, 292, *fac. 1*.
Rochelle (France): French send English captives to, 66.
Rock Creek (Md.): Ohio Co. storehouse, 146, 472, 622.
Rock Quarry: Christopher Gist takes sample for Ohio Co. from, 126, *fac. app. 14-15*; see also Copperas.
Rogers, Richard, clerk for John Mercer: 153, 187-88, 527.
Romanettos River. *See* Kiskiminetas River.
Romney (W. Va.): Job Pearsall home at, 597.
Rowland, Kate Mason: xix-xx.
Rozer, Henry: John Mercer attorney for, 222.
Ruff's Creek, branch of Ten Mile Creek: 518.
Russell, William: Gov. Dinwiddie's emissary to the French commandant on the Ohio (1753), 436, 579; John Mercer's criticism, 91, 226, *fac. 20*, 423-25; lands on the Youghiogheny surveyed, 69, 149, 241, *fac. 8*, 423-24, 573-74, 643-44; Ohio Co. enters caveats against, 69, 72, 241-42, *fac. 8, 10*, 426-27; Va. land grants, 51, 233, 249, 251, 289, *fac. 2, 6*, 568, 574.

Saguin's trading house on the Cuyahoga: 492.
St. Clair, Sir John: comments on Fort Cumberland, 628.
St. Pierre, Jacques le Gardeur, Sieur de: commandant at Fort Le Boeuf, 75-76, *fac. 14*, 585.
Salt Lick Creek (Ky.): 30, 119, *fac. app. 11*.
Salt Lick Creek (Ohio): 15, 105, *fac. app. 5*.
Salt Pond (Va.): 31, 120, *fac. app. 12*; see also Mountain Lake (Va.).
Saltsburg on the Ohio (Pa.): 147; see also Ohio Co. settlement and fort on Ohio River.
Sanders, Robert: 576; see also Albany, mayor of.
Sandy Gap (Md.): 32, 122, *fac. app. 13*, 508.
Sargent, John, member of the Grand Ohio Co.: 668.
Sassoonan. *See* Olumapies, Delaware chief.
Satana Indians: conquered by the Six Nations, 400; see also Shawnee Indians.
Scalp Creek (W. Va.): 38, *fac. app. 15*; see also Wheeling Creek.
Scarouady [Scaioady], Oneida chief:

· 724 ·

Index

agrees to go to S. C. to liberate Shawnee captives, 557; agrees with the Half King on policy toward French aggression on Ohio River, 548; asks Pa. for assistance against the French (1755), 483; asks Pa. to curb the excessive sale of rum, 558; attends Quaker conference at Philadelphia (1756), 484; of Logstown, 476-78; represents Ohio Indians at Winchester Treaty, 548; *see also* Monacatootha.

Schellsburg (Pa.), 474.

Schuyler, Myndert, Albany commissioner for Indian affairs: 70, 243-44, *fac. 9.*

Scioto River: Indian town on, 16, 17, 106, 256, *fac. app. 5.*

Sconohode, Seneca or Cayuga chief: confers with Thomas Cresap, 536.

Scotch Presbyterian schoolmasters: John Mercer's comments, 200-1.

Scott, James, member of the Ohio Co.: 3, 4, 5, 6, 143, 167, 168, 169, 170, 171, 172, 173, 174, 175, 176, 177, 179, 180, 181, *fac. 24, 25,* 465, 468, 569; opposes company merger with Grand Ohio Co., 321-22.

Seaclin's Creek (Va.): 41.

Sedgley & Hillhouse, London merchants: 208, 209.

Seneca Indians: 300.

Sewickley Bottom. See Youghiogheny Big Bottom.

Shamokin, Delaware Indian town: 484.

Shannopin, Delaware chief: 475.

Shannopin's [Shenapin's], Delaware Indian town: Christopher Gist visits, 9, 99, *fac. app. 2;* Delaware greet Va. commissioners (1752), 59, 131, 278, *fac. 19;* distance from Loyalhanna, 9, 99, *fac. app. 2;* population in 1750, 9, 99, *fac. app. 2.*

Sharpe, Horatio, gov. of Md.: 483, 627-29.

Shawnee Indian towns: on Pickaway Plains, 495; on the Scioto, 16, 106, 255-56, *fac. app. 5; see also* Hurricane Tom's, Lower Shawnee, Maguck, Old Town (Md.), Opessa's.

Shawnee Indians: accept Va.'s invitation to Logstown Conference, 17, 107, 256-57, *fac. app. 5-6;* at Logstown Conference, 56, 60, 61, 62, 63, 128, 131-32, 132-33, 135, 274-75, 278, 279, 282, *fac. app. 17-18, 19, 20, 21,* 544-45; captives in S. C., 556-57; confer with Virginians at Fort Cumberland, 649; desert to the French, 478-79, 502; friendship with the English, 16, 106, 256, *fac. app. 5,* 498-99, 500; marriage festival, 17, 107, 121-22, 257, 304-5, *fac. app. 6, 12;* move from headwaters of Potomac to Pa., 473; send message to Pa., 545; sketch, 497-98; solicit Pa. aid to help the Twightwee, 562, 564; threaten Md., 534-35; young king, 64, 135-36, 282, *fac. app. 21,* 431; *see also* Satana Indians.

Shawnee Warriors' Feather Dance: description, 23, 112-13, 262, *fac. app. 8.*

Shelburne, 2d earl of: on establishing a new colony in the western country, 641, 671; queries about the Ohio Co., 641.

Shelton, John: 250, 292, *fac. 4.*

Shenandoah River; 41.

Shickellamy [Shickallemo], Oneida chief: 303, 534, 535, 659.

Shingas, Delaware chief: 485, 518; abdication, 514; at Detroit Conference (1761), 516; at Logstown Treaty (1753), 431; made king of the Delaware, 62, 134, 280, *fac. app. 20,* 512; receives special present at Winchester Conference, 286; sketch, 558-61.

Shingas' Old Town, Delaware Indian town: 485-86, 560.

Shirley, William, gov. of Mass.: 591, 629.

Shirleysburg (Pa.): 512; *see also* Aughwick.

Silk raising on Ohio River: *fac. app. 26.*

Sinking Creek (Va.): 31, 120, *fac. app. 12.*

Six Nations Indians: accept Md.'s invitation to treat at Lancaster, 303; boundary of land according to Lancaster Treaty, 555; invited to treat with Virginians at Winchester (1753), 79, 541, 580; land returned by the Penns, 611; ownership of western land, 400; passports through Va., 555; place themselves under Dutch protection, 400; receive French and Delaware war belt, 73, 285, *fac. 11;* refuse to go to Fredericksburg (Va.) for treaty, 409, 494; release western lands to English by Lancaster deed, 246, *fac. 2;* unrest (1732-42), 401-2; Va. hostilities, 402, 535-36; *see also* Indian treaties, especially Lancaster (1744) and Logstown (1752), and Onondaga Council.

Slater, George: 41.

Slaughter, Robert: 249, 293, *fac. 1.*

Slaughter, Thomas: 249, 293, *fac. 1.*

Smith, Capt. John: conquers Indian tribes in Va., 400.

Smith, John: 233, 248, 289, 292, *fac. 1, 24.*

Smith, Miss (of Scarborough): reported affianced to George Mercer, 207.

Smith, Robert, Indian trader: 24, 25, 26, 113, 115, 116, 263, 264-65, *fac. app. 8, 9,* 503; employed by Ohio Co., 416.

Smith, Samuel, member of the Ohio Co.: 4, 5, 170, *fac. 24,* 470, 568, 620-21.

Index

Smiths Creek (Va.): 41.
Smiths Creek (W. Va.): 37.
Snelson, John: 250, 292, *fac. 4.*
Snickers, Edward, an overseer: dubious business tactics, 213-14.
Southampton Co. (Va.): erected, 299.
Spencer, Edward: 249, 292, *fac. 1.*
Spotswood, Alexander, lt. gov. of Va.: 400-1, 403.
Spotsylvania Co. (Va.): erected, 299.
Squissatego, Seneca child: imprisoned in Va., 661.
Stafford Co. (Va.): erected, 41.
Stafford County Courthouse: Ohio Co. meeting place, 3, 168, 171, 173, 176, 179, 182, 287, 296, 315.
Stanwix, Gen. John: 301, 521; assures Indians against white encroachment, 92, *fac. 21;* refuses Ohio Co. permission to lay out a town at Wills Creek, *fac. 29.*
Stedman [Sledmant], John: to procure German settlers for Ohio Co., 3, 167, 464.
Stephen, Adam: 613; letter to Gov. Fauquier, 613-14; presses claim for bounty land, 611-12; reports to Va. about Pa. trade policy at Fort Pitt, 93, 94, 95, 446-47; temporary command at Fort Cumberland, 629.
Stevens [Stephens], Arent: 585.
Stevenson, William: 250, 293, *fac. 4.*
Stewart, Henry, Indian trader: accompanies Washington to Fort Le Boeuf, 437.
Stewart, Robert: carries William Trent's letter to John Mercer, 578; presses claim for bounty land, 611-12.
Stobo, Robert, hostage at Fort DuQuesne: plan of Fort DuQuesne, 601.
Stoney Creek (Pa.): 474.
Stoney Gap (Ky.). *See* Pound Gap.
Stover, Jacob: 608.
Stoyestown (Pa.): 474.
Strettell, Amos: Pa. commissioner for Indian trade, 154.
Struther, Anthony: forwards treaty goods to Logstown, 494.
Stump, Frederick: 228, 645.
Suffering Traders Co. (1763): 572-73, 668.
Sugar Creek (Ohio): 489.
Sunbury (Pa.): 484.
Sussex Co. (Va.): erected, 299.
Syracuse (N. Y.), site of Onondaga Council: 402.

Tamany Buck, Shawnee chief: 503, 544.
Tanacharison. *See* Half King.
Tate, Henry: 250, *fac. 4.*
Tawa Indians: send message to English at Fort Pitt, 514-15.

Tayloe, John, member of Ohio Co.: 3, 4, 5, 168, 169, 170, 171, 177, 183, 191, 222, 224, *fac. 24,* 408, 468, 520, 521, 568, 569; executes release of John Mercer's bond, 190; letter to George Mercer, 211; purchases Mercer land, 40-45; sends letter of credit to George Mercer, 205; Va. land grant, 251, 291, 294, *fac. 4.*
Tayloe, John, Jr.: 249, 293, *fac. 1.*
Taylor, George: 249, 292, *fac. 1.*
Taylor, John, Indian trader: *fac. app. 22.*
Taylor, William: 250, 292, *fac. 4.*
Tcitahaia, Indian feather dance: 503.
Teaffe [Taaffe, Taaf, Teafe, Teaff], Michael, Indian trader: *fac. app. 22,* 576; losses at Lower Shawnee Indian town, 498; reports Ottawa in French interest, 13, 103, 254-55, *fac. app. 4;* robbed by Indians, 71, 242, *fac. 9;* trading house at Muskingum Indian town, 489-90.
Teedyuscung, Delaware chief: 513, 515; at Lancaster Treaty (1758), 297, 302, 659, 662.
Ten Mile Creek (Pa.): 518.
Ten Mile Creek (W. Va.): 519.
Tennessee [Hogohegee] River: 143; *see also* Cuttaway River.
Tepicon Indians: 501.
Thomas, George, gov. of Pa.: attends Lancaster Conference, 537-38.
Thomas, Job: 250, 292, *fac. 4.*
Thomson, Charles, sec'y of Pa.: 553.
Thonarissa, Six Nations chief: *fac. app. 22.*
Thornton, Francis, member of Ohio Co.: 2, 3, 168, 190, 206, *fac. 24,* 408; Va. land grant, 250, 293, *fac. 4.*
Thornton, Francis, Jr.: 250, 293, *fac. 4.*
Thornton, John: 250, 293, *fac. 4.*
Thornton, Presley [Presly], member of Ohio Co.: 3, 4, 5, 6, 168, 169, 170, 171, 174, 177, 183, 190, 197, 294, *fac. 24,* 468, 520, 521; executes release of bond to John Mercer, 190, 522; purchases Mercer land, 40-45.
Thornton, William: mentioned as member of Ohio Co., 2, 246, *fac. 2,* 568.
Thurlow, Edward: 669-70.
Togrondoara, Six Nations chief: *fac. app. 22.*
Tohiccon Creek: 302.
Tokintoa Molsinoughko, Wawiagta chief: 138-39, *fac. app. 23.*
Tostee, Peter, Indian trader: *fac. app. 22,* 478-79.
Treaties: Aix-la-Chapelle, 584, 598, 599; Breda, 400; Utrecht, 584; Westminster, 400; *see also* Indian treaties.
Trent, William: activities in the Ohio

· 726 ·

Index

Country (1753-54), 438-41, 599-600; and the Winchester Conference (1753), 428-31; authorized by Ohio Co. to employ workmen to build fort at mouth of Chartiers Creek, 148; builds Fort Prince [St.] George, 84, 623; complains about Ohio Co. traders, 531; confers with Indians at mouth of Pine Creek, 547; consulted by Va. at Logstown Conference, 56, 128, 274, *fac. 17;* delivers Va.'s present to Ohio Indians (1754), 480, 549, 592; extract of letter printed in *Pennsylvania Gazette* and in *Virginia Gazette,* 242-43; factor for Ohio Co., 631-32; Gov. Dinwiddie sends captain's commission to, 81, 82-83, *fac. 14-15;* Gov. Dinwiddie's personal envoy to the Ohio Country, 286, *fac. 11, 12,* 582, 624; holds conference with Indians at Logstown (1753), 651; informs Gov. Dinwiddie of French activities on the Ohio, 72-73, 284-85, *fac. 10;* informs Gov. Dinwiddie of French attack on Pickawillany, 569; land given him by Six Nations Indians, 668; leaves Fort Prince George to obtain supplies, 85, *fac. 16,* 440-41; letter from Nathaniel Walthoe to, 81, *fac. 13;* letter from Va. commissioners at conference at Logstown, 551; letter to George Washington, 84, *fac. 16;* letter to Gov. Dinwiddie, 71-72, 81, 244-45, *fac. 9;* letter to Lunsford Lomax, 94-95, *fac. 22;* letter to Robert Stewart, 578; letters from Gov. Dinwiddie, 73-74, 81-82, 284-85, *fac. 10-11, 15;* letters from William Fairfax, 78-80, *fac. 10, 11, 12;* loss at Lower Shawnee town, 498; named Ohio Co. factor, 68, *fac. 8;* obtains food for Va. militia, 83; petitions Va. for land on the Ohio, 290, 422, 569; recruits militia on frontier, 83, *fac. 16;* renews Va.'s promise to Ohio Indians, 587; reports English trader killed at Kuskuskies, 415; reports English traders captured by French, 71, 242-43, *fac. 9;* sketch, 569-73; takes Va.'s gift to Twightwee, 419-20, 494, 546-47; transports Va.'s gift to Logstown, 83, 589; witnesses Indian deed made at Logstown, *fac. app. 22.*

Trotter, John, Indian trader: 586.
Tucker, John: 250, 292, *fac. 4.*
Tucker, Robert: 250, 292, *fac. 4.*
Turkey Foot (Confluence, Pa.): 6, 142, 508.
Turner, Morris, Indian trader: 499.
Turpin, Thomas: 250, 292, *fac. 4.*
Turtle, The, Miami chief: 431, 562-63.
Tuscaloga, Delaware chief: 516-17.
Tuscarawas, Indian town: 515, 560.
Tuscarora Indians: 300.

Tussey Mt. (Pa.): Warriors' Path east of, 474.
Twightwee, Indian town: 18-19, 108-9, 257-59, 305, *fac. 8; see also* Pickawillany.
Twightwee Indians: 501; address Ottawa at Pickawillany, 22, 112, 261-62, *fac. app. 8;* admitted into English alliance (1748), 502, 562; answer Pa.'s invitation to treaty, 23, 113, 262-63, *fac. app. 8;* ask Va. for help against the French, 555; inform Va. and Pa. of French attack, 569; invited to conference at Winchester, 286, *fac. 12;* massacred by French, 66, 240, 305, *fac. 7, 8,* 419-20; receive part of Logstown treaty present, 58, 130, 275, *fac. app. 18;* receives Pa.'s gift, *fac. app. 7;* refuses to attend Winchester Conference, 78, 648; reported to have declared war on French, 68, 72, 240, *fac. 8;* speech of Gov. Dinwiddie sent to, 74, 285, *fac. 11; see also* Miami, Pickawillany, and Pict Indians.
Two Creeks: description, 38-39, *fac. app. 16; see also* Buffalo and Cross Creeks.
Tygart River (W. Va.): 524-25.

Unlawful settlement on Indian lands: causes frontier unrest, 644-45.
Upper Blue Lick: Great Warriors' Trail branches at, 504.
Utrecht, Treaty of (1713): 584.

Van Braam, Jacob: 597.
Vanceburg (Ky.): on Great Warriors' Trail, 504.
Van Meter, Isaac: 608.
Van Meter, John: 608.
Venango: John Fraser threatens to leave, 63, 135, 282, *fac. app. 21.*
Venice (Ohio): site of Huron Indian town, 489.
Virginia: acquires western land at Lancaster Conference, 403; acreage granted in, *fac. 24;* act to encourage western settlements discussed, 606-7; advertises methods of taking up land in colony, 89-90, *fac. 19-20;* Andrew Montour's service, 54, 143-44, 177, 271, *fac. 7,* 482-83, 539; asks Ohio Indians for friendship, 58-59, 130-31, 275 ff., *fac. app. 18;* authorizes warlike stores to Ohio Indians, 81, *fac. 13;* Carolina boundary line run, 467; commissioners at Logstown Conference, *see* James Patton, Joshua Fry, and Lunsford Lomax; condoles Indians at death of chief, 61, 133, 280; contribution to French and Indian War, 91-92, *fac. 21;*

· 727 ·

Index

denies settlers the right to settle west of the mountains (1745), 298; economic conditions, comments by John Mercer, 189 ff.; employs Christopher Gist to invite Ohio Indians to conference at Fredericksburg, 409; engages Conrad Weiser as Indian emissary and interpreter, 409; exempts foreign protestant settlers from certain taxes, 90, *fac. 20*; export duty on furs (1705) to support College of William and Mary, 466; frontier counties enumerated, 299; "headrights," method of taking up land, 527-28; Indian conference at Logstown (1753), 430-32, 438, 547-48, 592; Indian conference at Winchester (1753), 245, 286, *fac. 12*, 428-30, 433-34, 541, 557, 579; informed of French activities on Ohio by William Trent, 71-73, 284-85, *fac. 10*; invites Shawnee to conference at Logstown (1751), 16-17, 106-7, 256, *fac. app. 5*; laws for taking up land, 565; local taxes explained, 145-46; maps display route of Christopher Gist's explorations, 51, 237, *fac. 5*; Naturalization Act (1705), 621-22; offers to educate Indian children, 623; passes tax relief act for settlers in western country, *fac. 13*; Pa. boundary, 4, 92-93, 171, 235-36, *fac. 4*, 410-11; Pa. trade rivalry, 415-17; petitioners for land on Ohio (1745-53) enumerated, 292-94; plans fort at fork of Monongahela River [Pittsburgh], 77, 295-96, *fac. 17*; record of land grants made (1745-53), enumerated, 289-91; required to condone Six Nations for loss of warriors, 303; Six Nations controversy (1743), 402; special message to Shawnee at Logstown Conference, 60, 131-32, 278, *fac. app. 19*; speech to the Twightwee, 551, *see also* Logstown Treaty (1752); surveyor's fees, 46-47, 89-90, *fac. 20*, 523; to send ordnance to the Ohio, 82, *fac. 15*; veterans of militia denied land bonus, 526; whites murdered by Indians, 532-33; *see also* Robert Dinwiddie, Francis Fauquier, Thomas Lee, Lewis Burwell.

Virginia Executive Council: about Ohio Co. lands, 586-87; answers Half King's request for Va. aid, 598; opinion on Indian affairs (1753), 580-81; order about surveys (1749), 574; orders arms and ammunition for Ohio Indians, 587; orders for land grants (printed), 51, 248, 249, 250-51, *fac. 1, 2, 4, 6*; rule for taking up land (1699), 527-28; sends message to Catawba and Cherokee, 589.

Virginia Gazette: extracts printed, 68, 84, 85-86, 89-90, 242-43, *fac. 8, 12, 18, 19-20*.

Virginia Historical Society: owns French (Céloron) leaden plate, 554; photostat of "Articles of Agreement of Ohio Co.," 461.

Virginia House of Burgesses: fails to pass supply bill for support of militia (1753), 435; legislation on militia supply bill (1754), 590; memorial (1766), 397; passes bill remitting levies on protestant settlers on frontier, 435-36; petition to Privy Council mentioned, 212; petitions king to withdraw royal proclamation, *fac. 33*; rejects governor's plea for funds to equip militia, 245; Robert Dinwiddie asks appropriation for war supplies from, *fac. 13*; Robert Dinwiddie's speech to (1754), extract printed, *fac. 16-17*.

Virginia land grants: Aylett, Philip, 250, 292, *fac. 4*; Barnes, Richard, 249, 293, *fac. 1*; Barrett, Charles, 250, 292, *fac. 4*; Barrett, Robert, 250, 292, *fac. 4*; Baylor, John, 250, 292, *fac. 4*; Belfield, John, 249, 293, *fac. 1*; Beverley, William, 226, 248, 292, *fac. 1*, 567, 608, 642, 643; Blair, John, 51, 233, 249, 251, 289, *fac. 2, 6, 24*, 414, 567, 568; Blair, John, Jr., 249, 292, *fac. 1*; Borden, Benjamin, 298; Bowie, James, 249, 293, *fac. 1*; Buchanan, George, 249, 293, *fac. 1*; Burwell, Armistead, 250, 292, *fac. 4*; Butler, William, 293; Calmes, Mark, 51, 249, 251, 293, *fac. 2, 6*; Calvert, Cornelius, 250, 293, *fac. 4*; Calvert, Isaiah, 294; Calvert, Maximilian, 250, 292, *fac. 4*; Calvert, Robert, 294; Carrington, George, 250, 292, *fac. 4*; Carter, James, 294; Corbin, Richard, 72, 242, 251, 291, *fac. 10, 24*; Craig, John, 248, 292, *fac. 1*; Dalton, Samuel, 250, 293, *fac. 4*; Dansie, Thomas, 250, 292, *fac. 4*; Dick, Charles, 250, 292, *fac. 4*; Dixon, John, 250, 294, *fac. 4*; Downes, Henry, 233, 249, 289, 292, *fac. 1, 24*; Dunlop, Alexander, 249, 293, *fac. 1*; Ewin, James, 249, 293, *fac. 1*; Fontaine, Peter, Jr., 250-51, 293, *fac. 4*; Fry, Joshua, 250, 292, *fac. 4*; Fuller, Edward, 249, *fac. 1*; Garland, John, 250, 292, *fac. 4*; Gilchrist, Robert, 249, 294, *fac. 1*; Gilmer, George, 250, 292, *fac. 4*; Gilmer, Peachy, 250, 292, *fac. 4*; Glover, William, 293; Gordon, James, 249, 293, *fac. 1*; Graeme, John, 249, 293, *fac. 1*; Graham, Duncan, 250, 292, *fac. 4*; Green, Robert, 248, 293, *fac. 1*; Green, William, 249, 293, *fac. 1*; Harding, George, 294; Harding, Henry, 294; Harvey, John, 250, 292, *fac. 4*; Hedgman, Peter, 250, 293, *fac. 4*; Hill,

Index

Humphrey, 250, 294, *fac. 4*; Hite, Joist, 298; Hubbard, Benjamin, 250, 292, *fac. 4*; Hudson, William, 250, 293, *fac. 4*; Jackson, Robert, 249, 293, *fac. 1*; Jackson, William, 249, 293, *fac. 1*; Jefferson, Peter, 250, 294, *fac. 4*; Johnson, James, 249, 294, *fac. 1*; Jones, Richard, 250, 293, *fac. 4*; Lewis, Charles, 248, 292, 294, *fac. 1, 4*; Lewis, John, 248, 250, 290, 292, *fac. 1, 4, 24*; Lewis, Nicholas, 250, 293, *fac. 4*; Lewis Robert, 248, 292, *fac. 1*; Lewis, Thomas, 250, 293, *fac. 4*; Lewis, William, 248, 292, *fac. 1*; Lewis, Zachary, 248, 249, 292, *fac. 1*; Logan, George, 250, 293, *fac. 4*; Loyall, Paul, 250, 293, *fac. 4*; McKensie, Alexander, 250, 292, *fac. 4*; McMachon, John, 51, 249, 251, *fac. 2, 6*; McMachon, Richard, 51, 249, 251; *fac. 2, 6*; McMachon, William, 51, 233, 249, 251, 289, *fac. 2, 6, 24*; 414; Maddison, John, 250, 292, *fac. 4*; Martin, Robert, 250, 293, *fac. 4*; Maury, James, 250, 293, *fac. 4*; Meriwether, Francis, 250, 294, *fac. 4*; Meriwether, John, 250, 294, *fac. 4*; Meriwether, Nicholas, 250, 293, *fac. 4*; Meriwether, Thomas, 250, 292, *fac. 4*; Meriwether, Thomas, Jr., 250, 292, *fac. 4*; Moore, Bernard, 250, 290, 292, *fac. 4, 24*; Moore, John, 250, 293, *fac. 4*; Neal, William, 293; Neale, John, 51, 249, 251, 293, *fac. 2, 6*; Neale, William, 249, 251, 293, *fac. 2, 6*; Nelson, Thomas, Jr., 248, 292, 293, *fac. 1*; Ohio Co., 291; Parks, William, 249, 250, 251, 292, 293, *fac. 1, 4*; Patton, James, 233, 235, 249, 289, 293, *fac. 1, 4, 24, 567-68*; Pendleton, Edward, 250, 292, *fac. 4*; Pierce, John, 250, 293, *fac. 4*; Power, James, 250, 292, 294, *fac. 4*; Preston, John, 249, 293, *fac. 1*; Randolph, Peyton, 250, 290, 292, *fac. 2, 4*; Red, Samuel, 251, 293, *fac. 4*; Rice, Patrick, 293; Roberts, John, 249, 294, *fac. 1*; Robinson, Beverley, 248, 292, *fac. 1*; Robinson, George, 249, 293, *fac. 1*; Robinson, John, 233, 248, 289, 292, *fac. 1, 24*; Robinson, John, Jr., 248, 292, *fac. 1*; Russell, William, 51, 233, 249, 251, 289, *fac. 2, 6*, 568, 574; Shelton, John, 250, 292, *fac. 4*; Slaughter, Robert, 249, 293, *fac. 1*; Slaughter, Thomas, 249, 293, *fac. 1*; Smith, John, 233, 248, 289, 292, *fac. 1, 24*; Snelson, John, 250, 292, *fac. 4*; Spencer, Edward, 249, 292, *fac. 1*; Stevenson, William, 250, 293, *fac. 4*; Tate, Henry, 250, *fac. 4*; Tayloe, John, 251, 291, 294, *fac. 4*; Tayloe, John, Jr., 249, 293, *fac. 1*; Taylor, George, 249, 292, *fac. 1*; Taylor, William, 250, 292, *fac. 4*; Thomas, Job, 250, 292, *fac. 4*; Thornton, Francis, 250, 293, *fac. 4*; Thornton, Francis, Jr., 250, 293, *fac. 4*; Tucker, John, 250, 292, *fac. 4*; Tucker, Robert, 250, 292, *fac. 4*; Turpin, Thomas, 250, 292, *fac. 4*; Waddy, Samuel, 250, 292, *fac. 4*; Walker, Thomas, 250, 292, *fac. 4*; Weatheral, John, 249, *fac. 1*; Wetherburne, Henry, 248, 292, *fac. 1*; Williamson, Thomas, 250, 292, *fac. 4*; Willis, Henry, 250, 292, *fac. 4*; Willis, John, 249, 292, *fac. 1*; Willoughby, John, 250, 292, *fac. 4*; Wilson, John, 248, 292, *fac. 1*; Winslow, Richard, 249, 294, *fac. 1*; Winston, Edmund, 251, 293, *fac. 4*; Winston, Isaac, Jr., 250-51, 293, *fac. 4*; Winston, William, 290, *fac. 24*; Winston, William, Jr., 250-51, 293, *fac. 4*; Wood, James, 249, 251, 293, *fac. 1, 4*; Wood, William, 250, 293, *fac. 4*.

Virginia traders, Early, in Ohio Country: 531.

Wabash [Obache] River: 24, 113, 263, *fac. app. 8*.
Wachovia Tract: Moravian land in N. C., 608-9.
Waddy, Samuel: 250, 292, *fac. 4*.
Wales, ———: brewer for John Mercer, 190, 191, 192, 196.
Walhonding River (Ohio): 524.
Walker, Thomas: 250, 292, *fac. 4*.
Wallace, Paul A. W.: opinion on Lancaster Treaty, 403.
Wallace's Run (Pa.): Christopher Gist's cave, 510.
Walls, Burgess: 200.
"Walnut Bottom": Ohio Co. land in Md., 618-19.
Walpole, Thomas: 311, 668, 669, 674.
Walpole Co.: employs George Croghan, field agent on the Ohio, 326; George Mercer merges Ohio Co., 456-57; has access to Ohio Co. official documents, 470; king approves purchase of land, 324-25; memorial (1769), 397; to challenge legality of other grants in America, 311; William Trent, member, 573; *see also* Grand Ohio Co.
Walthoe, Nathaniel: 81, *fac. 13*.
Ward, Edward: capitulation of Fort Prince George (Pittsburgh), 85-88, *fac. 18*, 549, 592; Half King's special message, 88-89, *fac. 19*.
Wardrop [Woodrup, Woodrop], James, member of Ohio Co.: 3, 5, 167, 169, 177, 246, 294, *fac. 2, 24*, 468, 470.
Warriors' Path east of Tussey Mountain: 473-74.

Index

Warriors' Road: 28, 118, *fac. app. 10; see also* Big Sandy Creek and Bluestone River.

Washington, Augustine, member of the Ohio Co.: 2, 3, 5, 6, 168, 169, 170, 174, 177, 178, 246, 294, *fac. 2, 3, 24,* 468, 568; Robert Carter purchases Ohio Co. stock, 178.

Washington, George: advised by King Shingas, 559; at Fort Necessity, 483; at Winchester, 78, *fac. 10;* carries Va.'s ultimatum to Fort Le Boeuf, 74-75, 76, 245, *fac. 13-14,* 436-38, 583; commissioned by Va. to recruit militia, 81, *fac. 15;* confers with Half King at Logstown, 548; confers with Indians at John Fraser's, 599; confers with John Fraser, 591-92; corresponds with George Mercer about western lands, 520-21; defeats Jumonville, 609-10; disputes with Capt. John Dagworthy, 629; Indian request to march to the Ohio, 84; interpretation of Half King's speech to the governors of Pa. and Va., 604-5; letter to Thomas Cresap (heretofore unknown), 85, *fac. 17-18,* 442-43, 597; letters from Christopher Gist and William Trent, 84; meets William Trent and Ohio Co. settlers near Wills Creek, 76, 295, *fac. 14,* 570, 592; message to the Half King, 549; militia leaves Alexandria, 84-85, 597; praises Andrew Montour, 484; presses claim for bounty land, 611-12; requests transportation equipment from William Trent, 85, *fac. 17;* sends Half King's message to Gov. Dinwiddie, 648; to obtain supplies from the Ohio Co. store at Wills Creek, 85, *fac. 17;* to proceed to Redstone, 86, *fac. 18;* wheatgrower, 192-93.

Washington, Lawrence, member and head of the Ohio Co.: 2, 3, 5, 6, 168, 169, 170, 174, 177, 246, 293, *fac. 2, 24,* 465, 468, 568, 619; circulated company petition (1747), xi, 3; Lunsford Lomax purchases share in company, 176; opinion on company obtaining German Protestant settlers, 421; reimbursed for preparing Ohio Co. petition, 167, 168; to apply to the governor for muskets for the use of the company, 169; to purchase land for the company in Md., 142-43; transacts company business in England, 141, 169, 618, 631.

Washington (D.C.): 622.

Waterford (Pa.). *See* Fort Le Boeuf.

Wawiagta and Piankashaw Indians: 18, 22, 111-12, 257, 261; *see also* Wea Indians.

Wawiagta and Piankashaw Treaty: 24, 113, 138-39, 263, 300, *fac. app. 6, 8, 23,* 457.

Wea Indians: 501, 502.

Weatheral, John: 249, *fac. 1.*

Weatherhall, James: 294.

Wedderburn, Alexander: 669.

Weiser, Conrad: accused of misrepresenting Va. to the Six Nations, 298-300, *fac. app. 18, 21;* Andrew Montour, a companion, 481-82; conducts Logstown Conference for Pa. (1748), 57, 64, 129, 136, 276, 282, 449, 476, 485, 552-53, 570, 655; confers with Indians at Aughwick (1754), 559-60; corresponds with Thomas Lee, 409, 410; fails to persuade Six Nations to confer with Va. at Fredericksburg, 407, 485, 540; John Mercer's invective, 297, 298, 299; letter from Richard Peters, 434; sets price of liquor for Ohio Indians, 61, 133, 280, *fac. app. 20.*

Wequalia, Delaware chief: executed for murder, 657.

West, William, Indian trader: Pa. commissioner for Indian trade, 154, *fac. app. 22.*

West Liberty (Ohio): 501.

West Salem (Ohio): 486.

Western Country: description in Ohio Co. petition (1749), 246-48, *fac. 2-3.*

Western Indians: receive present from Pa., 20, 110, 260, *fac. app. 7.*

Wetherburne, Henry: 248, 292, *fac. 1.*

Wharton, Samuel, member of Walpole Co.: 324-26, 673-74, 668, 670.

Wheeling (W. Va.): French leaden plate buried, 553.

Wheeling [Wealin] Creek (W. Va.): 38, *fac. app. 15,* 520; *see also* Scalp Creek.

Whiskey Insurrection in Western Pa.: Fort Cumberland reactivated at time, 630.

White Eyes, Delaware chief: 515.

White settlers west of the Susquehanna River: Indians complain, 534.

White Woman's Creek: 14, 104, *fac. app. 4;* suggested natural boundary for Ohio Co. grant, 47.

White Woman's Indian town: 493.

Whiteport (Va.): Lord Fairfax's manor near, 587.

Wild rye in the Ohio Country: 497.

William and Mary College. *See* College of William and Mary.

Williamsburg (Va.): meeting place for Ohio Co., 179, 287.

Williamson, Thomas: 250, 292, *fac. 4.*

Williamson and Clifton: will contestation between, 184.

Williamsport (Md.): 622.

Willing, Thomas: Pa. commissioner for Indian trade: 154.

Index

Willis, Henry: 250, 292, *fac. 4.*
Willis, John: 249, 292, *fac. 1.*
Willoughby, John: 250, 292, *fac. 4.*
Wills Creek (Md.): Ohio Co. store at, 5, 142; projected Ohio Co. town at, 181-82, *fac. 29.*
Wills Mountain: Christopher Gist's remarks, 32, 122, *fac. app. 13.*
Wilson, John: 248, 292, *fac. 1.*
Winchester (Ky.): 576.
Windaughalah, Delaware chief: 15, 105, *fac. app. 5;* sketch, 496.
Winslow, Richard: 249, 294, *fac. 1.*
Winston, Edmund: 251, 293, *fac. 4.*
Winston, Isaac, Jr.: 250-51, 293, *fac. 4.*
Winston, William: 290, *fac. 24.*
Winston, William, Jr.: 250-51, 293, *fac. 4.*
Wood, James: 249, 251, 293, *fac. 1, 4.*
Wood, William: 250, 293, *fac. 4.*
Wyandott Indian town: 523-24; *see also* Conchake, Indian town.
Wyandott Indians: adopt Christopher Gist, 80, *fac. app. 3;* at Logstown treaties, 60, 132, 278, *fac. app. 19,* 431, 489; decline Va.'s invitation to go to Fredericksburg (Va.), 14, 104, *fac. app. 4,* 412; information from Christopher Gist, 101, 253, *fac. app. 3;* method of reckoning time, 13, 103, 254, *fac. app. 4;* protect whites at Muskingum, 84; put white woman captive to death, 13, 103, *fac. app. 4;* tell Conrad Weiser why they deserted the French, 555; *see also* Huron Indians.

Yadkin River (N. C.): Christopher Gist's home, 31, 121, 266, *fac. app. 12.*
Youghiogheny [Oswegle] Big Bottom (Pa.): George Croghan's trading house, 480, 493.
Youghiogheny [Youghogane, Youghyoughgane] River (Pa.): Delaware town on south fork, 33, 123, 267, *fac. app. 13;* description of land along middle fork (Castleman's River), 32, 33, 122, *fac. app. 13;* John Blair land grant, 233; Lewis Evans on navigation, *fac. app. 25;* Ohio Co. applies to Thomas Penn for land at three forks (Turkey Foot), 6, 142; Ohio Co. settlement, 68-69, 241, *fac. 8;* upper forks, 123.
Young, James, Indian trader: 499.

Zeisberger, David, Moravian missionary: 511.
Zinzendorf [Zinzendorff], Nicolas Ludwig, count von, Moravian: Wachovia tract in N. C. named for, 609.

· 731 ·

GEORGE MERCER PAPERS

Composed and printed for the University of Pittsburgh Press by Davis & Warde, Inc., of Pittsburgh; designed by THOS. C. PEARS, III; the text set in Linotype Baskerville; the illustrations reproduced in collotype by Meriden Gravure Company, Connecticut; text paper, 25 per cent rag, made especially for this book by the Curtis Paper Company of Delaware; the illustrations printed on stock made by the Lee Paper Company of Michigan; bound by Russell-Rutter Company, Inc., of New York.

EDITION LIMITED TO 1,000 COPIES